Encyclopedia of
SPECIAL EDUCATION
Second Edition

Encyclopedia of Special Education, SECOND EDITION
Cecil R. Reynolds and Elaine Fletcher-Janzen, Editors

Encyclopedia of
SPECIAL
EDUCATION

Second Edition

A Reference for the Education of the Handicapped and Other Exceptional Children and Adults

VOLUME 1

Edited by

Cecil R. Reynolds
Texas A & M University

Elaine Fletcher-Janzen
University of Northern Colorado

JOHN WILEY & SONS

NEW YORK · CHICHESTER · WEINHEIM · BRISBANE · SINGAPORE · TORONTO

ISBN 0-471-25323-5 (Volume 1)
ISBN 0-471-25324-3 (Volume 2)
ISBN 0-471-25325-1 (Volume 3)
ISBN 0-471-25309-X (three-volume set)

Printed in the United States of America.

10 9 8 7 6 5 4 3 2 1

CONTRIBUTORS

Susanne Blough Abbott
Bedford Central School District
Mt. Kisco, New York

Marty Abramson
University of Wisconsin at Stout
Menomonie, Wisconsin

Patricia Ann Abramson
Hudson Public Schools
Hudson, Wisconsin

Salvador Hector Achoa
Texas A & M University
College Station, Texas

Patricia A. Alexander
University of Maryland
College Park, Maryland

Nancy Algert
Texas A & M University
College Station, Texas

Thomas E. Allen
Gallaudet College
Washington, DC

Marie Almond
The University of Texas of the
   Permian Basin
Odessa, Texas

Geri R. Alvis
University of Tennessee
Memphis State University
Memphis, Tennessee

C.H. Ammons
Psychological Reports/
   Perceptual and Motor Skills
Missoula, Montana

Carol Anderson
Texas A & M University
College Station, Texas

Kari Anderson
University of North Carolina
Wilmington, North Carolina

Peggy L. Anderson
University of New Orleans,
   Lakefront
New Orleans, Louisiana

J. Appelboom-Fondu
Université Libre de Bruxelles
Brussels, Belgium

James M. Applefield
University of North Carolina
Wilmington, North Carolina

Pauline F. Applefield
University of North Carolina
Wilmington, North Carolina

John Arena
Academic Therapy Publications
Novato, California

Kim Ryan Arredondo
Texas A & M University
College Station, Texas

Gustavo Abelardo Arrendondo
Monterrey, Mexico

Bernice Arricale
Hunter College, City University
   of New York
New York, New York

H. Roberta Arrigo
Hunter College, City University
   of New York
New York, New York

Alfredo J. Artiles
University of California
Los Angeles, California

Michael J. Ash
Texas A & M University
College Station, Texas

Adel E. Ashawal
Ain Shams University
Cairo, Egypt

William G. Austin
Cape Fear Psychological Services
Wilmington, North Carolina

Anna H. Avant
University of Alabama
University, Alabama

Dan G. Bachor
University of Victoria
Canada

Rebecca Bailey
Texas A & M University
College Station, Texas

Timothy A. Ballard
University of North Carolina
Wilmington, North Carolina

Deborah E. Barbour
University of North Carolina
Wilmington, North Carolina

Russell A. Barkley
University of Massachusetts
   Medical Center
Worchester, Massachusetts

Charles P. Barnard
University of Wisconsin at Stout
Menomonie, Wisconsin

David W. Barnett
University of Cincinnati
Cincinnati, Ohio

Ellis I. Barowsky
Hunter College, City University
  of New York
New York, New York

Lyle E. Barton
Kent State University
Kent, Ohio

Vicki Bartosik
Stanford University
Stanford, California

Paul Bates
Southern Illinois University
Carbondale, Illinois

Anne M. Bauer
University of Cincinnati
Cincinnati, Ohio

Elizabeth R. Bauerschmidt
University of North Carolina
Wilmington, North Carolina

Michael Bauerschmidt
Brunswick Hospital
Wilmington, North Carolina

Monique Bauters
Centre d'Etude et de Reclassement
Brussels, Belgium

John R. Beattie
University of North Carolina
Charlotte, North Carolina

George R. Beauchamp
Cleveland Clinic Foundation
Cleveland, Ohio

Ana Yeraldina Beneke
University of Oklahoma
Norman, Oklahoma

Randy Elliot Bennett
Educational Testing Service
Princeton, New Jersey

Richard A. Berg
West Virginia University Medical
  Center, Charleston Division
Charleston, West Virginia

John R. Bergan
University of Arizona
Tucson, Arizona

Dianne E. Berkell
C.W. Post Campus, Long Island
  University
Greenvale, New York

Gary Berkowitz
Temple University
Philadelphia, Pennsylvania

Shari A. Stanton
Private Practice
Las Vegas, Nevada

Kristen Biernath
The Hughes Spalding International
  Adoption Evaluation Center
Georgia

Erin D. Bigler
Austin Neurological Clinic
University of Texas
Austin, Texas

Roseann Bisighini
The Salk Institute
La Jolla, California

L. Worth Bolton
Cape Fear Substance Abuse Center
Wilmington, North Carolina

Gwyneth M. Boodoo
Texas A & M University
College Station, Texas

Nancy Bordier
Hunter College, City University
  of New York
New York, New York

Jeannie Bormans
Center for Developmental Problems
Brussels, Belgium

Morton Botel
University of Pennsylvania
Philadelphia, Pennsylvania

Daniel J. Boudah
Texas A & M University
College Station, Texas

Michael Bourdot
Centre d'Etude et de Reclassement
Brussels, Belgium

Bruce A. Bracken
University of Memphis
Memphis, Tennessee

Mary Brady
Pennsylvania Special Education
  Assistive Device Center
Elizabethtown, Pennsylvania

Janet S. Brand
Hunter College, City University
  of New York
New York, New York

Don Braswell
Research Foundation, City
  University of New York
New York, New York

T. Berry Brazelton
Children's Hospital
Boston, Massachusetts

Warner H. Britton
Auburn University
Auburn, Alabama

Debra Y. Broadbooks
California School of
  Professional Psychology
San Diego, California

Michael G. Brown
Central Wisconsin Center for the
  Developmentally Disabled
Madison, Wisconsin

Robert T. Brown
University of North Carolina
Wilmington, North Carolina

Ronald T. Brown
Emory University School
  of Medicine
Atlanta, Georgia

Tina L. Brown
University of Tennessee
Memphis State University
Memphis, Tennessee

Robert G. Brubaker
Eastern Kentucky University
Richmond, Kentucky

Catherine O. Bruce
Hunter College, City University
  of New York
New York, New York

Andrew R. Brulle
Eastern Illinois University
Charleston, Illinois

Laura Kinzie Brutting
University of Wisconsin
Madison, Wisconsin

Donna M. Bryant
University of North Carolina
Chapel Hill, North Carolina

Milton Budoff
Research Institute for
  Educational Problems
Cambridge, Massachusetts

Carolyn Bullard
Lewis & Clark College
Portland, Oregon

Thomas Burke
Hunter College, City University
  of New York
New York, New York

Alois Bürli
Swiss Institute for Special Education
Lucerne, Switzerland

Thomas A. Burton
University of Georgia
Athens, GA

James Button
United States Department
  of Education
Washington, DC

Anne Campbell
Purdue University
West Lafayette, Indiana

Frances A. Campbell
University of North Carolina
Chapel Hill, North Carolina

Steven A. Carlson
Beaverton Schools
Beaverton, Oregon

Douglas Carnine
University of Oregon
Eugene, Oregon

Janet Carpenter
University of Oklahoma
Norman, Oklahoma

Tracy Calpin Castle
Eastern Kentucky University
Richmond, Kentucky

John F. Cawley
University of New Orleans
New Orleans, Louisiana

Constance Y. Celaya
Private Practice
Irving, Texas

James C. Chalfant
University of Arizona
Tucson, Arizona

Chris Cherrington
Lycoming College
Williamsport, Pennsylvania

Robert Chimedza
University of Zimbabwe
Havare, Zimbabwe

Kathleen Chinn
New Mexico State University
Las Cruces, New Mexico

LeRoy Clinton
Boston University
Boston, Massachusetts

Renato Cocchi
Pesaro, Italy

Shirley Cohen
Hunter College, City University
  of New York
New York, New York

Ginga L. Colcough
University of North Carolina
Wilmington, North Carolina

Christine L. Cole
University of Wisconsin
Madison, Wisconsin

Rhonda Collins
Florida State University
Tallahassee, Florida

Jennifer Condon
University of North Carolina
Wilmington, North Carolina

Jane Close Conoley
University of Nebraska
Lincoln, Nebraska

Vivian I. Correa
University of Florida
Gainesville, Florida

Lawrence S. Cote
Pennsylvania State University
University Park, Pennsylvania

Katherine D. Couturier
Pennsylvania State University
King of Prussia, Pennsylvania

J. Michael Coxe
University of South Carolina
Columbia, South Carolina

Anne B. Crabbe
St. Andrews College
Laurinburg, North Carolina

Sergio R. Crisalle
Medical Horizons Unlimited
San Antonio, Texas

Chara Crivelli
Vito de Negrar
Verona, Italy

Jack A. Cummings
Indiana University
Bloomington, Indiana

Jacqueline Cunningham
University of Texas
Austin, Texas

Susan Curtiss
University of California
Los Angeles, California

Rik Carl D'Amato
University of Northern Colorado
Greely, Colorado

Elizabeth Dane
Hunter College, City University
    of New York
New York, New York

Craig Darch
Auburn University
Auburn, Alabama

Jacqueline E. Davis
Boston University
Boston, Massachusetts

Raymond S. Dean
Ball State University
Indiana University School
    of Medicine
Muncie, Indiana

Jozi Deleon
New Mexico State University
Las Cruces, New Mexico

Bernadette M. Delgado
Puerto Rico

Randall L. De Pry
University of Colorado
Colorado Springs, Colorado

Lizanne DeStefano
University of Illinois,
    Urbana-Champaign
Champaign, Illinois

S. De Vriendt
Vrije Universiteit Brussel
Brussels, Belgium

Caroline D'Ippolito
Eastern Pennsylvania Special
    Education Resources Center
King of Prussia, Pennsylvania

Mary D'Ippolito
Montgomery County
    Intermediate Unit
Norristown, Pennsylvania

Marilyn P. Dornbush
Atlanta, Georgia

Susann Dowling
University of North Carolina
Wilmington, North Carolina

Jengjyh Duh
National Taiwan Normal University
Taiwan

Brooke Durbin
Texas A & M University
College Station, Texas

Mary K. Dykes
University of Florida
Gainesville, Florida

Peg Eagney
School for the Deaf
New York, New York

Ronald C. Eaves
Auburn University
Auburn, Alabama

Jana Echevarria
California State University
Long Beach, California

Amita Edran
California State University
Long Beach, California

John M. Eells
Souderton Area School District
Souderton, Pennsylvania

Stephen N. Elliott
University of Wisconsin
Madison, Wisconsin

Ingemar Emanuelsson
Goteburg University
Sweden

Carol Sue Englert
Michigan State University
East Lansing, Michigan

Christine A. Espin
University of Minnesota
Minneapolis, Minnesota

Rand B. Evans
Texas A & M University
College Station, Texas

Katherine Falwell
University of North Carolina
Wilmington, North Carolina

Stephen S. Farmer
New Mexico State University
Las Cruces, New Mexico

MaryAnn C. Farthing
University of North Carolina
Chapel Hill, North Carolina

Lisa Fashnacht Hill
California School of
    Professional Psychology
San Diego, California

Mary Grace Feely
School for the Deaf
New York, New York

John F. Feldhusen
Purdue University
West Lafayette, Indiana

Britt-Inger Fex
University of Lund
Sweden

Donna Filips
Steger, Illinois

Sally L. Flagler
University of Oklahoma
Norman, Oklahoma

Dennis M. Flanagan
Montgomery County
    Intermediate Unit
Norristown, Pennsylvania

David Fletcher-Janzen
Colorado Springs, Colorado

Elaine Fletcher-Janzen
University of Northern Colorado
Colorado Springs, Colorado

Wendy Flynn
Staffordshire University
England

Thomas A. Frank
Pennsylvania State University
University Park, Pennsylvania

Mary M. Frasier
University of Georgia
Athens, Georgia

Joseph L. French
Pennsylvania State University
University Park, Pennsylvania

Alice G. Friedman
University of Oklahoma Health
    Services Center
Norman, Oklahoma

Douglas L. Friedman
Fordham University
Bronx, New York

Douglas Fuchs
Peabody College, Vanderbilt
    University
Nashville, Tennessee

Lynn S. Fuchs
Peabody College, Vanderbilt
    University
Nashville, Tennessee

Gerald B. Fuller
Central Michigan University
Mt. Pleasant, Michigan

Rosemary Gaffney
Hunter College, City University
    of New York
New York, New York

Diego Gallegos
Texas A & M University
College Station, Texas
San Antonio Independent
    School District
San Antonio, Texas

Shernaz B. Garcia
University of Texas
Austin, Texas

Katherine Garnett
Hunter College, City University
    of New York
New York, New York

Melissa M. George
Montgomery County
    Intermediate Unit
Norristown, Pennsylvania

Phil Bless Gerard
University of Fribourg
Switzerland

Harvey R. Gilbert
Pennsylvania State University
University Park, Pennsylvania

Elizabeth Girshick
Montgomery County
    Intermediate Unit
Norristown, Pennsylvania

Joni J. Gleason
University of West Florida
Pensacola, Florida

Sharon L. Glennen
Pennsylvania State University
University Park, Pennsylvania

Rick Gonzales
Texas A & M University
College Station, Texas

Libby Goodman
Pennsylvania State University
King of Prussia, Pennsylvania

Carole Reiter Gothelf
Hunter College, City University
    of New York
New York, New York

Steve Graham
University of Maryland
College Park, Maryland

Jeffrey W. Gray
Ball State University
Muncie, Indiana

P. Allen Gray, Jr.
University North Carolina
Wilmington, North Carolina

Darielle Greenberg
California School of
    Professional Psychology
San Diego, California

Laurence C. Grimm
University of Illinois
Chicago, Illinois

Lindsay S. Gross
University of Wisconsin
Milwaukee, Wisconsin

Norma Guerra
Texas A & M University
College Station, Texas

John Guidubaldi
Kent State University
Kent, Ohio

Deborah Guillen
The University of Texas of the
    Permian Basin
Odessa, Texas

Steven Gumerman
Temple University
Philadelphia, Pennsylvania

Thomas Gumpel
The Hebrew University of Jerusalem
Israel

Terry B. Gutkin
University of Nebraska
Lincoln, Nebraska

Patricia A. Haensly
Texas A & M University
College Station, Texas

George James Hagerty
Stonehill College
North Easton, Massachusetts

Robert Hall
Texas A & M University
College Station, Texas

Winnifred M. Hall
University of West Indies
Jamaica

Richard E. Halmstad
University of Wisconsin at Stout
Menomonie, Wisconsin

Glennelle Halpin
Auburn University
Auburn, Alabama

Donald D. Hammill
Pro-Ed, Inc.
Austin, Texas

Harold Hanson
Southern Illinois University
Carbondale, Illinois

Elise Phelps Hanzel
California School of
  Professional Psychology
San Diego, California

Janice Harper
North Carolina Central University
Durham, North Carolina

Gale A. Harr
Maple Heights City Schools
Maple Heights, Ohio

Karen L. Harrell
University of Georgia
Athens, Georgia

Frances T. Harrington
Radford University
Blacksberg, Virginia

Karen R. Harris
University of Maryland
College Park, Maryland

Kathleen Harris
Arizona State University West
Arizona

Patti L. Harrison
University of Alabama
University, Alabama

Beth Harry
University of Miami
Miami, Florida

Lawrence C. Hartlage
Evans, Georgia

Patricia Hartlage
Medical College of Georgia
Evans, Georgia

Dan Hatt
University of Oklahoma
Norman, Oklahoma

Anette Hausotter
Bis Beratungsstelle Fur Die
  Intergration
Germany

Jeff Heinzen
Indianhead Enterprise
Menomonie, Wisconsin

Rhonda Hennis
University of North Carolina
Wilmington, North Carolina

Arthur Hernandez
Texas A & M University
College Station, Texas

E. Valerie Hewitt
Texas A & M University
College Station, Texas

Julia A. Hickman
Bastrop Mental Health Association
Bastrop, Texas

Craig S. Higgins
Stonehill College
North Easton, Massachusetts

Alan Hilton
Seattle University
Seattle, Washington

Delores J. Hittinger
The University of Texas of the
  Permian Basin
Odessa, Texas

Harold E. Hoff, Jr.
Eastern Pennsylvania Special
  Education
  Resources Center
King of Prussia, Pennsylvania

Elizabeth Holcomb
American Journal of
  Occupational Therapy
Bethesda, Maryland

E. Wayne Holden
University of Oklahoma Health
  Sciences Center
Norman, Ohlahoma

Ivan Z. Holowinsky
Rutgers University
New Brunswick, New Jersey

Thomas F. Hopkins
Center for Behavioral Psychotherapy
White Plains, New York

Wayne P. Hresko
Journal of Learning Disabilities
Austin, Texas

Charles A. Hughes
Pennsylvania State University
University Park, Pennsylvania

Jan N. Hughes
Texas A & M University
College Station, Texas

Kay E. Hughes
The Riverside Publishing Company
Itasca, Illinois

Aimee Hunter
University of North Carolina
Wilmington, North Carolina

Nancy L. Hutchinson
Simon Fraser University
Buraby, British Columbia

Beverly J. Irby
Sam Houston State University
Texas

Paul Irvine
Katonah, New York

Lee Anderson Jackson, Jr.
University of North Carolina
Wilmington, North Carolina

Markku Jahnukainen
University of Helsinki
Finland

Diane Jarvis
State University of New York
Buffalo, New York

Phillip Jenkins
University of Kentucky
Lexington, Kentucky

Elizabeth Jones
Texas A & M University
College Station, Texas

Gideon Jones
Florida State University
Tallahassee, Florida

Philip R. Jones
Virginia Polytechnic Institute
  and State University
Blacksburg, Virginia

Shirley A. Jones
Virginia Polytechnic Institute
  and State University
Blacksburg, Virginia

James W. Kalat
North Carolina State University
Raleigh, North Carolina

Maya Kalyanpur
Towson University
Towson, Maryland

Randy W. Kamphaus
University of Georgia
Athens, Georgia

Harrison Kane
University of Florida
Gainesville, Florida

Stan A. Karcz
University of Wisconsin at Stout
Menomonie, Wisconsin

Maribeth Montgomery Kasik
Governors State University
University Park, Illinois

Alan S. Kaufman
Yale University School of Medicine
New Haven, Connecticut

James Kaufman
Yale University
New Haven, Connecticut

Nancy J. Kaufman
University of Wisconsin
Stevens Point, Wisconsin

Kenneth A. Kavale
University of Iowa
Iowa City, Iowa

Hortencia Kayser
New Mexico State University
Las Cruces, New Mexico

Forrest E. Keesbury
Lycoming College
Williamsport, Pennsylvania

Barbara Keogh
University of California
Los Angeles, California

Kay E. Ketzenberger
The University of Texas of the
  Permian Basin
Odessa, Texas

Peggy Kipling
Pro-Ed, Inc.
Austin, Texas

Gonul Kircaali-Iftar
Anadolu University
Turkey

Margie K. Kitano
New Mexico State University
Las Cruces, New Mexico

F. J. Koopmans-Van Beinum
Amsterdam, The Netherlands

Mark A. Koorland
Florida State University
Tallahassee, Florida

L. Koulischer
Institut de Morphologie Pathologique
Belgium

Martin Kozloff
University of North Carolina
Wilmington, North Carolina

Howard M. Knoff
University of South Florida
Tampa, Florida

Thomas R. Kratochwill
University of Wisconsin
Madison, Wisconsin

James P. Krouse
Clarion University of Pennsylvania
Clarion, Pennsylvania

Louis J. Kruger
Tufts University
Medford, Pennsylvania

Timothy D. Lackaye
Hunter College, City University
  of New York
New York, New York

C. Sue Lamb
University of North Carolina
Wilmington, North Carolina

Nadine M. Lambert
University of California
Berkeley, California

Louis J. LaNunziata
University of North Carolina
Wilmington, North Carolina

Rafael Lara-Alecio
Texas A & M University
College Station, Texas

Franco Larocca
The University of Verona
Italy

Jeff Laurent
University of Texas
Austin, Texas

Samuel LeBaron
University of Texas Health
  Science Center
San Antonio, Texas

Yvan Lebrun
School of Medicine
Brussels, Belgium

Linda Leeper
New Mexico State University
Las Cruces, New Mexico

Ronald S. Lenkowsky
Hunter College, City University
  of New York
New York, New York

Mary Louise Lennon
Educational Testing Service
Princeton, New Jersey

Richard Levak
California School of
  Professional Psychology
San Diego, California

Allison Lewis
University of North Carolina
Wilmington, North Carolina

Collette Leyva
Texas A & M University
College Station, Texas

Elizabeth Lichtenberger
The Salk Institute
La Jolla, California

Ping Lin
Elmhurst College
Elmhurst, Illinois

Ken Linfoot
University of Western Sydney
Australia

Janet A. Lindow
University of Wisconsin
Madison, Wisconsin

Daniel D. Lipka
Lincoln Way Special Education
  Regional Resources Center
Louisville, Ohio

Cornelia Lively
University of Illinois,
  Urbana-Champaign
Champaign, Illinois

Jeri Logemann
Northwestern University
Evanston, Illinois

Charles J. Long
University of Memphis
Memphis, Tennessee

Linda R. Longley
University of North Carolina
Wilmington, North Carolina

Emilia C. Lopez
Fordham University
New York, New York

Patricia Lowe
Texas A & M University
College Station, Texas

Marsha H. Lupi
Hunter College, City University
  of New York
New York, New York

Ann E. Lupkowski
Texas A & M University
College Station, Texas

Pat Lynch
Texas A & M University
College Station, Texas

Philip E. Lyon
College of St. Rose
Albany, New York

Charles A. MacArthur
University of Maryland
College Park, Maryland

John MacDonald
Eastern Kentucky University
Richmond, Kentucky

Taddy Maddox
Pro Ed, Inc.
Austin, Texas

Ghislain Magerotte
Mons State University
Mons, Belgium

Susan Mahanna-Boden
Eastern Kentucky University
Richmond, Kentucky

Charles A. Maher
Rutgers University
Piscataway, New Jersey

Elba Maldonado-Colon
San Jose State University
San Jose, California

David C. Mann
St. Francis Hospital
Pittsburgh, Pennsylvania

Douglas L. Mann
V. A. Medical Center, Medical
  University of South Carolina
Charleston, South Carolina

Lester Mann
Hunter College, City University
  of New York
New York, New York

Donald S. Marozas
State University of New York
Geneseo, New York

Ellen B. Marriott
University of North Carolina
Wilmington, North Carolina

Tamara Martin
The University of Texas of the
  Permian Basin
Odessa, Texas

Patrick Mason
The Hughes Spalding International
  Adoption Evaluation Center
Georgia

Margo A. Mastropieri
Purdue University
Lafayette, Indiana

Deborah C. May
State University of New York
Albany, New York

Joan W. Mayfield
Baylor Pediatric Specialty Service
Dallas, Texas

Liliana Mayo
Centro Ann Sullivan
Peru

James K. McAfee
Pennsylvania State University
King of Prussia, Pennsylvania

Eileen F. McCarthy
University of Wisconsin
Madison, Wisconsin

Elizabeth McClellan
Council for Exceptional Children
Reston, Virginia

George McCloskey
The Psychological Corporation
San Antonio, Texas

Laura S. McCorkle
Texas A & M University
College Station, Texas

Linda McCormick
University of Hawaii, Manoa
Honolulu, Hawaii

Paul A. McDermott
University of Pennsylvania
Philadelphia, Pennsylvania

Phillip J. McLaughlin
University of Georgia
Athens, Georgia

James A. McLoughlin
University of Louisville
Louisville, Kentucky

Paolo Meazzini
University of Rome
Rome, Italy

Frederic J. Medway
University of South Carolina
Columbia, South Carolina

Brenda Melvin
New Hanover Regional
    Medical Center
Wilmington, North Carolina

James F. Merritt
University of North Carolina
Wilmington, North Carolina

Judith Meyers
San Diego, California

Danielle Michaux
Vrije Universiteit Brussel
Brussels, Belgium

Jennifer Might
University of North Carolina
Wilmington, North Carolina

Stephen Miles
Immune Deficiency Foundation
Towson, Maryland

James H. Miller
University of New Orleans
New Orleans, Louisiana

Ted L. Miler
University of Tennessee
Chattanooga, Tennessee

Norris Minick
Center for Psychosocial Studies
The Spencer Foundation
Chicago, Illinois

Anjali Misra
State University of New York
Potsdam, New York

Lisa Monda
Florida State University
Tallahassee, Florida

Linda Montgomery
The University of Texas of the
    Permian Basin
Odessa, Texas

Richard J. Morris
University of Arizona
Tucson, Arizona

Lonny W. Morrow
Northeast Missouri State University
Kirksville, Missouri

Sue Ann Morrow
EDGE, Inc.
Bradshaw, Michigan

Elias Mpofu
University of Zimbabwe
Harare, Zimbabwe

Tracy Muenz
California School of
    Professional Psychology
San Diego, California

Mary Murray
Journal of Special Education
Ben Salem, Pennsylvania

Jack Naglieri
Ohio State University
Columbus, Ohio

Sigamoney Naicker
Western Cape Educational
    SI Department
South Africa

Michael Nall
Louisville, Kentucky

Robert T. Nash
University of Wisconsin
Oshkosh, Wisconsin

Bonnie K. Nastasi
Kent State University
Kent, Ohio

Joyce Ness
Montgomery County
    Intermediate Unit
Norristown, Pennsylvania

Ulrika Nettelbladt
University of Lund
Sweden

Robert C. Nichols
State University of New York
Buffalo, New York

Etta Lee Nurick
Montgomery County
    Intermediate Unit
Norristown, Pennsylvania

Thomas Oakland
University of Florida
Gainesville, Florida

Festus E. Obiakor
Emporia State University
Nigeria

Masataka Ohta
Tokyo Gakujei University
Tokyo, Japan

John O'Neill
Hunter College, City University
    of New York
New York, New York

Alba Ortiz
University of Texas
Austin, Texas

Andrew Oseroff
Florida State University
Tallahassee, Florida

Lawrence J. O'Shea
University of Florida
Gainesville, Florida

Doris Paez
New Mexico State University
Las Cruces, New Mexico

Ellis B. Page
Duke University
Durham, North Carolina

Kathleen D. Paget
University of South Carolina
Columbia, South Carolina

Douglas J. Palmer
Texas A & M University
College Station, Texas

Hagop S. Pambookian
Elizabeth City, North Carolina

Ernest L. Pancsofar
University of Connecticut
Storrs, Connecticut

Sara Pankaskie
Florida State University
Tallahassee, Florida

Linda H. Parish
Texas A & M University
College Station, Texas

Daniel R. Paulson
University of Wisconsin at Stout
Menomonie, Wisconsin

Nils A. Pearson
Pro-Ed, Inc.
Austin, Texas

Mary Leon Peery
Texas A & M University
College Station, Texas

Olivier Périer
Université Libre de Bruxelles
Centre Comprendre et Parler
Brussels, Belgium

Joseph D. Perry
Kent State University
Kent, Ohio

Richard G. Peters
Ball State University
Muncie, Indiana

Faith L. Phillips
University of Oklahoma
Health Science Center
Norman, Oklahoma

Jeffry L. Phillips
University of North Carolina
Wilmington, North Carolina

Yongxin Piao
Beijing Normal University
Beijing, China

Sip Jan Pijl
Gion University of Groningen
Groningen, The Netherlands

John J. Pikulski
University of Delaware
Newark, Delaware

Sally E. Pisarchick
Cuyahoga Special Education
Service Center
Maple Heights, Ohio

Brenda M. Pope
New Hanover Memorial Hospital
Wilmington, North Carolina

John E. Porcella
Rhinebeck County School
Rhinebeck, New York

James A. Poteet
Ball State University
Muncie, Indiana

David P. Prasse
University of Wisconsin
Milwaukee, Wisconsin

Marianne Price
Montgomery County
Intermediate Unit
Norristown, Pennsylvania

Elisabeth A. Prinz
Pennsylvania State University
University Park, Pennsylvania

Philip M. Prinz
Pennsylvania State University
University Park, Pennsylvania

Antonio E. Puente
University of North Carolina
Wilmington, North Carolina

Krista L. Puente
University of North Carolina
Wilmington, North Carolina

Nuri Puig
University of Oklahoma
Norman, Oklahoma

Craig T. Ramey
University of North Carolina
Chapel Hill, North Carolina

Sylvia Z. Ramirez
University of Texas
Austin, Texas

Arlene I. Rattan
Ball State University
Muncie, Indiana

Gurmal Rattan
Indiana University of Pennsylvania
Indiana, Pennsylvania

Anne Reber
Texas A & M University
College Station, Texas

Robert R. Reilley
Private Practice
Atlanta, Georgia

Fredricka K. Reisman
Drexel University
Philadelphia, Pennsylvania

Kimberly M. Rennie
Texas A & M University
College Station, Texas

Daniel J. Reschly
Vanderbilt University
Nashville, Tennessee

Cecil R. Reynolds
Texas A & M University
College Station, Texas

Robert Rhodes
New Mexico State Unviersity
Las Cruces, New Mexico

William S. Rholes
Texas A & M University
College Station, Texas

James R. Ricciuti
United States Office of
Management and Budget
Washington, DC

Teresa K. Rice
Texas A & M University
College Station, Texas

Paul C. Richardson
Elwyn Institutes
Elwyn, Pennsylvania

Sylvia O. Richardson
University of South Florida
Tampa, Florida

Pamela Richman
University of North Carolina
Wilmington, North Carolina

Bert O. Richmond
University of Georgia
Athens, Georgia

Catherine Hall Rikhye
Hunter College, City University
of New York
New York, New York

Gary J. Robertson
American Guidance Service
Circle Pines, Minnesota

Kathleen Rodden-Nord
University of Oregon
Eugene, Oregon

Jean A. Rondal
Laboratory for Language,
Psychology, and Logopedics
University of Liege
Liege, Belgium

Sheldon Rosenberg
University of Illinois
Chicago, Illinois

Bruce P. Rosenthal
State University of New York
New York, New York

Kathy L. Ruhl
Pennsylvania State University
University Park, Pennsylvania

Joseph M. Russo
Hunter College, City University
of New York
New York, New York

Robert B. Rutherford, Jr.
Arizona State University
Tempe, Arizona

Anne Sabatino
Hudson, Wisconsin

David A. Sabatino
West Virginia College of
Graduate Studies
Institute, West Virginia

Lisa J. Sampson
Eastern Kentucky University
Richmond, Kentucky

Alfred Sander
Universitat des Saarlandes
Saarbruecken, Germany

Polly E. Sanderson
Research Triangle Institute
Research Triangle Park,
North Carolina

Scott W. Sautter
Peabody College, Vanderbilt
University
Nashville, Tennessee

Robert F. Sawicki
Lake Erie Institute of Rehabilitation
Lake Erie, Pennsylvania

Patrick J. Schloss
Pennsylvania State University
University Park, Pennsylvania

Ronald V. Schmelzer
Eastern Kentucky University
Richmond, Kentucky

Carol S. Schmitt
Eastern Kentucky University
Richmond, Kentucky

Sue A. Schmitt
University of Wisconsin at Stout
Menomonie, Wisconsin

Lyle F. Schoenfeldt
Texas A & M University
College Station, Texas

Eric Schopler
University of North Carolina
Chapel Hill, North Carolina

Fredrick Schrank
The Riverside Publishing Company
Itasca, Illinois

Louis Schwartz
Florida State University
Tallahassee, Florida

June Scobee
University of Houston, Clear Lake
Houston, Texas

Thomas E. Scruggs
Purdue University
Lafayette, Indiana

Denise M. Sedlak
United Way of Dunn County
Menomonie, Wisconsin

Robert A. Sedlak
University of Wisconsin at Stout
Menomonie, Wisconsin

John D. See
University of Wisconsin at Stout
Menomonie, Wisconsin

Sandra B. Sexton
Emory University School of Medicine
Atlanta, Georgia

Susan Shandelmier
Eastern Pennsylvania Special
Education Regional Resources
Center
King of Prussia, Pennsylvania

Alison Shaner
University of North Carolina
Wilmington, North Carolina

Deborah A. Shanley
Medgar Evers College, City
University of New York
New York, New York

William J. Shaw
University of Oklahoma
Norman, Oklahoma

Susan M. Sheridan
University of Wisconsin
Madison, Wisconsin

Naoji Shimizu
Tokyo Gakujei University
Tokyo, Japan

Ludmila Shipitsina
International University for
Family and Child
Russia

Edward Shirkey
New Mexico State University
Las Cruces, New Mexico

Dakum Shown
University of Jos
Nigeria

Lawrence J. Siegel
University of Texas Medical Branch
Galveston, Texas

Rosanne K. Silberman
Hunter College, City University
  of New York
New York, New York

Lissen Simonsen
University of North Carolina
Wilmington, North Carolina

Paul T. Sindelar
Florida State University
Tallahassee, Florida

Jerry L. Sloan
Wilmington Psychiatric Associates
Wilmington, North Carolina

Julie E. Smart
Utah State University
Logan, Utah

Craig D. Smith
Georgia College
Milledgeville, Georgia

Maureen A. Smith
Pennsylvania State University
University Park, Pennsylvania

Judy Smith-Davis
Counterpoint Communications
  Company
Reno, Nevada

Jane Sparks
University of North Carolina
Wilmington, North Carolina

Barbara S. Speer
Shaker Heights City School District
Shaker Heights, Ohio

Harrison C. Stanton
Private Practice
Las Vegas, Nevada

J. Todd Stephens
University of Wisconsin
Madison, Wisconsin

Cecelia Steppe-Jones
North Carolina Central University
Durham, North Carolina

Linda J. Stevens
University of Minnesota
Minneapolis, Minnesota

Rachael J. Stevenson
Bedford, Ohio

Mary E. Stinson
University of Alabama
University, Alabama

Roberta C. Stokes
Texas A & M University
College Station, Texas

Doretha McKnight Stone
University of North Carolina
Wilmington, North Carolina

Laura M. Stough
Texas A & M University
College Station, Texas

Michael L. Stowe
Texas A & M University
College Station, Texas

Edythe A. Strand
University of Wisconsin
Madison, Wisconsin

Elaine Stringer
University of North Carolina
Wilmington, North Carolina

Dorothy A. Strom
Ball State University
Indiana School of Medicine
Muncie, Indiana

Sheela Stuart
Georgia Washington University
Washington, DC

Sue Stubbs
Save the Children Fund
London, England

Kathryn A. Sullivan
Texas A & M University
College Station, Texas

Shelley Suntup
California School of
  Professional Psychology
San Diego, California

Emily G. Sutter
University of Houston, Clear Lake
Houston, Texas

Mark E. Swerdlik
Illinois State University
Normal, Illinois

Henri B. Szliwowski
Hôpital Erasme, Université Libre
  de Bruxelles
Brussels, Belgium

Pearl E. Tait
Florida State University
Tallahassee, Florida

Paula Tallal
University of California
San Diego, California

Mary K. Tallent
Texas Tech University
Lubbock, Texas

C. Mildred Tashman
College of St. Rose
Albany, New York

James W. Tawney
Pennsylvania State University
University Park, Pennsylvania

Ellen A. Teelucksingh
University of Minnesota
Minneapolis, Minnesota

Cathy F. Telzrow
Kent State University
Kent, Ohio

Spencer Thompson
The University of Texas of the
  Permian Basin
Odessa, Texas

Steven R. Timmermans
Mary Free Bed Hospital and
  Rehabilitation Center
Grand Rapids, Michigan

Gerald Tindal
University of Oregon
Eugene, Oregon

Francine Tomkins
University of Cincinnati
Cincinnati, Ohio

Carol Tomlinson-Keasey
University of California
Riverside, California

Bruce Thompson
Texas A & M University
College Station, Texas

Raymond Toraille
Public Education
Paris, France

Jose Luis Torres
Texas A & M University
College Station, Texas

Stanley O. Trent
University of Virginia
Charlottesville, Virginia

Timothy L. Turco
Louisiana State University
Baton Rouge, Louisiana

Lori E. Unruh
Eastern Kentucky University
Richmond, Kentucky

Cynthia Vail
Florida State University
Tallahassee, Florida

Greg Valcante
University of Florida
Tallahassee, Florida

Hubert B. Vance
East Tennessee State University
Johnson City, Tennessee

Aryan Van Der Leij
Free University
Amsterdam, The Netherlands

K. Sandra Vanta
Cleveland Public Shools
Cleveland, Ohio

Don Viglione
California School of
    Professional Psychology
San Diego, California

Judith K. Voress
Pro-Ed, Inc.
Austin, Texas

Emily Wahlen
Hunter College, City University
    of New York
New York, New York

Deborah Klein Walker
Harvard University
Cambridge, Massachusetts

Donna Wallace
The University of Texas of the
    Permian Basin
Odessa, Texas

Raoul Wallenberg
International University for
    Family and Child
Russia

Marjorie E. Ward
The Ohio State University
Columbus, Ohio

Sue Allen Warren
Boston University
Boston, Massachusetts

John Wasserman
The Riverside Publishing Company
Itasca, Illinois

Lauren Webster
University of North Carolina
Wilmington, North Carolina

Danny Wedding
Marshall University
Huntington, Virginia

Frederick F. Weiner
Pennsylvania State University
University Park, Pennsylvania

Marjorie Weintraub
Montgomery County
    Intermediate Unit
Norristown, Pennylvania

Bahr Weiss
University of North Carolina
Chapel Hill, North Carolina

Shirley Parker Wells
University of North Carolina
Wilmington, North Carolina

Louise H. Werth
Florida State University
Tallahassee, Florida

Catherine Wetzburger
Université Libre de Bruxelles
Brussels, Belgium

Larry J. Wheeler
Southwest Texas State University
San Marcos, Texas

Susie Whitman
Immune Deficiency Foundation
Towson, Maryland

Thomas M. Whitten
Florida State University
Tallahassee, Florida

J. Lee Wiederholt
Pro-Ed, Inc.
Austin, Texas

Saul B. Wilen
Medical Horizons Unlimited
San Antonio, Texas

Greta N. Wilkening
Children's Hospital
Denver, Colorado

Mary Clare Williams
Ramey, Pennsylvania

Diane J. Willis
University of Oklahoma Health
Sciences Center
Oklahoma City, Oklahoma

Victor L. Willson
Texas A & M University
College Station, Texas

John D. Wilson
Elwyn Institutes
Elwyn, Pennsylvania

Margo E. Wilson
Lexington, Kentucky

Joseph C. Witt
Louisiana State University
Baton Rouge, Louisiana

Bencie Woll
University of Bristol
Bristol, England

Bernice Y. L.Wong
Simon Fraser University
Buraby, British Columbia

Mary M. Wood
University of Georgia
Athens, Georgia

Diane E. Woods
World Rehabilitation Fund
New York, New York

Frances F. Worchel
Florida State University
Tallahassee, Florida

Eleanor Boyd Wright
University of North Carolina
Wilmington, North Carolina

Logan Wright
University of Oklahoma
Norman, Oklahoma

Karen F. Wyche
Hunter College, City University
of New York
New York, New York

Martha Ellen Wynne
Loyola University of Chicago
Chicago, Illinois

James E. Ysseldyke
University of Minnesota
Minneapolis, Minnesota

Roland K. Yoshida
Fordham University
New York, New York

Thomas Zane
Johns Hopkins University
Baltimore, Maryland

Lonnie K. Zeltzer
University of Texas Health
  Science Center
San Antonio, Texas

Paul M. Zeltzer
University of Texas Health
  Science Center
San Antonio, Texas

Kenneth A. Zych
Walter Reed Army Medical Center
Washington, DC

FOREWORD

After Cecil Reynolds and Elaine Fletcher-Janzen asked me to write the foreword for the second edition of the *Encyclopedia of Special Education,* I reread the original foreword, which was written in 1987 by Samuel A. Kirk. Dr. Kirk is regarded by most professionals as the "Father of Special Education," and I had the honor of working with him at the University of Arizona. I share his strong feelings about the value of special education and this encyclopedia. Although Dr. Kirk is deceased, the ideas he expressed in the original foreword are still true; thus I chose to retain most of his original text in this edition.

The creation of the *Encyclopedia of Special Education* represented the coming of age for a field of endeavor that not so many years ago drew little public interest or concern, both in society at large and within education in particular. Those of us who served in special education during its earlier years, when public commitment to its needs was minimal or even lacking, cannot help but be pleased with, and astonished at, the vast enterprise it has now become.

Special education has developed very gradually over the past 160 years. From approximately 1850 to 1900, the care, management, and education of children with disabilities was conducted primarily in facilities sponsored by religious organizations or in residential institutions for the deaf, the blind, the mentally deficient, and the delinquent. From 1900 to approximately 1950, public schools in large cities began to educate both gifted children and a small percentage of children with disabilities. After 1950, some states began providing subsidies to local public schools to encourage the establishment of special education and to decrease the demands made on overcrowded and dilapidated state residential schools. During this period, the federal government offered no financial assistance to the states, believing that education was a state responsibility and that federal aid would lead to federal control of education.

Later in the decade, the precedent of denying federal aid was discarded. Parents began to organize and demand services and funding for their children with disabilities—not just at the state level, but at the federal level as well. President Eisenhower responded by asking Congress to provide assistance, and Congress appropriated several million dollars to be used for research and for the preparation of professional personnel.

The major expansion and social revolution within special education came in the 1960s during the administration of John F. Kennedy, who dispatched task forces to various countries to survey their programs for children with disabilities. After hearing the task force reports, he presented Congress with a comprehensive research and training bill, the Mental Retardation Facilities and Community Mental Health Centers Construction Act of 1963, which was followed by a number of congressional acts that encompassed many different kinds of services. In 1975, Congress enacted P.L. 94-142, The Education for All Handicapped Children Act. Interestingly, the wording of this act follows the language of the United States Declaration of Independence. It has been paraphrased as follows:

> We hold these truths to be self-evident, that all children, handicapped and nonhandicapped, are created equal; that they are endowed by their creator with certain inalienable rights, among these are the right to equal education to the maximum of each child's capability. To secure these rights, Public Law 94-142 was established. We, the people of these United States, solemnly declare that all exceptional children shall be educated at public expense, and that their education will be in the least restrictive environment. (Kirk & Gallagher, *Educating Exceptional Children,* 3rd ed. 1979, xi)

During the following years, Congress and US presidents continued to pass legislation and provide additional funds to states, universities, colleges, and local education agencies. The most recent legislation—the Individuals with Disabilities Education Act Amendments of 1997 (P.L. 105-17), signed by President Clinton—recognized that most students with disabilities now spend most or all of their time in general education classrooms. Provisions included in these amendments specified that general education teachers participate in the creation of Individual Education Programs (IEPs) for students identified with disabilities.

It is particularly gratifying to see that a major public commitment has been made to special education for students with exceptionalities in the United States and throughout much of the world. This is true not only in Canada and western Europe (where achievements in many areas of special education service often preceded and inspired those in the United States) but also in Japan, Indonesia, and other less advanced and less affluent parts of the globe, all of which are represented in this encyclopedia. Worldwide, concerned professionals and parents have sought to provide for the education of children and youth with disabilities, often in spite of extremely limited resources.

This growth in special education, and the extraordinary commitment of financial and human resources to service and research over the past two decades, has meant an explosion of information scattered throughout a wide variety of journals and books. Thus, even with all the advances in media technology, professionals find it very difficult to obtain the information they need. Despite the contributions of abstracting services, databases, reviews, and handbooks to managing the special education knowledge base, coherent control and accessibility are still issues for professionals in related fields and interested lay persons.

The original *Encyclopedia of Special Education* was designed to present a comprehensive picture of special education in a readily understandable, usable, and summative form. The editors have successfully updated and expanded the award-winning first edition while continuing to preserve the original goals of clarity and completeness. By using it, individuals seeking special education information are able to understand both the broad scope of the field and also the detailed areas of endeavor within it. Comprehensive yet succinct, the *Encyclopedia* literally provides an A

to Z examination of special education. Furthermore, it does so through well-written explanations devoid of unnecessary detail. The *Encyclopedia* offers a scope and view of special education not readily obtained from other sources. In addition, the issuance of this second edition comes at a most propitious time, because special education has now taken innovative directions that are likely to continue well into the next century.

This work has become an essential reference tool, not only for professionals in special education, but also for lawyers, physicians, psychologists, social workers, school board members, and others who assist in or formulate policies for the education of individuals with disabilities and gifted persons. Its ultimate usefulness may be in its utility for the lay person, however: When all is said and done, it is informed citizens who are the guardians of special education. The *Encyclopedia of Special Education* has found a niche in many libraries—public, college, and professional. Dr. Cecil Reynolds and Dr. Elaine Fletcher-Janzen and their consulting editors should be congratulated for taking the time and effort to compile this gargantuan encyclopedia.

J. LEE WIEDERHOLT, EdD
President, Donald D. Hammill Foundation

PREFACE TO SECOND EDITION

The first edition of the *Encyclopedia of Special Education* was originally conceived to be a primary reference for many disciplines and professionals concerned with both the education of exceptional children and their special characteristics, needs, and problems. It was hoped that the *Encyclopedia* would serve as a desktop reference containing essential information for educators, psychologists, physicians, social workers, lawyers, ministers, and occupational, physical, and speech therapists. The *Encyclopedia* was also intended to be used by lay persons such as parents of exceptional children, school board members, advocates of handicapped persons, legislators, and other concerned individuals seeking to be more knowledgeable about the education of exceptional children.

The latter description turned out to be exactly how the *Encyclopedia* has been used over the past decade. There is always a need for a place to start researching a topic at hand and always a need for an in-depth reference point. The *Encyclopedia* entries were designed to define a subject, relate the history of the subject, explain the research and treatment of the subject in an objective manner, and relate the body of knowledge to everyday special education practices. This format hopefully leaves the reader with a solid overview of the subject and how research translates into practice. The references at the end of each entry help the reader explore the basis for the entry and direct the reader to further research. As with the first edition, the use of technical language was maintained at a minimum to maximize the readability of the text.

There are over two thousand entries in the second edition. They can be categorized much the same as the first edition: biographies, educational and psychological tests, interventions and service delivery, handicapping conditions, related services, legal, and miscellaneous. The miscellaneous grouping of entries has grown in the second edition, probably due to the addition of many more entries on subjects such as rare or orphan diseases, internet resources, and cultural perspectives on different subjects.

The number of staff members and contributors for the second edition is considerably smaller than that of the first edition. This was intentional. The first edition used over 400 authors, and even with the expertise of a large board of contributing and consulting editors, there was some redundancy and inconsistency in writing level and style. The board of consulting editors for the second edition consisted of seven individuals with extensive experience in both the field of special education and related fields. The consulting editors had considerably fewer authors writing for them. In addition, approximately half of the second edition was updated by the volume editors themselves. All in all, this arrangement changed the flow of the second edition into a tight, quality-controlled format.

As with the first edition, we hope that the *Encyclopedia* will serve in many functions:

1. a source of basic, summative information
2. a basic spot reference
3. a textbook
4. a continuing information-support system.

The second edition has changed, obviously, to reflect the times and preparation for the next century. Our experience of editing the first and second editions has given us a unique perspective on how special education has grown in the past fifteen years: A chance to look back and see what plans came to fruition, what promises were kept, and what developments were unforeseen. The following are some reflections on how the second edition is different in substance from the first edition:

1) Cultural competence: It is now mandatory that individuals involved in special education have training in cultural awareness and are working on the process of becoming culturally competent. This includes all special education (and regular education) personnel and materials. The terms "multicultural" and "minority" have been replaced with "culturally and linguistically diverse." This change reflects the huge increases in the Spanish-speaking school population and the recognition that "ethnicity" and "culture" are not synonymous terms. Cultural awareness does not denote competency; therefore, teacher training programs have included more than cursory introductions to working with diverse students and curricula. School psychologists can no longer receive certification and licensure that do not include competency in evaluating, developing, and interpreting tests that are culturally sensitive. Legislation and regulations about special education continue to ad-

dress cultural issues of long standing such as the underrepresentation of ethnic minorities in gifted programs and the overrepresentation of ethnic minorities in programming for mental retardation and behavior disorders, and newer issues such as the implementation of part H of the Individuals with Disabilities Education Act and culturally appropriate familial partnerships. The school population is changing rapidly, and special education is reflecting an appreciation of the diversity in a meaningful way.

2) Service delivery: The continuum of service delivery in special education has changed considerably in the past fifteen years. The first edition of the *Encyclopedia* discussed Deno's Cascade of Services and mainstreaming, and the second edition covers the evolution of the Regular Education Initiative into the Inclusion movement. As with all new ideas, there are extremists who insist on full inclusion for all special education students, extremists who refuse to embrace inclusion at all, and the moderate majority who are beginning to connect the individualistic nosology of recent IDEA amendments with including special education students based on the least restrictive placement mandate. Our only cause for concern with the Inclusion movement, however well-intentioned, is that it was brought about and put into operation in the public schools without pilot projects or the benefit of objective scientific evidence. Good ideas and moral thoughts are not enough for the basis of a revolution in service delivery. We hope that serious mistakes were not made with the education of so many children by good intentions. As we speak, there is still a scarcity of well-controlled studies to document the effectiveness of inclusion. This is somewhat ironic while another major change in special education is in full swing: the call for accountability.

3) Accountability: Accountability of programs has been another new movement in the 1990s. Federal legislation calls for accountability and, therefore, assessments of special education students focus on outcome. The field is no longer interested in the material that goes into the teaching process: Special education is interested in measuring student performance. Curriculum-based assessment and other alternative assessments are popular and indicative of this movement, but also fail to meet the test of research to back up their intuitively appealing claims.

4) Expansion of services: Special education services have expanded considerably since the first edition. Part H of IDEA spells out a considerable program of services for infants and toddlers, and Part B supports the three- to five-year-old students and their transition into kindergarten. All of these services must now actively involve the parents and/or family of the child to ensure support and generalization across settings.

5) The internet: The impact of the World Wide Web on special education has been considerable. The number of well-controlled and designed web sites that disseminate information about handicapping conditions, organizations, medical information, interactive groups, and research continues to grow. The average special education teacher or parent of an exceptional child can gain support and information about virtually any topic related to special education. Indeed, most special educators can now write an Individual Education Plan on a template and paste or insert objectives from extensive state or federal databases into the document. In fact, most special education files are computerized, which has led to a set of guidelines for handling electronic documentation. The dissemination of information from web sites such as the U.S. Department of Education, Deaf World Web, Educational Administration, and databases such as ERIC means that information is current and interactive. Such sources are powerful tools for special education.

There have been other salient events in the field as well. There have been many foreign adoptions in the past fifteen years, especially from eastern Europe. It has given us the opportunity to study the results of early deprivation in new ways. Unfortunately, the results of deprivation are faced by adoptive parents in the United States, who become all too aware of the sequelae of deprivation and the special education services needed to assist. The field is finding out more and more about rare diseases and databases on them are being developed. The growth of the internet has helped the spread of information about rare diseases, and has helped many families and professionals needing discourse.

James Flynn and others are tying to figure out why IQs have been increasing consistently for the past several decades. Different theories are being posed, such as improvements in nutrition, test sophistication, and cultural complexity. The debate on these phenomena will surely continue and be very interesting.

Attention-deficit/hyperactivity disorder has gained a place in the Other Health Impaired category of exceptionality. The incidence and prevalence of this disorder has caused much research and concern.

Traumatic Brain Injury (TBI) has gained its own place in an eligibility category for special services. The unique needs of TBI students were recognized legislatively in the 1990s. Unfortunately, the advent of managed care involvement in the restriction of services for TBI students means that TBI patients are often discharged from rehabilitation hospitals prematurely and left to seek out ad hoc services locally. Further, this means that school systems are encountering TBI students much earlier in their recovery and are far less prepared to manage the complex demands of TBI recovery.

Technology for the handicapped is currently in its heyday. Apart from access to the internet, software companies have revolutionized access to information and expression for the deaf, blind, and individuals with multiple handicaps. This accessibility has increased communication within exceptionalities and has contributed to the solidarity of deaf culture, blind athletes, and many more.

In terms of format for the second edition, for all entries that were written by the consulting editors and their teams, the first edition entry author's name was kept at the end of each entry. The second edition's author placed his or her name with the first edition author if the entry was just updated. Of course, if the entry needed complete revision, the second edition author name was placed by itself. For all of the other entries, we updated them ourselves. All entries that only have the first edition's author name at the end were reviewed and additions and deletions were made accordingly by the volume editors. We apologize to our first edition authors if we changed the intent of their work for the second edition. However, it was important that all work in this text be current and applicable to today's special education.

Over 200 entries in the second edition are completely new. Approximately 5 percent of the first edition entries were deleted because they were obsolete or redundant. Nearly 700 entries were updated or rewritten by the consulting editors and their teams. Over 300 biographies, journals, and organizations were updated and approximately 120 "See" entries were reviewed for better cross-referencing. The second edition, although not seminal, was still a massive project and therefore requires our thanks to many individuals. We would like to thank our contributing editors:

Bob Brown (University of North Carolina–Wilmington) for his experience in editing and for his breadth and depth of knowledge in the field of special education. Bob's entries for the first edition were superb and the culmination of his years of experience, insight, and humanism is evident in these volumes.

Jan Hasbrouck and Rich Parker (Texas A&M University) for their coverage of culturally and linguistically diverse and international students. This perspective is central to the updating of the *Encyclopedia* and is well represented.

Donald Hammill (Pro-Ed, Inc.) undertook the task of updating and reviewing many new tests and special education materials.

Kay Ketzenberger (University of Texas of the Permian Basin) took on the pursuit of biographees, journal editors, and organizations who had moved or changed their names. Her detective work is legendary!

Liz Lichtenberger (The Salk Institute) tackled the evaluation of many, many current tests and assessment instruments. As an editor, determining which tests were to be deleted, deemed historical, added, and evaluated was a formidable job indeed.

Robert Rhodes (New Mexico State University) gave his editorial perspective on the Speech/Language entries in the *Encyclopedia*. Robert's clarity of thought and organization were truly soothing in the chaos!

Of course, we offer many thanks to all of the authors of both first and second editions for their scholarly contributions and dedication to the field of special education.

There are other individuals who contributed to the *Encyclopedia* one entry at a time. We would like to thank Susie Whitman for her entry on Primary Immune Deficiency Disorder. This entry is the beginning of many articles that Susie will write during her career as a chronic illness counselor and as the mother of Amy, who has bravely managed Primary Immune Deficiency since birth. Krista Biernath, another contributor, is a physician spearheading research about post-institutionalized children at Emory University.

We must also thank Jennifer Simon for her guidance through the knotty problems that come up from time to time. Problems tend to snowball in a work of this size, and Jennifer kept us on the right path.

We do not get tired of thanking our families for their support during our hours away on our never-ending projects. Elaine would like to thank David, Emma, Leif, Win, and Peter for their tolerance and humor during the last mile of the project, especially when the computer blew up(!). Cecil continues to be appreciative of Julia for her support, tolerance, and guidance through the many briar patches of life he seems destined to discover!

We hope the second edition of the *Encyclopedia of Special Education* is of service to the many individuals in the field who help exceptional children. There have been many changes in the field over the past fifteen years, but some things will always stay the same: There are exceptional children and there are individuals with good will who wish to help them.

CECIL R. REYNOLDS
Texas A&M University

ELAINE FLETCHER-JANZEN
University of Northern Colorado

PREFACE TO FIRST EDITION

Exceptional children, i.e., handicapped or gifted individuals between the ages of birth and 23, constitute (depending on various types of estimation) nearly 10% of children and adolescents who receive educational services throughout the world. The field of endeavor concerned with this education is generally designated as special education.

Special education is a broad domain encompassing many different concerns and types of children. There long has been a need for a publication that provides ready access to authoritative and comprehensive, yet current and succinct, information about this category of education and its many related aspects. The *Encyclopedia of Special Education* is just such a publication. It is intended as a primary reference for many disciplines and professions concerned with the education of exceptional children and with their special characteristics, needs, and problems. The *Encyclopedia* will continue to serve for many years as a desktop reference containing essential information for educators, psychologists, physicians, social workers, occupational and physical therapists, lawyers, and ministers.

The *Encyclopedia of Special Education* is, however, more than just a professional reference book. It also is intended for use by intelligent lay people, including parents, school board members, advocates of handicapped persons' rights, legislators, and concerned citizens seeking to be more knowledgeable about the education of exceptional children. Indeed, as Raymond J. Corsini, editor of the *Encyclopedia of Psychology* (1984) (Wiley-Interscience) wrote in his preface to that valuable reference work, it can be argued that "professionals [themselves] are lay people when not reading in their own specialized field." It was on this basis that he sought to make his encyclopedia "understandable to the average intelligent layperson (Corsini, p. xxi). It is on this basis, too, that we have prepared the *Encyclopedia of Special Education* as a source of authentic and authoritative information expressed with clarity and conciseness. Though technical language is used, the level of presentation was carefully reviewed to achieve this goal of utility and readability.

The preparation of the *Encyclopedia of Special Education* presented many challenges. Among the foremost was the fact that over the past two decades or so, the needs and rights of exceptional children have moved from a position of relative obscurity and neglect to a position in the center of public consciousness and obligation to a degree unanticipated and even inconceivable in earlier generations.

Originally, special education was a small, poorly understood, and underfunded field that attempted to meet the needs of but a few children, first under the rubric of "the education of exceptional children" and then, in recent years, under that of "special education." Over the course of several decades, special education has become a massive multidimensional movement involving many different groups and interests and making important claims on public attention and funding. Thus, the *Encyclopedia of Special Education* has a broad scope. Though it is primarily concerned with the education and training of gifted and handicapped children, it also extends into psychology, medicine, and politics, to mention but a few of the noneducational fields. The inclusion of these fields is critical to an appreciation of special education. Indeed, the *Encyclopedia of Special Education* attempts to touch on all areas and fields deemed relevant to an understanding of what late twentieth century and early twenty-first century special education is about.

The volumes each follow a traditional encyclopedic structure and are organized alphabetically. Each topic is covered succinctly, giving the most crucial information and directing the reader to more extensive treatments of the issues. There are more than two thousand included in the work. Although presented alphabetically, the various entries can be grouped conceptually into seven major catagories.

1. *Biographies*—brief descriptions of key figures in the field, both living and deceased, and their key contributions to special education.

2. *Educational and psychological tests*—brief descriptions and commentary on tests with applications to special education are provided, but more extensive discussions are given of tests with widespread use or with a particularly complex structure. Tests are given under their proper titles and not by acronyms or popular titles. Acronyms are indexed and cross-referenced in most cases for ease of locating information.

3. *Interventions and service delivery*—techniques of intervention and the delivery of special education services to individuals are discussed and reviewed.

4. *Handicapping conditions*—conditions that require special education services are described.

5. *Related services*—services necessary to support the effectiveness of special education but not usually deemed to be special education services per se are described and their relevance to special education noted.

6. *Legal*—major court cases, legislation, and legal concepts related to the field of special education are noted and their implications for special education are reviewed.

7. *Miscellaneous entries*—this category includes special education topics that are not classified under the previous categories but that are substantive and relevant to the field (e.g., measurement terms, prevention projects, major works, journals, professional associations, and terms such as epidemiology, school psychology, vocational counselor, naturalistic observation, and effectiveness of special education).

These categories were derived primarily for the use of editors, consulting editors, and the publisher's staff. However, they are valuable to the users of the *Encyclopedia* as well as they help to locate items of interest. To address such a diverse array of topics and to maintain a balanced view on what can be a controversial field, two groups of advisers were formed: the Board of Consulting Editors, who had important writing and supervisory responsibilities shared with the editors, and the Editorial Advisory Board, professionals who advised the editors, did limited writing, and provided specialty reviewing for a variety of topics. These individuals were chosen to represent a host of theoretical positions, areas of expertise, disciplines (special education, psychology, medicine, speech pathology, physical therapy, educational psychology, and school psychology, to name a few), demographic and ethnic characteristics, and national origins. Practitioners, academicians, administrators, and others are represented here as well. Experts from many disciplines of science, education, politics, and philosophy contributed to the *Encyclopedia*. Each author is credited with a byline at the end of each entry. Those entries listed as authored by Staff were prepared by Elaine Fletcher-Janzen, E. Valerie Hewitt, Angela Baily, and Cecil Reynolds, with the assistance of various sources. Many of these entries are biographies in which the staff was assisted by the biographees. All living biographees were asked to review their entries for factual accuracy; most were extremely helpful and cooperative in this regard.

A great challenge in the creation of the *Encyclopedia of Special Education* was the recognition that special education is a worldwide concern rather than a concern narrowly defined and interpreted in terms of events proceeding within the boundaries of the United States. Fortunately, the *Encyclopedia* was able to draw on the expertise of authorities familiar with the international aspects of special education to assist in providing access to information worldwide about developments relevant to special education.

Still another challenge to the *Encyclopedia of Special Education* was to respond to the historical antecedents and roots of special education as well as to current issues. A significant effort, and a successful one was to ensure that the *Encyclopedia* would provide its users with succinct, pertinent information relative to the foundations of special education in addition to information bearing on its immediate concerns.

Indeed, the *Encyclopedia of Special Education* has gone to great lengths to give all of the aspects of special education their due. It is hoped that the *Encyclopedia* will serve as an efficient and effective aide for practitioners, scientists, parents, and intelligent laypersons alike, and for many years to come. We have been helped in this task by the expert opinions and advice of authorities across a broad range of disciplines. Recommendations for topics to be included in the *Encyclopedia* and opinions about those topics were sought from many experts, going far beyond even the insightful comments of our consulting editors and Editorial Advisory Board. Indexes of all major works in the field were examined, computer searches were conducted, and practitioners in special education were asked their opinion. Reference librarians throughout the United States were consulted. As preparation of the *Encyclopedia* proceeded, further topics were solicited and prepared as late as 2 weeks prior to the publisher's final deadline for submission. Inevitably, something will be missing and we, the editors, accept full responsibility for any such sins of omission.

As a consequence of the broad diversity of sources for the topics suggested, the *Encyclopedia* is an ecumenical work, a manifestation of many divergent streams of thought brought together in a flow of convergent achievement. There are more than 380 contributors all concerned, though often in quite different ways, with the education, training, and management of exceptional individuals. Users of the *Encyclopedia of Special Education* will find that it serves a variety of purposes. The *Encyclopedia* serves the profession and the public:

1. *As a source of basic summative information.* Users of the Encyclopedia of Special Education will find it valuable first and foremost as an immediate source of concise summative information about special education, rehabilitation, and childhood exceptionality; it covers topics in these areas literally from A to Z. The *Encyclopedia*'s information is presented in ways that make it very accessible. Readers seeking information will find it available in quick and easy to comprehend form, whether the information they seek concerns definitions or concepts, theories or histori-

cal personages, critical assessment techniques, issues of intervention techniques employed in special education, laws and regulations, or key projects and key persons. Great effort was made to ensure that the *Encyclopedia*'s entries are as contemporary as possible. In many instances, the *Encyclopedia*'s users will find the information offered on most topics to be sufficient for their purposes. When more extensive information is required, the *Encyclopedia* will guide its users to other sources of information both through cross-references within the *Encyclopedia* itself and to other texts as well.

2. *As a basic spot reference.* A most important use of the *Encyclopedia of Special Education* is to serve as a source for spot references. Using its entries or its extensive index, the user can look up and check out particular topics for names, definitions, and the like. The user can identify other topics related to a particular area and learn quickly how to access them. The *Encyclopedia* is more useful, in many ways, than abstracts or abstract services for tracking down information.

3. *As a textbook.* The *Encyclopedia* is not intended to serve as a primary text for a basic or core course in childhood exceptionality or special education. However, it will serve as a useful supplementary text for almost any course at either undergraduate or graduate levels, serving to amplify the topics in such courses or to extend the knowledge networks of concepts, practices, and research. The *Encyclopedia* also can serve as a primary text for advanced courses or seminars; as such, the student will be left with a set of books that will serve him or her long into a professional career. The *Encyclopedia* also should be helpful to students and scholars who need a concise yet precise guide to information in education, psychology, etc., for review purposes, either for comprehensives or licensure or certification. Graduate students approaching comprehensive exams should find the work useful, especially on their reference shelves as they move ahead toward the practice of special education.

4. *As a continuing information-support system.* Well beyond the immediate needs of knowledge and information, the *Encyclopedia of Special Education* will serve as a source of continuing education for its owners. Regular, even review of its contents will ensure its readers of a deeper understanding relative to special education and related fields. In professional and public libraries, it will serve as a network control system permitting the management of other resources concerning the education of exceptional children.

A project as massive as the *Encyclopedia* requires the joint work of an inordinate number of individuals. To our authors we must offer our first round of thanks. They worked in a timely manner, jovially revising their first efforts in many cases and under tight editorial guidelines. Our Editorial Advisory Board gave excellent advice in reviewing, writing, and generally advising at various stages of the project. All are listed in the front matter. The Board of Consulting Editors gave a yeoman's effort in all cases. Each consulting editor had significant supervisory and writing responsibilities; without their help we would still be struggling.

Many others desrve our thanks. Joan Kappus gave hours and hours to the development of the master list of entries. E. Valerie Hewitt began working with us only during the last 6 months of manuscript preparation, but was a godsend nevertheless. Mike Ash, Head of the Department of Educational Psychology at Texas A&M University, was instrumental in obtaining the university support necessary for such a large project. Mike's support, moral and professional, and as a friend, was necessary and welcomed—and very typical of this extraordinary department head. The Research Assistance Laboratory of the College of Education at Texas A&M University, under the direction of Victor Willson, graciously gave us cherished space for housing the *Encyclopedia* office and operations. Hugh J. Scott, dean of the Division of Programs in Education at Hunter College, provided an encouragement of scholarship in special education that was inspirational and deserving of our appreciation.

Angela Bailey was our administrative editor and was responsible for coordinating all aspects of the day-to-day operations of the office. She corresponded with hundreds of authors, cajoled the tardy, smoothed ruffled feathers, and served as chief operations officer, making everyone adhere to schedule, the editors included. She handled all with humor, aplomb, and efficiency. We could not have done it without her and consider ourselves fortunate to have had the insight to have hired her.

Elaine Fletcher-Janzen, senior editorial associate, read and edited every piece of manuscript for content and for style. She coordinated writing assignments and consistently performed well beyond the expected. Elaine prepared background material for more entries than any individual author and prepared her own entries, while also coordinating the review process. Elaine is truly the proverbial gem. She is the kind of graduate assistant and doctoral student that we came to academia hoping to mentor; we hope she has learned as much from us as we have learned from her while she progressed through her doctoral studies—and all while starting her family—another successful venture we are sure.

The overall guidance of the work can be ascribed to Dr. Martin Grayson, editor of the Encyclopedia Division of John Wiley & Sons. Martin believed in us and the project from the beginning. A journal and an encyclopedia editor as well as a scholar in his own field, Martin gave essential guidance, urging us on through inspiration as well as an occasional shove when our labors flagged. The staff of production editors at Wiley was most helpful as well, consistent with our experience with a half dozen other Wiley projects. In particular, Cary Weinberger and her predecessor April Kelliher deserve recognition for their coordination from the publisher's office. Margery Carazzone, Production Manager and Rosalind Greenberg, Production Editor, performed superbly.

To our families, our friends, and our secretaries, we needed your patience and understanding as we struggled to meet deadlines and asked more than we should have from you. You so graciously accommodated us. Thank you. And, Julia, thanks for the crucial times of sanity you bring to a very crazy life. CRR would like to express a special note of appreciation to his mentors, Alan S. Kaufman and E. Paul Torrance, who continue to inspire. To the users of the *Encyclopedia,* we await your comments on this work and hope that you will find it helpful to you in helping children grow and develop to the utmost of their potential.

CECIL R. REYNOLDS
LESTER MANN

College Station, Texas
New York, New York
April 1987

Encyclopedia of
SPECIAL
EDUCATION
Second Edition

A

AAAS

See AMERICAN ASSOCIATION FOR THE ADVANCEMENT OF SCIENCE.

AAMD CLASSIFICATION SYSTEMS

The American Association on Mental Deficiency (AAMD) was founded in 1876 to support and promote the general welfare of people who are mentally retarded through professional programs, dissemination of research and program advances, and development of standards for services and facilities. The organization is comprised of approximately 10,000 professionals from many different disciplines who are concerned with the prevention and treatment of mental retardation. The association publishes two research journals, *Mental Retardation* and *American Journal of Mental Deficiency*. A national conference, along with many regional and state conferences, is held each year to give professionals the opportunity to share significant information regarding the education and welfare of children and adults with mental retardation.

The first diagnostic and classification system was published in 1921. It was reviewed and revised in 1933, 1941, 1957, 1959, 1973, 1977, and 1983. In each case, the manual was revised based on new developments in philosophy and knowledge of the field. To make the revisions and clarify important issues, input is culled from presentations at national and regional meetings of the AAMD, national and local hearings, and discussions with representatives of many professional, social, and political action groups. All revisions are made by the AAMD's Terminology and Classification Committee after a careful examination of the present classification system and the new data. Major revisions over the years have centered around the presentation of a dual classification system, medical and behavioral; clarification of the definitions of adaptive and measured intelligence; the addition of an extensive glossary; an illustration of levels of adaptive behavior; and procedures for diagnosing mental retardation in the behavioral system. With this last example, it is important that clinicians understand, in diagnosing mental retardation, the concept of standard error of measurement and its use in making a clinical determination of retardation and level of functioning.

The 1983 AAMD classification system developed by the AAMD's Terminology and Classification Committee has been written to reflect current thinking in the field. This latest edition has three distinct purposes. First, the 1983 edition was an attempt to provide an acceptable system to be used worldwide. It was developed in coordination with the International Classification of Diseases-9 (ICD-9) of the World Health Organization, the American Psychiatric Association's *Diagnostic and Statistical Manual-III* (DSM-III), and the American Association on Mental Deficiency's Classification in Mental Retardation.

The second purpose was to improve opportunities to gather and disseminate information regarding diagnosis, treatment, and research activities. The third purpose of this classification system was to provide opportunities for the identification of causes of mental retardation with implications for prevention.

The definition of mental retardation accepted by most authorities is the one used by the American Association on Mental Deficiency. The definition was presented first by Heber in 1961 and later revised by Grossman in 1973 to read: "Mental retardation refers to significantly subaverage general intellectual functioning resulting in or associated with concurrent impairments in adaptive behavior and manifested during the developmental period." Based on the definition, to be classified mentally retarded, the person must be below average in both measured intelligence and adaptive behavior.

The AAMD classification of the retarded has been useful to professionals as well because it is based on the severity of retardation. The terms used by the AAMD are mild, moderate, severe, and profound.

The AAMD causal classification scheme centers around nine general groupings for mental retardation. These groups include infections and intoxication, trauma or physical agent, metabolism or nutrition, gross brain disease, unknown prenatal influence, chromosomal anomalies, other conditions originating in the perinatal period following psychiatric disorder, and environmental influences.

REFERENCES

Grossman, H. (Ed.). (1983). *Classification in mental retardation.* Washington, DC: American Association on Mental Deficiency.

CECELIA STEPPE-JONES
North Carolina Central University

AAMD ADAPTIVE BEHAVIOR SCALES MENTAL RETARDATION

AAMR ADAPTIVE BEHAVIOR SCALES–RESIDENTIAL AND COMMUNITY: SECOND EDITION (ABS–RC:2)

The *AAMR Adaptive Behavior Scales–Residential and Community: Second Edition* (ABS–RC:2) (Nihira, Leland, & Lambert, 1993) is the revision of the 1969 and 1974 *AAMD Adaptive Behavior Scales.* The latest version of the adaptive behavior scales is the product of a comprehensive review of the earlier versions of the rating scales relating to persons with mental retardation in the United States and other countries. The items of the ABS–RC:2 have undergone numerous modifications since the 1969 edition as a result of intensive item analyses over time, with different group results varying with respect to adaptive behavior levels. The scale items that survived this process were selected on the bases of their inter-rater reliability and their effectiveness in discriminating (a) among institutionalized persons with mental retardation and those in community settings who previously had been classified at different adaptive behavior levels according to the AAMD's Classification in Mental Retardation (Grossman, 1983) and (b) among adaptive behavior levels in public school populations. This scale is appropriate for individuals from ages 18 through 80.

Domain raw scores are converted to standard scores (M = 10, SD = 3) and percentiles. Factor raw scores are used to generate quotients (M = 100, SD = 15) and percentiles. The scale's normative sample consists of more than 4,000 persons from 43 states with developmental disabilities residing in the community or in residential settings. The test has been extensively examined regarding reliability and validity, and the evidence supporting the scale's technical adequacy is provided in the manual. Internal consistency reliabilities and stability for all scores exceed .8.

This scale was reviewed in *The Thirteenth Mental Measurements Yearbook* (Impara & Plake, 1998) by Carey (1998) and Harrison (1998). Carey stated that the scale is technically adequate for this type of assessment; Harrison reported that the ABS–RC:2 has many features that enhance the assessment of adults with developmental disabilities.

REFERENCES

Carey, K. T. (1998). Review of the AAMR Adaptive Behavior Scale–Residential and Community, Second Edition. In J. C. Impara & B. S. Plake (Eds.), *The thirteenth mental measurements yearbook* (pp. 3–5). Lincoln: Buros Institute of Mental Measurements, University of Nebraska Press.

Grossman, H. J. (Ed.). (1983). *Classification in mental retardation.* Washington, DC.: American Association on Mental Deficiency (now Retardation).

Harrison, P. L. (1998). Review of the AAMR Adaptive Behavior Scale–Residential and Community, Second Edition. In J. C. Impara & B. S. Plake (Eds.), *The thirteenth mental measurements yearbook.* Lincoln: Buros Institute of Mental Measurements, University of Nebraska Press.

Impara, J. C., & Plake B. S. (Eds.). (1998). *The thirteenth mental measurements yearbook* (pp. 1–3). Lincoln: Buros Institute of Mental Measurements, University of Nebraska Press.

Nihira, K., Leland, H., & Lambert, N. (1993). *AAMR Adaptive Behavior Scales–Residential and Community: Second Edition.* Austin, TX: Pro-Ed.

TADDY MADDOX
Associate Director of Research, PRO-ED, Inc.

AAMR ADAPTIVE BEHAVIOR SCALES–SCHOOL: SECOND EDITION (ABS–S:2)

The *AAMR Adaptive Behavior Scales–School: Second Edition* (ABS–S:2) (Lambert, Nihira, & Leland, 1993) is used for assessing the current adaptive functioning of children being evaluated for evidence of mental retardation, for evaluating adaptive behavior characteristics of children with autism, and for differentiating children with behavior disorders who require special education assistance. The scale is appropriate for children ages 3 years to 18 years 11 months.

This revision is divided into two parts. Part One focuses on personal independence; it is designed to evaluate coping skills considered important to independence and responsibility in daily living. The skills within Part One are grouped into nine behavior domains: Independent Functioning, Physical Development, Economic Activity, Language Development, Numbers and Time, Prevocational/Vocational Activity, Self-Direction, Responsibility, and Socialization. Part Two measures socially maladaptive behaviors. The behaviors assessed were identified through a survey of the social expectations placed upon persons with mental retardation in public and special schools, public and private residential institutions, and a wide range of local rehabilitative and recreational services. The descriptions of those expectations were obtained from an analysis of a large number of critical incident reports provided by personnel in residential, community, and school settings. The behaviors in Part Two are assigned to seven domains, which are measures of those adaptive behaviors that relate to the manifestation of personality and behavior disorders: Social Behavior, Conformity, Trustworthiness, Stereotyped and Hyperactive Behavior, Self-Abusive Behavior, Social Engagement, and Disturbing Interpersonal Behavior. The domains in Part One and Part Two are combined into five factors: Personal Self-Sufficiency, Community Self-Sufficiency, Personal-Social Responsibility, Social Adjustment, and Personal Adjustment.

Domain raw scores are converted to standard scores (M = 10, SD = 3) and percentiles. Factor raw scores are used to generate quotients (M = 100, SD = 15) and percentiles. The scale's normative sample consists of more than 2,000 persons from 31 states with developmental disabilities attending public schools and more than 1,000 students who have no disabilities. The test has been examined extensively regarding reliability and validity. Internal consistency reliabilities and stability for all scores exceed .8.

In *The Thirteenth Mental Measurements Yearbook*, Stinnett (1998) reviewed the instrument and concluded that the scale's psychometric qualities are good; Harrington (1998) stated that the ABS–S:2 makes a contribution to the area of adaptive behavior assessment. Both reviewers felt the test was improved from previous editions.

REFERENCES

Harrington, R. G. (1998). Review of the AAMR Adaptive Behavior Scale–School, Second Edition. In J. C. Impara & B. S. Plake (Eds.), *The thirteenth mental measurements yearbook* (pp. 5–9). Lincoln: Buros Institute of Mental Measurements, University of Nebraska Press.

Lambert, N., Nihira, K., & Leland, H. (1993). *AAMR Adaptive Behavior Scales–School: Second Edition.* Austin, TX: PRO-ED.

Stinnett, T. A. (1998). Review of the AAMR Adaptive Behavior Scale–School, Second Edition. In J. C. Impara & B. S. Plake (Eds.), *The thirteenth mental measurements yearbook* (pp. 9–14). Lincoln: Buros Institute of Mental Measurements, University of Nebraska Press.

TADDY MADDOX
Associate Director of Research,
Pro-Ed, Inc.

AAMD CLASSIFICATION SYSTEMS
ADAPTIVE BEHAVIOR

ABAB DESIGN

The ABAB design is one of the oldest and most widely used single-case designs developed in behavioral psychology. It was initially used in laboratory studies with animals (Sidman, 1960); however, as the applied behavior analysis movement got under way (Baer, Wolf, & Risley, 1968), it became a prototype for applied behavioral investigations conducted in the natural environment. Although the number of single-case designs has increased markedly since the early days of applied behavior analysis (e.g., Kazdin, 1980; Kratochwill, 1978), the ABAB design still occupies a prominent place in applied behavioral research. Moreover, because of the high degree of experimental control that it provides, it has been widely used with individuals manifesting various types of handicaps (Bergan, 1977). For example, the ABAB design has been particularly useful in studying environmental variables affecting language acquisition in retarded children (Bergan, 1977).

The ABAB design is intended to reveal a functional relationship between an experimental treatment and a behavior targeted for change. For example, it might be used to establish a functional relationship between the use of the plural form of a noun and a treatment such as praise following the occurrence of a plural noun. The demonstration of a functional relationship between praise and plural nouns would require an association between the frequency of plural-noun production and the occurrence of verbal praise. Given that a functional relationship were established, verbal praise could be assumed to function as a positive reinforcer increasing the probability of occurrence of plural nouns by the subject or subjects participating in the experiment.

The ABAB technique has often been referred to as a single-case design (e.g., Kratochwill, 1978). However, it may be applied with more than one subject. Thus, the term single case is a bit misleading. Glass, Wilson, and Gottman (1975) among others called attention to the fact that the ABAB design is a time-series design in that it reflects an effort to determine changes in behavior occurring across a series of points in time. Recognition of the ABAB design as a time-series design opened the way for linking the design to the statistical procedures associated with time-series analysis (see, for example, Glass, Wilson, & Gottman, 1975). Application of time-series analysis procedures affords a statistical test for hypotheses that may be investigated with the ABAB design. However, despite this advantage, time-series techniques have not been widely used in applied investigations involving the ABAB design. There are a variety of reasons for this. Among them is the fact that the graphing techniques suggested by behavioral psychologists (e.g., Parsonson & Baer, 1978) as an alternative to statistical analysis are easier to implement and to interpret than time-series statistics. Nonetheless, time-series procedures constitute a potentially powerful tool for applied behavioral research and their use can be expected to increase in the future.

As the letters in its name suggest, the ABAB design includes four phases. The initial A phase is a baseline period that records behavior across a series of points in time in the absence of intervention. The length of the baseline period varies depending on the variability of the behavior being recorded. If the behavior is highly variable, a longer baseline is required than if the behavior is highly stable. More data are required to get a sense of the fluctuations that may be expected without intervention for a highly variable behavior than for a highly stable behavior. The second phase, denoted by the letter B, is a treatment phase. During this phase the treatment is introduced. The treatment may be implemented in accordance with a variety of different schedules. For example, treatment may be implemented with every occurrence of the target behavior. For instance, praise might be given following every occurrence of a plural noun. On the other hand, treatment might be implemented in accordance with one of the many available partial reinforcement schedules. Thus, praise might be given after every third occurrence of a plural noun. The third phase, also denoted by the letter A, constitutes a return to baseline. The return to baseline may be brought about by various means. One is to withdraw the treatment. For instance, praise might not be given following plural-noun utterances during the return-to-baseline phase. Another procedure is to introduce another treatment intended to bring the target behavior back to baseline level. For example, reinforcement of a behavior that is incompatible with the target behavior may be introduced during the return-to-baseline phase. The final phase in the ABAB design, denoted by the second occurrence of the letter B, is a second implementation of the treatment. The second implementation is intended to demonstrate treatment control over the target behavior by minimizing the possibility that environmental influences occurring coincidentally with the treatment could be responsible for the observed behavior change.

The major advantage of the ABAB design lies in the fact that it minimizes the likelihood of coincidental environmental influences on the target behavior. There are two potential disadvantages to the approach (Kazdin, 1973). One is that some behaviors are not easily reversed. For example, a skill that has been well-learned may not be easy to unlearn. The second disadvantage is that there are cases in which it may not be practical to carry out a return-to-baseline even if it is possible to do so. For instance, a teacher may not want to return a child's performance of an academic skill to baseline even for a short period of time. Despite these shortcomings, the ABAB design has been shown to be useful in establishing a functional relationship between a treatment and behavior in countless appli-

cations. It is truly a mainstay in applied behavioral research and will continue to be used widely.

REFERENCES

Baer, D. M., Wolf, M. M., & Risley, T. R. (1968). Some current dimensions of applied behavior analysis. *Journal of Applied Behavior Analysis, 8,* 387–398.

Bergan, J. R. (1977). *Behavioral consultation.* Columbus, OH: Merrill.

Glass, G. V., Wilson, V. L., & Gottman, J. M. (1975). *Design and analysis of time-series experiments.* Boulder: Colorado Associated University Press.

Kazdin, A. E. (1973). Methodological and assessment considerations in evaluating reinforcement programs in applied settings. *Journal of Applied Behavior Analysis, 6,* 517–531.

Kazdin, A. E. (1980). *Research design in clinical psychology.* New York: Harper & Row.

Kratochwill, T. R. (1978). *Single-subject research: Strategies for evaluating change.* New York: Academic.

Parsonson, B. S., & Baer, D. M. (1978). The analysis and presentation of graphic data. In T. R. Kratochwill (Ed.), *Single-subject research: Strategies for evaluating change.* New York: Academic.

Sidman, M. (1960). *Tactics of scientific research.* New York: Basic.

JOHN R. BERGAN
University of Arizona

RESEARCH IN SPECIAL EDUCATION

ABECEDARIAN PROJECT

For the past quarter century, American education has been especially concerned with the academic performance of children from disadvantaged families. This special concern stems from the well-established fact that this group of children typically performs well below average on standardized tests of academic achievement. They also are overrepresented in special education classes. The root causes of this poor performance are not well understood but their consequences are costly, in terms both of economics and psychological dysfunction. Such consequences have frequently been called developmental retardation.

To ameliorate these costly consequences, a wide variety of special education programs have been investigated under the rubric of compensatory education. Most of these programs have concentrated on the so-called preschool and/or early elementary school years. The primary hypothesis has been that educational experiences that augment and/or supplement the educational experiences of the home will better prepare disadvantaged children for academic accomplishment in the public schools. The Abecedarian project has been such an experiment. Abecedarian means one learning the rudiments of something (the alphabet).

The specific aims of the Abecedarian project have been:

To determine whether developmental retardation and school failure can be prevented in children from socially and economically high-risk families by means of educational day care.

To determine whether a follow-through program for early elementary school is necessary to maintain preschool intellectual gains in high-risk children.

To determine whether school-age intervention alone can significantly improve academic and/or intellectual performance in children who did not have preschool intervention.

To identify a sample of families at high risk for having a developmentally retarded child, a high-risk screening index (Ramey & Smith, 1977) was developed. This index included social, environmental, and psychological factors judged on the basis of the developmental literature to be associated with poor intellectual and scholastic progress. Each factor was assigned a weight based on professional consensus as to its likely importance in determining intellectual and scholastic outcomes. Thirteen factors were included; among them were paternal and maternal education; family income; father's absence; retardation among other family members; family disorganization; maladaptive or antisocial behavior within the family; and unstable job history.

Based on the high-risk index, families were judged to be at elevated risk and eligible for inclusion in the study. Characteristics of the 109 families (111 children) eventually enrolled in the study are given in the following Table. As may be seen in the Table, the families in the sample were predominantly black (98%), were headed by a single female (72%) who was young (20 years) and who had less than a high school education (10.23 years).

It is a special feature of the Abecedarian project that participants were assigned to the preschool experimental educational treatment or control condition at random. Fifty-seven children were randomly assigned to the preschool experimental group, 54 were preschool controls. Ninety-six children remained in the study to be randomly assigned to a school-age treatment group.

At public school entry, Abecedarian children within the two preschool groups were rank-ordered according to 48-month Stanford-Binet IQ's; each consecutive pair was randomly assigned to the school-age experimental or control groups. All families accepted their school-age assignment, but three children assigned to the preschool control-school-

Entry Level Demographic Data for Experimental and Control Families

Experimental Variable	Group		
	Control (N = 55)	Experimental (N = 54)	Total (N = 109)
1. Mean high risk index	20.08 (5.72)	21.41 (5.88)	20.75 (5.81)
2. Mean maternal age (years)	19.62 (3.87)	20.28 (5.77)	19.94 (4.89)
3. Mean maternal education (years)	10.46 (1.75)	10.00 (1.89)	10.23 (1.83)
4. Mean maternal IQ (WAIS full scale)	85.49 (12.34)	84.18 (10.78)	84.84 (11.61)
5. Percent female-headed family	78%	65%	72%
6. Percent black families	96%	100%	98%

age experimental condition (CE) moved away and did not participate in the school-age phase.

Figure 1 gives the overall design of the Abecedarian study, including the preschool and school-age treatment programs and the number of children randomly assigned to each condition. The Abecedarian study can be conceptualized as a 2 × 2 factorial design. The factors are preschool educational treatment versus no preschool treatment and school-age educational treatment versus no school-age treatment. Thus, there were two preschool groups, the experimental (E) and control (C) groups, and four school-age conditions: preschool experimental school-age experimental (EE); preschool experimental school-age control (EC); preschool control school-age experimental (CE); and preschool control school-age control (CC). These groups varied in the intensity (defined as number of years) of intervention: 8 years for the EE group; 5 years for the EC group; 3 years for the CE group; none for the CC group.

The preschool program may be characterized as a comprehensive, whole child program. The aim was to create a rich, stimulating, yet orderly environment in which the children could grow and learn. The curriculum was designed to enhance cognitive and linguistic development and to provide the children with many opportunities for successful mastery experiences. The curriculum materials

Figure 1. Research design of Carolina Abecedarian Project.

included those for infants and preschoolers developed by Sparling and Lewis (1979). In addition, there was an enriched language environment that was responsive to the children's needs and interests (Ramey, et al., 1982).

In many ways the program was not unlike other high-quality infant daycare and preschool programs. Child/caregiver ratios ranged from 1:3 for infants to 1:6 for four year olds. Teachers typically had early childhood education experience and participated in an extensive in-service education program. The children's experiences became increasingly more structured over the preschool years, eventually coming to include prephonics programs and science and math experiences in addition to an emphasis on language and linguistic development. The presumption was that when the child left the preschool, he or she would be able to enter kindergarten without experiencing an abrupt transition.

Children attended the preschool program beginning between 6 weeks and 3 months of age. Children attended the daycare program 5 days per week, 50 weeks per year. The center was open from 7:30 A.M. to 5:15 P.M. Free transportation to and from the center was provided for families who needed it. Almost all of the children were transported by center staff. This portion of the program has been described in more detail by Ramey, MacPhee, and Yeates (1982).

The school-age intervention program began in kindergarten. It consisted of providing a home/school resource teacher to each child and family in the two Abecedarian school-age experimental groups (EE and CE) shown in Figure 1. These teachers filled many roles: they were curriculum developers who prepared an individualized set of home activities to supplement the school's basic curriculum in reading and math; they taught parents how to use these activities with their children; they tutored children directly; they met regularly with classroom teachers to ensure that home activities matched the skills being taught in the classroom; they served as consultants for the classroom teacher when problems arose; and they advocated for the child and family within the school and community. Thus, they facilitated communication between teacher and parent, providing an important support for disadvantaged parents who frequently lacked the skills and confidence needed to advocate for their children within the school system, an institution seen by many as both monolithic and difficult to comprehend. Each home/school resource teacher had a caseload of approximately 12 families per year. The home/school resource teachers were experienced educators familiar with the local school system.

The supplemental curriculum delivered as home activities concentrated on two basic subjects: reading and math. These subjects were emphasized because it seemed likely that high-risk children might need extra reinforcement of these basic concepts to master and to remember them. The program sought to provide such reinforcement, presuming that scholastic performance would best be enhanced by direct teaching and practice of needed basic skills. The curriculum packets contained teaching activities that parents and children could share and enjoy. In addition, work sheets to give extra drill and practice were often included.

Home/school teachers made approximately 17 school visits per year for each child. During these visits they met with the classroom teacher to identify the skills currently being taught and to learn which areas needed extra work or review. A variety of specialists within the system were contacted, including special education resource personnel, reading teachers, and school counselors. Efforts were made to coordinate the child's program and to make sure the best available resources were being used.

The home component of the program was equally intense. Home visits were made about 15 times each school year. A typical visit lasted approximately 30 to 45 minutes, with the mother being the most likely participant. Teachers reviewed the classroom situation and showed the parent the materials in the activity packet, explaining the purpose and directions for each activity. The child was present and participated in about one-quarter of the home visits; this was often helpful because it allowed the teacher to demonstrate how an activity was to be carried out. Parents reported spending an average of 15 minutes a day working with their children on home activities. Parent response to the activities was very positive; very few reported that they failed to use the activities although direct verification was not possible.

Many forces other than intellectual ability and encouragement to learn can have an impact on a child's scholastic performance: emotional upset within the home, parental unemployment, the death of a family member, or instability of living arrangements, to name a few. Home/school resource teachers sometimes helped families deal with personal crises. Extra home visits occurred if and when the home/school teacher attempted to help the family solve such real-life problems. Home/school teachers also helped to provide the children with a variety of summer experiences, including summer activity packets, summer camp, trips to the public library, and, for some children, a six-week tutorial in reading.

The results to be included here cover the intellectual and academic outcomes for Abecedarian children through the first 2 years in public school. Many other results are available, but these have been chosen because they represent the primary outcome hypotheses under investigation.

Figure 2 gives the IQ results for Abecedarian children from infancy through age 6½ years (78 months). In Figure 2, the mean IQs are graphed by preschool group up to the age of 60 months and by the four school-age groups thereafter. The scores are Bayley Mental Developmental Indices at 3, 6, 9, 12, and 18 months, Binet IQs at 24, 36, and 48 months, and full-scale IQs on the Wechsler Preschool and Primary Scale of Intelligence at 60 months and the Wech-

Figure 2. Mean mental development (MDI's) and IQ scores for randomly assigned high-risk children from 3 to 78 months of age in the Abecedarian Project.

sler Intelligence Scale for Children-Revised at 78 months.

The preschool intervention had a positive effect on intellectual development of the high-risk children in the experimental group, as may be seen in Figure 2. Throughout the preschool period, at every testing occasion after 12 months, significant mean differences on standardized test scores were found between the two Abecedarian preschool groups (Ramey & Campbell, 1984). The primary form of this effect was to reduce the drop in mental test scores evidenced by the control group. It is now apparent that this preschool effect persists up through 78 months (Ramey &

Campbell, in press). There is no evidence, however, that the school-age intervention significantly impacted children's intellectual performance during the first year and half of public school. No significant effect of the school-age program was found at 78 months. Thus regardless of school-age intervention status, the two groups who had preschool intervention maintained their relative superiority in tested intelligence over children who were preschool controls.

Figure 3 from Ramey and Campbell (in press) contains the kindergarten and first grade Peabody Individual

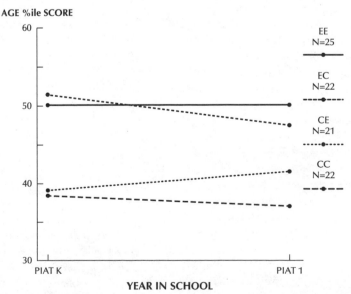

Figure 3. Mean age-referenced percentile scores on the Peabody Individual Achievement Test by year in school for the groups in the Abecedarian Project.

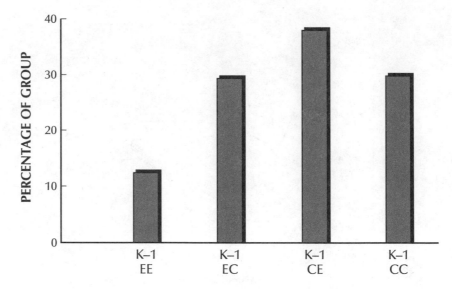

Figure 4. Percentage of high-risk children retained in grades as a function of experimental educational conditions.

Achievement Test results in terms of age-referenced percentile scores. Examination of this figure reveals that the preschool groups are near national average whereas the preschool control groups are below national average. Thus during the first 2 years in public school, positive preschool treatment effects on academic achievement were observed.

Figure 4 presents the percentage of children retained in either kindergarten or first grade for each of the four experimental conditions. One-eighth, or 12%, of the children in the EE group were retained in grade during the first 2 years of public school, compared with approximately one-third in the other three groups. Although it is very early in these children's public school careers, it is remarkable that the academic failure rate is so high in the groups that did not receive early and continuing supplemental education. The one-third grade retention rate is clearly costly and apparently reducible through intensive early education. Such a high retention rate also buttresses the initial judgment that these children were indeed at elevated risk for school failure.

Together, the data on IQs, academic achievement, and retention in grade suggest that preschool intervention exerts a positive influence on intelligence and school success in the first 2 years of public school. Preschool intervention supplemented by continued help in the early grades via a home/school resource teacher program shows promise for being the most effective intervention. This intensity of effort apparently enabled the high-risk children in this sample to maintain a level of achievement near the national average. In addition, the likelihood of being retained in grade was less by a factor of approximately three for children who had early and continued educational intervention.

We are currently in the process of analyzing data for the final year of the school-age intervention. When those analyses are completed and we have systematically examined the family, school, and child factors associated with academic performance, we hope to have a better understanding of the forces that are associated with the academic performance of children from disadvantaged families and the ability of educational intervention to ameliorate those forces.

REFERENCES

Ramey, C. T., & Campbell, F. A. (1984). Preventive education for high-risk children: Cognitive consequences of the Carolina Abecedarian project [Special issue]. *American Journal of Mental Deficiency, 88*(5), 515–523.

Ramey, C. T., & Campbell, F. A. (in press). The Carolina Abecedarian project: An educational experiment concerning human malleability. In J. J. Gallagher (Ed.), *The malleability of children.* Baltimore, MD: Brookes.

Ramey, C. T., MacPhee, D., & Yeates, K. O. (1982). Preventing developmental retardation: A general systems model. In L. A. Bond & J. M. Joffe (Eds.), *Facilitating infant and early childhood development* (pp. 343–401). Hanover, NH: University Press of New England.

Ramey, C. T., McGinness, G. D., Cross, L., Collier, A. M., & Barrie-Blackley, S. (1982). The Abecedarian approach to social competence: Cognitive and linguistic intervention for disadvantaged preschoolers. In K. Borman (Ed.), *The social life of children in a changing society.* Hillsdale, NJ: Erlbaum.

Ramey, C. T., & Smith, B. (1977). Assessing the intellectual consequences of early intervention with high-risk infants. *American Journal of Mental Deficiency, 81,* 318–324.

Sparling, J., & Lewis, I. (1979, February). Six learning games to play with your baby. *Parents* (pp. 35–38).

CRAIG T. RAMEY
FRANCES A. CAMPBELL
DONNA M. BRYANT
*University of North Carolina
at Chapel Hill*

HIGH RISK
MENTAL RETARDATION

ABILITY TRAINING

Many educators believe that most academic and social learning is based on factors such as student aptitudes or abilities, instructional environment, and teaching methodology. While these three variables do not form a complete structure capable of containing all those factors contributing to learning, they certainly account for many of the variables educators would agree are important to success in school.

Learner aptitudes or abilities are those personological variables that frequently are called intelligence(s), traits, gifts, and characteristics. Frequently, educators will talk about a child's potential to learn, using the term ability as if it were a predetermined factor waiting to be drawn on at some point. The logic, then, is that if learning is a result of the presence and development of certain mental abilities, school failure (both academic and social) may be the result of disabilities, with disability implying an academic or social handicap.

If regular (elementary and secondary) educators teach to the abilities of students to learn, then special educators may direct more of their instruction to the disabilities that inhibit learning, hence the term and concept of ability training. How valid is this construct of ability training? A short response to that question is impossible. Any field involving relatively newly defined services to persons, especially children, in particular handicapped children, will generate professional controversy. Any field struggling with the pressures associated with economic, political, social, legislative, litigative, and basic human rights and values will face diversity. Any field that requires its many disciplines to unite in purpose will experience communicative stress. But, few professionals will purposely question their field's major methodology to the degree special and remedial educators have, for the period of time they have done so, and in the face of such a degree of controversy.

Some special educators believe avidly in ability training of all types; some reject it totally; but almost all, no matter what they believe, practice ability training. The truth in that observation is vividly displayed when we recognize that the value of ability training to handicapped persons has been questioned repeatedly for over the last 100 years. What then is in ability training that has caused the field of special education to tenaciously and steadfastly maintain its cause? Ability training is routed in the historic search for the structure and function of the mind. Educators, in particular special educators, have sought to diagnose specific abilities and provide remediation to those abilities, or disabilities as the case may be.

Mental ability (aptitude), concerns those components that are assumed to constitute the mind, and therefore explain learning. Mental-ability structures, in more scientific parlance, may be referred to as information-processing behaviors. Mental processes or information processes are those theoretical or conceptual acts (processes) by which information is transmitted from the peripheral (to the central nervous system) sensory organs (i.e., eyes, ears, fingers [tactile], muscles, [kinesthetic]) perceived, labeled, stored, provided mediated meaning, conceptually associated, and expressed as language or motoric responses. It is not unusual for practitioners to reference most psychological functions synonymously with mental abilities. Hence, the very definition of learning disabilities refers to "basic psychological processes."

The history of man, at least those aspects related to the structures of the mind, how it works, and therefore how these processes can be measured, begins with the early Greek philosophers. Pythagoras placed the "mind" in the brain in the sixth century BC. Most of the processes described then were hypotheoretical, related to this assumed function. Therefore, the names given these processes sometimes sound as if they had been isolated neurologically or psychoneurologically. The truth is that the majority of the commonly referenced mental processes, that is, perception and language, are not simple, easily explained constructs. They are complex concepts that may contain hundreds of component subparts. The major issues relating to ability training have been the long-standing arguments regarding the mind, its disabilities, and the habilitation or rehabilitation needed. A case in point is that while simple tests are designed to ascertain visual perceptual-motor development, visual perception is not a simple discriminate function. In a general sense, perception requires the discrimination of distinctive features, wherein a specific symbolic meaning can be assigned each distinct stimuli. Logically then, once perceptual information has been discriminated, it may be stored for some short-term reference, or it may be assigned a permanent symbolism, then converted to a language concept. Logically then, too, there may be both visual and auditory perception. These two processes may need to be coordinated when auditory and visual information is presented in an integrated manner. Perception, however, is not logically complex in contrast to the explanations of the structure and function of language.

A mental ability may also be referred to as a faculty. Mann (1979) credits Aristotle for establishing the basis for modern faculty psychology. The Romans further refined and added descriptors such as intellect, attention, and language. St. Thomas Aquinas, during the Middle Ages, although poorly credited, began to amplify and extend faculty psychology by dividing it into two parts: the *intellectus,* which carries out abstractions and functions of the possible intellect; and the *ratio,* which is directed toward understanding, judgment, and reasoning. The intellect is active and creative, the ratio, passive and receptive, i.e., sensory stimuli must be perceptually assigned symbolic meaning/value before they have intellectual meaning.

Faculty psychology, the theoretical basis for mental process, was soundly criticized by many of the seventeenth-, eighteenth-, and nineteenth-century scholars. Hobbes (1558–1679) displaced it with his theories of automotion in the brain set off by sensory stimulation. Locke (1632–1704) was a sensationalist, and an arch antifacilist. Hume (1715–1776), also a sensationalist in the British tradition, condemned faculties, basing mental response solely in sensory stimulation. By the mid-nineteenth century, the psychologist and educator Herbart attempted to destroy for all time the residual of faculty psychology.

One of the predominate figures in mental measurement, Spearman, writing in 1927, notes that faculty psychology seems to persist, no matter what the criticism.

> One curious feature about these formal faculties has yet to be mentioned. The doctrine loses every battle—so to speak—but always wins the war. It will bend to the slightest breath of criticism; but not the most violent storm can break it. The attacks made long ago by the Herbartians appeared to be irresistible; no serious defense was even attempted. Yet the sole permanent effect of these attacks was only to banish the word "faculty," leaving the doctrine represented by this word to escape scot free. (pp. 38–39)

However, other early forces in the field such as Thorndike continued to be critical. As a quote from Mann (1979) notes,

> The science of education should at once rid itself of its conception of the mind as a sort of machine, different parts of which sense, perceive, discriminate, imagine, remember, conceive, associate, reason about, desire, choose, form habits, attend to.... There is no power of sense discrimination to be delicate or coarse.... There are only the connections between separate sense stimuli and our separate senses and human judgments thereof.... There is no memory to hold in a uniformly tight and loose grip the experiences of the past. There are only the particular connections between particular mental events and others. (Klein, 1970, p. 662)

Though an out-and-out antifaculist, Thorndike, interestingly enough, could not shake the ingrained habit of his times of speaking about "faculties." Thus, he described his bonds as faculties in the 1903 edition of *Education Psychology* (p. 30) "the mind is a host of highly particularized and independent faculties" (Spearman, 1927, p. 36).

Yet, it is faculty psychology that provided the definition for twentieth-century mental measurement. On the basis of his inquiries, Galton described what, in essence, is a superfaculty, which he called "general ability," assigning to this faculty the name intelligence (a term popularized by Spencer). Galton distinguished this superfaculty from special aptitudes. He was more interested in the first, since he believed that general ability inevitably set a limit to accomplishment of any kind. He complained that most writers emphasized specific aptitudes or skill, that they

> lay too much stress upon apparent specialties, thinking that because a man is devoted to some particular pursuit, he could not have succeeded in anything else; they might as well say that, because a youth has fallen in love with a brunette, he could not possibly have fallen in love with a blonde. He may or may not have had any more natural liking for the former type of beauty than for the latter; but it is as probable as not that the affair was mainly or wholly due to a general amorousness. It is just the same with intellectual pursuits. (Burt, 1955, p. 85)

Galton most certainly did not deny the existence of special capacities or their potential importance. He cited instances in which memory, musical ability, and artistic and literary talent ran within several members of the same family. Home environment or family tradition could not explain all such cases, for example, "prodigies of memory." However, his studies in the main had convinced him "in how small a degree intellectual eminence can be considered as due to purely special powers" (Burt, 1955, p. 85).

As to the measurement of both general and special abilities, Galton suggested that individual differences in both are distributed in accordance with the normal curve, much as other human characteristics such as size or height are distributed. He printed a tabular classification of frequencies which he held "may apply to special just as truly as to general ability" (Burt, 1955, p. 85). Thus we see the beginnings of psychometric assessment of both general ability and specific abilities.

About 1880, the German psychiatrist Kraeplin, one of Wundt's students, began to use different tests to describe higher cognitive functions (Guilford, 1967). His testing interests were directed to such processes as general memory, specific memory, attention, and task-directed behaviors. However, it was James McKeen Cattell who first formulated the term "mental tests." Cattell's extension of Galton's simple tests began the modern practice of psychometrics as we know it today. Others such as DeSanctis attacked the realms of higher cognitive functioning. DeSanctis published a series of six tests including (1) memory for colors, (2) recognition of forms, (3) sustained attention,

(4) reasoning involving relations, (5) following instructions, and (6) thinking.

At the turn of the twentieth century, the French Minister of Public Instruction was still wrestling with an age-old problem: how to consistently identify the handicapped. Having agreed on the terminology to be used (idiot for the lowest level; imbecile for the intermediate level; and moron for the mildly mentally retarded), a psychologist, Alfred Binet, and physician, Theodore Simon, were commissioned to develop a consistent means of classifying children. Binet and Simon (1905, 1908) produced, through a standardized procedure of observation, a psychological classification of quantifiable differences in children's intellectual characteristics (traits). By 1905 Binet and Simon had developed 29 such tests designed to measure specific traits; by 1908 they had developed a classification of tests beginning at age three and continuing through age 13. Thus, the work preceding 1905 established human intelligence as a comprehensive integration of several traits including memory, attention, comprehension, muscular coordination, spatial relations, judgment, initiative, and ability to adapt. Further, the criteria for measurement of these traits were standardized at various chronological age levels. From this procedure the measurement of human performance took a great leap forward.

Binet carried his interest in higher processes into his work of developing mental tests for use in Paris schools. He and his associates criticized tests of the Galton type as being too simple, too sensory-motor, and too dependent on associationistic dogma. They expressed their own preference for the complex cognitive functions, proposing that 10 categories be explored by mental tests: (1) memory, (2) imagery, (3) imagination, (4) attention, (5) comprehension, (6) suggestibility, (7) aesthetic appreciation, (8) moral sentiment, (9) muscular force, force of will, and motor skill, and (10) judgment of visual space.

Modern psychoeducational assessment and remedial practices, indeed the very content of most perceptual, motor, language, vocational, and academic remedial curricula, are based on Binet's work. Two of the major issues are the specificity with which mental ability processes can reliably be ascertained and the desirability of remediating the specific perceptual or language processes in terms of their transferability and ultimate academic and social learning transfer.

But, it is clear that abilities had been identified by tests and that ability training was to become a crucial issue facing the twentieth century. The main philosophic question is, do mental abilities really exist in nature? The second question is, do they respond to specific training once they are described, measured, observed, and, in short, isolated as specific mental abilities? These two questions constitute the major issues facing special educators today. Since mental abilities are developmentally linked to chronological growth, culture, and experience, they may be encouraged by structured educational experiences. Conversely, when developmentally arrested, culturally neglected, or denied sequenced experiential practice, they may become deficient. Mental ability deficiencies may then be the principal characteristics associated with handicapping conditions such as learning and behavioral disorders. The entire nervous system develops only when each aspect or component necessary to successfully decode information (perceive its symbolic features) provides that symbol a language construct and a mechanism by which encoding of the mediated concept through motoric or verbal language permits communication. Therefore, specific reference is made in the definition of mental retardation and learning disabilities, two of the largest categories of handicapping conditions, to dysfunction of perceptual, perceptual-motor, or language abilities.

Philosophically, then, it appears that a leap in logic is *not* required to assume that if a disability exists, relative to causing a handicap, it should be corrected. That is exactly what ability training implies. It would appear that it was incorrectly named to begin with. It should be called disability training.

The history of ability training parallels that of the field of special education. The pioneers in ability training were the pioneers of the field. Itard, Howe, Sequin, Montessori, Binet, Wepman, Kirk, Strauss, Fernald, Frostig, and Cruickshank were all advocates of special education as it grew, and responsible for advancing ability training simultaneously. Tests used to describe a disability were followed by commercially prepared curricula to train the ability and remove the disability. The logic is obvious. The problem is in the scientific validation, or lack of it.

The early 1960s brought with it a concern for neurologically impaired children. The mid-1960s added the term learning disabled as a category of handicapping conditions. Both of these conditions required an increased emphasis on psychoneurological and psychoeducational assessment. Those that developed psychoeducational and psychoneurological tests to diagnose these conditions fueled the fire for ability training by describing conditions which, by their description, must exist.

Curricula designed to modify and treat patterns of disability were soon commercially available. Whole classes of children were exposed to Montessori, Frostig, and Fernald techniques, and administered Frostig, Kephart, and Delaccato assessment procedures. Tests such as the Illinois Test of Psycholinguistic Abilities became common place, much as the Woodcock-Johnson test batteries of today. The prevailing belief was that specific mental processes must be diagnosed in order for modification of a specific disability to result in quantum jumps in academic remedial achievement and potential normalization. Thus, the so-called diagnostic-prescriptive process is one form of ability training.

What then is the difficulty with visual and auditory perceptual training, perceptual motor training, language training, and the other forms of sensory, motor, perceptual, and language ability training? The problem is that data arrived at through quasi-scientific means are controversial concerning the results of ability training. There are data to support ability training, if the objective to be achieved is a change in an ability, and that ability alone. There are relatively few data to support that transfer of training occurs between training of a perceptual or cognitive ability and an academic achievement skill, for instance reading.

It is not clear which age groups profit most; there are some data to suggest that perceptual motor training is most effective between 3 and 7 years of age, and language training, 18 months to 14 or 15 years of age. There is no clear pattern as to the intelligence level needed for a student to profit from ability training, since specific abilities constitute statements of global intelligence. Cultural and ethnic factors have been found: urban black children may need auditory perceptual training; Native Americans outperform age norms of Anglos on visual perceptual tests.

The overall interaction among these abilities being training and other abilities remains unknown, except it does seem that auditory perceptual training is related to language growth much more than visual perceptual training. Language training seemingly has the greatest transference to academic remediation. But even the search for generalities would produce only controversy. The fact is, ability training makes sense logically but has not been sufficiently researched devoid of other educational practices with school-age children to permit definitive statements. And yet, the practice does not only continue, it continues to thrive.

REFERENCES

Binet, A., & Simon, T. (1905). Methodes nouvelles pour le diagnostic du niveau intellectuel des anomaux. *L'anne psychologique, 11,* 191–244.

Binet, A., & Simon, T. (1908). Le developpement de l'intelligence chez les infants. *L'anne psychologique, 14,* 1–94.

Burt, C. (1955). The evidence for the concept of intelligence. *British Journal of Educational Psychology, 25,* 158–177.

Klein, D. B. (1970). *A history of scientific psychology.* New York: Basic Books.

Mann, L. (1970). *On the trail of process.* New York: Grune & Stratton.

Spearman, C. (1927). *The abilities of man: Their nature and measurement.* London: Macmillan.

DAVID A. SABATINO
*West Virginia College of
Graduate Studies*

DIAGNOSTIC-PRESCRIPTIVE TEACHING
FERNALD METHOD
ILLINOIS TEST OF PSYCHOLINGUISTIC ABILITIES
INTELLIGENCE
REMEDIATION, DEFICIT-CENTERED MODELS

ABNORMALITIES, NEUROPHYSIOLOGICAL

The human nervous system consists of the brain, the spinal cord, and an intricate network of nerve fibers projecting from the brain and spinal cord. Structurally, the brain is differentiated into the two cerebral hemispheres, the brain stem and the cerebellum. The brain, together with the spinal cord, traditionally has been conceptualized as the central nervous system (CNS). The entire network of nerve fibers is then referred to as the peripheral nervous system (PNS). The brief discussion regarding normal neurological structure and function that follows is meant as an aid in the appreciation of neurophysiological disorders. The intent here is to offer an overview; for a more detailed account of the nervous system, the reader is referred to one of a number of neurophysiological texts (e.g., Bickerstaff, 1978; Lindsley & Holmes, 1984).

Peripheral nerves are referred to by the direction the impulses flow and the site of their termination. Specifically, the direction of the impulses carried in relation to the CNS, the originating structure, or final destination of the impulse, and the nature of the impulse itself, are used to classify peripheral nerves. For instance, the PNS contains sensory nerves that carry impulses from the sense organs (eyes, ears, nose, etc.) to the CNS. By way of contrast, the motor nerves travel from the CNS to the periphery, exciting both skeletal (voluntary) and smooth muscle (involuntary) muscle into movement. Included in PNS, the cranial nerves arise from or travel to the brain stem (connecting structure between spinal cord and cerebrum). Similarly, the spinal nerves travel to or from the spinal cord. The group of peripheral nerves that carry impulses to smooth muscle (causing involuntary movements of the intestines, heartbeat, constriction of the pupils, etc.) and those that incite the secretion of glands cause automatic changes in the body. These peripheral nerves are sometimes referred to collectively as the autonomic nervous system.

Functionally, the fundamental building block of the nervous system is the neuronal circuit. The simplest neuronal circuit contains only two interconnected nerve cells, involving an input and an output cell (e.g., simple knee jerk reflex). Local circuits exist at all levels of the nervous system and, in fact, such circuits in the spinal cord connect the cerebral cortex, brain stem, and cerebellum. These connections can function as modules in more complex circuits. Indeed, these integrated networks are capable of sustaining complex behavior (Gaddes, 1985; Kandel, Schwartz, & Jessell, 1991).

As an example, sensory impulses traveling from the

various sense organs to the brain are integrated, recorded, recognized, stored or remembered, as interpreted by the cerebral cortex. Moreover, skeletal movement may be affected by motor nerves traveling by way of the spinal cord. Generally, the entire system works to regulate and coordinate bodily responses to both internal and external changes in the environment (Taber, 1970). A malfunctioning neurological system results in an impaired capacity for responding adaptively to a changing environment.

Neurophysiological abnormality may occur by means of many agents and during various stages of the life process; some stages offer more vulnerability than others. Antenatal agents (occurring before birth) described by Nelson (1969) include genetic factors, chromosomal aberrations, placental disease, maternal complications, number of previous pregnancies, age of both mother and father, intra-uterine infection, toxic agents (including certain drugs and alcohol), and radiation. Various organ systems begin and end their prenatal development at different times, therefore their sensitivity to agents varies with maturity of the fetus. The most vulnerable period for the brain is from 15 to 25 days of gestation but, clearly, damage can occur at any time during the development of the nervous system (Hetherington & Parke, 1979).

Perinatal (occurring just before or after birth) vulnerability to neurological insult is accentuated by premature birth. Inadequate oxygen during this stage, hemorrhage, trauma, and infection are the principal offenders (Nelson, 1969). Postnatal (occurring after birth) damage to the neurological system may include damage incurred after birth, during childhood, or throughout the various stages of adulthood. Infections, principally meningitis and encephalitis, injuries, and degenerative neurological disease have also been implicated (Nelson, 1969).

Weller, Swash, McLellan and Scholtz (1983) estimated that 40% of developmental malformations of the CNS arise from genetic abnormality. The most common genetic abnormality is Down's syndrome. This disorder is associated with a group of chromosomal aberrations involving the 21st chromosome pair. In the great majority of cases, a failure to join occurs during the meiosis process, resulting in a trisomy (additional chromosome) of the 21st chromosome pair. Translocation and mosaician represent less frequently occurring aberrations of the 21st chromosome pair, also associated with Down's syndrome (Kopp & Parmelee, 1979).

The incidence of Down's syndrome is between one and two per thousand live births for all races and ethnic groups (Gillberg, 1995; Norman, 1963). Although there is some variability in incidence, most researchers cite an increase in relation to maternal age (Benda, 1960; Lawrence, 1981; Weller et al., 1983). A gradual increase begins with maternal age of 35 and escalates drastically after 40. Metabolic or environmental factors in the mothers' ovaries have been suggested as causes for the syndrome (Benda, 1960;

Lawrence, 1981; Nelson, 1969; Norman, 1963; Weller, Swash, McLellan, & Scholtz, 1983). Structural inspection of the Down's syndrome brain suggests impairment of both growth and differentiation (Benda, 1960). The brain is generally low in weight and the normal convolutional pattern of the brain is simplified. The density of the nerve cells in the cerebral cortex is reduced (Weller et al., 1983).

Rate of mental development is not only slower than normal but also deteriorates progressively with age in Down's syndrome (Cornwell & Birch, 1969; Dicks-Mireaux, 1972; Gillberg, 1995). Many explanations, including neurophysiologic changes, have been offered as explanation for this progressive deterioration. Weller et al. (1983) noted that the microscopic study of brain tissue of Down's syndrome victims during autopsy reveals patterns of neurofibrillary tangles, senile plaques, and granulovacular degeneration such as are found in Alzheimer's disease (deteriorative disease of the elderly involving degeneration of the smaller blood vessels of the brain). Kopp and Parmelee (1979) suggest that the severe limitations in higher level integrative abilities evident in Down's syndrome may cause deficits in information processing (e.g., use of language) that could have progressive detrimental effects on the child's intellectual development over time. The child's capacity for responding adaptively to changing stimulus conditions, a necessity for proper intellectual development, may be impaired directly by the nature of the syndrome. However, the nature of the environment in which these children find themselves, whether it is enriched or impoverished, also can affect development.

In contrast to Down's syndrome, which is genetically related, spina bifida seems to be more influenced by environmental factors. Although genetic factors are suggested by the higher incidence in infants born to parents with a family history of such lesions, it seems that racial, geographical, and even seasonal factors also may be implicated (Kopp & Parmelee, 1979; Weller et al., 1983). Clearly, the interaction of genetic and environmental factors has recently been given prominence. Genetic predisposition combined with certain environmental factors may be the causal condition for spina bifida occurrence (Carter, 1974).

Spina bifida represents a malformation of the nervous system that appears to be more localized and variable in effect than that of Down's syndrome. This defect occurs as a result of faulty prenatal development, in which the lower end of embryotic CNS fails to close. The contents of the spinal column (nerve fibers, meninges, and fluid) may protrude from the lower back in a sac (meningomyelocele). Individual defects vary depending on the extent of damage to the nerve fibers and the existence of other associated conditions (Kleinberg, 1982). The spinal cord is frequently abnormal above and below the level of the spina bifida (Weller et al., 1983). Hydrocephalus, abnormal accumulation of cerebral spinal fluid, frequently is associated with spina bifida. Untreated hydrocephalus creates severe enlargement of the head, increased pressure, and subsequent damage to the brain (Kleinberg, 1982).

Intellectual levels of victims with spina bifida are variable, ranging from an IQ of 137 to severe subnormality (Gillberg, 1995; Hunt, 1981). More specifically, Spain (1974) associates mental retardation with protrusion of a portion of the brain (cranial meningocele and cephalocele), whereas infants with other forms are considered to have potentially normal intellect. Many individuals with spina bifida are incontinent of urine and feces, and have weakness of their legs with sensory loss below the level of the lesion (Kleinberg, 1982). Owing to the presence of the typical locomotor problems in spina bifida, it is unclear whether some deficits are due to neurological impairment or environmental influence. Spain's (1974) longitudinal spina bifida studies have revealed significant deficits in spatial and manipulative development. The fact that the disorder limits the individual's experience may, in fact, cause or influence the specific deficits in spatial and manipulative development. Among the educational problems noted are difficulties with arithmetic and perseveration in language, as well as emotionality and poor motivation (Kopp & Parmelee, 1979).

Primary disorders of the CNS, like Down's syndrome and spina bifida, represent a relatively small proportion of the neurological problems in infants (Horwitz, 1973). More frequently, the genetic programs for potentially normal neurological development are subverted by adverse prenatal or birthing conditions such as lack of oxygen (hypoxia). Cerebral hemorrhage often occurs during prolonged hypoxia. The accumulation of stagnate blood that follows circulatory collapse may cause bleeding and ultimate damage to brain tissue (Weller et al., 1983). Premature infants are especially vulnerable to hypoxia. Since the respiratory system is not fully perfected until the last four to six weeks of gestation, these infants are often born without an optimally functioning respiratory system. Postmortem studies on premature children show that the bleeding usually occurs within one of the cavities of the brain or the space below the arachnoid membrane that contains cerebrospinal fluid (subarachnoid space [Horwitz, 1973]). Later complications of such subarachnoid hemorrhage involve epilepsy, dementia, and hydrocephalus (Weller et al., 1983). Full-term infants are more likely to suffer from hemorrhage in the mid-brain stem (pons) and the posterior portion of the cerebral cortex (hippocampus). Cause for these differences are not, as yet, fully understood.

The location and size of brain lesions at or soon after birth are the primary determinants of the extent of nervous system impairment. The results may range from a gross alteration of brain organization to more minimal effects such as motor overactivity, shortened attention span, or slight muscle impairment (Pincus & Tucker, 1974; Teberg et al., 1982). Large injuries in infants tend to produce more widespread deficits in intellectual abilities than

similar injuries in adults. Dulling of many areas of intellectual functioning, as opposed to having an effect in specific functioning (e.g., language development, visual-spatial relationship comprehension), is also a hallmark effect of the diffuse damage that follows hypoxia (Rapin, 1982).

Neurological deficiencies from early injury are difficult to predict. The nervous system of the newborn infant is extremely immature, functioning largely at brain stem and spinal cord level. The neurologic reflexes such as Moro, grasping, and stepping represent primitive neuronal function that is largely uninhibited by higher cerebral control. Changes in these reflexes are usually not helpful in localizing the lesion, and may occur with either cortical or subcortical dysfunction (Horwitz, 1973). Damage to the cerebral cortex, for instance, may not be evident until the age when behavior dependent on the damaged part makes its developmental appearance. Thus, pathology of fine motor coordination, speech, and cognition is unlikely to be diagnosed in infancy (Rapin, 1982). However, changes in reflexes and disorganized activity of the subcortical structures expressed as a movement disorder or spasticity continue to be used as indicators of neurological damage. In Teberg et al.'s study of low birth weight infants (1982), spastic quadiplegia did, in fact, emerge as the indicative diagnosis of neurological handicap. Churchill, Masland, Naylor, and Ashworth (1974) support this finding.

Turkewitz (1974) contended that the standard methods used for the early identification of neurologic handicaps are insensitive to many forms of neurological involvement. Infants who have had difficulties shortly before or during the birth process frequently appear to recover in a few days. However, abnormalities in motor, language, and intellectual functioning become apparent later in infancy and childhood. Studies using indicators of higher levels of neurological organization (e.g., left/right preference) are being investigated in an effort to identify infants who have experienced neurological damage that is normally not expressed until later in life. However, normative patterns of left/right preference for infants must be established first, before atypical patterns can be interpreted.

The possibilities for neurophysiological dysfunction are limitless; the pathologies presented should not be considered as inclusive by any means. However, it is hoped that an appreciation of the complexity of cerebral neural structure and the corresponding intricacies of impairment resulting from neurophysiological dysfunction will encourage the reader to treat each impaired patient as a unique individual, for heterogeneity of outcome is common (Gaddes, 1985; Goldstein & Reynolds, 1999; Kopp & Parmelee, 1979).

REFERENCES

Benda, C. E. (1960). *The child with mongolism (congenital acromicria)*. New York: Grune & Stratton.

Bickerstaff, E. R. (1978). *Neurology* (3rd ed.). Bungay, England: Chaucer.

Carter, C. O. (1974). Clues to the aetiology of neural tube malformations: Studies in hydrocephalus and spina bifida. *Developmental Medicine and Child Neurology, 16*(Suppl. 32), 3–15.

Churchill, J. A., Masland, R. L., Naylor, A. A., & Ashworth, M. R. (1974). The etiology of cerebral palsy in pre-term infants. *Developmental Medicine and Child Neurology, 16*, 143–149.

Cornwell, A. C., & Birch, H. G. (1969). Psychological and social development in home-reared children with Down's syndrome (mongolism). *American Journal of Mental Deficiencies, 74*, 341–350.

Dicks-Mireaux, M. J. (1972). Mental development of infants with Down's syndrome. *American Journal of Mental Deficiencies, 77*, 26–32.

Gaddes, W. H. (1985). *Learning disabilities and brain function: A neuropsychological approach* (2nd ed.). New York: Springer-Verlag.

Gillberg, C. (1995). *Clinical child neuron psychiatry.* Cambridge: Cambridge University Press.

Goldstein, S., & Reynolds, C. R. (1999). *Handbook of neurodevelopmental and genetic disorders of children.* NY: Guilford.

Hetherington, E. M., & Parke, R. D. (1979). *Child psychology: A contemporary viewpoint* (2nd ed.). New York: McGraw-Hill.

Horwitz, S. J. (1973). Neurologic problems. In M. H. Klaus & A. A. Fanaroff (Eds.), *Care of the high risk neonate* (pp. 287–300). Philadelphia: Saunders.

Hunt, G. (1981). Spina bifida: Implications for 100 children at school. *Developmental Medicine and Child Neurology, 23*, 160–172.

Kandel, E., Schwartz, J., & Jessell, T. (1991). *Principles of neural science.* NY: Elsevier.

Kleinberg, S. B. (1982). *Educating the chronically ill child.* Rockville, MD: Aspen Systems.

Kopp, C. B., & Parmelee, A. H. (1979). Prenatal and perinatal influences on infant behavior. In J. D. Osofsky (Ed.), *Handbook of infant development* (pp. 29–75). New York: Wiley.

Lawrence, K. M. (1981). Abnormalities of the central nervous system. In A. P. Norman (Ed.), *Congenital abnormalities in infancy* (pp. 21–81). Oxford, England: Blackwell.

Lindsley, D. F., & Holmes, J. E. (1984). *Basic human neurophysiology.* Amsterdam: Elsevier Science.

Nelson, W. E. (Ed.). (1969). *Textbook of pediatrics* (9th ed.). Philadelphia: Saunders.

Norman, A. P. (1963). *Congenital abnormalities in infancy.* Philadelphia: Davis.

Pincus, J. H., & Tucker, G. J. (1974). *Behavioral neurology.* New York: Oxford University Press.

Rapin, I. (1982). *Children with brain dysfunction: Neurology, cognition, language and behavior.* New York: Raven.

Spain, B. (1974). Verbal performance ability in pre-school children with spina bifida. *Developmental Medicine and Child Neurology, 16*, 773–780.

Taber, C. W. (1970). *Taber's cyclopedic medical dictionary* (11th ed.). Philadelphia: Davis.

Teberg, A. J., Wu, P. Y. K., Hodgman, J. E., Mich, C., Garfinkle, J.,

Azen, S., & Wingert, W. A. (1982). Infants with birth weight under 1500 grams: Physical, neurological and developmental outcome. *Critical Care Medicine, 10*, 10–14.

Turkewitz, G. (1974). The detection of brain dysfunction in the newborn infant. In D. P. Purpura & G. P. Reaser (Eds.), *Methodological approaches to the study of brain maturation and its abnormalities* (pp. 125–130). Baltimore: University.

Weller, R. O., Swash, M., McLellan, D. S., & Scholtz, C. L. (1983). *Clinical neuropathology.* New York: Overwallop, Great Britain: BAS.

Dorothy A. Strom
Raymond S. Dean
Ball State University
Indiana University School
of Medicine

ADAPTED PHYSICAL EDUCATION
HEALTH MAINTENANCE PROCEDURES
PHYSICAL ANOMALIES

ABPP

See AMERICAN BOARD OF PROFESSIONAL PSYCHOLOGY.

ABROMS, KIPPY I. (1942–   )

Kippy I. Abroms received her BA in psychology from the University of New Hampshire in 1962, MEd in reading from Tulane University in 1973, and PhD in special education from the University of South Mississippi in 1977. Abroms also completed post doctoral training at the University of California, Riverside in 1977 where she worked with Jane Mercer on the System of Multiple Pluralistic Assessment (SOMPA). Abroms is presently an associate professor at Tulane University where she has been teaching since 1975. She has directed several projects for the Office of Special Education and Rehabilitation Services and the Bureau of Education for the Handicapped.

Abroms conducted research with J. W. Bennett (1981) that dispelled the well-entrenched notion of exclusive maternal etiology in Down's syndrome. Abroms and Bennett found that in a significant number of cases the extra #21 chromosome, the immediate cause of Down's syndrome, comes from the sperm. Thus there can be a maternal or paternal contribution to the etiology of Trisomy 21.

Her research has included a longitudinal study on the social development of preschool gifted children, and, as a member of the cranio-facial team at Tulane University Medical Center, she has been involved in investigations

Kippy I. Abroms

of the relationship between cognitive functioning, self-concept, and cranio-facial intervention. She has also become interested in how genetic disorders are manifested in children, and especially in facial deformities that are obvious in the classroom (Abroms, 1987).

REFERENCES

Abroms, K. (1987). Genetic disorders underlying facial deformities. *Topics in early childhood special education, 6,* 92–100.

Abroms, K. I., & Bennett, J. W. (1981). Parental contributions to Trisomy 21: Review of recent cytological and statistical findings. In P. Mittler (Ed.), *Frontiers of knowledge in mental retardation, Vol. 2. Biomedical aspects* (pp. 149–157). Baltimore: University Park.

ELAINE FLETCHER-JANZEN
University of Northern Colorado

ABSENCE OF SPEECH

See SPEECH, ABSENCE OF.

ABSENCE SEIZURES

Absence seizures (also known as petit mal seizures) are a form of epilepsy characterized by brief losses of consciousness unaccompanied by large convulsive movements. Ab-sence seizures are generalized; involving abnormal activity throughout the brain. They are characterized by lack of any aura (sensation that a seizure is to occur), brevity (absence seizures typically last 5–10 seconds [Menkes, 1985]), and abrupt termination. After an absence seizure has occurred, there is no postictal period, the individual does not complain of fatigue or the need to sleep, and he or she can resume the activity being engaged in prior to the seizure. Children with absence seizures often are unaware of their lapses of consciousness.

Although absence seizures are nonconvulsive during the seizure, some movement will be seen in about 70% of diagnosed children. When the seizure begins, an observer may notice a vacant look in the child's eyes. Minor motor movements such as lip smacking, eye blinking, or twitching of the eyelids or face sometimes occur. There may be a slight loss of body tone, with the child perhaps dropping something he or she is holding. Absence seizures often can be precipitated by sustained hyperventilation, and less frequently by photic stimulation.

Absence seizures are more common in girls, and onset is generally between 5 and 15 years of age. There frequently is a family history of a seizure disorder. Most often the neurologic exam and CAT scan is normal. The EEG shows a characteristic three-cycle per second spike and wave pattern during seizures. Generally IQs are reported to be within normal limits, though some studies suggest a mild depression when compared with siblings (Dreifuss, 1983). The most frequent school problem is difficulty in paying attention. There is some evidence that this is related to abnormal brain function (Mirsky, 1969). With frequent seizures, schoolwork often is disrupted.

The medications used in absence seizures include etho-suximide (Zarontin), valproate (Depakene), clonazepam (Clonopin), paramethadione (Paradione), and methsux-imide (Celontin). There are other types of seizures that include staring, but these are not simple absence seizures.

REFERENCES

Dreifuss, F. E. (1983). *Pediatric epileptology.* Boston: Wright.

Menkes, J. H. (1985). *Textbook of child neurology.* Philadelphia: Lee & Febiger.

Mirsky, A. F. (1969). Studies of paroxysmal EEG phenomena and background EEG in relation to impaired attention. In C. R. Evans & T. P. Mullholland (Eds.), *Attention in neurophysiology* (pp. 310–322). London: Butterworth.

GRETA N. WILKENING
Children's Hospital

ELECTROENCEPHALOGRAPH
GRAND MAL SEIZURES
SEIZURE DISORDERS

ABSENTEEISM/ATTENDANCE OF HANDICAPPED CHILDREN

Compulsory school attendance laws have been enacted in all states. The scope of those laws was narrowed in most states by the introduction of exemption clauses. These clauses excuse children considered unfit or uneducable because of physical or mental handicaps from school attendance. Legal challenges by handicapped children for extension and protection of the right established under state law of equal access to educational opportunity ensued during the early 1970s. Those cases were followed by federal and state laws that mandate free appropriate public education to handicapped children and ensure their right to attend school regardless of the severity or type of their disability.

Under IDEA and Section 504 of the Rehabilitation Act of 1973, a handicapped child must be educated in the least restrictive environment his or her needs allow. Children with serious, often chronic, health impairments who require special education and related services may receive instruction in hospitals or in the home. Schools use various approaches, including home visitations, school-to-home telephone communication, and interactive television to connect a homebound or hospitalized student with the classroom. Federal law recognizes that there are instances when, because of the nature or severity of a child's handicap, the child must be educated in a setting other than the regular classroom. However, the least restrictive environment provisions prohibit placement of a child on homebound instruction or other exclusion from the regular educational environment solely because the child is handicapped. Homebound instruction may not be appropriate for the instructional needs of that child.

There have been few studies of program and school attendance as a factor in the achievement of handicapped students. There is some evidence that handicapped students attending regular schools are no more likely to be absent from school than nonhandicapped students (Sullivan & McDaniel, 1983). High rates of school attendance do not necessarily ensure high rates of program attendance or achievement. Sullivan and McDaniel (1983) concluded that handicapped children served in resource rooms may be receiving up to one-quarter less schooling time than is prescribed in their individualized education programs because of competing school activities and absences of either the resource room teacher or the student during a scheduled period. In various studies involving handicapped or nonhandicapped learners (Ivarie, Hogue, & Brulle, 1984; Rosenshine, 1979), investigators in the area of academic learning time as it relates to academic achievement have found a positive correlation between the learning of basic skills and the number of minutes students spend on academically relevant tasks. Researchers are continuing their study of increased active learning time as a powerful intervention technique for handicapped and nonhandicapped students.

Under the IDEA and Section 504, mandatory procedural safeguards exist that allow parents to challenge school disciplinary actions that would interrupt a handicapped child's education. Expulsions, suspensions, and transfers to settings outside a regular classroom or school are considered placement changes since such measures remove students from their current school program or curtail attendance (Simon, 1984). A series of court decisions on this sensitive area have provided important guidelines for determining when and for what length of time handicapped students may be expelled or suspended under federal law (Reschly & Bersoff, 1999; Simon, 1984).

REFERENCES

Ivarie, J., Hogue, D., & Brulle, A. (1984). Investigation of mainstream teacher time spent with students labeled learning disabled. *Exceptional Children, 51,* 142 149.

Reschly, D., & Bersoff, D. (1999). Law and school psychology. In C. R. Reynolds & T. B. Gutkin (Eds.), *The Handbook of School Psychology* (3rd ed.) (pp. 1077–1112). NY: John Wiley & Sons.

Rosenshine, B. V. (1979). Content, time, and direct instruction. In P. L. Peterson & H. J. Walberg (Eds.), *Research on teaching* (pp. 28–56). Berkeley, CA: McCutchan.

Simon, S. G. (1984). Discipline in the public schools: A dual standard for handicapped and nonhandicapped students? *Journal of Law & Education, 13,* 209–237.

Sullivan, P. D., & McDaniel, E. A. (1983). Pupil attendance in resource rooms as one measure of the time on task variable. *Journal of Learning Disabilities, 16,* 398–399.

SHIRLEY A. JONES
*Virginia Polytechnic Institute
and State University*

**HOMEBOUND INSTRUCTION
INDIVIDUALS WITH DISABILITIES EDUCATION ACT
SUMMER SCHOOL FOR HANDICAPPED**

ABSTRACTION, CAPACITY FOR

Abstract reasoning refers to the ability to identify common features of two or more concepts, and has been considered an essential component of intelligence (e.g., Thorndike, 1927). Abstract reasoning ability can be assessed through at least three types of tasks: those which require a person to identify a general concept common to several exemplars, e.g., sorting objects according to categories; to state common features among different concepts, e.g, the Similarities subtest of the Wechsler Intelligence Scale for Children-III or to state examples or features of a given concept (Burger, Blackman, Clark, & Reis, 1982).

While general abstraction ability varies across persons, ability to reason abstractly in specific tasks appears to vary with subject area expertise. For example, in studying the superior memory of chess masters for the configuration of briefly presented game arrangements, Chi, Glaser, and Rees (1981) suggest that experts form abstract, organized representations of the field of play, while novices retain only the surface features of the problem. Adelson (1984) found that novice computer programming students actually had better recall for the details of a briefly presented program than did expert programmers, but that the experts had better recall for what the programs were designed to do. Ability to make abstractions about information seems to improve with experience; as one gains more experience with an area of knowledge, one becomes familiar with the organization of it, and is able to integrate new information with greater success.

Burger, Blackman, Clark, and Reis (1982) found that educable mentally retarded (EMR) adolescents could be trained to improve their abstract reasoning abilities. Context and instructional support also influence the application of abstract thinking skills (Alexander & Murphy, 1999).

REFERENCES

Adelson, B. (1984). When novices surpass experts: The difficulty of a task may increase with expertise. *Journal of Experimental Psychology: Learning, Memory, and Cognition, 10,* 483–495.

Alexander, P. A., & Murphy, P. K. (1999). What cognitive psychology has to say to school psychology: Shifting perspectives and shared purposes. In C. R. Reynolds & T. B. Gutkin (Eds.), *The Handbook of School Psychology* (3rd ed.) (pp. 167–193). NY: John Wiley & Sons.

Burger, A. L., Blackman, L. S., Clark, H. T., & Reis, E. (1982). Effects of hypothesis testing and variable format training on generalization of a verbal abstraction strategy by EMR learners. *American Journal on Mental Deficiency, 86,* 405–413.

Chi, M. T. H., Glaser, R., & Rees, E. (1981). Expertise in problem solving. In R. Sternberg (Ed.), *Advances in the psychology of human intelligence* (Vol. 1, pp. 7–75). Hillsdale, NJ: Erlbaum.

Thorndike, E. L. (1927). *The measurement of intelligence.* New York: Bureau of Publications, Teachers College, Columbia University.

JOHN MACDONALD
Eastern Kentucky University

EDUCABLE MENTALLY RETARDED INTELLIGENCE TESTING

ABSTRACT THINKING, IMPAIRMENT IN

Those who work with children having learning problems are interested in trying to understand their thinking processes. Three groups of children have been of particular interest—deaf, mentally retarded, and learning disabled. Children with these disorders have all exhibited difficulty acquiring academic skills. One hypothesis for their difficulty is that they may not be processing information normally. Some assert these children have deficiencies in abstract reasoning.

A theory of abstract reasoning hinges on the notion that human thinking is a process of conceptualization. Concept formation is the organization of data into categories. To know a concept is to know the characteristics of an entity that either include it or exclude it from a category. To know the concept of "dog" is to know that animals with four legs, hair, and the ability to bark belong together in a category. Some argue that forming a concept is a process of abstracting. To learn the concept of dog requires noticing common characteristics of different dogs, as well as noticing that cats have some characteristics that eliminate them from that category. However, not all concepts are created equally. Some are based on immediate, sensory experience. For example, a child may form a category of "doggy" by directly experiencing dogs and pictures of dogs. This is considered to be a concrete concept. On the other hand, there are concepts that are built from other concepts, for example, the notion of "mammal." A concept even further removed from direct experience is "democracy." The more removed the concept from direct experience, the more abstract it is. The term *abstract,* then, is used in two different ways. On the one hand, it is used to mean the process by which the salient characteristics of entities are identified in order to form concepts. On the other hand, it is used in contrast with the term *concrete* to indicate the role of direct experience.

Another factor related to abstract reasoning is the role of symbolization. Luria (1961) stated that the development of more abstract concepts was dependent on symbolization—more specifically the use of language. In fact, he felt that higher level concept formation was probably dependent on the mediation of language. For example, Luria would contend that a concept such as democracy more than likely requires language for acquisition.

Those dealing with children having difficulties with learning have tried to understand the role of conceptualization and symbolization in the development of abstract reasoning. Johnson and Myklebust (1967) were particularly interested in the conceptualization problems of learning-disabled children. They asserted that some have difficulties in the process of concept formation itself. They argued that any deficit in the processes of perception, imagery, symbolization, or abstracting could interfere with conceptualization. Others have difficulty not so much in the process of conceptualization as in dealing with the more abstract concepts. As Johnson and Myklebust point out, an individual with disturbances in the processes of abstracting or conceptualizing may be identified as a concrete thinker.

Myers and Hammill (1982) note that children who cannot form abstract concepts are generally labeled as being mentally retarded rather than learning disabled. Nonetheless, learning-disabled children are often described as having "concrete behavior characterized by a dependence upon immediate experience as opposed to abstract behavior that transcends any given immediate experience and results in the formation of conceptual categories" (p. 39). Many would argue that the difficulty exhibited by learning-disabled children is caused by a developmental lag and is not a permanent problem. In the case of mentally retarded children, however, the conceptualization problem may be permanent. Further, a body of research has been dedicated to trying to determine whether the conceptual behavior of mentally retarded children represents simply a delay or difference (Zigler & Balla, 1982). To understand this problem researchers may, for example, look at how mentally retarded children use the role of language as a mediation device for concept formation (Field, 1977).

It is not uncommon for those working with hearing-impaired children to describe their cognitive behavior as being concrete (Johnson & Myklebust, 1967). There are several difficulties with this notion, however. Hearing-impaired children, because of their limited input, may simply not have had a sufficient experiential base to adequately form concepts that would be expected of hearing children. Another problem in understanding the hearing-impaired child's conceptualization is that these children live in a visual linguistic world. What may appear to be concrete behavior on the part of the child may simply be an artifact of one of the underlying rules of natural sign language systems. The rule is that the structure of an utterance cannot violate the visual world. For example, the word order of the structure "I finished my work, then watched television" is directly translatable into American Sign Language. "I watched television after I finished my work" is not, because it violates the visual sequence of events. Difficulties that hearing-impaired children have with the latter structure, when encountering it in English, are sometimes interpreted as evidence that the child is a concrete thinker. In truth, it may be simply that the child is having difficulty in dealing with a structure that violates the child's linguistic rules (also see Braden, 1994).

It is important to note that the relationship between sensory information, concept formation, and symbolization is not well understood. Research has given us only the most sketchy idea of what the relationship among the three might be. One field of philosophy, epistemology, has been dedicated to trying to understand these relationships. Introspection and logical reasoning remain the most powerful tools available to both psychology and philosophy for describing concept development and abstract reasoning.

In summary, the notion of abstract reasoning is used in two different ways. It can mean the process by which one identifies the salient characteristics in entities for purposes of categorization. Abstract reasoning can also be the process by which individuals deal with concepts that are based on other concepts, rather than concepts that are based on direct experience. Children with learning problems can have difficulties with either type of abstract reasoning. When difficulties are exhibited, the question arises as to whether the difference is simply developmental delay or a difference in cognitive processing. Some people working with learning-disabled children contend that they eventually outgrow problems in these areas. Mentally retarded children may not necessarily do so. Children who are hearing impaired have also been described as "concrete" learners. However, their difficulties may be a result of too little experience and their use of visually based linguistic rules.

REFERENCES

Braden, J. P. (1994). *Deafness, deprivation, and IQ.* NY: Plenum Press.

Field, D. (1977). The importance of verbal content in the training of Piagetian conservation skills. *Child Development,* 1583–1592.

Johnson, D. J., & Myklebust, H. R. (1967). *Learning disabilities: Educational principles and practices.* New York: Grune & Stratton.

Luria, A. R. (1961). *The role of speech in the regulation of normal and abnormal behavior.* New York: Liveright (Pergamon Press).

Myers, P. I., & Hammill, D. D. (1982). *Learning disabilities: Basic concepts, assessment practices, and instructional strategies.* Austin, TX: Pro-Ed.

Zigler, E., & Balla, D. (1982). *Mental retardation: The developmental-difference controversy.* Hillsdale, NJ: Lawrence Erlbaum.

CAROLYN BULLARD
Lewis & Clark College

CONCRETE OPERATIONS
DEAF
LEARNING DISABILITIES

ABUSED CHILDREN

Today abused children are typically regarded as suffering from a primary illness (Quirk, 1980). A primary illness refers to the notion that living with a certain circumstance for a prolonged period of time creates a situation in the victim requiring primary treatment. The primary illness of child abuse has identifiable symptoms and etiology along with an official diagnosis and prescribed treatments.

An orderly treatment for abused children and adults who were abused as children involves the ability of the clinician to identify and diagnose properly the dilemma and its ramifications and to facilitate the natural healing process from trauma. Thus the first step in treatment is proper identification of child abuse as the problem to be treated.

Children who have been abused relive their abuse over and over in clear or symbolic ways. They dream abusive dreams, remember abusive situations, and in adulthood go so far as to recreate abusive relationships. They manifest little positive affect in interpersonal relationships, and they lack intimacy and express difficulty in trusting others (Herman, 1981). They are depressed and have difficulty in developing meaningful relationships or experiences in their lives. Adults who were abused children are often defensive, suspicious, nervous, and overly alert. They seem to be preoccupied with their bodily functions and are frequently labeled hypochondriacs. Insomnia is another frequently reported symptom, even in the absence of distressing nightmares. Abused children are also guilt-ridden, and experience much shame and self-hatred. Concentrating and following a task through to its completion is another problem area for this population (APA, 1994; Mrazek & Kempe, 1981; Williams & Money, 1980).

Acting out the abuse in self-destructive ways such as drug abuse is frequently observed in this population, which is disproportionately represented in chemical dependency treatment facilities. As teenagers, abused children often become runaways and act out their rage in criminal behavior. Abused children are also disproportionately represented in facilities for delinquents. A disproportionately large group in this population may attempt suicide, hallucinate, manifest seizures, and ultimately be placed in psychiatric hospitals. While these obvious problematic behaviors will occur at high rates, another observed phenomena of this population is the frequency with which they become quiet, good children who then marry an abusive partner. Other compulsive behaviors are frequently manifested by these children and subsequently they will be found as adults in Al-anon, Alcoholics Anonymous, Narcotics Anonymous, Overeaters Anonymous, Gamblers Anonymous, and other self-help treatment programs.

Abused children as adults have difficulty with parenting. Appropriate discipline is difficult for them because it is too restimulating. Consequently, they will abdicate their parenting until the children eventually become abusive toward them (Justice & Justice, 1976). This promotes another likely place for adult abused children to reflect inad-

equacies—as parents of children in trouble. On the other hand, adult abused children may become abusive parents themselves. The inordinate numbers of child abusers that were themselves abused has been widely documented.

Because young and abused children live and grow with a wounded and fragmented personality, they often need intensive treatment efforts. The client who clings or annoys the clinician, reporting that something is missing from treatment, will often be a person who was abused. This person will often complain about the deficiencies of treatment and report that he or she has not been responded to reasonably. This type of reporting should be expected in view of the fact that abused children are wounded people who will have difficulty objectifying their relations: after all, their primary objects, mom or dad, abused them.

Treatment programs and clinicians should routinely be sensitive in recognizing and treating child abuse. When working with clients the following questions should be a routine part of the interview. What was your childhood like? How did your parents treat you? How were you disciplined? What were the punishments employed by your parents? Were you ever raped or seduced? Those who report having difficulty recalling all or crucial parts of their childhood should definitely be regarded as potentially having been abused. This self-induced amnesia is a primitive form of defense against the pain and discomfort resulting from recall of an abusive situation. Naturally, this needs to be dealt with in a sensitive manner by the clinician, and the client should not be prematurely pushed into acknowledging information or feelings they are not prepared to confront.

Abused children often feel at fault for their experience of child abuse. They live with much guilt, shame, self-blame, and self-loathing. Often their abusers told them it was their fault. Child molesters use guilt as a tool with their victims in order to keep the secret, while parents who physically beat their children do so in the name of discipline. Yet, abused children mentally make their parents correct and good. Generally, therapists should enjoy relationships with people, but it is even more important for therapists of abused children to like their clients: While one might think that all therapists would like their clients, fragile clients often find themselves disliked by their therapists. Since they do not grow as the therapist expects, they experience rejection in the context of the therapeutic relationship.

Adults who were abused in childhood have unusual difficulty in establishing trust with the therapist, identifying and discussing feelings, and cooperating with the therapeutic process. Because their tormentors were often people they trusted (e.g., parents), abused children may recoil at the need to trust the therapist. Therefore, an unusually long working-through process is frequently required. This is often difficult for the novice therapist, educator, or other professional lacking information about child abuse and its symptoms.

Most children learn to cope by making decisions separate from the influence of their parents. Abused children have more to cope with, and fewer skills to do so. Reparenting applies here also. Regardless of age, abused children need to learn to live and cope in the real world, and come to recognize that not all people are as threatening as their abusive parents. Therefore, learning coping skills is essential to any successful treatment program. The following are examples of important coping skills to be addressed: learning to trust one's own instincts; learning to identify one's own needs; and learning to proceed to satisfy those needs. Another essential component to treatment is the development of an ability to identify and avoid close contact with abusive people.

Because abuse occurs in the context of an interpersonal relationship, the environment of a therapeutic group has proven itself a particularly helpful treatment modality. In view of the characteristics of this population, the following are important considerations for the leader of a group of abused children. The group should be initially supportive, gentle, homogeneous, and closed to new members after the group has begun. These elements are necessary to address the difficulty in trusting manifested by this population. The group needs to project an image of safety and members must be monitored from inappropriately expressing the rage some may possess. Confrontation must be kept well managed to further reduce regression that may be promoted by some of the more fragmented members. The group leader must monitor the development of any situation that may resemble the childhood abuse of any member in the group. A primary goal of the group is to develop understanding of the personal dynamics of abuse and coping skills that may prevent the development of similar abusive situations in the future.

REFERENCES

American Psychiatric Association. (1994). *Diagnostic and statistical manual of mental disorders* (4th ed.). Washington, DC: Author.

Herman, J. L. (1981). *Father-daughter incest.* Cambridge, MA: Harvard University Press.

Justice, B., & Justice, R. (1976). *The abusing family.* New York: Human Sciences.

Mrazek, P. B., & Kempe C. H. (Eds.). (1981). *Sexually abused children and their families.* New York: Pergamon.

Quirk, J. P. (Ed.). (1980). *Reading in child abuse.* Guilford, CT: Special Learning.

Williams, J. W., & Money, J. (Eds.). (1980). *Traumatic abuse and neglect of children at home.* Baltimore, MD: John Hopkins University Press.

Charles P. Barnard
University of Wisconsin at Stout

ACTING OUT
CHILD ABUSE
ETIOLOGY
NEGLECT

ACADEMICALLY TALENTED CHILDREN

Academically talented children usually possess superior intellectual ability or a specific subject matter aptitude. This point of view is supported by the continuing general acceptance of Witty's (1940) definition of giftedness as performance by a child that is consistently remarkable in a potentially valuable line of human activity. Included in the scope of Witty's definition are those who are academically talented, and, therefore, have the ability to do well in one or more academic subjects in school. This label distinguishes these children from those who may be talented in other areas designated by the U.S. Office of Education such as creative or productive thinking, leadership, visual and performing arts, and psychomotor activities (Renzulli, 1978).

Identification of academic ability can include the use of IQ tests, achievement test scores, evidence of academic achievement, and products successfully completed in an academic area. In addition, students who are academically talented are sometimes 2 to 8 years ahead of chronological age peers in academic subjects (Clark, 1983).

It must be noted that academic talent in one subject matter area does not always mean talent in another academic area. For example, children with a high mathematical aptitude may not perform equally well in other subject matter classes. Once identified, academically talented children require acceleration and/or enrichment in each area of strength.

REFERENCES

Clark, B. (1983). *Growing up gifted.* Columbus, OH: Merrill.

Renzulli, J. S. (1978). What makes giftedness? Reexamining a definition. *Phi Delta Kappan, 60,* 180–184.

Witty, P. (1940). Some considerations in the education of gifted children. *Educational Administration and Supervision, 26,* 512–521.

Mary K. Tallent
Texas Tech University

ACCELERATION OF GIFTED CHILDREN
GIFTED AND TALENTED CHILDREN
GIFTED CHILDREN

ACADEMIC ASSESSMENT

The global function of achievement testing is to assess a student's attainment of academic content areas. Reading, written language, and mathematical functioning are the major domains under the rubric of academic achievement. Anastasi (1982) notes that traditionally academic assessment has been differentiated from aptitude/ability testing by the degree to which a measure is designed to assess uniform versus diverse antecedent experiences. To be categorized as a measure of academic achievement, a measure is designed to test a fairly uniform previous experience (e.g., first grade instruction in reading). In contrast, an aptitude test would be designed to assess the impact of multiple or diverse antecedent experiences. Contemporary measurement specialists recognize that both achievement and aptitude tests assess acquired knowledge, but differ on the degree of specificity and abstraction.

Salvia and Ysseldyke (1981) have described four functions that achievement tests fulfill within the schools. They are used for screening students who may need more in-depth assessment to determine whether special services are appropriate; determining whether a child is eligible for placement in a special education class based on local criteria; assessing a child's strengths and weaknesses to facilitate decisions regarding his or her placement in an instructional sequence; and determining the impact of educational intervention on a class or group of students.

Achievement testing may be conceptualized along several lines: norm-referenced versus criterion referenced; individual versus group administered; and informal teacher-constructed versus standardized instruction. Each of these dimensions will be discussed to highlight the multifaceted construct of academic achievement assessment.

Norm-referenced testing (NRT) began to play a prominent role in American education after World War I. Army Alpha and Beta tests were used for the classification of recruits during the war. The Otis Group Intelligence Scale was published in 1918 by the World Book Company. This scale employed such advances as multiple choice questions, answer sheets, test booklets, and improved normative sampling procedures (Cunningham, 1986). These advances were adapted for the first norm-referenced, standardized measure of academic achievement, the Stanford Achievement Test, published in 1923.

The most salient characteristic of norm-referenced achievement tests is that an examinee's performance on the test is interpreted by comparing his or her relative standing to a given reference group. The reference group or standardization sample is usually composed of representative peers of the same chronological age, or peers in the same grade placement. Performance on a norm-referenced test is typically expressed in scores based on the normal curve such as stanines, T-scores, and/or standard scores (which usually have a mean of 100 and a standard deviation of 15, or sometimes 16). Performance on a norm-referenced test may also be expressed in percentiles, which tell a student's standing relative to a hypothetical group of 100 children. For instance, a score at the 86th percentile indicates that the examinee scored better than 86 out of 100 of his or her hypothetical same-aged peers.

The major norm-referenced group achievement tests include the California Achievement Test (CTB/McGraw-Hill, 1985); the Comprehensive Test of Basic Skills (CTB/McGraw-Hill, 1981); the Iowa Test of Basic Skills (Hieronymus, Lindquist, & Hoover, 1983); the Metropolitan Achievement Test (Barlow, Farr, Hogan, & Prescott, 1978); and the Stanford Achievement Test (Gardner, Rudman, Karlsen, & Merwin, 1982).

These group-administered tests have multiple levels, each designated for a specified grade range. For instance, the Stanford Achievement Test series has six levels: Primary Level 1 for grades 1.5–2.9; Primary Level 2 for 2.5–3.9; Primary Level 3 for 3.5–4.9; Intermediate Level 1 for 4.5–5.9; Intermediate Level 2 for 5.5–7.9; and Intermediate Level 3 for 7.0–9.9. Generally, these tests have gone through several revisions. The Stanford Achievement Test, for example, is in its seventh revision and has been in use in the public schools for over 60 years.

A primary difference between norm-referenced and criterion-referenced tests lies in the way they are interpreted. As noted, the norm-referenced achievement test is designed to give information on a given student's performance relative to a representative group of same-aged peers. In contrast, the criterion-referenced achievement test is designed to give information on a given student's performance in terms of whether he or she has learned a given concept or skill. Thus, the criterion-referenced measure is designed to tell what the student can and cannot do. For instance, the student can add single digit numerals with sums less than 10, but has not learned to regroup or perform simple subtraction problems. Since discrimination among students is not the purpose of a criterion-referenced test, the difficulty level of items and the power of items to separate students are not as important as they are in norm-referenced measures. The major issue in criterion-referenced measurement is whether items reflect a specified instructional domain. Most of the major group-administered achievement tests have been adapted to yield criterion-referenced information. The problem with adapting norm-referenced tests is that there are a multiplicity of instructional objectives (Cunningham, 1986). Since each objective requires several test items to achieve an adequate level of reliability, the length of the test becomes unmanageable.

Up to this point group-administered measures have been used to illustrate the norm- versus criterion-referenced dimensions of academic assessment. Academic achievement testing may also be examined from the viewpoint of the administration format, either individual or group. While group achievement tests are usually given to a whole class by the regular education teacher, individual achievement measures are administered by specially trained personnel (special education teachers, educational diagnosticians, and school psychologists) to a child on a one-to-one basis. Typically, the child has been referred for testing because of academic or behavioral problems manifested in the regular classroom. A general distinction between group and individual measures relates to their use in the decision-making process. Group measures are designed to make decisions about groups, while individual tests are more appropriate for decisions concerning an individual. Therefore, caution must be exercised when attempting to interpret the results of a single child's performance on a group-administered measure. There are many variables that may influence a child's performance on a group-administered measure and result in an inaccurate portrayal of that child's academic skills. Misunderstanding instructions, fatigue, random guessing, class distractions, looking on a neighbor's response sheet, etc., may invalidate a child's scores. When a child is being considered for placement in a special education program, a poor performance on a group-administered measure should be followed up with an individual assessment.

Finally, the academic achievement test may be approached by examining the degree to which the directions to students are standardized. The standardized test is one where the instructions and test questions are presented in the same manner to all examinees. On the other hand, in the teacher-constructed test, there is unlimited latitude in the construction and administration of test items. Both standardized and informal teacher-made tests have advantages and disadvantages. However, they should share certain attributes, i.e., clear directions to students, careful development of items based on a table of specifications, and the type or format of test items.

Whether the directions to an achievement test are standardized or constructed by the teacher, building a table of specifications represents the first step in test construction. A table of specifications contains a listing of instructional objects as well as the relative emphasis to be assigned to each objective. For standardized measures of achievement, the table of specification is based on an examination of major textbook series used across the country. For instance, when reading subtests are constructed, the most widely used basal reading series are reviewed by the test developer. Note is taken at what point in the curricula various concepts are introduced. Invariably, decisions and compromises have to be made regarding content, because all basal reading series are not identical. As such, the consumer of both individual and group standardized achievement tests must examine the available measures, not just in terms of quality of standardization and reliability, but also with respect to the match between the concepts assessed by the test and those taught within the framework of the local

Table 1. Selected objectives from the California Achievement Tests, Forms E and F

Visual Recognition
1. Single letters
2. Upper, lowercase letters
3. Letter combinations

Sound Recognition
4. Initial consonant sounds
5. Final consonant sounds
6. Rhyming

Word Analysis
7. Single consonants/oral
8. Consonant clusters, diagraphs/oral
9. Consonant clusters
10. Variant consonant sounds
11. Long vowels/oral
12. Long vowels
13. Short vowels/oral
14. Short vowels
15. Diphthongs, variant vowel sounds
16. Sight words
17. Compound words
18. Root words/affixes

Reading Comprehension
Literal comprehension
32. Passage details
33. Stated main ideas
Inferential Comprehension
34. Passage analysis/oral
35. Character analysis
36. Central thought
37. Interpreting events
Critical Comprehension
38. Forms of writing
39. Writing techniques

Spelling
40. Vowel sounds
41. Consonant sounds
42. Structural units

curriculum. See Table 1 for selected objectives covered by Forms E and F of the California Achievement Test.

A major difference between standardized and informal, teacher-developed tests is that the former usually represents many more hours of item development, refinement, empirical tryouts, and final selection of test items. In developing standardized achievement tests, considerable weight is placed on both content validity (the representativeness of the items to the domain being tested, and the appropriateness of the format and wording of items relative to the age level of the prospective examinees), and the empirical tryout of the items in terms of reliability. The advantage of the standardized test lies in its documented reliability (presented in an accompanying technical manual), and its ability to compare a student's performance with that of a reference group or specified criterion. Whereas standardized tests measure content that is common to reading and mathematics programs from around the country, the teacher-constructed tests can be specifically targeted to the content of the local curriculum, or to a specific teacher's class.

In addition to defining informal assessment as the administration of a teacher-constructed measure, the term may also be applied to diagnostic processes. These include error analysis, behavioral observation, and the learner's relations to various instructional strategies (Sedlak, Sedlak, & Steppe-Jones, 1982). This last process is flexible and dynamic. A psychoeducational examiner presents tasks to the student in a branching manner similar to the operation of a branching computer-assisted instructional program. Information about the student's mastery of various skills is gleaned from analysis of his or her errors. Error analysis

has been applied to reading, writing, mathematics, second language learning, and spelling (Bejar, 1984). The analysis is usually conducted within a "content" framework, such as an educational taxonomy.

Mathematical functioning is a key area where error analysis has been profitably employed (Brown & VanLehn, 1982). Ashlock (1976) offers useful exercises in a semiprogrammed text to help detect common error patterns in computation. See Table 2 for exemplars of common errors that give insight into the students' problems. Lankford (1974) demonstrated the value of having a student think aloud while solving arithmetic problems. Thus, when an error is made, the computation strategy used by the student becomes apparent. Roberts (1968) has noted four common error categories for arithmetic computation: selecting the wrong operation; erring in recalling a specific arithmetic fact; attempting the correct operation but using an inappropriate algorithm; and random responding that has no apparent relationship to the problem.

Another strategy that is being touted for assessment of academic skills is curriculum-based assessment (CBA). CBA attempts to link assessment more directly to classroom instruction and to provide a more direct assessment of a student's instructional needs (Shapiro & Elliott, 1999). Although touted as an alternative to traditional norm-referenced testing, CBA and NRT are seen best as complementary models, and not as competitive ones.

In summary, academic achievement assessment is used to make decisions about students. These decisions may be made from a normative perspective or in terms of students' mastery of a specified skill. Depending on the administration, format decisions can be made for an individual student or for groups of students. Norm-referenced achievement tests provide information about a student's relative standing compared with that of a reference group, while criterion-referenced tests and informal assessments may be used to make informed decisions about a student's future instructional needs. Specific achievement tests are described throughout this work.

Table 2 Samples of common arithmetic error patterns that give insight into the student's incorrect problem-solving strategy

Addition

$$\begin{array}{r} 56 \\ + 7 \\ \hline 513 \end{array}$$

$$\begin{array}{r} 24 \\ + 5 \\ \hline 11 \end{array}$$
(Addition of all numerals without regard for place value)

Subtraction

$$\begin{array}{r} 53 \\ - 5 \\ \hline 52 \end{array}$$
(Failure to group)

$$\begin{array}{r} 522 \\ - 101 \\ \hline 401 \end{array}$$
(Misunderstanding of zero as a subtrahend)

Multiplication

$$\begin{array}{r} 34 \\ \times 3 \\ \hline 122 \end{array}$$
(Addition of the regrouped number prior to multiplication)

$$\begin{array}{r} 93 \\ \times 8 \\ \hline 101 \end{array}$$
(Use of inappropriate algorithm)

Division

$$\begin{array}{r} 21 \\ 2\overline{)24} \\ 20 \\ \hline 4 \end{array}$$
(A right to left recording pattern is employed)

$$\begin{array}{r} 5 \\ 3\overline{)18} \end{array}$$
(Basic fact mistake)

REFERENCES

Anastasi, A. (1982). *Psychological testing* (5th ed.). New York: Macmillan.

Ashlock, R. B. (1976). *Error patterns in computation: A semi-programmed approach* (2nd ed.). Columbus, OH: Merrill.

Barlow, I. H., Farr, R., Hogan, T. P., & Prescott, G. A. (1978). *Metropolitan Achievement Tests* (5th ed.). New York: Psychological Corp.

Bejar, I. I. (1984). Educational diagnostic assessment. *Journal of Educational Measurement, 21,* 175–189.

Brown, J. S., & VanLehn, K. (1982). Toward a generative theory of "bugs." In T. P. Carpenter, J. M. Moser, & T. A. Romberg (Eds.), *Addition and subtraction: A cognitive perspective.* Hillsdale, NJ: Erlbaum.

CTB/McGraw-Hill. (1981). *The Comprehensive Tests of Basic Skills*. New York: Author.

CTB/McGraw-Hill. (1985). *California Achievement Tests*. New York: Author.

Cunningham, G. K. (1986). *Educational and psychological measurement*. New York: Macmillan.

Gardner, E. G., Rudman, H. C., Karlsen, B., & Merwin, J. C. (1982). *Stanford Achievement Test* (1982 ed.). New York: Psychological Corp.

Hieronymus, A. N., Lindquist, E. F., & Hoover, H. D. (1983). *Iowa Tests of Basic Skills*. Chicago: Riverside.

Jastak, S., & Wilkinson, G. S. (1984). *The Wide Range Achievement Test-Revised* (1984 revised ed.). Wilmington, DE: Jastak Associates.

Lankford, F. G. (1974). What can a teacher learn about a pupil's thinking through oral interviews? *Arithmetic Teacher, 21,* 26–32.

Roberts, G. H. (1968). The failure strategies of third grade arithmetic pupils. *Arithmetic Teacher, 15,* 442–446.

Salvia, J., & Ysseldyke, J. E. (1981). *Assessment in special and remedial education* (2nd ed.). Boston: Houghton Mifflin.

Sedlak, R. A., Sedlak, D. M., & Steppe-Jones, C. (1982). Informal assessment. In D. A. Sabatino & L. Mann (Eds.), *A handbook of diagnostic and prescriptive teaching*. Rockville, MD: Aspen Systems.

Shapiro, E., & Elliott, S. N. Curriculum based assessment and other performance based assessment strategies. In C. R. Reynolds & T. B. Gutkin (Eds.), *The Handbook of School Psychology* (3rd ed.) (pp. 383–408). NY: John Wiley & Sons.

JACK A. CUMMINGS
Indiana University

ACHIEVEMENT TESTS
CRITERION-REFERENCED TESTING
NORM REFERENCED TESTING
See also SPECIFIC TEST NAMES.

ACADEMIC LANGUAGE

Academic language (instructional discourse, cognitive-academic language, or school language) is the way teachers and students organize their communication interactions within educational environments. The purpose is to transmit scientific or logically based knowledge and skills. In contrast, everyday discourse (conversation, social discourse, or basic interpersonal communication) has as its general purpose the regulation of social interaction or interpersonal functions (Chamot & O'Malley, 1994; Wallach & Butler, 1994; Wallach & Miller, 1988; Westby, 1985).

Comprehending and producing academic language requires more cognitive and linguistic complexity than using social language. The transition from oral communication to literate communication marks the need for increased cognitive and linguistic complexity in the teaching-learning process (Cummins, 1983; Larson & McKinley, 1995; Merritt & Culatta, 1998; Naremore, Densmore, & Harman, 1995; Nelson, 1998; Ripich & Creaghead, 1994; Westby, 1997, 1998). Major cognitive, linguistic, and contextual characteristics of academic language include:

Cognitive: abstract concepts; cognitively demanding tasks (critical thinking [analytical and creative], problem solving, decision making); language-thinking and executive functions that are stabilizing (Nelson, 1998; Wallach & Butler, 1994; Wallach & Miller, 1988; Westby, 1998).

Linguistic: complex morphological markers, syntactic transformations, and semantic relationships and networks with explicit vocabulary, resulting in increased oral and text cohesion and coherence; the ability to project, predict, and infer; increased demand for oral and text *form* (pronunciation, spelling, punctuation, organization), *content* (accuracy, synthesis cohesion, and coherence), and *style* (advanced narrative levels and expository genres) (Hedberg & Westby, 1993; Hughes, McGillivray, & Schmidek, 1997; Naremore et al., 1995; Nelson, 1998; Tough, 1979; Wallach & Butler, 1994; Wallach & Miller, 1988).

Contextual: reduced contextual clues; indeterminate audience diffuse in time and space; often physical and temporal separation between sender (writer, speaker) and receiver (listener, reader) (Merritt & Culatta, 1998; Nelson, 1998; Wallach & Butler, 1994; Wallach & Miller, 1988).

Academic communication-learning problems are associated with many developmental and acquired disorders. Academic language use and rules vary from culture to culture. However, the consensus is that to succeed in mainstream educational settings in the course of life students must be able to understand and use the cognitive, linguistic, and contextual conventions associated with academic language.

REFERENCES

Chamot, A. U., & O'Malley, J. M. (1994). *The CALLA handbook: Implementing the cognitive academic language learning approach*. Reading, MA: Addison-Wesley.

Cummins, J. (1983). Language proficiency and academic achievement. In Oller, J. W., Jr. (Ed.), *Issues in language testing research*. Rowley: Newbury House.

Hedberg, N. L., & Westby, C. E. (1993). *Analyzing storytelling skills: Theory to practice*. Tucson, AZ: Communication Skill Builders.

Hughes, D., McGillivray, L., & Schmidek, M. (1997). *Guide to narrative language.* Eau Claire, WI: Thinking Publications.

Larson, V. L., & McKinley, N. (1995). *Language disorders in older students: Preadolescents and adolescents.* Eau Claire, WI: Thinking Publications.

Merritt, D. D., & Culatta, B. (1998). *Language intervention in the classroom.* San Diego, CA: Singular Publishing Group.

Naremore, R. C., Densmore, A. E., & Harman, D. R. (1995). *Language intervention with school-aged children: Conversation, narrative, and text.* San Diego: Singular Publishing Group.

Nelson, N. W. (1998). *Childhood language disorders in context: Infancy through adolescence* (2nd ed.). Boston, MA: Allyn and Bacon.

Ripich, D. N., & Creaghead, N. A. (Eds.). (1994). *School discourse problems* (2nd ed.). San Diego, CA: Singular Publishing Group.

Tough, J. (1979). *Talk for teaching and learning.* Portsmouth, NJ: Heinemann.

Wallach, G. P., & Butler, K. G. (1994). *Language learning disabilities in school-age children and adolescents: Some principles and applications.* New York: Merrill/Macmillan College Publishing.

Wallach, G. P., & Miller, L. (1988). *Language intervention and academic success.* College-Hill/Little, Brown.

Westby, C. E. (1998). Communicative refinement in school age and adolescence. In W. O. Haynes and B. B. Shulman (Eds.), *Communication development: Foundations, processes, and clinical applications* (pp. 311–360). Baltimore, MD: Williams and Wilkins.

Westby, C. E. (1997). There's more to passing than knowing the answers. *Language, speech and hearing services in the schools, 28,* 274–287.

Westby, C. E. (1985). From learning to talk to talking to learn: Oral-literate language differences. In C. Simon (Ed.), *Communication skills and classroom success: Therapy methodologies for language-learning disabled students.* San Diego: College-Hill.

STEPHEN S. FARMER
New Mexico State University

DISCOURSE

ACADEMIC SKILLS

While to some individuals the definition of academic skills conjours up the three Rs, to others the delineation of the academic skills most important to the process of special education is a task that poses an awesome definitional problem. To the preschool special educator, for example, certain fine motor skills may be defined as important academic skills. On the other hand, for the special educator working at the secondary level, the ability to accept positive and negative feedback (social skills), driving skills, or home economics may be considered important academic skills that warrant inclusion in the secondary special education curriculum.

A recent comprehensive sourcebook on research on teaching presents detailed analyses of seven academic skill areas: written composition, reading, mathematics, natural sciences, arts and aesthetics, moral and values education, and social studies (Wittrock, 1986). At least a few of these areas would be considered by most individuals to be core or basic academic skills. The fact that these academic skill areas have entire chapters devoted to them also indicates that there is enough research, theory, or perhaps controversy regarding them as to allow them to be studied and discussed extensively.

Beyond the issue of defining academic skills are the related issues of the rise and fall of skills across generations (which is constantly addressed by the popular media), and equally important, the procedures by which these skills are taught and acquired by students in special education. Cartwright, Cartwright, and Ward (1981) list several approaches used by special education teachers to impart academic skills; these include the diagnostic teaching model, remedial and compensatory education models, direct instruction, task analysis, perceptual-motor training, inquiry, modeling, media-based instruction, education games, and computer-assisted and computer-managed instruction. Two additional instructional approaches that were popularized in the 1970s include mastery learning and cooperative learning (Stallings & Stipek, 1986).

With regard to learner characteristics that affect the acquisition of academic skills, Wittrock (1986) suggests the following broad categories for consideration: students' perceptions and expectations, attention, motivation, learning and memory, comprehension and knowledge acquisition, learning strategies, and metacognitive processes. In summary, special educators must first define the academic skills that their students must acquire and then consider instructional, student, and other variables in planning for the optimal acquisition of academic skills.

REFERENCES

Cartwright, P. G., Cartwright, C. A., & Ward, M. E. (1981). *Educating special learners.* Belmont, CA: Wadsworth.

Stallings, J. A., & Stipek, D. (1986). Research on early childhood and elementary school teaching programs. In M. C. Wittrock (Ed.), *Handbook of research on teaching.* New York: Macmillan.

Wittrock, M. C. (1986). Students' thought processes. In M. C. Wittrock (Ed.), *Handbook of research on teaching.* New York: Macmillan.

RANDY W. KAMPHAUS
University of Georgia

MEMORY DISORDERS
METACOGNITION

ACADEMIC THERAPY

Academic Therapy was the first journal designed for specialists (special education teachers, educational diagnosticians, psychologists, resource room specialists, practitioners in speech, language, communication, vision, and hearing) who are in direct contact with children manifesting learning, language, and communication difficulties. Since 1965, it has established a reputation for easy-to-read and practical articles that focus on "what works" in the special clinical, therapeutic, or classroom setting. Contributors are teachers, professors, and specialists. Articles are short and are selected on the basis of their usefulness and ability to be put into immediate use by the journal reader. Each issue includes listings of new materials, current news on the national level, and ideas for home management. *Academic Therapy* is published five times during the year: September, November, January, March, and May.

JOHN ARENA
Academic Therapy Publications

ACADEMIC THERAPY PUBLICATIONS

Since 1965, Academic Therapy Publications (ATP) has served specialists, diagnosticians, private clinics and schools, teachers in mainstream and self-contained classes, and others who work in special settings. It has a wide variety of publications designed to address to classroom aids, auditory learning, language, math, vocational/career, secondary/adult, professional texts, parent brochures, and reading programs. Academic Therapy Publications has a computer software division for students and professionals, and a test division which offers diagnostic instruments for assessing academic achievement. The *Directory of Facilities and Services for the Learning Disabled* was published every two years for 34 years. The 17th edition, published in 1997, marked the *Directory*'s last and final publication. High Noon Books, a division of Academic Therapy Publications, publishes high-interest low-level mystery novels, written on a first through third/fourth grade reading level for individuals ages 10 through adult who have reading difficulties or limited English proficiency. Activity workbooks are also available.

REFERENCES

Kratowille, B. L. (Ed.). (1997). *Directory of facilities and services for the learning disabled* (17th ed.). Novato, CA: Academic Therapy.

ANNA M. ARENA
Academic Therapy Publications

ACALCULIA

Acalculia is defined by Hallahan, Kauffman, and Lloyd (1985) as "complete inability to use mathematic symbols and perform mathematical computations" (p. 267). Hallahan et al. distinguish acalculia from dyscalculia by stating that the term dyscalculia is "reserved for less severe problems in these areas" (p. 267).

One of the earliest uses of the term acalculia comes from the work of Henschen (Cohn, 1961). According to Cohn's description, Henschen used the term acalculia to include disturbances in number recognition as well as problems with specific arithmetic operations. This was reported by Henschen to be a manifestation of lesions in different regions of the brain, but primarily involved with the caudal portion of the left cerebral hemisphere (Cohn, 1961).

Strauss and Werner (1938) described acalculia as "deficiency in number operations" (p. 719) and provided evidence of the association between acalculia and finger agnosia (inability to recognize fingers on one's own hands), which was said to be caused by a lesion within an area around the angular gyrus. Strauss and Werner (1938) provided some evidence of a correlation between finger agnosia and acalculia.

According to Strauss and Lehtinen (1948), disturbance in visual perception was a major contributing factor to acalculia. They developed several principles for instruction based on organized perceptual experiences. Terms such as acalculia and dyscalculia have declined in popularity with the increasing attention given to more educationally relevant orientations. Generally, deficits in mathematical functioning have been remediated with the use of task-specific instructional strategies. Mercer (1979, chapter 8) provides an overview of some of these strategies. More recent nomenclature includes these disorders under the more general rubric of specific developmental disorders.

REFERENCES

Cohn, R. (1961). Dyscalculia. *Archives of Neurology, 4,* 301–307.

Hallahan, D. P., Kauffman, J. M., & Lloyd, J. W. (1985). *Introduction to learning disabilities* (2nd ed.). Englewood Cliffs, NJ: Prentice Hall.

Mercer, C. (1979). *Children and adolescents with learning disabilities.* Columbus, OH: Merrill.

Strauss, A. A., & Lehtinen, L. E. (1948). *Psychopathology and education of the brain-injured child.* New York: Grune & Stratton.

Strauss, A. A., & Werner, H. (1938). Deficiency in the finger schema in relation to arithmetic disability (finger agnosia and acalculia). *American Journal of Orthopsychiatry, 8,* 719–724.

THOMAS E. SCRUGGS
MARGO A. MASTROPIERI
Purdue University

ARITHMETIC REMEDIATION
DYSCALCULIA

ACCELERATION OF GIFTED CHILDREN

Acceleration is any process whereby a child makes educational progress faster than usual, whether measured by advancement in school grade or by actual achievement (Ward, 1980). Presently, there are numerous avenues for acceleration in schools for those students who exhibit general intellectual ability and/or outstanding aptitude in one or more subject areas.

For students who exhibit general intellectual ability, three of the existing options are telescoping, grade skipping, and early admission to formal schooling. Telescoping involves the completion of three years of schooling in two years or four years of schooling in three years (Fox, 1979). Those who skip grades are promoted two grade levels in one year. These children are usually given credit for the skipped year and are able to complete formal schooling in fewer years than usual. Early entrance to formal schooling occurs when children are allowed to enter kindergarten or first grade at an age lower than is usually allowed by the school or school system. These children may merit early entrance because of advanced scores on IQ or abilities tests.

For pupils with outstanding aptitude in one or more subject areas, six options exist: concurrent enrollment, correspondence courses, special schools or classes, independent study, tutorials, and credit by exam. Other options may be created within each individual class, school, or school system.

Concurrent enrollment for secondary school students occurs when high schools and universities cooperate to allow students to be concurrently enrolled both in a high school and in a college. These pupils receive college credit for courses taken on the college campus; in some cases they receive college credit for courses taught by a university faculty member on the high school campus. Correspondence courses provide another option for acceleration when secondary school students enroll through the continuing education division of participating universities. They receive lessons by mail, and, on completion of all requirements, receive a grade after taking a final examination graded by the same university professor who planned the lessons.

Another acceleration practice takes place in special schools or classes where students are allowed to complete more than one year of credit in a subject area class by working in a compacted curriculum and successfully passing examinations. One of the most well known of these special school and class arrangements is Julian Stanley's

Study of Mathematically Precocious Youth, conducted at Johns Hopkins University (Stanley, 1977). Students who have qualified for participation in this program by scoring at least 550 on the Scholastic Aptitude Test in mathematics have the opportunity to study higher level mathematics in college classes during the summer and/or complete college correspondence courses during the school year. Since the inception of the program at Johns Hopkins, it has expanded to include students with high verbal aptitude, and subjects other than mathematics are offered. Two other programs have replicated Stanley's work: the Midwest Talent Search at Illinois' Northwestern University and the Talent Identification Program at North Carolina's Duke University.

Talented students may also do independent study or be provided with a special tutor to complete course requirements in an advanced curriculum area. Finally, other credit-by-examination options are available to students who wish to advance beyond their peers through acceleration. These include advanced placement in secondary schools in states that provide their own examinations to receive credit for high school classes, advanced placement in college courses through the Advanced Placement Program, and the College Level Examination Program that allows students to receive credit in 15 fields by taking exams at university testing centers.

In the early 1900s the most frequent accommodation for gifted and talented children was to allow rapid acceleration through the standard curriculum (Whitmore, 1980). The popular belief that acceleration is socially detrimental to the child later curbed much of this acceleration. There are conflicting views on this subject. Kulik and Kulik (1984) concluded that the research they reviewed offered no real answers to this debate, with some studies showing small positive effects and some showing small negative effects in affective areas. However, following the work pioneered by Julian Stanley and his colleagues, acceleration has become more acceptable again.

Although there are no clear answers concerning the effects of acceleration on social and emotional growth, there are answers to questions about whether acceleration is beneficial academically. In a meta-analysis of 26 controlled studies, evidence showed that examination performance of accelerates surpassed by nearly one grade level the performance of nonaccelerates of equivalent age and intelligence. Furthermore, the examination scores of accelerates were equivalent to those of same-grade, but older, talented nonaccelerates (Kulik & Kulik, 1984).

REFERENCES

Fox, L. H. (1979). Programs for the gifted and talented. In A. H. Passow (Ed.), *The gifted and talented: Their education and development.* Chicago: National Society for the Study of Education.

Kulik, J. A., & Kulik, C. C. (1984). Effects of accelerated instruction on students. *Review of Educational Research, 54,* 409–425.

Stanley, J. C. (1977). Rationale of the study of mathematically precocious youth (SMPY) during its first five years of promoting educational acceleration. In J. C. Stanley, W. C. George, & C. H. Solano (Eds.), *The gifted and creative: A fifty-year perspective.* Baltimore, MD: Johns Hopkins University Press.

Ward, V. S. (1980). *Differential education for the gifted.* Ventura, CA: Ventura County Superintendent of Schools Office.

Whitmore, J. R. (1980). *Giftedness, conflict, and underachievement.* Boston: Allyn & Bacon.

MARY K. TALLENT
Texas Tech University

ACADEMICALLY TALENTED CHILDREN
GIFTED AND TALENTED CHILDREN
SIDIS, WILLIAM JAMES

ACCESSIBILITY OF BUILDINGS

The accessible building is a structure that is readily usable by individuals possessing a wide range of physical disabilities or other limitations (such as sensory handicaps). Although estimates vary widely as to the number of citizens whose temporary or permanent impairments inhibit their mobility, the U.S. Department of Housing and Urban Development (1978) projects that at least 30 million people possess conditions that demand barrier-free facilities. A building or other site designed to accommodate ambulant or sensorily disabled persons is equally convenient and accessible to the nonhandicapped population. The design criteria used to meet the needs of handicapped populations are essentially no different from those of the general, nondisabled citizenry; they are only more pronounced.

The generally accepted minimum standards for ensuring the accessibility of buildings are incorporated in the American National Standards Institute (ANSI) specifications. Originally adopted in 1961 and subsequently revised and expanded during 1970s, the ANSI standards serve as a foundation for state laws and federal guidelines concerning building accessibility. A federal entity, the National Commission on Architectural Barriers (CAB), was created by an act of Congress to promote and evaluate voluntary and, in the case of federally owned or subsidized buildings, mandatory compliance with the ANSI standards.

The CAB's primary function has been to oversee the implementation of the Architectural Barriers Act of 1968 and related federal legislation designed to foster the accessibility of buildings and other environments.

The economic and human benefits of a site design that is barrier free are substantial. Data from the U.S. Office of Housing and Urban Development (1978) suggest that the initial costs of remodeling existing structures or designing and constructing new, fully accessible facilities are minimal when compared with the benefits derived by the disabled, their families, friends and colleagues, educational and other service agencies, and employers. The initial, one-time investment in a barrier-free design provides long-term benefits in terms of personal comfort, mobility, maximization of educational, social and employment options, and (particularly important for business) an expansion in the pool of active consumers.

Guided by the ANSI standards, architects and facility planners must ensure that the entrances to and the interiors of buildings allow for the uninhibited mobility, orientation, comfort, and performance of all facility users. As reviewed by Cotler and DeGraff (1976), the structural dimensions, interior design, entranceways and the layout of furniture in all buildings should be integrated to accommodate the physical limitations in mobility, reach and posture experienced by most wheelchair users and individuals aided by crutches, walkers and canes. It is of equal importance to the sensorily handicapped population (e.g., individuals who are blind or deaf) that building environments offer a simple, regular, well-lighted and marked design that enhances orientation and ready access to sources of visual, aural and tactile information.

REFERENCES

Cotler, S. R., & DeGraff, A. H. (1976). *Architectural accessibility for the disabled on college campuses.* Albany, NY: State University Construction Fund.

U.S. Department of Housing and Urban Development. (1978). *Access to the environment.* Washington, DC: U.S. Government Printing Office.

GEORGE JAMES HAGERTY
Stonehill College

AMERICANS WITH DISABILITIES ACT
ARCHITECTURAL BARRIERS
ARCHITECTURE AND THE HANDICAPPED

ACCESSIBILITY OF PROGRAMS

Section 504 of the Rehabilitation Act of 1973, as amended, provides that

> no otherwise qualified handicapped individual . . . shall, solely by reason of his handicap, be excluded from participation in, be denied the benefits of, or be subjected to discrimination under any program or activity receiving federal financial assistance or under any program or activity conducted by any executive agency or the United States Postal Service.

The substantive provisions apply to two distinct sets of entities: recipients of federal financial assistance (federally assisted programs) and the operations of government agencies (federally conducted programs).

The concept of program accessibility is a key requirement of the implementing regulations for both federally assisted and federally conducted programs (U.S. Government, 1978; U.S. Government, 1985). In both cases, the requirement is not that every existing building or classroom be physically accessible, but rather that "the program or activity, when viewed in its entirety, is readily accessible to and usable by handicapped persons" (28 CFR 41.57(a)). All new buildings and facilities must be designed and constructed to be readily accessible to and usable by handicapped persons.

Since the late 1970s, federal court decisions and regulatory policy have interpreted and qualified the precise requirements of program accessibility. Of particular importance is the U.S. Supreme Court decision in *Southeastern Community College* v. *Davis* (1979), which held that the school was not required to modify a nurse training program as sought by a hearing-impaired individual because such modification would constitute "a fundamental alteration in the nature of the program." In discussing program modification, the Court also referenced attaining desirable goals "without imposing undue financial and administrative burdens" (pp. 410, 412).

In a prototype regulation distributed to all agencies as nonbinding guidance, and in its own regulation on federally conducted programs promulgated in 1984 (U.S. Government, 1985), the Department of Justice employs criteria from the *Davis* decision. The program accessibility requirement for existing programs explicitly does not "require the agency to taken any action that it can demonstrate would result in a fundamental alteration in the nature of the program or in undue financial and administrative burdens" (28 CFR 39.150(a)(2)).

Some commentators on the Department of Justice's proposed regulation objected to the inclusion of the *Davis* criteria. They argued that the language must be identical to the Department of Justice's government-wide coordinating regulation on federally assisted programs, which does not include such criteria (U.S. Government, 1985, p. 357). The Department of Justice's position is that "judicial interpretation of Section 504 [including circuit court decisions following *Davis*] compels it to incorporate the new language" and that the regulations for federally assisted programs must now be interpreted consistent with the federally conducted rule and *Davis* (U.S. Government, 1985, p. 357).

A good discussion of these issues is in the editorial note to 28 CFR 39 (U.S. Government, 1985). Other precedents have established the rights of all students to accessibility of educational programs (Sales et al., 1999).

REFERENCES

Sales, B., Krauss, D. A., Sacken, D., & Overcast, T. (1999). The legal rights of students. In C. R. Reynolds & T. B. Gutkin (Ed.), *The Handbook of School Psychology* (3rd ed.) (pp. 1113–1144). NY: John Wiley & Sons.

Southeastern Community College v. Davis (1979). United States Supreme Court, 442 U.S. 397.

U.S. Government. (1978). Code of Federal Regulations Title 28, Part 41. *Implementation of Executive Order 12250, Non-Discrimination on the Basis of Handicap in Federally Assisted Programs.*

U.S. Government. (1985). Code of Federal Regulations Title 28, Part 39. *Enforcement of Non-Discrimination on the Basis of Handicap in Programs or Activities Conducted by the Department of Justice.*

JAMES R. RICCIUTI
*United States Office of
Management and Budget*

ACCESSIBILITY OF BUILDINGS
AMERICANS WITH DISABILITIES ACT
SPECIAL EDUCATION, LEGAL REGULATION OF

ACCOMMODATION

Accommodation is one of two complementary processes proposed by Jean Piaget to account for an individual's adaptation to the environment; its counterpart is assimilation. Accommodation involves changing or transforming cognitive or sensorimotor schemes according to the demands of the environment; assimilation involves incorporating external elements into existing conceptual schemes.

The difference between accommodation and assimilation can be illustrated by an example of an infant's response to a rattle (Ginsburg & Opper, 1969). When a rattle suspended from an infant's crib begins to shake after the infant's arm movement causes it to move, the infant looks at and listens to the toy rattling, assimilating the event into his or her schemes of looking and listening. To repeat the movement of the rattle, the infant must make the necessary hand and arm movements, accommodating his or her actions according to the demands of the situation.

Assimilation and accommodation were viewed by Piaget as inseparable aspects of a single process of adaptation, separable only for purposes of discussion (Brainerd, 1978). Assimilation and accommodation occur simultaneously; a balance between the two is necessary for adaptation. A scheme must accommodate itself to the specific characteristics of the object or event it is attempting to assimilate;

accommodation guides the eventual change in structures (Gelman & Baillargeon, 1983).

REFERENCES

Brainerd, C. J. (1978). *Piaget's theory of intelligence.* Englewood Cliffs, NJ: Prentice-Hall.

Gelman, R., & Baillargeon, R. (1983). A review of some Piagetian concepts. In P. H. Mussen (Ed.), *Handbook of child psychology: Vol. III. Cognitive development* (pp. 167–230). New York: Wiley.

Ginsburg, H., & Opper, S. (1969). *Piaget's theory of intellectual development: An introduction.* Englewood Cliffs, NJ: Prentice-Hall.

LINDA J. STEVENS
University of Minnesota

ASSIMILATION
COGNITIVE DEVELOPMENT
PIAGET, JEAN

ACETYLCHOLINE

Acetylcholine (ACh) is a neurotransmitter, a chemical that is released from one neuron to pass a message to another neuron. Acetylcholine is naturally synthesized in living cells in cholinergic nerve terminals that are located primarily in the autonomic nervous system. It also is evident at parasympathetic postganglionic synapses, and at neuromuscular junctures (Cooper, Bloom, & Roth, 1982).

The autonomic nervous system is involved in what appears to be functionally reflexive responses directed toward energy conservation or preparation for possible trauma. Thus, with cholinergic stimulation, pupils contract, heart rate slows, and muscular contraction is facilitated (Katzung, 1982). Experimental work by Deutsch (1984) suggests the possibility of an indirect, environmental role for ACh in the development of memories. Results of animal studies indicate that drugs that block cholinergic action tend to increase low rates of response and decrease high rates of response among behaviors that were maintained through food reinforcers (Seiden & Dykstra, 1977). Such findings are consistent with the likelihood that ACh plays a role in creating a chemical environmental context for learning by mediating autonomic responsiveness. A role in pain perception also has been postulated (Cooper et al., 1982). Myasthenia gravis, a disease characterized by fluctuating muscle weakness, especially in muscles innervated by the motor nuclei of the brain stem (Adams & Victor, 1981), is a model of ACh dysfunction. Observed involvement of cholinergic systems in tardive dyskinesia,

Huntington's chorea, and Alzheimer's dementia has led to experimental administration of drugs that facilitate ACh; however, no consistent results have been observed in such studies (Cooper et al., 1982).

REFERENCES

Adams, R. D., & Victor, M. (1981). *Principles of neurology.* New York: McGraw-Hill.

Cooper, J. R., Bloom, F. E., & Roth, R. H. (1982). *The biochemical basis of neuropharmacology.* New York: Oxford University Press.

Deutsch, J. A. (1984). Amnesia and a theory for dating memories. In G. Lynch, J. L. McGaugh, & N. M. Weinberger (Eds.), *Neurobiology of learning and memory* (pp. 105–110). New York: Guilford Press.

Katzung, B. G. (1982). *Basic and clinical pharmacology.* Los Altos, CA: Lange Medical Publications.

Seiden, L. S., & Dykstra, L. A. (1977). *Psychopharmocology: A biochemical and behavioral approach.* New York: Van Nostrand Reinhold.

ROBERT F. SAWICKI
*Lake Erie Institute of
Rehabilitation*

CENTRAL NERVOUS SYSTEM

ACHIEVEMENT NEED

Achievement need is also known as achievement motivation, the need for achievement and n:Ach. The concept was first defined by Murray (1938) as the need, "to overcome obstacles, to exercise power, to strive to do something difficult as well and as quickly as possible" (pp. 80–81). Murray, however, chose not to attempt to conduct applied research in achievement motivation and the concept did not receive much attention until McClelland (1951) developed a cognitive theory of motivation in which the need for achievement is one element. McClelland's theory states that a person's tendency to approach a task (effort) is a function of the strength of the achievement need, the strength of the need to avoid failure, the person's subjective belief about the probability of success or failure, and the value of the incentives associated with either success or failure. According to McClelland (1951) and Atkinson (1964), achievement need is intrinsic. It is not associated with extrinsic rewards that accrue as a result of achievement. Achievement need is generally measured through the Thematic Apperception Test (TAT), although Hermans

(1970) developed a paper and pencil test for this purpose called n:Ach.

Many researchers have attempted to determine how achievement need develops. Crandall (1963) discovered that children with high achievement needs had mothers who rewarded achievement and achievement activities at an early age. These mothers also did not attend to their children's pleas for help when the children faced a difficult problem. Crandall further concluded that middle- and upper-class parents were more likely to engage in behaviors that develop achievement motivation than were parents of lower economic status.

A number of studies have been conducted to determine the effects of achievement on task performance and personality. Weiner (1970) found that high-need achievement persons persist in the face of failure while low-need achievement persons become more inhibited in their responses. He further found that low-need achievement persons will engage in achievement activity when success and reinforcement rates approach 100%, but high-need achievement persons work best when reinforcement is attained approximately 50% of the time. Weiner & Kukla (1970) related achievement need research to Rotter's (1966) research in locus of control. Using elementary school children, they concluded that high-need achievement children viewed their successes as resulting from their effort. Both high- and low-achievement need children attributed failure to themselves, but high-need achievement children attributed failure to lack of effort while low-achievement children attributed it to lack of ability.

REFERENCES

Atkinson, J. W. (1964). *An introduction to motivation.* Princeton, NJ: Van Nostrand.

Crandall, V. J. (1963). Achievement. In H. W. Stevenson (Ed.), *Child psychology* (pp. 416–459). Chicago: University of Chicago Press.

Hermans, H. J. M. A. (1970). A questionnaire measure of achievement motivation. *Journal of Applied Psychology, 54,* 353–363.

McClelland, D. C. (1951). *Personality.* New York: Dryden.

Murray, H. A. (1938). *Exploration in personality.* New York: Oxford University Press.

Rotter, J. B. (1966). Generalized expectancies for internal versus external control of reinforcement. *Psychology Monographs, 80.*

Weiner, B. (1970). New conceptions in the study of achievement motivation. In B. A. Maher (Ed.), *Progress in experimental personality research* (Vol. 5). New York: Academic.

Weiner, B., & Kukla, A. (1970). An attributional analysis of achievement motivation. *Journal of Personality and Social Psychology, 15,* 1–20.

JAMES K. McAFEE
Pennsylvania State University

LEARNED HELPLESSNESS
MOTIVATION
SELF-CONCEPT
SELF-CONTROL CURRICULUM

ACHIEVEMENT TESTS

Achievement tests are individually- or group-administered standardized instruments intended to measure the effectiveness of former training. Achievement tests are the dominant form of standardized assessment in education. Measures of achievement have been used to evaluate student performance, school instruction efficacy, candidates for scholarship awards, admission to academic programs, and applicants for industrial and government employment. Group administered achievement tests are more likely to be employed for the evaluation of a scholastic program, whereas individually administered achievement tests are typically used to assist in appropriate grade placement in schools and the identification and diagnosis of learning disabilities.

Traditional achievement tests were based on the principle of comparing examinees to their peers, or normative testing (classical test theory). Some more contemporary achievement tests are based on the premise that a prediction can be made about the performance of a person with a specified ability in regard to that person's probable success or failure on an item of specified difficulty (Anastasi, 1988). In other words, as the level of ability increases, the probability that an examinee will give a correct response increases (Hambleton, Swaminathan, & Rogers, 1991). Given the special characteristics of item response theory (IRT), computer adaptive testing is a desirable method to select different sets of items for each subject.

Some examples of commonly used normative achievement tests and their publishers include: Comprehensive Tests of Basic Skills (CTB/McGraw-Hill), Iowa Tests of Basic Skills (Riverside Publishing Company), Kaufman–Test of Educational Achievement (American Guidance Service), Stanford Test of Academic Skills (Psychological Corporation), and Tests of General Educational Development (GED Testing Service of the American Council on Education).

The use of computer aided testing and IRT represents a new era in achievement testing. For example, the ACCU-PLACER (College Board) computerized battery of achievement tests for college level placement was implemented in the placement of hundreds of thousands of students during the 1996–97 academic school year (Cole, Muenz, & Bates, 1998).

REFERENCES

Anastasi, A. (1988). *Psychological testing* (6th ed.). New York: Macmillan.

Cole, J. C., Muenz, T. A., & Bates, H. G. (1998). Age in correlations between ACCUPLACER's reading comprehension subtest and GPA. *Perceptual and Motor Skills, 86,* 1251–1256.

Hambleton, R. K., Swaminathan, H., & Rogers, H. J. (1991). *Fundamentals of item response theory.* London: Sage.

TRACY A. MUENZ
*California School of
Professional Psychology*

ASSESSMENT
CRITERION-REFERENCED TESTS
NORM-REFERENCED TESTS

ACHONDROPLASIA

Achondroplasia, also called chondrodystrophy, refers to a defect in the formation of cartilage in the epiphyses of long bones, such that a type of dwarfism results. This most common form of dwarfism is usually inherited as an autosomal dominant trait, or it may result from spontaneous mutation (Avioli, 1979; Magalini, 1971). Clinical features of achondroplasia include absolute diminution of extremities; normal trunk and head size; a prominent, bulging forehead; and a flattened, saddle nose. Hands and feet typically are short, and fingers tend to be nearly equal in length (trident hands). Adult height generally does not exceed 1.4 meters.

The intelligence of affected persons is reported to be normal (Avioli, 1979; Lubs, 1977), although there is evidence of occasional neurologic complications during early adulthood (Magalini, 1971). The fertility of achrondroplastic dwarfs is reported to be 30% of normal. Of offspring of two affected persons, two-thirds will exhibit the syndrome (Lubs, 1977). In educational settings, afflicted children may require adaptive equipment to accommodate their short stature. While there is no evidence to suggest that achondroplasia places individuals at increased risk for learning problems, a multifactored evaluation is appropriate for children who experience difficulty in school.

REFERENCES

Avioli, L. V. (1979). Diseases of bone. In P. B. Beeson, W. McDermott, & J. B. Wyngaarden (Eds.), *Cecil textbook of medicine* (pp. 2225–2265). Philadelphia: Saunders.

Lubs, M. (1977). Genetic disorders. In M. J. Krajicek & A. I. Tearney (Eds.), *Detection of developmental problems in children* (pp. 55–77). Baltimore, MD: University Park Press.

Magalini, S. (1971). *Dictionary of medical syndromes.* Philadelphia: Lippincott.

CATHY F. TELZROW
*Cuyahoga Special Education
Service Center*

CONGENITAL DISORDERS
MINOR PHYSICAL ANOMALIES

ACTING OUT

Acting out has been defined by Harriman (1975) as the "direct expression of conflicted tensions in annoying or antisocial behavior in fantasies" (p. 30). A child who exhibits acting-out behavior is one who cannot easily accept structural limits and is difficult to manage in the classroom. Acting-out behaviors are similar to conduct disorders, but not necessarily as severe. One reason for the similarity is that acting-out behavior is one of the characteristics clustered under the broader grouping of conduct disorders. Acting-out behaviors usually are of high frequency and of significant duration, and do not include minor daily misbehavior.

Usually, when a behavior is identified as an acting-out behavior, it is operationally defined, observed, and recorded by the classroom teacher in specific and observable terms. Some of the behaviors that can be identified as acting-out behaviors include fighting, lying, temper tantrums, pouting, stealing, hyperactivity, threatening, and bullying (Quay, 1979).

REFERENCES

Harriman, P. L. (1975). *Handbook of psychological terms.* Totowa, NJ: Littlefield, Adams.

Quay, H. C. (1979). Classification. In H. C. Quay & J. S. Werry (Eds.), *Psychopathological disorders of childhood* (2nd ed.). New York: Wiley.

MARIBETH MONTGOMERY KASIK
Governors State University

APPLIED BEHAVIOR ANALYSIS
CONDUCT DISORDER

ADAPTED PHYSICAL EDUCATION

Adapted physical education is a

> diversified program of developmental activities, games, sports, and rhythms suited to the interests, capacities, and limitations

of students with disabilities who may not safely and successfully engage in unrestricted participation in vigorous activities of the general physical education program. (Hurley, 1981, p. 43)

The focus of adapted physical education is on the development of motor and physical fitness and fundamental motor patterns and skills in a sportslike environment (Sherrill, 1985).

Adapted physical education implies the modification of physical activities, rules, and regulations to meet existing limiting factors of specific handicapped populations. By definition, adapted physical education includes activities planned for persons with learning problems owed to mental, motor, or emotional impairment, disability, or dysfunction; planned for the purpose of rehabilitation, habilitation, or remediation; modified so the handicapped can participate; and designed for modifying movement capabilities.

Adapted physical education primarily occurs within a school setting, but it may also occur in clinics, hospitals, residential facilities, daycare centers, or other centers where the primary intent is to influence learning or movement potential through motor activity (AAHPER, 1952).

In the school setting, adapted physical education differs from regular physical education in the following manner. It has a federally mandated base through PL 94-142. It serves students who are primarily identified as having a handicapping condition but may serve students such as the obese, who are not identified as handicapped but are in need of physical activity modification within a restricted environment. Adapted physical education classes are usually separate and educationally distinct from regular physical education owing to the need to modify the curriculum to suit the individual interests and capabilities of the student.

The basic elements in curriculum planning are individuality, flexibility, and educational accountability. Because of the intra-and intervariability of individual differences within and across handicaps, activities must be designed and programmed to fit each child's motor capabilities. For instance, children within a particular handicapped group may be able to throw a ball, but each within the group, because of motor limitations, may throw the ball differently while still achieving the objective of distance and accuracy. Second, adapted physical education activities are designed to be flexible enough to achieve educational goals. For instance, for basketball, a smaller ball is provided and baskets are lowered so that students may be able to score more baskets in a game, thereby increasing their enjoyment in the sport (Auxter & Pyer, 1985).

Adapted physical education for students classified as handicapped implies accountability via the individualized educational plan (IEP). Objectives stated on an IEP ensure that the student is receiving instruction in activities where there is the greatest physical, motor, and social need. The student is evaluated periodically to assess progress toward the short- and long-term goals stated in the IEP.

REFERENCES

AAHPER. (1952, April). *Guiding principles for a physical education journal of health, physical education, recreation.* Author.

Auxter, D., & Pyer, J. (1985). *Adapted physical education.* St. Louis: (1981, June). Mosby.

Hurley, D. (1981). *Guidelines for adapted physical education.* New York: *Journal of Health, Physical Education, Recreation, and Dance* (pp. 43–45).

Sherrill, C. (1985). *Adapted physical education and recreation* (3rd ed.). Dubuque, IA: Brown.

THOMAS R. BURKE
Hunter College

PHYSICAL EDUCATION FOR STUDENTS WITH DISABILITIES

ADAPTIVE BEHAVIOR

Adaptive behavior, or the daily activities required for personal and social sufficiency, is an integral part of the evaluation and planning for handicapped and nonhandicapped individuals. It is not a new concept and has its roots in historical views concerning the treatment of the mentally retarded. The increased emphasis now placed on the use of the adaptive behavior concept in special education and programs for the handicapped is resulting in attempts to better understand the characteristics of adaptive behavior and in the publication of many new instruments for measuring adaptive behavior (Meyers, Nihira, & Zetlin, 1979).

Present concepts of adaptive behavior are traced to early attempts to describe the mentally retarded (Harrison, 1985). As early as the Renaissance and Reformation, language and law defined mental retardation in terms of adaptive behavior, or a person's ability to take care of himself or herself and get along with others. Legal reforms for the mentally retarded during the 1800s resulted in continued attention to adaptive behavior. However, in the early 1900s, the development of the Binet intelligence scales and its counterparts led to a prevalent practice of defining mental retardation solely in terms of IQ; this practice continued for many years.

Edgar Doll, the major pioneer in adaptive behavior assessment, disagreed with the use of IQs only, and, in the 1930s, indicated that a person's social competence, or adaptive behavior, should be the first and most important criterion for mental retardation. It was not until 1959 that the American Association on Mental Deficiency published its official manual and formally included deficits in adaptive behavior, in addition to low intelligence, as an integral part of the definition of mental retardation (Heber, 1961). Subsequent editions of the manual have further emphasized the importance of adaptive behavior.

Several issues in the 1960s and 1970s precipitated an upsurge of interest in adaptive behavior and adaptive behavior assessment (Witt & Martens, 1984). A concern arose about "6-hour retarded children" or minority group and low socioeconomic status children who were labeled as retarded in the public schools but exhibited adequate adaptive behavior at home and in the community (Mercer, 1973). This concern eventually led to litigation such as the Guadalupe and Larry P. cases and court decisions that indicated that results of intelligence tests cannot be the primary basis for classifying children as mentally retarded and that adaptive behavior must be assessed. The 1960s and 1970s saw a trend toward the normalization of handicapped individuals and the awareness that effective programs for teaching adaptive skills allow handicapped individuals to participate as fully as possible in normal environments. A third issue was the need for a nonbiased and multifaceted assessment of all handicapped children to facilitate the fairness of decisions based on the results of tests and to investigate functioning in all areas related to a particular handicap.

The passage of the Education of All Handicapped Children Act of 1975 (Public Law 94-142) represented the culmination of the issues of the 1960s and 1970s. Public Law 94-142 and its successor, the current Individuals with Disabilities Education Act, commonly known as IDEA, have stringent guides for the assessment of handicapped children and stipulates that deficits in adaptive behavior must be substantiated before a child is classified as mentally retarded. Further, it recognizes the importance of adaptive behavior assessment for children other than the mentally retarded. Since the passage of the law, most states have developed guidelines for adaptive behavior assessment (Patrick & Reschley, 1982) and many have strict criteria for the types of adaptive behavior instruments and scores to be used.

Sparrow, Balla, and Cicchetti (1984) discuss several characteristics that are inherent in concepts of adaptive behavior. Adaptive behavior is an age-related construct; as normally developing children grow older, adaptive behavior increases and becomes more complex. Adaptive behavior is determined by the standards of other people, those who live, work, play, teach, and interact with an individual. Finally, adaptive behavior is defined as what an individual does day by day, not by an individual's ability or what he or she can do. If a person has the ability to perform a daily task, but does not do it, adaptive behavior is considered to be inadequate.

An important issue in the description of adaptive behavior is the distinction between adaptive behavior and intelligence (Meyers, Nihira, & Zetlin, 1979). Adaptive behavior and intelligence have several important differences. First, adaptive behavior focuses on everyday behavior and intelligence on thought processes. Adaptive behavior is based on concrete environmental demands while intelligence focuses on academic demands. Adaptive behavior assessment involves common, typical, and everyday behaviors, whereas intelligence scales attempt to measure a person's potential, or his or her best possible performance.

Since the passage of Public Law 94-142, a large number of adaptive behavior scales have been published or developed for local use. Most adaptive behavior scales are administered to a respondent such as a parent or teacher who is familiar with the daily activities of the person. Some are administered directly to the person whose adaptive behavior is being assessed. The Vineland Adaptive Behavior Scales (Sparrow, et al., 1984) measure adaptive behavior in the areas of communication, daily living skills, socialization, motor skills, and maladaptive behavior. The Adaptive Behavior Inventory for Children (Mercer & Lewis, 1977) assesses a child's adaptation to family, community, and peer social systems. The AAMD Adaptive Behavior Scale (Lambert & Windmiller, 1981) evaluates personal sufficiency, social sufficiency, responsibility, and personal and social adjustment. The Scales of Independent Behavior (Bruininks, Woodcock, Weatherman, & Hill, 1984) include measures of motor skills, social interaction and communication, personal and community independence, and problem behaviors. The Children's Adaptive Behavior Scale (Richmond & Kicklighter, 1980) contains scales for language, independent functioning, family roles, economic vocational activity, and socialization.

REFERENCES

Bruininks, R. J., Woodcock, R. W., Weatherman, R. F., & Hill, B. K. (1984). *Scales of independent behavior*. Allen, TX: DLM Teaching Resources.

Harrison, P. L. (1985). *Vineland Adaptive Behavior Scales, Classroom Edition Manual*. Circle Pines, MN: American Guidance Service.

Heber, R. F. (1961). A manual on terminology and classification in mental retardation (Monograph Suppl.). *American Journal of Mental Deficiency*.

Lambert, N., & Windmiller, M. (1981). *AAMD Adaptive Behavior Scale—School Edition*. Monterey, CA: Publishers Test Service.

Mercer, J. R. (1973). *Labeling the mentally retarded*. Berkeley, CA: University of California Press.

Mercer, J. R., & Lewis, J. E. (1977). *Adaptive Behavior Inventory for Children*. New York: Psychological Corporation.

Meyers, C. E., Nihira, K., & Zetlin, A. (1979). The measurement of adaptive behavior. In N. R. Ellis (Eds.), *Handbook of mental deficiency: Psychological theory and research* (2nd ed.) (pp. 215–253). Hillside, NJ: Erlbaum.

Patrick, J. L., & Reschley, D. J. (1982). Relationship of state educational criteria and demographic variables to school system prevalence of mental retardation. *American Journal of Mental Deficiency, 86,* 351–360.

Richmond, B. O., & Kicklighter, R. H. (1980). *Children's Adaptive Behavior Scale.* Atlanta: Humanics Limited.

Sparrow, S. S., Balla, D. A., & Cicchetti, D. V. (1984). *Vineland Adaptive Behavior Scales.* Circle Pines, MN: American Guidance Service.

Witt, J. C., & Martens, B. K. (1984). Adaptive behavior: Test and assessment issues. *School Psychology Review, 13,* 478–484.

PATTI L. HARRISON
University of Alabama

ADAPTIVE BEHAVIOR INVENTORY FOR CHILDREN
MENTAL RETARDATION

ADAPTIVE BEHAVIOR INVENTORY FOR CHILDREN (ABIC)

The Adaptive Behavior Inventory for Children (ABIC), a component of the System of Multicultural Pluralistic Assessment (SOMPA; Mercer & Lewis, 1977), is a 242-item rating scale for children ages 5 to 11 years. It provides an indication of a child's adaptation to social systems involving the family, peer group, and community. The ABIC items are administered to a child's parents or guardians; the questions are read to a parent and he or she indicates whether the child's role in the activity described by the item is latent, emergent, or mastered. The administration requires about 1 hour. The ABIC contains six scales: Family, Community, Peer Relations, Nonacademic School Roles, Earner Consumer, and Self-Maintenance. A measure of veracity (or a lie scale) is also included.

Scaled scores (with a mean of 50 and a standard deviation of 15) are available for each of the six scales; the ABIC Average Scaled Score, a measure of overall adaptive behavior, is the mean of the six scaled scores. The ABIC was standardized with a sample of 2085 California schoolchildren (696 black, 700 Spanish surname, and 689 white). The SOMPA *Technical Manual* reports average split-half reliability coefficients ranging from 0.82 to 0.89 for the six scales and a reliability coefficient of 0.97 for the ABIC Average Scaled Score. No validity data are reported in the manual, but the ABIC has been used in numerous studies that investigated, for example, the relationship between the ABIC and intelligence and achievement (e.g., Harrison, 1981; Oakland, 1983) and the representativeness of the ABIC norms (Oakland, 1979). Use of the ABIC has declined considerably as its parent system, SOMPA, has lost favor in the profession.

REFERENCES

Harrison, P. L. (1981). Mercer's adaptive behavior inventory, the McCarthy scales, and dental development as predictors of first grade achievement. *Journal of Educational Psychology, 73,* 78–82.

Mercer, J. R., & Lewis, J. E. (1977). *System of Multicultural Pluralistic Assessment.* New York: Psychological Corporation.

Oakland, T. (1979). Research on the adaptive behavior inventory for children and the estimated learning potential. *School Psychology Digest, 8,* 63–78.

Oakland, T. (1983). Joint use of adaptive behavior and IQ to predict achievement. *Journal of Consulting and Clinical Psychology, 51,* 298–301.

PATTI L. HARRISON
University of Alabama

ADAPTIVE BEHAVIOR
BEHAVIORAL OBSERVATION
SYSTEM OF MULTICULTURAL PLURALISTIC ASSESSMENT
VINELAND SOCIAL MATURITY SCALE

ADAPTIVE BEHAVIOR SCALE

See VINELAND ADAPTIVE BEHAVIOR SCALES.

ADAPTIVE DEVICES

Adaptive, assistive, augmentative, prosthetic, and orthotic devices are all aids to help those with a variety of disabilities to overcome problems of everyday living. Examples range from leg braces to highly sophisticated microcomputers adapted for the disabled. Included are hearing aids, Braille books, glasses, wheelchairs, specialized eating utensils, braces, positioning devices, page turners, tape recorders, typewriters, and the artificial larynx.

Two sources of information for this wide range of adaptive devices are *The Directory of Living Aids for the Disabled Person,* published by the Veterans Administration (U.S. Government Printing Office, 1982), which provides an extensive list of aids for daily living, and *The Information System for Adaptive, Assistive and Rehabilitative Equipment (ISAARE)* (Melichar, 1977, 1978), an information storage and retrieval system that lists devices by categories such as "travel" and "communication."

The type of adaptive devices currently experiencing the greatest technological advances as well as the greatest emphasis in rehabilitation is augmentative communication systems. Three general modes of nonvocal or augmentative communication have been developed for those for whom intelligible speech is not an option. They are manual communication, communication boards, and electronic systems. Manual communication includes gestures, signs, and finger spelling; it is used extensively with nonhearing-impaired as well as hearing-impaired populations, but it does not include an adaptive device. Communication boards are boards, or booklets, that come in a wide range of sizes, shapes, and materials, and make use of a variety of symbol systems. These symbols include objects, drawings and photographs, rebus symbols, Blissymbols, letters, and words. Sources of information on the design and use of communication boards include the *Language Board Instruction Kit* (Oaklander, 1980); Carlson, 1981; Musselwhite & St. Louis, 1982; Silverman, 1980; and *Non Oral Communication* (Plavan Schools, 1980).

The tremendous growth of computer technology is providing the impetus for the development of communication systems for the physically disabled that can be individually tailored to their abilities. Input devices for those who do not have sufficient motor control for direct selection (pointing or using a keyboard) include paddle switches, joy sticks, moisture switches, optical switches, eyebrow or tongue-controlled switches, sip and puff switches, and voice-controlled switches, among others. These augmentative systems are also tailored to the user's output needs and may include a combination of hard copy printout, synthesized speech output, display screens, and so on. The selection of an appropriate system to include the most effective and efficient symbol system, input technique, and output capabilities is a complex process requiring the services of a team of experts. The American Speech-Language-Hearing Association (ASHA) Ad Hoc Committee on Communication Processes and Non-Speaking Persons (1980) identifies possible team members as well as essential components of the assessment process. Depending on the individual's needs, most of the following people should be involved in the assessment and training process: speech-language pathologist, occupational therapist, physical therapist, parents, teacher, system user, psychologist, rehabilitation engineer, and social worker.

Ongoing research on the design and use of augmentative communication systems makes any list or discussion of specific systems quickly obsolete. The sources in the References list will provide further background reading. The most current information can be obtained through the following: *Communication Outlook,* a monthly publication from the Artificial Language Laboratory, Computer Science Department, Michigan State University, East Lansing, MI 48824; National Rehabilitation Information Center (NARIC), The Catholic University of America, 4407 8th Street NE, Washington, DC 20064; *The Resource Guide, Rehabilitation Engineering and Product Information* (Publication No. E-80-2205, September 1980), U.S. Dept. of Education, Office of Special Education and Rehabilita-

tion Services, Office for Handicapped Individuals, Washington, DC 20202; *Augmentative & Alternative Communication,* the official journal of the International Society for Augmentative and Alternative Communication, Baltimore: Williams & Wilkins; and the Trace Research and Development Center University of Wisconsin, Madison, WI.

REFERENCES

American Speech-Language-Hearing Association. (1980). Nonspeech communication: a position paper. *ASHA, 22,* 267–272.

Carlson, F. (1981). *Alternate methods of communication.* Danville, IL: Interstate.

Directory of living aids for the disabled person. (1982). U.S. Government Printing Office.

Fraser, B. A., & Hensinger, R. N. (1983). *Managing physical handicaps: A practical guide for parents, care providers, and educators.* Baltimore, MD: Brookes.

Haring, N. G. (Ed.). (1982). *Exceptional children and youth.* Columbus, OH: Merrill.

Melichar, J. F. (1977). *ISAARE,* San Mateo, CA: Adaptive Systems.

Melichar, J. F. (1978). *Challenges in mental retardation: Progressive ideology and sources.* New York: Human Services Press.

Musselwhite, C. R., & St. Louis, K. W. (1982). *Communication programming for the severely handicapped: Vocal and nonvocal strategies.* San Diego: College Hill Press.

Non Oral Communication: A Training Guide for the Child Without Speech. (1980). Plavan School, 9675 Warner Ave., Fountain Valley, CA 92708.

Oakander, S. (1980). *Language Board Instruction Kit.* Non-Oral Communication Center, 9675 Warner Ave., Fountain Valley, CA 92708.

Silverman, F. H. (1980). *Communication for the speechless.* Englewood Cliffs, NJ: Prentice Hall.

Margo E. Wilson
Lexington, Kentucky

AUGMENTATIVE COMMUNICATION SYSTEMS
BLISSYMBOLS
COMMUNICATION BOARDS

ADAPTIVE PE

See ADAPTED PHYSICAL EDUCATION.

ADDERALL

Adderall is a stimulant medication that is a different mixture of amphetamine isomers than the common stimulants such as dexedrine, benzedrine, methamphetamine, methylphenidate, and magnesium pemoline. It is available in 5, 10, 20, and 30 mg tablets. Adderall is used primarily in the treatment of attention-deficit hyperactivity disorder (ADHD) and narcolepsy. Adderall has been shown in clinical trials to increase alertness, improve attention span, decrease distractibility, and increase the ability to follow directions among children ages 3 years and up.

Adderall is popular among many children and families because it may need to be taken only once or twice a day, eliminating the need for dosing at school. Since it is a different chemical preparation, Adderall has been found to be effective with patients who do not respond to more popular stimulant treatments, such as Ritalin. However, Adderall may take as long as 3 to 4 weeks to become effective, while other stimulants tend to take effect more immediately. Adderall has a similar side-effect profile to other common stimulants, the most common of those being appetite suppression, growth retardation, insomnia, and headache. Less frequent side effects of this drug class include tics, dry mouth, irritability, cardiovascular acceleration, and, at high dosages, hallucinations and a disorder characterized as amphetamine psychosis. Adderall also interacts with a variety of drugs used in the treatment of depression and with drugs used to treat psychotic symptoms. Certain foods, especially those at extremes of acidity or alkalinity, may also alter dosage effects of Adderall.

Adderall may be habit-forming and is classified as a central nervous system stimulant. Monitoring of dose response, side effects, and polypharmacy by a physician is crucial to safe use of Adderall and other drugs in its class. Additional information is available in Arky (1998) and Cahill (1997).

REFERENCES

Arky, R. (1998). *Physicians desk reference.* Montvale, NJ: Medical Economies Data Production.

Cahill, M. (Ed.). (1997). *Nursing 97 drug handbook.* Springhouse, PA: Springhouse Corporation.

CECIL R. REYNOLDS
Texas A & M University

ADDITIVE-FREE DIETS

During the 1970s and 1980s, a very important and particularly controversial theory of the management of learning and behavioral disorders in children was the theory of the additive-free diet proposed by Feingold (1975). Specifically, Feingold has maintained that children with hyperactivity and other behavioral disorders have a natural toxic reaction to artificial food colors, flavorings, preservatives, and other substances that are added to food to enhance their shelf-life. The additive-free diet regimen proposed by Feingold purports to eliminate artificial flavors and salicylates (compounds naturally occurring in certain fruits and vegetables) from a child's diet as a treatment for hyperactivity and learning disabilities. It is also noteworthy that Feingold has advocated his additive-free diet for a number of other conditions, including mental retardation, early infantile autism, and delinquency (Barkley, 1990).

Despite the widespread appeal of the additive-free diet among the lay community and the Feingold Association, this treatment has been widely assailed in scholarly literature. On the basis of empirically unsubstantiated claims concerning the efficacy of this diet, Feingold has insisted that nearly 50% of hyperactive children in his clinical private practice sample displayed a complete remission of symptoms as a result of the additive-free dietary regimen. Such improved symptoms, according to the Feingold group, include markedly enhanced cognitive and academic functioning. Further, Feingold has insisted that the younger the child, the more expedient and complete the improvement that occurs. Nonetheless, several investigators (Harley & Matthews, 1980) have attributed this dramatic success to a placebo effect, or even the changed aspects of family dynamics that often result from the additive-free diet. Also contributing to widespread acceptance of the Feingold diet is our culture's current obsession with diet consciousness and health food fads.

The publicity and heated debate resulting from Feingold's claims have resulted in a proliferation of empirical studies among investigators in the scientific community that have assessed the efficacy of additive-free diets in hyperactive children (Conners, 1980; Conners, Goyette, Southwick, Lees, & Andrulonis, 1976). In a cogent summary of a series of studies conducted by these researchers, Conners (1980) has concluded that only a small number of children (less than 5%) respond specifically to the additive-free diet. More important, many investigators now recognize that those foods that Feingold has recommended be eliminated from children's diets are often high in important nutrients necessary for normal growth and development. Thus, placing children on the additive-free diet may even compromise their nutritional needs. Nonetheless, despite the "gross overstatements by Dr. Feingold" (Conners, 1980, p. 109) and the proliferation of weak studies in this area, one must be cognizant of the fact that for a small subgroup of hyperactive children (Ross & Ross, 1982) diet management may be a useful form of intervention. It remains unclear whether it is the additive-free diet itself that is responsible for the observed improvements or the behavioral regimen associated with this special diet. As a result, Conners (1980) has recommended that limited empirical investigations still be continued in this controversial area. Practitioners and researchers concerned with this topic will want to examine Conners' (1980) important work in this field, which is consistent with subsequent reviews (Brown, Dreelin, & Dingle, 1999; NIH, 1998).

REFERENCES

Brown, R. T., Dreelin E., & Dingle, A. D. (1997). Neuropsychological effects of stimulant medication on children's learning and behavior. In C. R. Reynolds & E. Fletcher-Janzen (Eds.), *Handbook of Clinical Child Neuropsychology* (2nd ed.). NY: Plenum Press.

Barkley, R. A. (1990). *Hyperactive children: A handbook for diagnosis and treatment* (2nd ed.). New York: Guilford.

Conners, C. K. (1980). *Food additives and hyperactive children.* New York: Plenum.

Conners, C. K., Goyette, C. H., Southwick, D. A., Lees, J. M., & Andrulonis, P. (1976). Food additives and hyperkinesis. *Pediatrics, 58,* 154–166.

Feingold, B. F. (1975). *Why your child is hyperactive.* New York: Random House.

Harley, J. P., & Matthews, C. G. (1980). Food additives and hyperactivity in children. In R. M. Knights & D. J. Bakker (Eds.), *Treatment of hyperactive and learning disordered children.* Baltimore, MD: University Park Press.

NIH. (1998). *NIH Consensus development conference on diagnosis and treatment of attention-deficit hyperactivity disorder.* Bethesda, MD: Author.

Ross, D. M., & Ross, S. A. (1982). Hyperactivity: Current issues, research and theory (2nd ed.). New York: Wiley-Interscience.

RONALD T. BROWN
*Emory University School
of Medicine*

**FEINGOLD DIET
HYPERACTIVITY**

ADJUSTMENT OF THE HANDICAPPED

By virtue of their "differentness," handicapped individuals and their families must make certain special adjustments to lead fulfilling and satisfying lives. The most obvious and important of these adjustments is the appraisal and acceptance of the handicapping condition itself. Such acceptance is prerequisite to seeking and obtaining appropriate care and services.

Another necessary adjustment requires recognizing and dealing with influences of a handicapping condition on all aspects of the individual's development. For example, a physical handicap affects social development and interactions in ways that have only recently been addressed scientifically and professionally, but have long been sources of confusion and frustration to the handicapped.

It has become fashionable among educators and devel-

opmental psychologists to refer to the "whole child" in nurturing and/or describing the development of "normal," i.e., nonhandicapped, children. Some (e.g., Shontz, 1980) have advocated this integrated approach in understanding the development of handicapped children and adolescents. However, two factors make it especially difficult to grasp specific implications of particular handicapping conditions for domains not directly affected by the conditions. One difficulty is that the interrelationships among the various developmental domains are subtle and complex; another is that the exceptional child's development is affected by special social and internal forces. Therefore, our ability to recommend theoretically based prescriptions for professional and parenting practices that will promote maximal development in indirectly affected domains is limited by the lack of empirical evidence comparing particular approaches to raising, treating, and educating the "whole" handicapped child.

The development of the child with a handicap occurs along the same lines as that of the nonhandicapped child. However, an individual handicapped child's development will exhibit qualitative variations from the norm. The specific deviations from typical development depend both on the nature and severity of the handicapping condition and on the level of adjustment achieved by the child and his or her family and teachers. Of particular significance in the adjustment of the handicapped child are personality and social development. Also of concern are possible physical and/or medical adjustments that may be required, and special educational adjustments.

Normal personal-social development includes the emergence of the individual's self-concept and self-esteem. These beliefs about one's characteristics, relative worth, and competence are acquired by internalizing an image of one's self as it is reflected by important adults and peers. Bartel and Guskin (1980) emphasize that the feedback one receives from the social environment is a crucial factor in the development of a positive self-concept and high self-esteem, for it creates an expectation and interpretive schema for self-evaluation of one's abilities and efforts. The self-concept of a handicapped child is at risk because society's negative evaluations of individuals who are different from the norm are systematically, if unconsciously, transmitted to him or her (Gliedman & Roth, 1980). Because the development of high self-esteem is based on what an individual *can* do, a handicapping condition may endanger a child's self-esteem by focusing attention on what the child cannot do.

The social side of personal-social development includes the acquisition of skills for interacting socially. Two forces interact to interfere with normal social experiences and therefore place the handicapped child at a disadvantage for acquiring appropriate social skills. On the one hand is a cultural tendency, described by Bartel and Guskin (1980), to stigmatize a handicapped individual; this often results in deliberate as well as unconscious social rejection of the child. Therefore, he or she may experience decreased opportunities to participate in the sorts of activities through which social skills are acquired and refined. On the other hand, some researchers (Field, 1980; Novak, Olley, & Kearney, 1980) have demonstrated that handicapped children are less likely to initiate social interaction with peers, preferring instead object-oriented activities. Such reserve is self-defeating, for the child denies himself or herself opportunities that are available. In sum, the rejection of others and the child's own reluctance to join in the usual social activities interfere with normal personal-social development by reducing opportunities for social participation.

A handicapping condition may limit a child's or adolescent's physical activities. The handicap may impose restrictions owing to physical limitations or medical complications that limit freedom to get about in the environment. Physical and/or medical limitations may reduce opportunities for interaction and exploration in both the physical and social realms and thus curtail experiences that stimulate and promote cognitive growth and personal-social development. Handicapped children must be encouraged not to retreat from any activities that are accessible, although inconvenient, because of physical restrictions. Professionals and others can help them to participate in an adapted way, if necessary, in order not to deprive them of beneficial experiences.

Handicapped children may have to adjust medical interventions or therapies such as drugs, braces, physical therapy, surgical procedures, hearing appliances, etc. The child's adjustment to the medical aspect of his or her program is absolutely essential because the child must cooperate in order to achieve the maximum benefits of the prescribed treatment(s).

A handicapped child is very likely to have to make an adjustment involving his or her educational programs. The adjustment may range from simply modifying his or her study habits or methods to full-time participation in a special self-contained program. Professionals who work with the child should strive to minimize whatever educational disadvantage(s) may be imposed by the handicap. The goals of the child's educational program should emphasize activities to compensate for and/or overcome his or her handicap.

The effectiveness of the child's program will be amplified by the active involvement of parents in consistently following through on behavioral and educational interventions in the home environment. Concrete benefits are derived from the parents' participation. Parents are able to provide additional reinforcement and practice for skills learned during the school day, helping their child consolidate gains more rapidly. In addition, their involvement is a signal to the child of their commitment to his or her development and the high value they place on educational achievement. These attitudes are highly motivating and will help see the child through difficult periods.

Parents who do not accept and adjust to the child's handicap escalate their child's difficulties. Maladaptive behavior patterns that emerge in the relationship between parents and their handicapped child can arise from either of two opposite, but equally harmful, reactions. Parents may either overestimate or underestimate their child's abilities and potential. Overestimates may be due to parents' denial of their child's problems. Such parents are prone to establish unreasonably high standards for their child's behavior or development. Because the child wants to please the parents but is not capable of fulfilling their expectations, he or she continually faces feelings of frustration, inadequacy, and other negative emotions such as guilt, disappointment, and uncertainty as to his or her place in the affections of the parents. On the other hand, some parents seem to overcompensate for their handicapped child. Some typical behaviors of these parents include setting goals that are too easily attained, praising or rewarding the child for work that is below his or her level of functioning, and intervening unnecessarily when the child is working on difficult tasks. Such behaviors convey the message, albeit indirectly, that the parents do not recognize or appreciate the child's actual abilities. These signals undermine the development of high self-esteem and a positive self-concept.

Adjusting to the child's handicap is difficult, but Kogan (1980) has shown that parents can learn and use techniques for interacting with their child in ways that promote an adaptive relationship. General guidelines for parents in nurturing optimum development include realistically accepting the child, including abilities and disabilities. Parents should be sympathetic, but must encourage independence in order to enhance the child's self-esteem and promote his or her success in the "real" world.

Parents also have a crucial role in setting the stage for good sibling relationships. They must not show favoritism toward any of their children. Although they may enjoy different activities with their individual children, they should not give their attention preferentially to any single child. In particular, parents must avoid making comparisons among their children, and instead emphasize each child's individual strengths. All children will benefit when parents provide experiences and delegate responsibilities in accordance with each child's developmental level and needs.

Due to increasing recognition of social and emotional problems that may be secondary to other disabilities, the IDEA requires a behavioral assessment of all children with a disability, regardless of their handicapping condition. It has become commonplace to use objective behavior rating scales and personality assessments during the initial referral and evaluation process (e.g., Reynolds & Kamphaus, 1992). Also, as a direct result of recognition of behavioral and emotional concomitants of various disabilities, IDEA now requires a behavioral assessment prior to disciplining a child with a disability, so that it can be determined whether the behavior of concern is a result of the child's disability. When behavioral problems are disability-related, children must be treated, not punished. Teachers will have the primary role to play in such interventions at school.

Over and above the special methods and materials teachers use in working with the handicapped child, perhaps the most important element of the handicapped child's educational experience is a positive social climate. Teachers can provide a model for accepting individual differences in general and specifically valuing each child's, including the handicapped child's, abilities and contributions. The child's classmates will imitate the teacher and assimilate the underlying nondiscriminatory attitudes. Being accepted by one's teachers and classmates nourishes the handicapped child's self-concept and self-esteem, thereby promoting not only social development, but also cognitive growth and educational achievement.

REFERENCES

Bartel, N. R., & Guskin, S. L. (1980). A handicap as a social phenomenon. In W. M. Cruickshank (Ed.), *Psychology of exceptional children and youth* (pp. 45–73). Englewood Cliffs, NJ: Prentice-Hall.

Field, T. (1980). Self, teacher, toy, and peer-directed behaviors of handicapped preschool children. In T. Field, S. Goldberg, D. Stern, & A. M. Sostek (Eds.), *High risk infants and children: Adult and peer interactions* (pp. 313–326). New York: Academic.

Gliedman, J., & Roth, W. (1980). *The unexpected minority: Handicapped children in America.* New York: Harcourt Brace Jovanovich.

Kogan, K. L. (1980). Interaction systems between preschool handicapped or developmentally delayed children and their parents. In T. Field, S. Goldberg, D. Stern, & A. M. Sostek (Eds.), *High risk infants and children: Adult and peer interactions* (pp. 227–247). New York: Academic.

Novak, M. A., Olley, G., & Kearney, D. S. (1980). Social skills of children with special needs in integrated separate preschools. In T. Field, S. Goldberg, D. Stern, & A. M. Sostek (Eds.), *High risk infants and children: Adult and peer interactions* (pp. 327–346). New York: Academic.

Reynolds, C. R., & Kamphaus, R. W. (1992). *Behavior assessment system for children.* Circle Pines, MN: American Guidance Service.

Shontz, F. C. (1980). Theories about adjustment to having a disability. In W. M. Cruickshank (Ed.), *Psychology of exceptional children and youth* (pp. 3–44). Englewood Cliffs, NJ: Prentice-Hall.

PAULINE F. APPLEFIELD
*University of North Carolina
at Wilmington*

BEHAVIOR ASSESSMENT SYSTEM FOR CHILDREN
FAMILY RESPONSE TO A HANDICAPPED CHILD
HANDICAPISM
INDIVIDUALS WITH DISABILITIES EDUCATION ACT
TEACHER EXPECTANCIES

ADLER, ALFRED (1870–1937)

Alfred Adler, an Austrian psychiatrist, severed an early connection with Freudian psychoanalysis to develop his more socially oriented Individual Psychology, which was a powerful influence in the development of the field of social psychology. Adler's work in education and child guidance is less well known, but it contributed greatly to the development of school services in Austria and it had worldwide significance for the education and treatment of children.

At the Pedagogical Institute of the City of Vienna, he helped to train thousands of teachers and established the first child guidance clinics in the Vienna school system. In 1935, with the coming of a fascist regime in Austria, Adler left Vienna for the United States, where he established a private practice and served as professor of medical psychology at the Long Island College of Medicine.

REFERENCES

Ansbacher, H. L. & R. R. (1956). *The individual psychology of Alfred Adler.* New York: Basic Books.

Watson, R. I. (1963). *The great psychologists.* New York: Lippincott.

PAUL IRVINE
Katonah, New York

ADMINISTRATION OF SPECIAL EDUCATION

Prior to the advent of public school programs for the handicapped in the late nineteenth and early twentieth centuries, administration of special education programs was usually executed by persons who were not administrators. Because many of the early programs were provided by religious organizations (Hewett & Forness, 1977), the earliest administrators were probably monks, nuns, or other religious figures (e.g., Pedro Ponce deLeon, a Spanish monk who worked with the deaf in the sixteenth century). During the late eighteenth and early nineteenth centuries, philosophical changes and a new attention to science changed attitudes toward the handicapped and their treatment. These changes, evidenced in the French and American revolutions, created a reverence for the individual and a belief that the lives of handicapped persons could be significantly improved through the application of science. Thus a new wave of administrators arose. These administrators were not interested primarily in running a program, but in teaching, scientific inquiry, and having an impact on contemporary thought through their writings. Thus a time was born in which most programs were managed by scientists, physicians, and philosophers such as Edouard Sequin, Valentin Hauy, and Samuel Gridley Howe. During the nineteenth century a great number of public and private residential schools/institutions were developed. For the most part, these institutions (which remained the dominant force in special education until the middle of the twentieth century) were administered by physicians. This was especially true for institutions for the mentally retarded, the emotionally disturbed, and the physically handicapped.

Public school services for exceptional children began in the latter part of the nineteenth century (Gearheart & Wright, 1979). By the middle of the twentieth century, public school classes became the primary mode of education for exceptional children. With this change, the administration of special education programs fell to educators and school psychologists. Although special education programs were held in public school buildings, they were usually separate, and writers of the time advocated separate administration and supervision systems (Ayer & Barr, 1928).

The rise of special education administration as a discipline occurred simultaneously with the rise of segregated public school programs. Special education administrators during the first quarter of the twentieth century were not trained generally as administrators; it was not until 1938 that any professional identity was established. In that year, the National Association of State Directors of Special Education was founded (Burrello & Sage, 1979). In 1951 the Council of Administrators of Special Education (CASE) convened as a special interest group within the Council for Exceptional Children (Burello & Sage, 1979).

During the 1950s, 1960s, and 1970s, special education administration grew as a result of the increase in public special-education programs brought about by the increased federal role in programs for the handicapped. In the 1950s, the U.S. Office of Education conducted several large-scale studies of special education and special-education administration (Mackie & Engel, 1956; Mackie & Snyder, 1957). These studies helped to establish the roles of administrators of programs for exceptional children and the need for professional training. Many more studies were conducted during the 1960s and 1970s (e.g., Kohl & Marro, 1971; Sage, 1968; Wisland & Vaughan, 1964). It was, however, the passage of PL 94-142, The Education of All Handicapped Children Act of 1975, that brought special education administration to its current state. This legislation, and others that followed, together with numerous lawsuits, created a demand for adminis-

trators who were specifically trained to manage special-education programs, a demand that has grown with subsequent programs (e.g., IDEA).

Although special education administration has developed a uniqueness and identity, there is considerable variety within the discipline. This variety is expressed across governmental levels and organizational arrangements. There are three governmental levels in special education administration: federal, state, and local. Within each level the tasks of the administrator may vary considerably depending on the specific role of the administrator, the organization of the agency for which the administrator works, and the ways in which the agency delivers services.

Presently, the federal role in special education administration is executed primarily by the Office of Special Education and Rehabilitation of the U.S. Department of Education. The administrative roles of this office include monitoring state compliance with IDEA; generating research; providing public information; formulating regulations; promoting personnel development; and drafting legislation. As a result of PL 94-142 and IDEA, the federal role in administration of special education has grown substantially. Nearly every administrative decision in special education must be made with consideration for the regulations propagated by IDEA. Because of this, the majority of the administrators at the federal level are involved in activities related to providing services to the states in order that they may carry out the provisions of IDEA, or in evaluating/monitoring the state's efforts.

Administration of special education programs at the state level occurs in three places: at the state education agency (SEA); at state-operated schools; and at state-operated regional centers. At the SEA, the roles of administration are to develop legislation; to develop state plans; to obtain and administer financial resources; to develop personnel preparation systems and standards; to develop plans for improving instruction; to enforce and monitor regulations; and to develop public relations (Gearhart & Wright, 1979; Podemski, Price, Smith, & Marsh, 1984). The SEAs also directly administer programs such as state schools for the deaf or blind (e.g., Pennsylvania). These programs are usually for low-incidence populations. In Georgia, the SEA administers both state schools and regional centers that provide direct service to low-incidence populations, especially in rural areas. Regional centers also serve as resource centers for local education agencies (LEAs).

Some state-operated programs in special education are not administered by the SEA. These programs, usually serving the mentally retarded or the emotionally disturbed, may be managed by state agencies such as a department of mental retardation, mental health, and juvenile services. Such programs are generally subject to the same regulations as programs operated by the SEA. In many instances, however, the programs are not managed by educators. The practice of employing physicians, psychologists, or social workers to manage state residential programs is a vestige of a tradition in state institutions and is justifiable for programs that are not chiefly educational.

At the local level, there are a number of different administrative arrangements and even more varied service delivery arrangements (Burello & Sage, 1979). The simplest administrative arrangement is the LEA. The LEA, also known as the local school district, provides direct services to exceptional children through various delivery systems. Administration at the local level may be centralized or decentralized. In a centralized system, persons (i.e., teachers) who provide services to exceptional children are managed by a district-wide special education director (coordinator). The special education director in a centralized system exercises a great amount of control over special education personnel and programs. In a decentralized system, the special education administrator serves in a coordinating/supporting/advising role. This administrator may have some authority over personnel but it is generally a building administrator (principal) who oversees daily operations.

More complex local administrative arrangements include intermediate educational units (IEU) and cooperative programs. Intermediate units exist in approximately 35 states (Podemski et al., 1984). In some states (e.g., Georgia) these units may be state-operated regional programs. In other states (e.g., New York, Texas, Wisconsin, Pennsylvania) the intermediate units are administered as a separate level of education agency. Intermediate units may be known by several names (e.g., Board of Cooperative Educational Services in New York, Regional Education Service Centers in Texas). According to Podemski et al. (1984), intermediate units were developed to pool resources and to share costs. In some states (e.g., Pennsylvania) intermediate units provide more than special education services and were developed for political as well as educational reasons during a time of district consolidation. Intermediate units have been criticized as arrangements that violate the principle of least restrictive environment because their services often require removing a child from his or her home school. Among the problems facing administrators of intermediate units are competition with LEAs for funds and students, potential conflict in lines of authority, communication gaps with the LEA, and salary variations that influence competition with LEAs for teachers.

Many rural school systems and suburban systems enter into cooperative agreements in order to provide more cost-effective programs, especially for low-incidence populations (Howe, 1981). Cooperative programs engender the same problems as do IEUs. Additionally, they must often contend with long distances for busing students.

The competencies of LEA and IEU special education administrators are similar. The differences are probably in terms of the amount of time devoted to different tasks rather than the tasks themselves. This may be true also for administrators of state-operated direct service programs (e.g., state schools). The competency areas for such administrators include organization theory and behavior; budget development; curriculum development; supervision; personnel administration; community relations; community resources; change processes; physical plant management; research; professional standards; and policy development.

IDEA requires all LEAs to have available the complete range of service-delivery options. This includes self-contained classes, resource rooms, part-time classes, residential programs, and other options (Deno, 1970). Before PL 94-142 it was possible for LEAs to offer only one service-delivery option (most often self-contained classes). This change and the variability of placement options has brought new problems to the forefront of special education administration. These problems include team-work with regular educators; appropriate placement; coordination with general education administrators; and increased parental involvement (Ysseldyke, Algozzine, & Allen, 1982; Mingo & Burrello, 1985).

Specialized graduate training for administrators of programs for exceptional children began in 1965. The impetus for such training was provided by a journal article by Milazzo and Blessing (1964). Subsequent to the publishing of that article, the U.S. Office of Education awarded grants to universities for the purpose of developing training programs (Burrello & Sage, 1979). Although these training programs have existed for 20 years, it is apparent that most persons in special education leadership positions have not come through such programs but rather have progressed through the ranks as teachers or as general education administrators (Burrello & Sage, 1979). Furthermore, as of 1971, only slightly more than 50% of the graduates of doctoral programs in special education administration actually became special education administrators (Vance & Howe, 1974). Although most states do have certification requirements for special education leadership positions, requirements can be met with a general administrative certificate or a collection of courses and experience. Because market demands are limited, most training programs have not reached a high degree of articulation, sophistication, or visibility. A number of writers have articulated the desired content of special education administration training programs. Among the more notable training programs is the Special Education Supervisory Training Project (SEST, 1974), which was based on a human/conceptual/technical model (Burrello & Sage, 1979).

REFERENCES

Ayer, F. C., & Barr, A. S. (1928). *The organization of supervision.* New York: Appleton.

Burrello, L. C., & Sage, D. D. (1979). *Leadership and change in special education.* Englewood Cliffs, NJ: Prentice-Hall.

Deno, E. (1970). Special education for the mildly retarded: Is much of it justifiable? *Exceptional Children, 37*(3), 229–237.

Gearheart, B. R., & Wright, W. S. (1979). *Organization and administration of educational programs for exceptional children* (2nd ed.). Springfield, IL: Thomas.

Hewett, F. M., & Forness, S. R. (1977). *Education of exceptional learners.* Boston: Allyn & Bacon.

Howe, C. (1981). *Administration of special education.* Denver: Love.

Kohl, J. W., & Marro, T. D. (1971). *A normative study of the administrative position in special education.* Grant No. OEG-0-70-2467 (607), U.S. Office of Education, Pennsylvania State University.

Mackie, R. P., & Engel, A. M. (1956). *Directors and supervisors of special education in local school systems.* U.S. Office of Education Bulletin 1955, No. 13. Washington, DC: U.S. Government Printing Office.

Mackie, R. P., & Snyder, W. E. (1957). *Special education personnel in state departments of education.* U.S. Office of Education Bulletin 1956, No. 6. Washington, DC: U.S. Government Printing Office.

Milazzo, T. C., & Blessing, K. R. (1964). The training of directors and supervisors of special education programs. *Exceptional Children, 31,* 129–141.

Mingo, J., & Burrello, L. C. (1985). *Determining the relationship between special education administrator, supervisor, and building principal role and responsibilities in the administration of educational programs for the handicapped.* Bloomington, IN: Council of Administrators of Special Education, Inc., Indiana University.

Podemski, R. S., Price, B. J., Smith, T. E. C., & Marsh, G. E. (1984). *Comprehensive administration of special education.* Rockville, MD: Aspen.

Sage, D. D. (1968). Functional emphasis in special education administration. *Exceptional Children, 35,* 69–70.

SEST Project (1974). *Professional supervisor competencies.* Austin, TX: University of Texas.

Vance, V. L., & Howe, C. E. (1974). Status of special education administration students who received USOE/BEH training grants. *Exceptional Children, 41*(2), 120–121.

Wisland, M. V., & Vaughan, T. D. (1964). Administrative problems in special education. *Exceptional Children, 31,* 87–89.

Ysseldyke, J., Algozzine, B., & Allen, D. (1982). Participation of regular education teachers in special education team decision making. *Exceptional Children, 48*(4), 365–366.

James K. McAfee
Pennsylvania State University

INDIVIDUALS WITH DISABILITIES EDUCATION ACT
POLITICS AND SPECIAL EDUCATION
SPECIAL EDUCATION PROGRAMS
SUPERVISION IN SPECIAL EDUCATION

ADOLESCENCE AND SPECIAL PROBLEMS OF THE HANDICAPPED

Adolescence is the period extending from puberty (about 12 years of age) to age 18 through 20. Crises during adolescence, according to McDowell (1981), generally involve two common elements, physiological and psychological development. Physiological development involves definition of concepts such as identity, relationships, and independence; psychological development involves definition of concepts such as identity, relationships, and independence. The physiological changes include development of sex characteristics. Changes in the body build and structure are very prominent during this period. Much of the stress and anxiety during this period revolve around a general lack of understanding about what adolescents can expect to happen; an impatience with nature in the developmental process; and possible ridicule if an adolescent does not meet certain standards.

Havinghurst (1972) outlined several tasks associated with adolescent development. They include the following:

> Achieving new and more mature relations with agemates of both sexes.
>
> Achieving a masculine or feminine social role.
>
> Accepting one's physique and using the body effectively.
>
> Achieving emotional independence of parents and other adults.
>
> Preparing for marriage and family life.
>
> Preparing for a career.
>
> Acquiring a set of values and an ethical system.
>
> Desiring and achieving socially responsible behavior (pp. 45–75).

These developmental tasks are considered crucial stages in development that require a great deal of adjustment and decision making. However, there are critical problems that many adolescents may be confronted with during this stage. According to McDowell (1981), one major problem adolescents have to deal with is the lack of support systems to meet their needs. Many programs for adolescents were originally designed for children or adults. Three major agencies that adolescents may be involved with are the public schools, mental health facilities, and the legal system. Only recently have the public schools begun to develop appropriate educational alternatives for handicapped adolescents. Many mental health agencies are still in the process of revising child and adult programs to meet the needs of adolescents. The legal system is confronted with deciding whether an adolescent is a child or an adult.

Other problem areas frequently encountered by adolescents include alcohol and drug abuse, crime, suicide, teenage pregnancy, and marriage. Alcohol and drug abuse has been a major problem for many years. Drug abuse surfaced during the late 1960s. The use of drugs by adolescents can lead to emotional and physical problems. Some youngsters may occasionally experiment with drugs; others may become drug abusers to escape from personal problems. Adolescent crime usually involves minor offenses. Only a small number of youngsters are brought to court for serious crimes such as assault, rape, or murder. Adolescent suicide is usually the result of extreme depression and is often related to a relationship problem. Teenage pregnancy can be a traumatic experience for a young girl. Information about sex and birth control are easily available, therefore many adults think adolescents have adequate knowledge. However, many adolescents are not educated about sex and birth control and tend not to admit their lack of knowledge.

Adolescence is often a difficult period for the nonhandicapped child, therefore it is reasonable to assume that it may be even more difficult for the handicapped child. The handicapped adolescent experiences all of the developmental stages and general needs characterized by this period of growth, plus problems relating to exceptionality (Smith & Payne, 1980). According to Cartwright, Cartwright, and Payne (1984), handicapped adolescents may be classified into two groups, the mildly vocationally handicapped and the seriously vocationally handicapped. Those individuals with a strong chance of becoming independent and self-supporting are classified as mildly vocationally handicapped. Those students will be able to get and maintain a job with the proper counseling, career and vocational training, and compensatory skills. Many others may be able to attend technical and trade schools. The seriously vocationally handicapped have severe disabilities that offer little hope for independent living. This group includes the severely and profoundly retarded, multihandicapped, and severely physically handicapped.

Prior to the 1970s, the educational programs for handicapped adolescents were very limited. During the 1950s and 1960s, educational programs for severely handicapped adolescents were minimal. During this time, handicapped youths who attended special classes in public schools were often socially promoted. Many dropped out of school at age 16. The impact of parent groups and the passage of PL 94-142 created many more special programs for handicapped adolescents of every level of severity and handicapping condition (Cartwright et al., 1984). Traditional secondary programs for handicapped adolescents are being rejected by many special educators. These programs are often inappropriate for handicapped students. The lack of relevant subject matter, materials, instructional practices, and testing methods are often major problem areas that offer little or no assistance in meeting the needs of the handicapped (Laurie, Buchwach, Silverman, & Zigmond, 1978).

Mandell and Gold (1984) emphasized that the handicapped adolescent's needs, skills, and future goals are essential components that must be considered when selecting the most appropriate service delivery model. The mildly handicapped student may be served in the mainstream with supplementary assistance. Some students may benefit from a combination of regular secondary and vocational education with supplementary assistance. The more severely handicapped student may benefit from self-contained and special classes or special vocational training centers.

Career and vocational education is an essential component of the secondary education program for the handicapped adolescent. McDowell (1979) stated that for handicapped adolescents, the following behaviors are essential for survival on the job and in today's society.

1. Be able to establish eye contact if required by the situation.
2. Demonstrate respect for others and their property.
3. Be attentive to authority figures in appropriate ways.
4. Exhibit good manners.
5. Use appropriate manners.
6. Discriminate between behaviors as to time and place (i.e., recognize that certain behaviors are appropriate at different times and places).
7. Achieve a reasonable balance between dependence and independence.
8. Learn to accept directions and take orders.
9. Learn to accept and follow the work schedule established by an employer.
10. See a task through to its completion (p. 2.).

A great deal of emphasis should be placed on helping the handicapped adolescent learn behaviors and skills essential to independence. However, many handicapped people are underemployed and unable to find jobs within their range of abilities (Razeghi & Davis, 1979). Another essential component of a secondary program for handicapped adolescents is social skills. Many handicapped children have problems developing appropriate social skills. Difficulties in these areas lead to problems with integration into the mainstream and peer relationships.

REFERENCES

Cartwright, G. P. (1984). *Educating special learners* (2nd ed.). Belmont, CA: Wadsworth.

Havinghurst, R. J. (1972). *Developmental tasks and education* (3rd ed.). New York: McKay.

Laurie, T. E., Buchwach, L., Silverman, R., & Zigmond, N. (1978). Teaching secondary learning disabled students in the mainstream. *Learning Disabilities Quarterly, 1*, 62–72.

Mandell, C. J., & Gold, V. (1984). *Teaching handicapped students*. St. Paul, MN: West.

McDowell, R. L. (1979). *The emotionally disturbed adolescent*. PRISE Reporter, No. 3, May 1979. King of Prussia, PA: Pennsylvania Resources and Information Center for Special Education.

McDowell, R. L. (1981). Adolescence. In G. Brown, R. L. McDowell, & J. Smith (Eds.), *Educating adolescents with behavior disorders*. Columbus, OH: Merrill.

Razeghi, J. A., & Davis, S. (1979). Federal mandates for the handicapped: Vocational education opportunity and employment. *Exceptional Children, 45,* 353–359.

Smith, J. E., & Payne, J. S. (1980). *Teaching exceptional adolescents*. Columbus, OH: Merrill.

JANICE HARPER
*North Carolina Central
University*

AFFECTIVE EDUCATION
FAMILY RESPONSE TO A HANDICAPPED CHILD
SOCIAL SKILLS
VOCATIONAL TRAINING OF HANDICAPPED

ADOPTEES

The practice of adoption is centuries old, but our understanding of the impact of this form of child care continues to be without definitive answers. At the theoretical level, adoption has often been associated with increased risk for psychological maladjustment. Psychoanalytic theory, for example, suggests that the experience of adoption sets the stage for disturbances in personality and identity development. This is especially true because of doubt surrounding the true circumstances of the child's origins, and because the child has two sets of parents instead of one with whom to identify. Bowlby's work (1969) suggests that adopted children are at risk for emotional problems, but only in cases where there is disruption in the development and continuity of primary attachment relationships. Consequently, infants adopted soon after birth and cared for continually by affectionate and competent parents would not be viewed as being at risk in terms of possible maladjustment. However, individuals raised by multiple caregivers, or separated from caregivers after a secure attachment has developed, would be perceived as being at risk.

In contrast to the theoretical literature, the results of empirical research have produced an inconsistent picture of the effects of adoption on an individual's psychological development. After reviewing the social work literature on the success of adoption placements, both Mech (1973) and Kadushin (1974) concluded that the majority of place-

ments were satisfactory. However, an examination of the records of mental-health clinics reveals that adopted children are referred to these clinics at disproportionate rates. Mech (1973) reported that while adopted children reared by nonrelatives constitute approximately 1% of the population, they account for over 4% of the children seen in clinics. Researchers have also reported that there are differences in types of problems presented by adopted children versus those who are nonadopted. Adopted children typically manifest more aggressive and acting-out problems, as well as learning-related difficulties. In fact, a recent study has even reported an elevated number of pediatric health conditions among adopted children (Dalby, Fox, & Haslam, 1982).

While there are those studies available that validate these findings, there are also those such as Aumend and Barrett's (1984) that provide a contrary set of findings. In their study of adult adoptees they reported the following: the majority of those in their study scored above the 60th percentile on the Tennessee Self Concept Scale; had positive scores on the Attitude Toward Parents Scales; were happy growing up, with only 12% reporting that they were unhappy; and did not report revelation of their adoptive status as being disruptive or traumatic. These findings were consistent with those of Norvell and Guy (1977), who determined there were no significant differences between self-concepts of an adopted and nonadopted population, aged 18 to 25. They concluded that problems of a negative identity seemed to stem more from problems within the home, rather than an association with adoption.

Because of a lack of definitive empirical information, the issue of open records, or allowing adopted children to learn about their biological parents at a particular point in time, continues to be controversial. As has been the case in the past, this issue will probably be resolved in the courts. Another issue unique to adoption is when children should be informed of their adoptive status. Currently, most specialists on adoption advocate telling children before they are 5 years of age. The specialists believe this promotes the development of a trusting relationship within the context of a warm and supportive family and eliminates the possibility that the child will hear of his or her unique family status from nonfamily members under less than desirable conditions. While many advocate telling the child during the preschool years, recent studies such as that by Brodzinsky, Schechter, Braff, & Singer (1984) suggest that a child's cognitive development during the preschool years may mitigate against his or her understanding of the nature of adoption. Their concern is that parents may relate this information to children and then feel the "job is done," failing to understand that advanced stages of cognitive development call for further explanations and sequential exploration of concerns the child might harbor.

While the data are not as definitive as might be liked, it certainly seems that adoption is a legitimate way of building families and caring for young children. It is superior to alternatives such as serial placements in a number of homes, or large-scale institutional care. Assuming the family is capable of providing a stable environment that is free of debilitating or otherwise pathological features, and relates the information on adoption in a facilitative fashion, there seems to be little reason to expect greater childhood problems than experienced in biologically created families. In families where psychological attachment between adoptee and parent fails, increased emotional and behavioral problems will occur (Ziegler, 1994).

REFERENCES

Aumend, S. A., & Barrett, M. C. (1984). Self-concept and attitudes toward adoption: A comparison of searching and nonsearching adult adoptees. *Child Welfare, 63,* 251–259.

Bowlby, J. (1969). *Attachment and loss: Volume 1 attachment.* New York: Basic Books.

Brodzinsky, D. M., Schechter, D. E., Braff, A. M., & Singer, L. M. (1984). Psychological and academic adjustment in adopted children. *Journal of Consulting and Clinical Psychology, 52,* 582–589.

Dalby, J. T., Fox, S. L., & Haslam, R. H. (1982). Adoption and foster care rates in pediatric disorders. *Developmental and Behavioral Pediatrics, 3,* 61–64.

Kadushin, A. (1974). *Child welfare services.* New York: Macmillan.

Mech, E. V. (1973). Adoption: A policy perspective. In B. Caldwell & H. Ricuitti (Eds.), *Review of child development research* (Vol. 3). Chicago: University of Chicago Press.

Norvell, M., & Guy, R. F. (1977). A comparison of self concept in adopted and nonadopted adolescents. *Adolescence, 12,* 443–448.

Ziegler, D. (1994). Adoption and adjustment. In B. James, *Handbook for treatment of attachment-trauma problems in children* (pp. 256–266). NY: Lexington Books.

CHARLES P. BARNARD
University of Wisconsin at Stout

CHILD CARE AGENCIES
CHILD CARETAKER
CHILD GUIDANCE CLINIC
POSTINSTITUTIONALIZED CHILDREN

ADULT BASIC EDUCATION (ABE)

Adult basic education (ABE), a part of the adult education movement, is designed and intended for those individuals who may lack the basic education needed to function appropriately in society. For many adults, particularly those with handicapping conditions, adult education serves as a substitute for the education that was missed in earlier years or never completed. For others, adult education implies further or continuing education.

Adult education encompasses all organized learning, including vocational education (Stubblefield, 1981). During the formative years of what became the adult education movement (mid-to-late 1920s), adult education revolved around a belief that individual growth and improvement was paramount; that is, individuals would respond to education that would assist in helping them to understand their life experiences and improve themselves through the acquisition of knowledge, enjoyment, power, etc.

Later, the adult education movement emphasized a variety of other themes, including psychological and physical maturity, service to society, and civic life. Those who have tried to identify a central focus within adult education have most often portrayed the adult learner as an individual who seeks out education and has a desire to accommodate to a changing society and value system. Thus one major issue has centered around whether the goal of adult education should be to satisfy individual needs or societal needs.

The content of adult education varies from the simple to the complex. In fact, any content that is reflective of the adult's interest and desire to know is legitimate (Schroeder, 1970). At times, content is selected to achieve cognitive objectives (i.e., facts, knowledge of principles) while, at other times, content is selected to achieve affective objectives (i.e., interests, values, or psychomotor objectives or skills). Similarly, adult education can involve hobby learning (e.g., learning to play golf or bridge), literacy learning (e.g., learning at the academic level of elementary and secondary schools), occupational learning (e.g., learning manual and clerical skills), and higher learning (e.g., learning beyond the secondary and vocational level) (Bowen, 1980). It is literacy learning that constitutes adult basic education.

There are many adult education service providers, although most can be assigned to one of four categories: (1) agencies that serve the needs of adults; (2) agencies that serve the needs of adolescents, but have some responsibility for serving the needs of adults; (3) agencies that serve the educational and noneducational needs of the community; and (4) agencies that serve the special interest needs of particular groups. In the first category are agencies such as proprietary schools (i.e., business schools, technical schools) and independent education centers. The second category consists of public schools, community colleges, and institutions of higher education. The third category includes libraries and museums, while the fourth category includes unions, churches, business and industry, and so on. In essence, adult education is found in a variety of organizations that provide education for adults.

There are numerous categories of individuals who provide potential populations of adult learners. These include:

Those desiring to overcome educational limitations

College and high school dropouts

Career changers or career updaters

Institutionalized populations

Elderly persons

Those who simply enjoy learning

The handicapped.

Adult basic education coupled with programs for speakers of other languages long have been features of adult education. The rationale behind ABE programs is based on the demonstrated correlation between years of schooling and income. That is, there is a presumed relationship between the length of time spent in school and the amount of income earned. Consequently, ABE programs are directed toward assisting individuals to enter or upgrade their skills for the labor market. A further rationale for ABE programs is that every adult has a basic right to acquire skills in written and verbal communication and computation. Therefore, ABE programs are directed toward undereducated adults. Although this can include those adult individuals having known handicapping conditions, the majority of clients are poor, from a minority background, and possibly defeatist.

All possible knowledge could be included in an ABE program. However, few programs have the resources to provide such an extensive range of services for all types of adult learners. Limiting services, however, tends to limit the types of individuals who can participate; thus, handicapped adults may not be recruited for ABE programs that require students who have needs that are linked to a program's goals or capacities. While some ABE programs for adult handicapped persons are available, they have not been a major focus of ABE programs.

REFERENCES

Bowen, H. R. (1980). *Adult learning, higher education, and the economics of unused capacity.* New York: College Entrance Examination Board.

Schroeder, W. L. (1970). Adult education defined and described. In R. M. Smith, G. F. Aker, & J. R. Kidd (Eds.), *Handbook of adult education.* New York: Macmillan.

Stubblefield, H. W. (1981). The focus should be on life fulfillment. In B. W. Kreitlow & Associates (Eds.), *Examining controversies in adult education.* San Francisco: Jossey-Bass.

Shworles, T. R., & Wang, P. H. (1980). Education for handicapped adults. In E. J. Boon, R. W. Shearon, & E. E. White (Eds.), *Serving personal and community needs through adult education.* San Francisco, Jossey-Bass.

MARTY ABRAMSON
University of Wisconsin at Stout

COMMUNITY-BASED SERVICES

REHABILITATION

VOCATIONAL VILLAGE

ADULT PROGRAMS FOR THE DISABLED

There are numerous programs of several types that serve adults with disabilities. Many such programs are financed by federal, state, and local governments; many others are funded by private business, private nonprofit organizations, and charities. The following is a summary of major programs organized by function and financing source. It will not capture the complexity and breadth of these programs, especially at the state and local level.

The Social Security Act authorizes several major programs providing cash payments and health insurance to adults on the basis of disability. The disability insurance (DI) program replaces in part income lost when a person with a work history can no longer work because of a physical or mental impairment. Many individuals, of course, have separate commercial disability insurance policies provided by an employer or purchased on their own. After receiving Social Security DI benefits for 24 months, regardless of age, an individual becomes eligible for government-provided health insurance under the Medicare program, which normally covers persons 65 and over. The Social Security Act also contains the Supplemental Security Income (SSI) program, which provides cash income support payments to needy individuals who are aged, blind, or disabled. Income is provided regardless of work history to those who meet means and asset requirements. In most states, with SSI eligibility comes eligibility for the Medicaid program (federal-state matching required), which provides health insurance for low-income individuals. Included in Medicaid is support for intermediate care facilities for the mentally retarded (ICFs/MR), which provide residential care and service programs. Many disabled individuals benefit from programs for which they may be eligible without regard to their disability, for example, Social Security Old Age and Survivors insurance payments and Medicare (persons 65 and older).

Finally, there are four other major federal programs of this type for special groups of disabled individuals. Veterans with service-connected disabilities are eligible for special cash payments under the Veterans Compensation program. Veterans of wartime service with nonservice-connected disabilities are eligible for a special pension program. Coal miners disabled by black lung or other lung disease are eligible for one of two separate special payment programs (one administered by the Social Security Administration, the other by the Labor Department), depending on circumstances.

Special programs of postsecondary education for the deaf and hearing impaired, supported with significant federal funding, are provided at Gallaudet College, the National Technical Institute for the Deaf, and four special regional postsecondary institutions. In addition, educational programs that are recipients of federal financial assistance at public and private colleges and universities must be accessible to and usable by individuals with disabilities of all types. Some schools are making adaptations and providing support services that go beyond legal requirements.

Rehabilitation and job training services are available from a number of sources. Under Title I of the Rehabilitation Act, the federal government and the states provide vocational rehabilitation services such as physical restoration, job training, and placement to persons with mental and physical disabilities, regardless of prior work history. Physical rehabilitation is covered by most accident and health insurance policies; vocational rehabilitation is sometimes covered. Rehabilitation is available and in fact required under some state workers' compensation laws. Rehabilitation services financed by various forms of insurance are provided by private, for-profit companies and facilities, private nonprofit agencies, and state agencies. Provision of rehabilitation services by private, profit-making (proprietary) firms has been a growing phenomenon (Taylor, et al., 1985) for many years now.

Private nonprofit entities play a significant role in providing job training, rehabilitation, and other skill development to adults with disabilities. Included in this group are organizations such as the Association for Retarded Citizens, Easter Seals, Goodwill Industries, and United Cerebral Palsy. Some activities of these organizations are financed by the government; others are funded by contracts with businesses for work performed.

Major employers, faced with rising costs of disability, will find it in their interest to pay greater attention to management, rehabilitation, and disability prevention (Schwartz, 1984). Many are increasing efforts in these areas, including rehabilitation, job, and work-site modification efforts to facilitate entry or return to jobs by individuals with disabilities. Contracts with the federal government of more than $2500 must operate with an affirmative action program to employ and advance individuals with disabilities.

Self-help, referral, and training services are available to people with very severe disabilities to improve their capacity for independent living. These services are available through a network of community-based nonprofit centers and from state rehabilitation agencies. In addition, supported employment is an important new program for individuals with disabilities so severe they were previously thought incapable of working. These individuals (especially those with mental impairments) are likely to need continual support, but they are able to work on regular jobs in integrated settings if given a highly structured training program and some support on the job site (Mank 1986).

Special housing and transportation programs are available for individuals with disabilities, financed by both the federal government and states and localities. The same is true for special recreation programs for the disabled, in which local governments, service organizations, charities, and private businesses play a large role. Therapeutic recreation is also part of some rehabilitation programs. In addition, many local recreation facilities and organizations, including those involved with the arts, are adapting programs so that the disabled can participate or attend with the general public.

REFERENCES

General Services Administration. (1985). *Catalog of federal domestic assistance*. Washington, DC: U.S. Government Printing Office.

Mank, D. (1986). Four supported employment alternatives. In W. Kiernan & J. Stark (Eds.), *Pathways to employment for developmentally disabled adults*. Baltimore, MD: Brooks.

National Council on the Handicapped. (1986). *Toward independence: An assessment of federal laws and programs affecting persons with disabilities*. Washington, DC: U.S. Government Printing Office.

Schwartz, G. (1984, May). Disability costs: The impending crisis. *Business and Health* (pp. 25–28).

Taylor, L. J., Golter, M., Golter, G., & Backer, T. (Eds.). (1985). *Handbook of private sector rehabilitation*. New York: Springer.

JAMES R. RICCIUTI
*United States Office of
Management and Budget*

**ACCESSIBILITY OF PROGRAMS
AMERICANS WITH DISABILITIES ACT
HABILITATION OF THE HANDICAPPED
REHABILITATION**

ADVANCED PLACEMENT PROGRAM

The Advanced Placement Program was established in 1955 as a program of college-level courses and examinations for secondary school students. It is administered by the College Board, a nonprofit membership organization composed of public and private secondary schools, colleges, and universities. This program gives high school students the opportunity to receive advanced placement and/or credit on entering college.

The essential premise of the Advanced Placement Program is that college-level courses can be successfully taught to high school students by high school teachers on high school campuses (College Entrance Examination Board, 1985). Descriptions and examinations on 26 introductory college courses in 14 fields are disseminated. These fields include art, biology, chemistry, computer science, English, French, German, government and politics, history, Latin, mathematics, music, physics, and Spanish. Course descriptions are prepared, with the help of the Educational Testing Service, by working committees of school and college teachers appointed by the College Board. Exams are administered by the Educational Testing Service.

Most participating high schools, offering one or more advanced placement courses (called AP courses) are larger schools with enough students to qualify for a class. Smaller schools usually provide independent study for those students wishing to take advanced placement exams. The AP course teachers are provided with course descriptions and teachers' guides that state curricular goals and suggest strategies to achieve them. Teachers are not required to follow a detailed plan of assignments and classroom activities; however, seven Advanced Placement Regional Offices and Advanced Placement Program conferences are available to assist teachers.

Advanced Placement courses offer demanding academic opportunities for abler students. Students who complete these courses are not required to take advanced placement examinations, but those who choose to take them and who receive a passing score, have the opportunity to receive advanced placement and/or credit on entering college.

REFERENCES

College Entrance Examination Board (1985). *School administrator's guide to the advanced placement program* (Edition G). New York: Author.

The College Board Review (quarterly publication)
The College Board
888 Seventh Avenue
New York, NY 10106

Advanced Placement Program
Harlan P. Hanson, Director
45 Columbus Avenue
New York, NY 10023-6917

MARY K. TALLENT
Texas Tech University

ACCELERATION OF GIFTED CHILDREN
GIFTED AND TALENTED CHILDREN

ADVANCE ORGANIZERS

Advance organizers are general overviews or conceptual models of new information presented to learners immedi-

ately prior to receiving new information. Ausubel (1960) originally proposed the concept of the advance organizer for use with reading material. The principle of advance organizers is that learning is enhanced when information is linked to learners' existing cognitive structures, thereby enabling the learner to organize and interpret new information (Mayer, 1979). Thus advance organizers prepare the learner for the meaningful reception of new learning. They can either present salient prerequisite knowledge not known to the learner (known as expository organizers), or help the learner establish connections between relevant dimensions of existing knowledge and the new information (known as comparative organizers) (Ausubel, Novak, & Hanesian, 1979).

Expository organizers draw the learner's attention to the internal organization of the body of new information by means of a rough overview that briefly presents general topics and concepts and how they are related. Outlines, models, and introductory paragraphs may serve this purpose. With comparative organizers, students' previous experiences or prior learning is tapped in such a way as to identify major points or dimensions of similarity between the new information and existing understandings. By providing external organization, or how new information is related to what students already know, comparative organizers establish a meaningful learning set.

Advance organizers may be either verbal or graphic, and can take a variety of formats, including overviews, outlines, analogies, examples, thought-provoking questions, concrete models, and figures such as cognitive maps (Alexander, Frankiewicz, & Williams, 1979; Mayer, 1984; Zook, 1991). Although originally conceptualized as abstract introductions, advance organizers tend to be more effective if they are concrete and if they are both familiar to the learner and well-learned. In this way, advance organizers provide frameworks or cognitive maps for new content. Corkill (1992) also emphasizes the importance of using examples that enable learners to identify the relationship between ideas in the organizer and the new information.

Eggen and Kauchak (1996) use the following example of an advance organizer from an elementary social studies lesson on governments.

The organization of a government is like a family. Different people in the government have different responsibilities and roles. When all the people work together, both families and governments operate efficiently (p. 214).

Current schema theory provides a theoretical basis for advance organizers, whose function can be viewed as both activating relevant schemata for to-be-learned material and revising the activated schemata to promote assimilation of the new material (Derry, 1984; Glover, Ronning, & Bruning, 1990). Advance organizers will benefit learners most when students lack the prerequisite knowledge for understanding, and when the transfer of learning to new problems is the desired outcome. To be maximally effective, they should be easy to acquire, as concrete as possible, and offer an integrated overview or model of the new material (Mayer, 1987).

REFERENCES

Alexander, L., Frankiewicz, R., & Williams, R. (1979). Facilitation of learning and retention of oral instruction using advance and post organizers. *Journal of Educational Psychology, 71,* 701–707.

Ausubel, D. P. (1960). The use of advance organizers in the learning and retention of meaningful verbal material. *Journal of Educational Psychology, 51,* 267–272.

Ausubel, D. P., Novak, J. D., & Hanesian, H. (1979). *Educational psychology: A cognitive view* (2nd ed.). New York: Holt, Rinehart & Winston.

Corkill, A. (1992). Advance organizers: Facilitators of recall. *Educational Psychology Review, 4,* 33–67.

Derry, S. J. (1984). Effects of an organizer on memory for prose. *Journal of Educational Psychology, 76,* 98–107.

Eggen P. D., & Kauchak, D. P. (1996). *Strategies for teachers: Teaching content and thinking skills* (3rd ed.). Boston: Allyn & Bacon.

Glover, J. A. Ronning, R. R., & Bruning, R. H. (1990). *Cognitive psychology for teachers.* New York: Macmillan.

Mayer, R. E. (1979). Can advance organizers influence meaningful learning? *Review of Educational Research, 49,* 371–383.

Mayer, R. E. (1984). Aids to text comprehension. *Educational Psychologist, 19,* 30–42.

Mayer, R. E. (1987). *Educational psychology: A cognitive approach.* Boston: Little, Brown.

Zook, K. B. (1991). Effects of analogical processes on learning and misrepresentation. *Educational Psychology Review, 3,* 41–72.

JAMES M. APPLEFIELD
*University of North Carolina
at Wilmington*

ADVENTITIOUS DISABILITIES

Disabilities may present themselves at birth or be acquired through disease or accident. Those acquired later in life are known as adventitious disabilities. Among these is brain damage produced by extremely high and consistent temperatures or a lack of needed oxygen to the brain. Adventitious disabilities may also be a consequence of trauma to the brain or injury to other parts of the body. A major cause of adventitious disabilities is child abuse. Child abuse is emotionally or physically damaging and can cause durable learning problems. An area of childhood ex-

ceptionality often associated with an adventitious disability is hearing impairment or deafness. Hearing losses may be present at birth or adventitiously acquired later on in life through disease or accident. Adventitious disabilities and congenital disabilities that appear similar (but are obviously of different etiologies) may well have different outcomes.

BRAIN DAMAGE/INJURY
CHILD ABUSE
POSTINSTITUTIONALIZED CHILDREN

ADVOCACY FOR CHILDREN WITH DISABILITIES

Advocacy for handicapped people has become a multifaceted reality in today's world of concern about the legal rights of those with disabilities. The term actually has a variety of meanings, depending on who is providing the advocacy. In its essence, advocacy refers to attempts by an individual handicapped person, by another person, or by a group to guarantee that all rights due a handicapped person are realized. Roos (1983) traces the origins of the advocacy movement to the 1930s, when parents of mentally retarded children began to react against neglectful or inappropriate actions by professionals who claimed to be helping these children and their families. Frustrated with the professionals' response, parents turned to each other for help.

In 1933, the Cuyahoga County (Ohio) Council for the Retarded Child was founded by parents as the forerunner of today's Association for Retarded Citizens (*ARC*). Other local, grass-roots organizations sprang up in different communities, and later, in 1950, joined together to form what was then known as the National Association of Parents and Friends of Mentally Retarded Children. At that time, similar organizational activity sprung up with parents of children with cerebral palsy.

Recently groups have been formed to advocate the interests of learning disabled, deaf, blind, and autistic children, and those with a variety of medical and physical anomalies. The early parent movements had at least three effects in the 1950s, at the same time as they formed a base on which later governmental and judicial action would be built. First, local ARCs extended emotional support to families with retarded members, providing information about available resources and bringing the issue of mental retardation into public view. This helped remove some of the stigma of having a handicapped child. Second, they encouraged state legislatures to adopt mandatory legislation for public school programs for retarded children, to enforce existing legislation, and to increase state appropriations for publicly funded programs. Third, parents developed preschool, school-age, and adult programs that became models for professionals, and public education and voluntary agencies (Lippman & Goldberg, 1973).

The role of ARC as a direct service provider has declined recently. Greater emphasis is now placed on information and public education services, advocacy, legislation, and funding (Roos, 1983). Advocacy efforts by ARC and other such groups today focus on citizen advocacy and self-advocacy. Professionals and volunteers have joined with parents to change the makeup of many groups formerly consisting exclusively of parents of handicapped children. Various advocacy groups and professional associations have formed coalitions to increase their political and public influence, with many organizations maintaining full- or part-time offices in Washington, DC, as well as in state capitals. These groups may be closely linked with legal advocacy agencies and may be represented on state and national advisory panels, accrediting boards, and monitoring bodies, often by state or federal regulation or court order. Advocacy groups have been instrumental in initiating litigation, often through the use of class-action suits, to guarantee that the existing rights of handicapped persons are safeguarded, to obtain new rights or services, or to enhance currently available programs. In some cases, international societies have been formed by national advocacy groups representing several nations (Roos, 1983).

Herr (1983) describes several different kinds of advocacy that have evolved from earlier movements. Though definitions and actual practice may vary, the following types of advocacy approaches for the handicapped can be identified:

1. *Self-advocacy*: "part consciousness-raising, assertiveness-training. . .and springboard to direct consumer involvement. . . ." (Herr, 1983).
2. *Family advocacy*: the oldest and most well understood.
3. *Friend advocacy*: personal, voluntary assistance by altruistic citizens; also referred to as *citizen advocacy*.
4. *Disability rights advocacy*: trained advocacy specialists dealing with individual needs and human service systems.
5. *Human rights advocacy*: usually citizen review committees composed of volunteers and professionals.
6. *Internal advocacy*: individuals within, rather than external to, human service agencies who attempt to guarantee clients' rights (sometimes referred to as ombudsmen).
7. *Legal advocacy*: primarily nonprofit, public-interest law projects, including some private or government lawyers (Herr, 1983).

Although individual special educators, acting alone or through professional organizations, may also view themselves as advocates for the handicapped children they serve, there may be inherent conflicts in attempting to play the two roles simultaneously (Bateman, 1982). Special educators must keep current on ethical practices and legal developments in their field, and on law and education in general.

REFERENCES

Bateman, B. (1982). Legal and ethical dilemmas of special educators. *Exceptional Education Quarterly, 2*(4), 57–67.

Herr, S. S. (1983). *Rights and advocacy for retarded people.* Lexington, MA: Lexington Books.

Lippman, L., & Goldberg, I. I. (1973). *Right to education: Anatomy of the Pennsylvania case and its implications for exceptional children.* New York: Teachers College Press.

Roos, P. R. (1983). Advocate groups. In J. L. Matson & J. A. Mulick (Eds.), *Handbook of mental retardation.* New York: Pergamon.

JOHN D. WILSON
Elwyn Institutes

ADVOCACY GROUPS, CITIZEN

A citizen advocacy group may be defined in general as any organization that has as its purpose to increase the quality of life for a specified handicapped population. Two examples of citizen advocacy groups containing both parents and professionals, and formally organized, are the Association for Children With Learning Disorders (ACLD) and the American Association on Mental Deficiency. These two groups have national headquarters but are organized state by state, having local chapters at county, city, or regional levels. They are not, however, classified as grass-roots advocacy groups.

An example of an informal organization is Youth Advocacy in the Washington, DC, area, a group of citizens (nonparents), with paid professional leadership, that provides services for adjudicated youths. They may represent an alternative to incarceration, providing community-based rehabilitation and supporting school, work, and living arrangements for youths in the area. Another example of a grass-roots nationally organized group is the Association for Autistic children. The chief characteristic of the organization is that the majority of local support groups are informally organized, and indeed are parents, while the leadership has national consolidation. There are formal and informal advocacy groups at national, regional, and local levels serving handicapped students representing all disability groups. The purposes for each group may vary considerably, depending on the perceived needs of the group.

The work of advocacy groups includes seeking federal or state legislation, developing policy or ordinances at the community level, supporting parental work, and intervening directly for students. One example of a community-based advocacy group is the Lion's Club, which supports the visually handicapped. Other social clubs support the hearing impaired (Rotary), the mentally retarded (Civitan), or orthopedically impaired (Shriners) by paying for services, prostheses, or therapy. Another example is the Junior Chamber of Commerce, a group that raises partial or full support for group homes, sheltered employment centers, or residential or day schools for the emotionally disturbed.

Providing funds for services or a community-support base are two of the major purposes of advocacy organizations. The definition of a community-support base varies with the particular advocacy group and community. Certainly, providing emotional support for parents is a major consideration. Obtaining legislation also is a primary function, given the fact that all legislation for the handicapped was provided and obtained by parents, not professionals. Advocacy groups may purchase direct services or even provide direct services, but that has not been their major role in the past. It is becoming more of a major role though, and represents a trend toward advocacy in the United States.

DAVID A. SABATINO
*West Virginia College
of Graduate Studies*

ADVOCACY ORGANIZATIONS

Advocacy organizations are organizations that devote themselves to advocacy for individuals or groups who have needs for which their own resources may not be sufficient. The establishment of these organizations has proceeded on "the assumption that classes of persons exist with similar needs and similar inability to speak effectively for themselves" (Sage & Burello, 1986).

Many, if not most, of the services currently available to handicapped children and adolescents either began or succeeded because of the efforts of advocacy groups. Much of special education history represents the efforts of advocacy groups, including church, parent, and charitable groups. The Association for Retarded Citizens, in its national, state, and local forms, is an example of an advocacy organ-

ization that has altered educational practices in major ways.

Increasing growth in all sorts of advocacy groups has taken place since the 1960s, with an acceleration in the last decade. Not all groups, of course, deal with the handicapped. There are environmental advocacy groups, groups concerned with product safety, with the elimination of drunk driving, etc. However, advocacy groups for the handicapped have been among the most vociferous and successful.

Many of these advocacy groups began and sustained themselves through grants from the federal government. This was particularly true during the 1960s and 1970s, when they were financially encouraged as part of the social legislation of the times. Some were started or supported through funds provided by foundations or their own fund-raising activities.

The nature of advocacy is such that agencies are likely to be activist, to aggressively seek to achieve long-range changes in the social system to benefit their clients, and to immediately help those clients. Thus they often seek to influence legislation. Some advocacy agencies have special service missions, but modern agencies are more likely to intercede with a particular service or political system so as to obtain services and other needed benefits for their clients rather than provide those benefits themselves. They also make efforts to educate both their clients and the systems with which they interact so as to facilitate their working relationships. Professional advocacy groups usually assume major informational roles. They provide forums for speakers and disseminate information and literature, including manuals that assist their audiences to assist themselves in achieving their goals.

Advocacy organizations often have been successful in obtaining services for their clients, either through their own intercessions or by educating and supporting the services' "consumers" or their representatives so as to make them more effective. Such organizations as Closer Look Information Center for the Handicapped and the National Center for Law and the Handicapped have been instrumental in making public schools more responsive to the needs of handicapped students. They also have played major roles in disseminating information to the individuals whose advocacies they are assuming, to the general public, and to the legislative bodies whose laws and regulations may affect their constituencies.

REFERENCE

Sage, D. D., & Burrello, L. C. (1986). *Policy and management in special education.* Englewood Cliffs, NJ: Prentice-Hall.

LESTER MANN
Hunter College

AFFECTIVE DISORDERS

Affect is the externally observable, immediately expressed component of human emotion (e.g., facial expression, tone of voice). Mood is considered to be a sustained emotion that pervades an individual's perception of the world. Affective disorders, as defined by the American Psychiatric Association (1994) are the class of mental disorders where the essential feature is a disturbance of mood.

Emotions and their expression are an integral part of human experience. It is only under certain conditions that the expression of emotion is considered maladaptive; in some instances, in fact, a lack of affect might be viewed as abnormal. It is only when an emotional reaction is disproportionate to the event, when the duration of the reaction is atypical, or when it interferes with a person's psychological, social, or occupational functioning that an emotional response may be labeled symptomatic of an affective disorder.

Affective disorders are comprised of two basic elements, depression and mania, which can be conceptualized as opposite ends of a continuum paralleling the normal happiness/sadness continuum. Both depression and mania have their counterparts in everyday life: The parallels for depression are grief and dejection; the experience corresponding to mania is less clear-cut, but probably could be described as the feverish activity with which people sometimes respond to stress.

Formally, both mania and depression can be characterized by symptoms at the emotional, cognitive, and somatic/motivational levels. The major emotional components of depression are sadness and melancholy, often accompanied by feelings of guilt and worthlessness. These emotions permeate the individual's total experience of life. Cognitively, depressed persons are characterized by a negatively distorted view of themselves, the world, and the future. Their outlook is generally one of unrealistic hopelessness. In terms of their physical functioning, depressed persons frequently suffer appetite and sleep disturbances, fatigue, apathy, and a general loss of energy.

In certain aspects, the symptoms of mania could be viewed as opposite to those of depression. For instance, people suffering a manic episode often are in a highly elevated mood, seeming to experience life with an intense euphoria. However, it generally takes little frustration to shift this elated enthusiasm to irritability or tears, which suggests that mania may be closer to depression than initially seems apparent. In fact, it has been suggested by a number of theorists that mania is a defense against depression, that it is an attempt to ward off depressive feelings through feverish activity.

Cognitively, manic individuals characteristically show wildly inflated self-esteem, believing themselves to be capable of great accomplishments or possessed of exceptional talent. Manic individuals act on their high opinion of themselves. They behave recklessly, involving themselves in unwise business deals or sexual liaisons, wasting large sums of money on shopping sprees or gambling. When experiencing a manic episode, individuals often have a decreased need for sleep, sometimes going for days without rest.

Within the affective disorders, there are two major syndromes: major depression (or unipolar depression as it has traditionally been called) and bipolar disorder (formerly manic-depressive disorder). In unipolar depression, an individual experiences one or more episodes of depression without ever experiencing an episode of mania. Approximately half of the people who suffer major depression will undergo only one episode of depression: Their first episode will be their last. In general, even without intervention, most people will recover from an occurrence of unipolar depression within 3 to 6 months.

In bipolar disorder, an individual experiences both manic and depressive episodes. In rare cases, an individual vacillates between manic and depressive episodes without an intervening period of normal functioning. More often, there are periods of normality interspersed between the manic and/or depressive episodes. There is no separate diagnostic category for persons who experience only manic episodes; this occurs only rarely. In such instances, an assumption is made that the person will ultimately experience a depressive episode, and a diagnosis of bipolar disorder will be made.

Of the two disorders, bipolar disorder is typically, but not always, the more serious and debilitating. People with bipolar disorder, in comparison with those with unipolar disorder, experience more episodes, and their interepisode functioning is worse. Further, such people are more likely to have serious alcohol abuse problems and attempt and commit suicide at a higher rate than persons with unipolar disorder.

Mood disorders have long been the most common of mental illnesses, but they are on the increase in modern society (Keller & Baker, 1992). Depression has been referred to as the common cold of mental illness. Around 10% of the males and perhaps 22% of the females living in the United States will at some point in their lives experience an episode of major depression. This one-to-two ratio has been found in many different cultures, in Europe and Africa as well as North America. (There are, however, a few notable exceptions such as the Amish in Pennsylvania.) It has been hypothesized that more women experience depression than men because it is more socially acceptable for women to respond to negative life experiences with passive, depressive symptoms. Men may be less likely to experience or express depressive symptoms because they may receive more social rejection (or less social reinforcement) than women for acting depressed. Instead, men may respond to stressful events more actively, with substance abuse (e.g., alcoholism) or antisocial behavior.

Bipolar disorder is much less common than unipolar

disorder; slightly less than 1% percent of the U.S. population will experience bipolar disorder at some point in their lives. Unlike unipolar disorder, bipolar disorder occurs with approximately the same frequency in men as in women. Both unipolar and bipolar disorder tend to run in families, though bipolar disorder probably has a significantly larger genetic component than unipolar disorder. At present, the nature of the genetic mechanisms underlying the affective disorders is not clear. It is known, however, that in both mania and depression there are abnormalities in the level of neurotransmitters in the brain.

Beyond the possibility noted that mania is a defense against depression, there has been relatively little psychological theorizing about the causes of mania and bipolar disorder. This is not the case with unipolar depression, for which a number of etiological theories have been developed. From a Freudian perspective, depression is viewed as the punishment an overly punitive superego inflicts on the ego for the ego's failure to properly treat a lost love. The superego's harshness is seen also as a means of preventing the ego's feelings of anger and aggression from being expressed (Freud, 1917).

From a more behavioral perspective, Lewinsohn (1974) has hypothesized that depression is the result of a low rate of response-contingent reinforcement, caused by either a lack of social skills or a deficient environment, which results in the person experiencing behavioral extinction. Rather than being a function of the rate of reinforcement, Seligman et al. (Abramson, Seligman, & Teasdale, 1978) believe that it is the individual's lack of control over his or her environment and the attributions that this person makes about this lack of control that results in depression. Seligman believes that a lack of control that is attributed to causes that are internal (the self), global (some general quality), and stable (not likely to change) will result in depression.

Most theorists believe that the cognitions that depressed persons experience are a consequence of depression. Beck (1967), however, believes that negative cognitions and thought patterns are the cause of unipolar depression rather than a consequence of depression. He has proposed that individuals prone to depression have negative schema that are activated by stress. Once activated, the individual tends to interpret his or her experience in the worst possible light, using errors of logic (e.g., drawing sweeping conclusions based on one or two events) to do so. This negative interpretation occurs even when more plausible explanations for experiences are available; the person chooses his or her explanation on the basis of its negativity rather than its validity.

From the viewpoint of the individual working with children, what may be most important regarding affective disorders is an awareness of and ability to recognize signs of childhood affective disorders. It should be noted first that it is rare for children, particularly prior to puberty, to experience manic episodes. When a young child exhibits overactive behavior that appears manic, it is probably more appropriately considered a symptom of hyperactivity. (It is also possible for overactive behavior to result from an endocrine dysfunction.) Depressivelike syndromes, on the other hand, have been reported in children 3 years of age and younger. The symptoms of these syndromes vary in part as a function of age; the older a depressed child, the more closely his or her symptoms will parallel those of adults. Consequently, this discussion will focus on the symptoms of younger school-aged children (i.e., approximately ages 6 to 14).

A major distinction between depressed children and adults is that children, in contrast to adults, seldom seek help or complain about feelings of depression. Instead, they may become apathetic regarding school or socially withdrawn, sometimes preferring to remain in their rooms at home rather than playing with friends. They may make vague physical complaints about head or stomach pains, seem overly self-conscious, and cry inexplicably. Older children may see themselves as bad kids—incompetent in school and unworthy of the love of adults or the friendship of other children. Some, but not all, depressed children may simply look sad, particularly in their facial expressions, for extended periods of time with little apparent fluctuation in mood. Overall, a child will usually exhibit only some of the symptoms noted, and the symptom pattern may vary across a period of weeks.

Such symptoms are expressed in what is essentially a passive manner. Though there is far from universal agreement on the issue, certain professionals believe that in some instances children may express depression through aggressive misbehavior. While it is usually difficult to distinguish between genuine misbehavior and misbehavior that is an expression of so-called masked depression, children who are acting out as a symptom of depression often are more responsive to firm (but not overly authoritarian) limit-setting than children who are misbehaving for other reasons.

A technique that is sometimes useful in determining if a child is feeling depressed is to ask the child where he or she stands on a scale of 1 to 10, with 10 being children who are very happy, and 1 being children who are very sad. (This technique presupposes a certain level of cognitive development in the child.) On an informal level, there are several things a teacher can do for a depressed child. With children who appear apathetic and low in self-esteem, it may be useful to set lower standards for praising their accomplishments in school, or to praise them for their efforts in addition to their finished products. It is important, however, to strike a balance between setting criteria that allow an increase in praise and avoiding reinforcement of the child's symptoms. The latter may lead to the child using the symptoms as an excuse to perform at a level significantly below his or her ability level. Children may also respond to messages from the teacher that suggest that the child is an important, valued person. Overall, it is important to make sure that such interactions with the child are honest and nonpatronizing; if it is not possible to do something in this manner, it is probably better not to do it. Psychologists use a variety of objective testing methods to assess the presence, absence, and degree of depression. Objective testing is necessary for accurate diagnosis.

If a teacher feels that a child needs more assistance than the teacher has the training or experience to render, there is a wide range of professional treatments for depression, many with proven efficacy (though the majority of treatment research has focused on adults rather than children). These treatments range from medication to psychotherapy and behavior therapy. Antidepressants are often prescribed in the treatment of unipolar depression, and they tend to be quite effective. Lithium carbonate is usually prescribed for bipolar disorder in adults; it has an effect on both the depressive and manic symptoms, and is probably the treatment of choice for bipolar disorder. The exact mechanism for lithium's action is unknown. In a few instances, lithium may be used to successfully treat adult unipolar depression.

The variety of psychological and behavioral therapies used in the treatment of depression is vast. Techniques such as social skills training, modification of negative cognitions through cognitive restructuring and reality testing, and the teaching of self-control strategies (to name just a few) have been used. Treatment may occur individually or in groups, and many of the therapies have been empirically tested, often with results supporting their value as treatments for depression. Cognitive-behavioral therapies have the greatest support in the scientific literature (e.g., Knell, 1998).

REFERENCES

Abramson, L. Y., Seligman, M. E. P., & Teasdale, J. D. (1978). Learned helplessness in humans: Critique and reformulation. *Journal of Abnormal Psychology, 87,* 49–74.

American Psychiatric Association. (1994). *Diagnostic and statistical manual of mental disorders* (4th ed.). Washington, DC: Author.

Beck, A. T. (1967). *Depression: Clinical, experimental, and theoretical aspects.* New York: Harper & Row.

Freud, S. (1976). Mourning and melancholia. In J. Strachey (Ed. and Trans.), *The complete psychological works.* New York: Norton. (Original work published 1917).

Keller, M., & Baker, L. (1992). The clinical course of panic disorder and depression. *Journal of Clinical Psychiatry, 53,* 5–8.

Knell, S. M. (1998). Cognitive-behavioral play therapy. *Journal of Clinical Child Psychology, 27,* 28–33.

Lewinsohn, P. M. (1974). A behavioral approach to depression. In R. J. Friedman & M. Katz (Eds.), *The psychology of depression:* *Contemporary theory and research.* Washington, DC: Winston-Wiley.

BAHR WEISS
*University of North Carolina
at Chapel Hill*

CHILDHOOD NEUROSIS
CHILDHOOD PSYCHOSIS
DEPRESSION
EMOTIONAL DISORDERS

AFFECTIVE EDUCATION

Affective education promotes emotional development by educating students about attitudes, thoughts, values, feelings, beliefs, and interpersonal relationships (Morse, Ardizzone, Macdonald, & Pasick, 1980). Through it, students are provided experiences in which cognitive, motor, social, and emotional elements are interrelated and balanced (Morse et al., 1980), leading to the enhancement of self-concept (what one is) and self-esteem (how one feels about what one is) and the development of social skills essential to meeting basic needs in a satisfying and socially responsible way (Wood, 1982). Affective education helps youngsters to establish value systems, morals, independence, a sense of responsibility, and self-direction (Morse et al., 1980; Wood, 1982). Although the need for affective education is not limited to students in special education programs, it is especially relevant for them because social skills are essential for success in mainstream placements.

Although most educators agree on the importance of affective education and understand its general purpose, there is less agreement among them on the specific objectives or how best to realize them. In part, this ambiguity derives from the persistent difficulty of defining such terms as self-concept, self-esteem, affect, and attitude. The general lack of systematic programming should not, however, be an indication that affective goals are unimportant (Francescani, 1982). Affective education is commonplace in regular education classrooms and is routinely addressed in teacher education programs (e.g., Woolfolk, 1995). Morse et al. (1980) have argued that affective education represents serious obligation and is an essential component of special education. Essentially, all children deserve the right to more "systematic assistance with their affective growth" (Morse et al., 1980, p. 6).

Nonetheless, affective goals are often subordinated to academic objectives, as the following example (Reinert, 1982) illustrates. Ann, age 10, was known by her teacher to display many different types of inappropriate behavior in the classroom. She talked out loud, pushed and shoved other children, would not share, and cried for no apparent reason. During evaluation, it was discovered that Ann was reading and spelling on a kindergarten level and her arithmetic skills were two years below grade level. In addition, Ann's parents were divorced and she was often absent from school because she had to babysit for her younger sister while her mother worked. She seldom came to school appropriately groomed or attired. Ann was either unwilling or unable to speak to adults or peers in a normal, conversational tone of voice; she had a poor self-concept and relatively few friends. Upon staffing, her Individual Education Plan (IEP) prescribed 60 minutes in a resource room for remedial help in arithmetic and reading skills, but no emphasis on affective problems. Although affective needs should be a part of an IEP, they are seldom systematically delineated.

Systematic instruction in the affective domain is especially important for emotionally handicapped students like Ann. Emotionally handicapped students include those who have not learned essential skills for social and emotional growth, or how to control their behavior in times of stress, how to communicate their feelings and needs in a socially acceptable manner, how to bring interpersonal problems to a satisfying solution, or how to encounter others without conflict (Francescani, 1982). It is difficult to imagine how a student with deficits as pervasive as these can survive in an environment for which he or she is so poorly equipped. Yet it is in the highly socialized classroom world in which affective education must occur, and most proponents recognize the need to integrate affective learning into everyday classroom life.

Integrated affective learning lies at one end of the intrinsic/extrinsic dimension of affective education. Morse et al. (1980) defined this dimension as the extent "to which (affective education) grows naturally out of what is going on in the educational life space versus how much is added as a special function" (p. 16). Ideally, affective lessons should derive naturally from school activities, using materials already in the curriculum in harmony with the philosophy of the program (Morse et al., 1980; Schlindler, 1982). Teachers should capitalize on naturally occurring opportunities spending time motivating the uninvolved student, resolving peer conflicts, encouraging a reluctant student to join in group activity, or trying to enliven a depressed student. A teacher should not rely on an added-on or extrinsic curriculum to accomplish affective goals.

Affective educators stress the need for developing empathetic relationships between teachers and students in order to convey fundamental human relationships where the "sense of relationship dominates authoritarianism" (Morse et al. 1980, p. 15). Teachers and students share responsibilities, goals, and rules for living together (Morse et al., 1980; Reinert, 1982; Sarason, 1971).

However, to expect all teachers to act at all times with the spontaneity, sensitivity, and astuteness that the ideal intrinsic approach requires is unrealistic. This expectation belies the human limitations of teachers and assumes a degree of training rare if not unknown in teacher preparation programs. Approximations to this intrinsic ideal may be found in curricular approaches to affective education and in strategies such as role playing and socio-drama (Wood, 1982) that allow for the exploration of new solutions to familiar problems.

Among the most popular and widely used curricula is DUSO (Developing Understanding of Self and Others). It is designed to be used by teachers or counselors as an add-on to the academic curriculum. Throughout the school year, eight themes (e.g., Developing Self-Concept, Understanding Peers) are explored through listening, modeling, discussion, and role-playing activities. Everyday problems of classroom life are described through pictures, stories, and puppetry, and solutions are discussed, modeled, and role played. The elements of the lessons are carefully prescribed and the materials are attractive and engaging to a primary-aged audience. Although the curriculum is extrinsic, it does provide a structure through which problems may be simulated and the values of alternative solutions weighed.

Only one of many such curricula, DUSO is singled out here for illustration only. Suffice it to say that they are diverse in objectives, activities, and the sophistication of their intended audiences. It is difficult to compare extrinsic programs because the materials themselves provide content and continuity in their individual components (Reinert, 1982). Most seek to enhance self-concept, encourage positive socialization, recognize and understand basic feelings, and model appropriate responses to given situations through practice and role playing. Few have substantial data bases.

Affective education has grown out of the school mental health movement, but has not yet evolved into a well-formulated program intrinsic to the ongoing school process (Morse, 1980). Instead it tends to be relegated to the periphery of the basic curriculum. If affective education is to realize its potential, deliberate efforts must replace the haphazard, casual, and indirect approaches currently in operation.

REFERENCES

Francescani, C. (1982). M A R C: An affective curriculum for emotionally disturbed adolescents. *Teaching Exceptional Children, 14,* 217–222.

Morse, W. C., Ardizzone, J., Macdonald, C., & Pasick, P. (1980). *Affective education for special children and youth.* Reston, VA: Council for Exceptional Children.

Reinert, H. R. (1980). *Children in conflict* (2nd ed.). St. Louis: Mosby.

Reinert, H. R. (1982). The development of affective skills. In T. L. Miller & E. E. Davis (Eds.), *The mildly handicapped student* (pp. 421–451). New York: Grune & Stratton.

Sarason, S. B. (1971). *The culture of schools and the problem of change*. Boston: Allyn & Bacon.

Schlindler, P. J. (1982). Affective growth in the preschool years. *Teaching Exceptional Children, 14,* 226–232.

Wood, F. H. (1982). Affective education and social skills training. *Teaching Exceptional Children, 14,* 212–216.

Woolfolk, A. E. (1995). *Educational Psychology* (6th ed.). Boston: Allyn & Bacon.

Louise H. Werth
Paul T. Sindelar
Florida State University

DEVELOPING UNDERSTANDING OF SELF AND OTHERS
SELF-CONCEPT
SOCIAL SKILLS

AFRICA: EAST AND SOUTHERN, SPECIAL EDUCATION IN

A brief history, statements on current status, and the future prospects of special education in twelve East and Southern African countries are presented here. The countries discussed include Botswana, Ethiopia, Eriteria, Kenya, Lesotho, Malawi, Namibia, Swaziland, Tanzania, Uganda, Zambia, and Zimbabwe. The availability of information on the aforementioned topics and between these countries differs widely. Thus, some countries are discussed in greater detail (Tanzania, Uganda, and Zimbabwe) than others (Eriteria, Malawi, and Swaziland).

Incidence of Handicapping Conditions within This Region

Reliable data on the incidence of childhood disorders within this region are unavailable. Various problems associated with incidence surveys preclude obtaining accurate data. Parents may need to register their disabled children in special centers, and they often are reluctant to admit their children display handicapping conditions (Kisanji, 1997; Whyte & Ingstad, 1995). Also, community attitudes toward the handicapped often are negative (Devlieger, 1995; Jackson & Mupedziswa, 1989). These and other qualities are believed to contribute to grossly underestimated incidence figures for handicapping conditions.

This large region in East and Southern Africa is home to an estimated 59,800,000 children. Population details for children ages 5 to 16 years for the year 1996 are provided below (UNICEF, 1996):

Botswana	700,000
Ethiopia	15,600,000
Eritrea	1,600,000
Kenya	12,100,000
Lesotho	600,000
Malawi	3,200,000
Namibia	700,000
Tanzania	8,700,000
Uganda	10,500,000
Zambia	2,900,000
Zimbabwe	3,200,000

If we accept the World Health Organization's general incidence estimate that 10% of a country's population is likely to be handicapped, almost six million children in this region can be expected to have one or more handicapping conditions. We believe this estimate substantially underestimates the number of handicapped children, given the region's sub-standard medical, health, and early childhood education facilities. Among children with handicaps, less than 1% attend formal school (Tungaraza, 1994; Kann, Mapolelo, & Nleya, 1989).

General History of Educational Services for Handicapped Children

The availability of special education services and other resources for children with physical, sensory, and cognitive disabilities occurred recently. Historically, native African societies integrated learning and other developmental activities within their everyday home and community activities (Kisanji, 1997). Home- and community-based activities provide various advantages: a favorable ratio between the young and elders, accommodations to match the child's developmental levels, and utilization of the child's natural milieu within which to promote development and transfer of training. The extent to which homes and communities provide appropriate adaptations to accommodate children with disabilities is unknown. The beneficial effects that professional services can have on children with disabilities are well-established.

The introduction and evolution of professional services for these children in East and Southern Africa closely follows a pattern found in other developing areas: first, national or regional institutions, often residential in nature and initiated by religious, humanitarian, and philanthropic agencies, are established. Professional services for middle-class children then develop in metropolitan centers. The widespread provision of services to children with disabilities in public schools occurs only after general education services, at least through the elementary level, are well-developed and nationally available. Children with handicapping conditions who reside in rural areas are least likely to receive professional services. Stronger special education services generally are found in countries with stronger and well-established regular education programs (Saigh & Oakland, 1989).

The majority of countries in this region have inadequate basic education programs (UNICEF, 1991, 1994), lack formal special education policies, and experience school dropout rates in the range of 15% to 60% involving disadvantaged children, which includes those with disabilities (Kann, Mapolelo, & Nleya, 1989; Stubbs, 1997; UNICEF, 1994).

The Role of Missionaries

Christian missionaries, often from Western Europe, initiated and provided almost all formal education within African communities during the colonial period. The development of special education services in this region is closely associated with their work. Trends in the development of special education facilities within individual countries generally followed a consistent pattern: Services were provided first for those with visual handicaps, and then for those with auditory, physical, and mental handicaps. This trend probably reflected the missionaries' beliefs as to the resources (like teaching expertise and materials) needed to serve each of these groups, as well as the family's willingness to admit one or more members have a disability. Because of their normal hearing ability, persons with visual impairments may have been thought to respond more favorably to the use of conventional instructional methods.

In Botswana, German missionaries opened special schools for the visually handicapped at Linchwe (in Mochudi) and the hearing impaired at Ramotswa (in Ramotswa) in the 1950s. A German couple opened residential centers named Rankoromane based on the Waldorf School model to educate children with mental handicaps in a number of towns in the late 1960s (Ingstad, 1995).

In Ethiopia, the Christofeblinden Mission opened a school for the blind and a training program for teachers of the visually handicapped in the early 1950s. Finnish missionaries were involved in developing Ethiopia's special education programs, and they opened a school for the deaf at Keren in the 1950s. The Church of Christ established the Mekanissa School for the Deaf in 1964. The Baptist Mission created the Alpha School for the Deaf in Addis Ababa in 1967. The Ethiopian Evangelical Mekaneyesus Church started the Hossana School for the Deaf in 1981.

In Eriteria, French Catholic, Swedish Lutheran and Italian Catholic churches provided school education to the natives since 1890 (Miran, 1998). The role of these organizations in founding schools for persons with disabilities could not be established. Eriteria, now an independent nation, was once a province of Ethiopia.

The first school in Kenya for the visually impaired, the Thika School, was opened by the Salvation Army in 1946 (Kristensen, 1987). Kenya's first full-time program to prepare teachers of students with visual handicaps and a school for deaf-blind children were founded by the Christofeblinden Mission in the 1980s.

In Malawi, education for the blind was started during the early 1940s when two primary residential special schools were established by missionaries at Kasungu and Lulwe. The Catholic Order of the Immaculate Conception (of the Netherlands) developed a program in 1964 that integrated students with and without visual impairments into regular classrooms within ordinary schools; resource rooms provided supportive services to the visually impaired. Fourteen resource rooms serving about 100 blind students were in operation by 1983 (Ross, 1988). The program at Montfort College, organized by the Catholic teaching brothers of the Order of the Immaculate Conception, prepared teachers for students with auditory and visual impairments for Malawi and some neighboring countries (namely, Lesotho, Swaziland, Tanzania, Zimbabwe, and Zambia) in the 1970s.

Tanzania established its first special education facility in 1950 when the Anglican Church opened a school for the blind, the Buigiri School. Two additional schools for the blind followed this school, one opened by the Swedish Free Mission, the Furaha, in 1962, and another by the Lutheran Church, the Irente School, in Lushoto in 1963. The first Tanzanian school for the hearing impaired, the Tabora Deaf-Mute Institute, was opened by the Roman Catholic Church in 1963. The Salvation Army opened the first school in Tanzania for the physically handicapped in 1967.

In Zambia, missionaries again pioneered special education services in the region (Csapo, 1987a). The Dutch Reformed Church established the first school for the deaf (Sichula, 1990) and one for the blind (Csapo, 1987a) at Magwero Mission in 1955. The Christian Mission of Zambia opened another school for the blind at Mambiling soon after. Other special schools were opened by missionaries and continue to exist today.

In Zimbabwe, the Dutch Reformed Church opened the Margaret Hugo School for The Blind, at Masvingo in 1927 (Peresuh, Adenigba, & Ogonda, 1997). Two schools for the hearing impaired opened in 1947, one in Loreto and another in Pamushana, founded by the Catholic Dominican Sisters and the Dutch Reformed Church respectively (Chimedza, 1994).

Information on missionary work and the opening of special education facilities in Lesotho, Namibia, Swaziland, and Uganda could not be located. However, the Dutch Reformed Church appears to have been involved in Namibia, and the Roman Catholic Church and Church of Uganda may have been involved in Uganda. Margaret Brown of the Church Missionary Society initiated Uganda's in-service teacher education for children with hearing impairment in 1962. Although Islam has a substantial following in some East African countries (namely, Tanzania, Uganda, Kenya, and Ethiopia), its role in establishing special education facilities in these countries could not be ascertained.

The Role of International Nongovernmental Organizations and Local Organizations

International nongovernmental organizations and local organizations advocating on behalf of students with disabilities also have had strong roles in developing and providing special education services. Their importance exceeds that of the colonial governments. The Danish International Development Agency (DANIDA), UNESCO Sub-Regional Project for Special Education in Eastern and Southern Africa, Swedish International Development Agency (SIDA), Royal Commonwealth Society for the Blind (now called the Sight Savers), International League for Persons with Mental Handicaps, and the British Red Cross are among the international agencies that have played significant roles in establishing special education programs in East and Southern Africa. DANIDA has been actively involved in promoting special education advising in Kenya, Uganda, and Zimbabwe for at least the past decade. SIDA has been involved in developing special education programs in all twelve Eastern and Southern African countries which comprise the focus of this paper. It helped establish Braille printing presses in Tanzania in 1971 (Tungaraza, 1994) and in Zimbabwe in 1994. In the early 1960s the Royal Commonwealth Society for the Blind started a rehabilitation center at Salama (in Uganda) for adults with visual impairments (Onen & Njuki, 1998).

Information on the involvement of local organizations in founding special education facilities in the East and Southern African countries is quite sparse. The Botswana Red Cross, with support from the Norwegian Red Cross, established a vocational training center for persons with physical disabilities in 1981. The Botswana Council for the Disabled has been unable to implement programs that enable children with disabilities to attend school (Ingstad, 1995). In Ethiopia, the Haile Selassie One Foundation established two special schools for blind students. They became government schools in the 1980s.

In Kenya, local voluntary organizations established two special schools for the mentally handicapped at St. Nicholas and Aga Khan in the late 1950s. These schools amalgamated in 1968 to form the Jacaranda School (Ross, 1988). The Kenya Society for the Mentally Handicapped and The Parents and Friends of Handicapped Children were formed by parents of children with disabilities to promote the education of persons with disabilities, improve the preparation for teachers of children with disabilities, and consolidate schools. The Tanzania Society for the Deaf established the first school for the hearing impaired at Buguruni in 1974. In 1955, the first school for children with visual impairment and blindness was started at Madera in Eastern Uganda by the joint effort of the then-local education committee (Teso education committee), the Ministry of Education, and Uganda Foundation for the Blind. The Uganda government later asked the Catholic Church to administer the school.

With the assistance of the Uganda Society for the Deaf, Sherali Bendali Jafer, Peter Ronald, and Mr. Semmpebwa were closely involved in developing awareness throughout Uganda of the need to educate children with hearing impairment (Onen & Njuki, 1998). As a result of their efforts, an integration unit for children with hearing impairment was started at Mengo Primary School. Subsequently, the Uganda School for the Deaf was started on Namirembe Hill in 1968. The following year, Ngora School for the Deaf was established.

Ugandan educational services for children with physical disabilities and mental handicaps both began in 1968, and both were largely the results of efforts of local self-help organizations. For instance, the Uganda Spastic Society was formed in 1968. Its membership consisted mainly of parents of children with spastic conditions and polio, and medical professionals. The society played a key role in the establishment of a school for the physically handicapped at Mengo (Onen & Njuki, 1998). Services for children with mental disabilities were available through the Uganda Association for Mental Health (UAMH). This association, established in 1968 by the Ministry of Health, had a short life due to the political turmoil in the country at the time and in subsequent years. In 1983, the Uganda Association for the Mentally Handicapped was founded, and it has been instrumental in the founding of many resource units for children with mental handicaps.

In Zimbabwe, the Jairos Jiri Association founded the Narran Center School for the Deaf and the Blind in Gweru in 1968, a school for the visually impaired at Kadoma in 1981, and a number of other schools for children with various physical, mental, and multiple handicaps at Bulawayo, Gweru, and Harare in the 1970s (Farquar, 1987). Zimbabwe's Council for the Blind has been involved in providing structural facilities and equipment to school-based integration units for children with visual disabilities since about 1980. Its Zimcare Trust has been actively involved in providing education for Zimbabwean children with mental handicaps since the 1980s.

Zambia's Council for the Handicapped has conferred with teachers and the Zambian government to promote effective ways of teaching children with disabilities since the 1970s. However, its role in the establishment of special education facilities in that country is unclear.

Information on the involvement of international nongovernmental agencies and local organizations advocating for those with disabilities and the establishment of special education facilities in Eriteria, Malawi, Namibia, and Swaziland could not be located.

The Role of Postcolonial Governments

Support for the development of special education by the postcolonial governments in each of the twelve East and Southern African countries differs widely. Support is strongest when elementary and secondary education is widely available and a commitment to the principle of universal education is widely held. Countries recently ravaged by civil war (Uganda, Eriteria, Ethiopia) currently are attempting to re-establish basic elementary and secondary education programs. Their programs in special education are in initial stages of development and support. In contrast, countries that have enjoyed relative political stability (Kenya, Tanzania, Zimbabwe) tend to have stronger regular education programs, as well as a longer history and stronger support for special education programs.

Although Botswana's National Development Plans (1973–1978; 1991–1997) identify the needs of disabled persons as a national priority (Ingstad, 1995), the government historically has viewed educational support to children with disabilities as a family responsibility rather than a state obligation (Ingstad, 1995; Kann et al., 1989). Children with disabilities are conspicuous in their absence from Botswana schools (Kann et al, 1989). Nonetheless, a special education unit was established within the Botswana Ministry of Education in 1984 with the support of SIDA. The University of Botswana has complemented government efforts by offering a two-year diploma course for specialist teachers for children with mental, visual, hearing, and learning handicaps, and is expected to launch a bachelor's degree in special education in August, 1998 (Abosi, C., pers. comm., February 2, 1998).

The Kenya government, through the Kenya Institute of Education, launched special needs teacher education programs at Jacaranda and Highridge Teachers Colleges in 1966–67 (Peresuh et al., 1997). The Kenya Institute of Special Education (KISE), founded by the Kenyan government with the assistance of DANIDA, has assumed responsibility for these programs. More than one thousand teachers have graduated from the KISE teacher education programs since 1987. KISE also is responsible for the educational placement of children with disabilities, community education, and teacher in-service education programs on disabilities.

Lesotho's government became involved in special education in 1987 when its Ministry of Education, with the financial support from the United States Agency for International Development (USAID), commissioned a comprehensive study of its special education programs and accompanying guidelines for its development (Csapo

1987b). The report recommended the infusion of special needs components to both pre- and in-service teacher preparation programs, adoption of an integration (resource room) model for educating children with special needs, and full community involvement in establishing and supporting special education facilities. The Lesotho Ministry of Education, Lesotho National Federation of Disabled People, Ministry of Social Welfare and Health, and Save the Children Fund (UK) created ten integration units. A special education unit was established in the Lesotho Ministry of Education in 1991 to coordinate the opening of integration units. The Lesotho National Teacher Training College assumed responsibility for introducing special education components in its pre-service programs in 1996, and the abovementioned special education unit within the Ministry of Education assumed responsibility for in-service education programs for teachers (Pholoho, Mariga, Phachaka, & Stubbs, 1995).

Namibia became politically independent in 1990 after a legacy of colonial rule under apartheid from South Africa, which left most of its Blacks with little or no education. Thus, the history of educating children with disabilities in Namibia is recent and short. According to Bruhns et al. (1995), Namibia established its first school for children with disabilities, the Dagbreek Special School, in 1970 as a racially segregated facility for White children. The school opened its doors to disabled students of other races after Namibia become independent. The Eluwa School for blind and deaf students was established at Ongwediva in 1973 with 20 deaf and 20 blind students. By 1995 the school enrolled 172 deaf, 70 blind, and eight physically disabled students. The Moreson School for children with severe learning difficulties was established by the Association of the Handicapped in 1976 and became a government school in 1990. It had 60 students along with seven teachers in 1995.

The Tanzania government, with the help of the Royal Commonwealth Society for the Blind, established the country's first integrated education program for children with visual handicaps, Uhuru Co-education School, in 1966, followed by a similar program for children with mental handicaps in 1982 (Tungaraza, 1994). The government also established a diploma-level teacher education program in 1976 and one for teachers of pupils with mental handicaps in 1983 at the Tabora Teacher Training College. In addition, the Mpwapwa Teacher Training College prepares teachers to work with students with visual handicaps. The number of special needs teachers who have graduated from the two Tanzania colleges could not be established.

Uganda's government involvement in special education came earlier than others in the region because of the lobbying efforts of Sr. Andrew Cohen, then-Governor of Uganda, to educate a blind relative (Atim, 1995). Government support to educate the blind was established through an act of Parliament in 1952. The first trial to integrate children with visual impairment was launched in 1962 at Wanyange Girls School in Eastern Uganda. In July 1973, a department of special education was established at the Uganda Ministry of Education headquarters in Kampala. This department was created to coordinate special education services in the Ministry and to work with other governmental and nongovernmental organizations providing services for persons with disabilities. The head start Uganda enjoyed in developing its special education programs was severely thwarted during two decades of dictatorships and civil war. Special education programs in Uganda began to rebuild after 1991.

The Ugandan government, with the help of DANIDA, founded the Uganda National Institute of Special Education (UNISE) in 1991 and save it the responsibility for coordinating the country's special education programs and teacher education programs at certificate, diploma, and degree levels. So far, about 255 teachers have received specialist training and attended awareness seminars, which are offered to ordinary primary school teachers in the districts throughout the country. The Special Education/Educational Assessment and Resource Services of Uganda (EARS-U) was formed in 1992. EARS-U, a division within the Uganda Ministry of Education, is responsible for evaluating programs for children with hearing, speech, learning, visual, mental, and physical impairments. EARS-U also is responsible for coordinating educational placements of children with disabilities, counseling services to their parents, community education, and prevention programs.

The Zimbabwe government, with the assistance of SIDA, established a Department of Special Education within the Ministry of Education in 1982, with its primary responsibility being educational placement of children with disabilities, pre-service and in-service training of teachers on special educational needs, and community education programs on disabilities. A teacher education program for teachers of children with visual, mental, hearing, and speech and language impairments was established by the government at the United College of Education in Bulawayo in 1983. About 300 special needs teachers graduated from the United College of Education since the establishment of its special education teacher education program. A two-year, post-diploma bachelor's degree in special education was launched at the University of Zimbabwe in 1993 and has graduated about 75 teachers of special needs children. The Zimbabwe Ministry of Education also has issued a number of documents to guide special education programs in the schools (Mpofu & Nyanungo, in press).

Government involvement in special needs programs in Zambia, Ethiopia, Eriteria, Malawi, and Swaziland could not be ascertained. However, respondents to a recent survey of special needs experts in these countries suggested that special education facilities in these countries are quite limited (Mpofu, Zindi, Oakland, & Peresuh, 1997).

Current Status of Special Education in East and Southern Africa

Special education services in East and Southern Africa generally follow a functional integration (resource room) model in which children with disabilities attend class part-time to full-time with their non-disabled peers and receive support of a full-time specialist teacher (Charema & Peresuh, 1997). Specialist teachers maintain the resource room, provide intensive individualized instruction to children with disabilities, and work closely with mainstream teachers in planning and effecting integration strategies for children with disabilities. A functional integration model generally is preferred for children with mild to moderate sensory, physical, and cognitive handicaps. Children with more severe handicaps generally attend special schools and rehabilitation centers, typically those residential in nature, which provide more specialized resources. With few exceptions, most integration units for the visually handicapped and hearing impaired are residential, whereas those for children with moderate to mild physical and cognitive handicaps are nonresidential.

Compared to current needs and potential demand, special education facilities in the twelve East and Southern countries of this survey are severely limited. Botswana has approximately 20 special schools and resource units for children with visual, auditory, mental, and physical handicaps (Abosi, C. O., pers. comm., February 2, 1998). Current enrollment figures by handicapping condition were unavailable. However, previous enrollment was vision (35 students), hearing (88), mental (176), and physical (18) (Kann et al., 1989). There are no facilities in the country for children with severe disabilities.

Lesotho has twelve special schools (Stubbs, 1997). Enrollment figures by handicapping condition were unavailable. Lesotho's Ministry of Education, with support from international nongovernmental organizations and United Nations agencies, recently opened integration units for children with a variety of handicaps in eight of the country's ten districts.

Namibia's school for children with visual impairments has 71 students and its school for the hearing impaired has 185 students (Bruhns et al., 1995). Twenty-four specialist teachers work in these schools. Two schools and 15 specialist teachers serve 125 children with severe learning disabilities. Two additional schools staffed by 67 teachers provide instruction to 733 children with mild learning difficulties. Twelve schools and 16 teachers offer remedial education to 385 children with specific learning disabilities. Namibia also has 28 integration units attended by 507 children with moderate to mild disabilities and taught by 40 teachers.

In Tanzania, services for students with visual impairments are provided in twelve special schools and 23 integrated (18 primary, 5 secondary) schools that offer education to 979 children with visual disabilities (Possi & Mkaali, 1995; Tungaraza, 1994). Sixty-four specialist teachers and 157 regular education teachers provide education to children with visual handicaps. Services for children with auditory impairments are provided through 14 special schools and three integrated primary (one residential and two nonresidential) schools to approximately 980 pupils and staffed by 100 specialist and 26 regular class teachers. In addition, 6 schools serve 305 deaf-blind students. About 930 children with physical disabilities attend 61 specialist and integration units staffed by 185 specialist and regular class teachers. The vast majority of children with physical disabilities either attend schools in their communities or do not attend school at all. Tanzania also has four residential special schools for children with moderate mental handicaps and 15 nonresidential integrated units that serve 980 children with moderate to mild mental handicaps. Sixty-seven specialist and 128 regular class teachers teach these children. Twelve children with autism and 14 with cerebral palsy attend four units taught by 6 specialist teachers. Thousands of children with severe mental handicaps do not receive any schooling. In contrast, more than 90% of Tanzanian children with epileptic conditions attend ordinary schools (Whyte, 1995).

Uganda has at least 6 special schools and one integration unit which serve about 500 children with visual impairments, two special schools for 150 children with hearing impairments, and one special school for 124 students with physical handicaps (Ross, 1988). An estimated 32,134 children with mild to moderate disabilities are attending ordinary schools (Onei & Njuki, 1998). The Ugandan government's goal was to have the country's estimated 325,000 children with disabilities attend school in 1997 (Kristensen, 1997; Uganda Ministry of Education, 1992). However, the country lacked the resources for meeting this highly ambitious target then, and it still does today (Mpofu et al., 1997).

Zimbabwe's twenty special schools provide educational and rehabilitation services to 5,000 children with visual, hearing, physical, and mental disabilities. The country also has 162 integrated resource units: 69 for those with hearing disabilities, 46 with mental disabilities, and 47 with visual disabilities. A total of 1,315 children with disabilities are served by the integrated resource units: 552 with hearing impairments, 409 with mental impairments, and 354 with visual impairments. Additionally, about 4,300 children with moderate to mild generalized learning difficulties attend 270 part-time special classes in regular education settings. At least 50,000 children with learning difficulties receive part-time remedial education in classes or clinics in general education schools.

The current status of special education programs in Swaziland, Eriteria, Kenya, and Zambia is unknown. However, information from respondents to a survey on school psychology practices in these countries (Mpofu et al., 1997) suggests special education programs may be better established in Kenya than in other East and Southern African countries. Such programs generally are limited to urban areas in Zambia, and may not exist to any significant degree in Swaziland and Eriteria.

Although the need for more special education facilities in all of the East and Southern African countries is quite apparent, a paradox exists in that attendance is below capacity in many existing special education schools and units in some countries, including Tanzania and Lesotho (Kisanji, 1995; Stubbs, 1997). This under-utilization exists because the facilities are not well-known to parents of children with disabilities and parents in some rural communities are suspicious of their intended purposes. In addition, government departments and international aid agencies often established special education schools and units in certain communities in response to requests by local politicians or parochial interest groups, but without adequate consultation with traditional and other community leaders. Thus, resistance to utilizing these facilities often occurs regardless of their need.

Some countries in this region have mounted comprehensive community outreach programs aimed at educating citizens on the nature of disabilities, their prevention, and appropriate educational interventions. In addition, teachers have walked from village to village to locate children with disabilities to attend school (Kisanji, 1995). The teachers' door-to-door, village-to-village approach can effectively reach families and significant community leaders, and it often yielded larger enrollments of children with disabilities in areas that seem to have few if any such children.

Future Prospects of Special Education in East and Southern Africa

Nearly all countries in East and Southern Africa provide some forms of special education programs. The work of Christian missionaries and nongovernmental agencies often resulted in the establishment of special education programs. The continued involvement of missionaries, although desired, is unlikely to match prior levels of involvement. Nongovernmental agencies increasingly are recognized by international agencies (like the United Nations and the World Bank) as effective implementers of needed social programs. Although their involvement is likely to continue for some years, their resources also are limited in time. Thus, special education programs in this large and important region must depend more heavily, if not exclusively, on local and regional resolve and resources.

A government's involvement in special education programs and teacher preparation programs (through policies enacted and funded by its legislature and implemented by its ministries of education) provides demonstrable evidence that they support special education as an essential component of its national education program. Although the degree to which federal governments are involved in special education programs differs among the twelve countries within this region, all are involved to some degree. However, beneficial policies often are enacted and either not funded or not implemented by ministries of education. For example, the governments of Uganda and Botswana both established policy underscoring the importance of school attendance among children with disabilities as a national priority. However, this policy remains to be implemented.

The adoption of the principle of universal primary education by these governments implicitly recognizes children with disabilities as having the right to education. This, and other positive trends in educational thinking, eventually can be expected to translate into more favorable policies and practices governing special education programs. Moreover, most governments continue to support the further development of their elementary and secondary regular education programs—conditions prerequisite to the strong support of special education programs. Thus, prospects for the continued growth and availability of special education programs in these countries are somewhat encouraging.

However, one should not underestimate impediments to the further development of sustainable special education programs in East and Southern Africa. These impediments include inadequate personnel and financial resources for the provision of basic and regular education and inadequate leadership from advocacy groups.

Given other pressing responsibilities, federal governments in this region are unlikely to prioritize special education programs without some form of external support. Uncertainty exists as to the willingness and commitment of some governments to fund special education programs at current or higher levels than that currently provided by international development agencies (like DANIDA and SIDA).

The sustainability of donor-supported special education programs in East and Southern Africa will depend on the extent to which donor agencies build into their aid packages policies and practices that cultivate a cadre of local personnel willing to lobby for future programs, to implement genuine partnerships with federal and regional government to establish and maintain special education programs, to employ phased donor-funding withdrawal, and to help developing vibrant self-advocacy organizations at the local and national levels. For example, the Swedish Federation for the Blind has financed an advisory project in Eastern Africa aimed at improving the organization and self-advocacy of persons with disabilities (Ross, 1988).

Greater involvement of parents and community members in founding special education schools and integration units would strengthen a sense of ownership for special ed-

ucation facilities in communities, leading to greater attendance and school retention. In addition, the importance of community education programs on disabilities to the future of special education programs in East and Southern Africa cannot be over-emphasized. Most parents of children with disabilities are not involved with any special interest groups or agencies providing special education services (Kisanji, 1995; Ross, 1988).

The significantly limited material and manpower resources within most of these countries constrain the establishment and growth of special education programs (Tungaraza, 1994; Ross, 1988). Most countries are grappling with the provision of basic education and health facilities. The countries have very few personnel specifically prepared to work with children with disabilities in either special or mainstream school settings. The future of special education programs in the region could be considerably enhanced if countries pooled resources to promote professional preparation and research on effective methods to promote basic education of students in special education.

REFERENCES

Atim, S. (1995). *Special education in Uganda.* Paper presented at the South-South-North Workshop. Kampala, Uganda.

Bruhns, B., Murray, A., Kanguchi, T., & Nuukuawo, A. (1995). *Disability and rehabilitation in Namibia: A national survey.* Windhoek: The Namibian Economic Policy Research Unit.

Farquhar, J. (1987). *Jairos Jiri–the man and his works.* Gweru: Mambo.

Charema, J., & Peresuh, M. (1997). Support services for special needs educational needs: Proposed models for countries south of the Sahara. *African Journal of Special Needs Education, 1,* 76–83.

Chimedza, R. (1994). Bilingualism in the education of the hearing impaired in Zimbabwe: Is this the answer? *Zimbabwe Bulletin of Teacher Education, 4,* 1–11.

Csapo, M. (1987a). *Perspectives in education and special education in southern Africa.* Vancouver: Center for Human Development and Research.

Csapo, M. (1987b). *Basic, practical, cost-effective education for children with disabilities in Lesotho.* Vancouver: University of British Columbia.

Devlieger, P. (1995). Why disabled? The cultural understanding of physical disability in an African society. In B. Ingstad & S. R. Whyte (Eds.), *Disability and culture* (pp. 94–106). Berkeley: University of California Press.

Ingstad, B. (1995). Public discourses on rehabilitation: From Norway to Botswana. In B. Ingstad & S. R. Whyte (Eds.), *Disability and culture* (pp. 174–195). Berkeley: University of California Press.

Jackson, H., & Mupedziswa, R. (1989). Disability and rehabilitation: Beliefs and attitudes among rural disabled people in a community based rehabilitation scheme in Zimbabwe. *Journal of Social Development in Africa, 1,* 21–30.

Kann, U., Mapolelo, D., & Nleya, P. (1989). *The missing children:*

Achieving basic education in Botswana. Gaborone: NIR, University of Botswana.

Kisanji, J. (1997). The relevance of indigenous customary education principles in the education of special needs education policy. *African Journal of Special Needs Education, 1,* 59–74.

Kisanji, J. (1995). Interface between culture and disability in the Tanzania context: Part 1. *International Journal of Disability, Development and Education, 42,* 93–108.

Kristensen, K. (1997). School for all: A challenge to special needs education in Uganda–A brief country report. *African Journal of Special Needs Education, 2,* 25–28.

Miran, J. (1998). *Missionaries, education and the state in the Italian colony of Eriteria 1980–1936.* Paper presented at the Third Annual Midwest Graduate Student Conference in African Studies. University of Wisconsin-Madison, February 27–March 1.

Mpofu, E., & Nyanungo, K. R. (in press). Educational and psychological testing in Zimbabwean schools: Past, present and future. *European Journal of Psychological Assessment.*

Mpofu, E., Zindi, F., Oakland, T., & Peresuh, M. (1997). School psychological practices in East and Southern Africa. *Journal of Special Education, 31,* 387–402.

Murray, J. L., & Lopez, A. D. (1996). *Global health statistics: A compendium of incidence, prevalence and mortality estimates for over 200 conditions.* Cambridge: Harvard University Press.

Onen, N., & Njuki, E. P. (1998). *Special education in Uganda.* Unpublished manuscript.

Peresuh, M., Adenigba, S. A., & Ogonda, G. (1997). Perspectives on special needs education in Nigeria, Kenya, and Zimbabwe. *African Journal of Special Needs Education, 2,* 9–15.

Pholoho, K., Mariga, L., Phachaka, L., & Stubbs, S. (1995). Schools for all: National planning in Lesotho. In B. O'Tootle & R. McConkey (Eds.), *Innovations in developing countries for people with disabilities.* Lancashire, England: Lisieux Hall Publications.

Possi, M. K., & Mkaali, C. B. (1995). *A brief report on special education services in Tanzania.* Paper presented at the South-South-North Workshop. Kampala, Uganda.

Ross, D. H. (1988). *Educating handicapped young people in Eastern and Southern Africa.* Paris: UNESCO.

Saigh, P. A., & Oakland, T. (Eds.). (1989). *International perspectives on school psychology.* Hillsdale, NJ: Erlbaum.

Sichula, B. (1990). *East African sign language report.* Helsinki, Finland: Finnish Association of the Deaf.

Stubbs, S. (1997). Lesotho integrated education programme. *African Journal of Special Needs Education, 1,* 84–87.

Tungaraza, F. D. (1994). The development and history of special education in Tanzania. *International Journal of Disability, Development, and Education, 41,* 213–222.

Uganda Ministry of Education. (1992). *Government white paper on the education policy review commission report.* Kampala, Uganda: Author.

UNICEF. (1996). *The state of the world's children: 1996.* Oxford: Oxford University Press.

UNICEF. (1994). *The state of the world's children: 1994.* Oxford: Oxford University Press.

UNICEF. (1991). *Children and women in Zimbabwe: A situation analysis update, July 1985– July 1990.* Republic of Zimbabwe: Author.

Whyte, S. R. (1995). Constructing epilepsy: Images and contexts in East Africa. In B. Ingstad & S. R. Whyte (Eds.), *Disability and culture* (pp. 226–245). Berkeley: University of California Press.

Whyte, S., & Ingstad, B. (1995). Disability and culture: An overview. In S. Whyte & B. Ingstad (Eds.), *Disability and culture* (pp. 3–32). Berkeley: University of California Press.

ELIAS MPOFU
University of Zimbabwe

THOMAS OAKLAND
University of Florida

ROBERT CHIMEDZA
University of Zimbabwe

AFRICA, SPECIAL EDUCATION IN

Special education is relatively new in most African countries. The need for a major commitment to special education by African countries to provide handicapped learners with a variety of programs and services has been recognized for some time now (Anderson, 1983; Joy, 1979; Shown, 1980; UNESCO, 1979, 1986), though progress toward realization has been slow and halting. The UNESCO definition of special education is one that generally adheres to western European and American expectations. Thus the Nigerian National Policy on Education (1981) has defined special education as "education of children and adults who have learning difficulties as a result of not coping with the normal school organization and methods" (Nigerian Year Book, 1984). In Nigeria's Plateau State (Nigeria), special education is defined as including "the course and content of education, including specially defined classroom, material, and equipment designed to meet the unique needs of a handicapped child" (Shown, 1986).

Despite such broad perspectives, special education in Africa is more likely to be concerned with children who are physically and sensorially handicapped rather than suffering from mild cognitive deficits. Children with more severe cognitive deficits are likely to be cared for in other contexts than those of formal special education. Expressing this fact, Shown observes: "To acquire education in the modern sense one must possess and make full use of all his senses. This is beside being fully mobile" (Shown, in press). Sambo (1981) has pointed out "when one loses two or more of these senses, then the acquisition of education in the normal sense becomes a problem entirely different from those problems normally encountered in the acquisition of education. For such a person, there is a need for a viable alternative for educating him."

Anderson (1973) observed that the majority of African teachers were not familiar with the special techniques and methods required to assist handicapped students to become educationally competent. Furthermore, as Shown (1986) has pointed out, a lack of clear educational objectives has hampered the delivery of educational services to handicapped learners.

Because most African nations have faced major fiscal difficulties for many years, improvements in special education have been difficult to achieve. Nations like Nigeria have, however, made serious efforts at both federal and both federal and local levels to teach the elements of special education in teacher training institutions (Nigeria Federal Ministry, 1977). Nigeria has established training programs at the universities of Jos and Ibadan. These universities provide training and research on scientific education of the handicapped at undergraduate and graduate levels.

In most places in Africa, there are not likely to be clearly defined admission policies for the handicapped or age limits for education of the handicapped as it now exists in Africa. It is not uncommon, therefore, to find a handicapped adult in a special education class with much younger students. Furthermore, the personnel providing special education services are likely to come from the middle or lower ranks of school staffs rather than the higher. The burden of education for handicapped students is thus frequently carried by less well-trained aides and members of the local community, rather than by highly skilled teachers.

Special education teachers working in regular school settings have been reported to be facing emotional and psychological problems (Joy, 1972). They may face neglect and even hostility on the part of other teachers who resent having handicapped students and special education teachers in regular schools. Also, nonspecialist teachers are often resentful of the fact that special education teachers receive extra pay.

Many of the special education services provided in Africa on a noninstitutional basis must be on an itinerant basis because of the scarcity of educational facilities able to serve handicapped students. A dearth of itinerant teachers has limited the extent and effectiveness of such education. Recent efforts have been made in certain African countries to mainstream handicapped students. Thus the Federal Ministry of Information, Lagos, Nigeria (1977) mandates that handicapped school children, where possible, should be mainstreamed along with their nonhandicapped peers. Some African educators have expressed disagreement with this policy (Shown, 1980). There is concern about the dangers that the physical hazards of African terrain may pose for mainstreamed handicapped students who are not carefully supervised, e.g., most parts of Nigeria have dangerous structures and hazards such as rocks, forests, and rivers. Also, the application of mainstreaming policies in Africa places an inordinate burden on most handicapped students unless they are able to use the same materials as their nonhandicapped peers or can be assisted to achieve comparable levels of attainment; this is difficult to achieve in light of the current dearth of trained professionals and the lack of proper facilities and materials. As UNESCO has pointed out (1979), mere physical placement in a mainstreamed school environment is not an answer to providing services to handicapped African children. Provisions at African colleges for handicapped students are essentially nonexistent. There are no ramps, suitable steps elevators, or toilet facilities with special accommodations.

Despite efforts to improve the education of the handicapped, the outlook of Africans respecting the needs of handicapped students and adults is not such as to raise hopes for serious concern regarding their transition into productive roles in society. As Shown has observed regarding the largest nation in Africa, "Nigerians are immensely practical people cauling something or someone only if it is seen to be economically useful. With this in mind, the outlook for the handicapped would seem to be bleak" (Shown, in press).

REFERENCES

Anderson, E. (1983). *The disabled school child. A study in integration.* Open University Set Book, Jos, Nigeria.

Federal Government of Nigeria. (1984). *Nigerian year book:* Lagos, Nigeria: Author.

Joy, D. C. (1979, August 9). Experiment with blind children. *New Nigerian.*

Nigeria Federal Ministry of Information. (1977). *The republic of Nigeria national policy on education,* Lagos, Nigeria: Author.

Sambo, E. W. (1981, April). *What is special education?* Paper presented at the workshop on the integration of elements of special education into teachers education curriculum in plateau state, University of Jos, Jos, Nigeria.

Shown, D. G. (1980). *A study of effectiveness of mainstreaming of visually handicapped children in Plateau State of Nigeria with a view toward determining quality education for these children.* Jos, Nigeria: University of Jos.

Shown, D. G. (1986, April). *Integrating handicapped children in Plateau State.* Paper presented at the workshop on the integration of elements of special education into teachers education curriculum in plateau state, University of Jos, Jos, Nigeria.

UNESCO. (1979, October 15–20). Expert meetings of special education, UNESCO headquarters, Paris. *Final Report.*

UNESCO. (1981, July 20–31). *Sub-regional seminar on planning for special education.* Nairobi, Kenya.

UNESCO. (1986, April). *Expert meeting on special education.* Plateau State, Nigeria: University of Jos.

DAKUM SHOWN
University of Jos, Nigeria

NIGERIA, SPECIAL EDUCATION IN

AGE-APPROPRIATE CURRICULUM

An age-appropriate curriculum is a special-education curriculum that consists of activities that are matched to both the students' chronological ages and their developmental or skill levels. This match has been difficult to achieve, especially for older trainable and severely handicapped students who continue to function on preschool levels. The older students with severe handicaps often need continued training in fine motor, cognitive, and language skills, but also need to acquire skills that can be used immediately and will transfer to later community and vocational placements (Drew, Logan, & Hardman, 1984).

Public law 94-142 has mandated an appropriate education for all handicapped students, but wide differences remain when defining this term. The justification for using an age-appropriate education lies in the principle of normalization, which Nirje (1979) has defined as follows: "Making available to all mentally retarded people patterns of life and conditions of everyday living which are as close as possible to the regular circumstances of society" (p. 73). Although it may appear unrealistic to teach age-appropriate behaviors to students with severe developmental delays, Larsen and Jackson (1981) argue that this is the mission of special education: "No, we will not be completely successful (but) . . . our goals for students will stress skills relevant to the general culture, rather than skills that have a proven value only in special-education classrooms" (p. 1).

Our current knowledge of developmental milestones, task analysis procedures, and behavior modification principles can be used in adopting this approach if we also examine the "age-appropriateness" of the materials, skills, activities, environments, and reinforcers used during instruction. For example, in learning visual discrimination of shapes, elementary-age students may use form boards and shape sorters, while older students use community signs and mosaic art activities. For other skills, calculators may be used instead of number lines; colored clothing can be sorted rather than colored cubes; and the assembly of vocational products may replace peg boards and beads (Bates, Renzaglia, & Wehman, 1981).

Because there are many skills that older severely handicapped youths will never acquire (e.g., reading a newspaper and buying groceries), the curriculum focuses on those abilities that can be learned (e.g., reading survival signs or following directions). To identify these skills for each group of students, Brown et al. (1979) employ an ecological inventory approach listing the environments and subenvironments where the students currently (or will eventually) function. An inventory of the activities in each environment and a listing of skills needed to participate in those activities provide the framework for selecting curriculum goals. In this approach, for example, the basic skill of matching pictures leads to finding grooming items in a drugstore, and identifying different foods leads to ordering in a fast-food restaurant.

Classroom design and decor also should reflect the chronological age of the students. For older youths, pictures of teen activities and movie celebrities are more age-appropriate decorations than cartoon characters. Many special-education classrooms have moved into secondary buildings, opening up opportunities to use age-appropriate training sites such as home economics rooms.

Severely handicapped students may have extremely slow learning rates and much difficulty in generalizing learned skills to new situations. Therefore, their education must include the teaching of critical skill clusters and opportunities to practice functional skills in natural settings such as sheltered workshops, supermarkets, and public transportation. For a more detailed description of curricular approaches to teaching functional skill clusters see Guess and Noonan (1982).

REFERENCES

Bates, P., Renzaglia, A., & Wehman, P. (1981). Characteristics of an appropriate education for severely and profoundly handicapped students. *Education & Training of the Mentally Retarded, 16,* 142–149.

Brown, L., Branston, M. B., Homre-Nietupski, S., Pumpian, I., Certo, N., & Grunewald, L. (1979). A strategy for developing chronological age appropriate and functional curriculum content for severely handicapped adolescents and young adults. *Journal of Special Education, 13,* 81–90.

Drew, C. J., Logan, D. R., & Hardman, M. L. (1984). *Mental Retardation: A Life Cycle Approach* (3rd ed.). St. Louis: Times Mirror/Mosby.

Guess, D., & Noonan, M. J. (1982). Curricula and instructional procedures for severely handicapped students. *Focus on Exceptional Children, 14,* 9–10.

Larsen, L. A., & Jackson, L. B. (1981). Chronological age in the design of educational programs for severely and profoundly impaired students. *PRISE Reporter, 13,* 1–2.

Nirje, B. (1979). Changing patterns in residential services for the mentally retarded. In E. L. Meyen (Ed.), *Basic Readings in the Study of Exceptional Children and Youth.* Denver: Love.

KATHERINE D. COUTURIER
Pennsylvania State University

ADAPTIVE BEHAVIOR
FUNCTIONAL INSTRUCTION
FUNCTIONAL SKILLS TRAINING
MENTAL RETARDATION

AGE AT ONSET

Age at onset refers to the point in an individual's life when a specific condition began. Age at onset can be compared with a child's chronological age to establish the duration of a condition. It is a significant variable in making diagnostic judgments and prognostic statements. Within a school setting, age at onset is typically a consideration in: (1) understanding behavioral disorders; (2) understanding the prognosis for adequate intellectual and learning performance in children with neurologic and chronic medical conditions; and (3) assessing and programming for children with learning disabilities.

In the assessment of behavioral difficulties, it is important to have an adequate history of the disorder, including an estimate of when the child began experiencing difficulties. Knowledge of age at onset allows one to assess the relationship between behavioral changes and other significant occurrences in the child's life (e.g., Did difficulties start when a sibling was born? When the child entered school?). Different psychopathologic conditions have different histories, ages at onset, and significance. For example, infrequent nightmares are not pathognomonic, in fact, they are normal in a three-year-old child (Lowrey, 1978). Infantile autism, by definition, has an age of onset prior to 30 months of age (*Diagnostic and Statistical Manual of Mental Disorders,* 1994). For many disorders, age of onset will influence diagnostic decisions, treatment choices, and prognostications.

REFERENCES

American Psychiatric Association. (1994). *Diagnostic and statistical manual of mental disorders* (4th ed.). Washington, DC: Author.

Lowrey, G. H. (1978). *Growth and development of children.* New York: Year Book Medical.

GRETA N. WILKENING
Children's Hospital

ASSESSMENT
MEDICAL HISTORY
MENTAL STATUS EXAM

AGGRESSION

Aggression is usually defined as any form of behavior designed to harm or injure some living being (Baron & Byrne, 1991), although some also include aggressive acts turned toward objects (intentional destruction of property) or toward the self (Ruhl & Hughes, 1985). This intentional definition of aggression includes two categories: hostile aggression and instrumental aggression. If the goal of an aggressor is to injure a victim, the behavior constitutes hostile aggression, whereas instrumental aggression involves acts perpetrated as a means to some end (to get an object or protect one's play space). Hollandsworth (1977) differentiates aggression from assertiveness by emphasizing the former's threatening, punitive, and coercive qualities.

Aggression is sometimes correlated with other disordered behavior patterns. It is frequently associated with hyperactivity and is also related to excessive distractibility and impulsivity. Positive correlations have been found between impulsive cognitive tempo and both aggression and lack of concern for the consequences of aggression (Messer & Brodzinsky (1979).

Children's aggression against others may be expressed as tantrums, verbal abuse, teasing, opposition (doing the opposite of what one is requested to do), and hitting, kicking, pinching, spitting and other forms of physical assault. There are several categories of high-frequency behaviors that are often exhibited as aggression, including yelling, harmful physical acts, the use of negative commands and threats to force compliance (Patterson, Cobb, & Ray, 1972; Patterson, Reid, Jones, & Conger, 1975).

While some instances of aggressive behavior are a common and normal part of the behavioral repertoire of children, it is only when the behavior occurs at high frequency or has extreme potential for harm that the aggressive child label is applied. What constitutes excessive aggression must be determined with reference to age, sex, form, and culture. For example, males in almost all cultures exhibit more physically aggressive behavior, although females exhibit more relational aggression (like excluding classmates from a group) (Crick & Grotpeter, 1995). Aggressive children also continue to exhibit aversive behaviors at a much later age than do normal children.

Explanations of aggressive behavior can be classified into five theoretical perspectives: (1) ethological/biological, (2) psychodynamic, (3) drive theory, (4) social learning theory, and (5) social-cognitive perspective. Lorenz (1966) has proposed the ecological view that aggression stems from an innate fighting instinct. Aggressive energy is thought to build up over time and must eventually be released directly or indirectly. But evidence for causative evolutionary or genetic factors in humans is weak. It is far more likely that environmental histories determine specific aggressive acts and targets (Simmel, Hahn, & Walters, 1983).

Biological approaches hold that aggression can be influenced by genetic factors (Olweus, 1980), biochemical factors (hormonal processes), or electrical activity in the central nervous system (Moyer, 1976). The extent of this influence varies, but most agree that the expression of biological tendencies is very much a function of the qualifying effects of the environment. Rather than providing a sufficient cause of aggression, it is more accurate to view biological factors as one of a multiple set of determinants (Parke & Slaby, 1983).

Freud believed that aggression is a basic instinctual force that creates a need for aggressive behavior. Thus aggression is viewed as a motivating force that causes behavior and may be expressed in either positive or negative ways. The demands of the environment and the controlling mechanisms of the ego and superego determine whether the expression of aggression is manifested in socially acceptable or unacceptable ways. This view continues to decline in influence because of its intestable hypotheses and because of far more persuasive alternatives.

The frustration-aggression hypothesis provides an historically important explanation of aggression. Frustration is hypothesized to be the cause of aggression (Dollard, Doob, Miller, Mowrer, & Sears, 1939; Berkowitz, 1962). Frustration, which is the result of the blocking or thwarting of some goal-directed activity, induces an aggressive drive that can only be reduced through the expression of aggressive behavior. Although it is certainly true that frustration can produce aggression, this explanation is far too simplistic to explain the myriad instances of aggression. Additional research has shown that aggression is not the inevitable consequence of frustration and that the frustration-aggression hypothesis has limited utility in accounting for either the onset or maintenance of aggressive behavior (Achenbach, 1982).

According to social learning theory (Bandura, 1973) acquiring aggressive behavior is a function of learning from models, the child's reinforcement history, and current contingencies of reinforcement that maintain aggression. It is well established that children can learn aggressive responses from live or filmed models, and from adults, peers, or cartoon characters. They are also more likely to imitate aggressive models who have high social status and who either receive no punishment or are reinforced for their behavior. Further, when specific or generalized imitation of aggression goes unpunished or is rewarded, a child will be more likely to engage in that behavior. Aversive stimulation in the form of taunts or threats, or the removal of salient reinforcers, may also evoke aggressive behavior.

Once aggression has become a regular aspect of one's behavioral repertoire, it will be perpetuated to the extent that it continues to be reinforced. Paradoxically, some uses of corporal punishment can increase the probability of future aggressive behavior (Axelrod & Apsche, 1983). Aggression can also be maintained through mental processes that serve to justify one's behavior. As Bandura has continued to develop this theory, primary emphasis has shifted from behavioral contributions to the importance of cognitive processes, including a person's thoughts, perceptions, attitudes and self-efficacy.

Cognitive analyses of aggression include interpersonal cognitive problem solving (Spivak & Shure, 1974; Shure and Spivak, 1978) and social information processing (Crick & Dodge, 1994). Both of these views link social cognition to social behavior by emphasizing how children's thoughts about themselves and others affect their behavior.

Interpersonal cognitive problem solving focuses on children's ability to generate multiple strategies for solving social problems. Skills associated with social problem solving include sensitivity to social problems, recognizing alternative solutions, identifying means to reach a social goal, considering the consequences of possible actions, and considering possible causes of other people's behavior. The more strategies children know for solving social problems and hence the greater their social competence, the less likely they are to resort to aggressive or impulsive behaviors. Training programs that increase children's cognitive problem-solving skills have been found to reduce children's aggressive behavior (Denham & Almeida, 1987; Shure, 1993).

A related approach emphasizes teaching children healthy ways to manage frustration (Fagen & Hill, 1987). By training children to recognize feelings of frustration, accept those feelings, tolerate frustrating experiences, and build coping skills, teachers can enable aggressive students to respond in more adaptive ways to inevitable frustrations.

According to the social information processing model, children's aggressive behavior is believed to be a function of the social schemas that they have gained from their experiences. Social schemas refers to memory structures that organized information, and it is proposed that aggressive children hold schemas that predispose them to interpret ambiguous behavior directed at them by their peers as having aggressive intent (Dodge & Frame, 1982). In other words, one's memories for specific events, private rules for interpreting behavior, and social schemas affect how children process information in specific social situations. Aggressive children use fewer cues in a social situation before drawing inferences than do nonaggressive children (Slaby & Guerra, 1990), and they pay more attention to aggressive cues (Gouze, 1987).

The model focuses on social judgments and interpretations of social cues. It calls attention to the attributions and inferences that are made about the motives of others. One must interpret social cues accurately in order to make correct attributions about whether another person's behavior is hostile or not. Cognitive mediators of aggression may affect how a child first determines which social cues are relevant and then evaluates those cues to interpret a peer's intentions. Other internally mediated events involve considering alternative responses to the situation, determining when to apply one's personal response rules, and deciding on the optimal response given the costs and benefits of various solutions. Therefore, this view of aggression seeks to reveal the cognitive and attributional underpinnings of personal decisions regarding the expression of aggressive behavior.

Studies based on this model indicate that aggressive children tend to have little interest in relationship goals, instead preferring to use their power to get what they desire. Also, they less often think of socially desirable responses (Dodge, Murphy, & Buchsbaum, 1984; Dorsch & Keane, 1994), in hypothetical situations will evaluate aggressive responses more positively, and have greater confidence about their ability to use aggression.

Approaches to the control of aggression vary according to theoretical persuasion. Psychodynamic interpretations of aggression invoke the concept of catharsis, the dissipation of built-up aggression that results from fantasy activities that permit one to vicariously express aggressive impulses (watching violent television programs or painting with aggressive themes), or through the psychodynamic processes of displacement and sublimation. Building trust, communicating total acceptance of the child, and creating a permissive, noncompetitive classroom environment are also recommended. Not only is there no empirical support for the efficacy of these approaches, but there is some evidence that such approaches may actually increase aggressive propensities (Lefkowitz, et al., 1977).

Procedures referred to as "psychoeducational" are distinctive for their focus on cognitive and affective contributions to behavior. The premise of most of these approaches is that cognitive awareness, feelings about aggression, and perceptions of others will influence the nature of one's behavior (Fagen, Long, & Stevens, 1975; Rezmierski, Knoblock, & Bloom, 1982; Dodge and Crick, 1994). Therefore, interventions should focus on training explicit skills for achieving self-control over aggressive behavior.

For example, the self-control curriculum of Fagen and Long (1979) taught skill clusters such as anticipating response consequences, managing frustration, inhibition and delay, and relaxation. A variety of strategies are used to teach these skills, including many used in cognitive-behavior modification (Mahoney, 1974). Research confirms that aggression can be decreased by altering a child's cognitive strategies and affective states (Goldstein, 1983). In a study of the social information processing model, Guerra and Slaby (1990), were able to improve adolescents' social information processing, change their beliefs about the ac-

ceptability of aggression and reduce the degree of aggressive, impulsive and inflexible behavior.

Interventions based on social learning theory also incorporate a variety of behavior modification techniques. All social learning strategies seek to modify the child's current social environment (Bandura, 1973; Patterson et al., 1975). Training consists of modeling or role playing (Chalmers, & Townsend, 1990). Children are taught non-aggressive behaviors for those situations most likely to elicit aggressive responses.

Strictly behavioral interventions are often effective in reducing aggression, even though adequate generalization to other environments and maintenance of behavior over time is sometimes problematic (Kazdin & Frame, 1983). To counter this challenge, careful effort is given to teach acceptable behavior, not merely eliminate aggressive responses. This may include building effective skills of social interaction, as well as cognitive or affective behaviors. As a consequence, there may be considerable overlap in the techniques used by proponents of behavioral and cognitive approaches to reducing aggressive behavior in children.

REFERENCES

Achenbach, T. M. (1982). *Developmental psychopathology* (2nd ed.). New York: Ronald.

Axelrod, S., & Apasche, J. (Eds.). (1983). *The effect of punishment on human behavior.* New York: Academic.

Bandura, A. (1973). *Aggression: A social learning analysis.* Englewood Cliffs, NJ: Prentice-Hall.

Bandura, A. (1986). *Social foundations of thought and behavior.* Englewood Cliffs, NJ: Prentice-Hall.

Baron, R. A., & Byrne, D. (1991). *Social psychology: Understanding human interaction* (5th ed.). Newton, MA: Allyn & Bacon.

Berkowitz, L. (1982). *Aggression: A social psychological analysis.* New York: McGraw-Hill.

Chalmers, J. B., & Townsend, M. A. R. (1990). The effect of training in social perspective taking on socially maladjusted girls. *Child Development, 61,* 178–190.

Crick, N. R., & Dodge, K. A. (1994). A reformulation of social information-processing mechanisms in children's social adjustment. *Psychological Bulletin, 115,* 74–101.

Crick, N. R., & Grotpeter, J. K. (1995). Relational aggression, gender and social-psychological adjustment. *Child Development, 66,* 710–722.

Denham, S. A., & Almeida, M. C. (1987). Children's social problem-solving skills, behavioral adjustment, and interventions: A meta-analysis evaluating theory and practice. *Journal of Applied Developmental Psychology, 8,* 391–409.

Dodge, K. A., & Frame, C. L. (1982). Social cognitive biases and deficits in aggressive boys. *Child Development, 53,* 62–635.

Dodge, K. A., Murphy, R. R., & Buchsbaum, K. (1984). The assessment of intention-cue detection skills in children: Implications for developmental psychopathology. *Child Development, 55,* 163–173.

Dorsch, A., & Keane, S. P. (1994). Contextual factors in children's social information processing. *Developmental Psychology, 30,* 611–616.

Fagen, S. A., & Long, N. J. (1979). A psychoeducational curriculum approach to teaching self control. *Behavioral Disorders, 4,* 68–82.

Fagen, S. A., Long, N. J., & Stevens, D. J. (1975). *Teaching children self-control.* Columbus, OH: Merrill.

Fagen, S. A., & Hill, J. M. (1987). Teaching acceptance of frustration. *Teaching Exceptional Children, 19,* 49–51.

Goldstein, A. P. (Ed.). (1983). *Prevention and control of aggression.* New York: Pergamon.

Gouze, K. R. (1987). Attention and social problem solving as correlates of aggression in preschool males. *Journal of Abnormal Child Psychology, 15,* 181–197.

Guerra, N. G., & Slaby, R. G. (1990). 1. Cognitive mediators of aggression in adolescent offenders. 2. Intervention. *Developmental Psychology, 26,* 269–277.

Hollandsworth, J. G., Jr. (1977). Differentiating assertion and aggression: Some behavioral guidelines. *Behavior Therapy, 8,* 347–352.

Kazdin, A. E., & Frame, C. (1983). Aggressive behavior and conduct disorders. In R. J. Morris & T. R. Kratochwill (Eds.), *The practice of child therapy* (pp. 167–192). New York: Pergamon.

Lefkowitz, M. M., Eron, L. D., & Walder, L. D., & Huesmann, L. R. (1977). *Growing up to be violent: A longitudinal study of the development of aggression.* New York: Pergamon.

Lorenz, K. (1966). *On aggression.* New York: Harcourt, Brace & World.

Mahoney, M. J. (1974). *Cognition and behavior modification.* Cambridge, MA: Ballinger.

Messer, S. B., & Brodzinsky, D. M. (1979). The relation of conceptual tempo to aggression and its control. *Child Development, 50,* 758–766.

Moyer, K. E. (1976). *The psychobiology of aggression.* New York: Harper & Row.

Olweus, D. (1980). Familial and temperamental determinants of aggressive behavior in adolescent boys: A causal analysis. *Developmental Psychology, 16,* 644–666.

Parke, R. D., & Slaby, R. G. (1983). The development of aggression. In P. Muessen & E. M. Heatherington (Eds.), *Handbook of child psychology. Vol. 4. Socialization, personality, and social development* (45th ed.) (pp. 547–641). New York: Wiley.

Patterson, G. R., Cobb, J. A., & Ray, R. S. (1972). Direct intervention in the classroom: A set of procedures for the aggressive child. In F. W. Clark, D. R. Evans, & L. A. Hammerlynck (Eds.), *Implementing behavioral programs in schools and clinics* (pp. 151–201). Champaign, IL: Research Press.

Patterson, G. R., Reid, J. B., Jones, R. R., & Conger, R. E. (1975). *A social learning approach to family intervention: Vol. 1. Families with aggressive children.* Eugene, OR: Castalia.

Rezmiersky, V. E., Knoblock, P., & Bloom, R. B. (1982). The psychoeducational model: Theory and historical perspective. In R. L. McDowell, G. W. Adamson, & F. W. Wood (Eds.), *Teaching emotionally disturbed children* (pp. 47–69). Boston: Little, Brown.

Ruhl, K. L., & Hughes, C. A. (1985). The nature and extent of aggression in special education settings serving behaviorally disordered students. *Behavioral Disorders, 10,* 95–104.

Shure, M. B. (1993). *I Can Problem Solve (ICPS): An interpersonal cognitive problem solving program for children.* Champaign, IL: Research Press.

Shure, M. B., & Spivack, G. (1978). *Problem-solving technique in child rearing.* San Francisco: Jossey-Bass.

Simmel, E. C., Hahn, M. E., & Walters, J. K. (1983). Synthesis and new direction. In E. C. Simmel, M. E. Hahn, & J. K. Walters (Eds.), *Aggressive behavior: Genetic and neural approaches* (pp. 183–190). Hillsdale, NJ: Erlbaum.

Slaby, R. G., & Guerra, N. G. (1988). Cognitive mediators of aggression in adolescent offenders: 1. Assessment. *Developmental Psychology, 24,* 580–588.

Spivack, G., & Shure, M. B. (1974). Social adjustment of young children: *A cognitive approach to solving real life problems.* San Francisco: Jossey-Bass.

JAMES M. APPLEFIELD
*University of North Carolina
at Wilmington*

COGNITIVE BEHAVIOR THERAPY
CONDUCT DISORDER
SOCIAL COGNITIVE THEORY

AGRAPHIA

The *Cyclopedia of Education* (1915) defines agraphia as a disorder of the associations of speech in which there is a partial or complete inability to express ideas by means of written symbols in an individual who had previously acquired this mode of speech expression. Agraphia is often associated with apraxia and with so-called motor aphasia.

Orton (1937) distinguished between motor agraphia and development agraphia, or special writing disability. Orton defined motor agraphia as the loss of ability to write restricted to the motor component of writing. Orton attributed this problem to dysfunction in relevant motor control areas of the brain without accompanying dysfunction in nearby speech functioning areas. Developmental agraphia was said to manifest itself in one of two ways: the first instance characterized by an unusually slow rate of writing; the second characterized by quality of writing. Orton suggested that "shifted sinistrals," or enforced training of the right hand in left-hand children, may result in slow writing. In other cases, the lack of dominant handedness was said to result in writing problems.

Strauss and Werner (1938) suggested that finger agnosia (inability to recognize one's own fingers) may be related to agraphia. Terms such as agraphia have declined in popularity in recent years, partly as a result of a trend toward the use of more educationally relevant orientations (see Hallahan, Kauffman, & Lloyd, 1985, for a historical overview). Deficits in writing performance are best defined and remediated in terms of task-specific behaviors (Mercer, 1979).

REFERENCES

Cyclopedia of Education (1915). New York: Macmillan.

Hallahan, D. P., Kauffman, J. M., & Lloyd, J. W. (1985). *Introduction to learning disabilities*. Englewood Cliffs, NJ: Prentice-Hall.

Mercer, C. (1979). *Children and adolescents with learning disabilities*. Columbus, OH: Merrill.

Orton, S. T. (1937). *Reading, writing, and speech problems in children*. New York: Norton.

Strauss, A. A., & Werner, H. (1938). Deficiency in finger schema in relation to arithmetic disability (finger agnosia and acalculia). *American Journal of Orthopsychiatry, 8,* 719–724.

Thomas E. Scruggs
Margo A. Mastropieri
Purdue University

DYSGRAPHIA
HANDWRITING

AICARDI SYNDROME (CALLOSAL DYSGENESIS)

Aicardi Syndrome (AS) is the most common of syndromes involving agenesis or dysgenesis of the corpus callosum and is sometimes used interchangeably with the designation *callosal dysgenesis*. The corpus callosum is the largest of the cerebral commissures and is the major communication link between the left and the right hemispheres of the brain.

Depending upon the level of dysgenesis, symptoms may vary considerably in their severity but among the most common are: mental retardation, autistic syndromes, severe obsessive compulsive disorders, seizure disorder, and macrocephaly (Gillberg, 1995). When limited to the extreme posterior portions of the corpus callosum, ADHD is a more common result. Girls tend to be overrepresented in callosal dysgenesis syndromes and in, Aicardi Syndrome proper, only girls occur since it is an X-linked, dominant mutation. As, among the callosal dysgenesis syndromes, is among the most severe and typically results in moderate to severe mental retardation and numerous physical abnormalities, especially of the spine and the orofacial area. Diagnosis is by CAT scan or MRI. Neuropsychological testing is recommended due to the possible range of reaction.

Treatment is entirely symptomatic and virtually all such children will require special education services and may qualify under multiple areas of disability. In less severe cases of callosal dysgenesis, asymptomatic presentations have been reported, emphasizing the need for ongoing neuropsychological follow-up and periodic reassessment of intervention plans. Symptoms not appearing by puberty typically do not occur and the disorder is not progressive. In the most severe forms of callosal agenesis, death in infancy is common.

REFERENCE

Gillberg, C. (1995). *Clinical child neuropsychiatry*. Cambridge: Cambridge University Press.

Cecil R. Reynolds
Texas A & M University

AIDES TO PSYCHOLINGUISTIC TEACHING

Psycholinguistics focuses on the interactions and psychological functions underlying communication. It attends to the processes by which a speaker or writer emits signals or symbols, and the interpretation of those signals by the receiver (Hammill & Larsen, 1974).

Language programs and assessment techniques have been derived from these psycholinguistic principles and have been applied to education. A basic tenet of psycholinguistics is that language is made up of discrete components that may be identified and measured; further, it is assumed that if one is deficient in a given component, the deficiency can be remediated. This leads to two more assumptions, that a child's failure to learn stems from his or her own weaknesses, and that strengthening weak areas will result in improved classroom learning (Hammill & Larsen, 1974). If these assumptions are valid, programs aimed at mitigating psycholinguistic weaknesses are both necessary and desirable. If the assumptions are invalid, however, a great deal of time and money is being wasted on the application of these programs in educational settings.

In their review of research, Hammill and Larsen (1974) showed that the efficacy of psycholinguistic training had not been adequately demonstrated. They pointed out that many exceptional children are being provided with training programs aimed at increasing their psycholinguistic competencies. On the basis of their review, the authors claimed that it is essential to determine whether the constructs are trainable by present programs. It is also necessary, they said, to identify the children for whom such training would prove worthwhile.

Arter and Jenkins (1977), in their examination of the

benefits and prevalence of modality considerations in special education, concluded that research evidence failed to support the practice of basing instructional plans on modality assessment. Thirteen of the 14 studies they reviewed indicated that students were not differentially assisted by instruction congruent with their modality strengths. Further, they stated that "increased efforts in research and development of test instruments and techniques may be warranted but, as far as the practitioner is concerned, advocacy of the (modality) model cannot be justified." (p. 295)

Recent reviews using a quantitative statistic known as effect size (ES) have been conducted to summarize educational research. This statistic is computed to quantitatively determine how much improvement occurs across different investigations, based on two indices: the direction of improvement (+ or −) and the amount of improvement with an ES of 1.00 revealing a 34% improvement. Kavale and Glass (1982) refer to a meta-analysis performed by Kavale in 1981 that investigated the effectiveness of psycholinguistic training. Kavale's studies yielded 240 effect sizes with an overall ES of 0.39. Kavale and Glass conclude by asserting that there are specific situations where psycholinguistic training is effective and that it should be included within a total remedial program. The findings from this research should be qualified, however, because of the lack of consideration of research methodologies across the different investigations. Furthermore, the outcome measures were based on performance on the process tests (i.e., Illinois Test of Psycholinguistic Abilities—ITPA), not on academic tests. Further analyses of studies using achievement outcomes have found negligible effect sizes. It remains open to question whether such improvement on psycholinguistic process tasks would translate into improved performance on academic tasks in the classroom.

REFERENCES

Arter, J. A., & Jenkins, J. R. (1977). Examining the benefits and prevalence of modality considerations in special education. *Journal of Special Education, 11*(3), 281–298.

Hammill, D. D., & Larsen, S. C. (1974). The effectiveness of psycholinguistic training. *Exceptional Children, 41,* 5–14.

Kavale, K. A., & Glass, G. V. (1982). The efficacy of special education interventions and practices: A compendium of meta-analysis findings. *Focus on Exceptional Children, 15*(4), 1–16.

KATHLEEN RODDEN-NORD
GERALD TINDAL
University of Oregon

FERNALD METHOD
ORTON-GILLINGHAM METHOD
PSYCHOLINGUISTICS

AIDS

See PEDIATRIC ACQUIRED IMMUNE DEFICIENCY SYNDROME.

AKINETON

Akineton is the proprietary name of *biperiden*, a skeletal muscle relaxant used in the treatment of Parkinson's disease (Modell, 1985). It is available in tablet and ampul form. Akineton is used in the treatment of all forms of parkinsonism, and it helps reduce movement disorders associated with this condition. It also is used in conjunction with antipsychotic drugs such as the phenothiazines to control extrapyramidal disturbances. Safe, effective use in children has not been established. Possible side effects associated with Akineton include dryness of the mouth, drowsiness, blurred vision, and urinary retention. Extreme adverse effects include mental confusion, agitation, and disturbed behavior. Teachers who have students with juvenile Parkinsonism may encounter those side effects in their students.

REFERENCES

Modell, W. (Ed.). (1985). *Drugs in current use and new drugs* (31st ed.). New York: Springer.

Physician's desk reference (37th ed.). (1983). Oradell, NJ: Medical Economics.

CATHY F. TELZROW
Cuyahoga Special Education Service Center

CHOREA
PHENOTHIAZINES

AL-ANON

Al-Anon originally was an adjunct of Alcoholics Anonymous, but in 1954 it incorporated as a separate fellowship. The central headquarters, known as the World Service Office (WSO), serves Al-Anon groups all over the world. The WSO is guided by a voluntary board of trustees, a policy committee, and an executive committee that makes administrative decisions. There is a paid staff with an executive director. Although there is a central headquarters, all local groups operate autonomously. The only requirement for membership is the belief that one's life has been or is being deeply affected by close contact with a problem drinker.

Al-Anon groups help affected by someone else's drinking to:

Learn the facts about alcoholism as a family illness

Benefit from contact with members who have had the same problem

Improve their own attitudes and personalities by the study and practice of the "twelve steps"

Reduce tensions and improve the attitudes of the family through attendance at Al-Anon meetings

Al-Anon is primarily a self-help/support group that focuses on assisting family members in dealing with the problems that an alcoholic brings to the family. It is based on anonymity and sharing.

PHILIP E. LYON
College of St. Rose

ALATEEN

Alateen is a self-help, self-support group for young Al-Anon members whose lives have been affected by someone else's drinking. Each Alateen group has an active, adult member of Al-Anon who serves as a sponsor and who is responsible for guiding the group and sharing knowledge of the twelve steps and traditions. The basis purpose of this group is to help Alateens to cope with the turmoil created in their lives by someone else's drinking. Meetings are voluntary and generally are held in community buildings. Alateen members openly discuss their problems, share experiences, learn effective ways to cope with their problems, encourage one another, and help each other to understand the principles of the Al-Anon program.

In a survey conducted by World Service Office it was found that 46% of the Alateens held membership for between 1 and 4 years, 57% were female, most were children of alcoholics, 27% were the brother, sister, or other relative of an alcoholic, and the average age of a member was 14, with 71% between the ages of 13 and 17. Furthermore, 31% of the Alateen members had participated in treatment/counseling before or since coming to Alateen. Fully 94% of the Alateen respondents indicated that personal influences were responsible for their attendance at their first Alateen meeting, with Alcoholics Anonymous members, Al-Anon/Alateen members, or family members being the most frequently identified influence.

PHILIP E. LYON
College of St. Rose

AL-ANON
ALCOHOL AND DRUG ABUSE PATTERNS

ALBINISM

Albinism is a genetic disorder that affects the pigmentation, of the skin, hair, or eyes or any combination of the three. Individuals with albinism often have significant visual impairment. Problems with acuity are common, as is pendular nystagmus. Central nervous system involvement may be present. Although one would typically require intense illumination for such problems, persons with albinism are severely photosensitive, i.e., intolerant of light. Special education services will often be necessary, particularly if the visual impairments so often accompanying albinism are severe. Social and behavioral problems related to the odd physical appearance concomitant with albinism are common, as are problems with anxiety and self-esteem. Children with albinism will vary as much as normal individuals in the vast majority of human characteristics. Some will not require special education.

CECIL R. REYNOLDS
Texas A & M University

ALBRIGHT'S HEREDITARY OSTEODYSTROPHY (PSEUDOHYPOPARATHYROIDISM)

Albright's hereditary osteodystrophy is believed to be an X-linked inherited disorder that results in a low level of calcium and a high level of phosphorus in the blood. Varying degrees of mental retardation, ranging from slight to severe, are associated with the condition, and hearing and vision problems are found in a number of afflicted children. At times, hyperthyroidism is associated with Albright's, therefore alterations in personality and behavior may be seen (Carter, 1978).

Children with this condition are usually short and stocky with skeletal abnormalities often observed in both upper and lower extremities and prominent foreheads. Calcium deposits may be present in the brain, skin, and organs. Calcification is often found in hands, wrists, and feet. Toes and fingers are short and stubby. There may be impairment in the sense of sour and bitter taste and the sense of smell. Glandular disorders may be seen and sexual glands may be poorly developed (Lemeshaw, 1982).

Neurological, sensory, and motor problems often accompanying this syndrome will require related attention. Developmental and mental status evaluations will be necessary to measure the degree of disability each child has. Because seizures may be present, drug therapy may be necessary and must be known and monitored.

REFERENCES

Carter, C. (Ed.). (1978). *Medical aspects of mental retardation* (2nd ed.). Springfield, IL: Thomas.

Lemeshaw, S. (1982). *The handbook of clinical types in mental retardation*. Boston: Allyn & Bacon.

Stonburg, J., & Wyngaarden, J. (1978). *Metabolic basis of inherited disease*. New York: McGraw-Hill.

Sally L. Flagler
University of Oklahoma

HYPERTHYROIDISM
See PHYSICAL ANOMALIES

ALCOHOL AND DRUG ABUSE PATTERNS

Alcohol and drug abuse patterns in contemporary American society should be viewed from many perspectives in an effort to understand the multidimensional nature of the problem. Patterns of alcohol and drug use, abuse, and dependence, particularly among adolescents, have changed radically in the past 20 years. Rates of use, abuse, and dependence have all increased at an alarming rate, as has the variety of substances indulged in by young and old alike. Many theories have been developed as social scientists seek to understand and explain the upsurge in adolescent alcohol and drug use. For example, in 1980, 50 theorists described 43 different theories on drug abuse (Lettieri, Sayers, & Pearson, 1980). Similarly, a plethora of research articles have appeared on the phenomenon of alcohol use and abuse (Maisto & Caddy, 1981; Roebuck & Kessler, 1972).

To explore and explain fully the complex nature of alcohol and drug use among youths, one must look at the theoretical constructs of anthropology, economics, medicine, politics, psychology, and sociology. In a recent review of the many determinants of alcohol and drug use, Galizio and Maisto (1985) call for a "biopsychosocial" model. Given the alarming rate of acceleration in alcohol and drug use and the complexity of the issue, such a model would allow theorists and scientists from varying disciplines to study and collaborate in an effort to understand and intervene in this escalating social issue.

The fourth edition of the *Diagnostic and Statistical Manual of Mental Disorders* (American Psychiatric Association, 1994) clearly distinguishes among the terms, use, abuse, and dependence. Although each category of psychoactive drug use (e.g., alcohol, barbiturate, opioid, co-caine, amphetamine, phencyclidine, hallucinogen, cannabis, and tobacco) is separated within the manual, the more general term substance use, is employed when referencing the disorder as a whole. Substance use is defined as a pattern of consumption of a psychoactive substance; (i.e., one that has a mechanism of action in the brain) that does not meet the definitive criteria that follow for abuse or dependence. Substance abuse is a pattern of pathological use, (i.e., impairment in social or occupational functioning that is related to the use of the substance) that lasts at least 1 month. Substance dependence is defined by the presence of body tolerance to the drug, or evidence of withdrawal symptoms (e.g., runny nose, goose flesh, fevers and chills, gastrointestinal discomfort, muscle cramping) after cessation of use. Tolerance is defined as a state of use in which larger and larger amounts of the particular substance are required to produce the user's desired outcome. Withdrawal symptoms can be physiological, psychological, or both; several drugs, notably alcohol, heroin, opioids, barbiturates, sedatives, and some types of stimulants, frequently create both. This point is significant regarding the establishment and maintenance of specific patterns of alcohol and drug use. Cessation of use by a chemically dependent person may create such great discomfort that the user feels compelled to return to use for relief.

Patterns of alcohol and drug use among adolescents are strongly linked with delinquent behavior. Indeed, delinquent behavior and substance abuse are consistently correlated (Elliott & Ageton, 1976). At the least, use of alcohol, illicit drugs, or prescription drugs not prescribed for the individual using them is illegal. Further, other unconventional or nonconforming actions such as sexual experiences, attenuated academic performance, and flagrant violations of minor and major laws often precede involvement with illicit substances. Not all youths who experiment with alcohol and other drugs will manifest the problems associated with chronic or continued substance abuse, but current research supports a high correlation between continuing drug and alcohol use and delinquent behavior (Clayton, 1981). Initial, or trial, use of alcohol and drug is likely to occur in youths who have already participated in other minor deviant activities; those who choose a high level of peer group involvement; and those who have seen both parent and peer use. Huba, Wingard, and Bentler (1980) found that prior behavior is a much stronger predictor of intended drug behavior than is either expressed interest or desire. This factor is significant in understanding the causal relationship between criminal behavior and drug and alcohol use. Initial research suggested that drug use precedes other forms of juvenile delinquent behavior (Single & Kandel, 1978), but more recent studies indicate that delinquent subgroups establish group acceptance of continued alcohol and drug use beyond the level of what could be considered normal adolescent experimentation and curiosity (Clayton, 1981).

Initiation of alcohol and drug use can be seen as either a developmental issue of adolescence (Kandel, 1975) or as an abnormal adaptation to frustration (Hendin, 1980), among other possibilities. Numerous theories have been posited about the initial or trial stage of drug use. However, consensus has been reached as to the critical role of peer-group pressure and the addictive nature, physically and/or psychologically, of the substances used in maintaining drug use. Thus regardless of the reason for beginning drug use, acceptance and support by peers to continue use, tolerance, and aversive withdrawal symptoms are essential factors in understanding the use, abuse, and dependence continuum. The addictive potential of the substance used, amount used, frequency and duration of use, and route of administration are key factors influencing adolescent's ability to start and stop their alcohol and drug use.

Adolescents seem to follow a predictable pattern in their continued alcohol and drug use. The use of legal drugs usually precedes the use of illegal drugs, irrespective of what age the use of illegal drugs is begun. Similarly, the use of illicit drugs like marijuana rarely takes place without prior experimentation or use. However, no evidence indicates that anything inherent in the pharmacologic properties of any substance necessarily leads from use of one to the use of another (the stepping stone theory of addiction). That is, the use of tobacco leads to alcohol, alcohol to marijuana, marijuana to stronger drugs, and finally addiction and dependency. Factors such as parental role models, peer pressure, and availability and access seem to be more important than anything pharmacological (Kandel, 1975).

A further complication is that adolescents who use and abuse substances that can produce tolerance may suffer the biomedical consequences of lifelong chemical affinity for continued abuse and dependency (Cohen, 1981). Also, evidence of a biogenetic predisposition to drug dependency can be seen in patterns of use and abuse in the offspring of alcoholics and, to a lesser degree, other substance-addicted parents (Crabbe, McSwigan, & Belknap, 1985). Children of addicted parents may become addicted with fewer episodes of intoxication, smaller amounts of substances, and fewer of the factors noted previously for adolescents. A word of caution is offered by Schuckit (1980), who states that even when a predisposition or affinity for substances is noted in an adolescent, the final picture must involve not only genetics but also the careful consideration of environment, culture, and other social factors.

The range and variation of the adolescent experience is an important final concern in understanding adolescent patterns of alcohol and drug use. The period of chronological growth beginning at age 12 and continuing through age 21 is marked by great physical, emotional, and intellectual development. Early, middle, and late phase adolescents respond differently to issues such as opportunity for first use, continued use, decision making, the ability to make choices, stress and anxiety, and prevalent patterns of communication within a given peer network. Cohen (1983) and Kandel (1975) substantiate concerns about the impact of the age of first use moving downward. Data on age of admission to treatment centers and survey responses both suggest that a large number of adolescents will become dependent at an earlier age. Further research is needed to determine the impact of this trend on the rapidly developing, but fragile, systems of young people. Although some studies suggest a decline in the frequency of adolescent drug and alcohol use in this society (Johnston, Bachman, & O'Malley, 1982), more specific information is needed about high-risk youths from isolated populations that are not routinely surveyed in national studies (e.g., high school dropouts, younger members of the armed forces, and residents of college dorms). Miller (1981) indicates that the "survellience function of epidemiological research" will best be served by closer attention to special "pockets" of substance-abusing youths who have escaped close scrutiny in the recent past.

REFERENCES

American Psychiatric Association. (1994). *Diagnostic and statistical manual of mental disorders* (4th ed.). Washington, DC: Author.

Clayton, R. R. (1981). The delinquency and drug use relationship among adolescents: A critical review. In D. J. Lettieri & J. P. Lundford (Eds.), *Drug abuse and the American adolescent* (pp. 82–98). Rockville, MD: National Institute on Drug Abuse.

Cohen, S. (1981). Adolescence and drug abuse: Biomedical consequences. In D. J. Lettieri & J. P. Ludford (Eds.), *Drug abuse and the American adolescent* (pp. 104–109). Rockville, MD: National Institute on Drug Abuse.

Cohen, S. (1983). *The alcoholism problems.* New York: Haworth.

Crabbe, J. C., McSwigan, J. D., & Belknap, J. K. (1985). The role of genetics in substance abuse. In M. Galizio & S. A. Maisto (Eds.), *Determinants of substance abuse* (pp. 13–54). New York: Plenum.

Elliott, J. D. S., & Ageton, A. R. (1976). The relationship between drug use and crime among adolescents. In Research Triangle Institute, *Appendix to drug use and crime: Report of the Panel on Drug Use and Criminal Behavior* (pp. 297–322). VA: National Technical Information Service.

Galizio, M., & Maisto, S. A. (1985). Toward a biopsychosocial theory of substance abuse. In M. Galizio & S. A. Maisto (Eds.), *Determinants of substance abuse* (pp. 425–427). New York: Plenum.

Hendin, H. (1980). Psychosocial theory of drug abuse. In D. J. Lettieri, M. Sayers, & H. W. Pearson (Eds.), *Theories on drug abuse* (pp. 195–200). Rockville, MD: National Institute on Drug Abuse.

Huba, G. J., Wingard, J. A., & Bentler, P. M. (1980). Framework for an interactive theory of drug use. In D. J. Lettieri, M. Sayers, & H. W. Pearson (Eds.), *Theories on drug abuse* (pp. 95–101). Rockville, MD: National Institute on Drug Abuse.

Johnston, L. D., Bachman, J. G., & O'Malley, P. M. (1982). *Student drug use, attitudes, and beliefs: National trends 1975–82.* Detroit, MI: Institute of Social Research.

Kandel, D. (1975). Stages in adolescent involvement in drug use. *Science, 190,* 912–914.

Lettieri, D. J., Sayers, M., & Pearson, H. W. (Eds.). (1980). *Theories on drug abuse: Selected contemporary perspectives.* Rockville, MD: National Institute on Drug Abuse.

Maisto, S. A., & Caddy, G. R. (1981). Self-control and addictive behavior: Present status and prospects. *International Journal of the Addictions, 16,* 109–133.

Miller, J. D. (1981). Epidemiology of drug use among adolescents. In D. J. Lettieri & J. P. Ludford (Eds.), *Drug abuse and the american adolescent* (pp. 25–35). Rockville, MD: National Institute on Drug Abuse.

Roebuck, J., & Kessler, R. (1972). *The etiology of alcoholism.* Springfield, IL: Thomas.

Schuckit, M. A. (1980). A theory of alcohol and drug abuse; A genetic approach. In D. J. Lettieri, M. Sayers, & H. W. Pearson (Eds.), *Theories on drug abuse* (pp. 297–302). Rockville, MD: National Institute on Drug Abuse.

Single, E., & Kandel, D. (1978). The role of buying and selling in illicit drug use. In A. Trebach (Ed.), *Drugs, crime and politics.* New York: Praeger.

L. Worth Bolton
*Cape Fear Substance Abuse
Center*

CHEMICALLY DEPENDENT YOUTH
DRUG ABUSE
SUBSTANCE ABUSE

ALEXANDER GRAHAM BELL ASSOCIATION FOR THE DEAF

The Alexander Graham Bell Association for the Deaf is a nonprofit membership organization established in 1890. The Association's mission is to empower persons who are hearing impaired to function independently by promoting universal rights and optimal opportunities to learn, use, maintain, and improve all aspects of their verbal communications, including their abilities to speak, speechread, use residual hearing, and process both spoken and written language. Towards this end, the Association strives to promote (1) better public understanding of hearing loss in children and adults, (2) detection of hearing loss in early infancy, (3) prompt intervention and use of appropriate hearing aids, (4) dissemination of information on hearing loss, including causes and options for treatment, and (5) inservice training for teachers of children who are deaf or hard of hearing. The organization also collaborates on re-

search relating to auditory/verbal communication and with physicians, audiologists, speech/language specialists, and educators to promote educational and social opportunities for individuals of all ages who are hearing impaired.

To accomplish these objectives, a wide variety of member-oriented programs, publications, and financial aid programs are offered, including school-age financial aid awards, scholarships, aid to parents to infants diagnosed with moderate to profound hearing loss, and arts and sciences awards.

The Alexander Graham Bell Association for the Deaf may be contacted by writing 3417 Volta Place, N. W., Washington, DC 20007-2778 or by calling (202) 337-5220 (Voice and TTY).

REFERENCE

Alexander Graham Bell Assn. for the Deaf. (1996). Washington, DC: Author.

Tamara J. Martin
*The University of Texas of the
Permian Basin*

ALEXIA

Alexia is used often in a general sense to refer to reading disabilities of adult onset (Lezak, 1995). As such, the term serves to differentiate between adult reading disorders and developmental reading disabilities commonly denoted by the term dyslexia. Literally, however, the term *alexia* derives from the Greek and can be approximately translated as "no reading." Thus, in a more precise sense, alexia denotes a total inability to read brought about by an abnormality in the central nervous system (Thomas, 1977). The term can be correctly applied to individuals regardless of age.

In most individuals, the perception of verbal material is mediated by cortical association areas found in the temporal lobe of the left hemisphere of the brain (Milner, 1971). Specifically, the perception of written words appears to be dependent on the proper function of a cortical area found in the posterior temporal lobe, the angular gyrus. As such, the presence of alexia is often seen as an indication of a cortical lesion or other abnormality associated with this particular brain region.

Not all researchers, however, agree that alexia should signify only a condition in which individuals demonstrate an inability to recognize words. It has been argued that individuals who cannot attach meanings to words that they can recognize (i.e., those who demonstrate a failure in word comprehension) are also alexic. Such an inability (whether or not one chooses to call it alexia) may also be related to cortical abnormalities in the left temporal lobe involving neural pathways connecting the angular gyrus to verbal comprehension centers such as Wernicke's area. Interestingly, individuals suffering from right temporal lobe lesions, although seldom demonstrating reading disorders, have been shown to experience related difficulties in nonverbal tasks calling for both spatial recognition and comprehension (Vignolo, 1969).

Given that the events that may lead to cortical damage (e.g., cardiovascular accident, toxic or other poisoning, head trauma) rarely are confined in their effects to any one specific brain location, alexia is generally observed in combination with related language dysfunctions, and rarely in pure form (Lezak, 1995). Dyslexia, defined as an impairment of reading ability of less than total magnitude, is a much more common occurrence.

REFERENCES

Lezak, M. D. (1995). *Neuropsychological assessment* (3rd ed.). New York: Oxford University Press.

Milner, B. (1971). Interhemispheric differences in the localization of psychological processes in man. *British Medical Bulletin, 27,* 272–277.

Thomas, C. L. (Ed.). (1977). *Tabor's cyclopedic medical dictionary.* Philadelphia: Davis.

Vignolo, L. A. (1969). Auditory agnosia: A review and report of recent evidence. In A. L. Benton (Ed.), *Contributions to clinical neuropsychology* (pp. 172–208). Chicago: Aldine.

RICHARD G. PETERS
Ball State University

RAYMOND S. DEAN
Ball State University
Indiana University School
of Medicine

DYSLEXIA

focused on the similarities between learning-disabled (LD) and low-achieving students. Algozzine contends that LD is a sophisticated term for low achievement and that it represents an oversophistication of a concept (Algozzine, Ysseldyke, & Shinn, 1982). He has shown that few differences exist in test profiles of LD and low-achieving students and that performance profiles of many normal students evidence significant discrepancies as well. He believes that schools need to spend less energy trying to identify exceptional students and place more effort on determining what to do with all students who fail to profit from their current educational placement (Algozzine & Ysseldyke, 1983).

Algozzine has written over 200 articles, research reports, monographs, final reports, and books. He has been a member of the Council for Exceptional Children, the American Educational Research Association, and the Florida Council for Children with Behavior Disorders. Currently, he is co-editor of the journal *Exceptional Children.*

REFERENCES

Algozzine, B., & Ysseldyke, J. E. (1983). Learning disabilities as a subset of school failure: The oversophistication of a concept. *Exceptional Children, 50,* 242–246.

Algozzine, B., Ysseldyke, J. E., & Shinn, M. (1982). Identifying children with learning disabilities: When is a discrepancy severe? *Journal of School Psychology, 20,* 299–305.

E. VALERIE HEWITT
Texas A & M University
First edition

KAY E. KETZENBERGER
The University of Texas of the
Permian Basin
Second edition

ALGOZZINE, BOB (1946–   )

After receiving a BS in economics in 1968 from Wagner College in New York, Bob Algozzine earned his MS in educational psychology from the State University of New York, Albany in 1970 and his PhD in the education of exceptional children from Pennsylvania State University in 1975. He was a professor at the University of Florida where he was involved with training regular class teachers to work with exceptional students. Currently, he is professor at the University of North Carolina Charlotte, in the Dept. of Educational Administration, Research & Technology.

Algozzine's main interest is in working with students who fail to profit in regular classes. Much of his work has

ALLERGIC DISORDERS

An allergy is a hypersensitivity to a specific substance (an antigen) that in a similar quantity does not affect other people. The abnormal reactions are usually in the form of asthma, hay fever, eczema, hives, or chronic stuffy nose (allergic rhinitis). Technically, the use of the term should be limited to those conditions in which an immunological mechanism can be demonstrated. Allergies are common to 20 to 25% of the children in the United States and are inherited. The tendency to develop allergies is present at birth but may appear at any age.

Allergies can be classified into two types: immediate hypersensitivity (such as allergic rhinitis, asthma, and food allergies) and delayed hypersensitivity (such as reactions to poison ivy). Patients with the former have more of the antibody IgE in their systems. This antibody reacts with whatever patients are allergic to, whether it is something that they breathe, eat, or have skin contact with. This reaction causes certain cells in the body to release chemical mediators such as histamine and serotonin. These chemicals cause the dilation of the small blood vessels, increased secretion from the mucous glands, and smooth muscle contractions that produce the allergy symptoms.

Allergic rhinitis is the commonest cause of nasal congestion in children. Epidemiological data indicate that in the United States alone allergic rhinitis occurs in 6 million children, accounting for 2 million days lost from school (Shapiro, 1986). An important complication of perennial allergic rhinitis is otitis media with effusion, an accumulation of fluid behind the eardrum in the middle ear. Patients usually have at least an intermittent loss of hearing and may complain of a sensation of fullness or popping and cracking noises.

Allergies often play a role in the etiology of asthma, especially in childhood. The chemical mediators released upon the allergic reaction cause contraction of the smooth muscles in the walls of the bronchial airways, swelling of the bronchial tubes, and an increase in the rate of secretion of mucous by submucosal glands. This produces obstruction and causes the characteristic wheezing and shortness of breath. Asthma may be mild (one or two mild attacks per year) or severe with intractable wheezing daily. The severe form may greatly restrict physical activity and make school attendance difficult for school-age children. Physical exertion may precipitate wheezing and become a problem in physical education classes.

Skin allergies are common, especially in younger children. Atopic dermatitis (eczema) may occur in 3 to 4% of infants and result in a dry, scaly, itchy rash involving the cheeks and extremities. While most children outgrow the rash, over 50% of them tend to develop respiratory allergies. Another common rash with an allergic origin is urticaria or hives. Possible causes are allergies to drugs like aspirin or penicillin and to foods.

Food allergies are perhaps the most controversial area of allergy study. Some allergists feel that allergic reactions to foods are rare, while others feel they are a common cause of illness. The frequency of food allergy seems to decrease as children grow older. The most common symptoms of food allergy include gastrointestinal symptoms such as abdominal pain, vomiting and diarrhea, and rashes such as hives. Food may play a role in other allergic conditions such as allergic rhinitis, asthma, and eczema, especially during the first 3 or 4 years of life. The most serious allergic reaction to foods and drugs is an anaphylactic one, in which the person experiences a shocklike reaction that can result in death. Any food can cause an allergic reaction, but the foods most apt to cause one in children include milk, eggs, fish, wheat, corn, peanuts, soy, pork, and chocolate.

Stinging insect allergies may cause a severe anaphylactic reaction to the sting of a bee, wasp, hornet, or yellow jacket. The reaction may occur within minutes after the sting and allergic persons need immediate medical attention.

A thorough history and physical examination are important components of a diagnosis. Seasonal patterns of symptoms, exposure to animals, and usual diet are useful information in identifying causes. Laboratory analysis of nasal secretions, sputum, and blood may establish the presence of eosinophil cells that appear in increased numbers with allergic reactions. Pulmonary function tests are also helpful. Scratch and intradermal skin tests for the suspected allergens can confirm a diagnosis. Another tool is the radioallergoabsorbant (RAST) test, which measures the level of IgE in the blood for a particular allergen (Tuft, 1973). The elimination-challenge diet is used for suspected food allergies; after avoiding a particular food for two to three weeks, the patient consumes it and is observed for reactions. Awareness of environmental conditions from change of seasons, foliage in different parts of the country, and environmental factors in homes, schools, and the work place also assists the diagnostician.

While there is no cure for allergies, symptoms may be controlled in a variety of ways. First, symptomatic treatment involves using medication. Antihistamines are the most commonly prescribed drugs for the treatment of allergic reactions. They inhibit some of the actions of histamine but frequently have negative side effects such as sedation, excitation, and insomnia. Antihistamines are often combined with decongestant drugs. Asthmatics are usually treated with bronchodilator drugs that cause relaxation of the smooth muscle surrounding the bronchial tubes. Acute asthmatic attacks and anaphylactic reactions are frequently treated with epinephrine. Both drugs may have negative side effects. For severe allergic problems, corticosteroids may be used, but on a limited basis because of adrenal suppression and limitation of physical growth in children.

The second method of treatment is environmental control, that is, removal of troublesome antigens such as pet hair, dust, and pollen. Good housekeeping practices, use of air conditioning at home and in the car, and other careful planning can prevent many allergic problems. A third and related approach is to teach self-regulation strategies to persons with asthma and other types of allergies. They include relaxation training, biofeedback procedures to modify physiological reactions, and general education about the medical condition (Creer, Marion, & Harm, in press). A fourth treatment is immunotherapy, which involves injecting the patient with small amounts of an antigen that has been processed into a dilute form. These injections stimulate the immune system to produce another type of antibody that inhibits the reaction between the allergic antibody and the antigen. While initially the shots are taken once or twice a week, the regimen is gradually phased out over a 2- to 3-year period (Patterson et al., 1978).

Allergies have been connected with specific learning disabilities through analyses of case studies (Rapaport & Flint, 1976). Allergic children are rated lower in reading, auditory perception, and visual perception (Harvard, 1975). Teacher and parent ratings as well as test scores indicated lower proficiency among allergic students in some areas (Rawls, Rawls, & Harrison, 1971). Learning-disabled students with recurrent otitis media may have more problems with allergies and verbal skills than non-disabled children (Loose, 1984). Geschwind and Behan (1982) associate left-handedness with reports of learning problems and immunological diseases such as thyroid and bowel disorders.

However, McLoughlin, et al. (1983) found no differences in parent reports concerning academic achievement, diagnosis for disabilities, and behavioral problems of allergic and nonallergic students. There was a tendency for children with asthma and chronic rhinitis to be rated lower in listening skills. Additionally, a comparison of group achievement scores of allergic and nonallergic students indicated no interaction of exceptional conditions and allergies (McLoughlin, Nall, & Petrosko, 1985). Some lower estimates of allergic children's school performance seem confused with the effects of socioeconomic factors.

Higher rates of school absenteeism are reported for asthmatic children and those with chronic rhinitis (Shapiro, 1986). Asthmatic children may be absent 10% of the time; such absenteeism is a direct cause of school problems. Additionally, the seasonal occurrence of allergic reactions (especially in the fall) and the typical pattern of frequent, brief absences are disruptive to classroom performance, attending skills, and social development. Milder forms of allergies may not cause significant school absenteeism, particularly with improved medical treatment, self-management programs, and parent education (McLoughlin, Nall, & Petrosko, 1985). Furthermore, some previous estimates of higher absenteeism of allergic children may have been confused with the effects of socioeconomic status.

Hearing difficulties are frequently associated with otitis media resulting from allergies (Northern, 1980). Among allergic students, Szanton and Szanton (1966) found many cases of intermittent hearing loss that had been undetected on screening measures. Articulation and/or vocal quality problems have also been reported among allergic students (Baker & Baker, 1980). Recurrent otitis media among three year olds has been associated with lower speech and language performance (Teele, et al., 1984).

Allergy history seems present among cases of behavioral and emotional disorders (Mayron, 1978). King (1981) estimated that 70% of students with such disorders have personal or family allergy histories; cognitive-emotional symptoms were noted after allergic exposure under double-blind conditions. Psychological and personality changes are frequently reported by asthmatic children and their parents (Creer, Marion, & Creer, 1983). However, comparisons of reports and ratings of behavioral problems, placement in services for behavior disorders, and school suspensions between allergic and nonallergic students have not yielded significantly different profiles (McLoughlin et al., 1985).

Hyperactivity has been particularly connected with food allergies. Feingold (1975b) drew attention to the ingestion of artificial food additives (color and flavors) and naturally occurring salicylates in food and proposed the Feingold Kaiser-Permanente (K-P) diet based on clinical observations and anecdotal accounts (Crook, 1977; Feingold, 1975a). However, reviews of controlled studies (Kavale & Forness, 1983; Mattes, 1983) dismiss these claims, as do the findings of the Consensus Development Conference sponsored by the National Institutes of Health (Office for Medical Applications of Research, 1982).

Allergy medication may have adverse effects on behavior and exacerbate existing behavioral problems (McLoughlin et al., 1983). Theophylline has been significantly correlated with inattentiveness, hyperactivity, irritability, drowsiness, and withdrawal behavior; the negative side effects increase with length of use. Furakawa and his colleagues (1984) found decreased test performances under the influence of theophylline. Terbutaline created socially inappropriate behavior in a comparison group (Creer, 1979), and corticosteroids negatively affected academic performance (Suess & Chai, 1981). Ladd, Leibold, Lindsey, and Ornby (1980) also reported euphoria, insomnia, and visual disturbances with corticosteroids. Antihistamines may cause sedation, dry mouth, and irritability (Weinberger & Hendeles, 1980). Visual hallucinations occur among some children receiving decongestants (Sankey, Nunn, & Sills, 1984).

Allergic disorders have important implications for the professional assessment and intervention of exceptionalities as well as for parental involvement. Certain types of allergies and/or the side effects of medication may be contributing factors in behaviors of concern and may require special consideration when designing special services. The self-monitoring and management skills taught in special education may be mutually beneficial in coping with this medical condition.

REFERENCES

Baker, M., & Baker, C. (1980). Difficulties generated by allergies. *Journal of School Health*, *50*, 583–585.

Creer, T. L. (1979). *Asthma therapy*. New York: Springer.

Creer, T. L., Marion, R. J., & Creer, P. P. (1983). The asthma problem behavior checklist: Parental perceptions of the behavior of asthmatic children. *Journal of Asthma, 20*, 97–104.

Crook, W. G. (1977, January). Letter to the editor. *News and Comment*. American Academy of Pediatrics.

Feingold, B. F. (1975a). Hyperkinesis and learning disabilities linked to artificial food flavors and colors. *American Journal of Nursing, 75,* 797–803.

Feingold, B. F. (1975b). *Why your child is hyperactive.* New York: Random House.

Furakawa, C. T., Shapiro, G. G., DuHamel, T., Weimer, L., Pierson, W. E., & Bierman, C. W. (1984, March). Learning and behavior problems associated with theophylline therapy. *Lancet,* 621.

Geschwind, N., & Behan, P. (1982). Left-handedness: Association with immune disease, migraine, and developmental learning disorders. *Proceedings of the National Academy of Science, USA, 79,* 5097–5100.

Harvard, J. G. (1975). Relationship between allergic conditions and language and/or learning disabilities. *Dissertation Abstracts International, 35,* 6940.

Kavale, K. A., & Forness, S. R. (1983). Hyperactivity and diet treatment: A meta-analysis of the Feingold hypothesis. *Journal of Learning Disabilities, 16,* 324–330.

King, D. S. (1981). Can allergic exposure provoke psychological symptoms? *Biology Psychiatry, 16,* 3–19.

Ladd, F. T., Leibold, S. R., Lindsey, C. N., & Ornby, R. (1980). RX in the classroom. *Instructor, 90,* 58–59.

Loose, F. F. (1984). *Educational implications of recurrent otitis media among children at risk for learning disabilities.* Unpublished doctoral dissertation, Michigan State University.

Mattes, J. A. (1983). The Feingold diet: A current reappraisal. *Journal of Learning Disabilities, 16,* 319–323.

Mayron, L. (1978). Ecological factors in learning disabilities. *Journal of Learning Disabilities, 11,* 40–50.

McLoughlin, J. A., Nall, M., Isaacs, B., Petrosko, J., Karibo, J., & Lindsey, B. (1983). The relationship of allergies and allergy treatment to school performance and student behavior. *Annals of Allergy, 51,* 506–510.

McLoughlin, J. A., Nall, M., & Petrosko, J. (1985). Allergies and learning disabilities. *Learning Disability Quarterly, 8,* 255–260.

Northern, J. L. (1980). Diagnostic tests of ear disease. In C. Bierman & D. Pearlman (Eds.), *Allergic diseases of infancy, childhood and adolescence* (pp. 492–501). Philadelphia: Saunders.

Office for Medical Applications of Research, National Institutes of Health. (1982). Defined diets and childhood hyperactivity. *Journal of the American Medical Association, 245,* 290–292.

Patterson, R., Lieberman, P., Irons, J., Pruzansky, J., Melam, H., Metzger, W. J., & Zeiss, C. R. (1978). Immunotherapy. In E. Middleton, Jr., C. Reed, & E. Ellis (Eds.), *Allergy principles and practice* (Vol. 2, pp. 877–897). St. Louis: Mosby.

Rapaport, H. G., & Flint, H. (1976). Is there a relationship between allergy and learning disabilities? *Journal of School Health, 46,* 139–141.

Rawls, D. J., Rawls, J. R., & Harrison, D. W. (1971). An investigation of 6 to 11 year old children with allergic disorders. *Journal of Consulting and Clinical Psychology, 36,* 260–264.

Sankey, R. J., Nunn, A. J., & Sills, J. A. (1984): Visual hallucinations in children receiving decongestants. *British Medical Journal, 288,* 1369.

Shapiro, G. (1986). Understanding allergic rhinitis. *Pediatrics in Review, 7,* 212–218.

Suess, W. M., & Chai, H. (1981). Neuropsychological correlates of asthma: Brain damage or drug effects? *Journal of Consulting and Clinical Psychology, 49,* 135–136.

Szanton, V. J., & Szanton, W. C. (1966). Hearing disturbances in allergic children. *Journal of Asthma Research, 4,* 25–28.

Teele, D. W., Klein, J. O., Rosner, B. A., & the Greater Boston Otitis Media Study Group. (1984). *Pediatrics, 74,* 282–287.

Tuft, L. (1973). *Allergy management in clinical practice.* St. Louis: Mosby.

Weinberger, M., & Hendeles, L. (1980). Pharmacologic management. In C. Bierman & D. Pearlman (Eds.), *Allergic diseases of infancy, childhood and adolescence* (pp. 311–332). Philadelphia: Saunders.

JAMES A. MCLOUGHLIN
University of Louisville

MICHAEL NALL
Louisville, Kentucky

ALLEY, GORDON R. (1934–   )

Gordon R. Alley received his BA (1959) from Augustina, Illinois, later earning his MA (1961) in Psychology and his doctorate (1967) in Special Education and School Psychology from the University of Iowa. Alley's contributions to the field of education include his service as teacher of the mentally retarded, school psychologist, and director of special education. He taught at the University of Utah (1967–1970), and has been professor of special education and a lecturer in pediatrics at the University of Kansas since 1970. Alley has been invited to present his papers to regional and national gatherings on numerous occasions.

Alley's work has emphasized learning strategies associated with the developmental characteristics of adolescents, with his research promoting alternatives to the traditional tutorial and remedial approaches to interventions for students with learning disabilities. While at the Institute for Research in Learning Disabilities at the University of Kansas, Alley published many of his writings pursuant to his interests, including a chapter in *Instructional Planning for Exceptional Children* (1979). Other important publications are his 1979 work, *Teaching the Learning Disabled Adolescent* and *The Effect of Advance Organizers on the Learning and Retention of Learning Disabled Adolescents within the Context of a Cooperative Planning Model,* a study conducted by Alley and Keith Lenz in 1983. Alley's study investigated whether advance organizers would help learning disabled adolescents process information on selected academic tasks more effectively. Results of the research indicated the efficacy of their use in secondary classrooms.

REFERENCES

Alley, G., & Deshler, D. D. (1979). *Teaching the learning disabled adolescent: Strategies and methods.* Denver: Love.

Alley, G., & Foster, C. (1979). *Instructional planning for exceptional children.* Denver: Love.

Lenz, B. K., & Alley, G. R. (1983). *The effect of advance organizers on learning and retention of learning disabled adolescents within the context of a cooperative planning model.* Lawrence, KS: Florida Atlantic University/Kansas University.

ROBERTA C. STOKES
Texas A & M University

TAMARA J. MARTIN
The University of Texas of the Permian Basin

ALPHABETIC METHOD

The alphabetic method of teaching children to read is historically connected with the development of an alphabet. Once letters and sounds were fixed in a structure (an alphabet), a method to master this structure emerged. The first recorded use of the alphabetic method was in ancient Greek and Roman civilizations. Reading instruction began by teaching children all the letters in their proper alphabetical order. After a complete mastery of the alphabet, children learned to group the letters to form syllables, words, and finally sentences. Reading instruction was considered primarily an oral process; the child recited the spelling of each syllable or word and then pronounced it. This progression of teaching letters, syllables, words, and sentences was the predominant method of teaching reading from Greek and Roman times until the late 1800s (Huey, 1908).

In using this method, sixteenth- and seventeenth-century teachers drilled children unmercifully on the names of the letters (Matthews, 1966). Instructional materials that presented lists of letters, syllables, and words to be memorized before advancing to the text were developed. The *New England Primer* was one of the most widely used reading texts in seventeenth-century America. Each reading selection focused on a moral or religious lesson, and was preceded by an alphabet, lists of the vowels and consonants, and lists of syllables such as ab, eb, and ib. The lists of words for spelling began with one-syllable words and progressed to two- and three-syllable words (Huey, 1980).

As the English language evolved, letter names no longer directly represented speech sounds; therefore, children became more and more confused as they tried to read modern literature by simply reciting the names of the letters. Realizing that this confusion hindered efforts to teach reading effectively, the alphabetic method was gradually replaced by phonetically based methods of reading instruction. By the beginning of the twentieth century, the classic alphabetic method was seldom used.

REFERENCES

Huey, E. B. (1908). *The psychology and pedagogy of reading.* New York: Macmillan.

Matthews, M. M. (1966). *Teaching to read.* Chicago: University of Chicago Press.

CHRIS CHERRINGTON
Lycoming College

DISTAR
READING REMEDIATION
WHOLE WORD TEACHING

ALTERNATIVE COMMUNICATION METHODS IN SPECIAL EDUCATION

Individuals with severe communication disorders are those who may benefit from AAC (augmentative and alternative communication)—those for whom gestural, speech, and/or written communication is temporarily or permanently inadequate to meet all of their communication needs. For those individuals, hearing impairment is not the primary cause for the communication impairment. Although some individuals may be able to produce a limited amount of speech, it is inadequate to meet their varied communication needs. Numerous terms that were initially used in the field but are now rarely mentioned include speechless, nonoral, non-vocal, nonverbal, and aphonic (ASHA, 1991, p. 10).

Beukelman & Ansel (1995) estimate 8 to 12 persons per 1,000 in the United States are in need of augmentative and alternative communication (AAC).

In the mid 1970s, alternative methods of communication began to be explored with the nonspeaking population. These methods are termed augmentative communication systems. They are currently being used with children and adults who have physical, mental, emotional, and linguistic handicaps. ASHA (1991) defines an AAC system as "an integrated group of components, including the symbols, aids, strategies, and techniques used by individuals to enhance communication" (p. 10). Unaided communication systems use only the physical body for communication. They include sign languages, gestures, and facial expressions. Aided systems require additional equipment for communication. There are many advantages to using unaided systems for communication. Social interaction is enhanced because the rate of communication is typically fast. Speaker-listener eye contact is maintained when using unaided systems. The meaning of many signs and gestures are concrete, making learning and recall of vocabulary easier. In addition, during training, sign and gesture response can be physically prompted and shaped by the instructor.

Sign languages such as American Sign Language (ASL) were originally developed for the hearing-impaired population. They are separate languages and not simply word-for-word manual translations of spoken English or other oral languages. Educational sign systems, or pedagogical sign systems, are designed to be manual equivalents of spoken English. Signed English is an educational sign system that is used frequently with the nonspeaking population (Bryen & Joyce, 1985). The differences between true sign languages and educational sign systems include differences in word order and sign representations and changes in grammatical structures. To use sign systems as an augmentative communication system, the nonspeaking person should have good motor control of the hands, arms, and face, along with good visual acuity and spatial orientation (Beukelman & Mirenda, 1998). Persons who routinely interact with a signing communicator will also need to learn the system. Gestures and facial expressions typically require less motor control than sign-language systems. Pantomime and natural gestures can often be used and understood without extensive training. Skelly and Schinsky (1979) developed a comprehensive gestural system known as Amer-Ind; it is based on American Indian hand talk. While gesture systems are initially less complex to learn, the information that can be conveyed is often constrained. Gestures and facial expressions are typically used as supplements to other communication systems, or as temporary communication methods.

Aided communication systems require additional devices or equipment for communication. Computers, writing with pen and paper, and communication boards are all examples of aided communication systems. An aided communication system consists of a communication aid, which is the mechanism used for communication, and a symbol system, which is the language used for communication.

The communication aid can consist of three major components: the interface, the communication device, and the output system. Complex electronic systems usually have all three components. Simple communication boards may consist of the communication device alone. The interface is used to control the system. A head stick, joystick, or computer keyboard are examples of interfaces. They are used to select symbols on the communication device. Direct selection allows the user to directly choose symbols for communication. Scanning systems present symbol choices to the user, who then activates a response when the desired symbol is reached. A scanning system resembles an ad-

A Hierarchy of Aided Communication Symbol Systems

Symbolically complex	Written alphabet orthography
	Linguistic pictographic systems (i.e., Blissymbols, Rebus, Piscyms)
	Black and white line drawings
	Colored drawings
	Photographs
	Miniature objects
Symbolically concrete	Real objects

vanced form of the guessing game "Twenty Questions." The communication device can display all of the available vocabulary options, or it can display a few symbols that are combined into codes to access vocabulary. Electronic devices often indicate, by small lights or LCD display screens, which symbol has been selected. Once the entire message to be communicated is completed, an output device such as a speech synthesizer, computer modem, or printer is used to convey the message to others.

Many symbol systems have been developed for use in aided communication systems. Symbol systems can be hierarchically ordered from linguistically simple concrete systems to complex written languages (see Table). Concrete linguistic systems are the easiest to learn. However, linguistically complex systems allow greater flexibility for communicative expression. The advantage of aided communication systems is flexibility. The communication aid and symbol system can be adapted to meet the physical and mental skills of almost any person. The symbol system can be permanently displayed to enhance symbol recall and memory. In addition, most aided communication systems can be easily understood by others without extensive listener training.

There are also many disadvantages to using aided communication systems. The devices themselves are often physically cumbersome and difficult to transport. Communication through a mechanical device also reduces speaker-listener eye contact and affects the location and distance from the speaker or a listener. The primary disadvantage of aided communication systems is an extremely slow rate of communication. Normal verbal communication rates range from 150 to 200 words per minute (Goldman-Eisler, 1986). Direct selection aided systems have rates that range from 6 to 25 words per minutes; scanning systems can be as slow as two words per minute (Foulds, 1980, 1987). This slow rate of communication tends to affect the style and amount of communicative interaction that occurs when using aided communication systems. Methods of increasing communication rate will be discussed later.

Before an augmentative communication system can be developed, a complete evaluation of the user's physical, linguistic, cognitive, and academic skills must be completed. This requires a team of professionals including speech-language pathologists, physical therapists, occupational therapists, and school psychologists. The physical evaluation should determine the user's gross motor skills, range of motion, adaptive posturing and seating, fine motor accuracy, and speed of movement. An evaluation of language skills should determine the user's current communication strategies and receptive language skills, and the communicative needs of the user (Beukelman & Mirenda, 1998). Academic and cognitive skills should be evaluated with a language specialist to determine a language symbol system that is within the user's capabilities. In addition, the academic and vocational skills and needs of the user should be identified. The evaluation results are then used to determine the communication aid, or unaided system, and symbolic system that best fits the user's needs.

When an aided communication system is being developed, the system should be designed to increase communication speed. Message cost can be used to analyze the communication speed of augmentative communication systems (Goodenough-Trepagnier, Tarry, & Prather, 1982; Higgenbotham, 1992). Message cost equals the number of separate motor movements necessary to encode a message. For example, the message cost of letter-by-letter encoding for "I want to go to the store" equals 25 when blank spaces between words are included. By using whole word symbols, message cost is reduced to seven. If unnecessary words are eliminated (i.e., "I want go store"), message cost is further reduced to four. Any system that requires more motor movements to encode messages will not result in effective communication.

Once an augmentative system is developed, extensive user training is required. There are two components to the training process. The first is augmentative system training. The user needs to learn how the augmentative system functions. Communication aid operation, vocabulary training, and the production of phrases and sentences are aspects of system training. The second component is communication training. Studies have documented that many nonspeaking persons who are trained to use their augmentative communication systems are unable to communicate effectively (Calculator & Bredosian, 1988; Light, 1988; Romski & Sevcik, 1988). Normal children learn how to interact communicatively and socially with others through experience. Nonspeaking persons have limited interactive experiences and need modeling of communicative and social interaction skills. Communication programming should concentrate on establishing the natural communication skills for the natural setting, in the same settings in which they will ultimately be used (Goosens, Crain, & Elder, 1995). Nonspeaking persons also need to learn how to respond to others, how to maintain conversations, and how to increase intelligibility in various contexts.

The ability to communicate with others is a binding element within members of a society. The development of augmentative communication systems has opened many avenues of communication for the nonspeaking population. While most augmentative systems are not yet perfect replacements for oral speech, they do provide a means of communication and interaction with others.

REFERENCES

American Speech-Language-Hearing Association. (1991). Report: Augmentative and Alternative Communication. *Asha, 33* (Suppl. 5), 9–12.

Beukelman, D. & Ansel, B. (1995). Research priorities in augmentative and alternative communication. *Augmentative and Alternative Communication, 11,* 131–134.

Beukelman, D. & Mirenda, P. (1998). *Augmentative and alternative communication.* Baltimore: Paul H. Brookes Publishing Co.

Bryen, D. & Joyce, D. (1985). Language intervention with the severely handicapped: a decade of research. *Journal of Special Education, 19,* 7–39.

Calculator, S. & Bredosian, J. H. (1988). *Communication assessment and intervention for adults with mental retardation.* San Diego: College-Hill Press.

Foulds, R. (1980). Communication rates of nonspeech expression as a function in manual tasks and linguistic constraints. In *Proceedings of the International Conference on Rehabilitation Engineering* (pp. 83–87). Toronto: RESNA Press.

Foulds, R. (1987). Guest editorial. *Augmentative and Alternative Communication, 3,* 169.

Goldman-Eisler, F. (1986). *Cycle linguistics: Experiments in spontaneous speech.* New York: Academic Press.

Goodenough-Trepagnier, C., Tarry, E., & Prather, P. (1982). Derivation of an efficient nonvocal communication system. *Human Factors, 24,* 163–172.

Goosens, C., Crain, S., & Elder, P. (1995). *Engineering the preschool environment for interactive symbolic communication.* Birmingham: Southeast Augmentative Communication Conference Publications.

Higgenbotham, D. J. (1992). Evaluation of keystroke savings across five assistive communication technologies. *Augmentative and Alternative Communication, 8,* 258–272.

Light, J. (1988). Interaction involving individuals using augmentative and alternative communication systems: State of the art and future directions. *Augmentative and Alternative Communication, 4,* 66–82.

Romski, M., & Sevcik, R. (1988). Augmentative and alternative communication systems: Considerations for individuals with severe intellectual disabilities. *Augmentative and Alternative Communication, 4,* 83–93.

SHARON L. GLENNEN
Pennsylvania State University

SHEELA STUART
George Washington University

AMAROUTIC FAMILIAL IDIOCY

See TAY-SACHS SYNDROME.

AMBLYOPIA

Amblyopia, also called suppression blindness (Harley & Lawrence, 1977), is a visual condition that occurs when an anatomically healthy eye cannot see because of some other defect (Eden, 1978). Amblyopia is commonly called "lazy eye"; however, this is a misnomer (Eden, 1978) because it implies that amblyopia results from a muscular problem. Actually, amblyopia can have a number of causes. For example, strabismus (a condition in which the two eyes are not parallel when viewing an object) can lead to amblyopia. The brain ignores the visual signals of one of the two eyes to reduce the annoyance of double vision. Other factors such as astigmatism can also lead to amblyopia.

The degree of visual impairment associated with amblyopia can vary a great deal from losses that are just below normal to those in which only large objects can be identified. Treatment of amblyopia consists of treating the causal factors. It must be accomplished early in life, (before the age of six) because the child is likely to permanently lose the ability to process a 20/20 image from the affected eye.

REFERENCES

Eden, J. (1978). *The eye book*. New York: Viking.

Harley, R. K., & Lawrence, G. A. (1977). *Visual impairment in the schools*. Springfield, IL: Thomas.

THOMAS E. ALLEN
Gallaudet College

BLIND
CATARACTS

AMERICAN ACADEMY FOR CEREBRAL PALSY AND DEVELOPMENTAL MEDICINE (AACPDM)

The American Academy for Cerebral Palsy, founded in 1947, changed its name in 1976 to the American Academy for Cerebral Palsy and Developmental Medicine (AACPDM). This is a professional organization of physicians, diplomates of specialty boards, and persons holding a Ph.D. degree in specialties concerned with diagnosis, care, treatment, and research into cerebral palsy and developmental disorders. The AACPDM's 1,200 members also include associate members from the fields of occupational and physical therapy and speech-language pathology.

The AACPDM's activities and services include the presentation of awards and grants for research, demonstration, and personnel preparation. The organization also supports or conducts continuing education activities. The AACPDM holds an annual convention. The office address is 6300 N. River Road, Suite 727, Rosemont, IL 60018.

SHIRLEY A. JONES
*Virginia Polytechnic Institute
and State University*
First edition

KAY KETZENBERGER
*The University of Texas of the
Permian Basin*
Second edition

AMERICAN ANNALS OF THE DEAF

The American *Annals of the Deaf* is a professional journal dedicated to quality in education and related services for hearing impaired children and adults. First published in 1847, the publication is the oldest and most widely read English language journal dealing with deafness and the education of deaf persons. The *Annals* is the official organ of the Convention of American Instructors of the Deaf and the Conference of Educational Administrators of Schools and Programs for the Deaf. Members of the executive committees of both organizations comprise the Joint *Annals* Administrative Committee charged with the direction and administration of the publication.

For 150 years, the *Annals* has primarily focused on the education of deaf students as well as dissemination of information for professionals associated with the educational development of this population. Concurrently, the *Annals* extends its range of topics beyond education, incorporating the broad interests of educators in the general welfare of deaf children and adults, and representing the diverse professional readership of the publication. Topics covered include communication methods and strategies, language development, mainstreaming and residential schools, parent-child relationships, and teacher training and teaching skills.

Four literary issues are published by the journal each year in March, July, October, and December. An annual reference issue, a comprehensive listing of schools and programs in the United States and Canada for students who are deaf or hard of hearing and their teachers, is also published by the *Annals*. In addition to the listings, the reference issue provides demographic, audiological, and educational data regarding students who are deaf and hard of hearing and the schools they attend. The data are compiled annually by the Center for Assessment and Demographic Studies, a component of the Gallaudet Research Institute.

CONFERENCE OF EDUCATIONAL
ADMINISTRATORS OF SCHOOLS
AND PROGRAMS FOR THE DEAF

AMERICAN ASSOCIATION FOR THE ADVANCEMENT OF SCIENCE (AAAS)

The American Association for the Advancement of Science (AAAS) was founded in Philadelphia in 1848, making it one of the oldest professional societies in the United States. AAAS is a nonprofit society dedicated to the advancement of scientific and technological quality across all fields of science, and to increasing the general public's understanding of science and technology. The mission of the organization, according to its Constitution, is to "further the work of scientists, facilitate cooperation among them, foster scientific freedom and responsibility, improve the effectiveness of science in the promotion of human welfare, advance education in science, and increase the public's understanding and appreciation of the promise of scientific methods in human progress" (AAAS, 1995).

Today AAAS's membership is international, and is composed of over 143,000 scientists, science educators, engineers, and interested others; membership is open to anyone interested in scientific and technological progress. There are 285 scientific and engineering societies that have chosen to affiliate themselves with the AAAS, and they include 238 other societies, 44 state and regional academies of science, and 3 city academies. AAAS is thus the world's largest federation of professional scientific organizations. The association is organized into 24 sections which represent the various fields of interest of members, and four regional divisions. Programs fall into one of three directorates: Education and Human Resources, International, and Science and Policy.

The Association publishes many science books and reference works, the most prestigious being the weekly *Science*, a highly respected publication which disseminates state-of-the-art scientific research.

REFERENCE

American Association for the Advancement of Science. (1995). General information. (http://www.aaas.org/aaas/geninfo.html.)

KAY E. KETZENBERGER
*The University of Texas of the
Permian Basin*

AMERICAN ASSOCIATION OF COLLEGES FOR TEACHER EDUCATION (AACTE)

The American Association of Colleges for Teacher Education is a national, voluntary association of colleges and universities with undergraduate and/or graduate programs committed to the preparation of professional educators, including teachers and other educational personnel. The Association is composed of over 700 member institutions representing both private and public colleges and universities of every size and located in every state, the District of Columbia, Puerto Rico, the Virgin Islands, and Guam. As a group, the AACTE institutions produce more than 85% of new educators each year.

The Association encourages major initiatives and innovations in teacher education, and serves as advocate for the profession on issues of interest to the membership, particularly in areas of certification, accreditation, and assessment. AACTE is a major influence in helping form federal and state educational policy, and is recognized as the primary representative of teacher education interests before Congress, state legislatures, other governmental agencies, and the media. The Association continues to advise the National Council for Accreditation of Teacher Education (NCATE) on issues of institutional standards and accreditation. AACTE publishes the biweekly newsletter *Briefs*, which reports on current happenings in the education, public policy, and government arenas to the teacher education community.

KAY E. KETZENBERGER
*The University of Texas of the
Permian Basin*

AMERICAN ASSOCIATION FOR MARRIAGE AND FAMILY THERAPY

The American Association for Marriage and Family Therapy (AAMFT), founded in 1942, is the national organization representing marriage and family therapists. The association seeks to (1) advance marriage and family therapy through increased understanding, research, and treatment, (2) establish and maintain standards for the education and training of marriage and family therapists, and (3) promote professional development, ethics, and conduct among marriage and family therapists. The AAMFT has over 23,000 members and offers four membership categories. Clinical, Associate, and Student members are mental health therapists or therapists-in-training who have met varying levels of AAMFT credential standards. Affiliate members are individuals in allied mental health professions who are interested in marriage and family therapy.

The AAMFT publishes three periodicals and a variety of books, videotapes, and brochures. The *Journal of Marital and Family Therapy* (the official journal of the association) offers current research findings in marriage and family therapy. The *Family Therapy News* provides the latest updates in the field of marriage and family therapy and *Practice Strategies* assists with practice management information and advice.

Each year the AAMFT sponsors an Annual Conference in early fall for training in family systems theory, practice, and research. Also, Summer Institutes are held for continued learning and professional development in marriage and family therapy. The association offices are located at 1133 15th Street, NW, Suite 300, Washington, DC 20005.

LINDA M. MONTGOMERY
The University of Texas of the Permian Basin

AMERICAN ASSOCIATION ON MENTAL RETARDATION (AAMR)

The American Association on Mental Retardation was founded in 1876, and claims over 9,500 members both in the United States and throughout the world. Its membership is composed of professionals from a large variety of academic disciplines who are interested in the field of mental retardation, as well as nonprofessionals who are involved in and care about mental retardation. One of its primary goals is to expand the possibilities for people with mental retardation to live fulfilling and productive lives.

The AAMR offers strong support to research in mental retardation in the service of increasing the knowledge and skills of all who are involved in the field of mental retardation, through the publication of two professional journals and the Association's newspaper *News and Notes*. The *American Journal on Mental Retardation* is a scholarly research journal, and *Mental Retardation* includes research, book reviews, and conceptual articles aimed at practitioners.

The AAMR is organized into 10 regions that cover the United States, Canada, and parts of the Pacific, and contains over 85 local, state, or provincial chapters. There are 16 divisions, the topics of which include, among others, administration, communication disorders, legal process and advocacy, medicine, psychology, occupational and physical therapy, and vocational rehabilitation. The Association also offers eight special interest groups, focused on creative arts therapies, direct support professionals, Down Syndrome, families, health promotions, mental health

services, multicultural concerns, and sexual/social concerns. Membership in the American Association on Mental Retardation is open to anyone concerned about mental retardation.

KAY E. KETZENBERGER
The University of Texas of the Permian Basin

AMERICAN BOARD OF PROFESSIONAL PSYCHOLOGY (ABPP)

Originally named the American Board of Examiners in Professional Psychology, this organization was renamed the American Board of Professional Psychology in 1968. Founded in 1947 with the support of the American Psychological Association, it is comprised of a board of 15 trustees with headquarters in Columbia, Missouri. This certification board conducts oral examinations and awards specialty certification in eleven specialties: behavioral psychology, clinical psychology, clinical neuropsychology, counseling psychology, family psychology, forensic psychology, health psychology, industrial/organizational psychology, psychoanalysis in psychology, rehabilitation psychology, and school psychology. Necessary for certification is 5 years of qualifying experience in psychological practice.

The ABPP annually presents the Distinguished Professional Achievement Award. This and other awards are presented at the annual convention of the American Psychological Association in August. Publications of the ABPP include the *Diplomate* newsletter and the *Directory of Diplomates* (biannual).

MARY LEON PERRY
Texas A & M University
First edition

KAY E. KETZENBERGER
The University of Texas of the Permian Basin
Second edition

AMERICAN BOARD OF PROFESSIONAL NEUROPSYCHOLOGY (ABPN)

The American Board of Professional Neuropsychology (ABPN) is a credentialing board that examines doctoral-level psychologists with specialized training in the field of clinical neuropsychology and awards diplomas if examination performance is satisfactory. Examinations consist of an essay exam concerning clinical casework, a work sample examination (wherein examinees submit for scrutiny two actual cases from their practice), and a 3-hour oral examination. Additionally, documentation of appropriate credentials and training is required. Incorporated in 1982, ABPN was the first (and as of this writing, the only) psychology credentialing board that has applied to be approved and certified by the National Commission of Certifying Agencies, the certification arm of the National Organization for Competency Assurance, an organization charged by the federal government with oversight and accreditation of health care certification bodies. The ABPN central office address is Care of the Executive Director, Dr. Michael Raymond, John Heinz Institute of Rehabilitation Medicine, Neuropsychology Services, 150 Mundy Street, Wilkes-Barre, PA 18702.

CECIL R. REYNOLDS
Texas A & M University

AMERICAN CANCER SOCIETY (ACS)

The American Cancer Society (ACS) is a voluntary organization committed to the elimination and control of cancer. This nationwide effort is conducted through 58 largely state-incorporated divisions and is accomplished through four major activities: (1) the public education program, which emphasizes regular, preventive care for adults, attention to specific warning signals, and information regarding positive outcomes when prompt diagnosis and preventive measures are adopted; (2) a comprehensive professional education program designed to stimulate health professionals to use the best cancer detection, diagnostic, and patient management techniques available, to exchange knowledge on the latest cancer-fighting techniques, and to disseminate new ideas and developments in the community; (3) a wide range of volunteer-based service and rehabilitation programs to assist cancer patients and their families with the necessary practical and emotional support so vital to coping with the wide-ranging effects of the disease; and (4) research into all aspects of cancer, from direct clinical investigations and training to prospective cancer prevention studies.

The ACS began in 1913, when fifteen physicians and business leaders gathered in New York City and founded the American Society for the Control of Cancer (ASCC). The Society's founders were aware that the disease, steeped in a climate of fear and denial, must be brought to the attention of the people. Articles were written for popular magazines and professional journals, a monthly bulletin providing information about cancer was published, and physicians were recruited throughout the United States in an attempt to increase public awareness.

In 1936, Marjorie G. Illig, an ASCC field representative and chair of the General Federation of Women's Clubs Committee on Public Health, proposed the creation of a legion of volunteers, with the sole purpose of waging war on cancer. The Women's Field Army, as this organization came to be known, was the driving force behind the agency's move to the forefront of voluntary health organizations.

Today, the core of the organization's effort resides in its 2 million volunteers who implement the society's public and professional education programs, service programs for patients and families, and raise funds for research programs.

The ASCC was reorganized in 1945, becoming the American Cancer Society (ACS), today's leader in the fight against cancer through its programs in research, patient services, prevention, detection and treatment, and advocacy. The Society strives to achieve this goal by promoting the early detection of cancer through education, intervention, and programs such as the Breast Cancer Network and Man to Man, a prostate cancer education and support group. In conjunction with these efforts, the ACS has increased its effort to protect children through comprehensive school health education and similar programs designed to discourage tobacco use and promote healthy living.

Scientists supported by ACS have successfully established the link between cancer and smoking, demonstrated the effectiveness of the Pap smear, developed cancer-fighting drugs and biological response modifiers, dramatically increased the cure rate for leukemia, and proved the safety and effectiveness of mammography. The American Cancer Society has committed almost $2 billion to research and funded 28 Nobel Prize winners.

CRAIG S. HIGGINS
Stonehill College
First edition

TAMARA J. MARTIN
*The University of Texas of the
    Permian Basin*
Second edition

AMERICAN EDUCATIONAL RESEARCH ASSOCIATION (AERA)

The American Educational Research Association (AERA) was founded in 1915 as the National Association of Directors of Educational Research. The AERA is an international organization of educators, professors, research directors, specialists, and graduate students interested in educational research. The objectives of AERA include improving the status and quality of research and promoting application and findings of research to educational problems (American Education Research Association, undated).

The AERA is divided into 12 divisions: administration, counseling and human development, curriculum studies, education in the professions, educational policy and politics, history and historiography, instruction and learning, measurement and research methodology, postsecondary education, school evaluation and program development, social context of education, and teaching and teacher education.

Journals published by the AERA include the American Educational Research *Journal, Educational Evaluation and Policy Analysis, Journal of Educational and Behavioral Statistics, Review of Educational Research, Educational Researcher, Review of Research in Education* (annual), *Encyclopedia of Educational Research*, and *Handbook of Research on Teaching* (both revised every 10 years).

The AERA holds an annual convention for the presentation of reports, papers, and awards. It also holds research training programs and monitors federal educational research activities.

REFERENCE

American Educational Research Association (Undated brochure). *American Educational Research Association: A membership for your discipline.* Washington, DC: Author.

Douglas L. Friedman
Fordham University

AMERICAN FOUNDATION FOR THE BLIND (AFB)

The American Foundation for the Blind (AFB), a nonprofit organization, was founded in 1921 to serve as the national partner of local services for the blind and visually impaired. The organization is a leading national resource for people who are blind or visually impaired, the organizations that serve them, and the general public. The mission of the organization is to enable people who are blind or visually impaired to achieve equality of access and opportunity in order to ensure freedom of choice in their lives.

The AFB traces its origins to a meeting of a group of professionals in Vinton, Iowa, in the summer of 1921 (Koestler, 1976). This meeting, comprised primarily of officers of the American Association of Workers for the Blind (AAWB), resulted in the recognition of the pressing need for a national organization that was not affiliated with special interest groups, professional organizations, or any local, regional, or state organization currently serving the needs of the blind (Hagerty, 1987).

Helen Keller was closely identified with AFB from the early 1920s until her death, and the organization is recognized as her cause in the United States. Working with AFB for over 40 years, she represented the organization in their efforts to educate legislators and the public about services needed for people who are blind.

AFB fulfills its mission through four primary areas of activity regarding the nonmedical aspects of blindness and visual impairment. Development, collection, and dissemination of information are accomplished by responding annually to 100,000 inquiries from people who are blind or visually impaired, their family and friends, professionals in the blindness field, and the general public requesting information about AFB's programs, services, and other topics related to blindness and visual impairment.

AFB activities in this area also include the publication of books, pamphlets, videos, and periodicals about blindness for professionals and consumers. The AFB publishes the leading professional journal of its kind, *Journal of Visual Impairment and Blindness*. In addition, the organization is responsible for maintaining and preserving the Helen Keller Archives, an invaluable collection of personal material donated by Helen Keller. AFB also houses the M. C. Migel Memorial Library, one of the world's largest collections of print materials on blindness.

Identification, analysis, and resolution of issues critical to people who are blind or visually impaired is achieved by setting priorities, analyzing policy options, and promoting feasible solutions in conjunction with experts and constituents in the field of blindness. Expertise is offered in program areas such as education, employment, aging, and technology; and policy research that positively affects the quality of life of people who are blind or visually impaired is conducted, evaluated, and published by the AFB. The organization also serves as an advocate for and evaluator of the development of assistive products and technology. Maintenance of the Careers & Technology Information Bank, a network of individuals who are blind from all 50 states and Canada who use assistive technology at home, school, or work and are able and willing to serve as mentors to others, is another function of the AFB.

In the accomplishment of its mission, the AFB also strives to educate policymakers and the public as to the needs and capabilities of people who are blind or visually impaired. Consulting on legislative issues and representing blind and visually impaired persons before Congress and government agencies accomplishes this goal. Corporate and public awareness of the capabilities of people who are blind or visually impaired is also increased through publications, audio/visual presentations, exhibits, and public service announcements.

AFB production and distribution of books and other audio materials includes recording and duplicating Talking

Books under contract to the Library of Congress. The organization also records and duplicates annual reports and other publications for various corporations and nonprofit organizations, thus making them accessible to print-handicapped employees, clients, and shareholders.

For more information about AFB, write the American Foundation for the Blind, 11 Penn Plaza, Suite 300, New York, NY 10001 or call 1-800-AFB-LINE (232-5463); in New York State, (212) 502-7657.

REFERENCE

Hagerty, S. J. (1987). American Foundation for the Blind. In C. R. Reynolds & L. Mann (Eds.), *Encyclopedia of Special Education* (1st ed.). New York, NY: Wiley.

Koestler, F. A. (1976). *The Unseen Minority*. New York: McKay.

TAMARA J. MARTIN
*The University of Texas of the
Permian Basin*

AMERICAN GUIDANCE SERVICE (AGS)

American Guidance Service, Inc. is an educational publishing company founded in 1957, and is an employee-owned company that encourages partnership and ongoing dialogue with the professionals that use its products. AGS publishes a wide variety of norm-referenced assessment instruments for the identification of special needs students, focusing primarily on cognitive ability, achievement, behavior, and personal and social adjustment, with many publications also available in Spanish. Their better-known tests include the Peabody Picture Vocabulary Test (PPVT-III), Vineland Adaptive Behavior Scales, the Kaufman Test of Educational Achievement (K-TEA), and the Developmental Indicators for the Assessment of Learning (DIAL-III). AGS also publishes The Behavioral Assessment System for Children, known popularly as the BASC, which became their best selling test during 1999, and is now used with over one million children annually.

In addition to testing materials, AGS publishes a great many instructional materials, including over 900 textbooks, as well as programs for parenting and family living. Much of their material is focused on children with learning/emotional problems or in special education, though they also publish material geared to all ages. AGS can be reached at 4201 Woodland Road, Circle Pines, MN 55014-1796, or by phone at (800) 328-2560 or (612) 786-4343.

TAMARA J. MARTIN
*The University of Texas of the
Permian Basin*

AMERICAN INSTITUTE—THE TRAINING SCHOOL AT VINELAND

The American Institute—The Training School at Vineland, is located in Vineland, New Jersey (Main Road and Landis Avenue, Vineland, NJ 08360). The school and training facility were founded in 1887; they are under the supervision and administrative management of Elwyn Institutes. The facility serves children and adults who are mentally retarded, brain damaged, emotionally disturbed, physically handicapped, and learning disabled.

The school programs are ungraded at the elementary and secondary levels. The school features education and training programs that are designed to train young people to return to the community. The training programs serve mildly handicapped to the severely retarded students. The range of educational programs and vocational training experiences are developed with individualized educational plans and rehabilitation services. The facility is internationally recognized for the pioneering works of Binet and Doll. The Stanford Binet tests were translated and norms were developed at the school. Dr. Edward Doll is recognized as the pioneer in the development of the Vineland Social Maturity Scale.

REFERENCE

Sargent, J. K. (1982). *The Directory for exceptional children* (9th ed.). Boston, MA: Porter Sargent.

PAUL C. RICHARDSON
Elwyn Institutes

AMERICAN JOURNAL OF MENTAL RETARDATION (AJMR)

Originally known as the *American Journal of Mental Deficiency, AJMR* is published on a bimonthly basis by the American Association on Mental Retardation (AAMR). The original title reflected the original name of the sponsoring organization, which was changed from the American Organization on Mental Deficiency (AAMD) to its current name in 1987. The primary purpose of the journal is to publish theoretical manuscripts and research in the area of mental retardation, with an emphasis on meterial of an objective, scientific, and experimental nature. Book reviews are included. The journal address is 1719 Kalorama Road, N.W., Washington, D.C. 20009.

STAFF

AMERICAN JOURNAL OF OCCUPATIONAL THERAPY (AJOT)

The *American Journal of Occupational Therapy (AJOT)* is an official publication of the American Occupational Therapy Association. *AJOT* is published monthly except for July/August and November/December, when it appears in bimonthly issues. Manuscripts are subjected to anonymous peer review. Accepted articles pertain to occupational therapy and may include reports of research, educational activities, or professional trends; descriptions of new occupational therapy approaches, programs, or services; review papers that survey new information; theoretical papers that discuss or treat theoretical issues critically; descriptions of original therapeutic aids, devices, or techniques; case reports that describe occupational therapy for a specific clinical situation; or opinion essays that discuss timely issues or opinions and are supported by cogent arguments. In addition, the journal contains letters to the editor, publication reviews, and product advertising.

AJOT is abstracted or indexed by Applied Science Index and Abstracts, Behavioral Medicine Abstracts, Cumulative Index to Nursing and Allied Health Literature, Exceptional Child Education Resources, Excerpta Medica, Inc., Hospital Literature Index, Index Medicus, Institute for Scientific Information, MEDLINE, OT BibSys, Psychological Abstracts, and Social Sciences Citation Index. Microfilms of complete volumes can be obtained from University Microfilms, Inc.

ELIZABETH HOLCOMB
*American Journal of
Occupational Therapy*

AMERICAN JOURNAL OF ORTHOPSYCHIATRY (AJO)

The *American Journal of Orthopsychiatry (AJO)*, is the quarterly journal of the American Orthopsychiatric Association. The association was founded in 1926 and began publication of *AJO* in 1930. The *AJO* is a quarterly, refereed, scholarly journal written from a multidisciplinary perspective. The *AJO* is dedicated to public policy, professional practice, and information that relates to mental health and human development. Clinical, theoretical, research, review, and expository papers are published in *AJO*. These papers are essentially synergistic and directed at concept and theory development, reconceptualization of major issues, explanation, and interpretation.

The *AJO* concentrates on many topics of concern to special educators. During its lifetime, *AJO*'s articles have cen-

tered around the topics of social issues and the handicapped, childhood psychosis, psychopharmacology, school phobia, depression, suicide, child abuse, mental retardation, and treatment of all of these disorders. The contributors' list and editorial board have, over the years, featured some of the finest scholars from developmental medicine, developmental psychopathology, child development, school psychology, clinical psychology, special education, neurology, psychiatry, and related mental health fields. The *AJO* is an influential journal that publishes top scholars' writing on special education.

CECIL R. REYNOLDS
Texas A & M University

AMERICAN ORTHOPSYCHIATRIC ASSOCIATION

AMERICAN JOURNAL OF PSYCHIATRY

The *American Journal of Psychiatry* began publication in 1844 as the *American Journal of Insanity*, changing to its current title in 1921. It is the official journal of the American Psychiatric Association, and is the most widely read psychiatric journal in the world. Published monthly, the *American Journal of Psychiatry* publishes peer-reviewed research studies and articles that focus on developments in the biological aspects of psychiatry, on treatment issues and innovations, and on forensic, ethical, social, and economic topics. Letters to the editor, book reviews, and official American Psychiatric Association reports are also included. Of special interest to many readers are the overview and special lead articles, which address major psychiatric syndromes and issues in depth.

KAY E. KETZENBERGER
*The University of Texas of the
Permian Basin*

AMERICAN OCCUPATIONAL THERAPY FOUNDATION

The American Occupational Therapy Foundation was founded in 1965 as the American Occupational Therapy Association's (AOTA) philanthropic sister organization. The foundation has devoted its energies to raising funds and resources in three program areas—publications, research, and scholarships—associated with the profession of occupational therapy and health-care delivery.

The foundation's publication program aims to increase

public knowledge and understanding of the occupational therapy profession. In addition to various reports and documents, it publishes *The Occupational Therapy Journal of Research*, and has produced a major bibliography of completed research in the field. The foundation supports the Occupational Therapy Library, which supplies requested materials through interlibrary loan.

A research program is conducted through the foundation's Office of Professional Research Services. Program services include the Academy of Research, support of researchers through grant awards (in association with the AOTA), and doctoral and postdoctoral fellowship awards to support researchers. The foundation widely disseminates scholarship information for undergraduate and graduate students in occupational therapy publications and through occupational therapy schools.

The American Occupational Therapy Foundation is located at 4720 Montgomery Lane, P.O. Box 31220, Bethesda, MD 20824.

SHIRLEY A. JONES
*Virginia Polytechnic Institute
and State University*
First edition

KAY KETZENBERGER
*The University of Texas of the
Permian Basin*
Second edition

AMERICAN ORTHOPSYCHIATRIC ASSOCIATION (ORTHO)

The American Orthopsychiatric Association (Ortho) was formed at the invitation of Herman Adler and Karl Menninger at the Institute for Juvenile Research in Chicago in 1924 under the name of the Association of American Orthopsychiatrists. The group operated informally, debating its name and purpose and finally founding Ortho a year later. In 1926 Ortho amended its constitution, which limited membership to physicians, to redefine membership to include psychiatrists, psychologists, social workers, and other professional persons "whose work and interests lie in the study and treatment of conduct disorders." According to Eisenberg and DeMaso (1985), the first published membership roster, published October 1, 1927, included 45 psychiatrists, 12 psychologists, 5 social workers, and several lawyers and penologists. Ortho had as its purpose the centralization of the techniques, objectives, and aspirations of psychiatrists, psychologists, and related mental health workers whose primary interests were in the area of human behavior, providing a common meeting ground for

students of behavior problems and for fostering scientific research and its dissemination. The early membership included names familiar to special educators, including such notables as Edgar Doll, Lightner Witmer, and Carl Murchison.

Lightner Witmer, noted among historians of psychology as the man who coined the term clinical psychology, founded school psychology and established the first psychological clinic; he also coined the term orthogenics and established the team approach to children's problems when he invited neurologists to collaborate on case studies (Eisenberg & DeMaso, 1985). Ortho subsequently became a major force in the establishment of the child guidance movement in the early 1900s. In 1930 Ortho established the *American Journal of Orthopsychiatry*, a widely read and respected journal that in its early years vigorously debated the roles and functions of various professionals (e.g., psychiatrists, psychologists, social workers, etc.) in the treatment of childhood mental health disorders.

Presently, many special educators belong to Ortho. It is a large, robust organization of more than 10,000 members. It is involved in social, scientific, and public policy issues, including diagnosis, evaluation, and treatment, relevant to the improvement of the lives of the handicapped. The *American Journal of Orthopsychiatry* is provided as a benefit of membership; it contains many articles of interest to special educators. The association is located at 330 7th Ave., 18th Floor, NY: NY 10001-5010.

REFERENCE

American Orthopsychiatric Association. (1998). *About Ortho.* http//www.amerortho.org/ortho2.htm.

Eisenberg, L., & DeMaso, D. R. (1985). Fifty years of the *American Journal of Orthopsychiatry*: An overview and introduction. In E. Flaxman & E. Herman (Eds.), *American Journal of Orthopsychiatry: Annotated index: Vols. 1–50. 1930–1980.* Greenwich, CT: JAI.

CECIL R. REYNOLDS
Texas A & M University

AMERICAN JOURNAL OF ORTHOPSYCHIATRY
WITMER, LIGHTNER

AMERICAN PHYSICAL THERAPY ASSOCIATION

The American Physical Therapy Association (APTA) endeavors to improve physical therapy services and education through accrediting academic programs in physical therapy; assisting states in preparing certification examinations; and offering workshops and continuing education courses for therapists at the national and local level. Information is available about careers in physical therapy, accredited preparation programs, sources of student financial aid, and employment opportunities. A variety of pamphlets are available on prevention of injuries and chronic or degenerative conditions. The association publishes a newsletter and journal. Bibliographies have been prepared on topics including resources for stroke victims, quadriplegics, paraplegics, amputees, parents, and educators. Members benefit from information on questions regarding practice and disabilities. The association also serves as a referral source for individuals who require physical therapy services. Association offices are located at 1111 North Fairfax Street, Alexandria, VA 22314. Telephone: (703) 684-2782; e-mail: www.apta.org.

PHILIP R. JONES
*Virginia Polytechnic Institute
and State University*

AMERICAN PRINTING HOUSE FOR THE BLIND (APH)

The American Printing House for the Blind (APH), the oldest private, nonprofit institution for the blind in the United States, was founded in Louisville, Kentucky in 1858. It is the world's largest company devoted solely to creating products and services for people who are visually impaired. The Act to Promote the Education of the Blind, mandated by Congress in 1879, enabled the American Printing House for the Blind to receive grants for education texts and aids for those with visual impairments from the federal government. Funds appropriated under the Act are used by each state to purchase educational materials from APH for their blind students below the college level (American Printing House for the Blind, 1998).

The Company's mission is to promote the independence of blind and visually impaired persons by providing special media, tools, and materials needed for education and life. A wide variety of products and services are available through APH, including braille, large type, recorded, computer disk, and tactile graphic publications as well as a wide assortment of educational and daily living products. Various services designed to assist consumers and professionals in the field of vision are also offered, including *Louis*, a database listing materials available from accessible media across North America and *Patterns*, a reading instruction program developed through APH research.

APH's Talking Books on cassette tape, produced in agency recording studios, are a popular reading medium for blind and visually impaired people of all ages. Fiction and nonfiction topics, ranging from romance to cookbooks, are produced by professional narrators who are also teachers, actors, and media personalities. Most Talking Books can be obtained on a free loan basis from the National Library for the Blind and Physically Handicapped, a division of the Library of Congress. Three magazines are offered by APH directly to eligible blind readers. They include *Readers Digest*, *Newsweek*, and *Weekly Reader*.

In addition to the publications and products provided to those who are visually impaired, APH maintains a national center for research and development, focusing on the creation of products for blind students and adults, and a museum, offering a look at the history of education of blind people.

REFERENCE

American Printing House for the Blind. (1998). What is the American Printing House for the Blind? Louisville, KY: Author.

TAMARA J. MARTIN
*The University of Texas of the
Permian Basin*

AMERICAN PSYCHIATRIC ASSOCIATION (APA)

The American Psychiatric Association was founded in 1844 as the Association of Medical Superintendents of American Institutions for the Insane, and changed to its current name in 1921. The APA is a national medical specialty society that had over 40,000 members in 1998; members are physicians who specialize in the diagnosis and treatment of mental, emotional, and substance abuse disorders. The Association's major focus areas include mental health, psychopharmacology, psychotherapy, and health professions development, and its primary objectives include the advancement and improvement of care for people with mental illnesses through the provision of nationwide education, public information, and awareness programs and materials.

The Association publishes the *American Journal of Psychiatry* (its official monthly journal), *Hospital and Community Psychiatry* (monthly), and *Psychiatric News* (twice monthly). The APA offers many continuing education workshops, seminars, and courses, as well as library services for members. The APA can be contacted at their national offices at 1400 K Street, NW, Washington, DC, 20005.

KAY E. KETZENBERGER
*The University of Texas of the
Permian Basin*

AMERICAN PSYCHOLOGICAL ASSOCIATION

The American Psychological Association (APA) is the nation's major psychology organization. The APA works to advance psychology as a science and a profession, and to promote human welfare. When the APA was established in 1892, psychology was a new profession and the organization had fewer than three dozen members. Over the years the organization has grown rapidly: In 1998 the APA had more than 155,000 members, 51 divisions in specialized subfields and interest areas, and 58 affiliated state, provincial, and territorial psychological associations.

The growth of the science and profession of psychology is reflected in the development of diverse programs and services administered by the association. These programs aim to disseminate psychological knowledge, promote research, improve research methods and conditions, and develop the qualifications and competence of psychologists through standards of education, ethical conduct, and professional practice.

The program and business activities of the APA are coordinated at the association's central office in Washington, DC. These offices are headquarters for APA's programs in governance affairs, national policy studies, public affairs, communications, and financial affairs. Through these programs, the central office staff provides information to members, other professionals, students, and the public through the publication of books, major journals, pamphlets, the monthly APA *Monitor* newspaper, and a growing spectrum of bibliographic and abstracting services covering the literature of psychology.

The affairs of the association are administered by the Board of Directors, which is responsible for the work of an executive officer who administers the affairs of the central office. The Board of Directors is composed of a president, past president, and president-elect, all of whom are elected by APA members at large, and a treasurer, a secretary, and six board members who are elected by the Council of Representatives. The Council of Representatives is composed of members of the association who are elected by their division and state members in proportion to the annual assignment of seats by the membership. The Council of Representatives sets policy for the association, and those policies are administered by the Board of Directors through the executive officer and the staff of the central office.

The governance affairs office of the association coordinates and directs psychology programs and activities such as accreditation of doctoral programs in professional psychology and predoctoral internship sites; supervision of educational affairs aimed at identifying and analyzing developments in higher education and training of psychologists; setting standards for scientific and professional ethics, professional affairs, scientific affairs, social and ethical responsibility of psychologists, and overseeing special issues concerning minority groups and women's programs.

The national policy studies of APA help to formulate and implement federal policy and legislative activities of the association. The Public Policy Office develops advocacy positions, informs Congress and federal agencies of psychology's concerns, keeps the APA membership and governance structure informed of related policy issues, and develops working coalitions with outside organizations on common legislative issues.

The Public Affairs Office works to provide overall direction on the ways organized psychology is presented to its national and international public. The office works with television, radio, and print media to demonstrate the contributions psychologists make to society and to improve public understanding of psychology's broad scope and application.

The APA publishes more than 30 periodicals and a variety of books, brochures, and pamphlets. Among these are *American Psychologist*, the official journal of the association, and *Psychological Abstracts*, which contains abstracts of the world's literature on psychology and related disciplines.

Each year more than 12,000 psychologists and other individuals attend the APA convention in late summer. This is the world's largest meeting of psychologists and one of the largest professional conventions in the United States. The week-long program features more than 3,000 presentations through symposiums, lectures, invited addresses, specialized workshops, and other forums. Through the convention, practitioners and the public are given the opportunity to learn of the latest findings from psychological research, their applications in society, and other professional, scientific, and educational issues.

From energy conservation and industrial productivity to child development, aging, and prevention of stress and related illness, hardly a personal or national problem exists that does not demand an understanding of human behavior. Even modern technological innovations emerge from the ability of the mind to transform observations and data into action. Because of their fundamental understanding of behavior, psychologists are increasingly consulted for ways to increase human progress and well-being.

NADINE M. LAMBERT
University of California

AMERICAN PSYCHOLOGIST

American Psychologist is the official journal of the American Psychological Association. Published monthly, it is the most widely circulated psychological journal in the world, going out to the more than 155,000 members of the Association around the globe. It is a primary source of discussion on cutting-edge issues in psychology, and it publishes empirical, theoretical, and practical articles on broad aspects of psychology. It is indexed in over 20 abstracting/indexing services, including PsycINFO, Index Medicus, Academic Index, Social Sciences Index, and Applied Social Science Index & Abstracts, making its contents easily discoverable and thus highly available to users. As the official journal of the association, it contains archival documents, including the minutes of the annual business meeting, and reports of the officers, directorates, and committees whose work involves policies and practices affecting members of the association. The journal also publishes a commentary section, obituaries of well-known psychologists, and (in each year's December issue) a listing of all APA-approved doctoral training programs in clinical, counseling, and school psychology in the United States and Canada.

In setting forth general editorial policy for the *American Psychologist*, past and present editors have agreed that the journal should (1) contribute to enlightened participation in the profession of psychology and thereby to effective function of the association, (2) provide a forum for the examination of the relationship between psychology and society, especially as historical, cultural, and societal influences have an impact on the science and practice of psychology, (3) foster the development of the diverse applications of psychological knowledge, and (4) present and disseminate psychological knowledge in a form and style suitable to the general membership and to the interested public.

The current editor is Raymond D. Fowler. All submissions for publication are mask reviewed in a peer-review process. The journal's offices are housed within the American Psychological Association's national headquarters, located at 750 First Street, NE, Washington, DC, 20002-4242.

Nadine M. Lambert
University of California
First edition

Kay E. Ketzenberger
The University of Texas of the Permian Basin
Second edition

AMERICAN SIGN LANGUAGE

During the past 20 years, there has been a rapid and widespread increase in the use of sign language as a viable means of communication by deaf and hearing individuals. American Sign Language (ASL), also known as Ameslan, has been recognized as a natural language with its own unique grammatical structure (Klima & Bellugi, 1979; Liddell, 1980; Wilbur, 1979). Approximately half a million deaf Americans and Canadians currently use ASL (Wilbur, 1979).

Systematic research on the linguistic bases of ASL and the importance of sign language to the cultural identity of the deaf community began less than two decades ago. In 1960 William Stokoe published the first linguistic analysis of American Sign Language, and in 1965 he and his associates published the first dictionary of ASL (Stokoe, Casterline, & Croneberg, 1976). The 1970s and early 1980s were an exceptionally active period in terms of deafness and sign language research. Much of the research during this period examined the linguistic aspects of ASL, while only a few studies investigated psycholinguistic, sociolinguistic, and/or developmental issues.

Sign language is composed of specific movements and shapes of the hands, arms, eyes, face, head, and body that correspond to the words and suprasegmental features of spoken languages. In delineating the major components of ASL, linguists find it useful to differentiate between manual and nonmanual aspects of signing. Sign formation, originally called "cherology" by Stokoe (1960), corresponds to the phonological system of oral languages. Each sign consists of four basic parameters: hand shape (dez); location or place of articulation (tab); movement in a particular direction (sig); and palm orientation occurring with various hand shapes.

Another way of classifying signs is on the basis of specific morphologic and/or lexical characteristics. One family of signs is that based on motion and direction differences. For example, the sign for "appear" is formed by bringing the right index finger up between the index and middle fingers of the left hand. By moving in the opposite direction, that is by drawing the right index finger down, the signer creates the sign for "disappear." Some families of signs are based on hand shape. Signs expressing emotion are produced with the open eight hand shape, where the middle fingertip touches the thumb to form the hand shape for the number eight. This hand shape occurs in the signs "excite," "depress," "feel," and "like."

Some families of signs are based on the location of the sign in space. Masculine and feminine signs are differentiated on the basis of location. For example, the sign for "man" is made at the forehead by grasping the imaginary brim of a hat with four fingers and the thumb and then bringing the flat hand, palm down, away from the head at the level of the imaginary hat. The sign of "woman" is produced at the level of the cheek by moving the inside of the thumb of the right "A" hand shape down along the right cheek toward the chin and then bringing the flat hand, palm down, away from the face.

There are similarities in some of the syntactic mechanisms used in ASL and English; others are specialized to accommodate communication in the visual—gestural mode. It has been argued that sign order is relatively flexible and that several built in syntactic devices help to convey information efficiently. One such device is the deletion of grammatical morphemes such as articles and the copular verb "to be." Information is preserved by establishing positions of reference in space and referring to them through pointing and eye gaze. A second device is the incorporation of location, number, manner, size, and shape of signs. A third syntactic device is the use of nonmanual signals, for example, facial expressions and body posture. These are important in terms of syntactic as well as semantic and pragmatic functions in ASL, and they frequently assume a role similar to the suprasegmentals in speech (Liddell, 1980). Eye gaze is used to perform indexic reference or even to establish the reference in a conversation. Raising the eyebrow is used as a topic marker and in forming questions. Eye blinking is relevant to the proper interpretation of conditional sentences and interrogatives. A head shake over part or all of a signed utterance may negate that part or the entire sign communication. Also, certain nonmanual behaviors are associated with particular lexical items. For example, the sign for "bite" is accompanied by a biting motion of the mouth. The sign for "relieved" is accompanied by rapid exhaling and a burst of air through pursed lips. Frequently, a combination of nonmanual signals is used to convey specific linguistic constructions and semantic relations.

In addition to studies of the linguistic bases of American Sign Language, the research of the previous decade focused primarily on psycholinguistic, neurolinguistic, and sociolinguistic aspects of sign language; and studies of the acquisition of sign language in deaf children. For a review of this and related research, the reader is referred to Lane and Grosjean (1980), Prinz (1981), and Strong (1987).

REFERENCES

Klima, E. S., & Bellugi, U. (1979). *The signs of language*. Cambridge, MA: Harvard University Press.

Lane, H., & Grosjean, F. (Eds.). (1980). *Recent perspectives on American Sign Language*. Hillsdale, NJ: Erlbaum.

Liddell, S. (1980). *American Sign Language syntax*. The Hague: Mouton.

Prinz, P. M. (1981). Recent perspectives on the development of sign language in deaf children. *Journal of the National Student Speech-Language-Hearing Association, 9*(1), 50–65.

Stokoe, W. C. (1960). Sign language structure: An outline of the visual communication systems of American deaf. *Studies in Linguistics, Occasional Papers, 8*.

Stokoe, W. C., Casterline, D. C., & Croneberg, C. G. (1976). *A dictionary of American Sign Language on linguistic principles* (2nd ed.). Silver Spring, MD: Linstok Press.

Strong, M. A. (Ed.). (1987). *Language learning and deafness*. Cambridge, England: Cambridge University Press.

Wilbur, R. B. (1979). *American Sign Language and sign systems*. Baltimore, MD: University Park Press.

PHILIP M. PRINZ
ELISABETH A. PRINZ
Pennsylvania State University

ALTERNATIVE COMMUNICATION METHODS IN SPECIAL EDUCATION
AUGMENTATIVE COMMUNICATION SYSTEMS

AMERICAN SOCIETY FOR DEAF CHILDREN (ASDC)

The American Society for Deaf Children is a national nonprofit organization of parents and families of deaf or hard of hearing children, founded in 1967. Its stated purpose is to provide support, encouragement, and information to families of deaf children, and to advocate for their total high-quality participation in education and the community. ASDC furnishes information upon request to help families base their decisions on current and accurate information, supports the use of signing, and promotes a positive attitude toward deaf culture.

The ASDC operates a Parents Hotline at (800) 942-ASDC, and their national offices are located at 1820 Tribute Road, Suite A, Sacramento, CA 95815. The ASDC can be contacted at (916) 641-6084 (Business V/TTY).

KAY E. KETZENBERGER
The University of Texas of the Permian Basin

AMERICAN SPEECH-LANGUAGE-HEARING ASSOCIATION (ASHA)

The American Speech-Language-Hearing Association is the professional and scientific association for more than 96,000 speech-language pathologists, audiologists, and speech, language, and hearing scientists in the United States as well as internationally. Its stated mission is to promote the interests of professionals in audiology and speech-language pathology, and work for the provision of the highest quality services for people with communication disorders.

In the early 1900's, a number of practitioners were actively engaged in the treatment of communication disorders. Unfortunately, there were also a few unscrupulous individuals who made claims about their ability to cure communication disorders for exorbitant fees. Those involved in the ethical treatment of speech disorders saw an immediate need to protect the public from this small minority of opportunistic individuals. This became the prime motivation for forming an organization of speech and hearing professionals.

The ethical practitioners of speech correction began working in public schools and publishing the results of their clinical work in the 1920's, with most belonging to the National Association of Teachers of Speech (NATS). They published in the *Quarterly Journal of Speech Education* and met as a special interest group at NATS meetings.

In 1925, a small group interested in communication disorders met in Iowa City, Iowa, to create an organization devoted entirely to the study and treatment of communication disorders, naming it the American Academy of Speech Correctionists. In 1935, the group's 87 members changed its name to the American Speech Correction Association. In 1947 the name was changed again, to the American Speech and Hearing Association (ASHA). The current name of the organization, American Speech-Language-Hearing Association, was adopted in 1978.

One of ASHA's most important actions was the development of standards for a Certificate of Clinical Competence in Speech Pathology (CCC-SP) and Audiology (CCC-A). Professionals in communication disorders must meet stringent training and experience standards in order to qualify for these prestigious certifications. ASHA continues to work actively with state governments on licensing procedures for communication disorder professionals, and remains the voice of the professions of speech-language pathology and audiology.

The ASHA offices are located at 10801 Rockville Pike, Rockville, MD 20852, and may be reached by telephone at (800) 498-2071, for hearing impaired individuals at (301) 897-5700 (TTY), or by fax at (301) 571-0457.

REFERENCE

Paden, E. P. (1970). *A history of the American Speech and Hearing Association, 1925–1958*. Washington, DC: American Speech and Hearing Association.

FREDERICK F. WEINER
Pennsylvania State University
First edition

KAY E. KETZENBERGER
The University of Texas of the Permian Basin
Second edition

AMERICANS WITH DISABILITIES ACT (ADA)

The Americans with Disabilities Act of 1990 (ADA) is a comprehensive civil rights law designed to prohibit discrimination against people with disabilities. ADA is a civil rights law; therefore, it preempts any other local, state, or federal law that grants lesser rights to individuals with disabilities (National Association of State Directors of Special Education [NASDSE], 1992). Federal funding is not provided to carry out the ADA mandates; however, a wide range of public and private institutions, including educational institutions, are required to comply with the ADA provisions. The purpose of ADA is "1) to provide a clear and comprehensive national mandate for the elimination of discrimination against individuals with disabilities; 2) to provide clear, strong, consistent, enforceable standards addressing discrimination against individuals with disabilities; 3) to ensure that the federal government plays a central role in enforcing the standards established in this Act on behalf of individuals with disabilities; and 4) to invoke the sweep of congressional authority, including the power to enforce the 14th Amendment, to address the major areas of discrimination faced by people with disabilities" (42 U.S.C. §§ 12101 Sec 2 [b] [1–4]). ADA derives its substance from Section 504 of the Rehabilitation Act of 1973, but its procedures from Title VII of the Civil Rights Act of 1964, amended in 1991 (First & Curcio, 1993).

In 1988, the ADA bill was first introduced in Congress in response to mounting evidence that Americans with disabilities, over 40 million strong, faced an inordinate number of inequities in different spheres of life (Jacob-Timm & Hartshorne, 1995). Moreover, congressional testimony had documented a strong link between disability and economic and social hardships, and limited educational opportunities (Burgdorf, 1991). Based on these inequities and disadvantages, congressional legislative action was taken to bring individuals with disabilities into the American social and economic mainstream through the enactment of ADA. The U.S. Congress approved the final version of the bill on July 13, 1990, and President George Bush signed it into law on July 26, 1990.

The ADA consists of five titles. The areas addressed in these five titles include employment, public services, public accommodations, telecommunications, and miscellaneous provisions. Title I prohibits discrimination in employment of persons with disabilities. Under this title, employers must reasonably accommodate the disabilities of the "otherwise qualified" applicants or employees unless "undue hardship" would result. An example of an "undue hardship" would be a significant difficulty or excessive expense to the employer associated with making alterations or modifications at the job site to accommodate a qualified applicant who is also an individual with a disability. All school districts, regardless of the number of personnel employed, are subject to Title I standards.

Title II prohibits discrimination in programs, activities, and services provided by state and local governments and their instrumentalities. Title II applies to all public entities, such as public schools, regardless of federal funding status. Under Title II, school facilities, whether existing facilities or under construction, must meet accessibility requirements for individuals with disabilities consistent with Section 504 of the Rehabilitation Act (First & Curcio, 1993). Public transportation, like buses and rail vehicles, must also meet accessibility requirements. Title II requires school districts to provide appropriate aids so that individuals with disabilities have equal opportunities to participate in available programs and services. Likewise, districts are required to give primary consideration to disabled individuals' requests and to ensure that individuals with hearing or visual impairments receive information in an appropriate and understandable format about available programs and services. Examples of public school programs, services, and activities covered by Title II include public entertainment or lectures sponsored by the school district, afterschool activities and social events offered by the schools, parent-teacher conferences, classroom activities, field trips, and any other service provided for students or staff (Office of Civil Rights [OCR], 1996).

Title III prohibits discrimination based on disability in privately owned public accommodations. Nonsectarian private schools and school bus transportation, as well as other privately owned public accommodations must make reasonable alterations in policies, practices, and procedures to avoid discrimination. Nonsectarian private schools must provide auxiliary aids and services to individuals with visual or hearing impairments. In addition, physical barriers must be removed unless readily unachievable. If not readily achievable, alternate methods of providing services must be offered. All new construction and alterations in existing facilities must be handicap-accessible. School bus transportation services, such as bus routes, must be comparable in duration and distance, for disabled and nondisabled individuals.

Title IV requires telephone companies to provide telecommunication relay services for hearing and speech impaired individuals. Closed-captioned public service announcements must also be provided. Under Title IV, schools must ensure that communication with disabled individuals is just as effective as communication with nondisabled individuals.

Title V consists of a variety of provisions. The title identifies the federal agencies responsible for the enforcement and technical assistance related to ADA. The federal agency responsible for the enforcement of Title II, Subtitle A, programs, activities, and services provided by state and local governments and their instrumentalities, which extends to all public school systems, is the Office of Civil

Rights (OCR) in the Department of Education. The OCR not only enforces the ADA provisions under Title II, Subtitle A, but it also handles complaints filed with regard to alleged violations of this title. Title V also dictates that state governments are not immune from legal actions related to ADA. In addition, individuals with disabilities have the right to accept or reject accommodations and services offered under ADA. Furthermore, individuals with or without disabilities cannot be coerced or retaliated against for exercising their rights under ADA. The title also addresses the relationship between ADA and other laws and its impact on insurance providers and benefits.

In examining the relationship between ADA and other federal laws affecting persons with disabilities, ADA is viewed as a complementary law (Conconan-Lahr, 1991). ADA does not diminish any of the rights of disabled individuals under the Civil Rights Act of 1964, as amended in 1991, Individuals with Disabilities Education Act (IDEA), or Section 504 of the Rehabilitation Act of 1973 (NASDSE, 1992).

Section 504 and ADA espouse the same underlying principle, which is that entities under their jurisdiction cannot discriminate against individuals with disabilities in their programs, activities, and services (Cunconan-Lahr, 1991). To eliminate discrimination, both laws stress the importance of equal opportunity, not just equal treatment, for disabled and nondisabled individuals. However, ADA does create a higher standard of nondiscrimination than does Section 504 in several respects. First, Section 504 applies only to recipients of federal funding, whereas ADA applies to employment, public services, public accommodations, and transportation, regardless of whether or not federal funding is received. Second, Section 504 covers qualified individuals with disabilities, whereas ADA extends protection to a person without a disability who is related to or associated with an individual with a disability (OCR, 1996).

With the aforementioned exceptions, Title II of ADA, which extends to public schools, does not impose any new major requirements on school districts (OCR, 1996). Much of the language in Title II and Section 504 are similar and school districts that receive federal funding have been required to comply with Section 504 for over the past 25 years. In the area of education, nondiscrimination requirements related to disabled individuals are detailed more specifically under Section 504 than under Title II. However, Title II requirements are not to be interpreted as applying a lesser standard or degree of protection for disabled individuals. In fact, if a rule issued under Section 504 imposes a lesser standard than the ADA regulation, the language in the ADA statute replaces the language in Section 504 (NASDSE, 1992).

The ADA statute does not directly specify procedural safeguards related to special education, evaluation and placement procedures, due process procedures, and responsibility and requirements under the provision of a free, appropriate public education (FAPE) as does Section 504 and IDEA. ADA incorporates the specific details of these concepts from Section 504 and IDEA into Title II, Subtitle A. ADA also provides additional protection in combination with the actions brought under Section 504 and IDEA. For example, reasonable accommodations must be made for eligible individuals with disabilities to perform essential functions of a job. Special education programs that are community-based and involve job training or placement are covered under the ADA statute. ADA protections are also applicable to nonsectarian private schools, but not to organizations or entities controlled by religious affiliations (Henderson, 1995).

Section 504 and IDEA provide specific details regarding procedural safeguards, whereas ADA does not. Procedural safeguards involve notification to parents regarding identification, evaluation, and placement of a child in special education programs and related services. ADA, on the other hand, specifies administrative requirements, complaint procedures, and consequences for noncompliance related to services (Henderson, 1995).

ADA does not specify evaluation and placement procedures as does Section 504 and IDEA. However, ADA does specify reasonable accommodations for individuals with disabilities across educational settings and activities. Reasonable accommodations are not limited to, but may include, modifying equipment, hiring one-on-one aids, modifying tests, providing alternate forms of communication, relocating services in more accessible areas, altering existing facilities, and constructing new facilities (Henderson, 1995).

ADA does not delineate specific due process procedures; however, IDEA and Section 504 do. IDEA and Section 504 require local educational agencies (LEAs) to provide hearings for parents who disagree with the identification, evaluation, or placement of a child. With the passage of the 1997 Amendments to IDEA, parents and LEAs or state educational agencies (SEAs) are strongly encouraged to participate in voluntary mediation to resolve disputes prior to conducting due process hearings. According to ADA, individuals with disabilities who are discriminated against in an educational setting have the same recourse that is available under Title VII of the Civil Rights Act of 1964, as amended in 1991. Individuals may file complaints with the OCR or sue in federal court. The OCR encourages informal mediation and voluntary compliance (Henderson, 1995). However, administrative remedies do not have to be exhausted prior to filing a lawsuit (28 C.F.R. § 35.172). Federal funds may be removed from schools for noncompliance with the ADA mandates and individuals with disabilities may be awarded attorney fees if they prevail in any action filed under ADA (28 C.F.R. § 35.175)

Title II, Subtitle A of ADA is the section of the statute pertaining to public schools. The statute prohibits discrimination against any "qualified individual with a disability."

ADA's definition of an individual with a disability is essentially the same as Section 504's definition. The ADA definition of a disability consists of three prongs. ADA defines a disability as "a physical or mental impairment that substantially limits one or more major life activities, a record of such an impairment, or being regarded as having such an impairment" (42 U.S.C. § 12102 [2]).

The first prong of the ADA definition, which is a physical or mental impairment, includes physiological disorders, cosmetic disfigurement, or anatomical loss that affects body systems as well as mental or psychological disorders (28 C.F.R. § 35.104 [1] [i]). Examples of physical or mental impairments under the ADA definition of a disability are epilepsy, muscular dystrophy, multiple sclerosis, cancer, heart disease, diabetes, mental retardation, emotional illness, specific learning disabilities, drug addiction, HIV disease (symptomatic or asymptomatic), alcoholism, and orthopedic, visual, speech, and hearing impairments (OCR, 1996). The preceding examples are not an exhaustive list of physical and mental impairments under the ADA definition of a disability.

Another key concept in the ADA definition of a disability is "a substantial limitation in a major life activity." A "major life activity" refers to a basic activity that the "average person performs with little or no difficulty" such as walking, speaking, seeing, breathing, working, and learning (28 C.F.R. § 35.104). A person who has "a substantial limitation" that is determined by the nature, severity, duration, and long-term or permanent impact of the impairment on a major life activity is protected under ADA (OCR, 1996).

In the second prong, a person with a record or history of an impairment that substantially limits a major life activity also meets ADA's definition of an individual with a disability (28 C.F.R. § 35.104 [3]). Examples include a person who has a history of a mental or emotional illness, drug addiction, alcoholism, heart disease, or cancer. An individual who has been misclassified as having an impairment, (such as a person misdiagnosed as being mentally retarded or emotionally disturbed) is also protected under ADA (OCR, 1996).

The third prong of the definition of a disability under ADA protects a person who has an impairment that does or does not substantially limit a major life activity, but is perceived by the public or public entity as being substantially limiting (28 C.F.R. § 35.104 [3]). For example, a girl who walks with a limp but is not substantially limited in her ability to walk is not allowed to participate on the school's soccer team out of fear by school personnel that she will be injured. Under ADA, the third prong of the definition of an individual with a disability applies and thus protects the girl. The third prong of the definition of a disability also protects an individual who does not have an impairment, but the public or public entity perceives the individual as having an impairment (28 C.F.R. § 35.104 [3]).

An individual who is covered under the second or third prong of ADA's definition of a disability is not necessarily entitled to special education and related services or regular education with supplementary services. If a student is protected under the second or third prong, but not under the first prong, then the student is not eligible for special education and related services. The fact that an individual has a disability does not automatically trigger an evaluation for special education and related services. For example, if a student has an attention deficit disorder (ADD) but is performing well in the classroom, then an evaluation for special education and related services at the present time is not needed. On the other hand, if a student's mental or physical impairment substantially limits the student's ability to learn in the classroom, then the student would be entitled to an evaluation, and special education and related services or regular education with supplementary services may follow (OCR, 1996).

Title II and Section 504 use the three-prong definition of a disability, whereas IDEA uses the 13 recognized disability categories and the "need" criteria, in other words there must be a need for special education and related services. Based on these differences in the definition of a disability, there may be some students who qualify for regular or special education and related services under Section 504 and Title II but do not have one of the 13 disabilities recognized by IDEA (OCR, 1996).

Protection under Title II, Subtitle A is afforded to *qualified* individuals with disabilities. An individual with a disability is qualified to receive services and/or participate in an elementary and secondary education program if the student meets the eligibility requirements of a qualified individual with a disability established under Section 504. As previously mentioned, Title II incorporates the more specific details and standards in Section 504. A qualified individual with a disability is an individual who has a disability and is of the appropriate age (school-aged), and "who, with or without reasonable modifications to rules, policies, or practices, the removal of architectural, communication, or transportation barriers, or the provision of auxiliary aids and services, meets the essential eligibility requirements for the receipt of services or the participation in programs or activities provided by a public entity" (28 C.F.R. § 35.104).

Parents or other associates of a student who are disabled themselves and who are invited to attend a school event or choose to participate in a school event open to the public are also qualified as individuals with disabilities and are protected under ADA. Under these circumstances, the school district must ensure program accessibility and provide auxiliary aids and services to ensure effective communication for these individuals with disabilities. For example, if a parent is deaf and is invited to attend a parent-teacher conference for his or her child, who may or may not be a student with a disability under ADA, then the school is responsible for providing an interpreter at the parent's request in order for the parent to participate in the meeting (OCR, 1996).

Title II also extends protection to, but does not provide accommodations for, an individual who is not disabled but who assists or lives with someone with a disability (28 C.F.R. § 35.130 [g]). Family members, friends, or any other person or entity who associates with an individual with a disability are protected under this federal regulation. Likewise, Title II extends protection to an individual with or without a disability who takes action to oppose any act or practice prohibited by the statute or assists or encourages others to exercise their rights under the ADA regulations (28 C.F.R. § 35.134). For example, if an educator encourages a family to exercise their rights under ADA regarding a school policy, then the educator and the family, including the individual with the disability, are protected under ADA from any coercion or retaliation from the school district.

To bring a school district into compliance with the ADA statute, five action steps must be taken by the district. First, the school district must designate a responsible employee to coordinate ADA compliance. Under Title II, if the school district has 50 or more employees, then at least one coordinator must be designated (28 C.F.R. § 35.107 [a]). The ADA coordinator's role includes planning and coordinating compliance efforts, implementing and ensuring completion of the five action steps, and receiving and investigating complaints of possible discrimination against individuals with disabilities. Second, the school district, regardless of size, must provide notice of ADA requirements to all interested parties including participants, beneficiaries, employees, applicants, and the public. Specific information on how Title II requirements apply to particular programs, services, and activities must be included (28 C.F.R. § 35.106). Appropriate methods to disseminate this information include publications, public posters, or media broadcast. The most effective methods for making people aware of their rights and protections under ADA, however, are determined by the head of the school district or delegated to the ADA coordinator. Third, school districts with 50 or more employees must adopt and publish grievance procedures providing for prompt and equitable resolution of complaints alleging violations of ADA (28 C.F.R. § 35.107). These grievance procedures are available to school district employees, students, or the public. Fourth, all school districts, regardless of size, must conduct a self-evaluation of its policies and practices, including communications and employment, and correct any inconsistencies in its policies and practices in relation to the ADA statute (28 C.F.R. § 35.105 [a]). However, if the school district has received federal funding and has conducted a self-evaluation as required under Section 504, then only those programs and new or modified policies or practices since the Section 504 self-evaluation must be reviewed and corrections made to be consistent with the ADA regulations (28 C.F.R. § 35.105 [c]). School districts should have completed Title II self-evaluations by January 26, 1993 (28 C.F.R. § 35.105 [c]) for current programs, policies, and practices in existence at that time. Fifth, a transition plan must be developed to bring existing facilities into structural compliance with the ADA statute. A transition plan is needed to ensure that programs, services, or activities are accessible to individuals with disabilities (28 C.F.R. § 35.150 [d] [1]). Structural changes outlined in the transition plan should have been completed by January 26, 1995 for existing facilities (28 C.F.R. § 35.150 [c]).

Nondiscrimination requirements are used to analyze the policies, programs, and practices of a public school district. Specific nondiscrimination requirements imposed on a school district under Section 504 are applicable under Title II. According to Section 504, a school district is obligated to provide a free, appropriate public education (FAPE) to school-aged children with disabilities. The school district's responsibilities are specifically described under Section 504 and are incorporated into the general provisions of Title II (28 C.F.R. § 35.130; 28 C.F.R. § 35.103 [a]; see 34 C.F.R. §§ 104.31-104.37).

Title II also requires a school district to ensure that qualified individuals with disabilities are not excluded from participation in or denied any benefits from the district's programs, services, or activities based on their disability (28 C.F.R. § 35.130 [a]). This requirement applies to programs, services, and activities operated or provided directly by the district as well as those operated or provided by another entity on behalf of the district under contractual agreement or other arrangements (28 C.F.R. § 35.130 [b]). For example, if a student with a disability is excluded from bus service by a private school bus company that is under contract with the school district to provide this service, then the school district would be liable for the alleged discriminatory act under Title II (OCR, 1996).

The school district must also ensure that qualified individuals with disabilities have an equal opportunity to participate in the district's programs as do nondisabled individuals. Likewise, individuals with disabilities must have an equal opportunity to benefit from any aids, benefits, or services provided by the school district as do nondisabled individuals. For example, if a student with a severe visual impairment is evaluated and it is determined, in order to provide FAPE, visual aids and services must be provided, and the school district refuses to pay for the visual aids, citing expenses, then under these circumstances, the school district is in violation of Title II standards because the district has denied related aids and services to the student. As a result, the student does not have an equal opportunity as does a nondisabled student to participate in or receive benefits from the school program (OCR, 1996). Similarly, a school district's benefits and services must be effective enough to afford equal opportunity to obtain the same results, benefits, or levels of achievement for both individuals with and without disabilities.

Under Title II, a school district may not operate different or separate programs or provide different or separate benefits or services, unless the programs, benefits, or services are needed to provide equal benefits to individuals with disabilities (28 C.F.R. § 35.103 [a]; 28 C.F.R. § 35.130 [b] [1] [iv]). If separate or different programs, services, or benefits are needed, then the school district must provide them in the most integrated setting for individuals with disabilities (28 C.F.R. § 35.103 [a]; 28 C.F.R. § 35.130 [d]). However, in the establishment of separate or different programs, services, or benefits, individuals with disabilities may not be denied participation in the regular programs or access to regular benefits and services.

Another nondiscrimination requirement under Title II includes the prohibition of surcharges. A school district is not allowed to place a surcharge on an individual with a disability to cover the costs of measures that are necessary to provide nondiscriminatory treatment (28 C.F.R§35.130 [f]). For example, if an evaluation is conducted and it is determined that a student with a disability should be placed in a regular education program with related aids and services, including a computer, then the school district cannot charge the student or his/her parents for the use of the computer, as the computer is a necessary aid in order to provide FAPE. Similarly, modifications that would fundamentally alter a specific benefit, program, service, or activity are prohibited. On the other hand, if failure to modify a specific benefit, program, service, or activity results in the denial of FAPE, then the school district must make modifications. However, a school district is not required to provide a personal device, such as wheelchair, or service of a personal nature, such as toileting, unless the device or service is necessary to provide FAPE to the student.

Nondiscriminatory requirements also apply to eligibility criteria. A school district may not use eligibility criteria to screen out individuals with disabilities from participation in its programs or receipt of its benefits or services (28 C.F.R. § 35.103 [a]; 28 C.F.R. § 35.130 [b] [8]). However, a school has the right to impose legitimate safety requirements needed for the safe operation of its services, benefits, or programs, but these safety requirements must be based on actual risks, not stereotypes. For example, if a school offers a course in scuba diving and demonstrates that a certain level of swimming ability is needed for safe participation in the class, then those individuals who cannot pass a swimming test, including some individuals with disabilities, could be screened out without violating the law (OCR, 1996).

Besides nondiscriminatory requirements, a school district must ensure that their programs, services, and activities are accessible to individuals with disabilities. This includes not only students, but parents, guardians, and members of the public with disabilities. According to Title II, two standards are used to determine program accessibility. One standard deals with existing facilities and the other standard deals with new construction and alterations. For existing facilities, when viewed in their entirety, the program or activity must be accessible to and usable by individuals with disabilities, unless a fundamental alteration in the program or undue financial or administrative burden would result (28 C.F.R. § 35.130). The burden of proof, according to Title II, is placed on the school district. For new or altered facilities, the same standard applies, however, the fundamental alteration or undue burden is not applicable.

Based on the program accessibility standard, numerous misconceptions have evolved, such as the view that buildings must be completely accessible and barrier-free. As long as the program, class, or function is accessible, Title II does not require that existing buildings offer a barrier-free environment. In other words, if the program can be held in another classroom or building, and this classroom or building meets accessibility requirements, then the school district's fundamental alteration in the program is in compliance with the standards set forth under Title II (OCR, 1996).

In addition to program accessibility requirements, transition services are also addressed under Title II as well as Title III of ADA. Transition services are defined as "a set of coordinated activities that promote movement from school to postschool activities" (Jacob-Timm & Hartshorne, 1995). Transition services for youth with disabilities are provided in more specific details under IDEA. The enactment of ADA is expected to lead to the expansion of opportunities for youth with disabilities in their transition to postschool activities (American Council on Education, 1993). Postschool activities may include vocational training, continuing education, integrated employment, independent living, community participation, and postsecondary education.

For postsecondary education, the enactment of ADA has translated into renewed attention focused on disability access to facilities and programs as well as employment and promotion issues. In addition, ADA has resulted in a greater number of opportunities for students with disabilities due to increased access to employment, public accommodations, transportation, and telecommunications. Thus, an expanded pool of qualified college-educated disabled workers is expected in the future to address anticipated manpower shortages in the next decade (American Council on Education, 1993).

Numerous implications exist for education officials under Title II. First, local agencies may witness an increase in the number of requests for public hearings to determine student eligibility for special education. A potential increase in the number of students served may occur. Second, parents and other adults' requests to participate in school activities may increase. Since public schools offer programs and opportunities to the community, many adults with disabilities may desire greater participation due to the enactment of the statute. As a result, the public school's responsibilities may increase in meeting program accessibility, service, and benefit requirements. Third, ADA encourages full participation in society of individuals with disabilities. Thus, parents' requests for their children with disabilities to participate in school activities (e.g., athletic events, field trips, recreational offerings, etc.) may increase and transportation issues will also need to be addressed (NASDSE, 1992).

The implementation of ADA has expanded the role of the schools in the preparation of students with disabilities to take full advantage of employment opportunities, to participate more fully in school programs, to achieve greater independence through the use of public transportation, and to learn and to communicate more effectively through the use of telecommunication systems (First & Curcio, 1993). ADA encourages the education system to become more actively involved in the lives of individuals with disabilities and to assist in the empowerment of students with disabilities. Educators and parents are challenged to bring real meaning into the lives of students with disabilities and to the school environment, not only for the students' benefit, but also for the benefit of all people.

PATRICIA A. LOWE
CECIL R. REYNOLDS
Texas A & M University

REFERENCES

American Council on Education (1993). *Americans with Disabilities* (Report No. H030C3002-94). Washington D.C.: HEATH Resource Center. (ERIC Reproduction Document Service No. ED 381 919)

Americans with Disabilities Act of 1990, 28 C.F.R. § 35; 34 C.F.R. §§ 104.31–104.37 (1993).

Americans with Disabilities Act of 1990, 42 U.S.C. § 12101 *et seq*. (West 1994).

Burgdorf, R. L. (1991). The Americans with Disabilities Act: Analysis and implications of a second-generation civil rights statute. *Harvard Civil Rights—Civil Liberties Law Review, 26,* 413–522.

Cuconan-Lahr, R. (1991). *The Americans with Disabilities Act: Educational implications and policy considerations.* (ERIC Document Reproduction Service No. Ed 333 665)

First, P. F. & Curcio, J. L. (1993). *Individuals with disabilities: Implementing the newest laws.* Newbury Park, CA: Corwin.

Henderson, Kelly (1995). *Overview of ADA, IDEA, and Section 504* (Report No. EDO-EC-94-8). Washington, D.C.: Office of Educational Research and Improvement. (ERIC Document Reproduction Service No. ED 389 142)

Jacob-Timm, S., & Hartshorne, T. (1995). *Ethics and law for school psychologists.* Brandon, VT: Clinical Psychology Publishing.

National Association of State Directors of Special Education. (1992). The Americans with Disabilities Act: New challenges and opportunities for school administrators. *Liaison Bulletin, 18*(4), 1–11.

Office of Civil Rights. (1996). *Compliance with the Americans with Disabilities Act: A self-evaluation guide for public elementary and secondary schools.* Washington DC: U.S. Government Printing Office.

PATRICIA A. LOWE
CECIL R. REYNOLDS
Texas A & M University

ADULT BASIC EDUCATION
ARCHITECTURAL BARRIERS
LEGISLATION

Louise Bates Ames

AMES, LOUISE BATES (1908–1996)

Born in Portland, Maine, Louise Ames received her BA in 1930 from the University of Maine. She then went on to receive her MA in 1933 and PhD in 1937 in experimental psychology from Yale University, where she studied with Arnold Gesell. Her relationship with Gesell resulted in the founding of the Gesell Institute in 1950, a project where Dr. Ames collaborated with Dr. Frances Ilg and Dr. Janet Learner. Ames was also an instructor. She was assistant professor at Yale Medical School (1936–1950) and curator of the Yale Films of Child Development (1944–1950).

Working with Frances Ilg and Arnold Gesell, Dr. Ames developed the important developmental theory that patterned, predictable behaviors are associated with chronological age, with the explicit implication that human development unfolded in discrete, recognizable stages. Such ideas were relatively novel at the time and have had great impact since their development. Her career interests and research in the behavior and development of normal children resulted in the development of standard references for psychologists working with children, and served to educate nonprofessionals as well through its coverage by the popular media.

Dr. Ames' greatest impact was in teaching parents and teachers about the course of child development, primarily through her prolific publications, which included *Infant and Child in the Culture of Today* (1940), *School Readiness* (1956), the syndicated newspaper column "Child Behavior" in collaboration with her colleagues (which later became a weekly half-hour television show in the 1950s), *Child Behavior* (1981), and *Don't Rush Your Preschooler (1980)*, co-authored with her daughter Joan Ames Chase. Ames also had a strong interest in projective assessment and provided normative data in *Child Rorschach Responses*

(1974). This interest extended to assessment of the elderly (*Rorschach Responses in Old Age*) and a series of articles developing test batteries for assessing deterioration of functions in old age.

Over her long career, Dr. Ames authored some 300 articles and monographs, co-authored/collaborated on 25 books, and received honorary degrees and many awards for service. One of the most publicized women in psychology, Louise Bates Ames died of cancer in November, 1996, at the age of 88.

REFERENCES

Ames, L. B. (1940). *Infant and child in the culture of today.* New York: Harper & Row.

Ames, L. B. (1974). *Child Rorschach responses.* New York: Brunner/Mazel.

Ames, L. B. (1981). *Child behavior.* New York: Harper Perennial.

Ames, L. B., & Chase, J. A. (1980). *Don't rush your preschooler.* New York: Harper & Row.

Ames, L. B., & Ilg, F. (1956). *School readiness.* Now York: Harper & Row.

Ames, L. B., Metraux, R. W., Rodell, J. L., & Walker, R. W. (1973). *Rorschach responses in old age.* New York: Brunner/Mazel.

ELAINE FLETCHER-JANZEN
Texas A & M University
First edition

KAY E. KETZENBERGER
The University of Texas of the Permian Basin
Second edition

AMNESIA

Amnesia is a disorder of memory that occurs in the absence of gross disorientation, confusion, or dementia. Amnesia may be retrograde, where the individual has difficulty remembering events and information learned prior to the onset of the amnesia, or it may be anterograde, where the individual is unable to learn new information from the point of onset of the amnesia. Amnesics do not have difficulty with immediate memory. Digit span and immediate repetition are intact. Rather, individuals with amnesia are unable to remember after a delay filled with interference.

Amnesia is fascinating because observation of amnesics may help us understand how new information is learned (e.g., what brain structures are involved and what processes facilitate new learning). Amnesics are also of interest because the sense of continuity and time passing, remembering experiences, and hence, self-identity (Walton, 1977) depend on continuous access to information about the remote and recent past. The difficulties that amnesic patients encounter in awareness of their own experiences emphasizes just how important memory is.

Amnesia as an isolated neurologic symptom can be mistaken for a psychiatric disorder (DeJong, Itabashi, & Olson, 1969). There are hysterical amnesias that are a consequence of psychiatric distress alone. Fugue states are 20 dissociative episodes during which an individual forgets his or her identity and past. Hysterical amnesia is discriminable from neurologic conditions causing amnesia in that the total loss of self-identity rarely occurs in neurologically based amnesias, and because the end of the fugue state is abrupt. In the neurologically based amnesias that remit, the cessation of memory loss is gradual, with the period of time for which the individual is amnesic shrinking only gradually.

Transient amnesia is a known consequence of electroconvulsive therapy (ECT shock treatment). Individuals receiving ECT have both retrograde amnesia for events occurring just prior to treatment, and anterograde amnesia for what happens subsequent to treatment. When compared with their own performance after recovery from amnesia, patients who are amnesic after receiving ECT forget more easily and at an abnormal rate (Squire, 1981). This suggests a deficit in consolidation and elaboration of memory. There is some disagreement as to whether memory loss secondary to ECT is cumulative. Transient amnesia also may occur when an individual receives general anesthesia.

Anterograde amnesia that gradually remits is a frequent occurrence after closed head injuries (Levin, Benton, & Grossman, 1982; Reynolds & Fletcher-Janzen, 1997). There often is a more limited retrograde amnesia for the period just prior to the injury. Anterograde amnesia secondary to closed head injury (also called posttraumatic amnesia) is a good index of the severity of the injury and

useful in the prediction of long-term recovery. After the amnesia has remitted, there is often a residual memory disorder.

Transient global amnesia is a neurologic condition that is now assumed to be a consequence of transient ischemia (Heathfield, Croft, & Swash, 1973). The presentation of an individual with transient global amnesia is characteristic. There is an abrupt onset of amnesia, both retrograde and anterograde, with perhaps only initial, mild clouding of consciousness, and no change in cognition or speech. Episodes typically last for several hours only, and the retrograde amnesia gradually shrinks, leaving individuals amnesic only for the period during which they had anterograde amnesia (Hecaen & Albert, 1978).

Amnesia is the hallmark of Korsakoff's disease (an entirely adult disease induced by alcohol consumption). Patients with Korsakoff's have a profound anterograde amnesia. Though immediate repetition is intact, remembering what they have been told after an interference (e.g., a brief conversation) is impossible. Patients hospitalized with Korsakoff's often reintroduce themselves to their physicians when the physician who has been caring for them reenters the room after a short interval. Korsakoff's patients are notable for their tendency to confabulate (i.e., fill in the blanks in their memory with imaginary accounts). The most common etiology of Korsakoff's is thiamine deficiency as a consequence of alcoholism. Head injury, anoxia, carbon monoxide poisoning, tumors, and other pathologies involving the same brain structure are other causes of the disorder (Walton, 1977).

A great deal has been learned about amnesia and memory through the study of groups of patients with unremitting forms of amnesia: amnesia secondary to Korsakoff's syndrome, amnesia secondary to neurosurgery for control of epilepsy, traumatic brain lesions resulting in amnesia, and generalized dementing processes (especially Huntington's disease and Alzheimer's disease) in which memory deficits are disproportionately problematic (at least during specific stages of the disease). Careful investigation of these patients clearly reveals that though the average clinician thinks of memory as a unitary phenomenon, memory loss is a multidimensional symptom with different etiologies resulting in characteristic, discriminable patterns of memory loss and skill (Butters, 1984).

One pattern of amnesia reflects hemispheric differences. Individuals with amnesia secondary to isolated damage to the right hemisphere have deficient skills in nonverbal memory when the information is presented visually. Those amnesic secondary to isolated left hemisphere damage have greater difficulty with verbal memory. Verbal memory deficits are seen regardless of the sensory modality used to present the information; e.g., visual presentation of verbal information (Hecaen and Albert, 1978).

The pattern of retrograde amnesia is not the same

across all amnesic populations. Butters (1984) compared remote memory functioning in Huntington's disease, Korsakoff's disease, and normal subjects by assessing their ability to recall famous people and events from past decades. Korsakoff's patients had more severe difficulties recalling past events, but there was a normal gradation in their ability to remember, with events that occurred further in the past recalled better than more recent past experiences. The Huntington's disease patients demonstrated a flat pattern. They were equally unable to remember any past event. This pattern of remote recollection occurs across the stages of Huntington's disease, though the severity increases as the disease progresses.

Amnesic patients of differing etiologies demonstrate differential responses to manipulations aimed at facilitating memory. For example, Korsakoff's amnesics are assisted in memorization by increasing rehearsal time, intertrial rest intervals, and a structured orientation procedure. They are not aided, however, by the provision of verbal mediation. Conversely, Huntington's disease patients are not assisted as are Korsakoff's patients; neither increased rehearsal time, increased intertrial intervals, nor general orientation aids their performance. They are assisted, however, by verbal mediation. Patients with Alzheimer's disease are not assisted by verbal mediation.

Another difference between amnesic syndromes is related to the ability to acquire procedural versus declarative memories (Squire, 1982). Declarative memory pertains to specific facts and data. Procedural memory refers to the rules for completing a specific type of task. Studies of amnesic patients indicate that patients with amnesia secondary to Korsakoff's disease acquire procedural information but have great difficulty in learning declarative data. Huntington's disease patients do not remember procedural rules, but do learn (or at least recognize) previously presented data of a declarative type.

The study of patient populations with known etiologies has been useful in increasing our understanding of what brain structures are involved in the elaboration and retrieval of memory. Evidence from neurosurgical intervention to control severe epilepsy has demonstrated that damage to the medial aspects of both temporal lobes, especially the hippocampus, results in profound amnesia (Hecaen & Albert, 1978; Squire, 1982). This amnesia is distinguished by rapid and abnormal forgetting. Other amnesics appear to have diencephalic damage with some disagreement as to exactly which structures are affected. The mammillary bodies and dorsal-medial nucleus of the thalamus are involved, though the relative contributions of either structure are not known. Damage to the dorsal-medial nucleus appears sufficient to cause amnesia (Squire, 1982). Amnesia secondary to diencephalic damage is notable for a normal forgetting curve, but difficulty with encoding. Identification of structures involved in memory is useful not only in terms of understanding specific syndromes, but also in considering pharmacologic manipulations to assist in treatment.

With the exception of posttraumatic amnesia, amnesia in its pure form is not reported to occur in children. Subsequent to head injuries, children do exhibit posttraumatic amnesia and have difficulty learning new information in school and remembering what they learned just prior to their injuries. Consequently, they will be confused in the school setting. Posttraumatic amnesia generally will remit. Such children should be allowed to recover after their injuries (with the most rapid recovery occurring in the first 6 months) without the expectation that by studying harder they will remember significantly better. Once the major recovery period is over (after 6 to 9 months), cognitive rehabilitation programs aimed at providing strategies to assist in memory may be useful. There are limited data available on how generalizable the effect of cognitive rehabilitation is in the adult population, and less data regarding children.

It should be clear that the short-term memory impairments described in the learning of disabled children bear little resemblance to amnesic disorders. Amnesic patients are capable of short-term memory performance. Children with severe brain injury may become amnesic, but it is most often within the context of general dementia with difficulties in a variety of areas.

REFERENCES

Butters, N. (1984). The clinical aspects of memory disorders: Contributions from experimental studies of amnesia and dementia. *Journal of Clinical Neuropsychology, 6,* 17–36.

DeJong, R. N., Itabashi, H. H., & Olson, J. R. (1969). Memory loss due to hippocampal lesion. *Archives of Neurology, 20,* 339–348.

Heathfield, K. W. G., Croft, P. B., & Swash, M. (1973). The syndrome of transient global amnesia. *Brain, 96,* 729–731.

Hecaen, H., & Albert, M. L. (1978). *Human neuropsychology.* New York: Wiley.

Levin, H. S., Benton, A. L., & Grossman, R. G. (1982). *Neurobehavioral consequences of closed head injury.* New York: Oxford University Press.

Milner, B., Corkin, S., & Teuber, H. L. (1968). Further analysis of the hippocampal amnesic syndrome: A 14-year follow-up study of H. M. *Neuropsychologia, 6,* 215–234.

Reynolds, C. R., & Fletcher-Janzen, E. (Eds.). (1997). Handbook of Clinical Child Neuropsychology. New York: Plenum Press.

Squire, L. (1981). Two forms of human amnesia: An analysis of forgetting. *Journal of Neurosciences, 1,* 635–640.

Squire, L. (1982). The neuropsychology of human memory. *Annual Review of Neurosciences, 5,* 241–273.

Walton, J. N. (1977). *Brain's diseases of the nervous system.* Oxford: Oxford University Press.

GRETA N. WILKENING
Children's Hospital

MEMORY DISORDERS

AMNIOCENTESIS

Amniocentesis is the sampling of amniotic fluid surrounding a fetus. A physician anesthetizes a small area of the pregnant woman's abdomen, inserts a small needle through the abdominal wall, and, with the aid of ultrasonography, enters the amniotic sac and removes 30 ccs (approximately 1 oz) of fluid. It is performed most frequently between 15 and 18 weeks gestation to detect hereditary disease or congenital defects in the fetus. One disadvantage is that analysis of the fluid takes 2 to 4 weeks. Damage to the fetus also may occur, but the risk is small (Pritchard, MacDonald, & Gant, 1985).

Midtrimester amniocentesis plays an important role in genetic and other prenatal counseling by providing potential parents with reproductive options. It should be considered when the pregnant woman is over 35, or a family history of genetic or congenital disorders is apparent (Kaback, 1979). Cytogenetic analysis of fetal fluid leads to prevention of birth of approximately 15,000 chromosomally abnormal infants each year in the United States alone (Pritchard et al., 1985).

Amniocentesis allows identification of about 300 chromosomal, single-gene, and other congenital abnormalities (Pritchard et al., 1985). The list grows with the discovery of new markers. Chromosomally based disorders are identified through karyotyping and resultant abnormal appearance of one or more chromosomes; other disorders are identified through elevated or reduced levels of particular substances. Among the disorders that can be reliably diagnosed are (1) all chromosomally based disorders such as Down's syndrome and cri du chat; (2) about 75 inborn errors of metabolism, including galactosemia, Tay-Sachs disease, and Lesch-Nyhan syndrome (X-linked), but not phenylketonuria; (3) some central nervous system defects including meningocele (a form of spina bifida) and anencephaly; (4) some fetal infections (cytomegalovirus, herpes simplex, and rubella); (5) and some hematologic disorders (e.g., sickle-cell anemia; Pritchard et al., 1985).

The widespread availability of amniocentesis forces many women to confront the decision to terminate an advanced pregnancy. Attachment grows throughout pregnancy, and confronting the decision of choosing termination at a late stage can be emotionally painful (Brewster, 1984). Many women are unprepared for the anxiety associated with both waiting several weeks for results of their amniocentesis and choosing between life and quality of life. Optimally, women in high-risk groups should weigh this decision and discuss other reproductive options with a genetic counselor prior to conception. Some counselors suggest that health caregivers be sensitive to pregnant women's emotional reactions and not use measures such as a doppler to hear the fetus's heartbeat or ultrasonography to take pictures of the fetus, that promote maternal attachment prior to amniocentesis (Brewster, 1984).

A new diagnostic technique, chorion-villus biopsy, usable as early as 8 weeks gestation, may be preferable in some cases because of the emotional and medical problems presented with a midtrimester abortion.

REFERENCES

Brewster, A. (1984). After office hours: A patient's reaction to amniocentesis. *Obstetrics & Gynecology, 64,* 443–444.

Kaback, M. M. (1979). Predictors of hereditary diseases or congenital defects in antenatal diagnosis (National Institute of Child Health and Human Development, U.S. Department of HEW, NIH Publication No. 79-1973). *Antenatal Diagnosis,* 39–42.

Pritchard, J. A., MacDonald, C., & Gant, N. F. (Eds.). (1985). *Williams obstetrics* (17th ed.) (pp. 267–293). Englewood Cliffs, NJ: Appleton-Century-Crofts.

BRENDA POPE
*New Hanover Memorial
Hospital*

CHRONIC VILLUS SAMPLING
GENETIC COUNSELING
INBORN ERRORS OF METABOLISM

AMPHETAMINE PSYCHOSIS

Amphetamine psychosis results from the neurochemical and behavioral interaction of large doses of amphetamines. The toxic reaction, induced by chronic amphetamine abuse or by an acute overdose, leads to transitory symptoms that are clinically indistinguishable from those of paranoid schizophrenia. Such symptoms, occurring as early as 36 to 48 hours after a large dosage, include vivid auditory, visual, and tactile hallucinations, changes in affect, loosening of associations with reality, and paranoid thought processes (Gilman, Goodman, & Gilman, 1980). Affected individuals may also show behavioral stereotypes such as continuous rocking or polishing motions, repetitive grooming activities (rubbing or picking of the skin), and other locomotor irregularities. Biochemical correlates of amphetamine psychosis, including increased dopaminergic activity, are similar to those of schizophrenia (Kokkinidis & Anisman, 1980).

In addition to reducing amphetamine intake, treatment includes sedatives, psychotherapy, and custodial care. Acidification of the urine will speed excretion of the amphetamines. The psychotic state usually clears in about a week after beginning treatment, with hallucinations being the first symptom to disappear (American Medical Association, 1980).

REFERENCES

American Medical Association. (1980). *AMA drug evaluations* (4th ed.). New York: Wiley.

Gilman, A. G., Goodman, L. S., & Gilman, A. (1980). *Goodman and Gilman's pharmacological basis of therapeutics* (6th ed.). New York: Macmillan.

Kokkinidis, L., & Anisman, H. (1980). Amphetamine models of paranoid schizophrenia: An overview and elaboration of animal experimentation. *Psychological Bulletin, 88,* 551–579.

VICKI BARTOSIK
Stanford University

CHILDHOOD SCHIZOPHRENIA
DRUG ABUSE
LSD
PSYCHOTROPIC DRUGS

AMSLAN

See AMERICAN SIGN LANGUAGE.

ANASTASI, ANNE (1908–   )

Anne Anastasi

Anne Anastasi obtained her BA from Barnard College in 1928 and her Ph.D. from Columbia University in 1930 at the age of 21. Influenced by H. L. Hollingworth and articles about early precursors of factor analysis by C. Searman, Anastasi changed her orientation from mathematics to psychology. She also extended her study of individual differences to include major group differences. These changes began her association with the development of differential psychology. Her major areas of study are the nature and identification of psychological traits, test construction and evaluation, and interpretation of test results with specific reference to the role of cultural factors in individual and group differences.

Anastasi's publication of *Psychological Testing*, in the most recent edition, continues to stress the responsibility of the test administrator in selecting appropriate tests and methods of testing, interpreting test scores, and using and communicating test results. Other major publications include *Differential Psychology* and *Fields in Applied Psychology*. She has published more than 170 journal articles and monographs and is the only author who has contributed to every edition of the *Mental Measurements Yearbook* since its inception in 1938.

Anastasi has received several honorary degrees and many awards such as the 1977 Educational Testing Service Award for Distinguished Service to Measurement, the E. L. Thorndike Award for Distinguished Psychological Contributions to Education (from APA Division 15), the American Psychological Association Distinguished Scientific Award for the Application of Psychology, the American Psychological Foundation Gold Medal, and the AERA award for Distinguished Contributions to Research in Education. Anastasi is also professor emeritus at Fordham University and is esteemed as the third female president of the American Psychological Association.

REFERENCES

Anastasi, A. & Urbina, S. (1997). *Psychological testing* (7th ed.). Upper Saddle River, NJ: Prentice-Hall.

Anastasi, A. (1979). *Fields of applied psychology* (2nd ed.). New York: McGraw-Hill.

Anastasi, A. (1958). *Differential psychology* (3rd ed.). New York: Macmillan.

ELAINE FLETCHER-JANZEN
University of Northern Colorado
First edition

DEBORAH B. GUILLEN
The University of Texas of the
    Permian Basin
Second edition

Nicholas J. Anastasiow

ANASTASIOW, NICHOLAS J. (1924–   )

Though he retired as Thomas Hunter professor at Hunter College, City University of New York, in 1992, Nicholas Anastasiow maintains his principal interest in early childhood special education and child development. He began his career as an elementary school teacher in the early 1950s and garnered various educational certifications until he received his PhD in child development and guidance from Stanford University in 1963. In 1967, he completed postdoctoral courses in neurology at Columbia University.

Anastasiow believes that "many at risk children can lead normal lives when they are provided remediation as well as support and education for their parents" (personal communication, August 2, 1985). This belief is well represented in the 200 articles, reports, and books he has published on a vast array of subjects such as language development. Some of his titles are *Language and Reading Strategies for Poverty Children* (Anastasiow, Hanes, & Hanes, 1982), *The At Risk Infant* (Harel & Anastasiow, 1984), and *Development and Disabilities* (Anastasiow, 1986). He is currently working on the 9th revision of the classic textbook *Exceptional Children*, which he co-authors with Samuel Kirk & Jim Gallagher.

Anastasiow is also interested in the "prevention of at risk children by educating future parents in knowledge of child development and the skills and strategies of parenting before they become parents" (personal communication, August 2, 1985). He has encouraged schools to establish child development courses for sixth and seventh graders in publications such as *The Adolescent Parent* (1982).

Anastasiow has served as a consultant to the Assistant Secretary on Human Development, the White House Conference on the Handicapped, and the President's Council for Exceptional Children—Early Childhood Division, and as an exchange delegate to the USSR.

REFERENCES

Anastasiow, N. J. (1982). *The adolescent parent*. Baltimore, MD: Brookes.

Anastasiow, N. J. (1986). *Development and disabilities*. Baltimore, MD: Brookes.

Anastasiow, N. J., Hanes, M. L., & Hanes, M. (1982). *Language and reading strategies for in text poverty children*. Austin, TX: Pro-Ed.

Harel, S., & Anastasiow, N. J. (Eds.). (1984). *The at risk infant*. Baltimore, MD: Brookes.

ELAINE FLETCHER-JANZEN
University of Northern Colorado

ANDERSON, META L. (1878–1942)

Meta L. Anderson, while a teacher in the New York City public schools, enrolled in a course in the education of mentally retarded children at The Training School at Vineland, New Jersey. There, Edward R. Johnstone and Henry H. Goddard, recognizing her unusual ability, recommended her to the Newark, New Jersey, Board of Education, which employed her to begin special classes for mentally retarded children. In 1910 she established two special classes and Newark joined the handful of school systems that provided special programs for handicapped students.

Anderson developed an instructional approach based on careful analysis of the abilities and limitations of each student and devised trade classes and a work experience program to provide vocational preparation. Her book, *Education of Defectives in the Public Schools* (1917), described the program and added impetus to the growing special class movement in the United States. In the closing months of World War I, Anderson was appointed head of reconstruction aid in Europe. After the war she served for a year in Serbia. She returned to the Newark schools in 1920 to become director of the city's comprehensive special education program. She received her PhD from New York University in 1922. She served as president of the American Association on Mental Deficiency in 1941.

REFERENCES

Anderson, M. L. (1917). *Education of defectives in the public schools*. Yonkers, New York: World Book.

Whitney, E. A. (1953). Some stalwarts of the past. *American Journal of Mental Deficiency, 57,* 345–360.

PAUL IRVINE
Katonah, New York

ANENCEPHALY

Anencephaly is a congenital disorder marked by the absence of the cerebral cortices. It belongs to a class of disorders that are termed neural tube defects (NTD) and results from the failure of the neural tube to close during embryogenesis. The neural tube, which is the precursor to the brain and spinal cord, usually closes by the 28th day after conception (Kloza, 1985). If this does not occur completely, various defects to the central nervous system (CNS) become manifest. If this occurs "lower" on the neural tube, spina bifida will be present. However, if the "top" of the neural tube remains open, anencephaly results. Anencephaly with spina bifida, rarely occurs (Swaiman & Wright, 1973).

As anencephaly is ostensibly marked by the absence of the cerebral cortices, the centers of higher cognitive functioning are absent. Therefore, while certain subcortical structures may remain intact (producing the reflex patterns and responses often indicative of neonates), higher cerebral activity is precluded by the absence of structures subserving those functions. Many anencephalics are stillborn, as they lack the brain structures necessary to maintain respiration and other functions vital to survival. On the occasion that the newborn is physiologically viable, it should be remembered that associative processes, reasoning, and cognitive and language development are not possible. Therefore, educational services are not a practical consideration and absolute custodial supervision and care are indicated. Ethical considerations pertaining to care must also come into play. Anencephaly remains a medical disorder where special educational services are not practical.

The development of anencephaly and other NTDs is believed to be multifactorial. The second most common group of congenital anomalies, with environment, intrauterine environment, and genetic factors implicated in their development are NTDs. Kandel, Schwartz, and Jessell (1991) provide a detailed review of the development of NTDs, including anencephaly. Geographically, anencephaly appears to be a more common occurrence on the East Coast of the United States and in the Rio Grande Valley of Texas. It is found more frequently in female births than male (two to one). It has been suggested that a higher prevalence of anencephaly is found in lower socioeconomic class families (James, Nevin, Johnston, & Merrett, 1981; Nevin, Johnston, & Merrett, 1981).

While treatment of anencephaly is not feasible, prenatal screening has been effective in identifying anencephaly prior to birth. With NTDs, a substance called alpha fetoprotein (AFP) occurs in higher concentration in the amniotic fluid surrounding the fetus (Adinolfi, 1985; Kloza, 1985). The AFP enters the mother's circulation either by the amniotic fluid or the placenta; it can then be measured in the mother's blood. Higher levels of AFP in the mother's blood at certain times in fetal gestation indicate NTDs. This method of identifying anencephaly has been shown to be 99% reliable, with a reliability of similar magnitude for other NTDs such as spina bifida.

REFERENCES

Adinolfi, M. (1985). The development of the human blood–csf–brain barrier. *Developmental Medicine and Child Neurology, 27*(4), 532–537.

James, W. H., Nevin, N. C., Johnston, W. P., & Merrett, J. D. (1981). Influence of social class on the risk of recurrence of anencephaly and spina bifida. *Developmental Medicine and Child Neurology, 23*(5), 661–662.

Kandel, S.; Schwartz, J., & Jessell, T. (1991). *Principles of neural sciences* (3rd ed.). NY: Elsevier.

Kloza, E. M. (1985). Prenatal screening: neural tube defects. *Disorders of Brain Development and Cognition*. Boston: Eunice Kennedy Shriver Center and Harvard Medical School.

Nevin, N. C., Johnston, W. P., & Merrett, J. D. (1981). Influence of social class on the risk of recurrence of anencephaly and spina bifida. *Developmental Medicine and Child Neurology, 23*(2), 151–154.

Swaiman, K. F., & Wright, F. S. (1973). Neurologic diseases due to developmental and metabolic defects. In A. B. Baker & L. H. Baker (Eds.), *Clinical neurology*. New York: Harper & Row.

ELLIS I. BAROWSKY
Hunter College

BABY JANE DOE

ANGELMAN SYNDROME

Angelman Syndrome is an emerging disorder, little studied, with no good population studies completed to allow proper prevalence or incidence estimates. Many, but not all, Angelman Syndrome individuals have deletions on chromosome 15 in maternally related regions (q11–q12) while others are of unknown pathogenic origin. The disorder is characterized by physical, motoric, and behavioral features. Physical features include a wide mouth, prominent lower jaw, and microbrachycephalia. Motor problems are related to diverse, jerky, sometimes rhythmic movements. Some children experience particular difficulties with inadequate control of chewing and swallowing which creates feeding problems. However, these problems abate after infancy in most cases. Acquisition of walking is delayed, and mild to severe ataxia after learning to walk is common.

A variety of behavioral and cognitive problems are evident. Most children with Angelman Syndrome have severe to profound levels of mental retardation, although some patients may reach moderate and, rarely, mild levels of mental retardation. Spoken language is absent in 75-80% of children with Angelman Syndrome, but receptive language is typically superior to expressive language. Some do develop skills in sign language but normal levels of communication have not been seen in any published case. Behavioral presentation of Angelman Syndrome often includes hyperactivity, impulsivity, episodic pica, random bursts of laughter (in nearly all cases), jerky nighttime movements, and a generally happy disposition.

Diagnosis is sometimes very difficult, as Angelman has similarities of presentation to Rett Syndrome and to Prader-Willi Syndrome in a number of cases. Detailed cytogenic studies are often necessary for proper diagnosis and even then the diagnosis may still be only inferred rather than confirmed. EEG is helpful as a common pattern with posterior slow wave activity used as a marker variable. CT and MRI are normal in 30–35% of cases, and others show mixed results with diffuse atrophy, deep white matter lesions (periventricular leukomalacia), and cerebellar growth retardation all having been documented in various cases.

At present 100% of children with Angelman Syndrome are believed to require special education services, typically as children with mental retardation, although numerous related services may be required. Intervention is largely related to symptom management and the teaching of fundamental adaptive behavior and communication skills. Sheltered employment is possible in many but not all cases. However, more and better longitudinal studies of Angelman Syndrome individuals are needed to document the long-term effects of interventions and general life outcomes.

CECIL R. REYNOLDS
Texas A & M University

PRADER-WILLI SYNDROME
RETT SYNDROME

ANIMALS FOR THE HANDICAPPED

Today, animals are being used to assist the handicapped with daily living. For centuries, the blind have used dogs to assist them in ambulation. Recently, pilot programs using domesticated monkeys to assist moderately to severely disabled persons in the home to perform rote chores has been a successful innovation. Horseback riding has emerged as a leisure-time pursuit for many types of disabled persons.

The benefits of human/animal interaction are now being realized, especially for special education purposes. Lowered blood pressure has been documented in studies where the participants had regular contact with dogs. In another study, Friedman (1980) found that the survival rate of hypertensive persons increased dramatically with pet ownership. Pets have been considered effective agents in the reduction of everyday stress. They provide a sense of relaxation (Kidd, 1981). They also provide a chance to exercise, and for many a sense of security (White & Watson, 1983).

Animals provide the opportunity to communicate. This is probably the most valuable attribute of the human/animal relationship. Levinson (1969) states that an animal can have a "very positive effect on a family and that they have the potential to bridge the gap between children and adults by providing a common object of responsibility."

According to Levinson (1969), the introduction of animals into a residential setting for the handicapped indicates that the staff believes that anything of possible treatment value to the handicapped can and should be used. It reveals an awareness of the potential healing properties of pet ownership, even if those benefits have not been scientifically documented in the laboratory.

A handicapped child is not constantly reminded of his or her handicap in the interaction with a pet. A deaf child can care for a dog competently and receive all of the rewards that a hearing child would for the same efforts. The same is true for a variety of handicaps; only the type of pet might have to be changed. A child confined to a wheelchair may interact well with a rabbit or an aquarium and achieve a sense of purpose and responsibility previously unrealized.

The teaching of the emotionally disturbed child provides a setting in which the use of animals may be especially beneficial. Typically, motivating this student to participate in class can be a difficult task for the teacher. Often, these students have never learned to care for or share with others. The animal in the class may provide both the subject matter and the motivation to learn. The child who had previously trusted no one can begin to trust the teacher for the first time when he or she sees the teacher's concern in dealing with the classroom pet. This could be the first step by the child in accepting the structure of the class (Levinson, 1969).

REFERENCES

Friedman, E. (1980, July/August). Animal companions and one year survival of patients after discharge from a coronary care unit. *Public Health Reports, 44*(4), 37–42.

Kidd, A. (1981). Dogs, cats and people. *Mills Quarterly, 23*(8), 23–28.

Levinson, B. (1969). Pet oriented child psychotherapy. Springfield, IL: Thomas.

White, B., & Watson, T. (1983). *Pet love, how pets take care of us.* New York: Pinnacle.

THOMAS R. BURKE
Hunter College

EQUINE THERAPY
THERAPEUTIC RECREATION

ANNALS OF DYSLEXIA

Originating in 1950 as the *Bulletin of the Orton Society* under the editorial leadership of June Lyday Orton, the annual periodical of the Orton Dyslexia Society was renamed the *Annals of Dyslexia* in 1981. It was designed as a means to enhance communication among the members of the Orton Dyslexia Society, an organization founded in 1949 to further research and work with children with specific language disabilities.

The journal was aimed at a professional multidisciplinary membership, consisting of neurologists, psychologists, pathologists, psychiatrists, educators, and social workers. Through concrete illustration of the practical applications of new knowledge, *Annals* served as a bridge between the researcher and the field worker.

The *Annals of Dyslexia* ceased publication in 1988.

ELIZABETH DANE
Hunter College
First edition

KAY E. KETZENBERGER
The University of Texas of the Permian Basin
Second edition

ANNUAL DIRECTORY OF EDUCATIONAL FACILITIES FOR THE LEARNING DISABLED

See BIENNIAL DIRECTORY OF EDUCATIONAL FACILITIES FOR THE HANDICAPPED.

ANNUAL GOALS

Annual goals describe expected student performance, are an important part of an individual education plan (IEP), and are in compliance with the Individuals with Disabilities Education Act. Each IEP must contain a statement of annual educational goals consisting of specific objectives indicating the condition under which desired performance should occur, a description of the desired performance, and a listing of the criteria for adequate performance. Short-term instructional objectives, which should be included in the IEP, break annual goals down into smaller components, sometimes using task analysis, to provide a logical progression of objectives in a given domain, while indicating the rate at which students are expected to progress toward mastery of goals. The proportion of IEP objectives achieved by each student at the end of the term divided by the total number written at the start of the term can be used as a measure of educational progress (Brinker & Thorpe, 1984).

Public Law 94-142 was first to mandate that pupils' rates of progress be continuously monitored so that educational programs can be reassessed and improved as students move toward goals. A common method used in instruction is the pretest, teach, posttest design. In assessing pupils, teachers in special education commonly rely on informal observation and develop curriculum-based measurement systems matched to annual goals.

Findings indicate that the use of more systematic measurement and evaluation systems than those currently in use result in better student achievement toward goals (Fuchs, Deno, & Mirkin, 1984). Another finding is that public goal setting between student and teacher is more effective than private goal setting in increasing on-task behavior in the classroom (Lyman, 1984). One suggested system is the Goal Attainment Scale (GAS), a method that can help special educators to become more accountable and effective and increase the likelihood that curricula will become student centered rather than method centered.

The method involves devising a set of goals with the involved persons, developing a set of expected outcomes for each goal, scoring the outcomes on a five-point continuum from worse than expected to better than expected, and calculating a summary score of outcomes across the goals. Mutual determination of goals and their importance by the persons involved ensures relevance and meaning to parents, students, and educators. This mutual determination also helps students to learn about alternative behaviors and helps to clarify expectations for both students and teachers. GAS is independent of theoretical predispositions and can be used by teachers to clarify specific problems, sharpen goal setting, and point out directions for action (Carr, 1979). Setting objective, observable goals and evaluating outcomes is crucial to student progress (Martens et al., 1999).

REFERENCES

Brinker, R. P., & Thorpe, M. E. (1984, October). Integration of severely handicapped students and the proportion of IEP objectives achieved. *Exceptional Children, 51,* 168–175.

Carr, R. A. (1979, October). Goal Attainment Scaling as a useful tool for evaluating progress in special education. *Exceptional Children, 46,* 88–95.

Fuchs, L. S., Deno, S. L., & Mirkin, P. K. (1984, Summer). The effects and frequent curriculum-based measurement and evaluation on pedagogy, student achievement and student awareness of learning. *American Education Research Journal, 21,* 449–460.

Gerardi, R. J., Grohe, B., Benedict, G. C., & Collidge, P. G. (1984, Fall). IEP—more paperwork and wasted time. *Contemporary Education, 56,* 39–42.

Jaffe, M. J., & Snelbecker, G. E. (1982, Summer). Evaluating independent education programs: A recommendation and some programmatic implications. *Urban Review, 14*(2), 73–81.

Lyman, R. D. (1984, September). The effect of private and public goal setting on classroom on-task behavior of emotionally disturbed children. *Behavior Therapy, 15,* 395–402.

Martens, B., Witt, J., Daly, E., & Vollmer, T. (1999). Behavior analysis: Theory and practice in educational settings. In C. R. Reynolds & T. B. Gutkin (Eds.), *The Handbook of School Psychology* (3rd ed.) (pp. 638–663). New York: John Wiley & Sons.

CATHERINE O. BRUCE
Hunter College

INDIVIDUAL EDUCATION PLAN
INDIVIDUALS WITH DISABILITIES EDUCATION ACT

ANOMALIES, PHYSICAL

See PHYSICAL ANOMALIES.

ANOREXIA NERVOSA

Anorexia nervosa (starvation due to nerves) is a condition in which an individual eats little or no food for prolonged periods. No physical basis for the abnormal eating can be found. This disorder can be life-threatening, is increasing in incidence, and is a serious problem for medical and psychological professionals.

Although famous and tragic cases such as that of singer Karen Carpenter have made anorexia familiar, little can confidently be said about specific etiology or overall effective treatment. Anorexics share certain personality characteristics and frequently have families with a particular complex of unhealthy attitudes and behaviors. The physical appearance of anorexics is emaciated.

Anorexia is largely a disorder of middle- and upper-class adolescent females. It occurs approximately nine times more often in women than in men, and may affect one in one hundred white women between the ages of 12 and 18 years (Newman & Halvorson, 1983). The most common age of onset for anorexia is early adolescence (Newman & Halvorson, 1983).

Diagnostic criteria for anorexia nervosa may be summarized as involving intense fear of becoming obese, which does not diminish as weight loss progresses; disturbed body image (e.g., feeling fat even when emaciated); refusal to maintain normal body weight; and in postmenarcheal females, amenorrhea (i.e., the absence of at least three consecutive menstrual cycles) (American Psychiatric Association, 1994).

Anorexics are subject to numerous additional complications, including malnutrition, edema, loss of hair, hyperactivity, hypoglycemia, vitamin deficiencies, constipation, weakness, and fatigue. In extreme cases, death may result from starvation, electrolyte depletion, or cardiac arrhythmia (Newman & Halvorson, 1983).

Anorexic sufferers share many behaviors and concerns among each other. They are terrified of becoming obese and measure their worth and self-esteem by how much they weigh and how much their stomachs protrude. They tend to be perfectionists, overdemanding of themselves, and very success-oriented. Low self-esteem and fear of rejection, especially by the opposite sex, are common. They have difficulty allowing anyone to become emotionally close to them.

Many anorexics were model children who were "people pleasers." They tend to be introverted, well-behaved, compulsive, self-critical, and very conscientious. As the disorder progresses, anorexics frequently become suspicious, indecisive, stubborn, unsociable, and disliking of any change. Phobic, depressive, or hysterical features are also common. Perceptions of events often become very distorted.

Studies indicate that children as young as 8 to 10 years old may be likely to be concerned with weight and body esteem. Shapiro, Newcomb, & Loeb (1997) found that 8- to 10-year-old children admitted to concern with their body weight and dieting. The investigators concluded that eating disorders or disregulated-restrained eating in vulnerable children and adolescents might be both expressed and internalized at an extremely early age. Brumberg (1997) report that studies have demonstrated that as many as 53% of 13-year-olds and 78% of 17-year-olds are dissatisfied with their bodies. *Seventeen* magazine in 1995 ran a headline in the July 1995 issue which asked: "Do You Hate Your Body? How to Stop." Although the article offered adolescents ways to stop hating their bodies, the author confessed that it is very difficult to do so in a culture where your body is very important. Wolf (1994) stated that the world never gives girls the message that their bodies are valuable simply because they themselves are inside them. Until our culture tells young girls that they are welcome in any shape—that women are valuable with or with the excuse of beauty—girls will continue to starve.

The specific etiologies of anorexia nervosa are not known, but are thought to be biopsychosocial diseases. Unknown biological predispositions may interact with both individual psychological states and needs and our culture's emphasis, especially for females, on thinness as a worthy or desirable characteristic (Wooley & Wooley, 1985). Several etiological factors can be described:

1. According to Bruch (1985), in the past 20 years the average female under 30 years of age has become heavier; at the same time, the ideal shape for women has been in the direction of being thinner. To be thin is to increase women's desirability both in their eyes and the eyes of others. The result is demonstrated in the mushrooming of the weight reduction industry and the numerous books and magazine articles that have appeared on losing weight and dieting.

2. Wooley and Wooley (1985) quote from Ambrose Bierce's Devil's Dictionary: "To men a man is but a mind, who cares what face he carries? Or what form he wears? But woman's body is the woman." For many centuries females' cultural conditioning has tied self-esteem to physical attractiveness. Many therapists think that recent cultural emphasis on "thinness is beautiful and good" has contributed to the increased incidence of eating disorders (Wooley & Wooley, 1985). The message to woman in particular is that in order to be popular, attractive, accepted, sexy, healthy, and desired in the world of work, they must be thin. The ideal of feminine beauty increasingly conforms each year to the adolescent male physique, implying emulation of men both behaviorally and physically (Wooley & Wooley, 1985). This change may be due to broader social changes involving competition between women and men for prestige and power. Also involved for many young women is the resolution of intense identification conflicts with their parents. Young women today are the first generation raised by extremely weight-conscious mothers who additionally view themselves as failures by current social standards of beauty.

3. Bruch (1985) says that cultural emphasis for slimness as determining factor does not explain the more severe disturbance of "frantic preoccupation with excessive slenderness of the anorexic." She believes that the changing status of expectations for women is important in understanding the etiology. Females, says Bruch, who have been raised as "clinging vines" and future wives, and who find themselves during their teens with the expectation to demonstrate that they are women of achievement, may find that they are filled with self-doubt and uncertainty. By bowing to the dictum to be thin, they are validating that they deserve respect.

Anorexia can begin with a stressful life situation for which the young woman does not possess appropriate coping skills. Real or perceived perfection, sexual engagements, or loss of some kind frequently precedes development of the disorder. Any change can be catastrophic for an anorexic. Worrying about performing perfectly and being socially accepted often results in situations in which anorexics find themselves out of control. Magical thinking is common.

According to Bemis and colleagues, who have studied hypothalamic functions in anorexics, starvation may actually damage the hypothalamus, and emotional stress may interfere with hypothalamic functioning. Further, psychological aberrations associated with anorexia may be relatively independent expressions of a primary hypothalamic deficiency that is of unknown origin (Bemis, 1978).

Women may be biologically more susceptible to eating disorders than men because women tend to demonstrate greater appetite fluctuations when confronted by stress. Also, through socialization, women are more likely than men to inhibit expression of negative feelings, leading to internal stress. This internal stress may exacerbate a biological predisposition.

Certain family factors facilitate the development of anorexia. If a parent has had the disorder or is either extremely thin or obese, the chances of a young woman becoming anorexic increase (Neuman & Halvorson, 1983). In families of anorexics, food is usually a primary issue. The family may use food for other than nutritional purposes. For example, eating may be a way of dealing with personal problems or negative or positive feelings, or it may be a method of presenting the appearance of a happy family. Power struggles over eating are extremely common.

Families of anorexics show certain personality patterns, although no one pattern appears consistently. Mothers are frequently intrusive and dominating and have experienced clinical depressions, whereas fathers appear passive and aloof from the family. Less frequently, these patterns may be reversed (Newman & Halvorson, 1983).

Family interpersonal dynamics are a significant contributing factor. Features that appear to be correlated with the development of the disorder are rigidity, lack of conflict resolution, overprotectiveness, and enmeshment (appearing to be a very close family). Keeping the peace at any cost is a high priority in these families; conflicts are not dealt with openly. In many families of anorexics, the anorexic generally feels powerless and ineffective, and behaves primarily on the basis of what other people want or need. Often the family has not encouraged or allowed the young woman to develop her autonomy or individuality. Only compliance is tolerated. Anorexia may develop as a result of a young woman's attempt to take control of her own life and achieve her own sense of identity. She learns that one thing she can control is her weight. Families must realize that this is an emotionally based disorder with the attempt to control, hide, avoid, and forget emotional pain. Nobody can make these anorexics eat, therefore it is important not to immediately focus on the food (Something Fishy Website).

In some cases the family unconsciously does not want the child to grow up. This message is received by the child, who in turn exhibits anorexic behavior, which then leads to failure to develop secondary sexual characteristics. Some anorexics enjoy being viewed as special by their families. Thus being anorexic can bring a great deal of attention, leading to self-perpetuation of the disorder.

Adolescent peer memberships are viewed as being critical in making the transition from childhood to adulthood. Some investigators have noted that anorexics have few if any close peer friendships (Neuman & Halvorson, 1983). Adolescent anorexics' overdependence and involvement with their families may prevent the formation of normal adolescent peer relationships. Thus, these youngsters may be at great disadvantage in making the essential developmental transition to adulthood.

Fifty percent of women diagnosed and treated for anorexia nervosa can be expected to recover completely within 2 to 5 years. Nutritional improvement or recovery can be expected in approximately two thirds of treated cases. Usually, after adequate body weight has been attained, menstruation will resume within a year.

As many as half of all anorexics experience a relapse. Approximately 38% may be re-hospitalized at some point during the next 2 years. Three to 25% of anorexia nervosa cases end in death from medical complications or suicide. This disorder has the highest death rate in psychiatry.

No consensus exits regarding the most effective form of treatment for anorexia nervosa (Vandereycken & Meermann, 1984). The course of treatment typically begins with stabilizing the patient's health, and then it is important that a course of therapy takes place (Something Fishy Website). Current treatment is aimed at first normalizing body weight, correcting the irrational thinking about weight loss, and finally preventing relapse. To obtain these goals, one must be admitted to a hospital or a day treatment program where the disorder can be monitored (Walsh & Devlin, 1998).

Many forms of treatment for anorexia are used. Therapists have used behavioral therapy, diet counseling, cognitive therapy, cognitive-behavioral treatment, drug treatment, and family therapy with varying degrees of success (Garner & Garfinkel, 1985). Whatever the treatment approach, the usual goals are aimed at increasing confidence and self-esteem, challenging irrational or "anorexic" thinking, developing autonomy, and teaching coping skills. Further, Vandereycken and Meermann (1984, p. 219) suggest that the "best guarantees of success in therapy are a constructive patient/therapist working relationship and an explicit but consistent treatment plan/contract." In the case of drug treatment, the therapist is not trying to treat the eating disorder with medication, but the emotional disorder that they are suffering from that causes the eating disorder (Something Fishy Website).

Hospitalization becomes necessary when outpatient therapy fails to reverse an impasse or a deteriorating physical or psychological course. The therapist assumes considerable physical and psychological control and responsibility for the care of the hospitalized anorexic. A weight restoration program is usually initiated in which the anorexic is expected to gain at least 1 pound a week until she achieves a target weight consisting of 95% of her ideal weight (Anderson, Morse, & Santmyer, 1985).

Psychotherapy combined with the restoration of weight through direct management of the anorexic's eating is effective in varying degrees. The anorexic has, through her disorder, avoided dealing with several important issues that need to be addressed in psychotherapy. These include individuation, assuming responsibility, separation, becoming an adult, making career and other decisions, and dealing with the loss of one's own life. A key factor in treating eating disorders is to develop a framework for intervention. One should begin prevention of eating disorders to help control the problem. Prevention should be aimed at the students who are susceptible to develop this disorder (Schwitzer, Bergholz, Dore, & Salimi, 1998). Prevention relies on educating individuals about anorexia nervosa. Educating these individuals by giving them facts increases knowledge, and that will likely change their attitude toward anorexia. If the individual continues to develop anorexia, it is assumed that this education will intrigue them to seek help for their existing problem.

Certain beliefs and values seem very important in the maintenance of these conditions. One of these is the belief that weight and shape are extremely important and need to be closely controlled at all cost. A change in these psychopathological beliefs and values concerning body weight and shape may be necessary for complete recovery. Self-help and support groups may be valuable. According to Garrett (1997), anorexics claim that events, people, and processes outside therapy were the most relevant things towards their recovery.

Because eating-disordered individuals are usually perfectionists, teachers can help by advising and encouraging them to take fewer courses and to balance academic loads by combining difficult classes with classes that are less demanding. If hospitalization becomes necessary, and the anorexic student expresses fear that she will be unable to maintain her academic standing, the teacher can point out that usually hospital personnel are more than willing to assist the patient by insuring that the patient will be provided the opportunity to continue uninterrupted with academic requirements. Major treatment centers as well as many hospitals have educational components and academic teachers on their staff.

REFERENCES

American Psychiatric Association. (1994). *Diagnostic and statistical manual of mental disorders* (4th ed.). Washington, DC: Author.

Anderson, A. E., Morse, C., & Santmyer, K. (1985). Inpatient treatment for anorexia nervosa. In Garner, D. M. & Garfinkel, P. E. (Eds.), *Handbook of psychotherapy for anorexia nervosa and bulimia* (pp. 311–343). New York: Guilford.

Bemis, K. M. (1978). Current approaches to the etiology and treatment of anorexia nervosa. *Psychological Bulletin, 35,* 395–617.

Bruch, H. (1985). Four decades of eating disorders. In D. M. Garner & P. E. Garfinkel (Eds.), *Handbook of psychotherapy for anorexia and bulimia* (pp. 7–18). New York: Guilford.

Brumberg, J. J. (1977). *The body project: An intimate history of American girls*. New York: Vintage.

Garner, D. M., & Garfinkel, P. E. (Eds.). (1985). *Handbook of psychotherapy for anorexia nervosa and bulimia*. New York: Guilford.

Garrett, C. J. (1998). Recovery from anorexia nervosa: A sociological perspective. *International Journal of Eating Disorders, 21,* 261–272.

Halmi, K. A. (1983). Advances in anorexia nervosa. In M. Wolrich & D. K. Routh (Eds.), *Advances in development and behavioral pediatrics* (Vol. 4, pp. 1–23). Greenwich, CT: Jai Press.

Hart, K. J., & Ollendick, T. H. (1985). Prevalence of bulimia in working and university women. *American Journal of Psychiatry, 142,* 851–854.

Johnson, C., & Flach, A. (1985). Family characteristics of 105 patients with bulimia. *American Journal of Psychiatry, 142,* 1321–1324.

Mitchell, J. E., Halsukami, D., Eckert, E. D., & Pyle, R. L. (1985). Characteristics of 275 patients with bulimia. *American Journal of Psychiatry, 142,* 251–255.

Newman, P. A., & Halvorson, P. S. (1983). *Anorexia nervosa and bulimia: A handbook for counselors and therapist*. New York: Van Nostrand Reinhold.

Schwitzer, A. M., Bergholz, K., Dore, T., & Salimi, L. (1998). Eating disorders among college women: Prevention, education, and treatment responses. *College Health, 45,* 199–207.

Shapiro S., Newcomb, M. & Loeb, T. B. (1997). Fear of fat, disregulated-restrained eating, and body-esteem: Prevalence and gender differences among eight- to ten-year-old children. *Journal of Clinical Psychology, 26(4)*.

Vandereycken, W., & Meermann, R. (1984). *Anorexia nervosa: A clinician's guide to treatment*. Berlin: de Gruyter.

Walsh, B. T., & Devlin, M. (1998). Eating disorders: Progress and problems. *Science, 280,* 1387–1391.

Wooley, S. C., & Wooley, O. W. (1985). Intensive outpatient and residential treatment for bulimia. In D. M. Garner & P. E. Garfinkel (Eds.), *Handbook of psychotherapy for anorexia nervosa and bulimia* (pp. 391–430). New York: Guilford.

C. Sue Lamb
*University of North Carolina
at Wilmington*

Wendy L. Flynn
Staffordshire University

**BULIMIA NERVOSA
EATING DISORDERS
OBSESSIVE-COMPULSIVE DISORDERS**

ANOSMIA

The term *anosmia* derives from the Greek *an* (without) and *osme* (odor); it refers to the absence or impairment of the sense of smell. Synonyms for this condition include anodmia, anosphrasia, and olfactory anesthesia (*Dorland's*, 1981). Organic forms of anosmia are categorized as afferent (related to impaired conductivity of the olfactory nerve), central (due to cerebral disease), obstructive (related to obstruction of the nasal fossae), and peripheral (due to diseases of peripheral olfactory nerves) (*Blakiston's*, 1979).

The most common cause of anosmia is a severe head cold or respiratory infection, which intranasal swelling blocks the nasal passages, preventing odors from reaching the olfactory region. This type of anosmia is temporary. Other organic causes of this condition include neoplasms (tumors), head injuries, or chronic rhinitis associated with granulomatous diseases (Levin, Benton, & Grossman, 1982; *Mosby's*, 1983; Thomson, 1979). Anosmia also is a characteristic of olfactogenital dysplasia, also known as *Kallman's syndrome* or anosmia-eunuchoidism. This condition, more prevalent in males, is associated with lack of development of secondary sexual characteristics and anosmia. The apparently *X*-linked autosomal dominant or recessive inheritable condition is associated with dysfunction of the hypothalamus and the pituitary (Magalini, 1971). Anosmia with these etiologies typically is a permanent condition. Decreased sense of smell, microsmia, is also common with aging and among smokers.

Psychological forms of anosmia, while less common, may occur. Phobias or fears have been identified as precipitating such forms of anosmia (*Mosby's*, 1983). Specific types of anosmia include anosmia gustatoria (loss of the ability to smell foods) and preferential anosmia (loss of the ability to smell certain odors) (*Dorland's*, 1981).

REFERENCES

Blakiston's Gould medical dictionary (4th ed.). (1979). New York: McGraw-Hill.

Dorland's illustrated medical dictionary (26th ed.). (1981). Philadelphia: Saunders.

Levin, H. A., Benton, A. L. M. & Grossman, R. G. (1982). *Neurobehavioral consequences of closed head injury*. New York: Oxford University Press.

Magalini, S. (1971). *Dictionary of medical syndromes*. Philadelphia: Lippincott.

Mosby's medical and nursing dictionary. (1983). St. Louis: Mosby.

Thomson, W. A. R. (1979). *Black's medical dictionary* (32nd ed.). New York: Barnes & Noble.

CATHY F. TELZROW
*Cuyahoga Special Education
Service Center*

ANOXIA

Anoxia literally means an absence of oxygen, a condition that is incompatible with life. Recent terminology more correctly uses the term hypoxia to refer to a condition of lowered oxygen intake. Although hypoxia is compatible with life, long-term sequelae may result depending on the degree and duration of the condition.

BRENDA POPE
*New Hanover Memorial
Hospital*

ASPHYXIA
HYPOXIA

ANTECEDENT TEACHING

Antecedent stimuli are those events that occur before a response that affect the probability of the occurrence of that response. In his book *Science and Human Behavior*, Skinner (1953) described the response sequence as having three parts: the antecedent events, the response, and the consequences. Although much has been written concerning the management of the consequences and their effects on a student's responses, Repp (1983) emphasized that teaching is actually the effective arrangement of both antecedent *and* consequent events in a manner that allows the student to learn to the full extent of his or her capabilities.

Teachers exert tremendous control over the antecedents to which their students are exposed. Some antecedent stimuli commonly seen in classrooms include instruction, curriculum, instructional objectives, commands, modeling, and materials (Repp, 1983; Snell, 1983). As teachers manipulate these antecedents, students learn to respond differentially to the differing stimuli. When their behaviors are consistently affected by the antecedents, their responses are considered to be under stimulus control. Kazdin (1975) noted one particularly effective antecedent strategy, response priming. He stated that "response priming refers to any procedure which initiates early steps in a sequence of responses" (Kazdin, 1975, p. 135). The use of various prompts or directions, while not inclusive of the total concept of response priming, is one area that has received considerable attention.

Snell (1983) identified four different types of prompts: verbal directions; modeling, which is the demonstration of all or parts of a behavioral sequence before the subject makes an attempt; cueing, which is a procedure that helps the student to focus on the task at hand without using physical contact (e.g., pointing to the relevant materials); and physical prompting, which is the actual physical manipulation of the subject's responses. In using prompting, Snell (1983) reported that prompts may be used by themselves, in combination with other prompts (e.g., physical prompting and verbal directions), or in a hierarchical pattern. When using prompting in a hierarchical manner, one may use the least to most intrusive order (i.e., verbal directions to modeling to cueing to physical prompting) or conversely, the most to least intrusive order, also known as graduated guidance. Snell (1983) stated that both hierarchies have advantages, with the graduated guidance order being the best choice for students with lower functioning levels (e.g., those labeled severely or profoundly retarded). Snell (1983) also noted that whenever artificial prompts are used, they must be gradually faded to allow the desired behaviors to come under the control of natural stimuli.

Kazdin (1975) described another effective subset of response priming, reinforcer sampling. In this procedure, the subject is allowed to experience a small portion of the reinforcer in an effort to have the subject initiate the full sequence of responses necessary to earn the entire reinforcer. Teachers could easily incorporate this procedure into their classrooms, particularly before difficult behavioral sequences are begun (e.g., a verbal description of a movie to be seen after the upcoming math quiz has concluded).

The curriculum and materials that are used in the classroom are other powerful antecedent stimuli that can be easily controlled. In an interesting exposition on classroom materials, Vargas (1984) proposed that many current textual materials actually have a number of errors that result in faulty stimulus control. She stated that if any one of five questions could be answered affirmatively concerning particular textual material, then that material would not be appropriate for use. The questions she listed were

1. Can students use pictures or diagrams instead of text to complete an exercise?
2. Does highlighting or physical layout give away answers, making it unnecessary to read through an assignment?
3. Are students able to answer questions on a passage without reading it?
4. Do all of the problems on a page require the same process for solution, making it unnecessary to discriminate between strategies?
5. Are the questions Jabberwocky comprehension questions—that is, can they be answered using grammatical cues alone? (p. 130).

Even a casual analysis of many commercially prepared and teacher-made materials will reveal that they provide improper antecedent stimuli for the responses they were designed to elicit.

The area of antecedent teaching is both broad and important. For more information on how this strategy blends with the area of behavioral teaching, the reader is referred to Skinner (1953; 1968), Repp (1983), and Martens et al. (1999).

REFERENCES

Kazdin, A. E. (1975). *Behavior modification in applied settings*. Homewood, IL: Dorsey.

Martens, B., Witt, J., Daly, E., & Vollmer, T. (1999). Behavior analysis: Theory and practice in educational settings. In C. R. Reynolds & T. B. Gutkin (Eds.), *Handbook of School Psychology* (3rd ed.) (pp. 638–663). NY: John Wiley & Sons.

Repp, A. C. (1983). *Teaching the mentally retarded*. Englewood Cliffs, NJ: Prentice-Hall.

Skinner, B. F. (1953). *Science and human behavior*. New York: Macmillan.

Skinner, B. F. (1968). *The technology of teaching*. New York: Appleton-Century-Crofts.

Snell, M. E. (1983). *Systematic instruction for the moderately and severely handicapped* (2nd ed.). Columbus, OH: Merrill.

Vargas, J. S. (1984). What are your exercises teaching? An analysis of stimulus control in instructional materials. In W. L. Heward, T. E. Heron, D. S. Hill, & J. Trap-Porter (Eds.), *Focus on behavior analysis in education*. Columbus, OH: Merrill.

ANDREW R. BRULLE
Eastern Illinois University

APPLIED BEHAVIOR ANALYSIS
BEHAVIOR MODELING

ANTHROPOSOPHIC MOVEMENT

The anthroposophic movement was founded by Rudolf Steiner (1861–1925). Steiner defined anthroposophy as knowledge produced by the higher self in man, and a way of knowledge that undertakes to guide man's spirit to communion with the spirit of the cosmos (Wannamaker, 1965). Anthroposophy postulates a spiritual world beyond man's sensory experiences. Steiner proposed that, through proper training, each person could develop an enhanced consciousness that would restore values and morality to materialistic society.

Steiner became involved in the education of both adults and children. Anthroposophic education for adults took place at the Goetheanum, a school for physical science, near Basal, Switzerland. The Waldorf School, founded in Stuttgart, Germany, in 1919, was the first of several schools for children that sought to reach the inner nature of the child and provide guidance to maturity. By 1965, 80 Waldorf Schools had been attended by more than 25,000 children in the United States and Europe (Wannamaker, 1965). Eurythmy (movement of speech and music) was used to develop concentration, attention, imitation, and an awareness of position in space (Zeigler, 1979). The schools included programming for the emotionally disturbed, socially maladjusted, and other exceptional children.

During a residential tutorship, Steiner began to apply anthroposophic training to the mentally handicapped. Karl Konig, a student of Steiner's, continued the application of Steiner's techniques in an approach known as curative education (Payne & Patton, 1981). In 1939 Konig founded the first integrated community for the mentally retarded, based on the anthroposophic philosophy in Aberdeen, Scotland (Payne & Patton, 1981). This "Camphill movement" formulated anthroposophy into the following four bases of curative education:

A right to education for all children

A humanistic/developmental perspective

An accepting milieu, providing the retarded with stability and support,

Group and individual instruction, providing the retarded with a sense of integration with mankind

Camphill communities are comprised of approximately equal numbers of retarded and normal citizens. These self-sufficient, monasticlike communes are comprised of "families" of no more than 15 persons, about half of whom are retarded. Criteria for admission include the ability to care for personal needs and adequate physical health (Zipperlen, 1975). Presently, there are 25 communities in Europe, South Africa, and the United states.

REFERENCES

Payne, J. S., & Patton, J. R. (1981). *Mental retardation*. Columbus, OH: Merrill.

Steiner, R. (1972). *Outline of occult science*. New York: Anthroposophical Society.

Wannamaker, O. D. (1965). *The anthroposophical society: The nature of its objectives*. New York: Anthroposophical Society.

Ziegler, E. F. (1979). *A history of physical education and sport*. Englewood Cliffs, NJ: Prentice-Hall.

Zipperlan, H. R. (1975). Normalization. In J. Wortis (Ed.), *Mental retardation and developmental disabilities, Volume VII*. New York: Brunner/Mazel.

ANNE M. BAUER
University of Cincinnati

CAMPHILL COMMUNITY MOVEMENT
HUMANISM AND SPECIAL EDUCATION

ANTICONVULSANTS

Anticonvulsants are medications used to control seizure activity. Investigation of the possible effects of anticonvulsant medications on a person's ability to function has been complicated by certain methodological difficulties, including the use of only normal controls, the interaction of a placebo with an active agent, and the use of a limited number of performance measures. Studies tend to fall into three different groups: those that have not distinguished among different drugs, those examining the effects of specific drugs, and those that have included the measurement of serum (blood) anticonvulsant levels (Corbett & Trimble, 1983).

Phenobarbital is perhaps one of the most widely investigated anticonvulsants with regard to effects on cognitive functioning. Lennox (1940) assessed the causes of mental deterioration in 1245 individuals with epilepsy and determined that in 15% of the cases, the anticonvulsant medication was the cause. In a later publication, Lennox and Lennox (1960) reduced this number to 5%. Relatively few studies on the effects of multiple drugs on children have been carried out. Of the investigations reported, the results have been conflicting. Chaudhry and Pond (1961) examined the causes of intellectual deterioration in 28 children with epilepsy and found no evidence to suggest that anticonvulsant medications were responsible for the noted declines in functioning. Rather, these authors suggested that such declines were related to seizure frequency. In a study of 117 children with seizures in regular public school classes, Holdsworth and Whitmore (1976) reported no differences in academic achievement depending on whether or not phenobarbital had been prescribed. These findings lend support to an earlier study that assessed the psychological performance of 26 epileptic patients over a three-month period and found little effect on total environmental adjustment caused by the use of anticonvulsants (Loveland, Smith, & Forster, 1957). There were, however, no controls in the study and the majority of patients had been receiving anticonvulsant medication for several years prior to the study.

Conversely, a number of studies of multiple drug effects have reported learning impairments with specific deficits noted in visual-spatial perception and performance (Cepeda, 1997; Rayo & Martin, 1959; Tchicaloff & Gaillard, 1970). In a study by Hutt, Jackson, Belsham, and Higgins (1968), phenobarbital was administered to normal subjects with serum level control. Decreases in abilities were noted that were related to phenobarbital blood serum levels. These effects were seen most prominently on tasks requiring sustained attention, psychomotor performance, and spontaneous speech. The drug effects became more prominent as the tasks became longer and more difficult and as the degree of external constraint (having the examiner in the room) was decreased. It was concluded that phenobarbital has effects maximally evident on tasks requiring attention and concentration, but that it also may have pronounced effects on motor coordination.

Unfavorable behavioral changes have been estimated to occur in 20 to 75% of children receiving phenobarbital as prophylaxis for febrile convulsions in infancy (Bennett & Ho, 1997; Heckmatt, Houston, & Dodds, 1976; Thorn, 1975; Wolf & Forsythe, 1978). Although no significant IQ differences were reported for groups of toddlers receiving a 8- to 12-month period of phenobarbital or placebo, there were effects on memory that were related to blood serum levels and effects on comprehension that were related to the duration of treatment (Camfield et al., 1979). There was no evidence of hyperactivity, although 15 of the 315 children on phenobarbital in the study did demonstrate an increase in "daytime fussiness and irritability."

Phenytoin (Dilantin) is the most widely used anticonvulsant in the world (Bennett & Ho, 1997; Dodrill, 1981; Hartlage & Hartlage, 1997). It has been shown to be effective with a broad range of attacks including generalized tonic-clonic seizures, most types of partial seizures, and some other less frequently observed seizure types. Acute intoxication with phenytoin leads to a confusional state, occasionally referred to as encephalopathy, which is associated with neurological symptoms of toxicity, especially ataxia and nystagmus (Corbett & Trimble, 1983). It also has been demonstrated that prolonged use of this medication, even in low doses (Logan & Freeman, 1969; Vallarta, Bell, & Reichert, 1974), may result in a clinical picture of a progressive degenerative disorder that may occur without the classic signs of such a disorder. Rosen (1968) and Stores (1975) have both reported impaired intellectual performance on long-term treatment with phenytoin. Dodrill (1975) reports that phenytoin has behavioral effects specifically related to motor performance decrements.

Ethosuximide (Zarontin), an anticonvulsant used with children for control of absence (petit mal) seizures, has been shown to impair memory and speech as well as result in affective disturbances (Guey et al., 1967). Soulayrol and Roger (1970) reported intellectual impairment in children treated with this medication; however, other studies have not confirmed this (e.g., Brown et al., 1975).

Carbamazepine (Tegretol) has been reported to have psychotropic effects. About half of 40 studies cited by Dalby (1975), in a major review of the literature, reported a beneficial psychologic effect. Typically, improvements in mood and behavior have been noted, as manifested by greater cooperativeness, reduced irritability, and a possible decrease in aggression. Increases in cognitive skill levels have been reported as well (Bennett & Ho, 1997). There have been no reported studies of the effects of primidone (Mysoline) on behavior in children, although adults occasionally have been reported to develop a florid confusional state on doses within the normal therapeutic range (Booker, 1972). It is well recognized that the drug initially may cause drowsiness and have effects similar to phenobarbital in causing restlessness in some children.

Trimble and Corbett (1980a, 1980b) studied the relationship between anticonvulsant drug levels and the behavior and cognitive performance of 312 children with seizures. The drug most commonly prescribed was phenytoin, followed by carbamazepine, valproic acid, primidone, and phenobarbital. A decrease in IQ was noted in 15% of the 204 children studied; these children had significantly higher mean phenytoin and primidone levels than other subjects. A distinct relationship between an increase in serum drug levels and a decline in nonverbal skills was reported.

Despite these side effects associated with anticonvulsants, they are recognized as essential in the management of epilepsy. According to Dodrill (1981), when anticonvulsant blood serum levels fall within therapeutic ranges and when there are no overt signs of toxicity, the chances of deleterious effects are minimal if detectable at all. Furthermore, the deleterious effects are distinctly offset by decreased seizure frequency, which has known effects on the deterioration of mental functions. It is far preferable to have modest drug side effects than seizures. Other, low incidence drugs used as anticonvulsants are reviewed in detail by Bennett and Ho (1997).

REFERENCES

Bennett, T. & Ho, M. (1997). The neuropsychology of pediatric epilepsy and antiepileptic drugs. In C. R. Reynolds & E. Fletcher-Janzen (Eds.), *Handbook of Clinical Child Neuropsychology* (2nd ed.) (pp. 517–538). New York: Plenum.

Booker, H. E. (1972). Primidone toxicity. In D. M. Woodbury, J. K. Penry, & R. P. Schmidt (Eds.), *Antiepileptic drugs* (pp. 169–204). New York: Raven.

Brown, T. R., Dreifuss, F. E., Dyken, P. R., Goode, D. J., Penry, J. K., Porter, R. J., White, B. J., & White, P. T. (1975). Ethosuccimide in the treatment of absence (petit mal) seizures. *Neurology, 25,* 515–525.

Camfield, C. S., Chaplin, S., Doyle, A. B., Shapiro, S. H., Cummings, C., & Camfield, P. R. (1979). Side effects of phenobarbitone in toddlers: Behavioral and cognitive effects. *Journal of Pediatrics, 95,* 361–365.

Cepeda, M. (1997). Nonstimulant psychotropic medication: Desired effects and cognitive/behavioral adverse effects. In C. R. Reynolds & E. Fletcher-Janzen (Eds.), *Handbook of Clinical Child Neuropsychology* (2nd ed.) (pp. 573–586). New York: Plenum.

Chaudhry, M. R., & Pond, D. A. (1961). Mental deterioration in epileptic children. *Journal of Neurology, Neurosurgery, & Psychiatry, 24,* 213–219.

Corbett, J. A., & Trimble, M. R. (1983). Epilepsy and anticonvulsant medication. In M. Rutter (Eds.), *Developmental neuropsychiatry* (pp. 112–129). New York: Guilford.

Dalby, M. A. (1975). Behavioral effects of carbamazepine. In J. K. Penry & D. D. Daley (Eds.), *Advances in neurology* (Vol. 11, pp. 130–149). New York: Raven.

Dodrill, C. B. (1975). Diphenylhydantoin serum levels, toxicity, and neuropsychological performance in patients with epilepsy. *Epilepsia, 16,* 593–600.

Dodrill, C. B. (1981). Neuropsychology of epilepsy. In S. B. Filskov & T. J. Boll (Eds.), *Handbook of clinical neuropsychology* (pp. 366–395). New York: Wiley.

Guey, J., Charles, C., Coquery, C., Roger, J., & Soulayrol, R. (1967). Study of the psychological effects of ethosuccimide on 25 children suffering from petit mal epilepsy. *Epilepsia, 8,* 129–141.

Hartlage, R. L., & Hartlage, L. C. (1997). The Neuropsychology of epilepsy: Overview and psychosocial aspects. In C. R. Reynolds & E. Fletcher-Janzen (Eds.), *Handbook of Clinical Child Neuropsychology* (2nd ed.) (pp. 506–516). NY: Plenum.

Heckmatt, J., Houston, A., & Dodds, K. (1976). Failure of phenobarbitone to prevent febrile convulsions. *British Medical Journal, 1,* 559–561.

Holdsworth, L., & Whitmore, K. (1976). A study of children with epilepsy attending ordinary schools. *Developmental Medicine & Child Neurology, 16,* 746–758.

Hutt, S. J., Jackson, P. M., Belsham, A., & Higgins, G. (1968). Perceptual motor behavior in relation to blood phenobarbitone levels: A preliminary report. *Development Medicine & Child Neurology, 10,* 626–632.

Lennox, W. G. (1940). Brain injury, drugs, and environment as a cause of mental decay in epilepsy. *American Journal of Psychiatry, 99,* 174–180.

Lennox, W. G., & Lennox, M. A. (1960). *Epilepsy and related disorders.* Boston: Little, Brown.

Logan, W. J., & Freeman, J. M. (1969). Pseudodegenerative diseases due to diphenylhydantoin intoxication. *Archives of Neurology, 21,* 631–637.

Loveland, N., Smith, B., & Forster, F. (1957). Mental and emotional changes in epileptic patients on continuous anticonvulsant medication. *Neurology, 7,* 856–865.

Rayo, D., & Martin, F. (1959). Standardized psychometric tests applied to the analysis of the effects of anticonvulsant medication on the proficiency of young epileptics. *Epilepsia, 1,* 189–207.

Rosen, J. A. (1968). Dilantin dementia. *Transactions of the American Neurological Association, 93,* 273–277.

Soulayrol, R., & Roger, J. (1970). Effets psychiatriques defavorables des medications antiepileptiques. *Revue de Neuropsychiatrie Infantile* (English abstract), *18,* 599–603.

Stores, G. (1975). Behavioral effects of anticonvulsant drugs. *Developmental Medicine & Child Neurology, 17,* 547–658.

Tchicaloff, M., & Gaillard, F. (1970). Quelques effets indesirables des medicaments antiepileptiques sur les rendements intellectuels. *Revue de Neuropsychiatrie Infantile* (English abstract), *18,* 599–603.

Thorn, I. (1975). A controlled study of prophylactic longterm treatment of febrile convulsions with phenobarbital. *Acta Neurologica Scandinavica, 60,* 67–70.

Trimble, M. R., & Corbett, J. A. (1980a). Behavioral and cognitive disturbances in epileptic children. *Irish Medical Journal, 73,* 21–28.

Trimble, M. R., & Corbett, J. A. (1980b). Anticonvulsant drugs and cognitive function. In J. A. Wada & J. K. Penry (Eds.), *Advances in epileptology: The X International Symposium.* New York: Raven.

Vallarta, J. M., Bell, D. B., & Reichert, A. (1974). Progressive encephalopathy due to chronic hydantoin intoxication. *American Journal of Diseases of Children, 128,* 27–34.

Wolf, S. M., & Forsythe, A. (1978). Behavior disturbance, phenobarbital, and febrile seizures. *Pediatrics, 61,* 728–730.

RICHARD A. BERG
*West Virginia University
Medical Center*

**DILANTIN
DRUG THERAPY
MEDICATION
PHENOBARBITOL
SEIZURE DISORDERS
TEGRETOL**

ANTIHISTAMINES

Antihistamines are a class of pharmaceutical agents that block the effect of histamine. Histamine is a naturally occurring body substance that is released in certain allergic reactions. Typically, antihistamines are more effective in preventing rather than in reversing the action of histamine. Unfortunately, antihistamines have not been found to have any dramatic effects in children with asthma or other severe diseases of an allergic nature (Markowitz, 1983). For pediatric populations, antihistamines may be effective in the treatment of hay fever or mild recurrent hives of unknown etiology. Some antihistamines, particularly Atarax and Vistaril, are used as safe, alternative antianxiety medications without withdrawal (Cepeda, 1997). Some research also has suggested the potential efficacy of antihistamines in the prevention of motion sickness in children (Macnair, 1983).

Typically, antihistamines are found in cold preparations prescribed for children (Pruitt, 1985). Children who are treated with antihistamines are likely to have less severe runny noses, yet the other features of the common cold are not significantly affected by this class of drugs. Antihistamines have atropine like effects that diminish the amount of secretions produced by the irritated lining of the nose or bronchial passages. Although some antihistamines have been marketed as cough suppressants, a number of studies have shown that antihistamines are no better than placebos in relieving children of the symptoms of the common cold (Markowitz, 1983).

Because the use of minor and major tranquilizers carries significant disadvantages in the treatment of behavioral and anxiety disorders in children (Popper, 1985), it has been suggested that antihistamines be used short term for calming acutely anxious children (Cepeda, 1997) and for controlling agitation in severely psychotic children (Popper, 1985). Risks of recreational abuse, management abuse, tolerance, and dependence are also lower than for anti-anxiety agents and major tranquilizers (Cepeda, 1997; Popper, 1985), making this class of drugs more appealing for use by the practicing physician. The enduring cognitive effects of antihistamines are not well documented in the empirical literature, although some recent research has suggested an amelioration of behavioral difficulties and improved academic performance in response to antihistamine therapy (McLoughlin, et al., 1983). Further, some investigators (Millichap, 1973; Mattes, 1979) have found antihistamines to be efficacious in the treatment and management of hyperactivity. While the effects of antihistamines on cognitive and learning outcome appear to be somewhat promising, more research must be mounted before any definitive conclusions can be made in this area. Moreover, while the use of antihistamines in the treatment of psychiatric disorders of children may provide a safer alternative than the use of other psychotropic agents, including neuroleptic agents and antianxiety drugs, it still entails some of the same risks and the physician must carefully weigh the potential benefits against any possible risks.

Although the long-term effects of antihistamines have received little systematic study, the use of these agents appear to provide primarily short-term benefits. They are typically safe and consequently are often sold without a prescription. They may have adverse effects, although these usually occur with higher doses. Sedation is the most common side effect in children, but some tolerance may develop. Combinations of antihistamines with other central nervous system depressants (e.g., alcohol) should be avoided. In high doses, or for children who are particularly sensitive to these agents, antihistamines may cause undesirable side effects. These may include excitation, nervousness, palpitations, rapid heartbeat, dryness of the mouth, urinary retention, and constipation. In rare instances, red blood cells can burst (hemolytic anemia) or bone marrow can be depleted of blood-forming cells (arganulocytosis) (Markowitz, 1983). Sustained antihistamine usage with pediatric populations may be associated with persistent daytime drowsiness, "hangover," or mild enduring effects on cognition (Popper, 1985). Although such side effects are better tolerated by younger children than by adolescents, the occurrence of these effects should result in the prompt cessation of antihistamine therapy.

REFERENCES

Cepeda, M. (1997). Nonstimulant psychotropic medication: Desired effects and cognitive/behavioral adverse effects. In C. R. Reynolds & E. Fletcher-Janzen (Eds.), *Handbook of Clinical Child Neuropsychology* (2nd ed.) (pp. 573–586). NY: Plenum Press.

Macnair, A. L. (1983). Cinnarizine in the prophylaxis of car sickness in children. *Current Medical Research Opinion, 8,* 451–455.

Markowitz, M. (1983). Immunity, allergy, and related diseases. In R. E. Behrman & V. C. Vaughn (Eds.), *Nelson textbook of pediatrics* (pp. 497–594). Philadelphia: Saunders.

Mattes, J. (1979). Trial of diphenpyraline in hyperactive children (letter). *Psychopharmacology Bulletin, 15,* 5–6.

McLoughlin, J., Nall, M., Isaacs, P., Petrosko, J., Karibo, J., & Lindsey, B. (1983). The relationship of allergies and allergy treatment to school performance and student behavior. *Annals of Allergy, 51,* 506–510.

Millichap, J. G. (1973). Drugs in management of minimal brain dysfunction. *Annals of the New York Academy of Science, 205,* 321–334.

Popper, C. W. (1985). Child and adolescent psychopharmacology. In R. Michels & J. O. Cavenar (Eds.), *Psychiatry* (Vol. 2, pp. 1–23). New York: Lippincott.

Pruitt, A. W. (1985). Rational use of cold and cough preparations. *Pediatric Annals, 14,* 289–291.

RONALD T. BROWN
*Emory University School
of Medicine*

DRUG THERAPY
TRANQUILIZERS

ANTISOCIAL BEHAVIOR

A study by Peterson (1961) considered a sampling of many behaviors of children that could be considered as antisocial. More than 400 representative case folders from files of a child-guidance clinic were inspected and the referral problems of each child noted. Peterson's results indicated that the interrelationship among 58 items could be reduced to two independent clusters: conduct problems and personality problems. The two dimensions of problems most frequently reported among the public school students in these two major clusters were aggression and withdrawal. Each child could be placed somewhere in these two dimensions regardless of the number of problem behaviors or other dimensions the child manifested. Children's behaviors differ quantitatively not qualitatively. The degree of quantitative difference between normal and abnormal is usually slight.

Definitions are particularly difficult to generate when context is general and critical, as is the case when the word "social" is used. While there is a need to convey with words what is meant by antisocial behavior, the intensity, timeliness, and impact of a behavior on others in the culture/society/group where the behavior is experienced determines the definition: therefore, a static meaning is not effective. Antisocial behaviors or misbehaving (disliked performances) are accepted daily by society. A behavior is labeled antisocial when the tolerance level of an observer is exceeded with respect to that observer's interpretation of societal rules.

For example, aggressive antisocial behavior is manifested when a student stands and yells a phrase of profanity during a school assembly. The consequences of such behavior could be removal from the audience (peer group), immediate verbal reprimand by adult authorities, a quick trip to the administrator's office, or dismissal from a school. In contrast, if the same pupil were to stand during a professional ball game and yell the same phrase of profanity, not only might the audience approve of the behavior, it might even reward the verbal expressiveness.

Variables in the environment that define the tolerance level of observers when a behavior is judged antisocial are many: time, social status, money, event, location, age, reputation, intensity, duration, frequency, and group expectations. When the cumulative effect of these variables is negative, exceeding the dynamic acceptable definition of the moment, a person's behavioral performance is judged antisocial. For example, when a behavior is poorly timed, appropriate social status is not recognized, intensity is high and loud, the behavior is against school rules, reputation is known, duration is long; frequency is perceived as too often, and other students are conforming to rules of the environment, an antisocial behavior is said to exist. To identify specific factors related to perceptions of antisocial behavior, recent investigation has emphasized those behaviors that teachers and students find most disturbing. Aggressive behavior is most often primary, but withdrawal behaviors such as fear, anxiety, and tension are also defined as antisocial.

This second type of antisocial behavior is reported to be more tolerable to society. The child suffering from withdrawal may be in deeper pain, despair, or depression than an aggressive individuals, however, such a child is less aversive to adults and peers, and less likely to excite the environment into action. These children have too little behavior rather than too much. Characteristics accompanying withdrawal are feelings of inferiority and self-consciousness, social withdrawal, shyness, anxiety, weeping, hypersensitivity, infrequent social smiles, nail chewing, depression and chronic sadness, drowsiness, sluggishness, daydreaming, passivity, short attention span, preoccupation, and somber quietness. These children are also picked on by others.

The term antisocial behavior is often applied when behaviors remain inflexible, or frozen, and the person performing the behaviors continues to react to the environment in a manner judged by the group to be displeasing, inappropriate and uncomfortable. The label antisocial behavior is attached to the person displaying the behavior and the definition itself magnifies the individual's differences. Not only does the behavior classify a person, but the antisocial definition itself accentuates differences. Only if classification leads to positive action through school programs on the behalf of the child is this definition constructive.

Characteristics

Patterns of antisocial behavior have received a variety of labels: e.g., unsocialized aggressive, conduct disorder, aggressive, unsocialized psychopathic, psychopathic delinquent, antisocially aggressive, and sadistically aggressive. Children exhibiting antisocial behaviors apparent to school officials and teachers may demonstrate one or more of the following characteristics:

1. An inability to learn that cannot be explained by conventional intellectual, sensory, or health factors. A learning-disabled child seldom escapes recognition. He or she is frequently labeled learning disabled, thus lowering self-esteem. The inability to learn is perhaps the single most significant characteristic of antisocial children, with the learning disability manifested as the inability to profit from social experiences and/or academic instruction.

2. An inability to build and maintain satisfactory interpersonal relationships with peers and teachers; to demonstrate sympathy and warmth toward others; to stand alone when necessary; to have close friends; to be aggressively constructive; to enjoy working and playing with others as well as working and playing alone. Children who are un-

able to build and maintain satisfactory interpersonal relationships are easily defined as different by teachers and peers.

3. "Inappropriate" behaviors or feelings that occur under normal conditions. What is appropriate is judged by the teacher and the student's peers. This judgment is sensed by children because their ability to profit from school experiences and relate to their teachers. Children classified as antisocial often cannot learn what is appropriate because of their inability to relate to and profit from cultural experiences. This amplifies the daily failures of children who fail to conform to social/cultural rules and exacerbates their lack of socialization.

4. Lack of flexibility. When behaviors become frozen into patterns of inappropriateness of such intensity, duration, and frequency that they interfere with social activities of a group, those behaviors are identified as antisocial.

5. Depression and general moods of unhappiness, characteristics of withdrawal. When children seldom smile and express unhappiness in play, art work, group discussions, and language arts, the observer should watch for antisocial expression.

6. A tendency to develop physical symptoms, pains, or fears, especially in reaction to school situations or authority figures. These symptoms may indicate potential antisocial behaviors.

7. Disobedience, disruptiveness, fighting, temper tantrums, irresponsibility, impertinence, jealousy, anger, bossiness, the use of profanity, attention-seeking behavior, boisterousness, defiance of authority, feelings of guilt and inadequacy, irritability, and quarrelsomeness. These descriptors are often associated with antisocial phenomena.

Behaviors described by these characteristics may formulate a pattern of active antisocial behavior that results in conflict with parents, peers, and social institutions. Children and adolescents who represent extreme patterns of antisocial behaviors are likely to have difficulty with law-enforcement agencies. Extreme antisocial behavior will be defined as criminal conduct and result in arrest, incarceration, recidivism, and failure to become a good citizen.

Acquisition

The possibility of hereditary or predispositional factors cannot be ignored, neither can the contributions of organic factors be ruled out. Prematurity, (birth weight less than 5 pounds,) is regarded as an important cause of brain damage in children. Epilepsy and cerebral palsy studies report higher prevalances of antisocial behaviors among those with known brain lesions. Situations where trait patterns of deviant behavior can be studied along with the mechanisms by which the acquisition of the traits occurs is very revealing. Sociological literature has emphasized social class, deviant social organization, and social inequalities as influential. The family is also a setting where deviant behavior has been studied. It is obvious making the acquisition of principal behavioral patterns of antisocial behavior more probable. Psychiatric illness in parents reflects an increased rate of behavior problems in children. Antisocial parents tend to rear antisocial children. Childhood behavior problems are more common among lower socioeconomic classes. To what extent the influence of parents' disturbances on the child's behavior is genetic and to what extent it is environmental, is speculative.

Children with antisocial behaviors are most visible when required to pay strict attention, follow directions, demonstrate control, exhibit socially acceptable behavior, and master academic skills. School, the primary socializing agency for society, emphasizes conformity and educational achievement. These expectations are basic to the order of formal training. When children are unable to meet these expectations, concerns frequently arise among teachers. Questions educators pose may include: How many children are there? How do they behave? How can they be controlled and managed in the classroom? How should they be classified to deduce effects created by labels? What support systems can provide these children with needed programs?

Terms used in educational settings to describe children with antisocial behaviors are emotionally disturbed, socially maladjusted, minimally neurologically impaired, culturally disadvantaged, behavior disordered, educationally handicapped, and conduct disturbed. Such labels represent different orientations that exist among educators confronted with the task of providing educational programs for children with antisocial behaviors. All these labels could be used collectively for a single child experiencing difficulty in school. For qualification for programs, labels and treatments should be closely related to how the antisocial child (in classroom, community, or at home) is perceived (by educators, social groups, or family). Educational offerings frequently depend on how a child is perceived and the attitude of the referring school toward the child.

Treatment

When an individual has appropriate behavioral responses in his or her repertoire and exhibits these responses under appropriate circumstances, antisocial behavior is interpreted. Through systematic and explicit application of the principles of learning, behavior management can be applied in educational settings to treat antisocial behaviors.

The individual can be helped to change deficient or maladaptive behavior by receiving assistance to modify his or her responses to specific sound cues. In the case of maladaptive behavior, for example, aggression could be modified to be elicited or emitted under appropriate circumstances only. This type of behavioral learning, unlearning,

or relearning is known as behavior management. The teacher or behaviorist operates on the assumption that the behavior can be modified without understanding why the behavior is antisocial. The antecedents to the behavior need not be reconstructed to initiate corrective action. Teaching the child to react more appropriately is the only relevant issue, not finding out how the child came to behave antisocially. The focus during behavior therapy is on teaching new behaviors and eliminating old ones. The first task of the therapist (teacher) is to decide which behavior should be modified. Once a target behavior is defined, the treatment goal can be specified. Treatments are based on principles of learning: respondent learning, operant conditioning, interrelationships of operation and respondent factors, social reinforcement, desensitization, and aversive and contingency control. The treatment goal is assessed when the antisocial behavior has become adapted. If in the process of identifying target behaviors the teacher discovers antecedents as causes, the organization of the classroom environment, stimuli, and consequences can be arranged so that the learning situation supports the child's development. An engineered, structured classroom with clear-cut expectations and rewarding consequences for appropriate behavior and academic accomplishment can result in definite academic and behavioral gains. Primary or tangible rewards, teacher attention, "game" approaches, and high-interest activities can become successful interventions for adapting antisocial behaviors. Precision teaching involves selecting a behavior, charting it on a graph, recording changes and occurrences, analyzing the child's performance, and changing the program according to program effects. Some schools use a resource room concept, in which the child participates part time in a special program and part time in a regular class program.

Completely self-contained classrooms for children with more severe learning and behavioral problems can be successful. The engineered classroom directs attention to the establishment of specific goals or develops a sequence of behavioral objectives, for example, attention, response, order, exploratoration, social activity, mastery, and achievement. This engineering translates behavior modification strategy into realistic use in the classroom. There is constant manipulation of stimuli and intervention in the class to assure a child's continued success.

There are limitless behaviors that can disturb, interfere, or interrupt. There are as many interventions to attempt to modify disturbing behaviors. The range of children's behaviors that are judged negatively is extensive, especially in the complex social system called school. Our tendency is to cause a child to internalize his or her problematic characteristics through inadvertent reinforcement.

Reactors classify, define, program, analyze, label, and provide some services to those identified as aggressive when threatening behaviors become a serious concern.

Seldom do educators recognize the responder as a contributor to the disturbances. The child judged as antisocial is the one who violates a large number of behavioral codes, yet some of the most seriously troubled go unrecognized and untreated as passive aggressors.

The intensity of observer reaction may be related to the observer's own social tolerance and his or her difficulty in controlling comparable tendencies. Certainly, the observer's tolerance plays a significant role in determining the services to be received by the antisocial performer.

If a tree crashes in the forest but there is no human ear to hear it, is there a noise? When an individual behaves in an antisocial fashion, does the disturbance exist without a reactor to register the event? Does the disturbance reside in the child or the reactor, or is it a product of both?

REFERENCE

Quay, H. C., & Werry, J. S. (1972). *Psychopathological disorders of childhood.* New York: Wiley.

ANNE SABATINO
Hudson, Wisconsin

CONDUCT DISORDER
EMOTIONAL DISORDERS
SERIOUSLY EMOTIONALLY DISTURBED

ANTISOCIAL PERSONALITY

The antisocial personality is characterized by a recurring pattern of antisocial behaviors and a general disregard for the rights of others. This pattern of behavior has, in the past been referred to as psychopathy or sociopathy. It emerges during childhood in the form of truancy and other school-related academic and behavior problems such as delinquency, lying, fighting, sexual promiscuity, substance abuse, and running away from home. The DSM-IV (American Psychiatric Association, 1994) requires at least four of the following nine manifestations of the disorder be present before a diagnosis of antisocial personality disorder (APD) is made: inability to sustain consistent work behavior; lack of ability to function as a responsible parent; failure to accept social norms with respect to lawful behavior; inability to maintain enduring attachment to a sexual partner; irritability or aggressiveness; failure to honor financial obligations; failure to plan ahead, or impulsivity; disregard for the truth; and recklessness. Cleckley (1976) has identified other characteristics such as lack of remorse or shame, failure to learn from experience, poor judgment, and absence of anxiety.

The diagnosis of APD is typically reserved for individuals age 18 and over. Younger children and adolescents who manifest signs of APD are diagnosed as conduct disorder. There are four subtypes of conduct disorder depending on the presence or absence of normal social attachments and aggressive behavior. Many, but not all, children who manifest conduct disorder go on to develop an antisocial personality disorder (Loeber, 1982). Research has identified five factors that appear to play a role in the etiology of APD including heredity, brain abnormalities, autonomic nervous system underarousal, and family, and environmental influences.

REFERENCES

American Psychiatric Association. (1994). *Diagnostic and statistical manual of mental disorders* (4th ed.). Washington, DC.

Cleckley, H. M. (1976). The mask of sanity (5th ed.). St. Louis: Mosby.

Loeber, R. (1982). The stability of antisocial and delinquent behavior: A review. *Child Development, 53,* 1431–1446.

ROBERT G. BRUBAKER
Eastern Kentucky University

AGGRESSION
CONDUCT DISORDER
PERSONALITY DISORDERS

ANXIETY

There is probably no aspect of the human experience more universal than that of anxiety. In every culture and throughout recorded time, the human organism has been subject to real and imagined threats that may produce the arousal state that is labeled anxiety. By the midpoint of the present century, many authors, philosophers, psychologists, and others were referring to the twentieth century as the age of anxiety. Auden (1947) explained that the age of anxiety was reflected in heightened feelings of loneliness. This increase in anxiety, or perhaps an increased awareness of its existence, was often attributed to loneliness, uncertainty, and bureaucratic interference with the individual's efforts toward self-recognition and self-realization. Anxiety may be both a symptom and a disorder.

Both Kierkegaard (1944) and May (1977) noted the potential for human growth inherent in a satisfactory response to anxiety-producing stimuli. In support of this notion is the considerable research and theory of Torrance (1965) affirming that creative problem solving serves as an antidote for anxiety. Thus anxiety is not always defined as a destructive or debilitating force in human behavior. Many psychologists and educators today describe a curvilinear relationship between learning and anxiety. Both very high and very low levels of anxiety are negatively related to learning, resulting in the well-known inverted or U-shaped curve between anxiety and performance on complex tasks.

One of the more prevalent conceptualizations of anxiety today embodies the state-trait distinction. Here we may refer to Spielberger (1972), who states the differences between state and trait anxiety very clearly. Essentially, state anxiety is a complex system of emotional reactions that arise when an individual perceives a situation as threatening, regardless of whether a real threat exists. Thus, state anxiety is a transitory condition and may vary greatly from individual to individual and from one condition to another. Not all conditions are equally threatening to all individuals.

In contrast, anxiety may be understood to be more of a personality trait. This notion suggests that it is a more permanent construct of the individual's usual manner of functioning. Trait anxiety is a term used to define the personality of one who frequently experiences anxiety, often where the strength of the stimulus for evoking anxiety is relatively weak. It refers to the propensity of the individual to feel anxiety. This trait appears to vary among persons on a continuum from highly infrequent to an almost constant level of anxiety. Several researchers, including Gottschalk and Gleser (1969), view anxiety as a multimodal concept. It has been theorized that such emotions as anger, guilt, shame, and shyness are really components of anxiety.

In an effort to understand more clearly the nature and impact of anxiety, several researchers have developed measures of anxiety. Some of these measures record physiological manifestations of anxiety such as changes in temperature or heart rate. Taylor (1951) is credited with an early effort to measure anxiety through a self-report technique. Behavior, task performance, clinical intuition, and stress responses are also used to measure anxiety.

Among the most widely researched measures of anxiety are the *State-Trait Anxiety Inventory for Children* (Spielberger, et al., 1973), the *State-Trait Anxiety Inventory* (Spielberger, et al., 1970) and the *Revised Children's Manifest Anxiety Scale* (Reynolds & Richmond, 1978, 1985), the latter being the most widely used measure of children's anxiety throughout the world. For behavioral representations of anxiety, the Behavior Assessment System for Children is widely used, especially in the public schools (Reynolds & Kamphaus, 1992). These and other instruments continue to be used by researchers and clinicians in their efforts to specify the nature of anxiety and to record and remediate its debilitating effects on the individual.

REFERENCES

Auden, W. H. (1947). *The age of anxiety*. New York: Random House.

Gottschalk, L. O., & Gleser, G. C. (1969). *The measurement of psy-chological states through the content analysis of verbal behavior*. Los Angeles: University of California Press.

Kierkegaard, S. (1944). *The concept of dread* (translated by Walter Lowrie). Princeton, NJ: Princeton University Press (originally published in Danish in 1844).

May, R. (1977). *The meaning of anxiety*. New York: Norton.

Reynolds, C. R., & Kamphaus, R. W. (1992). *Behavior assessment system for children*. Circle Pines, MN: American Guidance Service.

Reynolds, C. R., & Richmond, B. O. (1978). What I think and feel: A revised measure of children's manifest anxiety. *Journal of Abnormal Child Psychology, 6,* 271–280.

Reynolds, C. R., & Richmond, B. O. (1985). *Manual, revised children's manifest anxiety scale*. Los Angeles: Western Psychological Services.

Spielberger, C. D. (1972). Anxiety as an emotional state. In C. D. Spielberger (Ed.), *Anxiety: Current trends in theory and research* (p. 30). New York: Academic.

Spielberger, C. D., Edwards, C. D., Lushene, R. E., Montuori, I., & Platzek, D. (1973). *Manual, state trait anxiety inventory for children*. Palo Alto, CA: Consulting Psychologists Press.

Spielberger, C. D., Gorsuch, R. L., & Lushene, R. E. (1970). *Manual, for the state-trait Anxiety inventory*. Palo Alto, CA: Consulting Psychologists Press.

Taylor, J. A. (1951). The relationship of anxiety to the conditioned eyelid response. *Journal of Experimental Psychology, 41,* 81–92.

Torrance, E. P. (1965). *Mental health and constructive behavior*. Belmont, CA: Wadsworth.

BERT O. RICHMOND
University of Georgia

FEARS AND PHOBIAS
REVISED CHILDREN'S MANIFEST ANXIETY SCALE
TEST ANXIETY

ANXIETY DISORDERS

Anxiety is an emotional condition experienced by all children and adults to some degree. It results when people's responses to internal or external events produce a negative arousal state. It is a state of general emotional arousal that is experienced as unpleasant to some degree by the individual. Internal or external conditions that create fear are the most common sources of anxiety. When individuals experience anxiety to a significant degree, they often show a wide range of possible responses that are exaggerated in proportion to the objective situation. These diffuse effects may include emotional responses, including physiological changes; cognitive changes in perceptions of objects or thoughts about a situation; motor responses such as irritable behavior or hyperactivity, or the opposite including lethargy or withdrawn behavior. A certain degree of anxiety has motivating properties and can have a positive value such as enhancing performance on educational tasks. Anxiety becomes a clinical problem when it reaches a significant degree on a regular basis and interferes with normal adaptive behavior.

Anxiety can be specific to particular situations or even a specific object, or it can be generalized, undifferentiated, and "free-floating." Specific anxiety may give rise to phobias. Generalized anxiety would be part of a disorder such as an avoidant disorder, in which anxiety is part of a general response to social encounters.

The two general approaches to explaining the origins of anxiety disorders are psychoanalytic and behavioral, although the most common treatments are biological. According to the psychoanalytic approach, anxiety, in its more significant forms, represents intrapsychic conflict between a child's ego and unconscious sexual impulses. As the developing child attempts to defend himself or herself against the unconscious impulses, the accompanying anxiety is displaced or transferred into some other form that is the behavioral manifestation of one of the anxiety disorders. The particular form of the disorder may represent a personality difference in the individual child or be the result of a traumatic incident.

The behavioral approach traces the origins of the symptom behavior to specific environmental conditions. For example, phobias are often explained as conditioned responses in which a previously neutral stimulus (e.g., a dog) is paired with a noxious stimulus to produce fear, which then may be generalized (e.g., to other animals). The concept of reinforcement is also used by learning theorists. According to this point of view, the behavior is maintained because it serves to reduce the anxiety. For example, the child who avoids a fearful object, in the case of a phobia, controls anxiety in this way. Similarly, the child who is fearful of other people learns to control anxiety by withdrawing from social contacts and acting shy. The anxiety disorders have their own psychiatric classification (American Psychiatric Association, 1994).

Childhood Stress

Stress refers to environmental pressures and changes that produce emotional and physiological coping responses in the child. Circumstances often produce anxiety reactions. Changes that produce stress frequently occur in normal child development. For example, the young infant experiences anxiety in the form of separation anxiety from the mother. Healthy child development depends on the child's learning effective ways to cope with stressful changes so as to keep anxiety at manageable levels.

Much research exists on the effects of change and stressors on adults, and a variety of stress scales have been developed. Less is known about the clinical effects of stress and changes in child development, although Bowlby (1980) has studied the role of separation and loss on the development of childhood depression. Clinicians, teachers, and guidance counselors should be aware of the role of change, loss, and stress in the development of anxiety disorders. The loss of a parent through death or divorce, chronic illness, and school failure all place the child at risk of developing anxiety reactions. The Behavior Assessment System for Children (Reynolds & Kamphaus, 1992) includes standardized measures of stress in children of school age.

Separation Anxiety Disorder

The main symptom of this syndrome is excessive anxiety when the child is separated from a major attachment figure such as a parent. Common behaviors include fear that harm will come to the parent; worry that a major trauma such as an automobile accident will occur; refusal to go to school; sleep disturbance; reluctance to be left alone; physical symptoms, such as stomach aches, headaches, or dizziness; and withdrawal from normal social activities. This disorder may develop anytime from infancy through adolescence. It is usually not caused by a single event, but gradually emerges as a behavioral pattern stemming from a disturbed child-parent relationship. Cases often appear to have been set off by a particular upsetting event, but close examination reveals the longstanding pattern.

School Phobia

Children refusing to go to school or asking to leave school once they arrive is one of the most common and sometimes most difficult to treat of childhood disorders. Children sometimes develop a negative association based on a frustrating school experience and then refuse to go to school. This could be the case where a child has a serious learning disability of an attention deficit disorder in which self-esteem is adversely affected. Generally, however, a school-refusal or school-phobic child is acting out of anxiety relating to separation.

School phobic cases can be classified into two types. The first is generally seen in younger children with more cooperative parents; it responds better to intervention. The second type occurs in late childhood (ages 10 to 12) or adolescence. The parents tend to be less cooperative; there may be conflict in the marital relationship; and response to treatment is slower and may require hospitalization.

Two cases treated by the author demonstrate the two clinical subtypes. In one, an 8-year-old girl was referred by her pediatrician because she was showing anxiety about attending school and was frequently calling her mother from school in acute distress. She worried excessively and was concerned that her mother might be in an automobile accident (her mother did a good deal of traveling as part of her job). In her rural community, a number of fatal automobile accidents had been well publicized, and the child was focusing on those traumas as she verbalized her terror. She was the youngest child in the family and the mother had a long pattern of overinvolvement and protectiveness toward her. Treatment consisted of individual psychotherapy addressing the irrational fear that the mother may die in a traffic accident, and behavioral prescriptions for the mother to be less protective of the child. The parents were supportive and responsive to identifying the problem. The child responded well to insight-oriented therapy, and the fear and phobic behavior was gradually extinguished.

A case that reflects the second type of school phobia involved a 14-year-old boy. He was referred following involvement with a school truant officer because of refusal to go to school in the grade 8. A history revealed that the child had always been reluctant to attend school. The mother had worked as a teacher's aide in the child's elementary school during his early years; this served to reduce the child's separation anxiety. Mother and child had an extremely close, enmeshed relationship. When the family moved to a different city and the mother no longer was in the school during the day, the school refusal became acute. The parents had an extremely poor marital relationship, and the mother had been diagnosed as a paranoid personality disorder. The child, as an adolescent, felt compelled to stay home from school because of his mother's worry and agitation. This case required hospitalization of the adolescent to work intensely on the overinvolvement between mother and child and to address the family problems.

Avoidant Disorder of Childhood and Adolescence

This disorder occurs from age 2½ through adolescence. A behavioral pattern of shrinking away from social contacts and withdrawing from others is the central characteristic. Children with this disorder are not merely shy, they actively retreat from social contacts and are very cautious in dealing with peers. Nonverbal body movements may be characterized by the avoidance of eye contact, poor posture, and childlike mannerisms.

A clinical case treated by this psychologist illustrates this disorder. A 17-year-old female was referred with the suspected problem of bulimia. She had been vomiting daily for several months because of a preoccupation with the idea that she was overweight and unattractive to others. History revealed that this seemed to be a recent pattern of behavior stemming from a longstanding pattern of social isolation. This girl and her mother described her as being rejected and isolated from others since grade 1. Her peers had seen her as "weird" and different for 12 years and had ostracized her because of her unusual behaviors. She had

few friends and was performing poorly in school despite excellent academic skills and at least average intelligence. The decision to come to therapy resulted in the girl and her family finally admitting to the severity of her social isolation and unhappiness. It was followed by a suicidal gesture that resulted in hospitalization. In the hospital, the girl showed behaviors that impressed others as similar to those of schizophrenics. There was regressed, childlike behavior. As she began to adjust to the hospital setting, she showed nonverbal behaviors of avoidance of eye contact and stared at the wall when engaged in conversation with others. She would curl her legs into a fetallike position in the middle of a conversation. This case demonstrated behaviorally the psychological turmoil of the avoidant disorder. Children with this disorder are extremely sensitive to social acceptance and the judgment of others. Treatment was highly successful. A supportive hospital milieu and intensive individual psychotherapy produced fairly rapid changes in the longstanding behavioral pattern of avoiding contact with other people. The school environment was an important testing ground of the behavioral changes involving less sensitivity to the judgment of peers.

Overanxious Disorders

Children with this syndrome show excessive worry about performance, potential injuries, and acceptance by others. The difference between this disorder and the avoidant one is that the primary problem is worry or anxiety rather than avoidant behavior. Children who show this problem syndrome tend to come from families having a high emphasis on performance, achievement, and socially acceptable behavior. The worry tends to be generalized, not specifically associated with a particular situation. It often involves overconcern with being a highly competent individual and sensitivity to criticism. Children with this disorder also may show psychophysiological symptoms such as stomach aches or general nervousness. There are signs of obsessional thoughts about oneself, a tendency toward perfectionism, and approval-seeking behavior. Such children also are prime examples of people who are always imagining the worst; they may have fears of death or impending disaster. Children with this psychological problem share many of the same concerns as those with the avoidant disorder, but they persevere in their efforts to achieve or to please despite their excessive worry instead of withdrawing from social contacts.

Childhood Phobias

Phobias reflect intense anxiety associated with a fear about a specific object or situation that is out of proportion to the apparent objective danger. In this sense, phobias are irrational fears. In evaluating whether or not a childhood fear is a phobia, the clinician must keep in mind the fears that normally would be apparent at different developmental ages. For example, fear of loud noises and strangers are the norm in infancy; fear of animals and fear of darkness in toddlerhood; and fear of social embarrassment in adolescence. A phobia is distinguished by the severity of the anxiety and a sense of panic that seems to overwhelm the child when faced with the object or situation. There is an obsessional quality to the phobia as the child may spend unusual amounts of time worrying about exposure to the object. Common phobias include fear of animals, heights, and insects.

Psychoanalytic theory explains the development of phobias as a process in which internal conflicts produce anxiety and are displaced onto an external object, causing an intense fear reaction. In contrast, behavior therapy proposes a conditioning theory to explain the development of phobias. Wolpe (1969) suggests that a traumatic or frightening incident occurs when a neutral stimulus or object is present at the same time. Anxiety thereafter is evoked by the presence of the previously neutral object such as a dog; a phobia is born this way. There are other variations of these two general approaches in explaining the development of phobias, many of which emphasize the development of irrational cognitive beliefs from many sources including a child's imagination.

Behavior therapy has become the most popular approach to treating phobias because of fairly high success rates. The most common behavioral therapy technique remains Wolpe's (1969) systematic desensitization technique. In this approach, the clinician first constructs an anxiety hierarchy that consists of a list of objects or situations that are logically related to the phobic object and that gradually increase in the degree of anxiety that would be elicited. For example, in a social phobia, the list may begin with low levels of anxiety involving the introduction to an acquaintance and increase to a situation involving public speaking. The second step in the desensitization procedure is to train the person in techniques of relaxation. The final step in the procedure is to gradually introduce the individual to anxiety-producing objects while relaxation techniques are employed or alternated with the introduction to the objects, as it is assumed the relaxation is incompatible with anxiety.

The clinician hopes to teach the individual to control anxiety in the face of exposure to the objects, in this way desensitizing the subject to the phobic reaction. Visualization or imagery techniques are often applied. The individual is asked to visualize an anxiety-producing situation and then to practice relaxation. The person might at a later time be exposed to this actual situation. The hope is that the subject will have learned to control anxiety through practicing relaxation and also, with the help of a therapist, to be able to think through misconceptions about the irrational fear. This approach has proven effective in a wide variety of phobias, including school phobia.

REFERENCES

American Psychiatric Association. (1994). *Diagnostic and statistical manual of mental disorders* (4th ed.). Washington, DC: Author.

Bowlby, J. (1980). *Attachment and loss: Vol. 3. Loss: Sadness and depression.* New York: Basic Books.

Reynolds, C. R., & Kamphaus, R. W. (1992). *Behavior assessment system for children.* Circle Pines, MN: American Guidance Service.

Wolpe, J. (1969). *The practice of behavior therapy.* New York: Pergamon.

WILLIAM G. AUSTIN
*Cape Fear Psychological
Services*

BEHAVIOR ASSESSMENT SYSTEM FOR CHILDREN
CHILDHOOD PSYCHOSIS
DEPRESSION
EMOTIONAL DISORDERS
PSYCHONEUROTIC DISORDERS
SCHOOL PHOBIA

APGAR RATING SCALE

The Apgar Rating Scale was specifically designed to assess medical distress in newborns. Ratings are made by attending nurses or physicians at 1 minute after birth, with possible further ratings at 3, 5, and 10 minutes. Five vital signs, heart rate, respiratory effort, reflex irritability, muscle tone, and color, are rated on a 3-point scale: 2 if present, 1 if not fully present, and 0 if absent. Thus the range of possible scores is 0–10, with scores greater than 7 (about 70% of all newborns) indicating excellent condition, 3–7 (24% of all newborns) indicating a moderately depressed condition, and less than 3 (6% of all newborns) indicating a severely depressed condition (Apgar, 1953; Apgar, Holaday, James, & Weisbrott, 1958).

The Apgar Scale has been used extensively in research in anesthesiology, obstetrics, pediatric neurology, and developmental psychology. Apgar scores are predictive of infant mortality: 15% of neonates with severely depressed scores die within 7fi months, compared with 0.13% of those receiving scores of 10 (Apgar, et al., 1958). There is also a moderate relationship between Apgar scores and intellectual and motor development: Edwards (1968), for example, found an Apgar correlation of 0.251 with Stanford-Binet

IQ, 0.456 with a battery of fine-motor tasks, and 0.480 with gross-motor tasks at age 4. The 5-minute postnatal Apgar scores were more predictive than 1-minute scores in Edwards' study.

REFERENCES

Apgar, V. (1953). A proposal for a new method of evaluation of the newborn infant. *Current Researches in Anesthesia and Analgesia, 32,* 260–267.

Apgar, V., Holaday, D., James, L., Weisbrott, I., & Berrien, C. (1958). Evaluation of the newborn infant—second report. *Journal of the American Medical Association, 168,* 1985–1988.

Edwards, N. (1968). The relationship between physical condition immediately after birth and mental and motor performance at age four. *Genetic Psychology Monographs, 78,* 257–289.

JOHN MACDONALD
Eastern Kentucky University

LOW BIRTH WEIGHT INFANTS
NEONATAL BEHAVIORAL ASSESSMENT SCALE
PREMATURITY/PRETERM

APHASIA

Everyone with the diagnosis of aphasia has an acquired language disorder, but the type of language disorder (problems understanding talking, problems talking, problems reading, problems writing) and the severity of these difficulties vary, reflecting the different locations and the extent of the damage to the brain. There also are similarities in the type of problems using language among persons whose brain has been damaged in the same location. Aphasiologists are persons who study aphasia and attempt to provide a structure for understanding and diagnosing this language disorder upon the basis of these variations and similarities. As a result of their studies, there are many different definitions of aphasia and many different classification systems offering a means of subdividing aphasia (Chapey, 1994; Davis, 1993).

Literature within the last decade reflects a general agreement on the following: The term aphasia (acquired language disorder due to brain damage) applies to persons who formerly had intact, developed language functioning and, therefore, the term aphasia does not apply to language disorders experienced by children (Davis, 1993). Some aphasiologists (Darley, 1982; Schuell, 1972) set forth arguments against subdividing or classifying aphasia according to differences or similarities of symptoms. In the opinion of these experts, the variations in symptoms reflect

degrees of problems in the total, integrated brain function.

However, if classification is considered, one common basis is nonfluent versus fluent. In this case, separation is made on the basis of whether the symptoms of a person's language disorder result in a disruption of fluency (Hegde, 1994). Rosenbek, Wertz, & LaPointe (1989) define being fluent as producing five or more connected words. Obviously, persons who have aphasia and who cannot produce five or more connected words have nonfluent aphasia. Further common subdivision types within nonfluent aphasia include Broca's, global, isolation, and transcortical motor. Subdivisions of fluent aphasia include Wernicke's transcortical sensory and conduction.

Other common perspectives seen in the literature for defining symptoms of aphasia are those in terms of cognitive impairments (Chapey, 1981; Davis, 1993) and linguistic analysis of the disordered language (Jakobsen, 1971; Caplan, 1991). Cognitive definitions of aphasia are based on the idea that cognition underlies language and that if language is impaired, some aspects of cognition also must be impaired. Descriptions of symptoms are reported as impairments in long- and short-term memory for words, phrases, and sentences and as impairments in processing linguistic information (Hegde, 1994). Research done from the linguistic point of view is called "neurolinguistic," and it analyzes the symptoms from a perspective of whether a patient shows difficulties in linguistic units if they are shorter or longer, simple or complex, active or passive, embedded or unembedded, and so forth (Hegde, 1994).

The types of language disorders encountered by persons with aphasia include difficulties in comprehending spoken language (for example, the patient cannot point to a picture or object named, or the person may not know the meaning of ordinary words) and difficulties in talking (the patient may substitute sounds or words and create new words that do not mean anything to the listener, or the person may omit sounds within words or whole words). Persons with aphasia may struggle to get out any words and speak very little, or they may talk a great deal with ease, but the words and grammar do not have meaning for the listener. Persons with aphasia may also experience difficulties in reading or writing and doing number calculations (Hegde, 1994). In addition, there are often many related disorders that occur from the damage to the overall neurological network, such as motor speech problems or paresis of the oral structure and/or arm and leg.

Over one million people in the United States suffer from aphasia and each day almost 300 new cases occur. Rehabilitation requires commitment and support from professionals and family. In an effort to provide a better understanding of this disorder, a national organization, the National Aphasia Association has been formed (LaPointe, 1997). This organization can be reached at P.O. Box 1887, Murray Hill Station, New York, NY 10156-0611.

REFERENCES:

Caplan, D. (1991). Agrammatism is a theoretically coherent aphasic category. *Brain and Language, 40,* 274–281.

Chapey, R. (1981). Assessment of language disorders in adults. In R. Chapey (Ed), *Language intervention strategies in adult aphasia* (pp. 31–84). Baltimore: Williams & Wilkins.

Chapey, R. (1994). *Language intervention strategies in adult aphasia* (3rd ed.) Baltimore: Williams & Wilkins.

Darley, F. (1982). *Aphasia.* Philadelphia: W.B. Saunders.

Davis, G. (1993). *A survey of adult aphasia and related language disorders* (2nd ed.). Englewood Cliffs, New Jersey: Prentice Hall.

Hegde, M. (1994). *A coursebook on aphasia and other neurogenic language disorders.* San Diego: Singular.

Jakobsen, R. (1971). Two aspects of language and two types of aphasic disturbances. In R. Jakobson & M. Halle (Eds.), *Fundamentals of language* (2nd ed.). The Hague, Netherlands: Mouton.

LaPointe, L. (1997). *Aphasia and related neurogenic language disorders* (2nd ed.). New York: Thieme.

Rosenbek, J., LaPointe, L. & Wertz, R. (1989). *Aphasia: A clinical approach.* Austin, TX: Pro-Ed.

Schuell, H. (1972). *The Minnesota Test of Differential Diagnosis of Aphasia.* Minneapolis: University of Minnesota Press.

SHEELA STUART
George Washington University

DEVELOPMENTAL APHASIA
LANGUAGE DISORDERS

APHASIA, DEVELOPMENTAL

See CHILDHOOD APHASIA; LANGUAGE DISORDERS.

APNEA

Apnea is defined as a lack of respiration for a period of 20 to 30 seconds with or without an accompanied decrease in heart rate to ≤ 80 beats per minute with resultant cyanosis. Twenty-five percent of infants in premature nurseries, but only a small percentage of full-term infants, exhibit apnea. Apnea, therefore, appears in most cases to stem from actual immaturity of the neural mechanism responsible for regulation of respiration. When immature, this mechanism is vulnerable to metabolic disturbances in calcium and blood-sugar levels, changes in body temperature, or disturbances in brain-wave patterns that occur during seizures or normal REM (rapid eye movement)

sleep. The association between apnea and sleep is significant because premature sleep up to 80% of the time and REM sleep are the predominant sleep states of these infants (Parry, Baldy, & Gardner, 1985). Apnea is less frequently caused by actual obstruction of the airway itself either from excessive mucus or improper body positioning, as premature infants have very flexible tracheas.

Apnea owed to immaturity or genetic influences appears to be a possible cause of sudden infant death syndrome (SIDS). The fact that SIDS occurs most frequently in children less than 1 year of age supports this theory. Treatment focuses on prevention and involves general measures to promote adequate respiration until the infant "outgrows" the condition. Correction of existing chemical imbalances may be all that is required. Theophylline, a respiratory stimulant drug, decreases apnea and is widely used. Most infants reinstitute breathing with gentle tactile stimulation such as stroking or jostling, but at times they require manual ventilation to prevent prolonged anoxia and to restore breathing. Occasionally apnea becomes so severe that the child has to be temporarily placed on a respirator (Volpe & Koenigsberger, 1981). Generally, the heart and respiratory rates of premature infants should be closely monitored for signs of apnea. A home monitor may be necessary for infants with persistent apnea. Full-term infants who are at high risk for *SIDS* should also be monitored for apnea (Spitzer & Fox, 1984).

Prognosis is generally good for infants who do not experience prolonged apnea and who are otherwise healthy. It becomes less favorable with increased frequency and duration of apneic episodes (Parry, et al., 1984). However, at least one study suggests that infantile apnea may be associated with deficiencies in later gross motor, and perhaps some cognitive, functions and behavior (Deykin, Bauman, Kelly, Hsieh, & Shannon, 1984). Since apnea produces transient anoxia, it can, when extensive, cause many of the problems associated with that disorder.

REFERENCES

Deykin, E., Bauman, M., Kelly, D., Hsieh, C., & Shannon, D. (1984). Apnea of infancy and subsequent neurologic, cognitive and behavioral status. *Pediatrics, 73,* 638–645.

Parry, W., Baldy, M., & Gardner, S. (1985). Respiratory diseases. In G. B. Merenstein, & S. L. Gardner (Eds.), *Handbook of neonatal intensive care.* St. Louis: Mosby.

Spitzer, A., & Fox, W. (1984). Infant apnea, an approach to management. *Clinical Pediatrics, 23,* 374–380.

Volpe, J., & Koenigsberger, R. (1981). Neurologic disorders. In G. B. Avery (Ed.), *Neonatology: Pathophysiology and management of the newborn* (2nd ed.) (pp. 920–923). Philadelphia: Lippincott.

BRENDA M. POPE
*New Hanover Memorial
Hospital*

ANOXIA
INFANT STIMULATION

APPLIED BEHAVIOR ANALYSIS

Applied behavior analysis is an approach for changing behavior that involves the systematic application of a set of principles derived from psychological theories of learning. Applied behavior analysis has been demonstrated to be a highly effective, management system in both school (Alberto & Troutman, 1982; Martens et al, 1999) and home situations (Becker, 1971). Its principles have been successfully applied to a wide range of children's problems, including academic problems such as reading, handwriting, and task completion, and social and behavioral problems such as aggression, shyness, and school avoidance.

Applied behavior analysis and behavior modification are closely related terms. Both involve the application of principles of learning to the changing of behavior. Technically, behavior modification is the broader term, including behavior change strategies that are not based on learning principles (e.g., chemotherapy, the use of physical restraints, and brain surgery). Behavior modification in schools has become synonymous with reinforcement programs derived from operant conditioning principles. Operant conditioning procedures change behavior through changing the events that follow behaviors (i.e., consequences of behavior). Applied behavior analysis applies principles derived from operant conditioning, social learning theory, and respondent conditioning. The applied behavior analyst assesses and treats behavior in terms of both consequences and antecedents (i.e., events that precede behavior). These antecedent events may be environmental events or cognitive events (i.e., thoughts, attitudes, or perceptions) that are thought to influence behavior.

The principles of learning that are applied to problem behaviors include positive reinforcement, negative reinforcement, shaping, prompting, fading, extinction, punishment, modeling, discrimination learning, task analysis, and self-instructional talk. Most of these terms are described in more detail in separate entries in this encyclopedia but they are summarized here. Then the steps in behavior analysis are outlined. Finally, applied behavior analysis is illustrated with a case study.

Positive reinforcement involves presenting a reward to a child after the child performs a specific desired behavior. If that behavior occurs more frequently after the reward, positive reinforcement has occurred. A reinforcer, or reward, is defined in terms of its effect on the behavior it follows. If something (a stimulus) follows a specific behavior and the rate of that behavior increases, that stimulus is a reinforcer. There are no universal reinforcers; children can

react differently to such potential reinforcers as adult praise and bubble gum. Allowing a child 5 extra minutes of free time when he or she completes an arithmetic assignment with 80% accuracy is an example of positive reinforcement. It is important that the positive reinforcer be contingent on the specific desired behavior. If the behavior occurs, then the reinforcer is given. If the behavior does not occur, or does not occur at the specified frequency, then the reinforcer is not given. Sometimes teachers and parents will inadvertently follow an undesired behavior with a positive reinforcer. For example, when a child gets out of his or her seat, the teacher calls out that child's name. If the out-of-seat behavior occurs more frequently, the teacher calling out the child's name is a reinforcer. When reinforcement is used, the reinforcement can follow every appropriate behavior (continuous reinforcement schedule) or only a portion of the appropriate behaviors (intermittent reinforcement). Continuous reinforcement results in a quick increase in the rate of the reinforced behavior, and intermittent reinforcement results in maintenance of the behavior change when the behavior is no longer being reinforced.

When a behavior that has been followed by a reinforcer in the past no longer is reinforced, *extinction* has occurred. Often the immediate result of extinction is a temporary increase in the previously reinforced behavior. If a teacher who has attended to a child's temper tantrums begins to ignore the temper tantrums, the child is likely to increase the frequency and duration of tantrum behavior; however, if the teacher continues to ignore the tantrums (and there are no other reinforcers that follow the tantrums, like peer attention), the tantrums should decrease in frequency.

Negative reinforcement, like *positive reinforcement,* is a procedure for increasing the rate of a desired behavior. In negative reinforcement, some unpleasant event (stimulus) is terminated following the desired behavior. For example, a teacher tells students that children who complete their assignments at 85% accuracy will be relieved of their homework assignment.

Punishment is a process in which the consequences of a behavior reduce the future rate of that behavior. There are three types of punishment procedures. In the application of an unpleasant consequence, a behavior is followed by some unpleasant stimulus, such as extra work, a verbal reprimand, or physical punishment. In response cost, a teacher removes a reinforcer contingent on a specified behavior. Children may lose 3 minutes of recess each time they receive a check next to their names on the board. In *time out,* the child is denied the opportunity to participate in positive reinforcement for a specified period of time, contingent on a specified undesired behavior. Requiring a child to sit on a bench at recess when playing roughly or to sit on a mat during art are examples of time out.

When a child has learned to say "red" only to colors in the red spectrum, the response of saying "red" is under the *stimulus control* of the color red. This control is established by reinforcing the correct response and/or punishing the incorrect response. The reinforcer may be praise or a star. The punisher may be "no" or an X on the paper. When the child learns to respond differently to red and not red, this shows *discrimination learning*. The child who goes to the cookie box when Mother is occupied on the telephone has also mastered a discrimination learning task. Going to the cookie box is reinforced with a cookie when Mother is on the phone. When Mother is not on the phone, she either prevents the child from getting a cookie or reprimands the child.

Shaping involves reinforcing improvement in behavior. For example, a child may work only three math problems during a 30-minute period. The teacher would like the child to work 15 problems. (It is assumed the teacher has determined that the problems are at the appropriate level of difficulty for the child.) If reinforcement were contingent on the child working 15 problems, reinforcement would not occur. The teacher establishes a series of steps between the current level of performance and the goal behavior and applies differential reinforcement at each step. Only if the child performs the behavior at or above the behavioral criterion at the operative step in the hierarchy does the child receive the reinforcer. When the child is consistently successful at one step, the next step is operative, and the child's behavior must meet or exceed the criterion for reinforcement at that step. A related procedure is *task analysis,* which involves specifying the prerequisite behaviors to successful performance of a given behavior. Many instructional tasks are composed of several smaller steps that occur in a specific order. Often the difficulty of the task is the reason a child is having difficulty mastering the task. A *skill hierarchy* breaks a complex skill, such as two-digit multiplication, into sequential steps in which each step is a prerequisite for the next higher step in the hierarchy. Skill hierarchies exist in all areas of human learning, including reading, penmanship, dressing, and eating. Task analysis is a useful tool for selecting what skill to teach. Shaping procedures involve the application of reinforcement and extinction to teaching the selected skill.

Prompting involves the use of additional cues to increase the probability the child will respond appropriately to the discriminative stimulus. These extra cues increase the saliency of the discriminative stimuli and are phased out as soon as the behavior is under control of the discriminative stimulus. Prompts may be visual, verbal, or physical. The first-grade teacher who places pictures with letters of the alphabet is using visual prompts to increase the probability that the child will make the correct letter-sound association. The phasing out of prompts involves gradually decreasing the saliency of the prompt.

Modeling involves having a teacher or peer demonstrate the desired behavior to a child. Models can be live or filmed. When models are present at the time the child im-itates the modeled behavior, the model serves as a special type of visual prompt. The effects of modeling extend beyond the direct and immediate imitation of specific behaviors. Children can learn complex sequences of behavior (e.g., participating in a game or ordering a meal in a restaurant) through observation. Furthermore, modeling effects do not depend on the child or the model receiving reinforcement for the imitated behaviors. An impulsive child who is paired with a more reflective child to work on puzzles and games may later adopt a more reflective problem-solving approach.

In recent years behavior analysts have attempted to modify cognitions (i.e., thoughts, attitudes, and perceptions) that are thought to influence overt behavior (Meyers & Craighead, 1985). For example, an impulsive child may be instructed to imitate a model who talks out loud while solving a problem. The model provides the child with an example of helpful *self-instructional talk* (Hughes, 1999; Meichenbaum & Goodman, 1971).

Steps in Behavior Analysis

In applying the preceding principles, the behavior analyst follows a six step process.

1. Identify the target behaviors. Rather than being satisfied with the problem definition "Lucy is lazy," the analyst states the behavior in specific, observable, behavioral terms. Lazy does not tell us what Lucy does or does not do, and two people might have different ideas about what lazy means. Is Lucy daydreaming or is she turning in messy work? Unless the target behaviors are defined specifically and behaviorally, the existing antecedents and consequences of the behavior cannot be determined, and reinforcement and punishment cannot be administered consistently.

Once the problem, or undesired behavior, is stated in behavioral terms, the desired replacement behavior is stated. If the problem behavior is daydreaming, the desired behavior might be working on the task. The replacement behavior is incompatible with the undesired behavior. That is, Lucy cannot be daydreaming and working on the task at the same time.

2. Count the target behaviors. Since the undesired and replacement behaviors are incompatible, only one needs to be counted. Counting behaviors is necessary to evaluate the effectiveness of the behavior change intervention. This preintervention count is referred to as the baseline. It is preferable to count the target behavior continuously from the baseline until the intervention has been in effect for long enough to determine its effectiveness. A follow-up count following the intervention determines the durability of the behavior change. There are several different ways to count behavior. In a frequency count, each incidence of the target behavior is counted or tallied. The count may occur

during a part of the day only. Frequency counts are appropriate for discrete behaviors that either occur infrequently (e.g., hitting) or for a short duration (e.g., calling out answers in class). In a duration count, the percentage of time that a behavior occurs is estimated. Duration counts are best suited for behaviors that occur infrequently and have a duration of more than a few seconds. Owing to the difficulty of actually timing the amount of time a child is engaged in a behavior such as being off-task, a time sampling procedure is usually used to estimate the percentage of time the behavior occurs. The teacher may set a timer to go off at five randomly set intervals during a 30-minute work period or record whether the child was on-task or off-task each time the timer rang. If the child was on task at four out of five rings, the teacher estimates that the child was on task 80% of the time.

The results of the count are charted on a graph similar to the one in the following figure.

3. Assess the antecedents and consequences of both the desired and undesired behaviors. The purpose of this step is to determine the consequences and antecedents that may be maintaining the undesired behavior and to identify possible reinforcers for increasing the desired behavior and conditions under which the desired behavior is more likely to occur. The analyst determines what happens after the child engages in the undesirable behavior. How does the teacher respond? What is the reaction of peers? What is the effect of the undesirable behavior on the child's assignment? The analyst determines the conditions under which the undesired behavior is most likely to occur (antecedents). Are there certain task characteristics (i.e., presentation of materials, subject matter, amount of structure, length or difficulty of the assignment, response requirements), setting characteristics (i.e., independent seatwork, group discussion, certain persons nearby), or other conditions (i.e., time of day, medication levels) that are associated with the undesired behavior? The same investigation of consequences and antecedents surrounding the desired behavior is accomplished at this step. This assessment of antecedent and consequent events may uncover unintended reinforcers that are contingent on the undesired behavior (e.g., the child gets the play materials when pushing a peer, the teacher attends to whining behavior, or the child avoids the task by turning in incomplete work) as well as insufficient reinforcers or even punishers following the desired behavior (e.g., the child gets extra work after completing in-class assignments or the child receives no positive peer attention when he or she asks politely to play).

4. Based on the analysis at step 3, create a plan for changing antecedent and consequent events to result in an increase in the desired behavior and a decrease in the undesired behavior. Any of the learning principles previously discussed may be applied at this step. Prompts may be added, reinforcement and punishment contingencies

changed, shaping and extinction procedures implemented.

5. Implement the planned intervention. During implementation, counting of the target behaviors continues.

6. Evaluate the effectiveness of the intervention. Using the data obtained from the counting to compare the baseline performance with performance during the intervention, the intervention may be continued as is, modified, or terminated. If the intervention is having the desired outcome, the analyst will want to plan to gradually withdraw teacher-administered reinforcers (going from continuous to intermittent schedules), gradually phase out prompts, and select the next most important target behavior to improve or increase the difficulty of the reinforced behavior. To increase the probability the desired behavior will generalize to other settings, the intervention may be applied in different settings. If the intervention is not having the desired outcome, the analyst will reexamine hypotheses created at stage 3, resulting in a modified intervention plan at stages 4 and 5.

Illustrative case study. The hypothetical case of Andy illustrates the six steps of behavior analysis. Andy, a seven-year-old second grader, was aggressive on the playground, and his teacher asked the consultant for assistance in reducing Andy's aggressiveness.

1. Identify the target behaviors. The consultant helped the teacher state the problem behavior in behavioral terms by asking questions like "What would Andy be doing if I saw him act aggressively?" The specific undesired behaviors were hitting, pushing, grabbing, kicking, and threatening to hurt a child. Using questions like, "What would you like Andy to do instead of hitting, grabbing, etc?", the consultant helped the teacher define the desired behavior as participating nonaggressively.

2. Count the target behaviors. Because Andy's aggressive behavior tended to occur during outdoor play, the counting occurred during outdoor play. Because the aggressive behaviors occurred frequently and did not last over time, a frequency count was used. Aggressive behaviors were counted for five consecutive days to obtain a baseline (Figure 1).

3. Assess antecedents and consequences. Informal and formal observations of Andy indicated that aggressive behaviors were associated with the following antecedent events: unstructured play and teacher far away. Andy was more likely to participate when play was structured and the teacher was nearby. When Andy was aggressive, the following consequences were likely to occur: the teacher talked with him, he was sent to the principal's office (about one-third of the time), and he got to play with the equipment of his choice (the children he bullied gave in to him). When Andy participated without being aggressive, he received no teacher or principal attention and the other children rejected him.

Frequency of aggressive behavior during approximately 30 minutes of outdoor play.

4. As a result of the assessment at step 3, the following plan was selected. Andy was encouraged to play more structured games and the teacher stayed close to Andy during outdoor play. When Andy behaved aggressively, he was given one warning signal, a whistle. If he continued to play aggressively, he was given a second signal to go sit on a bench for 5 minutes. He received no verbal attention from the teacher or principal when he played aggressively. When Andy participated nonaggressively, he earned the privilege of being equipment monitor, responsible for bringing and returning all playground equipment. The teacher and principal praised Andy for participating nonaggressively, and his classmates were primed to react positively to Andy by the promise of a group reward, contingent on Andy's meeting the weekly goal for playing nonaggressively. The group reward was 10 extra minutes of recess time.

5. Implement the planned intervention. The intervention plan was explained to Andy and to the class before it was implemented.

6. Evaluate the effectiveness of the intervention. Figure 1 shows the results of the frequency count of aggressive behaviors during baseline and intervention. Owing to the decrease in aggressive behaviors, the plan was continued for 2 weeks. After the 2 weeks, the teacher gradually introduced less structure, supervised play less closely, and offered praise less frequently. The teacher counted the aggressive behaviors again on four occasions after the initial intervention was terminated. Based on results at these follow-up counts, the teacher removed the group contingency (day 22) and Andy was only occasionally permitted to be equipment monitor (day 26).

REFERENCES

Alberto, P. A., & Troutman, A. C. (1982). *Applied behavior analysis for teachers*. Columbus, OH: Merrill.

Becker, W. C. (1971). *Parents are teachers*. Champaign, IL: Research Press.

Hughes, J. N. (1999). *Child psychotherapy*. In C. R. Reynolds & T. B. Gutkin (Eds.), *The Handbook of School Psychology* (3rd ed.) (pp. 745–763). NY: John Wiley & Sons.

Martens, B., Witt, J., Daly, E., & Vollmer, T. (1999). Behavior analysis: Theory and practice in educational settings. In C. R. Reynolds & T. B. Gutkin (Eds.), *The Handbook of School Psychology* (3rd ed.) (pp. 638–663). NY: John Wiley & Sons.

Meichenbaum, D. N., & Goodman, J. (1971). Training impulsive children to talk to themselves: A means of developing self-control. *Journal of Abnormal Psychology, 77,* 115–126.

Meyers, A. W., & Craighead, W. E. (1985). *Cognitive behavior therapy with children*. New York: Plenum.

JAN N. HUGHES
Texas A & M University

BEHAVIORAL ASSESSMENT
BEHAVIORAL OBJECTIVES
BEHAVIOR MODIFICATION
TASK ANALYSIS

APPLIED PSYCHOLINGUISTICS

Applied Psycholinguistics publishes original articles on the psychological processes involved in language. Articles address the development, use, and impairment of language in all its modalities, including spoken, signed, and written. *Applied Psycholinguistics* is of interest to professionals in a variety of fields, including linguistics, psychology, speech and hearing, reading, language teaching, special education, and neurology. Specific topics featured in the journal include language development (the development of speech perception and production, the acquisition and use of sign language, studies of discourse development, second language learning); language disorders in children and adults (including those associated with brain damage, retardation and autism, specific learning disabilities, hearing impairment, and emotional disturbance); literacy development (early literacy skills, dyslexia and other reading disorders, writing development and disorders, spelling development and disorders); and psycholinguistic processing (bilingualism, sentence processing, lexical access).

In addition to research reports, theoretical reviews will be considered for publication, as will short notes, discussions of previously published papers, and book reviews. The journal will occasionally publish issues devoted to special topics within its purview. For further information about the journal, contact *Applied Psycholinguistics*, Harvard Graduate School of Education, Larsen Hall, 3rd Floor, Cambridge, MA 02138.

PHILIP M. PRINZ
Pennsylvania State University
First edition

APRAXIA

See DEVELOPMENTAL APRAXIA.

APTITUDE TESTING

The term *aptitude test* has been traditionally employed to refer to tests designed to assess the level of development attained by an individual on relatively homogenous and clearly defined segments of ability, such as spatial visualization, numerical aptitude, or perceptual speed. Aptitude tests measure the effects of learning under the relatively uncontrolled and unknown conditions of daily living. In this sense, they differ from achievement tests that measure the effects of a relatively standardized set of experiences encountered in an educational program. The two types of test differ in use as well. Achievement tests generally represent a terminal evaluation of an individual's status on the completion of training. Aptitude tests serve to predict subsequent performance. They are employed to estimate the extent to which an individual will profit from a specific course of training, or to predict the quality of achievement in a new situation.

The term "special aptitude" originated at a time when the major emphasis in testing was placed on general intelligence. Traditional intelligence tests were designed primarily to yield a single global measure of an individual's general level of cognitive development such as an IQ. Although they were comprised of a heterogeneous grouping of subtests, both practical and theoretical analysis soon revealed that intelligence tests were limited in their coverage of abilities, and that more precise measures were required. This development led to the construction of separate tests for measuring areas of ability that were not included in the intelligence batteries. Traditional intelligence tests oversampled abstract functions involving the use of verbal or numerical symbols; therefore, a particular need was felt for tests covering the more concrete or practical abilities. The earliest aptitude tests were those measuring mechanical aptitude, but soon tests to measure clerical, musical, and artistic aptitude were developed. These special aptitudes were regarded as supplementary to the IQ in a description of an individual, and were usually administered in conjunction with a standard intelligence battery.

A strong impetus to the construction of special aptitude tests was provided by the problems of matching job requirements with the specific pattern of abilities that characterize each individual, a task commonly faced by psychologists in career counseling or in the classification of industrial and military personnel. Intelligence tests were not designed for this purpose. Aside from the limited representation of certain aptitudes discussed earlier, their subtests or item groups were often too unreliable to justify the sort of intra-individual analysis required for classification purposes. To respond to this need, the testing field turned to the development of multiple aptitude batteries.

Like intelligence tests, multiple aptitude batteries measure a number of abilities, but instead of a total score, they yield a profile of scores, one for each aptitude; thus they provide a suitable instrument for making intra-individual analysis (Anastasi, 1997). In addition, the abilities measured by multiple aptitude batteries are often different than those measured by intelligence batteries. Aptitude batteries tend to measure more concrete skills, such as arithmetic reasoning, numerical aptitude, perceptual speed, and spatial visualization, thereby placing less emphasis on verbal skills than intelligence tests.

Nearly all multiple aptitude batteries have appeared since 1945. Much of the test research and development began in the armed forces during World War II, when the Air Force designed special batteries to select training candidates to be pilots, bombardiers, radio operators, and range finders. The armed services still sponsor a considerable amount of research in this area, but a number of multiple aptitude batteries have been developed for civilian use in educational and vocational counseling and in personnel selection and classification (Murphy, 1994).

The application of factor analysis to the study of trait organization provided the theoretical basis for the construction of multiple aptitude batteries. Factor analysis identified, sorted, and defined the abilities that were loosely grouped under the definition of intelligence. The tests that best measured the factors identified in the analysis were then included in the multiple aptitude battery. The Chicago Test of Primary Mental Abilities (1941) represents the first attempt to construct a battery based on factor analysis using the pioneer factor analytic work of Thurstone (1938). Most multiple aptitude batteries developed since that time have employed the use of factor analysis in construction.

About a dozen multiple aptitude batteries have been developed for use in a number of fields. These instruments vary widely in approach, technical quality, and the amount of available validation data. In business and industry, data gained from the administration of multiple aptitude test batteries may be used for institutional decisions regarding the assignment of personnel to different jobs. In education, multiple aptitude batteries such as the SRA Primary Mental Abilities Test (Hanna, 1992) are used to guide the admission of students to different educational curricula (Schutz, 1972). The armed services use aptitude data to assign specific job classifications to personnel after screening with a more general instrument (Weitzman, 1985). The Air Force pioneered this practice, but all branches of the armed services now use the Armed Services Vocational Aptitude Battery (ASVAB) (Bayroff, 1968).

A number of multiple aptitude batteries have been designed for use with high school students to aid in the transition from high school to work or postsecondary training. The most widely used of these tests is the Differential Aptitude Test (DAT; Bennett, Seashore, Wesman, 1974). Based on the factor analytic work of Thurstone (1938), the DAT is used in the educational and vocational counseling of students. It provides a profile of scores on eight subtests: Verbal Reasoning, Numerical Ability, Abstract Reasoning, Clerical Speed and Accuracy, Mechanical Reasoning, Spatial Relations, Spelling, and Language Usage. In the most recent fifth edition of the DAT, significant changes have occurred in the battery of tests. The fifth edition is divided into two parallel forms for grades 7–9 and 10–12. New items have been added, old items have been revised and updated, and the overall testing time has been shortened by reducing the length of some tests. Using the student's profile in conjunction with an interest inventory, a counselor can use a computer or casebook to predict the student's success in postsecondary education, or generate a list of potential careers. A vast amount of validity data is available for the DAT. The predictive validity coefficients are high, indicating that the DAT serves as a good predictor of high school achievement in academic and vocational programs (Schmitt, 1995). However, the differential validity of the separate tests is quite poor. The DAT should therefore be used cautiously for classification purposes (such as to identify possible fields of educational or occupational specialization) (Hattrup, 1995; Wise, 1995).

In 1987 the Computerized Adaptive Testing (CAT) edition of the DAT was developed, which allowed the test to be administered via Apple II or DOS-based IBM-compatible systems. However, the CAT has not been revised in light of recent technological innovations, and has therefore become somewhat obsolete (White, 1985). The Comprehensive Ability Battery (Hakstian & Cattell, 1977) and the Guilford-Zimmerman Aptitude Survey (Guilford & Zimmerman, 1956) are other multiple aptitude batteries that are often used in transition and vocational education (Biskin, 1995).

Many aptitude tests have been designed explicitly for counseling purposes in which classification decisions are preeminent. In a counseling situation, the profile of test scores is used to aid the counselor in choosing among several possible fields of educational or occupational specialization. The General Aptitude Test Battery (GATB; U.S. Department of Labor, 1980) was developed by the U.S. Employment Services (USES) for use by employment counselors in state employment services offices. The GATB is comprised of 12 tests that combine to yield nine factor scores: Intelligence, Verbal Aptitude, Numerical Aptitude, Spatial Aptitude, Form Perception, Clerical Perception, Motor Coordination, Finger Dexterity, and Manual Dexterity. The profile of these subtest scores can then be compared with profiles corresponding to a huge number of job categories. An alternative form is available for nonreading adults. A host of studies have been conducted on the GATB, which have consistently shown that the test is a valid predictor of performance across a range of jobs (Bemis, 1968).

Unlike the multiple aptitude batteries, special aptitude tests typically measure a single aptitude. Certain areas such as vision, hearing, motor dexterity, and artistic talents are often judged to be too specialized to justify inclusion in standard aptitude batteries, yet often these abilities are vital to a certain task. Special aptitude tests were designed to measure such abilities. They are often administered in conjunction with an aptitude battery, either to assess a skill not included in the battery or to further probe a skill or interest. Special aptitude tests may also be custom-made for a particular job, and be constructed using a simulation of the requisites of the job, such as the Minnesota Clerical Test (The Psychological Corporation, 1959), the Meier Art Judgment Test (Meier, 1942), or the Seashore Measure of Musical Talents (Seashore, 1938). Despite wide use in education, counseling, and industry, the development of aptitude tests has been slow (Murphy, 1994). Many of the aptitude tests currently in use were developed in the 1940s and 1950s and have been revised and reissued in subsequent years.

REFERENCES

Anastasi, A. (1997). *Psychological testing* (7th ed.). Saddle River, NJ: Prentice Hall.

Bayroff, A. G., & Fuchs, E. F. (1968). The armed forces vocational aptitude battery. *Proceedings of the 76th annual convention of the American Psychological Association, 3,* 635–636.

Bemis, S. E. (1968). Occupational validity of the General Aptitude Test Battery. *Journal of Applied Psychology, 52,* 240–244.

Bennett, G. K., Seashore, H. G., & Wesman, A. G. (1974). *Fifth edition manual for Differential Aptitude Tests, Forms S and T.* New York: Psychological Corporation.

Biskin, B. H. (1995). Review of the Guilford-Zimmerman Interest Inventory. In J. C. Conoley & J. C. Impara (Eds.), *The twelfth mental measurements yearbook* (pp. 442–443). Lincoln, NE: Buros Institute of Mental Measurements.

Guilford, J. P. & Zimmerman, W. S. (1956). *The Guildford-Zimmerman Aptitude Survey.* New York: McGraw-Hill.

Hakstian, A. R., & Cattell, R. B. (1977). *The Comprehensive Ability Battery.* Champaign, IL: Institute for Personality and Ability Testing.

Hanna, G. S. (1992). Review of the SRA Achievement Series Forms 1 & 2 and survey of Basic Skills Form P & Q. In J. J. Kramer & J. C. Conoley (Eds.), *The eleventh mental measurements yearbook* (pp. 859–861). Lincoln, NE: Buros Institute of Mental Measurements.

Hattrup, D. (1995). Review of Differential Aptitude Tests: Fifth Edition. In J. C. Conoley & J. C. Impara (Eds.), *The twelfth mental measurements yearbook* (pp. 302–304). Lincoln, NE: Buros Institute of Mental Measurements.

Meier, N. C. (1942). *Art in human affairs.* New York: McGraw-Hill.

Murphy, K. R. (1994). Aptitude interest measurement. In D. J. Keyser & R. C. Sweetland (Eds.), *Test critiques: Volume 10* (pp. 31–38). Austin, TX: Pro-Ed.

Schmitt, N. (1995). Review of Differential Aptitude Tests: Fifth Edition. In J. C. Conoley & J. C. Impara (Eds.), *The twelfth mental measurements yearbook* (pp. 304–305). Lincoln, NE: Buros Institute of Mental Measurements.

Schutz, R. E. (1972). S.R.A. primary mental abilities. *Seventh mental measurements yearbook* (Vol. 11, pp. 1066–1068).

Seashore, C. E. (1938). *Psychology of music.* New York: MacGraw-Hill.

The Psychological Corporation (1959). *Minnesota Clerical Test.* New York: Author.

Thurstone, L. L. (1938). Primary mental abilities. *Psychometric Monographs.* No. 1.

U.S. Department of Labor, Employment, and Training Administration. (1980). *Manual, USES General Aptitude Test Battery.* Washington, DC: U.S. Government Printing Office.

Weitzman, R. A. (1985). Review of the Armed Services Vocational Battery. In J. V. Mitchel (Ed.), *The ninth mental measurements yearbook* (Vol. 1, pp. 83–84). Lincoln, NE: Buros Institute of Mental Measurements.

White, K. R. (1985). Review of the Comprehensive Ability Battery. In J. V. Mitchel (Ed.), *The ninth mental measurements yearbook* (Vol. 1, pp. 377–379). Lincoln, NE: Buros Institute of Mental Measurements.

Wise, S. L. (1995). Review of Differential Aptitude Tests: Computerized Adaptive Edition. In J. C. Conoley & J. C. Impara (Eds.), *The twelfth mental measurements yearbook* (pp. 300–301). Lincoln, NE: Buros Institute of Mental Measurements.

LIZANNE DeSTEFANO
University of Illinois

ACHIEVEMENT TESTS
ASSESSMENT
CRITERION REFERENCE TESTING
VOCATIONAL TRAINING OF HANDICAPPED

APTITUDE-TREATMENT INTERACTION

Aptitude-treatment interaction refers to an educational phenomenon in which students who are dissimilar with regard to a particular aptitude perform differently under alternate instructional conditions. The alternate instructional conditions are specifically designed to reflect the students' aptitude differences. Thus, if a significant performance difference between the groups results under alternate instructional conditions, an aptitude by treatment interaction has occurred.

Aptitude-treatment interactions have been discussed at length by Bracht (1970), who defines an aptitude-treatment interaction as "a significant disordinal interaction between alternate treatments and personological variables" (p. 627). A personological variable is any measure of an individual characteristic such as learning style, intelligence, achievement anxiety, or locus of control. Disordinal interactions refer to performance differences between groups that denote the significantly better performance of one group under one set of conditions and the significantly better performance of the second group under alternate conditions. Figure 1 graphically displays a disordinal aptitude-treatment interaction.

Figure 1 depicts hypothetical data for two groups of students who differ on a particular aptitude, one group being high and the other being low. Alternate treatments, matched to the students' aptitude, were provided. Students with low aptitude performed better under treatment number 1. Students with high aptitude performed better under treatment number 2. The data confirm the occurrence of an aptitude-treatment interaction and support the use of different instructional approaches for these two groups of students.

Figures 2 and 3, respectively, display hypothetical experimental outcomes that are not indicative of an aptitude-treatment interaction. In Figure 2, both groups of students, despite the aptitude difference, performed better under treatment number 1. In Figure 3, treatment number

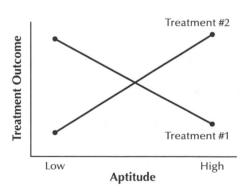

Figure 1. Disordinal aptitude-treatment interaction.

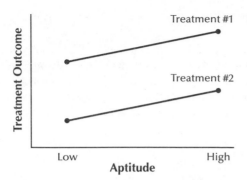

Figure 2. Hypothetical experimental outcome that is not indicative of an aptitude-treatment interaction.

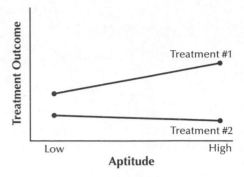

Figure 3. Hypothetical experimental outcome that is not indicative of an aptitude-treatment interaction.

1 was again superior for both groups of students. However, the differences for the low-aptitude students under treatment conditions number 1 and number 2 were not significant. The aptitude difference does not suggest the use of different treatments for the two groups; other factors may dictate the use of one or the other treatment for both groups. In this instance, the aptitude dimension did not clarify the choice between treatments.

Interest in aptitude-treatment interactions is fueled by the widely espoused commitment to individualization of instruction and the quest for teaching adaptations that enhance individual student performance. Appreciation for individual differences is a relatively recent development (Snow, 1977). Snow believes that the "recognition that individual differences in aptitude not only predict learning outcomes but also often interact with instructional treatment variations" (p. 11). This concept makes adaptive instruction a possibility. Teachers have long recognized individual differences and have accommodated such differences in a myriad of ways. Nowhere is the concern for individual differences greater than in special education. The Individual Educational Program requirement of PL 94-142 has mandated individualized educational planning for all exceptional children. Adaptation and accommodation to individual learner needs and characteristics is at the heart of the special education instructional process. Corno and Snow (1986), in a discussion of adapted teaching, view adaptations as involving either direct aptitude development or circumvention of inaptitude. In special education, the adage "teach to the strengths and remediate the weaknesses" prevails. Teachers generally seek intact or relatively strong abilities as avenues for instruction. Accompanying remediation is most often focused on specific skill or knowledge deficits that impede academic performance or independent functioning. Unfortunately, the commitment among educators, particularly teachers of the exceptional, to individualized instruction in practice is not matched by a strong commitment to educational research. "While it is clear that teachers adapt their behavior to students' individual differences at virtually all levels of edu-

cation, what is less clear is the underlying logic and intentionality that governs these adaptations" (Corno & Snow, 1986, p. 614).

The systematic experimental investigation of teaching adaptations in relation to student characteristics is the focus of aptitude-treatment interaction research. However, the research to date underscores the difficulties associated with investigations of this kind. Bracht's review of 90 aptitude-treatment interaction studies yielded only five in which disordinal interactions were found. However, Bracht's review did help to clarify the nature of the aptitude and treatment variables and to identify the variables that increase the probability of significant aptitude-treatment interactions. Bracht's review included five studies that involved handicapped learners; none of the studies yielded significant interactions. Bracht notes that the subjects in these five studies bore categorical labels such as mentally retarded and emotionally disturbed. Such broad categories tend to mask the considerable heterogeneity that exists within the groups—a factor that works against the probability of aptitude-treatment interactions. In another review, Ysseldyke (1973) discussed five aptitude-treatment interaction studies involving handicapped learners grouped for instruction according to modality differences. Auditory and/or visual functioning were the modalities under consideration. Instruction matched to modality strengths or preferences failed to yield evidence of significant interactions across a variety of academic outcome measures (e.g., reading achievement and word recognition skills) in any of these studies.

Another review of research specifically involving modality-instructional matching has been reported by Arter and Jenkins (1977). Preset criteria limited the number of studies reviewed in depth to 14. In all of the studies, the students were assigned to a modality group based on a statistical difference in modality functioning (modality assessments had adequate test-retest reliability and validity). Alternate instructional methods had a clear modality emphasis and outcome measures were constant across the groups. Only one study (Bursuk, 1971) demonstrated a significant modality-instruction interaction. This study involved tenth-grade below-average readers who were given instruction in listening and reading comprehension (reading comprehension lessons were given to the visual modality preference group only) over an entire school semester. The authors point out the specificity and control of subjects, treatments, and outcome measures that distinguish the Bursuk study from the remaining 13 research reports.

The meager results from studies specifically designed to demonstrate the interaction between modalities and instruction have not been a deterrent to practitioners. Despite the lack of supportive research, instruction based on the modality concept has been widely implemented. The instructional approach involved children who were tested to determine modality preferences and instruction provided via the preferred modality. It also involved training of perceptual and perceptual-motor skills to enhance the child's readiness for later academic instruction. An extensive body of literature relates to the efficacy of perceptual-motor training. Kavale and Mattson (1983) applied the technique of meta-analysis to 180 efficacy studies. Meta-analysis permits the integration of the results from a large number of independent research studies to reveal the presence of treatment effects that might be obscured in traditional research reviews with a narrative format. The authors found that perceptual-motor interventions were not effective in improving academic, cognitive, or perceptual-motor variables. The results of this review are consistent with the conclusions drawn by others in earlier reviews of perceptual-motor training (Hallahan & Cruickshank, 1973; Myers & Hammill, 1976). The negative or negligible results of efficacy studies should not be surprising in light of the paucity of aptitude-treatment interactions found in studies designed to demonstrate the efficacy of the modality-instructional match. The modality model of instruction is founded on aptitude-treatment interaction theory, but the applicability of aptitude-treatment interaction theory to modality-based instruction has yet to be demonstrated and validated.

Aptitude-treatment interaction research is by no means confined to special education or to investigations of modality-based instruction. Aptitude-treatment interaction research has been conducted in other academic areas such as math (Holton, 1982) and reading (Blanton, 1971). The results generally have been disappointing.

Even though the number of research studies that have successfully demonstrated aptitude-treatment interactions is extremely limited, the research has provided considerable insight into the complexities of the interaction phenomenon and the conditions that favor the occurrence of aptitude-treatment interactions. Bracht (1970) found that disordinal interactions were related to the degree of control over treatment tasks, the factorial makeup of the specific personological variables, and the nature of the dependent outcome variables. Controlled treatments, factorially simple personological variables, and specific, rather than complex, outcome variables favor aptitude-treatment interaction. Snow (1977) stresses the "essential importance of detailed description of specific instructional variables and specific groups of people" (p. 12) to aptitude-treatment interaction research. In retrospect, the few research reports that documented significant aptitude by treatment interactions displayed the prerequisite degree of control and specificity of critical variables that seem essential for aptitude-treatment interactions to occur.

In discussing the relationship of aptitude-treatment interaction research to instructional theory, Snow (1977) cautions educators not to expect general theories of instruction to evolve from aptitude-treatment interaction investigations. The research findings to date suggest that each aptitude-treatment interaction, when found, will be valid only in a specific context. Each finding will pertain to a particular group of students under particular instructional conditions. Generalizations, if made at all, will be limited. Educators should not anticipate general educational theories with potential for broad application to emerge from aptitude-treatment interaction research. Those who initiate "blanket treatments" (Snow, 1984) on the premise of aptitude-treatment interactions are likely to be disappointed, as were the proponents of perceptual-motor training. Rather, aptitude-treatment interaction theory implies ongoing evaluation of student and instructional variables and a constant readiness to adjust to meet changing conditions.

REFERENCES

Arter, J. A., & Jenkins, J. R. (1977). Examining the benefits of modality considerations in special education. *Journal of Special Education, 11*(3), 281–298.

Berliner, C. D., & Cohen, L. S. (1973). Trait-treatment interaction and learning. In F. N. Kerlinger (Ed.), *Review of research in education* (Vol. 1). Ithasca, IL: Peacock.

Blanton, B. (1971). Modalities and reading. *Reading Teacher, 25*(2), 210–212.

Bracht, G. H. (1970). Experimental factors related to aptitude-treatment interactions. *Review of Educational Research, 40*(50), 627–645.

Bursuk, L. A. (1971). Sensory mode of lesson presentation as a factor in the reading comprehension improvement of adolescent retarded readers. (ERIC Document Reproduction Service No. ED 047 435)

Corno, L., & Snow, R. E. (1986). Adapting teaching to individual differences among learners. In M. C. Wittrock (Ed.), *Handbook of research on teaching* (3rd ed.). New York: Macmillan.

Hallahan, D. P., & Cruickshank, W. M. (1973). *Psychoeducational foundations of learning disabilities*. Englewood Cliffs, NJ: Prentice-Hall.

Holton, B. (1982). Attribute-treatment-interaction research in mathematics education. *School Science & Mathematics, 82*(7),

593–601.

Kavale, K., & Mattson, P. D. (1983). "One jumped off the balance beam": Meta-analysis of perceptual-motor training. *Journal of Learning Disabilities, 16*(3), 141–188.

Myers, P. I., & Hammill, D. D. (1976). *Methods for learning disorders* (2nd ed.). New York: Wiley.

Snow, R. E. (1977). Individual differences and instructional theory. *Educational Researcher, 6*(10), 11–15.

Snow, R. E. (1984). Placing children in special education: Some comments. *Educational Researchers, 13*(3), 12–14.

Ysseldyke, J. E. (1973). Diagnostic-prescriptive teaching: The search for aptitude-treatment interactions. In L. Mann & D. A. Sabatino (Eds.), *The first review of special education*. Philadelphia: JSE.

LIBBY GOODMAN
Pennsylvania State University

DIAGNOSTIC-PRESCRIPTIVE TEACHING
DIRECT INSTRUCTION
REMEDIATION, DEFICIT-CENTERED MODELS OF
TEACHER EFFECTIVENESS

ARC, THE

The Arc was founded in 1950 as the National Association of Parents and Friends of Mentally Retarded Children. The organization has undergone several name changes, but its mission has remained constant: to improve the quality of life for children and adults with mental retardation, as well as their families, through education, research, and advocacy.

From 1952 to 1974, the organization was known as the Association for Retarded Children. The name was then changed to the National Association for Retarded Citizens (NARC) in order to reflect a growing service to adults as well as children. In 1980, NARC became the Association for Retarded Citizens of the United States. In 1991, the word "retarded" was removed, and the organization changed its name to The Arc.

Throughout its nearly 50-year history, The Arc has taken a leadership role in encouraging research into the causes and prevention of mental retardation, and in educating the public in the results of that research. Some of the research projects and developments funded by The Arc include a new screening test for phenylketonuria (PKU) in 1961, the Bioengineering Program launched in 1982, and ongoing research on fetal alcohol syndrome. The Arc has also spearheaded efforts to influence federal policy toward children and adults with mental retardation. Some of its successes include the expansion of Medicaid to finance res-

idential programs, Supplemental Security Income, the passage of Public Law 94-142, the passage of the "Baby Doe" Amendments to the Child Abuse Act protecting newborns with disabilities from the withdrawal of medical care, and the Fair Housing Act Amendment of 1988, which prohibits housing discrimination based on disability. The Arc also serves as a clearinghouse for information on subjects important in the field of mental retardation, from medical advances to education to setting up financial trusts. It also funds numerous publications, many of which can be downloaded from its website.

Among the association's goals are

- increasing the availability of health care for people with mental retardation
- helping people understand and comply with the public accommodations requirements of the Americans with Disabilities Act
- ensuring the legal rights of criminal offenders with mental retardation
- reducing the incidence of fetal alcohol syndrome
- providing all children, regardless of disability, with a free and appropriate public education
- protecting the rights of people with mental retardation to enjoy community living, obtain employment, vote, and be protected from abuse and neglect.

In 1998, The Arc had 1100 state and local chapters, with over 140,000 members. Information on membership, publications, and topics of interest can be obtained from The Arc National Headquarters, 500 E. Border Street, Suite 300, Arlington, TX, 76010.

REFERENCES

The Arc of the United States. [Organization Website]. Retrieved November 4, 1998: *http://thearc.org/*

DONNA WALLACE
*The University of Texas of the
Permian Basin*

ARCHITECTURAL BARRIERS

Recent efforts to fully integrate disabled individuals into the societal mainstream have demanded the elimination of physical barriers that impede access to facilities and the surrounding environment. Common barriers to facility or service accessibility confronted by handicapped citizens include constricted entranceways, ill-equipped public facilities (e.g., restrooms and parking areas), limited passageways, poor room spacing and layout, inadequate lighting, and limitations in the availability of supplementary mediums for providing public information (e.g., braille directions, visual warning or evacuation alarms).

Prior to the 1960s, the vast majority of buildings and thoroughfares were designed for the "ideal user" (i.e., an able-bodied young adult). However, over the past two decades, the National Center for Law and the Handicapped (1978) and the U.S. Department of Housing and Urban Development (1983) have reported that the confluence of federal and state legislation, judicial pronouncements, and publicly accepted standards of accessibility have brought about significant and permanent changes in the architectural design of structures and thoroughfares. These changes have prompted the removal of barriers that inhibit the accessibility (e.g., mobility and orientation) of physically and sensorily impaired citizens.

The American National Standards Institute (ANSI) specifications, originally adopted in 1961 and updated in the 1970s, establish barrier-free criteria for buildings, entraceways, and thoroughfares. These standards are designed to eliminate all architectural barriers that have historically impeded the access of the following populations:

Nonambulatory Disabled: People with physical impairments that confine them to wheelchairs.

Semiambulatory Disabled. People with physical impairments that cause them to walk with insecurity or difficulty and require the assistance of crutches, walkers, or braces.

Coordination Disabled. Those with impairments of muscle control result in faulty coordination and that create an increased potential for personal injury.

Sight Disabled. Those with impairments that affect vision, either totally or partially, to the extent that an individual functioning in the environment is insecure or liable to injury.

Hearing Disabled. People with impairments that affect hearing, either totally or partially, to the extent that an individual functioning in the environment is insecure or liable to injury.

Modifications that may be required to eliminate architectural barriers in facilities and along public accessways include, but are not limited to, the construction of ramps, wheelchair lifts, and curbing cutouts; the improvement of transfer areas and enlarged spaces for parking facilities; the enhancement of public facilities such as restrooms, telephones, physical education facilities, and dining areas; and the improvement of passageways, entrances (e.g., doors, doorways), room designs (e.g., spacing and layout), facility lighting, and public/user information systems.

REFERENCES

National Center for Law and the Handicapped. (1978, July/August). *Moving toward a barrier free society*: *Amicus*. South Bend, IN: Amicus.

U.S. Department of Housing and Urban Development. (1983). *Access to the environment*. Washington, DC: U.S. Government Printing Office.

GEORGE JAMES HAGERTY
Stonehill College

ACCESSIBILITY OF BUILDINGS
AMERICANS WITH DISABILITIES ACT
ARCHITECTURE AND THE HANDICAPPED

ARCHITECTURE AND THE HANDICAPPED

Approximately 10% of the population has some degree of physical handicap (Moe, 1977). These physical handicaps are of three general types: visual, hearing, and physical/orthopedic. Of these individuals 22 million persons in the United States have some limitation of mobility, with approximately 400,000 confined to wheelchairs. In addition, there are 5½ million individuals who are visually handicapped and 8 million deaf or hearing-impaired persons (Sorensen, 1979).

Apart from the visually handicapped/blind, hearing impaired/deaf, and physically/orthopedically impaired, are those individuals who have health impairments involving cardiopulmonary disorders or neuromuscular diseases. These disorders may permit some mobility but may result in diminished stamina, poor coordination, or limited grasping and manipulative capacity.

Architectural considerations vary and are dependent on whether the handicap is physical, visual, or aural. In fact, such considerations can involve competing requirements that necessitate the establishment of unique environments for the physically handicapped in comparison with the visually handicapped. For example, a physically handicapped person confined to a wheelchair may function best in spaces that are open and large. In contrast, individuals who are blind may do better in smaller spaces where key elements of the sensory environment are within close range. Similarly, an environment that reflects noises may be advantageous for the blind but a disadvantage to the hearing impaired, who have difficulty in attenuating to multiple acoustical cues.

There are a number of general factors to be considered in designing or adapting environments:

1. Many handicapped persons may be smaller or weaker than average; therefore, slopes, reach dis-

tances, and forces necessary to open and close objects should be reduced.

2. A number of individuals who use mobility-assist devices (e.g., wheelchairs) may have secondary disabilities that involve difficulty in strength, grasping, etc.

3. Most persons blind at birth, or shortly after birth, know braille, while those adventitiously blind often do not know braille.

4. Tactile signals and signs should be few in number and their location carefully considered to ensure uniformity of placement throughout a building.

5. Audible signals should be in the lower frequencies, because persons lose the capacity to hear higher frequencies with increasing age.

6. Many deaf and blind persons can hear and see in favorable environments such as acoustically "dead" surroundings for the deaf and well-lit and magnified print environments for the blind.

7. Visual and aural signals are best to provide redundancy of cues and to accommodate deaf or blind persons (Sorensen, 1979, p. 2).

Through the use of mobility training programs provided through special education classes or rehabilitation efforts, the blind are able to go virtually anywhere. While guide dogs are used by a small proportion of the blind population, most blind people are initially guided through a building and later follow a memorized route. As might be expected, the primary impediments for the blind are unanticipated hazards such as people or objects moving across their paths or objects placed temporarily in a familiar area. Some specific building modifications that can be of assistance to the blind include:

Providing steps and stairs that are not open and do not have square, extended nosings on each step.

Using sound-reflecting walls since such walls allow the blind to better use their sense of hearing as a guide (moreover, sounds reflected from surfaces assist in orienting the blind to their position in an area).

Changing the construction materials in walking surfaces to denote entrances, restrooms, stairs, and other potentially hazardous areas.

Identifying doors leading to dangerous areas by door knobs that are distinctive from that of hardware used throughout the remainder of a building.

Placing all signs and letters/numbers at a consistent height, usually between 5 feet and 5 feet, 6 inches from the floor, so that the blind will know where to find them.

Of all those having auditory deficits, few are totally deaf. Even with a large hearing loss, many of those who are legally deaf can hear and comprehend if the environment is devoid of ambient noises. Modifications that can be of assistance to the deaf include:

Warning and direction devices equipped with visual indicators, as well as audible signals.

Telephones equipped with amplifiers for the hard of hearing and telephone typewriters for those who cannot use a standard phone even with amplification.

Clear signs so the deaf do not have to ask for directions since some deaf individuals have a difficult time talking and being understood.

Those individuals who have physical disabilities can be divided into those who are ambulant (able to walk with canes, crutches, or braces) and the chair-bound. The architectural requirements for those two groups, while similar, differ in some respects.

The ambulant disabled frequently have difficulty in stooping or bending. Consequently, modifications may include:

Placing handles, controls, switches, etc., within the reach of a standing person so stooping is unnecessary.

Placing ramps with a maximum gradient of slope of 1:12.

Using steps and stairs with nonprotruding nosings so individuals with restricted joint movement or braces will not catch their toes as they climb.

Placing hand rails on both sides of steps and stairs that extend beyond the first and last steps.

Chairbound individuals evidencing high degrees of independence use collapsible adult-size wheelchairs. Apart from the greater space needed for wheelchair movement, the chair-bound individual may need:

Grab bars to transfer via the front of the wheelchair to the shower, bed, and so on.

Space alongside a chair or bed.

The placement of countertops, control devices, and so on within the low to middle range of a standing person's areas of reach.

Much of the impetus for the modification of buildings and facilities for the physically handicapped is attributable to the Architectural Barriers Act of 1968 (PL 90-480) and its subsequent amendments. The act specifies that buildings financed with federal funds must be designed and constructed to be accessible to the physically handicapped. In addition, the Rehabilitation Act of 1973 (PL 93-112) created the Architectural and Transportation Barriers Compliance Board, which has as its mission, in part, to:

Ensure compliance with the Architectural Barriers Act, as amended.

Examine alternative approaches to barriers that confront handicapped individuals in public settings.

Determine the measures that federal, state, and local governments should take to eliminate barriers.

Many states, by state statute, require that accessibility for the physically handicapped be provided in newly constructed, privately funded buildings that are open to the public. All states require that publicly funded buildings be accessible to the handicapped. A number of states require that when extensive remodeling is undertaken, such remodeling will include making the building accessible.

Funds for state education agencies have been appropriated for the removal of architectural barriers in schools. This one-time, nonrecurring appropriation was authorized by Section 607 of the Education for All Handicapped Children Act (PL 94-142) as amended by Section 5 of the Education of the Handicapped Act amendments of 1983, PL 98-199. The American with Disabilities Act requires accessibility.

REFERENCES

Harkness, S. P., & Groom, J. N. (1976). *Building without barriers for the disabled*. New York: Whitney Library of Design.

Moe, C. (1977). *Planning for the removal of architectural barriers for the handicapped*. Monticello, IL: Council of Planning Librarians.

Sorensen, R. J. (1979). *Design for accessibility*. New York: McGraw-Hill.

PATRICIA ANN ABRAMSON
Hudson Public Schools,
Hudson, Wisconsin

ACCESSIBILITY OF BUILDINGS
AMERICANS WITH DISABILITIES ACT
MOBILITY TRAINING

ARCHIVES OF CLINICAL NEUROPSYCHOLOGY (ACN)

Archives of Clinical Neuropsychology (ACN) is the official journal of the National Academy of Neuropsychology, a 4000+ member organization composed primarily of practicing clinical neuropsychologists. The journal was founded in 1985 under the NAN Presidency of Raymond Dean, who became its first editor. Originally a quarterly,

the journal increased to 8 times a year in 1996, and also enlarged its page format to accommodate more articles. It is free as a benefit of membership in the Academy and available by subscription to nonmembers. Cecil R. Reynolds assumed the role of editor-in-chief in 1990. The editorial address is care of Dr. Reynolds at the Department of Educational Psychology, Texas A & M University, College Station, TX, 77843-4225. The journal is owned by the Academy and published by Elsevier Science, the largest scientific publisher in the world today.

The journal publishes original research dealing with psychological aspects of the etiology, diagnosis, and treatment of disorders arising out of dysfunction of the central nervous system. Manuscripts that provide new and insightful reviews of existing literature or raise professional issues are also accepted on occasion. The journal reviews books and tests of interest to the field, and publishes the abstracts of the annual meeting of the Academy. A Grand Rounds section is also included that provides in-depth information about individual or small groups of patients with unique, unusual, or low incidence disorders. According to impact factors calculated by the Social Science Citation Index, the journal is one of the most influential in the field of clinical neuropsychology.

CECIL R. REYNOLDS
Texas A & M University

ARGENTINA, SPECIAL EDUCATION SERVICES FOR YOUNG CHILDREN IN

Among the countries of Latin America, Argentina has a well-established record of providing educational services to its citizens. Mandatory school attendance was established in 1884 and Argentina has the highest literacy rate (84%) in Latin America (UNESCO, 1984). The National Directorate of Special Education is responsible for the special instruction of mentally, physically, and socially handicapped students. Services are provided from preschool through adulthood.

Early intervention services for children from birth to age 3 were scarce in Argentina and poorly organized (UNESCO, 1981). There was a need for early educational intervention services for children and their families prior to enrolling a child in a nursery school or special center. As a result, services were developed for early stimulation and education. These services are divided by handicapping condition and are provided in infant consultation units. For children with slight to moderate mental handicaps, services focus on sensory and motor stimulation, socialization skills, and speech development. Parents are involved in these activities so that follow through can be done at home. For children with physical handicaps (blind, partially sighted, deaf or hard of hearing), the education is divided into two stages. The first stage is early neurological and sensory stimulation; it is continued until the child has reached a developmental level of 18 months (UNESCO, 1981). The next stage involves stimulation of sensorimotor activities, language development, and the development of self-care and socialization skills. Guidance and educational services also are given to the families.

The primary goal of these intervention programs is to raise the child's level of developmental functioning so that he or she can enter a prenursery special education program. Along with outreach to parents is the involvement and continuing education of special education teachers. There is a central registry of handicapped children so that they may be referred to the appropriate resources. Primary prevention programs are initiated via the media, with special programs for or articles on handicapped children. Public meetings on issues relating to handicapped students constitute an ongoing effort at general education as to the needs of handicapped children.

REFERENCES

UNESCO. (1981). *Handicapped children: Early detection, intervention and education in selected case studies from Argentina, Canada, Denmark, Jamaica, Jordan, Nigeria, Sri Lanka, Thailand, and the United Kingdom* (Report No. ED/MD/63). Paris: Author.

UNESCO. (1984). Wastage in primary education from 1970 to 1980. *Prospects, 14*, 348–367.

KAREN F. WYCHE
Hunter College

LATIN AMERICA, SPECIAL EDUCATION IN

ARITHMETIC INSTRUCTION

The Direct Instructional System for Teaching Arithmetic and Reading (DISTAR) is the foremost example of the directive teaching process. It is a highly structured, systematic program for teaching disadvantaged preschool and primary grade children. The method emphasizes structure, programmed learning, drill, and repetition. Basic skills and concepts are presented in a way that requires mastery of each step in the programmed sequence before proceeding to subsequent steps. A major goal of the DISTAR program is to reduce the correlation between IQ and achievement by ensuring that prerequisite skills are learned, designing motivational strategies to keep the student engaged in the learning activity, and accelerating the learning rate of the student mastering the learning task (Bereiter, 1976). The Bereiter–Engelmann model was designed to alleviate the language and conceptual deficits often displayed by disadvantaged children.

Baine (1978) points out that highly efficient instructional techniques are required to teach handicapped youngsters while accommodating individual needs within group instruction. He found the Distar materials to be well-suited for the purpose. The Engelmann–Becker model emphasized small-group instruction, using daily sequenced lessons in reading, arithmetic, and language. The objectives of the DISTAR program, which address language and reading development as well as arithmetic computation and concept skills, include knowledge of letters, numbers, forms, perceptual discrimination, relational concepts, grouping, ordering, reasoning and problem solving, and social skills. The arithmetic curriculum includes addition, subtraction, multiplication, division, measurement, and word problems.

Distar was the curriculum of Bereiter and Engelmann's (1966) Academic Preschool; it was designed to help low socioeconomic class children progress academically. The DISTAR teacher has aides to help with the delivery of instruction. Small-group lessons of 35 to 40 minutes employ techniques of positive reinforcement, correction procedures, and teaching to mastery. Criterion-referenced tests are administered periodically and are the basis for regrouping and staff training.

Teachers in the Academic Preschool in Champaign, Illinois, followed scripts in their interaction with students. The scripts were specified sequential programs of instruction. Teachers bombarded students with rapid-fire verbal interface involving a great deal of drill exercise. Children were expected to respond in like manner; this led to the tag "pressure cooker teaching." The underlying assumption was that the academic failure of the disadvantaged or middle-class child was due to a failure of instruction, and that if accelerated learning schedules were instituted, results of enriched instruction would be maintained.

To build on gains attained in preschool programs, several Follow Through programs were designed. They rely on the highly structured DISTAR materials for arithmetic, reading, and language. Structured programs described in the DISTAR literature involve students through third grade. These programs represent a cross-section of the country. The East Las Vegas Follow Through project incorporates a variety of basal reading and mathematics series along with the highly structured DISTAR system of instruction. In each subject, teachers work with small groups of students 90 minutes daily providing special correction procedures and frequent opportunity for student oral and written responses. Diagnostic assessment is frequent. Children with limited English are provided instruction in their native language. There is a strong parent program in establishing a bilingual language and homereading program.

The Uvalde, Texas, Direct Instruction program incorporates problem-solving skills for disadvantaged students so that at the end of three years students can compete with peers from higher socioeconomic levels. The design of this program allows students who already possess prerequisite skills to move ahead at accelerated rates. A classroom teacher, with the help of a paraprofessional, uses the Direct Instruction materials that include DISTAR language, reading, mathematics, and spelling mastery skills. Homogeneous groups are made up to 5 to 10 students. Those who need extra help are tutored by adults and peers. Criterion-referenced progress tests are administered every 2 weeks by trained diagnosticians. Instruction is monitored; to ensure quality, in-service instruction is provided continually throughout the year. There is an active parent group that supports the program. Since almost 70% of the students are Hispanic, DISTAR materials are in Spanish. The bilingual instruction is designed to encourage students to function in English as soon as possible.

The focus of the Cherokee, North Carolina, DISTAR program is planned learning that incorporates preserving the Cherokee language and customs. Students are instructed in language and folklore by a full-time Cherokee aide each week. They also make pottery, baskets, beadwork, and fingerweaving in the traditional ways. When the students have completed the three levels of the DISTAR program, they move into the regular program of the school's upper elementary grades, regardless of their age.

The DeKalb County Follow Through program in Smithville, Tennessee, addresses the needs of disadvantaged rural children. The program incorporates the DISTAR materials and methods: positive reinforcement, group responses, individual turns, teaching to mastery, and immediate correction of errors. The reading curriculum includes decoding and comprehension (Level I), reading for understanding (Level II), and comprehension and information acquisition skills (Level III). The arithmetic curriculum includes addition and subtraction (Level I), multiplication, complex addition and subtraction, and fractions (Level II), and column addition, long division, complex multiplication, and story problems (Level III). One teacher and two or three aides are assigned a maximum of 25 students in groups of 10 (those who learn at a rapid rate) or 5 (those who learn at a slower rate) for 35 minutes daily in each content area. Biweekly criterion-referenced tests are administered to monitor progress. Health and other support services, staff development, and parent involvement are also components of the DeKalb County program.

The Flippin, Arkansas, Follow Through program also relies on the structured DISTAR program. Flippin is a rural, mainly white, low-to-medium-income community. The goal of the Flippin Follow Through program is to build on Head Start gains. The DISTAR instructional system is the core of the program. On completion of the three programmed levels that comprise the DISTAR system, regardless of grade level, students move into the regular programs of the Flippin schools. Arithmetic is taught by a problem-solving approach, progressing from basic addition and subtraction to multiplication and fractions, renaming, long division, column addition, measurement, and story problems. One teacher and at least one aide staff each K-3 classroom. They are expected to incorporate all of the following instructional techniques: teaching to mastery, group response, positive reinforcement, immediate correction of errors, individual turns, and rapid pacing. DISTAR instruction occurs in the morning. Criterion-referenced tests are administered biweekly in arithmetic, reading, and language. The Flippin program also features health services, a strong parent support program, and continuous in-service training.

The Nichols Avenue Follow Through program in Washington, DC, also relies on the DISTAR program of highly structured, carefully sequenced instructional tasks that are designed to enhance skill mastery. In addition to DISTAR instruction, physical education, art, and science are taught by district resource teachers. Instruction to small groups of six to ten occurs for 30 to 35 minutes daily in each content area. Criterion-referenced tests are administered every 9 weeks and result in placement of students in the most appropriate learning environment. In-service training for teachers and a parent support group are other components of the Nichols Avenue program. Other Follow Through programs that incorporate the DISTAR materials and procedures include the following: Public School 137 in Brooklyn, New York; The Bandini Center, San Diego, California; and Williamsburg and County Schools in Kingstree, South Carolina.

Conclusions of evaluation studies regarding the effectiveness of the DISTAR approach are mixed. Generally reported were possible advantages in arithmetic computation achievement and disadvantages regarding word meaning, paragraph meaning, and arithmetic concept skills development. Elkind (1970) questioned the efficiency, economy, and learning benefits of formal instructional programs at the preschool level, particularly for middle-class children. Positive results were reported by Bereiter and Engelmann (1976, 1973, 1966a) and Schwartz (1974). Studies that reported no significant differences in effectiveness of the DISTAR program include Ogletree (1976), Ogletree and Ogletree (1976), and Mahan (1971). Kaufman (1972, 1974) reported mixed results—no difference in developing oral language ability but positive results in spelling, word-study skills, and arithmetic computation. Qualitative evaluations that surveyed teachers' opinions of the DISTAR program generally reported positive attitudes, particularly concerning slow learners and learning-disabled students (Fleischner & Garnett, 1980; Mayes, 1977; DiPasalegne & Ogletree, 1976; Moodie &

Hoen, 1972; Moodie, 1973; Guinet, 1971). Performance-based models involving direct instruction do appear to have a positive impact on school performance overall (Elliott, Busse, & Shapiro, 1999).

REFERENCES

Baine, D. (1978). Direct instructional techniques for young handicapped children. *Elements: Translating Theory into Practice, 9*(8), 6–8.

Becker, W. C., & Engelmann, S. (1976). Analysis of achievement data on six cohorts of low-income children from 20 school districts in the University of Oregon direct instruction Follow Through model. *Research in Education,* March 1978.

Bereiter, C. (1976). IQ differences and social policy. In N. F. Ashline, T. R. Pezullo, & C. I. Norris (Eds.), *Education, inequality, and national policy* (pp. 137–155). Lexington, MA: Lexington.

Bereiter, C., & Engelmann, S. (1966). *Teaching disadvantaged children in the preschool.* Englewood Cliffs, NJ: Prentice-Hall.

Bereiter, C., & Engelman, S. (1966a). Effectiveness of direct verbal instruction on IQ performance and achievement in reading and arithmetic. *Research in Education,* Nov. 1969.

DiPasalegne, R. W., & Ogletree, E. J. (1976). An assessment of DISTAR by Chicago innercity teachers. *Research in Education,* April 1978.

Elkind, D. (1970). The case for the academic preschool: Fact or fiction. *Young Children, 25*(3), 132–140.

Elliott, S. N., Busse, R., & Shapiro, E. S. (1999). Intervention techniques for academic performance problems. In E. R. Reynolds & T. B. Gutkin (Eds.), *The Handbook of School Psychology* (3rd ed.) (pp. 664–685). NY: John Wiley & Sons.

Fleischner, J., & Garnett, K. (1980). Arithmetic learning disabilities: A literature review. *Research in Education,* May 1982.

Guinet, L. (1971). Evaluation of DISTAR materials in three junior learning assistance classes. *Research in Education,* March 1972.

Kaufman, M. (1972). The effect of the DISTAR instructional system on first and second grade achievement: An evaluation of the 1971–1972 Title I program of Winthrop, Massachusetts. *Research in Education,* April 1973.

Kaufman, M. (1974). The effect of the DISTAR instructional system: An evaluation of the 1972–1973 Title I program of Winthrop, Massachusetts. *Research in Education,* Dec. 1975.

Mayes, B. (1977). What do reading teachers teach in first grade classes? A study of questions teachers ask. *Research in Education,* Jan. 1979.

Moodie, A. G. (1973). An evaluation of the DISTAR Language I program at Seymour Elementary School. *Research in Education,* July 1974.

Moodie, A. G., & Hoen, R. (1972). Evaluation of DISTAR programs in learning assistance classes of Vancouver 1971–1972. *Research in Education,* Oct. 1973.

Ogletree, E. J. (1976). A comparative study of the effectiveness of DISTAR and electric reading methods for innercity children. *Research in Education,* April 1978.

Ogletree, E. J., & Ogletree, G. S. (1976). Teachers' opinions of the DISTAR reading program. *Research in Education,* April 1978.

Schwarz, J. I. (1974). Effects of a structured pedagogy on children's language. *Research in Education,* June 1975.

FREDRICKA K. REISMAN
Drexel University

ACALCULIA
ARITHMETIC REMEDIATION
DIRECT INSTRUCTION
DISTAR
MATHEMATICS, LEARNING DISABILITIES IN

ARITHMETIC REMEDIATION

Remediation in arithmetic has evolved into an instructional system comprised of goals and objectives; tests at various levels and of kinds that assess the objectives; instructional activities that represent curriculum at the concrete, pictorial, and abstract levels; and summative evaluations. Instructional goals are based on the general mathematics goals of a school district or similar educational agency. These goals usually emerge from curriculum groups of teachers, supervisors, administrators, and content specialists from outside the school district. In some cases, goals are determined by available textbooks. Objectives are translations of the goals into observable performance statements.

According to the National Council of Supervisors of Mathematics (NCSM, 1979), the goal of the mathematics curriculum should be to ensure that each student is able to

1. Solve problems
2. Apply mathematics to everyday situations
3. Determine if results are reasonable
4. Estimate
5. Compute
6. Use geometry
7. Measure
8. Read, interpret, and construct tables, charts, and graphs
9. Use mathematics to predict
10. Understand the role of computers

Objectives used to assess each of the NCSM goals might be to

1. Generate a list of possible solutions for finding the difference between two integers
2. Purchase items from a store and use the correct amount of money

3. State whether a series of answers make sense
4. State whether a quantity is reasonable for a specified purpose
5. Add with renaming
6. Find the circumference of a circle
7. Find the volume of a container
8. Interpret a graph showing income of teachers compared to inflation rates over time
9. Use a graph to predict direction of a group of stocks over time
10. Describe the use of the computer as a mathematics tutor

Diagnostic assessments may include survey tests, concept tests, interviews, attitude scales, and learning style inventories. Survey tests tap broad ranges of mathematics competence and serve to present an overview of students strengths and weaknesses. Survey tests also are referred to as screening tests, where there are relatively few items for each of a great number of objectives. Survey tests have the following characteristics:

1. They may be group or individually administered
2. Test items are usually sequenced from easy to difficult
3. They are usually not timed
4. They may be machine scored
5. Test results indicate further areas of investigation in terms of student strengths and weaknesses

Concept tests may be used for diagnosing in more depth weaknesses identified in the survey test. Concept tests tap objectives with a greater number of items than survey tests. There may be five items on the concept test as compared with two on the survey test for each objective. Furthermore, a greater number of objectives are assessed on a concept test. Examples of concept tests include the *Diagnostic Test of Arithmetic Strategies*, *KeyMath Diagnostic Arithmetic Test*, and *Individual Assessment Battery: Standardized Form.*

Interviews are crucial to diagnostic assessment, which is the foundation for designing, developing, implementing, and evaluating remedial programs in mathematics. Interviews occur after the paper-pencil assessments and may accompany additional diagnosis at concrete and pictorial levels. Interviews provide a structure for probing how and what a student is thinking. The following types of data may emerge from interviews: (1) what the student is thinking; (2) the student's thought processes, e.g., whether the thinking is concrete or simplistic, whether cause-effect relations are apparent; (3) the problem-solving strategies being used by the student; (4) the mode of representation that appears most comfortable for the student: concrete,

pictorial, or abstract; (5) how the student's performance compares with age peers as well as with other things that the student can do, e.g., science, writing, art, music, sports, and social interaction. Interviews may be organized around topics such as whole numbers, fractions, geometry, measurement, and mathematical applications. The purpose of the interview is to collect data in a manner that is more thorough than from written tests. It is important to probe during an interview and to avoid correcting errors and instructing. If the student gets stuck, rephrase questions and move to a lower but related objective. The interview should allow the diagnostic teacher to identify error patterns, understand the student's thinking in regard to isolated errors, and observe whether the student's performance differs on the same objective with concrete models, or pictorial and abstract representations. Data from interviews should clarify performance on written assessments. The following matrix serves as a structure for selecting interview activities in terms of mode of representation of probe items:

The following are guidelines for conducting an interview:

1. Establish rapport to get to know the student and allow the student to relax.
2. Explain the purpose of the meeting as well as what you wish to learn. Ask the student whether he or she has any questions about the meeting.
3. Probe and learn about the student's strengths and weaknesses; do not teach.
4. Check to determine whether the student can perform prerequisite as well as corequisite skills. Prerequisites are subskills or components of a task; corequisites are parallel tasks. Multiplication and division may be considered corequisites by the time the student is in grade five; addition is prerequisite to multiplication, while subtraction is prerequisite to division.
5. Look for generic patterns of performance that may be trouble spots. Most errors in arithmetic are not random but represent patterns of misunderstanding.
6. Ask questions that serve different purposes to help identify different styles of thinking. Include divergent and convergent types such as "How many different ways can you use these materials to help you find an answer?" or "What is your favorite color?"

Attitude scales provide information about the student's interest in, fear of, or enjoyment of arithmetic. Often those students who do not do well in mathematics have high anxiety toward the subject and do not like mathematics. Thus since attitude often interacts with performance, it is necessary to gather information about the student's attitude as part of the diagnostic process. The following are some instruments that assess attitude toward mathematics: (1) Aiken Mathematics Attitude Scale (Aiken, 1972); (2) Dutton Mathematics Attitude Scale (Dutton, 1956); and (3) Mott Mathematics Student Survey (Mott, 1984).

Learning style inventories provide another view of how the student learns best. This type of inventory may assess preferences by the student such as grouping (e.g., small group, large group, or individual), or preferences concerning instruction (e.g., teacher explanations, peer tutoring, or self-instruction).

Cawley (1985), Reisman and Kauffman (1980), and Reisman (1981), presented a number of remedial instructional strategies. These include the following:

1. Present small amounts of a sequence to be learned in an organized format
2. Use visual or auditory cues that highlight what is to be learned
3. Use separating and underlining as cues
4. Emphasize patterns
5. Teach rehearsal strategies such as repetition, verbal elaboration, systematic scanning, and grouping material to be remembered
6. Reinforce attention to a relevant dimension
7. Point out relevant relationship
8. Emphasize differences in distinctive features of stimuli
9. Control irrelevant stimuli
10. Replace incidental learning tasks with structured intentional learning tasks
11. Reduce complexity of task
12. Use consistent vocabulary
13. Use a model whose competency in the task has been established
14. Encourage deferred judgment during problem solving
15. Use peer-team learning
16. Provide immediate knowledge of results
17. Plan for transfer in learning
18. Use short, simple sentences when giving directions
19. Use concrete examples of spatial and quantitative relationships
20. Use prompting

Summative evaluation should include broad objectives that allow students to demonstrate their ability to compare, summarize, classify, interpret, judge, imagine, hypothesize, and engage in decision making. Remediation is an integrated system of assessment and instruction. The concept of remediation described here goes beyond the diagnose-prescribe model that focuses on fixing with a remedy, to preventive model that implies doing it right the first time.

REFERENCES

Aiken, L. R. (1972, March). Research on attitudes toward mathematics. *Arithmetic Teacher, 19*(3), 229–234.

Brown, J. S., & Burton, R. R. (1978). Diagnostic models for procedural bugs in basic mathematical skills. *Cognitive Science, 2,* 155–192.

Cawley, J. F. (1985). *Cognitive strategies and mathematics for the learning disabled.* Rockville, MD: Aspen.

Dutton, W. H. (1956). Attitudes of junior high school pupils toward arithmetic. *School Review, 64,* 18–22.

Mott, T. (1984). *Mott Mathematics Student Survey.* Unpublished doctoral dissertation, University of Pittsburgh.

Reisman, F. K. (1981). *Teaching mathematics: Methods and content.* Boston: Houghton Mifflin.

Reisman, F. K. (1982). *A guide to the diagnostic teaching of arithmetic.* Columbus, OH: Merrill.

Reisman, F. K., & Kauffman, S. H. (1980). *Teaching mathematics to children with special needs.* Columbus, OH: Merrill.

Suydam, M. N. (1979, February). The case for a comprehensive mathematics curriculum. *Arithmetic Teacher, 26,* 10–13.

FREDRICKA K. REISMAN
Drexel University

ACALCULIA
ARITHMETIC INSTRUCTION
MATHEMATICS, LEARNING DISABILITIES IN

ARMITAGE, THOMAS RHODES (1824–1890)

Thomas Rhodes Armitage, an English physician forced by failing sight to leave the practice of medicine, founded the British and Foreign Blind Association in 1868. This organization, which became the Royal National Institute for the Blind, had as its major purposes the establishment of an effective educational program for the blind and the elimination of the existing confusion over printing systems of the blind.

Armitage established the Royal Normal College and Academy of Music to provide vocational preparation for blind students. Eighty percent of its graduates became self-supporting, a unique accomplishment in that time. After conducting an extensive study of printing systems for the blind, Armitage and his association became the leading English proponents of braille. They were instrumental in the ultimate adoption of that system throughout Britain.

REFERENCES

Armitage, T. R. (1886). *Education and employment for the blind* (2nd ed.). London: Harrison.

Ross, I. (1951). *Journey into light*. New York: Appleton-Century-Crofts.

PAUL IRVINE
Katonah, New York

ARMSTRONG v. KLINE (1979)

Armstrong v. Kline was filed on behalf of handicapped children seeking special education services during the summer term. The plaintiffs argued that handicapped children needed continuous, year-round programming in order to receive an appropriate education. The state countered that summer school was beyond the needs of these children and was not made available to nonhandicapped children free of charge and therefore was not required. In finding that some handicapped children are in need of year-round services, the court used the reasoning that "the normal child, if he or she has had a loss, regains lost skills in a few weeks, but for some handicapped children, the interruption in schooling by the summer recess may result in a substantial loss of skills previously learned."

The court was referring principally to the severely handicapped, concluding that they would most likely require summer sessions. Of particular importance is that the court's finding seems to shift the burden of proof from the parents (to show need) to the school district (to show a lack of necessity for year-round programming). These rulings have been upheld in the appeals process thus far. The court did not issue a blanket requirement for summer sessions for all handicapped children, but rather required a determination to be made on the basis of the needs of the individual child. This ruling ultimately forced the development of better techniques for assessing retention and regression among disabled students.

CECIL R. REYNOLDS
Texas A & M University

SUMMER SCHOOL FOR THE HANDICAPPED

ARMY GROUP EXAMINATIONS

The Group Examination Alpha, better known as the Army Alpha, was the first group test of intelligence for adults.

The examination was one of a battery of tests developed as a result of the armed forces's need during World War I to have an objective means of classifying vast numbers of recruits for military service.

The original examination, consisting of 13 subtests, was developed between June and September 1917 by the Committee on the Psychological Examining of Recruits. The committee was chaired by R. M. Yerkes and included W. V. Bingham, H. H. Goddard, A. S. Otis, T. H. Haines, L. M. Terman, F. L. Wells, and G. M. Whipple. Although experience among measurement experts with group examination procedures was rare, the committee relied heavily on A. S. Otis's group adaptation to the Binet scales for content and standards for administration (Yoakum & Yerkes, 1920). The committee worked continuously for almost a month developing, selecting, and adapting methods for the test content, and another month thoroughly testing the efficacy methods in military stations across the United States. The resulting version of the test consisted of eight subtests: (1) oral directions, (2) disarranged sentences, (3) arithmetic reasoning, (4) information, (5) Otis synonyms and antonyms, (6) practical judgment, (7) number series complete, and (8) analogies. There were five alternative forms provided and the average administration time was 40 to 50 minutes for groups of up to 500 recruits (Linden & Linden, 1968).

Between April 1 and December 1, 1918, Army Alpha was administered to approximately 1,250,000 military recruits. Contributing to its reliability and concurrent validity, the Army Alpha correlated with other ability measures as follows:

0.50 to 0.70 with officer ratings

0.80 to 0.90 with Stanford–Binet

0.72 with Trabue B and LC completion test combined

0.80 with Beta

0.94 with composite of Alpha, Beta, and Stanford-Binet.

Army Beta

The Army Alpha had more than adequately addressed the need for an instrument with which large numbers of individuals could be evaluated in a short period of time, but another problem quickly emerged. Army psychologists did not know what to do about the approximately 30% of the draftees who either could not read English or read so slowly that they could not perform on the Army Alpha. The Army Group Examination Beta, or Army Beta, was prepared to meet this need. The development of an instrument that could be group-administered without a heavy emphasis on reading or understanding verbal language presented special problems. These problems were mainly eliminated through the use of demonstration charts and pantomime to convey instructions (Yoakum & Yerkes, 1920).

The final version of the examination consisted of seven subtests: (1) maze test, (2) cube analysis, (3) X-O series, (4) digit symbol, (5) number checking, (6) pictorial completion, and (7) geometrical completion. The Beta also took approximately 50 minutes to administer and yielded the same type of numerical scores as the Alpha. Although the ability scores obtained on the Beta were somewhat less accurate than on the Alpha for the higher range of intelligence, the data obtained revealed the following correlations:

> 0.80 with the Alpha
>
> 0.73 with the Stanford–Binet
>
> 0.91 with the Stanford–Binet, Alpha, and Beta

The general administration procedure for the Army examinations soon became routine. Groups of draftees (100 to 500) reported to a special building to take the mental test(s). Based on whether the draftees could speak and/or write English, they were assigned to take either the Army Alpha for literates or Army Beta for illiterates or foreign-born recruits. Depending on the individual's performance on one of these tests, a decision was made regarding classification in the military or on the need for further testing to ascertain mental capacity for military service. Individuals failing the Alpha exam were automatically administered the Beta exam to factor out the possible role of reading and oral language in their poor performance. Anyone failing the Alpha exam and the Beta exam initially was given one of three individual performance examinations. Thus, no individual was designated as mentally incompetent solely based on performance on the group examinations.

The Army Alpha and the Army Beta yielded numerical scores of ability ranging from 0 to 212, which for military classification purposes were translated into the letter grades A, B, C, D, or E. Classifications were assigned as in the following examples:

Intelligence Grade	Probable Classification	Definition	Score (Alpha)
A	High officer type	Very superior	135–212
B	Commissioned / Noncommissioned officer	Superior	105–134
⋮			
D−	Considered fit for regular duty; rarely suited for tasks requiring special skill or alertness	Very inferior	0–14

The scores on the Alpha showed a high correlation with the individual's social status. The data also seemed to indicate a high correlation between an individual's Alpha score and level of occupational responsibility (Yoakum & Yerkes, 1920). These data were at least partially responsible for the soon to be widespread use of tests to predict vocational success, but as Matarazzo (1972) points out in reporting this data, there was a failure to highlight the considerable overlap in the scores obtained by individuals in the various occupational groups. More important, the vast amounts of data generated from the Army Alpha exams provided glimpses of the full range of adult abilities, confirming Galton's assumption that intelligence test scores are normally distributed in the population at large. Additionally, these data were largely responsible for the practice of using a fixed mental age for calculating adult intelligence.

The practical utility of the entire battery is expounded in terms of the number of men discharged from military service before the country wasted vast amounts of money, effort, and time training them. Yoakum and Yerkes (1920) report that between April and November 1918, 45,653 draftees were found deficient to serve in the military. From a measurement or psychometric perspective, the subtests and techniques developed and used for the army group examinations paved the way for the tremendous growth of group and individual testing in education and industry. Subtests developed for the army examinations are very much in evidence on most current tests of intelligence. For example, the most widely used individual tests of intelligence today, the Wechsler scales, are composed of subtests that are in many respects identical to the subtests on the Army Alpha and Beta. This is not surprising: the author of these scales, David Wechsler, participated in the army testing program during World War I.

The influence of the army group examinations is not all positive. Anastasi (1976) reminds us that often tests modeled after the army examinations failed to acknowledge and account for the limitations of the technical properties of the group examination methods. This failure resulted in much of the negative sentiment toward ability testing in the United States. That sentiment threatened the demise of psychological testing. Thus the army examinations may have done as much to retard as to advance the progress of psychological tests. The ease and efficiency of these group techniques also created a preference for impersonal testing as opposed to the more clinical, individual testing methods promoted by pioneers such as Binet (Matarazzo, 1972).

REFERENCES

Anastasi, A. (1976). *Psychological testing* (4th ed.). New York: MacMillan.

Linden, K. W., & Linden, J. D. (1968). *Modern mental measurement: A historical perspective*. Boston: Houghton-Mifflin.

Matarazzo, J. D. (1972). *Wechsler's measurement and appraisal of adult intelligence* (5th ed.). Baltimore: Williams & Wilkins.

Yoakum, C. S., & Yerkes, R. M. (1920). *Army mental tests*. New York: Holt.

Julia A. Hickman
University of Texas

INTELLIGENCE TESTS
MEASUREMENT

ARTHRITIS, JUVENILE

Juvenile rheumatoid arthritis (JRA) is a systemic disease that causes inflammation of one and usually more joints. The manifestations of JRA vary considerably among patients. The most common symptoms include joint swelling, warmth, tenderness, and pain, which may lead to stiffness, contractures, and retardation of growth. This disease is usually accompanied by fever bursts, rash, and visceral symptoms.

This form of arthritis is the most common connective tissue disease in children and is the most prevalent of the arthritic diseases. It has been estimated that around 250,000 Americans suffer from JRA with an incidence of 1.1 cases per year 1000 school-age children (Varni & Jay, 1984). The disease affects more girls than boys. It is similar to adult rheumatoid arthritis except that it typically appears before puberty and is more likely to stay in remission.

The causes of JRA are only recently known. Infection, autoimmune disorders, trauma, psychological stress, and heredity all have been considered, but evidence now supports the ideas that JRA is primarily an autoimmune disorder (Rennebohm, 1994). As there are no known causes, there are also no known cures. The most common treatment is the administration of large doses of aspirin. Other common drug treatments include gold salts, antimalarial drugs, corticosteroids, and penicillamine. Special exercises and sometimes periods of rest may also be employed. Different kinds of heat may be applied to reduce stiffness and pain, and a variety of other pain-control measures have been tried. Splints are often used to prevent deformity and enhance function. Surgery, including total joint replacement, may sometimes be necessary and can be beneficial.

There are basically three forms of JRA: systemic, polyarticular, and pauciarticular. The systemic form accounts for approximately 20% of the population with JRA. High fevers, rashes, stomach pains, and severe anemia are usually present in this type. Pauciarticular accounts for 30 to 40% of the cases. It begins by affecting only a few joints, usually the large ones (knees, ankles, or elbows). Polyarticular is the most common type, accounting for 40–50%

of children with JRA. This type affects several joints (five or more), usually small joints of the fingers and hands (Arthritis Foundation, 1983).

The long-term effects of JRA vary greatly depending on the type as well as the individual. There is no way to know the outcome of the disease in its early stages. However, the overall prognosis for children with JRA is good. Most will be able to go through adulthood without any severe physical limitations. Only about 25% will suffer any significant disability (Jay, Helm, & Wray, 1982). In most cases the disease will go into permanent remission but structural damages and functional limitations will remain. In other cases the disease may continue to be active throughout the individual's life (Rennebohm, 1994).

In addition to physical considerations, certain psychological aspects of JRA are also important. McAnarney, Pless, Satterwhite, and Friedman (1974) found that children who have JRA but no disabilities have more emotional problems than disabled arthritics. They also found that parents of the nondisabled children had a poorer understanding of the disease and were less likely to acknowledge its impact on the child's behavior, schooling, and social relations. Litt, Cuskey, and Rosenburg (1982) found that good self-image and greater autonomy coincided with higher compliance in treatment.

Wilkinson (1981) studied the emotional and social behavior of adolescents with chronic rheumatoid arthritis. She found that one of the major complaints among these adolescents was people's tendency to treat them as younger than their age because of their smaller size. She also reported a high anxiety level because of restricted mobility and fears about an uncertain future. Children with JRA are at increased risk of emotional and behavioral problems but there is considerable variability in the response to the disorder psychologically (Varni, Rapoff, & Waldrov, 1994).

Schaller (1982) has stressed the need to avoid an image of chronic invalidism. It is important to account for the limitations experienced by individuals with JRA; however, when not specifically restricted by the disease, they should be expected to perform as well as their peers.

The way children are treated by others affects their self-image; therefore, those working with these children should help them to avoid feelings of inferiority. Wilkinson (1981) reported that the adolescents in her study expressed a desire for more social contacts with able-bodied individuals and a desire to be in regular rather than special classes.

In the classroom as well as at home, children should not be unnecessarily restricted from activities. They should be encouraged to find alternatives when they cannot participate in regular play. Periodically calling on the child to do an activity requiring movement may help relieve stiffness whenever the child is not in pain. Beales, Keen, and Holt (1983) have stressed the importance of being aware of the child's perception of pain. Children may be less likely to interpret internal sensations as pain and therefore may fail to recognize it as a warning sign. Often, even when children know they are in pain they may not complain and may even try to conceal it. Some visible signs that may help determine the presence of pain are walking with a stiff gait, taking short steps, tense muscles, and inability to perform certain tasks. Cognitive behavior therapies may be useful in controlling chronic pain in JRA (see Varni, Rapoff, & Waldrov, 1994).

Another important consideration is JRA's erratic and unpredictable changes from day to day and even throughout the day. Usually the most severe stiffness occurs in the morning. Finally, it is very important for people supervising individuals with JRA to know the signs of aspirin overdose: rapid or deep breathing, ringing in the ears, decrease in hearing, drowsiness, nausea, vomiting, irritability, and unusual behavior.

REFERENCES

Arthritis Foundation. (1983). *Arthritis in children and When your student has childhood arthritis.* Atlanta, GA: Patient Services Department.

Beales, J. G., Keen, J. H., & Holt, P. L. (1983). The child's perception of the disease and the experience of pain in juvenile arthritis. *Journal of Rheumatology, 10*(1), 61–65.

Jay, S., Helm, S., & Wray, B. B. (1982). Juvenile rheumatoid arthritis. *American Family Physician, 26*(2), 139–147.

Litt, I. F., Cuskey, W. R., & Rosenberg, A. (1982). Role of self-esteem and autonomy in determining medication compliance among adolescents with juvenile rheumatoid arthritis. *Pediatrics, 69*(1), 15–17.

McAnarney, E. R., Pless, I. B., Satterwhite, B., & Friedman, S. B. (1974). Psychological problems of children with chronic juvenile arthritis. *Pediatrics, 53*, 523–528.

Rennebohm, R. M. (1994). Juvenile rheumatoid arthritis: Medical issues. In R. Olson, L. Mullins, J. Gillman, & J. Chang (Eds.), *The Sourcebook of Pediatric Psychology* (pp. 70–74). Boston: Allyn & Bacon.

Schaller, J. G. (1982). Juvenile rheumatoid arthritis. *Pediatric Annals, 11*(4), 375–382.

Varni, J., Rapoff, M., & Waldron, S. (1994). Juvenile rheumatoid arthritis: Psychological issues. In R. Olson, L. Mullins, J. Gillman, & J. Chang (Eds.), *The Sourcebook of Pediatric Psychology* (pp. 75–89). Boston: Allyn & Bacon.

Varni, J. W., & Jay, S. M. (1984). Biobehavioral factors in juvenile rheumatoid arthritis: Implications for research and practice. *Clinical Psychology Review, 4*, 543–560.

Wilkinson, V. A. (1981). Juvenile chronic arthritis in adolescence: Facing the reality. *International Rehabilitation Medicine, 3*, 11–176.

DAN HATT
NURI PUIG
LOGAN WRIGHT
University of Oklahoma

ARTHRITIS, JUVENILE
PHYSICAL HANDICAPS

ARTICULATION DISORDERS

Articulation involves the study of (1) the phonemes in a given language, (2) the manner in which they are produced, (3) the order in which they are acquired by the members of a culture, and (4) the disorders which may occur. There are forty phonemes in the English language, consisting of twenty-six consonants and fourteen vowels. (Bernthal & Bankson, 1998). A phoneme is defined as the smallest difference conveying a change of meaning. This is in contrast to an allophone which includes all of the acceptable productions of a given phoneme. Allophonic variations do not impact meaning.

The consonant sounds may be differentiated on the basis of three distinctive features: place, manner and voicing. A vowel varies according to tongue height, placement, and whether the tongue is tense or lax. There are also other characteristics of phonemes, known as suprasegmentals, that cause variations in sounds but do not signal a difference of meaning in English. Suprasegmentals are distinctive in some languages. For example, in tonal languages, the pitch of a phoneme signals a change in meaning.

If a traditional view of articulation development is taken, the age of emergence of specific phonemes may be identified. For example, /p/, / b/, and /m / are early developmental phonemes and are typically in a child's repertoire by age 3. In contrast, the /s/ phoneme may not emerge until a child is 8 years of age or older. Numerous studies, including one by Sander (1972), have examined the age of emergence of various phonemes. All children have articulation errors when they are young and are moving through the normal developmental process. The errors decrease in number as the child matures. Generally, articulation development is thought to be complete by age 8, although some children continue to develop articulation skills beyond this age.

When a child or adult has an articulation disorder, it is characterized by sound production errors, usually involving less than 10 phonemes. The individual's underlying rule system for combining sounds into words is thought to be intact. That is, the speaker understands how sounds are put together to make words which convey meaning, but the speaker is having trouble making individual sounds. The errors can further be classified as phonetic or phonemic in nature.

A listener will generally understand a person with articulation errors, although speech production will attract the listener's attention. The misarticulations may vary in severity from a mild distortion to omission. The least noticeable error is a mild distortion. The listener will recognize the sound as an /s/, for example, but its production will be just outside of the acceptable allophonic range. Only the skilled listener is likely to note this error. As the degree of distortion increases into the more severe range, the average listener will become aware of the error in production. Even though the phoneme is recognizable as a particular phoneme, it will call attention to itself. Further on the continuum of severity is substitution, in which another phoneme is used in place of the one that is intended. For example, a person may substitute a /t / for a /k /. The most severe error is an omission, in which the sound is left out.

The order of progression of severity is based on the impact the error has on intelligibility and the knowledge the speaker has about the phoneme. In regard to intelligibility, a distortion of a phoneme in a word generally does not impair the listener's understanding of a word. A substitution or omission may make it difficult for the listener to identify the word being used. The knowledge a speaker has about the phoneme is also reflected in the type of error used. When the phoneme is distorted, the speaker knows that for example, it is an /s/ but they are unable to correctly execute the production. When the error is a substitution, example /p/ for /s/, the speaker knows a sound is required in a particular location in a word but isn't sure which sound belongs there. In contrast, when a phoneme is omitted, the speaker doesn't realize a phoneme is needed. Thus, omission is the most severe type of error, followed by substitution and distortion.

The more common sources of articulation errors are (1) inaccurate learning, (2) incorrect speech models, (3) structural deficits of the speech and hearing mechanism, and (4) imprecise and/or poor coordination of motor movements. In the first instance, inaccurate learning, something interferes with the process as the child is acquiring a sound. For example, if a child has fluid in his or her ears or brain injury at a critical point in the acquisition of a phoneme, the child may not hear the sound or its replication accurately. It is thought that children rely heavily on the auditory modality when sounds are being learned, but later shift their focus to the proprioceptive/kinesthetic aspects for monitoring the accuracy of their productions. Thus, initially they focus on how their sound matches up auditorily to that produced by others, but later, once the phoneme is learned, they pay less attention to the auditory aspects and focus on how it feels both proprioceptively and kinesthetically. They then are thought to make the assumption that if the phoneme felt like last time, it must be correct. An erroneously learned production is thus maintained. Second, a child may have a family member or significant other who has an articulation error and is providing incorrect models for the child. Learning of faulty articulation is likely to occur because the child will imitate the errored

phoneme and incorporate it into his or her repertoire. Third, structural abnormalities of the speech and hearing mechanism may be a contributing factor to articulation errors. Examples are teeth that do not occlude properly or inadequate velopharyngeal closure. The structure may interfere with the ability to produce acceptable phonemes. Fourth, imprecise motor movements and/or the coordination of these movements may cause articulation errors. Correct articulation requires precise placement, timing, and accurate movement of the articulators. Persons with cerebral palsy, dysarthria, or apraxia, for example, have difficulty in these domains, and their speech production is affected to varying degrees.

The treatment for articulation errors generally consists of teaching the phoneme in isolation, and then assisting the client in generalizing the new sound throughout their sound system. Traditional strategies, such as those suggested by Van Riper (1978) or Bankson and Bernthal (1998), may be used. Minimal pairs and co-articulation strategies may also be utilized. Typically, the prognosis for resolving the errors is good.

REFERENCES

Bernthal, J., & Bankson, N. (1998). *Articulation and phonological disorders* (4th ed.). Boston, MA: Allyn & Bacon.

Sander, E. (1972). When are speech sounds learned? *Journal of Speech and Hearing Disorders, 37,* 55–63.

Van Riper, C. (1978). *Speech correction: Principles and methods* (6th ed.). Englewood Cliffs, NJ: Prentice Hall.

SUSANN DOWLING
University of Houston

COMMUNICATION DISORDERS
SPEECH AND LANGUAGE HANDICAPS

ART THERAPY

Art therapy is a technique developed by Margaret Naumberg (1917), who applied her experience as an art teacher and psychologist to treating children with behavior problems. Naumberg used the art of children as a tool to guide therapy. The techniques of art therapy are based on the knowledge that every person has the capacity to project his or her inner feelings into visual form.

Naumberg's first book was published in 1947; it describes the application of psychoanalytical principles to the use of art therapy (Detre, 1983). Naumberg is also credited with developing active teaching methods to facilitate artistic expression, i.e., the scribble technique and rhythmic exercises to enhance creativity and guide imagination.

Naumberg studied and worked with Maria Montessori and was partly influenced by the European painters, Matisse, Braque, and Picasso. The influences of Freud and Jung enabled her to apply the principles of psychology and psychiatry to art work; this led to the interpretation of drawings. This technique was then put to use in treating people with emotional problems.

There are two approaches to art therapy. The psychoanalytical approach, which was developed by Naumberg, uses art work to symbolize the unconscious. However, in 1958 Edith Kramer began using art therapy as a way of helping individuals to express current life experiences and to solve life problems (Dalley, 1984). Tukianen (1980) divided art therapy into three separate modalities. These are the supportive, active, and psychoanalytical elements. The supportive modality is aimed at social rehabilitation; the active form concentrates on ego development; and the analytical form uses patients' drawings as a diagnostic tool. All patients who participate in art therapy are required to draw. It is claimed that these techniques are useful in preventing suicide and in diagnosing depression and schizophrenia in adults.

Art therapy has also been used in special education. Art therapy has been helpful in treating children with learning disabilities (Mullin, 1974) as well as children who are mentally retarded. Mullin found that children who are mentally limited or too depressed to make even simple drawings can use pictures from magazines to stimulate their thought processes. Children are encouraged to communicate to one another through art work, which has been found to be helpful in reducing emotional stress. Salant (1974) used art therapy with preschool children to help them with their problems. The art therapist, a teacher, and a parent work together in helping children develop through their art work. Art therapy is based on the idea that man's most fundamental thoughts and feelings can be transferred from the unconscious into images rather than words (Dalley, 1984).

The work pioneered by Naumberg is now being used in schools, hospitals, and institutions. Art therapists must have advanced training (Rubin, 1984) and practical experience with supervision, working directly with patients from early childhood through adulthood. There is little research establishing the effectiveness of art therapy.

REFERENCES

Dalley, T. (1984). Art as therapy. The introduction to the use of art as a therapeutic technique. London: Tavistock.

Detre, K. C. (1983). Roots of art therapy. *American Journal of Art Therapy, 22,* 111–123.

Mullin, J. B. (1974). The expressive therapies in special education, *American Journal of Art Therapy, 13,* 54–58.

Naumberg, M. (1917). *A direct method of education* (Bulletin #4). New York: Bureau of Educational Experiments.

Rubin, J. A. (1984). *The art of art therapy.* New York: Brunner/Mazel.

Salant, E. G. (1975). Preventive art therapy with a preschool child. *American Journal of Art Therapy, 14,* 67–70.

Tukianen, K. (1980). Art therapy. *American Journal of Art Therapy, 32,* 300–314.

STEVEN GUMERMAN
Temple University

**PSYCHOANALYSIS AND SPECIAL EDUCATION
PSYCHOTHERAPY WITH THE HANDICAPPED
THERAPEUTIC RECREATION**

ASPHYXIA

Asphyxia is a medical emergency requiring immediate intervention to prevent infant mortality and morbidity (Golden & Peters, 1985). Asphyxia occurs with inadequate oxygenation and cellular perfusion. This article deals specifically with asphyxia that occurs during the time of birth or shortly thereafter. Many terms are associated with oxygen deprivation during this period; pertinent information can be found in different sources under the headings of neonatal asphyxia, asphyxia neonatorium, perinatal asphyxia, intrapartum asphyxia, and hypoxic ischemic encephalopathy (HIE). Asphyxia has been hard to define accurately, which has caused difficulty in research on its effects and prognosis for recovery. The classical definition of asphyxia has been a low Apgar score with more emphasis on the 5- or even 10-minute scores than on the 1-minute (Fitzhardinge & Pape, 1981). As low Apgar scores are not necessarily associated with asphyxia, however, this definition is not always accurate and is a poor predictor for neurological outcome. Predicting outcome is very difficult. Even infants with 0 Apgar scores at birth have survived after efficient intervention with no serious handicaps (Rosen, 1985). Incidence of damage is generally overestimated when compared with actual findings (Brann, 1985). HIE, whose description follows, is predictive of later deficits.

Four basic mechanisms underlie asphyxia during the immediate perinatal period: (1) interruption of umbilical blood flow; (2) failure of placental exchange because of premature separation of the placenta from the uterus; (3) inadequate perfusion or oxygenation of the maternal side of the placenta as in severe hypotension; and (4) infant failure to inflate the lungs and complete transition to extrauterine life. In early stages, asphyxia may reverse spontaneously if the cause is removed, but later stages require varying degrees of medical intervention because of circulatory and neurological changes (Fitzhardinge & Pape, 1981).

Asphyxia is a progressive yet potentially reversible process with severity and duration of the insult affecting later outcome. Severe asphyxia can result in death within 10 minutes without proper intervention (Fitzhardinge & Pape, 1981). Delayed intervention may exacerbate cellular injury in all organ systems, contributing to a poor outcome. The brain is the most vulnerable system and mediates the most pronounced effects on later life. Asphyxia not only affects the brain directly, but also impairs the autoregulation centers controlling cerebral blood flow, which may cause intraventricular hemorrhage with resultant complications (Golden & Peters, 1985). Premature infants appear to be particularly susceptible to this complication.

Cerebral palsy (CP) is the most frequent complication of asphyxia. Even then, risk is high only when the Apgar score is low (<3) for prolonged periods (>10 to 15 minutes) (Freeman, 1985). The incidence of CP may be as high as 38% in infants with Apgar scores of 0 to 3 at 20 minutes, and often occurs in conjunction with mental retardation and seizures. Asphyxia does not seem to be associated with severe mental retardation in the absence of CP (Paneth & Stark, 1983).

HIE may result from severe asphyxia. Children diagnosed with HIE show signs of neurologic dysfunction within 1 week, and often within 12 hours, after birth. The major signs of dysfunction include seizures, altered states of consciousness, and abnormalities in tone, posture, reflexes, and respiration. Infants who exhibit seizures have a 30 to 75% likelihood of long-term sequelae. Mortality is high among infants who had definite neurologic abnormality at discharge. Full-term infants with a history of asphyxia and an abnormal neurologic exam during the first week of life show a 7% incidence of early death and a 28% incidence of neurological handicaps. The most common deficits seen in severely affected children include spastic quadriplegia (a form of CP), severe mental retardation, seizures, hearing deficits, and microcephaly. Treatment for HIE is improving but research is difficult. Identification of infants at risk for neurological handicaps is becoming increasingly important as early intervention techniques improve (Brann, 1985).

Overall, the majority of asphyxiated infants suffer no detectable neurologic or intellectual sequelae. Prognosis is good even in relatively serious cases if neurologic examination is normal by 1 week of age. As would be expected, prognosis is poor when the asphyxia is long and severe or subsequent abnormal clinical features appear (Paneth & Stark, 1983). Much about asphyxia and its sequelae is still not well understood. However, adequate pre-natal care, careful monitoring during labor and delivery with prompt obstetrical intervention, and immediate intervention after delivery by professionals skilled in resuscitation all contribute to lowering the incidence of asphyxia and lessening its long-term effects (Phibbs, 1981).

REFERENCES

Brann, A., Jr. (1985). Factors during neonatal life that influence brain disorders. In J. Freeman (Ed.), *Prenatal and perinatal factors associated with brain disorders* (NIH Pub #85-1149, pp. 263–358). Bethesda, MD: National Institutes of Health.

Fitzhardinge, P. M., & Pape, K. E. (1981). Follow-up studies of the high risk newborn. In G. Avery (Ed.), *Neonatalogy: Pathophysiology and management of the newborn* (2nd ed.) (pp. 350–367). Philadelphia: Lippincott.

Freeman, J. (1985). Summary. In J. Freeman (Ed.), *Prenatal and perinatal factors associated with brain disorders* (NIH Pub #85-1149, pp. 13–32). Bethesda, MD: National Institutes of Health.

Golden, S., & Peters, D. (1985). Delivery room care. In G. Merenstein & S. Gardner (Eds.), *Handbook of neonatal intensive care* (pp. 31–54). St. Louis: Mosby.

Paneth, N., & Stark, R. I. (1983). Cerebral palsy and mental retardation in relation to indicators of perinatal asphyxia. *American Journal of Obstetrics & Gynecology, 146,* 960–966.

Phibbs, R. H. (1981). Delivery room management of the newborn. In G. Avery (Ed.), *Neonatalogy: Pathophysiology and management of the newborn* (2nd ed.) (pp. 350–367). Philadelphia: Lippincott.

Rosen, M. G. (1985). Factors during labor and delivery that influence brain disorders. In J. Freeman (Ed.), *Prenatal and perinatal factors associated with brain disorders* (NIH Pub #85-1149, pp. 13–32). Bethesda, MD: National Institutes of Health.

BRENDA M. POPE
New Hanover Memorial Hospital

APGAR RATING SCALE
CEREBRAL PALSY
LOW BIRTH WEIGHT INFANTS
PREMATURITY/PRETERM

ASSESSMENT, CURRICULUM BASED

See CURRICULUM BASED ASSESSMENT.

ASSESSMENT, EDUCATIONAL

The need for assessment of students' abilities was recognized long before Congress passed the Education of All Handicapped Children Act, PL 94-142. Thomas Jefferson saw the virtues of identifying gifted students and allotting financial aid to those who needed it in order to ensure that these students further their education (Cronbach, 1984). While the need for special services for exceptional children has been long recognized, little was done on a uniform basis in the United States until the passing of PL 94-142.

An important question should be asked: Why assess? Taylor (1984) answers this query by considering the stages assessment should take and explaining why. The first stage of assessment is to screen and identify those students with potential problems. This stage may be formal, as with group testing, or informal, as when conducting behavioral observations. The next reason for assessment is to determine and evaluate the appropriate teaching programs and strategies for a particular student. At this point it is possible to implement strategies in the classroom before making a formal referral. This stage also allows for information about previously successful strategies to be incorporated into teaching programs.

The third stage involves determining the current level of functioning and the educational needs of the student. Possible strategies for remediation and the student's strengths and weaknesses should be identified at this point. In the next stage, assessment is used to make decisions about placement within special education and student classification; i.e., what would be the least restrictive environment for the student? The last step is to develop individual educational programs (IEP) for the student using the information obtained in the assessment process.

This is not to imply that all students with educational problems must go through all of these stages of assessment. If a problem can be remediated within the regular classroom, then it is pointless to continue assessment. Evaluations should be done completely and carefully to ascertain exactly what the student needs and how to meet those needs in the best possible way.

A number of important historical events played a part in determining how the special needs of exceptional children are currently evaluated. These events have been outlined in a number of sources (Cronbach, 1984; Graham & Lily, 1984; Nitko, 1983; Nunnally, 1970; Sattler, 1982; Wisland, 1977). Several significant milestones are summarized here.

1837. A French physician, Sequin, established the first school to educate children who are mentally retarded. He was one of the first to advocate the idea that the mentally retarded could be educated. He also developed the Sequin Form Board, which was later adopted by others for assessing intelligence.

1856. The Chicago public schools implemented the use of written exams for promotion of elementary students and for admission to high school.

1861. In England, payment by results policy was instituted as arithmetic, reading, and writing tests were used to determine the government's funding of the schools.

1869. Francis Galton, considered to be the founder of in-

dividual psychology, made the first systematic and statistical investigation of individual differences and mental inheritance. By using subjects of all intellectual levels, including those at the extremes, he showed that psychological traits are normally distributed.

1890. James McKeen Cattell helped establish the foundations of mental measurements in the United States. He was also the first person to introduce the term mental test.

1904. A two-factor theory of intelligence was introduced by Charles Spearman. His theory maintained that an individual's capacity consists of a general factor of intelligence (g) and other specific factors or special abilities (s).

1905. In France, a means of systematically evaluating the needs of individual students within the educational system was needed, as concepts had been unclearly defined causing great variation from school to school. To meet this need, Alfred Binet and Theophile Simon developed the first practically applied, individually administered test of intelligence, the 1905 Binet-Simon scale.

1908. The first professionally developed standardized test of educational achievement was introduced by C. W. Stone.

1912. William Stern first suggested the concept of a mental quotient determined by the mental age and the chronological age of an individual (MA/CA). This idea of an intelligence quotient was adopted by Binet.

1914. The first commercially available standardized achievement test, the Courtis Standardized Research Test in Arithmetic, was published by Lewis Terman.

1916. The Stanford Revision of the Binet-Simon Scale of Intelligence was introduced by Lewis Terman.

1917. The first commercially available group intelligence test, the Absolute Point Scale, was developed by Arthur Sintor Otis.

1921. The Psychological Corporation was founded by L. M. Terman, G. M. Ruch, and T. L. Kelley.

1936. E. F. Lindquist designed the Iowa Every Pupil Test of Basic Skills, which was later renamed the Iowa Test of Basic Skills.

1938. The Bender Visual Motor Gestalt Test was introduced. It was purported to measure perceptual-motor abilities as well as psychological and personality components.

1939. David Wechsler introduced a new individually administered test of intelligence, the Wechsler-Bellevue Intelligence Scale.

1963. The theory of fluid intelligence, which is of a physiological base, and crystallized intelligence, which is influenced by educational factors, was proposed by Raymond B. Cattell.

1969. Arthur R. Jensen began publication of his controversial articles on the heritability of intelligence.

1975. Congress passed PL 94-142, the Education of All Handicapped Children Act, imposing guidelines and criteria that must be met by the educational systems to service all eligible students.

1983. Kaufman and Kaufman challenge the dominance of the Wechsler Scale.

1992. Reynolds and Kamphaus publish the first nationally normed system for evaluation and diagnosis of behavior problems in the schools.

Test publishing has become a flourishing and lucrative industry since World War I. With this growth has come some substantial advantages, the most significant of these being the increased emphasis on test standardization and the provision of norms for purposes of comparison of individuals with the populations within which they exist. This has been pervasive in all areas of assessment used with exceptional children in the education system.

Consideration of more than just a student's intellectual capacity has also become prevalent as other aspects of the individual and his or her capabilities are assessed in conjunction with this area. Other areas that are relevant to evaluation for special education are the student's current level of academic functioning, the level of adaptive behavior, and, in some cases, the evaluation of personality and behavioral factors. All of these areas play an integral part in the assessment of exceptional students.

Intellectual assessment has played a key role since the beginning of interest in special children. There have been many changes within the intellectual assessment field as well. With the growth of the test publishing industry, instruments used to assess intelligence have increased in number. Along with this increase have come changes in the content of the instruments as well as the way the concept of intelligence has been defined. While the Binet-Simon Intelligence Scale purported to measure an overall concept of intelligence, later instruments attempted to further refine this construct. Witness, for example, the sub-scores of the Wechsler scales, which give not only a full-scale score but also verbal and performance scores. The McCarthy Scales of Children's Abilities yield not only a general cognitive index but also information about a student's abilities in verbal, perceptual-performance, quantitative memory, and motor development areas. The Kaufman Assessment Battery for Children has drawn from past research to develop an instrument that yields not only a global mental processing composite score but also scores pertaining to the processing of information presented sequentially and simultaneously. With these changes has come the advancement of not only how the concept of intelligence is evalu-

ated, but also how intelligence test results relate to intervention in special education.

Tests of educational achievement are also an important aspect of the evaluation of the special education needs of children. There are numerous tests that have been developed to assess a child's level of academic functioning compared with other students of the same age or grade. The content of such measures is usually related to actual academic curricula. There are instruments available that assess many academic areas within one test, while others merely concentrate on one specific area. The number of available instruments of these various types is multitudinous and they have been compiled in various tests elsewhere (Compton, 1984). The relevance of such tests when assessing the needs of exceptional children is evident. Information gained from such measures can lead to more effective educational planning for individual students. These instruments allow for the careful scrutinization of students' strengths and weaknesses in academic areas to establish those who are in need of remediation.

Adaptive behavior may also be an integral part of the assessment of exceptional students. It is essential that this area be assessed for the classification of the mentally retarded as the American Association on Mental Deficiency (AAMD) defines mental retardation as not only low intellectual functioning but also subaverage functioning in adaptive behavior (Sattler, 1982). Other educational classifications such as emotionally disturbed and behavior disordered also make it necessary to evaluate this area of functioning. As with intelligence and achievement, there are a number of instruments available to use to assess adaptive behavior levels. Some examples are the AAMD Adaptive Behavior Scales and the Vineland Adaptive Behavior Scales. These allow specific behavior deficits or strengths to be evaluated; such information is imperative for designing proper behavior management or training programs within educational settings.

The evaluation of personality and emotional disorders also has benefited from the growth of the test publishing industry. While such tests play a role in the educational system, it is to a much lesser extent than those previously mentioned. The relevance of using such measures depends on the type of problem a particular student has. This type of instrument is most likely to be used in evaluating those students who may be classified as emotionally disturbed. While the other areas (intelligence, adaptive behavior, and academic achievement) are more likely to be assessed using instruments that are objective in nature, this has not necessarily been true of personality instruments.

Since the early 1990s, objective evaluation of behavior and personality has become the norm, whereas prior efforts in the affective domain relied heavily upon projective techniques and subjective interpretation. The use of behavior rating scales (e.g., Behavior Assessment System for Children; Reynolds & Kamphaus, 1992) and objective self-report (e.g., Reynolds & Richmond) is now commonplace in school settings, and has led to objective determination of emotional disability and stronger methods of intervention.

All of these types of assessments are an important part of special education evaluation. They can all give useful information about the students and their specific needs within the educational setting.

REFERENCES

Compton, C. (1984). *A guide to 75 tests for special education.* Belmont, CA: Lake.

Cronbach, L. J. (1984). *Essentials of psychological testing* (4th ed.). New York: Harper & Row.

Graham, J. R., & Lily, R. S. (1984). *Psychological testing.* Englewood Cliffs, NJ: Prentice Hall.

Nitko, A. J. (1983). *Educational tests and measurement: An introduction.* New York: Harcourt Brace Jovanovich.

Nunnally, J. C., Jr. (1970). *Introduction to psychological measurement.* New York: McGraw-Hill.

Reynolds, C. R., & Kamphaus, R. W. (1992). *Behavior assessment system for children.* Circle Pines, MN: American Guidance Service.

Reynolds, C. R., & Richmond, B. O. (1985). *Revised children's manifest anxiety scale.* Los Angeles: Western Psychological Services.

Sattler, J. M. (1982). *Assessment of children's intelligence special abilities* (2nd ed.). Boston: Allyn & Bacon.

Taylor, R. L. (1984). *Assessment of exceptional students: educational and psychological procedures.* Englewood Cliffs, NJ: Prentice Hall.

Wisland, M. V. (1977). *Psychological diagnosis of exceptional children* (2nd ed.). Springfield, IL: Thomas.

CAROL S. SCHMITT
Eastern Kentucky University

ACHIEVEMENT TESTS
BEHAVIOR ASSESSMENT SYSTEM FOR CHILDREN
"g" FACTOR THEORY
INTELLIGENCE TESTING
INTELLIGENT TESTING
KAUFMAN ASSESSMENT BATTERY FOR CHILDREN
VINELAND ADAPTIVE BEHAVIOR SCALES
WECHSLER ADULT INTELLIGENCE SCALE
WECHSLER INTELLIGENCE SCALE FOR CHILDREN

intellectual development; its counterpart is accommodation. Assimilation involves incorporating external elements (objects or events) into existing cognitive or sensorimotor schemes; incoming information is interpreted or adjusted in a manner consistent with current cognitive structures. In contrast, accommodation involves changing the structures that assimilate information (Brainerd, 1978).

The distinction between assimilation and accommodation can be illustrated by a physiological example: digestion of food (Ginsburg & Opper, 1969). Acids (or the body's current schemes or structures) transform the food into a form that can be used; thus elements of the external world are assimilated. Accommodation occurs in this example when, in order to deal with a foreign substance, stomach muscles contract, acids are released by certain organs, etc. Physical structures (the stomach and other organs) accommodate to an external element (food).

Assimilation involves both constraints on the nature and range of a child's interactions with the environment and the seeking out of new stimuli that can be assimilated into existing schemes (Gelman & Baillargeon, 1983). Piaget discusses three forms of assimilation: functional assimilation; which involves a basic tendency to use an existing structure such as a sucking reflex; recognitory assimilation, which involves recognizing particular situations in which the scheme should be applied; and generalizing assimilation, which involves a tendency to generalize a scheme to new objects and situations (Ginsburg & Opper, 1969).

REFERENCES

Brainerd, C. J. (1978). *Piaget's theory of intelligence.* Englewood Cliffs, NJ: Prentice Hall.

Gelman, R., & Baillargeon, R. (1983). A review of some Piagetian concepts. In P. H. Mussen (Ed.), *Handbook of child psychology: Vol. III. Cognitive development* (pp. 167–230). New York: Wiley.

Ginsburg, H., & Opper, S. (1969). *Piaget's theory of intellectual development: An introduction.* Englewood Cliffs, NJ: Prentice Hall.

LINDA J. STEVENS
University of Minnesota

ACCOMMODATION
PIAGET, JEAN

ASSIMILATION

Assimilation is one of two complementary processes of adaptation to the environment in Jean Piaget's theory of

ASSISTIVE DEVICES

The term assistive device has been applied to a wide range of highly specialized mechanical, electronic, and computer-based consumer tools that are now commonly used in rehabilitation and special education settings. The assistive device is typically designed to perform a particular prosthetic or orthotic function, but it is not a prosthesis or an orthosis in the traditional medical sense (Webster, Cook, Tompkins, & Vanderheiden, 1985). For example, an artificial arm that is operated by electric impulses generated by the user's nervous system (a myoelectric prosthesis) is not considered an assistive device in the same sense that a robotic arm is. The arm is completely separate from the user's body and can be operated by a number of alternative control mechanisms. While it may be configured or applied with a specific individual's needs in mind, it is essentially modular and noncustomized in nature. The myoelectric arm must be carefully designed and fitted to the individual using it (Caldwell, Buck, Lovely, & Scott, 1985; Apostolos, 1985).

Sensory aids such as hearing aids and tools for vision-impaired individuals are often considered assistive devices as well. In function, these are closer to the generally applied robotic arm than to the individually designed and fitted myoelectric arm.

The gray area of technological application between individualized medical uses and "off-the-shelf" technologies for rehabilitation and special education is the domain of communication aids, computer access devices, and aids to daily living that fall in neither category and share the functional categorization of assistive devices. The term was most likely coined by the Assistive Device Center of California State University in 1978 and has been imitated in recent years by similarly focused efforts internationally (MacDonald & Baillie, 1984; Coleman, Cook, & Meyers, 1982).

A communication aid is used with a person having limited or total inability to speak, usually from lack of motor control. This condition may be a result of congenital anomaly, accident, or a temporary condition.

Speechlessness may or may not be accompanied by cognitive language impairment; frequently nonspeaking students are multiply handicapped. Such students have needs in two of three areas: speech, mobility, and self-care. There is no typical candidate for a communication aid. The student may have cerebral palsy, mental retardation, or any of a number of disabilities that severely limit conversation, writing, and interaction with instructional or vocational materials. The communication device serves a prosthetic function, replacing natural speech, writing, and drawing with output in the form of audible speech (synthetic or recorded), written text, or graphics (Randal, 1983).

The terms nonvocal or nonverbal have been used to describe the student requiring an augmentative speech device. Such terms are not satisfactory because the student may have vocalizations, some intelligible speech that is functional, and even intact verbal skills including reading and writing. The term allolingual has been suggested by Baker (1982), but it has not found widespread acceptance. The most acceptable current term to describe students having no functional speech and those using augmentative communication systems is nonspeaking. Augmentative communication systems may incorporate any existing speech as one mode of communication.

The multiply physically handicapped student requires access not only to speaking and writing, but also to devices in the environment: appliances, lights, doors, alarm systems, telephones, and transportation systems. In this area, assistive devices provide control of such necessary implements through the same mechanism or control interface that the individual may use to obtain control of his or her communication aid.

The third area of assistive device application is in providing access to the large body of educational materials and vocational opportunities afforded by the computer. Many assistive devices, from simple mechanical keyguards to sophisticated high-technology devices such as keyboard emulators and infrared data transmitters, have been designed solely for this purpose and are now readily available. Computer technology and its availability has broadened the sophistication of assistive devices substantially, and change is now quite rapid.

REFERENCES

Apostolos, M. K. (1985). An application of aesthetics in the use of a robotic arm. *Proceedings of the Eighth Annual Conference on Rehabilitation Technology*. Memphis, TN: Rehabilitation Engineering Society of North America.

Baker, B. (1982). Is a rose a rose? *Communication Outlook, 4*(2), 3–18.

Caldwell, R. R., Buck, C. S., Lovely, D. F., & Scott, R. N. (1985). A myoelectric b/e prosthesis system for young children. *Proceedings of the Eighth Annual Conference on Rehabilitation Technology*. Memphis, TN: Rehabilitation Engineering Society of North America.

Coleman, C. L., Cook, A. M., & Meyers, L. (1982). *Final report: D.O.E. grant numbers 6007902261, field-initiated research project-enhancing the educational potential of non-oral children through matching communication device capabilities to children's needs*. Sacramento, CA: Assistive Device Center, California State University.

MacDonald, B. J., & Baillie, E. (1984). *Abstracts: Third international conference on augmentative and alternative communication*. Boston: Massachusetts Institute of Technology.

Randal, J. (1983). *Health technology case study 26: Assistive devices for severe speech impairments*. Washington, DC: U.S. Congress, Office of Technology Assessment, OTA-HCS-26.

Trefler, E., Romich, B., & Russel, N. (1985). Modular technology for the severely physically disabled—the Lainey system. *Proceedings of the Eighth Annual Conference on Rehabilitation Technology*. Memphis, TN: Rehabilitation Engineering Society of North America.

Webster, J. G., Cook, A. M., Tompkins, W. J., & Vanderheiden, G. C. (1985). *Electronic devices for rehabilitation.* New York: Wiley.

MARY BRADY
*Pennsylvania Special Education
Assistive Device Center*

AUGMENTATIVE COMMUNICATION SYSTEMS
COMMUNICATION BOARDS
ELECTRONIC COMMUNICATION AIDS

ASSOCIATION FOR CHILDHOOD EDUCATION INTERNATIONAL (ACEI)

Founded in 1892, The Association for Childhood Education International (ACEI) is a not-for-profit professional education association of educators, parents, and other caregivers interested in promoting quality education practices for children. The organization was originally conceived to provide a formal organization to promote the interest and professionalism of the kindergarten movement throughout the world. With over 11,000 members in the United States and Canada, ACEI is the oldest organization of its kind. Members participate in local and state group activities, including meetings, workshops, and regional conferences. Annual Study Conferences have been held each year since 1896 to share ideas and contribute to the standard of excellence in teaching in all arenas, such as public and private day care centers, kindergartens, elementary schools, middle schools, high schools, and university-level teacher education programs.

The mission of ACEI is to promote the inherent rights, education, and well-being of all children, from infancy through early adolescence, in the home, school, and community. The organization is member-driven and is guided by a dynamic philosophy of education that is flexible and responsive to human needs in a changing society. Members are dedicated to a holistic, child-centered approach to education that considers the child's experiences in the home, school, community, and world.

ACEI is interested in promoting good educational practices for children. By acting as a facilitator for the sharing and dissemination of information through publications and conferences, the organization provides a service to its members and to the education community as a whole. This is accomplished through the regular publication of two refereed professional journals, *Childhood Education* and *Journal of Research in Childhood Education.* Additionally, the Association publishes books, newsletters, pamphlets, position papers, and position statements that relate to the welfare of children, recommend sound, developmentally appropriate educational practice, and include practical application guidelines for educators.

Other contributions of the organization include the publication of *Childhood Education,* a professional journal of theory and practice in the field. The journal has consistently sought to make a thoughtful, multifaceted contribution to the growing body of knowledge concerning children and the learning process. In 1986 an additional publication, *Journal of Research in Childhood Education,* was created as a vehicle for sharing research knowledge as it is acquired. A catalog containing information regarding ACEI publications is available free upon request.

Improved standards for teacher preparation and others involved with the care and development of children are among the association's goals. ACEI was recently appointed to serve as the organization responsible for overseeing the folio review process of elementary teacher preparation programs offered at US colleges and universities seeking accreditation through the National Council for Accreditation of Teacher Education.

A library, including volumes on childhood and elementary education, is maintained at association headquarters. Association offices are located at 17904 Georgia Avenue, Suite 215, Olney, MD 20832.

TAMARA J. MARTIN
*The University of Texas of the
Permian Basin*

ASSOCIATION FOR CHILDREN AND ADULTS WITH LEARNING DISABILITIES (ACLD)

See LEARNING DISABILITIES ASSOCIATION.

ASSOCIATION FOR THE ADVANCEMENT OF BEHAVIOR THERAPY (AABT)

The Association for Advancement of the Behavioral Therapies was founded in 1966 and renamed the Association for the Advancement of Behavior Therapy (AABT) in 1968. Headquartered in New York City, the AABT is a not-for-profit organization of over 4,500 mental health professionals and students who utilize and/or are interested in empirically based behavior therapy and cognitive behavior therapy. Membership is interdisciplinary and consists of psychologists, psychiatrists, social workers, physicians, nurses, and other mental health professionals who treat over 90 mental health problems. AABT does not certify its members.

Among its activities, the AABT sponsors training programs and lectures aimed at professionals and semiprofessionals, provides communication accessibility among behavior therapists interested in similar areas of research or specific problems, and maintains a speaker's bureau. Affiliates of the Association conduct training meetings, workshops, seminars, case demonstrations, and discussion groups. In addition, the AABT holds committees on continuing and public education and provides referrals to the general public upon request (a $5 postage and handling fee is required). A Fact Sheet regarding the problem for which help is being sought and the pamphlet, *Guidelines for Choosing a Behavior Therapist*, are included with mailed referrals. Beginning in approximately September 1998, referrals can be obtained by visiting AABT's website at www.aabt.org/aabt.

The Association's Media & Community Connection Program assists the media with background information and news of the latest developments in the behavioral therapies. The program also helps locate suitable experts in the field for interviews or speaking engagements. Providing membership services to mental health professionals and students seeking to network with like-minded colleagues and to remain current in the behavioral therapies is another activity of the AABT.

AABT offers Full and Associate professional memberships and sponsors an Annual Convention every November, attracting approximately 2,000 participants. One to three smaller educational seminars are held each year as well. Two peer-reviewed journals, *Behavior Therapy* and *Cognitive & Behavioral Practice*, are published by the organization in addition to its newsletter, *The Behavior Therapist*. For a list of AABT publications or for information regarding upcoming educational programs, please call (212) 647-1890 or visit the AABT website at *www.aabt.org/aabt*.

MARY LEON PEERY
Texas A & M University
First edition

TAMARA J. MARTIN
The University of Texas of the Permian Basin
Second edition

ASSOCIATION FOR THE GIFTED, THE

Founded in 1958, The Association for the Gifted is one of the 17 divisions of The Council for Exceptional Children.

The purposes of this association are to (1) promote the welfare and education of children and youth with gifts, talents, and/or high potential; (2) improve educational opportunities for individuals from all diverse groups with gifts, talents, and/or high potential; (3) sponsor and foster activities to develop the field of gifted education, such as the dissemination of information, the conduct of research, and other scholarly investigations; (4) support and encourage specialized professional preparation for educators of individuals with gifts, talents, and/or high potential, as well as for professional persons in related fields; and (5) work with organizations, agencies, families, or individuals whose purposes are consistent with those of The Association for the Gifted.

The association distributes two publications to its membership. One, the *Journal for the Education of the Gifted*, is a forum for theoretical, descriptive, and research articles that analyze and communicate information about the needs of children and youth with gifts, talents, and/or high potential. The *Journal* also serves as a forum for the exchange of diverse ideas and points of view on the education of the gifted and talented. The second publication, *TAG Update*, is the association's newsletter, containing brief, timely information on the association's activities, upcoming events, workshops and institutes, reports on legislation, and relevant news from other organizations.

Membership inquiries should be made to The Association for the Gifted, The Council for Exceptional Children, 1920 Association Drive, Reston, VA 20191-1589. Only members of The Council for Exceptional Children are eligible to join. The Association for the Gifted. Special membership categories for students and parents and professionals are available for those who qualify for these discounted membership rates.

STAFF

ASSOCIATION OF BLACK PSYCHOLOGISTS

The Association of Black Psychologists (ABPsi) was founded in San Francisco in 1968 when a number of black psychologists from across the country met to discuss the serious problems facing black psychologists and the larger black community. The founding members began building an organization through which they could confront the long-neglected needs of black professionals. They also hoped to have a positive impact on the mental health of the black community through programs, services, training, and advocacy. The Association is organized into four regions as well as a student division. From the original group, the membership of ABPsi has grown into an international organization of over 1,300 psychologists and mental health professionals, committed to addressing the mental health issues of individuals throughout the African diaspora.

The main offices of the Association of Black Psychologists can be reached at P.O. Box 55999, Washington, DC 20040-5999, or by telephone at (202) 722-0808.

NADINE M. LAMBERT
University of California
First edition

KAY E. KETZENBERGER
The University of Texas of the Permian Basin
Second edition

ASSOCIATIVE LEARNING

Associative learning, as demonstrated in the classical conditioning experiments of Pavlov (1927), is based on the concept that events or ideas that are experienced at the same time tend to become associated with each other. When a new (conditioned) stimulus is presented with an old (unconditioned) stimulus, the conditioned stimulus assumes the capability of eliciting a (conditioned) response almost identical to the original (unconditioned) response. The conditioned stimulus should be presented about half a second before the unconditioned stimulus for maximum effectiveness.

Associative learning is routinely applied when students recognize words, spell, and recall math facts. A number of remedial techniques are also based on the associative principle. Multisensory approaches to reading, which presume the formation of associative bonds across sensory modalities, have been successful in remediating deficits in mildly and severely reading-disabled children and in retarded students (Sutaria, 1982). Visual imagery training, in which children learn to associate mental pictures with printed text, has been shown to improve learning-disabled students' reading comprehension (Clark, Warner, Alley, Deshler & Shumaker, 1981).

Retarded children, for whom associative skills are often an area of relative strength, have improved their memory performance when taught to pair words according to their conceptual similarity (Lathey & Tobias, 1981). Associative learning is a fundamental principle of teaching, and children's associative learning skills can be corrected and compensated for by using a variety of techniques (Woolfolk, 1995).

REFERENCES

Clark, F., Warner, M., Alley, G., Deshler, D., Shumaker, J., Vetter, A., & Nolan, R. (1981). *Visual imagery and self questioning.* Washington, DC: Bureau of Education for the Handicapped. (ERIC Document Reproduction Service No. ED 217 655)

Lathey, J. W., & Tobias, S. (1981, April). *Associative and conceptual training of retarded and normal children.* Paper presented at the annual meeting of the American Educational Research Association, Los Angeles. (ERIC Document Reproduction Service No. ED 206 139)

Pavlov, I. P. (1927). *Conditioned reflexes.* London: Oxford University Press.

Sutaria, S. (1982). *Multisensory approach to teaching of reading to learning disabled students.* Paper presented at the annual meeting of the World Congress on Reading, Dublin, Ireland. (ERIC Document Reproduction Service No. ED 246 600)

Woolfolk, A. E. (1995). *Educational psychology* (6th ed.). Boston: Allyn & Bacon.

GARY BERKOWITZ
Temple University

CONDITIONING

REVISUALIZATION

ASTHMA

Asthma has been recognized and described for more than 200 years and is one of the most common lung diseases of childhood. It is a difficulty in breathing caused by obstruction to the flow of air in the bronchial tubes because of swelling of the lining membranes, contraction of the surrounding musculature, and plugging of the tubes by mucus. This is inevitably accompanied by wheezing. Other symptoms are sometimes present such as a persistent cough and shortness of breath. The distress of asthma attacks is sometimes worsened by simple activities like laughing or lying down (Asthma and Allergy Foundation of America, 1980).

Asthma affects about 2 million children under 17 and as many as 4 to 7% of children in the United States may at some time suffer from asthma (Evans, 1981; Young, 1994). It accounts for 20 to 25% of school absences owing to chronic diseases. Asthma may appear at any age but it generally appears in the first 20 years of life. The frequency of onset diminishes rapidly after 40 years. In children there is an estimated ratio of 2:1 for boys over girls, but as asthmatics mature and approach adulthood, the sex ratio becomes essentially equal. There is little doubt that some asthma has a genetic basis but such is difficult to prove in a given case. Some symptoms diminish systematically with age. This is referred to as "growing out of asthma." The reason for this more or less spontaneous cure is not understood, but one should not consider it a total cure, since the symptoms may reappear later. Asthmatic patients may have at least minimal airway obstruction throughout their lives.

Asthma can be precipitated by a variety of triggers such as environmental pollution, exercise (especially when breathing cold air), viral infections, aspirin and related substances, emotional factors and allergens (the most common being pollen), animals or feathers, molds and fungus, insects, occupational dust, chemicals, house dust, and foods. To confirm the diagnosis of asthma, three steps can be followed: (1) provoke bronchio constriction by having the patient inhale stimuli thought to produce smooth muscle hyperactivity; (2) give bronchodilations to check on the reversibility of the attack; and (3) establish the chronicity and intermittency of attacks (Greer, Harm, & Marion, 1983).

Asthma can be classified on a continuum, with intrinsic or perennial asthma (a type of asthma that presents symptoms all year round) at one end and extrinsic or seasonal asthma (which tends to be aggravated during certain seasons, especially the fall) at the other (Greer, Marion, & Harm, 1985). Treatment for asthma must be continuously evaluated because of its variability. Medical treatment falls into two categories: the first is immunotherapy, which is the process of desensitizing the child's allergies by injecting the child with progressively increasing amounts of the allergen. Effectiveness of this treatment is limited by compliance to the administration of allergen shots. The second category is pharmacologic therapy. The most common drug prescribed is theophyllene, which is a bronchodilator that reduces the frequency and the severity of attacks. If this or other medication fails to control the attacks, then corticosteroids are used, but, because of their serious side effects, they should not be used unless all other forms of treatment fail.

Psychological factors are usually not sufficient by themselves to cause asthma. For this and other reasons psychotherapy is not used as a way to control the disease. It has, however, proven effective with psychological problems resulting from the disorder. Broncho constriction in asthmatic patients can result in anxiety in both patients and their parents. Relaxation techniques, biofeedback, and systematic desensitization have also proven effective in managing some cases. Parentectomy (Kapotes, 1977), the removal of patients from the home environment that appears to trigger the attack, is sometimes recommended. Recently, a number of comprehensive self-management programs for asthma have been developed. These are designed to provide patients with the skills to assume responsibility for controlling the affliction. Such programs as the *Living with Asthma* project (Greer, Backial, & Leung,

1984; Greer, Allman, & Leung, 1984; Greer, et al., 1984) evolved from the treatment and rehabilitation program established at CARIH. Patients are provided with information about the mechanics of breathing, the changes that occur during attacks, triggers of attacks, and the medication to control them. When an asthmatic knows his or her condition is due to allergies, then an effective way to control attacks is to avoid the allergens that he or she is sensitive to (Flod, Franz, & Yalant, 1976).

Asthmatic children in educational settings face the problem that teachers may be unfamiliar with the condition and frightened by attacks. It is very important that teachers have meetings with the parents, the child, and the physician to learn about the child's condition and to become familiar with procedures to be followed in case of an attack. Physical education teachers can usually respect a child's knowledge of his or her condition even though exercise can trigger attacks. Preexercise medication can sometimes be useful in preventing attacks. School absenteeism could be reduced by realizing that, through medication, attacks can be controlled. If asthma is under control, a child should be capable of participating in all educational activities. Children with asthma are at increased risk of behavioral and emotional problems but asthma is too complex to allow specification of specific outcomes without considering the individual child (Greer, 1994).

REFERENCES

American Lung Association. (1981). There are solutions for the student with asthma. *American Lung Association Publication Item 0083.*

Asthma and Allergy Foundation of America. (1980). Handbook for the asthmatic. *Asthma and Allergy Foundation of America Publication.*

Evans, H. E. (1981). What happens when a child has asthma. *American Lung Association Publication.*

Flod, N. E., Franz, M. L., & Yalant, S. P. (1976). Recent advances in bronchial asthma. *American Journal of Diseases of Children, 130,* 890–899.

Greer, T. (1994). Asthma: Psychological issues. In R. Olson, L. Mullins, J. Gillman, & J. Chaney (Eds.), *The sourcebook of pediatric psychology* (pp. 61–69). Boston: Allyn & Bacon.

Greer, T. L., Backiel, M., & Leung, P. (1984). *Living with asthma: Manual for teaching self-management skills to children.* Washington, DC: U.S. Department of Health and Human Services.

Greer, T. L., Marion, R. J., & Harm, D. L. (1985). Childhood asthma. In V. B. Hasselt, P. S. Strain, & M. Henson (Eds.), *Handbook of developmental and physical disabilities.* New York: Pergamon.

Greer, T. L., Ullman, S., & Leung, P. (1984). *Living with asthma: Manual for teaching adults the self-management of childhood asthma.* Washington, DC: U.S. Department of Health and Human Services.

Kapotes, C. (1977). Emotional factors in chronic asthma. *Journal of Asthma Research, 15,* 5–14.

Young, G. A. (1994). Asthma: Medical issues. In R. Olson, L. Mullins, & J. Fillman, & J. Chaney (Eds.), *The sourcebook of pediatric psychology* (pp. 57–60). Boston: Allyn & Bacon.

ANA YERALDINA BENEKE
LOGAN WRIGHT
University of Oklahoma

ALLERGIC DISORDERS
BIOFEEDBACK

ASTIGMATISM

Astigmatism is a refractive error that causes reduced visual acuity and a lack of sharply focused, clear vision. In astigmatism, the curve of the cornea is irregular. Because of this irregularity, some light rays may come to focus in front of the retina, some on the retina, and some at the theoretical point behind it. The result is distorted or blurred vision and headache or eye fatigue after intensive close work.

Astigmatism does not seem to be clearly related to difficulties in learning to read. In some cases it has even been associated with better than average reading (Lerner, 1985). The special educator should be aware of the symptoms of astigmatism (Rouse & Ryan, 1984): headaches; discomfort in tasks that demand visual interpretation; problems seeing far as well as near; red eyes; distortion in size, shape, or inclination of objects; frowning and squinting at desk tasks; and nausea in younger or lower-functioning students. Astigmatism is generally correctable with eyeglasses or contact lenses, which should be worn full-time by affected students. These students may be helped in the classroom by being moved closer to the front of the room and by a reduction in the amount of time spent on near tasks.

REFERENCES

Lerner, J. (1985). *Learning disabilities: Theories, diagnoses, and teaching strategies.* Boston: Houghton Mifflin.

Rouse, M. W., & Ryan, J. B. (1984). Teacher's guide to vision problems. *Reading Teacher, 38*(3), 306–317.

ANNE M. BAUER
University of Cincinnati

VISUAL ACUITY
VISUAL TRAINING

ASYMMETRICAL TONIC NECK REFLEX (ATNR)

Asymmetrical tonic neck reflex (ATNR) is one of a group of postural central nervous system reflexes that in the normal child is inhibited and incorporated into more sophisticated motor skills. The ATNR can be demonstrated easily in normal infants to about 40 weeks by placing the child on the back and turning the head to the left or right. As the face is turned to the left, the left arm extends and the right arm flexes, bringing the right hand flexed to the skull side of the head simultaneous with flexion of the leg on that and the opposite side. In the normal child with no pathology, this reflex is gradually inhibited; thus, children of 24 to 36 months can reach for toys in front of them; look to the side and still bring a cracker or spoon to the mouth when the head is in midposition; and cross the midline. Later on, the child can sustain weight on the arms and knees, and rotation of the head will not result in collapse or support on the skull side arm.

The child who has central nervous system damage above the level of the midbrain (usually considered to be in the basal ganglia, cerebral cortex, or both) will demonstrate a persistent ATNR well beyond the age of 1 year, with accompanying profound damage into adult life. The child with severe ATNR finds self-feeding impossible. Persistence of ATNR can interfere with sitting and standing balance and dressing and writing, and make voluntary motion difficult or impossible.

Some help can be provided to children with delayed inhibition of ATNR by positioning and adaptive motor responses in physical and occupational therapy. Proper classroom seating can help moderately to severely involved children learn to diminish uninhibited reflexive responses when they are relaxed and listening. Excitement, anxiety, and stress may override the child's ability to inhibit the reflexive movement, making controlled, purposeful movement difficult or impossible for the more severely involved young adult with persistent uninhibited ATNR.

RACHEL J. STEVENSON
Bedford, Ohio

CENTRAL NERVOUS SYSTEM

ATARAX

Atarax (hydroxyzine hydrochloride) may be used for symptomatic relief of anxiety and tension associated with psychoneurosis and as an adjunct in organic disease states in which anxiety is manifested. It also may be used as a sedative; the most common manifestation of overdosage is extreme sedation. Other uses include treatment of pruritis owed to allergic conditions such as chronic urticaria and dermatoses. Although not a cortical depressant, its action may be due to suppression of activity in certain key regions of the subcortical area of the central nervous system. Adverse reactions may include dryness of mouth and drowsiness, with the possibility of tremor, involuntary motor activity, and convulsions reported in cases where higher than recommended doses have been used.

A brand name of Roeris Pharmaceuticals, it is available in tablets of 10, 25, 50, and 100 milligrams, and as a syrup. The recommended dosage for children under 6 years of age is 50 mg daily in divided doses, and for children over 6 years of age 50 to 100 mg daily in divided doses. When used as a sedative, dosage is recommended to be 0.6 mg/kg (milligram per kilogram of body weight) at all childhood ages, and 50 to 100 mg for adults.

LAWRENCE C. HARTLAGE
Evans, Georgia

ANTIHISTAMINES
BENADRYL
DRUG THERAPY

ATAXIA

Ataxia is a type of cerebral palsy caused by the loss of cerebellar control. It is characterized by an unbalanced gait. An ataxic gait is often referred to as a drunken gait, as it resembles the walk of someone who is intoxicated.

According to Batshaw and Perret (1981), "The cerebellum coordinates the action of the voluntary muscles and times their contractions so that movements are performed smoothly and accurately" (p. 163). That is, the cerebellum senses where the limb is in space (based on input to the cerebellum), estimates where the target is, integrates the information, and then carries out the infinitesimal corrections necessary to compensate for inaccuracies in motor output, thereby maintaining fluid movement.

A child whose primary diagnosis is ataxia has poor righting and equilibrium reactions, and a staggering, lurching, irregular, and broad-based gait (Brown, 1973). According to Connor, Williamson, and Siepp (1978), the child has difficulty sustaining posture, as well as shifting posture in a coordinated manner. He or she often stumbles and falls. This postural instability may make the child overly cautious. The child may stiffen his or her trunk abnormally in order to increase stability. When walking, the child may visually fix on an object in the environment in an effort to maintain postural control. According to

Walsch (1963), when an older child attempts purposeful reaching, he or she often overshoots the mark because of the presence of a distal, wavering tremor. Nystagmus is often present.

It is important that physical therapy begin as early as possible. According to Connor, Williamson, and Siepp (1978), early intervention should concentrate on the development of proximal control and stability. Repetition and reinforcement of movement is necessary so that responses become reliable. Activities that increase tremors or stiffening must be avoided. However, since children with ataxia demonstrate variations in their movement behavior, individual program planning is necessary.

REFERENCES

Batshaw, M. L., & Perret, Y. M. (1981). *Children with handicaps: a medical primer*. Baltimore, MD: Brookes.

Bobath, B., & Bobath, K. (1976). *Motor development in the different types of cerebral palsy*. London: Heinemann Medical.

Brown, J. E. (1973). Disease of the cerebellum. In A. B. Baker & L. H. Baker (Eds.), *Clinical neurology, Vol. II*. New York: Harper & Row.

Connor, F. P., Williamson, G. G., & Siepp, J. M. (1978). *Program guide for infants and toddlers with neuromotor and other developmental disabilities*. New York: Teachers College Press.

Swaiman, K. F., & Right, F. S. (Eds.). (1982). *The practice of pediatric neurology* (2nd ed.). St. Louis, MO: Mosby.

Walsch, G. (1963). *Cerebellum, posture, and cerebral palsy* (Clinics in Developmental Medicine, No. 8). London: Heinemann Medical Books.

CAROLE REITER GOTHELF
Hunter College

CEREBRAL PALSY
CEREBELLAR DISORDERS

ATHETOSIS

Athetosis is a central nervous system disorder characterized by slow, writhing movements, most notable in the extremities. These involuntary muscle movements have been described also as wormlike or snakelike. The actual movements consist of alternating flexion–extension and supination–pronation of the limbs, and are usually associated with increased, though variable, muscle tone (Chow, Durard, Feldman, & Mills 1979).

Athetosis is most commonly form of cerebral palsy (CP) is childhood accounting for approximately 15 to 30% of children with that diagnosis; however, the overall incidence rate is declining, probably because of improved neonatal intensive care (Batshaw & Perret, 1981). The condition, also known as choreo-athetoid CP, often occurs in conjunction with other forms of CP, especially spasticity. As a form of cerebral palsy, athetosis is one of a group of nonprogressive neuromotor disorders caused by earlier brain damage. Unlike other common forms of CP, the athetoid type presents a problem of controlling movement and posture rather than a difficulty in initiating voluntary movement. The uncontrolled, purposeless, involuntary movements associated with athetosis are not evidenced during sleep. Although the precise nature of the central nervous system insult is often indeterminable, among known causes may be various prenatal factors (e.g., anoxia, blood group incompatibilities, excessive radiation dosage during gestation, physical injuries, various maternal infections); perinatal factors (e.g., prematurity, head trauma, asphyxia, kernicterus); and postnatal factors (e.g., head trauma, hemorrhage, infections of the brain or cranial linings). In the United States, one to two children per thousand may be affected by CP, including athetosis or mixed cerebral palsy with athetosis. It is believed that in the more pure athetoid type of CP, the site of lesion is generally in the basal ganglia or extrapyramidal track (Kandel, Schwartz, & Jessell, 1991; Vaughan, McKay, & Behrman, 1979).

Secondary problems important to the special educator frequently accompany athetosis. Early difficulties may be observed in sucking, feeding, chewing, and swallowing. Special techniques to deal with these problems may come from speech/language pathologists, occupational therapists, physical therapists, or physicians. Speech articulation is often impaired and drooling may be present. In addition, hearing loss, epilepsy, and mental retardation may exist simultaneously. However, careful assessment of cognitive functioning is essential because both speech and motor skills are affected.

Little, if any, in the way of curative action is successful with cerebral palsy. Early intervention, special education, and vocational rehabilitation will be important, but the exact nature of the treatment approach will depend largely on the presence, nature, and degree of concomitant disorders. As many of 70% of children with the athetoid type of CP may function in the mentally retarded range, so educational and habilitative services must take into account the child's developmental limitations. Because facial muscles are involved in athetosis, vision disorders, especially of the eye-muscle imbalance type, may be present in more than 40% of the affected group (Black, 1980). Hearing loss is also common, though less so than vision problems, necessitating early and continuous audiometric evaluations and the possible provision of amplification devices. Physical therapy, including bracing and splinting to help maintain balance and to control involuntary movements, may be indicated in many cases. Orthopedic surgery and neuro-surgery, though sometimes helpful with other forms of CP, have not yet shown promise for children with athetosis.

REFERENCES

Batshaw, M. L., & Perret, Y. M. (1981). *Children with handicaps: A medical primer*. Baltimore, MD: Brookes.

Black, P. D. (1980). Ocular defects in children with cerebral palsy. *British Medical Journal, 281,* 487.

Chow, M. P., Durand, B. A., Feldman, M. N., & Mills, M. A. (1979). *Handbook of pediatric primary care*. New York: Wiley.

Kandel, E., Schwartz, J., Jessell, T. (1991). *Principles of Neural Science* (3rd ed.). NY: Elsevier.

Vaughan, V. C., McKay, R. J., & Behrman, R. E. (1979). *Nelson textbook of pediatrics*. Philadelphia: Saunders.

JOHN D. WILSON
Elwyn Institutes

CENTRAL NERVOUS SYSTEM
CEREBRAL PALSY

ATTENTION-DEFICIT/HYPERACTIVITY DISORDER (ADHD)

Attention-Deficit/Hyperactivity Disorder (ADHD) is the most recent diagnostic label for children who exhibit developmentally inappropriate levels of inattention, impulsivity, and hyperactivity (American Psychiatric Association, 1994). Children with ADHD display diminished persistence of effort or have difficulty sustaining attention to tasks with little intrinsic value, exhibit excessive motor and/or vocal activity, and experience difficulty in inhibiting behavior to situational demands (Barkley, 1997). Behavioral disinhibition exhibited by these children is the sine qua non of the disorder (Barkley, 1998). Behavioral disinhibition, overactivity, and inattentiveness are the cardinal characteristics of this disorder, and these characteristics occur across a variety of settings (for example, home and school) with the magnitude of symptom presentation significantly fluctuating in different settings and with different caregivers (Barkley, 1998; Zentall, 1985).

Prevalence rates have been difficult to ascertain, as ADHD has not only been difficult to define but has also been difficult to precisely and objectively measure (Barkley, 1998). Prevalence estimates of ADHD in school-aged children have ranged from a low of 1% to a high of 12% (Frick, Strauss, Lahey, & Christ, 1993). Consensus among many experts in the field, however, suggests that approximately 3–5% of the school-aged population has ADHD (American Psychiatric Association, 1994).

Gender differences have also been reported. The proportion of males to females manifesting the disorder range from 2.5:1 to 5.1:1 with an average of approximately 3.4:1 among non-referred children (Szatmari, Offord, & Boyle, 1989). In clinic-referred samples, however, boys are six to nine times more likely than girls to be diagnosed with the disorder (Barkley, 1998). Research has found that girls with ADHD are more impaired in their intelligence, less hyperactive, and less likely to exhibit other externalizing symptoms (like aggression, defiance, and conduct problems) and internalizing symptoms (like anxiety, depression, and withdrawn behaviors) than boys (Gaub & Carlson, 1997).

From a historical perspective, the concept of ADHD and the terms used to describe the disorder have undergone a series of revisions. These revisions have been in response to changes in the conceptualization of the disorder among clinical researchers. ADHD was first described in the scientific literature in 1902 (Still, 1902). Still described a group of children whose major difficulties were in the control of their own behavior. These children were of normal intelligence and poor child-rearing techniques had been ruled out. Still believed the major defect displayed by these children was in the moral control of their behavior or volitional inhibition. According to Still, the most distinguishing attribute of these children was their inappropriate social conduct.

Ebaugh (1923) and Strecker and Ebaugh (1924) reported on a group of children who were described as inattentive, impulsive, and socially disruptive. These children had survived the encephalitis outbreak in 1917–1918 in North America, but were left with significant behavioral and cognitive sequelae as a result of brain damage. Many of the characteristics displayed by these children are now incorporated into the concept of ADHD.

Research on the disorder showed resurgence in the 1940s and 1950s with the work of Laufer, Denhoff, and Solomons (1957) and Strauss and Lehtinen (1955). Strauss and Lehtinen described a group of children who were restless, impulsive, overactive, distractible, and inattentive. The researchers attributed the children's problems to brain damage, although direct evidence was weak or nonexistent. The term Minimal Brain Damage (MBD) was coined during this period of time and used to describe these children of the postencephalitic period. These children's greatest problem was their excessive activity levels.

In the 1960s, a number of disagreements arose in the psychiatric community regarding the Minimal Brain Damage label. The crux of the disagreements was due to the fact that there was a lack of clear evidence demonstrating a link between organic impairment and excessive activity levels. Thus, the Minimal Brain Damage label was replaced with a new term, Minimal Brain Dysfunction. The rationale behind the change in terminology was that behavioral symptoms alone could not be used to imply neurological impairment (Copeland & Love, 1991).

The term Minimal Brain Dysfunction was replaced with the term Hyperkinetic Reaction of Childhood in 1968 in the revised nomenclature of the American Psychiatric Association, Diagnostic and Statistical Manual of Mental Disorders, Second Edition (DSM-II; American Psychiatric Association, 1968). The primary diagnostic symptom of ADHD in the DSM-II was hyperactivity.

In the next decade, however, a shift in focus occurred in which attention problems became the most salient symptom of ADHD. Research suggested the inability to sustain and regulate attention was the critical feature of this disorder, rather than hyperactivity (Douglas & Peters, 1979). As a result, the term and description of the disorder was changed to Attention Deficit Disorder (Diagnostic and Statistical Manual of Mental Disorders, Third Edition [DSM-III]; American Psychiatric Association, 1980). The DSM-III also recognized a dichotomy in the disorder in which some children displayed only attention problems, whereas others exhibited both inattention and hyperactivity. The children with attention problems and hyperactivity were given the diagnostic label of Attention Deficit Disorder with Hyperactivity. In contrast, those children with attention problems only were labeled Attentional Deficit Disorder without Hyperactivity. The essential features of Attention Deficit Disorder included inattention, impulsivity, and hyperactivity.

Later in the decade, the DSM criteria for ADHD was revised again (Diagnostic and Statistical Manual of Mental Disorders, Third Edition, Revised [DSM-III-R]; American Psychiatric Association, 1987). In the DSM-III-R, Attention Deficit Disorder with Hyperactivity became known as Attention-Deficit Hyperactivity Disorder and Attention Deficit Disorder without Hyperactivity was removed as a subtype and relegated to a vaguely defined category known as Undifferentiated Attention Deficit Disorder. Attention-Deficit Hyperactivity Disorder was now classified as a disruptive behavioral disorder along with conduct disorder and oppositional defiant disorder. In the revised diagnostic criteria, which were empirically derived, children with affective disorders were now eligible to receive the diagnosis of ADHD, whereas in the past, these children were excluded from the ADHD diagnosis. Moreover, the revisions stressed the importance of assessing the developmental appropriateness of a child's symptoms relative to his or her mental age in determining whether he or she met the diagnostic criteria for the disorder.

The current definition of ADHD is found in the Diagnostic and Statistical Manual of Mental Disorders, Fourth Edition (DSM-IV; American Psychiatric Association, 1994). In the DSM-IV, ADHD symptoms are divided into two main categories, inattention and hyperactivity-impulsivity. Children must exhibit six of the nine symptoms in one or both categories to meet the criteria for one of the three subtypes of ADHD: ADHD-Predominately Inattentive Type, ADHD-Predominately Hyperactive-

Impulsive Type, and ADHD-Combined Type. Moreover, the inattentive and/or hyperactive-impulsive symptoms must be present on a frequent basis for at least six months to be considered clinically significant. The symptoms must also be cross-situational (i.e., occur across two or more settings, such as the home and school settings). Some of the symptoms must also have been present before the age of seven.

Of the three subtypes, the ADHD-Combined Type is the most common. Children who meet the criteria for this subtype display both inattentive and hyperactive-impulsive behaviors. In contrast, the Predominately Inattentive Type describes those children who exhibit inattention but do not meet the diagnostic criteria for hyperactivity-impulsivity. These children have difficulty concentrating and completing work. Under the old DSM-III criteria, these children would have met the criteria for Attention Deficit Disorder without Hyperactivity. Currently, little is known about the third subtype, the Predominately Hyperactive-Impulsive Type. These children supposedly exhibit hyperactive-impulsive behavior but do not meet the diagnostic criteria for inattention. McBurnett, Lahey, and Pfiffner (1993) indicate a number of preschoolers fit this subtype.

Children with ADHD are at risk for developing comorbid disorders. Over 50% of the children with ADHD have at least one additional disorder (Barkley, 1998). The most prevalent comorbid psychiatric disorders seen with children with ADHD include conduct disorders, oppositional defiant disorders, anxiety disorders, major depression, bipolar disorders, and somatization disorders. Of these disorders, oppositional defiant disorders and conduct disorders are the most common disorders associated with ADHD. On the other hand, the co-occurrence of mood and anxiety disorders occurs somewhat less frequently in children with ADHD.

In addition to comorbid psychiatric disorders, children with ADHD are more likely to have significant social impairments. Poor peer relationships and misinterpretation of social cues have been reported (Barkley, 1998). These children are more likely to exhibit aggression toward their peers, which in turn, leads to peer rejection. In their relationships with adults, these children are less compliant to parental and teacher requests and receive a greater share of commands, reprimands, and punishment (Barkley, 1998). For parents, parent-training programs are available to address noncompliance. In addition, family therapy and individual counseling for children with ADHD are also available to address difficulties some children and families may encounter in association with the disorder.

A host of etiologies have been proposed throughout the years, including neurological aberrations (Werry et al., 1972), food additives (Feingold, 1975), fluorescent lighting (Frick et al., 1993), and environmental stressors (Barkley, 1981). Recently, neurological and genetic factors have received substantial empirical support as the greatest con-

tributors to this disorder (Barkley, 1998). Possible genetic and neurological etiologies include pregnancy and birth complications (Hartsough & Lambert, 1985), acquired brain damage (Cruickshank, Eliason, & Merrifield, 1988), exposure to environmental toxins (Needleman, Schell, Bellinger, Leviton, & Alfred, 1990), infections (Mick, Biederman, & Faraone, 1996), and genetic effects (Edelbrock, Rende, Plomin, & Thompson, 1995). Genetic and/or neurological factors are thought to disrupt a final common pathway in the nervous system known as the prefrontal cortical-striatal network, and this disruption in the neural pathway may give rise to the disorder (Barkley, 1998). Based on family aggregation studies, adoption studies, twin studies, and molecular genetic research, hereditary factors appear to play the major role in the occurrence of ADHD symptoms in children (Barkley, 1998). On the other hand, environmental factors, such as social adversity and family factors, have received some support in the literature as possible etiologies (Carlson, Jacobvitz, & Sroufe, 1995). Family dynamics, parental characteristics, and parenting styles have been highlighted in this line of research (Silverman & Ragusa, 1992). Barkley (1998), however, believes psychosocial factors play a secondary role to the genetic and neurological factors. According to Barkley, environmental factors are contributors to the persistence of the disorder over development, and may simply intensify the symptoms that already exist.

Perhaps the changing diagnostic nosology and the variability in prevalence rates for this very complex disorder have been a function of inadequate assessment techniques in child psychology, psychiatry, and special education. Although new assessment instruments have been developed, the search continues for accurate and reliable measures of ADHD, as no single test has been devised that definitely tells a clinician that a child has ADHD (Gordon & Barkley, 1998). Thus, a multimethod assessment approach has been recommended in which information from a variety of measures, sources, and settings is collected and analyzed (Bradley & DuPaul, 1997).

According to Barkley and Edwards (1998), a comprehensive evaluation of a child with ADHD involves three critical components: the clinical interview, the medical examination, and the completion of behavioral rating scales. When feasible, psychological tests and observations may be included to aid in differential diagnosis or yield additional information about the presence and severity of cognitive impairments associated with some cases of ADHD. Psychological tests incorporated into ADHD-related evaluations tend to fall into four categories: (1) intelligence /achievement measures, (2) neuropsychological batteries, (3) individual neuropsychological tests, and (4) projective/ personality measures (Gordon & Barkley, 1998).

Clinical interviews are conducted with parents and teachers to obtain highly descriptive information about the child and the child's psychological adjustment at home and at school. Information about school, family, and treatment histories are also gleaned from these interviews. The child is also interviewed, with the content of the interview being dependent upon the child's age. For a preschooler, the interview is a means of establishing rapport and noting the child's appearance, behavior, developmental characteristics, and general demeanor. For an older child or adolescent, the purpose of the interview is to obtain information about the child or adolescent's perspective of the reason for the referral, evaluation, and difficulties encountered (Barkley & Edwards, 1998).

In addition to the interview, it is imperative that a child has a complete medical examination. In the past, these examinations tended to be extremely brief and produced unreliable or invalid results (Costello et al., 1988). The pediatric medical examination should consist of two parts, the medical interview and the physical examination. The purpose of the medical interview is to focus on differential diagnosis, to evaluate possible coexisting medical conditions, and to determine if any physical conditions exist that preclude the use of medication in the treatment of a child with ADHD. The physical exam, on the other hand, includes numerous screening tests, a neurological examination, and a neurodevelopmental exam (Barkley & Edwards, 1998).

The third component of a comprehensive evaluation is the completion of behavioral rating scales. Child behavior checklists and rating scales provide a wealth of information with little investment of time required. Barkley and Edwards (1998) recommend that parents, teachers, and children, if applicable, complete a broad band rating scale, a narrow band rating scale, and additional scales depending upon the child's problems. Broad band rating scales provide coverage of the major dimensions of child psychopathology. Examples of broad band rating scales include the *Behavior Assessment System for Children*–Parent Rating Scale, Teacher Rating Scale, and Self-Report of Personality (BASC; Reynolds & Kamphaus, 1994) and the *Child Behavior Checklist*–Parent Report Form (Achenbach & Edelbrock, 1983), Teacher Report Form (Achenbach & Edelbrock, 1986a), and Youth Self-Report (Achenbach & Edelbrock, 1986b). In contrast, narrow band scales are used to assess specific symptoms of ADHD. Examples of narrow band scales include the *Disruptive Behavior Rating Scale* (Barkley & Murphy, 1998) and the *Child Attention Profile* (Barkley, 1990). Additional behavioral ratings may be included to address specific areas of concern, for example, peer relations or adaptive functioning.

Besides Barkley and Edwards's (1998) approach to assessing children with ADHD in a clinical setting, DuPaul (1992) presented a model for assessing ADHD within the school setting. DuPaul's model is based on a multimethod assessment approach and includes five stages. Following the initial referral of the child, Stage One of the model involves screening. The child's teacher is asked to complete teacher-rating scales, which assess ADHD symptomatol-

ogy. Stage Two involves the multimethod assessment of ADHD. Stage Two includes teacher and parent interviews and completion of behavior rating scales, a review of the child's educational records, observations of the child in the school setting, and a review of the child's academic portfolio. During Stage Three, the assessment data are evaluated and interpreted with respect to the DSM-IV diagnostic criteria for ADHD. A treatment plan is developed in Stage Four followed by an assessment of treatment outcome during Stage Five. Based on a multiassessment model, a variety of interventions may be developed and implemented to optimize the child's learning and educational success.

Various treatments for children with ADHD have been widely researched. Interventions have ranged from fluorescent lighting (Sprague, 1979) to dietary regimens (Feingold, 1975). Stimulant medication is the most common form of treatment for ADHD (Milich, Licht, Murphy, & Pelham, 1989). It has been estimated that between 1% and 2% of the school-age population receive stimulant medication for the treatment of ADHD, with methylphenidate (Ritalin) being the most commonly used medication (Safer & Krager, 1988). The primary response to stimulant medication has included an increase in attention and a decrease in impulsive, disruptive, and inappropriate behavior (DuPaul & Rapport, 1993). Collaboration among medical and school personnel and parents is needed to implement clinical drug trials to ensure that the optimal drug dosage level is obtained to optimize a child's learning (DuPaul, Barkley, & Connor, 1998). Research has demonstrated short-term enhancement of behavioral, academic, and social functioning of children with ADHD who are treated with stimulant medication (Pelham, 1993). In contrast, limited long-term effectiveness of stimulant medication has been reported (Evans & Pelham, 1991). The medication's failure to "normalize" children's behavior and academic performance relative to their peers has led to an active search to identify more viable alternatives (Evans & Pelham, 1991).

In 1991, the U.S. Department of Education recognized for the first time that children with ADHD may be entitled to special assistance at school under Section 504 of the Rehabilitation Act of 1973 or special education and related services under the category of "Other Health Impaired" of the Individuals with Disabilities Education Act (IDEA; Davila, William, & McDonald, 1991). Children with ADHD, however, do not automatically qualify for services under these two pieces of legislation. Significant impairment in school performance along with a diagnosis of ADHD is a necessary condition for children with ADHD to qualify for special services. Specifically, if it can be demonstrated that a child's handicap significantly interferes with learning, then the child can be classified under IDEA as Other Health Impaired. On the other hand, if the child is classified as handicapped and the child's handicap results in a substantial limitation in learning, but the child is not eligible for special education services, then the child qualifies for special services under Section 504. It is estimated that 35–57% of the children with ADHD receive special services, with the majority of these children receiving special services in the general education classroom or through "pullout" resource/content mastery programs (Barkley, DuPaul, & McMurray, 1990; Reid, Maag, Vasa, & Wright, 1994).

Children with ADHD are at risk for a number of cognitive and academic problems. In the cognitive domain, children with ADHD are more likely to be behind in comparison to their classmates in intellectual development. Academic difficulties in reading, spelling, mathematics, and handwriting have been reported (Barkley, 1998). It had been estimated that up to 80% of children with ADHD might have an associated learning disability or achievement problems (Semrud-Clikeman, et al., 1992). Deficits in both reading and mathematics have been reported in children with ADHD (Reid et al., 1994). Semrud-Clikeman et al. (1992) found 38% of children with ADHD have a reading disability. Students with ADHD may also have a poor sense of time, decreased nonverbal and verbal working memory, impaired planning ability, reduced sensitivity to errors, decreased attention span, difficulty with simultaneous and sequential tasks, and possible impairment in goal-directed behavior (Barkley, 1998; Reardon & Naglierli, 1992). Language and motor difficulties may be present as well (Barkley, 1998). Researchers have found these children are more likely to have academic difficulties, failing grades, grade retention, and dropping out (Barkley, 1990). Moreover, behaviorally, children with ADHD show increased motor and vocal behavior, poor response inhibition, limited persistence, and diminished compliance with rules (Pfiffner & Barkley, 1998). The question then arises whether the symptoms of ADHD interfere with a child's learning, or if a child with learning problems exhibits ADHD symptoms in response to his or her learning difficulties (Frick & Lahey, 1991). This may be the case for some children; however, researchers have noted that many children with ADHD achieve just as well academically as children without ADHD (Reid et al., 1994).

In the classroom, a child with ADHD can be a challenge. Educational success for a child depends not only on the child but on the teacher who is knowledgeable about ADHD and who is willing to develop and foster a positive teacher-student relationship with the child. Pfiffner and Barkley (1998) suggest teachers should be aware of the following:

1. Children with ADHD may experience some difficulty in their academic and social endeavors, even when intervention strategies have been implemented, due to the refractory nature of ADHD symptomatology.

2. Children with ADHD have difficulty sustaining attention, effort, and motivation, and inhibiting behavior in a consistent manner over time. Thus, children with ADHD may encounter difficulty in performing tasks due to limited attention and lack of motivation rather than lack of ability.

3. Children with ADHD need more structure, more frequent positive consequences, more consistent negative consequences, and modifications in assigned work.

4. Interventions implemented in the school setting must be applied with consistency.

Many schools have adopted collaborative consultation models whereby a consultant (i.e., a school psychologist) works with consultees (i.e., regular and special education teachers; see Kratochwill & Bergen, 1990; or parents and regular and special educators, see Conoley & Conoley, 1992; Sheridan, 1993) to address the difficulties encountered by a child, such as a child with ADHD (Dunson, Hughes, & Jackson, 1994). Through collaborative consultation, the consultant and consultees work together to improve the fit between the child's characteristics and the school and/or home settings. The consultant and consultees assess the child's needs and design and implement intervention strategies to increase the child's success in academic and nonacademic endeavors.

A variety of nonpharmacological interventions have been used with children with ADHD in the school and home settings. Modifications in the environment and/or task characteristics associated with a child's difficulties are one group of viable behavioral strategies (Bradley & DuPaul, 1997). These strategies focus on the antecedents of behavior. An example of these strategies may include moving a child's desk closer to the teacher and away from distractors to increase the opportunity for a child to maintain his or her attention.

Another approach used with children with ADHD is teacher administered consequences contingent upon children's performance of particular target behaviors. These strategies are the most commonly used behavioral interventions with students with ADHD. A combination of positive consequences (like teacher praise, tangible rewards, and token economies) and negative consequences (such as response costs, reprimands, and time out) administered immediately after the behavior, with more positive consequences than negative consequences being delivered, seem to be the most effective (Pfiffner & Barkley, 1998).

Peer strategies represent another group of behavioral interventions used with children with ADHD. Peer tutoring and classwide peer tutoring have produced positive effects on both classroom behavior and academic performance for students with ADHD (DuPaul & Henningson, 1993). Peer tutoring strategies appear to be most effective when children with ADHD are paired with well-balanced and conscientious students (Pfiffner & Barkley, 1998).

Home-school contingencies represent a fourth group of strategies used with students with ADHD. Home-school contingency programs are among the most widely used strategies (Pfiffner & Barkley, 1998). Home-school contingencies require collaboration between the home and school systems in order to implement and to produce effective results. A home-school note is an example of a home-school contingency program. The advantages associated with these interventions are that they address the behavior across a variety of settings, which increases the probability of generalization and maintenance of the desired behavior(s). These strategies are less labor-intensive for teachers as well (Kelley, 1990).

Self-management strategies are also used with children with ADHD. These strategies are derived from cognitive or cognitive-behavioral approaches. Self-management interventions emphasize the development of self-control and include self-monitoring, self-instruction, self-reinforcement, and problem-solving strategies. Self-management strategies, such as self-instruction and problem solving approaches, that focus on cognitive control rather than contingency management, such as self-monitoring and self-reinforcement, have shown less positive results with children with ADHD (DuPaul & Stoner, 1994). Overall, self-management strategies have fallen short of initial expectations (Abikoff & Gittelman, 1985; Braswell et al., 1997). Cognitive or cognitive-behavioral interventions are not as strong, durable, or generalizable as once believed, and these strategies are not superior to the traditional behavioral programs used with children with ADHD (Pfiffner & Barkley, 1998).

Based on the research to date, however, no single treatment has been documented to be overwhelmingly successful with children with ADHD (Bradley & DuPaul, 1997). Instead, research shows the need for multi-modal approaches implemented across a variety of settings (Abikoff, 1991). Multi-modal approaches may involve the integration of medication, such as Ritalin, with specific therapies. Studies have generally indicated that cognitive therapy in combination with stimulant medication is more efficacious than stimulant medication alone (Rapport, Carlson, Kelly, Pataki, 1993). Similarly, behavior therapy in combination with stimulant medication has been shown to be more effective than stimulant medication alone (Carlson, Pelham, Milich, & Dixon, 1992). Thus, multi-modal approaches offer a glimmer of hope in the empirical horizon to address the short- and long-term effects of this disorder.

The clinical myth that ADHD bears a benign prognosis in adolescence and adulthood has not been empirically supported. Over 70% of ADHD children are likely to display the ADHD symptomatology in adolescence (Barkley, Fisher, et al., 1990; Barkley, Anastopoulous, Guevremont, & Fletcher, 1991), but the symptoms dissipate to some ex-

tent with age (Hart, Lahey, Loeber, Applegate, & Frick, 1995). Lower levels of hyperactivity and improvement in attention span and impulse control have been reported among adolescents with ADHD (Hart et al., 1995). Cognitive and behavioral difficulties, however, persist with some adolescents. Oppositional and antisocial behavior have been reported in 25–45% of teenagers with ADHD (e.g., Biederman et al., 1996). Moreover, academic outcomes are considerably poorer for adolescents with ADHD in comparison to normal adolescents, as teenagers with ADHD are more likely to fail a grade, be suspended, or be expelled from school (Barkley, 1998). Contradictory findings for alcohol and drug use among adolescents with ADHD have been reported; however, more recent research indicates cigarette and alcohol use is more prevalent among these teenagers (Barkley, Fisher et al., 1990). Poorer social relationships have also been documented with these adolescents (Barkley, 1998). These results run contrary to the clinical lore that ADHD dissipates during the teenage years. For many, this disorder lasts a lifetime (Weiss & Hechtman, 1993).

REFERENCES

Abikoff, M. (1991). Cognitive training in ADHD children: Less to it than meets the eye. *Journal of Learning Disabilities, 24*(4), 205–209.

Abikoff, M., & Gittelman, R. (1985). Hyperactive children treated with stimulants: Is cognitive training a useful adjunct? *Archives of General Psychiatry, 42,* 953–961.

Achenbach, T. M., & Edelbrock, C. S. (1983). *Child Behavior Checklist–Parent Report Form.* Burlington, VT: University of Vermont.

Achenbach, T. M., & Edelbrock, C. S. (1986a). *Child Behavior Checklist–Teacher Report Form.* Burlington, VT: University of Vermont.

Achenbach, T. M., & Edelbrock, C. S. (1986b). *Child Behavior Checklist–Youth Self-Report.* Burlington, VT: University of Vermont.

American Psychiatric Association. (1968). *Diagnostic and Statistical Manual of Mental Disorders* (2nd ed.). Washington, DC: American Psychiatric Association.

American Psychiatric Association. (1980). *Diagnostic and Statistical Manual of Mental Disorders* (3rd ed.). Washington, DC: American Psychiatric Association.

American Psychiatric Association. (1987). *Diagnostic and Statistical Manual of Mental Disorders* (3rd ed., Revised). Washington, DC: American Psychiatric Association.

American Psychiatric Association. (1994). *Diagnostic and Statistical Manual of Mental Disorders* (4th ed.). Washington, DC: American Psychiatric Association.

Barkley, R. A. (1981). *Hyperactive children.* New York: Guilford.

Barkley, R. A. (1990). *Attention deficit hyperactivity disorder: A handbook for diagnosis and treatment.* New York: Guilford.

Barkley, R. A. (1997). *ADHD and the nature of self-control.* New York: Guilford.

Barkley, R. A. (1998). *Attention-deficit hyperactivity disorder*. New York: Guilford.

Barkley, R. A., Anastopoulos, A. D., Guevremont, D. C., & Fletcher, K. E. (1992). Attention-deficit hyperactivity disorder in adolescents: Mother-adolescent interactions, family beliefs and conflicts, and maternal psychopathology. *Journal of Abnormal Child Psychology, 20,* 263–288.

Barkley, R. A., DuPaul, G. J., & McMurray, M. B. (1990). A comprehensive evaluation of attention deficit disorder with and without hyperactivity as defined by research criteria. *Journal of Consulting and Clinical Psychology, 58,* 775–789.

Barkley, R. A., & Edwards, G. (1998). Diagnostic interview, behavior rating scales, and the medical examination. In R. A. Barkley (Ed.), *Attention-deficit hyperactivity disorder* (pp. 263–293). New York: Guilford.

Barkley, R. A., Fischer, J., Edelbrock, C., & Smallish, M. (1990). The adolescent outcome of hyperactive children diagnosed by research criteria: An eight year follow-up study. *Journal of the American Academy of Child & Adolescent Psychiatry, 29,* 546–557.

Barkley, R. A., Murphy, K. R. (1998). *Attention-deficit hyperactivity disorder: A clinical workbook* (2nd ed.). New York: Guilford.

Biederman, J., Faraone, S. V., Milberger, S., Curtis, S., Chen, L., Marrs, A., Ouellette, C., Moore, P., Spencer, T., Norman, D., Wilens, T., Kraus, I., & Perrin, J. (1996). A prospective 4-year follow-up study of attention-deficit hyperactivity and related disorders. *Archives of General Psychiatry, 53,* 437–446.

Bradley, K. L., & DuPaul, G. J. (1997). Attention-deficit/hyperactivity disorder. In G. G. Bear, K. M. Minke, and A. Thomas (Eds.), *Children's needs II: Development, problems and alternatives* (pp. 109–117). Bethesda, MD: National Association of School Psychologists.

Braswell, L., August, G. J., Bloomquist, M. L., Realmuto, G. M., Skare, S. S., & Crosby, R. D. (1997). School-based secondary prevention for children with disruptive behavior. *Journal of Abnormal Child Psychology, 25,* 197–208.

Carlson, E. A., Joacobvitz, D., & Stroufe, L. A. (1995). A developmental investigation of inattentiveness and hyperactivity. *Child Development, 66,* 37–54.

Carlson, C. L., Pelham, W., Milich, R., & Dixon, M. (1992). Single and combined effects of methylphenidate and behavior therapy on the classroom behavior, academic performance and self-evaluations of children with attention-deficit hyperactivity disorder. *Journal of Abnormal Child Psychology, 20,* 213–232.

Conoley, J. C., & Conoley, C. W. (1992). *School consultation: Practice and training* (2nd ed.). New York: Allyn and Bacon.

Copeland, E. D., & Love, V. L. (1991). *Attention please! A comprehensive guide for successfully parenting children with attention deficit disorders and hyperactivity*. Atlanta, GA: Southeastern Psychological Institute Press.

Costello, E. J., Edelbrock, C. S., Costello, A. J., Dulcan, M. K., Burns, B. J., & Brent, D. (1988). Psychopathology in pediatric primary care: The new hidden morbidity. *Pediatrics, 82,* 415–424.

Cruickshank, B. M., Eliason, M., & Merrifield, B. (1988). Long-term sequelae of water near-drowning. *Journal of Pediatric Psychology, 13,* 379–388.

Davila, R. R., William, M. L., MacDonald, J. T. (1991). *Memorandum of chief state school officers re: Clarification of policy to address the needs of children with attention deficit disorder within general or special education*. Washington, DC: U.S. Department of Education.

Douglas, V. I., & Peters, K. G. (1979). Toward a clearer definition of the attentional deficit in hyperactive children. In G. A. Hale & M. Lewis (Eds.), *Attention and the development of cognitive skills* (pp. 173–247). New York: Plenum.

Dunson, R. M. III, Hughes, J. N., & Jackson, T. W. (1994). Effect of behavioral consultation on student and teacher behavior. *Journal of School Psychology, 32*(3), 247–266.

DuPaul, G. J. (1992). How to assess attention-deficit hyperactivity disorder within school settings. *School Psychology Quarterly, 7,* 60–74.

DuPaul, G. J., Barkley, R. A., & Connor, D. F. (1998). Stimulants. In R. A. Barkley (Ed.), *Attention-deficit hyperactivity disorder* (pp. 510–552). New York: Guilford

DuPaul, G. J., Barkley, R. A., & McMurray, M. B. (1991). Therapeutic effects of medication on ADHD: Implications for school psychologists. *School Psychology Review, 20,* 203–219.

DuPaul, G. J., Henningson, P. N. (1993). Peer tutoring effects on the classroom performance of children with attention deficit hyperactivity disorder. *School Psychology Review, 22,* 134–143.

DuPaul, G. J., & Rapport, M. D. (1993). Does methylphenidate normalize the classroom performance of children with attention deficit disorder? *Journal of the American Academy of Child and Adolescent Psychiatry, 32,* 190–198.

DuPaul, G. J., & Stoner, G. (1994). *ADHD in the schools: Assessment and intervention strategies*. New York: Guilford Press.

Ebaugh, F. G. (1923). Neuropsychiatric sequelae of acute epidemic encephalitis in children. *American Journal of Diseases of Children, 25,* 89–97.

Edelbrock, C. S., Rende, R., Plomin, R., & Thompson, L. (1995). A twin study of competence and problem behavior in childhood and early adolescence. *Journal of Child Psychology and Psychiatry, 36,* 775–786.

Evans, S. W., & Pelham, W. E. (1991). Psychostimulant effects on academic and behavioral measures for ADHD junior high school students in a lecture format classroom. *Journal of Abnormal Child Psychology, 19,* 537–552.

Feingold, B. F. (1975). *Why your child is hyperactive*. New York: Random House.

Frick, P. J., Lahey, B. B. (1991). The nature and characteristics of attention-deficit hyperactivity disorder. *School Psychology Review, 20,* 163–173.

Frick, P. J., Strauss, C. C., Lahey, B., & Christ, M. (1993). Behavior disorders of children. In P. B. Sutker and H. Adams (Eds.), *Comprehensive Handbook of Psychopathology* (2nd ed.) (pp. 765–789). New York: Plenum.

Gaub, M., & Carlson, C. L. (1997). Gender differences in ADHD: A meta-analysis and critical review. *Journal of the American Academy of Child and Adolescent Psychiatry, 36,* 1036–1045.

Gordon, M., & Barkley, R. A. (1998). Tests and observational measures. In R. A. Barkley (Ed.), *Attention-deficit hyperactivity disorder* (pp. 345–372). New York: Guilford.

Hart, E. L., Lahey, B. B., Loeber, R., Applegate, B., & Frick, P. J. (1995). Developmental change in attention-deficit hyperactivity disorder in boys: A four-year longitudinal study. *Journal of Abnormal Child Psychology, 23,* 729–750.

Hartsough, C. S., & Lambert, N. M. (1985). Medical factors in hyperactive and normal children: Prenatal, developmental, and health history findings. *American Journal of Orthopsychiatry, 55,* 190–210.

Kelly, M. L. (1990). *School-home notes: Promoting children's classroom success.* New York: Guilford.

Kratochwill, T. R., & Bergen, J. R. (1990). *Behavioral consultation in applied settings: An individual guide.* New York: Plenum.

Laufer, M. W., Denhoff, E., & Solomons, G. (1957). Hyperkinetic impulse disorder in children's behavior problems. *Psychosomatic Medicine, 19,* 38–49.

McBurnett, K., Lahey, B. B., & Pfiffner, L. J. (1993). Diagnosis of attention deficit disorders in DSM-IV: Scientific basis and implications for education. *Exceptional Children, 60,* 108–117.

Mick, E., Biederman, J., & Faraone, S. V. (1996). Is season of birth a risk factor for attention-deficit hyperactivity disorder? *Journal of the American Academy of Child and Adolescent Psychiatry, 35,* 1470–1476.

Milich, R., Licht, B. G., Murphy, D. A., & Pelham, W. E. (1989). Attention-deficit hyperactivity disordered boys' evaluations and attributions for task performance on medication versus placebo. *Journal of Abnormal Psychology, 98,* 280–284.

Needleman, H. L., Schell, A., Bellinger, D. C., Leviton, L., & Alfred, E. D. (1990). The long-term effects of exposure to low doses of lead in childhood: An 11-year follow-up report. *New England Journal of Medicine, 322,* 83–88.

Pelham, W. E. (1993). Pharmacotherapy for children with attention-deficit hyperactivity disorder. *School Psychology Review, 22,* 199–227.

Pfiffner, L. J., Barkley, R. A. (1998). Treatment of ADHD in school settings. In R. A. Barkley (Ed.), *Attention-deficit hyperactivity disorder* (pp. 458–490). New York: Guilford.

Rapport, M. D., Carlson, G. A., Kelly, K. L., & Pataki, C. (1993). Methylphenidate and desipramine in hospitalized children: 1. Separate and combined effects on cognitive function. *Journal of the American Academy of Child and Adolescent Psychiatry, 32,* 333–342.

Reardon, S. M., & Naglieri, J. A. (1992). PASS cognitive processing characteristics of normal and ADHD males. *Journal of School Psychology, 30,* 151–163.

Reid, R., Maag, J. W., Vasa, S. F., & Wright, G. (1994). Who are the children with attention deficit-hyperactivity disorder? A school-based survey. *Journal of Special Education, 28,* 117–137.

Reynolds, C. R., & Kamphaus, R. W. (1994). *Behavior Assessment System for Children.* Circle Pines, MN: American Guidance Service.

Safer, D. J., & Krager, J. M. (1988). A survey of medication treatment for hyperactive/inattentive students. *Journal of the American Medical Association, 260,* 2256–2258.

Semrud-Clikeman, M., Bierderman, J., Sprich-Buckminster, S., Lehman, B. K., Faraone, S. V., & Norman, D. (1992). Comorbidity between ADHD and learning disability: A review and report in a clinically referred sample. *Journal of the American Academy of Child and Adolescent Psychiatry, 31,* 439–448.

Sheridan, S. M. (1993). Models for working with parents. In J. E. Zins, T. R. Kratochwill, S. N. Elliott (Eds.), *Handbook of consultation services for children* (pp. 110–133).

Silverman, I. W., & Ragusa, D. M. (1992). A short-term longitudinal study of the early development of self-regulation. *Journal of Abnormal Child Psychology, 20,* 415–435.

Sprague, R. L. (1979). Assessment of intervention. In R. L. Trites (Ed.), *Hyperactivity in children: Etiology, measurement, and treatment implications* (pp. 217–299). Baltimore, MD: University Park Press.

Still, G. F. (1902). The Coulstonian lectures on some abnormal physical conditions in children. *Lancet, 1,* 1008–1012.

Strauss, A. A., & Lehtinen, L. E. (1947). *Psychopathology and education of the brain-injured child.* New York: Grune & Stone.

Strecker, E., & Ebaugh, F. (1924). Neuropsychiatric sequelae of cerebral trauma in children. *Archives of Neurology and Psychiatry, 12,* 443–453.

Szatmari, P., Offord, D. R., & Boyle, M. H. (1989). Correlates, associated impairments, and patterns of service utilization of children with attention deficit disorders: Findings from the Ontario Child Health Study. *Journal of Child Psychology and Psychiatry, 30,* 205–217.

Weiss, G., & Hechtman, L. R. (1993). *Hyperactive children grown up* (2nd ed.). New York: Guilford.

Werry, J. S., Minde, K., Guzman, A., Weiss, G., Dogan, K., & Hoy, E. (1972). Studies on the hyperactive child–VII: Neurological status compared with neurotic and abnormal children. *American Journal of Orthopsychiatry, 42,* 441–451.

Zentall, S. S. (1985). A context for hyperactivity. In K. D. Gadow & I. Bialer (Eds.), *Advances in learning and behavior disabilities* (Vol. 4, pp. 273–343). Greenwich, CT: JAI Press.

PATRICIA LOWE
CECIL R. REYNOLDS
Texas A & M University

ATTENTION SPAN
HYPERACTIVITY
RITALIN

ATTENTION SPAN

Adequate attention span requires optimal arousal, selection of task-relevant information, maintenance of attention long enough to get a task done, and central processing of the task (Cohen, 1993; Posner & Boies, 1971). Arousal is assessed by heart rate, respiration, or other indicators of autonomic arousal, and there is a level that is optimal for learning. At very low levels of arousal, learning is inefficient and attention to environmental stimuli is diffuse; at very high levels, attention is narrowed but learning becomes inefficient, particularly for complex tasks. Teachers can increase arousal by increasing the novelty of classroom activities, by asking students questions to generate curiosity (Berlyne, 1960), by rotating students in and out of the "action zone" (the T-shaped front-row-and-center region of the classroom) (Piontrowski & Calfee, 1979), or by directing questions to students outside the action zone.

Selective attention is assessed most frequently by use of incidental learning tasks. The child is instructed to recall a specific set of items (e.g., pictures of animals), but other incidental items (e.g., household items) are actually paired with the target (central) items during presentation. After being given tests of recall for central items, the child is tested for recall of the central-incidental pairs. The assumption is that only items that are attended to will be recalled. Recall for central items increases steadily from preschool age through adolescence, while memory for incidental items remains stable. The correlation between central and incidental recall becomes increasingly negative between ages 6 and 13 in normal children, indicating an increasing ability to screen out distractions with age. Adolescents and adults appear to screen out distractors by rehearsing central stimuli (Hagen & Stanovich, 1977). Hallahan, et al. have found selective attention problems to be common in children with learning problems. They also found that these children can be trained to improve their attention to central stimuli by using task-relevant self-talk and by being reinforced for recall of central items (Hallahan & Reeve, 1980).

Maintenance of attention can be assessed by observation, by interviewing, by self-monitoring, or through formal testing (see Reynolds & Bigler, 1997, 1994). In observational methods, eye contact with assigned task materials, with the teacher during instruction, or during task-relevant interaction with peers, is scored as engaged (on-task); other activities are scored as nonengaged (Piontrowski & Calfee, 1979). Observed engaged time is related to achievement; for example, Leach reports that 58% of the variance in primary mathematics achievement is accounted for by academic engaged time (Leach & Dolan, 1985). Observed on-task attention increases from ages 5 to 11 (Higgins & Turnure, 1984), although students may become more adept at appearing to maintain attention with development (Hudgins, 1967). Self-monitoring of "paying attention" improved observed engaged time among second graders, and reinforcement for self-monitoring accuracy improved engaged time more than self-monitoring alone (Rooney, Hallahan, & Lloyd, 1984).

REFERENCES

Berlyne, D. (1960). *Conflict, arousal, and curiosity*. New York: McGraw-Hill.

Cohen, R. A. (1993). *The neuropsychology of attention*. NY: Plenum Press.

Hagen, J. W., & Stanovich, K. E. (1977). Memory: strategies of acquisition. In R. V. Kail & J. W. Hagen (Eds.), *Perspectives on the development of memory and cognition*. Hillsdale, NJ: Erlbaum.

Hallahan, D. P., & Reeve, R. E. (1980). Selective attention and distractibility. In B. K. Keogh (Ed.), *Advances in special education, Vol. 1*. Greenwich, CT: JAI Press.

Higgins, A. T., & Turnure, J. E. (1984). Distractibility and concentration of attention in children's development. *Child Development, 55*, 1799–1810.

Hudgins, B. B. (1967). Attending and thinking in the classroom. *Psychology in the Schools, 66*, 29–32.

Leach, D. J., & Dolan, N. K. (1985). Helping teachers increase student academic engagement rate: The evaluation of a minimal feedback procedure. *Behavior Modification, 9*, 55–71.

Piontrowski, D., & Calfee, R. (1979). Attention in the classroom. In G. A. Hale & M. Lewis (Eds.), *Attention and cognitive development* (pp. 297–329). New York: Plenum.

Posner, M. I., & Boies, S. J. (1971). Components of attention. *Psychological Review, 78*, 391–408.

Reynolds, C. R., & Bigler, E. D. (1994). *Test of memory and learning*. Austin, TX: Pro-Ed.

Reynolds, C. R., & Bigler, E. D. (1997). Clinical Neuropsychological assessment of child and adolescent memory with the Test of Memory and Learning. In C. R. Reynolds & E. Fletcher-Janzen (Eds.), *The Handbook of Clinical Child Neuropsychology* (3rd ed.) (pp. 296–319). NY: Plenum.

Rooney, K. J., Hallahan, D. P., & Lloyd, J. W. (1984). Self-recording of attention by learning disabled students in the regular classroom. *Journal of Learning Disabilities, 17*, 360–364.

JOHN MACDONALD
Eastern Kentucky University

ATTENTION DEFICIT HYPERACTIVITY DISORDER
HYPERACTIVITY
HYPERKINESIS
TEST OF MEMORY AND LEARNING

ATTITUDES OF STUDENTS WITH DISABILITIES

Attitudes are learned beliefs that develop over time. They are feelings that develop from experiences with others and the environment, and they influence the way people behave toward, feel about, and accept others. In addition, the attitudes of others will affect the way we view ourselves and our capabilities. People with a positive self-attitude or self-concept will have a much better chance of achieving success than people with a negative self-concept (Smith, Price, & Marsh, 1986). Unfortunately, handicapped students tend to have a lower self-concept than nonhandicapped students.

There are many reasons for the handicapped having lower self-attitudes, and they may vary from individual to individual. Generally, the handicapped encounter so many negative experiences that it is difficult for them to develop a positive self-attitude. A major negative experience is academic failure. While limited amounts of failure may inspire many children to overcome obstacles, it is difficult for handicapped students' self-concepts to be immune from repeated failures. Furthermore, the handicapped experience many negative reactions from others, and these reactions cannot be hidden. These negative experiences can result in a lack of confidence in abilities and a lower self-attitude. The handicapped's lack of confidence can lead to behavior problems, or to withdrawn, overly anxious, immature behaviors. These behaviors can further limit a student's academic progress, interactions with others, and self-attitude.

Since self-attitudes are essential for academic and social success, it is imperative that the handicapped develop positive self-attitudes. To establish positive attitudes in handicapped students, young children should develop a sense of self-importance, and older students should be encouraged to balance their failures with an appreciation of their specific talents and abilities (Polloway, Payne, Patton, & Payne, 1985).

REFERENCES

Polloway, E. A., Payne, J. S., Patton, J. R., & Payne, R. A. (1985). *Strategies for teaching retarded and other special needs learners* (3rd ed.). Columbus, OH: Merrill.

Smith, T. E. C., Price, B. J., & Marsh, G. E., II (1986). *Mildly handicapped children and adults*. St. Paul, MN: West.

LARRY J. WHEELER
*Southwest Texas State
University*

**LEARNED HELPLESSNESS
SELF-CONCEPT**

ATTITUDES TOWARD THE HANDICAPPED

With the passage of P.L. 94-142 and Section 504, the visibility of disabled children and adults increased in mainstream American society. This has precipitated a need for the examination of attitudes, reactions, and behaviors toward the disabled to foster their integration into a society that has traditionally excluded them (Hazzard, 1983).

Siller (1976) points out that attitudes and reactions to the handicapped are wide ranging and complex. They are based on variables considered related to and important to attitudinal formation (e.g., family background, culture, and personality). Age, sex, and other demographic variables appear to be significant determinants in the manner in which attitudes toward the disabled are expressed rather than in their formation. Generally, Siller (1976) found that women may have attitudes similar to those of men, but they are more likely to express them in ways influenced by their sex role. Voeltz (1980) found girls to be more nurturing and accepting than boys on psychological indices and more likely to respond in a socially desirable direction (Hazzard, 1983). Gottlieb and Gottlieb (1977) did not find this to be true. Siller (1976) found that adolescents of both sexes tend to be more rejecting than older or younger persons. Coie and Pennington (1976) and Hazzard (1983) support the notion that children's knowledge about and understanding of disabilities increase with age.

Personal contact with the disabled may either substantially improve or worsen attitudes, depending on the quality of the previous interaction. Voeltz (1980) and Fenrick and Petersen (1984) found that nonhandicapped children with the most contact with handicapped peers held the least negative attitudes and were the most accepting of their handicapped peers. Others (Cook & Wollersheim, 1976; Gottlieb, Cohen, & Goldstein, 1974) reported no difference according to the amount of contact.

As more handicapped children are both mainstreamed into regular classes (as in the case of the mildly handicapped) or placed within the elementary/secondary school setting (as with the more severely handicapped), attention must be placed on assisting regular teachers in accommodating these children in the general school program and on to fostering positive attitudes in nonhandicapped students. Reynolds, Martin-Reynolds, and Mark (1982) report that the most important ingredient in making mainstreaming work is teacher attitude. Some studies have indicated that it is difficult for regular classroom teachers to accept the handicapped in their classrooms (Alexander & Strain, 1978; Macmillan, Jones, & Meyers, 1976). This may be due to teachers' feeling inadequately prepared to serve the needs of handicapped children rather than any general negative attitude toward disability. Guerin and Szatlock (1974) and Harasiymiw and Horn (1975) found teacher attitude to be positively affected by experiences in in-service programs (Reynolds, Martin-Reynolds, & Mark, 1982).

Attitudes of children toward the handicapped have also been affected positively through a variety of programs aimed at increasing contact with the disabled and offering quality of interaction. Fenrick and Petersen (1984) successfully used a peer tutoring program designed to lessen negative attitudes toward moderately and severely handicapped students. Rynders, et al. (1980) also found that junior high school students had increased positive perceptions of their teammates who had Down's syndrome after an extended time period of bowling together.

Investigations by Gottlieb (1978) and others on the social effects of the integration of mildly handicapped children into classroom settings with nonhandicapped peers are inconclusive (Voeltz, 1980). Furthermore, it may be inaccurate to generalize data involving mildly handicapped children to the social integration of severely handicapped children (Voeltz, 1980). One may assume with confidence that negative attitudes toward the disabled represent a real barrier to their filling appropriate roles in society (Siller, 1976). Positive teacher intervention efforts and structured, long-term contact with handicapped peers (Fenrick & Petersen, 1984) may serve as viable means to breaking down barriers.

REFERENCES

Alexander, C., & Strain, P. S. (1978). A review of educators attitudes towards handicapped children and the concept of mainstreaming. *Psychology in the Schools, 15,* 390–396.

Coie, J., & Pennington, B. (1976). Children's perceptions of deviance and disorder. *Child Development, 47,* 407–413.

Cook, J., & Wollersheim, J. (1976). The effect of labeling of special education students on the perceptions of contact versus noncontact normal peers. *Journal of Special Education, 10,* 187–198.

Fenrick, N. J., & Petersen, T. K. (1984). Developing positive changes in attitude towards moderately/severely handicapped students through a peer tutoring program. *Education and Training of the Mentally Retarded, 19*(2), 83–91.

Gottlieb, J., Cohen, L., & Goldstein, L. (1974). Social contact and personal adjustment as variables relating to attitudes toward EMR children. *Training School Bulletin, 71,* 9–16.

Gottlieb, J., & Gottlieb, B. (1977). Stereotype attitude and behavioral intentions toward handicapped children. *American Journal of Mental Deficiency, 82,* 65–71.

Hazzard, A. (1983). Children's experience with, knowledge of, and attitude toward disabled persons. *Journal of Special Education, 17*(2), 131–139.

MacMillan, D. L., Jones, R. L., & Meyers, C. E. (1976). Mainstreaming the mildly retarded: Some questions, cautions, and guidelines. *Mental Retardation, 14,* 11–13.

Reynolds, B. J., Martin-Reynolds, J., Mark, F. D. (1982). Elementary teachers' attitudes toward mainstreaming educable mentally retarded students. *Education and Training of the Mentally Retarded, 17*(3), 171–177.

Rynders, J. E., Johnson, R. T. Johnson, D. W., & Schmidt, B. (1980). Producing positive interaction among Down syndrome and nonhandicapped teenagers through cooperative goal structuring. *American Journal of Mental Deficiency, 85,* 268–273.

Siller, J. (1976). Attitudes towards disability. In H. Rusalem & D. Malikin (Eds.), *Contemporary vocational rehabilitation* (pp. 63–79). New York: New York University Press.

Voeltz, L. M. (1980). Children's attitudes toward handicapped peers. *American Journal of Mental Deficiency, 84*(5), 455–464.

Marsha H. Lupi
Hunter College

SCAPEGOATING
TEACHER EXPECTANCIES

ATTRIBUTIONAL RETRAINING

Many handicapped pupils perceive themselves to be incompetent in a variety of school-related activities. While these self-perceptions may accurately reflect limited skills in these areas, they may also affect youngsters' willingness to engage in learning tasks. When presented with school tasks, even tasks in which they have evidenced recent success, many pupils will state that they cannot do the work and as a consequence will not even try. To address the learning needs of their pupils, special education teachers need to focus on their pupils' cognitive and motivational characteristics. An intervention procedure entitled attributional retraining has been used to influence pupils' self-perceptions and their subsequent motivation to learn.

Attribution retraining may be defined as a systematic set of procedures designed to influence individuals' perceptions concerning the causes of their performance on tasks. Many of the procedures are derived from research in the area of cognitive behavior modification. In attributional retraining the focus is on modifying learners' thoughts concerning why they have succeeded or failed on a task. Although attributional retraining procedures have been used in treatment programs for a variety of problems including alcoholism, anxiety, depression, and diet management, the focus on this presentation will be on the use of these procedures with youngsters who evidence severe learning problems.

Most of the attributional retraining programs focus on the role of effort on student achievement. This emphasis is due, in part, to the fact that pupils can choose to change their levels of effort. In addition, high achieving pupils tend to attribute successes to their ability and effort and ascribe their failures to lack of effort. When students perceive that increased effort will result in success, they persist; this, in turn, enhances their performance. In contrast, children who have learning problems frequently attribute their failures to lack of ability, and fail to persist on academic tasks.

One of the first attributional retraining studies was conducted by Dweck (1975). In this investigation, children identified as learned helpless were asked to solve arithmetic problems. One group of pupils was given math tasks in which they continually succeeded; another group was given tasks that they occasionally failed at. When pupils did not correctly respond on an arithmetic task, they were given attributional feedback indicating that they should have tried harder. All the youngsters in the study were subsequently given difficult math problems. Pupils who received the attributional feedback maintained or improved their performances after failure, whereas the performances of children who continually succeeded deteriorated if they failed on a math problem. Chapin and Dyck (1976) and Fowler and Peterson (1981) subsequently reported that persistence on academic tasks was jointly affected by reinforcement procedures and attribution retraining. Fowler and Peterson also reported that reinforcement/attribution retraining that involved direct attributional feedback to pupils was more effective in increasing reading persistence than other treatment procedures. Recently, educational researchers have reported that attribution training procedures may influence students' use of learning strategies (Johnson & Winograd, 1985; Palmer & Goetz, 1984). Attribution training may affect both pupils' achievement outcomes and how they learn.

Related to the attributional retraining research, DeCharms (1976) developed a two-part program to help teachers enhance personal causation of elementary-aged children. The project was designed to influence pupils' goal planning and ultimately produce a person who is in control of his or her achievements. The experiment involved two groups: one consisted of motivation-trained teachers using an experimental curriculum; a control group had untrained teachers and the regular curriculum. The first step involved a personal causation training course for all teachers in the experimental group, followed by a year-long implementation of a number of classroom exercises. Personal causation training did appear to affect pupil's self-confidence and their academic achievement scores. Four years later, a semistructured interview revealed higher personal goals and responsibility orientation for those children in the trained group over those in the untrained group. Five years later, it was found that more pupils from the trained group had graduated. While there were a variety of components to the training program, one of the crucial elements was teaching the pupils that they had control over their achievement outcomes.

Although additional research is needed to determine how and when to most effectively use attributional retraining procedures, it appears that teachers' direct attributional feedback to children does influence pupils' willingness to learn and their school achievement. Teachers' systematic feedback to their pupils that effort is important in determining their successes or failures may affect youngsters' persistence on school tasks and ultimately their achievement.

REFERENCES

Chapin, M., & Dyck, D. G. (1976). Persistence in children's reading behavior as a function of N length and attribution retraining. *Journal of Abnormal Psychology, 85,* 511515.

Decharms, R. (1976). *Enhancing motivation: Change in the classroom.* New York: Irvington.

Dweck, C. S. (1975). The role of expectations and attributions in the alleviation of learned helplessness. *Journal of Personality and Social Psychology, 31,* 674–685.

Fowler, J. W., & Peterson, P. L. (1981). Increasing reading persistence and altering attributional style of learned helpless children. *Journal of Educational Psychology, 73,* 251–260.

Johnson, P. H., & Winograd, P. N. (1985). Passive failure in reading. Unpublished manuscript.

Palmer, D. J., & Goetz, E. T. (in press). Selection and use of study strategies: The role of the studier's beliefs about self and strategies. In C. Weinstein, E. Goetz & P. Alexander (Eds.), *Learning and study strategies: Issues and assessments, instructions and evaluations.* New York: Academic.

DOUGLAS J. PALMER
NORMA GUERRA
Texas A & M University

LEARNED HELPLESSNESS
MOTIVATION

ATTRIBUTIONS

Attribution theorists assert that individuals seek causes for events in their environment and that these perceived causes influence subsequent behavior. The individual is seen as a naive psychologist searching for theories and cause and effect relationships that explain his or her behavior as well as the behavior of others. The father of modern attribution theory, Fritz Heider (1958), has argued that individuals' subjective experiences are essential for understanding how they perceive the world. Furthermore, Heider proposed that these causal ascriptions subsequently influence a person's behavior.

Weiner (1972, 1979) has extensively examined attributions for achievement outcomes. Within academic settings, content, ability, effort, task difficulty, and chance are among the most commonly investigated of individuals' attributions (Weiner, 1979). Weiner (1974) proposes that attributions for success and failure can be classified within a two-dimensional taxonomy: locus of control (internal or external) and stability (fixed or variable). Attributions of ability and effort are classified as internal, while luck and task difficulty are considered external. On the stability dimension, ability and task difficulty are viewed as fixed, and effort and luck are seen as variable.

Pupils systematically use a variety of achievement-related information to derive attributions for their school performance. The primary types of information that individuals use when deciding which factors caused their performance include their current performance outcome, their history of performance on similar tasks, and the performance of others on the same or similar tasks. For example, if a pupil with a history of learning difficulties in math just answered some arithmetic problems correctly, as did 95% of the other pupils in the class, that pupil is most likely to attribute success to an easy task. In contrast, if the pupil does poorly on a school task in which he or she has had a history of failure, yet most of the student's classmates or friends appear to understand, the pupil may attribute failure to a lack of competence. These illustrative vignettes reflect the attributional antecedents and attributions that differentiate many handicapped and nonhandicapped pupils. By definition, many special education pupils experience a history of failure prior to being referred and ultimately placed in special education classes. It is this background of failure, current achievement problems, and the recognition that other pupils are doing well on classroom assignments that leads to perceptions of lack of competence. In turn, these perceptions concerning lack of ability influence pupils' expectancy for future performance and their willingness to try new tasks and persist on difficult ones.

Recently there has been considerable interest generated concerning the consequences of repeated academic failure and its effect on the motivation and achievement of special education children. The repeated academic failure experienced by these students may cause them to doubt their abilities and reduce their persistence and effort when exposed to novel or familiar tasks. Researchers have found that learning-disabled (LD) children are less likely than nonhandicapped children to attribute their failures to insufficient effort and more likely to attribute their failures to their own inabilities. LD pupils also have exhibited less persistence on achievement tasks than nonhandicapped pupils. Investigators have found that LD pupils' tendency to attribute failure to ability is negatively related to persistence. It has also been reported that when LD children succeed at a task, they are less likely to attribute the success to their abilities and more likely to attribute the success to luck or ease of the task. These children appear to blame themselves when they fail and not give themselves credit when they succeed. Low levels of persistence and effort often result in additional failures, and the special education student, more frequently subjected to these difficulties, is caught in a vicious downward spiral of motivation and performance (Licht & Kistner, 1986). Measures of children's attributional styles are now included on several widely used assessment devices (Reynolds & Kamphaus, 1992).

REFERENCES

Heider, F. (1958). *The psychology of interpersonal relations*. New York: Wiley.

Licht, B. G., & Kistner, J. A. (1986). Motivational problems of learning disabled children: Individual differences and their implications for treatment. In J. K. Torgesen & B. W. L. Wong (Eds.), *Learning disabilities: Some new perspectives*. Orlando, FL: Academic.

Reynolds, C. R., & Kamphaus, R. W. (1992). *Behavior assessment system for children*. Circle Pines, MN: American Guidance Service.

Weiner, B. (1972). *Theories of motivation: From mechanism to cognition*. Chicago: Rand McNally.

Weiner, B. (1974). *Achievement motivation and attribution theory*. Morristown, NJ: General Learning.

Weiner, B. (1979). A theory of motivation for some classroom experiences. *Journal of Educational Psychology, 71*, 3–25.

DOUGLAS J. PALMER
MICHAEL L. STOWE
Texas A & M University

ACHIEVEMENT MOTIVATION

ATYPICAL CHILD SYNDROME

Atypical child syndrome is a term borrowed from the medical profession and is no longer in common usage. The current term referring to this group is exceptional children. An exceptional child is one who deviates from the norm and could be categorized on the basis of a set of physical and/or behavioral characteristics. There are a variety of specific disorders in the area of special education that use the term syndrome as a part of the classification. Hunter's syndrome, Down's syndrome, Turner's syndrome, Lesch-Neyhan syndrome, Cornelin deLange syndrome, Sturge-Weber syndrome, and Klinefelter's syndrome are but a few that are discussed in the special education literature.

A wide range of handicaps contribute to the atypical child's condition. That condition may range from mild to severe, physical to mental, educational to social, or any combination of those conditions. What is difficult is to fit an individual into a category, as each individual has a different combination and severity of disability. Handicapped classifications are set up according to the characteristics of the children that deviate from the average or normal child and should be used to help educational programs meet the individual's needs. Kirk (1972) describes five categories: (1) communication disorders (learning disabilities and speech handicaps); (2) mental deviations (gifted and retarded); (3) sensory handicaps (auditory and visual); (4) neurological, orthopedic, or other health problems; and (5) behavior disorders. Although these categories have been used by psychology, sociology, physiology, and the medical profession, they will be briefly addressed from the educational standpoint.

Learning disabilities is a recently developed classification for those individuals that have language difficulties, visual or auditory-perceptual problems, and memory or other cognitive disabilities. Usually the child has an average or above average IQ, although development will be hindered owing to the cognitive disability. Many times the learning problems contribute to behavior problems resulting from academic failure, unobtainable expectations, frustrations, etc. Although definitions have related these dysfunctions to the central nervous system (Clements, 1966), remediation is dealt with through educational intervention with a focus on academic, social, and emotional adjustment.

Mental retardation involves below average intellectual functioning with social and behavioral deficits. Grossman (1973) describes five levels of individuals with retardation, all of whom have IQs below 85 and engage in behaviors inappropriate for their age group. Individuals with borderline retardation (from 85 to 70 IQ) are frequently referred to as slow learners. Individuals with mild retardation (the educable mentally retarded) range from 69 to 55 IQs and have some potential to master basic academic skills. These individuals can live as independent or semiindependent adults. Moderately or trainable mentally retarded individuals with IQs of 54 to 40 have potential for learning self-help, social, and communication skills and simple occupational tasks. Severely mentally retarded individuals range from 39 to 25 IQs and need continual monitoring. They may be taught simple self-help skills, work tasks, and some type of communication system. The profoundly retarded, with IQs below 25, are totally dependent and require close supervision. Some may be able to perform self-help skills. Educational programs for the mentally retarded have made great gains. Depending on severity, educational programs range from self-contained classrooms to special schools and employ a great many management and instructional techniques (Snell, 1978). The goal is to teach these individuals skills to help them become as independent as possible.

Sensory handicaps range greatly from minimal visual defects and hard of hearing to blindness and deafness. Education can range from no special programming, to special part-time instruction from an itinerant teacher, to special schools. Focus in the public schools is on auditory and visual perception training.

Bleck and Nagel (1975) offer an excellent handbook for teachers of the physically handicapped. Basically, these individuals are disabled in motor abilities that do not affect educational achievement, although there may be some difficulties in social and emotional adjustment. The school needs to adapt the physical environment to accommodate wheelchairs, braces, etc. Teachers with neurologically impaired students need to be aware of complications, such as seizures.

Behavior disorders interfere with a child's growth and the development of relationships with others. Hewett and Jenkins (1945) define three types of behavior disorders involving those having unsocialized aggression (participating with peers in misdemeanors and crime) or overinhibition (overdependent and withdrawn). All involve social maladjustments and emotional disturbances. Although they are dealt with through the mental health fields, education has taken on prevention and treatment. The intervention, whether through resource rooms, itinerant teachers, special classes, special or residential schools, or hospitals, includes psychodynamics, behavior modification, and developmental, ecological, or psychoeducational strategies (Kirk, 1972).

REFERENCES

Bleck, E. G., & Nagel, D. A. (1975). *Physically handicapped children: A medical atlas for teachers*. New York: Grune & Stratton.

Clements, D. D. (1966). *Minimal brain dysfunction in children* (Public Health Service Publication N. 415). Washington, DC: Department of Health, Education, and Welfare.

Fliegler, I. A., & Bish, C. E. (1959, December). Summary of research on the academically talented student. *Review of Educational Research, 29,* 408–450.

Hewett, L. E., & Jenkins, R. L. (1945). *Fundamental patterns of maladjustment: The dynamics of their origin*. Springfield, IL: state of Illinois.

Gloss, G. H., & Jones, R. L. (1968). *Correlates of school district provisions for gifted children: A statewide study*. Paper presented at the annual meeting of the Council for Exceptional Children, New York.

Grossman, H. J. (Ed.). (1973). Manual on terminology and classification in mental retardation. *American Journal of Mental Deficiency* (Special issue. Series No. 2).

Kirk, S. A., (1972). *Educational exceptional children*. Boston: Houghton Mifflin.

Snell, M. E. (1978). *Systematic instruction of the moderately and severely handicapped*. Columbus, OH: Merrill.

DONNA FILIPS
Steger, Illinois

EVALUATION
LEARNING DISABILITIES
MENTAL RETARDATION

AUDIOGRAM

An audiogram is a graphic representation of the threshold of hearing for each ear, measured at discrete frequencies using pure-tone signals, and transduced through an earphone for determining air conduction (AC) and through a bone vibrator for determining bone conduction (BC) thresholds. The audiogram form and symbols plotted on the audiogram, representing hearing thresholds, have

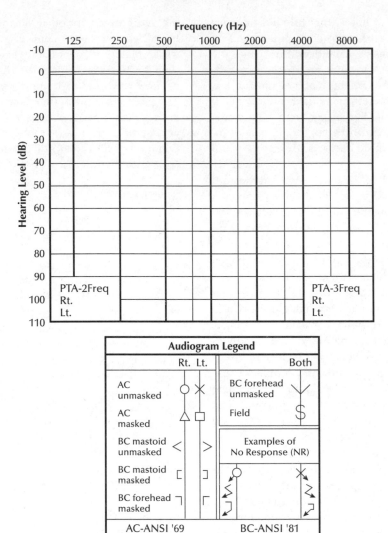

Audiogram Form and Symbols.

been standardized (ANSI S3.6–1996) and are shown in the figure. The abscissa of the audiogram shows frequency in hertz (Hz) from 125 to 8000 Hz. The ordinate shows hearing level (HL) in decibels (dB) from –10 to 120 dB. 0-dB HL for each frequency represents the statistical average of normal hearing. If an individual has normal hearing, all pure-tone thresholds would be plotted on the 0-dB HL line. Thresholds <zero-dB HL would mean better hearing than normal and thresholds >zero-dB HL would mean poorer hearing than normal, or the amount of hearing loss. AC hearing thresholds between –10 and 20 are considered within a normal range, while thresholds from 25 to 40 indicate a mild hearing loss; 41 to 55 dB, a moderate one; 56 to 70, moderate to severe; 71 to 90 severe, and greater than 91 dB, profound.

Air-conduction thresholds are obtained through earphones so that sound is conducted to the inner ear by the air in the ear canal and recorded as "O" for the right and "X" for the left ear. Bone-conduction thresholds are obtained through a bone vibrator, usually placed on the mastoid behind the ear so that sound is conducted to the inner ear by the cranial bones and recorded as "<" for the right and ">" for the left ear. When the possibility exists that a pure-tone presented to one ear may be heard in the other ear, a narrow-band masking sound is directed to the non-test ear to eliminate it from responding to the pure-tone presented to the test ear. AC and BC thresholds obtained with masking have different symbols than those obtained unmasked. Once thresholds have been obtained, the AC thresholds for each ear are connected with a solid line and BC thresholds are connected with a dotted line. Sometimes audiologists color code their symbols so that all right ear thresholds are plotted in red and left ear in blue.

REFERENCES

American National Standards Institute. (1996). *Specifications for audiometers*. S3.6-1996. New York.

Yantis, P. A. (1994). Puretone air-conduction threshold testing. In J. Katz (Ed.), *Handbook of clinical audiometry* (4th ed.) (pp. 97–108). Baltimore, MD: Williams & Wilkins.

THOMAS A. FRANK
Pennsylvania State University

AUDIOMETRY
AUDITORY ABNORMALITIES

AUDIOLOGY

Audiology is the study of hearing and hearing disorder, including assessment procedures, hearing conservation, and the habilitation and rehabilitation of individuals having impairment. The field of audiology can be differentiated into specialty areas.

Clinical audiology is concerned with assessing the degree, type, and site of lesion of hearing loss, and determining appropriate rehabilitation procedures. Emphasis is placed on testing, diagnostic procedures, interpretation of results, and counseling. Pediatric audiology is like clinical audiology, except emphasis is placed on special procedures for assessment of hearing in infants and young children. Experimental audiology concerns itself with investigations designed to advance testing, diagram procedures, and increase knowledge of normal and abnormal auditory systems. Educational audiology provides appropriate therapies to preschool and school-age children having educationally significant hearing impairments. Industrial audiology deals with the effects of noise on humans, hearing conservation programs, noise control, interpretation of state and federal programs, and noise standards. Rehabilitative audiology has as its primary goal providing therapies for children and adults with hearing impairments. Therapies include speech reading, auditory training, and speech-language therapy.

REFERENCES

Martin, F. N. (1997). *Introduction to audiology* (6th ed). Boston, MA: Allyn & Bacon.

Stach, B. A. (1998). *Clinical audiology: An introduction*. San Diego, CA: Singular Publishing Group, Inc.

THOMAS A. FRANK
Pennsylvania State University

AUDIOMETRY
AUDITORY ABNORMALITIES

AUDIOMETRY

Audiometry is the collection of techniques and procedures used for measuring hearing. Traditionally, measurements are done with a calibrated electronic instrument called an audiometer. Generally, two types of audiometry, called pure-tone and speech audiometry, and measurements of the middle ear, collectively called acoustic immittance measurements, are done during a audiological evaluation.

Pure-tone audiometry is the measurement of the threshold of hearing for air- and bone-conducted pure tones. Air-conducted pure tones are transmitted through an earphone so that sound is conducted to the inner ear by the air in the ear canal as part of the pathway. Bone-conducted pure tones are transmitted by a bone vibrator usually placed on the mastoid process behind the outer ear so that sound is conducted to the inner ear by the crania bones.

The American National Standards Institute (ANSI) has specified the methods for manual pure-tone audiometry (ANSI, S3.21-1978, R1992). As a result of pure-tone audiometry, the severity and type of hearing loss can be classified for each ear. Speech audiometry is concerned with determining the threshold of hearing for speech and with measuring speech discrimination ability. The threshold of speech can be measured by determining the lowest hearing level that causes an individual to detect speech. This level is known as a speech awareness threshold (SAT) or speech detection threshold (SDT). Another speech threshold measure, spondee threshold (ST), is found by determining the lowest level at which an individual can just hear and understand bisyllabic words spoken in spondaic stress 50% of the time. If speech stimuli other than bisyllabic words are used (e.g., body parts), this measure is known as a speech reception threshold (SRT). Speech discrimination testing is done to determine the percentage of words (usually monosyllabic) correctly identified when the words are presented loud enough to be heard at normal conversational level. This measure is also known as word or speech recognition or identification; it can be used to judge social adequacy, for hearing-aid fitting, and for diagnostic site-of-lesion testing.

Acoustic immittance measurements are done on a special instrument. It is not truly a measurement of hearing, but rather a test battery to obtain diagnostic information about eardrum mobility (tympanogram) and middle- and inner-ear function (acoustic reflex tests). The result of acoustic immittance measurements can be used alone for diagnostic purposes; however, when used in conjunction with pure-tone and speech audiometry results, the type, degree, site-of-lesion, and in some cases the underlying pathology of the hearing loss can be determined.

REFERENCES

American National Standards Institute. (1992). *Methods for manual pure-tone threshold audiometry* (1978, R 1992). New York: Author.

Block, M.G. & Wiley, T. L. (1994). Overview and basic principles of acoustic immittance measurements. In J. Katz (Ed.), *Handbook of clinical audiometry* (4th ed.) (pp. 271–282). Baltimore, MD: Williams & Wilkins.

Penrod, J. P. (1994). Speech threshold and recognition/discrimination testing. In J. Katz (Ed.), *Handbook of clinical audiometry* (4th ed.) (pp. 147–164). Baltimore, MD: Williams & Wilkins.

Yantis, P. A. Puretone air-conduction threshold testing. In J. Katz (Ed.), *Handbook of clinical audiometry* (4th ed.) (pp. 97–108). Baltimore, MD: Williams & Wilkins.

THOMAS A. FRANK
Pennsylvania State University

AUDIOLOGY
AUDITORY ABNORMALITIES

AUDITORY ABNORMALITIES

Auditory abnormalities are disorders or dysfunctions of the ear that affect the hearing mechanism or sense of hearing. Auditory abnormalities can occur in just one part of the ear or in several parts of the ear simultaneously.

A congenital abnormality of the outer ear is called a microtia. If a patient has a microtia and an intact ear canal, he or she usually does not have a hearing loss. A smaller than normal ear canal, common in Down's Syndrome, is known as a stenotic canal; it usually does not cause hearing impairment. An absent ear canal, or a canal that "deadends," is known as an atresia; it causes a moderate to severe conductive hearing loss. An overabundance of wax (cerumen) in the ear canal can cause a mild to moderate conductive loss if it is impacted.

The most common auditory abnormality in children is the presence of fluid in the middle ear space, usually due to Eustachian tube dysfunction; however, there are many causes of middle-ear fluid. Middle-ear fluid is especially prevalent in children having craniofacial disorders (Down's, cleft palate, etc.). Usually, middle-ear fluid can cause a mild to moderate educationally significant conductive hearing loss because movement of the eardrum and middle ear bones bones are restricted. A hole in the ear drum,

known as a perforation or rupture, can cause a mild to severe conductive hearing loss, depending on its location and size. A fixation of the stapes in the oval window of the inner ear is a condition known as otosclerosis, and this usually produces a progressive mild to severe conductive hearing loss. If the joint between the incus and stapes becomes disarticulated, usually by a blow to the head, a moderate to severe conduction hearing loss occurs. There are many congenital middle-ear abnormalities, including absent, fixed, or distorted middle-ear bone malformations. Generally, auditory abnormalities that involved the outer or middle ear and produced conductive hearing losses are amenable to drug therapy or surgical correction to restore hearing.

There are many auditory abnormalities that may be part of an overall syndrome involving other sensory systems, skeletal formation, internal organs, or the nervous system. Generally, inner-ear abnormalities affect the sensory hair cells in the Organ of Corti, causing a sensorineural hearing loss that can range from mild to profound and that can be unilateral (one ear) or bilateral (both ears). In children, about 50% of educationally significant inner-ear hearing losses are inherited and about 50% are acquired. If a child is born with an absent inner ear (cochlea), the condition is known as an inner-ear aplasia. Common genetic causes of inner-ear hearing loss are syndromes (such as Usher's or Waardenburg's Syndromes) and inter-family marriages. Common acquired causes are due to prematurity, meningitis, and birth injury. An inner-ear hearing loss owed to aging is called presbycusis. One from excessive noise exposure is called acoustic or noise-induced trauma.

Auditory abnormalities can also occur from a problem with the auditory nerve (VIII cranial nerve), a brainstem disorder, or a temporal lobe dysfunction. A tumor growing on the acoustic nerve or in the brainstem region usually causes poor speech discrimination ability, but does not always cause a loss of hearing sensitivity. A temporal lobe dysfunction usually produces poor understanding for speech on the ear contralateral to the lesion. Many children have trouble processing speech, especially in reference to auditory sequential memory, or hearing speech in a noisy background. These children are usually diagnosed as having a central auditory processing problem. The exact site of the lesion is not known; however, the temporal lobe and associated areas of the brain are suspected.

An auditory abnormality in any part of the ear can cause tinnitus, which is any sound perceived in the head. In most cases, it is a symptom of an inner-ear hearing loss. Abnormalities of the outer, middle, and inner ear can cause a feeling of fullness; however, most often this is a symptom of a middle-ear abnormality. Dizziness is another symptom of hearing loss, often from a dysfunction in the inner ear, but it can also occur from an outer- or middle-ear abnormality.

REFERENCES

Gelfand, S. A. (1997). *Essentials of audiology* (pp. 171–218). New York: Thieme.

Hayes, D., & Northern, J. L. (1996). *Infant and hearing.* San Diego, CA: Singular Publishing Group, Inc.

Northern, J. L. & Downs, M. P. (1996). *Hearing in children* (4th ed.). Baltimore: Williams & Wilkins.

Pappas, D. G. (1998). *Diagnosis and treatment of hearing impairment in children* (2nd ed.). San Diego, CA: Singular Publishing Group, Inc.

THOMAS A. FRANK
Pennsylvania State University

AUDIOGRAM
AUDIOMETRY

AUDITORY DISCRIMINATION

Auditory discrimination is the process of an individual's ability to recognize, interpret, and distinguish among auditory stimuli, and to respond appropriately. Most often, auditory discrimination is thought to involve the ability to differentiate speech sounds leading to an understanding of the speech message. However, auditory discrimination also involves an individual's ability to differentiate nonspeech sounds of varying intensities, frequencies, and durations. In part, the study of psychoacoustics is devoted to understanding human perception of acoustic stimuli.

Applied to speech, auditory discrimination is the process that enables an individual to recognize, interpret, and distinguish differences among all of the phonemes that make up speech segments. In a broader sense, it is the ability to distinguish and understand speech. Auditory discrimination also involves the process of selecting relevant stimuli from nonrelevant stimuli in the environment. This process is called auditory figure-ground, auditory differentiation, auditory selective listening, competing message integration, and listening in noise.

Auditory discrimination can be tested in several ways, using a variety of specially designed tests in quiet or noisy backgrounds using an open- or closed-set response. Some auditory discrimination tests employ a rhyming word format so that the individual has to hear a pivotal phoneme to distinguish between two words or to identify the stimulus word from rhyming word alternatives. Some auditory discrimination tests require the listener to hear key words in a sentence or phrase.

Generally, auditory discrimination is tested by presenting a list of monosyllabic words through an earphone or loudspeaker at various sound pressures or hearing levels corresponding to a normal conversational levels, most comfortable levels, or sensational levels above an individual's speech threshold. The monosyllabic word lists can be presented by tape or by monitored live voice. Usually the word lists are phonetically balanced, meaning that the phonetic elements of the words on the list are balanced in relation to their occurrence in normal speech. An auditory discrimination score is the percentage of words correctly identified. A normal discrimination score is usually considered to be 86% to 100% and in some cases 80% to 100%. A discrimination loss is the difference between an individual's score compared with a normal score under the same conditions; it can be classified in severity from mild to profound. Auditory discrimination tests can also be scored by determining the number of phonemes correctly and incorrectly identified.

REFERENCE

Stach, B. A. (1998). *Clinical audiology: An introduction* (pp. 229–249). San Diego, CA: Singular Publishing Group, Inc.

THOMAS A. FRANK
Pennsylvania State University

AUDITORY PERCEPTION
AUDITORY PROCESSING

AUDITORY PERCEPTION

Auditory perception relates to the processing of auditory stimuli though the auditory nervous system, including the brainstem and central auditory cortex. Perception follows a sequence of steps from detection of the acoustic signal to discrimination. Children with auditory perceptual and processing disorders often exhibit language and learning disabilities (Garstecki & Erler, 1997; Cherry, 1992).

The sequence of auditory processing includes detection of a single auditory event; temporal resolution of the offset of the first auditory event to the onset of a second; the discrimination of the two events (whether they are the same or different); and temporal order (which signal came first versus second) (Tallal & Piercy, 1973). The process with two signals may be followed by three or more auditory events depending on one's ability to store and recall (i.e., auditory memory).

Regarding auditory perception, Garstecki & Erler (1997) state:

> For auditory stimuli to be meaningful, there must be an intact auditory perceptual system that transmits, processes, stores,

and retrieves information provided by the peripheral hearing mechanism. It is the perceptual system that permits focusing on specific stimuli while blocking out irrelevant auditory information. It is the perceptual system that enables identification of a voice or that permits the recognition of "sit" as one of the "it" words that rhymes with "hit." Auditory perceptual disturbances involve the entire communication cycle, interfering with the complex interdependence of auditory sensitivity, auditory perception, language, and speech, The acoustic world is not perceived normally by children with deficits in these areas. The result is that the delicately balanced relationships between cognition and language and between language and subsequent academic behavior are disturbed (p. 223).

To that end, Tallal and others argued that specific deficits at stages in auditory processing could be related to specific deficits in both perceiving and producing speech sounds that would subsequently characterize children with specific language–related learning disabilities especially in reading (Tallal & Piercy, 1973; Tallal, Stark, & Mellits, 1985). For example, a rate processing deficit could result in an auditory memory disability. Furthermore, Stark and Tallal (1979) noted that a specific rate processing deficit produces a disability in perceiving and producing rapidly changing temporal cues characterized in the phonemes / ba /, /da /, /ga /, /pa /, /ta /, and / ka /.

In summary, auditory perception is the processing of auditory stimuli at the brain stem and cortical levels. There is a hierarchy of steps through which the stimulus is processed between detection of the signal to storing the auditory information in memory. Deficits in the perception processing steps have been linked to specific language and reading disabilities. It has been suggested that it is important to evaluate basic auditory perception separately from speech and language perception to pinpoint deficits. Afterward, it is the responsibility of educators and other related ancillary service providers to ensure that children with auditory processing deficits receive special accommodations or speech language services in order to ensure their classroom success.

REFERENCES

Cherry, R. (1992). Screening and evaluation of central auditory processing disorders in young children. In Jack Katz, Nancy Steckler, & Donald Henderson (Eds.), *Central auditory processing: A transdisciplinary view* (pp. 129–140). St. Louis MO: Mosby Year Book.

Garstecki, D. C., & Erler, S. F. (1997). Hearing loss management in children and adults. In G. T. Mencher, S. E. Gerber, & A. McCombe (Eds.), *Audiology and auditory dysfunction* (pp. 220–232). Needham Heights, MA: Allyn & Bacon.

Stark, R., & Tallal, P. (1979). Analysis of stop-consonant production errors in developmentally dysphasic children. *Journal of the Acoustical Society of America, 66,* 1703–1712.

Tallal, P. & Piercy, M. (1973). Developmental aphasia: Impaired rate of non-verbal processing as a function of sensory modality. *Neuropsychologia, 12,* 83–93.

Tallal, P., Stark, R., & Mellits, D. (1985). Identification of language impaired children on the basis of rapid perception and production skills. *Brain & Language, 25,* 314–322.

PAULA TALLAL
University of California
First edition

KATHLEEN M. CHINN
New Mexico State University
Second edition

AUDITORY ABNORMALITIES
AUDITORY DISCRIMINATION
AUDITORY PROCESSING

AUDITORY PROCESSING

Auditory processing is the means in which auditory information is collected, converted, and sent to the auditory portion of the brain (Bess & McConnell, 1981) where it is perceived as information, whether from speech or non-speech stimuli. In the educational environment the majority of information is conveyed via an auditory modality. If there is a breakdown in the auditory system, whether due to a specific hearing loss or a central auditory processing disorder, the learning process will be affected (Garstecki & Erler, 1997).

The auditory process can be briefly and clearly described. The acoustic signal is collected at the outer ear, channeled through the outer ear canal to the eardrum, the border of the middle and outer ear, where it is converted to mechanical energy. After transformation to mechanical energy in the form of ossicular vibration, the signal is transferred to the inner ear (the cochlea) at the point of the oval window. The cochlea is filled with fluid, and therefore the signal is then conducted via hydraulic energy. The hydraulic waves cause movement of the hair cells in the cochlea which in turn cause an electrical impulse to travel up the VIII Nerve, thus transferring the signal to the brain stem and then to the auditory cortex. At different points of the brain stem, the signal begins to be processed for temporal elements and localization. As the signal transfers further up to the temporal auditory cortex, decoding and information transfer for speech and language reception takes place.

Hearing loss may occur if there is a breakdown in any part of the system. Sometimes there are lesions in the neurological tract or in the cortex which do not result in a noticeable hearing loss, but which do result in disruptions in processing the signal at a higher level (i.e., the brain stem or auditory cortex). These processing disruptions may be manifested by disabilities in the following listening skill areas:

- discrimination—the ability to differentiate among sounds not having the same intensity, duration, or frequency
- auditory discrimination—the ability to differentiate between words and sounds that are similar
- auditory association—the ability to identify a sound with its source
- auditory closure—the ability to understand a word or message when part of the signal is missing
- auditory memory; sequential memory—the ability to store and recall auditory stimuli in exact order
- auditory localization—the ability to determine the source of a sound
- auditory figure-ground—the ability to discriminate a speaker's voice from background noise
- auditory attention—the ability to attend to sound, particularly speech, over a long period of time
- auditory blending—the ability to synthesize phonemes into words
- auditory analysis—the ability to identify phonemes or morphemes within words (Keith, 1988; Garstecki & Erler, 1997)

These areas are interrelated; thus, problems in one area may lead to problems in others. Many times, learning disabilities result from auditory processing skill disruptions (Garstecki & Erler, 1997; Cherry, 1992). These disabilities due to auditory skill disruptions may include, but may not be limited to, academic problems in areas such as reading, writing, spelling, and other areas (Rees, 1981). It is important to note that in some cases, auditory processing disruptions cause no learning disabilities. In either case, children who exhibit learning difficulties should be tested for auditory processing problems in the areas listed above. Further, educational accommodations, such as addressing different learning styles and alternative methods of presenting academic material, should be made.

Auditory processing is the sequence by which an acoustic signal is taken in through the outer ear, processed through the middle and inner ear, and transmitted via neurological pathways to the auditory cortex. Lesions or disruptions in the neurological pathways and auditory cortex can lead to problems in auditory discrimination, localization, attention, closure, analysis, figure-ground, and memory. These problems usually manifest in the form of learning disabilities. Thus, educators may need to provide learning style accommodations for children with disabilities related to auditory processing problems.

REFERENCES

Bess, F. H., & McConnell, F. E. (1981). *Audiology, education, and the hearing-impaired child*. St. Louis: Mosby.

Cherry, R. (1992). Screening and evaluation of central auditory processing disorders in young children. In Jack Katz, Nancy Steckler, & Donald Henderson (Eds.), *Central auditory processing: A transdisciplinary view* (pp. 129–140). St. Louis: Mosby.

Garstecki, D. C., & Erler, S. F. (1997). Hearing loss management in children and adults. In G. T. Mencher, S. E. Gerber, & A. McCombe. (Eds.), *Audiology and auditory dysfunction* (pp. 220–232). Needham Heights, MA: Allyn & Bacon.

Keith, R. W. (1988). Central auditory tests. In L. N. McReynolds & D. Yoder (Eds.), *Handbook of speech language pathology and audiology* (pp. 1215–1236). Toronto: BC Decker.

Rees, N. S. (1981). Saying more than we know: Is auditory processing a meaningful concept? In R.W. Keith (Ed.), *Central auditory and language disorders in children* (pp. 94–120). San Diego, CA: College Hill.

CAROLYN L. BULLARD
Lewis & Clark College
First edition

KATHLEEN M. CHINN
New Mexico State University
Second edition

AUDITORY DISCRIMINATION
CENTRAL AUDITORY DYSFUNCTION
LEARNING DISABILITIES

AUDITORY–VISUAL INTEGRATION

Auditory–visual perceptual integration is poorly understood; therefore, it is seldom measured and described in the psychoeducational diagnostic process. Instead, beginning in the 1920s with German psychology, and later (1930s) in clinical work, the focus fell almost solely on visual–motor perceptual development. Indeed, psychology in general, and Gestalt psychology in particular, drew heavily from the easily administered, easily scored visual motor tests. Bender's (1938) *Visual-Motor Gestalt Test*, an extension of Wertheimer's (1923) laboratory instrument, soon became the most commonly administered psychological test. Early on, these easily administered tests showed substantial correlations with intelligence (Armstrong & Hauck, 1960) as a diagnostic test for brain damage (Shaw & Cruickshank, 1956), academic achievement (Koppitz, 1958), emotional difficulties (Clawson, 1959), and perceptual development (Koppitz, 1962).

Auditory perception, which in many respects appears to

be a sensory–perceptual corollary of visual perception, remains relatively unexplored. The reason may be that the auditory perceptual structures are less well understood than visual perception, and more difficult to ascertain. For example, it is difficult to identify precisely where auditory sensorial function stops, perception begins, auditory perception ends, and receptive language begins.

The result has been that psychologists and special educators have generally limited the theoretical scope to an explanation of auditory–visual perceptual integration as an operational construct important to human learning. However, that fact also conveys a certain ambience, as remedial educators have been tenacious about the importance of auditory–visual integration within the reading process. They believe that reading would be a slow, awkward instructional process in the absence of integrating perceptual symbolic information from the primary sensory channels. Many reading experts are convinced that perceptual integration is critical to early learning of letters and letter phonemic symbolism. For example, the visual perceptual system may neurally code a "B" and a "D" as distinct symbols based on luminancy differences. A "B" uses a different neuronal subsystem than a "D" because it draws on lateral inhibition and activation associated with on-center neurons; "D" draws on off-center neurons. Symbolic clarity in the visual perceptual realm may be influenced by these factors, all of which have been well investigated: extent and organization of retinal area activities; transformation of receptive-field organization; and estimates of size of receptive field.

In reading, as in most visual tasks, the eye gathers information during the pauses between saccadic movements. Ultimately, stimulus letters are recognized; that is, an appropriate subvocal or auditory response (saying a letter) occurs. The recognition (perceptual) memory can hold at least three letters for a period of about 1 second, until they have been rehearsed.

A scan component is needed to transform the visual information in very short-term visual perceptual memory into motoric information, and then auditory information. Actually, the visual scan component has at least three distinguishable functions: deciding which areas of the visual field contain information; directing processing capacity to the locations selected by the prescan ("attention"); and converting the visual input from the selected locations into the forms of motor memory units and ultimately auditory information.

In principle, although not in detail, the auditory scan is exactly analogous to the visual scan. The auditory scan selects some contents of auditory memory (e.g., the sound representation of one letter) and converts them into motor information. A street address is remembered by placing it into auditory–perceptual memory. By means of this short-term loop, information can be retained in auditory short-

term memory. Subvocal rehearsal, the subvocal output of the rehearsal component, is entered into the auditory short-term memory just as though it had been a vocal output. Once that occurs, visual imagery results. The importance of visual–auditory or auditory–visual perceptual integration becomes paramount when confronting remedial reading difficulties. Critchley (1964) noted that children with so-called congenital word blindness failed to develop visual perceptual memory, while their auditory perceptual memory was unaffected.

A great deal of literature from the mid and late 1960s suggests a close interrelationship between the short-term storage mechanisms of vision and audition. Conrad (1959) has shown that subjects frequently make substitution errors when recalling lists of visually presented letters in which the letter substituted (e.g., ANQT) sounds similar to the correct letter (e.g., ANQE). Although these letters are highly dissimilar in appearance, they sound similar when spoken aloud. Thus, visual material, Conrad suggests, must have been translated and encoded in auditory storage.

Murray (1968) reports extensive studies of short-term storage for visual and auditory items. His results show how the similarity of sounds affected recall of the list (acoustic similarity). In Murray's experiment, conditions enabling the auditory system to assist in the coding and storing of incoming information tend to produce superior performances; this may indicate that the auditory mechanism is generally superior to the visual mechanism in this respect. Such a superiority has also been demonstrated by Murdock (1968).

Wickelgren (1965) has demonstrated that the presence of acoustic elements in visually presented material can influence the accuracy of recall. Subjects listened to four random letters. Next, eight letters were visually presented and copied by the subject. Finally, a test of the first four aural letters was administered. Even though the interpolated material had to be copied rather than spoken, if the eight letters were similar in sound to the aural letters, performance on auditory recall was poorer than when the visual letters were quite dissimilar in sound.

Ross (1969) developed a logical test of the audio–visual interaction in short-term storage by measuring the retention of simple symbols (+ and −) either organized in patterns (e.g., − + + − + − + −) or unpatterned (e.g., + − + + − + − − +). Blanton and Odom (1968) found a superiority in seeing and hearing children over deaf children in terms of the span of digits that could be recalled. However, this result may reflect greater experience with numbers on the part of the normal children.

In short, an integration of information from the visual and auditory perceptual channel seems to be occurring. How else, in fact, could a person read graphics, or listen to others read, and write the graphic symbol being received aurally? Reading is a dual process that, except for the handicapped learner who may be missing one of the sensory channels or have perceptual deficits, is an integrated function.

Of all the perceptual functions, perceptual integration is the most poorly understood. The result is that applied tests do not exist for the practitioner. One study illustrative of research in the area is by Birch and Belmont (1965), who administered a series of cards with three patterns of dots. The examiner first tapped out a pattern. The subject was to listen to the tapped pattern and then look at three sets of dot patterns. One set represented the tapped pattern, the others did not. The examiner than required the subject to point to the appropriate pattern, for instance, the pattern representing the previously tapped sound. Those children who had the greatest difficulty on this task were the most difficult to teach under remedial conditions of reading instruction. These subjects were found to be unable to deal effectively with tasks requiring judgments of auditory–visual equivalence. Thus, the ability to treat visual and auditory patterned information as equivalent differentiated the good reader from the poor reader.

In summary, auditory–visual integration would appear to be the internal stimulation of the opposite modality, for instance, visual perceptual information is received and a signal system translates the meaning to the auditory perceptual modality. Information on the assumed trait is limited, and awaits much research. It does seem likely that this function holds promise as a predictor of what modality may be used as a unisensory or multisensory receiving mechanism in planning an intervention.

REFERENCES

Armstrong, R. G., & Hauck, P. A. (1960). Correlates of the Bender-Gestalt scores in children. *Journal of Psychological Studies, 11*, 153–158.

Bender, L. (1938). *Visual Motor Gestalt Test and its Clinical Use*. American Ortho Psychiatry Association Research Monograph 3.

Birch, H. G., & Belmont, L. (1965). Auditory-visual integration in brain damaged and normal children. *Journal of Developmental Medicine and Child Neurology, 7*, 135–144.

Blanton, R. L., & Odom, P. B. (1968). Some possible interferences and facilitation effects of pronounciability. *Journal of Verbal Learning Behavior, 7*, 844–846.

Clawson, A. (1959). The Bender-Gestalt Visual Motor Gestalt Test as an index of emotional disturbance in children. *Journal of Project Technology, 23*, 198–206.

Conrad, R. (1959). Errors of immediate memory. *British Journal of Psychology, 50*, 349–359.

Critchley, M. (1965). *The dyslexic child*. London: Heineman.

Koppitz, E. M. (1958). The Bender Gestalt Test and learning disturbances in young children. *Journal of Clinical Psychology, 14*, 292–295.

Koppitz, E. M. (1962). Diagnosing brain damage in young children with the Bender Gestalt Test. *Journal of Consultative Psychology, 26*, 541–546.

Murdock, B. B., Jr. (1968). Modality effects in short-term memory: Storage or retrieval? *Journal of Experimental Psychology, 78*, 70–86.

Murray, D. J. (1968). Articulation and acoustic confusability in short-term memory. *Journal of Experimental Psychology, 78*, 679–684.

Ross, B. M. (1969). Sequential visual memory and the limited magic of the number seven. *Journal of Experimental Psychology, 80*, 339–347.

Shaw, M. C., & Cruickshank, W. M. (1956). The use of the Bender-Gestalt Test with epileptic children. *Journal of Clinical Psychology, 12*, 192–193.

Wertheimer, M. (1923). Untersuchanger zur Lehre von der Gestalt. II. *Psychol. forsch, 5*, 301–350.

Wickelgren, W. A. (1965). Acoustic similarity and intrusion errors in short-term memory. *Journal of Experimental Psychology, 70*, 102–108.

DAVID A. SABATINO
*West Virginia College of
Graduate Studies*

AUDITORY PERCEPTION
AUDITORY PROCESSING
VISUAL PERCEPTION AND DISCRIMINATION

AUGMENTATIVE COMMUNICATION SYSTEMS

Augmentative communication systems are methods of communication that are used as a supplement to vocal speech. These systems are used with persons who are unable to use speech as their primary communication method. They are used to compensate (either temporarily or permanently) for the impairment and disability patterns of individuals with severe expressive communication disorders (i.e., the severely speech-language and writing impaired) (ASHA, 1989, p. 107).

Augmentative communication systems are used with many types of persons to enhance communication and the development of language skills. A child or adult who is unable to communicate at a chronologically age-appropriate level due to physical or other disabilities is at risk for developing poor social interactions and language skills. Even when it seems likely that oral speech may eventually develop, augmentative communication systems are used to prevent delayed communication development. Several studies have shown that the use of augmentative communication systems can sometimes lead to improved oral communication skills (Silverman, McNaughton, & Kates, 1978).

There are two categories of augmentative communication systems: unaided and aided. Unaided communication systems use only the physical body for communication. Sign language, gestures, vocalizations, and facial expressions are unaided communication methods. Aided communication methods require additional tools or equipment to convey a message. Typewriters, communication boards, pen and paper, and computers can all be used as aided communication methods. Although aided communication systems are physically cumbersome, they have the advantage of being easily understood by most listeners. Unaided systems usually require familiarity with the nonspeaking person for the communication system to be understood.

Effective augmentative communication systems should promote social and communicative interactions. To enhance interaction across many social situations, more than one type of augmentative communication system may be needed. The person should be able to use a variety of augmentative communication methods and apply them appropriately. They might rely on a computer for lengthy conversations, school work, and phone calls through a modem. The same person may have a communication board to take shopping or to go outside. In addition, head nods, simple gestures, and vocalizations might be used for rapid communication with friends and family who are familiar with the person. Through using all available augmentative communication methods, social interaction can be enhanced and communication can become effective.

REFERENCES

American Speech-Language-Hearing Association (ASHA). (1989). Competencies for speech-language pathologists providing services in augmentative communication. *Asha, 31,* 107–110.

Silverman, H., McNaughton, S., & Kates, B. (1978). *Handbook of Blissymbolics.* Toronto, Ontario: Blissymbolics Communication Institute.

SHARON L. GLENNEN
Pennsylvania State University
First edition

SHEELA STUART
George Washington University
Second edition

ALTERNATIVE COMMUNICATION METHODS IN SPECIAL EDUCATION BLISSYMBOLS

AUSTRALIA, SPECIAL EDUCATION IN

Background and Context

Like many western countries, Australia's early provisions for children with special education needs were through institutions and schools established by charitable organizations for people with disabilities in vision or hearing. For example, in Sydney, New South Wales (NSW), a school for deaf children was opened by the Institution for Deaf, Dumb, and Blind in 1860 (Drummond, 1978; Snow, 1990). That organization continues today as the Royal NSW Institute for Deaf and Blind Children, providing a range of on-site and community-based services for dead, blind, deaf-blind and other multiply-handicapped children. Similar developments took place in other states, such as Victoria, where a school for the blind was established in 1866 by the Victorian Royal Blind Society, and in South Australia where a school for deaf children was established in 1874 (Drummond, 1978).

The separate development of Australia's states from beginnings as English colonies meant that each developed its own set of governmental powers and responsibilities, gradually emerging as sovereign states and agreeing to form the federation of states which became known as the Commonwealth of Australia in 1901. While the advent of federation meant that some governmental powers became the province of the new federal government, many, such as the responsibility for universal public education, remained within the jurisdiction of individual states. As a result, the states' public education systems, which were established independently in the late nineteenth century, continued to grow under their own administrations. Services for children with disabilities were slow to be introduced by these state governments, until influences such as the reorganization of schooling into primary and secondary levels and an age-grade placement model identified particular problems for schools in providing for students with intellectual disabilities. Not surprisingly for that time, a segregated special education model was widely adopted for those students (see Snow, 1990, for a fuller discussion of these events in one Australian state between 1880 and 1940).

Early Provisions

From these beginnings it has been possible to see the emergence in all Australian states and territories of a range of government-supported special education services. These included a rapid increase in the number of self-contained classes in regular schools, especially for children with mild intellectual difficulties (in the IQ range of 50/55 to 75/80 points); an initially small number of separate special schools along with limited support to voluntary organizations establishing their own special schools for children with moderate and severe disabilities. However, by the late 1970s, state governments moved to take over the ownership and running of voluntary association schools, under an initiative funded by the federal government (Karmel, 1973).

More recently, special education service provision has changed dramatically, to include mainly regular school-based or itinerant services to support those children and their teachers in regular classes. This applies for children with emotional or behaviour disorders (Conway, 1994), though some difficulty is often experienced in identifying the extent to which this problem should be seen as a concern of special education, or as part of the general student welfare/support services of the regular school system. Indeed, the very notion of special education as a separate parallel school system has also been questioned in a growing number of Australian states, as detailed below (Peach, 1991) and also as questioned in the United States (Will, 1986). Associated with this is increasing uncertainty in defining and diagnosing children as having a behavior problem or as being emotionally disturbed. While problems of definition are one issue, more important for schools is the matter of deciding on best educational provisions.

Varying forms of support have been offered to children with learning difficulties, a term used to describe children with deficits in skills of literacy and/or numeracy, in the absence of apparent causes associated with physical, intellectual, or sensory impairment. Support for these children over the years has included the special class, the resource room with a specially trained teacher for withdrawal lessons one or two times a week, and more recently, the support teacher (learning difficulties) who works in the classroom of the regular teacher on a team-teaching basis for a short period (Department of Education, Queensland, 1993; Directorate of School Education, Victoria, 1993; Northern Territory Board of Studies, 1994; NSW Department of School Education, 1992; Ministry of Education, Western Australia, 1993; Special Education Consultative Committee (South Australia), 1994).

Many children with severe intellectual and/or multiple difficulties had been confined to residential institutional settings, often with no access to identified educational programs until this situation was addressed through federal government initiatives in the late 1980s. As a result, the Children in Institutions program saw the introduction of teachers to institutional settings, caring for children with severe intellectual and multiple disabilities. More recently, many of those children have been moved to community-based residential settings, with their education taking place in either a special school or special class in a regular school.

A development in Australia from the early 1970s has been the growth of early intervention services for children with developmental disabilities and their families. Al-

though such services had been in place for many years through the institution-based programs offering services for the deaf or for the physically handicapped (Drummond, 1978), more widespread generic services commenced at university-affiliated research programs (Pieterse, Bochner, & Bettison, 1988), often based on models such as those of Hayden and Dmitriev (1975) at the University of Washington in the United States. These were gradually adopted by community-based groups across the country, often supported by other universities, or by government departments involved in early childhood matters (e.g., community services, health, education) (Linfoot, 1992; 1997).

Commonwealth or Federal Government Initiatives

This overview of the development of special education in Australia must acknowledge the significant influence of federal government initiatives introduced in the Australian parliament in the early 1970s. Initiatives were then taken nationally for the first time on school education in Australia, university education being already funded by the Australian government. From 1972 onward, following recommendations of a Commonwealth Parliament Standing Committee on the needs of physically and mentally handicapped persons in Australia, the national government undertook a program to provide supplementary funding to states to assist handicapped persons through initiatives involving preschool education, improved education for handicapped children and adolescents, special education teacher training, and the provision of vocational services (Drummond, 1978). Those activities resulted from a significant injection of funds for special education services across Australia, and made the most significant contribution of government support for special education services in government and nongovernment schools to that time. Those initiatives were first presented in recommendations of the Interim Committee of the Australian Schools Commission (Karmel, 1973). More recent statements of Australian government level support for special education can be found in an Australian government paper to the Organization for Economic Cooperation and Development (OECD) (Department of Education, Training & Development, 1991) and in the Australian government's current guidelines on Commonwealth Programs for Schools (Department of Employment, Education, & Youth Affairs, 1997).

Current State of Special Education and Emerging Trends

Special education services in Australia have been broadly influenced by developments in countries such as the United Kingdom, where the Warnock report publicized debate on special education services (Committee of Enquiry into the Education of Handicapped Children and Young People, 1978) and the United States, whose series of public laws prescribing educational provisions for students with disabilities are well-known (Ysseldyke, Algozzine & Thurlow, 1992). In Australia, there has been no equivalent national legislation on special education, nor a Bill of Rights-style document guaranteeing similar individual expectations of their society. In 1992, however, the Australian federal parliament passed the Disability Discrimination Act, making unlawful discrimination against people with disabilities in access to employment, housing, and education. While offering some protection to the access rights of students with disabilities to education in regular schools, the legislation also provides for *exemption* from its provisions to educational institutions which might suffer an unjustifiable hardship in providing the special services needed to sustain a particular student's enrollment (Commonwealth of Australia, 1992). Most Australian states have developed their own legislation in support of the Commonwealth's Disability Discrimination Act (for example, the Disability Services Act, 1993, in NSW) and these have been influenced by the principles and language of normalization (Wolfensberger, 1972). In most Australian states, the principle of the continuum of special education services is supported, involving the placement of each student in a setting best suited to individual needs but as close as possible to a least restrictive or regular class setting. Nevertheless, there is considerable variation between the states in the extent to which this principle is applied. This is most clearly seen in changing trends in special school enrollments as shown below.

Particularly Australian issues in special education services relate to the needs of indigenous Australians with special education needs and the problems of providing special education services in remote and rural areas, where a sparsely distributed population is scattered over an area the size of western Europe. The compounded disadvantage of disability, geographic isolation, and membership of marginalized groups including women and those of different ethnic and cultural backgrounds have been well described by Germanis-Koutsounadis (1990). The national government initiatives include the English as a Second Language Program; the Special Education Program (e.g., recurrent grants including integration support; pre-school special education; children in residential institutions; children with severe disabilities; other training services); the Disadvantaged Schools program (special projects in literacy, numeracy, money management, initiatives to improve retention rates) for schools meeting criteria in relation to socioeconomic disadvantage; and the Country Area program, designed to provide resources to attempt to "minimize the imbalance between rural and urban education" (Australian Education Council, 1989, pp. 156–158).

Towards Inclusion

Probably the most significant change to special education services in recent years, both in Australia as in other countries, has been the effect of the so-called inclusion movement (Foreman, 1996; Ysseldyke et al., 1992). A trend has emerged by which many more children with special needs are placed in regular classes, with greater expectations on the regular school to be responsible for the educational program. This has been accompanied by a trend to eliminate separate Directorates of Special Education from within Australia's state education departments but to attach special education school support responsibility to school district level administrators and consultancy services. An account of this process of administrative change was set out by Peach (1991), a Deputy Director General of Education in the Australian state of Queensland, in a paper to Australia's special education professional organization (Australian Association of Special Education). Citing support in the literature for the merger of regular and special education, Peach described the end of the

"dual state system of education . . . with separate schools for students with severe intellectual and multiple disabilities and separate special classes for students categorized as hearing impaired, visually impaired and mildly intellectually handicapped. . . ." (p. 358)

The closing of separate Directorates of Special Education has also been effected in other states. In NSW, this was accomplished at the end of 1997, with responsibility for special education statewide policy development subsumed within a division within the bureaucracy responsible for all student welfare issues in schools. Unlike Queensland, the state of NSW has disbanded its regional administration layer within the bureaucracy. Instead, administration of schools is supervised by small district offices headed by superintendents across the state. These, in turn, are closely directed by the central Head Office bureaucracy. Although the administrative reform process of education services was still underway in this state in 1998, it is apparent that more centralized control of schools and schooling is one overall result of the reforms.

Associated with these changes in NSW are trends towards the increasing use of inclusive education practices in the delivery of support services outlined in a recently commissioned report, *The Integration/Inclusion Feasibility Study* (McRae, 1996). Also interesting is that the data presented in that report show that changes have already occurred towards inclusion. For example, in the period 1985-98, there was a fall of 30% in NSW in the number of students enrolled in special schools, although the school population as a whole has remained static in that period. This is in line with the position nationally, where data cited from a study by DeLemos (1994) show a fall in special *school* enrollments of 37% nationally (p. 24). While some increase in the proportion of special *class* enrollments is noted in the data over that period, by far the greater increase is noted in enrollments of students with disabilities in *regular classes*. Some of these regular class enrollments would have been supported by state or federal government integration funds to schools to support those students in regular classes. However, many of those placements are likely to reflect the changing expectations of many parents that they wish their children with disabilities to be educated in regular classes irrespective of government policy changes.

Considerable differences exist between the various states' special education enrollment data for 1992. These show that special class provisions were rarely used at all (just 2%) by students in government schools in Victoria, with most students placed in special schools (44%), or in regular classes with support (54%). By contrast, in NSW, around 46% were in special classes, 21% in special schools and 33% in regular classes. Most other Australian states fell between these two positions, although South Australia reported 68% of its students with disabilities in regular schools, with special classes and special schools used for 19% and 13% respectively (McRae, 1996, p. 25). Nongovernment schools across Australia accounted in 1992 for 28% of the school population generally but under 17% of those students identified with disabilities. Of these, most were provided for in regular classes (Catholic schools) though 40% of the small number enrolled in independent schools (2,377 nationally) were in special schools (DeLemos, 1994, cited in McRae, 1996).

These data show, then, that there is quite some disparity between Australian states. The wish of state governments to maintain their responsibilities for public education administration suggests that these differences will continue as each tries to reflect its own community's attitude to issues such as special education services, while the national government role remains restricted to special initiative funding to extend state services to areas considered to have been overlooked by states. The extent to which national governments may continue such a role may well be limited in future years as current constraints on domestic public expenditure continue.

REFERENCES

Australian Education Council. (1989). *National report on schooling in Australia*. Canberra: Author.

Committee of Enquiry into the Education of Handicapped Children and Young People. (1978). *Special education needs*. London: HMSO.

Conway, R. N. F. (1994). Students with behavioural and emotional problems. In A. F. Ashman & J. Elkins (Eds.), *Educating children with special needs* (2nd ed). Sydney: Prentice Hall.

DeLemos, M. (1994). *Schooling for students with disabilities*. Melbourne: Australian Council for Educational Research.

Department of Education, Queensland. (1993). *Educational provision for students with disabilities: Policy statement and management plan*. Brisbane: Author.

Department of Employment, Education, & Training. (1991). *Country paper by Australia, on the project Active Life for Disabled Youth-Integration in the School*. Prepared for the Organization for Economic Co-operation and Development, Centre for Educational Research and Innovation. Canberra: Author.

Department of Employment, Education, Training and Youth Affairs. (1997). Special learning needs. *Commonwealth programmes for schools quadrennial administrative guidelines, 1997–2000*. Canberra: Author.

Directorate of School Education, Victoria. (1993). *Educational opportunities for students with disabilities and impairments*. Melbourne: Author.

Disability Discrimination Act. (1992). Section 22, Division 2-Discrimination in other areas. Canberra: Commonwealth of Australia. (Internet: http://www/austlii.edu.au/au/legis/cth/consol_act/dda1992264/s22.html)

Drummond, N. W. (1978). *Special education in Australia*. Sydney: Royal Far West Children's Health Scheme.

Foreman, P. (Ed.). (1996). *Integration and inclusion in action*. Sydney: Harcourt Brace.

Germanos-Koutsounadis, V. (1990). "Fair Go" access and equity issues for Australians with disabilities who are from non-English speaking backgrounds (NESB), aboriginal, Torres Strait Islanders, women and from remote areas. *Australian Disability Review, 3*(90), 3–10.

Hayden, A. H., & Dmitriev, V. (1975). The multidisciplinary preschool program for Down syndrome children at the University of Washington model preschool center. In B. Z. Friedlander, G. M. Sterritt, & G. E. Kirk (Eds.), *Exceptional infant: Assessment and intervention* (Vol. 3). New York: Brunner/Mazel.

Karmel, P. (1973). *Schools in Australia: Report of the interim committee for the Australian Schools Commission*. Canberra: Australian Government Publishing Service.

Linfoot, K. W. (1992). The delivery of early intervention services for infants and preschool children: A ten year retrospective. *The Australasian Journal of Special Education, 16*(1), 42–47.

Linfoot, K. W. (1997). *Access to early intervention for families of children with disabilities in rural areas of New South Wales: A research report*. Penrith, NSW: University of Western Sydney, Nepean.

McRae, D. (1996). *The integration/inclusion feasibility study*. Sydney: NSW Department of School Education.

Ministry of Education, Western Australia. (1993). *Social justice in education: Policy and guidelines for the education of students with disabilities*. Perth: Author.

NSW Department of School Education. (1992). *Special Education*. Sydney: Author.

Northern Territory Board of Studies. (1994). *Provision for stu-*

dents with disabilities in Northern Territory Schools. Darwin: Author.

Peach, F. (1991). Crossing boundaries—Present realities and future possibilities. Opening address to the 15th National Conference of the Australian Association of Special Education. *Proceedings of the 15th National Conference of the Australian Association of Special Education*. Brisbane, Q.: AASE.

Pieterse, M., Bochner, S., & Bettison, S. (Eds.). (1988). *Early intervention for children with disabilities: The Australian experience*. Sydney: Macquarie University.

Snow, D. (1990). Historicising the integration debate. *Australasian Journal of Special Education, 13*(2), 28–38.

Special Education Consultative Committee (South Australia). (1994). *Schools for all*. Adelaide: Author.

Wolfensberger, W. (1972). *The principle of normalization in human services*. Toronto: National Institute on Mental Retardation.

Ysseldyke, J. E., Algozzine, B., & Thurlow, M. L. (1992). *Critical issues in special education* (2nd ed.). Boston: Houghton Mifflin.

KEN LINFOOT
University of Western Sydney

NEW ZEALAND, SPECIAL EDUCATION IN

AUTISM

Leo Kanner's 1943 paper, "Autistic disturbances of affective contact," made autism a medical entity. It took twenty more years for autism to become a cultural entity—an intriguing (to outsiders) and devastating (to families) aberration of child development whose incidence, causes, and treatment were mysteries demanding solutions. Prevalence estimates for autism have ranged from the earlier figure of approximately 4 or 5 per 10,000 children to more recent findings of about 1 per 1,000 children (Bryson, 1996), with a ratio of 3 or 4 males to each female. Differences in rates over time may reflect expansion of the list of criteria that define autism, increased reporting (Coleman & Gillberg, 1985), environmental pollution, and iatrogenic (illness-producing) effects of antibiotics (Rimland, 1997). The onset of autism (the beginning of a child's atypical trajectory of psychosocial development) often occurs in the first months of the child's life (Coleman & Gillberg, 1985). Early abnormalities of development crystallize into autism around two and a half years (Folstein & Rutter, 1987).

The lives of many individuals with autism are characterized by marginality with respect to ordinary adolescent and adult activities. Several decades ago, for example, Rutter et al. (1967) stated that a minority of persons with autism reached a good level of social adjustment by adolescence, and even fewer entered paid employment. Recent research is more encouraging. As an autistic child grows through adolescence and adulthood, activity level decreases, ease at managing undesirable behavior increases, and language, sociability, and activities of daily living improve (Mesibov, 1983). Good outcomes (e.g., social relatedness and independent living) appear to be predicted by reactions to sound, less problem behavior at earlier ages, language, schooling, and higher IQ in early childhood (Coleman & Gillberg, 1985).

Characteristics of Autism

As indicated by the name itself, the most striking and pervasive feature of autism is a child's difficulty participating in the social world. Even with his or her parents, an autistic child may seem alone; in social relationships generally, he or she may be unattached or have a difficult time sustaining attachment. In particular, a child may (1) pay little attention to other persons; (2) avoid physical contact and even the gaze of other persons (Lord, 1993); (3) fail to initiate interaction with others, or initiate interaction in ritualized ways (Hauck, Fein, Waterhouse, & Feinstein, 1995); (4) fail to imitate simple routine actions, e.g., waving bye-bye (Coleman & Gillberg, 1985); (5) fail to follow simple instructions (Coleman & Gillberg, 1985); and (6) have much difficulty taking the role or standpoint of the other person (Schopler & Mesibov, 1995), as indicated by not sharing attention with others to the same task at hand, not displaying empathy, and seemingly not understanding emotions displayed by other persons (Lord, 1993). In summary, the child with autism, perhaps from infancy, is not geared into the patterns of interaction—the various forms of turn-taking during meals, play and other social activities—which are the vehicle that brings children into the already organized social world.

Second features of autism are overselectivity and overreactivity in attention and attachment. For example, a child with autism may (1) pay attention to stimuli that are irrelevant to a task (e.g., a shiny bolt on a refrigerator door, rather than the handle); (2) stare fixedly and for long periods at spinning objects and flapping hands; (3) have "bizarre attachments to certain objects, such as stones, curls of hair, pins, pieces of plastic toys, or metals," apparently on the basis of color or texture (Coleman & Gillberg, 1985, p. 21); and (4) pay little attention and underreact to relevant events (e.g., verbal, facial, and postural cues signifying intentions, expectations and feelings of other persons) (Green, Fein, Joy, & Waterhouse, 1995).

Third, individuals with autism show uneven levels of competence across functional domains (Dawson, 1996; Rutter, 1983). Approximately 75 percent of autistic children are mentally retarded (Rutter, 1983). For example, autistic children may have much skill with spatial relations and memory, along with severe impairments in the following areas:

1. *Language.* Autistic children generally acquire speech sounds in typical fashion and learn to form words, but are impaired with respect to comprehension and language use; e.g., sharing or requesting information and initiating or reciprocating in conversation (Green, Fein, Joy, & Waterhouse, 1995; Prizant, 1996; Rimland, 1964).

2. *Social skills;* e.g., greetings and goodbyes, understanding and following requests, jointly working at tasks, taking the role of another person.

3. *Abstract reasoning,* e.g., figuring out sequences and abstracting general principles from specific events; imagination.

4. *Typical or appropriate play;* e.g., imaginative and cooperative play (Lewis & Boucher, 1995; Lord, 1993). For example, a child with autism may sit for hours rocking back and forth, staring intently at his or her fingers or at shiny objects; or make hundreds of ritualistic gestures during the day, like moving his or her hands and fingers in a fixed pattern, pulling at his or her hair, or twisting his or her face into strange expressions.

Fourth, a child with autism may engage in self-injury or even self-mutilation, especially if he or she is nonverbal (Shodell & Reiter, 1968). Examples include pinching, scratching, biting or striking himself, raising callouses and welts, and sometimes tearing his or her flesh (Schopler, 1995).

Finally, as described below, substantial evidence indicates neurological abnormalities or differences in individuals with autism (Dawson, 1996). For example, Reichler and Lee (1987) comment that autism is generally seen as "the expression of some underlying brain dysfunction" that is "associated with multiple etiologies, any one of which could potentially cause central nervous systems dysfunction" (p. 15).

Approaches to Cause and Treatment

Until the mid-1960s, the psychodynamic or psychogenic approach provided the predominant explanation and treatment of autism (Rimland, 1964). Autism was presumed to be caused by early interactions with the parents. Kanner (1943) originally observed that the parents, particularly the mothers, appeared cold and hostile towards their children. Mothers were characterized with the phrase "refrigerator mothers." Bettelheim (1967) in particular adopted the position that autism owed to poor parenting and that therapy required removing autistic children from their hostile home environment. However, no basis for parental, or any other early social, cause of autism has been found. Unfortunately, therapists blamed parents for their children's autism for decades, itself an iatrogenic effect (e.g., Torrey, 1977).

Pharmacological/Medical

Suggested pathogenic agents underlying autism are many and varied, ranging from genetic factors to infectious processes during prenatal (e.g., rubella and possibly cytomegalovirus), perinatal, early postnatal (e.g., herpes simplex infection), and later occurring conditions Coleman, 1987; Reichler & Lee, 1987). Evidence for a genetic component in autism is strong (Bailey, Phillips, & Rutter, 1996): Identical twins have a higher probability than fraternal twins of both being diagnosed with autism, and the probability of autism in siblings is 50 times higher than in the general population (Silliman, Campbell, & Mitchell, 1989). However, the specific role of genetic factors in autism is not yet clear (Folstein & Rutter, 1987), although some children with autism test positive for Fragile X. In addition, recent medical research has found additional factors that may start a trajectory towards the diagnosis of autism and may help explain certain behavioral excesses and developmental deficits identified earlier. These factors include:

1. Elevated levels of serotonin and dopamine in the blood, immature patterns of circadian rhythms for corticosteroids, and abnormalities in brain-stem auditory evoked responses (Coleman & Gillberg, 1985; Volkmar & Anderson, 1989).

2. Abnormalities (e.g., reduced size, or hypoplasia) of the brain's cerebellar vermis, which may help explain difficulties in arousal, attention, speech, and motor output (Hashimoto et al., 1995).

3. Possible overactivation of the right hemisphere of the brain, which may help explain chronic high levels of arousal and therefore overselectivity to novelty and underattention to speech and social cues (e.g., facial expressions).

A variety of medications, vitamins, dietary changes, and psychiatric treatments have been used over the years—not as remedies for autism, but for specific symptoms and associated problems, such as seizures, destructive behavior, and stimulus overreactivity (Gualtieri, Evans, & Patterson, 1987). These include vitamin B6, Deanol, chlorpromazine, clozapine, gluten-free diets, lithium, haloperidol, fenfluramine, L-dopa, D amphetamine, Naltrexone, electroconvulsive therapy, insulin coma therapy, opiate antagonists, and leucotomy. Results have ranged from poor to good. The current situation with respect to medical explanations and treatments is perhaps best summarized by Waterhouse, Wing, and Fein (1989): "Despite clinical impressions of a unity among typically autistic children, investigations of the group, regardless of which set of diagnostic criteria has been used, have found no shared etiology, no shared uniquely pathognomic neural deficit, no shared cognitive deficit, no distinct shared behavioral pattern, no shared specific life course, and no shared response to drug treatment."

Behavioral Approaches

Currently, the behavioral approach (including applied behavior analysis and precision teaching) is the best choice for educating children with autism. The behavioral approach rests on about 75 years of behavioral science research, particularly social learning and the experimental analysis of behavior. For practitioners of the behavioral approach, a child's maladaptive behavior and development are the most pressing problems. Moreover, the most verifiable and reliable remedies to date are environmental operations, events of instruction, and patterns of communication in the child's environments, as described by Engelmann and Carnine (1991); Mattaini (1996); Schlinger and Blakely (1994); and Gagne, Briggs, and Wager (1992).

A sample of reportedly effective behavioral-educational programs for children with autism includes those described by Anderson, Avery, DiPietro, Edwards, and Christian (1987); Fenske, Zalenski, Krantz, and McClannahan (1985); Fox, Dunlap, and Philbrick (1997); Hamblin et al. (1971); Harris, Handleman, Kristoff, Bass, and Gordon (1990); Harris, Handleman, Gordon, Kristoff, and Fuentes (1991); Holmes (1998); Howlin and Rutter (1987); Hoyson, Jamieson, and Strain (1984); Koegel and Johnson (1989); Koegel and Koegel (1996); Koegel, Rincover, and Egel (1982); Kozloff (1994a, 1994b, 1998); Lord, Bristol, and Schopler (1993); Lovaas (1977, 1987); Maurice, Green, and Luce (1996); McClannahan and Krantz, (1997); McEachlin, Smith, and Lovaas (1993); Prizant and Wetherby (1989, 1993); Rogers (1996); Rogers and DiLalla (1991); Rogers and Lewis (1989); Schopler, Lansing, and Waters (1983); Smith, Eikseth, and Lovaas (1997); and Watson, Lord, Schaffer, and Schopler (1989).

The best educational programs seem to have the following features:

1. Programs for autistic children based on principles of learning are designed to foster competencies that will enable children to participate in family, peer group, church, school, and other environments. In general, child-teacher interaction is structured so that inappropriate behaviors are weakened (usually with combinations of extinction and time out) while developmentally feasible and socially functional behaviors (attention, cooperation, imitation, play, speech, activities of daily living) are strengthened via the systematic use of compliance training, modeling, prompting, errorless learning, response chaining, and differential reinforcement of desirable behavior.

Learning appropriate behavior (e.g., speech) as a substitute for inappropriate behavior (e.g., pulling and pushing) is a low process consisting of numerous steps. The teacher might first reinforce a mute child for making any sounds. Then when the child's rate of vocalizing has increased and she is emitting many different sounds, the teacher will reinforce the child only when the child repeats a particular sound after the teacher, i.e., when the child imitates the teacher. In this way, words, sentences, and conversation are shaped up as closer and closer approximations to functional speech are prompted and reinforced. The same shaping process is used to teach a child to name objects, to read and write, to play, and to cooperate. In other words, the teacher attempts to build up the child's repertoire of appropriate behavior as a substitute for autistic behavior.

2. Curricula in the better schools are a synthesis of contributions of many bodies of knowledge regarding psychosocial development. In particular, excellent programs pay attention to:

   a. *Respondent learning*—how movements are assembled into reflexive emotional and attention responses.

   b. *Operant learning*—how contingencies of reinforcement teach individuals to perform actions with more or less skill, frequency, intensity, generality, and duration.

   c. *Applied behavior analysis*—using principles of respondent and operant learning to assess an individual's behavioral repertoire and environments, and suggest how to foster beneficial change either in the context of "discrete-trials" (highly structured turn taking) or in more naturalistic ("free operant") environments.

   d. *Forms and processes of child-caregiver and child-peer interaction.*

   e. *Cognitive developmental psychology and ecological psychology*—on how routine tasks and activities in a person's round of daily life (akin to scripts, frames, templates, or scaffolds) help a person organize actions into larger classes and sequences (Barker, 1968; Fogel, 1992).

   f. *The personalization process* in families, schools, and neighborhoods, by which valued versus degraded social positions, roles, and identities are bestowed on children (Henry, 1966; Kozloff, 1994a).

3. Excellent educational programs work on all eight phases of learning. These phases are as follows.

a. *Acquisition* is the early phase when a child learns concepts, propositions, and operations (tool skills, learning channels), and strategies for assembling these elements them into more complex and successful or accurate composite sequences (e.g., solving problems).

b. *Fluency* means behavior is performed accurately, smoothly, and at effective and/or culturally desirable speeds, durations, and intensities (Binder, 1996; Dougherty & Johnson, 1996; Lindsley, 1996). For example, a child not only knows how to read words accurately (acquisition), but reads quickly and almost automatically.

c. *Endurance* means a person fluently (rapidly and accurately) performs a task for an extended period. Endurance is fostered by practicing and improving concepts and tool skills; increasing the duration of practice sessions; and shifting performances from practice environments to naturalistic environments.

d. *Behavioral momentum* (Plaud & Gaither, 1996) means a person fluently (rapidly and accurately) performs a task despite distractions; e.g., other students' talking. Momentum is fostered by practice to the point of fluency and beyond; practice in the presence of increasingly obtrusive distractors; and by introducing events that have been associated with reinforcement (e.g., music or a teacher's presence).

e. *Generalization* (sometimes called *application*) means a person learns to transfer concepts, propositions, strategies, and operations acquired in one environment to other environments. For example, generalization of reading would involve reading at home and in class; reading newspapers, posters, graffiti, TV screens, and computers as well as school books; reading different type faces; and reading for various purposes (e.g., pleasure, following recipes, and crossing streets) (Mundschenk and Sasso, 1995).

f. *Adaptation*, not to be confused with generalization, involves altering (not simply transferring) concepts, propositions, strategies, and operations to suit the circumstances. This could mean using different movements, tools, or sequences, or adding a side-sequence.

g. *Retention* means a performance is fluent despite time between practice or performance. Retention is a function of past fluency and endurance.

h. *Maintenance* means a person performs competently in the absence of instructional scaffolding or assistance; i.e., the person is a more independent learner.

4. The better programs have strong collaborative relationships with parents and offer training programs and support. Important activities include assessing children's competencies, impairments, and preferences; translating assessment information into program plans; conducting complementary home programs; and evaluating and revising children's programs (Anderson, Avery, DiPietro, Edwards, and Christian, 1987; Holmes, 1998; Huynen, Lutzker, Bigelow, Touchette, and Campbell, 1996; Koegel, Bimbela, and Schreibman, 1996; Kozloff, 1998; Kozloff, Helm, Cutler, Douglas-Steele, Wells, and Scampini, 1988; and Marcus and Schopler, 1989).

REFERENCES

Anderson, S. R., Avery, D. L., DiPietro, E. K., Edwards, G. L., & Christian, W. P. (1987). Intensive home-based early intervention with autistic children. *Education and Treatment of Children, 10,* 352–366.

Bailey, A., Phillips, W., & Rutter, M. (1996). Autism: Towards an integration of clinical, genetic, neuropsychological, and neurological perspectives. *Journal of Child Psychology and Psychiatry, 37,* 89–126.

Barker, R. (1968). *Ecological psychology.* Stanford, CA: Stanford University Press.

Bettelheim, B. (1967). *The empty fortress: Infantile autism and the birth of the self.* New York: Free Press.

Binder, C. (1996). Behavioral fluency: Evolution of a new paradigm. *The Behavior Analyst, 19,* 163–197.

Bryson, S. E. (1996). Brief report: Epidemiology of autism. *Journal of Autism and Developmental Disorders, 26,* 165–167.

Coleman, M. (1987). The search for neurological subgroups in autism. In E. Schopler & G. Mesibov (Eds.), *Neurobiological issues in autism* (pp. 163–178). New York: Plenum.

Coleman, M., & Gillberg, C. (1985). *The biology of the autistic syndromes.* New York: Praeger.

Courchesne, E. (1989). Neuroanatomical systems involved in infantile autism. In G. Dawson (Ed.), *Autism: Nature, diagnosis, and treatment* (pp. 119–143). New York: Guilford.

Engelmann, S., & Carnine, D. (1991). *Theory of instruction: Principles and applications* (Rev. ed.). Eugene, OR: ADI.

Fenske, E. C., Zalenski, S., Krantz, P. J., & McClannahan, L. E. (1985). Age at intervention and treatment outcome for autistic children in a comprehensive intervention program. *Analysis and Intervention in Developmental Disabilities, 7,* 7–31.

Fogel, A. (1992). Movement and communication in infancy: The social dynamics of development. *Human Movement Science, 11,* 387–423.

Folstein, S. E. & Rutter, M. (1987). Familial aggregation and genetic implications. In E. Schopler & G. Mesibov (Eds.), *Neurobiological issues in autism* (pp. 83–105). New York: Plenum.

Fox, L., Dunlap, G., & Philbrick, L. A. (1997). Providing individual supports to young children with autism and their families. *Journal of Early Intervention, 21,* 1–14.

Gagné, R. M., Briggs, L. J., & Wager, W. W. (1992). *Principles of instructional design* (4th ed.). Fort Worth: Harcourt Brace Jovanovich.

Gaultieri, T., Evans, R. W., & Patterson, D. R. (1987). The medical treatment of autistic people. In E. Schopler & G. Mesibov (Eds.), *Neurobiological issues in autism* (pp. 373–388). New York: Plenum.

Green, L., Fein, D., Joy, S., & Waterhouse, L. (1995). Cognitive functioning in autism. In E. Schopler & G. Mesibov (Eds.), *Learning and cognition in autism* (pp. 13–31). New York: Plenum.

Hamblin, R. L., Buckholdt, D., Ferritor, D., Kozloff, M., & Blackwell, L. (1971). *The humanization processes*. New York: John Wiley and Sons.

Harris, S., Handleman, J. S., Kristoff, B., Bass, L., & Gordon, R. (1990). Changes in language development among autistic and peer children in segregated and integrated preschool settings. *Journal of Autism and Developmental Disorders, 20,* 23–32.

Hashimoto, T., Tayama, M., Murakawa, K., Yoshimoto, T., Miyazaki, M., Harada, M., & Kurado, Y. (1995). Development of the brain stem and cerebellum in autistic patients. *Journal of Autism and Developmental Disorders, 25,* 1–18.

Hauck, M., Fein, D., Waterhouse, L., & Feinstein, C. (1995). Social initiations by autistic children to adults and other children. *Journal of Autism and Developmental Disorders, 25,* 579–595.

Henry, J. (1966). Personality and aging—with special reference to hospitals for the aged poor. In J.C. McKinney & F. T. DeVyver (Eds.), *Aging and social policy* (pp. 281–301). New York: Meredith.

Holmes, D.L. (1998). *Autism through the lifespan: The Eden model*. Bethesda, MD: Woodbine House.

Howlin, P., & Rutter, M. (1987). *Treatment of autistic children*. Chichester, England: Wiley.

Hoyson, M., Jamieson, B., and Strain, P.S. (1984). Individualized group instruction of normally developing and autistic-like children: A description and evaluation of the LEAP curriculum model. *Journal of the Division of Early Childhood, 8,* 157–171.

Huynen, K. B., Lutzker, J. R., Bigelow, K. M., Touchette, P. E., & Campbell, R. V. (1996). Planned activity training for mothers of children with developmental disabilities. *Behavior Modification, 20,* 406–427.

Kanner, L. (1943). Autistic disturbances of affective contact. *Nervous Child, 2,* 217–250.

Koegel, R. L., Bimbela, A., & Schreibman, L. (1996). Collateral effects of parent training on family interactions. *Journal of Autism and Developmental Disorders, 26,* 347–359.

Koegel, R. L. & Johnson, J. (1989). Motivating language use in autistic children. In G. Dawson (Ed.), *Autism: Nature, diagnosis, and treatment* (pp. 310–325). New York: Guilford.

Koegel, R. L., & Koegel, L. K. (1996). *Teaching children with autism: Strategies for initiating positive interactions and improving learning opportunities*. Baltimore, MD: Paul H. Brookes.

Koegel, R. L., Rincover, A., & Egel, A. L. (1982). *Educating and understanding autistic children*. San Diego, CA: College Hill Press.

Kozloff, M. A. (1998). *Reaching the autistic child* (Revised Edition). Cambridge, MA: Brookline Books.

Kozloff, M. A. (1994a). *Improving educational outcomes for children with disabilities: Principles of assessment, program planning and evaluation*. Baltimore, MD: Paul H. Brookes.

Kozloff, M. A. (1994b). *Improving educational outcomes for children with disabilities: Guidelines and protocols for practice*. Baltimore, MD: Paul H. Brookes.

Laski, K. E., Charlop, M. H., & Schreibman, L. (1988). Training parents to use the Natural Language Paradigm to increase their autistic children's speech. *Journal of Applied Behavior Analysis, 21,* 391–400.

Lewis, V. & Boucher, J. (1995). Generativity in the play of young people with autism. *Journal of Autism and Developmental Disorders, 25,* 105–121.

Lichstein, K. L. & Schreibman, L. (1976). Employing electric shock with autistic children: A review of the side effects. *Journal of Autism and Childhood Schizophrenia, 6,* 163–173.

Lindsley, O. R. (1996). The four operant freedoms. *The Behavior Analyst, 19,* 199–210.

Lord, C. (1993). Early social development in autism. In E. Schopler, M. E. Van Bourgondien, & M. M. Bristol (Eds.), *Pre-school issues in autism* (pp. 61–94). New York: Plenum.

Lord, C., Bristol, M., and Schopler, E. (1993). Early intervention for children with autism and related developmental disorders. In E. Schopler, M. E. Van Bourgondien, & M. M. Bristol (Eds.), *Preschool issues in autism* (pp. 199–221). New York: Plenum.

Lovaas, O. I. (1977). *The autistic child: Language development through behavior modification*. New York: Irvington.

Lovaas, O. I. (1987). Behavioral treatment and normal educational and intellectual functional of young autistic children. *Journal of Consulting and Clinical Psychology, 55,* 3–9.

Marcus, L. M. and Schopler, E. (1989). Parents as co-therapists with autistic children. In C. E. Schaefer & J. M. Briesmeister (Eds.), *Handbook of parent training: Parents as co-therapists for children's behavior problems* (pp. 337–360). New York: John Wiley and Sons.

Maurice, C., Green, G., & Luce, S. C. (1996). *Behavioral intervention for young children with autism*. Austin, TX: Pro-Ed.

Mattaini, M. A. (1996). Envisioning cultural practices. *The Behavior Analyst, 19,* 257–272.

McClannahan, L. E., & Krantz, P. J. (1997). In search of solutions to prompt dependence: Teaching children with autism to use photographic activity schedules. In D. M. Baer & E. M. Pinkston (Eds.), *Environment and behavior* (pp. 271–278). Westview Press.

McEachlin, J. J., Smith, T., & Lovaas, O. I. (1993). Long-term outcome for children with autism who received early intensive behavioral treatment. *American Journal on Mental Retardation, 97,* 359–372.

Mesibov, G. B. (1983). Current perspectives and issues in autism and adolescence. In E. Schopler & G. B. Mesibov (Eds.), *Autism in adolescents and adults* (pp. 37–53). New York: Plenum.

Mundschenk, N. A., & Sasso, G. M. (1995). Assessing sufficient social exemplars for students with autism. *Behavioral Disorders, 21,* 62–78.

Plaud, J. J., Gaither, G. A. (1996). Behavioral momentum: Implications and development from reinforcement theories. *Behavior Modification, 2,* 183–201.

Prizant, B. M. (1996). Brief report: Communication, language, social, and emotional development. *Journal of Autism and Developmental Disorders, 26,* 173–178.

Prizant, B. M., & Wetherby, A. M. (1989). Enhancing language and communication in autism. In G. Dawson (Ed.), *Autism: Nature, diagnosis, and treatment* (pp. 282–309). New York: Guilford.

Prizant, B. M., & Wetherby, A. M. (1993). Communication in preschool autistic children. In E. Schopler, M. E. Van Bourgondien, & M. M. Bristol (Eds.), *Preschool issues in autism* (pp. 95–128). New York: Plenum.

Reichler, R. J., & Lee, E. M. C. (1987). Overview of biomedical issues in autism. In E. Schopler & G. Mesibov (Eds.), *Neurobiological issues in autism* (pp. 13–41). New York: Plenum.

Rimland, B. (1964). *Infantile autism.* New York: Appleton-Century-Crofts.

Rimland, B. (1997, October). Historical perspectives and techniques that work. Paper presented at the International Symposium on Autism, Illinois Center for Autism, McKendry College, Lebanon, IL.

Rogers, S. L. (1996). Brief report: Early intervention in autism. *Journal of Autism and Developmental Disorders, 26,* 243–246.

Rogers, S. J., & DiLalla, D. L. (1991). A comparative study of the effects of a developmentally based preschool curriculum on young children with autism and young children with other disorders of behavior development. *Topics in Early Childhood Special Education, 11,* 29–47.

Rogers, S. J., & Lewis, H. C. (1989). An effective day treatment model for young children with pervasive developmental disorders. *Journal of the American Academy of Child and Adolescent Psychiatry, 28,* 207–214.

Rutter, M. (1983). Cognitive deficits in the pathogenesis of autism. *Journal of Child Psychology and Psychiatry, 24,* 513–531.

Rutter, M., Greenfield, D., & Lockyer, L. (1967). A five to fifteen year follow-up study of infantile psychosis. *British Journal of Psychiatry, 113,* 1183–1199.

Schlinger, H. D., & Blakely, E. (1994). A descriptive taxonomy of environmental operations and its implications for behavior analysis. *The Behavior Analyst, 17,* 43–57.

Schopler, E. (1995). *Parent survival manual.* New York: Plenum.

Schopler, E., Lansing, M., & Waters, L. (1983). *Individualized assessment and treatment for autistic and developmentally disabled children: Volume 3. Teaching activities for autistic children.* Austin, TX: Pro-Ed.

Schopler, E., & Mesibov, G. (1995). Introduction to learning and cognition in autism. In E. Schopler & G. Mesibov (Eds.), *Learning and cognition in autism* (pp. 3–11). New York: Plenum.

Silliman, E. R., Campbell, M., & Mitchell, R. S. (1989). Genetic influences in autism and assessment of metalinguistic performance in siblings of autistic children. In G. Dawson (Ed.), *Autism: Nature, diagnosis, and treatment* (pp. 225–259). New York: Guilford.

Stahmer, A. C. (1995). Teaching symbolic play skills to children with autism using pivotal response training. *Journal of Autism and Developmental Disorders, 25,* 123–141.

Tager-Flusberg, H. (1989). A psycholinguistic perspective on language development in the autistic child. In G. Dawson (Ed.), *Autism: Nature, diagnosis, and treatment* (pp. 92–115). New York: Guilford.

Tobias, M. (1959). The disturbed child—A concept: Usefulness of Deanol in management. *Amer. Practit. Dig. Treat. 10,* 1759–1766.

Torrey, E. F. (1977). A fantasy trial about a real issue. *Psychology Today, 10*(10), 24.

Volkmar, F. R., & Anderson, G. M. (1989). Neurochemical perspectives on infantile autism. In G. Dawson (Ed.), *Autism: Nature, diagnosis, and treatment* (pp. 208–224). New York: Guilford.

Vollmer, T. R., Northup, J., Ringdahl, J. E., LeBlanc, L. A., & Chauvin, T. M. (1996). Functional analysis of severe tantrums displayed by children with language delays. *Behavior Modification, 20,* 97–115.

Waterhouse, L., Wing, L., & Fein, D. (1989). Re-evaluating the syndrome of autism in the light of empirical research. In G. Dawson (Ed.), *Autism: Nature, diagnosis, and treatment* (pp. 263–281). New York: Guilford.

Watson, L., Lord, C., Schaffer, B., & Schopler, E. (1989). *Teaching spontaneous communication to autistic and developmentally handicapped children.* Austin, TX: Pro-Ed.

Wing, L., & Gould, L. (1979). Severe impairments of social interaction and associated abnormalities in children: Epidemiology and classification. *Journal of Autism and Developmental Disorders, 9,* 11–29.

MARTIN A. KOZLOFF
*University of North Carolina
at Wilmington*

AUTISTIC BEHAVIOR
NATIONAL SOCIETY FOR CHILDREN AND ADULTS
WITH AUTISM

AUTISM SOCIETY OF AMERICA (ASA)

The Autism Society of America was founded in 1965 to help parents, family members, professionals, and caregivers learn about autism and how to effectively deal with the disability. The Society has over 24,000 members joined through a network of 225 chapters in 46 states across the country. The mission of ASA is to promote lifelong access and opportunities for persons within the autism spectrum and their families to be fully included, participating members of their communities through advocacy, public awareness, education, and research related to autism. ASA believes that each person with autism is a unique individual, and its policies promote the active and informed involvement of family members and those with autism in the planning of individualized, appropriate services and supports.

The ASA provides current information about autism through distribution of free packets of materials on a variety of topics; a comprehensive, bimonthly newsletter, the *Advocate;* and an annual national conference each July. An extensive library of information on issues affecting children and adults with autism, Pervasive Developmental/Disorder-not otherwise specified (PDD-NOS), Asperger's, or other related disorders is maintained by the Society. In addition, ASA furnishes national legislators and government agencies with information about the needs of people with autism and their families and promotes medical research in the field.

Local chapters help families find trained professionals and service providers in their communities and organize parent support groups. Some chapters also host presentations by autism experts and advocate at the state level for improvements in programs and services specific to the disability.

A variety of information packets are available from the ASA national office, including materials dealing with general information about autism, facilitated communication, insurance, medications, education, and adult issues. Information provided assists families in appropriately matching the unique needs and potential of individuals with autism to treatments or strategies likely to be effective in moving the person closer to normal functioning. The Society promotes treatments supported by research while asserting that no one treatment exists which is equally effective for all persons. In doing so, they focus on important areas to consider when formulating a treatment plan, including social skill development, communication, behavior, and sensory integration.

Headquarters of the Autism Society of America are located at 7910 Woodmont Avenue, Suite 650, Bethesda, Maryland 20814-3015. ASA may be reached by phoning 1-800-3AUTISM or on the internet at http:/www.autism-society.org/.

TAMARA J. MARTIN
*The University of Texas of the
Permian Basin*

AUTISM TREATMENT OPTIONS (ATO)

Autism Treatment Options (ATO) is a nonprofit organization that was established in 1994 by parents of autistic children. The main objective of ATO is to provide parents and others interested in the field of autism with information on different types of treatments. ATO publishes the *Autism Options Guide—Resource Handbook,* a book that provides readers with a great deal of information on available autism resources.

ATO seeks to increase the awareness of available options for parents and professionals, and also to provide support for family members of autistic persons. Members of ATO are continually updated on current research and new treatments and finding in the field. Membership is open to parents, relatives, and professionals with an interest in autism. For further information about ATO, contact them at Autism Treatment Options Inc., P.O. Box 10772, Goldsboro, North Carolina 27532-0772.

JENNIFER MIGHT
*University of North Carolina
at Wilmington*

AUTISTIC BEHAVIOR

Autistic behavior is the name for those activities and characteristics frequently associated with the developmental disorder known variously as autism, early infantile autism, or Kanner's (1943) syndrome. Although autism is a specific syndrome having well-defined diagnostic criteria, a wide variety of behaviors are said to be autistic. Further, many of the behaviors are occasionally exhibited by children with other developmental syndromes and disorders such as mental retardation, cerebral palsy, and serious disorders of receptive and/or expressive language. A particular pattern of symptoms, including an early age of onset as well as social and language peculiarities, characterizes the syndrome known as autism and distinguishes it from all other childhood psychotic disorders. Thus, the mere presence of behaviors called autistic in a child's repertoire does not guarantee that autism is the appropriate diagnosis for that child. Further, it is very unusual for any child diagnosed as autistic to show all of the behaviors that have been associated with autism.

One of the first attempts to compile the range of behaviors observed among autistic children was made by Creak (1964) and her colleagues in Great Britain. Similar sets of observations have been reported since that time by others. The observations may be summarized as follows:

1. Unusual and/or self-stimulatory behaviors such as rocking to and fro, flicking fingers in front of the eyes, flapping arms or hands rapidly at particular frequencies, adopting unusual postures, or toe walking.

2. Reluctance to use the distance receptors of vision and hearing. This translates into an avoidance of eye contact and inattention to auditory and visual cues and information. By contrast there is often an excessive and age-

inappropriate reliance on near receptors such as taste, touch, and smell for exploration. The threshold for pain may also be unusually high.

3. A preoccupation with certain objects or the operations of objects, often without respect to their intended function. For example, a child may be fascinated by an empty record turntable spinning or may play with a toy truck only by turning it on its side to spin its wheels.

4. The absence of speech or, where speech exists, delays and/or peculiarities such as the use of jargon, the repetition of phrases or whole passages (echolalia), the reversal or misuse of personal pronouns, and idiosyncratic use of words (neologisms).

5. Unusual anxieties, often unrelated to actual environmental circumstances. For instance, a child may become unusually upset if furniture is rearranged in a room, but may remain calm and seemingly unconcerned while involved in an auto accident or while performing dangerous activities such as climbing or balancing at great heights.

6. An unwillingness to have familiar routines changed or delayed and a reluctance to participate in new activities or to process unexpected events. Thus a child may insist on walking exactly the same route to school daily, may wish to constantly possess a particular toy, or consume only certain foods. Any changes or interruptions of these routines produce extreme anxiety.

7. A pattern of uneven intellectual development characterized by general mental retardation with "islands" of near normal, normal, or even supranormal functioning. A child may not be able to answer simple questions (why, when, where, etc.), but the same child may perform complex mathematical calculations or read large and unfamiliar words, though this skill is usually not accompanied by adequate comprehension.

Several authors have attempted to provide rating scales as an aid in formulating a diagnosis to quantify the types and amounts of autistic behavior a child shows while being observed. Three scales in fairly widespread use are the BRIAAC (Ruttenberg, et al., 1966), the CARS (Schopler, et al., 1985), and the BOS (Freeman, et al., 1984). Such scales may be useful in planning educational or behavioral intervention programs because they focus on particular problem behaviors and they usually reliably disciminate among samples of normal, retarded, and autistic people. However, they are less useful in establishing individual diagnoses because they only tap behaviors observed within the relatively brief observation period. They tend to be of greatest use in the most severe cases of autism, where mental retardation is also likely to be quite marked. Nevertheless, the scales are very useful in the overall process of diagnosis and intervention.

REFERENCES

Creak, M. (1964). Schizophrenic syndrome in childhood: Further progress report of a working party. *Developmental Medicine and Child Neurology, 6,* 530–535.

Freeman, B., Ritvo, E., & Schroth, P. (1984). Behavior assessment of the syndrome of autism: Behavior Observation System. *Journal of the American Academy of Child Psychiatry, 23,* 588–594.

Kanner, L. (1943). Autistic disturbances of affective contact. *Nervous Child, 2,* 217–250.

Ruttenberg, B., Dratman, M., Fraknoi, J., & Wenar, C. (1966). An instrument for evaluating autistic children. *Journal of the American Academy of Child Psychiatry, 5,* 453–478.

Schopler, E., Reichler, R., & Renner, B. (1985). *Childhood Autism Rating Scale (CARS).* New York: Irvington.

JERRY L. SLOAN
*Wilmington Psychiatric
Associates*

AUTISM
NATIONAL SOCIETY FOR CHILDREN AND ADULTS WITH AUTISM

AUTOMATICITY

Automaticity is an aspect of perceptual and motor processing that occurs outside of conscious awareness. Factors such as stimulus novelty and response practice have been found to be related to automaticity in cognitive functioning (Neiser, 1976). When aroused by a novel or difficult stimulus, extensive cognitive processing occurs, forcing the event into conscious awareness. However, an habitual response elicited by an expected stimulus may be performed at an automatic level requiring little or no attention.

Since humans have a limited attention capacity, automatic functions add to the efficiency of the information processing system (Kutas & Hillyard, 1980). Many simple perceptual processes are innately automatic, while even complex activities such as reading can become automatic with sufficient practice. In fact, Hancock and Byrd (1984) state that reading efficiency is dependent on the extent to which decoding skills become automatized, and Garnett and Fleischner (1980) have related automatization to basic math facts acquisition.

Learning disabilities, and mental retardation, have been discussed in terms of deficient automatization processes. Learning-disabled children have been found to take longer to produce acquired math facts than their nondisabled peers (Garnett & Fleischner, 1980). Their inability to perform this well-drilled task at an automatic level suggests that learning-disabled children's thinking processes are more circuitous and attention demanding. Severely disabled readers have been found to have difficulty processing letters within words, while less impaired readers, who have automatized letter recognition, read whole words in a controlled, attention-demanding manner (Hancock & Byrd, 1984).

Other researchers have suggested that automatic functions may be available to learning-disabled and retarded students, but that other factors impede their effects. Thus, retarded children have been found to perform as well as their nonretarded peers on a measure of perceptual memory automatization (Stein, Laskowski, & Trancone, 1982). The retarded children, however, had more difficulty organizing new skills, thereby preventing the automatization of more complex processes. In another study, learning-disabled children were found to produce the correct definitions of familiar words at a rate equal to that of nondisabled children, but showed a rapid decline in rate and accuracy when unfamiliar words were introduced (Ceci, 1983). As more purposeful processing was required, the learning-disabled students failed to decode the words, and instead substituted words that could be processed at an automatic level.

REFERENCES

Ceci, S. J. (1983). Automatic and purposeful semantic processing characteristics of normal and language/learning disabled children. *Developmental Psychology, 19*(3), 427–439.

Garnett, K., & Fleischner, J. (1980). *Automatization and basic fact performance of normal and learning disabled children* (Technical Report No. 10). Washington, DC: Office of Special Education. (ERIC Document Reproduction Service No. ED 210 839)

Hancock, A. C., & Byrd, D. (1984, April). *Automatic processing in normal and learning disabled children*. Paper presented at the annual meeting of the Southwestern Psychological Association, New Orleans. (ERIC Document Reproduction Service No. ED 246 414)

Kutas, M., & Hillyard, S. A. (1980). Reading senseless sentences: Brain potentials reflect sementic incongruity. *Science, 207*, 203–204.

Neiser, U. (1976). *Cognition and reality*. San Francisco: Freeman.

Stein, D. K., Laskowski, M. A., & Trancone, J. (1982). *Automatic memory processes in mentally retarded persons*. Paper presented at the annual meeting of the American Psychological Association, Washington, DC. (ERIC Document Reproduction Service No. ED 227 604)

GARY BERKOWITZ
Temple University

COGNITIVE STRATEGIES
CONDITIONING
TRANSFER OF LEARNING

AUTOMUTISM

See ELECTIVE MUTISM.

AUTONOMIC REACTIVITY

The autonomic nervous system consists of the sympathetic nervous system and the parasympathetic nervous system. The sympathetic nervous system increases heart rate, adrenal secretions, sweating, and other responses that prepare the body for vigorous activity. The parasympathetic nervous system increases salivation, digestion, and other vegetative responses while antagonizing many effects of the sympathetic nervous system.

The sympathetic system can be activated by sudden sensory stimuli or by emotional experiences. The response to a stimulus depends on one's interpretation of the stimulus and not on just the stimulus itself. Shock believed to be escapable increases heart rate; shock believed to be inescapable decreases it (Malcuit, 1973). A task given to fifth-grade boys as a test increased heart rate; a similar task given to them as a game decreased it (Darley & Katz, 1973).

The sympathetic nervous system is apparently most reactive in early childhood, when gauged by variability of heart rate (Shields, 1983). Sympathetic reactivity is fairly stable over time and may be related to personality traits. Many people with an antisocial personality have a weak sympathetic response to frightening stimuli. Some authors link high sympathetic responsiveness with impulsiveness and distractibility (Shields, 1983).

REFERENCES

Darley, S. A., & Katz, K. (1973). Heart rate changes in children as a function of test versus game instructions and test anxiety. *Child Development, 44,* 784–789.

Malcuit, G. (1973). Cardiac responses in aversive situation with and without avoidance possibility. *Psychophysiology, 10,* 295–306.

Shields, S. A. (1983). Development of autonomic nervous system responsivity in children: A review of the literature. *International Journal of Behavioral Development, 6,* 291–319.

JAMES W. KALAT
North Carolina State University

CENTRAL NERVOUS SYSTEM
LEARNED HELPLESSNESS

AVERSIVE CONTROL

The use of aversive stimuli to control behavior is one of the most controversial techniques employed by teachers, researchers, psychologists, therapists, and others. The effectiveness of this procedure is defined by its effect on behavior: it suppresses the behavior that it follows. This definition is similar to that for punishment. Indeed, aversive control is one form of punishment.

The controversy surrounding the use of aversive control is illustrated by Wood and Lakin (1982). They indicate that, although most states approve of the use of moderate corporal punishment, it is specifically forbidden by statutes in others (e.g., Maine and Massachusetts).

The use of aversive consequences for behavior control generally is viewed as a technique to be used only when other techniques have not been successful. Snell (1983) indicates that:

> Aversive conditioning using strong primary aversion (such as electric shock and slapping) to eliminate behavior is very defensible in two general instances: when the behavior is so dangerous or self-destructive that positive reinforcement and extinction are not feasible and when all other intervention methods (reinforce competing response, extinction, milder punishment forms) have been applied competently and have been documented as unsuccessful. (p. 140)

Despite the reservations that have been expressed regarding the use of aversives, aversives have been used to control behavior, particularly self-injurious behavior (SIB). Lemon juice (Sajwaj, Libet, & Agras, 1974), noxious odors (Baumeister & Baumeister, 1978), and electric shock (McConaghy, Armstrong, & Blaszcynski, 1981) are examples of aversive methods that have been used.

At times and under certain conditions, aversive procedures have been found to be the treatment of choice. However, aversive control should be reduced or eliminated when the desired behavior change has occurred or when the target behavior responds to less severe techniques. Suppression, and not elimination, of targeted behavior may result from using this technique. Unexpected and unintended results often occur whenever a punishment procedure is used; it is possible that similar side effects may occur when aversive control is used.

The use of aversives to control behavior raises many ethical questions. The basic rationale for the use of aversives is that other methods have failed, the child is at risk, and the aversive to be used is not as harmful as the behavior that is targeted for change.

REFERENCES

Baumeister, A., & Baumeister, A. (1978). Suppression of repetitive self-injurious behavior by contingent inhalation of aromatic ammonia. *Journal of Autism & Childhood Schizophrenia, 8,* 71–77.

McConaghy, N., Armstrong, M., & Blaszczynski, A. (1981). Controlled comparison of aversive therapy and covert sensitization in compulsive homosexuality. *Behavior Research & Therapy, 19,* 425–434.

Sajwaj, T., Libet, J., & Agras, S. (1974). Lemon juice therapy: The control of life threatening rumination in a six-month old infant. *Journal of Applied Behavior Analysis, 1,* 557–566.

Snell, M. (Ed.). (1983). *Systematic instruction of the moderately and severely handicapped* (2nd ed.). Columbus, OH: Merrill.

Wood, F. H., & Lakin, K. C. (Eds.). (1982). *Punishment and aversive stimulation in special education: Legal, theoretical and practical issues in their use with emotionally disturbed children and youth.* Reston, VA: Council for Exceptional Children.

PHILIP E. LYON
College of St. Rose

BEHAVIOR MODIFICATION
OPERANT CONDITIONING
PUNISHMENT

AVERSIVE STIMULUS

An aversive stimulus, whether unconditioned (e.g., bright lights) or conditioned (e.g., a frown or gesture) is "an unpleasant object or event" (Sulzer-Azaroff & Mayer, 1986) that can be used to decrease or increase a behavior. When presented as a consequence of, or contingent on, a specific behavior, it may be used to reduce or eliminate the rate of that behavior. However, when an aversive stimulus is removed contingent on the emission of a behavior, it may increase the rate of that behavior. In any case, an aversive stimulus is typically referred to as a punisher.

The application of aversive stimuli to effectively reduce or eliminate severe self-destructive behaviors and/or severe chronic behaviors has been demonstrated by several researchers including Lovaas and Simmons (1969) and Risley (1968). However, the many disadvantages of applying aversive stimuli to reduce behaviors (e.g., withdrawal, aggression, generalization, imitation, negative self-statements; Sulzer-Azaroff & Mayer, 1986) seem to outweigh the advantages. Aversive stimuli to reduce behaviors should be reserved for serious destructive behaviors and employed only when other less aversive procedures have been tried. A more detailed presentation of the use of aversive stimuli may be found in Sulzer-Azaroff & Mayer (1986).

REFERENCES

Lovaas, O. I., & Simmons, J. O. (1969). Manipulation of self destruction in three retarded children. *Journal of Applied Behavior Analysis, 2,* 143–157.

Risley, T. (1968). The effects and side effects of punishing the autistic behaviors of a deviant child. *Journal of Applied Behavior Analysis, 1,* 21–35.

Sulzer-Azaroff, B., & Mayer, G. R. (1986). *Achieving educational excellence using behavior strategies.* New York: Holt, Rinehart, & Winston.

ALLISON LEWIS
LOUIS J. LANUNZIATA
University of North Carolina at Wilmington

BEHAVIOR MODIFICATION
PUNISHMENT

AVEYRON, WILD BOY OF

See WILD BOY OF AVEYRON.

AYLLON, TEODORO (1929–)

Teodoro Ayllon obtained his PhD in clinical psychology in 1959 at the University of Houston. His special areas of interest are in behavior and condition therapy and applied behavior analysis. His major field of interest is in clinical psychology. He has done extensive research in behavioral analysis and management and has published articles and books concerning this subject. He is currently working on a book on children and their families.

Some of his principal contributions include "Eliminating Discipline Problems by Strengthening Academic Performance," "The Elimination of Discipline Problems Through a Combined School-Home Motivational System," and "Behavioral Management of School Phobias." In these articles, Ayllon discusses a procedure in which discipline problems and school phobias can be remedied by having parents support the child with positive reinforcement to increase motivation to go to school and improve performance.

He continues his research in clinical psychology and behavioral management and remains involved in the field of psychology. Ayllon's work has been recognized with honors. He retired as a professor of psychology and special education in the psychology department at Georgia State University in 1997, and continues to live in Georgia.

REFERENCES

Ayllon, T. (1974). Eliminating discipline problems by strengthening academic performance. *Journal of Applied Behavior Analysis, 7,* 71–76.

Ayllon, T., Garber, S., & Pisor, K. (1975). The elimination of discipline problems through a combined school-home motivational system. *Journal of Behavior Therapy, 6,* 616–626.

Ayllon, T., Smith, D., & Rogers, M. (1970). Behavioral management of school phobia. *Journal of Behavioral Therapy & Experimental Psychiatry, 1,* 125–138.

REBECCA BAILEY
Texas A & M University

AYRES, A. JEAN (1920–1988)

A. Jean Ayres died on December 16, 1988 at the age of 68. Ayres obtained her BS (1945) and MS (1954) in Occupational Therapy, and went on to earn her Ph.D. (1961) in Educational Psychology from the University of Southern California. She worked as an occupational therapist in several California rehabilitation centers, and between 1955 and 1985, she taught and conducted research at the University of Southern California in the Departments of Occupational Therapy and Special Education, achieving the rank of emeritus professor after her retirement in 1985. Ayres was also in private practice in occupational therapy from 1977 to 1984.

Occupational therapy, particularly as related to perceptual and sensory integrative dysfunction and neuromuscular integration, was the focus of her work. From 1964 to 1966, she was a postdoctoral trainee at the University of California, Los Angeles Brain Research Institute, which led to her discovery of sensory integration dysfunction, a neurological disorder of the senses characterized by learning and behavioral problems as well as pain associated with the performance of even simple daily tasks. Ayres had struggled with learning problems similar to those caused

A. Jean Ayers

by the disease, ultimately identifying an inefficient organization of sensory information received by the nervous system as its cause. Perhaps her greatest contribution was the development of sensory-integrative therapy, a neurologically-based treatment for learning disorders widely used among occupational therapists. She is also credited with devising the Southern California Sensory Integration Tests and the Sensory Integration and Praxis Tests, tools used for identifying the disorder.

Distinguishing her work from others, Ayres (1972) used a neurological as opposed to an educational or psychodynamic approach to learning and behavior disorders, emphasizing the normalization of the sensory integration process in the brain stem while not excluding cortical integrative processes. Her research found that students with certain identifiable types of sensory integrative dysfunctions who received occupational therapy specifically for the integrative dysfunction, showed greater gains in academic scores than those who received an equal amount of time in academic work.

During her distinguished career, Ayres published over 50 tests, articles, and films. She was the recipient of the Eleanor Clarke Slagle Lectureship and the Award of Merit, the highest honors conferred by the American Occupational Therapy Association, and she was named to the 1971 edition of *Outstanding Educators of America*. Ayres was a charter member of the honorary Academy of Research of the American Occupational Therapy Association.

REFERENCES

Ayres, A. J. (1972). Improving academic scores through sensory integration. *Journal of Learning Disabilities, 5,* 338–343.

E. VALERIE HEWITT
Texas A & M University
First edition

TAMARA J. MARTIN
*The University of Texas of the
Permian Basin*
Second edition

**OCCUPATIONAL THERAPY
SENSORY-INTEGRATIVE THERAPY**

B

BABINSKI REFLEX

The Babinski reflex was first recognized in 1896 by a French neurologist of Polish descent, Joseph Francois Felix Babinski. Babinski was a pupil of Charcot and was the first to differentiate between a normal and pathologic response of the toes. The Babinski sign, or extensor plantar response, is a phenomenon observed when the sole of the foot is stroked from below the heel toward the toes on the lateral (outside) side. The big toe turns upward or toward the head with the other toes fanned out and extended and the leg is withdrawn.

As the nervous system matures and the pyramidal tract gains more control over spinal motorneurons, the Babinski reflex will not be observed. Indeed, scratching the sole of the foot of a normal person with a dull object will produce a downward flexion of all toes. The presence of Babinski's reflex after the first year of life is an indication of damage to cortical motor neurons and a dysfunction of the pyramidal tract, and further neurological evaluation is required.

There has been controversy over the pathophysiologic interpretation of the Babinski sign or reflex; however, it is considered the single most important sign in clinical neurology because of its reliability. The clinical utility of the Babinski reflex has remained unchanged for over 100 years after its initial description.

REFERENCES

Bassetti, C. (1995). Babinski and Babinski sign. *Spine, 20*(23), 2591–2594.

Estanol, V. B., Huerta, D. E., & Garcia, R. G. (1997). 100 years of the Babinski sign. *Review Invest Clinical, 49*(2), 141–144.

van Gijn, J. (1995). The Babinski reflex. *Postgraduate Medical Journal, 171*(841), 645–648.

Rothenberg, M. A., & Chapman, C. F. (1994). *Dictionary of medical terms* (3rd ed.). Hauppauge, NY: Barron's.

ELAINE FLETCHER-JANZEN
University of Northern Colorado

APGAR RATING SCALE
DEVELOPMENTAL MILESTONES
PLANTAR REFLEX

BABY DOE

The term *Baby Doe* has come to signify the issue of denying life-sustaining treatment to infants born with permanent handicaps combined with life-threatening but surgically correctable conditions. These infants are the focus of a debate that tests the limits of medical certainty in diagnosis and raises profound ethical and legal issues.

A major stimulus to the ethical and legal debate on foregoing life-sustaining treatment for newborns was provided by Duff and Campbell (1973). Their article describes how and why nontreatment was chosen for 43 out of 299 infants during a 30-month period in the intensive care nursery at Yale New Haven Hospital.

The term *Infant Doe* was first used on April 9, 1982, when a baby boy with Down's syndrome and esophageal atresia (a defect that prevents normal feeding) was born in Bloomington, Indiana. His parents refused to give consent for surgery to correct the tracheoesophageal defect. The courts refused to intervene and Infant Doe died 6 days later. The Reagan administration responded by informing hospitals that Section 504 of the Rehabilitation Act of 1973, which prevents discrimination against individuals with handicaps in programs receiving federal funds, protects imperiled newborns. The administration issued an Interim Final Regulation in March 1983 that articulated this policy of nondiscrimination and established procedures to implement it. This regulation was overturned by a federal court because of the administration's failure to follow established notice and comment on procedures in promulgating it.

In July 1983 the Reagan administration issued a second similar proposed rule. It stated that treatment of an infant with a handicap was mandatory unless treatment was "medically contraindicated." It ruled that the denial of treatment on the basis of a potentially disabling or handicapping condition constituted unlawful discrimination. It was also specified that this regulation was not intended to mandate futile therapies that would only prolong an infant's process of dying.

On October 11, 1983, "Baby Jane Doe" was born in Port Jefferson, New York. She was born with myelomeningocele, hydrocephaly, microcephaly, bilateral upper extremity spasticity, a prolapsed rectum, and a malformed brain stem. Her parents chose a course of conservative treatment as an alternative to surgery. Based on anonymous information, the Department of Health and Human Services filed a complaint with the state Child Protection Agency. The July, 1983 ruling made it clear that the federal government was ready to step in if the decision of a state agency was considered insufficient. This case focused attention on the question of the federal government's right to intrude into the private realm of family decision-making.

In 1983, the President's Commission for the Study of Ethical Problems in Medicine and Biomedical Research issued, as part of its report, a statement on the decision to forgo life-sustaining treatment in critically ill newborns. It contrasted the presumption that parents are the appropriate decision makers for their infants with the *parens patriae* power of the state. That is, while laws concerning the family protect a substantial range of discretion for parents, the state may supervise parental decisions before they become operative to ensure that the choices made are not neglectful or abusive to the child. It concluded that public policy should resist state intervention into family decisions unless serious issues are at stake and the intervention is likely to achieve better outcomes. Additionally, the commission suggested that infants with handicaps be treated no less vigorously than their nonhandicapped peers. However, it also suggested that futile therapies that merely delay death without offering a reasonable probability of saving a baby's life should be avoided. Finally, in ambiguous cases, where the course of action that would benefit the infant is not chosen by the parents, authorized persons acting for the state as *parens patriae* must step in.

On April 15, 1985, the Department of Health and Human Services issued the final rule and model guidelines that encouraged hospitals to establish infant care review committees (ICRCs). This was part of the child abuse and neglect prevention and treatment program included in the Child Abuse Amendments of 1984 (PL 98-457). This legislation attempted to protect the rights of infants with disabilities and limit governmental intervention into the practice of medicine and parental responsibilities. The purpose of the ICRCs was to educate hospital personnel and families of infants with disabilities and life-threatening conditions, to recommend guidelines concerning the withholding from infants of medically indicated treatment (including appropriate hydration, nutrition, and medication), and to offer counsel and review in cases involving infants with disabling and life-threatening conditions.

Recent research (Carter, 1993) has surveyed military and civilian neonatologists and found that, despite frequency of potential cases for review, ICRCs were seldom consulted. In fact, 67% of neonatologists surveyed indicated that the Baby Doe regulations has affected neither their thinking about ethical issues nor their practice.

The practice of decision making continues to be primarily led by the parents and neonatologist or by multidisciplinary conferences that typically do not include the nurses who deliver care (Martin, 1989). The use of multidisciplinary conferences predates the Baby Doe regulations.

The Child Abuse Amendments of 1984 (PL 98-45) state three circumstances under which treatment is not considered medically indicated: the infant is chronically and irreversibly comatose, the treatment would prolong dying but not be effective in ameliorating life-threatening conditions, and the treatment itself would be futile and inhumane. However, when even one of these three circumstances exists (and therefore failure to provide treatment would not be considered withholding medically indicated treatment), the infant must be provided with appropriate hydration, nutrition, and medication. Additionally, the law states that the withholding of treatment must not be based on subjective opinions about the future quality of life of such a person but is to be based on the treating physicians' "reasonable medical judgment." These guidelines are advisory and not mandatory in any way because Congress did not make the rules binding on the states. Rather, it conditioned the receipt of federal funds upon incorporation of the rule into each state's law. Most states have accepted the condition, largely through rulemaking by state child abuse agencies. The rules continue to be vigorously debated (Newman, 1989).

REFERENCES

Carter, B. S. (1993). Neonatologists and bioethics after Baby Doe. *Perinatol, 13*(2), 144–150.

Duff, R. S., & Campbell, A. G. M. (1973). Moral and ethical dilemmas in the special-care nursery. *New England Journal of Medicine, 289,* 890–894.

Federal Register. (1985, April 15). Child abuse and neglect prevention and treatment program; final rule. Model guidelines for health care providers to establish infant care review committees, *50,* 14878–14901.

Martin, D. A. (1989). Nurse's involvement in ethical decision-making with severely ill newborns. *Issues in Pediatric Nursing, 12*(6), 463–473.

Newman, S. A. (1989). Baby Doe, Congress and the states: Challenging the federal treatment standard for impaired infants. *American Journal of Law and Medicine, 15*(1), 1–60.

President's Commission for the Study of Ethical Problems in Medicine and Biomedical and Behavioral Research. (1983). *A report on the ethical, medical and legal issues in treatment decisions.* Washington, DC: Author.

Rhoden, N. K., & Arras, J. D. (1985). Withholding treatment from Baby Doe: From discrimination to child abuse. *Milbank Memorial Fund Quarterly/Health and Society, 63,* 27–50.

Vitiello, M. (1984). The Baby Jane Doe litigation and Section 504: An exercise in raw executive power. *Connecticut Law Review, 17,* 95–164.

CAROLE REITER GOTHELF
Hunter College
First edition

ELAINE FLETCHER-JANZEN
University of Northern Colorado
Second edition

LEGISLATION REGARDING THE HANDICAPPED
PARENTS OF THE HANDICAPPED

BACKWARD READERS

Backward readers is an archaic term that was commonly used in the first quarter of the twentieth century; its use gradually declined. The term still appears in the literature occasionally and as late as 1970 was one of the 50 most frequently appearing technical terms in psychological reports prepared by school psychologists. It is used far less frequently by teachers and psychologists in contemporary special education settings.

In its broadest usage, backward reader referred to anyone with a significant reading problem. The term was derived from the tendency of young children with reading problems to reverse letters and words. Many children will read *was* for *saw* and frequently confuse d, b, p, and q during the early stages of learning to read. If such reversals persist past the age of nine, they are highly significant as indicators of dyslexia. Such reversals have also been termed strephosymbolia. Applied in a technically correct sense, backward readers should only be used to refer to children who have reversal problems, though this specific meaning has been largely lost over the years. When encountering the term in evaluations, reports, or school records, it is a good idea to query the individual using the term to clarify the specific meaning intended. Backward readers has been found to be a frequently misinterpreted term in both educational and clinical settings.

CECIL R. REYNOLDS
Texas A & M University

DYSLEXIA
READING DISORDERS
STREPHOSYMBOLIA

BAER, DONALD M. (1931–)

Donald M. Baer received his BA degree in liberal arts from the University of Chicago in 1950 and his PhD in experimental psychology in 1957. He is currently with the Department of Human Development of the University of Kansas at Lawrence.

He is most noted for his work with retarded children and reinforcement of appropriate behavioral imitativeness. He has explored environmental situations in which retarded individuals can be taught imitation and language through the use of behavioral reinforcement and shaping techniques. He found that after reinforcement for appropriate imitation, generalization to similar situations was enhanced. Much of Baer's research has focused on the learning process as it relates to social and personal adaptation in young children. He has published more than 100 journal articles and edited several books, which address how societal and environmental influences are essential to the understanding of human development.

REFERENCES

Baer, D. M., & Pinkston, E. M. (Eds.). (1997). *Environment and behavior.* Boulder, CO: Westview.

Baer, D. M. et al. (1967). The development of imitation by reinforcing behavioral similarity to a model. *Journal of the Experimental Analysis of Behavior, 10,* 405–416.

Bijou, S. W., & Baer, D. M. (1978). *Behavior analysis of child development.* Englewood Cliffs, NJ: Prentice Hall.

RICK GONZALES
Texas A & M University
First edition

DEBORAH B. GUILLEN
The University of Texas of the Permian Basin
Second edition

BANDURA, ALBERT (1925–)

Albert Bandura is a David Starr Jordan Professor of Social Science in Psychology at Stanford University. He received his bachelor's degree from the University of British Columbia in 1949 and his PhD degree from the University of Iowa in 1952. After completing his doctorate, Bandura joined the faculty at Stanford University where he has remained throughout his career. He has served as the school's chairman of the Department of Psychology, and was honored by Stanford as the recipient of an endowed chair.

Albert Bandura

Influenced by K. L. Spence and the Hullian research tradition, Bandura is recognized as one of the founders of social learning theory. He proposes that human thought, affect, and behavior are strongly influenced by vicarious learning, and he is a proponent of social cognitive theory. This theory accords a central role to cognitive, vicarious, self-regulatory, and self-reflective processes in sociocognitive functioning. According to Bandura, psychology, through its research, bears an obligation to society for the betterment of humanity.

Bandura has authored nine books and countless articles on a wide range of issues in psychology. In addition, he serves on numerous editorial boards of journals and serials. His recent book, *Social Foundations of Thought and Action: A Social Cognitive Theory*, provides the conceptual framework for and analyzes the large body of knowledge bearing on social cognitive theory. *Self-Efficacy: The Exercise of Control*, his latest book, presents efficacy belief as the foundation of action, and in it Bandura asserts that unless people believe they can produce desired effects by their actions, they have little incentive to act. Other publications include *Social Learning and Personality Development*, *Social Learning Theory*, *Aggression: A Social Learning Analysis*, *Principles of Behavior Modification*, and *Psychological Modeling, Conflicting Theories*.

Bandura's contributions to psychology have been recognized in the honors and awards he has received. He was elected to the presidency of the American Psychological Association (APA) in 1974 and the Western Psychological Association in 1980. His numerous awards included the Distinguished Scientific Contributions Award of the American Psychological Association; the Distinguished Scientist Award, Division 12 of the APA; the William James Award for outstanding achievements in psychological science of the American Psychological Society; the Distinguished Contribution Award of the International Society for Re-

search on Aggression; and a Guggenheim Fellowship.

Bandura has been elected to the American Academy of Arts and Sciences and the Institute of Medicine of the National Academy of Sciences, and is the recipient of 11 honorary degrees. He has also served as chairman of the Board of Directors for the APA, trustee for the American Psychological Foundation, and chairman of the Western Psychological Association.

REFERENCES

Bandura, A. (1969). *Principles of behavior modification*. New York: Holt, Rinehart, & Winston.

Bandura, A. (1971). *Psychological modeling, conflicting theories*. Chicago: Aldine-Atherton.

Bandura, A. (1973). *Aggression: A social learning analysis*. Englewood Cliffs, NJ: Prentice Hall.

Bandura, A. (1977). *Social learning theory*. Englewood Cliffs, NJ: Prentice Hall.

Bandura, A. (1986). *Social foundations of thought and action: A social cognitive theory*. Englewood Cliffs, NJ: Prentice-Hall.

Bandura, A., & Walters, R. H. (1963). *Social learning and personality development*. New York: Holt, Rinehart, & Winston.

Bandura, A. (1997). *Self-efficacy: The exercise of control*. New York: Freeman & Company.

MARY LEON PEERY
Texas A & M University
First edition

TAMARA J. MARTIN
*The University of Texas of the
Permian Basin*
Second edition

SOCIAL LEARNING THEORY

BANNATYNE, ALEXANDER D. (1925–　　)

Alexander Bannatyne received his BA in education and philosophy at Auckland University in New Zealand in 1949. He obtained his PhD in psychology at the institute of Psychiatry at the University of London in 1953. As a professor, he taught on learning disabilities to doctoral students at the University of Illinois, 1566 to 1969.

Bannatyne's major areas of work are in dealing with learning-disabled children and their reading, writing, and spelling abilities. Bannatyne believes that to understand abnormal, one must be knowledgeable about what is normal. Only through presentation of the abnormal in conjunction with a knowledge of the normal can we work out what has gone wrong; only then do we have standards against which to measure degrees and types of abnormalities (Bannatyne, 1971). Bannatyne did studies on the relationships among learned and unlearned handedness, spelling ability, mirror imaging, motor functioning, balance, memory for designs, and auditory vocal sequencing in terms of hemispheric activity and dominance. He found that three types of brain functions may exist: (1) an efficient balanced brain associated with unlearned handedness, balance ability, and competent spelling; (2) a less verbally efficient right hemisphere dominant brain that seems to give mirror imaging, spatial competence, and left-handedness; and (3) a brain that is visuospatially inept even though it is not given to the drawing of mirror images.

Some of his major works include *Language, Reading, and Learning Disabilities, Bannatyne System: Reading, Writing and Spelling, Body Image,* and *How Children Can Learn to Live Rewarding Lives.*

REFERENCES

Bannatyne, A. D. (1971). *Language, reading, and learning disabilities.* Springfield, IL: Thomas.

Bannatyne, A. D. (1973a). *Body image: Communication program.* Lafayette, LA: Learning System.

Bannatyne, A. D. (1973b). *How children can learn to live rewarding lives.* Springfield, IL: Thomas.

Bannatyne, A. D. (1973c). *Reading: An auditory-vocal proceso.* San Rafael, CA: Academic Therapy.

Bannatyne, A. D. (1975). *Bannatyne system: Reading, writing, and spelling.* Lafayette, LA: Learning System.

ELIZABETH JONES
Texas A & M University

Jack I. Bardon

BARDON, JACK I. (1925–1993)

Jack I. Bardon earned his BA in psychology at Cleveland College of Western Reserve University in 1949, with a minor in education. He continued his professional education at the University of Pennsylvania, earning the MA in psychology in 1951 and a PhD in clinical psychology in 1956. From 1952 until 1958, Bardon was a school psychologist in the Princeton, New Jersey schools and served as coordinator of special education services from 1958 to 1960. In 1960 he became director of the Rutgers University doctoral program in school psychology with the academic rank of associate professor. He was promoted to professor in 1963 and became head of the department in 1968.

During his tenure at Rutgers, Bardon began to have an impact nationally on the delivery of school psychological services to handicapped children. His program in school psychology at Rutgers was one of the early pioneering programs in the field and, along with the University of Texas program, had a major influence on the development of doctoral schools of psychology. The Rutgers program reflected Bardon's own prominent, driving interest: to determine how the body of knowledge and the methods and techniques of psychology can be applied to the improvement of schooling generally, and to meeting the special needs of exceptional children in schools specifically. Bardon was instrumental in developing the primary role definitions of school psychologists (Bardon, 1982; Bardon & Bennett, 1974). Bardon was involved in work to help differentiate school psychology from other disciplines (Bardon, 1983). His work has benefited special education and regular education by improving the ability of school psychologists to provide services to children at all levels. In Bardon's most recent work (1992), he discussed the rationale for successes and failures in educational undertakings and how they relate to the field of school psychology.

Bardon left Rutgers in 1976 to accept a professorship at the University of North Carolina at Greensboro, where he became an Excellence Foundation Professor in 1983. Bardon was editor of the *Journal of School Psychology* from 1968 to 1971, was president of the Division of School Psychology of the American Psychological Association in 1969, and served on the board of directors of the American Orthopsychiatric Association from 1981 to 1984.

Jack Bardon retired from the University of North Carolina at Greensboro in 1991, and died in November, 1993. He worked hard throughout his career to apply psychological theory, principles, and practice to the field of education, and is credited by his colleagues with having made a substantial impact in the definition of school psychology, professional organizational issues, and in the debate over levels of training in school psychology.

REFERENCES

Bardon, J. I. (1992). Solving educational problems: Working across institutional, cultural and political differences. *School of Psychology Quarterly, 7,* 137–147.

Bardon, J. I. (1982). The psychology of school psychology. In C. R. Reynolds & T. B. Gutkin (Eds.), *The handbook of school psychology.* NY: Wiley.

Bardon, J. I. (1983). Psychology applied to education: A specialty in search of an identity. *American Psychologist, 38,* 185–196.

Bardon, J. I., & Bennett, V. C. (1974). *School psychology.* Englewood Cliffs, NJ: Prentice Hall.

CECIL R. REYNOLDS
Texas A & M University
First edition

DEBORAH B. GUILLEN
*The University of Texas of the
    Permian Basin*
Second edition

Natalie C. Barraga

BARRAGA, NATALIE C. (1915–   )

Natalie C. Barraga obtained her BA in home economics from North Texas State University in 1938; her MEd from the University of Texas, Austin, in 1957; and her EdD in special education for the visually handicapped from George Peabody College for Teachers in 1963. Barraga's entry into the study of the visually handicapped originated from a prior interest in child development and a concern for her daughter, who had a severe visual impairment. Years of teaching focused her objectives on those learners who had low vision. She experimented with ways to help students learn and read visually when they had a desire to do so.

Barraga's research documented that the use of vision (when impairment is present) is learned and not determined by acuity measurements, and that functional academic visual tasks could be taught with a sequential progressive learning program. She developed visual assessment tools and published a systematic instructional program, *Development of Efficiency in Visual Functioning.*

Professor emerita at the University of Texas at Austin, Barraga has published several books, monographs, assessment instruments, and articles. She has lectured extensively overseas, and maintains an interest in promoting interdisciplinary communication and an international exchange of information, especially with Third World countries.

Her publications include "Innovations in Teacher Education" (1981), reviewing trends associated with visually handicapped children; "Perspectives on Working with Visually Impaired Persons Worldwide" (1989), examining differences in philosophies of education; and "Infusion of Research and Practice into Personnel Preparation" (1990), discussing challenges related to personal preparation for the field of vision disabilities.

REFERENCES

Barraga, N. C. (1981). Innovations in teacher testing. *Journal of Visual Impairment & Blindness, 75,* 96–100.

Barraga, N. C. (1989). Perspectives on working with visually impaired persons worldwide: Looking forward. *Journal of Visual Impairment & Blindness, 83,* 84–87.

Barraga, N C. (1990). Infusion of research and practice into personnel preparation. *Peabody Journal of Education, 67,* 10–21.

ELAINE FLETCHER-JANZEN
University of Northern Colorado
First edition

TAMARA J. MARTIN
*The University of Texas of the
    Permian Basin*
Second edition

BARRIER-FREE EDUCATION

The delivery of special education services to all handicapped children in the least restrictive environment means that school buildings and facilities must be designed or altered to make those services accessible. Barrier-free design standards typically give technical specifications that cover building entrances and exits, parking, curbs, stairs, elevators, lavatories, drinking fountains, hazard warnings, and building elements and fixtures. In both new construction and modifications of existing facilities, buildings may be subject to a variety of definitions and design standards (Redden, 1979). In 1973, the American National Standards Institute (ANSI) criteria were cited in the regulations for Section 504 of the Rehabilitation Act of 1973 as the minimum access standard to assure compliance with nondiscrimination provisions. The design standards set forth in the Uniform Federal Accessibility Standards (UFAS, 1984) generally were consistent with federal standards in effect, major model building codes, and most state and local codes; they were based on ANSI A117.1-1980. The 1984 UFAS criteria were geared to adult dimensions and anthropometrics. Some states, however, developed design guidelines for special education facilities that considered the total learning environment for children with all types of handicaps (Abend, et al., 1979). A barrier-free environment require the removal of all architectural barriers to accessibility (Redden, 1979). It should be noted that the regulations for Section 504 (which were applicable to recipients of funds from the U.S. Department of Education or Health and Human Services) did not require barrier-free environments. Section 504 required "program accessibility"—that is, a recipient's program or activity, when viewed in its entirety, was to be readily accessible to and usable by handicapped persons. Access to each facility was not required. While the program accessibility standard could be achieved by a number of effective methods, including structural changes, priority was to be given to methods that provide the most integrated setting appropriate. Under Section 504, it was not permissible to isolate handicapped students in a single accessible building.

The passage of the Americans with Disabilities Act of 1990 (ADA) substantially supported the intent of accessibility spelt out in Section 504. Title II of the ADA did not impose any major new requirements on school districts because school districts received federal funds and were required to provide accessibility under Section 504 as far back as 1973. However, as the ADA expanded nondiscriminatory protection to school students, it also took precedent over any lesser stringent rules in Section 504. The ADA reiterated that

"A school district must ensure that students with disabilities are not excluded from participation in, or denied the benefits of, its services, programs, and activities. It must also ensure that they are not subjected to discrimination by the school system." (Office for Civil Rights, p. 45).

The ADA provided new guidelines and self-evaluation surveys based on the Americans with Disabilities Act Accessibility Guidelines for Buildings and Facilities (ADAAG) (U.S. Department of Education, 1996).

The Office for Civil Rights (OCR) enforces Title II of the ADA and Section 504 of the Rehabilitation Act of 1973. The OCR investigates complaints filed by individuals or their representatives, who believe that they have been discriminated against because of a disability. The OCR can be reached at U.S. Department of Education, Office for Civil Rights, 330 C Street, S.W., Room 5000, Washington, D.C. 20202. Their telephone is (202) 205-5413 and TDD number is (800) 358-8247.

In addition, an internet resource designed to accommodate specific disabilities that can help teachers, parents, and students overcome educational obstacles is called "Barrier Free Education." The creators of the web site initiated the internet resource because they believe that "the academic community has a responsibility to take a leadership role in making accessible environments a reality" (Ira, 1998).

REFERENCES

Abend, A. C., Bedner, M. J., Froehlinger, V. J., & Stenzler, Y. (1979). *Facilities for special educational services: A guide for planning new and renovated schools.* Reston, VA: Council for Exceptional Children.

Ira, V. (1998). Barrier free education. *The Exceptional Parent, 28,* 30.

Redden, M. R. (Ed.). (1979). *Assuring access for the handicapped.* San Francisco: Jossey-Bass.

Uniform Federal Accessibility Standards. (1984, August 7). 49 F.R. 31528-31621.

U.S. Department of Education, Office for Civil Rights. (1996). Compliance with the Americans with Disabilities Act: A self evaluation guide for Public Elementary and Secondary Schools. Washington, DC: U.S. Government Printing Office.

SHIRLEY A. JONES
*Virginia Polytechnic Institute
and State University*
First edition

ELAINE FLETCHER-JANZEN
University of Northern Colorado
Second edition

ACCESSIBILITY OF BUILDINGS
ACCESSIBILITY OF PROGRAMS
AMERICANS WITH DISABILITIES ACT OF 1990

BARRIERS, ARCHITECTURAL

See ARCHITECTURAL BARRIERS.

BARSCH, RAY H. (1917–   )

Ray H. Barsch earned his BA in special education in 1950 and MEd in school psychology in 1952 from the University of Wisconsin, Milwaukee. He went on to receive his PhD in educational psychology from Northwestern University in 1959 under the direction of Claude Mathis, Paul Witty, and Helmer Myklebust.

Barsch is principally known for his development of a curriculum called movigenics, a theory of movement developed from "the study of origin and development of patterns of movement in man and the relationship of those movements to his learning efficiency." He regards movigenics as "orientation—a cognitive map to guide practitioners toward a goal of practical synthesis" (Barsch, 1976).

As an ardent supporter of interdisciplinary approaches to assessment and teaching in special education, Barsch defines learning disabilities as a concept that focuses on learning rather than "a frantic but seldom fruitful effort to delineate a uniform and specific set of characteristics" (Barsch, 1976).

Barsch became a professor in the department of special education at California State University, Northridge in 1970, and in the division for continuing education at the University of Santa Clara. Among other positions and consultantships, Barsch directed teacher preparation programs in the department of counseling and behavioral studies at the University of Wisconsin (1963–1966) and the Easter Seal Development Center in Milwaukee, Wisconsin (1950–1964).

From the early 1970s to the early 1980s, Barsch was a professor in the School of Education at the California State University, Northridge. He also directed the Ray Barsch Center for Learning, where he specialized in one-on-one therapy for children with specific learning problems and counseled parents. In addition, he has supervised the development of the Special Education Teacher Program in Ventura, California, as well as the training of graduate students in various evaluation and therapy techniques.

His (1995) book, *Fine Tuning: An Auditory-Visual Training Program,* describes exercises for developing students' listening skills, and a 1992 reprint in the *Journal of Learning Disabilities* of Barsch's article, "Perspectives on Learning Disabilities," has generated substantial debate, highlighting the absence of progress in defining, classifying, and providing appropriate interventions for learning disabilities. This piece, originally published in 1968, examines learning disabilities from the perspective of history, viewing them as a concept rather than a category, promoting interdisciplinary convergence, evaluating various delivery systems, and noting a new recognition of human divergence.

Of his many awards, in 1974 Barsch received the International Milestone Award of the International Federation of Learning Disabilities at its world congress in the Netherlands.

REFERENCES

Barsch, R. H. (1976). *Achieving perceptual motor efficiency: A space oriented approach to learning* (Vol. 1). Seattle, WA: Special Child.

Barsch, R. H. (1992). Perspectives on learning disabilities: The vectors of a new convergence. *Journal of Learning Disabilities, 25,* 6–16.

Barsch, R. H. (1995). *Fine tuning: An auditory-visual training program.* Novato, California: Academic Therapy.

ELAINE FLETCHER-JANZEN
University of Northern Colorado
First edition

TAMARA J. MARTIN
*The University of Texas of the
   Permian Basin*
Second edition

BASC

See BEHAVIOR ASSESSMENT SYSTEM FOR CHILDREN.

BASAL READERS

Basal reader programs are comprehensive, meaningfully sequenced collections of stories, frequently arranged in groups according to a central theme or topic. Smith and Johnson (1980) described these programs as being based on the belief that a controlled vocabulary of high-frequency words, coupled with the presentation of easily decodable pattern words, facilitates learning to read and the improvement of reading skills.

Basal reader programs are intended to be used to instruct children from the stage of nonreading, through the acquisition of developing skills, to the level of mature, flexible reading. Typically, these programs include various correlated and supplementary materials including teachers' manuals, workbooks, skills sheets, activity boxes, criterion-referenced monitoring systems, and even computer software management programs. This self-contained aspect of basal reader programs is intended to provide all that is necessary for a core reading program. Teachers are carefully guided through instructional directed reading activities as outlined in the accompanying manuals. The structure of these lesson plans, explained by both Stauffer (1969) and Harris (1970), follows the sequence of prereading preparation, guided silent reading, oral rereading and comprehension assessment, skill development activities, and enrichment. In addition, teachers are usually provided with suggestions for choosing related books and other materials to use in conjunction with the basal reader. A survey of 500 educators by Bauman and Heubach in 1996 found that teachers believed that these materials have an empowering effect by providing additional instructional ideas to draw from, adapt, or extend (Bauman & Heubach, 1996).

Of course, the reading books themselves constitute the essential materials in any basal program. Usually there is a set of readiness materials for use with children at the beginning stages of reading instruction. These are followed by readers considered to be at the preprimer and primer levels of difficulty. The readers contain a limited number of frequently repeated words that assist in the development of a basic sight vocabulary. These basic reading books are followed by progressively more difficult readers extending through all the elementary grades and frequently into the middle and junior high grades as well. Many of these higher level basal readers consist of comprehensive literary anthologies and, according to Ringler and Weber (1984), may include a variety of narrative types such as realistic fiction, fantasy, science fiction, folklore, poetry, and plays.

In recent years basal readers have been analyzed in terms of cultural competence. Foley and Boulware (1996) found that gender equity reflected in basal readers has not essentially changed since the 1960s. In addition, analyses of basal readers regarding race and ethnicity indicate that these aspects of culture are omitted from the majority of basal texts. The omission of race and/or ethnicity from basal selections and teacher manuals may not meet the needs of many children (McDermott, 1997). Other criticisms of basal readers suggest that publisher censorship still exists and essential components of literary works are being eliminated by widespread anthologization (Reutzel & Larsen, 1995). However, others (Risner & Nicholson, 1996) applaud the addition of questions to the readers that support higher levels of comprehension than previously found. Therefore, research still suggests that basal readers support the development of additional teacher materials and engaging activities that, in turn, elevate student reading comprehension. Cultural competence appears to be the most important future development for basal readers.

REFERENCES

Bauman, J. F., & Heubach, K. M. (1996). Do basal readers deskill teachers? A national survey of educator's use and opinions of basals. *Elementary School Journal, 96,* 511–526.

Foley, C. L., & Boulware, B. J. (1996). Gender equity in 1990 middle school basal readers. *Reading Improvement, 33,* 220–223.

Harris, A. J. (1970). *How to increase reading ability* (5th ed.). New York: McKay.

McDermott, P. (1997). The illusion of racial diversity in contemporary basal readers: An analysis of teacher manuals. Evaluative/feasibility report: speech/conference paper. Abstract from: ERIC Item No. ED407473.

Reutzel, D. R., & Larsen, N. S. (1995). Look what they've done to real children's books in the new basal readers. *Language Arts, 72,* 495–507.

Ringler, L. H., & Weber, C. K. (1984). *A language-thinking approach to reading.* New York: Harcourt Brace Jovanovich.

Risner, G. P., & Nicholson, J. I. (1996). *The new basal readers: What levels of comprehension do they promote? Evaluative/feasibility report.* (ERIC Item No. ED403546)

Smith, R. J., & Johnson, D. D. (1980). *Teaching children to read* (2nd ed.). Reading, MA: Addison-Wesley.

Stauffer, R. G. (1969). *Directing reading maturity as a cognitive process.* New York: Harper & Row.

JOHN M. EELLS
Souderton Area School District,
Souderton, Pennsylvania
First edition

ELAINE FLETCHER-JANZEN
University of Northern Colorado
Second edition

READING DISORDERS
READING REMEDIATION

BASELINE DATA

A baseline measurement occurs prior to the beginning of an intervention. It involves precise counting of the target behavior (i.e., dependent variable) during whatever current conditions exist. A common misconception is that baseline data can only be gathered in the absence of any intervention. This is not true. Baselines are measures of behavior under current conditions. If these conditions are not ones in which there is no intervention, then this information should be stated in the program outline. If there is an informal intervention that currently is ongoing (e.g., telling a child to "stop"), then this response should continue. If one were to attempt to stop intervening with a behavior and then take baseline data, that person would be defeating the purpose of the baseline procedure because removing the intervention procedure acts as an intervention itself. Data gathered during this time would be intervention data and different from those that were representative of the behavior during the condition in which the behavior became important enough to the practitioner to attempt intervention aided by data collection.

Baselines are meant to be representative measures of the target behavior. As such they should also be reliable and valid. Reliability should be scored by having two persons simultaneously record the data and by comparing those data records using different calculation procedures (e.g., Kappa), dependent on which recording technique was used (e.g., momentary time sampling) and the properties of the data. Validity, in its simplest form, requires that a measure be that which was purported. If after writing the behavioral definition of the target behavior the definition was compared to the behavior to determine whether the behavior written was that which the student exhibited, the primary form of validation would be completed. If the definition is given to another person and he or she is asked whether the written definition was observable in he student's behavior, and if that person found it to be so, the second form of validation would be completed.

Baseline data should be stable prior to the initiation of intervention. Stability is said to have occurred when there is an absence of directionality or trend in the data and when there is restricted variation in the pattern of the data. Trend is said to occur when there are three or more data points patterned in a specific direction. This is also referred to as celeration and is illustrated by data that accelerated or decelerated. Baseline data that are either accelerating or decelerating are generally not useful as preintervention data. The trend in the data suggests that there is already something that is influencing the target behavior. However, when the trend is countertherapeutic (i.e., moving in the undesired direction), the need for protracted baseline data collection is negated. Therefore, if the trend of the baseline data is therapeutic, continuation of the baseline is indicated until such time as the behavior becomes acceptable or until it levels off and becomes stable. If the data are countertherapeutic, this is not necessary and intervention can be begun in 5 to 10 sessions or days.

Variability in the data during baseline in the absence of a significant trend must be measured by examining its degree to determine its effect on the baseline. Baseline data should be stable so that the practitioner can say with reasonable certainty that the target behavior occurred in a specific condition prior to intervention. Stability is measured as the degree of variability about the mean. In research and teaching with humans we would look for +/– 50% variability about the baseline mean (Alberto & Troutman, 1982). For example, if we gathered 10 days of baseline data and then summed each day's score and divided by 10 we would have the mean of the baseline. If this mean were 40%, then all data should fall between 60% and 20% during the baseline as that is the range established by the +/– 50% rule. A single (or perhaps 2) data point(s) falling outside this range could be judged to be an oddity; it should not hamper the identification of these data as

stable. However, more than this number would indicate a lack of stability and a longer baseline would be required. Baseline stability or countertherapeutic trend is a basic requirement prior to the initiation of intervention programming.

REFERENCE

Alberto, P. A., & Troutman, A. C. (1982). *Applied behavior analysis for teachers.* Columbus, OH: Merrill.

LYLE E. BARTON
Kent State University

APPLIED BEHAVIOR ANALYSIS
BEHAVIOR MODIFICATION

BASE RATE

A base rate is a baseline measurement of a target behavior's rate of responding. This measurement is useful when the student's behavior of interest is one for which frequency recording is the appropriate recording strategy and for which rate of responding is the appropriate datum. The latter case is true when the response frequency dependent on duration of observation is important. For example, should the target behavior be either units of "X" assembled in a workshop or incidences of aggressive behavior, frequency would be an appropriate recording strategy. If, in addition, the issue of importance is this number within a specified time frame, then rate of response becomes the appropriate datum. If this period of observation tends to vary, then rate of response is the only appropriate datum. Therefore, the special education practitioner would record the frequency of student response and then divide the frequency by the number of minutes (or hours) of observation. The resultant figure (e.g., 1.56, 0.75, 0.05) would be indicative of the relative frequency of responding per unit of measurement (e.g., minutes, hours) and would be reported as rate per minute (rpm) or rate per hour (rph).

To determine the base rate, these data would be gathered over a period of days or sessions and would be examined to meet the criterion for stability for any baseline data; that is, the data must be stable (have limited variability) or countertherapeutic. Stability is said to occur when the data vary no more than +/– 50% of the baseline mean (Alberto & Troutman, 1982). A countertherapeutic trend is said to occur when the data are not stable but moving in the opposite direction. Base-rate data are usually reported as a mean figure (e.g., "the mean base rate was. . ."), however, these data may be reported as including the range and the usual data display via a graph.

REFERENCE

Alberto, P. A., & Troutman, A. C. (1982). *Applied behavior analysis for teachers.* Columbus, OH: Merrill.

Lyle E. Barton
Kent State University

APPLIED BEHAVIOR ANALYSIS
BEHAVIOR MODIFICATION

BASIC SKILLS TRAINING

Historically, the term "basic skills" refers to the traditional disciplines of reading, writing, and arithmetic that are stressed in the early years of formal education. These areas of study are those that are seen as necessary for an individual to become a contributing member of society. Without at least a rudimentary proficiency in these basic areas, individuals experience difficulty in developing independence and self-esteem.

The exceptional child or adult, however, may require a completely different type of basic skill training than the traditional disciplines deemed necessary for normal functioning within society. Depending on the severity of the handicapping condition, basic skills for special education may vary little or greatly from those of regular students and adults. Basic skills training for exceptional children could best be termed those activities and subject areas that provide for each child's individual learning abilities (allowing for his or her weaknesses) in such a way that deviation from the norm is as limited as possible. This training allows children to accomplish what Blake (1981) refers to as "cultural tasks," in which needs are met through means that are acceptable to society.

Specifically, basic skills for the exceptional child might include those skills noted by Berdine and Blackhurst (1981): training in attention skills, increased memory capacity, the ability to transfer and generalize recently learned skills, and language. In addition, study skills, self-management skills and computer competence are needed as basic skills. Therefore, for the special education student, the basic skills required for academic success are more process-orientated than for regular education students.

In recent years, inclusive programming has sought to assist the special education student in the acquisition of basic skills. Instead of pulling special education students out of the content classes, they have remained with specialized assistance (McCollum & Tindal, 1996). Unfortunately, little data exists to support the effectiveness of this programming for basic content skills at this time.

There is some evidence that computer assisted learning takes place by online computer services. These services assist high school special education students enter career-focused activities that require basic processing skills that reflect organization, problem-solving, and attention.

REFERENCES

Berdine, W. H., & Blackhurst, A. E. (1981). *An introduction to special education.* Boston: Little, Brown.

Blake, K. A. (1981). *Educating exceptional pupils: An introduction to contemporary practices.* Reading, MA: Addison-Wesley.

McCollum, S., & Tindal, G. (1996). Supporting students in content areas classes using an outcome-based system of collaboration. *Special Services in the Schools, 12,* 1–17.

353 Project (1996). *Advancing basic skills through the use of online services 1995–1996 special 353 project.* (ERIC Item No. ED402488)

James H. Miller
University of New Orleans
First edition

Elaine Fletcher-Janzen
University of Northern Colorado
Second edition

BASIC EDUCATIONAL SKILLS INVENTORY—DIAGNOSTIC
FUNCTIONAL DOMAINS
FUNCTIONAL INSTRUCTION

BATEMAN, BARBARA (1933–   )

Barbara Bateman received her BA (1954) in psychology from the University of Washington, her MA (1958) from San Francisco State College, and her PhD in special education (1962) from the University of Illinois. In the early years of her professional career, she taught mentally retarded and emotionally disturbed blind children at Washington State Hospital and a variety of exceptional children in the Oregon public schools. Bateman continued in the field teaching at the university level and became professor of education at the University of Oregon in 1969.

She has always been a strong advocate of direct instruction, and has urged the field of education to accept the direct instructional philosophy, methods, and materials in publications such as *Essentials of Teaching* (1971) and *Teaching Reading to Learning Disabled and Other Hard-to-Teach Children* (1979). In the 1970s, Bateman's interests broadened to the legal aspects of special education; she received her JD from the University of Oregon Law School in 1976, and has published on law and special education including her recent publication, *Better IEPs.*

Barbara Bateman

REFERENCES

Bateman, B. (1971). *Essentials of teaching.* Sioux Falls, SD: Adapt Press.

Bateman, B. (1979). Teaching reading to learning disabled and other hard-to-teach children. In L. Resnick & P. Weaver (Eds.), *Theory and practice of early reading.* Hillsdale, NJ: Erlbaum.

Bateman, B. D. (1996). *Better IEPs.* Longmont, CO: Sopris West.

STAFF

BATTERED CHILD SYNDROME

In 1962, pediatrician C. Henry Kempe published an article entitled "The Battered Child Syndrome." This marked the first official recognition by the medical establishment of the problem of child abuse. Kempe's article focused on abuse as a deliberate, violent attack on a child by a malicious adult and criticized the medical profession for failing to diagnose and report such cases. Child abuse is a broad term currently used to describe incidents of violent attack, neglect, or sexual abuse that may result in psychological and behavioral disturbances as well as physical or even life-threatening injury. Ellerstein (1981) states that between 1 and 3% of children in the United States are abused. Figures vary depending on laws governing reporting and definitions of child abuse. Indeed, the incidence of severe violence against children declined in the mid to late 1980s. Possible reasons cited for the lower rate were an increased reluctance to report, differences in the methods of study, years of prevention and treatment efforts, and effects of changes in American society and family patterns that produce lower rates of violence towards children (Gelles & Straus, 1987). However, regardless of decline, about 4,000 children die each year as a result of abuse.

Researchers have investigated several factors associated with child abuse. Various models, each emphasizing the importance of particular factors, have been formulated to explain the phenomenon. The psychopathological model focuses on the personality characteristics of the perpetrator. Attributes such as personal history of abuse, low self-esteem, and inability to cope with frustration are seen as important contributing factors (Gil, 1970). In the sociological model, environmental factors such as poverty, acceptance of corporal punishment, and overcrowding in the home receive emphasis (Gil, 1970). The cognitive-behavioral model takes into account style of responding to stress and the belief systems of abusive parents (Green, 1984). A broader model encompassing the preceding elements and accounting for the significance of interactions between parents and children is referred to as the ecological model (Roscoe et al., 1985).

Investigators have found that some children are more likely than others to become victims of child abuse. Children at increased risk for abuse often come from larger than average families, have low birth weights or were premature as infants, and fail to form attachment bonds with a caregiver. A comparison of incidence rates suggests that age, family income, and ethnicity were risk factors for both sexual and physical abuse. Gender was a risk factor for sexual abuse but not physical abuse (Cappelleri, Echenrode, & Powers, 1993). Males are more likely to be abused, as are handicapped, retarded, and otherwise different or difficult children (Newberger, 1982).

Kempe's early article on the battered child syndrome achieved considerable public notoriety and drew the attention of legislators, resulting in the passage of mandatory reporting of child abuse in all 50 states. Physicians and other health professionals are legally required to report suspected child abuse. Additionally, most states require other professionals having contact with children to report suspected cases of abuse. These professionals include teachers, social workers, and child-care workers.

In 1997, child protection professionals were surveyed regarding their opinions about the best papers and chapters on child abuse available. Kempe's 1962 article was cited as one of the best resources on child abuse and a seminal work (Oates & Donnelly, 1997).

REFERENCES

Cappelleri, J. C., Echenrode, J., & Powers, J. L. (1993). The epidemiology of child abuse: Findings from the second national incidence and prevalence study of child abuse and neglect. *American Journal of Public Health, 83,* 1622–1624.

Ellerstein, N. S. (Ed.). (1981). *Child abuse and neglect: A medical reference.* New York: Wiley.

Gil, D. (1975). Unraveling child abuse. *American Journal of Orthopsychiatry, 45,* 345–356.

Green, A. (1984). Child maltreatment: Recent studies and future directions. *Journal of the American Academy of Child Psychiatry, 23,* 675–678.

Kempe, C. H. (1962). The battered child syndrome. *Journal of the American Medical Association, 181,* 17–24.

Newberger, E. H. (Ed.). (1982). *Child abuse.* Boston: Little, Brown.

Oates, R. K., & Donnelly, A. C. (1997). Influential papers in child abuse. *Child Abuse and Neglect, 21,* 319–326.

Roscoe, B., Callahan, J., & Peterson, K. (1985). Who is responsible? Adolescents' acceptance of theoretical child abuse models. *Adolescence, 20,* 188–197.

BERNICE ARRICALE
Hunter College
First edition

ELAINE FLETCHER-JANZEN
University of Northern Colorado
Second edition

CHILD ABUSE
CHILD CARE AGENCIES
CHILD CARETAKER

BAUMEISTER, ALFRED A. (1934–   )

Born in Fairbanks, Alaska, Alfred A. Baumeister received his BA from the University of Alaska (1957) and his MA (1959) and PhD (1961) in psychology from George Peabody College. He is presently a professor at Vanderbilt University and George Peabody College, and directs the John F. Kennedy Center for Research on Education and Human Development at Vanderbilt University.

Baumeister has presented over 150 papers and published over 200 original investigations, literature reviews, and theoretical reports, many of which are concerned with learning and memory processes among mentally retarded children. He found that there are quantitative and structural differences in the short-term information processing capabilities of retarded and nonretarded subjects (Baumeister, Runcie, & Gardepe, 1984). Another major effort has been directed at understanding the treatment of aberrant behavior such as stereotyped movements and self-injurious actions.

Baumeister has been active in the improvement of psychological services to the mentally retarded. He has written about the role of the psychologist in public institutions (Baumeister & Hillsinger, 1984) and has served as a consultant to several state and federal agencies. He is a member of the Psychology Review Committee for the Joint Committee of the Accreditation of Hospitals.

Baumeister has been president of both the American Academy on Mental Retardation and the Division of Mental Retardation of the American Psychological Association.

Alfred A. Baumeister

For several years, he served as a witness before the U.S. House and Senate appropriations subcommittees. He has received awards for research contributions from the American Association on Mental Deficiency (1979) and the American Academy on Mental Retardation (1986). He continues to publish on a variety of special education topics (Baumeister, 1996; 1997).

REFERENCES

Baumeister, A. A., & Bacharach, V. R. (1996). A critical analysis of the infant health and development program. *Intelligence, 23*(2), 79–104.

Baumeister, A. A., Bacharach, V. R., Baumeister, Alan A. (1997). "Big" versus "little" science: Comparative analysis of program projects and individual research grants. *American Journal on Mental Retardation, 102*(3), 211–227.

Baumeister, A. A., & Hillsinger, L. B. (1984). The role of psychologists in public institutions for the mentally retarded revisited. *Professional Psychology, 15,* 134–141.

Baumeister, A. A., Runcie, D., & Gardepe, J. (1984). Processing of information in iconic memory: Differences between normal and retarded subjects. *Journal of Abnormal Psychology, 93,* 433–447.

E. VALERIE HEWITT
Texas A & M University

BAYLEY SCALES OF INFANT DEVELOPMENT— SECOND EDITION

The Bayley Scales of Infant Development—Second Edition (BSID-II; Bayley, 1993) is an individually administered test of developmental functioning. It is designed to be administered to infants and children between the ages of 1 month through 42 months. The first edition of the BSID (BSID; Bayley, 1969) was derived from several scales of infant development including the California First-Year Mental Scale (Bayley, 1933a), the California Preschool Mental Scale (Jaffa, 1934), and the California Infant Scale of Motor Development (Bayley, 1936). The revision of the Bayley Scales includes restandardization to update the norms, extending the age range (formerly ranged from 2 to 30 months), and addressing the shift in interest among clinicians and researchers from assessing normal infants to assessing high risk and developmentally delayed infants. However, a majority of the content of the BSID was retained; items were added to expand the age range and content coverage. Items were changed or deleted if they were considered difficult to administer, identified as biased against racial/ethnic groups, or were redundant with other items.

The BSID-II consists of three scales: the Mental Scale, Motor Scale, and Behavior Rating Scale, formerly called the Infant Behavior Record in the first edition of the Bayley Scales. The Mental Scale assesses the child's current level of cognitive, language, and personal social development and includes items that measure memory, problem solving, early number concepts, generalization, classification, vocalizations, language, and social skills. The Motor Scale measures the child's level of gross and fine motor development via items associated with crawling, sitting, standing, walking, and so on, for gross motor movement and items related to the use of writing, grasping, and imitation of hand movements for fine motor movement. The Behavior Rating Scale is completed by the examiner regarding the child's behaviors during the test administration and assesses the child's attention/arousal (for children under 6 months of age), orientation/engagement toward the tasks and the examiner, emotional regulation, and quality of motor movement. The Mental and Motor Scales each yield a raw score that is converted to a standard score ($M = 100$, $SD = 15$) to determine the child's Mental Developmental Index (MDI) and Psychomotor Developmental Index (PDI), respectively. Also provided are four descriptive categories ranging from Accelerated Performance to Significantly Delayed Performance. The Behavior Rating Scale yields percentile ranks and three classifications (Non-Optimal, Questionable, and Within Normal Limits), but no standard scores.

Both the Mental and Motor Scales combined take between 25 and 60 minutes to administer, with estimated time for children under age 15 months between 25 and 35 minutes. To determine which items to administer to a child, sets of items, called "item sets," are specified depending upon the child's chronological age or, under certain circumstances, upon the child's current level of functioning. Therefore, traditional basal and ceiling rules are not used (e.g., five consecutive failures for ceiling). Instead, if a child has at least 5 correct items and at least 3 failed items in the item set, the item set is considered to be an appropriate set of items for that child.

The BSID-II was standardized on a sample of 1,700 children, including 100 children (50 boys and 50 girls) in each of the 17 age groups between 1 month and 42 months of age. Data from the 1988 U.S. Census Bureau was used to stratify the sample on the following variables: age, gender, race/ethnicity, geographic region, and parent education variables. The BSID-II Manual (Bayley, 1993) contains specific characteristics of the sample. Data regarding reliability and validity of the BSID-II appear to be good and are described in detail in two chapters of the BSID-II Manual. However, BRS stability coefficients are consistently lower than coefficients for the Mental and Motor scales. This is addressed in the BSID-II Manual.

The BSID-II, like its predecessor, is likely the most widely used scale of infant development. Its primary use remains as a classification tool to describe normal child development and identify children with developmental delays. Several strengths of the BSID-II are important to mention. First, items are based from a wide range of theory and research on infant development. Second, it has the best, most updated norms of the available scales for assessing very young children. Last, it offers flexible administration of items, yet still allowing examiners to follow standardized procedures. Thus, while there is a specified set of items to administer, the order in which one administers the items can be modified, which helps to maintain the child's attention and rapport during the testing. The most notable limitations of the BSID-II include the following: (1) Many of the items require either expressive language or a good understanding of spoken language for success. However, many high risk and developmentally delayed young children have speech and/or language delays or impairments, making it difficult to assess their cognitive abilities using the BSID-II. (2) Mental and Motor Development Indices do not go below 50. Therefore, only mild mental retardation can be accurately assessed. (3) Noted by Dunst (1998) is "the implicit assertion that the scales have value for developing Individualized Family Service Plans (IFSPs). . . ." However, he notes that the Bayley Scales have not demonstrated treatment utility and they "are not appropriate as instruments for identifying behavior goals for intervention." Thus, although the BSID-II has diagnostic utility and is an excellent measure for assessing infant development, it should not be used to plan specific interventions.

REFERENCES

Bayley, N. (1933). *The California First-Year Mental Scale*. Berkeley: University of California Press.

Bayley, N. (1936). *The California Infant Scale of Motor Development.* Berkeley: University of California Press.

Bayley, N. (1969). *Manual for the Bayley Scales of Infant Development.* San Antonio, TX: Psychological Corporation.

Bayley, N. (1993). *Bayley Scales of Infant Development—Second Edition Manual.* San Antonio, TX: Psychological Corporation.

Dunst, C. J. (1998). Bayley Scales of Infant Development, Second Edition. In J. C. Impara & B. S. Plake (Eds.), *The Thirteenth Mental Measurements Yearbook.* Lincoln, NE: Buros Institute of Mental Measurements.

Jaffa, A. S. (1934). *The California Preschool Mental Scale.* Berkeley: University of California Press.

DEBRA BROADBOOKS
*California School of
Professional Psychology*

BECHTEREV (BEKHTIAREV) VLADIMIR M. (1857–1927)

Vladimir M. Bechterev was born in Viatka province, Russia. He was a noted physiologist and neuropathologist and the founder of the School of Reflexology. He was also the founder of the first Russian experimental psychological laboratory at the University of Kazan. Bechterev obtained his PhD at the Military Medical Academy in St. Petersburg (Petrograd, now Leningrad) in 1881. He continued postgraduate studies at the universities of Leipzig, Berlin, and Paris. At Leipzig he became familiar with the work of Wilhelm Wundt, considered to be the founder of experimental psychology. In 1885 Bechterev became professor at the University of Kazan and in 1893, professor at the Military Medical Academy. The same year he began to publish a journal, *Neurological Review.* Bechterev was also interested in the education of exceptional children. His work in this area is referred to as pedagogical reflexology. In 1911 he addressed the International Congress of Pedology in Brussels, Belgium. His pioneering work contributed immensely toward the future development of Soviet defectology.

Bechterev made an important contribution to the knowledge of anatomy and physiology of the nervous system. He conducted research on localization function of the brain and became famous for his work on nerve currents. He also identified the layer of fibers in the cerebral cortex known as Bechterev's fibers.

Bechterev was a prolific writer who produced over 135 publications and papers, including *General Principles of Reflexology* (1918) and *Objective Psychology* (1913).

REFERENCES

Bechterev, V. M. (1913). *Objective psychologie oder psycho-reflexologia.* Leipzig/Berlin: Verlag Teubner.

Bechterev, V. M. (1918). *Obshtchie osnovi reflexologii* (General principles of reflexology). St. Petersburg.

Debus, A. G. (Ed.). (1968). *World who's who in science.* Chicago: Marquis.

Prokhorov, A. M. (Ed.). (1970). *Bolshaya Sovetskay Entsyklopedia* (Major Soviet encyclopedia) (3rd ed.). Moscow: Soviet Encyclopedia Publishing.

IVAN Z. HOLOWINSKY
Rutgers University

BECKER, WESLEY C. (1928–   )

A native of Rochester, New York, Wesley C. Becker received his BA (1951), MA (1953), and PhD (1955) from Stanford University in psychology, statistics, and learning theory, respectively. Originally a child clinical psychologist, Becker's initial research interest was in how behavior problems and personality characteristics develop as a function of parental child-rearing practices. This developed into an interest in applications of behavior analysis to changing parent and child behaviors. His book, *Parents Are Teachers,* has been published in German, Portuguese, and Spanish. Becker's interest shifted to applications of behavior analysis to teachers and problem students (Becker, 1986; Becker, Engelmann & Thomas, 1975). In the late 1960s, he became interested in effective instructional practices, especially as they applied to hard-to-teach children. This is still his major interest, but he has become more active in disseminating research findings on effective instructional practices; such as the direct instruction (DI) follow-through model and its long-term effects on students (Becker, 1984; Gersten, Keating & Becker, 1991).

Becker has been a member of Phi Beta Kappa and a consultant to the Australian Association for Direct Instruction and has been included in *Who's Who in America.*

REFERENCES

Becker, W. C. (1986). *Applied psychology for teachers: A behavioral cognitive approach.* Chicago: Science Research Associates.

Becker, W. C. (1984, March 18–23). *Direct Instruction—A Twenty year review.* Paper presented at the 16th Annual Banff International Conference on Behavioral Science Honoring B. F. Skinner's 80th birthday.

Becker, W. C., Engelmann, S., & Thomas, D. R. (1975). *Teaching 1: Classroom management.* Palo Alto, CA: Science Research Associates.

Becker, W. C. (1971). *Parents are teachers.* Champaign, IL: Research.

Gersten, R., Keating, T., & Becker, W. C. (1991). The continued impact of the direct instructional model: Longitudinal studies of follow through students. *Education & Treatment of Children, 11*(4), 318–327.

E. Valerie Hewitt
Texas A & M University
First edition

Deborah B. Guillen
The University of Texas of the Permian Basin
Second edition

BEERS, CLIFFORD W. (1876–1943)

Clifford W. Beers founded the mental hygiene movement following 3 years as a patient in mental hospitals in Connecticut in the early part of the twentieth century. Because of the abuses that he suffered, he left the hospital determined to reform the system, to see harsh custodial care replaced with medical treatment. His book, *A Mind that Found Itself,* published in 1908, gives a vivid account of his experiences, and at the time created a public outcry against inhumane treatment of mental patients.

A gifted speaker and organizer, Beers obtained the support of eminent psychiatrists and other prominent people to form the Connecticut Society for Mental Hygiene in 1908, the National Committee for Mental Hygiene in 1909, and the International Committee for Mental Hygiene in 1930.

Beers's influence on the mental hygiene movement has been a lasting one, both through the work of the outstanding people he enlisted in the movement, and the continued popularity of *A Mind That Found Itself,* still in print after more than three-quarters of a century.

REFERENCE

Beers, C. W. (1981). *A mind that found itself* (5th ed.). Pittsburgh: University of Pittsburgh Press.

Paul Irvine
Katonah, New York

BEERY-BUKTENICA DEVELOPMENT TEST OF VISUAL-MOTOR INTEGRATION

The Beery-Buktenica Development Test of Visual-Motor Integration (VMI; Beery, 1997) assesses a child's ability to integrate visual and motor skills. The VMI consists of 27 geometric forms that increase in complexity, which the examinee is asked to copy in a space provided underneath each item. Group and individual administrations are equally acceptable. Administration time varies depending upon the age and ability of the examinee, but usually takes 15 minutes. Supplemental tests of Visual Perception and Motor Coordination represent the newest additions to this test, and are recommended by the author for use in individuals that perform poorly on the VMI. These supplemental tests (containing the same geometric figures as the VMI) separate the visual from the motor aspects of the VMI, allowing the examiner to identify which area contributes most to poor performance. The author advises that these tests should be given in the order for which they were normed: VMI, Visual Perception, and Motor Coordination.

The latest version of the VMI has returned to an earlier, unweighted scoring method. The manual provides the examiner with precise passing criteria as well as examples of both passing and failing items. All items on the VMI are scored and are only included in the raw score only if they precede the discontinuation rule of three non-pass items.

Reliability of the VMI and its supplemental tests are reported as high. The manual reports internal consistency at .88 for the VMI, .85 for the Visual Perception Test and .87 for the Motor Coordination Test. Test-retest at a 3 week interval for the VMI, Visual Perception, and Motor Coordination, were reported at .87, .84, and .83, respectively. Concurrent validity is reported through moderate median correlation with the Bender Gestalt (Armstrong & Knopf, 1982; Wesson, 1986) and significant correlations with WISC-R performance IQ (Breen et al., 1985). Predictive validity was established through relation of low VMI scores and grade failure (Fowler et al., 1986) and academic readiness (Weerdenburg & Janzen, 1985; Simner, 1983).

The VMI and its supplemental tests were normed in 1996 on 2,614 children aged 3 through 18 and representative of the 1990 U.S. Census. Ease of administration, simplistic score structure, and its culture-free nature have facilitated its wide use as a screening and research measure.

REFERENCES

Armstrong, B. B., & Knopf, K. F. (1982). Comparison of the Bender-Gestalt and Revised Developmental Test of Visual-Motor Integration. *Perceptual and Motor Skills, 55,* 164–166.

Beery, K. E. (1997). *The Beery-Buktenica Developmental Test of Visual-Motor Integration Administration Scoring and Teaching Manual.* Modern Curriculum Press, Parsippany, NJ.

Breen, M., & Carlson, M., & Lehman, J. (1985). The Revised Developmental Test of Visual-Motor Integration: Its relation to the VMI, WISC-R, and Bender Gestalt for a group of elementary aged learning disabled students. *Journal of Learning Disabilities, 3,* 136–138.

Fowler, M. G., & Cross, A. W. (1986). Preschool risk factors as predictors of early school performance. *Journal of Developmental and Behavioral Pediatrics, 4,* 237–241.

Simner, M. L. (1983). The warning signs of school failure: An updated profile of at risk kindergarten child. *Topics in Early Childroom Special Education, 3,* 17–27.

Weerdenburg, G., & Janzen, H. L. (1985). Predicting grade 1 success with a selected kindergarten screening battery. *School Psychology International, 1,* 12–23.

Wesson, M. D., & Kispert, K. (1986). The relationship between the Test for Visual Analysis Skills (TVAS) and standardized visual-motor tests in children with visual perception difficulty. *Journal of the American Optometric Association, 11,* 844–849.

ROSEANN BISIGHINI
The Salk Institute

BEHAVIORAL ASSESSMENT

Behavioral assessment is distinguished from other types of assessment by the assumptions on which it is based and the purposes for which it is designed (Nelson & Hayes, 1979). It has been used in the assessment of problems as varied as social withdrawal, insomnia, learning disabilities, and seizure disorders (Mash, & Terdal, 1981). Behavior domains assessed include cognitive and affective as well as motor behaviors (Cone, 1979). Techniques include interviewing, observation, checklists, psychophysiological and mechanical measurement, self-monitoring, and behavioral products. An argument has even been made for the inclusion of intelligence tests in behavioral assessment (Nelson, 1980).

Assessment is performed to generate treatment plans. This means that the quality of assessment is judged by the effectiveness of the intervention plans that it generates (treatment utility). Internal consistency, stability, interrater agreement, criterion-related validity, content validity, and construct validity are all necessary to establish treatment utility, and thus are as important as traditional assessment.

Although prior history and biological status affect the kinds of behaviors a person does or does not demonstrate, the occurrence of behaviors and their continuation are a function of immediate environmental events. In other words, behavior is purposeful within an environment. Because of this association between environment and behavior, behavioral assessment takes place in the natural setting in which the behavior occurs. In assessing bedtime tantrums, for example, child and parent behavior at bedtime may be observed by a professional on a home visit or by the parents themselves.

There is an emphasis on assessing publicly observable events such as specific motor behaviors or statements made by a client. This emphasis exists to reduce the need for inference (and possible bias) by the clinician. Besides the technical advantage of producing data of assessable reliability, it has the additional advantage of allowing clients, clinicians, parents, and other change agents to see directly the effects of treatment. Covert events (thoughts and feelings) can be incorporated by having clients observe and report their own internal behavior, or by teaching clients to perform a specific cognitive behavior and observing changes in behavior products or other overt behavior (Kendall & Braswell, 1985).

Identifying behaviors targeted for change is done by interviewing the person making a referral, generally the client or a person responsible for the client's welfare. Selection of target behaviors must be made with serious consideration of the ethics of changing behaviors (Harris & Kapche, 1978). It is generally easier for the client to identify behaviors that should be reduced than behaviors to be increased; however, replacement behaviors may be inappropriate unless treatment plans explicitly include increasing specific appropriate behaviors. The target may be to change the frequency (rate), form (topography), duration, intensity, setting, or latency of a behavior (the amount of time between a cue for a behavior and the onset of the behavior). These characteristics may be more or less salient in a specific problem and must be assessed. For example, temper tantrums generally have both frequency and duration as salient features: the rate of tantrums may be reduced from 10 per day to 1 per day, but duration may increase from 10 minutes each episode to 4 hours if duration is not targeted.

Controlling events are events that precede the behavior signaling its occurrence (antecedents), and that follow the occurrence of the behavior and have either the effect of strengthening or weakening the behavior (consequences). Different characteristics of a single target behavior may be under different controls. For example, tantrum behavior may be precipitated by the presentation of a frustrating task and the demand to perform it, but duration may be maintained by staff attention. Controlling events can be identified if changes in the occurrence of controlling events are made and the target behavior changes. The goal is to link assessment with intervention by determining what supports and what compromises a child's performance (Westbury, Stevens, & Oetter, 1996).

Skill deficits may preclude a desirable behavior from being performed. Techniques of task analysis (Resnick, Wang, & Kaplan, 1973) decompose behaviors into the simple parts that are necessary for performing the behavior. The client is assessed for performance of these prerequisite behaviors, thus yielding information that can be used to train the more complex skill. Among other methods, information from criterion-referenced tests can be useful for this purpose.

To evaluate intervention effects, data about the target

behaviors must be collected prior to the start of an intervention, during a baseline period, as well as after the intervention has begun. Because a behavioral intervention may have inadvertent side effects, it is important for the clinician to hypothesize these and to assess them as well as intended treatment effects. For example, a plan may be to reduce a child's inappropriate talking out in class; the clinician should consider that talking out in class discussions and talking out on the playground may reduce also. Behavior change is evaluated using experimental designs that attempt to remove the threats to validity encountered in single-subject research (Barlow & Hersen, 1984).

Three of the most commonly used behavioral assessment techniques are interviewing, observation, and behavior products. Techniques that are occasionally used include self-monitoring, psychophysiological assessment, checklists and questionnaires, sociometry, and psychoeducational assessment. Interviewing may be the only assessment method available when the behavior is covert, occurs at a low rate, or occurs in a setting in which it is not feasible to observe. Also, the selection and definition of target behaviors must take place in an interview with the client or with someone responsible for the client's welfare. The clinician must decide who will be most informative regarding the client's behavior, and must consider interviewing several persons if any one person's knowledge of the problem is incomplete. Behavioral interviews proceed from an initial phase of problem identification, in which the clinician attempts to elicit all problems of concern to the interviewee, to problem specification, in which the problem behaviors are sufficiently specified so that the clinician and interviewee would agree on occurrences of the behavior if it were observed. Then comes the problem analysis phase, in which the clinician and interviewee attempt to identify controlling events and skill deficits. In consultation and some forms of direct service, the interview also may be used to generate plans for intervention. A fifth phase of interviewing involves evaluating the effectiveness of an intervention. Of these five phases, the most important for successful problem solution appears to be problem specification. The success of this phase depends on the clinician's ability to ask questions eliciting specific descriptions of behavior and controlling events while at the same time maintaining rapport (Haynes, 1978; Tombari & Bergan, 1978).

Observations serve two main purposes in behavioral assessment: to assess characteristics of target behaviors as they change following intervention, and to identify the controlling events of a behavior. In addition, observations can be used to identify goals for behavior change by identifying group norms for behavior. For example, a teacher may want to increase a child's participation in class discussions, but 100% would be too much. Observations reveal that classmates spend 4% of class time participating in discussions; therefore, reaching this level may be a suitable goal. Observation methods vary according to the rate of the behavior, the characteristics being assessed, the training and experience of the observer, and the observer's purpose. Behaviors that are low-rate (e.g., less than one occurrence an hour) will usually need to be recorded by participant observers (e.g., parents, staff) and be tallied on a daily or weekly basis to yield a measure of behavior frequency. Duration and latency of behaviors will need to be timed. Intensity can be rated by an observer, and topography can be described in a verbal narrative. Identifying controlling events requires being able to track immediately preceding and following events. These events, if observers are trained to look for them, can be recorded in an anecdotal record, a narrative report of each occurrence of a behavior. A houseparent, reporting an incident of running away, can note the time and setting of the occurrence, immediately preceding events, the chain of running-away behaviors, the duration of the incident, and likely consequent events. Current observational methods many times rely on computer programs such as the Direct Observation Data System (DODS). These programs save time, increase reliability and validity, and are user friendly (Munoz & Garcia, 1996).

Sampling is required in observation of high-rate behaviors because it is not convenient or possible to observe target behaviors continuously. In time sampling, a decision must first be made about the length of an observation session (e.g., 20 minutes). This will depend on the rate of the behavior; the session should be long enough to observe many occurrences. A second decision concerns dividing the observation session into smaller units (intervals), deciding on the length of each interval and the interval sampling method to be used. Interval length needs to be short (e.g., 3 seconds) for high-rate behaviors, but can be long (e.g., 1 hour) for low-rate behaviors. The shorter the interval length, the closer the agreement between time sampling and continuous monitoring, but the more tedious observation becomes. In whole-interval sampling, a behavior is recorded only if it has been occurring during the entire interval. In partial-interval sampling, a behavior is recorded if it occurred at any time during the interval. Compared with continuous monitoring, whole-interval sampling consistently underestimates time, while partial-interval sampling overestimates time (Powell, 1984). A method of sampling that provides an unbiased estimate of frequency is momentary time sampling. In this method, an observation is made at the precise onset of an interval. If the behavior is occurring at the moment, it is recorded. Each method generates a summary score indicating the proportion of intervals in which the behavior occurred. If intervals are short (much shorter than average behavior duration), an estimate of behavior duration can be made if one counts consecutive intervals in which the behavior occurred.

Behavior products, such as a math worksheet completed by a student or number of pounds gained by a person with an eating disorder, are less reactive than interviews, observations, self-monitoring, or client-completed checklists (Webb et al., 1966). Such measures are most often used as measures of behavior change in addition to more reactive measures. Although in many instances producing little information about controlling events, some products may produce clues about such events. For example, examination of a child's math worksheet may reveal consistent misapplications of a math rule (Brown & Burton, 1978); or an examination of absentee records may reveal that a child's nonattendance tends to occur following weekends and holidays.

REFERENCES

Barlow, D. H., & Hersen, M. (1984). *Single case experimental designs.* New York: Pergamon.

Brown, J. S., & Burton, R. R. (1978). Diagnostic models for procedural bugs in basic mathematical skills. *Cognitive Science, 2,* 155–192.

Cone, J. D. (1979). Confounded comparisons in triple response mode assessment research. *Behavioral Assessment, 1,* 85–95.

Harris, A., & Kapche, R. (1978). Behavior modification in schools: Ethical issues and suggested guidelines. *Journal of School Psychology, 16,* 25–33.

Haynes, S. N. (1978). *Principles of behavioral assessment.* New York: Gardner.

Johnson, H., Brady, S., & Larson, E. (1996). A microcomputer-based system to facilitate direct observational data collection and assessment in inclusive settings. *Journal of Computing in Childhood Education, 7,* 3–4.

Kendall, P. C., & Braswell, L. (1985). *Cognitive-impulsive therapy for impulsive children.* New York: Guilford.

Mash, E. J., & Terdal, L. G. (Eds.). (1981). *Behavioral assessment of childhood disorders* (pp. 441–482). New York: Guilford.

Munoz, A. M., & Garcia, J. (1996). The Direct Observation Data System (DODS). *Journal of Computing in Childhood Education, 8,* 14–18.

Nelson, R. O. (1980). The use of intelligence tests within behavioral assessment. *Behavioral Assessment, 2,* 417–425.

Nelson, R. O., & Hayes, S. C. (1979). Some current dimensions of behavioral assessment. *Behavioral Assessment, 1,* 1–16.

Powell, J. (1984). On the misrepresentation of behavioral realities by a widely practiced direct observation procedure: Partial interval (one-zero) sampling. *Behavioral Assessment, 6,* 209–220.

Resnick, L. B., Wang, M. C., & Kaplan, J. (1973). Task analysis in curriculum design: A hierarchically sequenced introductory math curriculum. *Journal of Applied Behavior Analysis, 6,* 679–709.

Tombari, M. L., & Bergan, J. R. (1978). Consultant cues and teacher verbalizations, judgments, and expectancies concerning children's adjustment problems. *Journal of School Psychology, 16,* 212–219.

Webb, E. J., Campbell, D. T., Schwartz, R. D., & Sechrest, L. (1966). *Unobtrusive measures: Nonreactive research in the social sciences.* Chicago: Rand McNally.

Westby, C. E., Stevens, D. M., & Oetter, P. (1996). A performance/competence model of observational assessment. *Language, Speech, and Hearing in The Schools, 27,* 144–156.

JOHN MacDONALD
Eastern Kentucky University

BEHAVIORAL CONSULTATION
BEHAVIOR CHARTING
BEHAVIOR MODIFICATION

BEHAVIORAL CONSULTATION

Over the last three decades, consultation has become an increasingly important tool in the provision of psychological services to children and youths in educational settings (Meecham & Peckham, 1978; Ramage, 1979). School-based consultation may be rendered from a variety of theoretical perspectives. These include mental health consultation, which is linked to psychodynamic theories of personality (Caplan, 1970), organization development consultation (Schmuck, 1982), which has its origins in social psychological theory strongly influenced by the Lewinian perspective, and behavioral consultation, which is linked to behavioral theory (Bandura, 1977; Skinner, 1953). The following discussion describes the behavioral approach to consultation services.

There are no characteristics that uniquely define consultation. Consequently, there are no features that uniquely characterize behavioral consultation. Nonetheless, there are features that tend to be associated with consultation services. Perhaps the most widely shared attribute of consultation activities is that they generally involve indirect service (Bergan, 1977). Typically, service is rendered by a consultant (e.g., psychologist) to a consultee (e.g., teacher), who in turn provides services to one or more clients (e.g., students). The indirect approach to service characteristic of consultation is generally regarded as a major advantage of this form of service delivery. A consultant providing services to a number of consultees can bring expertise to many more clients than could be served by a direct-service approach. There is a multiplier effect in which the skills of the consultant can be brought to bear on client problems without the extensive time commitment required when the consultant provides direct services to the client.

A second attribute of consultation is that it is generally a problem-solving venture in which the consultant provides expert advice related to a problem presented by the consultee (Bergan, 1977). The consultant usually elicits a description of the problem from the consultee, assists in the development of a plan to solve the problem, and participates in an evaluation to determine the extent to which the problem has been solved.

A third feature of consultation is that it is typically assumed to involve a collegial relationship between the consultant and the consultee (Bergan, 1977). This means that the consultant has no direct authority over the consultee and the consultee has no direct authority over the consultant. Rather, each has an area of professional responsibility with respect to the services provided to the client. The consultant serves as an adviser. The consultee uses consultant advice in making and implementing decisions aimed at solving the problem(s) presented in consultation.

The three attributes discussed in the preceding paragraphs are not unique to behavioral consultation. Yet, they are a part of consultation rendered from a behavioral perspective. What distinguishes behavioral consultation from other varieties of consultation is the use of a behavioral perspective in providing consultation services (Bergan, 1977; Feld, Bergan, & Stone, in press). The behavioral viewpoint affects consultation in three important ways. First, it dictates that problems presented in consultation be conceptualized from a behavioral perspective. Second, it calls for the use of behavioral principles in designing interventions to solve problems. Third, it assumes an empirical approach to determining the effectiveness of consultation interventions.

Consultation services are generally rendered in a series of stages, each of which is designed to address a particular aspect of the problem-solving endeavor. Four stages are generally recognized in consultation (Bergan, 1977; Dorr, 1979; Goodwin & Coates, 1976; Tombari & Davis, 1979). They are (1) problem identification, (2) problem analysis, (3) plan implementation, and (4) problem evaluation.

Problem identification sets the direction that consultation will take. Within the behavioral perspective, a problem is defined in terms of a discrepancy between observed behavior and desired behavior. The problem is to eliminate the discrepancy. Determining the existence of a discrepancy between observed and desired behavior requires that the concerns communicated by the consultee be expressed in behavioral terms. During problem identification, the consultant assists the consultee to describe current client functioning and desired functioning in terms of current behaviors and desired behaviors. Data are generally collected to document the status of current behavior. A problem exists if the data reveal a difference between current and desired behavior that the consultee regards as a significant discrepancy.

Problem analysis follows problem identification. During this stage of consultation, the factors that may be influencing client behaviors of concern are identified and a plan is formulated to effect desired changes in behaviors. Behavioral principles are heavily relied on in determining influences on behavior. Problem analysis generally begins with the specification of antecedent and consequent environmental conditions that may be affecting behavior. However, client skills and behavioral patterns may also be the subject of analysis (Piersel, 1985). After hypothesized influences on client behavior have been identified, a plan is formulated to change client behavior. The consultant is generally responsible for specifying the strategies that may be used to achieve behavior change. However, the consultee often plays a major role in identifying specific tactics that may be useful in implementing a plan. For example, a consultant may determine that positive reinforcement may be useful in increasing a particular behavior of concern to the consultee. The consultee may then identify the type of reinforcement to be used with the behavior.

After a suitable plan has been formulated, it is implemented. Implementation is generally the responsibility of the consultee. However, the consultee may direct an implementation effort in which others actually carry out the plan. For instance, a teacher may direct a peer tutoring program designed to increase the reading skills of a group of children. The principal role of the consultant during implementation is one of monitoring what is occurring and of assisting the consultee to make minor revisions in the plan in those instances in which the plan is not working as expected.

The final stage in consultation is problem evaluation. During this phase of consultation, the consultant and the consultee determine the extent to which the goals of consultation have been achieved and the extent to which the plan implemented to attain goals has been effective. Evaluation data guide the course of consultation. If the goals of consultation have been achieved, a new problem may be identified or services may terminate. If the goals of consultation have not been achieved, consultation generally returns to problem analysis.

Behavioral consultation has been most widely applied in solving learning and/or adjustment problems manifested by children and youths in educational settings (Bergan, 1977). In the typical case, services are directed toward one client (e.g., a student). However, there have been many applications involving groups. For example, consultation may be used to modify the behavior of all of the children in a class (Bergan, 1977). It has also been suggested that behavioral consultation could be useful for organization development including all of the individuals associated with an educational setting (Piersel, 1985). However, applications of behavioral consultation for this purpose are lacking.

Piersel (1985) has outlined procedures for using behavioral consultation in special education programs. He points out that consultation is ideally suited to meeting the goal of providing students eligible for special services with a program that reflects the least restrictive alternative environment for rendering services. Piersel indicates that consultation should begin with an attempt to solve problems manifested by the child in the regular classroom environment. When evidence is gathered indicating that a solution cannot be achieved in the classroom, placement in a special program is considered. It is at this point that assessment and case conferences with the family and other professionals occur.

There is a large body of research documenting the effectiveness of behavioral consultation (Feld, Bergan, & Stone, 1984). Research on the effectiveness of behavioral consultation is of two types. The first involves studies of the application of behavioral principles in consultation to achieve changes in behavior. Research of this kind has shown the behavioral approach to be effective in remediating a large variety of behavioral and academic problems (Bergan & Tombari, 1976; Conoley & Conoley, 1982; Medway, 1979; Medway & Forman, 1980).

The second body of research on the effectiveness of the behavioral approach compares the effectiveness of behavioral consultation with that of other forms of service. Many of the comparative studies have methodological flaws (Medway, 1979) and therefore results and generalization are inconclusive.

Recent developments in behavioral consultation focus on collaborative arrangements between parents of special education students and educators. Specific emphasis has been placed on the cultural-ethnic lifestyle considerations (Fine & Gardner, 1994).

REFERENCES

Bandura, A. (1977). *Social learning.* Englewood Cliff, NJ: Prentice-Hall.

Bergan, J. R. (1977). *Behavioral consultation.* Columbus, OH: Merrill.

Bergan, J. R., & Tombari, M. L. (1976). Consultant skill and efficiency and the implementation of outcomes of consultation. *Journal of School Psychology, 14,* 3–13.

Caplan, G. (1970). *The theory and practice of mental health consultation.* New York: Basic Books.

Conoley, J. C., & Conoley, C. W. (1982). The effects of two conditions of client-centered consultation on student teacher problem descriptions and remedial plans. *Journal of School Psychology, 20,* 323–328.

Dorr, D. (1979). Psychological consulting in the schools. In J. J. Platt & R. J. Wicks (Eds.), *The psychological consultant.* New York: Grune & Stratton.

Feld, J. D., Bergan, J. R., & Stone, C. A. (1984). Behavioral approaches to school based consultation: Current status and future directions. In C. A. Maher (Ed.), *Behavioral approaches to providing educational services in schools.* Hillsdale, NJ: Erlbaum.

Fine, M. J., & Gardner, A. (1994). Collaborative consultation with families of children with special needs: Why bother? *Journal of Educational and Psychological Consultation, 5,* 283–308.

Goodwin, D. L., & Coates, T. J. (1976). *Helping students help themselves.* Englewood Cliffs, NJ: Prentice-Hall.

Meacham, M. L., & Peckham, P. D. (1978). School psychologists at three-quarters century: Congruence between training, practice, preferred role and competence. *Journal of School Psychology, 16,* 195–206.

Medway, F. J. (1979). How effective is school consultation: A review of recent research. *Journal of School Psychology, 17,* 275–282.

Medway, F. J., & Forman, S. G. (1980). Psychologists' and teachers' reactions to mental health and behavioral school consultation. *Journal of School Psychology, 18,* 338–348.

Piersel, W. C. (1985). Behavioral consultation: An approach to problem solving in educational settings. In J. R. Bergan (Ed.), *School psychology in contemporary society.* Columbus, OH: Merrill.

Ramage, J. C. (1979). National survey of school psychologists: Update. *School Psychology Digest, 8,* 153–161.

Schmuck, R. A. (1982). Organizational development in the schools. In C. R. Reynolds & T. B. Gutkin (Eds.), *The handbook of school psychology.* New York: Wiley.

Skinner, B. F. (1953). *Science and human behavior.* New York: Macmillan.

Tombari, M. L., & Davis, R. A. (1979). Behavioral consultation. In G. D. Phye & D. J. Reschly (Eds.), *School psychology: Perspectives and issues.* New York: Academic.

JOHN R. BERGAN
University of Arizona

**BEHAVIOR ASSESSMENT
CONSULTATION
CONSULTATION, MENTAL HEALTH**

BEHAVIORAL DEFICIT

The terminology associated with behavioral deficit has become confused as a result of various incomplete usages. The original usage was associated with the 1961 American Association on Mental Retardation inclusion of adaptive behavior in their definition of mental retardation. Adaptive behavior implies that many educational, psychological, sociological, and biological influences interact on the child, affecting function and performance. Principally, it is a term designed to offset the dependence the public schools, mental health agencies, and social welfare institutions had placed on measured intelligence.

The original concept was closely associated with developmental disabilities. Work in the late 1950s, and early 1960s with handicapped children resulted in a description of developmental lag, placing the emphasis for the disability on irregular test protocols and subtest patterns clinically thought to reflect possible neurological insult. The search had begun by psychoeducational researchers to specify the nature of these so-called behavioral deficits through the use of test and subtest patterns. In 1966, S. D. Clements placed into motion, through the committee he chaired on minimal neurological impairment, the search for neurological damage as an explanation of specific learning disabilities.

Tests designed to measure visual and auditory perceptual, perceptual-motor, and other cognitive abilities began to flood the market. The term specific added to learning disabilities accentuated that a deficit in one or more of the psychological processes was accountable for the condition.

In 1974, Gleason and Haring provided the first general behavioral definition of learning disabilities and in so doing used the term behavioral deficit as the principal construct associated with the concept learning disabilities. "We define a learning disability as a behavioral deficit almost always associated with academic performance and that can be remediated by precise, individualized instructional programming" (p. 226).

There are two major issues that surround the construct of behavioral deficits. The first is the possibility or utility of cognitive skills being broken into specific component parts. It should be remembered that all assumed cognitive behaviors are named, usually after a test or subtest designed to measure them. They are not occurrences in nature that are directly observable. The second issue is the reliability of most tests designed to ascertain or describe a basic behavior and therefore illustrate a behavioral deficit. As the reliability decreases, so does the validity.

A behavioral deficit then is a concept suggesting that human abilities are not all the same, and in some cases fall to a deficit level. Operationally defining a deficit has not been well done through the use of tests or subtests in terms of when a deficit statistically or clinically exists. Therefore, while the concept itself has driven several major thrusts (both diagnostic and treatment), including the term developmental disability to some degree, and theoretically is responsible for describing learning disability, it remains an incomplete term, less than fully developed by those who use it on a clinical basis.

REFERENCES

Clements, S. D. (1966). *Task force I: Minimal brain dysfunction in children. Monograph No. 3.* Washington, DC: U.S. Government Printing Office.

Gleason, C., & Haring, N. (1974). Learning disabilities. In N. G. Haring (Ed.), *Behavior of exceptional children* (pp. 245–295). Columbus, OH: Merrill.

DAVID A. SABATINO
*West Virginia College of
Graduate Studies*

ABILITY TRAINING
BEHAVIORAL OBJECTIVES

BEHAVIORAL DISORDERS

Behavioral Disorders is the official journal of the Council for Children with Behavioral Disorders (CCBD) of the Council for Exceptional Children. Founded in 1975, *Behavioral Disorders* serves as a resource for those professionals interested in the education and treatment of behaviorally disordered children and youth.

The journal, with a quarterly distribution to the 8,400 members of CCBD and hundreds of individual and institutional subscribers, was developed under the editorships of Albert Fink of Indiana University (1975–1978), Denzil Edge of the University of Louisville (1978–1981), and Robert B. Rutherford, Jr., of Arizona State University (1981–1987) into a forum for the publication of manuscripts derived from documented thought and empirical evidence. These data-based articles are presented in several forms: experimental research (either original or replications), research and practice reviews and analyses, program or procedure descriptions, and scholarly reviews of texts, films, and other media. The editorial process of the journal is designed to thoroughly and professionally analyze submitted manuscripts in terms of originality, relevance of topic, importance of the findings or concepts, content organization, and documentation.

Historically, *Behavioral Disorders* evolved from an early dependence on cosponsored thematic issues and reliance on solicited manuscripts to an open journal relying on unsolicited manuscripts submitted by professionals in the field. *Behavioral Disorders* has contributed significantly to the professional literature on behavioral disorders of children and youths.

ROBERT B. RUTHERFORD, JR.
Arizona State University

BEHAVIORAL OBJECTIVES

In the broadest sense, an objective is a statement of an aim or desired outcome. In an educational sense, an instructional objective may be a quantifiable and/or an observable academic or social achievement that specifies the enabling steps necessary to accomplish the objective in a stated period of time. All instructional or behavioral objectives must have observable or measurable outcomes. The difference between an instructional and a behavioral objective is the result to be achieved. The latter may be broader in scope and not confined to an educational effort; it may rather include a wide range of specified behavioral outcomes, for example, speech, language, perceptual development, motor training, and social skill development.

Behavioral objectives and instructional (teaching) objectives are frequently used interchangeably. While each impacts on the other, these two sets of objectives address two different performances. A behavioral objective focuses on any visible activity displayed by a learner (student). It has at its core the terminal behavior, or what the learner can demonstrate has been learned. An instructional objective may include the desired learner outcomes; it will specify the criteria acceptable for success in attaining that outcome, but it focuses on what will be taught and how it will be taught.

The purpose for developing behavioral objectives is to increase teaching efficiency by having educators and behavioral scientists determine what it is that will be learned, how it will be taught, what materials will be used, and the length of time within which it should be learned against a predetermined criteria or standard. Behavioral objectives become targets to which teachers can direct their instruction. In the process of instruction, their use requires educators to determine whether outcomes or observations of performance are being effectively and efficiently provided and creating an exactness for what is learned and how it is taught. Thus, a teaching methodology may be used for a specified amount of time under conditions that will permit the educator to judge the amount of progress being made. Mager (1962) notes, "An instructor will function in a fog of his own making until he knows what he wants his students to be able to do at the end of the instruction" (p. 2).

One of the most common points of confusion is between a course description (or what a course is about) and behavioral objectives (those specific, measurable, or observable performances a student will demonstrate at the completion of a course). Behavioral objectives must contain statements of concrete, measurable, or observable performances. In contrast, nonbehavioral goals are broad, abstract statements; they are not derived from previous observations or performance test data. They do not consider the skills necessary to enter into a next level of work. Nonbehavioral objectives are based on philosophy, ideology, and attitude, not the proficiency of task to be taught.

Popham and Baker (1970) note five different considerations necessary in the preparation and use of behavioral objectives. They are

1. *Systematic instructional decision making.* The use of behavioral objectives and the measured outcome to determine the most efficient method of instruction and how effective a specified method was in achieving an objective.

2. *Behavioral and/or educational objectives.* Determine what is to be accomplished, in what time period, and how it is to be accomplished.

3. *Selection of appropriate educational objectives.* Selecting significant and meaningful objectives is not easy; indeed, the task tends to be elusive and difficult. Educators must choose between the content (e.g., a math score, read-

ing score from a formal or informal test, new words to be learned) and behaviors that are reasoned to influence the process of learning (e.g., time on task). Many times the two intersect and both become important elements in achieving a goal.

4. *Establishing performance standards.* One of the most difficult tasks is to set the criteria that denote whether a behavioral objective has been achieved successfully. There are no absolutes or clear rules for achieving that purpose. Some guidelines exist, such as the 80/80 criterion, which states that 80% of what has been taught must be demonstrated as a successfully learned outcome at an 80% minimal level of performance. Thus, if 10 words were taught, on measurement eight words must be learned before the next list of words is taught. Many educators use the 80% criterion as a minimal standard for instructional or subject matter content objectives. A large percentage of these same practitioners believe that a 90% criterion is useful with behavioral objectives. The establishment of performance standards addresses the sophistication or precision of the objective. While performance standards may largely be intuitive, a performance standard frequently addresses the knowledge the educator has of the learner.

5. The curriculum rationale. Educators spend their professional lives developing and implementing the curriculum. Countless hours are spent discussing curriculum questions each school year through school-district, building-level, and grade-level curriculum committees; in addition, thousands of curriculum guides exist in the United States. Combine those teacher-made curricula and guides with the innumerable commercially printed materials, and it would appear the curricular-planning process is complete. It is not. Despite all these efforts, 20 to 30% of schoolchildren fail academically or socially each year. Why?

A simple and very clear explanation is that most curricula are targeted at theoretical learners who are ready to learn and have no disabilities. An educator using a general curricular guide or commercial material is exclusively concerned with determining the objectives for the educational system, and not any one typical or atypical youth in that system. There are basically two kinds of decisions that educators must make. First, they must decide what the objectives (the ends) of the instructional system should be; second, they must decide on the procedures (the means) for accomplishing those objectives. This is, the curricular rationale for using behavioral or instructional objectives. This point becomes critical when individualization of instruction is sought. The use of behavioral objectives suggests the teacher is selecting and evaluating instructional procedures to accomplish those objectives. Thus teachers are engaged in instructional decision making. Herein resides the critical difference between using a curriculum and an instructional objectives process. Instructional objectives require stated levels of success, and measured and/or observable outcomes. In short, they are empirical solutions requiring data. Curricular structures are generally value-based.

How then are behavioral objectives established? Usually by determining a behavioral characteristic such as inattentiveness, or a score on a test, or a set of facts or things to be learned, e.g., words or numbers. Behavioral objectives specify what it is to be learned and place a comfortable floor beneath the learner by dropping below what the learner can do initially and ending with what the learner can comfortably learn in a given period of time. A sound behavioral objective does not test the learner's limit, unless designed to do so for good reason.

A behavioral objective is one activity in a series of, or sequence of, activities to be learned. That sequence can become the curriculum. The principal reason for having many small, tightly sequenced steps in the curriculum is that learner performance is examined frequently. More important, the learner is provided with corrective feedback after every trial. That point is critical. What the learner knows does not fall to an assumption that cannot be proven. Behavioral or instructional objectives, once sequenced, become important interlocking steps. Because the ability of children to learn varies widely, particularly when materials change, each objective permits the individual student the necessary time on tasks.

The three major advantages of a behavioral objective are

1. Students are not compared with others, but with themselves and the speed with which they may learn a given task comfortably.

2. Each tightly sequenced step is validated in the curricular process; all assumptions about learning rate or about what has been learned are rejected.

3. There is a starting point, something the student knows, and a stopping point, a task within the comfort level to be learned.

A curriculum based on a series of behavioral objectives is a scientific approximation of the art of teaching. For that reason, P.L. 94-142 (1975), and its revision in 1990 called the Individuals with Disabilities Education Act (PL 101-476) required that an individual educational program (IEP) be written for every handicapped child served under this legislation. An IEP is a behavioral objective and/or an instructional objective that requires a specific diagnostic process (with a multidisciplinary team) and a preparation procedure. It ensures the availability of data for accountability.

REFERENCES

Mager, R. F. (1962). *Preparing instructional objectives*. Palo Alto, CA: Fearon.

Popham, W. J., & Baker, E. (1970). *Establishing instructional goals*. Englewood Cliffs, NJ: Prentice-Hall.

DAVID A. SABATINO
*West Virginia College of
Graduate Studies*

AGE APPROPRIATE CURRICULUM TEACHING STRATEGIES

BEHAVIORAL OBSERVATION

Behavior observation is at the core of behavioral assessment. Behavior observation is a procedure for categorizing motor and verbal behavior into an organized permanent record. A behavior observation system meets three criteria (Jones, Reid, & Patterson, 1974). These include "recording of behavioral events in their natural settings at the time they occur, not retrospectively; the use of trained impartial observer-coders, and descriptions of behaviors which (sic) require little if any inference by observers to code the events" (p. 46). Excluded from this definition are narrative recordings, anecdotal records, checklists and rating scales, and procedures that require a person to observe and record his or her own behavior.

Behavior observations occur in diverse settings and for numerous purposes. In educational settings, behavior observations are used for purposes of diagnosing individual students, planning an intervention to modify a pupil's behavior, evaluating interventions, consulting with teachers, and conducting research.

Although specific observational procedures and instruments vary in many important ways, they all require selectivity. The observation instrument structures the observer's attention to those selected aspects of behavior and the setting that are presumed to be most relevant to the purposes of the observation. Behavior occurs in a continuous stream, yet the observer must categorize behavior into objectively defined behavioral codes and encode it into an organized, permanent record. Care in defining what is to be observed is critical to measurable results. Narrative recordings and checklists can assist in selecting the most significant behavioral codes as well as the contextual, or environmental, events thought to be associated with the selected behaviors. Data on these antecedent and consequent events are useful in designing a plan for modifying the behaviors of concern.

To minimize observer subjectivity, the selected behaviors are defined as objectively as possible. "Aggressive behavior" is not as objective a definition as "hits, shoves, grabs, and tackles." Although "aggressive behavior" can serve as useful shorthand in coding behavior, the clear specification of the behaviors encompassed by this term

Observer: Cathy Snow (consultant)
Date: November 5, 1985
Student: Julie
Circumstance: Math seatwork

Behavior																	Total
Noise	II	I	I	III		I	III	I	I	II	IIII	II	III	I	I		26
Physi- cal contact			I		II			I	I			III			I		9
Out of seat								I					I		I		3

Frequency recording sheet.

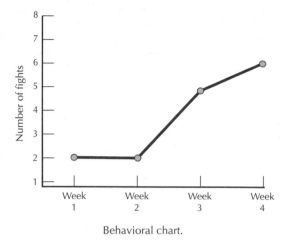

Behavioral chart.

gives the observer an objective definition of aggression. When the behavioral codes are objectively defined, any two trained observers should agree on the presence or absence of a behavior. Behavior observations can occur in natural settings (e.g., classroom, peer group, or home) or in simulated or role playing settings.

Observational instruments vary in their degree of formality from homemade teacher-used instruments to published instruments requiring highly trained observers. Three major types of observational procedures are frequency recordings, duration recordings, and interval recordings (Barton & Ascione, 1984). In frequency recordings, the number of times a behavior occurs within the observational period is recorded. Frequency recordings are best suited to behaviors that have a discrete beginning and end, that last approximately the same amount of time each time they occur, and that do not occur so frequently that separating each occurrence becomes difficult. Hand raises, inappropriate noises, bed-wetting, and hitting are examples of frequency target behaviors. The Figure shows the results of a frequency recording of a disruptive student's behavior. Each block represents 1 minute, and each observational period lasts 15 minutes. The totals at the end of each row are the frequencies of that target behavior in a 15-minute period. Observations should continue over several days to obtain a reliable measure.

A duration recording is a direct measure of the amount of time an individual engages in the target behavior. Duration recordings are most appropriate for behaviors that have a clear beginning and ending and that last for more than a few seconds. If a child gets out of his or her seat and stays out of the seat for periods of time ranging from 1 to 6 minutes, a duration count would indicate the percentage of time the child was out of the seat during the observational period.

In interval recordings, the occurrence or nonoccurrence of selected behaviors during a series of equal time intervals is recorded. Interval recording is recommended when several behaviors need to be observed, when behaviors occur at a high rate, or when behaviors do not have clear-cut beginnings and ends. There are several variations of interval recording procedures. Typically, some sort of signaling device (e.g., an audio timer or beeps on a prerecorded cassette) cues the observer to make a recording. The observer records which target behavior occurred during the preceding interval (usually 10 seconds).

Frequency, duration, and interval recordings can be adapted to a format that allows recording of selected antecedents and consequences of the behavioral codes. At the same time the observed child's behavior is coded, the antecedent and consequent circumstances are coded. Barton and Ascione (1984) provide examples of these different observational instruments.

Observational procedures are measurement procedures, and their reliability and validity need to be established. An important part of establishing reliability is determining the extent to which two observers agree in their use of the instrument while observing the same behavior and context. Recent advances in computer technology have supported reliable data collection by the use of software such as the Direct Observation Data System (DODS). This program saves time, standardizes input, and is preferred by educators over other methods (Johnson, Brady, & Larson, 1996). Validity issues include the relationship of the behavioral code to the referral problem (face validity) and the normality of the observed behavior. One way of determining whether a child's behavior in particular settings (e.g., a classroom) is atypical is to observe other children in the same settings. If the observer alternates between observing the target child and observing other children in a classroom, the observer will have a composite observation of the typical child to compare with the referred child. The observer must also be culturally competent so as to include the sociocultural context to the observation process.

REFERENCES

Barton, C. J., & Ascione, F. R. (1984). Direct observation. In T. H. Ollendick & M. Hersen (Eds.), *Child behavioral assessment* (pp. 166–194). New York: Pergamon.

Johnson, H., Brady, S., & Larson, E. (1996). A microcomputer-based system to facilitate direct observation data collection and assessment in inclusive settings. *Journal of Computing in Childhood Education, 7,* 3–4.

Jones, R. R., Reid, J. B., & Patterson, G. B. (1974). Naturalistic observation in clinical assessment. In P. McReynolds (Ed.), *Advances in psychological assessment.* San Francisco: Jossey-Bass.

JAN N. HUGHES
Texas A & M University

APPLIED BEHAVIOR ANALYSIS
BEHAVIOR THERAPY

BEHAVIORAL SUPPORT

See SUPPORT, BEHAVIORAL.

BEHAVIOR ANALYSIS, APPLIED

See APPLIED BEHAVIOR ANALYSIS.

BEHAVIOR ASSESSMENT SYSTEM FOR CHILDREN (BASC)

The BASC (Reynolds & Kamphaus, 1992) is a multidimensional, multimethod coordinated system of instruments (that may be used collectively or as individual instruments) designed to evaluate the behaviors, thoughts, and emotions of children and adolescents from ages 2.5 years up to the age of 19 years. The BASC uses both traditional norm-referenced, standardized behavior checklists and omnibus self-report personality scales, interview/questionnaire data, and structured student observations. Designed to provide a comprehensive view of children's and adolescents' behavior and affect when used as a system, each instrument is also designed to stand alone as an individual component when necessary.

The BASC consists of the following components:

1. *Parent Rating Scale (PRS).* Available in three forms, Preschool (ages 2.5 through 5 years), Child (ages 6 through 11 years), and Adolescent (ages 12 to 19 years), the PRS is a traditionally formatted behavior rating scale completed by a parent or other caregiver in 10 to 20 minutes. Broad and narrow bands of behavior and externalizing and internalizing dimensions are all represented. Specific scales are also devoted to school problems and the BASC PRS assesses positive behavioral dimensions through its Adoptive Skills scales. Table 1 reviews the scales and constructs assessed by the BASC by age level.

2. *Teacher Rating Scale (TRS).* The TRS is available in parallel forms to the PRS from ages 2.5 to 19 years and measures primarily the same sets of behaviors as the PRS (adding scales for Learning Problems and Study Skills) but from the perspective of the teacher. The TRS scales are noted in Table 1 as well.

3. *Self-Report of Personality (SRP).* The SRP is an omnibus self-report of thoughts, feelings, and behaviors completed by children (ages 8 through 11 years) and adolescents (ages 12 to 19 years) in about 15–20 minutes. Traditional concepts such as anxiety and depression are assessed alongside newer concepts such as sensation seeking and sense of inadequacy. Other scales with special relevance to the school setting are included as well. Table 2 lists the scales and constructs assessed by the BASC SRP.

4. *Student Observation Scale (SOS).* The SOS can be used in any structured setting with ages 2.5 years and up as long as the individual is in a learning environment. The SOS is a carefully, conveniently structured observation and coding system that uses an efficient time-sampling approach to observing and counting behaviors. The SOS encourages coding of positive as well as negative behaviors and interactions in classrooms and other structured settings. A child can be assessed with the SOS in about 15 minutes.

5. *Structured Developmental History (SDH).* The SDH is a comprehensive review of developmental, personal, medical, and social histories provided by a knowledgeable caregiver. The SDH is designed so that most caregivers can complete the form independently, but it has also been designed for use as a structured interview. The SDH provides the examiner or clinician with a comprehensive review of the examinee's lifelong developmental path and key family and social history information enhancing diagnostic accuracy and choice of interventions.

The BASC PRS is available in Spanish at all age levels. For those who prefer it, the PRS and SRP are also avail-

Table 1. Composites and Scales in the BASC Teacher Rating Scales and Parent Rating Scales

Composite/Scale	Teacher Rating Scales			Parent Rating Scales		
	Preschool	Child	Adolescent	Preschool	Child	Adolescent
Externalizing Problems	•	•	•	•	•	•
Aggression	•	•	•	•	•	•
Hyperactivity	•	•	•	•	•	•
Conduct Problems		•	•		•	•
Internalizing Problems	•	•	•	•	•	•
Anxiety	•	•	•	•	•	•
Depression	•	•	•	•	•	•
Somatization	•	•	•	•	•	•
School Problems		•	•			
Attention Problems	•	•	•	•	•	•
Learning Problems		•	•			
Other Problems						
Atypicality	•	•	•	•	•	•
Withdrawal	•	•	•	•	•	•
Adaptive Skills	•	•	•	•	•	•
Adaptability	•	•		•	•	
Leadership		•	•		•	•
Social Skills	•	•	•	•	•	•
Study Skills		•	•			
Behavioral Symptoms Index	•	•	•	•	•	•

able on audiotape. The Spanish translations were field tested in all four geographic regions of the United States and in Puerto Rico. They have since been used successfully with a variety of Hispanic and Latino populations including several in South America.

Each of the norm-referenced components of the BASC (each level of the PRS, TRS, and SRP) is available in a hand-scored version, computer-entry scored version, and on scannable forms, all for Windows or Macintosh users. Earlier DOS programs are no longer supported.

The BASC was designed to: (a) facilitate the objective identification of children who are emotionally disturbed according to special education placement criteria; (b) facilitate differential diagnosis among various clinical disorders of behavior, mood, or affect that may affect children; (c) facilitate treatment planning and monitor treatment effectiveness; (d) assess important traditional emotional and behavioral constructs as well as newer constructs that have strong research support; and (e) assess behavioral and emotional strengths as well as the presence of psychopathology.

The psychometric characteristics of the BASC are particularly strong. During 7 years of development, earlier versions of the BASC were administered to nearly 33,000 children.

Normative Data. The BASC scales were standardized on just over 19,000 children and youth from the United States and southern Canada, drawn in a double randomized stratified sampling plan designed to mimic the 1990 U.S. Bureau of the Census population statistics. The sample matched population demographics on the basis of ethnicity, socioeconomic status, parent's educational level, gender, geographic region of residence, and community size. This is overall the largest known standardization sample for an individually administered test.

Table 2. Composites and Scales in the BASC Self-Report of Personality

Composite/Scale	Child	Adolescent
Clinical Maladjustment	•	•
Anxiety	•	•
Atypicality	•	•
Locus of Control	•	•
Social Stress	•	•
Somatization		•
School Maladjustment	•	•
Attitude to School	•	•
Attitude to Teachers	•	•
Sensation Seeking		•
Other Problems		
Depression	•	•
Sense of Inadequacy	•	•
Personal Adjustment	•	•
Relations with Parents	•	•
Interpersonal Relations	•	•
Self-Esteem	•	•
Self-Reliance	•	•
Emotional Symptoms Index	•	•

Scaling. The BASC composite scores and individual scale raw scores are converted to T-scores via a linear transformation. T-scores have a mean of 50 and a standard deviation of 10. Percentiles corresponding to each T-score are provided.

Unlike most tests, the BASC provides the user with multiple sets of T-scores based on 4 normative samples. BASC users have the option of using scores based upon a combined gender sample, gender specific norms (male and female separately), and norms based on a separate sample of children with clinical diagnoses.

Reliability. Scores on the various BASC scales are assessed in the BASC Manual (Reynolds & Kamphaus, 1992) for internal consistency and for temporal stability. Internal consistency reliability estimates for the individual BASC scales are high, averaging about .80 for each gender for the SRP, with composite scores averaging above .90. Test-retest reliability is high as well. The TRS and PRS have comparable reliability associated with their scores as well and follow a common pattern in the research literature, scores on externalizing scales tend to be more reliable than scores on the internalizing scales.

Validity. The BASC Manual provides extensive data regarding the content, construct, and criterion-related validity of score interpretations on the various BASC scales. Follow-up research published since 1992 along with data in the manual are strongly supportive of the use of the BASC in determination of eligibility for special education services. The BASC has proven to be particularly effective, relative to other popular scales, in the differential diagnosis of attention deficit hyperactivity disorder. Although the BASC is more accurate in the diagnosis of all forms of this disorder, it performs especially well in detecting attention deficit hyperactivity disorder, primarily inattentive type.

The BASC has achieved widespread use in the public schools and is used with over 1 million children per year at this time. A growing presence in the private clinical market is also apparent. The BASC is being employed as the major assessment tool in several longitudinal studies including the Minnesota long-term study of ADHD children and the CHAMPUS study of the effectiveness of residential treatment for adolescents. The BASC affords the clinician with reliable and valid scores, comprehensive assessment that is developmentally sensitive to age-related changes in behavior, and with flexible choices of assessment devices.

REFERENCE

Reynolds, C. R., & Kamphaus, R. W. (1992). *Behavior assessment system for children.* Circle Pines, MN: American Guidance Service.

CECIL R. REYNOLDS
Texas A & M University

BEHAVIOR CHARTING

Behavior charting is a term commonly used as an equivalent to describe a graphic representation of behavioral data. Graphing behavioral data allows the special educator to see changes easily in target behaviors (behaviors that are to be increased or decreased in frequency or duration). The ordinate, or vertical line, of the graph is labeled with the behavioral measurement scale (see Figure). This could be the number of occurrences of off-task behavior, the number of fights a child has, or the percentage of time that a child follows instructions. The abscissa, or horizontal line, is labeled with the unit of time. This could be treatment sessions, days, weeks, minutes, or other intervals over which changes in behavior can be measured (Sulzer-Azaroff & Mayer, 1977). A graph of a child's fighting behavior is shown in the accompanying Figure. As can be seen from the figure, this particular child's incidences of fighting are getting more frequent with time. This behavioral chart will allow the special educator to evaluate the effectiveness of any treatment that may eventually be implemented.

REFERENCE

Sulzer-Azaroff, B., & Mayer, G. R. (1977). *Applying behavior-analysis procedures with children and youth.* New York: Holt, Rinehart and Winston.

RANDY W. KAMPHAUS
Eastern Kentucky University

APPLIED BEHAVIOR ANALYSIS

BEHAVIOR, DESTRUCTIVE

See DESTRUCTIVE BEHAVIORS.

BEHAVIOR DISORDERS

The terms behaviorally disordered, emotionally disturbed, emotionally handicapped, and socially maladjusted are used synonymously by practitioners in special education. One of the reasons that different terms are used interchangeably is that various states use a variety of terms in their legal language to describe students who are drawing attention to themselves in matters of personal/social adjustment.

Special education has in the last 50 years developed a repertoire of interchangeable terms. While the terms may be interchangeable, the meanings of these terms are not always the same. Behavioral disorder implies that a student's social/personal regulative and adjustive mechanisms are poorly defined and generally faulty, given a specific social or environmental condition. The relativity of the term behavioral disorders begins with the displaying situationally and socially of unacceptable behaviors. There are sharp contrasts in what may reflect acceptable behaviors in such settings as urban, rural, large school, small school, etc. In addition, young teacher, old teacher, autocratic or democratic philosophy of the principal, type of community, etc. affect acceptable behaviors. In short, immediate cultural-linguistic circumstances of the child and community are all relative factors.

The concept of social relativity comes into play when we see actual cases of students with well-defined social values seemingly respecting those values, but then rejecting them to embrace the culture and mores of the urban gang, or, the reverse situation. The point is that adjustment capabilities are devastated by the perceptions and distortions of the student in regard to the social order, and, in turn, of the social order in regard to the student. Additionally, the judgments of peers and adults concerning the fitness of a person in regard to the social order is not a constant, but influenced by age, sex, status, and ethnicity, and a number of other variables. When there is drug usage, violent behavior, verbal aggressiveness, a wide range of asocial, dysocial, and antisocial, antischool behaviors, status crimes, and even criminally punishable offenses, these may be judged to be disordered.

When do we say a student is failing to make a satisfactory adjustment? The words satisfactory adjustment should signal a recognition that such an expression requires a socially relative value judgment. What goes into that value judgment rests on many factors, including the proximity to the rules being broken and whose rules are being broken.

Revolutionary thinking in regard to all handicapped persons, and in particular the mentally ill, developed in the wake of the French Revolution. The great French psychiatrist Phillipe Pinel was the first to separate criminals from the insane. The lag in services, if not consideration for the mentally ill, resided in a collection of many superstitions. Emotional difficulties have been attributed to every conceivable cause: biological, physiological, sociological, religious, psychological, and genetic, to name just a few.

There can be little question that Freud and his observations, records, and theories raised the level of excitement in the field and stimulated an international response to theoretical explanation and treatment. The cost for such predominance by one person was that the early to mid-twentieth century was dominated by his thinking, and two camps were formed: the Freudians and the neo-Freudians. The influence of this one man was so powerful that he still influences, if not overwhelms, classic psychoanalytic thinking. Freud's theories were his direct contribution to child psychiatry. He believed his theories were supported by his observations from treatment. He proposed that psychological development must proceed through four sequentially related childhood psychosexual stages. Any inhibition of development critical to those stages would fixate the emotional structures needed for adult adjustment and result in stunted emotional development. Fixation in some stage would result in faulty emotional defense mechanisms, permitting the person to be flooded by anxieties. Neurosis was, according to Freudian psychology, the presence of more anxiety than the emotional defense structures can cope with comfortably. Psychosis was the loss of reality owing to the operational incapacitation of the mental defense structures.

Freud's emphasis on childhood, and the growth and development of the mind as a parallel to the biological development of organs, bones, and muscle, was a major contribution for the wrong reasons. These biologically metaphoric hypotheses of emotional development did provide a universal understanding of the importance of child-rearing practices, and a set of constructs that permitted an explanation of emotional disturbance scientifically was appealing. A mixed blessing is that Freud's theories far outran any data that any science could produce. Constructs such as the three major components of the mind—the id, ego, and super ego—are without substantiation.

The neo-Freudians of the post-World War II period extended Freud's biologically based metaphors to include socioenvironmental consideration. The slow, deliberate treatment processes associated with psychoanalytic theory soon gave way to the so-called client-centered theories that drew on principles of self-worth and self-actualization, and were then extended into public school counseling and classroom environments.

By the late 1950s, in response to Clifford Beer's book, *The Mind that Found Itself,* the two world wars, and the spectacular results achieved by the Veterans' Administration in treating emotionally disturbed soldiers, a national emphasis was placed on curing mental illness. However, emotional disturbance is not an acute disease. It is a chronic long-term adjustment disorder, found especially in children.

The 1960s were, however, a period when three significant phases occurred. The national mood in favor of treating mental illness took on a strong mental health dimension aimed at the public schools. There was a gradual development of classes for emotionally disturbed children in the public schools, and many of these classes were transferred from residential facilities in the beginning. The most promising factor was a change in the attitude of community and public policy makers toward treatment for emotionally disturbed children in the public schools by the public schools. However, the growth of programs was slow and awkward, and in contrast to programs and services for other handicapped populations (e.g., the mentally retarded), programs and services for the emotionally disturbed were practically nonexistent. However, state after state began to require teaching credentials and legislate monies for programs. The issues, once again, were why people are emotionally disturbed, how many are emotionally disturbed, and what can be done for them?

The public schools wanted a quick fix. Wolpe (1976) provided educators with behavior therapy. The behavior therapy and behavior modification content for controlling, regulating, and shaping acceptable behaviors in populations of norm-violating, chronically disruptive children was well timed. It opened the door to mechanical practices, based on simple principles that most any teacher could comprehend with little formal training. No longer was it necessary to comprehend the theories associated with the structure of the mind. It was a simple case of identifying, through observation, those student behaviors that were in deviation of the code or norm for the classroom or corridor, or that drew unfavorable attention to the student. Those behaviors became the target for treatment and the term behavioral disorders came into vogue.

None of the older terminologies were replaced; in 1977, Epstein, Cullinan, and Sabatino attempted to survey the use of the definition behavior disorders among states. The District of Columbia and 45 states replied. The component most prevalent in state definitions was disorder of emotion/behavior; the least common component was prognosis.

These researchers (Epstein, Cullinan, & Sabatino, 1977) identified two definitive types of definitions:

> First, numerous authoritative individuals or groups have defined behavior disorders; these statements generally reflect the theoretical positions and professional experiences of their authors and are often intended to structure an exposition of behavior disorders or to provoke thoughtful exploration of a particular position. Another (the second) kind of definition functions primarily to guide the delivery of resources or services to behaviorally disordered children—for example, a state educational agency's definition. (p. 418)

Fifteen definitional components were identified and reported in the data from the study.

Three components, disorders of emotion/behavior, interpersonal problems, and learning/achievement problems, appeared to be separate major areas of child functioning in which problems could occur. Disorders of emotion/behavior was found in all definitions, but the language of the definitions hardly indicated widespread agreement across states. For example, 15 definitions used the word emotion and/or a related reference to interpersonal or mental condition, excluding reference to behavior problems; 18 definitions used behavior and/or alluded to various overt behavior problems, with no mention of difficulties of emotion; 16 definitions referred to both types of problems. Among those definitions that referred to emotional or behavioral disorders, a wide variation in terms and emphases was evident. A majority of state definitions included the components interpersonal problems and learning/achievement problems. A wide range of terms were employed, representing quite different viewpoints that in turn emphasized treatment forms and even expected results.

The components deviation from norm, chronicity, severity, etiology, prognosis, and exclusions functioned as qualifiers in the majority of definitions. The fact that deviation from norm appeared in almost half of the definitions indicated awareness that emotional or behavioral disorders must not only consider the home, school, and social environment, but any discrepancy between a particular child's functioning and that of other pupils of that age in a particular environment. Absent from the definitions were specific statements addressing normal behavioral and emotional patterns. This means the boundaries of diagnosing these behavioral patterns do not have many boundaries wherein the deviation from norm components can be consistently considered. Severity and chronicity components appeared in well over one-third of the definitions. These were apparently intended to distinguish the mild from severe: those in need of in-class support and/or in-school therapy from those who require institutionalization.

The intent of the etiology component may have been to assure that children receiving special education for the behaviorally disordered were truly behaviorally disordered, i.e., that their disturbed functioning arose from some of the classical causes of a behavioral disorder such as organic damage, parental pathology, family breakdown, cultural deprivation, etc. Across the eight definitions that contained this component, however, divergent and even contradictory etiologies were emphasized. Prognosis apparently was included to provide special education primarily to the mildly behaviorally disordered in contrast to the more severely involved. This component is at odds with severity, a principal identification factor in behavioral disorders that affords a reduced likelihood of favorable response to treatment. Over one-third of the definitions contained an exclusions component, which stated that a child should not be identified as behaviorally disordered, regardless of emotional and behavioral problems, if he or she manifests concomitant handicaps. The most common of these handicaps are mental retardation, sensory disabilities, orthopedic disabilities, brain damage, delinquency, social maladjustment, and drug abuse.

Special education needed and certification components require that before formal identification is accomplished, certain individuals or groups designated as official labelers have to verify that a pupil is behaviorally disordered. Specific assessment procedures were not recommended by many states. In fact, diagnostic procedures were rarely addressed.

Behavioral disorders is a practical term, favored currently by many educators instead of more clinical or medically oriented (psychological/psychiatric) terminology. The reason is that all children and youths display a wide range of behaviors, the majority of which are normal. That is, children learn to respond by displaying an acceptable repertoire of behaviors to social cues. Children need the latitude to select a behavior in the learning process and try it; if acceptability or appropriate behaviors are displayed, normal adjustment is assumed to be manifest. A behavioral disorder exists when chronic, or inappropriate persistence is practiced. Certainly, home conditions, intelligence, appropriate modeling, and all important classroom management can inhibit or inadvertently reinforce many unwanted behaviors.

Behavioral disorders are transitory, temporal responses, many of which disappear with age and changes in environmental conditions. Therefore, definitions of behavioral disorders must distinguish between those that are referencing age-specific developmental periods and those that persist over time. There is the stigma and social learning significance of a pejorative label that serves no other purpose but to classify a child diagnostically. Generally, social interaction and self-concept research has shown these labels to set negative self-fulfilling prophecies into motion. Behavioral disorder is not meant to be anything more than a vague categorical descriptor of a handicapping condition for legal and educational purposes. The importance of this definition educationally is that it promotes defining precisely those targeted behaviors that are in need of modification. The term suggests that the educator must observe what is drawing unfavorable attention to the child, or delaying social and academic learning, and prepare specific behavioral objectives to combat the problem.

Behavioral disorders is a useful construct for the current state of knowledge that guides current special educational practices. It contains many improvements over earlier classification systems. It is not, however, a replacement for sophisticated statistical and clinical nomenclatures such as those found in the fourth edition of the *Diagnostic and Statistical Manual of Mental Disorders* (1980; DSM-IV) prepared by the American Psychiatric Association. A number of subclassification systems exist within the broad category of behavioral disorders. Most of these attempt to suggest, if not prescribe, the general course of diagnosis and treatment. The DSM-IV is a psychiatrically derived classification system for use with children and adults with emotional disorders. It is the standard classification system within mental health facilities in the United States, though it has far less official influence in public education.

Behaviorally disordered children may constitute one of the major national issues confronting the schools and society. Observation, diagnosis, and intervention strategies are poorly defined nationally. There is evidence that aggressive children are often detected. Unfortunately, there is also evidence that withdrawn children may not be recognized. The validity of treatment, indeed the value of any one approach may be questioned. Services too frequently are based on eliminating a problem student, not on teaching appropriate behaviors. Behavioral disorders as a loose configuration of symptoms may be the least developed special educational practice at this time. These disorders have the capability of being larger in incidence than any other, and most costly in both resources needed and loss of productivity. In addition, the pressure to place students with behavior disorders in inclusive programming has not borne any research results that suggest inclusion is appropriate for severe behavioral problems (MacMillan, 1996).

Finally, behavioral disorders are difficult to distinguish from learning disabilities. Frequently, the terms are used together. Certainly, children do react to the frustration of school failure by displaying inappropriate behaviors. There is no question that the symptoms of restlessness, aggressiveness, conflict, and other manifestations of behavioral disorders influence academic learning. Algozzine and Korinck (1985) note a national expansion, if not explosion, in learning disabilities, and fewer behavioral disorders (about 10% of the school-age population). Why? Probably because behavioral disorders remain an unsavory, mixed-bag issue, poorly understood by the schools and community and therefore threatening. Behavioral disorders, unlike learning disabilities, is not yet a concept whose time has come.

REFERENCES

Algozzine, B., & Korinck, L. (1985). Where is special education for students with high prevalence handicaps going? *Exceptional Children, 51,* 388–394.

American Psychiatric Association. (1980). *Diagnostic and statistical manual of mental disorders* (3rd ed.). Washington, DC: Author.

Epstein, M. H., Cullinan, D., & Sabatino, D. A. (1977). State definitions of behavior disorders. *Journal of Special Education, 11,* 417–425.

MacMillan, D. L., Gresham, F., & Forness, S. (1996). Full inclusion: An empirical perspective. *Behavior Disorders, 21*(2), 145–159.

DAVID A. SABATINO
West Virginia College of Graduate Studies

DIAGNOSTIC AND STATISTICAL MANUAL OF MENTAL DISORDERS (DSM-IV)
EMOTIONAL DISORDERS

BEHAVIORISM

The root of behaviorism is the term behavior, which may be defined as the set or universe of things an organism can do, or more simply, what an organism does. Typically, behavior is a term used in the fields of psychology or sociology to describe human or animal activity, but it is important to note that the term can be, and is, applied to a wide range of other things, including plants, simple microorganisms, machines, and even subatomic particles. The critical attribute is that the activities or functions of the organism must be observable and therefore capable of being measured. Just as it is possible to speak of the behavior of single organisms of varying complexity and composition, it is also possible to examine the behavior of organisms in groups. The empirical emphasis of the term behavior is especially prominent in the United States, where the term is associated with a particular school of psychology known as behaviorism. Behaviorism has its philosophical roots in the radical empiricist traditions of early thinkers such as John Locke and David Hume in Europe and in the twentieth-century movement known as logical positivism. The common thread philosophically is that behavior may be (and, for some, must be) understood purely as a lawful phenomenon in itself, without reference to intervening variables such as will, mind, volition, or motivation, which purport to explain why behavior occurs.

Early in the twentieth century, the young discipline of psychology was quite concerned with such concepts as will and mind, notably in the work of introspectionists such as Titchner. However, when Pavlov and his colleagues demonstrated that learning was a process whose parameters could be empirically specified and whose results could be reliably predicted, psychologists such as John Watson saw that human behavior could be studied in a simpler, more elegant way, as other sciences were being studied. Watson articulated his position as follows: "Psychology, as the behaviorist views it, is a purely objective, experimental branch of science which needs introspection as little as do the sciences of chemistry and physics. . . ." (1913, p. 176). Watson's fervent rejection of the idea of introspection, mental states, or any other nonempirical behavior analysis has earned him general recognition as the founder of behaviorism.

It remained for later thinkers, notably Edward L. Thorndike and B. F. Skinner, to refine and clearly articulate behaviorism. Watson had emphasized stimulus conditions (following Pavlov's respondent conditioning principles) in his work; the most famous example was his introduction of the fear of a white rat in a young boy (Watson & Rayner, 1920). Thorndike (1935), through is Law of Effect, and Skinner (1953), through his Principle of Reinforcement, argued that the consequences of response determine much of what we learn. Skinner in particular has written extensively of the many ways in which this oper-

ant conditioning can be observed and applied in our daily affairs. Like Watson before him, Skinner adamantly rejects the need for a psychology of the mind or any other attempt to understand behavior in subjective terms. For Skinner, behavior is conditioned by external events, and as such it can be controlled, predicted, and studied by empirical methods. The wide range of studies of both human and animal learning (Kazdin, 1975; Kimble, 1961) as a function of behavioral methods demonstrate how powerful the principles of behaviorism can be when effectively applied.

More recently, behaviorists cautiously have begun to reexamine the role of mental processes in determining behavior. Members of this new school of thought, sometimes called cognitive behaviorism, include psychologists such as Albert Bandura (1977) and Donald Meichenbaum (1977). Reconsideration of the role of mental process in behavior has come about for two reasons. First, certain kinds of learning, such as modeling, occur in the absence of typical observable consequences. It is thought that in some cases a form of self-reinforcement (or perhaps self-punishment) through language is responsible for strengthening the behavior (Bandura, 1977). Others (e.g., Meichenbaum, 1977) have noted that traditional behavioral learning paradigms have been too simplistic to account for the wide array of individual differences in behavior, especially among humans. Even unyielding behavioral analyses such as Skinner's make use of variables such as reinforcement history, which imply some sort of cognitive process in mediating across gaps in time.

The influence of behavioristic thought in psychology is undeniable. The emphasis on empirical research conditions that seemed so strident and incongruous in Watson's time is now taught as the basis of good research, and the importance of both Pavlovian and Skinnerian conditioning has been observed even in popular literature. Behavioristic methods of treatment occupy a prominent place in the study of psychopathology, and behavioral principles are being applied in industrial/organizational settings. As the school of thought broadens its consideration of variables involved in behavior, it holds even brighter promise as a tool for understanding what we do and why we do it.

REFERENCES

Bandura, A. (1977). Self-efficacy: Toward a unifying theory of behavioral change. *Psychological Review, 84,* 191–215.

Kazdin, A. (1975). *Behavior modification in applied settings.* Homewood, IL: Dorsey.

Kimble, G. A. (1961). *Hilgard and Marquis' conditioning and learning* (2nd ed.). New York: Appleton-Century-Crofts.

Meichenbaum, D. (1977). *Cognitive behavior modification: An integrative approach.* NY: Plenum.

Skinner, B. F. (1953). *Science and human behavior.* NY: Free Press.

Thorndike, E. L. (1935). *The psychology of wants, interests and attitudes.* New York: Appleton-Century.

Watson, J. (1913). Psychology as the behaviorist views it. *Psychological Review, 20,* 1958–1977.

Watson, J., & Rayner, R. (1920). Conditioning emotional responses. *Journal of Experimental Psychology, 3,* 1–14.

JERRY L. SLOAN
*Wilmington Psychiatric
Associates*

BEHAVIOR MODIFICATION
PSYCHOANALYSIS
SOCIAL LEARNING THEORY

BEHAVIOR MODELING

Modeling is a training intervention that was popularized by social learning theory and the works of Albert Bandura (Bandura, 1971). When using this procedure, the practitioner physically demonstrates or shows a visual representation (e.g., photo sequence, videotape, movie) of the production of the behavior. In essence, the practitioner shows the student the appropriate way to respond. The demonstration often includes secondary informational sources such as feedback about the model's success and the environmental and contextual cues that led the model to behave in the particular fashion demonstrated.

The effectiveness of this procedure can be enhanced through attention to several variables. Of primary consideration are the characteristics of the person providing the model. In some cases the person who demonstrates the behavior could be another student. This would be appropriate when the other student is (1) competent to do the behavior; (2) someone the student can identify with (i.e., someone similar to himself or herself); (3) someone held in high esteem by the target student; (4) able to demonstrate the appropriate behavior clearly; (5) able to demonstrate novel responses that the target student has not yet learned to do; and (6) reinforced for the performance of the target behavior.

Student factors are also important to the modeling process. First, the student must be sufficiently motivated to become an active participant in the modeling process. An absence of sufficient motivation will negate the qualities of the model and the modeling event. Second, the attention of the student must be keyed to the relevant properties of the modeled behavior. Third, the student must have sufficient motor abilities to replicate the modeled behavior. Finally, the ability of the student to remember and recall the modeled act will greatly affect the general and functional utility of the modeled behavior. This retention is based on two processes: imagination and verbalization. In the first case, when stimuli are consistently paired, the occurrence of one of the paired stimuli will signal the other. In the second case, labeling of an event (a verbal process whether vocalized or not) lends saliency to the event.

Factors related to the instructional variables can also affect the effectiveness of modeling. Reinforcement for the modeled behavior must be sufficient in quantity and quality to bring about student participation. For example, Lovaas (1967) has shown that children imitate precisely when they are rewarded for precise replication of modeled behaviors. However, when children are reinforced nondifferentially (i.e., for approximations of the response), they produce poorly matched responses. Modeled behavior is most effectively acquired and maintained when the modeled behaviors are familiar and functional to the target student. Overt rehearsals of the modeled response can considerably enhance the acquisition and maintenance of the modeled behavior.

Modeling, therefore, is a useful instructional procedure. As a technology for instruction, it requires that its users follow specific procedures to produce maximum results. These procedures are neither esoteric nor difficult to follow. Because modeling is thought to be a "least restrictive" instructional prompting procedure, and because it is usable in most environments, it should be considered to be an instructional procedure of choice under most circumstances.

REFERENCES

Bandura, A. (1971). Analysis of modeling processes. In A. Bandura (Ed.), *Psychological modeling: Conflicting theories.* Chicago: Aldine-Atherton.

Lovaas, O. I. (1967). A behavior therapy approach to the treatment of childhood schizophrenia. In J. P. Hill (Ed.), *Minnesota symposia on child psychology* (Vol. 1). Minneapolis: University of Minnesota Press.

LYLE E. BARTON
Kent State University

COGNITIVE BEHAVIOR THERAPY
SOCIAL LEARNING THEORY
THEORY OF ACTIVITY

BEHAVIOR MODIFICATION

Behavior modification is generally regarded as a term that encompasses the various methods derived from learning theory that are used to alter the response patterns of humans and other animals. The term has been used in this way by Bandura (1969); he and other behaviorists such as Skinner (1965) have enumerated a wide variety of learning principles that have been translated into methods for learning or changing behavior.

Although behavior modification is sometimes considered as a unitary position in discussions of certain issues in psychology, the techniques involved are derived from several different theoretical approaches to learning. Each approach tends to emphasize environmental determinants, as opposed to person-based determinants, of individual differences among organisms in the way in which they learn behavior. On the other hand, each approach also emphasizes the importance of determining the specific environmental variables that influence the behavior of an individual.

One such approach (Wolpe, 1982) is based on classical or respondent conditioning, which was studied extensively early in the twentieth century by Ivan Pavlov, the Russian psychologist, and John Watson, the American sometimes known as the father of behaviorism. In this type of learning, a neutral stimulus is paired in time with another stimulus (called the unconditioned stimulus) already able to elicit a particular response, usually unlearned, from an organism's repertoire. Through repeated pairings, this neutral stimulus also acquires the capability of eliciting the original (or unconditioned) response; this neutral stimulus is called the conditioned stimulus. For example, Watson and Rayner (1920) performed a classic study in which a neutral stimulus (a white rat) took on fear-inducing properties for a young boy when it was presented to the child paired with a sudden loud noise (an unconditioned stimulus) that startled and frightened the child (the unconditioned response). Soon the child began attempting to avoid the white rat because of its newly acquired association with the loud noise. Classical conditioning is apparently important in establishing subtle types of learning such as attitudes, basic emotional states such as love, fear and trust, and other similar behaviors acquired over long periods of time.

A second major approach to behavior modification (Skinner, 1965) is based on operant or instrumental conditioning. The basis of this approach is the so-called law of effect articulated by Thorndike (1935). He proposed that responses followed by pleasurable consequences would be strengthened, whereas responses followed by unpleasant consequences would be weakened. This formulation was refined and greatly expanded by others, notably Skinner, who had demonstrated that consequences (Thorndike would have called them effects) are important in learning a wide variety of behaviors. Most of these behaviors involve some activity or operation (hence the term operant conditioning) in the form of a skill the organism learns. An important derivative of operant conditioning has been described by Premack (1965). He showed that the opportunity to perform a desirable activity may be used as a consequence to reinforce or strengthen the performance of a less preferred activity. Thus a person may be willing to do

something relatively unpleasant (perhaps balancing a checkbook or reading a boring book) if this activity is followed soon thereafter by a pleasurable activity (perhaps a movie or a golf outing).

The modification of behavior using the outlined principles of operant conditioning is sometimes called applied behavior analysis. Usually this involves detailed empirical specification of the behavior to be changed (or to be learned), careful observation of the contributing conditioning elements, and the development of a strategy (changing antecedent stimulus conditions, response consequences, or both) to achieve the desired results. It is important to note that the use of behavior modification techniques does not require the use of terms such as normal or abnormal to describe the behavior being examined. In fact, the learning theorists who have contributed to the development of behavior modification techniques assume that behavior is learned according to principles that operate nearly identically in all situations, even though a given observer may have a higher or lower value to place on a particular learned behavior. As a result, descriptive terms such as abnormal are frequently rejected because their use tempts us to infer that different laws of learning have governed the behavior so described.

REFERENCES

Bandura, A. (1969). *Principles of behavior modification.* New York: Holt, Rinehart, & Winston.

Premack, D. (1965). Reinforcement therapy. In D. Levine (Ed.), *Nebraska symposium on motivation.* Lincoln: University of Nebraska Press.

Skinner, B. F. (1965). *Science and human behavior.* New York: Free Press.

Thorndike, E. L. (1935). *The psychology of wants, interests and attitudes.* New York: Appleton, Century.

Watson, J., & Rayner, R. (1920). Conditioning emotional response. *Journal of Experimental Psychology, 3,* 1–14.

Wolpe, J. (1982). *The practice of behavior therapy* (3rd ed.). New York: Pergamon.

JERRY L. SLOAN
Wilmington Psychiatric Associates

APPLIED BEHAVIOR ANALYSIS
OPERANT CONDITIONING

BEHAVIOR PROBLEM CHECKLIST, REVISED

The Revised Behavior Problem Checklist (RBPC; Quay & Peterson, 1983) is a widely researched rating scale for the clinical evaluation of deviant behavior. The original Behavior Problem Checklist (BPC) was developed in 1967 and the RBPC is the revised version of this scale. The RBPC consists of four major scales and two minor scales. The major scales include: Conduct Disorder (22 items), Socialized Aggression (17 items), Attention Problems–Immaturity (16 items), and Anxiety–Withdrawal (11 items). The two minor scales are Psychotic Behavior (6 items) and Motor Tension–Excess (5 items). In addition, twelve items are included for research purposes, and do not contribute to the overall score.

The revised version uses a weighted scoring system (2 = severe problem; 1 = mild problem; 0 = not a problem, no opportunity to observe, don't know). One problem associated with this scoring system is the failure to discriminate between the three possible zero responses (Roberts, 1986). Thus a score of zero does not necessarily indicate the absence of a behavior problem. Checklists and scoring templates are included with the manual. The checklists can be completed in approximately 15 minutes by any observer who is familiar with the subject. Scoring templates provide raw scores for each of the four major and two minor scales, and can be completed in 5–10 minutes.

Estimates of internal consistency reliability range from .68 to .95. Interrater reliabilities range from .52 to .85. Test-retest reliabilities (two-month interval) range from .49 to .83 (N = 149). Support for validity includes a substantial relationship between the RBPC and the BPC, discrimination between normal children and clinical groups, and support from numerous studies for many facets of validity (Dezolt, 1992; Hinshaw et al, 1987; Lahay & Piacentini, 1985). The authors do not provide representative norms based on Census data, but recommend developing local norms. However, the use of local norms without reference to a normative sample may be complicated by such things as cultural variation within communities and transient populations. The manual provides means and standard deviations for scale scores from clinical and nonclinical samples, and from parent and teacher ratings. However, little demographic information is included; thus, it is unclear whether these samples are representative.

The RBPC is a useful screening instrument for assessing behavior problems along four independent dimensions commonly associated with emotional disturbance (Quay, 1983). However, the absence of a well-defined normative sample is cause for some concern (Shapiro, 1992).

REFERENCES

Dezolt, D. M. (1992). Review of the Revised Behavior Problem Checklist. In J. J. Kramer & J. C. Conoley (Eds.), *The eleventh mental measurements yearbook* (pp. 764–765). Lincoln, NE: Buros Institute of Mental Measurements.

Hinshaw, S. P., Morrison, D. C., Carte, E. T., & Cornsweet, C. (1987). Factorial dimensions of the Revised Behavior Problem Checklist: Replication and validation within a kindergarten sample. *Journal of Abnormal Child Psychology, 15,* 309–327.

Lahay, B. B., & Piacentini, J. C. (1985). An evaluation of the Quay-Peterson Revised Behavior Problem Checklist. *Journal of School Psychology, 23,* 285–289.

Quay, H. C. (1983). A dimensional approach to behavior disorder: The Revised Behavior Problem Checklist. *School Psychology Review, 12,* 244–249.

Quay, H. C., & Peterson, D. R. (1983). *Interim manual for the Revised Behavior Problem Checklist.* Coral Gables, FL: University of Miami.

Roberts. T. (1986). Revised Behavior Problem Checklist. In D. L. Keyser & R. C. Sweetland (Eds.), *Test critiques: Volume 5* (pp. 371–377). Kansas City, MO: Test Corporation of America.

Shapiro, E. S. (1992). Review of the Revised Behavior Problem Checklist. In J. J. Kramer & J. C. Conoley (Eds.), *The eleventh mental measurements yearbook* (pp. 765–766). Lincoln, NE: Buros Institute of Mental Measurements.

LIZANNE DESTEFANO
University of Illinois

BEHAVIOR THERAPY

Behavior therapy encompasses a broad range of philosophical, theoretical, and procedural approaches to the "alleviation of human suffering and the enhancement of human functioning" (Davison & Stuart, 1975, p. 755). An approach to assessment, therapy, ethics, and professional issues, it has been used successfully with a variety of populations (adults, children, adolescents, mentally retarded, etc.) in diverse settings (schools, hospitals, psychiatric facilities, mental health centers, etc.) and for various problems (anxiety, depression, addictive disorders, social skills deficits, psychotic behaviors, marital dysfunction, academic skills, parent-child problems, etc.). There are probably few human behaviors that have not been addressed by behavior therapists.

A number of terms with somewhat different origins and connotations have been used almost interchangeably to denote the field. These terms include behavior therapy, behavior modification, applied behavior analysis, social learning theory, cognitive-behavior therapy, clinical behavior therapy, and multimodal behavior therapy. Attempts to clarify or standardize the meaning of the various terms based on the populations served (e.g., individual or group), techniques used (e.g., systematic desensitization, contingency management), methodologies (e.g., single-subject designs), or theoretical bases (e.g., classical conditioning, operant conditioning) have failed to gain wide acceptance (Franzini & Tilker, 1972; Wilson, 1978).

Several formal definitions of behavior therapy have

been proposed. For example, Wolpe (1982) defined behavior therapy as "the use of experimentally established principles and paradigms of learning to overcome unadaptive habits" (p. 1). Whereas Wolpe's definition emphasizes a theoretical basis of behavior therapy, other definitions stress the methods of inquiry used by behavior therapists. For example, Ross, in his presidential address to the Association for Advancement of Behavior Therapy, defined behavior therapy as "the empirically controlled application of the science of human behavior to the alleviation of psychological distress and the modification of maladaptive behavior" (Ross, 1985, p. 196). This definition reflects the growing acceptance of methodological behaviorism, which focuses on the methods used in obtaining psychological information. Such a definition, however, does not delineate behavior therapy from other construct systems that might also use empirical methods of inquiry.

The difficulty of arriving at a single definition of behavior therapy was well summarized by Kazdin and Wilson (1978):

> Contemporary behavior therapy is marked by a diversity of views, a broad range of heterogeneous procedures with different theoretical rationales, and open debate about conceptual bases, methodological requirements, and evidence of efficacy. In short, there is no clearly agreed upon or commonly accepted definition of behavior therapy. (p. 1)

This lack of consensus reflects both the continuous development of behavior therapy and the various models within the behavioral construct system.

At least four major models within behavior therapy can be identified: (1) applied behavior analysis, (2) neobehavioristic mediational model, (3) social learning theory, and (4) cognitive-behavior therapy (Agras, Kazdin, & Wilson, 1979). The models differ on the bases of historical tradition, fundamental principles, and therapeutic procedures.

Applied behavior analysis draws heavily from the Skinner tradition of operant conditioning. Behavior is assumed to be under the control of environmental stimuli. These controlling stimuli include the consequences of behavior as well as the antecedent events that are associated with differential consequences. Intervention involves the manipulation of the controlling environmental stimuli in order to modify overt behavior. Therapeutic procedures are based on principles derived from operant conditioning such as reinforcement, punishment, extinction, and stimulus control. The token economy, in which appropriate behaviors earn tokens that later can be exchanged for desired activities, consumable goods, and privileges, is a procedure representative of applied behavior analysis.

The neobehavioristic mediational model is based primarily on the principles of classical conditioning derived from the learning theories of Pavlov, Hull, and Mowrer (Wolpe, 1982). The model emphasizes the role of anxiety as a conditioned emotional response. For example, the anxiety response can be elicited by previously neutral stimuli as a result of pairing those neutral stimuli with noxious stimuli. Therapeutic procedures such as systematic desensitization and flooding are designed to reduce the anxiety underlying behavioral disorders by exposing the individual to the conditioned, feared stimulus in the absence of the noxious stimulus.

According to the third model, social learning theory (Bandura, 1977), three interacting systems regulate behavior. The first system is external stimulus control, which regulates behavior either through the association of stimuli, as in classical conditioning, or through antecedent stimuli reliably predicting differential consequences of behavior. Response feedback, primarily in the form of reinforcing consequences, provides a second regulatory system. Finally, cognitive processes mediate the effect of external events by influencing which events are attended to and how those events are perceived and interpreted. An important cognitive mediator of behavior change is self-efficacy, the expectation that the behavior required to produce an outcome can be performed. Social learning theory further posits that human functioning is a result of the reciprocal interaction among behavior, the environment, and a person's cognitions (Bandura, 1981). That is, not only does the environment influence behavior, but a person's behavior also influences the environment. Modeling of the desired behavior by the therapist, either with or without the client's subsequent performance, is a therapeutic procedure derived from social learning theory's emphasis on cognitive processes such as the capacity to learn through observation.

The most recent development in behavior therapy is the emergence of cognitive-behavior therapy (Beck, 1976; Mahoney, 1974). According to this model, it is the perception of events rather than the events themselves that most influence behavior. Further, adaptive and maladaptive patterns are acquired through cognitive processes. Thus irrational beliefs, errors of logic, faulty self-talk, dysfunctional attributions, and mental representations of one's self and one's world contribute to behavioral and emotional disorders. Cognitive restructuring, in which clients are taught to examine and change faulty cognitions, is a representative procedure used in cognitive-behavior therapy. Cognitive behavior therapy has become the treatment of choice for several adult and childhood disorders, including panic, phobic, and obsessive-compulsive disorders. It has also dominated outcome research on psychological therapy (Wilson, 1997).

Despite the diversity of models in the behavioral construct system and the inability to provide a single definition of behavior therapy, a number of characteristics and assumptions of behavior therapy can be delineated (Agras et al., 1979; Haynes, 1984; Kazdin & Hersen, 1980). No one of these characteristics is definitive of the field, nor does any one necessarily differentiate behavior therapy from other systems. Nevertheless, taken together, they represent the common core of behavior therapy.

One set of characteristics concern methods of inquiry:

1. There is a commitment to empiricism and scientific methodology as the primary basis for developing and evaluating concepts and therapeutic techniques.
2. There is a commitment to an explicit, testable, and falsifiable conceptual foundation.
3. Therapeutic procedures and hypotheses with sufficient precision to make evaluation, replication, and generalization possible are specified.
4. There are close ties to the experimental findings of the science of psychology.
5. There is a low level of inference about data so as to minimize biases.

These epistemological principles imply that behavior therapy will continue to evolve as new knowledge is gained from empirical findings.

A second set of characteristics concerns the assumptions about behavior and behavioral disorders.

1. There is a deterministic model of behavior in which environmental antecedents and consequences are assumed to have the greatest impact on behavior. Recently, interactional models have been introduced in which behavior, the environment, and the person (most notably cognitive events and physiological conditions) are all presumed to influence one another.
2. There is an emphasis on current determinants of behavior as opposed to historical determinants (i.e., early childhood experiences).
3. The same principles that govern normal behavior also govern abnormal behavior. That is, no qualitative difference separates normal from abnormal behavior.
4. There are multiple determinants of behavior. The determinants of behavioral disorders may vary from individual to individual, and from one disorder to another.
5. Both the disease model of abnormal behavior and the implication that dysfunctional behavior is a sign or symptom of an underlying illness are rejected. Instead, dysfunctional behavior is construed as a "problem in living" or as learned, maladaptive behavior. Thus the dysfunctional behavior itself is targeted for behavior change.
6. Psychological disorders can be expressed in behavioral, cognitive, and affective modes. These modes can covary to differing degrees owing to situational factors and individual differences.

7. There is the relative specificity of behavior to the situation in which it occurs as opposed to the belief that behavior is consistent across situations.

A third set of characteristics concerns the methods of behavior change:

1. Therapeutic procedures are derived from experimental-clinical psychology.
2. Therapy is conceptualized as an opportunity to unlearn maladaptive behaviors and to learn adaptive behaviors.
3. The importance of tailoring therapy to the individual based on an assessment of the idiosyncratic determinants of the individual's dysfunctional behavior is emphasized.
4. The importance of the therapist-client interaction as one source of behavior change is emphasized.
5. There is an ongoing evaluation of intervention results in order to modify procedures as needed.
6. Intervention results are generalized from the intervention setting to the client's natural environment.

In conclusion, behavior therapy is a multifaceted and diverse system linked by a common core of assumptions. It is a viable system that has withstood numerous criticisms to emerge as a major approach within the psychological treatment field.

REFERENCES

Agras, W. S., Kazdin, A. E., & Wilson, G. T. (1979). *Behavior therapy: Toward an applied clinical science.* San Francisco: Freeman.

Bandura, A. (1977). *Social learning theory.* Englewood Cliffs, NJ: Prentice-Hall.

Bandura, A. (1981). In search of pure unidirectional determinants. *Behavior Therapy, 12,* 30–40.

Beck, A. T. (1976). *Cognitive therapy and the emotional disorders.* New York: International Universities Press.

Davison, G. C., & Stuart, R. B. (1975). Behavior therapy and civil liberties. *American Psychologist, 30,* 755–763.

Franzini, L. R., & Tilker, H. A. (1972). On the terminological confusion between behavior therapy and behavior modification. *Behavior Therapy, 3,* 279–282.

Haynes, S. N. (1984). Behavioral assessment of adults. In M. Hersen & G. Goldstein (Eds.), *Handbook of psychological assessment.* New York: Pergamon.

Kazdin, A. E., & Hersen, M. (1980). The current status of behavior therapy. *Behavior Modification, 4,* 283–302.

Kazdin, A. E., & Wilson, G. T. (1978). *Evaluation of behavior therapy: Issues, evidence, and research strategies.* Cambridge, MA: Ballinger.

Mahoney, M. J. (1974). *Cognition and behavior modification.* Cambridge, MA: Ballinger.

Ross, A. O. (1985). To form a more perfect union: It is time to stop standing still. *Behavior Therapy, 16,* 195–204.

Wilson, G. T. (1978). On the much discussed nature of the term "behavior therapy." *Behavior Therapy, 9,* 89–98.

Wilson, G. T. (1997). Behavior therapy at century close. *Behavior Therapy, 28*(3), 449–457.

Wolpe, J. (1982). *The practice of behavior therapy* (3rd ed.). New York: Pergamon.

JEFFREY L. PHILLIPS
*University of North Carolina
at Wilmington*

APPLIED BEHAVIOR ANALYSIS
BEHAVIOR MODIFICATION
DESENSITIZATION
SOCIAL LEARNING THEORY

BEHAVIOR THERAPY

Behavior Therapy is the journal of the Association for Advancement of Behavior Therapy. The journal is an interdisciplinary publication for original research of an experimental and clinical nature that deals with theories, practices, and evaluation of cognitive-behavior therapy, behavior therapy, or behavior modification. The major emphasis of the journal is on empirical research, but methodological and theoretical papers are also published. The format for publication includes articles, brief reports of approximately eight pages, invited book reviews, case studies, and clinical replication series. *Behavior Therapy* is published in four issues (Winter, Spring, Summer and Fall) and edited by J. Gayle Beck, Ph.D., Department of Psychology, State University of New York at Buffalo, Buffalo, NY 14260-4110.

CRAIG D. SMITH
Georgia College
First edition

KAY E. KETZENBERGER
*The University of Texas of the
Permian Basin*
Second edition

BELL, ALEXANDER GRAHAM (1847–1922)

Alexander Graham Bell, inventor of the telephone, educator, and spokesperson for the deaf, was born and educated in Scotland. Emigrating first to Canada and then to the United States, Bell, whose father and grandfather were authorities in the field of speech, and who had himself specialized in the anatomy of the vocal apparatus, opened a school in Boston for the training of teachers of the deaf in 1872; he became a professor at Boston University and married one of his students, Mabel Hubbard, who was deaf, as was his mother.

Widely acclaimed for his numerous inventions, Bell used his vast influence to foster his major interest, the teaching of the deaf. An avid proponent of oral methods of teaching the deaf, Bell became the acknowledged leader of the oral movement in the United States. He also campaigned tirelessly for the establishment of day schools for the deaf to provide an alternative to residential school placement. Bell was a founder of the American Association to Promote the Teaching of Speech to the Deaf, later renamed the Alexander Graham Bell Association for the Deaf, and of the *Volta Bureau,* which he established for the dissemination of knowledge about the deaf.

REFERENCE

Bruce, R. V. (1973). *Alexander Graham Bell and the conquest of solitude.* Boston: Little, Brown.

PAUL IRVINE
Katonah, New York

BELL, TERREL H. (1921–1996)

Terrel H. Bell died at his home in Salt Lake City on June 23, 1996 at the age of 74. Bell was born in Lava Hot Springs, Idaho, and received a master's degree from the University of Idaho in 1954 and a PhD in Educational Administration from the University of Utah in 1961. He was the recipient of 21 honorary doctorates conferred by various colleges and universities throughout the United States during his lifetime.

After serving in World War II as a U.S. Marine, Bell was a superintendent of schools in Idaho, Wyoming, and Utah. He was U.S. Commissioner of Education from 1974 to 1976 and secretary of the U.S. Department of Education from 1981 to 1984. He appointed members, wrote the national charter, and provided support and leadership for the work of the National Commission on Excellence in Education. The commission report, "A Nation At Risk," found serious flaws in the education system and concluded that schools were mired in mediocrity. Twelve national forums were sponsored to disseminate the commission report, which is credited with prompting a movement to overhaul education. Over 12 million copies of the report have been printed, reprinted, and widely distributed.

Bell's numerous honors and awards include the Department of Defense Distinguished Public Service Medal awarded by Secretary of Defense Casper Weinberger in 1984. He authored numerous books and publications, and remained active in promoting education and learning after leaving the government. He subsequently taught Educational Administration at the University of Utah, and founded the educational consulting firm of T. H. Bell and Associates. In 1991, he wrote *How to Shape Up Our Nation's Schools: Three Crucial Steps for Renewing American Education.*

REFERENCES

Bell, T. H. (1956). *The prodigal pedagogue.* New York: Exposition.

Bell, T. H. (1960). *A philosophy of education for the space age.* New York: Exposition.

Bell, T. H. (1972). *Your child's intellect: A parent's guide to home based preschool education.* Salt Lake City, Utah: Olympus.

Bell, T. H. (1974). *Active parent concern.* Englewood Cliffs, NJ: Prentice-Hall.

Bell, T. H. (1984). *Excellence.* Salt Lake City, Utah: Deseret.

ROBERTA C. STOKES
Texas A & M University
First edition

TAMARA J. MARTIN
*The University of Texas of the
    Permian Basin*
Second edition

BELLEVUE PSYCHIATRIC HOSPITAL

The history of psychiatric care at Bellevue Hospital Center and the history of psychiatric care in the United States are closely interwoven. Bellevue has been at the vanguard of treatment for the mentally ill since the eighteenth century, pioneering methods of identifying and categorizing patients, training psychiatrists and psychiatric nurses, and developing out-patient as well as in-patient courses of treatment.

The Public Workhouse and House of Correction, which opened in 1736, ultimately became Bellevue Hospital. It contained a six-bed unit designed to provide care for "the infirm, the aged, the unruly, and the maniac." By 1826, a total of 82 of the 184 patients were listed as insane. In 1879 a pavilion for the insane was erected within hospital grounds. The concept of including the care and treatment of psychiatric patients in a general hospital rather than entirely apart from the treatment of the physically ailing was revolutionary.

In 1902 the Department of Bellevue and Allied Hospitals appointed a resident physician, two assistants, and trained nurses to provide medical attention for psychiatric patients, thereby providing the framework for the development of a modern psychiatric service. During the early 1900s, the primary function of the department of psychiatry at Bellevue was to "afford temporary care and treatment for those patients who are to be transferred to the state hospital for mental diseases within 10 days." Perhaps a more important function than maintaining patients on remand was to "provide care for another group of patients which had hitherto been neglected, patients whose psychoses are of such a character that they are not suitable for commitment to a hospital for the insane nor are they acceptable in a general hospital, e.g., cases of mild mental disorders, psychoneuroses, epilepsy, deliria, transitory attacks of confusion or excitement." Simultaneously, in an effort to discourage long-term hospitalization, the department of psychiatry at Bellevue established mental health clinics and the practice of ongoing contact with patients' families.

The Children's Inpatient Psychiatric Service began at Bellevue in 1920. Separate male and female adolescent wards were maintained providing for 30 patients each. In 1935 the New York City Board of Education established a special school for emotionally disturbed children at Bellevue. Now designated as P.S. 106, the school continues to function at Bellevue.

In establishing itself as a psychiatric prison ward, Bellevue has contributed to forensic medicine via the Psychiatric Clinic of the Court of General Sessions, established in 1931. This psychiatric prison ward encouraged the development of rigid safeguards for the rights of all psychiatric patients, including prisoners.

Among many firsts at Bellevue, in 1936 Karl Murdock Bowman was the first physician in the country to use insulin shock therapy for treatment of mental illness. In 1939 David Wechsler developed the Wechsler-Bellevue Scale of Intelligence, later called the Wechsler Adult Intelligence Scale, a test still widely used today. Wechsler went on to develop a number of intelligence tests often used with handicapped children including the Wechsler Intelligence Scale for Children and the Wechsler Pre-School Scale of Intelligence. Loretta Bender, a pioneer in work with autistic children and youths, worked at Bellevue during the 1950s and 1960s. In 1984, when its facilities in the New Bellevue Hospital at 27th Street and East River Drive in New York City were completed, Bellevue's psychiatric department was united for the first time with the rest of Bellevue. Psychiatry was truly integrated into a full-service hospital setting.

In recent years, Bellevue has continued to lead the field of psychiatric treatment. In the 1990s Bellevue was innovative in developing treatment modalities for individuals with substance abuse and mental illness with peer-led milieu therapy (Bellevue, 1993). In addition, "social marketing" was promoted by developing educational print materials for immigrant, low-literate, and other hard-to-reach groups (Dooley, 1996). The institution also developed a model for hospital-based alcoholism outpatient treatment services for homeless alcoholics (Miescher & Galanter, 1996). A vivid portrait of the everyday life of the staff and patients at Bellevue is portrayed in the 1995 book by the chief psychologist at Bellevue, Frederick Covan, and is entitled *Crazy All the Time: Life, Lessons, and Insanity on the Psych Ward of Bellevue Hospital.*

REFERENCES

Bellevue Hospital Center. *Bellevue hospital center.* New York: Author.

Covan, F. L., & Kahn, C. (1995). *Crazy all the time: Life, lessons, and insanity on the psych ward of Bellevue Hospital.* New York, NY: Simon & Schuster.

Dooley, A. R. (1996). A collaborative model for creating patient education resources. *American Journal of Health Behavior, 20,* 15–19.

Miescher, A., & Galanter, M. (1996). Shelter-based treatment of the homeless alcoholic. *Journal of Substance Abuse Treatment, 13,* 135–140.

New York City Health and Hospitals Corporation. (1984). *The nation's largest municipal health care system: directory of services.* New York: Author.

Walsh, James (Ed.). (1982). *Bellevue.* New York: Bellevue Hospital Center.

CATHERINE HALL RIKHYE
Hunter College
First edition

ELAINE FLETCHER-JANZEN
University of Northern Colorado
Second edition

BENADRYL

Benadryl (diphenhydramine hydrochloride) is used for perennial or seasonal (hay fever) allergic rhinitis, motion sickness, and allergic conjunctivitis owed to inhalant allergens and foods. An antihistamine, it has anticholinergic (drying) and sedative side effects. In isolated cases, it has been used as a sedative for treatment of hyperactivity. Adverse reactions include diminished mental alertness in both adults and children, with occasional excitation in the young child. A 1993 study (Vuurman, van Veggel, Uiterwijk & O'Hanlon, 1993) found that allergic reaction reduces learning ability in children. In addition, this effect is aggravated by diphenhydramine. Therefore, parents and educators should be aware that while Benadryl relieves some of the uncomfortable symptoms of allergies it increases problems in learning. Accommodations for the child with allergies should be specifically targeted to sedation if the child is taking Benadryl. These accommodations could include decreasing workload, increasing time for rehearsal of learning material and communications with parents on a daily basis to assist in the monitoring of side effects and learning retention.

A brand name of Parke-Davis Company, it is available in capsules of 25 and 50 ms; as an elixir for oral use; and in injectable syringes. Dosage for children (over 20 pounds) is 12.5 to 25 mg three to four times daily, with maximum daily dosage not in excess of 300 mg. For adults, dosage is 25 to 50 mg three to four times daily. Overdose with this or other antihistamines may cause hallucinations, convulsions, and death.

REFERENCES

Physician's desk reference (1997). Oradell, NJ: Medical Economics.

Vuurman, E. F., van Veggel, L. M., Uiterwijk, M. M., Leutner, D., & O'Hanlon, J. F. (1993). Seasonal allergic rhinitis and antihistamine effects on children's learning. *Annals of Allergy, 71*(2), 121–126.

LAWRENCE HARTLAGE
Evans, Georgia
First edition

ELAINE FLETCHER-JANZEN
University of Northern Colorado
Second edition

BENDER, LAURETTA (1897–1987)

Born in Butte, Montana, in 1897, Lauretta Bender obtained her BS and MA degrees from the University of Chicago in 1922 and 1923, respectively. She obtained her MD degree at the State University of Iowa in 1926 and returned to Chicago (Billings Hospital) for her internship (1927–1928) and residency in neurology (1928). A residency in psychiatry at Boston's Psychopathic Hospital preceded another psychiatric residency, in 1929–1930, at Johns Hopkins' Phipps Clinic. She also received postgraduate training in neuroanatomy, physiology, and pathology at the University of Amsterdam on a Rockefeller grant in 1926–1927.

Bender held numerous appointments, including assistant instructor of neuropathology at Iowa (1923–1926) and several psychiatric positions in the New York City area. These include senior psychiatrist at Bellevue Hospital (1930–1956), director of the Child Guidance Clinic at the New York City Infirmary (1954–1960), principal research scientist of Child Psychiatry at New York State Department of Mental Hygiene (1956–1960), director of Psychiatric Research at the Children's Unit of Creedmor State Hospital (1960–1969), and attending psychiatrist at the

New York Psychiatric Institute (1969–1973). She held teaching positions at New York University, Adelphi College Graduate School, and Columbia University. She retired in 1973 and moved to Annapolis, MD, where she remained until her death on January 4, 1987, at the age of 89.

Bender received numerous awards during her career, among them the Adolph Meyer Award in 1953 for her contributions to the profession's knowledge base on schizophrenic children, and was named Medicine's Woman of the Year for New York in 1958. She was a fellow of the American Medical Association, American Psychiatric Association, American Neurological Association, and American Orthopsychiatric Association.

With over 100 chapters and articles, Bender is widely published in the fields of child psychiatry, neurology, and psychology. She is best known for her Visual Motor Gestalt Test (1937), several books, including *Psychopathological Disorders of Children with Organic Brain Disease* (1956), and studies of learning disabilities (1970). Her theory of the role of brain pathology in the development of childhood schizophrenia is less known but also important. In addition, she developed the Face-Hand Test, which examines double simultaneous tactile sensation (face and hand). A variation of this test, the Fink-Green-Bender Test, has been used to discriminate between children with neurologic and schizophrenic disorders.

REFERENCES

Bender, L. (1937). *A visual motor gestalt test and its clinical use.* New York: American Orthopsychiatric Association.

Bender, L. (1956). *Psychopathological disorders of children with organic brain disease.* Springfield, IL: C. Thomas.

Bender, L. (1970). Use of the visual motor gestalt test in diagnosing learning disability. *Journal of Special Education, 4,* 29–39.

ANTONIO E. PUENTE
University of North Carolina at Wilmington
First edition

KAY E. KETZENBERGER
The University of Texas of the Permian Basin
Second edition

BENDER GESTALT

BENDER GESTALT

The Bender Gestalt is a brief, nonverbal, perceptual-motor assessment instrument. Originally developed by Lauretta Bender (1938) as a measure of visual-motor maturation in children, the test has become one of the most widely used assessment techniques for individuals of all ages. The Bender has, for example, been used with adults as a projective personality technique, and with children as an indicator of school readiness, emotional problems, and learning difficulties. However, it has been most widely used as a screening measure for brain dysfunction in both adults and children. (Figures 1 and 2.)

The test consists of nine figures, each of which is printed on a separate 4-inch by 6-inch card. Cards are presented one at a time and subjects are instructed to copy each figure as accurately as possible. Variations on this basic procedure include having subjects reproduce the figures from memory, embedding the figures in distracting backgrounds, and placing time limits on performance (Dana, Field, & Bolton, 1983). The test is typically administered individually, however, group administration procedures have also been developed (Koppitz, 1975). Although Bender did not provide a formal scoring method for the test, a number of objective scoring systems have since been devised (Lacks, 1984). The Developmental Bender Test Scoring System (Koppitz, 1963) has become the preferred scoring method for children's protocols. Designed for use with children between ages 5 and 10, the system identifies 30 scoring items (errors in the drawings; for example, rotations, distortions in shape, and failure to integrate the components of the design; see Figures 1 and 2). Each item

Figure B-1. Bender drawings of a normal ten year old female.

Figure B-2. Bender drawings indicating some impulsivity and visual motor/perceptual problems.

is worth one point and enters into a composite developmental score that may then be compared with age-appropriate norms provided by Koppitz (1975). A review of 31 studies revealed high interrater reliability for the developmental system (correlations ranged from .79 to .99; 81% of the correlations were at .89 or above). Despite the availability of objective scoring techniques, many practitioners prefer a global, intuitive interpretation based on clinical judgment (Dana, Field, & Bolton, 1983).

Although the Bender Gestalt has been an integral part of standardized test batteries for the past 50 years, there has been considerable criticism on issues of inappropriate admission, scoring, and interpretation (Pitrowski, 1995). However, recent studies indicate reliability of group and individual administration (Brannigan & Brannigan, 1995), reliability of scoring systems (Fuller & Vance, 1995), neuropsychological clinical utility (Bowers, 1994) and intellectual assessment of adults (Bobic, Pavicevic, Lukrecija & Drenovac, 1997). In recent surveys of test use, the Bender Gestalt remains ranked in the top ten assessment instruments (Pitrowski, 1995).

REFERENCES

Bender, L. (1938). *A visual motor Gestalt test and its clinical use.* New York: American Orthopsychiatric Association.

Bobic, J., Pavicevic, L., Drenovac, M. (1997). Intellectual deterioration in alcoholics. *European Journal of Psychiatry, 11*(1), 21–26.

Bowers, W. A. (1994). Neuropsychological impairment among anorexia nervosa and bulimia patients. *Eating Disorders: The Journal of Treatment and Prevention, 2*(1), 42–46.

Brannigan, G. G., & Brannigan, M. J. (1995). Comparison of individual versus group administration of the modified version of the Bender Gestalt Test. *Perceptual & Motor Skills, 80*(3), 1274.

Dana, R. H., Field, K., & Bolton, B. (1983). Variations of the Bender-Gestalt Test: Implications for training and practice. *Journal of Personality Assessment, 47*(1), 76–84.

Fuller, G. B., & Vance, B. (1995). Interscorer reliability of the modified version of the Bender Gestalt. *Psychology in the Schools, 32*(4), 264–266.

Koppitz, E. M. (1963). *The Bender Gestalt Test for young children.* New York: Grune & Stratton.

Koppitz, E. M. (1975). *The Bender Gestalt Test for young children. Vol. 2: Research and application. 1963–1973.* New York: Grune & Stratton.

Lacks, P. (1984). *Bender Gestalt screening for brain dysfunction.* New York: Wiley.

Pitrowski, C. (1995). A review of the clinical and research use of the Bender Gestalt Test. *Perceptual and Motor Skills, 81*(3), 1272–1274.

ROBERT G. BRUBAKER
Eastern Kentucky University
First edition

ELAINE FLETCHER-JANZEN
University of Northern Colorado
Second edition

VISUAL MOTOR PROBLEMS
VISUAL PERCEPTION AND INTEGRATION

BENNETT, VIRGINIA C. (1916–)

Virginia C. Bennett, a former nurse, studied elementary education at Rutgers University, earning a BA in this field in 1956. She subsequently was awarded an MEd in educational psychology (1961) and the EdD in school psychology (1963), both from Rutgers University, where she was on the faculty from 1963 until her retirement in 1983. During the years 1960 to 1963, Bennett was a W. S. Grant Foundation fellow.

Bennett has worked in school psychology as both a practitioner and a trainer of school psychologists since 1963. Her primary interest has been identification of children with learning problems, with emphasis on the remediation process, for those identified, through planning programs for teachers to implement within the regular classroom setting. She pioneered the mainstreaming of children identified for special educational resources in her practice in the New Jersey schools. With her doctoral students, she planned and implemented a program for the early identification (screening) of kindergarten children in the public schools of Trenton, New Jersey, a school district with a high proportion of minority group and Hispanic children.

Although always interested in the problems of school-children, and always convinced that the public schools are the most effective milieu for dealing with those problems, Bennett's interests throughout 25 years as a school psychologist and a trainer in a highly urban state have focused in recent years on the problems of poor black children and youths, as well as on those of the increasing numbers of Hispanic children in the schools. These latter interests are exemplified in her publication of work with school-age parents and in the development of a doctoral program geared to the application of psychological knowledge and skills to the solution of educational problems.

Bennett has long been recognized for her leadership in school psychology, where she is perhaps best known for her work with Bardon (Bardon & Bennett, 1974; Bennett & Bardon, 1976). With Bardon, she pioneered the development of professional preparation programs for school psychologists. In 1977 the Division of School Psychology of the American Psychological Association recognized her with the Distinguished Service Award. Bennett is now professor emeritus at Rutgers—The State University.

REFERENCES

Bardon, J. I., & Bennett, V. C. (1974). *School psychology*. Englewood Cliffs, NJ: Prentice Hall.

Bennett, V. C., & Bardon, J. I. (1976). Applied research can be useful. *Journal of School Psychology, 14,* 67–73.

CECIL R. REYNOLDS
Texas A & M University

BENZEDRINE

Benzedrine is a psychostimulant that acts on the central nervous system. It was the subject of widespread abuse and distribution under the slang term "bennies" until the 1970s. Its previous legitimate uses included, at times, the treatment of hyperactivity and obesity. Recent study indicates some evidence to support the judicious use of psychostimulants in "selected clinical instances of several adult psychiatric syndromes." It is no longer in use in the treatment of childhood or adolescent disorders.

REFERENCE

Chiarello, R. J., & Cole, J. O. (1987). The use of psychostimulants in general psychiatry: A reconsideration. *Archives of General Psychiatry, 44,* 286–295.

STAFF

ATTENTION DEFICIT DISORDER
DEXEDRINE

BEREITER, CARL (1930–   )

Carl Bereiter received his BA (1951) and MA (1952) in comparative literature and his PhD (1959) in education from the University of Wisconsin. He was a research associate at Vassar College (1959–1961) and then joined the faculty at the University of Illinois (1961–1967). Since 1967, Bereiter has been a professor at the Ontario Institute for Studies in Education.

In the early 1960s, Bereiter and Siefried Engelmann taught reading, mathematics, and logical skills to young disadvantaged children. Out of this effort came the method they called direct instruction, an approach that was often misperceived as behavioristic rather than rational analysis of difficulties of understanding.

Most of Bereiter's work has been in collaboration with Marlene Scardamalia. Through research on composing and comprehension processes, they have identified an immature strategy that seems to reflect a general way of coping superficially with academic tasks. This discovery led to Bereiter's broadening his studies to intentional learning: how it develops, how it is influenced by school practices, and how a higher level of intentional control over learning can be fostered in students. His most recent work, in this area, has been in using Computer Supported Intentional Learning Environment (CSILE) software. CSILE is intended to create a knowledge-building society by linking diverse participants, including school children and parents, teacher education and medical students, project researchers, and software developers.

REFERENCES

Bereiter, C., & Engelmann, S. (1966). *Teaching disadvantaged children in the preschool*. Englewood Cliffs, NJ: Prentice Hall.

Bereiter, C., & Scardamalia, M. (1985). Cognitive coping strategies and the problem of "inert" knowledge. In S. S. Chipman, J. W. Segal, & R. Glaser (Eds.), *Thinking and learning skills: Research and open questions* (Vol. 2, pp. 65–80). Hillsdale, NJ: Erlbaum.

Scardamalia, M., & Bereiter, C. (1996). Engaging students in a knowledge society. *Educational Leadership, 54*(3), 6–10.

DEBORAH B. GUILLEN
*The University of Texas of the
Permian Basin*

BETTELHEIM, BRUNO (1903–1990)

Bruno Bettelheim received his doctoral degree from the University of Vienna in 1938. He was strongly influenced by Freudian thought. Bettelheim was a psychiatrist who gained his fame from work with emotionally disturbed children, particularly those with autism.

During his long association with the University of Chicago, Bettelheim acted as principal of the University of Chicago's Sonia Shankman Orthogeneic School, a residential treatment center for severely emotionally disturbed children. The philosophy and operation of the Shankman School are described in Bettelheim's book *Love Is Not Enough* (1950), and four case studies of the treatment there are covered in his *Truants from Life* (1955).

Bettelheim sought in his treatment of severely disturbed children to create a particular social environment, a society with its own definite set of mores, closely paralleling those of society at large. He believed that social norms and standards are important to the treatment of emotionally disturbed children just as they are important in normal populations.

Bettelheim published many books, including *Children of the Dream* (1969) and *The Empty Fortress* (1967). He died in 1990 at the age of 87.

REFERENCES

Bettelheim, B. (1950). *Love is not enough: The treatment of emotionally disturbed children.* Glencoe, IL: Free Press.

Bettelheim, B. (1955). *Truants from life: The rehabilitation of emotionally disturbed children.* Glencoe, IL: Free Press.

Bettelheim, B., (1967). *The empty fortress: Infantile autism and the birth of the self.* London: Collier-Macmillan.

Bettelheim, B., (1969). *Children of the dream.* New York: Macmillan.

REBECCA BAILEY
Texas A & M University

BIALER, IRVING (1919–   )

Irving Bialer received his BA (1943) from Brooklyn College and his PhD (1960) in clinical psychology from George Peabody College, with a minor in education of exceptional children. His major field of interest is in clinical psychology; mental retardation and clinical child psychology are two special areas of interest.

His publications have dealt with issues of assessment and diagnosis in the areas of mental retardation and neurological impairment, personality and motivational development in retarded individuals, and drug-related treatments for behavior problems in neuropsychiatrically impaired children. He has over 30 publications to his credit, including books, articles, and book chapters. Some of his most significant publications include a chapter in *Social-Cultural Aspects of Mental Retardation,* discussing the relationship of mental retardation to emotional disturbance and physical disability, and *The Psychology of Mental Retardation: Issues and Approaches* (coedited with Manny Sternlicht), which focuses on the theoretical, practical issues and approaches to dealing with the psychology of mentally retarded people. Bialer and R. L. Cromwell wrote an article entitled "Failure as Motivation with Mentally Retarded Children," which was published in the *American Journal of Mental Deficiency.*

Bialer has held many academic positions in psychology and special education and has been a consulting editor to the *American Journal of Mental Deficiency* as well as the journal's book review editor from 1971 to 1981.

REFERENCES

Bialer, I. (1970). Relationship of mental retardation to emotional disturbance and physical disability. In H. C. Haywood (Ed.), *Social-cultural aspects of mental retardation* (pp. 607–660). New York: Appleton-Century-Crofts.

Bialer, I., & Cromwell, R. L. (1965). Failure as motivation with mentally retarded children. *American Journal of Mental Deficiency, 69,* 680–684.

Bialer, I., & Sternlicht, M. (Eds.). (1970). *The psychology of mental retardation: Issues and approaches.* New York: Psychological Dimensions.

REBECCA BAILEY
Texas A & M University

BIBLIOTHERAPY

Bibliotherapy is an approach to helping pupils understand themselves and their feelings and to providing in-classroom counseling to meet their emotional and social needs (Lerner, 1985). Readings and other media materials in which the characters learn to cope and deal effectively with problems similar to those which are, or will be, encountered by the students are used. The materials range from student selected readings to teacher chosen books, magazines, or articles designed to emphasize or illustrate a particular point or issue (Ysseldyke & Algozzine, 1984). Bibliotherapy may be used in either a remedial (dealing with current pupil distress) or preventive (anticipating future problems children may face) form, for children with physical, emotional, social, learning, or other handicaps (McKinnon & Kiraly, 1984).

As with psychotherapy, bibliotherapy includes three main components: identification, catharsis, and insight.

Identification with characters, situations, or elements of a story enables the reader to view his or her problem from a new and different perspective and thus gain hope and tension release (catharsis). Such tension reduction allows the student to gain insight into his or her motivations and actions and allows for positive change in attitude and behavior. This process is structured and guided by the teacher through the use of classroom discussion, example, and illustration (Lenkowsky & Lenkowsky, 1980).

Bibliotherapy offers many advantages for special education. It is effective in the reduction and management of the stress that often accompanies and impairs learning, development, and adjustment in handicapped children (Humphrey & Humphrey, 1985). It may be used individually or with small groups or classes of children. Bibliotherapy can be modified to the needs of children at any age and little formal training or experience is required for teachers to become proficient bibliotherapists. There is a large body of literature available that presents the problems, feelings, and situations faced by handicapped children and adolescents. In addition, research application demonstrates the potential for bibliotherapy to be a powerful agent for behavior change (Lombana, 1982; Cuijpers, 1997).

REFERENCES

Cuijpers, P. (1997). Bibliotherapy in unipolar depression: A meta-analysis. *Journal of Behavior Therapy & Experimental Psychiatry, 28*(2), 139–147.

Humphrey, J. H., & Humphrey, J. N. (1985). *Controlling stress in children.* Springfield, IL: Thomas.

Lenkowsky, B., & Lenkowsky, R. (1980). Bibliotherapy for the learning disabled adolescent. In C. H. Thomas & J. L. Thomas (Eds.), *Meeting the needs of the handicapped: A resource for teachers and librarians.* Phoenix, AZ: Oryx.

Lerner, J. (1985). *Learning disabilities* (4th ed.). Boston: Houghton Mifflin.

Lombana, J. H. (1982). *Guidance for handicapped students.* Springfield, IL: Thomas.

McKinnon, A. J., & Kiraly, J. (1984). *Pupil behavior, self-control and social skills in the classroom.* Springfield, IL: Thomas.

Ysseldyke, J. E., & Algozzine, B. (1984). *Introduction to special education.* Boston: Houghton Mifflin.

RONALD S. LENKOWSKY
Hunter College

COUNSELING THE HANDICAPPED
SOCIAL SKILLS

BIELSCHOLWSKY SYNDROME

See JUVENILE CEREBROMACULAR DEGENERATION.

BIENNIAL DIRECTORY OF EDUCATIONAL FACILITIES FOR THE LEARNING DISABLED

The *Biennial Directory of Educational Facilities for the Learning Disabled* is published by Academic Therapy Publications. It contains a listing of nonpublic educational facilities that specialize in programs for the learning disabled. The directory lists facilities in alphabetical order by state. Following the name, location, director, and number of staff members is coded information describing the following: type of facility—educational, related professional service (diagnostic, optometric, etc.), or summer camp; age ranges accepted; boys only, girls only, or coeducational; full day, part day, or residential; and fee information. A copy of the directory can be obtained from Academic Therapy Publications for a small fee to cover postage and handling (currently $5.00), at 20 Commercial Boulevard, Novato, CA 94949.

DANIEL R. PAULSON
University of Wisconsin at Stout

BIJOU, SIDNEY W. (1908–   )

Born in Baltimore, Maryland, Sidney W. Bijou received his BS in business administration from the University of Florida in 1933. He received his MS (1937) from Columbia University and his PhD (1941), both in psychology, from the University of Iowa. Professor emeritus at the University of Illinois, Bijou has been an adjunct professor of special education and psychology at the University of Arizona, and more recently the University of Nevada.

Although he was the coauthor of the *Wide Range Achievement Test* (Bijou & Jastak, 1941), his major interest is in the behavioral analysis of child development (Bijou, 1976; Bijou & Baer, 1965, 1978). He also coauthored a book on the behavior analysis and modification of children (Bijou & Ruiz, 1981). One of his major contentions is that the child and the environment are always interacting and maintaining a symbiotic relationship. He emphasizes the commonality of a general goal for children, normal and retarded, in early childhood education, regardless of age or degree of handicapping condition, while stressing individualization of education and treatment.

Bijou has been a National Institute of Mental Health senior fellow, a Fullbright-Hays fellow, president of the Midwestern Association of Behavior Analysis, and president of the American Psychological Association's Division of Developmental Psychology. He has also received the Research Award from the American Association of Mental Deficiency, and the G. Stanley Hall Award in child development from the American Psychological Association. The sum of Bijou's vast experience in the field is reflected in his 1996 article, "Reflections on Some Early Events Related to Behavior Analysis of Child Development."

REFERENCES

Bijou, S. W. (1976). *Child development: The basic stage of early childhood.* Englewood Cliffs, NJ: Prentice Hall.

Bijou, S. W. (1996). Reflections on some early events related to behavior analysis of child development. *Behavior Analyst, 19*(1), 49–60.

Bijou, S. W., & Baer, D. M. (1965). *Child development: Universal stage of infancy* (Vol. 2). New York: Appleton-Century-Crofts.

Bijou, S. W., & Baer, D. M. (1978). *Behavior analysis of child development.* Englewood Cliffs, NJ: Prentice Hall.

Bijou, S. W., & Jastak, J. F. (1941). *Wide range achievement test.* New York: Psychological Corporation.

Bijou, S. W., & Ruiz, R. (Eds.). (1981). *Behavior modification: Contributions to education.* Hillsdale, NJ: Erlbaum.

E. Valerie Hewitt
Texas A & M University

BILINGUAL ASSESSMENT AND SPECIAL EDUCATION

The assessment of children who are culturally and linguistically diverse for special education services has been a controversial issue for nearly thirty years. This controversy first received national attention via the case of Diana *v.* California in 1970 involving the identification of Spanish-speaking children as mentally retarded on the basis of being assessed in English. The safeguards decreed in this case had an impact on both legal requirements and professional ethical standards. Public Law 94-142 mandated that children be assessed in their primary language. Chapter 13 of the American Psychological Association's *Standards for Educational and Psychological Testing* (1985) acknowledges the need for assessing the native language of children.

Legal requirements and ethical standards, however, have not resolved the issue of disproportionate representation of culturally and linguistically diverse children in special education. The problem of disproportionate representation across different special education categories pertains both to overrepresentation (Artiles & Trent, 1994; Chinn & Hughes, 1987; Ortiz & Yates, 1983; Robertson, Kushner, Starks, & Drescher, 1994; Tucker, 1980; Wright & Cruz, 1980) and underrepresentation (Chinn & Hughes, 1987; Gersten & Woodward, 1994; Ortiz & Yates, 1983; Robertson et al., 1994).

There are many possible factors that contribute to the disproportionate representation of linguistically diverse students in special education. Ochoa, Powell and Robles-Pina (1996) state that the following are among some of the reasons why this problem continues today: "(a) socioeconomic status of minorities students, (b) test bias associated with cultural differences, (c) factors associated with second language acquisition, and (d) inappropriate referrals" (p. 251).

In addition to these four aforementioned variables, the role of the school psychologist with respect to appropriately conducting and interpreting test results is a critical factor that can reduce the probability of misdiagnosing bilingual and/or limited-English-proficient (LEP) children. While experts (Barona & Santos de Barona, 1987; Caterino, 1990; Esquivel, 1988; Figueroa, 1990; Hamayan & Damico, 1991; Wilen & Sweeting, 1986) have provided the field of school psychology with recommended procedures and factors to consider when conducting bilingual assessment, recent research indicates that practitioners have not been exposed to this information. Ochoa, Rivera, and Ford (1997) found that 83% of the school psychologists who conducted bilingual assessment self-reported that they had not received adequate training in this area by their university training program. "Moreover, 56% stated that they [school psychologists] had received no or very little training on interpreting results of bilingual assessments" (Ochoa, Rivera, & Ford, 1997, p. 341).

Given this lack of training, it is critical that the assessment practices school psychologists use with bilingual and/or LEP children be reviewed. These include the following: (a) use of interpreters, (b) the extent to which and how language proficiency is assessed, (c) methods used to assess intellectual functioning, academic achievement, and adaptive behavior, and (d) compliance with Section Four of the exclusionary clause of Public Law 94-142.

Use of Interpreters

The use of interpreters is common practice in bilingual assessment. This is not surprising due to the many different low-incidence language groups school psychologists have to assess (Ochoa, Gonzalez, Galarza, & Guillemard, 1996). Ochoa, Gonzalez et al. (1996) reported that 53% of school psychologists use interpreters. They found that 77% of school psychologists who use interpreters self-reported that they were clearly not trained by their university training program on how to do so. Moreover, approximately two-thirds of the interpreters used by the school psychologists did not have training to work in this capacity. Ochoa, Gonzalez et al. (1996) and Nuttall (1987) state the need for interpreter training. When school psychologists must resort to using interpreters, they should review the literature pertaining to the skills they should acquire in this situation (Figueroa, Sandoval, & Merino, 1984) as well as the skills that the interpreter should possess (Chamberlain & Medeiros-Landurand, 1991; Medina,

1982; Miller & Abudarham, 1984; Scribner, 1993; Wilen & Sweeting, 1986).

Language Proficiency Assessment

Language proficiency assessment is an essential component of bilingual assessment because it provides the school psychologist with information about (a) the appropriateness of the child's current educational placement with respect to his/her language development (Ochoa, Galarza, & Gonzalez, 1996) and (b) the child's native and second language development with respect to whether the student has achieved Cognitive Academic Language Proficiency (CALP). Cummins (1984) states that it is important to differentiate between CALP, which takes 5 to 7 years to acquire and is the type of proficiency which one needs to be successful in an academic context, and Basic Interpersonal Communication Skills (BICS), which is the proficiency one needs in social settings and only takes about two years to acquire. If a bilingual student does not have CALP in English, he or she will find the linguistic demands of his instructional arrangement to be difficult, which could result in academic failure. Ochoa, Galarza, and Gonzalez (1996) concluded from their study of the language proficiency assessment practices of school psychologists when conducting bilingual assessment that they". . . are not implementing the following recommended language proficiency practices: (a) conducting their own testing rather than relying on external data, (b) obtaining information about the LEP child's CALP level, and (c) utilizing informal language assessment methods . . ." (p. 33).

Intellectual Functioning, Academic and Adaptive Behavior Assessment

With respect to intellectual functioning, Ochoa, Powell, and Robles-Pina's (1996) study noted the following assessment trends used with bilingual and LEP students: (a) multiple measures are utilized; (b) nonverbal measures are commonly used; and (c) formally, informally translated tests and alternative/dynamic methods (i.e., Learning Potential Assessment Device and System of Multicultural Pluralistic Assessment) are often not used. In the area of academic assessment of second language learners, approximately 75% of school psychologists reported that they used the Woodcock instruments in both English and Spanish (Ochoa, Powell, & Robles-Pina, 1996). Moreover, the use of curriculum-based measurement (66% of school psychologists) and criterion reference testing (49% of school psychologists) in Spanish are also common practice to assess achievement (Ochoa, Powell, & Robles-Pina, 1996). With respect to adaptive behavior, the most commonly used measure with bilingual students is the Vineland Adaptive Behavior Scales–Survey Edition (Ochoa, Powell, & Robles-Pina, 1996).

Section Four of the Exclusionary Clause

Section Four of the exclusionary clause of Public Law 94-142 states that a student should not be identified as learning disabled if the "discrepancy between ability and achievement is primarily the result of environmental, cultural, or economic disadvantage" (U.S. Office of Education, 1977). Ochoa, Rivera, and Powell's (1997) study examined how school psychologists complied with this legal requirement. They identified 36 factors that school psychologists used which could be summarized by the following six major themes: "(a) family and home factors, (b) language instruction and language-related factors, (c) assessment instrument and procedural safeguards, (d) educational history factors, (e) general educational factors, and (f) other" (p. 163). Ochoa, Rivera, and Powell (1997) conclude that "the extent to which many of these factors are used, however, appears to be low. Moreover, many additional important factors are completely overlooked by school psychologists" (p. 163).

Conclusion

A review of the aforementioned research concerning the assessment practices used with bilingual and/or LEP students suggests that this area will continue to be controversial. Perhaps the words of Chinn and Hughes' (1987) words best summarize this situation: "The assessment of minority children for educational placement continues to be one of the more volatile issues in special education" (p. 45).

REFERENCES

American Psychological Association. (1985). *Standards for educational and psychological testing.* Washington, DC: American Psychological Association.

Artiles, A. J., & Trent, S. C. (1994). Overrepresentation of minority students in special education: A continuing debate. *The Journal of Special Education, 27*(4), 410–437.

Barona, A., & Santos de Barona, M. (1987). A model for assessment of limited English proficiency students referred for special education services. In S. H. Fradd & W. J. Tikunoff (Eds.), *Bilingual education and bilingual special education* (pp. 183–209). San Diego, CA: College Hill Press.

Caterino, L. C. (1990). Step-by-step procedure for the assessment of language minority children. In A. Barona & E. E. Garcia (Eds.), *Children at risk: Poverty, minority status, and other issues in educational equity* (pp. 269–282). Washington, DC: National Association of School Psychologists.

Chamberlain, P., & Medeiros-Landurand, P. (1991). Practical considerations in the assessment of LEP students with special needs. In E. V. Hamayan & J. S. Damico (Eds.), *Limiting bias in the assessment of bilingual students* (pp. 111–156). Austin, TX: Pro-Ed.

Chinn, P. C., & Hughes, S. (1987). Representation of minority students in special classes. *Remedial and Special Education, 8,* 41–46.

Cummins, J. (1984). *Bilingual special education issues in assessment and pedagogy.* San Diego: College-Hill.

Cummins, J. (1992). Bilingual education and English immersion: The Ramirez report in theoretical perspective. *Bilingual Research Journal, 16,* 91–104.

Esquivel, G. B. (1988). Best practices in the assessment of limited English proficient and bilingual children. In A. Thomas & J. Grimes (Eds.), *Best practices in school psychology* (pp. 113–123). Washington, DC: The National Association of School Psychologists.

Figueroa, R. A. (1990). Best practices in the assessment of bilingual children. In A. Thomas & J. Grimes (Eds.), *Best practices in school psychology II* (pp. 93–106). Washington, DC: The National Association of School Psychologists.

Figueroa, R. A., Sandoval, J., & Merino, B. (1984). School psychology and limited-English-proficient (LEP) children: New competencies. *Journal of School Psychology, 22,* 131–143.

Gersten, R., & Woodward, J. (1994). The language-minority student and special education: Issues, trends, and paradoxes. *Exceptional Children, 60*(4), 310–322.

Hamayan, E. V., & Damico, J. S. (Eds.). (1991). *Limiting bias in the assessment of bilingual students.* Austin, TX: Pro-Ed.

Medina, V. (1982). *Issues regarding the use of interpreters and translators in a school setting.* (ERIC Reproduction No. ED 161191)

Miller, N., & Abudarham, S. (1984). Management of communication problems in bilingual children. In N. Miller (Ed.), *Bilingualism and language disability: Assessment and remediation* (pp. 177–198). San Diego: College-Hill.

Nuttall, E. V. (1987). Survey of current practices in the psychological assessment of limited-English-proficiency handicapped children. *Journal of School Psychology, 25,* 53–61.

Ochoa, S. H., Galarza, A., & Gonzalez, D. (1996). An investigation of school psychologists' assessment practices of language proficiency with bilingual and limited-English-proficient students. *Diagnostique, 21*(4), 17–36.

Ochoa, S. H., Gonzalez, D., Galarza, A., & Guillemard, L. (1996). The training and use of interpreters in bilingual psychoeducational assessment: An alternative in need of study. *Diagnostique, 21*(3), 19–40.

Ochoa, S. H., Powell, M. P., & Robles-Pina, R. (1996). School psychologists' assessment practices with bilingual and limited-English-proficient students. *Journal of Psychoeducational Assessment, 14,* 250–275.

Ochoa, S. H., Rivera, B., & Ford, L. (1997). An investigation of school psychology training pertaining to bilingual psychoeducational assessment of primarily Hispanic students: Twenty-five years after Diana v. California. *Journal of School Psychology, 35,* 329–349.

Ochoa, S. H., Rivera, B., & Powell, M. P. (1997). Factors used to comply with the exclusionary clause with bilingual and limited-English-proficient pupils: Initial guidelines. *Learning Disabilities Research & Practice, 12,* 161–167.

Ortiz, A., & Yates, J. (1983). Incidence of exceptionality among Hispanics: Implications for manpower planning. *National Association of Bilingual Education Journal, 7,* 41–54.

Robertson, P., Kushner, M. I., Starks, J., & Drescher, C. (1994). An update of participation rates of culturally and linguistically diverse students in special education: The need for a research and policy agenda. *The Bilingual Special Education Perspective, 14*(1), 3–9.

Scribner, A. P. (1993). The use of interpreters in the assessment of language minority students. *The Bilingual Special Education Perspective, 12*(1), 2–6.

Tucker, J. A. (1980). Ethnic proportions in classes for the learning disabled: Issues in nonbiased assessment. *Journal of Special Education, 14,* 93–105.

U.S. Office of Education. (1977). Assistance to states for education of handicapped children: Procedures for evaluating specific learning disabilities. *Federal Register, 42,* 65083.

Wilen, D. K., & Sweeting, C. V. M. (1986). Assessment of limited English proficient Hispanic students. *School Psychology Review, 15,* 59–75.

Wright, P. & Cruz, R. S. (1983). Ethnic composition of special education programs in California. *Learning Disability Quarterly, 6,* 387–394.

HECTOR SALVIA OCHOA
Texas A & M University

BILINGUAL SPECIAL EDUCATION

BILINGUAL SPECIAL EDUCATION

By the year 2025, approximately 40% of the total United States population will be African American, Hispanic, or Asian American (Townsend, 1995) and by 2080, non-Hispanic Whites will be a minority. Every region of the country has experienced significant increases in the number of individuals from minority backgrounds, and schools are reporting dramatic increases in the number of language minority students they serve. "Language minority" refers to students who come from homes or communities where a language other than English is spoken. A subset of this population are limited English proficient (LEP) students, whose English skills are so limited they cannot profit from instruction delivered entirely in English and thus require the support of special language programs such as bilingual education or English as a second language instruction. LEP students represent some 200 language groups with Spanish being the most common language spoken (approximately 75%), followed by Vietnamese, Hmong, Cantonese, Cambodian, and Korean.

There is substantial evidence that educational services currently being provided to language minority students are not sufficient to meet their needs. These students experience higher rates of retention and school attrition, score poorly on standardized tests, are underrepresented in colleges and universities, and complete post-secondary studies at low rates. They are also disproportionately represented in special education.

Disproportionate Representation in Special Education

The prevalence of disabilities among language minority students is difficult to determine because local, state, and federal education agencies do not usually report disabilities by language proficiency level. Representation is affected by such factors as definitions, eligibility criteria, geographic location, percentage of minority enrollment, district size, and available program options. Consequently, in some states, LEP students are underrepresented, while in others they are seriously overrepresented in programs for students with special needs (Harry, 1992). Patterns of over- and under-identification suggest that some students are inappropriately placed in special education, but that others are neither being identified nor receiving the services they need and to which they are entitled. Because bilingual special education is a new field, research on second language learners with disabilities is limited and, consequently, when LEP students are identified as being eligible for special education, school districts struggle with how to best address disability- and language-related needs simultaneously.

Prevention and Prereferral

With increasing frequency, service delivery models such as the Assessment and Intervention Model for the Bilingual Exceptional Student (Ortiz & Wilkinson, 1991) emphasize proactive steps to ensure that all students are academically successful by creating school climates which reflect awareness and acceptance of diversity, high expectations for all students, a challenging curriculum, quality bilingual education and ESL programs, and involvement of parents and communities. Prereferral interventions are designed to strengthen teachers' abilities to provide appropriate educational opportunities to a diverse student population. This is accomplished through professional development, which focuses on helping teachers understand the characteristics of language minority students, instructional practices known to be effective for these learners, and by giving teachers access to consultants or problem solving teams which help them design interventions to address students learning difficulties. If LEP students are ultimately referred for a comprehensive individual assessment, prereferral data help document that external factors such as limited English proficiency or lack of appropriate instruction have already been eliminated as possible causes of problems.

Assessment

Although inappropriate assessment is one of the primary causes of disproportionate representation of language minority students in special education, research on best practices in assessment of these students is still limited (Ortiz, 1997). Adaptation of standardized procedures is quite common (e.g., translations, use of interpreters, modification of test content). However, such adaptations invalidate the test, making scoring and interpretation of outcomes difficult and error-prone (Hamayan & Damico, 1991). Only those instruments which include appropriate samples of language minority students in the norming sample should be used in making eligibility decisions. If test norms are not appropriate, or if standardized administration procedures are violated, it is recommended that patterns of performance be described and used diagnostically to support eligibility decisions rather than reporting test scores. If performance on the formal and informal measures are positively correlated, multidisciplinary teams can be more confident that the student has a disability.

Students with disabilities demonstrate skills and abilities significantly deviant from those of students from similar language and cultural backgrounds. In the case of LEP students assessed only in English, assessments should document that the student's performance is discrepant with that of other LEP students who have had similar exposure to native language and/or English as a second language instruction. Behaviors are not deviant unless they are significantly different from the student's reference group.

Instruction

Individualized education programs (IEPs) for language minority students specify goals and objectives for native language and ESL instruction and include instructional recommendations that reflect understanding of cultural differences, socioeconomic background, preferred modalities, learning styles, and appropriate reinforcements (Yates & Ortiz, 1998). Because of the need to accommodate students' limited English proficiency, a combination of "reciprocal interaction" teaching approaches and basic skills instruction seem to be most beneficial for LEP students with disabilities (Robertson, Wilkinson, & Ortiz, 1991; Willig, Swedo, & Ortiz, 1987; Cummins, 1984). Approaches which focus solely on teaching discrete skills in English are problematic for LEP students because activities that are simplified to focus on specific skills are frequently stripped of context and lose their meaning and purpose, becoming incomprehensible to the second language learner. Lessons which focus on specific skills (e.g., phonology or grammar) and accuracy may actually interfere with the second language acquisition process, since instruction attempts to correct "errors" which are, in reality, developmental. Reciprocal interaction approaches, on the other hand, are characterized by genuine dialogue between students and teacher, in both oral and written communication, opportunities for meaningful language use, collaborative learning groups, the teaching of basic skills in the context of lessons which focus on higher order thinking, and the incorporation of language use and development across the curriculum.

Service delivery models and alternative instructional arrangements are being explored in an effort to ensure that language minority students are served by special educators who have expertise in how language and culture influence learning (Yates & Ortiz, 1998). For example, students who are limited English proficient can be served by: (a) bilingual special educators (i.e., teachers whose certification program focused specifically on the education of language minority students with disabilities); (b) special education teachers with dual certification in special education and bilingual education or English as a second language; or (c) by bilingual education teachers with the support and consultation of the special education teacher. For effective service delivery, linkages between special education, special language programs, and general education must be established, instructional and related services must be coordinated, and the roles and responsibilities of all personnel who work with these students must be defined. Additionally, teacher education programs must prepare both monolingual and bilingual special educators to serve linguistically and culturally diverse learners. The content of pre-service teacher education which leads to licensure and certification, and perhaps even more importantly, professional development and graduate teacher training programs, must reflect competencies that promote the interface between linguistic and culturally diversity and disabilities.

REFERENCES

Cummins, J. (1984). *Bilingualism and special education: Issues in assessment and pedagogy*. Clevedon, Avon, England: Multilingual Matters Ltd.

Damico, J. S. (1991). Descriptive assessment of communicative ability in limited English proficient students. In E. V. Hamayan & J. S. Damico, *Limiting bias in the assessment of bilingual students* (pp. 157–217). Austin, TX: Pro-Ed.

Harry, B. (1992). *Cultural diversity, families, and the special education system: Communication and empowerment*. New York: Teachers College Press.

Ortiz, A. A. (1997). Learning disabilities occurring concomitantly with linguistic differences. *Journal of Learning Disabilities, 30*(3), 321–332.

Robertson-Courtney, P., Wilkinson, C. Y., & Ortiz, A. A. (1991). Reciprocal interaction-oriented strategies for literacy development: Teacher training outcomes. *The Journal of the New York State Association for Bilingual Education, 7*(1), 95–109.

Townsend, W. A. (1995). *Pocket digest: Digest of education statis-tics for limited English proficient students*. Washington, D.C.: Office of Bilingual Education and Minority Languages Affairs.

Ortiz, A. A., & Wilkinson, C. Y. (1991). Assessment and intervention model for the exceptional bilingual student (AIM for the BESt). *Teacher Education and Special Education, 14*(1), 11–18.

Willig, A. C., Swedo, J. J., & Ortiz, A. A. (1987). *Characteristics of teaching strategies which result in high task engagement for exceptional limited English proficient Hispanic students*. Austin, TX: The University of Texas, Handicapped Minority Research Institute on Language Proficiency.

Yates, J. R., & Ortiz, A. A. (1998). Developing individualized educational programs for the exceptional bilingual student. In L. Baca & H. Cervantes (Eds.), *The Bilingual Special Education Interface* (3rd ed.) (pp. 188–212). Columbus, OH: Merrill Publishing Company.

HECTOR SALVIA OCHOA
Texas A & M University

ALBA ORTIZ
SHERNAZ B. GARCÍA
University of Texas

BILINGUAL ASSESSMENT & SPECIAL EDUCATION

BILINGUAL SPEECH LANGUAGE PATHOLOGY

Bilingual speech language pathology is an emerging field within the profession of speech language pathology. It is recognized as an area of the field that serves individuals who are bilingual and have a communication disorder. There are graduate programs in the United States that train bilingual clinicians and adhere to the profession's position statement on academic and clinical competencies. The American Speech-Language Hearing Association approved a position statement that defines who can be a bilingual speech language pathologist and/or audiologist. This position statement includes the language proficiency required in the minority language and also the academic competencies necessary to provide services (Kayser, 1995). The definition states (ASHA, 1989): "Speech-language pathologists or audiologists who present themselves as bilingual for the purposes of providing clinical services must be able to speak their primary language and to speak (or sign) at least one other language with native or near-native proficiency in lexicon (vocabulary), semantics (meaning), phonology (pronunciation), morphology/syntax (grammar), and pragmatics (uses) during clinical management." (p. 93). The academic requirements (ASHA, 1985) include the following: (1) language proficiency: native or near native fluency in both the minority language and the

English language; (2) normative processes: the ability to describe the process of normal speech and language acquisition for both bilingual and monolingual individuals and how those processes are manifested in oral and written language; (3) assessment: the ability to administer and interpret formal and informal assessment procedures to distinguish between communication difference and communication disorders; (4) intervention: the ability to apply intervention strategies for treatment of communicative disorders in the minority language; and (5) cultural sensitivity: the ability to recognize cultural factors that affect the delivery of speech-language pathology and audiology services to the minority language speaking community.

REFERENCES

American Speech-Language-Hearing Association. (1995). Clinical management of communicatively handicapped minority language populations. *Asha, 27*(6), 29–32.

American Speech-Language-Hearing Association. (1989). Definition: Bilingual speech-language pathologists and audiologists. *Asha, 31*(3), 93.

Kayser, H. (1995). An emerging specialist: The bilingual speech-language pathologist. In H. Kayser (Ed.), *Bilingual speech-language pathology: An Hispanic focus* (pp. 1–14). San Diego: Singular Publishing Group, Inc.

HORTENCIA KAYSER
New Mexico State University

BILL OF RIGHTS FOR THE DISABLED

The Bill of Rights for the Disabled is a codification by the United Cerebral Palsy Association of rights that have been won for the handicapped in court cases and before legislatures during the 1960s and 1970s. These rights are as follows:

1. The right to prevention, early diagnosis, and proper care.
2. The right to a barrier-free environment and accessible transportation.
3. The right to an appropriate public education.
4. The right to necessary assistance, given in a way that promotes independence.
5. The right to a choice of lifestyles and residential alternatives.
6. The right to an income for a lifestyle comparable to that of the able-bodied.
7. The right to training and employment as qualified.
8. The right to petition social institutions for just and humane treatment.
9. The right to self-esteem.

STAFF

BINET, ALFRED (1857–1911)

Alfred Binet, the founder of French experimental psychology, became director of the Laboratory of Physiological Psychology at the Sorbonne in Paris in 1895. In the same year, he and a colleague founded the first French journal of psychology, *Année psychologique*. He was cofounder of the Société Libre pour l'Étude Psychologique de l'Enfant, which after his death became the Société Alfred Binet.

Binet's investigations took him outside the laboratory. He observed children in schools and camps and used questionnaires and interviews to collect data. In 1904, the minister of public instruction appointed him to a commission created to formulate methods for identifying mentally retarded children in the public schools so that these children could be given a special school program. Out of Binet's work with this commission came the first scale for measuring intelligence, based on the idea of classifying children according to individual differences in performance of tasks requiring thinking and reasoning. On the assumption that intelligence increases with age, he employed the concept of mental age. Results were expressed both as mental age and by a score obtained by subtracting mental age from chronological age. The German psychologist William Stern proposed an improved way of expressing the test results: dividing mental age by chronological age, yielding an intelligence quotient.

The scale was first published by Binet and Theodore Simon in 1905 and was revised in 1908 and 1911. It was translated into English by H. H. Goddard in the United States. In 1916, L M. Terman at Stanford University published his *Stanford Revision of the Binet Scales*. For half a century dozens of translations and revisions of Binet's scales dominated the field of intelligence testing; they are still extensively used.

Alfred Binet had a variety of other interests in the field of psychology. One of his earliest works was a book on hypnosis. In addition, he developed, with Simon, a classification of mental disorders. He also used pictures and inkblots to study thought processes, foreshadowing later projective techniques.

REFERENCES

Varon, E. J. (1935). The development of Alfred Binet's psychology. *Psychological Monographs* (No. 207). Princeton, NJ: Psychological Review.

Watson, R. I. (1963). *The great psychologists.* New York: Lippincott.

PAUL IRVINE
Katonah, New York

BIOCHEMICAL IRREGULARITIES

It has been long recognized that a large number of metabolic diseases have characteristic clinical, pathological, and biochemical irregularities that can be attributed to the congenital deficiency of a specific enzyme. This inadequacy is in turn owed to the presence of a particular abnormal gene. The identification and consequent understanding of such biochemical problems began in the early part of the twentieth century with the first demonstration of Mendelian inheritance in humans. A. E. Garrod (Roberts, 1967) derived the basic concept of these disorders through studies on the rare condition known as alcaptonuria (Garrod, 1909). His classical investigation of this abnormality has provided an elegant and simple model for the interpretation of a great variety of different inherited diseases subsequently discovered.

Alcaptonuria is a condition in which large quantities of homogentisic acid are excreted into the urine, which turns black on standing. Under normal conditions, the amino acid tyrosine is converted through a series of enzymatic reactions to fumarate and acetoacetate (La Du, 1966). Garrod noted that when homogentisic acid, a normal intermediary metabolite of tyrosine, was fed to alcaptonuric subjects, it was excreted quantitatively in urine, whereas when given to normal subjects it appeared to be readily metabolized. Additionally, the administration of tyrosine or proteins containing it to alcaptonurics augmented the excretion of homogentisic acid.

The other striking feature of alcaptonuria to which Garrod drew attention was its familial distribution. After studying the characteristic pedigrees of these subjects, he concluded that they implied a hereditary or genetic basis for the condition. Garrod pointed out that the homogentisic acid must be derived from tyrosine and that the essential feature of alcaptonuria was a block in the metabolism of this substance, whereby breakdown could proceed only as far as homogentisic acid.

Eventually Garrod described a number of metabolic peculiarities of this kind and called them inborn errors of metabolism. He viewed the inborn errors as conditions in which the specific enzyme deficiency effectively blocked at a particular point a sequence of reactions that form part of the normal course of metabolism. As a result, metabolites immediately preceding the block would accumulate and metabolites subsequent to the block would not be formed (Harris, 1975). The various biochemical, clinical, and pathological manifestations of the condition could be regarded as secondary consequences of this primary metabolic defect. These secondary changes might be complex and widespread and would depend in general on the nature and the biochemical effects of the metabolites that tended to accumulate or whose formation was restricted (Harper, Rodwell, & Mayes, 1977).

It is now understood that the end products of gene action are proteins, either structural cell components, elements of extracellular matrices, or enzymes. Since genes are potentially mutable units, a change in a gene will disturb the synthesis of the specific protein for which it is responsible. This results in the formation of a different protein (or no protein at all), which alters the process or processes that depend on it. When the protein is absent or deficient, the normal process is impaired. The expression of such a mutation is a phenotypic effect of more or less consequence to the individual. Such defects in cellular enzyme formation are most often characterized by abnormal protein, carbohydrate, or fat metabolism.

All biochemical processes are under genetic control and each consists of a complex sequence of reactions. Part (*a*) of the following Figure schematically represents a portion of a normal metabolic pathway. A substrate, the substance on which an enzyme acts, is converted into a product through the activity of a specific enzyme. A metabolic pathway consists of many such reactions or steps, each being dependent on the previous reaction and each catalyzed by a specific enzyme (Jenkins, 1983). Part (*b*) of the figure illustrates how a change in a gene that interferes with the synthesis of an essential enzyme interrupts this process. A block in the normal pathway may produce an accumulation of the substances preceding the block, such as the monosaccharide (simple sugar) galactose in galactosemia or the amino acid phenylalanine in phenylketonuria. In other cases, the block may create a deficiency in the normal product, such as the pigment melanin in albinism or the hormone thyroxine in familial cretinism. Sometimes alternative metabolic pathways are used that result in an increase in the products of these processes such as phenylketones in phenylketonuria. The effects of defective gene action are often observable in the individual as diseases.

There are many inherited disorders caused by an inborn error of metabolism that involves either the accumulation or degradation of metabolic processes. For the most part, they are rare diseases, and the mode of transmission is almost always autosomal recessive genes. This may be best understood by considering the double-dose effect as it relates to the concept that one gene is responsible for one enzyme. If a specific gene controls the formation of an essential enzyme, and each individual has two such genes (the normal homozygote), then the enzyme is produced in normal amounts. The heterozygote, who has only one gene

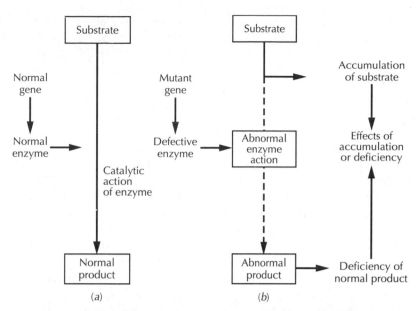

Alternative metabolic pathways. (*a*) formation of a normal product. (*b*) accumulation of substrate or deficiency of product as a result of an abnormal metabolic pathway (adapted from Whaley and Wong, 1983).

with a normal effect, is still capable of producing the enzyme in sufficient amounts to carry out the metabolic function under normal circumstances. However, the abnormal homozygote, who inherits a defective gene from each parent, has no functional enzyme and is, thus, clinically affected. It is becoming increasingly possible to detect and, therefore, to screen for a large variety of such inborn errors of metabolism. This should lead to the detection of the presence of the disease in the heterozygote (who is a carrier), the newborn, and the fetus before birth, thus allowing for proper genetic counseling of the parents and successful treatment of affected individuals (Goodenough, 1978).

REFERENCES

Garrod, A. E. (1909). *Inborn errors of metabolism.* New York: Oxford University Press.

Goodenough, U. (1978). *Genetics* (2nd ed.). New York: Holt, Rinehart, & Winston.

Harper, H. A., Rodwell, V. W., & Mayes, P. A. (1977). *Review of physiological chemistry* (16th ed.). Los Altos, CA: Lange Medical.

Harris, H. (1975). *The principles of human biochemical genetics* (2nd ed.). New York: American Elsevier.

Jenkins, J. B. (1983). *Human genetics.* New York: Benjamin/Cummings.

La Du, B. N. (1966). Alcaptonuria. In J. B. Stanbury, J. B. Wyngaarden, & D. S. Fredickson (Eds.), *The metabolic basis of inherited diseases.* New York: McGraw-Hill.

Roberts, J. A. F. (1967). *An introduction to medical genetics* (4th ed.). New York: Oxford University Press.

Whaley, L. F., & Wong, D. L. (1983). *Nursing care of infants and children* (2nd ed.). St. Louis: Mosby.

TIMOTHY A. BALLARD
*University of North Carolina
at Wilmington*

CONGENITAL DISORDERS
CRETINISM
INBORN ERRORS OF METABOLISM
PHENYLKETONURIA

BIOFEEDBACK

Biofeedback is a highly structured form of therapy that provides immediate feedback about involuntary biological functions such as heart rate, blood pressure, or brain waves. The feedback generally uses visual and auditory devices to show the subject what is happening to normally autonomic bodily functions as the patient attempts to influence them.

The classical animal experiments conducted by Neal Miller and his colleagues in the 1960s demonstrated that involuntary actions such as heart rate, blood pressure, and salivation could be altered by making rewards and punishments contingent on changes in these involuntary responses. This research suggested that people could be taught to control a number of physiological responses formerly thought to be involuntary (Miller, 1978).

In the field of special education, the effectiveness of biofeedback has been exaggerated, but a few procedures do seem to offer promise. The two most frequently used types of biofeedback with learning-disabled and gifted populations are passive and active. During passive electromyographic (EMG) biofeedback, the subject is asked to maintain a signal indicating a low level of tension or other required response. During active electromyographic biofeedback, the subject is asked to produce different levels of tension and or other required responses and to perform differential relaxation. For example, in biofeedback treatment of migraine headaches, patients are taught to warm their hands through temperature feedback. This hand warming is associated with increased blood flow to the hands which in turn leads to a lessening of arterial pressure in the brain (Allen & Shriver, 1997; Blanchard et al., 1978).

Electromyographic biofeedback has been used as an intervention strategy for hyperactivity (Braud, Lupin, & Braud, 1975; Christie, Dewitt, Kaltenbach, & Reed, 1984; Kaduson & Finnerty, 1995; Omizo & Michael, 1982; Rivera & Omizo, 1980). Braud et al. (1975) studied the effects of biofeedback on muscular activity and tension in a hyperactive boy. When the child's forehead muscle group exceeded a certain point, a tone sounded and the child was instructed to "keep the tone off" by sitting and relaxing. Muscular tension and activity decreased both within and across training sessions. It was found that continued practice using laboratory techniques was needed to maintain treatment results. Without parent and school cooperation, the treatment effects deteriorated.

Omizo and Michael (1982) demonstrated through the use of biofeedback-induced relaxation training increased attention to task and reduced impulsivity among hyperactive boys, but no effect on locus of control; this is also supported by the findings of Rivera and Omizo (1980). The basic treatment package asked the boys, seated in a reclining position, to induce the biofeedback unit to register a pattern of low activity while relaxation tapes were played for them.

Bhatara, Arnold, Lorance, & Gupta (1979) reviewed the literature on EMG biofeedback and concluded that there is insufficient evidence to support the clinical utility of EMG feedback in hyperactive children. Biofeedback is seen as a promising technique in this area but the problems found in the research to date must be solved (Kaduson & Finnerty, 1995).

There must be more tightly controlled designs to rule out the influence of task-motivated suggestions and expectant attitudes. There must be adequate follow-ups carried out on larger populations. Researchers must question the influence of suggestion, motivation, and emotion. Finally, most of the successful results with biofeedback techniques are closely related to relaxation therapies. Thus it would be fruitful to combine biofeedback with older proven therapies.

Progressive muscle relaxation and EMG biofeedback training were used to study the treatment effects on anxiety for 30 gifted children (Roome & Romney, 1985). The biofeedback group was connected to an Inner Tell EMG and told to experiment with various mental images to reduce the meter reading. The progressive muscle relaxation group listened to tapes in a chair. The results indicated neither treatment to be more effective than the other. Both groups showed a significant reduction in stated anxiety and a shift toward internal locus of control as compared with the control group. This study, like so many others (Zimet, 1979), is contradictory and the results are inconclusive owing to the limited number of sessions and lack of follow-up testing. There is still no conclusive evidence that a person's ability to learn self-control through biofeedback can be predicted from locus of control orientation. The instructional set, not biofeedback itself, appears to be the pivotal variable.

A relatively recent area of investigation is the use of urodynamic biofeedback with children with myelomeningocele (spina bifida), the most common congenital central nervous system defect. Neurogenic urinary and fecal incontinence is prevalent in the majority of these children. The impact of the physical and psychosocial difficulties associated with chronic incontinence in spina bifida children can cause great distress (Hunt, 1981).

Rectosphincteric biofeedback was used to reduce the number of accidents in eight spina bifida children with chronic fecal incontinence. Six of the eight children reduced the number of accidents and two children became continent (Varni, 1983). Wald (1981) used a similar procedure and found four of eight children had a good clinical response, defined as the disappearance of fecal soiling or a greater than 75% reduction in the frequency of soiling. The results of these studies are encouraging.

In the Killam, Jeffries, and Varni (1985) study using urodynamic biofeedback training, six of eight children demonstrated improved self-regulation of detrusor or sphincter functioning, but only one child demonstrated improvements in urinary incontinence. Unexpectedly, chronic neurogenic fecal incontinence was reduced in four children owing to placement of the surface electrodes in the perianal position.

Recent studies have suggested the clinical utility of biofeedback with children in the reduction of anxiety (Wench, Leu, & D'Amato, 1996), chronic pain management (James, Sharpley, & Sullivan, 1997), and asthma (Culpert, Kajander, & Reaney, 1996).

REFERENCES

Allen, K. D., & Shriver, M. D. (1997). Enhanced performance feedback to strengthen biofeedback treatment outcome with childhood migraine. *Headache, 37,* 169–173.

Bhatara, V., Arnold, L. E., Lorance, T., & Gupta, D. (1979). Muscle relaxation therapy in hyperkinesis: Is it effective? *Journal of Learning Disabilities, 11,* 182–186.

Blanchard, E. B., Theobald, D. E., Williamson, D. A., Silver, B. V., & Brown, D. A. (1978). Temperature biofeedback in the treatment of migraine headaches. *Archives of General Psychiatry, 35,* 581–588.

Braud, L. W., Lupin, M. N., & Braud, W. G. (1975). The use of electromyographic biofeedback in the control of hyperactivity. *Journal of Learning Disabilities, 8,* 420–425.

Christie, D. J., Dewitt, R. A., Kaltenbach, P., & Reed, D. (1984). Using EMG biofeedback to signal hyperactive children when to relax. *Exceptional Children, 50,* 547–548.

Culpert, T. P., Kajander, R. L., & Reaney, J. B. (1996). Biofeedback with children and adolescents: Clinical observations and patient perspectives. *Journal of Developmental and Behavioral Pediatrics, 17,* 342–350.

Hunt, G. M. (1981). Spina bifida: Implications for 100 children at school. *Developmental Medicine & Child Neurology, 23,* 160–172.

James, R. J., Sharpley, C. F., & Sullivan, M. F. (1997). The effects of self-efficacy and gender upon ability to increase and decrease heart-rate. *Scandinavian Journal of Behaviour Therapy, 26,* 11–16.

Kaduson, H. G., & Finnerty, K. (1995). Self-control game interventions for attention-deficit hyperactivity disorder. *International Journal of Play Therapy, 4,* 15–29.

Killam, P. E., Jeffries, J. S., & Varni, J. W. (1985). Urodynamic biofeedback treatment of urinary incontinence in children with myelomeningocele. *Biofeedback & Self-Regulation, 10,* 161–171.

Miller, N. E. (1978). Biofeedback and visceral learning. *Annual Review of Psychology, 29,* 373–404.

Omizo, M. M., & Michael, W. B. (1982). Biofeedback-induced relaxation training and impulsivity attention to task, and locus of control among hyperactive boys. *Journal of Learning Disabilities, 15,* 414–416.

Rivera, E., & Omizo, M. M. (1980). An investigation of the effects of relaxation training on attention to task and impulsivity among male hyperactive children. *Exceptional Child, 27,* 41–51.

Roome, J. R., & Romney, D. M. (1985). Reducing anxiety in gifted children by inducing relaxation. *Roeper Review, 7,* 177–179.

Shapiro, D., & Surwit, R. S. (1976). Learned control of physiological function and disease. In H. Leitenberg (Ed.), *Handbook of behavior modification and behavior therapy* (pp. 74–123). Englewood Cliffs, NJ: Prentice-Hall.

Varni, J. W. (1983). *Clinical behavioral pediatrics: An interdisciplinary biobehavioral approach.* New York: Pergamon.

Wald, A. (1981). Use of biofeedback of treatment of fecal incontinence in patients with myelomeningocele. *Pediatrics, 68,* 45–49.

Wenck, L. S., Leu, P. W., & D'Amato, R. C. (1996). Evaluating the efficacy of a biofeedback intervention to reduce children's anxiety. *Journal of Clinical Psychology, 52,* 469–473.

Zimet, G. D. (1979). Locus of control and biofeedback: A review of the literature. *Perceptual & Motor Skills, 49,* 871–877.

DEBORAH A. SHANLEY
Medgar Evans College
First edition

ELAINE FLETCHER-JANZEN
University of Northern Colorado
Second edition

HYPERACTIVITY
SPINA BIFIDA

BIOGENIC MODELS

Biogenic, or organic, models present causes of human actions in terms of the biological substrate that underlies behavior. Thus to predict, explain, and control behavior, the various activities of the nervous system and other bodily organs must be understood and manipulated. Implicit in this model is the notion that effective therapies will primarily involve biological manipulations such as drugs or surgery. This approach can be contrasted with psychogenic models that emphasize psychological constructs as explanatory mechanisms of behavior (Bootzin, 1984; Franzblau, Kanadanian, & Rettig, 1995).

Contemporary models of behavior are rarely in absolutely biological or psychological terms, but when a model is primarily biogenic in nature there are important implications for the user's conceptual framework in understanding behavior and implementing behavioral change programs. Biogenic models place the locus of the cause of problem behavior squarely within the individual's biological status and give only minimal roles to other parts of the ecosystem such as family or school. Most contemporary biogenic models are reductionistic and pin their ultimate hopes on an understanding of the relationships among biological, biochemical, and behavioral phenomena. Alterations, which are observed in cognitions or social relations, can be viewed as symptoms of physiological actions. Although our current understanding of biological factors may not allow for biochemical cures for all behavioral problems, the ultimate direction of the biogenic approach lies in biomedical interventions (Engel, 1977).

Critics of the biogenic model have difficulty denying that in a physical sense all behavior can ultimately be traced to biological processes. They do contend, however, that reductionist approaches may not always be the most fruitful guides to practice in education. Biogenic models tend to blame the victim by emphasizing changing the organism and not the environment or situation in which the individual exists (Albee, 1980; Millon & Davis, 1995). It is often the case that concepts of the biogenic model are confused with those of the medical or disease model. Engel (1977), however, proposed a disease model that replaced a biomedical with a biopsychosocial approach to the understanding of disordered behavior.

The organic (biogenic) model represents one of the major historical threads in the understanding of the etiology of abnormal behavior. This model has been advanced at least since the time of the Greek physician Hippocrates (Brown, 1986), and is still seen in such concepts as minimal brain dysfunction (Bootzin, 1984). Indeed, for thousands of years, it was the only viable alternative to magical or supernatural explanations of exceptional behavior. It should be noted, however, that biogenic models have not always resulted in more humane treatment or exacting scientific research into the nature of behavior disorders. For example, the warehousing of patients in the late nineteenth- and early twentieth-century psychiatric hospitals was the result in part of a belief that dealing with mental disease was hopeless until science found a biological cure (Erickson & Hyerstay, 1980).

Biogenic models may be of value to the classroom special education teacher as the basis for planning interventions. Reed (1979) noted the role of neuropsychological diagnoses in developing educational techniques that take into account deficits in brain function. In a rejoinder, Balow (1979) pointed out that such biogenic models were of limited use to the classroom teacher because of their lack of relevance for educational practice and their unclear specification of the link between specific biological dysfunctions and differential educational planning.

REFERENCES

Albee, G. (1980). A competency model to replace the deficit model. In M. Gibbs, J. Lachenmeyer, & J. Sigal (Eds.), *Community psychology: Theoretical and empirical approaches* (pp. 213–238). New York: Gardner.

Balow, B. (1979). Biological defects and special education: An empiricist's view. *Journal of Special Education, 13,* 35–40.

Bootzin, R. (1984). *Abnormal psychology: Current perspectives* (4th ed.). New York: Random House.

Brown, R. T. (1986). Etiology and development of exceptionality. In R. T. Brown & C. R. Reynolds (Eds.), *Psychological perspectives on childhood exceptionality: A handbook* (pp. 181–229). New York: Wiley.

Engel, G. (1977). A need for a new medical model: A challenge for biomedicine. *Science, 96,* 129–136.

Erickson, R., & Hyerstay, B. (1980). Historical perspectives on treatment of the mentally ill. In M. Gibbs, J. Lachenmeyer, & J. Sigal (Eds.), *Community psychology: Theoretical and empirical approaches* (pp. 29–64). New York: Gardner.

Franzblau, S. H., Kanadanian, M., & Rettig, E. (1995). Critique of reductionistic models of obsessive compulsive disorder. *Social Science and Medicine, 41,* 99–112.

Millon, T., & Davis, R. D. (1995). The development of personality disorders. *Developmental Psychopathology,* Vol. 2. New York, NY: Wiley.

Reed, H. (1979). Biological defects in special education: An issue in personnel preparation. *Journal of Special Education, 13,* 9–33.

Lee Anderson Jackson, Jr.
*University of North Carolina
at Wilmington*

**BIOLOGICAL BASIS OF EMOTIONAL DISTURBANCE
BIOLOGICAL BASIS OF LEARNING AND MEMORY
MEDICAL MODEL, DEFENSE OF**

BIOLOGICAL BASIS OF EMOTIONAL DISORDERS

Biological factors contribute to emotional disorders in various ways. A genetic predisposition has been strongly implicated for schizophrenia, depression, and manic-depressive illness. There is at least moderate evidence of a genetic contribution to childhood autism, obsessive-compulsive disorder, (Franzblau, Kanadanian, & Rettig, 1995) panic disorder, disability (Heubner & Thomas, 1995) and other conditions.

Whether because of genetics, improper nutrition, or other sources, certain areas of the nervous system can misfunction in ways that lead to behavioral abnormalities. For example, individuals who are subject to panic disorder have an overresponsive sympathetic nervous system. Even at rest, they have an elevated heart rate and blood epinephrine level compared with controls (Nesse et al., 1984). They may respond with anxiety, agitation, and palpitations to injections that produce only mild signs of arousal in other people (Charney, Heninger, & Breier, 1984; Liebowitz, et al., 1984).

Many types of emotional disorders have been linked to abnormalities affecting one or more synaptic transmitter systems in the brain. One example is depression. Most antidepressant drugs prolong the activity of the monoamine transmitters (dopamine, norepinephrine, and serotonin) in the brain. One interpretation of the effect of antidepressant drugs has been that they counteract an initial deficiency in the activity at monoamine synapses. That interpretation may be incorrect, however; a prolonged increase in the abundance of synaptic transmitter molecules at a synapse leads to a compensatory decline in the later release of that transmitter and to a decline in the number of receptors sensitive to that transmitter. Because of the multitude of effects, it is uncertain whether the antidepressant drugs help to repair an initial overactivity or underactivity of the monoamine synapses. Nevertheless, it is likely that some disorder of those synapses is responsible for many manifestations of depression.

Another probable example of a behavioral disorder linked to abnormalities at synapses is Gilles de la Tourette's syndrome. This uncommon condition affects mostly boys and has its onset in childhood. The symptoms include tics, repetitive movements, repetitive sounds, and learning disabilities (Golden, 1977). Although the cause is not known, the usual treatment is haloperidol and other drugs that block dopamine synapses in the brain.

The biological basis of an emotional disorder need not be a permanent chemical disorder of the brain, however, and drugs are not always the best remedy even for a biological disorder. Many cases of depression have been linked to inadequate or poorly timed sleep. Occasionally, individuals suffer from winter depressions as a result of inadequate sunlight. Uncorrected visual problems may lead to headaches. Many adolescents experience moodiness and aggressive outbursts that may be triggered by hormonal changes. A lack of exercise may predispose the body to overreact to stress. Malnutrition can aggravate psychological disorders as well. In certain cases, emotional disorders can be alleviated by altering sleep, diet, exercise, and other habits without resorting to tranquilizers, antidepressant drugs, or other medical interventions. For further information, see Kalat (1984), Pincus and Tucker (1985), or Snyder (1980).

REFERENCES

Charney, D. S., Heninger, G. R., & Breier, A. (1984). Noradrenergic function in panic anxiety. *Archives of General Psychiatry, 41,* 751–763.

Franzblau, S. H., Kanadanian, M., Rettig, E. (1995). Critique of the reductionist models of obsessive compulsive disorder. *Social Science and Medicine, 41,* 99–112.

Golden, G. S. (1977). Tourette syndrome. *American Journal of Diseases of Children, 131,* 531–534.

Heubner, R. A., & Thomas, R. The relationship between attachment, psychopathology, and childhood disability. *Rehabilitation Psychology, 40,* 111–124.

Kalat, J. W. (1984). *Biological psychology* (2nd ed.). Belmont, CA: Wadsworth.

Liebowitz, M. R., Fyer, A. J., Gorman, J. M., Dillon, D., Appleby, I. L., Levy, G., Anderson, S., Levitt, M., Palij, M., Davies, S. O., & Klein, D. F. (1984). Lactate provocation of panic attacks: Vol I. Clinical and behavioral findings. *Archives of General Psychiatry, 41,* 764–770.

Nesse, R. M., Cameron, O. G., Curtis, G. C., McCann, D. S., & Huber-Smith, M. J. (1984). Adrenergic function in patients with panic anxiety. *Archives of General Psychiatry, 41,* 771–776.

Pincus, J. H., & Tucker, G. J. (1985). *Behavioral neurology* (3rd ed.). New York: Oxford University Press.

Snyder, S. H. (1980). *Biological aspects of mental disorder.* New York: Oxford University Press.

JAMES W. KALAT
North Carolina State University

DIAGNOSTIC AND STATISTICAL MANUAL OF MENTAL DISORDERS (DSM-IV)
EMOTIONAL DISORDERS

BIOLOGICAL BASIS OF LEARNING AND MEMORY

To understand the biological basis of learning and memory, two largely independent questions must be dealt with: (1) How does a pattern of experience alter the future properties of cells and synapses in the nervous system? (2) How do populations of altered cells work together to produce adaptive behavior?

Striking progress has been made toward answering the first question. According to studies of invertebrates, short-term increases in behavior can be induced by chemical changes that block the flow of potassium across the presynaptic membrane of certain neurons. Longer lasting changes in behavior require the synthesis of proteins in the neurons to be changed (Kandel & Schwartz, 1982). Protein synthesis also appears to be necessary for learning by vertebrates, especially for long-term retention (Davis & Squire, 1984).

Certain of the brain changes associated with learning or the ability to learn are large enough to be visible under a light microscope. Enhanced learning ability is associated with a proliferation of glial cells and increased branching of dendrites (Uphouse, 1980). Impaired learning associated with the opposite anatomical changes. The extent of branching of dendrites is highly correlated with the number of synapses found in the brain.

Memory, on the other hand, is "attention" that leaves tracks or traces in the brain. Biologically, memory functions at two broad levels, one at the cellular level and one at a systems level. The creation of memories changes individual cell membranes and synaptic physiology (Reynolds & Bigler, 1997).

Investigators have not determined how the changed neurons operate together to produce the overall changes in behavior identified as learning. They have, however, identified areas of the mammalian brain that are necessary for certain aspects of learning. The famous neurological patient H. M. had most of his hippocampus removed as a treatment for severe epilepsy. He can recall very few events that have occurred since that operation, although he has been able to learn new skills such as reading material written in mirror fashion and working the Tower of Hanoi puzzle (Cohen & Squire, 1980; Milner, Corkin, & Teuber, 1968). Experiments with animals have indicated that amnesia is most severe if damage to the hippocampus is combined with damage to the amygdala. Damage to those two areas impairs animals' ability to store sensory information and respond to it a few minutes later (Zola-Morgan & Squire, 1985). Various other patterns of learning and memory loss occur after damage to the frontal lobes of the cerebral cortex and to numerous subcortical structures.

Majovski (1997) has suggested that:

Data collected from studies of heredity and environment show that morphogenetic development of the brain's intellectual nature is attributable to both genetic and social environmental influences, the former having slightly greater effect than the latter. What this suggests is that several different cortical and cortical-subcortical systems are operative during the process of learning and information storage. What the infant senses, then, may be in part the result of what is neurally "set" to sense or competent to sense via a selective attention process. (p. 83)

The interactive process of learning and memory with the environmental and physical factors in childhood suggests a highly interactive biological set.

Impaired learning and memory among children and adolescents are not generally caused by discretely localized brain damage. Exposure to alcohol and other toxins in utero can greatly impair brain development, as can phenylketonuria, severe malnutrition, or a chronic lack of social stimulation in early childhood. Head injury leading to a temporary loss of consciousness is a commonly overlooked source of minor, diffuse brain damage. These factors coupled with the process of brain development and acculturation makes the diagnosis of learning and memory problems very difficult.

REFERENCES

Cohen, N. J., & Squire, L. R. (1980). Preserved learning and retention of pattern-analyzing skill in amnesia: Dissociation of knowing how and knowing that. *Science, 210,* 207–211.

Davis, H. P., & Squire, L. R. (1984). Protein synthesis and memory: A review. *Psychological Bulletin, 96,* 518–559.

Kandel, E. R., & Schwartz, J. H. (1982). Molecular biology of learning: Modulation of transmitter release. *Science, 218,* 433–443.

Majovski, L. V. (1997). Development of Higher Brain functions in children: Neural, Cognitive, and Behavioral Perspectives. In C. R. Reynolds & E. Fletcher-Janzen (Eds.), *Handbook of Clinical Child Neuropsychology* (2nd ed.) (pp. 63–101). New York: Plenum.

Milner, B., Corkin, S., & Teuber, H. L. (1968). Further analysis of the hippocampal ammesic syndrome: 14-year follow-up study of H. M. *Neuropsychologia, 6,* 215–234.

Moscovitch, M. (1985). Memory from infancy to old age: Implications for theories of normal and pathological memory. *Annals of the New York Academy of Sciences, 444,* 78–96.

Reynolds, C. R., & Bigler, E. D. (1997). Clinical neuropsychological assessment of child and adolescent memory with the Test of Learning & Memory. In C. R. Reynolds & E. Fletcher-Janzen (Eds.), *Handbook of Clinical Child Neuropsychology* (2nd ed.) (pp. 296–329). New York: Plenum.

Uphouse, L. (1980). Reevaluation of mechanisms that mediate brain differences between enriched and impoverished animals. *Psychological Bulletin, 88,* 215–232.

Zola-Morgan, S., & Squire, L. R. (1985). Medial temporal lesions in monkeys impair memory on a variety of tasks sensitive to human amnesia. *Behavioral Neuroscience, 99,* 22–34.

JAMES W. KALAT
North Carolina State University
First edition

ELAINE FLETCHER-JANZEN
University of Northern Colorado
Second edition

BIOLOGICAL FACTORS AND SOCIAL CLASS

See SOCIAL CLASS AND BIOLOGICAL FACTORS

BIRCH, HERBERT G. (1918–1973)

Herbert G. Birch was born in New York City on April 21, 1918. He graduated from New York University (NYU) in 1939, and received the PhD degree in psychology in 1944. In 1960 Birch received the MD degree from the New York College of Medicine. He served as a research associate at the Yerkes Laboratories for Primate Biology from 1944 to 1946, as an instructor in psychology at NYU the next year, and as an assistant and associate professor at the City College of New York from 1947 to 1955. For the following 2 years, Birch was research associate at Bellevue Medical Center in New York City. From the time he received the MD degree in 1960 until his death, he was a member of the faculty of the Albert Einstein College of Medicine in New York City, first as an associate research professor and then as a full professor of pediatrics and director of the Center for Normal and Aberrant Behavioral Development. Concurrently, he was professor of psychology and education at the Ferkauf Graduate School of Humanities and Social Sciences, Yeshiva University.

Herbert G. Birch

Eisenberg, L. (1971). Herbert Birch 1918–1973. *International Journal of Mental Health, 1,* 80–81.

PAUL IRVINE
Katonah, New York

An internationally known researcher in child development and brain injury, Birch was the author of 200 articles and coauthor of six books, the latter including *Brain Damage in Children* (1964), *Disadvantaged Children: Health, Nutrition, and School Failure* (1970), and *Children with Cerebral Dysfunction* (1971). He served in an editorial capacity for a number of journals, including the *Journal of Special Education,* the *American Journal of Mental Deficiency,* the *American Journal of Child Psychology and Human Development,* and the *International Journal of Mental Health.* In 1971 he received the Kennedy International Award for Scientific Research for outstanding scientific research contributing to the understanding and alleviation of mental retardation.

Birch died at his home in Suffern, New York, on February 4, 1973. In his eulogy, Dr. Leon Eisenberg said of Birch, "Those who knew Herbert Birch recognized that they were in the presence of authentic genius. His knowledge was encyclopedic; his intellect, prodigious; his productivity, unmatched." In May 1973, Birch was posthumously granted the Research Award of the American Association on Mental Deficiency.

REFERENCES

Birch, H. G. (Ed.). (1964). *Brain damage in children.* Baltimore, MD: Williams & Wilkins.

Birch, H. G., & Diller, K. (1971). *Children with cerebral dysfunction.* New York: Grune & Stratton.

Birch, H. G., & Gussow, J. D. (1970). *Disadvantaged children: Health, nutrition and school failure.* New York: Grune & Stratton.

BIRCH, JACK W. (1915–1998)

A native of Glassport, Pennsylvania, Jack W. Birch began his career as an elementary education teacher after receiving a BS (1937) with majors in English and science and a minor in special education from California University of Pennsylvania. He later went on to earn his MEd from Pennsylvania State University (1941) and a PhD in Psychology from the University of Pittsburgh (1951).

Birch taught classes for educable mentally retarded children, and was a psychologist and supervisor of special education. From 1948 to 1958 he was director of special education for the Pittsburgh Public Schools, and spent the remainder of his career at the University of Pittsburgh as a professor of psychology and education, chairman of the Department of Special Education, and an associate dean in the School of Education. He was among the initial faculty organizers of the University Senate and served as its vice president. Birch became an emeritus professor in 1985 at the age of 70. He was active in the field of education and community service until his death on April 1, 1998.

As a young teacher in Eastern Pennsylvania in the 1930s, Birch was aghast at the ineptitude of a book about remedial reading he had purchased. He wrote the publisher, complaining of the money he had wasted buying the book and indicating that he could do a better job himself. The response from the publisher encouraged him to go ahead and try, so he did. His first book was published by that same company, beginning a long career combining his interests in research, writing, and special education. He published over 120 articles and books on topics including gifted and talented persons and individuals with mental retardation, speech handicaps, blindness, deafness, and physical handicaps. *Teaching Exceptional Children in All America's Schools* and *Reports on the Implementation and Effects of the Adaptive Learning Environments Model in General and Special Education Settings* are two of his major books. His writings also included books related to aspects of academia, including writing better dissertations and how to make the best use of retired professors.

Believing that students with handicaps should have an opportunity to display skills society assumed they were incapable of developing, Birch was among early advocates of mainstreaming students with handicaps. In 1978 he reviewed the process of mainstreaming in a national sample of school systems, concluding that expansion of individualized education was a necessity and recommending ways to effectively implement mainstreaming. Four essential conditions were cited for successful mainstreaming: (1) regular educators must be oriented to the adaptation requirements for the inclusion of pupils with handicaps; (2) teachers must learn to use the specialized instructional materials exceptional children may need; (3) regular classroom teachers must be able, through an overt arrangement, to obtain help for pupils from special education teachers; and (4) regular classroom teachers must receive immediate assistance (with no loss of face) if a crisis in class or individual management occurs. Birch's research also indicated that many young people who were believed to have mental disabilities actually suffered from hearing problems, and that their ability to learn would be enhanced by first addressing the hearing problem.

During his lifetime, Birch traveled to numerous countries, frequently as a consultant in special education to various foreign governments and schools, and from 1985 to 1986, he was the Belle van Zuijlen professor of clinical child psychology and pedagogy at the University Utrecht, Netherlands. Among his memberships, he was a fellow of the American Psychological Association; regional chairman of the Commission on Psychology, Education, Nomenclature, and Standards of the American Association of Mental Deficiency; and president of both the Council for Exceptional Children and the Foundation for Exceptional Children. For his contributions to special education and rehabilitation, Birch received an award from the Pennsylvania Federation of the Council for Exceptional Children, and he was also honored for his service with an award from The National Accreditation Council of Services to the Blind and Visually Handicapped.

REFERENCES

Birch, J. W. (1978). Mainstreaming that works in elementary and secondary schools. *Journal of Teacher Education, 29,* 18–21.

Reynolds, M. C., & Birch, J. W. (1982). *Teaching exceptional children in all America's schools.* Reston, VA: Council for Exceptional Children.

Wang, M. C., & Birch, J. W. (1985). *Reports on the implementation and effects of the adaptive learning environments model in general and special education settings.* Pittsburgh, PA: University of Pittsburgh.

E. VALERIE HEWITT
Texas A & M University
First edition

TAMARA J. MARTIN
*The University of Texas of the
Permian Basin*
Second edition

BIRTH INJURIES

Birth injuries are the traumatic injuries to the brain, skull, spinal cord, peripheral nerves, and muscle of the newborn that occasionally occur during the birth process. These injuries include cephalohematoma, skull fracture, central nervous system hemorrhage, spinal cord injury, peripheral nerve injury, bony injury, abdominal injury, cerebral palsy, and seizure disorders. The frequency of these birth injuries has greatly decreased with the declining use of high and midforceps, better monitoring during labor, and decreased vaginal breech deliveries (Brann, 1985). However the frequency of birth injuries may vary depending on the introduction of new techniques to assist delivery such as vacuum extraction (Hes, de Jong, Paz, & Avezaat, 1997).

Cephalohematoma usually refers to a benign traumatic lesion to the skull in which blood pools under the periosteum and is confined by suture boundaries. But 10 to 25% of all cephalohematomas are associated with an underlying skull fracture. These fractures rarely pose major problems but if depressed can result in compression of the skull (Menkes, 1984).

Central nervous system hemorrhage may be caused by mechanical trauma to the infant's brain during the birth process. The hemorrhage may occur in the subarachnoid space, the subdural space, or the dural space, or it may be intracerebral. The most common type of traumatic central nervous system hemorrhage is the subarachnoid hemorrhage resulting from tears in the meninges. Usually this is a benign condition unless it is associated with perinatal hypoxia or meningitis (Oxorn, 1986).

Subdural hemorrhage, now uncommon, may result in hydrocephalus and seizures. Intracerebral hemorrhage, one of the rarest types of traumatic central nervous system hemorrhage in the newborn, may result in increased intracranial pressure, hemiparesis, and convulsions. Hemorrhage into the dural space is also rare, but it usually results in massive hemorrhage and early neonatal death (Brann, 1985).

Traumatic spinal cord injuries are unusual. The most common sites of damage are the lower cervical and upper thoracic regions. These injuries can lead to stillbirth, respiratory failure, paralysis, or spasticity (Oxorn, 1986).

Peripheral nerve injuries can involve trauma to the brachial plexus, the phrenic nerve, the facial nerve, or the radial nerves. The nerve injuries are usually caused by traction or direct compression of the nerve itself. Trauma to the brachial plexus may cause muscle atrophy, contractures, and impaired limb growth (Menkes, 1984).

Trauma to the phrenic nerve may cause diaphragm paralysis and mimic congenital pulmonary or heart disease, resulting in long-term ventilatory support. Damage to the facial nerve results in weakness of the muscles to the affected side of the face, causing failure on the affected side of the mouth to move and the eyelid to close. Radial nerve injury may result in wrist drop and the inability to extend the fingers and the thumb (Menkes, 1984).

Traumatic bony injuries include fractures of the clavicle, humerus, and femur. Fracture of the clavicle is the most common bony injury; it usually occurs in association with shoulder dystocia. Fractures of the humerus and femur are rare and result from traumatic delivery (Oxorn, 1986).

Traumatic abdominal injuries are uncommon but they can have serious consequences. The traumatic abdominal injuries include hepatic or splenic rupture; they result from traumatic delivery. These injuries are usually life-threatening conditions (Oxorn, 1986).

Cerebral palsy is a chronic nonprogressive disorder of the pyramidal motor system resulting in lack of voluntary muscle control and coordination. The cause is uncertain but cerebral anoxia during the perinatal period has been associated with the resulting cerebral damage (Rosen, 1985).

There are several types of cerebral palsy: spastic, dyskinetic, ataxic, and mixed-type. Spastic cerebral palsy, the most common clinical type, is characterized by hypertonicity, uneven muscle tone, persistent primitive reflexes, lack of normal postural control, and incomplete spastic paralysis (Whaley & Wong, 1983).

Dyskinetic cerebral palsy is characterized by slow, writhing movements that involve the entire body. There is also high-frequency deafness associated with this type of cerebral palsy. Ataxic cerebral palsy is manifested by irregular muscle action and failure of muscle coordination. Mixed-type cerebral palsy is manifested by a combination of spaticity and atethosis, the slow writhing movements (Whaley & Wong, 1983).

Disabilities associated with cerebral palsy include mental retardation, seizure disorders, impaired behavioral and interpersonal relationships, and impairment of other senses. Approximately two-thirds of those diagnosed with cerebral palsy are also mentally retarded. About 50% of those with cerebral palsy have some type of seizure disorder. Those with impaired behavioral relationships usually have poor attention spans and hyperactive behavior. Impairment of the other senses include both visual and hearing defects (Batshaw & Perret, 1981). Cerebral palsy is a lifelong affliction. Most of those with the disorder live to adulthood but only 10% become self-supporting. The other 90% need support both medically and socially (Batshaw & Perret, 1981).

Seizure disorders may result from many causes, including perinatal asphyxia, intracranial hemorrhage, infection, congenital defects, metabolic disorders, drug withdrawal, inherited defects, and kernicterus. Perinatal asphyxia is the most frequent cause of seizures in the pre- and full-term infant. Perinatal asphyxia as the cause of neonatal seizures has the poorest prognosis. Approximately 60% of those infants with seizures caused by perinatal asphyxia have permanent neurologic sequelae and lifelong seizure disorders (Brann, 1985).

REFERENCES

Batshaw, R. L., & Perret, Y. M. (1981). *Children with handicaps: A medical primer.* Baltimore, MD: Brookes.

Brann, A. W. (1985). Factors during neonatal life that influence brain disorders. In J. M. Freeman (Ed.), *Prenatal and perinatal factors associated with brain disorders* (NIH Publication No. 85-1149, pp. 263–358). Bethesda, MD: U.S. Department of Health and Human Services.

Hes, R., de Jong, T. H., Paz, D. H., & Avezaat, C. J. (1997). Rapid evolution of a growing skull fracture after vacuum extraction. *Pediatric Neurosurgery, 26,* 269–274.

Menkes, J. H. (1984). Neurologic evaluation of the newborn infant. In M. E. Avery & H. W. Taeusch (Eds.), *Schaffer's diseases of the newborn* (5th ed.) (pp. 652–661). Philadelphia: Saunders.

Oxorn, H. (1986). *Human labor and birth* (5th ed.). Norwalk, CT: Appleton-Century-Crofts.

Rosen, M. G. (1985). Factors during labor and delivery that influence brain disorders. In J. M. Freeman (Ed.), *Prenatal and perinatal factors associated with brain disorders* (NIH Publication No. 85-1149, pp. 359–440). Bethesda, MD: U.S. Department of Health and Human Services.

Whaley, L. F., & Wong, D. L. (1983). *Nursing care of infants and children* (2nd ed.). St. Louis: Mosby.

ELIZABETH R. BAUERSCHMIDT
*University of North Carolina
at Wilmington*

ABSENCE SEIZURES
BRAIN DAMAGE
CEREBRAL PALSY
GRAND MAL SEIZURES

BIRTH ORDER

Birth order, or sibling status, refers to a child's ordinal position in the family. There has been much speculation about the effects of birth order on important variables such as personality characteristics, mental illness, intelligence, achievement, and occupational status; but consistent relationships have been difficult to establish unequivocally. The study of birth order can be traced at least as far back as *English Men of Science* (1874), in which Galton reported that firstborns were considerably overrepresented among the scientists of his day. Alfred Adler (1958) was also convinced of the influence of family position on development, and stated that ". . . position in the family leaves an indelible stamp upon the style of life." (p. 154) In contrast, Craig (1996) concludes that there are no consistent personality characteristics associated with birth order.

There is an intuitive appeal to the view that each ordinal position is accompanied by unique family environments and patterns of family interactions. It is congruent with a social theory of personality development, one that emphasizes the interpersonal relationships that stem from the dynamics of a child's ordinal position. Over the course of childhood, any consistent differences in social learning experiences might well produce varied personality and achievement profiles or distinctive behavioral traits for children within the same family (Forer, 1976). For example, the amount of time that parents have available for a particular child is a function of birth order. Parents spend almost twice as much time in direct contact with firstborns as they do with succeeding children (White, Kaban, & Attanucci, 1979). Further, the older child in a typical American family is accorded more opportunities to practice language skills and take responsibility for and teach younger siblings (Harris, 1973; Smith, 1984).

Harris (1973) describes the firstborn as being adult-civilized; parents are more actively involved in nurturing and guiding their firstborn child. Younger children in the family are more likely to be peer-civilized. Therefore, the firstborn or only child would be expected to identify more closely with the parents and hold more traditional values than laterborn children (Schacter, 1959; Sutton-Smith & Rosenburg, 1970). As subsequent children are added to the family, parents spend less and less time in direct care, and older siblings assume more responsibility for child care. The opportunity to teach younger siblings and assignment of more responsible roles within the family may enhance firstborns' intellectual development. It is also possible that firstborns receive more intellectual stimulation during infancy and more direct achievement training during the preschool years than laterborns do (Bradley & Caldwell, 1984; Rothbart, 1971).

Various personality profiles, though sometimes overlapping and inconsistent, have been suggested for prominent ordinal positions. The proposed profiles follow:

Firstborn. Firstborns are said to exhibit higher standards of moral honesty, have higher need for achievement, earlier social maturation, better work habits, and higher need for recognition and approval (Forer, 1976; Harris, 1973). Firstborns are also considered to rate higher in leadership, independence, and sensitivity to stress (Sutton-Smith & Rosenberg, 1970), and tend to be dominant, more aggressive, ambitious and conservative (Koch, 1955).

Secondborn. Secondborns are believed to have good social skills, seek out group activities, and maintain better relationships in life than do firstborns. They also show more dependency behavior and seek more adult help and approval (Forer, 1976; McGurk & Lewis, 1972).

Middleborn. Middleborns, like secondborns, show better interpersonal skills and tend to express greater sensitivity to the feelings and needs of others (Falbo, 1981; Miller & Maruyama, 1976). Middle children generally have the fewest behavior problems, enjoy a healthier adjustment to life and as adults experience less anxiety in new or threatening situations (Touliatos & Lindholm, 1980; Yannakis, 1976). They also show more concern for peer norms and consequently accept peer advice more readily (Harris, 1973).

Lastborn. The youngest child is more likely to exhibit dependency and be peer oriented (Schacter, 1959). This birth order also has been associated with higher propensity to use alcohol and cigarettes (Ernst & Angst, 1983).

Onlyborn. Only children have a tendency to be leaders rather than joiners and show considerable affinity for independent behavior (Falbo, 1981). Schacter (1959) reports that only children experience more fear and anxiety during adolescence and adulthood than laterborn children. Conventional wisdom that singletons are selfish, lonely, and uncooperative is unsupported (Falbo, 1984).

Many factors affect a child's perception of ordinal position and associated family dynamics. Sex of siblings and spacing are important, as is the status of adopted children and stepchildren. For example, Adler (1958) has suggested that the male child with all female siblings may place more emphasis on his masculinity. A secondborn might assume the responsibilities of a firstborn who is developmentally delayed. With adopted children or stepchildren, previous family interactional patterns may have consequences for adjustment to new ordinal positions.

Several large-scale studies have found relationships between birth order and intelligence and achievement. (Belmont & Marolla, 1973; Zajonc & Markus, 1975; Berbaum & Moreland, 1980). On the average, oldest children have higher IQ's and have higher achievement in school and in careers. Only children also tend to be high achievers (Zajonc & Markus, 1975). However, a more recent study using a large data set from 1973 found that birth-order effects, when measured by educational attainment (i.e., total years of education), are negligible for small sib sizes, such as one to four children. For large families, it was found that lastborns and next-to-lastborns did considerably better than firstborns (Blake, 1990). Birth order and SAT data showed virtually no correlation. When these data were collected, presumably more resources were available for the lastborn child and more educational opportunities were afforded them.

Zajonc and Markus (1976) developed a model to make predictions concerning the relationship of birth order and intellectual ability. The confluence model uses an estimate of the average intellectual environment (AIE) of the family to predict the intelligence of each child, where AIE is equal to the total intellectual level of the family divided by the number of family members. According to the model, in a family with two children spaced only a few years apart, the second child is expected to have a lower IQ. In a family where the spacing between first and secondborn exceeds 7 years, the prediction would be reversed. The model also predicts that children from father-absent families and twins should have lowered IQ's, as will laterborns from larger families.

There is no support in the literature for the confluence model. Reported birth order effects appear to be artifacts of sibship size or socioeconomic status; birth order is essentially random (Steelman, 1985). Furthermore, children raised in single-parent families do not show the poor intellectual performances that confluence theory predicts (Entwistle & Alexander, 1990).

Page and Grandon (1979) proposed the admixture theory as an alternative interpretation of the reported correlation of birth order with intellectual functioning. In their view, social class, race, and family size interact to determine birth order effects. Furthermore, their analysis indicates that social class and race are the dominant factors, while family size and birth order are actually negligible in their effects.

It must also be remembered that even the reported differences in IQ correlated with birth order are quite small and have been obtained only when large numbers of families are compared. It is therefore unwise to make predictions for individuals on the basis of birth order. Family size, family structure and income have far greater effects on IQ than birth order. Wide spacing of siblings also tends to eliminate any evidence of birth order effects (Shaffer, 1993). To the degree that birth order may have consequences for achievement, it should not be assumed that such effects occur cross-culturally (LeVine, 1990).

As for personality, some research has found that firstborn infants, preschoolers, and adults are more socially outgoing and more interested in peer contacts than laterborns (Schachter, 1959; Snow, Jacklin, & Maccoby, 1981; Vandell, Wilson, & Whalen, 1981). There is some evidence that laterborn children tend to be somewhat more popular on average than firstborn children (Miller & Maruyama, 1976). And birth order may be a factor that contributes to children's acceptance by peers. One rationale offered is that laterborn children must learn to negotiate with older, more powerful siblings, and hence learn how to cooperate. Acquiring and using more conciliatory interpersonal skills may enable laterborns to be more popular than firstborns, who may use their greater power to dominate their

younger siblings and use coercive ways with peers (Berndt & Bulleit, 1985).

However, as with correlations reported between birth order and measures of intelligence, ordinal position effects reported for sociability are quite small. Thus, one must conclude that birth order plays at best only a minor role in determining how sociable a child is likely to become. The same is true for effects on peer popularity. More research is needed before we can understand how children's experiences in their families are translated into patterns of behavior and social standing outside the family.

There is by no means unanimity of thinking about the value of birth order for understanding personality (Schooler, 1972; Ernst & Angst, 1983; Dunn & Plomin, 1990). That birth order may be significant for some individuals is not in dispute. Rather, the contention of critics of the birth order variable is that its significance is wholly unpredictable and certainly far less important than other social or genetic variables. Ernst and Angst concluded their extensive analysis of birth order and personality by saying:

> Birth order and sibship size do not have a strong impact on personality. The present investigation points instead to a broken home, an unfriendly educational style, and a premature disruption of relations with parents as concomitants of neuroticism and to higher income and social class . . . and an undisturbed home as concomitants of higher achievement. . . . Birth order influences on personality and IQ have been widely overrated. (p. 242)

And Dunn & Plomin (1990) assert that birth order "plays only a bit-part in the drama of sibling differences" (p. 85).

However, Frank Sulloway (1996), in his book *Born to Rebel,* marshals persuasive evidence for the contributions of birth order to personality development. His meta-analysis leads him to conclude that for the personality dimension of openness to experience, laterborns are more nonconforming, adventurous, and unconventional. And firstborns tend to be more responsible, achievement-oriented, and organized; in a word, conscientious. They also tend to be more emotionally unstable, anxious, and fearful. In short, "firstborns tend to be dominant, aggressive, ambitious, jealous, and conservative" (p. 79). He also claims that birth order effects are 5 to 10 times greater for the key personality dimensions of openness to experience, conscientiousness, agreeableness, and neuroticism than they are for academic achievement and IQ.

It does appear that birth order, at certain times and in some cultures, has been a significant developmental variable. In societies where primogeniture has been important, the life experiences of firstborn males were vastly different from those of other siblings and were no doubt instrumental in promoting their success. There is also some evidence to support the influence of birth order, as mediated through the complex dynamics of family experience, on certain dimensions of human personality. Although birth order can affect developmental outcomes, its importance cannot be systematically predicted, and thus should be considered with reasonable caution as a potential contributor to personality development.

REFERENCES

Adler, A. (1958). *What life should mean to you.* New York: Capricorn.

Belmont, L., & Marolla, F. A. (1973). Birth order, family size, and intelligence. *Science, 182,* 1096–1101.

Berbaum, M. L., & Moreland, R. I. (1980). Intellectual development within the family: A new application of the confluence model. *Developmental Psychology, 16,* 506–518.

Berndt, T. J., & Bulleit, T. N. (1985). Effects of sibling relationships on preschoolers' behavior at home and at school. *Developmental Psychology, 21,* 761–767.

Blake, J. (1989). *Family size and achievement.* Berkeley: University of California.

Bradley, R. H., & Caldwell, B. M. (1984). 174 children: A study of the relationship between home environment and cognitive development during the first 5 years. In A. W. Gottfried (Ed.), *Home environment and early cognitive development. Longitudinal research.* Orlando, FL: Academic.

Craig, G J. (1996). *Human development.* Upper Saddle River, NJ: Prentice Hall.

Dunn, J., & Plomin R. (1990). *Separate lives: Why siblings are so different.* New York: Basic Books.

Entwistle, D. R., & Alexander, K. L. (1990). Beginning school math competence: Minority and majority comparisons. *Child Development, 61,* 454–471.

Ernst, C., & Angst, J. (1983). *Birth order: Its influence on personality.* Berlin: Springer-Verlag.

Falbo, T. (1981). Relationship between birth category, achievement, and interpersonal orientation. *Journal of Personality & Social Psychology, 41,* 121–131.

Forer, L. K. (1976). *The birth order factor.* New York: McKay.

Galton, F. (1874). *English men of science.* London: McMillan.

Harris, I. D. (1973). Differences in cognitive style and birth order. In J. C. Westman (Ed.), *Individual differences in children* (pp. 199–210). New York: Wiley.

Koch, H. L. (1955). Some personality correlates of sex, sibling position, and sex of sibling among five- and six-year old children. *Genetic Psychology Monographs, 52,* 3–50.

LeVine, R. A. (1990). Enculturation: A biosocial perspective on the development of self. In D. Cicchetti & M. Beeghly (Eds.), *The self in transition: Infancy to childhood* (pp. 99–117). Chicago: University of Chicago.

McGurk, H., & Grandon, G. M. (1979). Birth order: A phenomenon in search of an explanation. *Developmental Psychology, 7, 33,* 366.

Miller, N., & Maruyama, G. (1976). Ordinal position and peer popularity. *Journal of Personality & Social Psychology, 33,* 123–131.

Page, E. B., & Grandon, G. M. (1979). Family configuration and mental ability: Two theories contrasted with U.S. data. *American Educational Research Journal, 16,* 257–272.

Rogers, J. L. (1984). Confluence effects: Not here, not now! *Developmental Psychology, 20,* 321–331.

Rothbart, M. K. (1971). Birth order and mother-child interaction in an achievement situation. *Journal of Personality and Social Psychology, 17,* 113–120.

Schacter, S. (1959). *The psychology of affiliation.* Stanford, CA: Stanford University.

Schooler, C. (1972). Birth order effects: Not here, not now. *Psychological Bulletin, 78,* 161–175.

Shaffer, D. R. (1993). *Developmental psychology: Childhood and adolescence* (3rd ed.). Pacific Grove, CA: Brooks/Cole.

Smith, T. (1984). School grades and responsibility for younger siblings: An empirical study of the teaching function. *American Sociological Review, 49,* 248–261.

Snow, M. E., Jacklin, C. N., & Maccoby, E. E. (1981). Birth-order differences in peer sociability at thirty-three months. *Child Development, 52,* 589–595.

Stagner, R., & Katzoff, E. T. (1936). Personality as related to birth order and family size. *Journal of Applied Psychology, 20,* 340–346.

Steelman, L. C. (1985). A tale of two variables: A review of the intellectual consequences of sibship size and birth order. *Review of Educational Research, 55,* 353–386.

Sulloway, F. J. (1996). *Born to rebel: Birth order, family dynamics, and creative lives.* New York: Pantheon.

Sutton-Smith, B., & Rosenberg, B. G. (1970). *The sibling.* New York: Holt, Rinehart, & Winston.

Touliatos, J., & Lindholm, B. W. (1980). Birth order, family size, and children's mental health. *Psychological Reports, 46,* 1097–1098.

Vandell, D. L., Wilson, K. S., & Whalen, W. T. (1981). Birth-order and social experience differences in infant-peer interaction. *Developmental Psychology, 17,* 438–445.

White, B. L., Kaban, B. T., & Attanucci, J. S. (1979). *The origins of human competence.* Lexington, MA: Heath.

Yiannakis, A. (1976). Birth order and preference for dangerous sports among males. *Quarterly Research, 47,* 42–67.

Zajonc, R. B., & Markus, G. B. (1975). Birth order and intellectual development. *Psychological Review, 82,* 74–88.

JAMES M. APPLEFIELD
*University of North Carolina
at Wilmington*

**PERSONALITY ASSESSMENT
SOCIOECONOMIC STATUS
TEMPERAMENT**

BIRTH TRAUMA

According to Freudian psychodynamic theory, early traumatic and painful events produce memories that, when repressed into the unconscious, may affect later life. Otto Rank (1929) elaborated on the proposition that birth is itself traumatic: It suddenly and painfully thrusts the infant from the warm, secure womb into a cold, hostile, and frustrating world. When frustrated later in life, people may in some ways behave as though they wished to return to the womb.

More recently, Leboyer (1975) has argued that birth should be as gentle as possible for both mother and infant. In his birthing technique, the shock of birth is reduced by, among other things, keeping light and noise levels in the delivery room low. At birth, the newborn is placed on the mother's breast, massaged to decrease initial crying, and placed in a warm bath. The father attends and assists in handling the newborn.

Although some physicians initially suggested that Leboyer's method put both newborn and mother at risk, research indicates that the procedure is safe. Relative to those conventionally delivered, Leboyer infants evidence normal physiological functioning (Kliot & Silverstein, 1984) and no differences in either maternal or infant morbidity or infant behavior (Nelson et al., 1980). At present, with the exception of shorter active labors among mothers expecting a Leboyer delivery (Nelson et al., 1980), advantages of the method appear more psychological than physiological (Grover, 1984). Indeed, evidence of long-term consequences of both conventional and Leboyer births are notably lacking, and the concept of birth trauma, particularly the Rankian version, is largely in disrepute.

Considering the other side of the issue, Handley et al. (1997) asked whether infants who had endured traumatic near-death births showed any later adverse effects. They longitudinally compared the development from 4 to 8 years of age of a group who had nearly suffocated during birth with a group who had experienced a normal birth. The two groups had comparable familial characteristics. The group that suffered the traumatic birth experience did not show meaningful deficits in cognitive and motor development, health, or general behavior.

Evidence of long-term effects of birth experiences, varying from Leboyer's gentle technique through traumatic ones, is notably lacking. Although it still has adherents, the concept of birth trauma, particularly the Rankian version, is largely in disrepute.

REFERENCES

Grover, J. W. (1984). Leboyer and obstetric practice. *New York State Journal of Medicine, 84,* 158–159.

Handley, D. M., Low, J. A., Burke, S. O., Wuarick, M., Killen, H., & Derrick, E. J. (1997). Intrapartum fetal asphyxia and the oc-currence of minor deficits in 4 to 8 year old children. *Developmental Medicine and Child Neurology, 39,* 508–514.

Kliot, D., & Silverstein, L. (1984). Changing maternal and newborn care. *New York State Journal of Medicine, 84,* 169–174.

Leboyer, F. (1975). *Birth without violence.* New York: Knopf.

Nelson, N. M., Enkin, M. W., Saigal, S., Bennett, K. J., Milner, R., & Sackett, D. L. (1980). A randomized clinical trial of the Leboyer approach to childbirth. *New England Journal of Medicine, 302,* 655–60.

Rank, O. (1929). *The trauma of birth.* New York: Harcourt, Brace.

ROBERT T. BROWN
SHIRLEY PARKER WELLS
*University of North Carolina
at Wilmington*
First edition

AIMEE R. HUNTER
*University of North Carolina
at Wilmington*
Second edition

BLATT, BURTON (1927–1985)

Burton Blatt, widely known as a leader in the movement for deinstitutionalization of people with mental retardation, began his professional career as a special class teacher in the public schools of New York City. After earning the doctorate in special education at Pennsylvania State University in 1956, he served on the faculties of Southern Connecticut State College and Boston University before joining the faculty of Syracuse University in 1969, where he served as dean of the School of Education from 1976 until his death in 1985.

In 1971 he formed the Center on Human Policy at Syracuse University, devoted to the study and promotion of open settings for people with mental retardation and other disabilities. His work was characterized by an inspirational humanism that contributed greatly to his effectiveness as a leader.

REFERENCES

Blatt, B. (1984). Biography in autobiography. In B. Blatt & R. J. Morris (Eds.), *Perspectives in special education: Personal orientations* (pp. 263–307). Glenview, IL: Scott, Foresman.

Blatt, B., & Kaplan, F. (1966). *Christmas in purgatory: A photographic essay on mental retardation* (2nd ed.). Boston: Allyn & Bacon.

Semmel, M. I. (1985). In memoriam: Burton Blatt, 1927–1985. *Exceptional Children, 52,* 102.

PAUL IRVINE
Katonah, New York

BLIND

Blind is a term used to refer to those students who have either no vision or, at most, light perception (the ability to tell light from dark) but no light projection (the ability to identify the direction from which light comes) (Faye, 1970; Colenbrander, 1977; NICHCY, 1998). Educationally, one who is blind learns primarily through tactual, auditory, and kinesthetic experiences, without the use of vision. The legal term for blindness is corrected visual acuity of 20/200 or less in the better eye and/or field of vision of 20 degrees or less (Goble, 1984; NICHCY, 1998). Severe visual impairments (legally or totally blind) occur at a rate of .06 per 1,000 (NICHCY, 1998). Individuals classified as blind under this legal definition receive certain benefits such as special educational materials and an extra income tax deduction.

The degree to which blindness or any type of visual impairment affects development depends on the type of visual loss, the severity of the loss, the age of onset, intellectual abilities, and environmental experiences. Lack of vision results in delays or limitations in motor, cognitive, and social development.

Blind children are limited in their ability to get about. Without visual input, the blind infant is not motivated to reach and move toward interesting objects in the environment. As soon as the blind infant finds it exciting to hear sounds, he or she will begin to reach and move toward the objects in the environment that produce sound. This does not occur for several months, because hearing sound does not motivate movement toward objects as soon as seeing objects (Fraiberg, 1977). As a result of the limitation in mobility, an older blind student cannot change his or her surroundings and activities as freely as a sighted one. Blind students, therefore, are dependent on assistance from others; this affects their attitudes and social relationships (Lowenfeld, 1981).

Cognitively, blind children are restricted in their range and variety of experiences. They cannot perceive objects in the environment that are beyond their grasp, including those that are too large or too small, or those that are moving. Blind children who use their tactual sense cannot directly observe such objects as the sun, the moon, and the clouds. Large buildings, mountains, and rivers cannot be observed as a whole. Other examples of objects that are inaccessible are flies, ants, butterflies, and spider webs: they are too fragile. Other objects such as burning wood or boiling water, cannot be touched under certain circumstances. Hearing, while it gives clues such as distance and direction, does not give a concrete idea of an object. If a blind child hears a bird, he or she can learn its sound and identify its location, but cannot perceive its shape, size, or other physical characteristics (Lowenfeld, 1981).

Socially, blind children are limited in interaction with the environment. They cannot see facial expressions of parents, teachers, and peers; they cannot model appropriate social behavior through imitation; and sometimes they are unaware of the presence of others unless a sound is made. While touch provides direct information, it is often socially unacceptable (Division for the Visually Handicapped, Council for Exceptional Children, 1982).

Historically, academically oriented blind and low-vision students have been mainstreamed successfully into regular classes. They obtain their specialized skills in a variety of placement options. These include

1. *Itinerant Program.* The blind or low-vision student is enrolled in the regular class in the neighborhood school and an itinerant teacher who travels from school to school provides direct instruction and serves as a consultant to the regular teachers several times a week.

2. *Resource Room Program.* The blind or low-vision student is enrolled in the regular class in a school within the district or town and a resource room teacher is housed in the school and is readily available to work with the student on a daily basis at regularly scheduled times and when needed.

3. *Special Class.* The blind or low-vision student is enrolled in a self-contained class in a public or private school setting for most of the day. Usually, those students with multiple impairments in addition to a visual handicap are placed in this type of setting.

4. *Residential School.* The blind or low-vision student enrolled in this placement usually has additional disabilities and/or cannot be cared for adequately at home. Sometimes blind students attend residential schools for short periods of time to develop intensive skills in such areas as orientation and mobility, vocational training, and technology (Cartwright, Cartwright, & Ward, 1981).

The unique curriculum for blind students includes reading and writing braille; typing; listening skills using human and synthetic speech; map and chart reading; domestic skills; orientation and mobility; career education; and instruction in the use of special aids and equipment such as the Cranmer abacus, talking calculators, cassette tape recorders, electronic reading machines, and other hardware and software adaptations that access computers (Heward & Orlansky, 1984).

Major resources relevant to blind students cited by the National Information Center for Children and Youth with Disabilities (1998) are:

American Council of the Blind Parents
c/o American Council of the Blind
1155 15th Street N.W., Suite 720
Washington, D.C. 20005
(202) 467-5081; 1-800-424-8666
Web Address: *http://www.acb.org*

American Foundation for the Blind
11 Penn Plaza, Suite 300
New York, NY 10001
1-800-AFBLIND (Toll Free Hotline)
To order publications, call: 1-800-232-3044
E-mail: *afbinfo@afb.org*
Web Address: *http://www.afb.org/afb*

Blind Children's Center
4120 Marathon Street
Los Angeles, CA 90029-0159
(213) 664-2153; 1-800-222-3566
E-mail: *info@blindcntr.org*
Web Address: *http://www.blindcntr.org/bcc*

Division for the Visually Handicapped
c/o Council for Exceptional Children
1920 Association Drive
Reston, VA 22091-1589
(703) 620-3660

National Association for Parents of the Visually
Impaired, Inc.
P.O. Box 317
Watertown, MA 02272
(817) 972-7441
800-562-6265

National Association for Visually Handicapped
22 West 21st Street, 6th Floor
New York, NY 10010
(212) 889-3141
E-mail: *staffnavh@org*
Web Address: *http://www.navh.org*

National Braille Association, Inc. (NBA)
3 Townline Circle
Rochester, NY 14623
(716) 427-8260

National Braille Press
88 St. Stephen Street
Boston, MA 02115
(617) 266-6160; 1-800-548-7323

National Eye Institute
National Institutes of Health

U.S. Department of Health & Human Services
Building 31, Center Drive, MSC2510
Bethesda, MD 20892-2510
(301) 496-5248
Web Address: *http://www.nei.nih.gov*

National Federation of the Blind, Parents Division
c/o National Federation of the Blind
1800 Johnson Street
Baltimore, MD 21230
(410) 659-9314
E-mail: *epc@roudley.com*
Web Address: *http://www.nfb.org*

National Library Services for the Blind and
Physically Handicapped
Library of Congress
1291 Taylor Street, N.W.
Washington, D.C. 20542
(202) 707-5100; 1-800-424-8567
E-mail: *nls@loc.gov*
Web Address: *http://www.loc.gov/nls*

Prevent Blindness America
500 E. Remington Road
Schaumburg, IL 60173
(708) 843-2020; 1-800-221-3004 (Toll Free)
E-mail: *info@preventblindness.org*
Web Address: *http://www.prevent-blindness.org*

The Foundation Fighting Blindness
(formerly National Retinitis Pigmentosa Foundation)
Executive Plaza One, Suite 800
11350 McCormick Road
Hunt Valley, MD 21031-1014
1-800-683-5555 (Toll Free)
(410) 785-1414; (410) 785-9687 (TT)
Web Address: *http://www.blindness.org*

REFERENCES

Cartwright, G. P., Cartwright, C. A., & Ward, M. (1981). *Educating special learners*. Belmont, CA: Wadsworth.

Colenbrander, A. (1977). Dimensions of visual performance. *Archives of American Academy of Ophthalmology, 83,* 332–337.

Division for the Visually Handicapped, Council for Exceptional Children. (1982). *Visual impairments fact sheet*. Reston, VA: ERIC Clearinghouse on Handicapped and Gifted Children.

Faye, E. E. (1970). *The low vision patient*. New York: Grune & Stratton.

Fraiberg, S. (1977). *Insights from the blind*. New York: Basic Books.

Goble, J. L. (1984). *Visual disorders in the handicapped child*. New York: Marcel Dekker.

Heward, W. L., Orlansky, M. D. (1984). *Exceptional children.* Columbus, OH: Merrill.

Lowenfeld, B. (1981). *Berthold Lowenfeld on blindness and blind people.* NY: American Foundation for the Blind.

National Information Center for Children and Youth with Disabilities (NICHCY). (1998). General information about visual impairments Fact Sheet Number 13. Washington, DC: Author.

ROSANNE K. SILBERMAN
Hunter College

AMERICAN PRINTING HOUSE FOR THE BLIND
BLINDISMS
BRAILLE
ELECTRONIC TRAVEL AIDS

BLIND INFANTS

An increase in the birth of blind infants can be related to four major factors: (1) prematurity; (2) family history of a visual defect; (3) infection during pregnancy; and (4) difficult or assisted labor (Ellingham et al., 1976). With increasing medical advances in saving premature infants, the incidence of retinopathy of prematurity (previously termed retrolental fibroplasia) is rising (Morse & Trief, 1985). In fact, it is estimated that in the 1990s there will be somewhere between 12,000 and 19,000 visually impaired preschoolers (up to 5 years of age) (Hill et al., 1984).

The increase of visually impaired infants demands focused attention toward early intervention efforts. Unfortunately, many of the infants born prematurely are also born with deafness, mental retardation, and blindness (Morse & Trief, 1985). Programs for both normally developing blind infants and multiply handicapped infants require intervention in areas including motor, sensory, communication, and conceptual development. Parent involvement is a critical component in the early intervention of blind infants (Moore, 1984; CEC, 1987). As an example, Ferrell (1985) developed a training handbook for parents of visually impaired and multiply handicapped children, describing several intervention strategies. Research is clearly needed in this area because much of what we know about the development of blind infants is currently based on research efforts from the 1960s (Fraiberg, 1977). Other and more current research has focused on orientation and motility training for infants (CEC, 1987).

REFERENCES

Council for Exceptional Children. (1987). *Orientation and mobility for blind infants.* Reston, VA: Author.

Council for Exceptional Children. (1992). *Visual Impairments.* (ERIC Digest No. E511)

Ellingham, T., Silva, P., Buckfield, P., & Clarkson, J. (1976). Neonatal at risk factors, visual defects and the preschool child: A report from the Queen Mary Hospital multidisciplinary child development study. *New Zealand Medical Journal, 83,* 74–77.

Ferrell, K. (1985). *Reach out and teach: Meeting the training needs of parents of visually and multiply handicapped young children.* New York: American Foundation for the Blind.

Fraiberg, S. (1977). *Insights from the blind.* New York: Basic Books.

Hill, E., Rosen, S., Correa, V., & Langley, M. B. (1984). Preschool orientation and mobility: An expanded definition. *Education of the Visually Handicapped, 16,* 58–72.

Moore, S. (1984). The need for programs and services for visually handicapped infants. *Education of the Visually Handicapped, 16,* 48–57.

Morse, A., & Trief, E. (1985). Diagnosis and evaluation of visual dysfunction in premature infants with low birth weight. *Journal of Visual Impairment and Blindness, 79,* 248–251.

VIVIAN I. CORREA
University of Florida

BLIND
VISUAL IMPAIRMENT

BLINDISMS

Blindisms is a term used to describe a group of simple or complex repetitive behaviors that involve both small movements of various parts of the body, such as eye rubbing, head turning, and hand flapping, and large body movements such as rocking or swaying (Warren, 1984). This term is actually a misnomer, since these behaviors occur in other types of children as well, including those who are autistic, retarded, and even normal. More appropriate terms that do not single out blind children are stereotypic behaviors or mannerisms.

One of the most common mannerisms in blind children is pressing on one or both eyes. Pressure on the eyeball results in a pleasurable sensation to the child, i.e., the child may find it entertaining and relaxing. The most active eye pressers are children with retinal disorders (Scott, Jan, & Freeman, 1985). Children who are continual eye pressers tend to have deeply depressed eyes and black circles around their eyes; this detracts from their overall appearance. Another common mannerism, not considered by parents to be unusual when it first develops, is rocking. Whereas sighted children find other pleasurable activities to replace rocking, blind children tend to persevere in this activity.

Mannerisms frequently occurring in children with low vision, particularly those with rubella, are light gazing at the sun or fluorescent lights and waving of fingers in front of their eyes against the lights. Many become so involved in these behaviors that it is extremely difficult to direct their attention to more appropriate activities within the environment (Scott, Jan, & Freeman, 1985).

There are several theories regarding the causes of stereotypic behaviors in blind children. One of them is that these behaviors are efforts to increase the level of sensory stimulation (Burlingham, 1967; Curson, 1979; Scott et al., 1985). It has also been suggested that stereotypic repetitive behaviors are pleasurable because of the motor discharge (Burlingham, 1965). Another theory related to cause of stereotypic behaviors is that the behaviors are a result of social rather than sensory deprivation (Warren, 1984). However, according to Webster (1983), one cannot separate the sensory stimulation factor from the social stimulation factor in the case of blind infants. Williams (1978) has indicated that mobility plays a role in inhibiting stereotypic behavior patterns, and that lack of early mobility causes these behaviors to perpetuate.

Stereotypic behaviors tend to increase in both sighted and blind children when they are under stress. However, these repetitive patterns are fewer, and more intensely practiced, in blind children (Warren, 1984). They continue because they become self-reinforcing and therefore self-sustaining (Eichel, 1979). Research studies have shown that behavior modification approaches can reduce or eliminate some stereotypic behaviors in visually handicapped children (Caetano & Kaufman, 1975; Miller & Miller, 1976; Williams, 1978).

Parents and teachers are advised to work together to help blind and low-vision children develop positive exploratory and mobile behaviors. These efforts will enable this population to become more socially accepted by their peers, to attend more to the outside environment, and to prevent possible physiologic damage caused by excessive eye poking or rubbing, or head banging (Warren, 1984).

REFERENCES

Burlingham, D. (1965). Some problems of ego development in blind children. *Psychoanalytic Study of the Child, 20*, 194–208.

Burlingham, D. (1967). Developmental considerations in the occupations of the blind. *Psychoanalytic Study of the Child, 22*, 187–198.

Caetano, A. P., & Kaufman, J. M. (1975). Reduction of rocking mannerisms in two blind children. *Education of the Visually Handicapped, 7*, 101–105.

Curson, A. (1979). The blind nursery school child. *Psychoanalytic Study of the Child, 34*, 51–83.

Eichel, V. J. (1979). A taxonomy for mannerisms of blind children. *Journal of Visual Impairment and Blindness, 72*, 125–130.

Jan, J. E., Freeman, R. D., & Scott, E. P. (1977). *Visual impairment in children and adolescents*. New York: Grune & Stratton.

Miller, B. S., & Miller, W. H. (1976). Extinguishing "blindisms": A paradigm for intervention. *Education of the Visually Handicapped, 8*, 6–15.

Scott, E. P., Jan, J. E., & Freeman, R. D. (1985). *Can't your child see?* Austin, TX: Pro-Ed.

Smith, M. A., Chethik, M., & Adelson, E. (1969). Differential assessments of "blindisms." *American Journal of Orthopsychiatry, 39*, 807–817.

Warren, D. H. (1984). *Blindness and early childhood development.* New York: American Foundation for the Blind.

Webster, R. (1983). What—no blindisms in African blind children? *Imfama, 7*, 16–18.

Williams, C. E. (1978). Strategies of intervention with the profoundly retarded visually-handicapped child: A brief report of a study of stereotypy. *Occasional Papers of the British Psychological Society, 2*, 68–72.

ROSANNE K. SILBERMAN
Hunter College

BLIND
SELF-STIMULATION
VISUAL IMPAIRMENT
VISUAL TRAINING

BLIND LEARNING APTITUDE TEST (BLAT)

The Blind Learning Aptitude Test (BLAT) was developed in 1969 by T. Ernest Newland as a nonverbal, individually administered multiple aptitude battery for use with blind and partially sighted children and adolescents. The age range of BLAT is from 6 to 20 years, but it is most often recommended for use between the ages of 6 and 12. The test was designed to objectively measure learning process rather than learning product in blind children by minimizing the influence of experiences to which the sighted child is subjected. In fact, the majority of the items were taken from tests designed to minimize cultural bias. The BLAT items are presented in an embossed format involving dots and lines similar to those used in braille; however, no knowledge of braille is required to complete the test. The test consists of 61 tactile stimulus items, and 49 of those are scored while 12 are used for training purposes. The items measure abilities such as discrimination, generalization, and sequencing (Buros, 1978).

The BLAT manual (Newland, 1971) provides detailed directions for administering the test, including techniques for introducing the examinee to the test, guiding the examinee's fingers across stimulus items, and dealing with special situations that may arise. No formal time limits are provided, though the manual states that examinees typically respond to individual items within two minutes (Herman, 1985). The scoring procedure is deceptively simple. Items are scored right or wrong, and the number of correct items serves as the total raw score. Complications may arise, however, as the response sheet is laid out in such a way that training items are not clearly differentiated from actual test items. The BLAT yields a learning aptitude test quotient with a mean of 100 and a standard deviation of 15 points, making it similar to the IQ. The BLAT also yields a learning aptitude age, which is defined as the midpoint of an age range for a given score.

Standardized on a sample of 961 blind students in a number of residential and day schools for the blind across the United States, the author reports reliability coefficients ranging from 0.86 to 0.93. However, much of the reliability data is indeterminate, as many tables lack information such as Ns, means, and standard deviations. Data on the validity of the BLAT is also incomplete. Factor analysis indicated some tendency for the items to fall into groups that relate to the six different items used in the test. However, information is not provided on the nature or size of the sample, nor how the factors were extracted or rotated.

Although it was welcomed as an alternative to traditional tests for the blind on its development in 1969, the BLAT is not widely used in education or research today.

REFERENCES

Buros, O. K. (1978). *The eighth mental measurements yearbook.* Highland Park, NJ: Buros Foundation.

Herman, D. O. (1985). Blind Learning Aptitude Test. In D. L. Keyser & R. C. Sweetland (Eds.), *Test critiques* (Vol. 3, pp. 32–36). Kansas City, MO: Test Corporation of America.

Newland, T. E. (1971). *Manual for the Blind Learning Aptitude Test: Experimental edition.* Urbana, IL: Author.

LIZANNE DESTEFANO
University of Illinois

BLIND
VISUAL IMPAIRMENT
VISUAL PERCEPTION AND DISCRIMINATION

BLISSYMBOLS

Blissymbols, or Blissymbolics, is a graphic symbol system that was originally created by Charles K. Bliss in 1942 (Bliss, 1965). Blissymbols consist of 100 meaningful picture symbols that are combined in a logical manner for communication. Not simply a set of symbols, Blissymbolics is a language that has its own linguistic rule system. Blissymbolics was originally developed to be a language that could be easily learned and understood for international communication. In 1971, Blissymbols were first used as an augmentative communication symbol system for non-speaking handicapped persons at the Ontario Crippled Children's Center in Toronto, Canada (Silverman, McNaughton, & Kates, 1978). Currently, Blissymbolics is one of many picture graphic symbol systems that have been developed for use with augmentative communication systems.

In Blissymbolics, the symbols are designed to depict the semantic concepts they represent. The meaning of the symbol can be pictographic, ideographic, or arbitrary (Figure 1). Pictographic symbols physically look like the concept they represent. Ideographic symbols represent feelings or ideas about a concept. Arbitrary symbols are usually used only as semantic grammatical markers. Some symbols are mixed, with one or more categories of meaning combined.

House	Woman	Happy	Sad	Plural	Action
Pictographic		Ideographic		Arbitrary	

Figure 1. Categories of Blissymbol concept representation.

By combining the basic 100 symbols together, many word concepts can be communicated. For example, the symbols for *happy* and *thing* are combined to create *toy*, a thing that can make someone happy (Figure 2).

thing marker   Happy   Toy

Figure 2. Combining Blissymbols to create new word concepts.

Blissymbolics uses semantic indicators to convey complex linguistic concepts such as plurality, action, number, and tense. In addition, the meaning of a symbol can change through changes in symbol size, orientation, position, or by adding pointers. The Blissymbolics Communication Institute (BCI), in Toronto, Canada, has developed an international standardized vocabulary of Blissymbols that is published in a user's dictionary (Hehner, 1980). New symbols are added after they are approved by BCI. Symbols that are newly created but are not approved should be designated with the combined symbol until they are approved (Figure 3).

Spaceship
(combine) flying plane to (the) stars (combine)

Figure 3. Use of the combined symbol to create new words.

There are many methods of teaching the symbols. Shepard and Haaf (1995) distinguished that teaching the composite meaning of a symbol as well as the meaning of the elements from which it was comprised was superior to a paired association method.

Many studies have documented the effectiveness of using Blissymbols with individuals who are nonspeaking and who have physical handicaps (Silverman, McNaughton, & Kates, 1978). In addition, they have been used with individuals who are mentally retarded, autistic (Kozleski, 1991), hearing impaired, and adults with aphasia. Blissymbols are best suited for persons who are unable to use traditional written language as an alternative communication method but are capable of learning large vocabularies.

REFERENCES

Bliss, C. K. (1965). *Semantography-Blissymbolics.* Sydney, Australia: Semantography.

Hehner, B. (1980). *Blissymbols for use.* Toronto, Canada: Blissymbolics Communication Institute.

Kozleski, E. B. (1991). Visual symbol acquisition by students with autism. *Exceptionality, 24*(4), 173–194.

Shepard, T. A., & Haaf, R. B. (1995). Comparison of two training methods in the learning and generalization of Blissymbolics. *Augmentative and Alternative Communication, 11*(3), 154–164.

Silverman, F., McNaughton, S., & Kates, B. (1978). *Handbook of Blissymbolics.* Toronto, Canada: Blissymbolics Communications Institute.

SHARON L. GLENNEN
Pennsylvania State University

ALTERNATIVE COMMUNICATION METHODS IN SPECIAL
  EDUCATION
AUGMENTATIVE COMMUNICATION SYSTEMS

BLOOM, BENJAMIN S. (1913–   )

Bloom obtained his BA and MS degrees from Pennsylvania State University, and went on to earn his PhD from the University of Chicago in 1942. He is noted for his work with taxonomies of educational objectives, the impact of environment and heredity on intelligence, and mastery learning.

Bloom's *Taxonomy of Educational Objectives* (1956) classifies cognitive behaviors according to a hierarchy of domains, providing a framework for viewing the educational process, classifying goals of the educational system, and specifying objectives for learning experiences. The hierarchy includes knowledge, comprehension, application, analysis, synthesis, and evaluation.

Bloom's (1964) book, *Stability and Change in Human Characteristics,* refuted the commonly held assumption that learning occurs in a regular, ascending line, demonstrating the developing function of intelligence as well as the increased stability of measured intelligence with age. In terms of intelligence measured at the age of 17, his correlational data and absolute scale of intelligence development indicated that approximately 50% of IQ development occurs before age 4, with 80% of the development of adult IQ taking place by 8 years of age. His findings also demonstrated that changes in relevant environmental factors have the greatest effect on a specific characteristic during its most rapid period of change. Bloom's research in this area resulted in an educational shift, with increased focus on the early years of development.

His interest has also included the identification and availability of highly favorable learning conditions. In his research, he has found that mastery learning, including detailed trial tests and a variety of feedback correctives, can be used to improve levels of learning of groups of students, with trial test/feedback correctives helping students discover and correct learning errors (Brandt, 1979).

Bloom's career has included positions as the Charles Swift Distinguished Service professor emeritus at the University of Chicago from 1970 and professor of education at Northwestern University, Evanston, Illinois from 1983 to 1989. He has served as an education advisor to the governments of India and Israel and as vice-chairman of the Meeting of Experts on Curriculum of General Education in Moscow in 1968. He is the recipient of the John Dewey award of the John Dewey Society (1968), the Teachers College medal for distinguished service of Columbia University (1970), and the award for distinguished contributions to education of the American Educational Research Association (1970). Bloom's numerous writings include *All Our Children Learning: A Primer for Parents, Teachers, and other Educators* (1980); *The State of Research on Selected Alterable Variables in Education* (1980), and *Developing Talent in Young People* (1985).

REFERENCES

Bloom, B. S. (Ed.). (1956). *Taxonomy of educational objectives. The classification of educational goals-Handbook I, cognitive domain.* New York: McKay.

Bloom, B. S. (1964). *Stability and change in human characteristics.* New York: Wiley.

Bloom, B. S. (1980). *The state of research on selected alterable variables in education.* Chicago: University of Chicago.

Bloom, B. S., & Sosniak, L. A. (1985). *Developing talent in young people.* New York: Ballantine.

Brandt, R. (1979). A conversation with Benjamin Bloom. *Educational Leadership, 37*(2), 157–161.

ANN E. LUPKOWSKI
Texas A & M University
First edition

TAMARA J. MARTIN
*The University of Texas of the
Permian Basin*
Second edition

BOBATH METHOD

Karel Bobath, a neuropsychiatrist, and Berta Bobath, a physiotherapist, developed an assessment and treatment program in England based on central nervous system (CNS) functioning. Their approach focuses on the whole child and is referred to as neurodevelopmental treatment (NDT).

Central nervous system functioning is regarded as the basis of all motor functioning. It provides the individual with the ability to perform all posture and movement tasks, from the most simple to the most highly integrated complex ones. The individual is able to maintain the head and trunk in a mid-line or balanced position while pursuing a motor task because of the working of the CNS.

If for some reason—as in cerebral palsy, other developmentally delaying conditions of childhood, or stroke—the working of the CNS is impaired, a therapist trained to use the NDT method would work with the person to improve the quality of tone and movement. Problems related to tone, posture, and fluidity of movement are the focus of the therapy.

Treatment has two basic goals: (1) the inhibition of primitive and postural reflexes that are abnormally present, and (2) the facilitation of insufficiently developed normal postural reactions. All therapy is developmentally oriented and is determined by the unique, specific needs of the individual.

Through therapy the individual experiences the feeling of more normal movement patterns and works to maintain these new, more efficient motor patterns. The treatment is dynamic in that there is interaction as the therapist makes constant changes in handling to match the individual's postural and movement responses.

It is the normal postural reflex mechanism that provides the basis for the individual to exhibit normal postural tone and variety in movement patterns. Through the process of co-contraction, the trunk and head (proximal parts) are stabilized, thus allowing for more finitely graded motor activity to be performed by the arms, hands, legs, and feet (distal parts). It is important for the individual to develop a more normal postural reflex mechanism so that efficient, purposeful actions can increase. The righting and equilibrium reactions are the bases of the normal postural reflex mechanism.

A major emphasis of NDT when employed with children is that parents and teachers be taught appropriate handling techniques by the therapist with the physician's approval. For carryover and integration of new skills to occur, the same handling procedures used by the therapist should be used at home and in the classroom. The Bobath method has been criticized as being "insufficient in meeting the special cognitive, social, and emotional problems and integrating these variables into patient examination and physical rehabilitation" (Rasmussen, 1994).

REFERENCES

Bobath, K. (1980). *A neurophysiological basis for the treatment of cerebral palsy.* Philadelphia: Lippincott.

Levitt, S. (1982). *Treatment of cerebral palsy and motor delay.* Oxford, England: Blackwell Scientific.

Morrison, D., Pothier, P., & Horr, K. (1978). *Sensory-motor dysfunction and therapy in infancy and early childhood.* Springfield, IL: Thomas.

Rasmussen, G. (1994). A new approach to physical rehabilitation. In A. L. Christensen & B. Uzzell (Eds.), *Brain injury and physical rehabilitation.* Hillsdale, NJ: Erlbaum.

Scherzer, A., & Tscharnuter, I. *Early diagnosis and therapy in cerebral palsy.* New York: Marcel Dekker.

MARY K. DYKES
University of Florida

CEREBRAL PALSY
OCCUPATIONAL THERAPY
PHYSICAL THERAPY

BODER TEST OF READING-SPELLING PATTERNS

The Boder Test of Reading-Spelling Patterns (the Boder Test) is subtitled "A diagnostic test for subtypes of reading disability," a designation that reflects the medical orientation of the test's senior author and the need for a typology of dyslexia. Boder and Jarrico (1982), in devising the Boder Test, relied on several assumptions about children and about reading.

The first assumption is that each dyslexic reader has a distinctive pattern of cognitive strengths and weaknesses across the two primary factors of the reading process: the visual gestalt and the auditory analytic functions. In Boder's scheme, the former underlies the development of a sight vocabulary and the latter the development of phonic word analysis or word attack. The Boder Test thus gives the following as its operational definition of developmental dyslexia:

> A reading disability in which the reading and spelling performance gives evidence of cognitive deficits in either the visual gestalt function or auditory analytic function, or both. A corollary of this definition is that when the reading-spelling pattern of poor readers gives no evidence of such cognitive deficits, the reading disability is regarded as nonspecific rather than dyslexic. (Boder & Jarrico, 1982, p. 5)

Accordingly, the Boder Test is intended to allow for differential diagnosis of developmental dyslexia by analyzing together a child's reading and spelling performances as interdependent functions. The manual describes what is offered as "a systematic sequence of simple reading and spelling tasks . . ." giving "an essentially qualitative analysis of the ability to learn to read and spell, for which quantitative criteria are provided" (Boder & Jarrico, 1982, p. 5).

Four subgroups of reading disability are then identified: (1) *dysphonetic dyslexics,* children with strong visual-gestalt reading functions and weak phonic analysis; (2) *dyseidetic dyslexics,* children with strong phonic analysis functions and weak visual gestalt areas; (3) *mixed dysphonetic-dyseidetic,* children who are weak in visual gestalt and phonic analysis; and (4) *nonspecific reading disability,* children strong in visual gestalt and phonic analysis function but not reading well. According to Boder and Jarrico (1982, p. 6), these patterns exist only among reading-disabled children, for "strengths and deficits in the gestalt and analytic functions of dyslexic children are manifested in three characteristic reading-spelling patterns not found among good readers who are at or above grade level in both reading and spelling." Significant reading retardation is defined in the Boder Test as reading two or more years below normal expectancy for grade level or mental age, although it is noted that performance one year below may be diagnostically significant. The authors further assert (p. 9) that the "test can make a reliable early diagnosis of a reading disability and identify the child's preferred modality, either visual or auditory, in learning how to read."

The test proper consists of an oral reading test (word recognition) and a written spelling test. The spelling words are determined from the results of the reading test. The test is individually administered in not more than about 30 minutes. According to the manual, the test may be administered by teachers, reading specialists, psychologists, physicians, and speech therapists.

The reading test consists of 13 "graded" word lists of 20 words each; half of each list contains words that are phonetically regular and half words that are not phonetic. Word lists are presented twice, in timed (1 second) and untimed (10 seconds) conditions. Reading level is determined to be the grade level corresponding to the highest graded word list at which the students read 50% or more of the words correctly. A more precise reading level is obtained by giving 2 months of additional credit for each word read correctly from the flash presentation above this basal level. Two other scores are yielded by the Boder Test, reading age (reading level -5) and reading quotient (RA/CA) × 100; if the child's overall mental ability is substantially above or below average, this quotient is to be corrected for MA by use of the following formula: $RQ = (2RA/(MA + CA)) \times 100$ or, by using $RQ = (3RA/(MA + CA + Grade Age)) \times 100$. A set of rules is provided based on the RQ and the pattern of spelling errors to allow classification of each child as normal, dysphonetic, dyseidetic, mixed, or nonspecific in reading skill.

Although the Boder Test is the product of much clinical experience with children and reflects great insight into abnormal reading processes, the technical development of the Boder Test was inadequate to support its use in other than research settings. The use of antiquated quotients for scaling, the failure to collect normative data, and significant problems with the development of reliability and validity data (Flynn, 1992) all argue strongly against use of the scale. Boder's model of reading disabilities may still be useful in the conceptualization and treatment of children's reading difficulties, particularly in learning disabilities placements where differentiated instruction is possible, although the visual learner–auditory learner aspects of the approach are antiquated and have not been supported over the years (Reynolds, 1981). The use of the Boder Test in the diagnosis or evaluation of dyslexia or other reading difficulties is insupportable at this time and other means of implementing Boder's model of dyslexia should be pursued.

REFERENCES

Boder, E., & Jarrico, S. (1982). *Boder Test of reading-spelling patterns.* New York: Grune & Stratton.

Flynn, J. M. (1992). Electrophysiological correlates of dyslexic subtypes. *Journal of Learning Disabilities, 25*(2), 133–141.

Reynolds, C. R. (1981). Neuropsychological basis of intelligence. In G. Hynd & J. Obrzunt (Eds.), *Neuropsychological assessment and the school aged child: Issues and procedures.* New York: Grune & Stratton.

CECIL R. REYNOLDS
Texas A & M University

GRADE EQUIVALENTS
RATIO IQ
READING DISORDERS

BODY IMAGE

Body image as defined by Galloway and Bean is "the individual's awareness and knowledge of the physical and spatial characteristics" of his or her own body (1974, p. 126). Included in this definition is the idea of knowing body parts and the relationships among body parts. Thus, laterality and directionality stem from body image (Marshall, 1975). In addition, body image is often considered a component of self-concept.

The body awareness and knowledge of an exceptional child may be distorted because of sensory, perceptual, or cognitive dysfunctions inherent in the handicapping condition. Visual or hearing impairments, for example, may deprive a developing child of sensory information necessary for a complete and functional body image. Children with learning disabilities may have problems with body image that influence their learning and development (Cruickshank, 1977). Mentally retarded children, when compared with normal children, have been found to express body images of larger size and less detail and symmetry (Wysocki & Wysocki, 1973). Children and adolescents who are cancer survivors may experience body image issues as far as seven years post incident (Pendley, Dahlquist, & Dreyer, 1997). Body image distortions may also be culturally bound as researchers are finding that Anglo and Mexican-American female students are more likely to develop body image distortion that leads to eating disorders than Black American female students (Guinn, Semper, Jorgenson, & Skaggs, 1997; Greenberg & LaPorte, 1996).

Typically, body image is assessed by a student's drawing of a person; problems in body image are suspected when a student evidences laterality and directionality confusion. When such basic problems are encountered, the educational plan may include developmental approaches typically associated with preschool education and physical motor development.

Beyond a definition of body image emphasizing body awareness and knowledge, a more popular definition includes the feelings that accompany a person's body knowledge. Conceptualized in this light, body image is a precursor to self-concept (Morse, 1975). Thus, accurate body image is not only necessary for foundations basic to learning, but also essential for self-concept development and, ultimately, self-acceptance.

When a concern about a student's body image emerges, there may be more than on etiology. It is very important that an appropriate assessment that includes not only neurological/developmental information but psychological evaluation is performed. In the instance of body image, the mind-body connection is well established.

REFERENCES

Cruickshank, W. M. (1977). *Learning disabilities in home, school, and community.* Syracuse: Syracuse University Press.

Galloway, H. F., & Bean, M. F. (1974). The effects of action songs on the development of body-image and body-part identification in hearing-impaired preschool children. *Journal of Music Therapy, 11,* 125–134.

Greenberg, D. R., & LaPorte, D. J. (1996). Racial differences in body type preferences of men for women. *International Journal of Eating Disorders, 19*(3), 275–278.

Guinn, B., Semper, T., Jorgenson, L., & Skaggs, S. (1997). Body image perception in female Mexican-American adolescents. *Journal of School Health, 67,* 112–115.

Marshall, E. D. (1975). Teaching materials for children with learning disabilities. In W. M. Cruickshank & D. P. Hallahan (Eds.), *Perceptual and learning disabilities in children* (Vol. 1, pp. 279–307). Syracuse: Syracuse University Press.

Morse, W. C. (1975). The learning disabled child and considerations of life space. In W. M. Cruickshank & D. P. Hallahan (Eds.), *Perceptual and learning disabilities in children* (Vol. 1, pp. 337–353). Syracuse: Syracuse University Press.

Pendley, J. S., Dahlquist, L. M., & Dreyer, Z. (1997). Body image and psychosocial adjustment in adolescent cancer survivors. *Journal of Pediatric Psychology, 22,* 29–43.

Wysocki, B. A., & Wysocki, A. C. (1973). The body-image of normal and retarded children. *Journal of Clinical Psychology, 29*(1), 7–10.

STEVEN R. TIMMERMANS
*Mary Free Bed Hospital and
Rehabilitation Center*

DRAW-A-PERSON
MENTAL STATUS EXAMS

BODY TYPES

Typology is the attempt to take complex observations of people and reduce them to a few salient characteristics or classifications in order to make human behavior more understandable and predictable. Classifying or typing people according to their body build, and using these classifications for predicting other phenomena such as personality or disease acquisition, is deeply rooted in the history of western civilization. The Greek physician Hippocrates, before the time of Christ, categorized people according to body types and claimed that certain diseases were associated with each type. It was believed, for example, that short, thick people were more likely to have a stroke, whereas, tall, thin people were liable to contract tuberculosis. More recently, Kretschmer (1925), using a similar classification of body type, hypothesized a relationship between body build and mental illness: long, lean people were more likely to succumb to schizophrenia while short, blocky individuals were apt to become manic-depressives.

The most recent and notable attempt to classify people according to bodily characteristics and their associated personality types was conducted by the American psychologist and physician William Sheldon. A system was developed to measure and classify the human body along three dimensions (Sheldon, 1940); this provided an individual's somatotype. A person receives a score ranging from one to seven on each of three bodily characteristics: endomorphy, mesomorphy, and ectomorphy. Endomorphy refers to a soft and rounded appearance. The extreme endomorph would be rated as 7-1-1 on the three components; the associated personality type would be considered viscerotonic, meaning a love of comfort and relaxation, sociability, and extroversion. The typical stereotype would be the jolly, gregarious fat person.

The second bodily characteristic, mesomorphy, refers to a strong muscular anatomy. At the extreme it would be rated as 1-7-1. Somatotonia is the related personality. This denotes a physically active individual who is assertive and adventuresome. The stereotype is a loud, aggressive athlete.

Ectomorphy is the third bodily characteristic. It gets rated as 1-1-7 at the extreme and refers to the thin, delicate person. Cerebrotonia is the associated personality type. This includes individuals who are restrained, private, and intellectually intense. The stereotype would be that of a shy, introverted scholar. The three bodily characteristics can vary along a seven-point scale, creating the possibility of many different combinations of these types with a hypothetically average person rated at 4-4-4.

Originally, Sheldon's theory hypothesized a relatively direct relationship between body type and behavior. Once the body build is created through genetic, biochemical, and physiological processes, certain behavior tends to follow. Even though there is some support for a correlation between body type and behavior (Shasby & Kingsley, 1978; Sheldon, Lewis, & Tenney, 1969; Walker, 1963), current authors (Cortes & Gatti, 1972; Glueck & Glueck, 1956; McCandless, 1961) have modified the genetic and physiological explanation by emphasizing a reciprocal relationship between people with different body types and the social-cultural milieu. Certain body types may arouse negative or positive social reactions in others; this fosters differential personality development (Collins, & Plahn, 1988; Butler & Ryckman, 1993; McCandless, 1961). In support of this social learning explanation, several studies (Brodsky, 1954; Lerner & Korn, 1972; Staffieri, 1967) have verified the existence of a body build-behavior stereotype. People with certain physiques create stereotype expectations in others of how they will behave.

REFERENCES

Brodsky, C. (1954). *A study of norms for body form-behavior relationships*. Washington, DC: Catholic University of America.

Butler, J. C., & Ryckman, M. (1993). Perceived and ideal physiques in male and female university students. *Journal of Social Psychology, 133,* 751–752.

Collins, J. K., & Plahn, M. R. (1988). Recognition accuracy, stereotypic preference aversion, and subjective judgment of body appearance in adolescents and young adults. *Journal of Youth and Adolescence, 17,* 317–334.

Cortes, J., & Gatti, F. (1972). *Delinquency and crime: A biopsychosocial approach.* New York: Seminar.

Glueck, S., & Glueck, E. (1956). *Physique and delinquency.* New York: Harper.

Kretschmer, E. (1925). *Physique and character* (W. J. H. Sprott, Trans.). London: Routledge & Kegan.

Lerner, R. M., & Korn, S. J. (1972). The development of body-build stereotypes in males. *Child Development, 43,* 908–920.

McCandless, B. (1961). *Children and adolescents.* New York: Holt, Rinehart, & Winston.

Shasby, G., & Kingsley, R. F. (1978). A study of behavior and body type in troubled youth. *Journal of School Health, 48,* 103–107.

Sheldon, W. H. (1940). *The varieties of human physique: An introduction to constitutional psychology.* New York: Harper & Brothers.

Sheldon, W. H., Lewis, N. D. C., & Tenney, A. M. (1969). Psychotic patterns and physical constitution: A thirty-year follow-up of thirty-eight-hundred psychiatric patients in New York State. In D. V. Siva Sanker (Ed.), *Schizophrenia: Current concepts and research.* New York: PJD.

Staffieri, J. (1967). A study of social stereotype of body image in children. *Journal of Personality & Social Psychology, 7,* 101–104.

Walker, R. (1963). Body build and behavior in young children. *Child Development, 34,* 1–23.

JOHN O'NEILL
Hunter College

HEREDITY
PHYSICAL ANOMALIES

BONET, JUAN P. (1579–1629)

Juan Pablo Bonet, a Spanish philologist, instructed deaf students in language and articulation, and taught them a manual alphabet and system of signs that he had developed. He wrote the first book on the education of the deaf, *Simplification of the Letters of the Alphabet and Method of Teaching Deaf-Mutes to Speak.* This work, which appeared in 1620, provided a basis for the developments relating to the education of the deaf in Europe and Great Britain during the eighteenth century (Lane, 1984).

REFERENCE

Lane, H. (1984). *When the mind hears.* New York: Random House.

PAUL IRVINE
Katonah, New York

BORDERLINE PERSONALITY DISORDER

Borderline personality disorder is a diagnostic classification included in the *Diagnostic and Statistical Manual of Mental Disorders* (DSM-IV; American Psychiatric Association, 1994). In the past, various borderline disorders were described in ambiguous terms as mild (or latent) forms of schizophrenia (falling somewhere between psychosis and neurosis). With the publication of the DSM III, the disorder received official recognition as a distinct diagnostic entity, closer in form to the affective disorders than schizophrenia (Archer, 1985); however, questions have recently been raised about the reliability and validity of the borderline diagnosis (Widiger, 1982).

The diagnosis of borderline personality disorder requires the presence of at least five of the following: impulsive or unpredictable behavior, unstable interpersonal relationships, difficulty in controlling anger or inappropriate anger, identity disturbance, unstable mood (including depression, anxiety, and irritability), physically self-damaging acts, chronic feelings of boredom, and intolerance of being alone. As is the case with other personality disorders, the borderline disorder represents a chronic, pervasive pattern of behavior that emerges during late childhood/adolescence and interferes with social and occupational functioning for much of the individual's adult life. Despite the presence of symptoms during adolescence, the DSM-IV recommends that this diagnosis be reserved for individuals 18 years of age and older. For those under 18, the diagnosis of identity disorder, characterized by a similar clinical picture (e.g., mild depression, anxiety, self-doubt, negative/oppositional behavior), is preferred. Identity disorder reflects an inability to establish an acceptable sense of self and includes uncertainty about such issues as career goals, sexual orientation or behavior, moral values, friends, and long-term goals. Contrary to DSM-IV recommendations, however, the borderline diagnosis is often used with children and adolescents (Bradley, 1981), a practice that has recently received some empirical support (Archer et al., 1985).

The advent of managed care companies has severely restricted the ability of the helping professions to give significant and long-term care to individuals with this condition. Consequently many individuals with borderline personality disorder are left to fend for themselves after short-term treatment. Hopefully this poor state of affairs will change in the future.

REFERENCES

American Psychiatric Association. (1994). *Diagnostic and statistical manual of mental disorders* (4th ed.). Washington, DC: Author.

Archer, R. P. Ball, J. D., & Hunter, J. A. (1985). MMPI characteristics of borderline psychopathology in adolescent inpatients. *Journal of Personality Assessment, 49,* 47–55.

Bradley, S. J. (1981). The borderline diagnosis in children and adolescents. *Child Psychiatry & Human Development, 12*(2), 121–127.

Gabbard, G. O. (1997). Borderline personality disorder and rational managed care policy. *Psychoanalytic Inquiry, 10,* 17–28.

Widiger, T. A. (1982). Psychological tests and the borderline diagnosis. *Journal of Personality Assessment, 46,* 227–238.

ROBERT G. BRUBAKER
Eastern Kentucky University

CHILDHOOD PSYCHOSIS
CHILDHOOD SCHIZOPHRENIA
DIAGNOSTIC AND STATISTICAL MANUAL OF MENTAL
DISORDERS (DSM-IV)

BOWER, ELI M. (1917–1991)

Eli M. Bower obtained a BS degree from New York University in 1937 and an MA from Columbia University in 1947. He continued his education at Stanford University, receiving his EdD in counseling psychology in 1954. He was Professor Emeritus and president of the American Orthopsychiatry Association at the University of California, Berkeley. Bower was a pioneer in the field of early childhood education of handicapped children. Serving as a member of the California Governor's Advisory Committee on Children and Youth, he assumed an important role in the development of state policy on the education of emotionally handicapped and gifted children. He also held the position of deputy director of the California Department of Mental Hygiene in the early 60s.

His major areas of study included orthopsychiatry, enhancing growth and learning for the disabled, and engaging children in the school setting with games. By bringing together mental health professionals and parents of dis-

Eli M. Bower

BRACKEN BASIC CONCEPT SCALE-REVISED

The Bracken Basic Concept Scale (BBCS; Bracken, 1984) was designed to assess children's (ages 2½ to 8 years) understanding of 258 foundational language terms in eleven distinct conceptual domains. After 14 years of clinical use and research by early childhood educators, speech-language pathologists, and psychologists, the BBCS was revised (BBCS-R; Bracken, 1998). The revised instrument retained many of the characteristics of the previous test, but added several significant improvements (e.g., larger, full-color stimulus manual, 50 additional concepts, minor reorganization of content and subscales, Spanish form) and was renormed. The BBCS-R, like its predecessor, assesses children's conceptual knowledge in eleven categorical areas (i.e., colors, letters, numbers/counting, sizes, comparisons, shapes, direction/position, self/social awareness, texture/material, quantity, and time/sequence).

A considerable time before the recent edumetric emphasis on functional assessment and curriculum-based assessment, the BBCS was developed to provide a thorough sampling and functional assessment of foundational language concepts—concepts that are integrated throughout typical early childhood curricula. Additionally, the BBCS was, and remains, one of few instruments that is linked directly to a remedial or instructional curriculum, the Bracken Concept Development Program (Bracken, 1986). As such, the BBCS-R, like the BBCS, provides diagnosticians with an assessment of important, functional language concepts that is directly linked to a curriculum with which concept deficiencies can be remediated. That is, the BBCS-R was designed to provide educators and psychologists with a direct assessment/intervention linkage.

The BBCS-R was normed on a nationally representative sample of children from across the United States. The sample included 200 children from each year level, for a total of 1,100 children. Also included in the normative sample were proportionate samples of exceptional children (e.g., developmentally delayed, learning disabled, autistic). A separate sample of Spanish-speaking children (i.e., Caribbean, Mexican, Puerto Rican, Central American, South American) was tested to establish the technical qualities of the instrument for use with Hispanic youth.

The BBCS-R demonstrates strong psychometric qualities. Subtest internal consistencies across the age levels range from .78 to .98. Total test internal consistencies range from .96 to .99 across the age span for the English speaking sample and .95 to .99 for the Spanish speaking sample. BBCS-R stability coefficients similarly range from .78 to .88 for the subtests, and .94 for the total test. The Examiner's Manual documents several sources of validity, including content, construct, criterion-related, and treatment validity. For example, total test correlations between the BBCS-R and comprehensive intelligence tests (WPPSI-R and DAS) reported in the examiner's manual

abled children, orthopsychiatry was founded in 1924. Orthopsychiatry is defined as the science of the study and treatment of behavior disorders, particularly those involving young people.

Bower's interest in this area was focused on behavioral and social problems and their daily resolution (Bower, 1971). He also believed that games should be encouraged as teaching devices, allowing children the freedom to be involved while learning to relate to the real world. Bower looked at the question of whether children with learning disabilities could be helped in an economical, effective, and institutionally acceptable manner early enough to change their course of school development.

Bower wrote several books and more than 100 articles. Some of his major works include *Games in Education and Development, Early Identification of Emotionally Handicapped Children in School,* and *Orthopsychiatry and Education.* Eli Bower died at his home in Alameda, California, on December 20, 1991 at the age of 74.

REFERENCES

Bower, E. M. (1971). *Orthopsychiatry and education.* Detroit: Wayne State University Press.

Bower, E. M. (1974). *Early identification of emotionally handicapped children in school.* Springfield, IL: Thomas.

Bower, E. M., & Shears, L. M. (1974). *Games in education and development.* Springfield, IL: Thomas.

ELIZABETH JONES
Texas A & M University
First edition

TAMARA J. MARTIN
*The University of Texas of the
Permian Basin*
Second edition

(.85 and .88, respectively) are comparable to correlations typically found between the two respective intelligence tests and other tests of intelligence.

The BBCS-R is intended to be used as a language measure, school readiness screener, and intellectual screener, in addition to its primary use as a measure of basic concept acquisition. When used with the Bracken Concept Development Program (Bracken, 1986), the BBCS-R also can be employed as a curriculum-based measurement tool.

REFERENCES

Bracken, B. A. (1984). *Bracken Basic Concept Scale.* San Antonio, TX: The Psychological Corporation.

Bracken, B. A. (1986). *Bracken Concept Development Program.* San Antonio, TX: The Psychological Corporation.

Bracken, B. A. (1998). *Bracken Basic Concept Scale-Revised.* San Antonio, TX: The Psychological Corporation.

BRUCE A. BRACKEN
University of Memphis

BRAIDWOOD, THOMAS (1715–1806)

Thomas Braidwood, a Scottish teacher, established Great Britain's first school for the deaf in Edinburgh in 1760. Unaware of the methods of teaching the deaf that had been developed on Europe by Heinicke, Epée, and others, Braidwood developed his own techniques, through which his students learned to speak and lip read, and to read and write. Once he had established the effectiveness of his methods, Braidwood published a proposal for the provision of public funds for the education of those deaf students whose families could not afford to pay for schooling, and for the training of teachers in his methods. When public funding was not granted, Braidwood declared that the system would remain his property, and swore to secrecy the family members and others at the school who had learned his techniques (Bender, 1970).

Braidwood moved his school to Hackney, near London, in 1783. Because of his obsession with secrecy, it was not until after Braidwood's death that the details of his methods became known. The writings of his nephew, Joseph Watson, who assisted him at Hackney and later established England's first school for the indigent deaf, showed that Braidwood had developed an elaborate oral method of instruction that generally paralleled the development of the oral approach elsewhere. Braidwood's great contribution was the initiation of education for the deaf in Great Britain (Bender, 1970).

REFERENCE

Bender, R. (1970). *The conquest of deafness.* Cleveland: Case Western Reserve University.

PAUL IRVINE
Katonah, New York

BRAILLE

Braille is a tactile system that individuals who are blind use to read and write. The basis of braille is a rectangular "cell" consisting of six raised dots, two vertical rows of three dots each. The official code, Standard English Braille (Grade 2), consists of alphabet letters, numbers, punctuation, composition signs, and 189 contractions and short-form words, both of which are abbreviations of whole words to increase the speed of reading and writing braille. The Nemeth Braille code is used to transcribe mathematics and science; other codes are used to transcribe foreign languages and musical notation.

The first tactually perceptible code was developed in the early nineteenth century by Charles Barbier, a French army officer; its purpose was to send and receive messages at night. Louis Braille modified Barbier's code and published his system in 1829, while he was a professor at the Paris School for the Blind. Although Braille was permitted to teach his system outside of school hours, it was not officially accepted by the school until 1854, two years after he died. In the United States, the first school to adopt Braille's code was the Missouri School for the Blind, in 1869.

Reading and writing braille is taught to blind students by educators specifically trained to teach these skills to visually handicapped pupils placed in a variety of settings, including resource room or itinerant programs within the public school, or a residential school for the blind. The majority of experienced braille readers use two hands. A skilled two-handed reader usually begins reading a line of braille by placing both hands at the beginning of the line; when the middle of the line is reached, the right hand continues across the line, while the left hand moves in the opposite direction and locates the beginning of the next line. After the entire first line has been read by the right hand, the left hand reads the first several words on the next line, while the right hand moves quickly back to meet the left hand (Mangold, 1982). Important mechanical skills needed by braille readers include light finger touch, finger curvature, smooth independent hand movements, and page turning.

A major disadvantage of braille reading is that its average speed is two to three times slower than that of print reading. An average speed of 90 words per minute has been reported as typical for readers in the upper elementary grades (Harley, Henderson, & Truan, 1979). Braille books are also large and cumbersome, and they require large amounts of storage space. However, Mellor (1979) reports that braille as a medium for reading and recording information is superior to other mediums for providing random access to a page; skimming a page; labeling; filing; writing memorandums; reading tables and diagrams; reading technical or difficult material; allowing the reader to be an active participant in reading; and providing deaf-blind individuals with their only means of reading. In addition, braille-reading students have been found to be significantly ahead of their sighted peers in spelling; braille students make less than half the spelling mistakes of their sighted peers. (Grenier, D., & Giroux, N., 1997)

Young blind children learn to write braille using a Perkins Brailler, a six-keyed device that has similarities to a typewriter. Once blind students become proficient in reading braille and in using the Brailler, they are taught to use the slate and stylus, a more complex procedure in which braille dots are punched out one at a time by hand, from right to left. While the Brailler is easier to use, the slate and stylus is smaller, easier to carry, and more useful for taking short notes.

There have been several innovations in braille reading, writing, and production. One of them is an electronic braille device that can send and retrieve information to and from a computer. This device can store information on audio cassette tapes and present it in a braille display of 20 or more characters in a single line of movable pins representing braille dots. The blind individual presses on a keyboard similar to the Brailler and the information is converted to a digital code that is recorded on the tape in a cassette. The encoded information moves the six pins up and down so that the reader can read the configurations on the one-line display. When the reader gets to the end of the line, he or she touches a switch, which then presents the next line of braille stored on the cassette. Blind students can write and edit their papers with ease using one of these machines. (Olson, 1981; Ruconich, 1984). The electronic braille device reduces considerably the storage space needed for braille materials since an ordinary 60-minute audio cassette tape can store the equivalent of 400 pages of bulky paper braille. It is marketed by several commercial companies.

Another recent invention is an electronic braille printer that enables a person to produce hard-copy braille in either six- or eight-dot computer code. It also provides an onboard Grade 1 translator. Using translation software, the user can produce Grade 2, Nemeth, or music braille codes in six-dot computer braille code mode.

Another innovation is a paperless braille device that provides access to the screen of a computer by directly reading the computer's memory. It enables the blind person to access information on a full screen in increments of up to 20 characters while maintaining orientation to screen format through the use of auditory and tactile cues.

While the cost of such electronic braille devices is currently extremely high, their benefits are overwhelmingly positive in enabling blind individuals to access the available technology. As a result, more and more of this equipment will become available for use by blind students in special education programs yearly.

REFERENCES

Grenier, D., & Giroux, N. (1997). A comparative study of spelling performance of sighted and blind students in senior high school. *Journal of Visual Impairment and Blindness, 91,* 393–400.

Harley, R. K., Henderson, F. M., & Truan, M. B. (1979). *The teaching of braille reading.* Springfield, IL: Thomas.

Mangold, S. (1982). Teaching reading via braille. In S. Mangold (Ed.), *A teachers' guide to the special educational needs of blind and visually handicapped children.* New York: American Foundation for the Blind.

Mellor, C. M. (1979). Technical innovations for braille reading, writing, and production. *Journal of Visual Impairment and Blindness, 73,* 339–341.

Olson, M. R. (1981). *Guidelines and games for teaching efficient braille reading.* New York: American Foundation for the Blind.

Ruconich, S. (1984). Evaluating microcomputer access technology for use by visually impaired students. *Education of the Visually Handicapped, 15,* 119–125.

ROSANNE K. SILBERMAN
Hunter College

BLIND
VERSABRAILLE

BRAILLE, LOUIS (1809–1852)

Louis Braille, blinded in an accident at the age of three, developed his system of reading and writing for the blind while serving as a teacher at the Institution National des Jeunes Aveugles, the school for the blind in Paris. Dissatisfied with earlier approaches that were cumbersome and difficult to read, Braille developed a code employing one or more raised dots in a cell three dots high and two wide. An accomplished musician, he also worked out an application of his system to musical notation. Ironically, his school did not accept his system and actually forbade its use. Braille feared that his invention would die with him, but it survived, although it did not immediately flourish. It was not until 1916 that braille was officially adopted by the schools for the blind in the United States. A universal braille code for the English-speaking world was adopted in 1932.

REFERENCE

Kugelmass, J. (1951). *Louis Braille: Windows for the blind.* New York: Messner.

PAUL IRVINE
Katonah, New York

BRAIN DAMAGE/INJURY

The expression brain injury denotes a condition where extragenetic influences arrest or impair the normal structure, growth, development and functioning of brain tissue (Cruickshank, 1980). Damage to the brain can be either congenital or acquired after birth, with acquired damage resulting most frequently from trauma (Rourke, Bakker, Fisk, & Strang, 1983). The severity of dysfunction and prognosis for recovery following trauma depend on many variables, including the nature, location, and extent of the injury, the developmental level, and demographic factors such as age and sex (Rourke et al., 1983).

Brain damage does not always impair learning ability; conversely, impaired learning ability is not always caused by brain damage. Thus it is interesting that explanations of learning impairment often suggest underlying brain dysfunction. In many cases, brain dysfunction is inferred from behavior in the absence of any hard neurological signs. Speculative diagnoses such as minimal brain damage (MBD) neither clarify the cause of the learning impairment nor specify rehabilitation strategies (Rutter, 1983). Such diagnostic labels minimize the importance of individual differences. Even classification of children into large diagnostic groups such as retarded or learning disabled probably generates more confusion than clarification and does not provide sufficient focus to aid in remediation.

Brain damage is but one of many important variables that influence behavior. To understand a child's learning problems, nonneurological factors must be investigated carefully. Even in a case of documented brain injury, learning impairment may reflect an impoverished home environment, problems in emotional adjustment, poor motivation, systemic health problems, developmental lags, and genetic predispositions (Figure 1).

Brain damage may be the most important factor in a given case, but the label brain injury offers no clarification unless the nature, location, and extent of the damage are understood. There is also considerable danger in labeling a child brain damaged. To do so implies permanence, encourages drug treatment, minimizes the importance of ed-

ucation or remediation, and shifts responsibility to physicians (Gaddes, 1980). Given such a label, important and remediable strengths may be ignored. However, the label of traumatic brain injury entered the official handicapping conditions list in 1990 with the advent of the Individuals with Disabilities Act (IDEA), a revision of Public Law 94-142. The official label mandated that school personnel resist old nosology of "damage" and look more towards recovery and rehabilitation.

Clinical neuropsychological assessment of a child involves the elucidation of brain-behavior relationships in a developing human organism; consequently, this is a unique area of inquiry with problems quite different from those encountered in investigating the mature brain (Rourke et al., 1983). The developing brain undergoes rapid changes, and brain damage during childhood may impair future development of certain cognitive and behavioral capacities.

The brain of a child shows a capacity for development and recovery of function following brain injury. It has been argued (the Kennard principle) that early brain damage produces less dramatic behavioral effects and better prospects for recovery than damage in later life. This claim is only partially correct. The prognosis of early brain damage depends on many variables, including the type, location, and extent of the injury (Rourke et al., 1983). Most brain-injured children show some capacity for development of functions or recovery of functions, although it is difficult to predict the extent, rate, and degree of improvement because it depends on a number of neurological and psychological factors (Kolb & Fantie, 1997; Rourke et al., 1983).

Early brain damage may produce permanent dysfunction, delayed onset of dysfunction, or no dysfunction, depending on the maturational status of the system (Teuber & Rudel, 1962). For example, the effect of brain damage initially may be mild until functions subserved by damaged tissue become crucial for behavioral performance during development.

The term growing into a deficit has been used to emphasize the importance of the maturational status of the brain area at the time of damage (Rourke et al., 1983).

Organic	Genetic
	Neurological
	Systemic
Individual	Cognitive
	Emotional
	Cultural
	Achievement
Social/	Family
Situational	Social
	Academic

Figure 1. Factors that influence behavior.

Rourke (1983) argues that attentional deficits are a special problem for the young brain-damaged child, while older brain-damaged children show cognitive deficits. Rourke contends the young brain-injured child also has cognitive deficits, but they may not be apparent because of the generalized effects of attentional deficits. As attentional deficits resolve, the previously masked cognitive deficits become evident. Part of the process of recovery may involve the brain-injured child's learning to solve old problems in new ways by reorganizing functional elements of the behavioral repertoire (Luria, 1973). Thus one important premise of neuropsychology is that if the nature and extent of the deficit can be identified early in life, effective remediation can be instituted to minimize the consequences of brain damage on future learning.

In summary, consequences of brain lesions must be assessed in light of the dynamic nature of the developing brain and its emerging anatomical and functional asymmetries. Only by looking at these factors can we hope to understand the apparent paradox that the immature brain is simultaneously characterized by both a greater vulnerability to cerebral impairment and an apparently enhanced potential for recovery of function (Chelune & Edwards, 1981).

There are few common behavior patterns characterizing brain damage. However, most changes suggest a loss of the normal inhibitory influence of the cortex on behavior (Rutter, 1983). There is also frequently a deficit in attention that can lead to perseveration, hyperactivity, and impaired sensory processing (Cruickshank, Bentzen, Ratzeburg & Tannhauser 1961; Gordon, White, & Diller, 1972; Haskell, Barrett, & Taylor, 1977).

Attention deficit disorders or hyperactivity represent early and common consequences of brain injury. Such behaviors may reflect a deficit in planning and regulation of behavior, a deficit in memory, or loss of inhibitory control on the brain stem reticular system. In cases where a major behavioral component of the dysfunction is attention deficits, other deficits may not be observable or may not be easily measured.

Deficits affecting primarily the diencephalon often produce impaired memory consolidation. Individuals with such deficits may be able to attend to a task but they do not benefit from their experiences. As with attentional deficits, memory deficits can be pervasive and lead to more generalized deficits unless effectively remediated.

Higher level functions involve more complex cortical processing of information. The left hemisphere processes verbal material and deals with material in a discrete manner. The right hemisphere deals with nonverbal and new material in a more global manner. Functions can be divided further in each hemisphere; thus cortical damage can have dramatically different effects on behavior and learning depending on the brain area damaged. Cognitive functions relate primarily to cortical processing and in-

clude a broad range of behaviors. Early deficits in acquired brain damage may be generalized, but most pronounced recovery is noted in sensory and motor function and speech comprehension. Often recovery of language is given precedence and other functions may suffer. Left hemisphere damage is likely to impair syntactical functions, although with increasing severity, more general language processing may be involved. Furthermore, right-sided sensory and motor deficits may be observed as well as processing of verbally labeled material. Right hemisphere impairment results in deficits in visuo-spatial functions and spatial memory. Recovery of these functions is likely to lag behind language. Developmental changes appear to shift from right hemisphere global functions to left hemisphere linguistic functions. Rourke (1983) postulates that the left hemisphere functions in an automated manner, thus freeing the right hemisphere to deal with novelty, complexity, and intermodal integration.

Brain damage not only attenuates intellectual functions but also increases the chance of problems in emotional adjustment (Rutter, 1981). While brain damage can cause emotional lability, emotional problems are usually secondary or reactive to intellectual impairment, physical handicaps, or altered peer relations. The emotional consequences of brain injury are substantially influenced by the child's level of preinjury functioning as well as post-injury social support systems. Social learning is a complex cognitive function that involves learning social cues and gestures and modifying social behavior. Head-injured children are most likely to retain characterological deficits that limit full remediation (Lezak, 1976).

Neuropsychological assessment in the schools is a topic that has received much support during the last decade. Literature in the fields of special education, school psychology, and, recently, child neuropsychology has espoused understanding neuropsychological principles when assessing and planning educational intervention for children who are experiencing significant learning or behavioral problems in school (Hynd & Obrzut, 1981; Rourke et al., 1983).

Impaired learning may reflect the influence of multiple factors; therefore, an initial step in understanding the nature of learning impairment is to explore carefully the various potential contributing factors in each case. Once these factors are identified they can be prioritized in terms of their assumed significance (Long, 1985). In this way a framework is established for diagnosing the significance of brain-damage effects in each individual case.

An adequate evaluation involves assessing intelligence (verbal and nonverbal), memory, academic achievement, and emotional adjustment. In some cases more specific neuropsychological functions also must be tested (Figure 2). In addition, consideration must be given to social/environmental factors and their contribution to overall performance. The assessment must produce a valid and reli-

Basic sensory and motor functions
Perceptual and perceptual-motor functions
Attention
Language abilities
Intelligence
Problem-solving and abstract reasoning
Memory
Emotional adjustment

Figure 2. Essential areas of neuropsychological assessment.

able picture of the individual's strengths and weaknesses, and allow inferences about underlying brain functions to be made. It is important to differentiate between behavioral problems that reflect structural lesions and behaviors having no direct relationship to the brain's continuity.

Determining the nature (e.g., acute vs. chronic) and extent of brain damage of the child presents a much more difficult task for the neuropsychologist than the diagnosis of adult brain injury. The major difficulty concerns the role of age and development in children. Children change quickly in the kinds of skills we can expect them to acquire, and all children with the same chronological age are not at the same developmental level. It is necessary to take developmental factors into account. A basic rule in assessing children is to use multiple tests so that patterns and changes can be seen. The resulting profile then can be used to determine whether the hypothesis of delayed development is tenable (Golden & Anderson, 1979).

Assessment of intellectual and academic strengths and weaknesses for remedial or rehabilitative purposes, such as constructing an individual educational program (IEP), is maximally useful only when certain requirements are met (Hartlage, 1981). First, a majority of the child's educationally related cognitive abilities and methods of higher order information processing skills must be assessed in a quantifiable, replicable, and valid manner. Second, the assessment should be translated into a relevant and valid educational plan. Third, the assessment procedures should be reasonably efficient in terms of time and effort needed to administer and interpret them. In essence, the neuropsychological assessment process should be designed to test the specific referral problem and to provide the information needed to devise an appropriate program for the child in question (Hartlage, 1981).

Comprehensive neuropsychological batteries developed for use with children such as the Reitan-Indiana Neuropsychological Battery and the Luria-Nebraska Neuropsychological Battery-Children's Revision add significantly to the evaluation and remedial planning process (Berg et al., 1984; Lezak, 1976). The major drawback to the use of these and similar batteries is the great deal of time and training required for administration and interpretation (Hartlage, 1981; Reynolds, 1981).

Hartlage (1981) suggests an alternative approach in the application of neuropsychological principles to the interpretation of developmental, behavioral, and test data that can provide a systematic framework for understanding patterns of learning strengths and weaknesses and for making direct translations of the findings into intervention strategies that are uniquely relevant to the child's cerebral organization. By knowing the neuropsychological implications of common psychoeducational tests, such as the Wechsler Intelligence Scale for Children—III (WISC-III), Bender-Gestalt, Wide Range Achievement Test, and Peabody Picture Vocabulary Test, the neuropsychologist can determine which additional tests, if any, are needed to complete an adequate neuropsychological diagnostic profile (Hartlage, 1981). Detection with an accurate description of dysfunction leads to a remediation program to enhance the child's acquisition of skills using the child's intact areas and capitalizing on the child's neuropsychological strengths.

There are basically two approaches to the development of educational intervention based on psychoeducational test data: the strength model and the deficit model (Clark & Reynolds, 1984; Hartlage & Telzrow, 1984; Reynolds, 1981). The deficit model is the one most familiar to educators. This model is based on the premise that greater use of an impaired function will increase competency in that area (Hartlage & Telzrow, 1984) or restore dysfunctional neurological systems to their normal capacity (Clark & Reynolds, 1984). When neurological or genetic bases exist for the child's problem, the deficit approach to remediation is doomed to failure since it attempts to identify damaged or dysfunctional areas of the brain and focuses training specifically on those areas.

An academic intervention plan that focuses on deficits is not only ineffective, it is also more frustrating for the child, teacher, and parents (Hartlage & Telzrow, 1984). According to Reynolds (1981), this approach could be harmful to the child in that there is a high likelihood for failure and subsequent loss of self-esteem. To date there is limited empirical evidence to suggest any significant gains in academic or general behavioral functioning as a result of these efforts (Clark & Reynolds, 1984).

Remediation based on strengths has received little emphasis in educational settings primarily because eligibility for special education services is tied directly to the identification of deficits and treatments to restore those deficits (Hartlage & Telzrow, 1984). Reynolds (1981) has proposed the adoption of a habilitative or a strength model for the remediation of learning or behavioral problems. This approach involves designing instructional strategies that are based on or capitalize on the cognitive and neuropsychological strengths that are sufficiently intact so as to enable the child to successfully complete steps in an educational program (Clark & Reynolds, 1984; Reynolds, 1981). The strength model has been found to be effective in rehabilitation programs for adults, and preliminary research

(Reynolds, 1981) shows great promise in its application with children.

To develop an individualized remediation strategy, careful attention must be given to the level of functioning and the role that various brain systems play in such functions. Luria's model of hierarchical systems is a convenient conceptual framework. The foundation for learning is based, at the lowest level, on attention. While the whole brain is involved in attention, in most cases the brain stem is of primary importance and brain-stem lesions can disrupt attention significantly. The child must be able to - select salient cues and attend to them in order to learn effectively. When attention deficits are present, other intervention strategies may be ineffective. Attention deficits can be managed to some extent by (1) restricting distractors in the environment, (2) presenting more potent stimuli, and (3) dividing study into shorter periods of time. If these strategies are unsuccessful, consideration should be given to referral to pediatric neurology for psychopharmacological treatment.

Like attention, memory is related to total brain function and memory stores are located throughout the central cerebrum. However, the diencephalon and limbic system are particularly important for memory consolidation (storage of information). Deficits in memory obviously impair learning and severely limit acquisition of information. Intervention can be enhanced by (1) aiding the child in strategies for processing information by presenting it in discrete units, (2) increasing incentives, as most are strongly linked to memory consolidation, (3) sustaining practice, and (4) using multimodal sensory input. In memory rehabilitation in children, it is important to understand areas of weakness and assist in resorting to alternative methods of input and storage.

Remediation strategies must take into account strengths and deficits in higher level or cortical processing. With a comprehensive assessment, including neuropsychological assessment, not only modality but material specific weaknesses can be identified and remediation can be established to bypass such weaknesses.

Intervention and remediation in brain-impaired children involve standard procedures with adjustment in manner or mode of presentation. These children need sustained study on material where they receive effective feedback, and where material is interesting and presented on their level. Computer systems are an ideal tool for special education with such children, as they can provide individualized courses of study. Such systems should be viewed as an adjunct rather than a replacement for the educator.

REFERENCES

Berg, R. A., Bolter, J. F., Chien, L. T., Williams, S. J., Lancster, W., & Cummins, J. (1984). Comparative diagnostic accuracy of the Halstead-Reitan and Luria-Nebraska neuropsychology adult and children's batteries. *International Journal of Clinical Neuropsychology, 6,* 200–204.

Chelune, G. J., & Edwards, P. (1981). Early brain lesions: Ontogenetic-environmental consideration. *Journal of Consulting & Clinical Psychology, 49,* 777–790.

Clark, J. H., & Reynolds, C. R. (1984, August). *Habilitation or rehabilitation: Strength versus deficit.* Paper presented at the meeting of the American Psychological Association, Toronto, Canada.

Cruickshank, W. M. (Ed.). (1980). *Psychology of exceptional children and youth.* Englewood Cliffs, NJ: Prentice-Hall.

Cruickshank, W. E., Bentzen, F. A., Ratzeburg, E. H., & Tannhauser, M. T. (1961). *A teaching method for brain-injured and hyperactive children: A demonstration-pilot study.* Syracuse, NY: Syracuse University Press.

Gaddes, W. H. (1980). *Learning disabilities and brain function: A neuropsychological approach.* New York: Springer-Verlag.

Golden, C. J., & Anderson, S. (1979). *Learning disabilities and brain dysfunction: An introduction for educators and parents.* Springfield, IL: Thomas.

Gordon, R., White, D., & Diller, L. (1972). Performance of neurologically impaired preschool children with educational material. *Exceptional Child, 38,* 428–437.

Hartlage, L. C. (1981). Neuropsychological assessment techniques. In C. R. Reynolds & T. Gutkin (Eds.), *Handbook & School Psychology* (pp. 296–320). New York: Wiley.

Hartlage, L. C., & Telzrow, C. F. (1984). Neuropsychological basis of educational assessment and programming. In P. E. Logue & J. M. Schear (Eds.), *Clinical neuropsychology: A multidisciplinary approach* (pp. 297–313). Springfield, IL: Thomas.

Haskell, S. H., Barrett, E. K., & Taylor, H. (1977). *The education of motor and neurologically handicapped children.* New York: Wiley.

Hynd, G. W., & Obrzut, J. E. (1981). *Neuropsychological assessment and the school-age child.* New York: Grune & Stratton.

Kolb, B., & Fantie, B. (1997). Development of the child's brain and behavior. In C. R. Reynolds & E. Fletcher-Janzen (Eds.), *Handbook of Clinical Child Neuropsychology.* New York, NY: Plenum.

Lezak, M. D. (1976). *Neuropsychological assessment.* New York: Oxford University Press.

Long, C. J. (1985). Neuropsychology in private practice: Its changing focus. *Psychotherapy in Private Practice, 3,* 45–55.

Luria, A. R. (1973). *The working brain: An introduction to neuropsychology.* New York: Basic Books.

Otto, W., McMenemy, R. A., & Smith, R. (1973). *Corrective and remedial teaching.* Boston: Houghton Mifflin.

Reitan, R. M., & Davison, L. A. (1974). *Clinical neuropsychology: Current status and applications.* New York: Wiley.

Reynolds, C. R. (1981). Neuropsychological assessment and the habilitation of learning: Considerations in the search for the aptitude × treatment interaction. *School Psychology Review, 10,* 343–349.

Rourke, B. P. (1983). Reading and spelling disabilities: A developmental neuropsychological perspective. In U. Kirk (Ed.), *Neuropsychology of language, reading and spelling* (pp. 209–234). New York: Academic.

Rourke, B. P., Bakker, D. J., Fisk, J. L., & Strang, J. D. (1983). *Child neuropsychology: An introduction to theory, research, and clinical practice.* New York: Guilford.

Rutter, M. (1981). Psychological sequelae of brain damage in children. *American Journal of Psychiatry, 138,* 1533–1544.

Rutter, M. (1983). *Developmental Neuropsychiatry.* New York: Guilford.

Stevens, M. M. (1982). Post concussion syndrome. *Journal of Neurosurgical Nursing, 14,* 239–244.

Teuber, H. L., & Rudel, R. (1962). Behavior after cerebral lesions in children and adults. *Developmental Medicine & Child Neurology, 4,* 3–20.

CHARLES J. LONG
TINA L. BROWN
*University of Tennessee
at Memphis
Memphis State University*

NEUROPSYCHOLOGY

BRAIN DISORDERS (DEGENERATIVE MOTOR DYSFUNCTION)

Degenerative disorders of the central nervous system are a group of diseases of unspecified etiology leading to progressive deterioration and, eventually, death. Many of these disorders demonstrate a familial pattern and for some there is evidence of heritability (Slager, 1970; Gelbard, Boustany, & Shor, 1997). Recent studies that began with attempts to understand cell loss during normal development have now began to contribute to the understanding of the process of pathological cell loss (Gelbard, Boustany, & Shor, 1997). Specific degenerative disorders are characterized by their unique clinical and pathological features associated with age of onset and type and progression of symptoms (Alpers & Mancoll, 1971; Slager, 1970).

Major degenerative brain disorders such as Alzheimer's disease, Pick's disease, and Creutzfeldt-Jakob disease have their onset during the middle to late adult years. The same is typically true of the major motor neuron disease, amyotrophic lateral sclerosis, and Huntington's chorea, a major, degenerative disease of the basal ganglia. The remainder of this chapter will describe briefly several degenerative disorders that affect children and hence have relevance for special education.

Several genetically determined disorders are associated with progressive cerebral degeneration in children. Major types are the lipid storage disease, the leukodystrophies, and progressive degeneration of the gray matter (Sandifer, 1967). Tay-Sachs disease, a major example of cerebral lipidosis that is confined to children of Jewish descent, is an infantile variety of cerebromacular degeneration (Walton, 1971). Symptoms, which emerge during early infancy and result in death during the second or third year of life, include spastic paralysis, epilepsy, dementia, and optic atrophy leading to blindness (Sandifer, 1967). Alper's disease is an example of a disorder characterized by gray matter degeneration. Onset of symptoms occurs during infancy or early childhood. Symptoms include mental deficiency, cerebral palsy, ataxia, blindness, and epilepsy (Slager, 1970). Death typically occurs within a few months to several years (Sandifer, 1967). Hallervorden-Spatz disease encompasses a group of degenerative disorders that affect boys more than girls (Halliday, 1995; Sandifer, 1967). Symptoms occur between the ages of 8 and 10 and include spastic paralysis, choreo-athetosis, and slowly developing dementia (Sandifer, 1967). The development of magnetic resonance imaging has increased the number of reports of this disease and the case-to-case variability is considerable. Demyelinating leukodystrophies are disorders associated with progressive paralysis and increased mental impairment (Conway, 1977). One example in metachromatic leukodystrophy, inherited as an autosomal recessive trait. Apparently normal development up until about 2 years is followed by onset of symptoms that include ataxia, impairment in swallowing and speaking, tonic seizures, and mental regression (Conway, 1977). Other examples of the demyelinating leukodystrophies include Krabbe's disease, Grienfield's disease, and Alexander's disease (Conway, 1977).

Spinocerebellar ataxias are a group of degenerative disorders involving the cerebellum and associated pathways. Friedreich's ataxia is an autosomal recessive disorder with symptoms developing between ages 7 and 15 (Conway, 1977). Early symptoms include ataxia, gait disturbances, and poor coordination, including frequent falling (Rosenberg, 1979). Other cerebellar signs, including nystagmus, dysarthria, and sensory impairments distally may be evident. Other forms of progressive ataxia affecting children include Ramsay Hunt syndrome, hereditary cerebellar ataxia, and Louis-Bar syndrome (Conway, 1977).

Demyelinating encephalopathies are a group of progressive degenerative disorders resulting in death. One example is Leigh's disease (subacute necrotizing encephalopathy), an autosomal recessive condition with onset occurring during infancy. Characteristics of this disorder include hypotonia, ataxia, and spasticity. Respiratory or feeding problems may be associated with this condition, resulting in failure to thrive (Conway, 1977; Slager, 1970). Schilder's disease is another example of the demeylinating encephalopathies. The progressive deterioration associated with this condition may result in significant behavioral disturbance in children during the middle years of childhood (Conway, 1977). More advanced symptoms of Schilder's disease include ataxia, cortical blindness, seizures, and deafness.

Some authors include among the degenerative diseases

of the nervous systems neurocutaneous syndromes such as neurofibromatosis and tuberous sclerosis (Rosenberg, 1979; Walton, 1971). Such disorders may be expressed with wide degrees of severity, hence individual monitoring is essential. In summary, degenerative disorders of the nervous system are progressive, frequently hereditary conditions that produce significant mental, motor, and behavioral impairments that frequently result in death. Because of the genetic component associated with the transmission of many of these conditions, genetic counseling may be advisable for parents who have one affected child. Special education and related services may be required for children with degenerative disorders who survive to school age. The assistance of a variety of social service agencies may be of value to the families of afflicted children for counseling and group and individual support.

REFERENCES

Alpers, B. J., & Mancoll, E. L. (1971). *Clinical neurology* (6th ed.). Philadelphia: Davis.

Conway, B. L. (1977). *Pediatric neurologic nursing*. St. Louis: Mosby.

Gelbard, H. A., Boustany, R. M., & Shor, N. F. (1997). Apoptosis in childhood neurologic disease. *Pediatric Neurology, 16,* 93–97.

Halliday, W. (1995). The nosology of Hallervorden-Spatz disease. *Journal of the Neurological Sciences, 134,* 84–91.

Rosenberg, R. N. (1979). Inherited degenerative diseases of the nervous system. In P. B. Beeson, W. McDermott, & J. B. Wyngaarden (Eds.), *Cecil textbook of medicine* (15th ed.) (pp. 764–772). Philadelphia: Saunders.

Sandifer, P. H. (1967). *Neurology in orthopaedics*. London: Butterworths.

Slager, U. T. (1970). *Basic neuropathology*. Baltimore, MD: Williams & Wilkins.

Walton, J. N. (1971). *Essentials of neurology* (3rd ed.). Philadelphia: Lippincott.

CATHY F. TELZROW
*Cuyahoga Special Education
Service Center*

CONGENITAL DISORDERS
GAIT DISTURBANCES
HEREDITY
NEUROPSYCHOLOGY
PHYSICAL ANOMALIES

BRAIN GROWTH PERIODIZATION

Brain growth periodization refers to the rapid unequal development of the central nervous system (CNS) in general and the brain in particular. Following the moment of conception, neuronal cells begin an accelerated developmental course of division and reorganization (Gardner, 1969). This process involves the sequence of neuronal cell proliferation, migration, differentiation, axonal growth, formation of synapses, process of elimination, and, finally, myelination. Complexity of this emerging system is immense, and it grows within the context of plasticity and modifiability that exists throughout prenatal, perinatal, and early postnatal development (Moore, 1985).

The formation of the neural plate, which is marked by rapid neuronal cell proliferation, is evident within 16 days following conception. This plate then folds over into a tube shape. After a month, it closes toward the front and rear. The majority of cells attach themselves to the front of the tube and eventually form the brain.

Cell differentiation occurs at variable rates, as dictated by the location of cells within the CNS, where the cortical areas change rapidly and other areas mature more slowly. Next, the axonal growth and dendritic formations of the cells expand to make synaptic connections to one another. This highly ordered circuitry, which links up the brain electrochemically, is controlled by genetic programming and is largely influenced by the environment. One function of the synapses is related to specificity of action, which changes relative to location in the CNS (Sidman & Rakic, 1982). The primary sensory and motor structures are examples of highly specific functioning areas.

Genetic programming initiates the processes of brain growth, but environmental influences modify its form and function. Myelination can be thought of as insulating the neuronal cells to increase the conductivity of sending or receiving electrochemical messages. Early influences of nutrition and mother's health and lifestyle impinge on prenatal development; social, cultural, and economic factors further refine brain growth through postnatal life (Avery, 1985; Freeman, 1985).

Epstein (1978) has postulated that periodic growth spurts of the brain occur at predictable ages, and that rapid growth periods are associated with increases in mental age. Further, complementary curricula employed during rapid growth periods would maximize the individual's biological capacities to facilitate learning. Although the theory appears logical, research has not yet decided its empirical efficacy. Indeed, studies challenging pace of growth (McCall, 1988), continuity as opposed to "spurts of growth" (Thornburg, Adey, & Finnis, 1986) and practicality of the concept to everyday academics (McCall, 1990) have been presented.

The observation of a growing and changing system that is adapting to environmental influences before and after birth complicates the prediction of any pathological outcome (i.e., early insult resulting in later specific learning disorders). Special educators should be aware of the periodic growth of the brain in the framework of a dynamic interaction between genetics and environment. Recognition of this complex process promotes understanding of students' individual differences and necessitates the development of unique perspectives for intervention.

REFERENCES

Avery, G. (1985). Effects of social, cultural and economic factors on brain development. In J. M. Freeman (Ed.), *Prenatal and perinatal factors associated with brain damage* (Publication No. 85–1149) (pp. 163–176). Washington, DC: National Institutes of Health.

Epstein, H. T. (1978). Growth spurts during brain development: Implications for educational policy and practice. In J. S. Chall & A. F. Mirsky (Eds.), *Education & the brain* (pp. 343–370). Chicago: University of Chicago Press.

Freeman, J. M. (1985). *Prenatal and perinatal factors associated with brain damage* (Publication No. 85-1149). Washington, DC: National Institutes of Health.

Gardner, E. (1968). *Fundamentals of neurology*. Philadelphia: Saunders.

McCall, B. (1988). Growth periodization in mental test performance. *Journal of Educational Psychology, 80,* 217–233.

McCall, B. (1990). The neuroscience of education: More research is needed before Application. *Journal of Educational Psychology, 82,* 885–888.

Moore, R. Y. (1985). Normal development of the nervous system. In J. M. Freeman (Ed.), *Prenatal and perinatal factors associated with brain damage* (Publication No. 85–1149, pp. 33–51). Washington, DC: National Institutes of Health.

Sidman, R. L., & Rakic, P. (1982). Development of the human central nervous system. In W. Haymaker & R. D. Adams (Eds.), *Histology and histopathology of the nervous system* (pp. 3–145). Springfield, MA: Thomas.

Thornburg, H. D., Adey, K. L., & Finnis, E. (1986). A comparison of gifted and nongifted early adolescents' movement toward abstract thinking. *Journal of Early Adolescence, 6,* 231–245.

SCOTT W. SAUTTER
Vanderbilt University

BRAIN DAMAGE
BRAIN DISORDERS (DEGENERATIVE MOTOR
   DYSFUNCTION)
NEUROLOGICAL ORGANIZATION

BRAIN INJURY ASSOCIATION (BIA)

The Brain Injury Association (BIA), formerly the National Head Injury Foundation, was founded in 1980 by concerned parents and professionals as the first national organization to advocate for persons with head injuries and their families. Today its mission is "to promote awareness, understanding, and prevention of brain injury through education, advocacy, research grants, and community support services that lead toward reduced incidence and improved outcomes for children and adults with brain injury." The BIA is the only national nonprofit organization working on behalf of those with brain injury, maintaining 42 state affiliates and several hundred local support groups nationwide (BIA, 1998).

With 4.5 million persons living with brain injury, the physical and emotional effects on individuals, their families, and communities are overwhelming. Brain injury is the single, most prevalent cause of death and disability of our youth, with one infant, child, or adult sustaining this type of injury every 15 seconds as a result of motor vehicle accidents, falls, sports and recreational activities, abuse, or violence (BIA, 1998).

Increasing awareness, education, and prevention of brain injury is accomplished through the organization's work in conjunction with a diverse group of individuals, including persons with brain injury and their families, rehabilitation providers, physicians, attorneys, educators, therapists, case managers, counselors, government organizations, corporate partners, and citizens. Prevention and education is attained through public awareness initiatives, training seminars, and publications, while advocacy results from work with government entities at all levels. BIA efforts in these areas have resulted in such important measures as safety belt and car seat legislation and heightened awareness of the dangers of drinking and driving. Also in the area of education, the Violence and Brain Injury Institute, founded by the BIA in conjunction with other institutions, is currently developing the Headsmart® Schools Program, a brain injury and violence prevention program for elementary and preschools focusing on brain development and both intentional and unintentional injuries (BIA, 1998).

Veterans and military personnel are assisted by the recent adoption of the Defense and Veterans Head Injury Program (DVHIP), a program established in 1992 representing a collaborative effort among the Department of Defense, the Department of Veterans Affairs, and the Brain Injury Association. The program ensures that veterans and military personnel with brain injury receive the best medical services, collecting and compiling outcome data on the effectiveness and cost of various treatments and rehabilitation regimens in furtherance of this goal (BIA, 1998).

Information on brain injuries is provided by the organization's interactive multimedia software program, the Brain Injury Resource Center‰, available in certain emergency and trauma centers as well as state association offices throughout the nation. The BIA also publishes *Brain Injury Source,* a magazine devoted to professionals in the field, and a catalog of current educational resources. The organization annually confers several prestigious awards to those who have made outstanding contributions to the field of brain injury. The Brain Injury Association headquarters are located at 105 North Alfred Street, Alexandria, VA 22314 (BIA, 1998).

REFERENCE

The Brain Injury Association. (1998, October 1). *Welcome to the Brain Injury Association, Inc.* web site. Retrieved December 29, 1998 from http://www.biausa.org/.

TAMARA J. MARTIN
*The University of Texas of the
Permian Basin*

BRAIN ORGANIZATION

See NEUROLOGICAL ORGANIZATION.

BRAIN STEM AUDIOMETRY

Brain stem audiometry is an electrophysiologic measurement of hearing function currently known as auditory brain stem response (ABR) audiometry. As a diagnostic procedure, brain stem audiometry is used for the assessment of a peripheral hearing function (especially for high-risk infants, (Durieux-Smith, Picton, Edwards, & MacMurray, 1987) the retarded, and those individuals who are unable to respond appropriately to traditional tests) and to determine the neurological integrity of the auditory nerve and brain stem (especially for adults suspected of having an auditory nerve or brain stem tumor or other neural pathology). Brain stem audiometry can be done when the patient is lightly sedated, asleep, or awake.

Brain stem audiometry is possible because the neural reaction of the brain stem is time-locked to an acoustic stimulus while higher level ongoing brain stem neural activity is random. Consequently, with the use of an averaging computer, the time-locked brain stem neural response to an acoustic stimulus can be extracted from the random ongoing higher level brain stem neural activity.

A brain stem audiometer contains an averaging computer that triggers stimulus-generating instrumentation that transduces an acoustic stimulus through an earphone, loudspeaker, or bone vibrator. The patient is fitted with an active surface electrode along the midline of the head (usually at the vertex) and reference surface electrodes (usually on each mastoid or earlobe). The output of the electrodes are amplified, filtered, and directed to the averaging computer, which is programmed to present many repetitions of the same stimulus and average the re-

sponse of the neural activity for each stimulus for a period of about 10 milliseconds following the onset of the stimulus. The resultant pattern, known as the ABR waveform, is characterized by six to seven identifiable peaks having different latencies and amplitudes. Each peak is thought to originate from a neural generator starting with the auditory nerve through the brain stem. Peak I and especially Peak V are the most robust in reference to stimulus level and procedural variables.

If brain stem audiometry is done to determine the existence of a peripheral hearing impairment, an ABR waveform is obtained to high level auditory stimuli and to the same stimuli at lower levels until an ABR waveform cannot be determined for each ear. Then the latency of Peaks I and V at each stimulus level (intensity) are usually plotted on an intensity-latency graph referenced to age-appropriate norms. This procedure allows for determining the degree and type of peripheral hearing loss. When used to determine neurological integrity, an ABR waveform is usually obtained for one or two high-level auditory stimuli for each ear. The amplitude and latency of the ABR peaks are analyzed individually and compared across ear and to norms to determine whether a pathologic condition exists.

REFERENCES

Davis, H. (1976). Principles of electric response audiometry. *Annals of Otology, Rhinology, & Laryngology, 85*(28), 1–96.

Durieux-Smith, A., Picton, T., Edwards, C. G., & MacMurray, B. (1987). Brainstem electric-response audiometry in infants of a neonatal intensive care unit. *Audiology, 26,* 284–297.

Fria, T. (1980). The auditory brain stem response: Background and clinical applications. *Maico Monographs in Contemporary Audiology, 2,* 1–44.

Glasscock, M. E., Jackson, G. G., & Josey, A. F. (1981). *Brainstem electric response audiometry.* New York: Thieme-Stratton.

Jacobson, J. T. (1983). Auditory evoked potentials. *Seminars in Hearing* (Vol. 4). New York: Thieme-Stratton.

THOMAS A. FRANK
Pennsylvania State University

AUDIOLOGY
AUDIOMETRY

BRAIN TUMORS

Brain tumors are the most frequent type of childhood cancer, after leukemia. Over half of the brain tumors in childhood occur in the area of the cerebellum and brain stem; the rest occur higher in the brain, primarily in the cerebrum. Presenting symptoms for children with cerebellar tumors include early morning headaches, nausea and vomiting, vision problems, and loss of balance. Children with tumors located higher in the brain may experience more focal symptoms such as weakness on one side of the body or vision problems. For any child with a brain tumor, these symptoms are often accompanied by changes in mood and academic performance. These findings can easily lead parents or teachers to assume that the child is developing a school phobia or behavioral problems.

Many brain tumors are treated successfully with various combinations of surgery, radiation, and chemotherapy. Depending on the type and location of the tumor, and the treatment, most children are able to resume schooling (at least on a limited basis) within a few months following treatment. Teachers need to be aware of the treatment regimen and possible side effects for a child recovering from a brain tumor. For a period of 2 to 4 months following surgery, mood and behavior changes are frequently observed, presumably a result of cranial irradiation and the psychological impact of having been diagnosed with a severe illness (Katz, 1980; Mulhern, Crisco, & Kun, 1983). Some of these children will receive chemotherapy for 1 to 3 years following surgery. Most children experience at least one of the following side effects: hair loss (usually reversible), nausea, behavioral changes, and painful mouth sores. Cortisone, taken to reduce the traumatic effects of surgery, also may cause changes in mood and physical appearance.

A decline in academic performance following surgery (compared with their previous performance) can be expected for most of these children (Hirsch et al, 1979; Walther & Gutjahr, 1982; Radcliffe, Bunin, Sutton & Goldwein, 1994). After returning to school, children may improve gradually in school performance. Other children experience a continued decline in academic performance as a result of the various treatment side effects. A continued decline also could signal a recurrence of the tumor. Regular communication with the child's primary physician is important to obtain information regarding the medical treatment and, in turn, to inform the physician about the child's functioning at school.

As these children resume school, they need regular, detailed assessment of their abilities and deficits. A complete neuropsychological assessment should be obtained every few years. There have not been enough studies to predict what specific deficits will occur; however, available data suggest that most children recovering from brain tumors suffer from at least one of the following: (1) poor coordination, (2) poor memory, (3) difficulty in acquiring and integrating new concepts, (4) a decline in overall IQ (ranging from only a few to 20 or more points), (5) emotional problems, especially somatic worries and low self-esteem (Mulhern, Crisco & Kun, 1983). Most of these children will require either special education placement and a learning program that emphasizes gradual acquisition and practice of basic skills or placement in a regular classroom with the ready availability of additional resources. Parents can play

a significant role in helping the child to perform at a maximal level.

Students who had previously done well in school often are frustrated by their inability to work as quickly and efficiently as before (Paviour, 1988). Teachers need to offer reassurance and encouragement, as well as extra time to learn and practice new material. Some students with impaired efficiency can continue to learn and use new information, but they may require more time than usually allowed on a timed exam to demonstrate their true levels of ability.

REFERENCES

Hirsch, J. F., Renier, D., Czernichow, R., Benveniste, L., & Pierre-Kahn, A. (1979). Medulloblastoma in childhood. Survival and functional results. *Acta Neurochirurgica, 48,* 1–15.

Katz, E. R. (1980). Illness impact and social reintegration. In J. Kellerman (Ed.), *Psychological aspects of childhood cancer* (pp. 14–46). Springfield, IL: Thomas.

Mulhern, R. K., Crisco, J. J., & Kun, L. E. (1983). Neuropsychological sequelae of childhood brain tumors: A review. *Journal of Clinical Child Psychology, 12*(1), 66–73.

Paviour R. (1988). Walking in the valley of death: The impact of brain tumors on children. *Child & Adolescent Social Work Journal, 5,* 315–324.

Radcliffe, J., Bunin, G. R., Sutton, L. N., & Goldwein, J. (1994). Cognitive deficits in long term survivors of childhood medulloblastoma and other noncortical tumors age dependent effects of whole brain radiation. *International Journal of Developmental Neuroscience, 12,* 327–334.

Walther, B., & Gutjahr, P. (1982). Development after treatment of cerebellar medulloblastoma in childhood. In D. Voth, P. Gutjahr, & C. Langmaid (Eds.), *Tumours of the central nervous system in infancy and childhood* (pp. 389–398). Berlin: Springer-Verlag.

SAMUEL LEBARON
PAUL M. ZELTZER
*University of Texas Health
Science Center*

**BRAIN DISORDERS (DEGENERATIVE MOTOR
    DYSFUNCTIONS)
CHEMOTHERAPY**

BRAZELTON, THOMAS B. (1918–   )

A native of Waco, Texas, Thomas B. Brazelton received his BA (1940) from Princeton University and his MD from Columbia College of Physicians and Surgeons in 1943. He served his internship (1944) at Roosevelt Hospital in New York City, and completed his residency (1947–1950) in child psychiatry at Putnam Children's Center, Roxbury, Massachusetts. Brazelton was an instructor in pediatrics (1951–1972) and clinical professor of pediatrics (1972–1986) at Harvard University Medical School, and served as director of the Child Development Unit, Children's Hospital Medical Center, Boston, Massachusetts from 1972 to 1992.

Brazelton's research has focused on early attachment of infants to their primary caregivers as well as cross-cultural research on child-rearing practices in Kenya, Guatemala, Mexico, and Greece. His comparison of interactional behaviors of African and American mothers' age-appropriate teaching tasks indicated that while techniques differed, both groups demonstrated positive interactions (Dixon et al., 1984). Brazelton views these findings as important in terms of culture-specific values, expectations for children, and goals and assumptions of the teaching process.

Brazelton (1973) developed the Brazelton Behavioral Assessment Scale, a tool for behavioral evaluation of newborn infants that measures interactions between the infant and social or potentially social stimuli, the infant's various reflexes, and physiologic responses to stress. Additional research led to his finding that term infants are more likely than preterm infants to lead interactions with their mothers, thus offering a possible explanation for later reported differences in children's development (Lester, Hoffman, & Brazelton, 1985).

For his work with infants, Brazelton received an award from the Child Study Association of America, and *Parent's Magazine* has awarded him a medal for outstanding service to children. He is the recipient of an Emmy award for Daytime Host (1994) for his cable television program, "What Every Baby Knows." Brazelton has served as president of the National Center for Clinical Infant Programs (1988–1991), president of Zero to Three (1989–1991), and member of the National Commission on Children (1989–1992). He has authored numerous books and articles, including *The Earliest Relationship* (1991), *Touchpoints: Your Child's Emotional and Behavioral Development* (1995), and *Going to the Doctor* (1996).

REFERENCES

Brazelton, T. B. (1973). *Neonatal behavioral assessment scale.* Philadelphia: Lippincott.

Brazelton, T. B. (1995). *Touchpoints: Your child's emotional and behavioral development.* London: Penguin.

Brazelton, T. B. (1996). *Going to the doctor.* Reading, Mass: Addison-Wesley.

Brazelton, T. B., & Cramer, B. G. (1991). *The earliest relationship: Parents, infants, and the drama of early attachment.* London: Karnac.

Dixon, S. D., LeVine, R. A., Richman, A., & Brazelton, T. B. (1984). Mother-child interaction around a teaching task: An African-American comparison. *Child Development, 55*(4), 1252–1264.

Lester, B. M., Hoffman, J., & Brazelton, T. B. (1985). The rhythmic structures of mother-infant interaction in term and preterm infants. *Child Development, 56*(1), 15–27.

E. Valerie Hewitt
Texas A & M University
First edition

Tamara J. Martin
The University of Texas of the Permian Basin
Second edition

BRIDGMAN, LAURA DEWEY (1829–1899)

Laura Dewey Bridgman, deaf and blind from the age of 2, entered the Perkins Institution and Massachusetts School for the Blind at the age of 7. The director of the institution, Samuel Gridley Howe, developed an educational program for Bridgman and she quickly learned to read from raised letters and to communicate with manual signs. She related well to people and developed into a cheerful, intelligent woman who used her talents to teach other deaf-blind students at Perkins.

Bridgman was the first deaf-blind person to become well educated, and her achievement received wide attention. Charles Dickens visited her and published an account of their meeting. That publication led Helen Keller's mother to appeal to Howe to find a teacher for Helen; the teacher he recommended was Anne Sullivan Macy, who, as

Laura Dewey Bridgman

a student at Perkins had lived in the same house as Bridgman. What Bridgman accomplished was later repeated by Helen Keller and other similarly handicapped persons. But Bridgman was the first to demonstrate that proper education could enable a deaf-blind person to lead a happy and productive life.

REFERENCE

Ross, I. (1951). *Journey into light.* New York: Appleton-Century-Crofts.

PAUL IRVINE
Katonah, New York

BRIGANCE DIAGNOSTIC INVENTORIES

The Brigance Inventories are a comprehensive set of individually administered criterion-referenced tests. There are several inventories, each covering a specific age range, that are used for assessment, diagnosis, record keeping, and instructional planning. The following paragraphs briefly describe the intended use of each of the inventories.

The Brigance Diagnostic Inventory of Early Development, Revised (Brigance, 1991) is designed to assess infants and children under age seven. In addition to being an assessment instrument, an instructional guide, a record-keeping tracking system, and a tool for developing individualized education programs, it can also serve as a resource for training parents and professionals. The Inventory of Early Development-Revised offers a variety of possible assessment methods: parent interview, teacher observation, group administration, or informal appraisal of the child's performance in the school setting. The goal of the assessment of the child under age seven is to identify those segments of the curriculum objectives that have been mastered. The following skill areas are assessed: Preambulatory Motor Skills and Behaviors, Gross-Motor Skills and Behaviors, Fine-Motor Skills and Behaviors, Self-Help Skills, Speech and Language Skills, General Knowledge and Comprehension, Social and Emotional Development, Readiness, Basic Reading Skills, Manuscript Writing, and Basic Math.

There are two Brigance measures that assess only kindergarteners and first graders. The Brigance Diagnostic Inventory of Basic Skills (Brigance, 1977) is designed for students in kindergarten and the first grade and assesses basic readiness and academic skills with the following subtests: Readiness, Reading, Language Arts, and Math. The Brigance K and 1 Screen-Revised (Brigance, 1992) is designed for students in kindergarten and first grade and assesses pupils' basic skills in order to identify

special service referrals, determine appropriate pupil placement, and assist in planning individual pupil programs. The following basic skills are evaluated with the K and 1 Screen-Revised: personal data response, color recognition, picture vocabulary, visual discrimination, visual motor skills, standing gross motor skills, ability to draw a person (body image), rate counting, identification of body parts, ability to recite alphabet, comprehension of verbal directions, numeral comprehension, recognition of lower and upper case letters, auditory discrimination, print personal data, syntax and fluency, and numerals in sequence.

The Brigance Diagnostic Comprehensive Inventory of Basic Skills (Brigance, 1983) is designed to assess students in kindergarten through the ninth grade. The Comprehensive Inventory of Basic Skills contains 203 skill sequences to be assessed in the areas of reading, listening, research and study skills, spelling, language, and mathematics. The Brigance Diagnostic Inventory of Essential Skills (Brigance, 1981) is designed for students with special needs in fourth through twelfth grade and assesses basic academic (Reading, Language Arts, and Mathematics) and applied skills relevant to functioning as citizen, consumer, worker, and family member. Ten rating scales cover traits, behaviors, attitudes, and skills.

Reviewers of the Brigance Diagnostic Inventories consistently have noted that the lack of reliability or validity data for these measures is troubling (Berk, 1995; Carpenter, 1995; Watson, 1995). Also questioned by one reviewer was the appropriateness of the instruments for students who do not speak English as a first language (Berk, 1995). The instruments are generally viewed as viable tool because of their flexibility and planning utility (Carpenter, 1995). One reviewer viewed the Brigance Inventories as positive methods for identifying a child's strengths and weaknesses (Penfield, 1995). Because of the lack of validity data, these inventories are perhaps best used as informal screening measures to provide assistance to teachers in planning curriculum objectives. Also because of the lack of data, placement decisions based on the inventories are inappropriate (Watson, 1995).

REFERENCES

Berk, R. (1995). Review of the Revised Brigance K & 1 Screen for Kindergarten and First Grade Children-Revised. In J. C. Conoley & J. C. Impara (Eds.), *The twelfth mental measurements yearbook* (pp. 133–134). Lincoln, NE: Buros Institute of Mental Measurements.

Brigance, A. H. (1977). *Brigance Diagnostic Inventory of Basic Skills.* North Billerica, MA: Curriculum Associates.

Brigance, A. H. (1981). *Brigance Diagnostic Inventory of Essential Skills.* North Billerica, MA: Curriculum Associates.

Brigance, A. H. (1983). *Brigance Diagnostic Comprehensive Inventory of Basic Skills.* North Billerica, MA: Curriculum Associates.

Brigance, A. H. (1991). *Brigance Diagnostic Inventory of Early Development, Revised*. North Billerica, MA: Curriculum Associates.

Brigance, A. H. (1992). *Brigance K and 1 Screen-Revised*. North Billerica, MA: Curriculum Associates.

Carpenter, C. D. (1995). Review of the Revised Brigance Diagnostic Inventory of Early Development. In J. C. Conoley & J. C. Impara (Eds.), *The twelfth mental measurements yearbook* (pp. 852–853). Lincoln, NE: Buros Institute of Mental Measurements.

Penfield, D. A. (1995). Review of the Revised Brigance Diagnostic Inventory of Early Development. In J. C. Conoley & J. C. Impara (Eds.), *The twelfth mental measurements yearbook* (pp. 853–854). Lincoln, NE: Buros Institute of Mental Measurements.

Watson, T. S. (1995). Review of the Revised Brigance K & 1 Screen for Kindergarten and First Grade Children-Revised. In J. C. Conoley & J. C. Impara (Eds.), *The twelfth mental measurements yearbook* (pp. 134–135). Lincoln, NE: Buros Institute of Mental Measurements.

ELIZABETH O. LICHTENBERGER
The Salk Institute

CRITERION-REFERENCED TESTING

GRADE EQUIVALENTS

BRITTLE BONE DISEASE (OSTEOGENESIS IMPERFECTA)

Osteogenesis imperfecta appears in several forms, one that is nearly always fatal to the neonate (osteogenesis imperfecta congenita), and a later appearing variation (osteogenesis imperfecta tarda) in which the affected individual may live a normal life (Behrman & Vaughan, 1983). The congenital variety results from an autosomal recessive gene; the later appearing from an autosomal dominant gene.

The later appearing type (OI Type I) is present in 1 out of 30,000 births. Bone fractures are present at birth about 10% of the time and scoliosis is seen in about 20% of affected adults. There is a distinct blue coloring and bulging appearance of the white portion of the eyes (sclera). One-third of this group will show hearing impairment after age 10; earlier onset is uncommon. "Occurrence of neonatal fractures does not predict more deformity or more handicap" (Behrman & Vaughan, 1983).

In the second type (OI Type II), the condition is generally fatal. Half of the infants survive the birth process but expire soon afterward, usually to respiratory difficulties associated with the skeletal anomalies. The limbs are usually severely deformed. There is no effective treatment for Type II.

Management of the disorder centers around proper support and support of skeletal growth. Parents must learn first aid for fractures. The youngster must learn to engage in activities that minimize the risk of fracture without becoming inactive. Nutrition and genetic counseling are essential, as is a careful monitoring of the hearing loss (Bennett, 1981).

Recent studies have suggested that early diagnosis is very important to prevent families from being suspected of child abuse (Brodin, 1990). A 30-year-old Nigerian woman in England had her 3-week-old infant removed from her care when the infant was presented at a hospital with multiple fractures of the femurs and ribs. It was only several months later that osteogenesis imperfecta was diagnosed. The disruption in the mother-child bonding was not measurable (Minnis, Ramsay, Ewije, & Kumar, 1995).

REFERENCES

Behrman, R., & Vaughan, V. (1983). *Nelson textbook of pediatrics* (12th ed.). Philadelphia: Saunders.

Bennett, P. (1981). *Diseases, The nurse's reference library series*. Philadelphia, Pennsylvania: Informed Communications Book Division.

Brodin, J. (1990). Children with osteogenesis imperfecta and their daily living. *Handicap Research Group Report, 4*, 2.

Minnis, H., Ramsay, R., Ewije, P., & Kumar, C. (1995). Osteogenesis imperfecta and non-accidental injury. *British Journal of Psychiatry, 166*, 824–825.

JOHN E. PORCELLA
Rhinebeck Country School

OSTEOPOROSIS

BROCA, PIERRE PAUL (1824–1880)

Pierre Paul Broca, a French surgeon and physical anthropologist noted for his studies of the brain and skull, was a member of the Academy of Medicine in Paris and professor of surgical pathology and clinical surgery. Through postmortem examinations he learned that damage to the third convolution of the left frontal lobe of the brain (Broca's convolution) was associated with loss of the ability to speak; this was the first demonstration of a connection between a specific bodily activity and a specific area of the brain. His announcement of this finding in 1861 led to a vast amount of research on cerebral localization.

Broca was a key figure in the development of physical

anthropology in France. He founded a laboratory, a school, a journal, and a society for the study of anthropology. He originated techniques and invented instruments for studying the skull, and helped to establish that the Neanderthal man discovered in his time was a primitive ancestor of modern man.

REFERENCE

Talbott, J. H. (1970). *A biographical history of medicine: Excerpts and essays on the men and their work*. New York: Grune & Stratton.

PAUL IRVINE
Katonah, New York

BROCA'S APHASIA

Broca's aphasia is one of several subdivisions of nonfluent aphasia. Originally the symptoms associated with this acquired language disorder were believed to occur as a result of damage to Broca's Area, the posterior-inferior (third) frontal gyrus of the left hemisphere, also known as Broadman's area 44 (Hegde, 1994). Kearns (1997) reports that as modern neuroradiographic techniques obtain sophisticated data related to symptoms characteristic of damage to this area, it is often evident that many different parts of the brain may be damaged while still resulting in the type of symptoms classified as Broca's. Obviously, as our knowledge base expands, the model of brain function from a purely localized perspective is yielding to an overall view of brain function as a total system with localized areas and a myriad of vital pathways.

The major language characteristics most often associated with this diagnosis are: nonfluent and effortful speech, many inappropriate pauses, short mean length of utterance, telegraphic speech limited to nouns and verbs, omission of grammatical function words (articles, pronouns, auxiliary verbs, and some prepositions), impaired repetition of words and sentences, and impaired confrontation naming. Although these persons may have some problems in the area of auditory comprehension, silent reading comprehension, and writing, these persons most often have better skills in these areas and than in their expressive communication (Kearns, 1997, Hegde, 1994). Other types of nonfluent aphasia include the following.

Transcortical Motor Aphasia

Originally the symptoms associated with this acquired language disorder were believed to occur as a result of damage to the watershed regions between the middle cere-

bral and anterior arteries and in the premotor area in front of the motor cortex. However, as Kearns reports (1997), as modern neuroradiographic techniques obtain sophisticated data related to symptoms characteristic of damage to this area, it is often evident that many different parts of the brain may be damaged while still resulting in the type of symptoms classified as transcortical motor aphasia.

The major language characteristics most often associated with this diagnosis are nonfluency, paraphasia, agrammaticisms, telegraphic (similar to those described in Broca's aphasia) and intact repetition (differing from Broca's aphasia), and echolalia. Comprehension may be impaired for complex speech but is generally good for simple conversation (Chapey, 1994; Hegde, 1994).

Global Aphasia

Originally, the symptoms associated with this acquired language disorder were believed to occur as a result of damage to the entire perisylvian region. All the so-called language centers are believed to be affected with destruction of the left fronto-temporoparietal regions. This disorder reflects a depth of neural destruction to the point that damage to cortical white matter was assumed even prior to the new view of systemic brain function (pathways vs. localization) (Hegde, 1994).

Persons with this diagnosis have profoundly impaired language skills in all ways, and fluency is greatly reduced (naming, repetition, auditory comprehension, reading, and writing are impaired). Language is limited to a few words, exclamations or automatic speech. (Chapey, 1994; Hegde, 1994).

Isolation Aphasia

This is a rare type of nonfluent aphasia with severe impairment to all language functions except preservation of the skill to repeat words. It is this characteristic that discriminates between global aphasia and isolation aphasia. This subdivision is not acknowledged by all aphasiologists (Hegde, 1994).

REFERENCES

Chapey, R. (1994). *Language intervention strategies in adult aphasia* (3rd ed.). Baltimore: Williams & Wilkins.

Hegde, M. (1994). *A coursebook on aphasia and other neurogenic language disorders*. San Diego: Singular Publishing Group, Inc.

Kearns, K. P. (1997). Broca's aphasia. In L. L. LaPointe (Ed.), *Aphasia and related neurogenic language disorders* (pp. 1–41). New York: Thieme.

SHEELA STUART
George Washington University

BRONFENBRENNER, URI (1917–   )

Uri Bronfenbrenner was born in Moscow, Russia in 1917, and came to the United States at an early age. He received his BA degree from Cornell University in 1938, his EdM from Harvard in 1940, and his PhD in developmental psychology from the University of Michigan in 1942. After World War II, Bronfenbrenner returned to the University of Michigan as assistant professor. In 1948, he joined the faculty of Cornell as professor of psychology, child development, and family relationships, and currently holds the position of Jacob Gould Schurman Professor Emeritus of Human Development and Family Studies and Professor Emeritus of Psychology.

Bronfenbrenner has written extensively in the field of developmental psychology. He is perhaps best known for his ecological approach to developmental psychology. The ecological environment, according to Bronfenbrenner, is like a set of nested Russian dolls in which one doll contains another which contains another and so forth. He recognizes three levels of ecological environment in psychological development. "At the innermost level is the immediate setting containing the developing person. This can be the home, the classroom, or...the laboratory" (Bronfenbrenner, 1979).

Involving influences beyond the immediate setting and the relationships among them, the school and peer group exemplify the next level. Bronfenbrenner (1979) contends that a "child's ability to learn to read...may depend no less on how he is taught than on the existence and nature of ties between the school and the home." The third level consists of influences from events that occur in settings in which the child is not directly involved. According to Bronfenbrenner, our industrialized society, in which both parents are employed, has a direct influence on how children develop.

Bronfenbrenner is also well-known for his comparison of education in the United States and the former Soviet Union. He has authored 15 books and countless articles. His most recent book, *The State of Americans: This Generation and the Next*, was published in 1996. Other publications include *The Ecology of Human Development: Experiments by Nature and Design and Two Worlds of Childhood: U.S. and USSR*.

Bronfenbrenner's writing interests range from developmental behavioral genetics to practical aspects of memory. His numerous awards include six honorary doctorates from various colleges and universities, the Lifetime Contribution to Developmental Psychology in the Service of Science and Society Award of the American Psychological Association (APA), Division 7; the James McKeen Cattell Award for Distinguished Scientific Contribution of the American Psychological Society; the Award for Distinguished Scientific Contributions in Child Development of the Society for Research in Child Development, and the Camille Cosby "World of Children" Award.

REFERENCES

Bronfenbrenner, U. (1972). *Two worlds of childhood: U.S. and USSR*. New York: Simon & Schuster.

Bronfenbrenner, U. (1979). *The ecology of human development: Experiments by nature and design*. Cambridge, MA: Harvard University Press.

Bronfenbrenner, U., McClelland, P., Wethington, E., Moen, P., & Ceci, S. J. (1996). *The state of Americans: This generation and the next*. New York: Free Press.

TAMARA J. MARTIN
*The University of Texas of the
Permian Basin*

BROWN, ANN L. (1943–   )

Ann Brown received the BA in psychology with first-class honors in 1964 from Bedford College of the University of London, and her PhD in psychology in 1967, also from the University of London. She is currently a Professor of Cognition and Development in the Graduate School of Education at the University of California, Berkeley, and was previously on the faculty at the University of Illinois.

Brown's research has focused in the area of cognitive psychology, including cognition, metacognition, cognitive development, intentional learning, and transfer of learning. She has distinguished between knowledge, or *cognition*, and how that knowledge is understood, or *metacognition*, and is an acknowledged leader in the field of metacognition. Major works include *Knowing When, Where, and How to Remember* (1978) and *Metacognition Reconsidered* (Reeve & Brown, 1984), the latter describing modifications Brown views as necessary for successful interventions based on metacognitive principles, including increased attention to pertinent developmental issues, and understanding transition from other-regulated to self-regulated thought. She is one of the founders and principal researchers of the Learning and Development Program, a research center within the Graduate School of Education at UC Berkeley. Her most recent articles have focused on the integration of psychological theory and the design of innovative learning environments, and guided discovery.

Brown has been highly active within the profession throughout her career. She is the current (1998) president of the National Academy of Education, and a past president of the American Educational Research Association (1993–94). Between 1976 and 1979, she was associate editor for the journal *Child Development*, and later a member of the Harvard University Press *Cognitive Science Series* and the MIT Press *Learning and Development and Conceptual Change Series*. Other editorial activities include serving as consulting editor for numerous scholarly journals, including the *Journal of Experimental Psychology, Developmental Psychology, American Journal of Mental Deficiency*, and the *American Journal of Psychology*. She has also served as a member of the governing board of the Cognitive Science Society.

In 1997, Brown received the American Psychological Society James McKeen Catell Fellow Award for Distinguished Service to Applied Psychology, and was the recipient of AERA's Distinguished Research Award in 1991.

REFERENCES

Brown, A. L. (1978). Knowing when, where and how to remember: A problem in metacognition. In R. Glasser (Ed.), *Advances in instructional psychology*. Hillsdale, NJ: Erlbaum.

Reeve, R. A. & Brown, A. L. (1984). *Metacognition reconsidered: Implications for intervention research*. Champaign, IL: University of Illinois.

TAMARA J. MARTIN
*The University of Texas of the
Permian Basin*

BROWN, LOU (1939–   )

Lou Brown received BA and MA degrees in Social Studies Education and Clinical Psychology from East Carolina University and a PhD degree in Special Education from Florida State University in 1969. Since 1969 he has been a professor in the Department of Rehabilitation Psychology and Special Education at the University of Wisconsin.

His efforts in the field of education have focused on the development of service delivery models, curricula, and values that prepare individuals with disabilities to live, work, and play in integrated society. His dream is that some day in the near future all such persons will live in decent family-style settings that contain no more than two unrelated persons with disabilities, perform real work in the real world next to nondisabled coworkers, enjoy rich and varied recreation and leisure lives with their nondisabled friends and neighbors, and have access to and use all community environments.

Brown's strong belief that individuals with disabilities can become productive members of integrated society, as well as his call for the termination of institutions, special schools and classes, sheltered workshops, activity centers, enclaves, group homes, and other manifestations of segregation, caused many in the past to consider his views radical and extreme. Such views are common today. He believes that many educational and vocational training programs do not adequately prepare persons with and without disabilities to function in integrated society. Thus, he contends that massive changes are needed in the ways we serve and prepare others to serve those with disabilities.

Brown has lectured, consulted, and served as a technical advisor for various organizations, school districts, colleges, and universities throughout the United States and abroad. He has written countless books and articles, and has been as a member of several editorial boards of publications including *The Journal of Special Education*, the *Encyclopedia of Special Education* (First Edition), and *The Journal of the Association for Persons With Severe Handicaps*. Recent publications by Brown include *Generating Meaningful Experiences for a Student With Disabilities and Nondisabled Classmates in Regular Education Settings (1994), Middle to High School Transition Plans for Students With Disabilities (1996), and Research Team Experiences for Students With and Without Disabilities (1997)*. He is currently writing *Work-Pay Relationships and Individuals With Disabilities* and *The 1998 Version of The Madison Vocational Evaluation*.

REFERENCES

Brown, L. (1997). *Work-pay relationships and individuals with disabilities*. Unpublished manuscript, University of Wisconsin-Madison.

Brown, L. (1997). *The 1998 version of The Madison Vocational Evaluation Strategy*. Unpublished manuscript.

Brown, L., Kluth, P., Suomi, J., Causton, J., Houghton, L., & Jorgensen, J. (1997). *Research team experiences for students with and without disabilities*. Madison, WI: University of Wisconsin and Madison Metropolitan School District.

Brown, L., Mueller, A., Kluth, P., Suomi, J., Houghton, L., & Jorgensen, J. (1996). *Middle to high school transition plans for students with disabilities*. Madison, WI: University of Wisconsin and Madison Metropolitan School District.

Brown, L., Shiraga, B., York, J., Kessler, K., Strohm, B., Rogan, P., Sweet, M., Zanella, K., Van Deventer, P., & Loomis, R. (1985a). Integrated work opportunities for adults with severe handicaps: The extended training option. *Journal of the Association for Persons with Severe Handicaps* (pp. 262–269).

Brown, L., Shiraga, B., York, J., Udvari Solner, A., Z. Albright, K., Rogan, P., McCarthy, E., & Loomis, R. (1985b). *Educational programs for students with severe intellectual disabilities*. Madison, WI: Madison Metropolitan School District.

Brown, L., Udvari Solner, A., Temple, J., Kluth, P., Suomi, J., & Ross C. (1994). *Generating meaningful experiences for a student with significant disabilities in regular education settings*. Madison, WI: University of Wisconsin and Illinois Benedictine College.

TAMARA J. MARTIN
*The University of Texas of the
Permian Basin*

Robert T. Brown

BROWN, ROBERT T. (1940–   )

Born in 1940 in Greenwich, Connecticut, Robert T. Brown obtained his BA degree from Hamilton College in 1961 and his PhD in experimental psychology from Yale University in 1966. At Yale he worked with Allan R. Wagner and Frank A. Logan before conducting his dissertation research under the supervision of William Kessen. After a USPHS postdoctoral fellowship at the University of Sussex, he was on the faculty of William and Mary and then the University of North Carolina, Chapel Hill. He is now professor of psychology at the University of North Carolina, Wilmington.

His research on the effects of rearing environments on problem solving in rats and on imprinting in chicks and ducklings has influenced theories of early experience and critical periods. In addition to being a consulting editor of the *Encyclopedia of Special Education,* he coedited two books of relevance to special education, *Perspectives on Bias in Mental Testing* (Reynolds & Brown, 1984) and *Psychological Perspectives on Childhood Exceptionality: A Handbook* (Brown & Reynolds, 1986). He coedits, with Cecil R. Reynolds the Plenum Perspectives on Individual Differences, a series of professional books.

More recent publications include "Exercise Demonstrating a Genetic-Environment Interaction (Brown, 1989), providing instruction for introducing and conducting an interaction between genetics and environment, and "Ex-huming an Old Issue" (Brown & Jackson, 1992), an article reviewing research on inductive reasoning errors.

REFERENCES

Brown, R. T., & Reynolds, C. R. (Eds.). (1986). *Psychological perspectives on childhood exceptionality: A handbook.* New York: Wiley.

Brown, R. T. (1989). Exercise demonstrating a genetic-environment interaction. *Teaching Psychology, 16,* 131–.

Brown, R. T., & Jackson, L. A. (1992). Ex-huming an old issue. *Journal of School Psychology, 30,* 215–221.

Reynolds, C. R., & Brown, R. T. (Eds.). (1984). *Perspectives on bias in mental testing.* New York: Plenum.

CECIL R. REYNOLDS
Texas A & M University
First edition

TAMARA J. MARTIN
The University of Texas of the Purmian Basin
Second edition

BROWN v. BOARD OF EDUCATION

In 1954, *Brown v. Board of Education* was brought to the Supreme Court by a Kansas City black family, the Browns. It was joined by other cases from South Carolina, Virginia, and Delaware (Alexander, Corns, & McCann, 1969; Zirkel, 1978). The plaintiffs, black students from various states, were seeking admission to public schools that had been restricted to white students. Black students had been denied admission to attend these schools under the "separate but equal" doctrine that had been adopted in a previous court case (Bolmeier, 1973). Under this doctrine, schools claimed that black students were being treated equally through the provision of equal facilities, even though these facilities were separate. The plaintiffs claimed that, by being denied equal facilities, they were also being deprived of their right to an equal education.

The *Brown v. Board of Education* 347 U.S. 483 decision (1954) was unanimously in favor of the plaintiffs. The Court declared that separate educational facilities were unequal because they violated the black students' right to an equal education under the Fourteenth Amendment of the Constitution, which guarantees equal protection of the law to all American citizens. As delivered by Justice Warren, the Brown decision follows (Fellman, 1976):

> Today . . . [education] is a principal instrument in awakening the child to cultural values, in preparing him for later professional training, and in helping him to adjust normally to his environment. In these days, it is doubtful that any child may reasonably be expected to succeed in life if he is denied the opportunity of an education. Such an opportunity, where the state has undertaken to provide it, is a right which must be made available to all on equal terms. (p. 137)

Because of the complexities of this case, the U.S. attorney general and the attorneys general of the different states involved in the case were recalled for a second deliberation in 1955. The 1954 decision was sustained and the Court ordered that immediate steps were to be taken to eliminate segregation in public schools, with local school authorities given the responsibility of implementing the Court order.

Today, this Court decision is regarded as a landmark in the history of the U.S. educational system because it set a direction for future Court decisions that emphasized that children cannot be discriminated against on the basis of race, sex, or national origin.

The complexities of case law and practice in the nearly fifty years after the decision suggest that the Brown case represented a significant shift in the national attitude towards students from ethnic minorities. However, studies of the effect of desegregation on intergroup attitudes are generally inconclusive and inconsistent (Schofield, 1989). The fortieth anniversary of the Brown decision brought forth discussion groups that analyzed the promise of *Brown* and strategies for achieving the promise in a more current context (Johnson, 1995). The Department of Education stated that the "Brown decision was a crowbar for change, and we are all the better for it" (Riley, 1994). However others (Ruiz, 1994) suggested that although 500 school districts were ordered to desegregate, very few of those schools were found by the courts to have completed the process. Ruiz (1994) suggests that the central tenet of *Brown* is in danger of being lost amidst "voluminous paperwork and clever legal arguments." Race discrimination issues are still prominent, however the issues have evolved into conflicts about ability grouping, bilingual education, harassment, educational services for undocumented immigrants and different kinds of educational remedies in school desegregation cases (*Milliken II*) (Heubert, 1994).

REFERENCES

Alexander, K., Corns, R., & McCann, W. (1969). *Public school law: Cases and materials*. St. Paul, MN: West.

Bolmeier, E. C. (1973). *Landmark decisions on public school issues*. Charlottesville, VA: Michie.

Felman, D. (1976). *The Supreme Court and education* (3rd ed.) New York: Teachers College, Columbia University.

Heubert, J. P. (1994). *"Brown" at 40: The tasks that remain for educators and lawyers*. (ERIC Clearinghouse No. EA026514)

Johnson, D. (1995). *The promise of Brown: Has it been fulfilled?* New York, NY: Metropolitan Center for Urban Education.

Riley, R. W. (1994). *Fulfilling the promise of Brown*. Washington DC: Department of Education.

Ruiz, C. M. (1994). *Equity, excellence and school reform: A new paradigm for desegregation*. (ERIC Clearinghouse No. EA026648)

Zirkel, P. A. (1978). *Supreme Court Decisions affecting education*. Bloomington, IN: Phi Delta Kappa.

EMILIA C. LOPEZ
Fordham University

CULTURE FAIR TESTS
DISPROPORTIONALITY
SOCIOECONOMIC STATUS

BRUININKS-OSERETSKY TEST OF MOTOR PROFICIENCY

The Bruininks-Oseretsky Test of Motor Proficiency (Bruininks, 1978) is an individually administered test of gross and fine motor functioning of children from 4½ to 14½ years of age. It is the latest revision of the Oseretsky tests of motor proficiency published in Russia in 1903 (later translated into English by Edgar Doll in 1946). The complete battery comprises 46 items subdivided into 8 subtests: Running Speed and Agility (1 item), Balance (8 items), Bilateral Coordination (8 items), Strength (3 items), Upper-Limb Coordination (9 items), Response Speed (1 item), Visual-Motor Control (8 items), and Upper Limb Speed and Dexterity (8 items). In addition to subtest scores, composite scores are available for the gross motor subtest scores, the fine motor subtests, and the total battery. The complete form takes from 45 to 60 minutes to administer. There is also a 14-item short form, requiring 15 to 20 minutes, which provides a single index of general motor proficiency.

Subtest and composite scores can be expressed in terms of age-based standard scores, percentile ranks, and stanines. Age equivalents are available for each subtest. The battery was standardized on a sample of 765 children, and was distributed across ten age groups from 4–6 to 14–15 years. The sample was stratified by age, sex, race, community size, and geographic region according to the 1970 U.S. Census. Test-retest reliability coefficients for the separate subtests range from .58 to .89 for Grade 2, and from .29 to .89 for Grade 6. The lower reliability scores for Grade 6 are probably a result of the maximum point scores achieved by many older children (Anastasi, 1997). Validity was investigated using factor analysis of items, age differentiation, and comparative studies with retarded and learning-disabled children.

The Bruininks-Oseretsky Test is a useful tool for measuring gross and fine motor skills, developing and evaluating motor training programs, and screening for special purposes (Sabatino, 1985). It should be noted, however, that the test is a product measure of motor development as opposed to a process measure. Product measures focus on the outcome of movement, while process measures emphasize the movement of the body when performing particular motor tasks or skills (Harrington, 1985). Thus the Bruininks-Oseretsky is best combined with other measures of sensory and motor development in order to provide an appropriate indication of motor development.

REFERENCES

Anastasi, A. (1997). *Psychological testing* (7th ed.). Saddle River, NJ: Prentice Hall.

Bruininks, R. H. (1978). *Bruininks-Oseretsky Test of Motor Proficiency*. Circle Pines, MN: American Guidance Services.

Doll, E. A. (1946). *The Oseretsky Tests of Motor Proficiency*. Minneapolis, MN: American Guidance Service.

Harrington, R. G. (1985). Bruininks-Oseretsky Test of Motor Proficiency. In D. L. Keyser & R. C. Sweetland (Eds.), *Test critiques* (Vol. 3, pp. 99–110). Kansas City, MO: Test Corporation of America.

Sabatino, D. (1985). Review of the Bruininks-Oseretsky Test of Motor Proficiency. In J. V. Mitchel (Ed.), *The ninth mental measurements yearbook*. (Vol. 1, pp. 235–236). Lincoln, NE: Buros Institute of Mental Measurements.

LIZANNE DeSTEFANO
University of Illinois

BRUNER, JEROME (1915–   )

Bruner obtained his BA from Duke University in 1937 and his PhD in Psychology from Harvard University in 1941. For almost three decades he was Professor of Psychology at Harvard University (1945–1972), and also served as Director of the Center for Cognitive Studies there, founded by him in the 1960s. He was professor at both Oxford and Cambridge Universities in England, and has held the positions of George Herbert Mead Professor at the New School for Social Research and fellow of the Institute for the Humanities at New York University.

Known by some as the only real intellectual in modern cognitive psychology, in his long career as a psychologist and teacher, Bruner has frequently rejected prevailing views, becoming a major influence in moving American psychology towards a more cognitive approach in the process. His principal areas of research have focused on the knowledge acquisition processes, including perception, memory, learning, thought, language, and literary and scientific creation.

In the 1950s Bruner demonstrated that perceptions are not merely mental photographs, but are actively shaped by the meaning to the individual of what is perceived. This research gave rise to the widely criticized "New Look" movement in psychology, which focused on factors such as how perception is affected by individual intentions or emotions. This movement was the precursor of cognitive psychology, a theory that continues to thrive today. Bruner's research in this area was later expanded to include studies conducted in Senegal in the 1960s of cultural influences on individual perception, an element he concluded was missing from Jean Piaget's child development model.

Another of Bruner's major contributions involved infant learning and the formerly prevalent notion that children's learning occurs entirely as a result of what they experience. This "blank slate" theory was challenged by his study indicating that infants could control whether slides of a woman's face were in or out of focus via their sucking patterns, suggesting a sense of intention as a factor in their intellectual development. These findings were the beginning of his conception for the development of the Head Start programs for preschool children in the United States.

Bruner's effort to bridge the gap between psychology and the humanities is reflected throughout his work. Believing that psychology, particularly cognitive psychology, has become excessively narrow, he has attempted to expand the discipline into the realms of philosophy, the arts, and literature, thus providing a broader perspective of the human mind. Some have criticized Bruner's (1990) call for a "renewed cognitive revolution," arguing that he fails to specify the direction of the movement as well as the obstacles that must be overcome for its success (Shanker, 1992).

His more recent work has focused on the study of narrative modes of thought, analyzing the words and construction used by individuals as they relate the story of their lives. Bruner argues that how the stories are told "becomes so habitual that they finally become recipes for structuring experience itself, for laying down routes into memory," therefore shaping the way people experience life itself.

His numerous publications include *A Study of Thinking* (1956), centering on problem-solving and thinking; *The Process of Education* (1960), a controversial study of the underlying structure of science curriculum; *Actual Minds, Possible Worlds* (1986), dealing with narrative modes of thought; and *Child's Talk* (1985), a summation of his findings and arguments regarding language learning. Bruner has served on two presidential commissions and received numerous awards and honorary degrees. In 1987 in Bern, Switzerland, he was awarded the prestigious Balzan Prize, previously given to Jean Piaget and Jorge Luis Borges, and only rarely presented to an American.

REFERENCES

Bruner, J. S. (1961). *The process of education*. Cambridge, Mass: Harvard University Press.

Bruner, J. S. (1986). *Actual minds, possible worlds*. Cambridge, Mass: Harvard University Press.

Bruner, J. S. (1990). *Acts of Meaning*. Cambridge, MA: Harvard University Press.

Bruner, J. S., Goodnow, J. J., & Austin, G. A. (1956). *A study of thinking*. New York: Wiley.

Bruner, J. S., & Watson, R. (1985). *Child's talk: Learning to use language*. New York: Norton.

Shanker, S. (1992). In search of Bruner. *Language and Communications, 12,* 53–74.

TAMARA J. MARTIN
*The University of Texas of the
Permian Basin*

BRUXISM AND THE HANDICAPPED STUDENT

Bruxism can be defined as "the nonfunctional gnashing and grinding of teeth occurring during the day or night" (Richmond, et al., 1984). The adverse effects of bruxism include severe dental wear, damage to the alveolar bone, temporomandibular joint disorders, and hypertrophy of masticatory muscles, as well as occasional infection. It can also result in significant pain, permanent damage to the structures of the mouth and jaw, and lost teeth (Richmond et al., 1984; Rugh & Robbins, 1982). Dental wear is the most commonly used measure to determine the extent of bruxism.

Estimates of the frequency of bruxism in the nonretarded population have ranged between 5% (Reding et al., 1966) to a high of 21% (Wigdorowicz-Makowerowa et al., 1977), with no significant differences between sexes (Bober, 1982) or age groups (Lindqvist, 1971).

Investigators have reported more dental wear as a consequence of bruxism in severely mentally retarded children than in nonretarded children (Lindqvist & Heijbel, 1974). An informal survey by Blount et al. (1982) indicated that 21.5% of a profoundly retarded group engaged in bruxism. The study of Richmond et al. of some 433 mentally retarded individuals in a state institution revealed a rate of 41 to 59% in this group based on a questionnaire used with direct-care staff who were asked to observe the residents. Higher rates were reported for deaf retarded individuals. Older patients were more likely to grind teeth and wear into the dentin than younger patients.

A variety of explanations for bruxism have been advanced. The etiology of bruxism has been approached along lines of local, psychological, neurophysiological and systemic causes (Glaros & Melamed, 1992). An example of a local cause is occlusive abnormalities. Glaros and Rao (1977) believe that stress is a major cause. Systemic explanations include heredity factors and endocrinal or neurological dysfunction. It has been suggested (Lindqvist & Heijbel, 1974) that bruxism may be a form of stereotypy among retarded populations. It has also been suggested (Richmond et al., 1984) that it can be considered a form of self-injurious behavior.

While such methods as deep muscle relaxation and massed practice have been found to assist individuals of normal intelligence, these methods require a certain level of cognitive ability to be successfully deployed and may not be suited for bruxists who have cognitive difficulties or retardation. Behavioral methods to reduce bruxism have been favored in recent years (Rugh & Robbins, 1982). Thus positive reinforcement has been used to reduce its incidence in retarded individuals (i.e., to reinforce nonbruxist behaviors) and to encourage incompatible behaviors such as keeping the mouth open. Problems with positive reinforcers include the fact that social and tactile reinforcers usually do not have strong effects with severely retarded individuals. Edibles result in further chewing, thus reinforcing behaviors that are not compatible with efforts to reduce bruxism.

Hence behavioral treatment has sometimes been of an aversive nature (e.g., using a contingent sound blast). Such treatment, however, involves expensive equipment. Blount et al. (1982) were able to use a much simpler method, known as icing, with two profoundly retarded women. They greatly reduced their bruxism and successfully generalized their improvements beyond the training sessions. In icing there is a brief contingent application of ice to cheeks or chin as an aversive stimulus. Another, similar method of aversive control of bruxism in a mentally retarded nonverbal child in a class for trainable mentally retarded children was accomplished by Kramer (1981). The method involved the use of a contingent verbal "no" accompanied by the teacher's finger to the child's jaw. Unfortunately, the treatment ideology and modalities has been haphazard for bruxism; therefore, most treatment effects are short-lived (Glaros & Melamed, 1992).

REFERENCES

Blount, R. L., Drabman, R. S., Wilson, N., & Stewart, D. (1982). Reducing severe diurnal bruxism in two profoundly retarded females. *Journal of Applied Behavior Analysis, 15,* 565–571.

Bober, H. (1982). Cause and treatment of bruxism and bruxomania. *Dental Abstracts, 3,* 658–659.

Glaros, A. G., & Melamed, B. G. (1992). Bruxism in children, Etiology and treatment. *Applied and Preventive Psychology, 1,* 191–199.

Glaros, A. G., & Rao, S. M. (1977). Bruxism: A critical review. *Psychological Bulletin, 84,* 767–781.

Heller, R. F., & Strang, H. R. (1973). Controlling bruxism through automated aversive conditioning. *Behavior Research & Therapy, 11,* 327–328.

Kramer, J. J. (1981). Aversive control of bruxism in a mentally retarded child: A case study. *Psychological Reports, 49,* 815–818.

Lindqvist, B. (1971). Bruxism in children. *Odontologisk Revy, 22,* 413–424.

Lindqvist, B., & Heijbel, J. (1974). Bruxism in children with brain damage. *Acta Odontologica Scandinavica, 32,* 313–319.

Reding, G. R., Rubright, W. C., & Zimmerman, S. O. (1966). Incidence of bruxism. *Journal of Dental Research, 45,* 1198–1204.

Richmond, G., Rugh, J. D., Dolfi, R., & Wasilewsky, J. W. (1984). Survey of bruxism in an institutionalized retarded population. *American Journal of Mental Deficiency, 88,* 418–421.

Rugh, J. D., & Robbins, W. J. (1982). Oral habit disorders. In B. Ingersoll (Ed.), *Behavioral aspects in dentistry* (pp. 179–202). New York: Appleton-Century-Crofts.

Wigdorowicsz-Makowerowa, N., Grodzki, C., & Maslanka, T. (1977). Frequency and etiopathogenes of bruxism (on the basis of prophylactic examinations of 1000 middle-aged men). *Czaopismo-Stomatologiczne, 25,* 1109–1112.

DAVID C. MANN
St. Francis Hospital

DENTISTRY AND THE HANDICAPPED CHILD
SELF-INJURIOUS BEHAVIOR

BUCKLEY AMENDMENT

See FAMILY EDUCATIONAL RIGHTS & PRIVACY ACT (FERPA).

BULIMIA NERVOSA

Bulimia nervosa (a term of Greek origin meaning "ox hunger") is an eating disorder that is also referred to as the binge-purge syndrome. It is a condition in which an individual alternately binges (grossly overeats) and purges (rids the body of food or fluids). Although difficult to comprehend, bulimics apparently may ingest as many as 20,000 calories in one binge episode. Bulimics commonly chew and spit out food (Mitchell, Halsukami, Eckert, & Pyle, 1985). Bingeing is mainly on foods rich in carbohydrates; purging may be through vomiting, abuse of laxatives or diet tablets, or excessive exercise, regardless of fatigue (Garner & Garfinkel, 1985). No physical basis for the abnormal eating can be found. This disorder can be life-threatening, is increasing in occurrence and is a serious problem for medical and psychological professionals who are attempting to treat it. Unlike anorexia, which has been known for centuries, bulimia is of relatively recent origin. Indeed, professional journals have commonly reported on bulimia only since the 1970s. This recency is partly responsible for the relatively little firm knowledge about bulimia and the absence of generally effective treatments. Incidence rates that vary with age, race, job status, and ethnic background further hamper general understanding of the disorder.

Bulimia characteristically is largely a disorder of wo-men, with 9–17 times more women than men hospitalized for an eating disorder (Goetestan, Erikson, Heggestad, & Neilson, 1998). It is largely restricted to white women from middle- and upper-class social classes, although it is becoming more common among women from lower social economic status. Further, incidence is increasing among African American women as they become acculturated into the dominant White society. Although mainly a western cultural problem, eating disorders do occur in other cultures. For example, Srivivasan, Suresh, and Jayaram (1998) found that eating disorders occur in India but in milder form without the severe escalation found in Western countries. Onset of bulimia is generally between 18 and 20 years of age, with a peak onset at about the age of 18 years of age (Neuman & Halvorson, 1993). Bulimia is more common than anorexia nervosa and may affect 5% of college women and 1% of young employed women (Hart & Ollendick, 1985). Twenty to 30% of college women may occasionally engage in bulimic behavior.

Although primarily affecting women, bulimia also is seen, and in some areas increasingly, in men. Reasons for the disorder appear to be quite different in men and women except in sports (eg., gymnastics) or vocations (e.g., modeling or dancing) that impose comparable demands on members of both sexes. Those engaged in high-powered sports such as running and wrestling or vocations are particularly at risk. One study (McNulty, 1997) reported that Navy servicemen showed prevalence rates of 2.5% for anorexia and 6.8% for bulimia. In men, bulimia may be driven by individual competition where weight or appearance and goals of "perfection" are important. Male bulimics may need a high calorie intake for energy but at the same time fear not being able to burn off the fat. If a Naval officer wants high scores on body measurements and fitness tests, then he may find purging an effective means, in the short term.

Although bulimia is more common than anorexia, it is harder to recognize because affected individuals do not show severe weight loss and are usually of normal or slightly above normal weight. The stereotypical bulimic's physical appearance may not be apparent to anyone else, possibly not even the sufferer's spouse, as was the case of Princess of Wales, Diana.

However, some general etiological factors and occasionally effective treatments have been described. Bulimics share personality characteristics and have families with a particular complex of unhealthy attitudes and behaviors. Bulimics can suffer from gastrointestinal problems and serious potassium depletion and damage to their teeth due to the acid nature of the regurgitated food. In extreme cases, death may result. As is the case with anorexia, bulimia is viewed as a biopsychosocial disorder.

DSM-IV (American Psychiatric Association, 1994) criteria for bulimia include: (a) recurrent episodes of secretive binge eating (rapid consumption of a large amount of food in a short period of time); (b) termination of bingeing because of abdominal pain, sleep, or social interruptions; and (c) recurrent episodes of purging as an attempt to lose weight or avoid gaining weight through self-induced vomiting, severe diets, abuse of laxatives, cathartics, or diuretics, or excessive exercise. The bulimic suffers frequent weight fluctuations owing to alternating binges and fasts, awareness that the eating pattern is abnormal, and fear of not being able to stop eating voluntarily. Depression and self-deprecating thoughts may follow eating binges (American Psychiatric Association, 1994). DSM-IV distinguishes between purging and non-purging types of bulimia. A purging type periodically engages in the act of self-induced vomiting or the use of laxatives, whereas a non-purging type uses diets, exercise, and fasting instead of regular self-induced vomiting.

Considering biological aspects, bulimia leads to a variety of physiological complications, including cardiac irregularities, kidney dysfunction, neurological abnormalities, gastrointestinal pain, salivary gland enlargement (appearance of a chipmunk), edema and bloating, electrolyte imbalance, amenorrhea, dermatological disorders, and finger clubbing or swelling. Finger abnormalities result from the pressure against the mouth during self-induced vomiting. Abuse of laxatives can lead to permanent nerve damage in the colon, chronic stomach overloading, and potential of stomach rupture. Several of these complications can result in death.

Psychologically, bulimics share many behaviors and concerns. They are terrified of becoming obese, and measure their worth and self-esteem by how much they weigh and how little their stomachs protrude. They tend to be perfectionists, overdemanding of themselves, and very success-oriented. Low self-esteem and fear of rejection, especially by the opposite sex, are common. They are typically helpless, ineffective, nonassertive, have maturity fears, tension management problems, and difficulty in identifying or describing internal states (Johnson & Flach, 1985). Their relationships tend to be superficial and lack genuineness, as they have difficulty allowing others to become emotionally close to them. They are very good at distancing themselves from people while seeming to be friendly and sociable. A common underlying fear is, "If this person really gets to know me, he or she won't like me." They frequently fear sexual rejection or not being good enough to please a sexual partner. Bulimics may additionally overidentify with femininity. Drug abuse among bulimics and their families occurs at a high rate (Herzog, 1982). Motivation for change is extremely difficult to maintain, making therapy difficult.

Bulimics commonly report that their disorder originated out of possible "comfort eating" stemming from loneliness, stress, or some other self-induced inadequacy, such as low self-esteem. Suicide can also be a fatal result of either lack of observation from family and friends, lack of support (as interpreted by the bulimia), or the lack of help from themselves or possibly from the therapist (Hsu, 1990). Not surprisingly, both depression and anxiety are comorbid conditions (Cooper & Fairburn, 1986).

The third aspect of the biopsychosocial triad model of bulimia is social factors. Many bulimics spend so much time in their eating rituals that they do not have time for a normal social life. In one study (Mitchell, et al, 1985) 70% had interpersonal relations difficulties, 53% had family problems, and 50% had work-related interpersonal difficulties. Bulimics can also use their eating habits to shut out the world. They can avoid engaging with others or becoming involved in a situation that could potentially be out of their control. Eating rituals are one thing that bulimics (and anorexics as well) believe they can continue to control, even though it is evident to those who know them that they have actually lost control. The specific etiology of bulimia is not known.

The biopsychosocial model suggests that unknown biological predispositions may interact with both individual psychological states and needs and society's emphasis, especially for women, on thinness as a desirable characteristic (Wooley & Wooley, 1985). Families of bulimics are characterized by a paradoxical combination of enmeshment and disengagement, showing high family conflict with little emphasis on self-expression, especially over conflict. Intellectual achievement is emphasized at the expense of social activities (Johnson & Flach, 1985).

Much of the bulimic's perceived control simply does not exist. The social world exposes vulnerable people to things that, depending on their perception, can exploit their fears. Mass communication can intensify people's low self-esteem and fear of rejection. Consider, for example, size 6 models in fashion shows; Sarah Ferguson, the Duchess of York, saying how easy it is to lose weight; and advertisements for weight-loss programs such as Weight Watchers. Supermodels or representatives of diet programs frequently suffer from serious eating disorders themselves. Numerous media messages instill an unrealistic view of the human form that may enhance fear of "fatness." At the same time, of course, the average weight of American children and adults continues to increase—the average dress size of American adult women is size 12–14.

Treatment can be very difficult. Usually, the longer the bulimic has been ill, the more difficulty she will have in overcoming the disorder. Also, as mentioned previously, lack of motivation for change makes working with bulimics on an outpatient basis difficult. The drive for a weight loss or the perfect body may outweigh the drive for being cured. Numerous difficulties in addition to the motivation problem interfere with recovery. Bulimia nervosa seems to have an addictive quality that is usually not seen in anorexia nervosa. Many therapists believe that treatment is likely to fail if this addictive quality is not addressed. Unfortunately, both bingeing and purging behaviors may have strong and immediate reinforcement qualities. Finally, continual dieting often results in compensatory overeating which appears to have a physiological component. Whether or not inpatient treatment is necessary depends on factors as weight, self-harm tendencies, and other comorbid symptoms.

Cognitive behavior therapy has at least short-term success, although dropout rates vary from 0 to 34% (Robin et al., 1998). Long-term follow-up studies indicate that approximately 33% of patients remain symptom-free (Robin, Gilroy, & Dennis, 1998). Cognitive behavior therapy has the further advantage of being demonstrably effective in dealing with comorbid factors such as anxiety and depression. Family therapy has been discussed as another way of assisting patients with bulimia nervosa, but little research supports its effectiveness. As a recurring theme, no matter what kind of therapy is offered, whether cognitive behavioral, interpersonal, psychodynamic, or pharmacological, without sufficient and persistent motivation, bulimics will probably find treatment unsuccessful.

No consensus exists regarding the most effective form of treatment for eating disorders (Vandereycken & Meermann, 1984). Therapists have used behavioral therapy, diet counseling, cognitive therapy, cognitive-behavioral treatment, drug treatment, and family therapy with varying degrees of success (Garner & Garfinkel, 1985). Whatever the treatment approach, the usual goals are aimed at increasing confidence and self-esteem, challenging irrational or anorectic thinking, developing autonomy, and teaching coping skills. Unfortunately, group therapy sessions may provide an environment in which bulimics can feed on each other's effective purging techniques and become essentially schools for training better bulimics. Further, Vandereycken and Meermann (1984, p. 21) suggest that the "best guarantees of success in therapy are a constructive patient/therapist working relationship and an explicit but consistent treatment plan/contract."

Certain beliefs and values seem to be very important in the maintenance of these conditions. One of these is the belief that weight and shape are extremely important and need to be closely controlled at all costs. A change in these psychopathological beliefs and values concerning body weight and shape may be necessary for complete recovery. Self-help and support groups such as Overeaters Anonymous may be valuable.

Because eating-disordered individuals are usually perfectionists, teachers can help by advising and encouraging them to take fewer courses and to balance academic loads by combining difficult classes with classes that are less demanding. If hospitalization becomes necessary and the student expresses fear that she will be unable to maintain her academic standing, the teacher can point out that hospital personnel are usually more than willing to assist the patient by administering academic tests and by making arrangements to assist meeting other academic requirements. Major treatment centers, as well as many hospitals, have educational components and academic teachers on their staff.

REFERENCES

American Psychiatric Association. (1994). *Diagnostic and statistical manual of mental disorders* (4th ed.). Washington, DC: Author.

Anderson, A. E., Morse, C., & Santmyer, K. (1985). Inpatient treatment for anorexia nervosa. In D. M. Garner & P. E. Garfinkel (Eds.), *Handbook of psychotherapy for anorexia nervosa and bulimia* (pp. 311–343). New York: Guilford.

Bemis, K. M. (1978). Current approaches to the etiology and treatment of anorexia nervosa. *Psychological Bullentin, 35,* 593–617.

Bruch, H. (1985). Four decades of eating disorders. In D. M. Garner & P. E. Garfinkel (Eds.), *Handbook of psychotherapy for anorexia and bulimia* (pp. 7–18). New York: Guilford.

Cooper, P. J., & Fairburn, C. G. (1986). The depressive symptoms of bulimia nervosa. *British Journal of Psychiatry, 148,* 234–246.

Garner, D. M., & Garfinkel, P. E. (Eds.). (1985). *Handbook of psychotherapy for anorexia nervosa and bulimia.* New York: Guilford.

Goetestan, K. G., Erikson, L., Heggestad, T., & Neilson, S. (1998). Prevalence of eating disorders in Norwegian general hospitals 1990–1994: Admissions per year and seasonality. *International Journal of Eating Disorders, 23,* 57–64.

Halmi, K. A. (1983). Advances in anorexia nervosa. In M. Wolraich & D. K. Routh (Eds.), *Advances in development and behavioral pediatrics* (Vol. 4, pp 1–23). Greenwich, CT: Jai Press.

Hart, K. J., & Ollendick, T. H. (1985). Prevalence of bulimia in working and university women. *American Journal of Psychiatry, 142,* 851–854.

Herzog, D. B. (1982). Bulimia: The secretive syndrome. *Psychosomatics, 23,* 481–487.

Hsu, T. (1990). *Eating disorders.* New York: Guilford.

Johnson, C., & Flach, A. (1985). Family characteristics of 105 patients with bulimia. *American Journal of Psychiatry, 142,* 1321–1324.

Mitchell, J. E., Halsukami, D., Eckert, E. D., & Pyle, R. L. (1985). Characteristics of 275 patients with bulimia. *American Journal of Psychiatry, 142,* 251–255.

Neuman, P. A., & Halvorson, P. S. (1983). *Anorexia nervosa and bulimia: A handbook for counselors and therapists.* New York: Van Nostrand Reinhold.

Robin, A. L., Gilroy, M., & Dennis, A. B. (1998). Treatment of eating disorders in children and adolescents. *Clinical Psychology Review, 18,* 421–446.

Srinivasan, T. N., Suresh, T. R., & Jayaram, V. (1998). Emergence of eating disorders in India: Study of eating distress syndrome and development of a screening questionnaire. *International Journal of Social Psychiatry, 44,* 189–198.

Vandereycken, W., & Meermann, R. (1984). *Anorexia nervosa: A clinician's guide to treatment.* Berlin: de Gruyter.

Wooley, S. C., & Wooley, O. W. (1985). Intensive outpatient and residential treatment for bulimia. In D. M. Garner & P. E. Garfinkel (Eds.), *Handbook of psychotherapy for anorexia nervosa and bulimia* (pp. 391–430). New York: Guilford.

C. SUE LAMB
*University of North Carolina
at Wilmington*

WENDY L. FLYNN
Staffordshire University

BUREAU OF EDUCATION FOR THE HANDICAPPED (BEH)

The Bureau of Education for the Handicapped (BEH) was created in 1966 to administer all U.S. Office of Education programs designed for the handicapped. During the late 1960s and early 1970s, BEH administered newly created federal programs for the handicapped, including regional resource centers that provided testing to determine the special education needs of handicapped children. It also administered service centers for the deaf-blind; offered technical assistance on programs for the gifted and talented; provided funds for recruiting and training special education personnel; created experimental preschool and early education programs that could serve as models for school districts; and mounted research projects concerning the handicapped. Eventually, BEH's responsibility was extended to include the provision of technical assistance, compliance monitoring, and evaluation of state education agency and local school district implementation of PL 93-380, the Education Amendments of 1974, and PL 94-142, the Education of All Handicapped Children Act of 1975. The BEH was succeeded in name but not in authority and responsibility by the Office of Special Education when the U.S. Department of Education was created in 1980. For a more detailed description of federal legislation and the role of BEH, see Weintraub, Abeson, Ballard, and LaVor (1976).

REFERENCE

Weintraub, F. J., Abeson, A., Ballard, J., & LaVor, M. L. (1976). *Public policy and the education of exceptional children.* Reston, VA: Council for Exceptional Children.

ROLAND K. YOSHIDA
Fordham University

BUREAU OF INDIAN AFFAIRS: OFFICE OF INDIAN EDUCATION PROGRAMS

The mission of the Office of Indian Education Programs (OIEP) is to:

> provide quality education opportunities from early childhood throughout life in accordance with the Tribe's needs for cultural and economic well-being in keeping with the wide diversity of Indian Tribes and Alaska Native villages as distinct cultural and governmental entities. OIEP manifests consideration of the whole person, taking into account the spiritual, mental, physical, and cultural aspects of the person within a family and Tribal of Alaska Native village contexts. (OIEP, 1998)

The OIEP has developed an extensive list of goals and benchmarks for the year 2000. These goals do not address exceptional children per se, but do include goals that pertain to areas that overlap with special education programs such as behavioral management, alcohol and drug abuse, culturally appropriate assessment instrument for reading and language arts, attendance issues, and staff development (OIEP, 1998).

The OIEP supervises the Branch of Exceptional Education (BEE). The mission of this branch is to assure that:

> Indian children with disabilities, who are between the ages of 5 and 22 are enrolled in Bureau funded schools and have available to them a free appropriate education in the least restrictive environment in accordance with an Individual Education Program. This mission includes: Monitoring to assure the rights of children with disabilities and their parents or guardians are protected; providing technical assistance to provide for the education of all children with disabilities; and assessing the effectiveness of efforts to educate children with disabilities. (OIEP, 1998)

In 1994, 7,933 students with disabilities were served. Those children with severe disabilities requiring residential care were also provided services through contracts with state or private institutions. In 1993, 371 students received residential services. The Branch of Exceptional Education (BEE) also provides programs for gifted and talented students. In 1994, 4,703 students were served in Gifted and Talented Programs (Branch of Exceptional Education, 1998).

The Branch participates in the Very Special Arts Festival that is facilitated by the Kennedy Foundation. Regional festivals have been held to facilitate greater participation by students. Students with disabilities from 21 Bureau funded schools representing 5 states have participated in the Festival (BEE, 1998).

The Bureau of Indian Affairs Office of Indian Education Programs maintains an informative webpage at http://shaman@unm.edu. An extensive newsletter *American*

Indian Education News is available from this website. The information in this entry was taken from the OIEP webpage with gracious permission from the BIA.

ELAINE FLETCHER-JANZEN
University of Northern Colorado

**CULTURAL BIAS IN TESTING
SPECIAL EDUCATION, LEGAL REGULATIONS OF**

BURKS' BEHAVIOR RATING SCALES (BBRS)

The Burks' Behavior Rating Scales (BBRS), Preschool and Kindergarten Form and Grades One–Nine Form, are rating inventories used to identify the type and severity of problem behaviors exhibited by referred children ages 2 to 15. The scales may be completed by parents, teachers, or any responsible person who knows the rated child well. Raters use a five-point scale ranging from 1 ("You have not noticed this behavior at all") to 5 ("You have noticed this behavior to a very large degree") to render quantitative judgments about the severity of observed negative behaviors.

Individual items are clustered together to form 19 (18 for the Preschool and Kindergarten Form) factor-analytically derived behavior categories bearing diagnostic labels such as excessive withdrawal, excessive dependency, poor coordination, poor academics, poor impulse control, poor reality contact, or excessive aggressiveness. Items are summed for each behavior category (usually by someone other than the rater) and transferred to a profile sheet. The profile sheet orders each category score along a continuum indicating the degree of significance of the presence of each negative behavior. Significance ratings can be used in differential diagnosis and in prioritizing intervention needs. Comparison of score profiles obtained from various raters can help broaden the scope of understanding and interpretation of the child's behavior patterns. The BBRS manual includes a lengthy discussion of the possible meanings of category scores and intervention suggestions for each problem behavior area. The BBRS has received favorable reviews as a clinical tool to aid in behavior assessment (Lerner, 1985).

REFERENCES

Burks, H. F. (1977). *Burks' Behavior Rating Scales*. Los Angeles: Western Psychological Services.

Lerner, J. V. (1985). Review of the Burks' Behavior Rating Scales. In D. J. Keyser & R. C. Sweetland (Eds.), *Test critiques. Vol. II* (pp. 108–112). Kansas City, MO: Test Corporation of America.

GEORGE MCCLOSKEY
American Guidance Service

**BEHAVIOR PROBLEM CHECKLIST, REVISED
CHILD BEHAVIOR CHECKLIST**

BUROS, OSCAR K. (1905–1978)

Oscar K. Buros is remembered internationally as the foremost proponent of critical analyses of educational and psychological tests. Buros attended the State Normal School in Superior, Wisconsin, from 1922 to 1924 and completed his undergraduate education at the University of Minnesota in 1925. Buros received his graduate degree from the Teachers College, Columbia University. He accepted a faculty appointment at Rutgers University in 1932 and was a member of that faculty until his retirement in 1965. During World War II, he was in charge of testing for the U.S. Army's specialized training program, and later an adviser on the assessment of leadership at West Point.

He married Luella Gubrud who, an accomplished artist in her own right, later shared with him the responsibilities for the famous *Buros Mental Measurements Yearbook* (MMY) series. It was she who saw the last edition through to its completion following his death on March 19, 1978. Buros published the first *MMY* in 1938. Seven other *Yearbooks* followed, as well as the *Mental Measurements Yearbook* monographs series (1968, 1970, and 1975a–i) and the *Tests in Print* series (1961, 1974).

He was the recipient of many professional honors and awards. Some of these were citations in 1953 from both the American Educational Research Association and the American Psychological Association for excellence in contributions to measurement; a senior Fulbright lectureship in statistics at Makerere University College, Uganda, 1956–1957; the 1965 Phi Delta Kappa research award; and in 1973 both an honorary Doctor of Science degree from Upsala College and the Distinguished Service to Measurement Award from the Educational Testing Service. Buros was a fellow of the American Statistical Association and the American Psychological Association. Rutgers University's Graduate School of Applied and Professional Psychology established a professorship in Buros's honor in 1985.

In 1979, the Buros Institute of Mental Measurements was moved to the University of Nebraska-Lincoln. The institute has continued the Buros tradition by publishing *Tests in Print III* (Mitchell, 1983) and up to twelve *Mental Measurements Yearbooks* (Conoley, Impara & Murphy, 1995).

REFERENCES

Buros, O. K. (1938). *The 1938 mental measurements yearbook*. Highland Park, NJ: Gryphon.

Buros, O. K. (1961). *Tests in print*. Highland Park, NJ: Gryphon.

Buros, O. K. (1968). *Reading tests and reviews I*. Highland Park, NJ: Gryphon.

Buros, O. K. (1970). *Personality tests and reviews I*. Highland Park, NJ: Gryphon.

Buros, O. K. (1974). *Tests in print II*. Highland Park, NJ: Gryphon.

Buros, O. K. (1975a). *Personality tests and reviews II*. Highland Park, NJ: Gryphon.

Buros, O. K. (1975b). *Reading tests and reviews II*. Highland Park, NJ: Gryphon.

Buros, O. K. (1975c). *Intelligence tests and reviews II*. Highland Park, NJ: Gryphon.

Buros, O. K. (1975d). *English tests and reviews*. Highland Park, NJ: Gryphon.

Buros, O. K. (1975e). *Foreign language tests and reviews*. Highland Park, NJ: Gryphon.

Buros, O. K. (1975f). *Mathematics tests and reviews*. Highland Park, NJ: Gryphon.

Buros, O. K. (1975g). *Science tests and reviews*. Highland Park, NJ: Gryphon.

Buros, O. K. (1975h). *Social studies tests reviews*. Highland Park, NJ: Gryphon.

Buros, O. K. (1975i). *Vocational tests and reviews*. Highland Park, NJ: Gryphon.

Conoley, J. C., Impara, J. C. & Murphy L. L. (Eds.). (1995). *The twelfth mental measurements Yearbook*. Lincoln, NE: Buros Institute of Mental Measurements.

Mitchell, J. V. Jr. (1983). *Tests in print III*. Lincoln, NE: Buros Institute of Mental Measurements.

Mitchell, J. V. Jr. (1985). *The ninth mental measurements yearbook*. Lincoln, NE: Buros Institute of Mental Measurements.

JANE CLOSE CONOLEY
University of Nebraska

TESTS IN PRINT

gent consumer choice and use of tests. The most recent *MMY* (Conoley, Impara, & Murphy, 1995) contains descriptive information on new or revised tests, test reviews, extensive listings of test references and reviewer references, several indexes including indexes of test titles, classified subject areas, publishers, scores, and names of test authors and reviewers. In addition, the Buros Library of Mental Measurements provides qualitative reviews on computer-based test interpretation systems (Conoley, Impara, & Murphy, 1995; Plake, Conoley, Kramer, & Murphy, 1989).

The books are published by the Buros Institute of Mental Measurements, located since 1979 at the University of Nebraska, Lincoln, Department of Educational Psychology. The institute, established originally by Oscar K. Buros, has published over 20 volumes (edited by Buros) relating to test description and review.

REFERENCES

Buros, O. K. (1938). *The 1938 mental measurements yearbook*. Highland Park, NJ: Gryphon.

Conoley, J. C., Impara, J. C., & Murphy, L. L. (Eds.). (1995*). The twelfth mental measurements yearbook*. Lincoln, NE: Buros Institute of Mental Measurements.

Plake, B. S., Conoley, J. C., Kramer, J. J., & Murphy, L. L. (1989). Buros bulletin. *Educational Measurement: Issues & Practices, 8,* 20–21.

JANE CLOSE CONOLEY
University of Nebraska
First edition

ELAINE FLETCHER-JANZEN
University of Northern Colorado
Second edition

BUROS, OSCAR K.
TESTS IN PRINT

BUROS MENTAL MEASUREMENTS YEARBOOK

There are twelve *Mental Measurements Yearbooks* (MMYs) The yearbooks, which originated in 1938 (Buros, 1938), provide test users with factual information on all known tests published separately in the English-speaking countries of the world. In addition, the books contain test reviews written by professional people representing a variety of viewpoints. The volumes are also sources of comprehensive bibliographies for specific tests, and references relevant to the tests.

The purpose of all the *MMYs* is to provide a forum in which tests can be reviewed candidly to facilitate intelli-

BURT, SIR CYRIL (1883–1971)

Sir Cyril Burt became the first psychologist in the world to be employed by a school system when he was appointed to the position of psychologist with the London County Council in 1913. Burt's career centered around the application of psychology to the study and education of children. He made pioneering investigations in the areas of mental retardation, delinquency, and the genetics of intelligence, and conducted studies that served as models of the application of the scientific method to the study of human characteristics. Burt developed numerous tests for use by school psychologists and published his influential *Factors of the Mind* in 1941. He was co-editor of the *British Journal of Statistical Psychology*.

From 1931 until his retirement in 1950, Burt was professor of psychology at University College, London, where he devoted most of his attention to the training of psychologists and the continuation of his research and writing. He was knighted in 1946.

Sadly, Burt's work and reputation are marred by recent findings that he deliberately fabricated data in some of his best known studies. These acts of fraud cast doubt on his research findings, but do not erase his great contributions to psychology as a clinician, theoretician, and teacher (Hearnshaw, 1979).

REFERENCES

Burt, C. (1941). *The factors of the mind: An introduction to factor analysis in psychology*. New York: Macmillan.

Hearnshaw, L. S. (1979). *Cyril Burt, psychologist*. Ithaca, NY: Cornell University Press.

PAUL IRVINE
Katonah, New York

C

CAFÉ AU LAIT SPOTS

Café au lait spots are areas of patchy pigmentation of skin, usually light brown in color. They are so-named because of their resemblance in color to coffee with cream. They are of diagnostic significance because they may indicate the presence of serious disease such as neurofibromatosis, polyostotic fibrous dysplasia, or tuberous sclerosis (*Blakiston's*, 1979; Johnson, 1979). Café au lait spots may be found in normal individuals.

When six or more café au lait spots are present and they are larger than 1.5 cm in diameter, neurofibromatosis is suspected (Johnson, 1979). Neurofibromatosis, also known as Von Recklinghausen's disease, is a genetic disorder inherited as an autosomal dominant trait (Batshaw & Perret, 1981). In addition to the presence of café au lait spots, which exist at birth and hence aid in the diagnosis of this condition, other symptoms include multiple skin-colored tumors or nodules and freckles of the axillae (armpits), which represent the Crowe's sign of neurofibromatosis.

Neurofibromatosis may have numerous neurological, psychological, and educational implications. Tumors or neurofibromas typically develop prior to puberty. These tumors may be associated with the spinal or cranial nerves and hence may result in sensory deficits such as visual or hearing impairment. Enlargement and deformation of the bones and scoliosis (curvature of the spine) may occur. Hypertension may be present in young victims of this condition. There is reported to be an increased incidence of mental retardation (Johnson, 1979) and school problems associated with neurofibromatosis (Batshaw & Perret, 1981). In severe cases, the presence of multiple contiguous tumors produces elephantiasis neuromatosa, a cosmetically disfiguring condition. While skin tumors may be removed, there is some evidence these may recur and multiply (*Fact Sheet,* 1983).

In addition to neurofibromatosis, café au lait spots also have been observed in other neurocutaneous syndromes such as tuberous sclerosis (Bourneville's disease) (Rosenberg, 1979). Also inherited as an autosomal dominant trait, tuberous sclerosis is characterized by nevi or moles on the face, epilepsy, and mental retardation (Rosenberg, 1979). The course of tuberous sclerosis begins with the onset of epilepsy and declining mental ability during the first decade, with development of facial lesions around the cheeks and nose several years later (Rosenberg, 1979).

Café au lait spots occurring in the size and number as noted previously are considered diagnostically significant in neurofibromatosis. Ninety percent of afflicted individuals are reported to exhibit them at birth (Johnson, 1979). Because their presence is associated with serious medical conditions such as neurofibromatosis and tuberous sclerosis, identification of numerous café au lait spots in children without medical diagnoses warrants referral to a physician. Educational management of children who have been diagnosed as having neurofibromatosis or tuberous sclerosis should be conducted on an individual basis because the severity and expression of symptoms vary widely.

REFERENCES

Batshaw, M. L., & Perret, Y. M. (1981). *Children with handicaps: A medical primer*. Baltimore, MD: Brookes.

Blakiston's Gould medical dictionary (4th ed.). (1979). New York: McGraw-Hill.

Fact Sheet: Neurofibromatosis. (1983). Bethesda, MD: National Institute of Neurological and Communicative Disorders and Stroke.

Johnson, M. (1979). Certain cutaneous diseases with significant systemic manifestations. In P. B. Beeson, W. McDermott, & J. B. Wyngaarden (Eds.), *Cecil textbook of medicine* (15th ed.) (pp. 2266–2312). Philadelphia: Saunders.

Rosenberg, R. N. (1979). Inherited degenerative diseases of the nervous system. In P. B. Beeson, W. McDermott, & J. B. Wyngaarden (Eds.), *Cecil textbook of medicine* (15th ed.) (pp. 764–772). Philadelphia: Saunders.

CATHY F. TELZROW
*Cuyahoga Special Education
Service Center*

**MINOR PHYSICAL ANOMALIES
NEUROFIBROMATOSIS**

CALDWELL, BETTYE M. (1924–   )

Bettye M. Caldwell received her BA (1945) from Baylor University, her MA (1946) from the University of Iowa, and

Bettye M. Caldwell

her PhD (1951) in psychology from Washington University. Caldwell's career, which has spanned more than 30 years, reflects her interest in early childhood education and development. Currently, she is a Donaghey Distinguished Professor of Education at the University of Arkansas at Little Rock.

Since the late 1960s, when Caldwell was a member of the National Advisory Committee for Research and Evaluation for Project Head Start, she has maintained an interest in the impact of research on social policy. She has devoted her efforts to early intervention programs for very young handicapped children, demonstration daycare centers, and training parents and others who work with young children. By studying the impact of day care on factors such as intellectual and social development and mother-child attachment, Caldwell has shown that day care can have a significant, positive impact on children, especially those from disadvantaged backgrounds (Caldwell, 1977).

One of Caldwell's major research interests has been the measurement of the quality of a child's home environment. The HOME (Home Observation for Measurement of the Environment) Inventory, which resulted from this work, is used worldwide as a measure of the learning environment within the home. Having such information available is vital both for the determination of the extent to which atypical development is due to inadequate or inappropriate environmental stimulation, and for the design of intervention programs (Bradley & Caldwell, 1984).

For the last 9 years, Caldwell has been involved as one of the major investigators in a large, 10-site study concerned with the effects of different patterns of child care during early infancy. She has also developed a unique training program for caregivers in educare settings that integrates knowledge and skills from both nursing and education. The training is based on contemporary research on brain development and early experience. Caregivers are taught to introduce learning activities that will meet the needs of the developing brain at each chronological age pe-

riod and thereby facilitate emotional and cognitive advances in the children.

A leader in her field, Caldwell has been president of the National Association for the Education of Young Children (1982–1984) and editor of the journal *Child Development* (1968–1971). She has served on the editorial board and the board of directors for other journals and organizations. She also has earned international notice, serving as a U.S. delegate to the U.S.S.R. and the People's Republic of China to study early education programs in those countries.

REFERENCES

Bradley, R. H., & Caldwell, B. M. (1984). 174 Children: A study of the relation between home environment and mental development in the first five years. In A. Gottfried (Ed.), *Home environment and early cognitive development* (pp. 5–56). New York: Academic.

Caldwell, B. M. (1977). Child development and social policy. In M. Scott & S. Grimmett (Eds.), *Current issues in child development*. Washington, DC: National Association for the Education of Young Children.

Ann E. Lupkowski
Texas A & M University
First edition

Tamara J. Martin
*The University of Texas of the
Permian Basin*
Second edition

CAMP, BONNIE W. (1931–   )

Bonnie Camp received her BA from Mississippi State College for Women in 1948, and her MA and PhD in clinical psychology from Indiana University in 1954. She went on to receive her MD in 1965 from the University of Colorado School of Medicine and pediatric training from the University of Colorado Health Sciences Center. In 1972, she received a Research Career Award from NIMH for her studies on learning disabilities. She also served on the faculty of Pediatrics and Psychiatry at the University of Colorado School of Medicine, and was director of the JFK Child Development Center at the University of Colorado Health Sciences Center before retiring in 1993.

While employed as a pediatrician in the Denver Health and Hospitals Neighborhood Health Center, Camp organized a tutorial reading program for children with severe reading delay in the center's catchment area using community aides, older students, and volunteers. The program was eventually extended to schools throughout the Denver School District.

Camp is best known for her development of the Think

Aloud Program (Camp & Bash, 1981, 1985; Bash & Camp 1985a, 1985b, 1986). Think Aloud is a cognitive behavior modification program designed to improve social and cognitive problem-solving skills in young children. It was conceived as a training program to decrease impulsivity, encourage consideration of alternatives, and plan a course of action. It emphasizes the use of cognitive modeling as a teaching tool whereby teachers model their own strategies for thinking through problems. Camp is currently professor emeritus of pediatrics and psychiatry at the University of Colorado School of Medicine.

REFERENCES

Camp, B. W. and Bash, M. A. S. (1981). *Think Aloud: Increasing social and cognitive skills—a problem-solving program for children*. Champaign, IL: Research Press.

Camp, B. W. and Bash, M. A. S. (1985). *The Think Aloud Classroom Program for grades 1 and 2*. Champaign, IL: Research Press.

Bash, M. A. S. and Camp, B. W. (1985a). *The Think Aloud Classroom Program for grades 3 and 4*. Champaign, IL: Research Press.

Bash, M. A. S. and Camp, B. W. (1985b). *The Think Aloud Classroom Program for grades 5 and 6*. Champaign, IL: Research Press.

Bash, M. A. and Camp, B. A. Training teachers in the Think Aloud Classroom Program. In G. Cartledge & J. Milburn (Eds.). (1986). *Teaching social skills to children: Innovative approaches*. Pergamon Press.

STAFF

CAMPBELL, SIR FRANCIS JOSEPH (1832–1914)

Francis J. Campbell was born on a farm in Tennessee on October 9, 1832. Blinded in an accident at the age of 3, he was educated at the newly opened Tennessee State Institution for the Blind, where he later served as a teacher of music while studying at the University of Tennessee. Following a period as a student at Harvard University and then as a teacher of the blind in Wisconsin, he became an instructor at Perkins Institution and Massachusetts Asylum for the Blind, where he served for 11 years as head of the music department.

A talented pianist, Campbell left Perkins to continue his music education in Europe and to study methods of teaching the blind. While in London he met Thomas Rhodes Armitage, a blind physician who had just completed joining together Britain's numerous organizations for the blind into a federation that ultimately became known as the Royal National Institute for the Blind.

Campbell's account of the large number of students at

Perkins whom he had helped prepare for successful careers as professional musicians led Armitage to establish a music school to train blind children, with Campbell as headmaster. Starting in 1872 with two students, the school ultimately became the Royal Normal College and Academy of Music, with an enrollment, by 1885, of 170 students. Campbell's original faculty included a number of teachers from Perkins, and through the years he maintained a continuing exchange of teachers with Perkins and other schools in the United States. As a result, the Royal Normal College and Academy of Music probably had more influence on American teaching methods than any other foreign school. The institution, under Campbell, combined general education and physical training with careful vocational preparation, job placement, and follow-up after graduation. Between 80 and 90% of the graduates became self-supporting, mostly as musicians, teachers, and technicians trained in piano tuning and repair. This unprecedented achievement stimulated an emphasis on vocational preparation in schools for the blind throughout the world.

Campbell believed strongly in the value of physical exercise, and took great pride in his own physical prowess— he once scaled the formidable Mont Blanc, a feat that he considered one of the crowning achievements of his life. He viewed physical training as an essential ingredient in any educational program preparing the blind for active and productive lives and developed an extensive physical education program that greatly influenced other schools for the blind.

In recognition of his work on behalf of the blind, Campbell was knighted by King Edward VII in 1909. Campbell retired as headmaster in 1912. He died on June 30, 1914.

Sir Francis Joseph Campbell

REFERENCES

Koestler, F. A. (1976). *The unseen minority: A social history of blindness in America*. New York: McKay.

Ross, I. (1951). *Journey into light*. New York: Appleton-Century-Crofts.

PAUL IRVINE
Katonah, New York

CAMPHILL COMMUNITY MOVEMENT

The Camphill Community (movement) was founded by Karl Koenig (1902–1966) after he fled the Nazi powers of central Europe in 1939. The name Camphill refers to the group's first house in Aberdeen, Scotland (Baron & Haldane, 1991).

The Camphill Community is based on the writings of Rudolph Steiner (1861–1925). It works for a full understanding of people's spiritual being, eternal purpose, and earthly tasks. The goals of Steiner's work (known as anthroposophy) include allowing all human beings, handicapped or not, to develop to their potential and to find a productive place in society. The fostering and development of individual human dignity is of paramount importance.

Camphill villages are currently found in 11 countries, with 5 in the United States. Despite minor differences, village life centers around the family, community, and productive, meaningful work. The family typically consists of parents, children, and a number of mentally handicapped individuals living and working together, free from labels and distinctions. Mutual responsibility is stressed; no salaries are paid but individuals have their needs met by the community.

The Camphill Special School, Glenmoore, Pennsylvania, currently serves 72 children from elementary through high school age. Its program complements the philosophies of the larger Camphill Community and provides the "structure, rhythm, regularity, and consistency" needed for curative education. Each child works from an individual education program based on an adaptation of the Waldorf School movement. The education of the whole child is stressed; specific therapies (painting, speech, medicine, music) are provided depending on need. Older students are prepared vocationally for life after graduation through training in groundskeeping, woodwork, and household activities.

A 4-year training seminar is currently offered in the Beaver Run, Pennsylvania school. It is designed to train the individual in curative education using the Waldorf curriculum, as well as in all aspects of community living in the Camphill tradition.

Persons interested in joining or learning more about the Camphill communities are encouraged to contact them directly.

Camphill Special Schools Beaver Run Glenmore, PA 19343	Camphill Village USA Copake, NY 12516
Camphill Village USA Kimberton Hills PO Box 155 Kimberton, PA 19442	Camphill Village Minnesota Route 3 PO Box 249 Sauk Centre, MN 56378

REFERENCES

Baron, S., & Haldane, D. (1991). Approaching Camphill: From the boundary. *British Journal of Special Education, 18*, 2, 75–78.

JOHN E. PORCELLA
Rhinebeck Country School

CAMPING FOR THE HANDICAPPED

Camping for the handicapped is divided into two types—individual and organized camping. The camping areas used for individualized camping are either in developed or wilderness states. Developed campsites are usually near conveniences that facilitate their use by handicapped campers, e.g., they offer amenities such as tent pads, electrical and water outlets, and restroom facilities. Their nature paths are wide and smooth to facilitate travel for children and youths who are wheelchair-bound or impaired in motor functioning (Gerstein, 1992; Sessoms, 1984).

Wilderness campgrounds have cruder facilities and fewer activity programs for the handicapped than developed camping areas. Most are designed for a low level of human use. They lack conveniences such as smooth paths and picnic facilities. As a rule, they are considered closed to the physically handicapped, though there are no limitations to all other persons.

Organized camping has been defined as the merging of outdoor recreation and education in a campsite setting (Sessoms, 1984). Organized camping is carried out on day and residential bases. Activities at organized camps for the handicapped range from general activities (such as sports and games, hobbies, arts and crafts, and drama) to special-purpose activities such as computer training and weight control. Such camps are also likely to emphasize education and rehabilitation (Wiseman, 1982). Major emphases in organized camps are to foster socialization skills, the acceptance of responsibilities, and the learning of leisure skills, and to facilitate living in communal atmospheres.

Organized camping programs for the handicapped are sponsored by the following types of agencies: (1) private or commercial campers agencies, whose fees come from their clients; (2) quasipublic agencies, some of whose funds come from donations and endowments, while the balance is paid by the participants, e.g., Easter Seals and American Red Cross camps; and (3) public-camping programs supported and sponsored by either local or municipal parks and recreation systems, or by organizations serving the handicapped and parent groups.

Four different types of organized camping programs for the handicapped may be distinguished. One type is camps that are located within communities where campers participate on a daily basis; these have accessible toilets, play, and eating areas. Another type is resident camps for the handicapped. These have cabins, dining halls, staff quarters, and indoor and outdoor recreation facilities. Their sessions last from 1 to 8 weeks. A third type is combination resident and daycamping opportunities that permit some campers to attend daily while others remain overnight. Finally, there are special purpose camps that promote a single concept or activity such as a specific sport or religion (Wiseman, 1982).

Since 1975, some programs have adopted noncategorical approaches, i.e., involving all handicapped campers in a normalized integrated camp program. Handicapped campers are evaluated for an integrated camping program on the basis of their level of functioning in camp activities. The handicapped camper is placed in integrative, halfway, or special groups in such integrated camps depending on his or her capabilities.

In integrative camping, handicapped campers participate in all activities together with able-bodied campers. Handicapped campers in the halfway group may have the potential for regular group participation but still lack some ability to fully engage in activities. Usually, they engage in the same activities as the regular group and share the same facilities, but they do so separately (Sessoms, 1984).

Handicapped campers in the special group require a segregated and supervised program because of the severity and complexity of their condition. All camping activities are modified to the capabilities and interests of this group.

REFERENCES

American Camping Association standards for persons with special needs (Part IIC). (1980). Martinsville, IN: Bradford Woods.

Choosing a summer camp. (1985). *Exceptional Children, 14*(3), 37–39.

Gerstein, J. (1992). *Direction of experiential therapy and adventure-based counseling programs.* (ERIC Clearinghouse No. ED39 80 21)

Physical Education for the Handicapped. (1982). *Involving impaired and handicapped persons in regular camp programs.* Washington, DC: IRUC.

Sessoms, H. (1984). *Leisure services* (3rd ed.). Englewood Cliffs, NJ: Prentice-Hall.

Wiseman, D. (1982). *A practical approach to adapted physical education.* Reading, MA: Addison-Wesley.

THOMAS BURKE
Hunter College

EQUINE THERAPY
RECREATIONAL THERAPY

CANADA, SPECIAL EDUCATION IN

Canada is one of the few countries in the world that does not have a national education system; education is the exclusive jurisdiction of the 10 provinces and 2 territories[1] that make up the country. The only common vehicle that exists to discuss educational policy at the national level is the Council of Ministers of Education, Canada;[2] however, this body serves only as a mechanism to discuss issues of concern to the provinces and territories as it has no regulatory power over special education. The lack of a Canadian office of education results in considerable diversity in the organization and governance of special education across the country.

Within each province and territory, there is, in most cases, a provincial or territorial act designed to regulate education. This legislation is broad in scope and typically includes such things as the definitions of responsibilities for personnel associated with educational delivery, the organization and structure of schools and their governing bodies, and policies regarding fiscal matters. The result is that education differs from province/territory to province/territory. Special education is subsumed under the various political jurisdictions, and its profile in each province/territory varies as a function of the current legislation and policies that are in place, the financial resources committed to service provision, and regional priorities. In sum, there is no Canadian picture of special education; rather, there is a kaleidoscope of legislation, policy, and practice that varies across the country.

A combination of geographical and language factors continue to influence special education in Canada (Hutchinson & Wong, 1987). The majority of Canada's population is concentrated in the southern portion of the country, which results in a reasonable efficient pool of services for the majority of the population, which tends to be clustered in urban areas. Using geography as a framework, however, providing special education services for the minority of the population is both costly and inefficient. For example, there are several areas of the country where school authorities serve a sparse population spread over several hundred miles. Within such a service area there may be only a few people who require special education support service; however, they may be located in opposite ends of the catchment area. This geographic spread might be further complicated by the language(s) spoken and by an increasing cultural diversity. In addition to the two national official languages (English and French), a growing number of individuals have another native language and speak English or French only secondly or thirdly. There also are areas of the country where the majority cultural group is, for example, Indo-Canadian or Inuit. The change in cultural diversity is not limited to the sparsely populated regions of the country; because of immigration, English has now been reduced to a minority language status in Vancouver and Richmond, British Columbia ("English," 1998). The end result of this amalgamation is that service providers must be aware of diverse cultural values and be sensitive to the possibility that different languages are spoken at home, at school, and in the community, while providing the required services at a reasonable cost in an era of diminished fiscal resources.

The history of special education in Canada was described as follows by Hutchinson and Wong (1987).

1. Until 1969, special education developed more rapidly in larger cities than in rural communities; however, there was considerable interprovincial/interterroritial variation in service provision.

2. As of 1969, there were offices of special education in half of the provincial Ministries or Departments of Education, with approximately 3% of school-aged students receiving special education services.

3. From 1969 to 1972, special education developed rapidly, with seven provinces (British Columbia, Alberta, Saskatchewan, Manitoba, Ontario, Quebec, and Newfoundland) advancing new or revised legislation or policy and the remainder committing to change their special education legislation or policy.

4. An important trend during 1969 to 1972 was increasing concern over finding alternatives to special class placement and the beginning of service provision, through integration, in regular classrooms.

5. During the early to mid-1970s, two key reports were issued. First came the Standards for Educators of Exceptional Children (Hardy, McLeod, Minto, Perkins, & Quance, 1971), in which both a set of minimum standards and a model of training for teachers of exceptional children were advanced, which were translated in provincial and territorial guidelines. Second, a committee of the Council for Exceptional Children in Canada (Treherne, Dice, Grigg, & Sanche, 1974) prepared a report that advanced principles to govern legislation for children with special needs, which had a variable degree influence over the legislation proposed in different provinces/territories.

6. During the mid-1980s, it was estimated that 12% of the school population required special education; however, the accuracy of this estimation was questioned since there was no national office of education in Canada and provinces reported incidence data differently. By this time, every province had published legislation, regulations, policies, and/or guidelines for special education. The predominant models of service delivery were adapted from the United States and ranged from segregation to integration.

During the mid to late 1980s, the trends established during the middle of the decade continued; however, some new significant Canadian developments occurred as well. One of the most significant influences on Canadian special education was introduced in 1982. The full impact of the Canadian Charter of Rights and Freedoms (1982), however, was not felt by special educators until Section 15 was implemented in 1985 (MacKay, 1987). Section 15 of the Charter contained this key clause: "Every individual is equal before and under the law and has the right to the equal protection and equal benefit of the law with discrimination and, in particular, without discrimination based on race, national or ethnic origin, colour, religion, sex, age, or mental or physical disability." MacKay noted that Section 15 could provide the legal grounds on which to request the provision of well-funded special education programs and to challenge the segregation of children. Provinces/territories, however, can sidestep the implications of the Charter by invoking the "notwithstanding" clause, declaring that the education statute operates notwithstanding the Charter. There were also shifts in the preparation of materials to prepare special educators that had a Canadian flavor. For the first time, Canadian special educators introduced professional texts that initially were adaptations of work published in the United States (for example, Hammill, Bartel, & Bunch, 1984) but subsequently were written specifically for Canadian audiences (for example, Bachor & Crealock, 1986). This trend has continued with both adapted (Friend, Bursuck, & Hutchinson, 1998) and unique texts (for example, Andrews & Lupart, 1993; Crealock & Bachor, 1995) continuing to be published.

During this period, policies and practices established in the United States and (to a lesser extent) Europe, continued to influence service delivery models adopted in Canada as well. One notable example was the regular education initiative which led to the introduction of the full-service school (school-based service provision). Further, partly as a result of a British influence, Canadian schools have changed to school-based management, which has resulted in increased parental advocacy for all children and, in some provinces, the establishment of parent advisory councils. Deinstitutionalization gained momentum with the closure of provincial schools for the deaf and/or blind, with services being shifted to local school jurisdictions and of provincial institutions for the mentally disabled, and with accommodation and services being provided in the local community through group homes.

During the 1990s, the dominant theme in special education at the school level has been the evolution of services known as inclusion, in which most students remain in the regular classroom. Current policies across the country have been designed to support inclusion. For example, the policy of the Northwest Territories includes the following statement: "Inclusive schooling is both a philosophy and a practice. However, including all students in regular classrooms with their age peers, and responding to individual needs and strengths, requires a number of conditions and practices. . . ." A listing of territorial, regional, and school-based requirements for inclusion is given in the policy. (Northwest Territories, Department of Education, Culture, and Employment, 1998). As a consequence, the regular classroom has become the home base of most children and adolescents with special needs, and curriculum adaptations are made if required. Given this trend, it is not possible to estimate realistically the percentage of individuals with special educational needs being served in total; however, about 1 to 3 percent of students are still being provided services within non-graded special education classrooms.

Within the community, an important change that has been taking place over the last five to eight years is an increase in transportation options and environmental accessibility. Notable examples are the emergence of a paratransit systems such as minibuses that are wheelchair accessible; modifications in sidewalk curbs by rounding them so that they are accessible to wheelchairs, and the introduction of sound-signal cues at traffic lights for the visually impaired. Finally, increasingly sophisticated assistive technology—such as high-speed computers with voice input, adapted keyboards allowing individuals to attain full employment, and specialized telephone systems to facilitate communication—has become available, which has resulted in increased accessibility for individuals with special needs. Each of these shifts at the school and community levels needs to be tempered by the emergence of conservative budget policies by provincial/territorial governments. This fiscal policy has meant that the major priority has been on balanced budgets, and all service provision within the school system and the community has been judged against this budgetary standard.

As the 21st century approaches, the scope and substance of special education in Canada has changed substantially, and likely will continue to reform in at least two ways. First, special education no longer applies to school-aged children exclusively. It has been expanded to include services for younger children and to respond to meeting the needs of adults. Second, the substance of special education is being expanded to address a wider mandate of social and economic issues that affect the quality of life of both children and adults with special needs. As noted above, however, this expanded mandate comes in a period of fiscal conservatism and the impact on social services generally and on service provision for people with various challenges is unknown.

NOTES

[1]The provinces in Canada from east to west are Newfoundland and Labrador, Prince Edward Island, Nova Scotia, New Brunswick, Quebec, Ontario, Manitoba, Saskatchewan, Alberta, and British Columbia. Currently there are two Canadian territories, from west to east the Yukon and the Northwest Territories. It should be noted, however, that in 1993, there was an agreement passed to separate the Northwest Territories (NWT) into two independent jurisdictions. This agreement will come into effect on April 1, 1999. The new territories are Nunavut and an as yet unnamed western section of NWT, now the Mackenize Delta area.

[2]This Canadian federal agency has its own webpage and can be found at http://www.cmec.ca/ in both English and French.

REFERENCES

Andrews, J. & Lupart, J. (Eds.). (1993). *The Inclusive Classroom: Educating Exceptional Children* (pp. 293–329). Toronto: Nelson Canada.

Bachor, D. & Crealock, C. (1986). *Instructional strategies for students with special needs*. Scarborough, Ontario: Prentice Hall, Canada.

Canadian Charter of Rights and Freedoms. (1982). Schedule B of *Canada Act*, 1982 (U.K.) c. 11 (1982).

Crealock, C. & Bachor, D. (1995). *Instructional strategies for students with special needs* (2nd ed.). Scarborough, Ontario: Allyn and Bacon.

English now minority tongue. (1998, March 3). *The Globe and Mail*, p. A3.

Friend, M., Bursuck, W., & Hutchinson, N. (1998). Including exceptional students: A practical guide for classroom teachers (Canadian ed.). Scarborough, Ontario: Prentice Hall, Canada.

Hardy, M., McLeod, J., Minto, H., Perkins, S., & Quance, W. (1971). *Standards for Educators of Exceptional Children*. Toronto: Crainford.

Hammill, D. D., Bartel, N. R., & Bunch, G. O. (Eds.). (1984). *Teaching children with learning and behavior problems* (Canadian ed.). Toronto: Allyn & Bacon.

Hutchinson, N. L., & Wong, B. (1987). Special education in Canada. In C. R. Reynolds & L. Mann (Eds.), *Encyclopedia of special education: A reference for the education of the handicapped and other exceptional children and adults*. New York: Wiley.

MacKay, A. W. (1987). The charter of rights and special education: Blessing or curse? *Canadian Journal for Exceptional Children, 3*, 118–127.

Northwest Territories, Department of Education, Culture, and Employment. Inclusive schooling. http://siksik.learnnet.nt.ca/DOCS/juniorHandbook/InclusiveSchooling.html, retrieved March 11, 1998.

Treherne, D., Dice, T. L., Grigg, E. E., & Sanche, R. P. (1974). *A matter of principle: Standards governing legislation for services for children with special needs.* Regina, Saskatchewan: Council for Exceptional Children.

DAN G. BACHOR
University of Victoria

HUMANISTIC SPECIAL EDUCATION
POLITICS AND SPECIAL EDUCATION

CANCER, CHILDHOOD

Cancer is actually a group of diseases. It originates from a single malignant cell that has potentially unlimited growth. In cancer, the malignant cells invade noncancerous parts of the body in a systematic way, changing normal cells so that they lose control of their own growth processes and themselves become cancerous. This process is called metastasis. Injury or destruction of normal cells is a consequence (Pendergrass, Chard, & Hartmann, 1985). As the growth of cancer proceeds, cells sometimes break away from the original concentration of malignant cells to be carried to other parts of the body, which then also become cancerous. Cancerous symptoms appear because of the injury to or destruction of normal cells. The symptoms are frequently subtle, particularly during initial stages.

Cancer is a leading cause of mortality in children between the ages of 1 and 15 years, exceeded only by accidents as a cause of death in this age group. The incidence is 130 cases for each 1 million children who are under the age of 15. Approximately 40% of these cases will be leukemia.

The medical treatment of cancer involves radiation, chemotherapy, and—rarely in children—surgery. The treatment often causes weight loss, fatigue, nausea, and emotional distress, among other significant problems (Link, 1982). The physical discomfort suffered by the child and the resulting irritability require extremely sensitive attitudes on the part of teachers. Additionally, the disease, both in its manifestations and the time required to treat it, may result in lost time from school or instruction (Armstrong & Horn, 1995; Bigge & Sirvis, 1986).

Children who have cancer are likely to be referred for instruction and related services of a special education nature when they are unable to deal with the demands of regular school work. Under the guidelines established by IDEA they would receive these under the category of health impairments and would partake of inclusionary services as much as they are able (Peckham, 1993).

REFERENCES

Armstrong, D. F., & Horn, M. (1995). Educational issues in childhood cancer. *School Psychology Quarterly, 10,* 4, 292–304.

Bigge, J., & Sirvis, B. (1986). Physical and health impairments. In N. G. Haring & L. McCormick (Eds.), *Exceptional children and youth* (4th ed.). Columbus, OH: Merrill.

Link, M. P. (1982). Cancer in childhood. In E. E. Bleck & D. A. Nagel (Eds.), *Physically handicapped children: A medical atlas for teachers* (2nd ed.) (pp. 121–144). New York: Grune & Stratton.

Peckham, V. C. (1993). Children with cancer in the classroom. *Teaching Exceptional Children, 26,* 1, 26–32.

Pendergrass, T. W., Chard, R. L., & Hartmann, J. R. (1985). Leukemia. In N. Hobbs & J. M. Perrin (Eds.), *Issues in the care of children with chronic illness* (pp. 324–343). San Francisco: Jossey-Bass.

DON BRASWELL
*Research Foundation, City
University of New York*

CHEMOTHERAPY
CHRONIC ILLNESS

CANTRELL, ROBERT P. (1938–)

Robert P. Cantrell received his BA (1960) and MA (1962) in psychology from Baylor University. He received his PhD in 1969 from George Peabody College for Teachers with a major in experimental child psychology and a minor in special

Robert P. Cantrell

education. Since 1980, he has been an adjunct professor in the department of special education, Kent State University, an adjunct professor in the department of specialized instructional programs, Cleveland State University, the codirector of the Institute for Ecological Study of Children and Youth, and the director of research, Positive Education Program, Cleveland, Ohio. He has remained at the Positive Education Program, and is currently a Research Fellow with them.

Early experiences as a psychologist on a special education diagnostic team taught him that teachers of special children demand practical solutions to their special teaching problems. Partly from these experiences, he became an advocate of a heuristic, ecological system of problem solving (Cantrell & Cantrell, 1977). Although many professionals learn over time to develop solutions to these practical problems, he recognized that there are inadequate means by which we transmit this knowledge of effective intervention strategies to the next generation of professionals.

Cantrell has worked towards the identification of intervention strategies that produce the most efficient and effective changes in the ecologies of behavior-disordered children (Cantrell & Cantrell, 1980) and continues to focus much of his research on the analysis of and interventions with troubled behavioral ecologies. His most recent published work describes an ecological treatment program for emotionally or behaviorally disordered children, with the goal of creating "a single, coordinated system of care of each child and family" (Cantrell, Cantrell, & Smith, 1998).

REFERENCES

Cantrell, M. L., Cantrell, R. P., & Smith, D. A. (1998). Coordinating care through connections' liaison staff: Services, costs, and outcomes. In M. Epstein & K. Kutash (Eds.), *Outcomes for children and youth with emotional and behavioral disorders and their families: Programs and evaluation best practices* (pp. 205–229). Austin, TX: Pro-Ed.

Cantrell, R. P., & Cantrell, M. L. (1977). Evaluation of a heuristic approach to solving children's problems. *Peabody Journal of Education, 54*(3), 168–173.

Cantrell, R. P., & Cantrell, M. L. (1980). Ecological problem solving: A decision-making heuristic for prevention-intervention education strategies. In J. Hogg & P. Mittler (Eds.), *Advances in mental handicap research* (Vol. 1). New York: Wiley.

E. VALERIE HEWITT
Texas A & M University
First edition

KAY E. KETZENBERGER
*The University of Texas of the
Permian Basin*
Second edition

CARDIAC DISORDERS

Congenital cardiac disorders, with their subsequent physical impairments, constitute some of the most common and serious childhood illnesses. Congenital cardiac disorders are those in which defects in the structure of the heart and/or great vessels alter the normal flow of blood through the cardiorespiratory system. Whaley and Wong (1983) report the incidence of congenital heart disease to occur in approximately 8/1000 to 10/1000 live births. They also report that congenital anomalies are the major cause of death outside of prematurity. However, with the evolution of palliative and varied surgical techniques, the percentage of those infants who survive cardiac malformations/lesions in the neonatal period has dramatically increased; therefore, serious complex defects currently account for a large number of individuals passing through infancy and childhood into full maturity (Nelson, Behrman, & Vaughn, 1983). Surgically corrected congenital defects constitute the largest group of those surviving until adulthood.

The cause of congenital cardiac anomalies is still relatively unknown at this time; however multifactorial patterns have been associated with an increased incidence of the disease. The following prenatal factors have been identified as having causal relationships of varying degrees: maternal rubella infection and other viruses such as cytomegalovirus, coxsackle virus B, and nerpesvirus nomines B (Nelson, Behrman, & Vaughn, 1983; Nora, 1971); poor maternal nutrition (Reeder, Mastroianni, & Martin, 1983); alcohol, dextroamphelamine, lithium chloride, progesterine/estrogen, and warafin, which are suspected teratogenic agents, as well as maternal overexposure to radiation (Taybi, 1971).

Genetic factors have also been associated with an increased incidence of cardiac disorders. Those parents who already have a child with a cardiac defect have a higher incidence of a second child with a cardiac malformation than parents with an unaffected child (King, 1975). Although this incidence is higher than the general population, it is still quite low (2 to 5%) (King, 1975, p. 87; Nelson, et al., 1983, p. 1121). Other factors predisposing children to congenital heart disease are parents who have congenital cardiac disease themselves or chromosomal aberrations such as Down's syndrome and/or other noncardiac anomalies. Rowe and Uchida (1961) found that between 30 and 40% of all children with Down's syndrome have heart defects of some kind.

The general signs and symptoms associated with congenital cardiac defects in children have been outlined by Miller (1985): (1) dyspnea, especially on exertion; (2) feeding difficulties or a general failure to thrive; (3) stridor or choking spells; (4) increased heart and respiratory rate (tachypnea) with retractions when the ribs show with each breath; (5) numerous respiratory tract infections; (6) in older children, delayed or poor physical and/or mental development with a decreased exercise tolerance; (7) cyanosis, posturing (particularly a squatting position and clubbing of fingers and toes); (8) heart murmurs; and (9) dyaphoresis.

Cardiac lesions have been classified into two broad categories: acyanotic and cyanotic. "Acyanotic defects are those in which the blood flows from the arterial (left, oxygenated) side of the heart to the venous (right, deoxygenated) side as a result of a connection between the two sides and/or from a pressure gradient (left-to-right shunt)" (Carroll-Johnson & Neal, 1985, p. 605). Most acyanotic disorders are asymptomatic. There are six acyanotic defects demonstrating the left to right shunting of blood. The blood flows from the left ventricle to the right ventricle, where it mixes with venous blood with ventricular-septal defects (VSD). Watson (1968) has cited ventricular-septal defects as the most common cause of cardiac mortality. Atrial-septal defects (ASD) have blood flowing from the left atrium to the right atrium, then through the right ventricle before moving into the pulmonary artery and pulmonary circulation. Patent ductus arteriosus (PDA) is signified when the ductus arteriosus, which normally closes after birth, remains patent, thus recirculating blood repeatedly through the lungs, and, in essence, overoxygenating the blood. The fourth acyanotic lesion is a coarctation of the aorta. Narrowing of the aorta in this lesion manifests itself with an increased blood pressure in the upper extremities with a reciprocal decrease in pressure in the systemic circulation. Aortic stenosis is the narrowing or general inflexibility of the aortic valve, which increases the workload of the left ventricle with subsequent left ventricular hypertrophy resulting. Pulmonary stenosis in a like manner is the narrowing of the pulmonary valve. However, this narrowing results in decreased blood flow to the lungs and an increase in right ventricular pressure.

There are four cyanotic defects, with the outstanding clinical feature being cyanosis. The tetralogy of Fallot, with its four associated defects, has been described by Sacksteder, Gildea, and Dassy (1978, p. 267) as "(1) a large membranous ventricular septal defect; (2) right ventricular outflow obstruction; (3) right ventricular hypertrophy; and (4) dextroposition or overriding of the aorta." The outstanding clinical feature is cyanosis, along with associated features such as clubbing of nailbeds and squatting posture.

In addition to the tetralogy of Fallot, transposition of the great arteries is another cyanotic disorder. In this instance, the aorta arises from the right ventricle and the pulmonary artery from the left ventricle. Hence, two parallel and separate circulatory systems exist, one pulmonary and one systemic. This condition is incompatible with life unless coexisting lesions allow a mixture of blood to sustain life until the heart can be surgically repaired (Sacksteder, Gildea, and Dassy, 1978, p. 266).

The type of medical intervention or surgical treatment required for congenital heart disease depends on the type or severity of the cardiac lesion. The majority of children with mild congenital heart disease require no treatment. Children with severe heart defects may develop congestive heart failure, which is frequently treated with a cardiac glycoside (digoxin) and furesmide (lasix). Selective palliative surgical procedures may be done to improve oxygenation temporarily until the child grows. Total correction of the heart defect is usually postponed until the benefits of surgery outweigh the risks, or until the child is between the ages of 3 and 5 years (Rowe, 1978).

Parents of children with congenital heart defects are encouraged to treat their children normally. In all but the most severe cases (Morris 1993), a normal life can be expected. Restriction of the child's activities is rarely suggested, but it is often implemented as a control measure by parents. Discipline problems are common, and sibling rivalry is seen frequently because of the attention given the child with the cardiac disorder by parents, health care workers, and educators. The best means of avoiding overprotection of the child is to have a functional knowledge of the child's unique disorder. Overprotection frequently results in increased anxiety in the child and interferes with a normal lifestyle. Parents are recommended to manage their child's heart condition by providing a well-balanced diet, prevention of anemia, and the usual childhood immunizations.

Those children whose lesions are moderate to severe need not severely restrict their activities. Nelson, Behrman, and Vaughn (1983, p. 1167) suggest merely tailoring the child's activities to his or her ability to participate; however, rough competitive contact sports should be avoided. Generally, the child will establish his or her own limits. Nelson et al. (1983) also suggests that transportation to and from school may help school performance by eliminating excessive fatigue.

Additional, but imperative, guidelines for all children with cardiac lesions include treating bacterial infections vigorously but not prophylactically to prevent infective endocarditis. Specifically, cyanotic children should be alert for dehydration and iron deficiencies, which may interfere with activity tolerance. As maturity is achieved, women should be counseled regarding the risks of childbearing and the use of contraceptives.

REFERENCES

Carroll-Johnson, R. M., & Neal, M. C. (Eds.). (1985). *American Journal of Nursing, 1985 nursing boards review* (pp. 605–607). Pacific Palisades, CA: Nurseco.

King, O. M. (Ed.). (1975). *Care of the cardiac surgical patient*. St. Louis: Mosby.

Miller, A. (Ed.). (1985). *Mosby's comprehensive review of nursing* (11th ed.) (pp. 400–405). St. Louis: Mosby.

Morris, R. D. (1993). Neuropsychological, academic, and adoptive functioning in children who survive in-hospital cardiac arrest and resuscitation. *Journal of hearing Disabilities, 26*, 1, 46–51.

Nelson, W. E., Behrman, R. E., & Vaughn, V. C. (Eds.). (1983). *Textbook of pediatrics* (12th ed.) (pp. 1121–1167). Philadelphia: Saunders.

Nora, J. J. (1971). Etiologic factors in congenital heart diseases. In S. Kaplin (Ed.), *Pediatric clinics of North America* (Vol. 18, pp. 1059–1074). Philadelphia: Saunders.

Reeder, S. J., Mastroianni, L., & Martin, L. (Eds.). (1983). *Maternity nursing* (15th ed.). Philadelphia: Lippincott.

Rowe, R. D. (1978). Patent ductus arteriosus. In J. Keith, R. Rowe, & R. Vlad (Eds.), *Heart disease in infancy and children* (3rd ed.). New York: Macmillan.

Rowe, R. D., & Uchida, I. A. (1961). Cardiac malformation in mongolism: A prospective study of 184 mongoloid children. *American Journal of Medicine, 31*, 726–735.

Sacksteder, S., Gildea, J. H., & Dassy, C. (1978, February). Common congenital cardiac defects. *American Journal of Nursing*, 266–272.

Taybi, H. (1971). Roentgen evaluation of cardiomegaly in the newborn period and early infancy. In S. Kaplin (Ed.), *Pediatric clinics of North America, 18*(4), 1031–1058. Philadelphia: Saunders.

Watson, H. (Ed.). (1968). *Pediatric cardiology*. London: Lloyd-Luke.

Whaley, L. F., & Wong, D. L. (1983). The child with heart disease. In L. F. Whaley & D. L. Wong (Eds.), *Nursing care of infants and children* (2nd ed.) (pp. 1279–1337). St. Louis: Mosby.

MARY CLARE WILLIAMS
Ramey, Pennsylvania

PHYSICAL EDUCATION OF THE HANDICAPPED
PHYSICAL HANDICAPS

CAREER EDUCATION FOR THE HANDICAPPED

Career education is a comprehensive educational program aimed beyond work. It includes the whole person, who functions in a society in a variety of roles such as citizen, family member, student, and advocate (Kokaska, 1980). Career education is often thought of as an introduction to vocational education. In context, it is much broader than vocational education. This comprehensive and functional orientation in career education has received wide acceptance as a major curricular emphasis in special education (Clark, 1980).

Career education is divided into three phases: elementary career awareness, junior high or middle school career exploration, and high school and postsecondary career preparation (Phelps & Lutz, 1977). Career awareness can begin in the earliest years of schooling using the young child's curiosity for the adult world. It focuses on the various ways people work. At this level, children are exposed to a wide variety of vocations, the work ethic, and self-awareness. Phelps and Lutz (1977) characterize this phase as relying heavily on basic academic skills. Each successive phase shifts from a classroom orientation and basic skills to simulations and practical natural experiences. Yet each phase of the career education sequence emphasizes communication skills, language, computation, and socialization.

The next phase of career education, career exploration, provides opportunities to explore the world of work with simulated and hands-on experiences. Students learn work values and personal values through activities that give them a taste of the work environment. Career preparation often begins at the high school level in vocational programs or as a preparation for postsecondary training in a university, vocational-technical school, or on-the-job training program. Kokaska (1980) added career placement as a fourth phase, but also emphasized that each phase can and does continue throughout life. A handicapped person can be working at one job while continuing education and exploring another field of possible employment.

There are three major elements within each phase of career education: the school, the family, and community experiences. Career education creates and uses educational experiences in the community, business and industry, the family, and the school for each phase and level in career education sequence. The list of potential sources of assistance and experiences is extensive (Brolin & Kokaska, 1979). This functional, community-based educational emphasis forms the foundation for programs for severely handicapped individuals (Wilcox & Bellamy, 1982).

The infusion of career education into the curriculum creates a systematic curriculum organized through the postsecondary levels that emphasizes process rather than content Miller and Schloss (1982) believe that the integrated curriculum enhances the likelihood that instructional goals will be achieved and maintained.

A major question in designing curriculum in career education programs is, "What skills are essential to the individual to make him a more effective person?" (Brolin & Kokaska, 1979, p. 106). Boyan (1980) poses two questions in developing career education curriculum, "Where will the student live when he or she finishes schooling?" and "Where will he or she work?" From these questions the following curriculum outline is generated for the moderately handicapped:

Personal hygiene and grooming

Care and selection of clothing

Health and safety practices

Cooking, meal planning, and related kitchen skills

Home management and housekeeping

Socialization skills (manners and interpersonal relations)

Eating habits

Use of the telephone

Leisure-time skills

Physical training and sensory-motor integration (including regular exercise)

Language

Reading and writing for survival

Math/money skills

Time telling

Mobility in the community

Shopping

Use of community resources and public facilities

Family life education

Specific occupational skills

Brolin and Kokaska (1979) identified 22 career education competencies in three major clusters: daily living skills, personal/social skills, and occupational guidance and preparation. It is reported that these competencies represent the major goals and outcomes that should be completed by students if they are to be successful in community life. Although many local school jurisdictions create their own career counseling programs, successful programs such as "Pathways" (Hutchinson and Freeman, cited in Hutchinson, 1995) are recommended because outcomes for special education students have already been established (Hutchinson, 1995).

Career education is a concept that provides an alternative curricular orientation for educating handicapped students. While encompassing all of the basic skills, social skills, and content areas, it provides a functional, practical, and still holistic orientation to developing curriculum and instruction for handicapped students. It is much more than the mere preparation for vocational training. Career education is general curriculum development orientation that holds great promise for not only secondary aged and postsecondary handicapped students, but all handicapped individuals.

REFERENCES

Boyan, C. (1980). Curriculum considerations in career education for moderately handicapped. In G. M. Clark & W. J. White (Eds.), *Career education for the handicapped: Current perspectives for teachers*. Boothwyn, PA: Educational Resources Center.

Brolin, D. E., & Kokaska, C. J. (1979). *Career education for handicapped children and youth*. Columbus, OH: Merrill.

Clark, G. M. (1980). Career education: A concept. In G. M. Clark & W. J. White (Eds.), *Career education for the handicapped: Current perspectives for teachers*. Boothwyn, PA: Educational Resources Center.

Hutchinson, N. L. (1995). *Career counseling of youth with learning disabilities*. (ERIC Digest No. ED 400470)

Kokaska, C. J. (1980). A curriculum model for career education. In G. M. Clark & W. J. White (Eds.), *Career education for the handicapped: Current perspectives for teachers*. Boothwyn, PA: Educational Resources Center.

Miller, S. R., & Schloss, P. (1982). *Career-vocational education for handicapped youth*. Rockville, MD: Aspen.

Phelps, L. A., & Lutz, R. J. (1977). *Career exploration and preparation for the special needs learner*. Boston: Allyn & Bacon.

Wilcox, B., & Bellamy, G. (Eds.). (1982). *Design of high school programs for severely handicapped students*. Baltimore, MD: Brookes.

DANIEL R. PAULSON
University of Wisconsin at Stout

REHABILITATION

VOCATIONAL EVALUATION

CARIBBEAN, SPECIAL EDUCATION IN

Recognition of special education is a relatively recent phenomenon in the Caribbean. Although services for persons with special needs were evident in the first half of the twentieth century, increased government involvement began in the second half of the century. Nongovernmental organizations and individuals with humanitarian concerns were the architects of special education services in the region, and these groups are still involved. Consequently, national associations for the deaf and local chapters of the Salvation Army, for example, continue to play indispensable roles in educating persons with hearing and visual impairments. Activities relating to physical disabilities, mental retardation, learning disabilities, and multiple disabilities have gained prominence over the years.

There is no island with a legislated policy exclusively for special education. However, interest groups use existing legislation relating to general education, as well as statements made by governments relating to "education for all," as fuel in their quest for appropriate support. Governments are committed, therefore, to the concept of equal educational opportunities for children with special needs in the school system. This commitment is displayed in special education units (departments responsible for national special education affairs) in the Education Ministries of the Republic of Trinidad and Tobago and Jamaica, and at least one special education officer in some of the other islands. Education officers work in close collaboration with special and mainstream schools and other relevant institutions. Most of the special education schools and institutions are incorporated into the public system; therefore, governments are responsible for recurrent expenditure including the payment of salaries. There are, however, some institutions operating independently by private sector and nongovernmental organizations.

In the Caribbean, most of the children with special needs are in mainstream schools without adequate support. For example, in the Republic of Trinidad and Tobago, the Ministry of Education (1993) reports that approximately "13.1% of special needs children are not in school; 5.8% are in preschool; 5.1% are attending special schools; 6.7% are in other facilities, while 67.2% are in mainstream schools in which there are no provisions for them." The implication is that only 2.1% of children with special needs are in the mainstream with adequate support.

A similar situation is also evident in Jamaica, where persons attending either government-aided special schools or enrolled in facilities operated by nongovernmental agencies comprise 0.64% of the 680,700 individuals in the mainstream preschool to secondary population (Planning Institute of Jamaica, 1996). However, using census data for four of fourteen parishes, obtained from the Statistical Institute of Jamaica, Hall and Figueroa (in press) note that persons with disabilities comprised 4.8% of the population in these parishes, and that approximately 1.8% or 4,364 were in the 10–19 age group. From this group, 1000 were attending secondary schools. A survey of secondary schools in the four parishes mentioned indicate that both students with special needs and their teachers believed that support was either absent or inadequate (Hall & Figueroa, in press).

Overall, the support provided in the region is at varying levels of quality and organization, both within schools and institutions. In Jamaica, for example, there is a national braille and large print service, and to date over 400 texts have been printed and distributed to schools. Furthermore, at the Mona Campus of the University of the West Indies (UWI), there is a very active committee for students with special needs comprised of students and staff. Over the years, the committee has been acquiring resource materials to enhance the learning environment of the students. In January 1998, a member of the committee, who is blind and also a graduate student, created history when he was appointed Senator by the Jamaican Prime Minister.

Throughout the region, the current decade has witnessed intense efforts by persons with and without disabilities to pass local legislation relating to special needs. For example, in Jamaica, the Combined Disabilities Association is finalizing a draft of a policy for disabled persons in Jamaica for submission to the government. The basic tenets are grounded in the "Standard Rules on the Equalization of Opportunities," published by the United Nations. Education is one of the eleven policy issues addressed in the draft (Combined Disabilities of Jamaica, 1997).

The training of special education teachers began in 1971 with the introduction of a one-year certificate program at UWI Mona Campus for teachers of the deaf. In 1976, Mico Teachers College began offering a 3-year program in mental retardation, learning disabilities, hearing impairment, and physical disabilities. These initial training program are still available, and recently visual impairment was included. In 1986, Mico, in collaboration with UWI, began a Bachelor in Education program in special education. Each of the program mentioned has had large financial support from the Government of the Netherlands and regional governments, and is accessed by students throughout the region. In 1994, a B.Ed. in "Managing Learning Difficulties" began at Mona, UWI. The program focuses on learners in mainstream classes. Graduate level courses in special education are offered at Mona, and Cave Campus in Barbados introduced a Master in Education in special education during the 1997–98 academic year. In Trinidad and Tobago the local teachers' association, working in collaboration with a university in the United Kingdom, offers graduate level training to its teachers.

There are other training programs throughout the region. For example, the Caribbean Association for the Mental Retarded or Developmental Disabilities (CAMRODD), a regional association, has a 3-year Parent Empowerment Program for 1997–99. In a recent session, pairs of parents and professionals from several islands including Antigua, Saba, St. Lucia, Barbados, St. Vincent, and Trinidad and Tobago were involved (CAMRODD, 1997). The general plan is for participants involved in training to implement parent training workshops in their communities.

The major challenge in the region is economic constraint, and this manifests itself in part in limited resources including personnel. Identifying persons without overt disabilities continues to be a challenge in the absence of appropriate assessment measures and in the inability of educators to employ nontraditional or alternative measures. There is also the need for general education for parents and professionals as well as urging agencies to collaborate so that limited resources can be maximized.

Future directions in the field must encompass aspects of early identification of special needs, more community involvement, inclusion, giftedness, and public education. In Barbados, for example, there are plans to assess annually children in the 3 to 7 year age group for visual, hearing, and speech impairments (Ministry of Education, Youth Affairs, & Culture, 1995). The Republic of Trinidad and Tobago has plans to establish regional diagnostic prescriptive centers. The Mico College Centre for Child Assessment and Research, a diagnostic and therapeutic center, is committed to intensify its efforts in the area of research and its dissemination. The UWI, working with both governmental and nongovernmental agencies, is continuing to set standards and respond to needs with the delivery of relevant research and pedagogy. Finally, if work in progress in the area of special needs continues unabated, and plans articulated are implemented, interest groups within the region can greet the end of the millennium with optimism.

REFERENCES

Caribbean Association for the Mentally Retarded or Developmental Disabilities. (1997). *CAMRODD's parent empowerment programme*. Jamaica: 3D's Documentation Unit.

Combined Disabilities of Jamaica. (1997). *Draft national policy for persons with disabilities*. Jamaica: Author.

Hall, W. M., & Figueroa M. (in press). Jamaican children with special needs: concerns, realities and possibilities. *Disability and Society, 13*(2).

Ministry of Education. (1993). *Education Policy Paper: 1993–2003*. Trinidad and Tobago: Author.

Ministry of Education, Youth Affairs, & Culture. (1995). *White Paper on education reform: preparing for the 21st century*. Barbados: Government of Barbados.

Planning Institute of Jamaica. (1996). *Economic and social survey of Jamaica*. Jamaica: Author.

WINNIFRED M. HALL
University of the West Indies,
Jamaica

COLLETTE LEYVA
Texas A & M University

KIMBERLY M. RENNIE
Texas A & M University

CARNINE, DOUGLAS W. (1947–   )

A native of Sullivan, Illinois, Douglas Carnine obtained his BS (1969) in psychology from the University of Illinois, Urbana, the MA (1971) in special education from the University of Oregon, Eugene, and PhD (1974) in educational psychology from the University of Utah, Salt Lake City. In 1975 Carnine became an assistant professor in the Department of Education at the University of Oregon, Eugene, where he achieved the rank of full professor in 1987.

As an undergraduate student, Carnine began working with Wesley Becker to conduct research on classroom management, and later assisted Siegfried Englemann in the development of DISTAR arithmetic as well as the implementation, in 10 school districts in eight states, of the direct instruction model of teaching (Silbert, Carnine, & Stein, 1981). These experiences led to his belief that curriculum, staff development, and administrative leadership must be addressed in any program intended to improve schools.

Carnine's focus shifted from the notion that administrators should take the lead in introducing school effectiveness programs to an emphasis on teaching variables (Engelmann & Carnine, 1982). Discouraged about excessive demands on teacher's time, he has also investigated the effects of technology on the quality of instructional programs and improving teacher effectiveness (Carnine, 1983).

Douglas W. Carnine

Writing extensively on school-improvement programs, his publications include *Theory of Instruction* (1982) and *Learning Pascal* (1988) as well as chapters in *School Improvement Programs: A Handbook for Educational Leaders* (1995) and *Changing School Reading Programs* (1988). He was a featured speaker at the 1994 Summit on Learning Disabilities of the National Center for Learning Disabilities, Inc., and is recognized in *Who's Who in American Education* (3rd ed).

REFERENCES

Carnine, D. (1983). Direct institutional: In search of instructional solutions for educational problems. In D. Carnine & D. Elkind (Eds.), *Interdisciplinary voices in learning disabilities and remedial education* (pp. 1–66). Austin, TX: Pro-Ed.

Carnine, D. (1988). How to overcome barriers to student achievement. In S. J. Samuels & P. D. Pearson (Eds.), *Changing school reading programs: Principles and case studies*. Newark, DE: International Reading Association.

Carnine, D. W., Grossen, B., & Silbert, J. (1995). Direct instruction to accelerate cognitive growth. In J. H. Block, S. T. Everson, & T. R. Guskey (Eds.), *School Improvement programs: A handbook for educational leaders*. New York: Scholastic.

Englemann, S., & Carnine, D. W. (1982). *Theory of instruction*. New York: Irvington.

Niedelman, M. S., & Carnine, D. (1988). *Learning Pascal*. Glenview, IL: Scott-Foresman.

Silbert, J., Carnine, D., & Stein, M. (1981). *Direct instruction mathematics*. Columbus, OH: Merrill.

E. VALERIE HEWITT
Texas A & M University
First edition

TAMARA J. MARTIN
The University of Texas of the
Permian Basin
Second edition

CARROW ELICITED LANGUAGE INVENTORY (CELI)

The Carrow Elicited Language Inventory (CELI; Carrow, 1974) is a diagnostic test of expressive language, containing 51 sentences and one phrase that the child is required to repeat. The mean sentence length is 6 words. The sentences were selected to include basic sentence types, specific grammatical morphemes, and select transformational rules. The grammatical morphemes include nouns, plurals, verbs, adjectives, adverbs, pronouns, articles, negatives, prepositions, demonstratives, conjunctions, and contractions. The child's responses are audio taped to assist the examiner in scoring errors on substitutions, omissions, additions, transpositions, and reversal. The manual provides mean total error scores and mean subcategory error scores for children between the ages of 3 years and 7 years 11 months at one year intervals. Percentile and stanine scores are also available.

The CELI was normed in 1973 on 475 White middle-class Texans between 3 years and 7 years 11 months. Children who were identified with speech or language disorders were excluded from the normative sample. Validity of the CELI has been established by its ability to discriminate between children with and without language disorders and to identify children at high risk for learning disorders (Blau, 1984; Swift, 1984). Test-retest reliability at 2 week intervals is reported at .98, but this should be interpreted with caution because of the small sample size employed.

A major assumption underlying the CELI is that a child's imitations of model sentences will closely resemble his or her proficiency in spontaneous speech. However, numerous studies question the validity of the sentence imitation tasks as a valid measure of spontaneous language (Kuczaj, 1975; Haniff, 1975; Connell, 1982; Prutting, 1975; McDale, 1983). A weakness of this test is that the normative data is limited (small sample size, restricted geographic region, and limited SES) and out of date.

REFERENCES

Blau, A. F., & Lahey, M., Oleksiuk-Velez, A. (1984). Planning goals for intervention: Language testing or language sampling? *Exceptional Children, 1,* 78–79.

Carrow, E. (1974). *Carrow Elicited Language Inventory.* Boston: Teaching Resources Corporation.

Connell, P. J., & Myles-Zitzer, C. (1982). An analysis of elicited imitation as a language evaluation procedure. *Journal of Speech and Hearing Disability, 47,* 390–396.

Haniff, M. H., & Seigel, G. M. (1981). The effect of context on verbal elicited imitation. *Journal of Speech and Hearing Disability, 46,* 27–30.

Kuczaj, S., & Maratsos, M. (1975). What children can say before they will. *Merrill-Palmer Quarterly, 21,* 89–112.

McDade, H. L., & Simpson, M. .A. (1983). Reply to Carrow-Woolfolk. *Journal of Speech and Hearing Disorders, 3,* 334–335.

Prutting, C. A., Gallagher, T. M., & Mulac, A. (1975). The expressive portion of the NSST compared to a spontaneous language sample. *Journal of Speech and Hearing Disabilities, 40,* 40–48.

Swift, C. (1984). Sentence imitation in kindergarten children at risk for learning diability: A comparative study. *Language, Speech, & Hearing Services in Schools, 1,* 10–15.

MARGO E. WILSON
Lexington, Kentucky
First edition

ROSEANN BISIGHINI
The Salk Institute
Second edition

CARTWRIGHT, G. PHILLIP (1937–)

G. Phillip Cartwright received his BS (1960) in psychology and MS (1962) in special education from the University of Illinois. He received his PhD (1966) in special education and educational research from the University of Pittsburgh. Currently, he is professor and head of the Division of Special Education and Communication Disorders, Pennsylvania State University.

In the 1960s, Cartwright became convinced that the American education system was not providing an adequate education for handicapped children. He attempted to implement the then heretical idea of training regular educators to identify handicapped youngsters in their

G. Phillip Cartwright

early years and to help those youngsters to succeed in a regular classroom. Cartwright also proposed that the training of both regular and special education teachers be modified to include learning the use of alternative training approaches (Cartwright, 1977). One such approach is the use of computer technology in the process of training teachers. With this philosophy, Cartwright developed a series of computer-assisted instruction (CAI) courses.

Cartwright continues his work in the field of computer-assisted instruction, recently writing pieces for *Change* promoting an increase in expertise and technology through partnerships between business and higher education (Barton & Cartwright, 1997) and outlining a technology program using a computer program to deliver courses at universities (Sedlak & Cartwright, 1997).

Cartwright has been recognized in *American Men and Women in Science, Who's Who in the East,* and *Leaders in Education.*

REFERENCES

Barton, Lyle, & Cartwright, G. P. (1997). Reciprocal technology transfer: Changing partnerships. *Change, 29,* 44–47.

Cartwright, G. P. (1977). Educational technology. In S. Tarver & R. Kneedler (Eds.), *Changing perspectives in education.* Columbus, OH: Merrill.

Cartwright, G. P. (1984). Computer applications in special education. In D. F. Walker & R. D. Hess (Eds.), *Instructional software for design and use.* Belmont, CA: Wadsworth.

Cartwright, G. P., Cartwright, C. A., & Robine, G. C. (1972). CAI course in the early identification of handicapped children. *Exceptional Children, 38,* 453–459.

Sedlak, R. A. (1997). Two approaches to distance education: Lessons learned. *Change, 29,* 54–56.

E. VALERIE HEWITT
Texas A & M University

CASCADE MODEL OF SPECIAL EDUCATION SERVICES

The Cascade Model of Special Education Services is a conceptualization of the range of placement and service options that used to be available for handicapped children. The placement options were presented in hierarchical form and ranged from the least restrictive placement in the regular education classroom to the most restrictive placement in hospital or institutional settings. The Cascade Model was first proposed by Reynolds in 1962 and an amended version was proposed by Deno in 1970. Both proposals predated the passage of the Education of All Handicapped Children Act of 1975 (PL 94-142), a time when placement and service options for the handicapped were scarce. Reynolds and Birch (1977) characterized the pre-PL 94-142 administrative arrangements as a two-box system in which parallel but separate educational programs for regular and special education were in operation within school buildings. Interaction and movement of children between the two systems was difficult at best, and more often, nonexistent. The Cascade Model helped create understanding of and support for a better system that "facilitates tailoring of treatment to individual needs rather than a system for sorting out children so they will fit conditions designed according to group standards not necessarily suitable for the particular case" (Deno, 1970, p. 235).

The Cascade Model visually appeared as a triangular form that contained two essential elements: the degree of placement specialization and the relative number of children in the various placement options. The base of the triangle coincided with regular classroom placement, the preferred placement for the largest number of handicapped students. Progressively more specialized placements were included as the triangle extended toward the apex. The decreasing width of the triangle reflected the decreasing numbers of children to be placed in progressively more restrictive environments. Deno's Cascade Model was widely cited and reproduced; it has become a fundamental concept

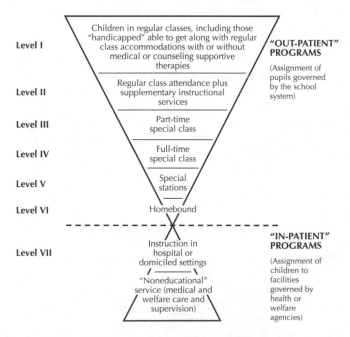

Figure 1. The cascade system of special education service. The tapered design indicates the considerable difference in the numbers involved at the different levels and calls attention to the fact that the system serves as a diagnostic filter. The most specialized facilities are likely to be needed by the fewest children on a long-term basis. This organizational model can be applied to the development of special education services for all types of disabilities.

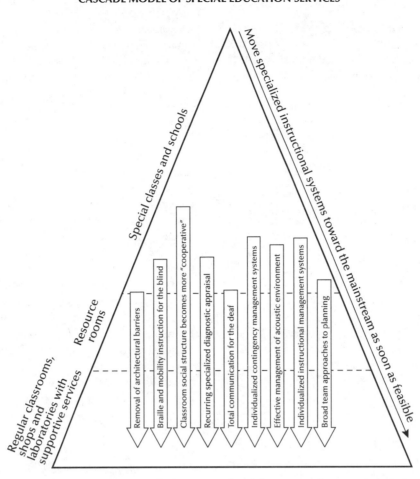

Figure 2. Changes occurring in the cascade (fewer specialized places; more diverse "regular" places)

for the field of special education. (See Figure 1 for an example of the Cascade Model.)

The basic concepts of specialization embodied in the Cascade Model were subsequently incorporated into federal and state laws as the least restrictive environment principle (Peterson, Zabel, Smith, & White, 1983). Variations of the Cascade Model have been presented by other authors (Cartwright, Cartwright, & Ward, 1985). However, the basic elements of degree of restrictiveness and relative numbers of children in the different placement options were retained.

Despite its popularity and utility, the Cascade Model was criticized. Reynolds and Birch (1977) viewed the original Cascade Model as "too place oriented" because of its "clearest focus on administrative structures and places." They offered an alternative conceptualization of the Cascade Model in which instructional diversity was emphasized. (See Figure 2.)

The Instructional Cascade envisioned the regular education classroom as the primary and optimal setting for the delivery of specialized services to handicapped children. Children were seen as moving among the levels of

the cascade for educational purposes. Ideally, a child would be moved to a more restrictive setting only for compelling educational reasons and was moved back as quickly as possible. The introduction of inclusive programming in the past few years has created a debate as to whether special education should abolish the Cascade Model. On one hand are conservative educators who believe in the original model that provided integration on a case by case method. On the other hand are abolitionists who believe in full inclusion for all special education students. At this time, federal law still supports individualization and many follow its lead (Fuchs, 1994). Outcome evaluation studies in the next few years will probably determine the debate and also determine how the cascade of services will change.

REFERENCES

Cartwright, G. P., Cartwright, C. A., & Ward, M. E. (1985). *Educating special learners* (2nd ed.). Belmont, CA: Wadsworth.

Deno, E. (1970). Special education as developmental capital. *Exceptional Children, 37*(3), 229–237.

Fuchs, D. (1994). *Best practices in school psychology: Peabody reintegration project*. (ERIC document No. ED378774)

Peterson, R. L., Zabel, R. H., Smith, C. R., & White, M. A. (1983). Cascade of services model and emotionally disabled students. *Exceptional Children, 49*(5), 404–408.

Reynolds, M. C. (1962). A framework for considering some issues in special education. *Exceptional Children, 28*(7), 367–370.

Reynolds, M. C., & Birch, J. W. (1977). *Teaching exceptional children in all America's schools*. Reston, VA: Council for Exceptional Children.

LIBBY GOODMAN
Pennsylvania State University

INCLUSION
LEAST RESTRICTIVE ENVIRONMENT
PHILOSOPHY OF EDUCATION FOR THE HANDICAPPED
SPECIAL CLASS

CASE HISTORY

Case histories serve several purposes: to provide information about rare disorders, individual differences in treatment responsiveness, or the natural course for a disorder (Kratochwill, 1985); to provide information necessary to plan and monitor appropriate treatment; to provide data needed by external agencies; to illuminate pitfalls to be avoided; and to provide information for scientific, administrative, and instructional purposes.

Identification information in a complete case history should include client's name, date of birth, sex, ethnicity, dominant language, marital status, guardians' names if a minor, residence, phone number, persons to notify in an emergency, medical status, and current program status (e.g., grade or placement if an educational setting); this information should be in an easily located part of the record. Historical data, as determined relevant for client welfare by a multidisciplinary committee, should include developmental, health, and educational history; work history if an adult; and significant family events.

Specific statements of the concerns of the referral agent should be included. The client's status at the time of referral should include information about current health, including current medications; sensory or perceptual abilities; motor abilities; language skills; current adaptive behavior; intellectual abilities and academic skills; other cognitive data, such as current belief systems or attributions as may be pertinent to the referral problem; emotional behavior; social skills and behavior; family status; and vocational aptitudes, skills, and interests. A descrip-tion of the client's current status with respect to the referring problem should always be included. The preintervention frequency of the problem behavior should be recorded to establish treatment effectiveness at a later time.

The case history should contain not only the treatment goals for a client, but the process by which those goals were determined, including dates of meetings for discussing goals, those who were present, alternative plans discussed, costs and benefits of alternative plans, and the final treatment plan agreed on. Records should also be maintained of the course of treatment implementation, including the goal to which the treatment session was directed, what was done during the session, and the clinician's notes about difficulties or unexpected results.

To establish intervention effectiveness, a record must be maintained of changes in the client's behavior or level of skill. Data from observations, self-monitoring, or other methods can be collected and recorded and effectiveness assessed by means of single-subject designs (Barlow & Hersen, 1984). These techniques have the advantage of demonstrating that specific treatments have been tried and have been effective or noneffective; of being sensitive to subtle changes in behavior; and of allowing the comparison of several alternative treatments.

REFERENCES

Barlow, D. H., & Hersen, M. (1984). *Single-case experimental designs: Strategies for studying behavior change* (2nd ed.). New York: Pergamon.

Kratochwill, T. R. (1985). Case study research in school psychology. *School Psychology Review, 14,* 204–215.

JOHN MACDONALD
Eastern Kentucky University

MEDICAL HISTORY
MENTAL STATUS EXAM

CATALOG OF FEDERAL DOMESTIC ASSISTANCE

The *Catalog of Federal Domestic Assistance* is a compendium of over 1,300 programs, projects, and activities of the federal government that provide benefits or assistance to the public (U.S. Government Printing Office, 1985). The catalog provides basic descriptive information on each program or activity, such as the purposes of the program, eligible applicants, total funds available, examples and dollar range of prior awards, and person to contact. The catalog covers programs providing both financial and nonfinancial forms of assistance (e.g., information, technical assistance, transfer of real property). It is updated and published twice a year by the General Services Administration, an agency of the federal government.

Programs are organized by sponsoring agency, but are also indexed across all agencies by subject area, by the type of entity or individual eligible to apply for assistance, and even by application deadline. The indexes make the catalog a useful reference guide for someone trying to locate potential sources of assistance for a particular project or in a specific subject area (e.g., mental retardation, early childhood education).

The catalog is distributed free of charge on a limited basis to state and local officials. It can be purchased on machine readable tape, diskettes and/or CD ROM from the General Services Administration, Ground Floor, Reporters Building, 300 7th Street, SW, Washington, DC 20407. Their telephone number is 202-708-5126.

REFERENCE

General Services Administration. (1998). *Catalog of federal domestic assistance.* Washington, DC: Author

JAMES R. RICCIUTI
United States Office of
Management and Budget

CATARACTS

A cataract is an imperfection in the clarity or a clouding of the lens of the eye. It will be experienced by a majority of people who live to an old age (Eden, 1978). Surgically removing the affected lens is the only treatment.

Eden (1978) defines three types of cataracts. Senile cataracts are those that occur as part of the normal aging process. Cell layers form around the lens as people grow older; this is similar to rings forming in the trunks of trees. The lens becomes opaque and loses its resiliency. Secondary cataracts are those that result from some other trauma or disease. For example, persons with diabetes often develop cataracts. Secondary cataracts can also result from excessive radiation, electrical shock, and the side effects of some drugs. Excessive use of cortisone, for example, has been related to the development of lens opacity. Congenital cataracts are those that are present from birth. This type of cataract is very rare. Illnesses during pregnancy such as German measles (rubella) can cause congenital cataracts (Harley & Lawrence, 1977).

It was once thought that cataracts had to be "ripe" before the lens could be removed. For example, *Melloni's Illustrated Medical Dictionary* (Dox, Melloni, & Eisner, 1979) defines a mature cataract as one in which the entire lens substance has become opaque and thus easy to separate from its capsule. However, Eden (1978) reports that such ripening is not necessary before surgery is possible.

Some cataracts get progressively worse; others do not. Some cataracts involve only the periphery of the lens; others may be more centrally located (Harley & Lawrence, 1977). Therefore, the symptoms can vary a great deal from patient to patient, and, although surgery is the only cure, it is often not necessary.

Post operative treatment of cataract removal involves the use of regular glasses or contact lenses, or the insertion of artificial plastic lenses in the eye itself. Such treatments are effective in restoring vision to the affected eye.

REFERENCES

Dox, I., Melloni, B. J., & Eisner, G. (1979). *Melloni's illustrated medical dictionary.* Baltimore, MD: Williams & Wilkins.

Eden, J. (1978). *The eye book.* New York: Viking.

Harley, R. K., & Lawrence, G. A. (1977). *Visual impairment in the schools.* Springfield, IL: Thomas.

THOMAS E. ALLEN
Gallaudet College

AMBLIOPIA
BLIND

CATEGORICAL EDUCATION

Categorical education was the practice of separating handicapped children into subgroups representing different types of disability. Each subgroup had a specific categorical designation and its members were reviewed as a cohesive group for instructional purposes. The traditional categorical group structure presumed that there were significant homogeneity of student characteristics within each subgroup and that there was significant heterogeneity among the groups. That is, the members of one group shared common qualities that distinguished them from the members of all other groups. The assumptions of homogeneity within categories and heterogeneity among categories were not well founded (Iano, 1972; Hallahan & Kauffman, 1977; Kirk & Elkins, 1975; Leland, 1977), particularly for the mildly handicapped.

Various categorical labels have been used to designate the separate subgroups of handicapped children. Different labels were frequently used to apply to essentially the same children (e.g., perceptually impaired, minimally brain damaged, and minimal cerebral dysfunction were terms that have been subsumed under the term learning disabilities). Dementia, feeblemindedness, and idiot were terms that originally, gave way to the general label of mental retardation. The Education for All Handicapped Children Act of 1975 (PL 94-142) stipulated 11 handicapping conditions: mentally retarded, hard of hearing, deaf, speech impaired, deaf-blind, learning disabled, visually handicapped, seriously emotionally disturbed, orthopedically handicapped, other health impaired, and multihandicapped. These categories became the prototype for the nation and were reflected in state and local plans for the education of handicapped children. They also continue to grow and change.

Although the categories of disabilities recognized by states and school districts was more consistent as a result of PL 94-142, the specific criteria actually used to identify handicapped children varied greatly from state to state and among local school districts. The variability in identification and placement criteria created the phenomenon that the same child could be placed in different categories in different states or school systems. Under a categorical system, the child invariably was, and still is labeled with a disability designation. The process of labeling has been studied and the negative consequences of labeling for the child, family, and school community have been discussed at length. Discussions of the pros and cons of categorical labels are available in numerous works (Hewitt & Forness, 1977; Kirk & Gallagher, 1979; Lilly, 1979; Reschley, 1996).

A long-term disaffection with traditional categorical education has led to the development of alternative practices. Critics of traditional categorical labels such as mentally retarded, learning disabled, or socially emotionally disturbed emphasize that such labels are of little use to the teacher who must plan appropriate instructional programs. Therefore the shift to inclusive practices of placement has placed emphasis on outcome rather than diagnosis or label. Alternate assessments (such as curriculum-based assessment) has also de-emphasized labels and classification, and have attempted to individualize instructions to learner needs as opposed to label.

REFERENCES

Hallahan, D. P., & Kauffman, J. M. (1977). Labels, categories, behaviors: ED, LD, and EMR reconsidered. *Journal of Special Education, 11*(2), 139–149.

Hewett, F. M., & Forness, S. R. (1977). *Education of exceptional learners*. Boston: Allyn & Bacon.

Iano, R. P. (1972). Shall we disband special classes? *Journal of Special Education, 6*(2), 167–177.

Kirk, S. A., & Gallagher, J. J. (1979). *Educating exceptional children*. Boston: Houghton Mifflin.

Kirk, S. A., & Elkins, J. (1975). Characteristics of children enrolled in the child service demonstration centers. *Journal of Learning Disabilities, 8*(10), 630–637.

Leland, H. (1977). Mental retardation and adaptive behavior. *Journal of Special Education, 6*(1), 71–80.

Lilly, M. S. (1979). *Children with exceptional needs*. New York: Holt, Rinehart & Winston.

Reschley, D. J. (1996). Identification and Assessment of Students with Disabilities. *Future of Children, 6,* 1, 40–43.

LIBBY GOODMAN
Pennsylvania State University

CASCADE MODEL OF SPECIAL EDUCATION SERVICES

CATECHOLAMINES

Epinephrine (adrenaline) and norepinephrine (noradrenaline) are hormones of the sympathetic division of the autonomic nervous system. Epinephrine was the first hormone to be isolated, and by 1897 Abel had separated it from the adrenal gland and found it to be represented by the formula C17 H15 No4. By 1905, the Japanese chemist Takamine treated Abel's abstract and named the product adrenaline, with the formula C9 H13 No3 (Krantz & Carr, 1961). Norepinephrine was not identified until 1942; it derives its name from the German expression Nitrogen ohne radikal, referring to the fact that the molecule is identical to that of epinephrine except for missing the methyl group on the nitrogen atom.

Epinephrine produces a variety of metabolic effects useful in an emergency: increased epinephrine levels result in what is often called the "fight, flight, or fright" reaction (West & Todd, 1963). Epinephrine stimulates the effector cells of the pilomotor nerves to cause hair erection, and also causes pupillary dilation, giving rise to the picture of a fright reaction. By also causing a rapid rise in blood pressure and an increase in the rate and amplitude of respiration, it prepares for more effective fright or flight from danger. The metabolic behavioral effects of epinephrine and norepinephrine are in some ways opposite, in that while epinephrine is associated with tachycardia (rapid heartbeat), norepinephrine is associated with brachycardia (slow heart action) (Eranko, 1955). In children, normal levels in plasma are 3–6 m/l for norepinephrine, and >1 m/l for epinephrine (Cone, 1968).

REFERENCES

Cone, T. E. (1968). The adrenal medulla. In R. Cooke & S. Levin (Eds.), *The biologic basis of pediatric practice* (pp. 1171–1177). New York: McGraw-Hill.

Eranko, O. (1955). Distribution of adrenaline and noradrenaline in the adrenal medulla. *Nature, 88,* 175.

Krantz, R. C., & Carr, C. J. (1961). The *pharmacologic principles of medical practice* (5th ed.). Baltimore, MD: Williams & Wilkins.

West, E. S., & Todd, W. R. (1963). *Textbook of biochemistry* (3rd ed.). New York: Macmillan.

LAWRENCE C. HARTLAGE
Evans, Georgia

EPINEPHRINE

CAT SCAN

Computerized axial tomography (CAT) scanning is an imaging technique (Binder, Haughton, & Ho, 1979) that permits visualization of many of the important landmarks and structures of the brain (see Figure 1). This is a recent technique that did not become commercially available until 1973 (Hounsfield, 1973). The importance of this breakthrough in diagnostic neuroradiology is exemplified by the fact that the 1979 Nobel Prize in Medicine was awarded to the scientists G. N. Hounsfield and A. M. Cormack, who established the theoretical physics and radiographic basis for CAT scanning. The fascinating history behind these monumental breakthroughs is reviewed in the text by Oldendorf (1980).

CAT scanning is accomplished by passing a narrow X-ray beam directed toward a detector on the other side through the patient's head (or body). The detector is sensitive to the number of X-ray beam particles that pass through the tissue; this in turn is related to the density of the tissue (e.g., the greater the density the fewer the X-ray particles that pass through). The X-ray beam is passed through the head (or body) in numerous planes so as to examine the same point from multiple directions, thus allowing a specification of density for any given point on the surface of a plane. Next, each density point is color-coded depending on the degree of density; these various density points are used to computer generate an "image" of the tissue being examined (see Figure 2).

CAT scanning has numerous useful applications. The CAT image approximates an actual anatomic specimen taken in a similar plane; thus significant structural abnormalities can be detected. This is particularly true in cases of cerebral trauma, vascular infarctions, congenital and neoplastic disorders, and degenerative brain diseases (see Figure 3). For children with developmental disorders, CAT scanning may reveal any major structural anomalies of the brain, but it has not been found to be routinely diagnostic in children in which the only problem is a learning disability (Denkla, LeMay, & Chapman, 1985). These observations suggest that, in general, there is no gross anatomic derangement associated with learning disorders.

Figure 1. CAT scan image of the brain in horizontal plane. The two upside down L-shaped dark areas represent the anterior horns of the lateral ventricles. The light area just adjacent and lateral to these structures is the caudate nucleus. The centrally located dark area just below the anterior horns in this figure represents the third ventricle. On either side of the third ventricle is the thalamus. The angular slightly darker area that runs from the outside top of the candate nucleus down and adjacent to the outside of the thalamus is the internal capsule. Lateral to the internal capsule is the putamen-globus pallidus complex.

Figure 2. Diagrammatic representation of the position of the view of the CAT image.

Figure 3. Representative CAT scan depicting different types of organic pathology. Left: tumor (meningioma). Middle: gunshot wound. Right: stroke (dark area on right side).

REFERENCES

Binder, G. A., Haughton, V. M., & Ho, K-C. (1979). *Computed tomography of the brain in axial, coronal and sagittal planes* Boston: Little, Brown.

Denkla, M. B., LeMay, M., & Chapman, C. A. (1985). Few Ct scan abnormalities found ever in neurologically impaired learning disabled children. *Journal of Learning Disabilities, 18,* 132–135.

Hounsfield, G. N. (1973). Computerized transverse axial scanning (tomography). I. Description of system. *British Journal of Radiology, 46,* 1016–1022.

Oldendorf, W. H. (1980). *The quest for an image of brain.* New York: Raven Press.

ERIN D. BIGLER
*Austin Neurological Clinic
University of Texas*

NUCLEAR MAGNETIC RESONANCE (NMR) X-RAY SCANNING TECHNIQUES

CATTELL, JAMES MCKEEN (1860–1944)

James McKeen Cattell was educated at Lafayette College in Pennsylvania and the University of Leipzig in Germany. He worked under Wilhelm Wundt at Leipzig and at Sir Francis Galton's psychological laboratory in London. He held the world's first professorship in psychology, at the University of Pennsylvania, and later was professor of psychology and head of the department of psychology at Columbia University (Woodworth, 1944).

A devoted researcher, Cattell conducted significant investigations in areas such as reaction time, perception, association, and individual differences. He developed numerous tests and coined the term mental tests. He studied the backgrounds and characteristics of eminent scientists, and published the widely used directory *Biographical Dictionary of American Men of Science.* To promote the practical application of psychology, he founded the Psychological Corporation and served as its president for many years. He also edited a number of influential journals, including the *American Journal of Psychology, Psychological Review,* and *Science.* Cattell, through his students, research, and writing and editing, was a major figure in the development of psychology as a profession in the United States (Watson, 1968).

REFERENCES

Watson, R. I. (1968). *The great psychologists.* New York: Lippincott.

Woodworth, R. S. (1944). James McKeen Cattell, 1860–1944. *Psychological Review, 51,* 201–209.

PAUL IRVINE
Katonah, New York

CAWLEY'S PROJECT MATH

Project MATH (Mathematics Activities for Teaching the Handicapped) is a comprehensive developmental mathematics program for children with special needs. The program was developed by Dr. John Cawley and his associates at the University of Connecticut under a federal grant operated from 1970 to 1975. The project was entitled "A Program Project Research and Demonstration Effort in Arithmetic Among the Mentally Handicapped"; it is available commercially.

The teaching model used in the curriculum is called the *Interactive Unit* (IU). This teaching model allows for the presentation of information to the learner in four different ways and also allows the learner to respond to questions or information in four different ways. There are 16 possible interactions that can take place between the teacher and the learner for any concept being taught. No interaction is considered to be cognitively superior to another. The interactive unit teaching model offers several advantages for the instructor. Chief among these advantages is that the model allows an instructor to teach around a disability. Learners who have difficulty in reading or writing may be taught by any of the remaining nine interaction possibilities. The instructor components of the IU are state, construct, present, and graphically symbolize. The learner components are state, construct, identify, and graphically symbolize.

The goal of the curriculum is to give a balanced emphasis to the development of skills, concepts, and social growth. The content of the math strands addressed are patterns, numbers, operations, measurements, fractions, and geometry. There are multiple lessons and support materials for concepts taught in each strand. A math concept inventory accompanies each level of the curriculum. This inventory is essentially a criterion-referenced test used to make initial placement decisions in the curriculum and to measure growth.

The verbal problem solving component of the curriculum is unique in that problem solving is introduced at the lowest level of the curriculum (Level I) and is carried out in an increasingly complex manner in the remaining levels. Problem solving is viewed as the ultimate objective of the mathematics curriculum. Unlike most mathematics programs, reading is not an essential prerequisite for entry into the verbal problem-solving exercises; the need for computational skills is also minimized. The focus of the verbal problem-solving component is on the processing of information necessary for the solution, not on the practice of computational skills. Levels I and II use sets of pictures, cards, and prepared scripts to guide a teacher and learner through the problem-solving activities. In Level III, reading is required for the first time. The use of extraneous information and language plays a major role in the problem-solving activities.

The final component of the Cawley's Project MATH curriculum consists of *Social Utilization Units*. These units are real-life extensions of the verbal problem-solving exercises; they require teams of learners to use mathematics to solve real-life problems. The units also stress social responsibility in that each member of the team is responsible for performing a task or gathering information so that the team's problem can be solved.

Two years of field testing, from 1972 to 1974, was undertaken. It involved 1917 children instructed by 116 teachers in seven states. In addition to the curricular development thrust of the project, a large number of research studies were undertaken and published, primarily in the area of verbal problem solving. Cawley has continued to build on the Project MATH materials and to expand the basic model so that it can be used by a wide variety of special educators (Thornton, 1995). Cawley continues to develop ways to reduce the inconvenience between special and general education mathematics instruction (Palmer & Cawley, 1995).

REFERENCES

Cawley, J. F. (Ed.). (1984). Developmental teaching of mathematics for the learning disabled. Rockville, MD: Aspen Systems.

Cawley, J. F. (Ed.). (1985). *Secondary school mathematics for the learning disabled*. Rockville, MD: Aspen Systems.

Cawley, J. F., Goodstein, H. A., Fitzmaurice, A. M., Lepore, A., Sedlak, R. A., & Althaus, V. (1976, 1977). *Project MATH: Mathematics activities for teaching the handicapped: Levels I–V*. Tulsa, OK: Educational Progress Corporation.

Goodstein, H. A. (1981). Are the errors we see the true errors? Error analysis in verbal problem solving. *Topics in Learning and Learning Disabilities, 1*(3), 31–45.

Palmer, R. S., & Cawley, J. F. (1995). Mathematics curricula frameworks: Goals for general and special education. *Focus on Learning Problems in Mathematics, 17*, 2, 50–66.

Thornton, C. A. (1995). Promising Research, programs, and projects. *Teaching Children Mathematics, 2*, 2, 134–135.

ROBERT A. SEDLAK
University of Wisconsin at Stout

MATHEMATICS, LEARNING DISABILITIES IN

CENTER FOR APPLIED SPECIAL TECHNOLOGY (CAST)

The Center for Applied Special Technology (CAST) is a nonprofit organization founded in 1984, with the mission of expanding opportunities for people with disabilities through the development of and innovative uses of technology. Center activities include research, product development, and work with educational settings in the service of furthering universal design for learning. In its early years, CAST sought to help people with disabilities through the development and provision of assistive technology on the individual level; however, they realized that this approach by itself kept the burden of adapting to a disability on each individual, and failed to address systemically the many barriers that the vast majority of learners with disabilities encounter.

As a result, CAST now works from the premise that the most effective way to expand educational opportunities is ". . .through universal design for learning. The phrase 'universal design' refers to the creation of computer software and learning models that are usable by everyone, including individuals of all ages, whether they are gifted, are typical learners, or have special needs." (CAST, 1998).

The CAST offices are located at 39 Cross Street, Suite 201, Peabody, MA 01960, and may be reached at (978) 531-8555, or (978) 538-3110 (TTY).

REFERENCE

Center for Applied Special Technology. (1998). About CAST—Mission and history.

KAY E. KETZENBERGER
*The University of Texas of the
Permian Basin*

CENTILE SCORES

See PERCENTILE SCORES.

CENTRAL AUDITORY DYSFUNCTION

Central auditory dysfunction is a term used to describe a broad spectrum of difficulties that may arise when an individual attempts to process an auditory signal. This disorder occurs even in people without measurable hearing loss. The term implies that when an individual has normal hearing status, but exhibits certain difficulties in correctly interpreting an auditory signal, there is some type of damage in the brain.

During the past two decades, a number of tests were devised to evaluate the integrity of the central auditory processing mechanism. These measures were used to evaluate the auditory processing of adults with anatomical lesions. Generally, these tests presented speech signals that reduced redundancy and made listening more difficult. It was found in a series of correlational studies that the performance of adults with known lesions was poorer than that of normal adults (Berlin & Lowe, 1972). It was then assumed that children who also performed poorly on similar tests suffered from some type of central auditory dysfunction (Keith, 1988). In the past 25 years, there have been attempts to determine whether children with lan-

guage disorders also have a central auditory dysfunction. If they did, the question pertains to the relationship between the two and what remedial strategies could be used successfully. Language acquisition, language disorders of various types, and learning disabilities have all been considered to be directly related to various types of central auditory dysfunction (Cherry, 1992; Garstecki & Erler, 1997).

Two basic types of tests are given to evaluate the central auditory functioning of an individual. The first type is designed to evaluate the auditory neuromaturational level of the individual. Keith (1981) suggests that these tests should (1) not be loaded with language comprehension items; (2) not require linguistic manipulation of the signal; (3) not require, or least minimize, cross-modal input or response; (4) use nonlinguistic signal; and (5) be primarily a speech imitative task using nonmeaningful material or speech material so familiar that comprehension plays no role in the process. To that end, Keith (1986) developed a Central Auditory Processing Disorder (CAPD) assessment instrument called the SCAN: A Screening Test for Auditory Processing Disorders. The SCAN includes three subtests: a filtered word test, an auditory figure-ground test, and a competing word test. The SCAN was originally normed on children ages 3 to 11 (Cherry, 1992). Another CAPD test, the Selective Auditory Attention Test (SAAT) was developed by Cherry (1980). The SAAT is used to assess auditory distractibility and Attention Deficit Hyperactivity Disorder. The SAAT includes two subtests, a monosyllabic word test given in quiet and a similar monosyllabic word list with a semantic distractor. Keith (1988) also suggested that tests of CAPD include:

1. *Auditory localization.* Generally children are able to localize at a very early age so any normal child past infancy should be able to localize without difficulty.

2. *Binaural synthesis.* An example of this test is the Rapidly Alternating Speech Perception Test, where sentences are switched rapidly from one ear to the other. If the child has difficulty with this test, there may be a lesion located in the brainstem.

3. *Binaural separation.* The Staggered Spondaic Word Test is used to determine whether the child shows ear dominance or whether the left ear score increases with age. Dichotic listening tests are also included in this category to determine whether children are establishing hemispheric dominance. A failure to do so may imply a neurological basis for a learning, reading, or language problem.

4. *Resistance to distortion.* Three types of tests are generally used in this category: speech in noise, filtered speech, and time-compressed speech. Individuals with normal central auditory functioning generally

have no difficulty with these tasks, but when there is a specific lesion or other auditory abnormality, the individual will have difficulty in understanding speech with reduced redundancy.

Keith (1988) notes that these tests are only to be used after language has emerged. He also notes that the tests have substantial maturational effects up until about age of 12. Research has indicated that there are children with no apparent language or learning difficulties who perform poorly on these tests. Likewise, there are children with such difficulties who have no problems with the tests. Keith cautions that while these tests might find some indication of the neurologic status of a child, they do not indicate specific language, learning, or reading deficits. Further, they do not in themselves suggest any particular remediation strategy.

The second type of test can be categorized as auditory-language tests. These tests are heavily loaded both cognitively and linguistically. Examples are tests in which the child must point to a series of pictures in the order in which the words are heard. It should be noted that this task is not simply a single-factor auditory-perceptual test, but requires memory and comprehension. Another example of an auditory-language test is one that asks the child to listen to a word with a phoneme missing, and then identify the missing phoneme. This is a complex language-mediated task requiring the child to analyze a distorted signal. Another frequently administered test, the Goldman-Fristoe-Woodcock Test of Auditory Discrimination Noise Subtest, contains a similarly difficult task. The child must use visual perception, auditory-visual association, and an auditory-visual-motor response with a vocabulary that may not be familiar.

While noting that a number of children with language problems do poorly on tests of central auditory functioning, Rees (1981) observes that it is not at all clear whether the deficits actually produce the language disorders or whether they are simply behavioral correlates of these and other disabilities. She further criticizes these tests, stating that "no one has developed an intelligible account of how these central auditory processing skills, or the lack of them, relate to language acquisition or academic learning" (p. 118). She considers the tests that are heavily loaded with linguistic and cognitive material to be tests designed more to evaluate an individual child's metalinguistic ability (the ability to analyze and talk about language) than to measure directly the child's ability to learn language. While these tasks may be good indicators of the individual child's ability to function successfully in school, she questions whether they have a fundamental relationship with central auditory processing. Rees notes that in some ways all the phenomena that have been clustered under the rubric of central auditory functioning have only one thing in common. They all involve data taken in through the ear.

In summary, central auditory dysfunction refers to problems individuals may exhibit in processing an auditory signal even when they have no specific hearing loss. When adults with known brain lesions were asked to perform specific tasks, related to auditory functioning, it was found that they exhibited specific problems. Some children with learning problems performed similarly on tests of auditory processing. It was presumed they also might have some kind of brain damage. Two types of tests are given to test auditory functioning. The first evaluates auditory maturational level. The second tests language-related auditory functions. It is not clear whether there is a cause-and-effect relationship between auditory functioning and learning disorders.

REFERENCES

Berlin, C. & Lowe, S. S. (1972). Temporary and dichotic factors in central auditory testing. In J. Katz (Ed.), *Handbook of clinical audiology*, 4th edition. Baltimore, MD: Williams and Wilkins.

Cherry, R. (1980). *Selective Auditory Attention Test (SAAT)*. St. Louis: Auditec of St. Louis.

Cherry, R. (1992). Screening and evaluation of central auditory processing disorders in young children. In J. Katz, N. Steckler, & D. Henderson (Eds.), *Central auditory processing: A transdisciplinary view* (pp. 129–140). St. Louis: Mosby.

Garstecki, D. C., & Erler, S. F. (1997). Hearing loss management in children and adults. In G. T. Mencher, S. E. Gerber, & A. McCombe (Eds.), *Audiology and auditory dysfunction* (pp. 220–232). Needham Heights, MA: Allyn & Bacon.

Keith, R. W. (1981). *Central auditory and language disorders in children*. San Diego, CA: College Hill.

Keith, R. W. (1986). *SCAN: A screening test for auditory processing disorders*. San Diego: The Psychology Corp.

Keith, R. W. (1988). Central auditory tests. In L. N. McReynolds & D. Yoder (Eds.), *Handbook of speech language pathology and audiology* (pp. 1215–1236). Toronto: BC Decker.

Rees, N. S. (1981). Saying more than we know: Is auditory processing a meaningful concept? In R. W. Keith (Ed.), *Central auditory and language disorders in children* (pp. 94–120). San Diego, CA: College Hill.

CAROLYN L. BULLARD
Lewis & Clark College
First edition

KATHLEEN M. CHINN
New Mexico State University
Second edition

AUDITORY ABNORMALITIES
AUDITORY DISCRIMINATION
AUDITORY PERCEPTION
AUDITORY VISUAL INTEGRATION

CENTRAL NERVOUS SYSTEM

The central nervous system (CNS) refers to the brain, including the cerebral cortex, cranial nerves, cerebellum, spinal cord, and other subcortical structures contained within the cranial vault. It consists of more than 12 billion neurons and approximately 10 times that number of glial cells. The cerebral cortex represents the CNS structure underlying most adaptive behavior, including sensation, perception, judgment, intellective functioning, and purposeful movement. Divided into two cerebral hemispheres, the respective cerebral cortices tend to be differentiated in terms of functions. As with other CNS structures that develop embryologically from the prosencephalon, the cerebral hemispheres have contralateral representation, i.e., the left side of the cortex controls the right side of the body, and vice versa. Each cerebral hemisphere is divided into anterior and posterior regions by the central sulcus or fissure of Rolando. Those cortical areas just anterior to the Rolandic fissure are specialized for motor functions, with motor enervation proceeding from superior areas of the motor strip, which control lower extremity movement, downward to more inferior areas, which control movement of the face. Just posterior to the Rolandic fissure is the sensory area, which controls such phenomena as sensitivity to stimulation for body areas corresponding to those enervated by the motor strip.

In addition to lateralized representation of motor and sensory functions, the cerebral cortex areas are also specialized for processing given types of information, and for processing information in given ways. In essentially all right-handed and in most left-handed individuals, the left cerebral hemisphere is more efficient in processing verbal or linguistic types of information, with the right hemisphere more specialized for the processing of spatial types of information. This specialization of function can be demonstrated in normal individuals by injecting fast-acting barbiturate types of drugs such as sodium amytal into a selected cerebral hemisphere. Following such an injection to the left cerebral hemisphere, for example, individuals will normally experience a brief period of aphasia, during which they are both unable to comprehend spoken language and to formulate verbalizations. Within a few minutes, all verbal functions return to preinjection levels. Similar temporary impairment of spatial function is demonstrated on right hemisphere injection (Hartlage & Flanigin, 1982).

In addition to specialization for type and process of cognitive information processing, the cerebral hemispheres also mediate differentiated emotional functions. Damage, deprivation of blood supply, unilateral electroconvulsive treatment, and depressant medication all have been shown to result in different emotional responses for each cerebral hemisphere. Insult to the right cerebral hemisphere produces what has been called the "la belle indif-ference syndrome," characterized by poor monitoring of behavior and euphoria. Insult to the left hemisphere produces the "catastrophic reaction," characterized by depression (Robertson & Inglis, 1973; Schwartz, Davidson, & Maer, 1975; Tucker, 1981).

Anatomically, the cerebral hemispheres are divided into four lobes. The frontal lobes are separated posteriorly from the parietal lobes by the central sulcus, and from the temporal lobes by the Sylvan fissure, which also separates the superiorly located parietal lobes from the temporal lobes. The occipital notch, at the posterior end of the parietal lobes, divides the parietal lobes from the occipital lobes. An approach to further subclassification of the cerebral hemispheres is the cytoarchitectural system of Brodmann, in which discrete areas of the cerebral cortices are divided into 52 Brodmann areas (Krieg, 1957) and are referred to and identified by numbers corresponding to those locations. For example, "Brodmann's area 8" corresponds to the frontal eye fields.

There is good evidence that in most individuals the cerebral hemispheres are not symmetrical (Geschwind & Levitsky, 1968; Von Bonin, 1962). This asymmetry has been related to differences in facility with processing certain types of information and other psychological characteristics (Lansdell & Smith, 1975; Levy, 1974; Reynolds, 1981; Reynolds, Kamphaus, Rosenthal, & Hiemenz, 1997). This hemispheric asymmetry has been postulated as being etiologic in certain mental disorders such as schizophrenia (Gruzelier, 1984; Newlin, Carpenter, & Golden, 1981), autism (Colby & Parkinson, 1977; Dawson, Warrenburg, & Fuller, 1982), and a number of other maladaptive behaviors (Sandel & Alcorn, 1980).

Separating the right and left cerebral hemispheres is the corpus callosum, which contains many fibers that convey impulses between the hemispheres. Right-handed individuals have a somewhat smaller corpus callosum than do individuals who are left handed or with mixed hand dominance. This phenomenon may be related to greater hemispheric specialization in strongly right-handed individuals (Witelson, 1985). Differential specialization has been suggested as a possible explanation of such conditions as dyslexia, on the basis that the lack of specialization in the language hemisphere may preclude the refinement of sophisticated processes involved in reading (Witelson, 1977).

Although much adaptive behavior is attributed to the cerebral hemispheres, other portions of the central nervous system mediate behaviors of crucial importance to the individual. The 12 cranial nerves (olfactory, optic, oculomotor, trochlear, trigeminal, abducens, facial, acoustic, glossopharyngeal, vagus, accessory, and hypoglossal) control such functions as smell, visual acuity, eye movement, facial sensation and movement, and hearing.

The cerebellum, located posteriorly and partially under the occipital lobe, with connections to many portions of the cerebral cortex, is involved with balance and with coordination of some motor activities (because some areas of the cerebellum are uniquely sensitive to the effects of alcohol, law enforcement officers often check some aspects of cerebellar function when screening drivers suspected of intoxication). A number of brain areas often referred to as subcortical (e.g., amygdala, hippocampus, thalamus) because of their location under the cortex, have been identified as playing important roles in such behaviors as emotion, memory, movement, and the integration of information from diverse cortical areas (Riklan & Levita, 1965). The medulla, that portion of the central nervous system that bridges with the spinal cord, is more involved with lower sensory and motor functions than with higher cognitive abilities.

Although some areas of the CNS have been shown to be crucial for the performance of given tasks, the CNS functions in an interrelated way for the execution of most complex tasks. Damage to the CNS will almost always result in a complex disorder requiring special educational services.

REFERENCES

Colby, K. M., & Parkinson, C. (1977). Handedness in autistic children. *Journal of Autism and Childhood Schizophrenia, 7,* 3–9.

Dawson, G., Warrenburg, S., & Fuller, D. (1982). Cerebral lateralization in individuals diagnosed as autistic in early childhood. *Brain and Language, 15,* 353–368.

Geschwind, N., & Levitsky, W. (1968). Human brain: Left-right asymmetries in temporal speech region. *Science, 161,* 186–187.

Gruzelier, J. H. (1984). Hemispheric imbalances in schizophrenia. *International Journal of Psychophysiology, 1,* 227–240.

Hartlage, L. C., & Flanigin, H. (1982, October). *An abbreviated intracarotical amytal testing procedure.* Paper presented at the annual meeting of the National Academy of Neuropsychologists, Atlanta, GA.

Krieg, W. J. S. (1957). *Brain mechanisms in diachrome* (2nd ed.). Evanston, IL: Brain Books.

Lansdell, H., & Smith, F. J. (1975). Asymmetrical cerebral function for two WAIS factors and their recovery after brain injury. *Journal of Consulting and Clinical Psychology, 43,* 931.

Levy, H. (1974). Psychological implications of bilateral asymmetry. In S. J. Dimond & J. G. Beaumont (Eds.), *Hemispheric function in the Human Brain.* London: Elek Science.

Newlin, D. B., Carpenter, B., & Golden, C. (1981). Hemispheric asymmetries in schizophrenia. *Biological Psychiatry, 16,* 561–581.

Reynolds, C. R. (1981). The neuropsychological basis of intelligence. In G. Hynd & J. Obrzut (Eds.), *Neuropsychological assessment of the school aged child: Issues and procedures.* New York: Grune & Stratton.

Reynolds, C. R., Kamphaus, R. W., Rosenthal, B. L., & Hiemenz, J. R. (1997). Applications of the Kaufman Assessment Battery for Children (K-ABC) in Neuropsychological Assessment. In C. R. Reynolds & E. Fletcher-Janzen (Eds.), *Handbook of Clinical Child Neuropsychology* (2nd ed.). New York: Plenum.

Riklan, M., & Levita, E. (1965). Laterality of subcortical involvement and psychological functions. *Psychological Bulletin, 64,* 217–224.

Robertson, A. D., & Inglis, J. (1973). Cerebral asymmetry and electroconvulsive therapy. *Proceedings of the 81st Annual Convention of the American Psychological Association, 8,* 431–432.

Sandel, A., & Alcorn, J. (1980). Individual hemispherity and maladaptive behaviors. *Journal of Abnormal Psychology, 9,* 514–517.

Schwartz, G. E., Davidson, R. J., & Maer, F. (1975). Right hemisphere lateralization for emotion in the human brain: Interactions with cognition. *Science, 190,* 286–288.

Tucker, D. M. (1981). Lateral brain function emotion, and conceptualization. *Psychological Bulletin, 89,* 19–46.

Von Bonin, G. (1962). Anatomical asymmetries of the cerebral hemispheres. In V. B. Mountcastle (Ed.), *Interhemispheric relations and cerebral dominance* (pp. 1–6). Baltimore, MD: Johns Hopkins Press.

Witelson, S. (1977). Developmental dyslexia: Two right hemispheres and none left. *Science, 195,* 309–311.

Witelson, S. F. (1985). The brain connection: The corpus callosum is larger in left handers. *Science, 229,* 665–668.

LAWRENCE C. HARTLAGE
Evans, Georgia

APHASIA
BRAIN ORGANIZATION
CEREBRAL DOMINANCE
CEREBRAL FUNCTION
LEFT BRAIN-RIGHT BRAIN

CENTRAL PROCESSING DYSFUNCTIONS IN CHILDREN

The world is a colorful, noisy, and interesting place. To learn and respond to the world around them, infants, children, adolescents, and adults receive information about their world through the senses of vision, hearing, smell, touch, and bodily movement.

The brain serves as a center for (1) receiving incoming sensations from the eyes, ears, skin, muscles, and internal organs; (2) analyzing and organizing sensory information; (3) interpreting or giving meaning to the sensory information that is being received; (4) generating messages to send to all parts of the body for purposes of responding; and (5) storing information for later use (Chalfant & Scheffelin, 1969).

When the brain does not function properly in receiving, analyzing, and storing sensory information or sending messages to the bodily parts, a dysfunction is said to exist. Because the brain is part of the central nervous system, which processes sensory information, a breakdown in this system is often referred to as a central processing dysfunction.

Central processing dysfunctions can be caused by damage to the brain, but brain damage is not always the cause. There are many cases in which individuals behave as if they had a central processing dysfunction, but show no evidence of brain damage. All of the causes of central processing dysfunctions are not yet known.

There are three major systems in which a central processing dysfunction might occur: the visual processing system, the auditory processing system, and the haptic processing system. Symptoms of dysfunctions in these systems follow.

With visual processing dysfunctions, a student may have normal visual acuity but have difficulty processing and obtaining meaning from visual information. Some of the major characteristics of visual processing dysfunctions are difficulty in (1) attending to or focusing on what is seen; (2) seeing the difference between printed numbers, letters, and words; (3) learning spatial relationships such as left-right, up-down, far-near; (4) distinguishing a figure or object from the background within which it is embedded; (5) reorganizing a whole when one or more of its parts are missing, as in constructing a puzzle; (6) remembering what has been seen; and (7) responding quickly to visual stimuli. Visual processing dysfunctions may result in academic learning disabilities in reading, writing, and arithmetic (Kirk & Chalfant, 1984).

In auditory processing dysfunctions, a student may have normal hearing, but have difficulty in processing what is heard. Auditory processing dysfunctions are characterized by difficulty in (1) listening or attending to sound; (2) locating the origin or source of sound; (3) hearing the differences or similarities between pitch, loudness, rhythm, melody, rate, or duration of sounds; (4) listening to a teacher's instructions (figure) through the interferences of classroom noises (background); (5) reorganizing a spoken word when only part of the word is heard, e.g., telepho—; (6) remembering what has been heard; and (7) associating sounds to experiences such as "ding-dong" to a bell. Dysfunctions in auditory processing may result in learning disabilities in understanding spoken language, expressing oneself through oral language, forming concepts, and developing abstract thinking skills (Kirk & Chalfant, 1984).

In the haptic processing system, the term haptic processing refers to the information received from both touch and movement. Dysfunctions in the haptic system will result in difficulty in performing fine motor tasks such as writing, manipulating tools and equipment, or learning motor performance skills. There are two subsystems for haptic processing (Gibson, 1965). The first subsystem is the tactile or cutaneous one. If a dysfunction exists in the tactile system, difficulties may be experienced in (1) being sensitive to the presence of pressure or textures on the skin; (2) reorganizing objects through the sense of touch;

(3) perceiving information about surface areas, sizes, shapes, boundaries, angles, etc.; and (4) being sensitive to pressure or aware of pain. Children with difficulties in the tactile system will have difficulty performing any task that requires the coordinated use of fingers such as learning to button or use a knife, fork, or spoon, or writing.

The second subsystem is the kinesthetic one. Bodily movement such as the movement of fingers, toes, arms, legs, head, lower jaw, tongue, and trunk, provides information about the body itself. Movement also provides information about direction and the location of objects in the environment in relation to the body itself. Muscular efforts such as lifting, pulling, and pushing objects give information about the weight of objects and gravity. Dysfunctions in the kinesthetic system result in difficulty in learning movement patterns such as crawling, walking, eating, dressing, undressing, writing, and riding a bicycle, or those needed for competing in sports activities (Kirk & Chalfant, 1984).

In summary, central processing dysfunctions can have a wide range of impact on a child or student. Young children often will be delayed in developing an understanding of and the use of oral language, visual-motor coordination, and/or cognitive abilities such as attention, discrimination, memory, conceptualization, and problem-solving skills. Students of school age may present academic disabilities in reading, writing, spelling, or arithmetic.

REFERENCES

Chalfant, J. C., & Scheffelin, M. A. (1969). *Central processing dysfunction in children: A review of research* (NINDS Monograph No. 9). Washington, DC: U.S. Department of Health, Education, and Welfare.

Gibson, J. J. (1965). *The senses considered as perceptual systems.* Boston: Houghton Mifflin.

Kirk, S. A., & Chalfant, J. C. (1984). *Academic and developmental learning disabilities.* Denver: Love.

JAMES C. CHALFANT
University of Arizonia

BRAIN DAMAGE
LEARNING DISABILITIES
LEARNING DISABILITIES, PROBLEMS IN DEFINITION OF
LEARNING STYLES

CENTRAL TENDENCY

Measures of central tendency are used to describe the typical or average score in a sample or population of scores. Many measures of central tendency exist, but the three most popularly used in the behavioral sciences are the mean, the median, and the mode.

The mean is the most widely used measure of central tendency. It is the arithmetic average of a given set of scores. For example, given the set of scores 87, 96, 98, 110, 113, 114, 119, the mean is 105.29, the sum of the seven scores divided by the number of scores, seven.

The median of a set of scores is the score that divides the set into two groups with each group containing the same number of scores. To compute the median, first rank the set of scores from smallest to largest. When the number of scores is odd and there are no ties, the median is the middle score. For example, the median of the above scores is 110. When the number of scores is even, with no ties, the median is the average of the two middle scores. Thus, the median score of 87, 96, 98, 110, 113, 114, 119, 120 is 110 + 113/2 = 111.50.

The mode is the score that occurs most frequently in a set of scores. For the scores 87, 96, 98, 98, 98, 110, 113, 114, 119, the mode is 98. When there are two modes, the distribution of scores is said to be bimodal. All three measures may be used when the data are quantitative. The median and mode are used with ranked data, whereas only the mode is applicable to nominal data.

The mean is the preferred measure of central tendency when the variable measured is quantitative and the distribution is relatively symmetric. It is relatively stable and reflects the value of every score in the distribution and, unlike the median and the mode, it is amenable to arithmetic and algebraic manipulations. These qualities make the mean useful not only for describing the average of a set of scores, but also for making inferences about population means. We can infer the value of the population mean from the sample mean, and also make inferences about the differences between population means for the same or different groups of individuals on one or more variables. When the distribution of scores is skewed, or the variable being measured is qualitative, the mean is not the preferred measure of central tendency.

For skewed distributions, the median is used. This is because the median is not affected by the scores falling above and below it. For example, the median of the scores 109, 108, 107, 106, 60 is 107; it more accurately reflects the typical score than the mean of 98. Inferences about the population median may also be concluded (see Marascuilo & McSweeney, 1977).

When the distribution is symmetric and unimodal, the median, mean, and mode are the same. When the distribution is skewed, however, the median and mean are unequal with median > mean in negatively skewed distributions and mean > median in positively skewed distributions.

REFERENCES

Glass, G. V., & Hopkins, K. D. (1984). *Statistical methods in education and psychology* (2nd ed.). Englewood Cliffs, NJ: Prentice-Hall.

Hays, W. L. (1981). *Statistics* (3rd ed.). New York: Holt, Rinehart and Winston.

Kirk, R. E. (1984). *Elementary statistics* (2nd ed.). Monterey, CA: Brooks/Cole.

MacGillivray, H. L. (1985). Mean, median, mode, and skewness. In S. Kotz, N. L. Johnson, & C. B. Read, *Encyclopedia of the statistical sciences* (Vol. 5). New York: Wiley.

Marascuilo, L. A., & McSweeney, M. (1977). *Nonparametric and distribution-free methods for the social sciences*. Monterey, CA: Brooks/Cole.

GWYNETH M. BOODOO
Texas A & M University

STANDARD DEVIATION

CEREBELLAR DISORDERS

The cerebellum is an oval-shaped portion of the brain under the occipital lobe of the cerebrum and behind the brain stem. It has a right and left hemisphere and a central section. The cerebellum integrates information vital to the control of posture and voluntary movement. The cerebellum is responsible for maintaining equilibrium and trunk balance; regulating muscle tension, spinal nerve reflexes, posture, and balance of the limbs; and regulating fine movements initiated by the frontal lobes.

Persons with cerebellar dysfunction may show any or all of the following deficits: wide-based clumsy gait; tremor on attempted motion; clumsy, rapid alternating movements; inability to control the range of voluntary movements with overshooting the goal most common; low muscle tone; and scanning speech with inappropriate accenting of syllables. Rapid alternating eye movements (nystagmus) may be observed as a component of closely associated vestibular involvement.

Tumors of the cerebellum, heavy metal poisoning, repeated high fever or head trauma, and hypothyroidism can affect the cerebellum directly. Since the cerebellum receives postural and movement information from many parts of the brain, integrates them and sends information out to motor coordinating areas, the function of the cerebellum may be impaired by a wide range of neurological conditions. Multiple sclerosis, blood clots, and congenital anomalies of other parts of the brain can influence the cerebellum via input/output tracts as well. The spinocerebellar diseases are a family of degenerative hereditary diseases that affect (to varying degrees) the cerebellum, spinal cord, brain stem, and other parts of the nervous system. Most of these diseases have their onset in childhood, are slowly progressive, and have no known specific inheritance patterns, cause, or treatment, although in some individual family studies clinical findings and inheritance patterns are consistent. It is believed that inherited biochemical abnormalities are causal, and some have been identified. Some diseases in this category with early onset, rapid progression, and strong familial tendencies are Marie's ataxia, Roussy-Levy syndrome, and Friedreich's ataxia. Although progression results in clumsiness, poor balance, later use of a wheelchair for safety, slurred speech, and loss of skilled hand function, there is usually no related impairment to intelligence.

Friedreich's ataxia is a hereditary disease of unknown origin with symptoms of frequent falling, clumsiness, and incoordination (ataxia) beginning between age 5 and 25. Slurred speech, swallowing difficulty, contractures, deformities, and weakness typically result in the need to use a wheelchair within 5 to 10 years. The lack of intellectual impairment is often in considerable contrast to the severity of the physical impairments, a circumstance that represents a challenge to educators to provide stimulating instruction within the limitations presented by the child's deteriorating physical condition. Occupational, physical, and speech therapists can provide useful adaptive support techniques to the child's teachers and family so that optimal function can continue as long as possible. Clinical experience has shown that these children are vulnerable because of their insight into the progressive nature of their disease. Anxiety, anger, and depression may occur, and such feelings may be exacerbated by observing the struggles and deaths of elder siblings. The impact on family life when several siblings have Friedreich's ataxia is profound. Since the average onset age is 13 years, a family may have a number of children before the eldest has symptoms and is diagnosed. Clinical experience suggests that early admission of all symptomatic family members to special education programs where supportive related services are available can help normalize adaptive responses and provide maximum comfort, safety, deformity prevention, and learning opportunities while prolonging activity. Estimates suggest that with proper management there may be 10 to 20 years of productivity following onset. Death frequently is due to progressive heart failure, medical complications, or effects of inactivity rather than the disease itself.

Dr. John C. Eccles (1973), a recognized authority on the cerebellum, believes that the relative simplicity of neuronal design, together with its well-defined action in control of movement, will result in the cerebellum becoming one of the first parts of the brain where linkage between structure and function can be documented. The rapid growth of specific knowledge about cerebellar diseases suggests that differential diagnosis by a skilled neurologist together with genetic studies when indicated are imperative in children with cerebellar disorders, as there are treatable conditions that may present symptoms similar to the degenerative disorders.

REFERENCES

Berkow, R. (Ed.). (1982). *The Merck manual of diagnosis and therapy* (14th ed.). Rahway, NJ: Merck, Sharp & Dohme.

Eccles, J. C. (1973). *The understanding of the brain.* New York: McGraw-Hill.

Stolov, W. C., & Clowers, M. R. (Eds.). (1981). *Handbook of severe disability* (stock #017-090-00054-2). Washington, DC: U.S. Government Printing Office.

RACHAEL J. STEVENSON
Bedford, Ohio

ATAXIA
BRAIN ORGANIZATION
FRIEDREICH'S ATAXIA

CEREBRAL DOMINANCE

Cerebral dominance refers to the asymmetrical lateralization of language and perceptual functions in the human brain. Cerebral dominance, or hemispheric specialization, was initially applied to language functions that are served by the left hemisphere in most individuals. However, the term was later expanded to include cognitive functions of nonverbal reasoning and visual-spatial information processing that are associated with the right hemisphere. In short, functions associated with the left hemisphere involve processing linguistic, analytical, and sequential information while the right hemisphere is responsible for processing nonlinguistic or spatial information in a holistic fashion (see Witelson, 1976).

Early reference to cerebral dominance can be traced back to Dax in 1836 and Broca in 1861; they found that damage to the left hemisphere results in disorders of speech and language. They believed that the left hemisphere is the dominant side for most people in that it controls the functions of language (Gaddes, 1980). The notion of cerebral dominance was further delineated by the writings of Jackson, who postulated that the left hemisphere is the dominant or the leading side and right hemisphere is the automatic and minor side (Dean, 1984). The emphasis in determining cerebral dominance for language was also noted by Orton (1937). He speculated that delayed or incomplete lateralization for linguistic functions by the left hemisphere results in the types of language disorders often seen in children.

Methods for assessing specializations of each hemisphere have employed invasive techniques such as direct electrical stimulation of the brain, hemispheric anesthetization, and split-brain studies. *Noninvasive procedures* have involved dichotic listening and split-visual field research.

Research using direct electric stimulation of the brain was pioneered by Penfield (Penfield & Roberts, 1959). This technique was developed to map the centers of the brain that controlled specific functions prior to surgical procedures. Since the brain does not contain pain receptors, the patient was conscious when a small electrical current was applied to the surface of the brain to determine areas of the brain associated with such functions as vision, hearing, olfaction, or haptic sensations. Applications of electrical stimulation to areas believed to control speech would be verified by the patient's inability to talk. These "aphasic arrests" would occur only when areas of the brain associated with speech were electrically stimulated. In this way, hypotheses about other functions of the brain could also be verified if responses associated with those functions were absent during stimulation.

Another invasive technique to study brain functioning has been to anesthetize one hemisphere by injecting sodium amytal in the carotid artery located on either the right or left side of the patient's neck. This procedure, known as the Wada test, quickly anesthetized that side of the brain. For example, if the left side or the side dominant for language was infused, the individual would become speechless while the drug was in effect, while the functions of the right hemisphere would remain intact. Wada and Rasmussen (1960) hypothesized that the left hemisphere is dominant for processing verbal information and the right hemisphere for nonverbal information. To demonstrate this, Wada and his associate injected sodium amytal into the left hemisphere and asked the patient to sing "Happy Birthday"; the patient was able to hum the tune without producing the words. When the right hemisphere was anesthetized and the patient was required to perform the same task, the patient was only able to recite the words of "Happy Birthday" in a monotone without producing a tune. Using this procedure, Milner (1974) found that 95% of right-handed and 70% of left-handed individuals are left hemisphere dominant for language.

Split-brain surgery or commissurotomy is another invasive technique used to study cerebral dominance. A commissurotomy is a surgical procedure used to stop the spread of seizure activity from a focal point in one hemisphere to the other hemisphere via the corpus callosum. This procedure involves the severing of the corpus callosum, a large band of nerve fibers that connects the left and right hemispheres, thereby preventing any communication between the hemispheres.

Much research was conducted by Speery in the 1950s. Researchers were able to localize functions of language, motoric control of the same or opposite sides of the body, and visual discrimination (Hacaen, 1981). In one study that examined visual perception, Levy and her associates (Levy, Trevarthen, & Speery, 1972) used stimulus figures in which the left half of one face was joined with the right half of another. The patient was required to gaze at a dot on the center of the screen before a figure was flashed on the screen. The presentation was such that each half of the face would be projected to only one hemisphere. When the patient was asked to respond by pointing to the correct picture from available alternatives, the left sides of faces, which are processed by the right hemisphere, were correctly chosen more often than the right sides regardless of the hand used for pointing. However, when the patient was required to verbally identify the picture, the face on the right side (left hemisphere) was chosen, although the number of errors made by this response mode was much higher. These results were subsequently replicated using other stimuli, suggesting that the right hemisphere is superior in processing nonverbal visual stimuli.

A noninvasive technique in the study of brain-behavior relationships has been dichotic listening. This procedure involves the simultaneous presentation of verbal or nonverbal information to each ear. Similar but different information is presented to each ear and the subject's task is to identify or recall what was heard. This technique was initially developed by Broadbent (1954) to study auditory attention and later adapted by Kimura (1961) to study cerebral lateralization. Studying normal individuals, Kimura found that subjects were more able to identify correctly verbal information when it was presented to the right ear (left hemisphere). If the information was nonverbal, however, a left-ear advantage (right hemisphere) was found. Kimura also showed that if patients having neurological disorders were found to be left hemisphere dominant for language (via the Wada test), a right-ear advantage was noted for verbal information. Similarly, if the patient was right hemisphere dominant for language, a left-ear advantage (right hemisphere) was found for verbal information. These findings suggested that superiority for each ear varies with the specialization in function for the opposite hemisphere.

Studies that have examined language lateralization for dyslexic children using a dichotic listening paradigm have found mixed results. Dyslexic or reading-disabled children are usually characterized by a two-year lag in reading achievement despite average intelligence and an absence of any sensory-motor, neurological or emotional difficulties (Hynd & Cohen, 1983). Some studies (e.g., Witelson & Rabinovitch, 1972) have reported that dyslexic children show a left-ear advantage for verbal information. Other researchers (e.g., Leong, 1976) have demonstrated a right-ear advantage for verbal information for both dyslexic and normal readers. Differential findings may be partially due to differences in methodology and criteria of subject selection.

Another noninvasive technique in studying cerebral dominance has been split-visual field research. This involves a tachistoscopic presentation of verbal or spatial information to either the right-half or left-half visual fields. The visual pathways are such that information perceived in the left-visual field is processed by the right hemisphere while right-visual field information is processed by the left hemisphere. Studies have demonstrated that while word recognition levels were lower for the dyslexic children when compared with normal readers, both readers showed a right-visual field superiority for words (Marcel & Rajan, 1975). However, when pictures were presented to either visual field, Witelson (1976) reported that while normal readers had a significant left visual-field advantage, this difference was not significant for a dyslexic group. These results suggest that while dyslexic readers, like normal readers, have a left-hemisphere representation for language, the dyslexic group appears to lack right-hemisphere specialization for visual-spatial information.

In sum invasive and noninvasive techniques have made significant contributions in mapping functions of the brain. However, our knowledge of hemispheric specializations is far from complete. Given the inter-individual differences in cognitive processing, the brain's ability to compensate for damage, and developmental factors, the assessment of hemispheric specializations remains a complex and sometimes chaotic (Reynolds, Kamphaus, Rosenthal, & Hiemenz, 1997) endeavor.

REFERENCES

Broadbent, D. E. (1954). The role of auditory localization in attention and memory. *Journal of Experimental Psychology, 47,* 191–196.

Dean, R. S. (1984). Functional lateralization of the brain. *Journal of Special Education, 18,* 239–256.

Gaddes, W. H. (1980). *Learning disabilities and brain function: A neuropsychological approach.* New York: Springer-Verlag.

Hacaen, H. (1981). Apraxias. In S. B. Filskov & T. J. Boll (Eds.), *Handbook of clinical neuropsychology.* New York: Wiley.

Hynd, G., & Cohen, M. (1983). *Dyslexia: Neuropsychological theory, research, and clinical differentiation.* New York: Grune & Stratton.

Jackson, J. H. (1874). On the duality of the brain. *Medical Press Circulator, 1,* 19, 41, 63.

Kimura, D. (1961). Cerebral dominance and the perception of verbal stimuli. *Canadian Journal of Psychology, 15,* 166–171.

Leong, C. K. (1976). Lateralization in severely disabled readers in relation to functional cerebral development and synthesis of information. In R. M. Knights & D. J. Bakker (Eds.), *Neuropsychology of learning disorders: Theoretical approaches.* Baltimore, MD: University Park Press.

Levy, J., Trevarthen, C., & Speery, R. W. (1972). Perception of bilateral chimeric figures following hemispheric disconnection. *Brain, 95,* 61–78.

Marcel, T., & Rajan, P. (1975). Lateral specialization of recognition of words and faces in good and poor readers. *Neuropsychologia, 13,* 489–497.

Milner, B. (1974). Hemispheric specialization scope and limits. In F. O. Schmitt & F. G. Warden (Eds.), *The neurosciences: Third study programme.* Cambridge, MA: MIT Press.

Orton, S. T. (1937). *Reading, writing, and speech problems in children.* New York: Norton.

Penfield, W., & Roberts, L. (1959). *Speech and brain mechanisms.* Princeton, NJ: Princeton University Press.

Reynolds, C. R., Kamphaus, K. W., Rosenthal, B. L., & Hiemenz, J. R. (1997). Applications of the Kaufman Assessment Battery for Children in neuropsychological assessment. In C. R. Reynolds & E. Fletcher-Janzen (Eds.), *Handbook of Clinical Child Neuropsychology* (2nd ed.). New York: Plenum.

Wada, J. A., & Rasmussen, T. (1960). Intracarotid injection of sodium amytal for lateralization of cerebral speech dominance: Experimental and clinical observations. *Journal of Neurosurgery, 17,* 266–282.

Witelson, S. F. (1976). Abnormal right hemisphere specialization in developmental dyslexia. In R. M. Knights & D. F. Bakker (Eds.), *Neuropsychology of learning disorders: Theoretical approaches.* Baltimore, MD: University Park Press.

Witelson, S. F. & Rabinovitch, M. S. (1972). Hemispheric speech lateralization in children with auditory-linguistic deficits. *Cortex 8,* 412–426.

GURMAL RATTAN
*Indiana University of
Pennsylvania*

RAYMOND S. DEAN
*Ball State University
Indiana University School
of Medicine*

CEREBRAL FUNCTION, LATERALIZATION OF

The human brain is divided longitudinally into two distinct hemispheres. Research over the past century has confirmed early speculations (Broca, 1861; Dax, 1865) that each of these cerebral hemispheres serve specialized functions (Dean, 1984). Although anatomical differences have been identified between hemispheres at birth, more complex patterns of functional specialization may well continue to develop throughout childhood (Dean, 1985).

Our present understanding of the lateralization of functions in the cerebral cortex owes much to the early efforts of investigations of the late nineteenth century (e.g., Broca, 1861; Dax, 1865; Jackson, 1874). Based on case studies of patients with confirmed brain damage, a number of researchers (e.g., Broca, 1861) argued in favor of the localization of individual functions (e.g., speech) to specific structures of the brain. Moreover, it was generally reported during this time that with damage to the left cerebral hemisphere, one could expect impaired language functions (Broca, 1861; Dax, 1865). These early underpinnings of the notion of lateralization were further extended by Jackson (1874), who suggested that a lateralization of functions corresponds to the two hemispheres of the brain.

Jackson (1874) argued that the left cerebral hemisphere is responsible for language-related functions, while the right hemisphere is the more automatic side, responsible for sensation and perception. The notion of hemispheric dominance grew out of such early arguments, which equated language lateralization in the left hemisphere with control functions. Although rather naive some hundred years later, the idea of hemispheric dominance continues in the literature. Clearly, these early case studies, which attempted to draw conclusions concerning the neuropsychology of normal individuals based on observations of patients with brain damage, were limited. However, the scientific interest stimulated by these reports in tandem with increasingly sophisticated approaches in research is responsible for the wealth of our present knowledge about the functioning of the brain.

While the differences in hemispheric functioning are acknowledged by most neuroscientists, the specific mechanism underlying these differences continues to be debated. At this point, it is not clear whether functional lateralization is related to differences in processing (e.g., Geschwind & Levitsky, 1968), storage (e.g., Dean, 1984), or attention (e.g., Kinsbourne, 1975). However, most researchers have found the arguments attributing observed differences to processing predisposition for the individual hemispheres compelling. From this point of view, the differences in functioning for the sides of the brain are due to biological differences in processing information that implicate the left hemisphere in language-related tasks and the right side in nonverbal elements.

Although communication between hemispheres is acknowledged, specific functional differences may be attributed to the individual hemispheres. Indeed, it is rather well established that the left hemisphere of the brain best processes information in a sequential, temporal, and analytic fashion. This may be likened to a verbal-sequential mode of thought in which information is represented, processed, and encoded with the aid of linguistic units (Dean, 1983; Paivio, 1971).

A second mode of thought may be seen to correspond to the functions of the right hemisphere. This mode is most clearly oriented toward processing visual information in a concrete, simultaneous, or holistic fashion (e.g., Sperry, 1974). Rather primitive when compared with the left, the right hemisphere seems predisposed to represent, reorganize, and encode visual-spatial elements (e.g., Dimond & Beaumont, 1974). Indeed, the use of imagery seems to be the most idiosyncratic expression of its processing (Seamon & Gazzaniga, 1973).

Hemispheric lateralization has been argued to be an interactive process in which the mode is dependent on the degree of cognitive reformulation, constraints of attention, and actual hemispheric differences in function (Dean, 1984; Gordon, 1974; Kinsbourne, 1997; Paivio; 1971). It has been suggested that normal individuals can employ different strategies that make differential use of one hemisphere or the other regardless of the form of the original stimulus (Dean, 1984). Clearly, information presented in a visual fashion may be encoded almost entirely in semantic terms (Conrad, 1964). So, too, it has been shown that verbal stimuli may be encoded and recalled as visual memory traces (Bower, 1970; Dean, 1983). As Dean (1984) points out, "even young learners can generate visual or verbal encoding strategies which correspond to hemispheric specific abilities regardless of the form of the original stimulus array" (p. 249). This point of view acknowledges independent cognitive processes served by each hemisphere while it stresses the importance of interhemispheric communication. It seems, therefore, that the verbal-nonverbal or left-right hemispheric differences may well be an exaggeration of reality. That is, cerebral lateralization may be more heuristically attributed to modes of processing information than to lateralization for specific stimuli. Therefore, the total task demands for the process of a given bit of information are necessary prior to assuming hemispheric lateralization.

The lateralization of functions is dependent in part on the degree to which cognitive processing is necessary for interpretation and encoding (e.g., Gordon, 1974). Indeed, few differences have been found between hemispheres for lower level information processing. For example, in the discrimination of sensory elements such as brightness, color, pressure, sharpness, pitch, and contour, little lateralization exists in processing (e.g., Dean, 1984; Rabinowicz, 1976). However, when learners are required to form generalizations, categorize, reorder, or integrate, or when they are called on to abstract common elements, clear hemispheric differences emerge. As would be expected, cerebral lateralization is dependent on the amount of interpretation or prior knowledge that the subject must draw on in dealing with the incoming information. Such cognitive processing enhances the degree to which functionally lateralized abilities are relied on (e.g., Moscovitch, 1979).

Although less than complete agreement exists among neuroscientists, it would seem that functional lateralization of cerebral hemispheres of the brain corresponds to the developmental pattern of consolidation that occurs from birth and progresses through adolescence (Dean, 1985). Dean (1984) argues that the rate of lateralization in the child varies with the specific function being examined. In keeping with this hypothesis, Krashen (1973) has offered data favoring a progressive decrease in the role played by the right cerebral hemisphere in verbal-analytic tasks with the child's increasing neurological development. The progressive lateralization of cerebral functions seems concomitant with the rate and variable progression in the maturation of the commissure-association cortex (Sperry, 1969).

Gender differences have been reported for the lateralization of cerebral functions. The force of the data in this area suggests less secure hemispheric specialization for females than for males (e.g., Witelson, 1976). Although anatomical gender differences exist (e.g., MacLusky & Naftolin, 1981), the functional differences found for males and females seem more heuristically attributed to organizational factors than differences in structure (e.g., Kolata, 1979). A convincing argument may be made for a genetic-hormonal cultural locus for observed gender differences (Dean, 1984).

In sum, the functioning of the left hemisphere seems predisposed to process information in a sequential, temporal, or analytic fashion; as such, language is an excellent tool for such forms of cognition. The right hemisphere, in contrast, is best prepared to function in a more simultaneous, holistic, or nonverbal fashion, with spatial reasoning and imagery being the most consistently reported mode of thought. This pattern corresponds with a large body of research in both cognitive psychology and the neurosciences. A good deal of interhemispheric communication should be recognized and functional lateralization is exhibited only as the individual must employ higher order cognitive skills in an attempt to comprehend or learn the incoming information.

REFERENCES

Bower, G. H. (1970). Analysis of a mnemonic device. *American Scientist, 58,* 496–510.

Broca, P. (1861). Nouvelle observation d'aphemie produite par une lesion de la moite posterieure des deuxieme et troiseme circonvolutions frontales. *Bulletin de la Society Anatomique de Paris, 36,* 398–407.

Conrad, R. (1964). Accoustic confusions in immediate memory. *British Journal of Psychology, 55,* 75–83.

Dax, G. (1865). Lesions de la moitie gauche de l'encephale coincident avec l'oubli des signes de la pensee. *Gazette Hebdomadaire de Medicine et de Chirurgie, 2,* 259–262.

Dean, R. S. (1983, Feb.). *Dual processing of prose and cerebral laterality.* Paper presented at the annual meeting of the International Neuropsychological Society, Mexico City, Mexico.

Dean, R. S. (1984). Functional lateralization of the brain. *Journal of Special Education, 18*(3), 239–256.

Dean, R. S. (1985). Foundation and rationale for neuropsychological bases of individual differences. In L. C. Hartlage & C. F. Telzrow (Eds.), *The neuropsychology of individual differences: A developmental perspective.* New York: Plenum.

Dimond, S., & Beaumont, J. (1974). *Hemisphere function in the human brain.* London: Elek Scientific Books.

Geschwind, N., & Levitsky, W. (1968). Human brain: Left-right asymmetries in temporal speech region. *Science, 161,* 186–187.

Gordon, H. W. (1974). Auditory specialization of the right and left hemispheres. In M. Kinsbourne & W. L. Smith (Eds.), *Hemispheric disconnection and cerebral function.* Springfield, IL: Thomas.

Jackson, J. H. (1874). On the duality of the brain. In J. Taylor (Ed.), *Selected writings of John Hughlings Jackson, Vol. 2.* London: Hodder & Stoughton.

Kinsbourne, M. (1975). Cerebral dominance, learning, and cognition. In H. R. Myklebust (Ed.), *Progress in learning disabilities.* New York: Grune & Stratton.

Kinsbourne, M. (1997). Mechanisms and development of cerebral lateralization in children. In C. R. Reynolds and E. Fletcher-Janzen (Eds), *Handbook of Clinical Child Neuropsychology* (2nd ed.) New York: Plenum.

Kolata, G. B. (1979). Sex hormones and brain development. *Science, 205,* 985–987.

Krashen, S. D. (1973). Lateralization, language learning, and the critical period: Some new evidence. *Language Learning, 23,* 63–74.

MacLusky, N. J., & Naftolin, F. (1981). Sexual differentiation of the central nervous system. *Science, 211,* 1294–1302.

Moscovitch, M. (1979). Information processing and the cerebral hemispheres. In M. S. Gazzaniga (Ed.), *Handbook of behavioral neurobiology, Vol. 2: Neuropsychology.* New York: Plenum.

Paivio, A. (1971). *Imagery and verbal processes.* New York: Holt, Rinehart, & Winston.

Rabinowicz, B. H. (1976). *A non-lateralized auditory process in speech perception.* Unpublished master's thesis, University of Toronto.

Seamon, J. G., & Gazzaniga, M. D. (1973). Coding strategies and cerebral laterality effects. *Cognitive Psychology, 5,* 249–256.

Sperry, R. W. (1969). A modified concept of consciousness. *Psychological Review, 76,* 532–536.

Sperry, R. W. (1974). Lateral specialization in the surgically separated hemispheres. In F. O. Schmitt & F. G. Worden (Eds.), *The neurosciences: Third study program,* New York: Wiley.

Witelson, S. F. (1976). Early hemisphere specialization and inter-hemisphere plasticity: An empirical and theoretical review. In S. Segalowitz & F. Gruber (Eds.), *Language and development and neurologic theory.* New York: Academic.

RAYMOND S. DEAN
Ball State University
Indiana University School
of Medicine

HEMISPHERIC ASYMMETRY
HEMISPHERIC FUNCTIONS
LATERALITY
LEFT BRAIN-RIGHT BRAIN
NEUROPSYCHOLOGY

CEREBRAL INFARCTION

Cerebral infarction refers to the death of brain tissues resulting from a sudden onset of a circulation disorder that often leads to a neurological deficit. Infarction is caused by conditions of anoxia, hypoglycemia, or ischemia (Toole, 1984; Toole & Patel, 1974). Anoxic infarction results from a lack of oxygen to the brain, whereas hypoglycemic infarction occurs when an insufficient level of blood glucose exists for a prolonged period of time despite normal circulation. The most prevalent of the infarctions, however, is ischemic infarction, which results from a sudden interruption of blood supply owed to an obstruction in an artery. Cerebral infarction can occur in any of the cerebral blood vessels of the carotid (anterior portion of the brain) or vertebral basilar (posterior portion of the brain) systems. It may be confused with symptomology resulting from cerebral hemorrhage, tumor, or other space-occupying lesions. Because ischemic infarctions are the most common, they will be the focus of the remaining discussion.

Transient ischemic attack (TIA) refers to a temporary obstruction of blood vessels; this is frequently caused by platelet-fibrin emboli or blood clots. An embolus is an aggregate of blood particles and tissue overgrowth (thrombus), fatty deposits, clumps of bacteria, or obstructive gas bubbles that block the blood vessels. Other causes of TIAs are acute high blood pressure and vasospasm or spasmodic constriction of blood vessels.

Transient ischemic attacks always have a sudden onset and peak in intensity within 2 to 5 minutes. Symptoms quickly disappear, within 30 minutes, but if symptoms persist past 24 hours, the diagnosis changes to a complete stroke or a cardiac vascular accident. The extent to which TIAs result in temporary or permanent neurological damage in unclear. Symptoms of carotid TIA include monocular blindness or blurring of vision in a previously normal eye; aphasic reactions such as difficulty with writing, reading, arithmetic, receptive and expressive language; and contralateral weakness and numbness of the face, arm, and leg, which may occur either simultaneously or separately. Weakness is characterized by heaviness or clumsiness of the extremities, while numbness can be described as a numbing sensation or a pins or needles sensation. These sensations do not spread or "march" to the various anatomical parts, but occur simultaneously. Vertebral basilar TIAs, however, have the following symptomology: vertigo (spinning movement of the environment); intermittent diplopia (double vision); visual blurring of both eyes; espisodic ataxia (gait problems); and spells in which sudden loss of strength in the lower extremities causes the patient to fall to the ground without loss of consciousness.

Transient ischemic attacks may occur sporadically or regularly, either in a short time span or over several months or years. More than one-third of the patients with diagnosed TIAs sustain a complete stroke within one year, while more than one-half of these patients eventually sustain a major stroke during their lifetime. Patients with TIAs may suffer mild cognitive impairments, especially on delayed recall tasks (Lezak, 1983). Patients suspected of having a TIA can have the diagnosis confirmed by an an-

giography, which enables a radiological visualization of the blood vessels.

Medical therapy usually involves a regimen of drugs that have the properties of inhibiting the formation or aggregation of red blood cells and the narrowing of arteries. Such drugs consist of aspirin, Anturane, Persantine, and Conmadin (Lubic & Palkovitz, 1979).

REFERENCES

Lezak, M. D. (1983). *Neuropsychological assesment* (2nd ed.). New York: Oxford University Press.

Lubic, L. G., & Palkovitz, H. P. (1979). *Discussions in patient management: Stroke.* New York: Medical Examination.

Toole, J. F. (1984). *Cerebrovascular disorders* (3rd ed.). New York: Raven.

Toole, J. F., & Patel, A. N. (1974). *Cerebrovascular disorders* (2nd ed.). New York: McGraw-Hill.

GURMAL RATTAN
*Indiana University of
Pennsylvania*

RAYMOND S. DEAN
*Ball State University
Indiana University School
of Medicine*

ANOXIA

CEREBRAL LESION, CHRONIC

A chronic cerebral lesion is one that has been in existence beyond what might be considered to be the amount of time required for recovery of lost function.

Chronic cerebral lesions, much like acute cerebral lesions, are likely to influence behavior in ways related to their location and extent or size. Unlike acute cerebral lesions, however, chronic cerebral lesions may have greater effects on behavior than effects related to their location and extent. Increased effects on behavior can result from two conditions. The primary behavioral loss can be due to the interruption of developmental schemata, whereby a child who sustains a chronic cerebral lesion at an early age may be precluded from development of the normal repertoire of behaviors dependent on the integrity of the area of lesion. Since the normal sequence of ontogenetic recapitulation of phylogenetic phenomena is interrupted, not only is there limitation of the behavior dependent on the specific area of cerebral tissue that sustains a lesion, but also of the subsequent behaviors dependent on the development of that initial behavior. The secondary loss from a chronic cerebral lesion results from a disuse atrophy phenomenon, whereby deterioration of muscle tissue or degeneration of neurotransmitter receptor sites, resulting secondary to the lesion, inhibits the development, performance, or acquisition of given behavioral skills.

Chronic cerebral lesions, especially those acquired after the developmental sequence is completed, may have lesser behavioral effects than those of acute lesions, in that the individual over time may acquire compensatory skills that help overcome some of the behavioral limitations imposed by the lesion.

Although chronic cerebral lesions can have onset at any age, many such lesions of congenital or prenatal onset result in death or profound developmental handicap. Onset age appears to be related to the severity of the handicap imposed by the lesion. Although it has been traditional to believe that the effects of chronic brain lesions are less severe in children because of presumed greater plasticity in the organization of their central nervous systems (Lyons & Matheny, 1984), there is accumulating evidence that a chronic cerebral lesion acquired early in childhood may have more severely debilitating effects (Cermak, 1985; Levin, Benton, & Grossman, 1982). There is also evidence that such lesions limit the development of memory and intellectual ability to a greater extent with early age onset than with later age onset (Levin, Eisenberg, Wigg, & Kobayashi, 1982). Further, there is evidence to suggest a greater likelihood of emotional problems resulting from chronic cerebral lesions at an early age (Rutter, 1981). These problems may interact with cognitive problems, depending on the age at which the lesion was acquired (Lyons & Matheny, 1984). The selective results of unilateral cerebral lesions on such specific aspects of behavior as language development, previously thought to be less specific when acquired at an early age, have been found to be similar in early childhood onset to those of later age onset (Aram et al., 1985). Even for those children who appear to show good recovery from early onset chronic cerebral lesions, there is a strong likelihood that special educational placement may be necessary (Lehr, 1984). The etiology of the chronic cerebral lesion, whether from head injury, brain tumor, or radiation therapy, appears to be unrelated to the neuropsychological outcome (Bruce, 1982).

Although recent developments in neurochemistry suggest that neurochemical adaptations at surviving synapses may mediate behavioral changes over time, which would account for frequent observations that behavioral consequences of chronic cerebral lesions change as time following the injury increases (Marshall, 1984), there is no generally accepted explanation for why this change over time should occur.

REFERENCES

Aram, D. M., Ekelman, B. L., Rose, D. F., & Whitaker, H. A. (1985). Verbal and cognitive sequelae following unilateral lesions acquired in early childhood. *Journal of Clinical and Experimental Neuropsychology, 7,* 55–78.

Bruce, D. A. (1982). Comment. *Neurosurgery, 11,* 672–673.

Cermak, L. A. (1985, Feb.). The effects of age at onset and causal agent of brain injury on later adaptive functioning in children. Paper presented at the International Neuropsychological Society, San Diego. Abstract in *Proceedings* (p. 10).

Lehr, E. (1984, August). Good recovery from severe head injury in children and adolescents. Paper presented at American Psychological Association meeting, Toronto, Ontario.

Levin, H. S., Benton, A. L., & Grossman, R. G. (1982). *Neurobehavioral consequences of closed head injury.* New York: Oxford University Press.

Levin, H. S., Eisenberg, H. M., Wigg, N. R., & Kobayashi, K. (1982). Memory and intellectual ability after head injury in children and adolescents. *Neurosurgery, 11,* 668–672.

Lyons, M. J., & Matheny, A. P. (1984). Cognitive and personality differences between identical twins following skull fracture. *Journal of Pediatric Psychology, 9,* 485–494.

Marshall, J. F. (1984). Brain function: Neural adaptations and recovery from injury. *Annual Review of Psychology, 35,* 277–308.

Rutter, M. (1981). Psychological sequelae of brain damage in children. *American Journal of Psychiatry, 138,* 1533–1544.

LAWRENCE C. HARTLAGE
Evans, Georgia

BIRTH INJURIES
BRAIN DAMAGE
CEREBRAL INFARCTION
HEAD INJURY

CEREBRAL PALSY (CP)

Cerebral palsy (CP), sometimes called congenital spastic paralysis, is characterized by varying degrees of disturbance of voluntary movements caused by damage to the brain. Cerebral refers to the brain and palsy refers to weakness or lack of control. Cerebral palsy was originally called Little's disease after the English surgeon William John Little, who first described it. Later, Winthrop Phelps, an orthopedic surgeon, coined the term cerebral palsy and brought it into common usage as a result of his extensive work with this population in the United States.

There is agreement among experts in the field that cerebral palsy is a complex of characteristics attributed to brain injury. It has been defined by the United Cerebral Palsy Research and Educational Foundation as having the following elements: (1) being caused by injury to the brain; (2) causing motor disturbance, including paralysis, weakness, and uncoordination; (3) consisting of a cluster of symptoms; (4) usually originating in childhood; and (5) perhaps including learning difficulties, psychological problems, sensory defects, convulsions, and behavioral disorders of organic origin. In addition to these elements, cerebral palsy is nonprogressive, static, and unamenable to treatment.

There are two major types of CP: spastic, characterized by sudden, violent, involuntary muscular contractions, and athetosic, characterized by ceaseless, involuntary, slow, sinuous, writhing movements. The physical symptoms of CP can be so mild that they are detected only with difficulty, or they can be so profound that the affected individual is almost complete physically incapacitated. It is not unusual for a cerebral palsied individual to function normally intellectually. However, this intelligence is often masked (at least to the lay person) by uncontrolled physical characteristics, involuntary movements of the body and extremities, speech disorders, and drooling. Cerebral palsy is not a disease, and it is not curable.

The incidence of cerebral palsy varies; a conservative estimate of its occurrence is 1.5 to 2.0 cases per 1000 live births. It has been estimated that the incidence may be higher in areas where there is inadequate prenatal care and accompanying prematurity. It is estimated that there are 500,000 children and adolescents with cerebral palsy in the United States (UCP, 1998). While CP occurs at every socioeconomic level, it is more prevalent among lower socioeconomic groups. Children born in poverty situations have a greater chance of incurring brain damage from factors such as malnutrition, poor prenatal and postnatal care, and environmental hazards during infancy. Cerebral palsy occurs slightly more frequently in males than in females, and more white than black children are affected. Cerebral palsy makes up the largest category of physical disabilities, representing 30 to 40% of all children in programs for the physically disabled.

In most cases, cerebral palsy is congenital (approximately 85% of all cases), meaning damage to the brain occurs during pregnancy or at birth. However, infectious diseases or severe head injuries can cause cerebral palsy at any time in life. Postnatal causes are said to be acquired, whereas those present at birth are congenital. It is generally agreed that CP cannot be inherited.

Prenatal causes of CP include German measles in the mother, pH incompatibility, maternal anoxia, use of drugs, and metabolic disorders such as maternal diabetes. Faulty growth of the fetal brain may occur if the mother is malnourished during pregnancy. In addition, maternal exposure to the toxic substances in X-rays may also damage the brain of the fetus. Perinatal (birth process) causes include prolonged labor, breech delivery, anoxia, and prematurity. High fever, poisonings, and other related factors may cause harm immediately following birth. After birth (postnatal) causes include anoxia, direct trauma to the brain, and infection. Poisonings also may contribute to brain damage during the postnatal period. In some cases, severe and consistent child beating has caused CP.

It is estimated that as many as three-quarters of all persons with CP have additional disabilities such as retardation, seizures, auditory and visual handicaps, or communication disorders (UCP, 1998). Approximately 50 to 60% of CP children are retarded. Mental retardation has been difficult to diagnose in the population since intelligence tests were standardized on children with adequate speech, language, and motor abilities. Seizures are associated with approximately 25 to 35% of individuals with cerebral palsy and are much more prevalent with spastic CP persons. Strabismus (squinting) occurs in approximately 30 to 35% of cerebral-palsied individuals. Some athetotic CPs experience farsightedness while spastic CPs are nearsighted. Visual field reduction also can occur in some types of CP (Capute, 1975).

Speech and/or language problems can range from normal speech and reception processing and expression to that which is nonfunctional. Speech in the two major types of CP has been characterized by Berry and Eisenson (1956) as (1) spastic speech, e.g., "slow, labored rate, lack of vocal inflection, gutteral or breathy quality of voice, uncontrolled volume, and, most important, grave articulatory problems which reflect the inability to secure graded, synchronous movement of the tongue, lips, and jaw"; and (2) athetoid speech, e.g., "varying gradations of a pattern of irregular, shallow, and noisy breathing; whispered or hoarse phonation, and articulatory problems varying from the extremes of complete mutism of extreme dysarthria (impaired articulation) to a slight awkwardness in lingual movement."

Speech disorders are found in 70% of cerebral-palsied children. It has been reported that speech defects are found in 88% of persons with athetosis, 85% of those with ataxia, and 52% of those who are spastic. Most of the speech problems are caused by problems controlling the muscles used to make speech sounds.

Minear (1965) developed a classification scheme for cerebral-palsied individuals based on motor characteristics as well as the area of the body where the problem is located. The six types within the motor component were adopted by the American Academy for Cerebral Palsy and have been described by others (Bleck, 1975; Denhoff, 1976; Healy, 1983). The six types include spasticity, athetosis, ataxia, rigidity, tremor, and mixed.

Spasticity is the most common type of CP, occurring in approximately 40 to 60% of the total. Stiffness of the muscles in spastic children occurs when the injury is on the brain surface or when it involves those nerves leading from the surface through the substance of the brain and onto the spinal cord. The spastic type is characterized by a loss of voluntary motor control. When the child initiates voluntary movement, it is likely to be jerky, with lack of control in the body extremities. This disability may affect any or all limbs. Involvement in the upper extremities may include varying degrees of flexing of the arms and fingers, depending on the severity of the disability. When lower extremities are involved, there may be a scissoring movement of the legs, caused by muscle contractions.

Athetosis is the second largest group in the CP population, occurring in approximately 15 to 20% of the total. This type is caused by injury to the brain's motor switchboard. Athetoid children are characterized by involuntary jerky, writhing movements, especially in the fingers and wrists. The head is often drawn back with the neck extended and mouth open. There are generally two types of athetosis: tension and nontension. The tension athetoid's muscles are always tense; this reduces contorted movement of limbs. The nontension athetoid has contorted movements without muscle tightness. Unlike the spastic child, all movements cease during sleep. The movements occur only in a conscious state; when emotionality increases, athetosis movements become intensified. Athetoids are usually higher in intelligence than spastic CP victims.

Ataxia is less prevalent than spasticity and athetosis. Together with tremor and rigidity, it makes up approximately 8% of the total CP population. The injury is in the cerebellum. Ataxic children are characterized by a lack of coordination and sense of balance. The eyes are often uncoordinated and the child may stumble and fall frequently.

Rigidity and tremor types of CP are extremely rare. Rigidity is unlike the other types in that the lower level of muscles stiffen and a rigid posture is maintained. The rigid type is usually severely retarded with a high incidence of convulsions. In tremor, there is involuntary movement in one extremity, usually one hand or arm. The motion may vary in its consistency and pattern. In intention tremor, the involuntary movement happens only when the child attempts an activity while in constant tremor. The involuntary movement is continuous.

Mixed is another variation of CP. It is a combination of the other five types with one type predominating. Approximately 30% of individuals with CP have more than one type.

The movement or motor component of the clinical classification system is composed of two types, pyramidal and extrapyramidal. The pyramidal type refers to the spastic cerebral-palsied group because the usual nerve cell involved in this disorder is shaped like a pyramid. Extrapyramidal refers to all other types of CP, athetosis, rigidity, tremor, ataxia, and mixed, in which the area of the brain affected is composed of conglomerates of nerve cells (Capute, 1975).

In addition to describing CP by type of neuromuscular or motor involvement, Denhoff (1976) also characterized this multihandicapped population by the body parts that are affected. This is also known as topographical classification, with (generally) seven types. With hemiplegia, one half, either the right side or left side, of the body is involved. Of cerebral-palsied individuals 30 to 40% fall into this category. The legs are involved to a greater extent than the arms with diplegia. Of all cerebral-palsied children 10 to 20% are diplegic. Quadriplegia involves all four limbs accounts for 15 to 20% of the total CP population. With paraplegia, occurring in 10 to 20% of all cerebral cases, only the legs are involved. Monoplegia involves only one limb and triplegia involves three limbs. These two types rarely occur. With double hemiplegia, both halves of the body are involved, but unlike quadriplegia, the two sides are affected differently. This type, too, rarely occurs.

Also CP can be classified by the severity of the motor involvement. Deaver (1966) described the CP child based on the mild, moderate, and severe classification scheme. Even though the descriptions were formulated several years ago, they are still useful today because of the explicitness of the activity level included in each category. In the mild category, no treatment is needed. The individual has no speech problem, is able to care for himself or herself, and can walk without the aid of appliances. In the moderate category, treatment is needed for speech problems and/or difficulties in ambulation and self-care. Braces and other equipment are needed. In the severe category, treatment is needed, but the degree of involvement is at a level wherein the prognosis for speech, self-care, and ambulation is poor.

Educational programs for children with cerebral palsy in the public schools gained momentum in the early 1970s with the emphasis on deinstitutionalization and normalization. Prior to this, many of these children, with multiple handicaps and not adequately diagnosed, remained in institutions for the mentally retarded.

It is generally agreed by experts in the field that treatment and educational considerations are extremely important and more complicated because cerebral-palsied children are multihandicapped. Not only must special equipment and facilities be provided to accommodate their physical disabilities, but additional special education techniques are needed to accommodate other handicaps (mental retardation, learning disabilities, auditory and visual disabilities).

When planning and implementing educational programs for cerebral-palsied individuals, a cadre of persons working in a multidisciplinary approach must be used. Many educators and physicians (Capute, 1975; Gearheart, 1980; Healy, 1983) have delineated the specific roles of the individuals who must work together in the education of cerebral-palsied children. The degree of CP and physical characteristics will determine the extent of participation by the physician. The physician may prescribe drugs for the patient to relax and to control the convulsions as well as treat overall health problems. Braces and other mechanical devices that provide support and allow children to walk are usually prescribed by medical doctors. The physical therapist works to facilitate motor development, to prevent or slow orthopedic problems, and to improve posture and positioning so that the child may benefit from other intervention activities. The occupational therapist uses creative, educational, and recreational activities to enhance self-help skills and teach parents to handle the child's daily living activities. The speech pathologist will monitor the child's progress in speech and language and provide therapy if the child is able to benefit from it. The speech therapist also may work with parents and other educational personnel on how to stimulate language development. An audiologist, learning disabilities specialist, and teacher of the mentally retarded may be needed to provide some direct and indirect services to the primary teacher when required. Biofeedback clinicians may be useful in teaching the individual what muscle groups are voluntarily effected (UNC, 1998).

A variety of specialized equipment is available to teachers, including adapted typewriters, pencil holders, book holders, page turners, and special desks to make cerebral-palsied individuals more self-sufficient.

The success achieved by the cerebral-palsied child depends largely on the extent of his or her physical and mental disability. While some cerebral-palsied people will need constant care in a protected environment, many can lead relatively normal lives and become productive citizens if given the opportunity.

REFERENCES

Berry, M. F., & Eisenson, P. (1956). *Speech disorders.* New York: Appleton-Century-Crofts.

Bleck, E. E. (1975). Cerebral palsy. In E. E. Bleck & D. A. Nagel (Eds.), *Physically handicapped children: A Medical atlas for teachers.* New York: Grune & Stratton.

Capute, A. J. (1978). Cerebral palsy and associated dysfunctions. In R. H. Haslam & P. G. Valletutti (Eds.), *Medical problems in the classroom.* Baltimore, MD: University Park Press.

Cruickshank, W. M. (1976). *Cerebral palsy: A developmental disability.* Syracuse, NY: Syracuse University Press.

Deaver, G. G. (1955). Cerebral palsy: Methods of evaluation and treatment. *Institute of physical medicine & rehabilitation, 9.*

Denhoff, E. (1978). Medical aspects. In W. M. Cruickshank (Ed.), *Cerebral palsy: A developmental disability* (3rd ed.). Syracuse, NY: Syracuse University Press.

Gearheart, B. R. (1980). *Special education for the 80s.* St. Louis: Mosby.

Healy, A. (1983). Cerebral palsy. In J. A. Blackman (Ed.), *Medical aspects of developmental disabilities in children—birth to three.* Iowa City, IA: University of Iowa Press.

Minear, W. L. (1956). A classification of cerebral palsy. *Pediatrics, 18,* 841–852.

United Cerebral Palsy. (1998). *Comments on biofeedback.* www.ucpa.org.

CECELIA STEPPE-JONES
North Carolina Central University

HABILITATION OF HANDICAPPED
HIGH INCIDENCE HANDICAPS CONDITIONS

MULTIPLE HANDICAPPING CONDITIONS
PHYSICAL HANDICAPS
UNITED CEREBRAL PALSY

CERTIFICATION/LICENSURE ISSUES

With only a few exceptions, the issues and standards involving special education programs do not differ from those that apply to teacher education programs nationwide. These issues include teacher testing, the use of teaching personnel having college degrees but lacking teacher preparation courses, standards used to approve teacher education programs, and state certification requirements.

A number of states have moved toward, or implemented, the use of tests as part of the certification process. Some states require a test of basic skills prior to entering a teacher education program (e.g., California, Missouri), while other states require teachers to achieve a passing score on a content area test. It has been suggested that such tests will have a significant impact on the qualifications of individuals desiring to become teachers, particularly minority populations (Feistritzer, 1983). Feistritzer (1983) has suggested that the number of minority candidates entering teacher preparation programs has declined considerably in recent years. The Center for Minority Research in Special Education (COMRISE, 1998) is attempting to increase the number and research capacity of minority scholars in institutions of higher education with high minority enrollments and is trying to improve the quality and effectiveness of these programs.

An issue that has importance to special education is that of appropriate certification in the actual field of teaching. While most teachers are certified to teach in some field, not all teachers have been trained and certified to teach in the field to which they are assigned. For example, large numbers of special education teachers are not certified in special education or are not teaching the types of handicapped children and youths for which they hold a special education certificate. Thus teachers who are qualified to teach nonhandicapped children in elementary schools may be teaching learning-disabled, emotionally disturbed, or some other type of handicapped children. While emergency, temporary, or provisional certificates permit regular education teachers to teach handicapped learners, there is some question as to whether this constitutes the most appropriate and effective instruction for these students. An analysis of the changes made in the past twenty years to special education coursework for regular educators seeking recertification shows dramatic advances (Patton & Braithwaite, 1990).

Many teacher-training programs are competency-based

and result in program graduates receiving generic teaching licenses or endorsements. While this affords local school districts considerable flexibility for serving students, there is concern that distinct differences exist among differing handicapping conditions that cannot be met through the preparation of a generic teacher. While the needs of some handicapped students can be served using generic teaching personnel, the use of resource rooms for mildly/moderately handicapped learners (learning disabled, etc.) often results in placement with a noncategorically certified teacher rather than a teacher who holds a categorical (learning disabled, etc.) certificate.

Certification and licensure are also affected by supply and demand. In the past, special education teachers have been in short supply and the use of temporary or provisional certificates, as noted earlier, became common. This led to the development of teacher preparation programs that prepare teachers to meet temporary endorsement requirements as well as to meet full certification requirements. In many respects, programs become defined by the certification standards they parallel and are not being designed to promote excellence. Teachers, or prospective teachers, tend to enroll in programs that most expeditiously meet the minimum standards necessary for them to maintain or gain employment. For this reason, preparation programs in competitive situations (i.e., with other institutions of higher education) may feel compelled to meet minimum training requirements, which, in turn, become maximum training requirements.

The development of inclusionary education has changed the requirements of teacher preparation from a focus of individual mastery to a consultation/collaboration format. The inclusion of special education students in the regular classroom has mandated teacher preparation to prepare students for collaborative teaching arrangements (Campbell & Fyfe, 1995). Programs that involve students in practicum supervision involving regular-education cooperating teachers, special-education cooperating teachers, and university supervisors are growing in number (Ludlow, Wienke, Henderson, & Klein, 1998). The reflection of educational service delivery trends such as inclusion in teacher preparation, however, is not uniform and assessing competency is difficult at best.

REFERENCES

Campbell, D. M., & Fyfe, B. (1995). *Reforming teacher education: The challenge of inclusive education.* Paper presented at the Annual Meeting of the Association of Independent Liberal Arts Colleges for Teacher Education (Washington, DC, February 12, 1995).

COMRISE. (1998). *Center of Minority Research in Special Education.* Charlottesville, VA: University of Virginia, Curry School of Education.

Council for Exceptional Children. (1983). Code of ethics and standards for professional practice. *Exceptional Children, 50,* 205–218.

Feistritzer, C. E. (1983). *The condition of teaching.* Lawrenceville, NJ: Princeton University Press.

Ludlow, B. L., Wienke, W. D., Henderson, J., & Klein, H. (1998). A collaborative program to prepare mainstream teachers: Using peer supervision by general and special educators. In American Council on Rural Special Education Conference Proceedings *Coming together: Preparing for Rural Special Education in the 21st Century.* March 25–28.

Maple, C. C. (1983). Is special education certification a guarantee of teaching excellence? *Exceptional Children, 49,* 308–313.

Patton, J. M., & Braithwaite, R. (1990). Special education certification/recertification for regular educators. *Journal of Special Education, 24,* 117–124.

PATRICIA ANN ABRAMSON
Hudson Public Schools,
Hudson, Wisconsin

PROFESSIONAL STANDARDS FOR SPECIAL EDUCATORS PERSONNEL TRAINING IN SPECIAL EDUCATION SPECIAL EDUCATION, LEGAL REGULATION OF

CHALFANT, JAMES C. (1932–   )

A native of Fremont, Ohio, James Chalfant obtained his BS (1954), MS (1958) and EdD (1965) from the University of Illinois. Early in his career, Chalfant's interest focused on an integrated training program for children with Down's Syndrome. Made available by the state of Illinois to all teachers of children with Down's Syndrome, the program involved intensive behavior shaping of self-help skills and the development of language, motor, and social skills (Chalfant, Silikovitz, & Tawney, 1977).

Chalfant is also noted for his extensive work on the development of teacher assistance teams, a team problem-solving model designed to assist and support individual teachers in managing situations for which the teacher needed additional help that was otherwise unavailable. This work is detailed in a chapter written by Chalfant in *Critical Issues in Gifted Education: Programs for the Gifted in Regular Classrooms (1993).*

During his distinguished career, Chalfant has been head of the Division of Special Education, Rehabilitation, and School Psychology at the University of Arizona, where he remains an active researcher and teacher with the rank of full professor. His most current research involves the study of self-concept in the visually impaired, and he teaches courses in learning disabilities, program development/service delivery, self-esteem, and cognitive abilities.

Chalfant was a member of a U.S. Department of Education task force focusing on issues and practices related to the identification of students with learning disabilities, and he was honored with a Presidential Citation for Outstanding Services for his work with the U.S. Office of Education's Division of Handicapped Children and Youth. Chalfant is also the recipient of the Award of Honor of the South African Association for Children with Learning Disabilities as "the international educator who has most influenced the field of learning disabilities in South Africa."

REFERENCES

Chalfant, J. C. (1993). Teacher assistance teams: Implications for the gifted. In C. J. Maker (Ed.), *Critical issues in gifted education: Programs for the gifted in regular classrooms.* Austin, TX: Pro-Ed.

Chalfant, J. C., & Pysh, M. V. (1982). *Teacher assistance teams: A procedure for supporting classroom teachers* (filmstrip; audiocassette; handout). New Rochelle, NY: Pem Press/Pathescope Educational Media.

Chalfant, J. C., Silikovitz, R. G., & Tawney, J. W. (1977). *Systematic instruction for retarded children: The Illinois program.* Danville, IL: Interstate.

E. VALERIE HEWITT
Texas A & M University
First edition

TAMARA J. MARTIN
The University of Texas of the Permian Basin
Second edition

CHALL, JEANNE S. (1921–   )

Jeanne S. Chall earned her BBA from the City College of New York in 1941. She went on to do her graduate work at Ohio State University, receiving her PhD in 1952. Chall taught at the City College of the City University of New York for 15 years. She joined the faculty at Harvard in 1965, and is currently Professor Emeritus of Education and Director of the Reading Laboratory in the Harvard Graduate School of Education.

Chall has long been active in the fields of education, reading, and language-related learning disabilities. She has served on numerous national committees and acted in a consulting capacity to various government education agencies. In addition, she has been a member of the editorial boards of several journals in the fields of reading, education, and educational psychology, including *Reading Research Quarterly* and the *Journal of Educational Psychology.* Three major books on reading have been authored by Chall, one currently in its third edition (1967, 1983a, 1983b, 1996a, 1996b). In earlier work, she authored two columns on the readability of instructional materials. She has also published diagnostic instruments to aid in the diagnosis of reading and other language-related disorders.

Jeanne S. Chall

The *Roswell-Chall Diagnostic Reading Test of Word Analysis Skills* (1997) is the most notable of these instruments.

Chall has also published widely on readability of instructional materials and other texts, coauthoring the Dale-Chall formula in 1948 and the New Dale-Chall formula in 1996. In 1996, she wrote a book entitled *Qualitative Assessment of Text Difficulty: A Practical Guide for Teachers and Writers.*

In addition to her diagnostic instruments, Chall's major contributions to the field of special education have been in her research in reading and learning disabilities and in teacher training in these closely related areas. She has received many honors for her outstanding achievements. In 1979, Chall was elected to the Reading Hall of Fame and the National Academy of Education. In 1982, Chall received both the American Educational Research Association Award for Distinguished Contributions to Research in Education and the American Psychological Association Edward L. Thorndike Award for Educational Psychology. In 1996, she received the Samuel T. Orton Award from the Orton Dyslexia Society. Currently, Chall continues to pursue her research interests in reading and language development and in diagnostic testing of reading disorders.

REFERENCES

Chall, J. S. (1967, 1983a, 1966a). *Learning to read: The great debate* (3rd ed.). Fort Worth, TX: Harcourt Brace.

Chall, J. S. (1983b, 1996b). *Stages of reading development* (2nd ed.). Fort Worth, TX: Harcourt Brace.

Chall, J. S., Jacobs, V. A., & Baldwin, L. E. (1990). *The reading crisis: Why poor children fall behind.* Cambridge, MA: Harvard University Press.

Chall, J. S. & Dale, E. (1995). *Readability revisited and the New*

Dale-Chall Readability Formula. Cambridge, MA: Brookline Books.

Chall, J. S., Bixxes, G., Conard, S., & Harris-Sharples, S. (1996). *Qualitative assessment of text difficulty: A practical guide for teachers and writers.* Cambridge, MA: Brookline Books.

Roswell, F. G., & Chall, J. S. (1997). *Roswell-Chall diagnostic test of word analysis skills* (4th ed.). Cambridge, MA: Educators Publishing Company.

KATHRYN A. SULLIVAN
Texas A & M University
First edition

TAMARA J. MARTIN
The University of Texas of the Permian Basin
Second edition

CHEMICALLY DEPENDENT YOUTHS

Chemically dependent youths are children and adolescents who want and need continued use of a psychoactive substance to sustain or maintain a chronic state of euphoria or intoxication. Alcohol and drug use by young people must be viewed not in isolation but in concert with that period of life known as adolescence. Substance use and addiction have profound effects on development and have serious implications for the future functioning of the abuser (Cohen, 1983).

The period of life commonly referred to as adolescence generally runs from 12 to 22 years of age. Adolescents are often described by age groupings: early (12 to 15), middle (15 to 18), and late (18 to 22). Although these divisions are convenient, they do not adequately describe the complex period of adolescence. More important are the biological, emotional, social, academic, and intellectual changes that young people undergo as they move from childhood to adulthood. Because these phases vary widely across adolescents and even within the same adolescent, no one variable, including age, is sufficient. The complex interplay of these dynamic phases in youth and the distinct stages of movement from drug use to chemical dependency best explain chemical dependency. Newman and Newman (1975) note that the physical development that accompanies puberty leads to a heightened awareness of body sensations. Drugs, especially marijuana and the hallucinogens, accentuate pleasurable bodily sensations and may be used by adolescents in an attempt to increase the sense of physical arousal. Cohen (1984) warns that adolescence, a period of critical psychosocial development when adaptive responses are being learned, is much more vulnerable to the loss of learning time than is adulthood.

Two types of chemical dependency occur, physical and psychological. Some substances induce tolerance and cre- ate a physical craving and addiction cycle, whereas others create a psychological dependency in which the user experiences changes in mood. Further, some compounds create both a physical and psychological dependency. In the latter case, chemically dependent youths may undergo detoxification to treat the physical craving and resultant withdrawal symptoms, but may continue to experience a craving or felt need to use again. This process sets up a cycle of dependency, detoxification, and return to use that accounts for the recidivism rate among addicted youths.

Psychological dependence is characterized by a drive to continue taking a drug when the user feels the effects of the drug are needed to maintain his or her sense of well being at an optimal level. The complex interaction of drug effects, personality, and stage of development constitute the degree of psychic craving or compulsion the user may experience. Drug-seeking behavior or compulsive drug use develops when the user comes to believe that the drug can produce pleasure and deter discomfort such that continuous or periodic administration of the drug is required. This mental state is the most powerful of all the factors involved in chronic intoxication with psychoactive drugs (Adesso, 1985).

Physiological dependence is characterized by reliance of body tissue on the continued presence of a drug within the user's system. Its presence is unknown to the user as long as the drug continues to be taken and is of no immediate consequence until the drug is withdrawn or no longer available. The magnitude of the dependence and the severity of the withdrawal symptoms vary directly with the type, amount, frequency, and duration of the drug use. Physiological dependence manifests itself as severe and immediate physical pain and discomfort, commonly referred to as withdrawal symptoms or abstinence syndrome. Symptoms may include fever, chills, gastrointestinal cramps, watery eyes, runny nose, and muscle cramping or spasms. They are frequently accompanied by psychological dependence. For drugs like alcohol, barbiturates, narcotic analgesics (morphine, Percodan, heroin) and cocaine, withdrawal symptoms and accompanying psychological dependence are so uncomfortable and threatening that they motivate young drug users to continue to seek and administer the drug. For drugs like stimulants (speed), and to a lesser degree marijuana and hallucinogenics (LSD, mescaline, psilocybin, peyote), the primary disturbance is psychological rather than physiological. But it should be noted that although the symptoms are not as severe as with physiological withdrawal, the user does experience discomfort of a mental or emotional nature (Bardo & Risner, 1985).

Different drug compounds act on different youths in different ways, both psychologically and physiologically. A 13-year-old pubescent male who is smoking two to three joints of high-grade (THC potent) marijuana daily over a 5- to 6-month period is likely to develop a psychological compulsion while not experiencing physical withdrawal symptoms on cessation. However, evidence suggests that THC lowers levels of the male hormone testosterone in the young male's system, retarding development of secondary sexual characteristics. Additionally, an amotivational syndrome from chronic cannabis intoxication results in lethargy, restlessness, and increased irritability (Cohen, 1984). Conversely, the same male drinking 1 to 3 ounces of alcohol (beer, wine, or hard liquor) over the same period of time will most likely experience both psychological and physiological withdrawal symptoms. Although medical complications may be more severe in the latter case, emotional, social, and intellectual complications occur in both.

Kandel (1984) proposes that culturally determined developmental stages of drug behavior are observed in adolescents. Initiation, progression, and regression in drug behavior are related to factors like prior delinquent behavior, high levels of drug-using peer affiliations, and parental models who use or abuse alcohol and drugs. The role of genetics in the development of substance abuse is also a major area of concern (Crabbe et al., 1985). Extensive research, primarily using animal models, indicates a strong predisposition to addiction in the offspring of addicted parents, particularly those using alcohol and sedative compounds. In sum, environment, psychosocial variables, and genetics are important concepts for consideration in adolescent substance abuse.

A single episode of intoxication does not produce either physical or psychological dependency. Several stages occur in the move from no use to dependency. The initial reason to try any drug depends more on the value the youth places on its use than on its pharmacological properties. Curiosity and availability, key factors at this stage, are influenced by the social factors of peer pressure and acceptance, adult role models, and family norms or values. Adolescents with learning disabilities are at particularly high risk for chemical dependency (Karacostas & Fisher, 1993). The majority of youthful experimenters do not proceed through all stages to dependence because of the drug effects themselves not being valued and the fact that most peer-group norms do not support continued use (Kandel, et al., 1978).

Experimental use may proceed to casual or occasional use, frequently referred to as socio-recreational use. This pattern usually involves imitation of adult role models who drink during social gatherings or use other drugs as mood enhancers. The youthful user may use drugs while at a party once or twice a month, or while attending a movie or listening to music with friends. Such use tends to be spontaneous and in a social context where drugs are readily available. Reasons for use are primarily social in that friends use and approve of use. Also, the drugs enhance self-confidence and social interaction during the identity phase of adolescence. The youthful user does not avidly seek drugs at this stage but will participate with a group if drugs are available.

The third stage, regular use, is distinguished from sociorecreational use by several features. The user at this stage actively seeks drugs, and is rarely seen in a social context without being intoxicated. Psychological dependence occurs. The user perceives that he or she functions better in social gatherings while intoxicated. Regular use also may involve physiological dependence if the user develops tolerance to a drug and experiences physical discomfort with cessation. The pharmacological properties of the drug become critical at this point. Whether the user proceeds into the final stage, dependency, is partly a function of what the drug does for the user's personality and the user's stage in adolescence.

The final stage is physical and/or psychological reliance on the drug to produce the user's desired effect. Heavy or compulsive use implies daily intoxication, although the user may indulge in binge-type use. Although only a minority of users become chemically dependent youths, the central factor is the degree to which use dominates the life of the adolescent. Intoxication may avoid other critical issues of adolescence (e.g., responsibilities of school and family, stress, lack of self-confidence) or mask the pain and discomfort of other pathological personality or mental disorders. Psychological and physical dependence are critical at this stage because regardless of reasons for continued use, the youthful user will have to continue to take the drug in order to avoid the newly acquired set of symptoms and difficulties associated with chemical dependency (Kandel, 1984). Although chemical dependency is not an official handicapping condition under federal legislation, it has been considered (Williams, 1990), and specialized programs for individuals with disabilities have been developed (Campbell, 1994).

REFERENCES

Adesso, V. J. (1985). Cognitive factors in alcohol and drug use. In M. Galizio & S. A. Maisto (Eds.), *Determinants of substance abuse* (pp. 179–208). New York: Plenum.

Bardo, M. T., Risner, M. E. (1985). Biochemical substrates of drug abuse. In M. Galizio & S. A. Maisto (Eds.), *Determinants of substance abuse* (pp. 65–99). New York: Plenum.

Campbell, J. (1994). Issues in Chemical dependency treatment and aftercare for people with learning differences. (1994). *Health and Social Work, 19,* 1, 63–70.

Cohen, S. (1983). *The alcoholism problems.* New York: Haworth.

Cohen, S. (1984). Adolescence and drug abuse: Biological consequences. In D. J. Lettieri & J. P. Ludford (Eds.), *Drug Abuse and the American adolescent* (pp. 104–109). Rockville. MD: National Institute on Drug Abuse.

Crabbe, J. C., McSwignan, J. D., & Belknap, J. K. (1985). The role of genetics in substance abuse. In M. Galizio & S. A. Maisto (Eds.), *Determinants of substance abuse* (pp. 13–54). New York: Plenum.

Kandel, D. B. (1980). Developmental stages in adolescent drug involvement. In D. J. Lettieri, M. Sayers, & H. W. Pearson (Eds.),

Drug abuse and the American adolescent (pp. 120–127). Rockville, MD: National Institute on Drug Abuse.

Kandel, D. B. (1984). Drug use by youth: An overview. In D. J. Lettieri & J. P. Ludford (Eds.), *Drug abuse and the American adolescent* (pp. 1–24). Rockville, MD: National Institute on Drug Abuse.

Kandel, D. B., Kessler, R. C., & Margulies, R. (1978). Adolescent initiation into stages of drug use: A developmental analysis. In D. B. Kandel (Ed.), *Longitudinal research in drug use: Empirical findings and methodological issues* (pp. 73–99). Washington, DC: Hemisphere.

Karacostas, D. D., & Fisher, G. L. (1993). Chemical dependency in students with and without hearing disabilities. *Journal of hearing Disabilities, 26,* 491–495.

Newman, B. M., & Newman, P. R. (1975). *Development through life: A psychosocial approach.* Homewood, IL: Dorsey.

Williams, R. W. (1990). Adolescent chemical dependency as a handicapping condition: An analysis of state regulations. *Journal of Chemical Dependency, 1,* 1, 69–82.

L. Worth Bolton
Cape Fear Substance Abuse Center

ALCOHOL AND DRUG ABUSE PATTERNS
DRUG ABUSE
SUBSTANCE ABUSE

CHEMOTHERAPY

The treatment of cancer in children usually includes chemotherapy, which consists of drugs that are administered to the child intravenously, intramuscularly, or orally on a repeated schedule (e.g., every 10 days or every month). The purpose of chemotherapy is to poison the cancer cells. Unfortunately, it also is toxic to healthy cells of the body. As a result, many children receiving chemotherapy experience unpleasant side effects.

Two common side effects of chemotherapy are nausea and vomiting. Children differ in the extent to which they have these symptoms. Furthermore, the degree of nausea and vomiting for a given child may vary widely from one course of chemotherapy to the next, even when there are no changes in chemotherapy. Many children feel intensely ill during the days they receive chemotherapy and for a few days afterward. Other children are able to carry on with play and other normal activities to varying degrees (Zeltzer, LeBaron, & Zeltzer, 1984).

Another possible side effect is a temporary susceptibility to bacterial infection or excessive bleeding. During such a period, physicians usually will advise the child not to participate in any contact sports or activities (e.g., gymnastics) that might increase the risk of bleeding. Because children on chemotherapy also are sometimes at risk for severe illness with certain viral infections, doctors often advise these children to stay home from school for a period of time if there is an outbreak of chicken pox. However, for the majority of time the child is receiving chemotherapy, the doctor usually will permit the child to engage in all normal school activities, including sports.

Another problem related to chemotherapy is that total hair loss may occur. Baldness is the most troublesome side effect of chemotherapy for many children. Bald children may feel so embarrassed that they refuse to go to school. Many children cope with this problem by wearing a cap, kerchief, or wig; others explain to their friends the reason for the baldness. Fortunately, in almost all cases, the hair grows back once chemotherapy is completed.

What are the effects of chemotherapy on the child's behavior and academic performance? Many of these children are absent from school at regular intervals because of medical appointments and chemotherapy side effects. Some children also stay home because of embarrassment over hair loss and fear of being rejected by peers. A further reason for school absence is a fear of failure because of the large amount of school material missed (Deasy-Spinetta, 1981; Deasy-Spinetta & Spinetta, 1980; Katz, Kellerman, Rigler, Williams, & Siegle, 1977).

For some children, radiation to the head produces cognitive deficits, especially when combined with injections of chemotherapy into the spinal canal. Many children with cancer show little or no evidence of cognitive deficits, but these are problems that can occur gradually and may be long-lasting. During the acute phase of radiation therapy, there often is transient swelling of the brain, which could produce additional temporary cognitive deficits.

There are several ways educators can be helpful to the student who is receiving chemotherapy. A teacher or counselor needs to contact the student's parents to discuss ways in which the student's educational needs can be met. For example, if the student is in the hospital, a few books and short assignments could be sent. If the child is likely to be at home for some time, homebound education may be indicated. A student who would not otherwise qualify for special education can qualify on the basis of the illness and can benefit greatly from both home and hospital teacher visits combined with regular school attendance.

With the permission of the child's parents, it usually is helpful to contact the student's physician to learn about the doctor's expectations regarding the student's capabilities during the period of treatment. The teacher also can ask the student how he or she feels about returning to school. A discussion of the student's needs and feelings with classmates can give the class an opportunity to discuss their misconceptions and worries about the student, as well as to ask questions. Children who are unable to return to school for a period of time usually appreciate receiving cards, drawings, or letters from classmates at school.

Educators need to be aware that hospitalization or confinement to bed at home because of nausea and vomiting does not necessarily preclude school work. On the contrary, involvement in school work, at least at a minimal level, can have therapeutic value. By attending school a few hours a day, having a homebound teacher, or doing some school work in the hospital, children can be distracted from unpleasant physical symptoms or worries. Some adolescents who receive chemotherapy in the morning prefer to come to school in the afternoon rather than to spend the rest of the day at home feeling sick. If the student experiences some nausea, he or she may need to leave the class abruptly. If these considerations are discussed in advance, then involvement in school can be therapeutic for the many children and may reduce the severity of nausea and vomiting.

Teachers can be most helpful to children receiving chemotherapy by maintaining a flexible attitude and realistic expectations. Most children receiving chemotherapy can maintain a normal educational load. However, specific expectations regarding homework and exams need to be flexible because of the intermittent nature of treatment-related problems. Frequent consultation with the student and parent will help to define reasonable and appropriate education goals.

REFERENCES

Deasy-Spinetta, P. (1981). The school and the child with cancer. In J. J. Spinetta & P. Deasy-Spinetta (Eds.), *Living with childhood cancer* (pp. 153–168). St. Louis: Mosby.

Deasy-Spinetta, P. M., & Spinetta, J. J. (1980). The child with cancer in school: Teachers' appraisal. *American Journal of Pediatric Hematology/Oncology, 2,* 89–94.

Katz, E. R., Kellerman, J., Rigler, D., Williams, K., & Siegle, S. E. (1977). School intervention with pediatric cancer patients. *Journal of Pediatric Psychology, 2,* 72–76.

Zeltzer, L. K., LeBaron, S., & Zeltzer, P. M. (1984). The adolescent with cancer. In R. Blum (Ed.), *Chronic illness and disabilities in childhood and adolescence* (pp. 375–395). Orlando, FL: Grune & Stratton.

Samuel LeBaron
Lonnie K. Zeltzer
*University of Texas Health
Science Center*

**CANCER, CHILDHOOD
HOMEBOUND INSTRUCTION**

Stella Chess

CHESS, STELLA (1914–)

Stella Chess was born and educated in New York City. She received her BA from Smith College in 1935 and MD from New York University School of Medicine in 1939. She served several internships, including psychoanalytic training, and became a diplomate of the American Board of Psychiatry and Neurology in Child Psychiatry in 1959. A member of the staff at New York Medical College from 1945, she became Professor and Director of the Division of Child Psychiatry in 1964. In 1966 Chess moved to a full professorship at New York University, a position she has held to the present.

Chess is best known for her collaboration (1956–present) with her husband, Alexander Thomas, and Herbert Birch (deceased) on a longitudinal study of the individual characteristics of children. This study found early differentiable temperament factors that persist and strongly influence child-environment interaction and later behavior. Additional longitudinal studies by Chess include behavioral patterns and child care practices of Puerto Rican families in New York City (1956–1970), children with multiple handicaps and congenital rubella (1970–1981), and children with mild mental retardation (1963–1968).

For her book, *How to Help Your Child Get the Most Out of School* (1974), Chess was awarded the Family Life Book Award of the Child Study Association of America. Her many awards and honors include the Honors Award from the Society for Research in Child Development for Distinguished Contributions to Psychiatric Theory (1993), the Adolph Myers Award of the American Psychiatric Association for Scientific Contributions to Psychiatric Theory and Practice (1996), and the George Tarjan Award from the

American Academy of Child and Adolescent Psychiatry for Significant Contributions to Mental and Developmental Disabilities.

Chess and Thomas were editors of the series *Annual Progress in Child Psychiatry and Child Development* from 1968 to 1970. Recent books include *Origins and Evolution of Behavior Disorders: From Infancy to Early Adult Life* (1984/1987) and *Temperament: Theory and Practice* (1996). With well over 50 publications spanning 25 years, including journal articles, authored books, and edited books, Chess remains highly active and productive in her fields of interest.

REFERENCES

Chess, S. & Thomas, A. (1974). *Annual progress in child psychiatry and child development*. New York: Brunner/Mazel.

Chess, S. & Thomas, A. (1987). *Origins and evolution of behavior disorders: Infancy to early adult life*. Cambridge, MA: Harvard University Press.

Chess, S. & Thomas, A. (1996). *Temperament: Theory and practice*. New York: Brunner/Mazel.

Chess, S. & Whitbread, J. (1974). *How to help your child get the most out of school*. Garden City, NY: Doubleday.

ELAINE FLETCHER-JANZEN
University of Northern Colorado
First edition

TAMARA J. MARTIN
The University of Texas of the Permian Basin
Second edition

CHILD ABUSE

The age-old phenomenon of child maltreatment has only recently attracted the attention of mental health professionals. Psychiatric and psychological exploration of child battering has lagged two decades behind the pioneering efforts of pediatricians and radiologists in establishing medical diagnostic criteria for physical abuse in children. Between 1963 and 1965, the passage of laws by all 50 states requiring medical reporting of child abuse ultimately subjected the abusing parents to legal process; these laws were also the catalyst for the formation of child protective services throughout the nation. The first psychological studies of abusing parents were carried out during this period.

Child abuse is currently regarded as the leading cause of death in children and a major public health problem. The proliferation of child abuse and neglect might bear some relationship to the alarming general increase of violence in our society demonstrated by the rising incidence of violent crimes, delinquency, suicide, and lethal accidents. In the last 20 years, child abuse has become a major focus of research and clinical study. A concerted effort is being made by federal, state, and local governments to develop programs for the study, prevention, and treatment of child abuse.

Owing to its complexity and far-reaching consequences, the problem of child abuse has attracted the attention of professionals from widely divergent backgrounds. Contributions to this area have come from the fields of pediatrics, psychiatry, psychology, social work, sociology, nursing, education, law, and law enforcement. Such multidisciplinary involvement has been essential in tracking down cases, locating medical treatment, and arranging for protective intervention and long-term planning with families. At the same time, it has become a source of confusion as a result of the differing roles, frames of reference, and terminology of each specialty. Exclusively cultural, socioeconomic, psychodynamic, and behavioral interpretations of the child abuse syndrome have failed to present the full picture.

The definition of child abuse has been continually expanding in recent years. In a classic paper, "The Battered Child Syndrome," (Kempe et al. (1962) described child abuse as the infliction of serious injury on young children by parents or caretakers. The injuries, which included fractures, subdural hematoma, and multiple soft tissue injuries, often resulted in permanent disability and death. Fontana's concept of the "maltreatment syndrome" (1964) viewed child abuse as one end of a spectrum of maltreatment that also included emotional deprivation, neglect, and malnutrition. Helfer (1975) recognized the prevalence of minor injuries resulting from abuse and suspected that abuse might be implicated in 10% of all childhood accidents treated in emergency rooms. Gil (1974) extended the concept of child abuse to include any action that prevents a child from achieving his physical and psychological potential.

Child protective services are specialized agencies existing under public welfare auspices; they are responsible for receiving and investigating all reports of child abuse or maltreatment for the purpose of preventing further abuse, providing services necessary to safeguard the child's well-being, and strengthening the family unit. These agencies are responsible for maintaining service until the conditions of maltreatment are remedied. They also have the mandate to invoke the authority of the juvenile or family court to secure the protection and treatment of children whose parents are unable or unwilling to use their services.

The wide variety of behavior and personality traits observed in abusing parents suggests that a specific abusive personality does not exist. Rather, individuals with a certain psychological makeup operating in combination with the burden of a painfully perceived childhood and immediate environmental stress might be likely to abuse the offspring who most readily elicits the unhappy childhood imagery of the past.

While environmental stress has often been suggested as a prominent etiological factor in child abuse, the precise definition of this relationship has eluded most investigators. One author has attributed child abuse almost exclusively to socioeconomic determinants (Gil, 1968, 1970), but most researchers agree that environmental stress is only the catalyst, in many instances, for an abuse-prone personality.

The stress argument has at least in part been predicated on the high percentage of low socioeconomic status (SES), multiple problem families in child abuse registers throughout the country. It is probable that reporting procedures themselves have led to the greater emphasis on socioeconomic determinants. Any controlled study that matches for SES is compelled to look beyond such variables as family income for the origins of child abuse. The conclusion that Spinetta and Rigler (1972) reach in their review of the literature is far more likely—that environmental stress is neither necessary nor sufficient for child abuse but that it does, in some instances, interact with other factors such as parent personality variables and child behaviors to potentiate child battering.

Environmental stress includes current events that widen the discrepancy between the limited capacity of the parents and increased child-rearing pressures. The stress may consist of a diminution of child-rearing resources owing to a spouse's illness or desertion, or to the unavailability of an earlier caretaker such as a neighbor or some other family member.

Environmental stress also includes the actual or threatened loss of a key relationship that provides the parent with emotional security and dependency gratification. This may occur when the spouse becomes physically or emotionally unavailable or when ties with parents or important relatives are severed owing to estrangement, illness, or death. Additional child-rearing pressures such as the birth or illness of another child, or the assumption of temporary care of other children, create environmental stress that may also lead to child abuse.

Justice and Duncan (1975) described the contribution of work-related pressures to environmental stress in situations of child abuse. They cited four types of work-related situations: unemployed fathers caring for children at home; working mothers with domestic obligations; overworked husbands who neglect their wives; and traumatic job experiences resulting in undischarged tension. Justice and Justice (1979) were able to document the importance of stress in terms of excessive life changes in child-abusing families by means of the *Social Readjustment Rating Scale* developed by Holmes and Rahe (1967).

The greatest area of agreement in the field of child abuse has pertained to the history and background of the abusive parents themselves. These individuals have usu-

ally experienced abuse, deprivation, rejection, and inadequate mothering during childhood. As children they were subjected to unrealistic expectations and premature demands by their parents. Parents with these characteristics are said to have "abuse-prone" personality traits.

The psychodynamics in a given case of child abuse are largely determined by the abuse-prone personality traits of the parent. The relationship between the abusing parent and his or her child is distorted by the cumulative impact of the parent's own traumatic experiences as a child reared in a punitive, unloving environment. Individuals who abuse their children cannot envision any parent-child relationship as a mutually gratifying experience. The task of parenting mobilizes identifications with the parent-aggressor, child-victim dyad of the past. The key psychodynamic elements in child abuse are role reversal, excessive use of denial and projection as defenses, rapidly shifting identifications, and displacement of aggression from frustrating objects onto the child.

Role reversal occurs when the unfulfilled abusing parent seeks dependency gratification, which is unavailable from his or her spouse or family, from the "parentified" child. It is based on an identification with the child-victim. The child's inability to gratify the father or mother causes the youngster to be unconsciously perceived as the rejecting mother. This intensifies the parent's feelings of rejection and worthlessness, which further threaten his or her narcissistic equilibrium. These painful feelings are denied and projected onto the child, who then becomes the recipient of the parent's self-directed aggression.

Any plan for the prevention or treatment of child abuse must be designed to create a safe environment for the child and to modify the potentiating factors underlying abuse. Therefore, an effective treatment program must deal specifically with the parental abuse proneness, those characteristics of the child that make him or her vulnerable for scapegoating, and the environmental stresses that trigger the abusive interaction.

A wide range of psychotherapeutic and educational techniques have proven successful in reducing the symptoms and problems of abused children. In general, these children present with ego deficits and cognitive impairment to such a degree that an emphasis on ego integration, reality testing, containment of drives and impulses, and strengthening of higher level defenses (similar to those techniques applied to borderline and psychotic children) proves necessary.

The ideal objective in studying and treating child abuse on a nationwide scale is, as with any major public health problem, the development of a strategy for prevention. Thus far, early case findings and protective intervention in abusing families have been the primary areas of interest for workers in this field. As more basic knowledge is accumulated about the child-abuse syndrome, through clinical experience and research, one can envision a logical shift in focus from treatment and rehabilitation (secondary prevention) to primary intervention.

REFERENCES

Fontana, V. (1964). *The maltreated child.* Springfield, IL: Thomas.

Gil, D. (1968). Incidence of child abuse and demographic characteristics of persons involved. In R. E. Helfer & C. H. Kempe (Eds.), *The battered child.* Chicago: University of Chicago Press.

Gil, D. (1970). *Violence against children.* Cambridge, MA: Harvard University Press.

Gil, D. (1974). *A holistic perspective on child abuse and its prevention.* Paper presented at the Conference on Research on Child Abuse, National Institute of Child Health and Human Development, Washington D.C.

Helfer, R. E. (1975). *The diagnostic process and treatment programs.* Washington, DC: U.S. Department of Health, Education and Welfare, National Center for Child Abuse and Neglect.

Holmes, T., & Rahe, R. (1967). The social readjustment rating scale. *Journal of Psychosomatic Medicine, 11,* 213–218.

Justice, B., & Duncan, D. (1975). *Child abuse as a work-related problem.* Paper presented at American Public Health Association, Chicago.

Justice, B., & Justice, R. (1979). *The broken taboo: Sex in the family.* New York: Human Science Press.

Kempe, C. H., Silverman, F., Steele, B., Droegemueller, W., & Silver, H. (1962). The battered child syndrome. *Journal of the American Medical Association, 181,* 17–24.

Spinetta, J., & Rigler, D. (1972). The child abusing parent: A psychological review. *Psychological Bulletin, 77,* 296–304.

CHARLES P. BARNARD
University of Wisconsin at Stout

ABUSED CHILDREN
BATTERED CHILD SYNDROME
CHILD CARE AGENCIES

CHILD ANXIETY SCALE (CAS)

The Child Anxiety Scale (CAS) is a 20-item self-report inventory of anxiety for young children. The CAS was published in 1980 by the Institute for Personality and Ability Testing.

Items for the CAS were selected based on their relationship to items on a "second-order anxiety factor" of the Early School Personality Questionnaire (ESPQ). Of 320 items tried out, the 20 items correlating most highly with this factor were selected.

The norms for the CAS were derived from a standardization study involving 2105 cases (1097 boys and 1008

girls). The test manual does not do an adequate job of describing the standardization sample. The manual also admits that the geographic representation of the sample did not mimic the national population. The authors tested for significant score differences by region by randomly selecting 30 cases from each region and testing for differences with an ANOVA (Analysis of Variance procedure). The results were insignificant but this may be due to a lack of statistical power because of small sample sizes rather than a lack of real differences. The match of the CAS sample to U.S. Census statistics by socioeconomic status or ethnic group is not shown. In light of other evidence, one cannot help but assume that the sample was selected on a convenience basis as much as on the basis of important stratification variables.

Results of a test-retest study were favorable with coefficients ranging from .82 at grade 1 to .92 at grade 3. Estimates of internal consistency were somewhat lower.

A variety of types of validity evidence are reported in the manual. First, the correlations between each of the 20 items and the ESPQ are reported. These range from .17 to .49. In addition, a study was conducted correlating CAS scores with parent mobility but a significant relationship was not found. In addition, the CAS scores of children in single versus dual parent families were compared and no significant differences between the groups were reported. Taken together, the results of these validity studies appear mixed at best and unimpressive at worst.

In summary, as a brief measure of children's anxiety the CAS shows some potential but suffers from problems with a poor standardization sample and poor evidence of validity.

REFERENCE

Gillis, J. S. (1980). *Child Anxiety Scale.* Champaign, IL: Institute for Personality and Ability Testing.

RANDY W. KAMPHAUS
Eastern Kentucky University

REVISED CHILDREN'S MANIFEST ANXIETY SCALE

CHILD BEHAVIOR CHECKLIST/4–18

The Child Behavior Checklist/4–18 (CBCL; Achenbach, 1991) is a standardized measure designed to elicit information from parents regarding their child's competences and problems. The checklist contains 20 competence items which target domains such as activities, school performance, and ability to establish and maintain friendships. These items yield a standardized T-score (mean of 50 and standard deviation of 10) on three scales: Activities, Social, and School. The remaining 118 problem items are rated on a 3-point Likert scale (not true, sometimes true, very true). These items yield standardized T-scores on 8 syndrome scales (Withdrawn, Somatic Complaints, Anxious/Depressed, Social Problems, Thought Problems, Attention Problems, Delinquent Behavior, and Aggressive Behavior). Combinations of these subsets comprise two other broader indices, Internalizing and Externalizing, as well as an overall Total Problem score. Cutoffs are provided in the manual for interpretation of scores in the clinical, borderline clinical, and normal ranges.

The CBCL was normed on 2,368 individuals from 4 to 18 years of age, representing 48 states. These individuals were stratified according to socioeconomic status, ethnicity, region, and CBCL respondent. Individuals receiving professional services for behavioral or emotional problems within the year prior to data collection, were excluded.

Detailed reliability and validity data are provided. Test-retest reliability at 7-day and one-year intervals for the competence and problem scales are reported at .87, .89, and .62, .75, respectively. Inter-rater reliability (agreement between mother's and father's ratings) is .75 for the Competence scale and .70 for the Problem scale. Criterion-related validity was established through its ability to discriminate between referred and nonreferred children. Although well-established as an effective clinical and research tool, the author emphasizes that the CBCL's utility is enhanced when used in combination with other measures and clinical observations (Achenbach, 1991; Lowe, et al. 1998).

REFERENCES

Achenbach, T. M. (1991). *Manual for the Child Behavior Checklist/4–18 and 1991 Profile*. Burlington, VT: University of Vermont Department of Psychiatry.

Achenbach, T. M. (1991). *Integrative guide for the 1991 CBCL/4–18, YSR, and TRF profiles*. Burlington, VT: University of Vermont Department of Psychiatry.

Lowe, L. A. (1998). Using Behavior Checklists in assessing conduct disorder: Issues of reliability and validity. *Research on Social Work Practice, 8*, 286–301.

ROSEANN BISIGHINI
The Salk Institute

CHILD DEVELOPMENT

Since its inception in 1930, *Child Development* has been published six times a year by the University of Chicago Press. It is a professional journal sponsored by the Society for Research in Child Development. As an interdisciplinary group, the Society for Research in Child Development uses the *Child Development* journal to publish manuscripts from all academic and professional disciplines that study developmental processes. The articles range from empirical and theoretical to reviews of previous research. The scholarly papers that appear in *Child Development* focus on the growth and development of children from conception through adolescence, including the development of language, thinking and reasoning, moral judgment, social skills, and family relationships.

The distribution of the journal, while primarily North American, is international. The editorial board is made of world renowned scholars. *Child Development*, clearly the most comprehensive journal in this field, is read by psychologists, pediatricians, anthropologists, social workers, and others who wish to obtain information related to research in child development.

The editor of *Child Development* is Marc H. Bornstein and subscription information can be obtained from The University of Chicago Press Journals Division, P.O. Box 37005 Chicago, IL 60637.

MICHAEL J. ASH
JOSE LUIS TORRES
Texas A & M University

CHILD FIND

Child Find is a term used since 1974 to describe a federal requirement for states to institute systematic procedures in order to locate all children with disabilities or at risk for disabilities from birth to age 21. In 1986, Congress expanded support for early intervention by creating the Infants and Toddlers with Disabilities Program, authorized under Part H of the Individuals with Disabilities Education Act (IDEA). The Part H program promotes a comprehensive and culturally appropriate approach to meeting the needs of infants and toddlers with disabilities through statewide systems of coordinated, comprehensive, multidisciplinary and interagency programs. In any given state, there are about half a dozen state agencies that participate in the financing and delivery of early intervention services under the Part H umbrella. Unfortunately, each state has created its own definition of developmental delay; therefore, variation in eligibility exists across the United States. Today, about 155,000 infants and toddlers birth through age 2 and their families are receiving early intervention services under Part H.

A comprehensive child find system includes many different aspects and methods of locating at-risk infants and toddlers. Interagency Coordinating Councils (authorized by Part H of IDEA) reveal that a wide variety of public awareness and child-find strategies have been utilized to improve program participation of culturally/linguistically diverse groups (Bernstein & Stettner-Eaton, 1994). Low-cost strategies such as mailings, home visit, and on-site questionnaires have had success in identifying children (Squires, 1996). Programs such as the Infant Follow Along Program (Lytwyn, 1992) combines agencies for referral and follow-up of identified children. In addition, training for physicians about developmental delays is becoming commonplace (Solomon, 1995).

Feasibility studies about Part H of IDEA are being conducted by state departments of health and education departments (Hawaii Department of Health, 1993; Michigan Department of Education, 1991). The effectiveness of child find and Part H of IDEA is addressed regularly in state annual reports (Colorado Evaluative Report, 1993) and annual reports to Congress (Eighteenth Annual Report, 1996).

REFERENCES

Bernstein, H. K., & Stettner-Eaton, B. (1994). Cultural inclusion in Part H: Systems development. *Infant-Toddler Intervention: The Transdisciplinary Journal, 4,* 1, 1–10.

Colorado Evaluative Report. (1993). Part H of the Individuals with Disabilities Education Act (IDEA) for Infants, Toddlers, and Their Families. *Annual Performance Report, Year V* (1991–1993).

Eighteenth Annual Report to Congress on the Implementation of the IDEA. (1996). Washington, DC: U.S. Department of Education.

Hawaii Department of Health. (1993). *A feasibility study for an evaluation of family needs in early intervention.* Hawaii: Author.

Lytwyn, P. (1992). *Infant follow along program: A computer assisted child find system using parent completed questionnaires.* Project description. (ERIC Document No. ED350734)

Michigan Department of Education. (1991). *Barriers and resources underlying Part H implementation: A utilization-focused evaluation study.* Michigan: Author.

Squires, J. (1996). Parent-completed developmental questionnaires: A low-cost strategy for child-find and screening. *Infants and Young Children, 9,* 1, 16–28.

Soloman, R. (1995). Pediatricians and early intervention: Everything you need to know but are too busy to ask. *Infants and Young Children, 7,* 3, 38–51.

ELAINE FLETCHER-JANZEN
University of Northern Colorado

EARLY IDENTIFICATION OF HANDICAPPED CHILDREN

EDUCATION FOR ALL HANDICAPPED CHILDREN ACT OF 1975

CHILD GUIDANCE CLINIC

Child guidance clinics are the result of the blending of several historical forces. The feminist movement was instrumental in opening the way for the *Century of the Child* (Key, 1909). This was precipitated by a new interest in child psychology that occurred at the turn of the century. Concern for children was also evidenced at this time in the passage of child labor laws. Also, as compulsory education gained momentum, problem children could no longer be hidden away at home and school-related problems became more prominent. In fact, the first clinic created for children (Lightner Witmer, at the University of Pennsylvania in 1896) was primarily concerned with the adaptation of children to the school situation. In 1891, America's earliest child psychologist of renown, G. Stanley Hall, designed the first journal devoted to child psychology; it served as a record of educational literature, institutions, and progress.

A second major force in the development of child clinics was the mental hygiene movement that was stimulated by the publication of *The Mind That Found Itself* (Beers, 1908). Beers and his associates set out to disprove the age-old dictum that suggested once insane, insane forever. This proved to be a significant step in the direction of acknowledging that if mental hygiene held value for adults, the same must hold true for children.

Another significant force was the influence of the psychiatrists that came to be known as the Boston Group. They viewed mental disorders as maladjustments of the personality rather than as diseases of the nervous system. Adolf Meyer (1928), a member of this group, believed that all possible factors should be considered, including original endowment, personality traits, home influences, habits, bodily ailments, and environmental stresses. Meyer is also believed to be the initiator of psychiatric social work as his wife visited the homes of his patients to determine emotional histories and information about their personalities and other illnesses. Meyer's wife was also concerned with preparing families for the return of the patient to the home setting. This interest in families and the childhood experiences of adult patients established a precedent for similar interest in the families and experiences of child patients.

By 1921 there were a number of clinics for children that were attached to mental hospitals, social agencies, schools, and colleges. Child guidance clinics were formally organized under that name in 1922 by the National Committee for Mental Hygiene and the Commonwealth Fund. These early clinics emphasized a team approach to the diagnosis and treatment of children's problems. A social worker and psychologist (under the supervision of a psychiatrist) constituted the treatment team. Thus, the interdisciplinary team concept was initiated, and it was revolutionary for its time. While interdisciplinary teams today have considerable overlap in role and function, the early teams were regimented so that the psychologist did the necessary testing, the social worker dealt with the parents (typically just the mother), and the psychiatrist worked with the child.

The Philadelphia Child Guidance Clinic was one of these early clinics; it has survived the years and seems reflective of the changes that have evolved. This is the clinic that is identified strongly with one of the major orientations to working with families: primarily structural family therapy as developed by Salvador Minuchin (1974). As Minuchin was an employee of the Philadelphia-based clinic, so were other influential persons in the development of family therapy such as Jay Haley, Harry Aponte, and Braulio Montalvo. This clinic also demonstrates the great overlap of functioning by various disciplines; social workers, psychologists, and psychiatrists all share equally in the delivery of services. In fact, a project supervised by Haley and Minuchin in the early 1970s focused on the training of lay people as significant helpers with troubled families. The Philadelphia Child Guidance Clinic, with its emphasis on one-way mirrors, live supervision, and video taping has also distinguished itself as a significant training institution. While not on the same scale as the Philadelphia clinic, many other clinics have followed the lead and developed themselves as centers of treatment and training (Chandra, Srinath & Kinshore, 1993). Certainly, the early child guidance clinics initiated the development of a far more elaborate treatment delivery system, but their influence still seems easily distinguishable as one considers the many community mental health centers that feature the multidisciplinary treatment teams that are now considered standard practice.

REFERENCES

Beers, C. (1908). *The mind that found itself.* New York: Longmans, Green.

Chandra, P. S., Srinath, S., & Kinshore, A. (1993). Disturbed children grown up: Follow up of a child guidance clinic population into adulthood. *NIMHANS Journal, 11,* 1, 43–47.

Key, E. (1909). *The century of the child.* New York: Putnam.

Meyer, A. (1928). Presidential address: 35 years of psychiatry in the United States and our present outlook. *American Journal of Psychiatry,* LXXXV, 1–32.

Minuchin, S. (1974). *Families and family therapy.* Cambridge, MA: Harvard University Press.

CHARLES P. BARNARD
University of Wisconsin at Stout

CHILD CARE AGENCIES
CHILD PSYCHIATRY
CHILD PSYCHOLOGY

CHILDHOOD APHASIA

Childhood aphasia, a label used in the pediatric and neurologic literature to describe disorders of speech and language in children, covers various disorders of communication. It is applied to children who have impairment of previously normal language and to children who failed in the normal acquisition of language.

The term aphasia derives from adult pathology in which an acute or progressive lesion produces a characteristic language disorder; it is "a clinical term that denotes the loss or impairment of language following brain damage and therefore, by definition, aphasia is a neurologic disorder" (Benson, 1979). When the brain has reached maturity, all the cerebral areas have their specialized activities. The language function is localized in the left hemisphere in right-handed people but also in the majority of left-handed persons. The cerebral hemispheres are not symmetrical anatomically or functionally. The asymmetry is already present in the fetus, but it becomes more marked in adult life. The planum temporale (superior temporal cortex) is larger on the left side of the brain and corresponds to an auditory association area which, in the adult, is included in the receptive area for language, called Wernicke's area. The left hemisphere is preponderant for language but its activities result from relations with different areas of the same hemisphere and also with the right hemisphere, which participates in language function.

An exhaustive study of cerebral lateralization, cerebral dominance, and asymmetrical functions in the nervous system has been recently reviewed by Geschwind and Galaburda (1985). Many classifications of the adult aphasias are known. Benson (1979) describes in detail eight different types of acquired aphasia that are based on the possibility of the patient expressing himself or herself in a fluent way or not, of understanding spoken language or not, of repeating, reading, and writing. In the adult there are mainly two groups of aphasia. The first, in which the patient is more affected in the comprehension of oral language, is called receptive, sensory, or Wernicke's aphasia. The patient is able to speak fluently but speech may have no connection with the questions asked. The pathology involves the posterior-superior portion of the first temporal gyrus (Wernicke's area). In the second group, the aphasic patient has great difficulties with speech but is able to write or to show the answers indicating that comprehension is correct. This is expressive, motor, or Broca's aphasia. The underlying pathology affects mainly the prerolandic region of the brain (frontal operculum or Broca's area).

Acquired aphasia in children is defined as impairment of previously normal language. Even in similar pathologic processes, as in adults, the clinical symptoms of aphasia in children depend on the degree of language development prior to cerebral insult. Childhood aphasia is characterized by an absence of spontaneous expressive language (oral, written, and gestural), producing a clinical syndrome of nonfluent speech or mutism (Wright, 1982). In all cases, the lexicon is reduced and the syntax is simplified; there is no logorrhea and even the lesion is temporal. Recovery is more frequent and rapid than in the adult, but when children regain language they rarely return to the premorbid level. Guttmann (1942) showed that disorders of language are mainly a reduction of the verbal expression of speech (thus, mainly a motor disorder). The prognosis is good unless there are simultaneous expressive and comprehension disorders.

Basser (1962) supported hemispheric equipotentiality because pre- or perinatal hemiplegia does not produce language impairment if the lesion is left or right; there is a possible transfer to the other hemisphere of the processes responsible for language when the damage is early, before language development. But if language is already acquired at the time of the hemiplegia, there is a persistent language deficit. Alajouanine and Lhermitte (1965) studied acquired aphasia in 32 children ages 6 to 15 years. The lesion was always in the left hemisphere, either traumatic or vascular. In all cases, they observed a reduction in expression in oral language, written language, or gestures; spontaneous language was nearly absent. Lenneberg (1967) suggested that up to age 11, language function could be assumed by the right hemisphere. However, Hecaen (1976) showed that 88% of acquired aphasias in children are due to left hemisphere lesions, while only 33% have right hemisphere lesions. Woods and Teuber (1978) confirmed that less than 10% of acquired aphasia results from right hemisphere lesions; if left-handedness is excluded, only 5% are due to right hemispheric lesions. Recovery, more frequent than in adults, is less evident if there are bilateral lesions. Recovery is better and more likely to occur with early lesions, before age 8. The recovery is never complete in comparison with normal controls, even when the child is no longer aphasic. In children with an injury prior to 12 months, there is no deficit in language, but the verbal IQ is significantly lower than that of sibling controls, showing that hemispheric specialization for language is very early. If the injury to the left hemisphere is made after 1 year, there is a persistent aphasic deficit as well as impaired cognitive function (Woods & Carey, 1979).

A syndrome of aphasia with convulsive disorders has been described in childhood by Landau and Kleffner (1957). This syndrome occurs in children who have had normal language development. It may begin between 18 months of age and 13 years, but the peak is reached between 3 and 7 years. The affected children may develop acutely or progressively (over days to months) a severe impairment of verbal comprehension as well as a loss of expressive language. At times, they appear deaf. The deficit has been ascribed to a verbal auditory agnosia (Rapin et al., 1977). The aphasic disorder may fluctuate with complete recovery and relapse. Intelligence remains normal. Outcome is variable with complete recovery or persistence of a mild or moderate deficit. Epileptic fits usually precede the language disorder, but they are not always present even though the electroencephalogram (EEG) always shows paroxysmal epileptic activity. The clinical fits usually disappear before 15 years and the EEG also becomes normal. No organic lesion has been shown in this syndrome.

Developmental language disorders or dysphasias are seen in children who have never acquired normal language function. They have been described under various terms: congenital or developmental aphasias, specific language disorders, and dysphasias. From the literature it appears that the capability for human language is partially an innate cognitive skill (Mayeux & Kandel, 1985). The process of acquisition of normal language function (Rapin, 1982; Wright, 1982) starts at birth. Infants with normal hearing are sensitive to sounds and react to them; they progressively become able to discriminate the acoustically subtle phonetic cues crucial for the comprehension of human language. This sensitivity is lost as language is acquired. Children learn to associate meaningful visual precepts (visual memory) with discriminable auditory ones (auditory memory), and to demonstrate this by pointing to objects on verbal command. Therefore, language acquisition is not a passive operation based on imitation. The child will only start to repeat syllables and words when he or she is able to segment speech sounds and elemental units of meaningful language extracted from the casual conversation all around. Auditory comprehension precedes speaking. An infant understands the meaning of a word before vocalizing it and initially learns to comprehend the spoken symbol of a word (decoding). When the child comprehends the word, he or she is able to express the language symbol (encoding) (Wright, 1982). Children progressively acquire the rules of grammar and form sentences by age 4. It will take a child much longer to perfect articulatory skills and to learn to produce highly complex sentences. The addition of new words throughout the vocabulary continues throughout life. The process of acquisition follows a progression related to the overall maturation and development of the infant, but it also requires normal functioning and control of the structures involved in sound production.

The acquisition of language by children in all cultures follows a similar series of stages. Some children progress through these stages faster than others, but the average age for each stage is the same for all cultures, with peaks of development at certain age. At 3 to 6 months, an infant is able to do cooing, then babbling at 6 to 9 months. At 9 to 12 months, the baby imitates sounds and says the first intelligible words. By 14 months, the first word is given in a specific sense, usually "mommy" and "daddy." By 18 months, the vocabulary has 10 to 15 words. At 2 years, the child is able to make some sentences containing two or three words. At 3 years, speech contains questions and statements, as well as some emotional tone. Questions are of importance as they show the interest of the child in the surrounding world. At 4 years, complex sentences of a few words are used and the child knows his or her first and last names.

Developmental language disorders traditionally have been divided into two groups. The first is disorders of receptive language, in which impaired comprehension is the essential feature; however, one may find some degree of verbal language and articulation dysfunction. The second group is expressive language disorders, characterized by delayed talking; poverty of words (especially in naming); and agrammatical spontaneous speech but normal comprehension, provided the child has no deafness, no mental retardation, no cerebral palsy and is not psychiatrically disturbed and did not suffer from environmental deprivation. As this type of classification has not satisfied clinicians or linguists, other subgroups have been proposed (Aram & Nation, 1975; Bishop & Rosenbloom, in press; Rapin, 1982, 1985). The classification presented by Rapin (1985) takes into account the input–central processing–output stages of language operation as well as the level of language most severely affected; it is based on the various levels of acquisition of language. The levels are phonology (concerned with sounds used as linguistic symbols), grammar (syntax and morphology, or the arrangement of words into meaningful sentences), semantics (the representation of meaning in language), pragmatics (how language is used).

In verbal auditory agnosia (word deafness), one is incapable of decoding the sounds around him or her (phonologic level, first necessary step to comprehension of language). The child does not understand phonemes or verbal words; therefore, he or she cannot reproduce them, is mute, or utters single words with phonologic distortion. The syntax is poor. These children learn gestural language and can express themselves through drawings. Their comprehension of symbols and cognitive functions is good and is expressed through games. They will benefit from teaching techniques for deaf children.

In semantic-pragmatic syndrome, the child has an impaired comprehension of the meaning and intent of communication but has good phonology and syntax. The child has a fluent language and often reproduces what is said, but is echolalic for even well-constructed sentences. As the deficit affects comprehension and use of language, the syndrome will be mainly observed with sophisticated questions. If these are put in a simply way, the child can answer yes or no, showing the deficit is not a cognitive one. These children have good auditory memory and are able to repeat long sentences, but their spontaneous speech often lacks precision. As pragmatics is affected in this syndrome, the subject cannot read facial expression or recognize tone of voice, so speech can be unadapted to the situation, creating difficulties in social contacts and behavioral problems. These children also can learn to read, but they do not totally understand what they read.

In semantic-syntactic-organizing syndrome, the deficit lies at two levels: syntax, necessary to organize words into meaningful sentences, and semantics, which is concerned with the meaning of sentences. Therefore, children are dysfluent using incorrect words in an inadequate order. The repetition of words is better than spontaneous speech.

Mixed receptive-expressive (phonologic-syntactic) syndrome is the most frequently seen syndrome of the developmental dysphasias. Comprehension is always better than expression, and can even be normal. The children are dysfluent, have a reduced vocabulary, and an elementary syntax. The phonology is also impaired, producing some distortions of poorly articulated words. Speech may be telegraphic.

In severe expressive syndrome (verbal apraxial), children with normal comprehension have a deficiency in coding language symbols into words. Their speech is extremely poor; often the children are mute. They learn to read and sign.

Phonological programming deficit syndrome is a subgroup of severe expressive syndrome. Children have a good comprehension, are fluent, and are able to speak in sentences. Phonologic disorder produces distorted pronunciation with substitutions or omissions in words; speech is uncomprehensible to other than family members.

The classifications used in developmental language disorders are still descriptive and the anatomic clinical correlations are less well understood than in adult or childhood acquired language disorders. The mechanisms involved are not only dependent on the left hemisphere, they have still to be elucidated.

REFERENCES

Alajouanine, T., & Lhermitte, F. (1965). Acquired aphasia in children. *Brain, 88,* 653–662.

Aram, D. M., & Nation, J. E. (1975). Patterns of language behavior in children with developmental language disorders. *Journal of Speech & Hearing Research, 18,* 229–241.

Basser, L. S. (1962). Hemiplegia of early onset and the faculty of speech with special reference to the effects of hemispherectomy. *Brain, 85,* 427–460.

Benson, D. F. (1979). Aphasia. In K. M. Heilman & E. Valenstein (Eds.), *Clinical neuropsychology.* New York: Oxford University Press. 22–58.

Bishop, D. V. M., & Rosenbloom, L. (in press). Childhood language disorders: Classification and overview. In W. Yule, M. Rutter, & M. Bax (Eds.), *Language development and disorders. Clinics in developmental medicine.* Blackwell Scientific & Lippincott.

Geshwind, N., & Galaburda, A. M. (1985). Cerebral lateralization. Biological mechanisms, associations and pathology. *Archives of Neurology, 42–I,* 428–459; 42–II; 521–552; 42–III, 634–654.

Guttmann, E., (1942). Aphasia in children. *Brain, 65,* 205.

Hecaen, H. (1976). Acquired aphasia in children and the ontogenesis of hemispheric functional specialization. *Brian & Language, 3,* 114–134.

Landau, W. M., & Kleffner, F. R. (1957). Syndrome of acquired aphasia with convulsive disorder in children. *Neurology, 7,* 523–530.

Lenneberg, E. H. (1967). *Biological foundations of language.* New York: Wiley.

Mayeux, R., & Kandel, E. R. (1985). Natural language, disorders of language, and other localizable disorders of cognitive functioning. In E. R. Kandel & J. H. Schwartz (Eds.), *Principles of Neural Science.* New York: Elsevier.

Rapin, I. (1982). *Children with brain dysfunction: Neurology, cognition, language and behavior.* New York: Raven.

Rapin, I. (1985). Communication disorders in children. In H. Szliwowski & J. Bormans (Eds.), *Progrès en neurologie pédiatrique.* Brussels: Prodim.

Rapin, I., Mattis, S., Rowan, A. J., & Golden, G. G. (1977). Verbal auditory agnosia in children. *Developmental Medicine & Child Neurology, 19,* 192–207.

Woods, B. T., & Carey, S. (1979). Language deficits after apparent clinical recovery from childhood aphasia. *Annals of Neurology, 6,* 405–409.

Woods, B. T., & Teuber, H. L. (1978). Changing patterns of childhood aphasia. *Annals of Neurology, 3,* 273–280.

Wright, F. S. (1982). Disorders of speech and language. In K. F. Swaiman & F. S. Wright (Eds.), *The Practice of pediatric neurology.* St. Louis: Mosby.

HENRI B. SZLIWOWSKI
CATHERINE WETZBURGER
*Hôspital Erasme, Université
Libre de Bruxelles*

APHASIA
LANGUAGE DISORDERS
LEFT BRAIN, RIGHT BRAIN
MUTISM

CHILDHOOD NEUROSIS

See PSYCHONEUROTIC DISORDERS.

CHILDHOOD PSYCHOSIS

Researchers in child psychology and psychiatry agree that there exist identifiable clinical syndromes where children are out of touch with reality, withdraw from the social world around them, and show unusual and bizarre behaviors. These psychotic children present great challenges to their caretakers: parents who try to provide for the psychotic child's needs and integration into the family system; teachers who try to educate the child and provide basic social skills training; and mental health professionals who try to treat the child clinically.

Consider the following case that the author supervised at a community mental health center. A 9-year-old boy was referred by foster parents following a sudden onset of bizarre destructive behavior and hallucinations. He thought monsters lurked behind doors, heard voices, and displayed bizarre speech during psychotic episodes. This child had been placed in several different foster homes since being abused and neglected as an infant. Two of his siblings were being legally adopted by one set of foster parents, but this child's behavior had led them to decide not to adopt him. He showed poor social skills, was intrusive with others (i.e., did not keep his hands to himself), and had a short attention span. He tolerated stress poorly and would sometimes lash out at others in a violent manner when frustrated. Several psychiatric hospitalizations had only temporarily stabilized self-control and reality orientation. This child was psychotic.

Other clinical cases make the important point that highly unusual and even bizarre behavior does not necessarily imply that a child is psychotic. During the clinical evaluation, for example, one 8-year-old boy freely launched into colorful descriptions of monsters and secret fantasy worlds. His conversation was marked by bizarre verbalizations with little distinction between reality and illusion. He mixed grandiose and paranoid ideas with characters of fantasy and real significant others from his life. Taken out of context, these verbalizations might be construed to reflect an active psychotic delusional state. However, on other occasions, the child was able to perceive reality accurately and to describe his delusions as a fantasy game. This child was not psychotic, but used fantasy as a retreat from high conflict and turmoil in his life. His family history did suggest that he was at risk for developing a psychotic state under stress since his mother had been diagnosed as schizophrenic.

Incidence of childhood psychosis is estimated at a maximum of 6 in 10,000 children (Werry, 1972), with a more probable estimate of 1 in 1,000 children (Quay & Werry, 1979). Unfortunately, methodological difficulties impede accurate estimates of incidence. However, research consistently shows that more boys than girls are diagnosed for each of the psychotic disorders. Estimated differences vary considerably, but it appears that at least twice as many boys are diagnosed as psychotic (Wing, 1968).

Early interest in psychotic states in children appeared near the turn of the twentieth century in the writings of Kraepelin and Bleuler, who introduced the terms dementia Praecox (early insanity) and schizophrenia (split mind), respectively. Both of these pioneers felt that the onset of many of their adult patients' psychotic disorders had been in their childhood. Thus childhood psychosis was seen as essentially identical symptomatically to adult schizophrenia. The concept of childhood psychoses gained greater acceptance as a result of articles by Potter (1933), Bender (1942), and Bradley and Bowen (1941) on childhood schizophrenia; Kanner (1943) on early infantile autism; Rank (1949) on atypical child psychosis; Mahler (1952) on symbiotic psychosis. These early writings were uniformly based on medical model or disease conception of mental abnormality and were marked by conceptual ambiguity and a lack of specific diagnostic criteria (Wing, 1968).

The evolution of theoretical syndromes points to three general types of childhood psychosis: (1) childhood schizophrenia, (2) early infantile autism, and (3) atypical or symbiotic psychosis.

Interest in childhood schizophrenia followed Potter's (1933) paper. The schizophrenic child was seen as someone who was disinterested in the environment, manifested disturbed thought processes and frequently poor verbal skills, had difficulty in forming emotional attachments to others, and showed bizarre behaviors with a tendency to perseverate in various activities. This view of childhood schizophrenia was modeled after adult schizophrenia.

Research on childhood autism was pioneered by Kanner (1943), who described autistic children as generally having a limited ability to relate to other people beginning in infancy, a language disturbance making it difficult to communicate with others, and conspicuous and obsessive behavior for repetition and maintaining sameness.

Symbiotic psychosis is a rare subtype described by Mahler (1952) as a disturbance owed to intense resistance by the child to becoming psychologically independent of the mother. The number of cases reported is small. The syndrome may be due to repeated early traumatic events and also may stem from a constitutional predisposition to fail to see the mother as a separate object (Mahler, 1965). The onset of this syndrome occurs between 2½ and 5 years of age, preceded by fairly normal development during the first 2 years of life. The onset of symptoms can be set off by such events as illness of a mother, birth of a sibling, or the beginning of school. The following Figure shows the general distribution of cases (not necessarily according to Mahler's theory) of childhood psychoses given on age of onset.

The child manifests the behaviors of extreme separation anxiety, emotional withdrawal, and distortions of reality similar to autism. Threats of separation create panic. Frustration tolerance is low, and even minor disruptions in routine create panic. There is a craving for sameness. This type of environmental disinterestedness diminishes contact with reality. This syndrome produces hypoactivity or hyperactivity, peculiar thoughts and abnormal speech, and aggressive behavior such as biting and hitting. The central symptom is profound anxiety to the point of panic over the possibility of separation from the mother. When this bond is threatened, the symbiotic child may show excessive screaming and temper tantrums. These episodes may be followed by disturbed thinking and the expression of bizarre ideas. Following the onset of the psychotic state, the child may show regression in previously acquired

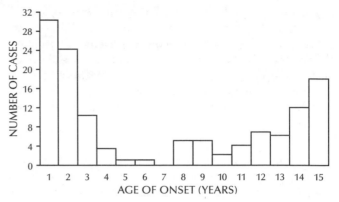

Distribution of cases of childhood psychosis given by age of onset (first detection)

habits such as toilet training and disturbances in other behaviors such as eating and sleeping.

The *Diagnostic and Statistical Manual of Mental Disorders* (DSM-IV; American Psychiatric Association, 1994) attempted to integrate the various approaches to childhood psychosis. This was not an easy task because of the complexity of the subject matter and the distinct points of view on such disorders as childhood schizophrenia. The resulting classification system is organized under the concept of pervasive developmental disorders, with separate subcategories for infantile autism and childhood onset pervasive developmental disorder. This latter category is very general and appears to reflect early research on childhood schizophrenia represented by the work of Lauretta Bender; it excludes work on symbiotic psychosis by Mahler. A separate less specifically defined category, atypical pervasive developmental disorder, allows the clinician to use diagnostic flexibility in describing the individual case, including a symbiotic psychotic child. The clinician can draw on the diagnostic criteria for adult schizophrenia in determining the appropriateness of this category for a child. The DSM-IV represents the most current thinking of the mental health profession on these disorders, and contains specific criteria for each psychotic disorder.

Treatment Approaches

Psychotherapy. Individual psychotherapy has been widely used in the treatment of childhood psychosis. Treatment approaches differ depending on the clinician's theory of the causes of the disorder, but they have in common an attempt to resolve psychic turmoil. Psychoanalytic-based approaches focus on the individual child and the presumed intrapsychic conflicts created by a fractured mother-child relationship (Mahler, 1965). Other approaches focus more on interpersonal skills and involve other family members in the treatment (Reiser, 1963).

Research on the effectiveness of psychotherapy with

psychotic children has produced differing estimates of improvement. Most writers agree that it often helps to improve symptoms, but there is disagreement on how much it contributes beyond an untreated recovery rate. Some reported recovery rates have been astoundingly high, but the research is difficult to evaluate because of differing criteria used to measure success and lack of untreated control groups.

Milieu and Educational Therapy. This approach manipulates the total environment in a residential setting. It addresses impairments to all areas of functioning and employs multiple treatments (individual, educational, and group therapy). Children referred for these programs are usually the most disturbed; this may partly explain why clinical improvement occurs in a high percentage of cases. Milieu therapy often focuses on improving adaptive self-care skills and improving reality orientation to facilitate better relatedness to others (Zimmerman, 1994). Research on the effectiveness of such programs is difficult to evaluate owing to lack of experimental controls, diverse groups of psychotic children, and small sample sizes. However, more structured programs appear to be more effective (Schopler, 1974).

Behavior Therapy. Principles of learning theory have been successfully applied to treating the symptoms of psychotic children, especially autism (Fester, 1961). The application of behavioral contingencies has helped child care workers and parents to shape the behavior of disturbed children in positive ways, but research suggests that the effects are not easily generalizable across settings.

Organic Treatments. A wide variety of physical treatments have been attempted. Electroconvulsive shock therapy, sensory deprivation, vitamin therapy, hallucinogenic drugs (LSD), and antipsychotic drugs all have been used. Campbell (1973) concluded that little success can be attributed to any of these treatments though antipsychotic drugs are effective in alleviating the worst of some symptoms such as aggressiveness and hallucinations.

In summary, biological, genetic, (Crow, Done & Sacker, 1995) and family factors combine to produce psychotic disturbance in children. A small percentage of children appear to be at risk of developing psychotic symptoms owed to these etiological factors when exposed to extreme environmental stress. Although a variety of treatments may produce some positive changes, long-term prognosis is generally poor for psychotic children. A high percentage continue to show psychotic symptoms or minimal social adjustment over time. With onset before age 10, the prognosis appears to be particularly poor. When a therapist and/or parent demonstrates a high degree of emotional involvement over time, the prognosis improves.

REFERENCES

American Psychiatric Association. (1994). *Diagnostic and statistical manual of mental disorders* (4th ed.). Washington, DC: Author.

Bender, L. (1942). Schizophrenia in childhood. *Nervous Child, 1,* 138–140.

Bradley, C., & Bowen, M. (1941). Behavior characteristics of schizophrenic children. *Psychiatric Quarterly, 15,* 296–315.

Campbell, M. (1973). Biological interventions in psychoses of childhood. *Journal of Autism & Childhood Schizophrenia, 3,* 347–373.

Crow, T. J., Done, D. J., & Sacker, A. (1995). Childhood precursors of psychosis as clues to its evolutionary origins. *European Archives of Psychiatry & Clinical Neuroscience, 245,* 2, 61–69.

Ferster, C. (1961). Positive reinforcement and behavioral deficits of autistic children. *Child Development, 32,* 437–456.

Kanner, L. (1943). Autistic disturbances of affective contact. *Nervous Child, 2,* 217–250.

Mahler, M. (1952). On child psychosis in schizophrenia: Autistic and symbiotic infantile psychosis. *Psychoanalytic Study of the Child, 7,* 286–305.

Mahler, M. (1965). On early infantile psychosis: The symbiotic and autistic syndromes. *Journal of the American Academy of Psychiatry, 4,* 554–568.

Potter, H. W. (1933). Schizophrenia in children. *American Journal of Psychiatry, 12,* 1253–1270.

Quay, H. C., & Werry, J. S. (1979). *Psychopathological disorders of childhood* (2nd ed.). New York: Wiley.

Rank, B. (1949). Adaptation of the psychoanalytic technique in the treatment of young children with atypical development. *American Journal of Orthopsychiatry, 19,* 130–139.

Reiser, D. (1963). Psychosis of infancy and early childhood. *New England Journal of Medicine, 269,* 790–798, 844–850.

Schopler, E. (1974). Changes of direction with psychotic children. In A. Davids (Ed.), *Child personality and psychopathology: Current topics* (Vol. 1). New York: Wiley.

Werry, J. S. (1972). Childhood psychosis. In H. D. Quay & J. S. Werry (Eds.), *Psychopathological disorders of childhood.* New York: Wiley.

Wing, J. (1968). Review of B. Bettelheim, *The empty fortress. British Journal of Psychiatry, 114,* 788–791.

Zimmerman, P. D. (1994). Bruno Bettelheim: The mysterious other: Historical reflect on the treatment of childhood psychosis. *Psychoanalytic Review, 81,* 3, 411–413.

WILLIAM G. AUSTIN
Cape Fear Psychological Services

AUTISM
BORDERLINE PERSONALITY DISORDER
DEPRESSION
EMOTIONAL DISORDERS
MENTAL STATUS EXAMS
PSYCHONEUROTIC DISORDERS

CHILDHOOD SCHIZOPHRENIA

The term childhood schizophrenia is one that is, at present, the subject of considerable dispute among authorities in the fields of child psychiatry and psychology. The dispute has mainly to do with the boundaries of this term and the validity of the concept of a childhood onset schizophrenic disorder. As a result of the uncertainty and differences of opinion, firm conclusions have not been reached, and the variation in interpretation of the term childhood schizophrenia has made compilation of a data base problematic.

A large part of the current confusion about childhood schizophrenia results from changes in the definition of the term itself. As Walk (1964) has noted, most authors prior to 1930 tended to diagnose schizophreniclike disorders in children much as they would have diagnosed them in adults. Typical of this literature is De Sanctis's (1906) use of the term *dementia precocissimia*, which apparently was a variant of Kraepelin's concept of *dementia praecox* in adults.

By about 1935, several major clinics had been established in the United States for the study and treatment of severe children's disorders. The directors of these clinics (Bender, 1947; Kanner, 1943; Potter, 1933) all published descriptions of their samples of children and follow-up studies delineating the children's progress. Throughout the period 1930 to 1960, the terms infantile psychosis, autism, and childhood schizophrenia tended to be used interchangeably, although Kanner and his colleagues (Kanner, 1949; Kanner & Eisenberg, 1955) tended to define autism as a separate category that was seen as the earliest form of schizophrenia. Most of these early authors also agreed that schizophrenic disorders closely resembling the adult disorder could occur in childhood, although adult symptoms such as delusions and hallucinations did not occur before about age six. Creak (1961) provided a working definition of childhood schizophrenia that included nine basic characteristics. However, this definition included a substantial overlap into both the autistic and schizophrenic syndromes. Early analytic writers such as Bettelheim (1950) and Szurek (1956) also tended to lump a wide variety of disorders under the rubric of childhood psychosis. In contrast to earlier authorities who were uncertain about etiology, psychoanalytic writers felt that the etiology of the disorder was always psychogenic.

By the end of the period 1965 to 1980, it became clear that some important and distinct subpopulations were emerging. Barbara Fish and her colleagues (Fish et al., 1968) developed a classification system based on language and the ability to integrate basic functions in infancy, and Rutter (1978) presented his findings from long-term studies at Maudsley Hospital in London. In addition, Kolvin (1971), Vrono (1974), and others had published epidemiological data that demonstrated that two major peaks occurred in the distribution of cases across age. The first, at about 2 to 3 years consisted of cases of autism and autisticlike disorders. The second, occurring in early adolescence, consisted of cases resembling adult schizophrenia with delusions, hallucinations, and a thought disorder of form or content. It was also clear that a mixed or residual group with unclear symptoms existed, and most writers clearly acknowledged that some crossover cases existed that did not follow the age of onset distinction. This tripartite division of severe childhood disorders is the basis of the third edition of the *Diagnostic and Statistical Manual of Mental Disorders* (DSM-IV) (American Psychiatric Association, 1994) classification of pervasive developmental disorders.

In DSM-IV, childhood schizophrenia is not set apart as a separate category, but is diagnosed using the adult criteria for schizophrenia. These include

A. Characteristic symptoms: Two (or more) of the following, each present for a significant portion of time during a 1-month period (or less if successfully treated):

(1) delusions

(2) hallucinations

(3) disorganized speech (e.g., frequent derailment or incoherence)

(4) grossly disorganized or catatonic behavior

(5) negative symptoms, i.e., affective flattening, alogia, or avolition

B. *Social/occupational dysfunction*: For a significant portion of the time since the onset of the disturbance, one or more major areas of functioning such as work, interpersonal relations, or self-care are markedly below the level achieved prior to the onset (or when the onset is in childhood or adolescence, failure to achieve expected level of interpersonal, academic, or occupational achievement).

C. *Duration*: Continuous signs of the disturbance persist for at least 6 months. This 6-month period must include at least 1 month of symptoms (or less if successfully treated) that meet Criterion A (i.e., active phase symptoms) and may include periods of prodromal or residual symptoms. During these prodomal or residual periods, the signs of the disturbance may be manifested by only negative symptoms or two or more symptoms listed in Criterion A present in an attenuated form (e.g., odd beliefs, unusual perceptual experiences).

D. *Schizoaffective and Mood Disorder exclusion*: Schizoaffective Disorder and Mood Disorder with Psychotic Features have been ruled out because either (1) no Major Depressive, Manic, or Mixed Episodes have occurred concurrently with the active-phase symptoms; or (2) if mood episodes have oc-

curred during active-phase symptoms, their total duration has been brief relative to the duration of the
active and residual periods.

E. *Substance/general medical condition exclusion*: The
disturbance is not due to the direct physiological effects of a substance (e.g., a drug of abuse, a medication, or a general medical condition.

F. Relationship to a Pervasive Developmental Disorder: If there is a history of autistic disorder or another pervasive developmental disorder, the additional diagnosis of Schizophrenia is made only if
prominent delusions or hallucinations are also present for at least a month (or less if successfully
treated). (DSM-IV, 1994, p. 285–286)

DSM-IV suggests that this approach is controversial.
Part of the problem involves the inherent difficulty in identifying delusions, hallucinations, and thought disorders in
children whose language abilities are very limited. Another shortcoming involves the inability to diagnose organic disorders in children, especially at an early age. Finally, a number of authors (e.g., Fish & Ritvo, 1979) have
noted the crossover of children from one category to another. This crossover does not occur often in samples of
more retarded children, who tend to show more autistic
symptoms, but it occurs often enough among samples with
average intelligence to prompt concern about the diagnostic criteria.

Demographic data using the DSM-IV criteria for schizophrenia in children are virtually nonexistent except insofar as they may be inferred from data obtained for adults.
The overall incidence of schizophrenia is thought to range
between 15 and about 1% of the population, with an equal
sex distribution and a higher incidence rate in lower socioeconomic classes. It also appears to have a higher incidence in some families, but the concordance rate, even in
monozygotic twins, is not perfect, implying intervening environmental and/or biological factors. The lower limit for
the age of onset using the DSM-IV criteria appears to be 8
or 9 years, but there are isolated reports of much earlier
onset. As Rutter (1974) notes, the differences in age of onset between autism and schizophrenia and the low incidence of any severe disorder between ages three and early
adolescence suggest that both autism and schizophrenia
are etiologically distinct and valid syndromes. Unfortunately, little of substance can be said regarding the prognosis or etiology of schizophrenia in children or adults.
Whereas autism has been linked to a number of organic
and/or genetic conditions, the changing definition of childhood schizophrenia has prevented the compilation of a
large enough data base to permit inferences about etiology.
The same general state of affairs exists concerning prognosis, although in adults, schizophrenia is thought to have

a very poor outcome and a high relapse rate, as noted in
DSM-IV.

As noted previously, early in this century it was common to lump all severe childhood disorders together diagnostically; it was assumed that these were earlier forms of
adult schizophrenia. In the last 20 years, however, it has
become clear that distinctions should be made among
these disorders. The most important differential diagnoses
are between schizophrenia and disorders such as autism,
mental retardation, and pervasive developmental disorders or disintegrative diseases of organic origin such as
Heller's syndrome. Some of these disorders are documented in DSM-IV and some are not, but delineation of
the differences among them may illuminate the nature
of schizophrenia in children.

Both schizophrenia and mental retardation may coexist in the same individual, and DSM-IV is careful to
point out that some of the social isolation and odd behavior
seen in retarded children, especially at a very early age,
may be mistaken for symptoms of schizophrenia. In general, however, among the retarded one may expect to find
a steady, unremitting course to the disorder, whereas
schizophrenics will usually show a prolonged period of
normal development. In addition, many retarded persons
have physical (particularly facial) stigmata that permit
their identification into basic syndromes, but the presence
of such stigmata is rare in child schizophrenia of later onset. Goldfarb (1967) has noted stigmata present in early
onset psychoses and Bender (1947) also noted their presence among psychotic children, but it is not clear how their
samples correspond to current DSM-IV categories. Hall-
marks of schizophrenia such as delusions and hallucinations are rarely found in individuals who are diagnosed
only as retarded. It is generally possible to distinguish between retardation and schizophrenia when careful psychological testing is done to establish the subject's mental age
as a baseline for judging the appropriateness of language
and social behavior.

By far the most effort has been expended to differentiate schizophrenia from infantile autism. Kanner (1943)
initially described autism as the earliest form of schizophrenia, but it has become clear that there are marked differences between the two disorders. First, Rutter (1974)
points out that there is a great difference in the distribution of the age of onset between the two disorders, with a
peak at 2 to 3 years for the onset of autism and a much
later peak in adolescence for schizophrenia. In addition,
the course of the two disorders differs sharply, with schizophrenic children having a period of normal development
followed by an uneven course, whereas autistic children
show deviant development from birth and a consistent
course. The symptoms themselves differ: schizophrenic
symptoms such as delusions and hallucinations are rare in
autism, whereas the autistic child's need for sameness and

frequent seizures (in about 25% of cases) are not usual features of schizophrenia. Although most major studies of schizophrenia show a familial loading for schizophrenia and an equal sex distribution, schizophrenia is rare in the families of autistic children and autism occurs more frequently in boys than girls by a ratio of about 4:1 (Rutter, 1985). In most cases (a few exceptions have been reported) children who are diagnosed as autistic do not resemble schizophrenics as adults (Kanner & Eisenberg, 1955).

Some authorities have noted that distinguishing between autism and other disorders is particularly difficult when the child is of average intelligence and does not show many of the characteristic language and behavior peculiarities of the younger and/or more limited autistic child. Asperger (1944) proposed that these children constitute a separate diagnostic group characterized by normal intellect, restricted and obsessive interests in certain subjects or activities, and constricted emotional and social responses. However, this description also applies to many children who have been diagnosed as autistic at an earlier age, especially those with better intelligence and/or language skills.

Schopler (1985) has pointed out that until some behavior distinction between higher level autism and so-called Asperger's syndrome can be demonstrated, confusion might be reduced if Asperger's syndrome were not regarded as a distinct diagnostic category. Most cases could adequately be classified as autistic or as schizoid disorders of adolescence (Rutter & Schopler, 1985). Both high-level autism and the adolescent schizoid disorder differ from schizophrenia, however, since the former disorders do not have hallucinations as a major feature and have an earlier age of onset with a fairly even course marked by the failure to develop normal social relationships.

Heller (1930) described a disorder in which an initial period of 3 to 4 years of apparently normal development is followed by a gradual and widespread disintegration of behavior involving areas as diverse as receptive and expressive language and bowel and bladder training. Social impairment and a general loss of interest in the outside world follow. Other disorders such as tuberous sclerosis may, in the early stages, show some features similar to schizophrenia. However, the early onset age of these latter disorders and the broad deterioration (including social skill areas such as toileting), accompanied in some cases by seizures and other physical problems, are the distinguishing features for differential diagnosis. The etiology is thought to be organic.

Because of the heterogeneity of the cases that have been labeled as schizophrenia, a wide variety of treatments have been employed, as has been the case with autism. Insofar as schizophrenic children may have more intact intellectual/language skills than children with other severe disorders, the traditional play, insight-oriented, and "talking" therapies might be expected to be more effective. Unfortunately, no good studies documenting the utility of this approach are available, again owing in part to differences in diagnostic terminology over the years. Similarly, since drugs such as the phenothiazines have demonstrated value with adult schizophrenic populations, one might expect them to be effective with younger patients diagnosed with schizophrenic symptoms. Campbell (1975), Fish (Fish et al., 1968), and others have noted the favorable effects of such drugs with children, but it is again not clear how their samples fit into the DSM-IV scheme. It is noteworthy that most antipsychotic drugs are apparently not especially effective in reducing the symptoms of autism, except in isolated cases (Rutter & Schopler, 1985). The most common form of treatment today involves parental support, counseling, and special psychoeducational strategies, much as with autistic children. In fact, many classes for severely disturbed or psychotic children contain a mix of autistic, schizophrenic, and other types of children. Whether the use of DSM-IV nosology will lead to enhanced and differentiated treatment for these diagnostic groups remains to be seen.

REFERENCES

American Psychiatric Association. (1994). *Diagnostic and Statistical Manual of Mental Disorders* (4th ed.). Washington, DC: author.

Asperger, H. (1944). Die autistischen psychopathen im kindersalter. *Archives Fur Psychiatrie und Nervenkrankheiten, 117,* 76–136.

Bender, L. (1947). Childhood schizophrenia. Clinical study of one hundred schizophrenic children. *American Journal of Orthopsychiatry, 17,* 40–56.

Bettelheim, B. (1950). *Love is not enough.* Glencoe, IL: Free Press.

Campbell, M. (1975). Pharmacotherapy in early infantile autism. *Biological Psychiatry, 10,* 399–423.

Creak, M. (1961). Schizophrenia syndrome in childhood: Progress report of a working party. *Cerebral Palsy Bulletin, 3,* 501–504.

DeSanctis, S. (1906). On some varieties of dementia praecox. Translated and reprinted in J. G. Howells, *Modern perspectives in international child psychiatry.*

Fish, B., & Ritvo, E. (1979). Psychoses of childhood. In J. Noshpitz (Ed.), *Basic handbook of child psychiatry.* New York: Basic Books.

Fish, B., Shapiro, T., & Campbell, M. (1968). A classification of schizophrenic children under five years. *American Journal of Psychiatry, 124,* 1415–1423.

Goldfarb, W. (1967). Factors in the development of schizophrenic children: An approach to subclassification. In J. Romano (Ed.), *The origins of schizophrenia.* New York: Excerpta Media Foundation.

Heller, T. (1930). About dementia infantilis. Reprinted in J. Howells (Ed.), *Modern perspectives in international child psychiatry.* Edinburgh: Oliver & Boyd.

Kanner, L. (1943). Autistic disturbances of affective contact. *Nervous Child, 2,* 219–230.

Kanner, L. (1949). Problems of nosology and psychodynamics of early infantile autism. *American Journal of Orthopsychiatry, 19,* 416–426.

Kanner, L., & Eisenberg, L. (1955). Notes on the follow-up studies of autistic children. In P. Hoch & J. Zubin (Eds.), *Psychopathology of childhood.* New York: Grune & Stratton.

Kolvin, I. (1971). Psychoses in childhood—A comparative study. In M. Rutter (Ed.), *Infantile autism: Concepts, characteristics and treatment.* London: Churchill-Livingstone.

Potter, H. (1933). Schizophrenia in children. *American Journal of Psychiatry, 12,* 1253–1270.

Rutter, M. (1974). The development of infantile autism. *Psychological Medicine, 4,* 147–163.

Rutter, M. (1978). Diagnosis and definition. In M. Rutter & E. Schopler (Eds.), *Autism: A reappraisal of concepts and treatment.* New York: Plenum.

Rutter, M. (1985). Infantile autism and other pervasive developmental disorders. In M. Rutter & L. Hersov (Eds.), *Child and adolescent psychiatry: Modern approaches.* Oxford: Blackwell Scientific.

Rutter, M., & Schopler, E. (1985). Autism and pervasive developmental disorders: Concepts and diagnostic issues. Paper prepared for National Institute of Mental Health Research Workshop, Washington, DC.

Schopler, E. (1985). Convergence of learning disability, higher-level autism, and Asperger's syndrome. *Journal of Autism and Developmental Disabilities, 15*(4), 359.

Szurek, S. (1956). Childhood schizophrenia symposium 1955: Psychotic episodes and psychotic maldevelopment. *American Journal of Orthopsychiatry, 25,* 519–543.

Vrono, M. (1974). Schizophrenia in childhood and adolescence. *International Journal of Mental Health, 2,* 7–116.

Walk, A. (1964). The pre-history of child psychiatry. *British Journal of Psychiatry, 110,* 754–767.

Eric Schopler
*University of North Carolina
at Chapel Hill*

Jerry L. Sloan
*Wilmington Psychiatric
Associates*

AUTISM
CHILDHOOD PSYCHOSIS
PSYCHONEUROTIC DISORDERS

CHILD PSYCHIATRY

Child psychiatry is a subdiscipline of psychiatry, a branch of medicine focusing on human emotional development and pathology. As a subspeciality, child psychiatry is approximately 75 years old, with Freud's treatment of a young boy in 1909 marking its genesis (Jones, 1959). The practitioner of child psychiatry must have comprehensive training both in general psychiatry and child development. This includes a firm understanding of trends in cognitive, language, and motor development. Training in neurology is also essential in understanding which developmental delays may be attributed to organic as opposed to psychogenic etiology.

Initial involvement of the child psychiatrist is focused on the mentally retarded and an assessment of them for the purpose of deciding on entrance to state schools and hospitals for the mentally retarded. This may have been influenced by European trends in determining which children were able to benefit from a public education and which were ineligible as a result of deficient mental abilities (Wolman, 1972). This focus has been greatly expanded to areas of treatment and prevention, with assessment being regarded as the role of a multidisciplinary team.

While the earliest child psychiatrists often acted in a unitary fashion, more contemporary approaches have included psychiatrists as team members. This has also been reflected in their involvement in a larger variety of agencies than traditionally noted. Earlier trends in child psychiatry have placed the psychiatrist in medically oriented facilities such as hospitals, state homes for the retarded, and pediatric services. Recent trends have included child psychiatric services in child-guidance clinics, community mental health facilities, and, with the introduction of PL 94-142, in community-based schools.

Along with this shift in orientation, child psychiatrists have attained more of a consultant status (Knapp & Harris, 1998); they are no longer seen as the sole practitioner for the young child. Their presence is observed throughout the progression from the mainstream classroom to the residential facility. For example, if the child with special needs is educated within the mainstream class, resource room, or special education class, the child psychiatrist may consult to assist in determining developmental needs requiring medical attention. This assessment is made in conjunction with other members of the multidisciplinary team. As the placement shifts to a more restrictive milieu, as with residential placement, the multidisciplinary team remains the functional unit for developing the individual education plan (IEP), with the child psychiatrist maintaining a consultant and team-member status and contributing from his or her area of expertise.

Another domain of child psychiatry includes participation on recommendations of Committees for the Handicapped (COH) and school-based guidance and support teams. Within his or her area of expertise, this new consultant to the educational system contributes in a unique manner, evaluating the child for possible psychopharmacological intervention to assist in the learning process.

With the advent of medications focusing on attentional deficit disorders, disruptive behaviors, and childhood depression syndromes, new tools interface the educational and the medical approaches with child development and treatment. This required the special knowledge that the child psychiatrist is trained to possess. Transcending traditional training in dynamic psychotherapy, the knowledge of more contemporary behavioral management techniques has also become part of the armamentarium of this profession, thus allowing for additional assistance in structuring the child's environment for facilitating growth. In conjunction with significant school personnel and the family, the child psychiatrist may assist in developing treatment plans geared to maximize the child's educational experience. To carry out this role, the practitioner must have a sound foundation of knowledge about child development, assessment of personality and its pathology, therapeutic intervention, and prevention (Noshpitz, 1979).

REFERENCES

Jones, E. (Ed.). (1959). *Sigmund Freud: collected papers* (5 vols). New York: Basic Books.

Knapp, P. K., & Harris, E. S. (1998). Consultation—liaison in child psychiatry: A review of the past 10 years. *Journal of the American Academy of Child and Adolescent Psychiatry, 37,* 2, 139–146.

Noshpitz, J. D. (1979). *Basic handbook of child psychiatry* (4 vols). New York: Basic Books.

Wolman, B. B. (Ed.). (1972). *Manual of child psychopathology.* New York: McGraw-Hill.

ELLIS I. BAROWSKY
Hunter College

CASCADE MODEL OF SPECIAL EDUCATION SERVICES
MENTAL STATUS EXAMS
MULTIDISCIPLINARY TEAMS

CHILD PSYCHOLOGY

Child psychology is concerned with answering two basic questions: How do children change as they develop, and what are the determinants of these developmental changes? (Hetherington & Parke, 1979). Modern child psychology is particularly concerned with understanding the processes that produce and account for age-related changes in children. Child psychology is concerned with development from conception to adolescence.

Historically, modern child psychology can be traced to the work of G. Stanley Hall, president of Clark University and one of the founders of the American Psychological Association (Kessen, 1965). In 1893 Hall published *The Contents of Children's Minds*, the first systematic study of large groups of children using a questionnaire method to obtain information about children's and adolescents' behaviors, attitudes, and interests. During the early years of this century, research in child psychology was primarily atheoretical and focused on the description of age changes in physical, psychological, and behavioral characteristics. Child psychologists in the past several decades, however, have been primarily interested in studying the basic processes underlying development. Some of the earliest researchers and theorists who had great impact on the expansion of the field of child psychology were Binet, who developed the first test of intelligence, Gesell, who investigated perceptual-motor abilities in young children, Freud, who proposed a theory of personality development, and Piaget, who published an influential theory of children's cognitive development.

Biologists and geneticists have made important contributions to an understanding of some of the processes and mechanisms related to development (Rosenthal, 1970). Behavior geneticists have been concerned with the mechanisms by which genetic factors contribute to a wide range of individual differences observed in human behavior across the entire life span. Research suggests that genetic factors play a role in the development of many physical and physiological characteristics, in intelligence, sociability, emotional responsiveness, and in some types of psychopathology.

Developmental changes in sensory capacities, visual-perceptual abilities, and fine and gross motor skills are major areas of study by child psychologists during the period of infancy. Among the specific areas studied are sound discrimination, visual stimulus preferences, and depth perception. Another important focus of child psychologists during infancy has been the effects of early experiences on their cognitive, motor, and social-emotional development. Among the issues addressed are the timing of experiences (i.e., early versus later experiences; the existence of critical periods) and concerns with the plasticity of development (i.e., previously acquired behavior patterns be modified by later experience?; Bower, 1977).

Child psychologists recognize the influence of heredity on setting the foundation for the course of development. These genetic factors interact with the child's learning experiences to determine actual developmental outcomes. Learning processes (e.g., conditioning mechanisms, imitation), are therefore an important area of study by child psychologists.

During the past two decades, five areas of development have received considerable attention by child psychologists. These areas are emotional development, language development, cognitive development, moral development, and the development of sex role behaviors (Mussen, 1970).

In the area of emotional development, research has

focused on the manner in which positive and negative emotions originate and how the expression of emotions changes with age (Yarrow, 1979). Another area that has attracted considerable interest is the development of attachment, in which infants show a specific desire to be near particular caretakers in their environment. Related to this issue is the study of the development of fears in the young child, particularly the fear of strangers. Child psychologists also have been interested in the ways that children learn to label and recognize their own and other people's emotions.

Language development represents one of the most significant achievements of childhood because of its importance in communication, thinking, and learning. Child psychologists differ on their views of the mechanisms underlying the development of language. Some argue that language is innate while others contend that language can be accounted for by traditional principles. A third view, which is held by most current theorists, is that both genetic and learning factors play a role in language development (Dale, 1976).

Research in children's cognitive development has dominated the field of child psychology. The area of cognition pertains to the mental activity and behavior through which knowledge is acquired and processed, including learning, perception, memory, and thinking. The psychological processes that underlie cognitive development are of particular interest to the child psychologist, including the operations involved in receiving, attending to, discriminating, transforming, storing, and recalling information.

Piaget (1952) developed the most comprehensive and influential theory of cognitive development. His theory emphasized developmental changes in the organization and structure of intelligence, and how differences in those structures are reflected in the learning of children at different ages. Another component of Piaget's theory involved his approach to the development of social cognition, i.e., the way in which children perceive, understand, and think about themselves, other people, and social interactions. Piaget's provocative theory probably has stimulated more research by contemporary child psychologists than any other theory.

In addition to investigating the basic processes by which children learn, researchers also have investigated how children retain information and recognize, recall, and use it when needed. A distinction is made between two types of memory: short term and long term. Developmental changes in various strategies used by children to facilitate memory such as rehearsal, mental imagery, and organization, also have been investigated by child psychologists.

Child psychologists have noted individual differences in the cognitive styles that children use to process information. One of the most frequently studied dimensions of swcwcognitive style is reflectivity-impulsivity. Reflectivity-impulsivity is associated with a number of intellectual, social, and personality factors.

Cognitive problem-solving abilities, as reflected in the concept of intelligence, have attracted the attention of psychologists for nearly a century. Child psychologists have addressed such issues as whether intelligence is a unitary, generalized ability, or a group of relatively separate abilities. In addition, the modifiability of intelligence has attracted much research attention in recent years (Lewis, 1976). There have been debates between those groups who argue that intelligence is genetically determined and, therefore, not alterable, and those who suggest that intelligence is more dependent on learning experiences. Similarly, the development and use of intelligence tests has generated considerable controversy within the field, with some investigators arguing that such tests are culturally biased toward white middle-class experiences. Intelligence tests, based on the concept of global intelligence, yield a single IQ score and continue to be widely used by practicing psychologists in clinical and academic settings. Tests of intellectual ability generally have been shown to be good predictors of achievement in academic settings.

The development of sex roles also has been an area of study in child psychology. Sex-role typing is the process by which children acquire the values and behaviors that are regarded as appropriate to either males or females in a specific culture. Characteristics of masculinity and femininity appear to be developed very early in life and are stable over time. Research indicates that the development of sex roles and sex differences in behavior is a complex phenomenon that involves the interaction of biological, social, and cognitive factors (Maccoby & Jacklin, 1974).

One component of the socialization process of children that has been of particular interest to child psychologists is the development of moral values and moral behaviors. Psychological research has focused on three basic aspects of morality: (1) cognitive factors including knowledge of ethical rules and judgments about whether various acts are right or wrong; (2) behavioral factors involving negative acts such as cheating, lying, resisting temptation, and controlling aggression, and behaviors involved in prosocial acts such as sharing, cooperation, altruism, and helping; and (3) emotional factors of morality such as feelings of guilt following a transgression (Hoffman, 1979).

Children are intimately involved in a number of social systems including the family, peer group, and school. Child psychologists have investigated the influence of these social systems on various aspects of the development of children (Hartup, 1979).

There is a long history of interest by child psychologists in the family's role in the socialization process. Of particular interest has been the relationship between child-rearing attitudes and practices and children's cognitive, personality, and social development. Contemporary issues pertaining to the family that have been investigated by

Uchild psychologists include the effects of child abuse, divorce, single-parent families, and maternal employment on the child's development.

Relationships with age mates are another important influence on the development of children. Age-related changes in peer interactions and the role of play behaviors have been the focus of much research. The influence of peers as models for negative and prosocial behaviors, and factors affecting peer group acceptance, also have been investigated.

Finally, child psychologists have studied the influence of the school as a socializing agent with children. In particular, the effects of teachers on children's academic achievement as well as social and emotional development has been examined. One area of interest has been an investigation of the impact of teacher expectations on children's performance in the classroom.

The major research interests in child psychology have changed over the course of time, often in response to social and historical pressures. Much of the knowledge that has accumulated in this field has been used to meet the needs of children in today's society and improve their well being through the implementation of various programs and services. In recent years, child psychologists have become increasingly interested and influential in the formulation of social policies affecting children (Seitz, 1979). A review of development in child psychology from the 1960s to 1990s can be found in Reese (1993).

REFERENCES

Bower, T. G. R. (1977). *A primer of infant development*. San Francisco: Freeman.

Dale, P. S. (1977). *Language development: Structure and function* (2nd ed.). New York: Holt, Rinehart, & Winston.

Hartup, W. W. (1979). The social worlds of childhood. *American Psychologist, 34,* 944–950.

Hetherington, E. M., & Parke, R. D. (1979). *Child psychology: A contemporary viewpoint* (2nd ed.). New York: McGraw-Hill.

Hoffman, M. L. (1979). Development of moral thought, feeling, and behavior. *American Psychologist, 34,* 958–966.

Kessen, W. (1965). *The child*. New York: Wiley.

Lewis, M. (Ed.). (1976). *Origins of intelligence*. New York: Plenum.

Maccoby, E. E., & Jacklin, C. N. (1974). *The psychology of sex differences*. Stanford, Stanford University Press.

Mussen, P. H. (Ed.). (1970). *Carmichael's handbook of child psychology*. New York: Wiley.

Piaget, J. (1952). *The origins of intelligence in children*. New York: International Universities Press.

Reese, H. W. (1993). Developments in child psychology from the 1960s to the 1990s. *Developmental Review, 13,* 4, 503–524.

Rosenthal, D. (1970). *Genetic theory and abnormal behavior*. New York: McGraw-Hill.

Seitz, V. (1979). Psychology and social policy for children. *American Psychologist, 34,* 1007–1008.

Yarrow, L. J. (1979). Emotional development. *American Psychologist, 34,* 951–957.

LAWRENCE J. SIEGEL
*University of Texas Medical
Branch, Galveston*

**CHILD PSYCHIATRY
CLINICAL PSYCHOLOGY
PEDIATRIC PSYCHOLOGIST**

CHILDREN OF A LESSER GOD

Children of a Lesser God is a play by Mark Medoff that was a hit on the Broadway stage in 1980. It is about the meeting, courtship, and marriage of James Leeds, a speech teacher at a state school for the deaf, and Sarah Norman, a maid at the school who has been deaf from birth and who refuses to lip read or speak. Sarah wishes to be left alone in her silent world; James insists that she learn to lip read and speak if she is to achieve first-class citizenship in the hearing, speaking world. He repeats aloud everything he and Sarah sign in an attempt to teach Sarah to lip read. The two cannot reconcile their differences, and, in the end, they separate. James asks Sarah to return, but it is left unclear whether or not the marriage will be successful.

Mark Medoff, the author of *Children of a Lesser God*, found sign language an interesting theatrical device, and used deafness as a symbol for the problems inherent in all human communication. He wrote the play for Phyllis Frelich, a founding member of the National Theater of the Deaf, in response to her difficulty in finding roles. The play was developed based on situations suggested by Medoff and improvised by Frelich and her husband Robert Steinberg, who originally played the role of James in workshop and regional productions of the play.

REFERENCES

Guernsey, O. L., Jr. (Ed.). (1980). *The best plays of 1979–1980*. New York: Dodd, Mead.

Kakutani, M. (1980, April 1). Deaf since birth, Phyllis Frelich became an actress and now a star. *New York Times, III* 7:1.

Medoff, M. (1980). *Children of a Lesser God*. New York: Dramatists Play Service.

CATHERINE O. BRUCE
Hunter College

**DEAF
DEAF EDUCATION
SIGN LANGUAGE**

CHILDREN OF THE HANDICAPPED

Parents have the responsibility of providing care, love, and social training for their children. It is commonly assumed that many of a child's developmental abilities (e.g., expressive language, reasoning, social and emotional) will be enhanced through formal and informal activities initiated by parents. This may not be assumed for children of handicapped individuals who may grow up in environments where stimulation in communication areas and training in the socialization processes are less accessible. However, this does not mean that a child of a handicapped person will be deficient in cognitive and affective development. It may mean that the child will have to adapt to different methods of learning and rely more on relatives, teachers, and others who can provide the necessary stimulation. Individual differences in intelligence, physical abilities, and temperament will play an important role in how well children adapt to the environment and how growth and development proceed when confronted with obstacles. The type of disability of the parent, the parent's intellectual ability, and the parent's motivation to rear children properly are also crucial factors.

A great deal of literature has emerged regarding the effects of deaf parents' speech on their children's speech and language development. Some studies note that children of deaf parents have developed normal speech and language (Lenneberg, 1967; Mayberry, 1976), while other studies report that these children have not developed normal speech because of the manual sign procedures used in the home (Sachs, Bard, & Johnson, 1981; Sachs & Johnson, 1976).

Evidence indicates that children of parents who are intellectually handicapped (Rosenberg & McTate, 1982; Schilling, Schinke, Blythe, & Barth, 1982) and emotionally disturbed (Goodman, 1984) have a tendency toward physical abuse and neglect of their children and may be delinquent in providing the kind of stimulation necessary for normal growth and development. Children of mildly handicapped parents and parents with some forms of acquired handicaps are generally born with the capacity for normal development. Early attention to these deficits and delays will ensure more wholesome human and physical environments. Because of inadequate knowledge of good parenting skills, parents of handicapped children may make errors in judgment and fail to provide proper care.

To minimize the probability that children of handicapped parents will experience developmental deficits, emphasis must be placed on adequate parenting and improving the quality of the child-rearing environment. This can be done through parent training that emphasizes effective parenting skills. This training will not only eliminate developmental disabilities in some children, but also make individuals with disabilities more responsible and effective parents.

REFERENCES

Goodman, S. (1984). Children of emotionally disturbed mothers: Problems and alternatives. *Children Today, 13,* 6–9.

Lenneberg, E. (1967). *Biological foundations of language.* New York: Wiley.

Mayberry, R. (1976). An assessment of some oral and manual language skills of hearing children of deaf parents. *American Annals of the Deaf, 121,* 507–512.

Rosenberg, S., & McTate, G. A. (1982). Intellectually handicapped mothers: Problems and Prospects. *Children Today, 11,* 24–26.

Sachs, J., Bard, B., & Johnson, M. (1981). Language learning with restricted input: Case studies of two hearing children of deaf parents. *Applied Psycholinguistics, 2,* 33–54.

Sachs, J., & Johnson, M. (1976). Language development in a hearing child of deaf parents. In W. von Raffler-Engel & Y. Lebrun (Eds.), *Baby talk and infant speech.* Lisse, Netherlands: Swets & Zeitlinger.

Schilling, R. F., Schinke, S. P., Blythe, B. J., & Barth, R. P. (1982). Child maltreatment and mentally retarded parents: Is there a relationship? *Mental Retardation, 20,* 201–209.

CECELIA STEPPE-JONES
North Carolina Central University

FAMILY RESPONSE TO A HANDICAPPED CHILD

CHILDREN'S DEFENSE FUND (CDF)

The Children's Defense Fund (CDF) is an advocacy organization for poor, minority, and handicapped children. The mission of the CDF is to "Leave No Child Behind" (CDF, 1999). Efforts are undertaken on behalf of large numbers of children as opposed to individual children. Relevant to special education, the organization has addressed exclusion of children from school as well as the labeling and treatment of children with special needs (Staff, 1974). The CDF maintains a lobbying organization, pursuing an annual legislative agenda in the U.S. Congress; works with state and local child advocates, providing information, technical assistance, and support; monitors the development and implementation of federal and state policies; and litigates selected cases (Children's Defense Fund, undated).

The CDF also develops information on key issues affecting children. It has published books and handbooks of interest to special education, including *94-142 and 504: Numbers that Add Up to Educational Rights for Handicapped Children, How to Help Handicapped Children Get an Education.* A monthly newsletter, *CDF Reports*, is also published.

The CDF was founded in 1973. Until 1978 CDF was

known as the Children's Defense Fund of the Washington Research Project. It is a private organization, with its main office in Washington DC at 25 E. Street NW, Washington DC 20001. The CDF has a very informative website at www.childrensdefense.org.

REFERENCES

Children's Defense Fund. (1999). *About the Children's Defense Fund*. Washington, DC: Author.

Staff. (1974). An interview with Marian Edelman Wright. *Harvard Educational Review, 44*, 53–73.

DOUGLAS L. FRIEDMAN
Fordham University

CHILDREN'S EARLY EDUCATION DEVELOPMENTAL INVENTORY

See BATTELLE DEVELOPMENTAL INVENTORY.

CHILDREN'S MANIFEST ANXIETY SCALE (CMAS)

Originally published in 1956 by Castaneda, McCandless, and Palermo as a downward extension of Taylor's Manifest Anxiety Scale for adults (Taylor, 1951), the Children's Manifest Anxiety Scale (CMAS) was substantively revised in 1978 (Reynolds & Richmond). The *Revised Children's Anxiety Scale* (RCMAS) was published in 1985 (Reynolds & Richmond). Since its first publication, more than 150 articles using the CMAS or the RCMAS have been published in various scholarly journals. These scales have been used in studies of the effects of anxiety on children's learning, behavior in the classroom, and response to a variety of treatment programs, and in descriptive studies of anxiety and its relationship to behavior, gender, ethnicity, age, socioeconomic status, and other variables.

Designed to measure anxiety of long-standing duration (i.e., trait as opposed to state or situational anxiety), the RCMAS has four empirically derived subscales titled: Concentration/Social, Worry and Oversensitivity, Physiological Anxiety, and Lie or Social Desirability. Standard scores are provided for a total anxiety score and for each subscale. Reliability data are good with most studies reporting internal consistency estimates in the .80s across age (5 to 19 years), gender, and race (black, white, and Hispanic). Extensive validity data are provided in the test manual (Reynolds & Richmond, 1985).

The RCMAS is used principally by school, child clinical, and pediatric psychologists in the screening and diagnosis of various anxiety-related emotional disorders in children, and by researchers interested in children's anxiety. Learning-disabled and other groups of children in special education programs have been shown to display higher than normal levels of anxiety on the RCMAS (Paget & Reynolds, 1984), while students in programs for the intellectually gifted demonstrate lower than average anxiety levels when compared with the normal population (Scholwinski & Reynolds, 1985).

REFERENCES

Castaneda, A., McCandless, B., & Palermo, D. (1956). The children's form of the Manifest Anxiety Scale. *Child Development, 27*, 327–332.

Paget, K. D., & Reynolds, C. R. Dimensions, levels, and reliabilities on the Revised Children's Anxiety Scale with learning disabled children. *Journal of Learning Disabilities, 17*, 137–141.

Reynolds, C. R., & Richmond, B. O. (1978). What I think and feel: A revised measure of children's manifest anxiety. *Journal of Abnormal Psychology, 43*, 281–283.

Reynolds, C. R., & Richmond, B. O. (1985). *Revised Children's Manifest Anxiety Scale*. Los Angeles: Western Psychological Services.

Scholwinski, E. & Reynolds, C. R. (1985). Dimensions of anxiety among high IQ children. *Gifted Child Quarterly, 29*, 125–130.

Taylor, J. A. (1951). The relationship of anxiety to the conditioned eyelid response. *Journal of Experimental Psychology, 41*, 18–92.

CECIL R. REYNOLDS
Texas A & M University

ANXIETY

CHILD SERVICE DEMONSTRATION CENTERS (CSDC)

Child Service Demonstration Centers (CSDCs) (1971–1980) were federally funded operations that, in their totality, represented the largest single national commitment specifically made to the education of the learning disabled (Mann et al., 1984).

Their beginnings are to be found in several pieces of legislation. PL 88-164, passed in 1963, which predated the introduction of the modern term learning disabilities (LD), provided assistance to learning-disabled children in a bill directed at the educational needs of handicapped children under the rubric of "crippled and other health impaired." Then, under PL 91-230, passed in 1969, the U.S. commissioner of education was enjoined by Congress "to seek to make equitable geographic distribution of training programs, and train personnel throughout the nation, and . . . to encourage the establishment of a model training center in each of the states." This was to be done by making grants or contracts available to public schools, state educational agencies, nonprofit organizations, and colleges and universities. Such model centers for the learning disabled were then authorized, and ultimately created, under PL 91-230, Title VI-G.

This law made possible Child Service Demonstration Centers to serve learning-disabled students. Under the law, the to-be-created centers were to (1) provide testing and educational evaluation to identify learning-disabled students; (2) develop and conduct model programs designed to meet their special educational needs; (3) assist appropriate educational agencies, organizations, and institutions "in making such model programs available to other children with learning disabilities"; and (4) disseminate new methods or techniques for overcoming learning disabilities and evaluate their effectiveness.

From 1971 to 1980, 97 CSDCs were created in all, with each of the 50 states being served by at least one during that time. The majority operated under the auspices of state educational agencies (SEAs). A good number also operated out of universities, and sometimes out of local educational agencies (LEAs), often on the basis of their serving as agencies of the states. The private sector was only minimally represented.

Many of the CSDCs were to carry out state as well as federal mandates. Often they were supported by state and local funds and resources that allowed them to augment their efforts far beyond the limits allowed by their relatively meager funds. Thus the hopes of the federal government that state and local education agencies would contribute to the support of the CSDCs with their own funds were realized.

The federal government had high hopes for the CSDCs. They were expected to assume major responsibility for trailblazing in the creation of service models, programs, and technologies; the identification, diagnosis, and remediation of learning disabilities; and the training of regular as well as special education teachers, specialists, and administrators. They were also expected to play a major role in research on the learning disabled. Furthermore, they were cast as both transformation instigators and partners for state educational agencies. In these roles they were expected to help the state agencies to plan and implement statewide learning disabilities programs and services; indeed, the initial CSDCs were granted to state educational agencies to further this expectation.

While every state had at least one project, as did the Commonwealth of Puerto Rico, some states had multiple centers operating at the same time under their state educational departments (e.g., California, New York). Most centers operated for 3 years; reapplication and competition

for further funding was needed for subsequent years. The strategy was that the first year would involve planning, the second year the actual operation of the center, and the third year replication and dissemination. Some states, however, put projects together to create longitudinal efforts of some duration.

During their tenure, the CSDCs served a mix of urban, suburban, and rural areas. Most of the services were rendered, however, to rural children. This was in large part the result of the federal government's insistence that unserved and underserved learning-disabled students, who were in greatest abundance in rural areas at the time, be given priority in the provision of services.

For much the same reason, the racial composition of the learning-disabled students served by the CSDCs included a disproportionate number of minority students. Two projects were directed to American Indians and two to Puerto Rican students, while many of the urban and rural centers were oriented to the needs of black students. This is an interesting point in light of the fact that some advocacy groups at the time were claiming that learning disabilities were a white middle-class syndrome, with minority students being consigned to classes for the mentally retarded or having their academic problems neglected.

The CSDCs emphasized elementary school-aged children since the LD movement is generally oriented to this stage of education. There were some preschool and secondary efforts as well. Interest and efforts in the latter accelerated during the later years of funding as the federal government increased its emphasis on secondary school programming.

The CSDCs were in the vanguard of mainstreaming and the provision of special education services in the least restrictive environment. They also did much to relate special education services for learning-disabled pupils to those of general education. In these respects they clearly fulfilled the federal government's expectations. Their major service delivery models were those of resource rooms, consulting teachers, and regular classrooms.

The assessment and diagnostic efforts of the CSDCs were traditional. They were strictly secondary to the service and training functions assumed by the centers. Furthermore, they eventually resulted in controversies that still percolate in education. Although the CSDCs were expected to identify appropriately handicapped children who had specific learning disabilities, as per federal definitions, their screening and identification efforts were such as to assign children to their services on the basis of academic failure and other school problems rather than on the basis of any precise learning disability criteria. It was on such bases that a position was taken by some critics that the concept of learning disabilities, as a defensible independent diagnostic entity apart from and different from school failure, could not be sustained.

The intervention models stressed by the CSDCs were

strongly academic, as might be expected since students receiving services from the CSDCs usually had been referred because of academic problems. Remedial reading was the treatment of choice, on similar grounds. Perceptual motor training, including ITPA-based interventions, held the second highest priority, particularly in the early projects, when perceptual motor training was still the vogue. Surprisingly, the behavioral movement that so dominated special education during much of the CSDCs' sway does not appear to have greatly influenced most of the CSDCs, though some had strong behavioral emphases. While only several projects have averred ecological orientations, there was an ecological shift over the course of CSDC operations. Earlier projects were committed to overcoming learning disabilities through direct intervention, while later ones were more likely to emphasize helping learning-disabled students to adjust to academic and school environments and assisting schools in their accommodations to the special needs of learning-disabled students.

One of the major efforts made by CSDCs was in respect to training. Some of this was at the college and university level. Most, often representing an introduction to LD concepts and practices, was of an in-service nature directed at regular as well as special education teachers, administrators, paraprofessionals, and parents.

The CSDCs' efforts at replication were considerable. Most of the replications were at the local level, with far fewer at the state level. Impressive is the fact that there were 16 national replications. The CSDCs generated an extraordinary number of screening, remedial, and curricular materials and training manuals for teachers and parents. Because these were in the public domain, many were adapted by schools subsequent to the CSDCs' close, though often without awareness of their origins.

While there were some exemplary research efforts, the CSDCs remained essentially service agencies and, generally speaking, did not assume the research leadership originally expected of them. This was not surprising since neither their funding, personnel capabilities, nor the nature of local conditions were such as to encourage earnest research. The Learning Disability Institutes, funded in 1977, were created in response the federal government's recognition of these facts and a desire to seek wider research efforts from other sources.

Public Law 91-239 also authorized the creation of the Leadership Training Institute (LTI) at the University of Arizona (1971–1974). The institute was supposed to assist the CSDCs in addition to carrying out its own research and training missions. It was later replaced by the National Learning Disabilities Assistance Project (1975–1979), which was entirely devoted to providing support functions for the CSDCs.

The federal government clearly expected the CSDCs to have a major national impact on LD practices. That they did not fulfill such expectations can be attributed to a va-

riety of causes. One was the fact that their allocation of funds was far below original authorizations. Another was that individual centers came on line too slowly and irregularly, thus any collaborative thrust on their part was weakened. Still another reason was that they did not affect state educational policies as had been hoped, the states usually pursuing their own LD agendas rather than those of the federal government or of the CSDCs. Furthermore, the demands made on the CSDCs regularly changed as a consequence of changes in federal direction and because of disagreements among recognized LD specialists as to the nature of learning disabilities and the goals of intervention. Finally, most of the projects were funded for only 3 years, and several were funded for 2 or less, hardly time to create forceful and enduring efforts. Nevertheless, they did sensitize many areas of the nation and its schools to the needs of learning-disabled children and provided them with guidance, training, programs, materials, and direct services during a period when the field of learning disabilities was still emerging as an area of educational concern in the United States. Undoubtedly, they also shaped current concepts and services.

The CSDCs were subject to a number of external evaluations. A study of the CSDCs' intervention efforts was carried out by Kirk and Elkin in 1975. In 1976 a major yearlong effort was made by the American Institute of Research to examine the operations of the CSDCs. In 1979 Ysseldyke et al. began their studies of the CSDCs' assessment approaches (Thurlow & Ysseldyke, 1979). At the final closing of the CSDCs, Mann et al. published several summative articles reviewing the status and contributions of the CSDCs (Boyer et al., 1982; Mann et al., 1983; Mann et al., 1984).

REFERENCES

Boyer, C. W., Mann, L., Davis, C. H., Metz, C. M., & Wolford, B. (1982). The Child Service Demonstration Centers: Retrospect of an age. *Academic Therapy, 18,* 171–177.

Kirk, S. A., & Elkin, V. (1975). Characteristics of children enrolled in the Child Service Demonstration Centers. *Journal of Learning Disabilities, 16,* 63–68.

Mann, L., Davis, C. H., Boyer, C. W., Metz, C. M., & Wolford, B. (1983). LD or not LD, that was the question: A retrospective analysis of the Child Service Demonstration Centers' compliance with the federal definition of learning disabilities. *Journal of Learning Disabilities, 16,* 14–17.

Mann, L., Cartwright, G. P., Kenowitz, L. A., Boyer, C. W., Metz, C. M., & Wolford, B. (1984). The Child Service Demonstration Centers: A summary report. *Exceptional Children, 50,* 532–540.

Thurlow, M. L., & Ysseldyke, J. E. (1979). Current assessment and decision making practices in model LD programs. *Learning Disability Quarterly, 4,* 15–24.

JONI J. GLEASON
University of West Florida

DIAGNOSIS IN SPECIAL EDUCATION
LEARNING DISABILITIES

CHILD VARIANCE PROJECT

The Conceptual Project in Child Variance was undertaken from 1970 to 1972 at the University of Michigan under the direction of William C. Rhodes. It was funded as a special project by the (then) Bureau of Education for the Handicapped to "order and organize the vast but scattered literature on emotional disturbance and other types of variance in children" and to "serve as a prototype for combining the functions of graduate training and professional research" (Rhodes & Tracy, 1974, p. 1). The product of this prodigious undertaking is a series of five volumes in which the literature on explanations of variance, intervention with variant children, and service provision are integrated and synthesized.

The first volume, *Conceptual Models,* has had a significant impact on subsequent treatments of childhood emotional disturbance and the education of disturbed children. The volume is comprised of papers in which explanatory models from five perspectives are presented. These models include biological, behavioral, psychodynamic, sociological, and ecological accounts of deviance. A paper on countertheoretical perspectives is included, as is a paper by Rhodes establishing a framework for understanding and synthesizing these diverse accounts.

The organization of the second volume, *Interventions,* derives from the first. In it, intervention with variant children is considered from biophysical, behavioral, psychodynamic, environmental, and countertheoretical perspectives. (The paper on environmental intervention explores approaches derived from both the sociological and ecological perspectives.) Of course, the rapid and multifaceted advance in the treatment of disturbed children in the decade since the publication of this volume has limited its usefulness. Nonetheless, the logic of its organization has endured. The idea that intervention must be understood in the context of the explanatory system has influenced scholars and teacher trainers to this day.

In the third volume, *Service Delivery Systems,* the development of contemporary services for deviant children provided by educational, correctional, mental health, and social welfare systems and religious institutions is analyzed from a historical perspective. The current services provided by these systems in a representative American community are examined and evaluated through a series of case studies. The fourth volume, *The Future,* is a treatise by Rhodes on the somewhat profound cultural and philosophical changes that must be realized for our society to fulfill its caretaking role. The fifth volume, *Exercise Book,* presents a series of exercises through which the sometimes complex and abstract content of the previous volumes may be brought to life for students.

Although the project has not yet realized the ultimate and far-reaching goals set forth by Rhodes in *The Future,* its impact on our thinking about emotional disturbance, the education of emotionally disturbed children, and the training of teachers of the emotionally disturbed has been significant and enduring. The organization of explanatory theory and its application to the understanding of intervention approaches are legacies of the Child Variance Project. Furthermore, its emphasis on the understanding of problems in their broadest context provided impetus to the subsequent development of ecological theory and intervention approaches.

REFERENCES

Rhodes, W. C. (1975). *A study of child variance. Exercise book.* Ann Arbor: University of Michigan Press.

Rhodes, W. C., & Tracy, M. L. (1974). Preface. In W. C. Rhodes & M. L. Tracy (Eds.), *A study of child variance. Vol. 2. Interventions* (pp. 1–15). Ann Arbor, MI: University of Michigan Press.

Rhodes, W. C., & Tracy, M. W. (Eds.). (1974). *A study of child variance. Vol. 1. Conceptual models.* Ann Arbor, MI: University of Michigan Press.

Rhodes, W. C., & Tracy, M. L. (1974). *A study of child variance. Vol. 2. Interventions.* Ann Arbor, MI: University of Michigan Press.

Rhodes, W. C., & Tracy, M. W. (Eds.). (1974). *A study of child variance. Vol. 3. Service delivery systems.* Ann Arbor, MI: University of Michigan Press.

Rhodes, W. C., & Tracy, M. L. (1974). *A study of child variance. Vol. 4. The future.* Ann Arbor, MI: University of Michigan Press.

PAUL T. SINDELAR
Florida State University

AFFECTIVE EDUCATION
EMOTIONAL DISORDERS

CHINA, SPECIAL EDUCATION IN

History of Special Education Services

China has a history of civilization exceeding five thousand years. The description of disabled people (deaf and blind) was first documented in the fourth century BC in Zuo. The progressive thought that all people with disabilities should be well taken care of was explicitly stated in the Book of Rites, in the second century BC. In 1859, Hong Rengan proposed that institutions for disabled people be established. However, the first school for the blind was founded by a British missionary named William Murray in Beijing, in 1874. Thirteen years later (1887), an American, C. R. Mills, became the founder of the first school for the deaf in Shandong. It was not until 1916 when the first Chinese, Zhang Jian, opened Nantong School for the Deaf in Jiangsu, which is still in operation. By 1948, there were a total of 42 special schools for the deaf and blind, with an enrollment of 2,380 students and 360 faculty/staff members. Among these schools, eight were funded by the public. At that time, special education was categorized as social education.

After the People's Republic of China was founded in 1949, the government integrated special education into the general educational system and new special education programs were created in the Department of Education. The number of schools for the deaf and blind increased significantly from 64 to 253 between 1953 and 1963. According to statistics in 1984, the enrollment of deaf and blind students was 33,055, served by 8,000 faculty and staff. Meanwhile, four schools for students with other disabilities came into existence. In 1997, there were a total of 1,440 special education schools—27 higher education institutions, 845 schools for the deaf, 143 schools for the deaf and blind, and 425 schools for children with disabilities. The number of disabled students enrolled also increased to 340,621, along with 43,296 faculty and staff members.

In 1987, the survey results showed that there were 52 million disabled people in China, 4.9% of the national population. It was estimated that 60 million people were handicapped out of 1.2 billion Chinese; among them 12.3 million were under 18, which was 2.58% of the total population. The enrollment rate of school-age children with visual, hearing, speech, and mental disabilities increased from 20% (1991) to nearly 60% (1995).

Legal Rights and Public Policy

A legal regulation system regarding special education has been developing since 1980. Provision No. 45 of the Constitution of People's Republic of China (1982) states that all disabled persons have the right to be educated. In response to the Constitution, provincial governments support special education through various ways to meet their local needs. Special education is also touched upon in specific legal regulations. It is stipulated in Provision No. 9 of the Law of Compulsory Education (1986) that the government is obligated to set up and support special education schools or classes for disabled children, and any individuals are encouraged to found schools. Special law—Law of the PRC on the Protection of Disabled Persons—was constituted in 1990. This law declares that the educational rights of the disabled are protected, and classifies special education as one of the components of general education. Nine provisions in Regulation No. 3 of the 1990 law stipulate the responsibilities, policies, funding, approaches, adult education, training of faculty/staff, and so on in special education. Rules and regulations were also established for various departments in the government, specifying how they comply with the laws. Fifty-two provisions in Educational Regulations for the Disabled Persons specifically define the education of the disabled at different stages. In addition, other relevant laws such as Law of Teachers and Law of Vocational Education also relate to special education.

The following aspects are highlighted in the laws and regulations. It is clearly stated that teaching disabled children is one of the important components in compulsory education, which must be insured and enforced by the government. The educational policy regarding disabled people observes the principle of keeping a balance of popularization and advancement, with the former as the focus. While the priority is to improve compulsory and vocational education, preschool education should be strengthened and secondary and higher education should gradually be developed. It is stipulated that multiple methods should be applied in the education of disabled children. The guiding principle in special education is that general education schools function as the backbone, and learning in regular classrooms and special education classes/programs constitute the main body. The training of faculty and staff should be emphasized and the supply for special education should be assured.

Present Structure

Special education can be defined in the following two ways: (a) in a broad sense, it may indicate the education of all children who have special needs including the gifted and talented and juvenile criminals, or (b) in a narrow sense, it may imply the education of all kinds of mentally and physically disabled people. Currently, the emphasis in special education is placed on the training of people, especially children, with various disabilities, though the study of all who need special care in education is being conducted simultaneously.

China is developing a special education system with its own characteristics, responding to the situation of a large number of disabled children, a developing economy, and a developing educational foundation. This system is neither complete segregation nor mainstreaming and inclusiveness; it is a combination of general education and special education—each is independent but also integrated. Special education is in one of three forms: special education schools, special education programs, and learning in regular class. However, the majority of the students are enrolled in either special programs or regular classes in general education schools.

The focus of special education is within the nine-year compulsory education. Early childhood education is considered critical and the early intervention and training of deaf and mentally disabled children have received a great deal of attention. Meanwhile, disabled adult vocational education also grows rapidly. In 1997, 610 adult vocational education institutions were registered and 1.5 million disabled people were trained. In addition to advancing their education in regular higher educational institutions, disabled people also enjoy the privilege of attending two universities founded exclusively for them. Although the national educational department established standard curriculum and instruction materials in special education, local educational institutions are encouraged to make any changes to accommodate their specific needs.

Financing

As is the general nine-year compulsory primary and secondary education, special education is run and supported by local governments. On the other hand, noncompulsory early childhood and higher education is supported by the central government and by individuals. The central government has increased its budget to improve and further develop special education in the past decade. In 1994, the national financial budget for special education reached ¥28 million, a 142% increase of the budget in 1990. A special allowance was provided by relevant central government departments for the purpose of enhancing special education in 1989—¥14 million were allocated between 1989 and 1995. Consequently, local governments followed the example, creating their special allowance for special education. Another financial source for special education is donations and fund raising. Economically disadvantaged students are supported with assistantship and scholarship awarded by the government.

Education and Training of Educators

There was no special institution where faculty and staff were trained for special education in P.R. China until 1980. Special education majors received their training at secondary normal schools in several provinces in the early 1980s. The special education program was created at Beijing Normal University in 1986. At present, there are 34 secondary special education normal schools in operation. Special education programs are offered in five nationally and two provincially affiliated normal universities, where teacher candidates pursue bachelor's degrees. Graduate programs are also available at institutions such as Beijing Normal University. Bachelor's degrees can be completed in four years, and master's degrees in three years. Special education classes are opened in general secondary normal schools to train special education candidates in a regular classroom setting. Various workshops and long distance learning also are part of the overall training system. In addition, the National Educational Committee often entrusts relevant institutions with seminars for different types of education professionals, such as principals and special education administrators. Experts from home and abroad are invited to lecture and teach at these seminars. Moreover, professional special education research institutions and mass research organizations have been developed. Journals such as *Modern Special Education* and *Special Education in China* are published periodically. Lastly, special educators are entitled to a special allowance which equals to 15–25% of their base salary.

Relationship to Other Social Services

Special education touches all walks of life. In 1993, the State Council Coordinating Committee on Disability was organized, with chief officers from 34 departments as its members. The central government issued *Work Program for Disabled Persons During the 9th Five-Year Plan Period, 1996–2000*. Specific requirements and implementation plans have been proposed in early intervention community services, compulsory education, vocational education, employment, culture, appliances for the handicapped, immunization, legality, reduction of expenses, and organization. A series of special regulations are also included in laws and policies. For instance, Electoral Law states that disabled people have equal rights to vote, Inheritance Law stipulates that the disabled have equal property and civil rights, and Criminal Law and Civil Law insure that the disabled are protected in human rights and lawsuits. In employment, a quota of 1.5–2% is assigned for any institution to hire the disabled. Nontax or tax deduction is applicable to any enterprise whose employees are handicapped. The blind enjoy mailing reading materials free of charge and free urban transportation. It is also regulated that the third Sunday of May each year is the national Individuals with Disabilities' Day.

Trends and Goals for the Present and Near Future

A Chinese-style special education system is being established on the basis of adapting models from other countries to serve the needs of China. The national government has set the following five priorities in developing special education for the near future.

1. The expansion of special education in rural areas will be emphasized before the year 2000. For those places where special education has been available, the focus will be placed on educational improvement and reform. The goal is to increase the enrollment rate of disabled children to that of regular children. By the year 2000, approximately 80% of all blind, deaf, and mentally handicapped children are expected to attend schools.
2. Early childhood special education will be improved considerably, and families and communities are encouraged to participate in early intervention.
3. Vocational training for the disabled will be strengthened, with short-term training as the primary means.

4. Promotions systems will be established for special education teachers to improve their benefits.

5. Further research will be conducted on the education of children with learning disability, autism, and other disabilities.

Due to historical reasons, special education in Taiwan, Hong Kong, and Macao shares similar cultural tradition and background with that in P.R. China. However, each has formed its own characteristics in classification, standards, and educational methods in their process of development. In December of 1997, a symposium was held at Taibei Normal University to discuss special education in mainland China and Taiwan. The theme of the conference was to create a brand new world of special education with love and wisdom. The interaction among Chinese and international special education professionals has increased significantly in recent years. These educators' interactions enhance mutual understanding and advance the knowledge of special education by all nations.

REFERENCES

Law of the People's Republic of China on the Protection of Disabled Persons. (1991). Beijing, China: Hua Xia.

Mao, Y. (1993). Viewpoints gleaned from participating early intervention in China. Early Child Development and Care, 84, 59–74.

Piao, Y. (Ed.). (1995). Special pedagogy. Fuzhou: Fujian Education Press.

Piao, Y. (1987). China, People's Republic of. In J. Van Cleve (Ed.), Gallaudet encyclopedia of deaf people and deafness (Vol. 1, pp. 181–184). New York: McGraw-Hill.

Piao, Y., Gargiulo, R., & Yun, X. (1995). Special education in the People's Republic of China: Characteristics and Practices. International Journal of Special Education, 10(1), 52–65.

State Council. (1994). The provisions on the education of disabled persons. People's Daily. August 27.

State Education Commission. (1995). Documents of special education, 1990–1995. Beijing: Author.

State Statistics Bureau. (1987). First national sampling of the handicapped. Beijing, China: Author.

Work Program for Disabled Persons During the 9th Five-Year National Development Plan (1996–2000). (1992). Beijing, China: Hua Xia.

Yang, H., & Wang, H. (1994). Special education in China. Journal of Special Education, 28(1), 93–105.

Yun, X. (1994), China. In K. Mazurek & M. Winzer (Eds.), Comparative studies in special education (pp. 163–178). Washington, DC: Gallaudet University Press.

YONGXIN PIAO
Beijing Normal University

PING LIN
Elmhurst College

CHLAMYDIA TRACHOMATIS INFECTIONS

Chlamydia trachomatis is the most prevalent sexually transmitted infection in the United States today. The annual incidence is estimated to be as high as 3 million (Washington, Gove, Schachter, & Sweet, 1985). Of sexually active adolescents who were examined, about 22% had a chlamydia infection (Fraser, Rettig, & Kaplan, 1983).

Chlamydia is spread by intimate and/or sexual contact, and affects both women and homosexual/heterosexual men in all socioeconomic classes. The disease is especially alarming because it is often silent, having no symptoms. Up to 70% of women and 25% of men with chlamydia may be relatively asymptomatic (Washington et al., 1985).

The bacteria can cause painful urination and pelvic, urinary, eye, and respiratory infections in both sexes. Additional symptoms in women may include vaginal discharge, lower abdominal pain or sensitivity, abnormal Pap smear (often described as heavy or moderate inflammation), vaginal bleeding between periods even when taking birth-control pills regularly, and uterine infection. Symptoms in men may include penile discomfort and/or discharge.

If silent or not correctly diagnosed and treated, the disease can lead to such serious complications as pelvic inflammatory disease, ectopic (tubal) pregnancy, infertility, and, possibly, cervical cancer in women and urethritis and sterility in men. Though common, the disease may not be recognized among the mentally handicapped, often thought of as asexual by many medical or social work personnel. Mentally retarded adolescents, and young adults in particular, should receive education in the recognition of chlamydia and other venereal diseases.

Chlamydia infections are curable with a full 21-day treatment with tetracycline. A 7-day treatment may be effective for men, but not for women. Sulfisoxazole and erythromycin are also effective, but penicillin is not.

REFERENCES

Fraser, J., Rettig, P., & Kaplan, D. (1983). Prevalence of cervical chlamydia trachomatis and Neisseria gonorrheae in female adolescents. Pediatrics, 71, 333–336.

Washington, E., Gove, S., Schachter, J., & Sweet, R. (1985). Oral contraceptives, chlamydia trachomatis infection, and pelvic inflammatory disease. Journal of the American Medical Association, 253, 2246–2250.

C. SUE LAMB
GINGA L. COLCOUGH
University of North Carolina
at Wilmington

JAPAN, SPECIAL EDUCATION IN

HERPES

CHLORPROMAZINE

Chlorpromazine (CPZ) is the generic name for Thorazine, a phenothiazine used in the treatment of psychoses and other psychiatric disorders (Conley, Tamminga, Bartro, Richardson, Peszke, Lingle, Hegerty, Love, Gounaris, & Zaremba, 1998). Though CPZ was synthesized by Charpentier in 1950 during research intended to produce an antipsychotic medication, the endeavor began in 1949 with a French surgeon Laborit, who was seeking a medication to reduce shock during surgery (Leavitt, 1982). Chlorpromazine is used primarily in the treatment of schizophrenia, but also has been used at low dosages to treat nausea and seasickness.

Though the actions of CPZ on the central nervous system (CNS) are not completely understood, it tends to produce the following behavioral changes: decreases apparent agitation, decreases perceptions of anxiety, decreases reports of hallucinatory experiences, produces mild to moderate sedating effects that appear to be both dosage and clinical condition dependent, and decreases spontaneous motor activity.

Because CPZ and all phenothiazines appear to block dopamine receptors in the CNS, a number of motor-related adverse effects are noted, especially during initial usage, chronic usage, or at high dosages. Three general reactions may be observed: dystonic reactions (most often with children, especially during acute infections or while dehydrated; these include spasms of neck muscles, rigidity with extension of back muscles, jaw tics, difficulty in swallowing or talking, and facial spasms with tongue protrusion, and may be accompanied by sweating or pallor); feelings of motor restlessness (e.g., agitation, inability to sit still, tapping of feet, insomnia, strong desire to move about without reported anxiety; often occurs within 2 to 3 days of initiating treatment); parkinsonlike symptoms (most frequent with elderly persons; include masked facial appearance, increased salivation/drooling, motor slowing, including slowed speech, swallowing difficulties, and cogwheel rigidity) (McEvoy, 1985). In addition, blurred vision and dry mouth are reported during early stages of treatment. A persistent motor syndrome called tardive dyskinesia, characterized by rhythmic involuntary movements of facial and oral musculature and occasionally the limbs, may develop in conjunction with CPZ administration. The elderly, especially females, on high dosages are reported as most at risk for this condition.

REFERENCES

Conley, R. R., Tamminga, C. A., Bartro, J. J., Richardson, C., Peske, M. Lingle, J., Hegerty, J., Love, R., Gounaris, C., & Zaremba, S. (1998). Olanzapine compared with chlorpromazine in treatment-resistant schizophrenia. *American Journal of Psychiatry, 155,* 7, 914–920.

Leavitt, F. (1982). *Drugs and behavior.* New York: Wiley.

McEvoy, G. K. (1985). *American hospital formulary service: Drug information 85.* Bethesda, MD: American Society of Hospital Pharmacists.

Robert F. Sawicki
*Lake Erie Institute of
Rehabilitation*

PHENOTHIAZINES
STELAZINE

CHOLINESTERASE

Neurons are the basic information processing and transmitting elements of the central nervous system. The transmission of impulses across these nerve cells is a biochemical process. As such, a neurochemical process is the foundation of all human behavior.

Impulses travel from one neuron to another across a biochemical junction (synapse). Specifically, when an impulse reaches the terminal button of a neuron, it releases a transmitter substance called acetylcholine (ACh), which causes a temporary change in the membrane of the receiving neuron. If there is sufficient chemical stimulation, the second neuron will subsequently fire. Following the alteration of the membrane potential, the enzyme *cholinesterase* (ChE) neutralizes (destroys) the transmitter substance and thus restores the synapse to a resting state. In this way a single impulse is transmitted through the nervous system.

Neuroscientists have long hypothesized that this biochemical process underlies learning and memory functioning in the brain (Hillgard & Bower, 1975). While a clear relationship has not been established between cholinesterase activity and memory functioning, a number of investigators have consistently found a cholinergic deficit in dementia patients (e.g., Giacobini, Gracon, Smith, & Hoover, 1997; Perry et al., 1978). Based on postmortem examination, these investigators found reduced cholinesterase levels in those areas of the brain typically associated with memory (e.g., the hippocampus). Thus, it appears that a reduction in cholinesterase activity may be related to memory dysfunctions. Research efforts are presently under way that examine the relationship between increased cholinergic activity and memory and learning functions, and the role of cholinesterase in obsessive-compulsive disorder (Erzegovesi, Bellodi & Smeraldi, 1995).

REFERENCES

Erzegovesi, S., Bellodi, L., & Smeraldi, E. (1995). Serum cholinesterase in obsessive-compulsive disorder. *Psychiatry Research, 58,* 3, 265–268.

Giacobini, E., Gracon, S., Smith, F., & Hoover, T. (1997). Cholinesterase inhibitors in Alzheimer disease treatment. In R. E. Becker & E. Giacobini (Eds.), *Alzheimer Disease: From molecular biology to therapy*. Boston, MA: Birkhauser.

Hillgard, E. R., & Bower, G. H. (1975). *Theories of learning*. Englewood Cliffs, NJ: Prentice-Hall.

Perry, E. K, Tomlinson, B. E., Blessed, G., Bergmann, K., Gibson, P. H., & Perry, R. H. (1978). Correlation of cholinergic abnormalities with senile plaques and mental test scores in senile dementia. *British Medical Journal, 2,* 1457–1459.

JEFFREY W. GRAY
Ball State University

RAYMOND S. DEAN
Ball State University
Indiana University School
of Medicine

NEUROLOGICAL ORGANIZATION
SYNAPSES

CHOMSKY, NOAM (1928–   )

Noam Chomsky was born on December 7, 1928 in Philadelphia, Pennsylvania. His undergraduate and graduate years were spent at the University of Pennsylvania, where he received his BA in 1949 and his PhD in Linguistics in 1955. From 1951 to 1955, Chomsky was a Junior Fellow of the Harvard University Society of Fellows. It was during this time that he completed his doctoral dissertation entitled *Transformational Analysis*. The major theoretical viewpoints of the dissertation were published in the monograph *Syntactic Structure* in 1957, which was later expanded in a more extensive work published in 1975, *The Logical Structure of Linguistic Theory*.

Chomsky joined the staff of the Massachusetts Institute of Technology (MIT) in 1955, and in 1961 was appointed full professor in the Department of Modern Languages and Linguistics, currently the Department of Linguistics and Philosophy. From 1966 to 1976, he was the Ferrai P. Ward Professor of Modern Languages and Linguistics, and he was appointed Institute professor in 1975.

Chomsky is famous for the construction of a system of generative programs developed out of his interest in modern logic and mathematics. His theory proposes that the grammatical rules for any given language are, in general, similar in all languages. He is best known for his work on the "Chomsky hierarchy," which classifies language groups according to the different types of grammars that generate them. In particular, he was the first linguist to identify what are today thought of as "context-free" grammars.

Among his earlier works are *Cartesian Linguistics* (1966) and *Language and Mind* (1968).

Chomsky became interested in politics and the dynamics of governmental power during the Vietnam War, and has subsequently written much on language, politics, philosophy, and the media. Among the best known are *Manufacturing Consent* (1988), *Necessary Illusions* (1989), and *Deterring Democracy* (1992). He has also written and lectured widely on contemporary issues, international affairs, intellectual issues, and U.S. foreign policy.

From 1958 to 1959, Chomsky was in residence at the Institute for Advanced Study at Princeton, New Jersey. He delivered the John Locke Lectures at Oxford in 1969, the Bertrand Russell Memorial Lecture at Cambridge University in 1970, the Nehru Memorial Lecture in New Delhi in 1972, and the Huizinga Lecture in Leiden in 1977. His numerous honors include honorary degrees from the University of London, University of Pennsylvania, Georgetown University, and Cambridge University. He is a Fellow of the American Academy of Arts and Sciences as well as a member of other professional and learned societies including the National Academy of Science. In addition, he is a recipient of the Distinguished Scientific Contribution Award of the American Psychological Association (APA). Chomsky remains on the faculty at MIT, and continues to be actively involved in the wide variety of interests that have marked his career as a highly productive scholar and citizen.

REFERENCES

Chomsky, A. N. (1957). *Syntactic structures*. 'S-Gravenhage: Mouton.

Chomsky, A. N. (1966). *Cartesian linguistics: A chapter in the history of rationalist thought*. New York: Harper & Row.

Noam Chomsky

Chomsky, A. N. (1968). *Language and mind.* New York: Harcourt, Brace and World.

Chomsky, A. N. (1975). *Logical structure of linguistic theory.* New York: Plenum.

Chomsky, N. (1992). *Deterring Democracy.* New York: Hill & Wang.

IVAN Z. HOLOWINSKY
Rutgers University
First edition

KAY E. KETZENBERGER
TAMARA J. MARTIN
*The University of Texas of the
Permian Basin*
Second edition

CHOREA

Choreiform movement is a term used to describe a disorder characterized by quick, sudden, random, purposeless, jerky, irregular, spasmodic movement. Choreiform movement can occur in any body part and often is observed in shoulders, arms, and hands, or in the tongue and face as grimaces. Clark (1975) reports a hemichorea may occur on one side of the body with vascular lesions of the basal ganglia of the brain. There are a number of diseases in which choreiform movement is a part of the descriptive syndrome, including hysterical chorea, which is a kind of conversion hysteria with the movement disorder a primary symptom (Hensyl, 1982).

Two major kinds of chorea are of primary interest to school personnel because of their possible school-age onsets and their markedly different outlook for recovery or prognosis. Sydenham's chorea (also known as chorea minor, rheumatic chorea, or St. Vitus's dance) is a disease of the central nervous system that usually occurs following streptococcal inflammation. Its slow start, often several months after the initial infection, begins with choreiform movements after the initial infection, begins with choreiform movements involving all muscles except those of the eyes, and may involve obsessive-compulsive symptoms (Swedo & Leonard, 1994). There are seldom any specific laboratory findings. There is no specific treatment except for sedation and protection from injury, together with prophylactic follow-up for identified residual infection. Recovery is slow and spontaneous, usually within 3 to 6 months, with no permanent damage to the central nervous system. Medical follow-up is recommended, and return to regular school is encouraged as soon as the transitory motor symptoms permit. The disease is reported to be more common in girls, with onset most frequent in summer and early fall (Berkow, 1982).

The second major type of chorea is Huntington's chorea (also known as chorea degenerative, progressive, or hereditary). The age of insidious onset of Huntington's chorea is reported by most sources to be between 30 and 50 years (Barr, 1979; Chusid, 1976; Clark, 1975). However, a subtype of this disease has been described with onset in childhood, with initial symptoms of stiffness (rigidity), slowed movement (bradykinesia), and later choreiform movement (Berkow, 1982). The disease is characterized by progressive choreiform movement, progressive mental deterioration, and marked personality changes. Swallowing becomes difficult, walking impossible, and dementia profound with progression. Death usually follows within 10 to 15 years. Treatment is symptomatic for motor symptoms. There is no known treatment for the dementia.

Huntington's chorea is transmitted as an autosomal dominant trait, which means that half of the children of an affected parent are at risk for developing the disease. Those who do not have the disease do not transmit it. In cases where the family history is not known, affected individuals with onset after childbearing years may transmit the disease to offspring before their own onset. Research has been directed toward a chemical identification of those with the disease, but at present the only conclusive evidence is family history, and *all* potential known carriers are advised not to have children. Chusid (1976) suggests that most American cases have been traced to two brothers who emigrated from England.

Clinical experience suggests that the subtypes with early childhood onset appears to progress more rapidly to early death. The presence of several children with the disorder in one family is a devastating experience. The serious implications of Huntington's chorea should serve to reinforce the importance of differential diagnosis of choreiform movement disorders by a skilled neurologist with appropriate medical follow-up. Supportive special education services should be provided.

REFERENCES

Barr, M. L. (1979). *The human nervous system* (3rd ed.). Hagerstown, MD: Harper & Row.

Berkow, R. (Ed.). (1982). *The Merck manual of diagnosis and therapy* (14th ed.). Rahway, NJ: Merck, Sharp & Dohme.

Chusid, J. G. (1976). *Correlative neuroanatomy and functional neurology* (16th ed.). Los Angeles: Lang Medical.

Clark, R. G. (1975). *Manter and Gatz's essentials of clinical neuroanatomy and neurophysiology* (5th ed.). Philadelphia: Davis.

Hensyl, W. R. (1982). *Stedman's medical dictionary* (24th ed.). Baltimore, MD: Williams & Wilkin.

Stolov, W. C., & Clowers, M. R. (Eds.). (1981). *Handbook of severe disability* (stock #017-090-00054-2). Washington, DC: U.S. Government Printing Office.

Swedo, S. E., & Leonard, H. (1994). Childhood movement disorders and obsessive compulsive disorder. *Journal of Clinical Psychiatry, 55,* 3, 32–37.

RACHAEL J. STEVENSON
Bedford, Ohio

GENETIC COUNSELING
HEREDITY
HUNTINGTON'S CHOREA

CHORIONIC VILLUS SAMPLING (CVS)

Chorionic villus sampling (CVS), sometimes called chorionvillus biopsy, is a relatively new technique that allows diagnosis of chromosomal abnormalities, many inborn errors of metabolism, and other disorders, in the first trimester of pregnancy. Conducted before organogenesis is complete, it cannot detect reliably disorders such as neural tube defects; they may be assessed with later maternal serum alpha-fetoprotein (AFP) screening.

CVS has clear advantages over amniocentesis as a technique for antenatal (prenatal) diagnosis. It can be performed optimally at 9 weeks of pregnancy as opposed to 16 to 18 weeks, and results, including chromosomal analyses, are available in about a week after testing, as opposed to the 2 to 4 weeks for amniocentesis (*Lancet*, 1986). Thus genetic counseling can be provided early in pregnancy in cases where disorders are identified, avoiding some of the ethical and emotional concomitants of later abortion.

In CVS, 10–50 mg of placental tissue are removed. Enzyme assay and DNA analysis are performed directly on this tissue; chromosomal analysis is generally done on cultures of the CVS tissue. Most CVS assays are done transcervically, with a small percentage conducted abdominally (*Lancet*, 1986).

Risk of CVS is not established, although the likelihood of it infecting the embryo appears low. Of particular concern is the suggestion of greater risk of test-induced abortion following CVS than following amniocentesis (Clarke, 1985), although at least one study has found no difference between the two techniques (Jahoda, Vosters, Sacks, & Galjaard, 1985). A number of questions, particularly regarding safety, remain unanswered (*Lancet*, 1986). Widespread availability of CVS will depend on the outcome of large-sample controlled studies of risk and accuracy. Research reports are appearing frequently, and coordinated evaluation studies in Europe, Canada, and the United States began in 1985 (Clarke, 1985).

REFERENCES

Clarke, M. (1985). Fetal diagnosis trial. *Nature, 315,* 269.

Jahoda, M. G., Vosters, R. P. L., Sacks, E. S., & Galjaard, H. (1985). Safety of chorionic villus sampling. *Lancet, 2,* 941–942.

Staff. (1986). The potential of chorionic villus sampling. *Lancet, 1,* 76.

ROBERT T. BROWN
*University of North Carolina
at Wilmington*

BRENDA M. POPE
*New Hanover Memorial
Hospital*

AMNIOCENTESIS
CHROMOSOMAL ABNORMALITIES
MATERNAL SERUM ALPHA-FETROPROTEIN (AFP)
SCREENING

CHROMOSOMES, HUMAN, ANOMALIES AND CYTOGENETIC ABNORMALITIES

Chromosomal (cytogenetic) abnormalities are the most frequent cause of congenital (present at birth) malformations, affecting some 1 in 200 newborns (Moore, 1982). Their importance is reflected in the fact that they account for at least 10 to 15% of individuals with mental retardation severe enough to require institutionalization (Moore, 1982; Pueschel, 1983) and for about 8 to 10% of newborn and early infant deaths (Sperling, 1984). Further, some 30% of spontaneously aborted embryos/fetuses had a chromosomal abnormality, an incidence 50 times higher than that in live births, meaning that incidence in all pregnancies must be about 5% (Sperling, 1984).

Because chromosomal abnormalities involve disruption in the action of many genes, most are associated with severe and varied effects (Brown, 1986). These frequently, but not always, involve general and specific intellective deficits, particular facial anomalies and cardiovascular, digestive, and pulmonary defects. Further, people with a chromosomal abnormalities usually have such characteristic phenotypes (physical appearance and physiological and behavioral functioning) that they frequently look more like unrelated persons with the same chromosomal abnormality than like their own siblings (Moore, 1982). The common characteristics that differentiate individuals with one abnormality from normal people or those with a different abnormality are called syndromes. Some two dozen chromosomally based syndromes have been identified. Although some, particularly the familiar Down's, Klinefelter's, and Turner's syndromes are relatively common, others are so rare that only 50 or so cases have been reported (Smith, 1982).

This entry will address general issues about abnormalities, provide background information for more specialized reading, and address similarities and differences among currently identified syndromes. As is the case with other genetically based disorders and congenital and perinatal abnormalities, new research routinely leads to significant changes in knowledge.

Vogel and Motulsky (1979, p. 18) elegantly describe human cytogenetics as "a successful late arrival." Although the chromosome theory of inheritance had been proposed in 1902, cytogenetics really began in 1956 with the discovery that the diploid number of human chromosomes was 46 instead of the commonly accepted 48. To give an idea of past attitudes toward the handicapped and their behavior, the diploid number 48 had been found by Painter (1923) in studies of spermatogenesis in testes of three inmates of the Texas State Insane Asylum who had been castrated because of, among other things, their excessive masturbation. When in 1959 researchers discovered chromosomal bases for three common and well-established human syndromes (Down's, Klinefelter's, and Turner's), human cytogenetics really came into its own. Since then, a variety of

chromosomally based syndromes have been discovered on the basis of now routine cytogenic analysis of spontaneously aborted fetuses, early death newborns and infants, and individuals with physical and behavioral abnormalities. A number of children traditionally labeled by diagnosticians as "syndromish in appearance" (something looks wrong but no etiology is known) now are identified as having a chromosomal abnormality. In most cases, the description of the physical and behavioral characteristics of the syndrome has followed, rather than preceded, chromosomal analysis. Further, subsequent studies have identified multiple chromosomal bases for syndromes such as Down's, Klinefelter's, and Turner's that help to account for high variability among and even within affected individuals. A variety of technical advances account for much of our knowledge about these abnormalities (Sperling, 1984; Vogel & Motulsky, 1979).

Normal and Abnormal Karyotypes

Normal humans have 23 pairs of chromosomes in all body cells, 22 pairs of autosomes, and one pair of sex chromosomes. Females normally have two long X sex chromosomes and males one long X and one shorter Y sex chromosomes. Chromosomes (colored bodies) are visible only early in mitosis, when cell samples are subjected to certain stains. A karyotype is a picture of chromosomes arranged by pair. The 22 autosomal pairs are arranged from the

Figure 1. Karyotype for a normal human male. Twenty-two pairs of autosomes have been ordered and numbered according to convention from largest to smallest. Sex chromosomes are labeled X and Y.

— SHORT (p) ARM

— CENTROMERE

— LONG (q) ARM

Figure 2. Standard nomenclature for describing parts of a chromosome, after Cohen and Nadler (1983).

longest (1) to the shortest (22), followed by the sex chromosomes. A karyotype, showing chromosomal bands, of a normal human male is shown in Figure 1. Figure 2 shows a typical chromosome pair; the short arm is termed "p" and the long arm, "q"; the two arms are held together at the centromere, or primary constriction. Cohen and Nadler (1983) suggest the useful mnemonic of associating "p" with petite. Chromosomes are grouped into three types: metacentric (e.g., numbers 1 and 3), where the arms are nearly equal in length; submetacentric (e.g., numbers 4 and 5), where the "p" arm is distinctly shorter than the "q"; and acrocentric (e.g., numbers 14 and 21), which have a secondary constriction and abbreviated and apparently genetically inactive satellite "p" arms.

Normal Cell Division. During mitosis, the process of duplication of body cells, each of the 46 chromosomes divides and one member of each migrates to a pole of the cells. When the cell divides, each offspring cell contains the same 23 pairs of chromosomes. Thus mitosis is a process of chromosome duplication. In meiosis, the process of production of germ cells (sperm and eggs), each of the 23 chromosome pairs divides and one member of each pair migrates to a pole of the cell. When the cell divides, each offspring has 23 chromosomes. Thus each germ cell has 23 chromosomes. Meiosis is a process of chromosome reduction. Women's eggs will all have 22 autosomes and an X chromosome; men's sperm all have 22 autosomes and can have either an X or Y. In sexual recombination, when a sperm penetrates an egg, the resulting zygote normally has the appropriate 46 chromosomes. Thus gender of offspring is determined by the father's sperm.

Abnormal Karyotypes. Abnormalities can be: (1) an abnormal total number of chromosomes in an individual's body cells; (2) structural aberrations resulting from breakage in one or more chromosomes; or (3) populations of cells of different chromosome numbers in the same individual (mosaicism).

Aneuploidies refers to deviations, greater or fewer, in number of chromosomes from the normal 46. The most common aneuploidy is trisomy 21, which accounts for the greatest number of chromosomal abnormalities in spontaneous abortions as well as in live births. Trisomies on most pairs are prenatally lethal. Similarly, monosomy, absence of one of a pair, resulting in fewer that 46 chromosomes, is virtually always prenatally lethal, except for Turner's syndrome, in which one X chromosome is missing (45,X). Even then, only one in 150 to 200 45,X embryos survives to full-term birth. The most common cause of aneuploidy is nondisjunction, the failure of a chromosome pair to split during formation of germ cells in meiosis. Thus one offspring germ cell will have a "double dose" of one chromosome and the other will have none. Anaphase lag can also produce monosomy.

Mosaicism results from nondisjunction occurring mitotically in a cell in an embryo in an early stage of development. As a result, if the embryo survives and continues to develop, it will have both normal and abnormal, generally trisomic, cell populations. Because of the presence of normal cells, individuals with mosaicism will generally show less severe symptoms than those with the pure syndrome.

The basis for nondisjunction is not known, but is presumed to be manifested biochemically. In nondisjunction Down's syndrome, approximately 80% of the cases result from maternal and 20% from paternal nondisjunction (Sperling, 1984). Since all autosomal trisomies (not just Down's syndrome) increase dramatically with maternal age, research focuses on factors that correlate with aging, including potential problems with aging oocytes themselves. Hypothesized links with irradiation, chemical agents, methods of birth control, and endocrine factors have not been fully confirmed, but some evidence suggests they play a role (Hassold & Jacobs, 1984).

Chromosomes may break, with material being either lost or attached to another chromosome. The most common structural aberrations are translocations, which result when two chromosomes break and parts of one are transferred to another. A reciprocal translocation occurs when two nonhomologous chromosomes exchange pieces. Individuals with such translocation chromosomes themselves have an appropriate balance of chromosomes and are phenotypically normal. Since they are carriers of a translocation chromosome, their offspring may suffer from duplication-deficiency syndromes, notably partial trisomies.

Important because of clinical implications are centric fusions, or Robertsonian translocations. Centric fusion occurs when two acrocentric chromosomes each break near the centromere and rejoin. Generally, the short arms of both and the centromere of one are lost. Again, individuals may be unaffected, although they have one fewer than normal chromosome, but they are carriers. Their offspring may have a trisomy syndrome. Monosomies are also possible, but appear to be prenatally lethal. The best known translocation is Down's syndrome, resulting from centric fusion of chromosome 21 with chromosome 14 or, less frequently, 15.

Several other structural aberrations also may occur. Simple loss of part of a chromosome may result in a deletion syndrome. Isochromosomes occur when instead of a chromosome pair dividing longitudinally through the centromere, it divides horizontally, producing two chromosomes with identical arms. Fertilization will produce a cell with three "p" or "q" arms and only one of the other. When the segment between two breaks in a chromosome becomes inverted, reversing the gene order, an inversion results. Ring chromosomes occur when both ends of a chromosome break off and the tips of the centric segment rejoin. The resulting circular chromosome is unstable and has material from both ends deleted.

Standard Nomenclature. Normal and abnormal human karyotypes are described using a standard system, general aspects and examples of which are given here. More detailed descriptions are in Cohen and Nadler (1983), Smith (1982), Vogel and Motulsky (1979), and most human genetics textbooks.

As shown in Table 1, the order of information is (1) total number of chromosomes; (2) sex chromosomes; and (3) any abnormalities. Extra or missing chromosomes are indicated by "+" and "−", respectively, before the affected chromosome's number; extra or missing parts are indicated by "+" and "−", respectively, after the affected part. Structural aberrations are indicated by a standard abbreviation followed, parenthetically, by the number of the affected chromosome(s). Then, also parenthetically, the affected arm(s) and, if known, the chromosomal band numbers, are stated. Mosaics are indicated by a (/) mark separating descriptions of the two cell populations.

Abnormalities and Their Characteristics

Although chromosomal syndromes vary widely in their effects, the various types share some characteristics. Because much genetic material has been either added or is missing, many are lethal and most of the rest involve multiple and severe complications. However, as normal individuals vary in their physical and behavioral characteristics, so do those affected by chromosomal abnormalities. Not all will show even all of the major effects.

The description and characteristics of major cytogenic abnormalities occurring in live births are in Tables 2 and 3. It is important that different sources vary in their estimates of incidence and specification of major characteristics. In a number of cases, subsequent cases have led to changes in what were initially thought to be defining characteristics. For example, Cat-eye syndrome (trisomy 22p) was named for the striking coloboma of the iris seen originally. However, it has occurred only in a minority of the 40 cases that had been reported at the time of Smith's summary (1982).

Chromosomal Aneuploidies. The most common abnormalities are aneuploidies, involving an added or missing chromosome (Table 2). Multiple forms of some may occur. By far the most common is Down's syndrome (trisomy 21), but several others have been reported. Early death is common in all, and in some types virtually all die in early infancy. Although each has individual characteristics, all involve brain damage generally resulting in moderate to severe mental retardation, congenital heart disease, and malformed ears. Specific facial, limb, and digit abnormalities are also common. All increase dramatically in incidence with maternal age (Vogel & Motulsky, 1979).

Turner's and Klinefelter's syndromes have clear phenotypic characteristics and were described before the development of modern cytogenic techniques. Both are associated with absence of puberty and sterility. Unfortunately, as pointed out by Brown (1986), textbook authors have frequently described sex-chromosome aneuploidies in chapters on mental retardation. However, standard forms are associated with low average intelligence (IQ ≈ 90), not mental retardation, although incidence of mental retardation is higher than among the normal population. Many affected individuals will complete high school and college. Mosaic Turner females and Klinefelter males will be less affected. Klinefelter males and Poly-X females with extra X chromosomes above trisomy for sex chromosomes are much more adversely affected and likely to be retarded.

Klinefelter and Poly-X syndromes increase with maternal age (Hassold & Jacobs, 1984). However, incidence of neither Turner's nor XYY syndrome correlates with ma-

Table 1. Examples of Karyotype Nomenclature

Karyotype	Description
46,XX; 46,XY	Normal female and male
47,XX,+21	Female with trisomy 21 (Down's syndrome)
46,XY/47,XY+21	Male with mosaic trisomy 21 (Down's syndrome)
46XY,+t(14q21q)	Male with Down's syndrome owed to centric-fusion type translocation between chromosomes 14 and 21
46,XX,del(5p) or 46,XX,5p—	Female with cri du chat owed to deletion of part of short arm of chromosome 5
46,XY,fra X(q27)	Male with fragile X syndrome, involving constriction at distal end of long arm of chromosome

Table 2. Chromosomal Aneuploidies and Characteristics

Syndrome	Incidence (live births)	Source	Characteristics
Autosomal Trisomies			
Trisomy 8	Very Rare	Mosaicism (mainly)	Variable height; MR (M → S); CHD; poor coordination; prominent forehead; deep-set eyes; digital abnormalities
Trisomy 9	Very rare	Mosaicism (mainly)	LBW; MR (S); CHD; low-set malformed ears; joint contractures; majority die in infancy
Trisomy 13 (Patau syndrome)	1:7000 to 20,000	Nondisjunction	LBW; MR (S); CHD; apnea; seizures; bilateral cleft lip and/or palette; failure to thrive; majority die in infancy
Trisomy 18 (Edwards syndrome)	1:8000	Nondisjunction	Three times more frequent in females; LBW; MR (S); failure to thrive; CHD; prominent occiput, majority die in infancy
Trisomy 21 (Down's syndrome)	1:650–800	Nondisjunction—94% Mosaicism—2.4% Translocation—3.3%	MR (M → Mod); CHD; hypotonia; flat occiput; epicanthic fold; large tongue; above average infant death rate
Trisomy 22	Very rare	Nondisjunction (?)	MR; growth retardation; microcephaly; CHD; cleft palate; digit abnormalities; majority die in infancy
Sex Chromosome Aneuiploidies			
Turner's syndrome	1:10,000	Various	Short stature; sterility; short webbed neck; broad, flat chest; IQ ≈ 90
(45,X)	57% of cases	Missing paternal X	
(45,X/46XX, others)	12% of cases	Mosaicism	
(45,X/46,XY)	4% of cases	Mosaicism	
(other)	27% of cases	Inversion and deletion	
Klinefelter's syndrome	1:1000	Various	Sterility; hypogonadism; decreased facial and pubic hair; IQ ≈ 90; behavior problems
(47,XXY)	82% of cases	Nondisjunction	
(48,XXXY)`	3% of cases	Nondisjunction	More problems with added X chromosomes
(49,XXXXY)	<1% of cases	Nondisjunction	
(47,XXY/46,XY)	8% of cases	Mosaicism	
(Others)	6% of cases		
Poly X Syndrome	1:1000	Nondisjunction	No characteristic features; some delayed speech and motor development; more problems with added X chromosomes
(47,XXX)	98+% of cases		
(48,XXXX)	Rare		
47,XYY syndrome	1:1000	Nondisjunction	Variable features; tall; impulsive behavior; IQ ≈ 90

MR = mental retardation (S = severe; Mod = moderate, M = mild); CHD = congenital heart disease; LBW = low birth weight. Information from Cohen and Nadler (1983), Gerald and Meryash (1983), and Smith (1982).

Table 3. Syndromes Involving Abnormal Part of Chromosomes

Syndrome	Incidence	Source	Characteristics
Autosomal Partial Trisomies			
Trisomy 9p	Rare	Translocation (?)	MR (S); delayed growth and puberty; delayed language; digital abnormalities
Partial trisomy 10q	Rare	Translocation (?)	LBW; MR (S); flat occiput; digital abnormalities; CHD; 50% die in infancy
Trisomy 20p	Rare	Translocation (?)	MR (M → Mod); hypotonia; facial abnormalities; digital deformities
Cat-eye syndrome (trisomy 22p)	Rare	Translocation (?)	MR (M); emotional retardation; normal growth; CHD; coloboma of iris; other eye defects
Autosomal Partial Deletion			
4p-	Rare(?)	Partial deletion	LBW; MR (S); beaked nose; microcephaly; cleft palate; hypotonia; seizures; early death
Cri du chat (5p-)	Rare	Partial deletion	LBW; MR (S); catlike cry; hypotonia; epicanthal folds; microcephaly
9p-	Rare	Partial deletion	Normal growth; MR (S); micronathia; trignocephaly; wide-spaced nipples
11p- (Andiria-Wilms Tumor Association)	Rare	Partial deletion	MR (Mod → S); growth deficiency; microcephaly; eye defects: micronathia; andiria; Wilms tumor
13p-	Rare	Partial deletion	LBW; MR (S); failure to thrive; microcephaly; CHD; facial and digital abnormalities
18p-	Rare	Partial deletion	Variability in effect; LBW; MR (variable); epicanthal folds; large, floppy ears
18q-	Rare	Partial deletion	LBW; MR (S); seizures; CHD; microcephaly; limb, digital, and genital abnormalities
21q-	Rare	Partial deletion	MR; hypertonia; growth retardation; microcephaly; micrognathia; large ears
22q-	Rare	Partial deletion	MR; hypotonia; microcephaly; epicanthal folds; digital abnormalities
Constriction Syndrome			
Fragile X	1:1000 males	Constriction at distal end of long arm of X chromosome	Long face; prominent chin; MR (M → S); developmental delay; language problems; specific learning problems

MR = mental retardation (S = severe; Mod = moderate, M = mild); CHD = congenital heart disease; LBW = low birth weight. Information from Cohen and Nadler (1983), Gerald and Meryash (1983), and Smith (1982).

ternal age, consistent with largely paternal origin (Hassold & Jacobs, 1984; Simpson, 1982).

Abnormal Parts of Chromosomes. Several partial trisomy syndromes, involving extra chromosomal material, and deletion syndromes are known, as shown in Table 3. Mental retardation of some degree is common to all. Low birth weight and specific facial and digital anomalies are also frequent.

Of particular current interest is Fragile X syndrome, resulting from a constriction in the X chromosome, which cy-togenic studies reveal to be relatively common. Associated with mental retardation in affected males, it appears to be second only to Down's syndrome as a cytogenic cause of mental retardation.

Implications for Special Educators

As cytogenic analyses become more standard, increasing numbers of children will be identified as having some chromosomal disorder. Many minor ones will have few implications for teachers. Others will be associated with general and specific intellectual deficits, coordination problems, and emotional disorders. Special educators and others in education generally may need to become familiar with the syndrome and standard nomenclature. Further, research will doubtless render some current knowledge incorrect and we must be ready to accept new information. It should be kept in mind that syndromes can induce stereotypes, and that affected children should be treated on the basis of their individual characteristics, not the general ones of a syndrome.

REFERENCES

Brown, R. T. (1986). Etiology and development of exceptionality. In R. T. Brown & C. R. Reynolds (Eds.), *Psychological perspectives on childhood exceptionality: A handbook* (pp. 181–229). New York: Wiley.

Cohen, M. M., & Nadler, H. L. (1983). Chromosomes and their abnormalities. In R. E. Behrman & V. C. Vaughn, III (Eds.), *Nelson textbook of pediatrics* (12th ed.) (pp. 288–310). Philadelphia: Saunders.

Gerald, P. S., & Meryash, D. L. (1983). Chromosomal disorders other than Down syndrome. In M. D. Levine, W. B. Carey, A. C. Crocker, & R. T. Gross (Eds.), *Developmental-behavioral pediatrics* (pp. 346–353). Philadelphia: Saunders.

Hassold, T. J., & Jacobs, P. A. (1984). Trisomy in man. *Annual Review of Genetics, 18,* 69–97.

Moore, K. L. (1982). *The developing human* (3rd ed.). Philadelphia: Saunders.

Painter, T. S. (1923). Studies in mammalian spermatogenesis. II. The spermatogenesis of man. *Journal of Experimental Zoology, 37,* 291–321.

Pueschel, S. M. (1983). The child with Down syndrome. In M. D. Levine, W. B. Carey, A. C. Crocker, & R. T. Gross (Eds.), *Developmental-behavioral pediatrics* (pp. 353–362). Philadelphia: Saunders

Scarr, S., & Kidd, K. K. (1983). Developmental behavior genetics. In P. W. Mussen, M. M. Haith, & J. J. Campos (Eds.), *Handbook of child psychology: Infancy and developmental psychobiology* (4th ed.) (Vol. 2, pp. 345–433). New York: Wiley.

Simpson, J. L. (1982). Abnormal sexual differentiation in humans. *Annual Review of Genetics, 16,* 193–224.

Smith, D. W. (1982). *Recognizable patterns of human malformation* (2nd ed.). Philadelphia: Saunders.

Sperling, K. (1984). Frequency and origin of chromosome abnormalities in man. In G. Obe (Ed.), *Mutations in man* (pp. 128–146). Berlin and New York: Springer-Verlag.

Vogel, F., & Motulsky, A. G. (1979). *Human genetics.* Berlin and New York: Springer-Verlag.

ROBERT T. BROWN
*University of North Carolina
at Wilmington*

CHROMOSOMAL ABNORMALITIES
CRI DU CHAT
DOWN'S SYNDROME

ETIOLOGY
FRAGILE X SYNDROME
KLINEFELTER'S SYNDROME
TURNER'S SYNDROME
XYY SYNDROME

CHRONIC ILLNESS IN CHILDREN

There are many chronic illnesses that children may suffer from. They include some but not all of the conditions regarded as being within the traditional scope of special education. Among important chronic illnesses are asthma, cystic fibrosis, diabetes, epilepsy, leukemia, juvenile rheumatoid arthritis, muscular dystrophy, sickle cell anemia, and thalassemia.

Each group within the broad constituencies of chronic illness by itself may not constitute a large number of children, but together they represent a large group. Thus, Gortmaker (1985) and Pless and Roghmann (1975) have estimated that some 10 to 15% of children have chronic health impairments of some sort. While many of these impairments are mild, others are severe and debilitating. Hobbs, Perrin, and Ireys (1985) estimate that at least 1 million children have severe diseases and that many of these diseases are chronic. This number expands if Hobbes et al. include children who might otherwise be considered physically handicapped, e.g., children with spina bifida, and others who have suffered severe and catastrophic trauma from injuries.

Many of the children who suffer from chronic illness, e.g, asthma or diabetes, have their health needs reasonably well met within the mainstream of society (by medical practitioners and public health agencies). The more severe of these illnesses, however, require more persistent, pervasive, and demanding care. The severity of a child's medical condition does not directly relate to the type and severity of the problem encountered. Some children with severe medical conditions may have little difficulty in participating within the mainstream of everyday living, including at school. Others with relatively mild physical or physiological disturbances may have their lives severely affected by their problems. There is no direct correlation between chronic illness and poor psychosocial functioning (Midence, 1994).

Educationally, some chronically ill children will be served under PL 94-142, either because their conditions are directly diagnosed as constituting handicaps requiring special education services, or because the consequences of their illnesses or injuries result in handicapping conditions that require such services. They are often served under the rubric of "other health impaired."

Where a chronically ill child's health condition, rather than the problems or limitations posed by a handicap, is a main consideration, and the child is not able to effectively participate in special education services within school settings, the child is likely to receive special education services via instruction in the home. In this situation, medical services are likely to be emphasized in their service delivery models.

Despite the fact that some chronically ill children are being effectively served under current special education laws and regulations, there are those who believe that the parents and policy makers who were the prime movers in the creation of state and federal programs for the education of the handicapped largely overlooked the needs of chronically ill children (Walker & Jacobs, 1985). Hobbes, Perrin, and Ireys claim that chronically ill children and youths have "shared in relatively little of the sustained attention given to children with other handicapping conditions, such as mentally retardation" (1985, pp. 4–5).

REFERENCES

Gortmaker, S. L. (1985). Demography of chronic childhood diseases. In N. Hobbes & J. M. Perrin (Eds.), *Issues in the care of children with chronic illness: A sourcebook on problems, services and policies*. San Francisco: Jossey-Bass.

Hobbs, N., Perrin, J. M., & Ireys, H. T. (1985). *Chronically ill children and their families*. San Francisco: Jossey-Bass.

Midence, K. The effects of chronic illness on children and their families: An overview. *Genetic, Social, & General Monographs, 120*, 3, 309–326.

Pless, I. B., & Pinkerton, P. (1975). *Chronic childhood disorder: Promoting patterns of adjustment*. Chicago: Year Book Medical.

Pless, I. B., & Roghmann, K. J. (1971). Chronic illness and its consequences: Some observations based on three epidemiological surveys. *Journal of Pediatrics, 79*, 351–359.

Walker, D. K., & Jacobs, F. (1985). Public school programs for chronically ill children. In N. Hobbes & J. M. Perrin (Eds.), *Issues in the care of children with chronic illness: A sourcebook on problems, services and policies*. San Francisco: Jossey-Bass.

Douglas L. Mann
*V. A. Medical Center, Medical
University of South Carolina*

ASTHMA
DIABETES
OTHER HEALTH IMPAIRED

CHURCH WORK WITH THE HANDICAPPED

During the early development of Christianity, the influence of Christ's healing works and the Apostle Paul's writings shaped the Christian attitude toward handicapped persons. However, as Christianity spread across Europe, especially during the Middle Ages, Christian attitudes varied. Religious teaching led to persecution (witnessed in the Inquisition), isolation (lest a clean person be tainted), and protection (many monasteries tended to the handicapped) (Hewett & Forness, 1977; Scheerenberger, 1982). It was during this time (1377 AD) that the first asylum (Hospital of St. Mary of Bethlehem, known as Bedlam) was founded. In the early part of the seventeenth century, St. Vincent dePaul initiated a program for "idiots." In the eighteenth century William Tuke, a Quaker, established a program for the humane treatment of the mentally retarded and the mentally ill (Scheerenberger, 1982). Also in the eighteenth century, the charitable work that had been the purview of the church began to receive attention from governments (Hewett & Forness, 1977). Religious organizations such as the St. Vincent dePaul Society, and much later the YMCA and YWCA, provided services, but their roles were diminished. Kowalski (1978) believes that today the government has nearly totally replaced the church as a provider of services to the handicapped.

According to Parks (1975), the doing of good works is viewed as one path to Christian salvation. It is this belief that has marked the history of church work with the handicapped. Recent changes can best be characterized as moving from provider of services to facilitator of integration. For example, the World Council of Churches (National Council of Churches, 1978) stated that the disabled ought to be full members of the church. The United Presbyterian Church in the United States (1979) committed the church to full integration and mandated physical adaptations for accessibility. In 1978 the U.S. Catholic bishops declared that the role of the church was to function as an advocate for handicapped persons (U.S. Catholic Conference, 1978).

In addition to the hundreds of religious schools that provide special education and residential services for handicapped children, and the hundreds of hospitals and medical care facilities that are church supported, there are a large number of organizations dedicated to service/advocacy for the handicapped. The following is a list of some of these organizations.

1. Board of Missions, Ministry of the Deaf, Lutheran Church–Missouri Synod
2. Department of Urban Ministries, Board of Missions, United Methodist Church
3. Ephphatha Missions for the Deaf and Blind
4. Episcopal Conference of the Deaf
5. International Catholic Deaf Association
6. National Congress of Jewish Deaf
7. Xavier Society for the Blind
8. National Apostolate with Mentally Retarded Persons
9. Advisory Committee on Ministry with Handicapped Persons, United States Catholic Conference

10. Task Force on Church and Disability, World Council of Churches

REFERENCES

Hewett, F. M., & Forness, S. R. (1977). *Education of exceptional learners*. Boston: Allyn & Bacon.

Kowalski, A. P. (1978). The church and the handicapped. *America, 138*(9), 426–427.

National Council of Churches. (1978). *The handicapped and the wholeness of the family of God*. New York: Author.

189th General Assembly of the United Presbyterian Church (1979). Overture 16: On responding to the concerns of the handicapped. *Church and Society, 69*, 22–34.

Parks, L. D. (1975). Barriers to normality for the handicapped adult in the United States. *Rehabilitation Literature, 36*, 108–111.

Scheerenberger, R. C. (1982). Treatment from ancient times to the present. In P. T. Cegelka & H. J. Prehm (Eds.), *Mental retardation: From categories to people* (pp. 44–75). Columbus, OH: Merrill.

Stine, E. (1979). The disabled, the new community and the world. *Church and Society, 69*(3), 10–19.

United States Catholic Conference. (1978). *Pastoral statement of the U.S. Catholic bishops on handicapped people*. Washington, DC: USCC Publications.

JAMES K. MCAFEE
Pennsylvania State University

CITIZEN ADVOCACY GROUP

See ADVOCACY GROUP, CITIZEN.

CIVIL RIGHTS OF THE HANDICAPPED

A handicapped person has certain rights guaranteed by law that relate to education, employment, health care, senior citizen activities, welfare, and any other or private services, programs, or activities that receive federal assistance.

Diamond (1979) has summarized the need for services and the specific rights of handicapped individuals from a personal perspective. She reports that handicapped persons have a right to private and public education at the elementary, secondary, and postsecondary levels. In addition to the education curriculum, supportive or rehabilitative services should be made available. When requiring a service, e.g., when dining out or shopping, the same courtesies should be extended to handicapped individuals as to others.

People with disabilities have the right to travel assisted or unassisted on airplanes, trains, buses, and taxi cabs. Persons with disabilities have a right to gain entrance to public facilities without being inconvenienced, and buildings should be free of architectural barriers. Handicapped individuals have a right to receive equal treatment by doctors and hospitals. This will require that medical personnel acquire understanding and knowledge of disabilities. Handicapped persons have a right to apply for any license (e.g., marriage, fishing) made available to nonhandicapped individuals without additional requirements or embarrassment. It is unlawful to discriminate against the handicapped regarding employment practices. It is also unlawful for the owner of commercial property to refuse to sell, rent, lease, or in any way discriminate because of a disability. As important as the services needed is the right to feel assured that the members of society will look on the handicapped as responsible people capable of making a contribution to society.

It is the responsibility of the Office for Civil Rights in the Department of Education and the Office for Civil Rights in the Department of Health and Human Services to enforce federal laws prohibiting discrimination against persons on the basis of race, color, national origin, sex, age, or handicap in federally assisted programs or activities, and to investigate discrimination complaints brought by individuals under these statutes (Office of Civil Rights, 1998).

REFERENCES

Diamond, S. (1979). Developmentally disabled persons: Their rights and their needs for services. In R. Wiegerink & J. Pelosi (Eds.), *Developmental disabilities: The DD movement* (pp. 15–25). Baltimore, MD: Brookes.

Office of Civil Rights. (1998). Mission Statement. Washington, DC: U.S. Department of Education.

CECILIA STEPPE-JONES
North Carolina Central University

ACCESSIBILITY OF BUILDINGS
ACCESSIBILITY OF PROGRAMS
AMERICANS WITH DISABILITIES ACT
ATTITUDES TOWARDS THE HANDICAPPED
SOCIAL BEHAVIOR OF THE HANDICAPPED

CLASS-ACTION SUITS

Class actions are lawsuits in which a class of persons is represented by one or more of its members. In federal and in most state courts, groups of persons who have similar interests in the law and fact of the lawsuit can sue or be sued through a representative who acts on their behalf. A class action offers the following: the benefits of a clear resolution of a specific issue; the convenience of a useful method to assert legal rights in cases that have common interest where small individual claims might otherwise preclude judicial relief; and the saving of time, money, and effort by eliminating repetitious lawsuits (Redden & Vernon, 1980).

General requirements of a class action follow: the representative class must be large, although no specific number has been determined, so that it would be impractical to name each individual as a party to be brought before the court; the court must be able to clearly recognize the group as a class by virtue of its well-defined interests; and members of the class must raise the same questions of law and fact. The existence of an ascertainable class is evidenced by its certification by the court, which is necessary for the maintenance of a class action. All persons who will be affected by a judgment in a class action must be notified that such an action has commenced; each is provided an opportunity to present his or her side of the case. The court's ruling in a class-action suit applies to all members of that class unless a member has requested an option indicating that he or she does not wish to be bound by the specified court action (Payne & Patton, 1980; Redden & Vernon, 1980).

Court rulings in class-action suits have stimulated both litigation and legislation on behalf of handicapped individuals. During the 1950s courts were confronted with class actions concerning the civil rights of handicapped children and adults. The majority of the actions were focused on the public's responsibility to provide education and treatment for handicapped citizens. The legal doctrines which courts have relied in substantiating the right to an education for the handicapped stem, in part, from the Supreme Court ruling in *Brown v. Board of Education*. The Supreme Court ruled in this landmark decision that all children are constitutionally entitled to an equal educational opportunity (Abeson & Bolick, 1974; Kirp, 1976). Subsequent class-action suits addressed the enforcement of the ruling in *Brown v. Board of Education* (Martin, 1980). Handicapped children were no longer denied a public education, however, many issues remained unresolved, and new issues surfaced in the courts, as well. For example, several state laws still regarded the severely handicapped as uneducable and thereby excluded this group from public schools. Questions regarding racial overrepresentation in special programs were also subjects of extensive litigation (Kirp, 1976).

The major legislation that governs our present delivery of services to exceptional children, Individuals with Disabilities Education Act (IDEA), precipitated litigation that was more diverse and more individualized, thereby decreasing the numbers of representative classes. With the advent of the earlier version of IDEA, PL 94-142, class-

action suits declined and individual legal claims were filed in matters of due process, Individual Education Plan (IEP) challenges, placement, and related services.

REFERENCES

Abeson, A., & Bolick, N. (1974). *A continuing summary of pending and completed litigation regarding the education of handicapped children*, Reston, VA: Council for Exceptional Children.

Kirp, D. (1976). *Trends in education: The special child goes to court*. Columbus, OH: University Council for Educational Administration.

Martin, R. (1980). *Educating handicapped children the legal mandate*. Champaign, IL: Research Press.

Patten J., & Patton J. (1981). *Mental retardation*. Columbus, OH: Merrill.

Redden, K. & Vernon, E. (1980). *Modern legal glossary*. Charlottesville, VA: Michie.

FRANCES T. HARRINGTON
Radford University

BROWN V. BOARD OF EDUCATION
EDUCATION FOR ALL HANDICAPPED CHILDREN ACT
   OF 1975
LARRY P.

CLASSROOM MANAGEMENT

Broadly conceived, classroom management refers to the orderly organization of materials and activities and the development of acceptable student behavior within the school learning environment. Although a deceptively simple concept, any consideration of the purposes and techniques of classroom management suggests numerous other educational concerns. Classroom management techniques must be in harmony with the school's perception of the nature and purpose of instruction and must satisfy a significant number of ethical and legal concerns. Similarly, the school's organizational structure must be constructed in a manner that will allow meeting the psychoeducational assumptions implicit in any selected alternative. For these reasons, classroom management techniques must be selected with regard to many considerations. Few authors advocate a single approach as optimal for all settings.

Although classroom management can be broadly conceived, the usual topic of interest is the behavior of students and, specifically, discipline in the classroom. Clearly, the control of student behavior receives far more emphasis than other potential events that could be associated with classroom management. Public opinion consistently notes school discipline, often described as student control, to be a major problem in schools. In addition, a 1981 survey of teachers conducted by the National Education Association found 90% of the respondents indicating negative instructional outcomes as a result of student misbehavior. Cruickshank (1981) found similar results in that the control of students was seen to be one of the five most important issues identified by teachers throughout the course of a 15-year longitudinal study. Clearly then, classroom management is now virtually synonymous with discipline. Why discipline is a problem in contemporary U.S. schools is not fully understood. However, Charles (1985) and Jones and Tanner (1981) offer an analysis of the origin of the problem.

Given the widespread concern for discipline in the schools, it is not surprising that many models of classroom management have emerged. Since most of the efforts of classroom management techniques are devoted to redirecting atypical behavior, most currently advocated procedures were derived from intervention strategies used in laboratory or clinical settings. Relatively few of the available procedures were initially developed within the classroom (Gunter & Denny, 1996), although there are exceptions (e.g., Cantor & Cantor, 1976; Kounin, 1977). In conceptualizing variations in individuals, Rhodes and Tracy (1972) enumerated several general models that emphasize a perspective on the causes and alteration of behavior.

Almost all current approaches to classroom management are derived from one of the following perceptions. The *biophysical model* emphasizes the role of biology as a determinant of behavior. Interventions drawn from this model emphasize the control of environmental stimuli to a limited extent, and tend to rely more on the effects of diets, the elimination of environmental hazards to biological processes, genetic counseling, and the use of psychotropic drugs. The *sociological model* emphasizes the context of the school in society. This approach stresses the role of society in determining the nature of behaviors in need of control and the social forces operating to promote or inhibit specific behaviors (Tierno, 1991). Classroom management techniques drawn from this viewpoint tend to emphasize the influence of, for example, community and peer group on individual behavior. The *behavioral model* emphasizes, in particular, the immediate consequences of behavior for its role in the subsequent occurrence or lack of occurrence of behavior. Classroom management strategies drawn from this influence generally emphasize the role of the teacher (or other significant individuals) in the provision of consequences to particular behaviors. Control is sought by the careful manipulation of consequences. The *ecological model* emphasizes the context of behavior, noting that behavior never occurs in isolation and that naturally occurring events coerce specific types of behavior, e.g., a chair promotes sitting behavior, close proximity may promote speaking behavior. Finally, *the psychodynamic model* represents many alternative viewpoints that conceptualize the individual as possessing a dynamic intrapsychic life.

The personality emerging from these inner forces becomes the basis for behavior. Personality formation and its ultimate effect on behavior is interpreted differently across the many models. However, virtually all psychodynamic models see the basis for behavioral change as the personal realization of the causes of one's behavior.

All of the above models have had significant influence on the development of techniques for classroom management. The sociological and ecological models, though theoretically suggesting great promise, have generally not spawned specific procedures widely placed into practice. The biophysical model has largely remained the purview of physicians. Both the psychodynamic and the behavioral models have, however, demonstrated immense appeal to educators and have generated many variations in approach. Of the two, the behavioral model is now the more dominant in the special education literature, but is now taking into account social constructivist classrooms (Brophy, 1998). Early conceptualizations that relied on the teacher's control of contingencies have been augmented in recent years through the widespread use of modeling techniques (e.g., Bandura, 1969), cognitive behavior modification (e.g., Meichenbaum, 1977), group contingency programs (e.g., Litow & Pumroy, 1975), and other advances. Significant problems in transfer of training and generalization of learned behaviors remain obstacles to the use of the approach. An excellent overview of representative classroom management techniques can be found in Charles (1985) and Walker and Shea (1984).

REFERENCES

Bandura, A. (1969). *Principles of behavior modification*. New York: Holt.

Brophy, J. (1998). Classroom management as socializing students into clearly articulated roles. *Journal of Classroom Interaction, 33,* 1, 1–4.

Cantor, L., & Cantor, M. (1976). *Assertive discipline. A take charge approach for today's educator*. Seal Beach, CA: Cantor and Associates.

Charles, C. M. (1985). *Building classroom discipline: From models to practice* (2nd ed.). New York: Longman.

Cruickshank, D. (1981). What we know about teachers' problems. *Educational Leadership, 38,* 402–405.

Jones, R. S., & Tanner, L. N. (1981). Classroom discipline: The unclaimed legacy. *Phi Delta Kappan, 62,* 494–497.

Gunter, P. L., & Denny, R. K. (1996). Research issues and needs regarding teacher use of classroom management strategies. *Behavior Disorders, 22,* 1, 15–20.

Kounin, J. (1977). *Discipline and group management in classrooms*. New York: Holt.

Litow, L., & Pumroy, D. K. (1975). A brief review of classroom group-oriented contingencies. *Journal of Applied Behavior Analysis, 8,* 341–347.

Meichenbaum, D. (1977). *Cognitive-behavior modification: An integrative approach*. New York: Plenum.

Rhodes, W. L., & Tracy, M. L. (Eds.). (1972). *A study of child variance: Conceptual models*. Ann Arbor, MI: University of Michigan.

Tierno, M. J. (1991). Responding to the socially motivated behaviors of early adolescents: Recommendations for Classroom Management. *Adolescence, 26,* 103, 569–577.

Walker, J. E., & Shea, T. M. (1984). Behavior management: *A practical approach for educators* (3rd ed.). St. Louis: Times Mirror/Mosby.

TED L. MILLER
University of Tennessee

APPLIED BEHAVIOR ANALYSIS
BEHAVIOR ASSESSMENT
DISCIPLINE

CLAUSEN, JOHS (1913–   )

Johs Clausen was born in Bergen, Norway. He is a psychophysiologist and researcher in mental retardation. In 1939 he obtained his MA at the University of Oslo and in 1956 his PhD at the Faculty of Medicine, University of Oslo. Between 1949 and 1951, Clausen was a research fellow at Columbia University. He participated in the Columbia Greystone Project and the New York State Brain Research Project. He was also a research fellow with the Norwegian Research Council from 1953 to 1955; an associate scientist at the New York Psychiatric Institute from 1955 to 1966; and research psychologist, chief of psychological research, and research administrator at the Training School at Vineland (American Institute of Mental Studies). Clausen conducted research on ability structures and autonomic nervous functions in mentally retarded individuals. From 1966 to 1984, Clausen was chief research scientist, department of psychology, New York State Institute for Basic Research in Mental Retardation.

Among his numerous professional affiliations, Clausen has been a member of the American Psychological Association, Eastern Psychological Association, American Association for the Advancement of Science, American Association on Mental Deficiency, and the American Academy on Mental Retardation. He is the author of *Ability Structure and Subgroups in Mental Retardation* as well as more than 55 scientific studies.

REFERENCE

Clausen, J. (1966). *Ability structure and subgroups in mental retardation*. Washington, DC: Spartan.

IVAN Z. HOLOWINSKY
Rutgers University

CLEFT LIP/PALATE

The phenomenon of cleft lip and palate is a rather frequent one all over the world: 0.1% of all neonates are born with a more or less severe cleft, ranging from a cleft uvula or a partly cleft upper lip to a two-sided complete cleft of upper lip, jaw, and hard and soft palate. Normally, three main groups are discerned: cleft lip only (CL), cleft palate only (CP), and cleft lip and palate combined (CLP). Cleft lip and palate malformations are congenital and originate in the fourth to seventh week (CL) and in the seventh to twelfth week (CP) of embryonic development. Although in some cases viral, medical, and X-ray influences may play a role in causing these malformations, they are generally believed to have a hereditary basis. The chance of cleft lip and palate increases accordingly as the occurrence of clefts in a family are more frequent and more severe, and with the closeness of the relationship (mother or father). The occurrence of clefts is more frequent in boys than in girls, and, moreover, types of clefts are not equally divided between the sexes.

Problems arising from being born with a cleft lip and palate are highly dependent on the part of the world in which the baby is born. In Third World countries, where no surgery is done on cleft lip and palate children, the main problem is survival and nourishment. In highly developed countries, the problems for cleft lip and palate children mainly concern communication and socialization. But even in these countries, a large differentiation can be found in the treatment of children with cleft lip and palate depending on the scientific ideas and theories of the treating medical team. However, for all newborn babies with cleft lip and palate, the first problem encountered is the feeding, because of the difficulties in sucking and swallowing. In Third World countries, infants depend entirely on breast feeding; if the baby is kept in a somewhat deviant feeding position (almost vertically sitting on the mother's lap or nearly horizontally held against the body of the mother), breast feeding is generally considered to be successful. Breast feeding is advisable in highly developed countries as well, because apart from other advantages, it is highly beneficial to the mother-child bond. In case of insurmountable breast feeding problems, feeding by means of special spoons and cups is preferred to bottles with long nipples (so-called lamb's nipples). Sometimes the infant will be provided with an obturator, a small plastic plate covering the cleft in the palate. This may help normal sucking, but it must be frequently renewed and readjusted because of the growing of the infant's mouth.

In most countries where surgery is applied, the child passes through a whole program of treatment and rehabilitation during the first years of life, often starting with healing of the lip followed by closure of the soft palate some months later, and sometimes the hard palate as well. The schedule and type of treatment depends to a large extent on the philosophy of the medical team. For example, the plastic surgeon will stress the aesthetic and visible aspects, the orthodontist the dental aspects, the speech pathologist the importance of the development of language and speech, and so on. Nevertheless, it will be clear that the best results are achieved by an interdisciplinary team of experts in close cooperation, all aiming to establish normal appearance, normal dental function, and good language and communication skills. The whole rehabilitation program is normally spread over more than 15 years.

As for the intellectual abilities of cleft lip and palate children, many prejudices have to be disproved. Visible congenital deformations, especially of the head, are often wrongly associated with poor intellectual capacities. In recent research, children with cleft lip and palate were found to have at least average general intelligence, with no intellectual differences between boys and girls. The lowest scoring group are children with cleft palate only (CP), the group with no visible abnormalities.

As for the speech and language development and related verbal expression abilities of children with cleft lip and palate, a clear delay is found compared with the average population. One of the causes might be hearing problems, since children with cleft lip and palate have increased chances of inflammation of the middle ear combined with hearing impairment. Nevertheless, these possible hearing losses are not considered to be the main cause of the speech and language delays. Nor are the pronunciation problems that result from the abnormalities of the speech production mechanism, although a thorough speech training program will nearly always be necessary. No one-to-one relationship can be found between the severity of the malformation or the proportions of the cleft and the degree of delay in language and speech development. More and more, the psychosocial development of the child is believed to be a ground for speech and language problems.

Because interaction between parent and child is the cradle of the development of communication, it is clear that acceptance of the infant and his or her difficulties is a must. The birth of a child with a cleft lip and palate will undoubtedly cause the parents a degree of concern. The questions of the parents, their anxieties and concerns, require immediate professional counseling to create safe and adjusted surroundings for the child. Well-balanced interaction between parents and infant provides the possibility for the cleft palate child to develop normal linguistic, communicative, and social skills.

REFERENCES

Brookshire, B. L., Lynch, J. I., & Fox, D. R. (1984). *A parent-child cleft palate curriculum*. Tigard, OR: C. C. Publications.

Heineman-de Boer, J. A. (1985). *Cleft palate children and intelligence*. Lisse, Netherlands: Swets & Zeitlinger.

McWilliams, B., Morris, H., & Shelton, R. (1990). *Cleft palate speech* (2nd ed.). Philadelphia, PA: B. C. Decker.

Moller, K. & Starr, C. (1993). *Cleft palate: Interdisciplinary issues and treatment: For clinicians by clinicians*. Austin, TX: Pro-Ed.

F. J. Koopmans-Van Beinum
Amsterdam The Netherlands
First edition

Robert L. Rhodes
New Mexico State University
Second edition

LANGUAGE DEFICIENCIES AND DEFICITS
LANGUAGE DISORDERS, EXPRESSIVE
PHYSICAL ANOMALIES

CLELAND, CHARLES C. (1924–   )

Charles Cleland received his BS in political science in 1950, and his MS in educational psychology in 1951, from Southern Illinois University. Cleland's doctoral work in educational psychology and general and industrial management at the University of Texas, Austin (1957), presented a theme that has been reflected in most of his work.

After a year as chief psychologist at the Lincoln State School (Illinois), Cleland returned to Texas to the Austin State School. In 1959 he was promoted to superintendent of the Abilene State School, where he stayed for four years until joining the faculty in the educational psychology department at the University of Texas, Austin.

Since that time, Cleland has been a professor of special education and educational psychology, teaching courses primarily in the areas of mental retardation, residential care, and management of service facilities. Although Cle-

Charles C. Cleland

land does not view himself as researcher (personal communication, June 26, 1985), his 250 articles, chapters in books, monographs, and books on a wide variety of subjects may prove otherwise. His principal publications include *Mental Retardation: Developmental Approach, Exceptionalities Through the Lifespan, Mental Retardation Approaches to Institutional Change,* and *Mental Retardation.*

REFERENCES

Cleland, C. C. (1978). *Mental retardation: A developmental approach.* Englewood Cliffs, NJ: Prentice-Hall.

Cleland, C. C. (1992). *Mental retardation.* New York, NY: Wiley.

Cleland, C. C., & Schwartz, J. D. (1969). *Mental retardation approaches to institutional change.* New York: Grune & Stratton.

Cleland, C. C., & Schwartz, J. D. (1982). *Exceptionalities through the lifespan.* New York: Macmillan.

ELAINE FLETCHER-JANZEN
University of Northern Colorado

CLERC, LAURENT (1785–1869)

Laurent Clerc, deaf from the age of one, was educated at the Institution Nationale des Sourdes Muets in Paris; following graduation served as a teacher there. He traveled to the United States with Thomas Hopkins Gallaudet to open the nation's first school for the deaf, now the American School for the Deaf, at Hartford, Connecticut, in 1817. Schooled in the teaching methods of Epée and Sicard, Clerc was the school's first teacher and was responsible for the training of new teachers.

Clerc was the first educated deaf person to be seen in the United States. He exemplified the potential of education for the deaf, and was influential in the movement to establish public responsibility for the education of the deaf.

REFERENCES

Lane, H. (1984). *When the mind hears.* New York: Random House.

Turner, W. W. (1871). Laurent Clerc. *American Annals of the Deaf, 15,* 14–25.

PAUL IRVINE
Katonah, New York

CLINICAL EVALUATION OF LANGUAGE FUNDAMENTALS

The Clinical Evaluation of Language Fundamentals, Third Edition (CELF-3) is an individually administered diagnostic battery designed for the identification, diagnosis, and follow-up evaluation of language skill deficits in the areas of listening (receptive) and speaking (expressive). The CELF-3 can be administered to persons aged 6 through 21 and takes approximately 30 to 45 minutes to administer. The full battery contains 11 subtests, but only 6 are needed to obtain the global standard scores for Receptive Language, Expressive Language, and Total Language Scores. The CELF-3 is comprised of sentence structure, word structure, concepts and directions, formulated sentences, word classes, recalling sentences, sentence assembly, semantic relationships (core subtests) and word associations, listening to paragraphs, and rapid, automatic naming (supplementary subtests). The third edition of the CELF contains updated norms, revised subtests and items, and color stimuli. Individuals with suspected or known deficits in the use of word meaning (semantics), word and sentence structure (morphology and syntax), and recall and retrieval of spoken language (memory) would be appropriate candidates for the use of the CELF-3.

The CELF-3 was standardized on 2450 students ranging in age from 6 to 21 years. The entire standardization sample consisted of normally achieving children. Thus, an issue of generalizability results from the use of the test to identify those who are impaired. Tests of internal consistency ranged from .83 to .95 for the global standard scores and from .54 to .95 for the individual subtests. Test-retest reliability (based on repeated administration with 152 of the examinees form the standardization set) ranged from .52 to .90 for the individual subtests and from .80 to .91 for the global standard scores. Validity was examined through the comparison of the CELF-3 with the Wechsler Intelligence Scale for Children (WISC-III). A strong correlation of $r = .75$ resulted. Gillam noted that the CELF-3's relationship to the WISC-III supports of the idea that the CELF-3 is a good measure of verbal ability but leaves much to be desired, as a measure of criterion-related validity (relating the CELF-3 to an achievement test) would have been more convincing (1998).

REFERENCES

Gillam, R. B. (1998). Review of the Clinical Evaluation of Language Fundamentals, Third Edition. In J. C. Impara & B. S. Plake (Eds.), *The thirteenth mental measurements yearbook* (pp. 261–263). Lincoln, NE: Buros Institute of Mental Measurements.

Semel, E. M., Wiig, E. H., & Secord, W. A. (1995). *Clinical Evaluation of Language Fundamentals, Third Edition.* San Antonio, TX: The Psychological Corporation.

TRACY A. MUENZ
*California School of
Professional Psychology*

CLINICAL INTERVIEW

Assessment interviews are conducted to identify and define current problems, to collect information concerning why current problems exist, or to make a diagnostic decision. The focus can be on information the client provides directly (content interviews), or on information that the client's behavior provides (process interviews, also known as mental status exams), or both. Manuals for conducting process interviews with children include Beiser's (1962), Goodman & Sours' (1967), and Greenspan's (1981). Content interviews have been emphasized in the literature on behavioral assessment of adult disorders (e.g.; Haynes, 1978); prior to 1975, however, there were few references to content interviews with children. Since then, a number of studies have demonstrated that children can directly provide reliable information (e.g., Abu-Saad & Holzemer, 1981; Herjanic & Campbell, 1977), particularly when describing publicly observable events.

As with any assessment instrument, the quality of an interview depends on getting accurate information with the least amount of error. Three major sources of error are present in the interview: the interviewer, the interviewee, and the interview setting. One obvious interviewer error is the failure to ask for necessary information. It is unlikely that information that is not specifically asked for will be obtained; thus the information needed from an interview should be well planned. Some interviews are highly structured (e.g., the Vineland Adaptive Behavior Scales); others use rough organizing frameworks such as BASIC ID (Lazarus, 1973) or S-O-R-K-C (Kanfer & Saslow, 1969); the interview also may be organized ad hoc by the clinician. Several structured interviews for the assessment of child psychopathology exist (e.g., Edelbrock & Costello, 1984; Orvaschel, Sholomskas, & Weissman, 1980). The specific plan an interviewer uses will depend on the interviewer's purpose and theoretical model (Ventura, Lieberman, Green, Shaner & Mintz, 1998). The interviewer, however, must be careful not to lead the client's responses; only information to which the client has access should be asked for, and it should be clear to the client that no one response is favored by the interviewer. A second information-gathering error is the failure to recognize and clarify ambiguous responses. This source of error can be reduced by asking questions that clarify contradictory information.

A great deal of information can be given during interviews; thus, the storage and retrieval system used by the clinician is a third potential source of error. Audio or video recording ensures that all information given is stored, but recordings are cumbersome to review, may have adverse effects on rapport, and are not readily available in some settings. Notetaking is more efficient and can be more easily organized, but notetaking can also detract from rapport with some clients. Notetaking also has the effect of implicitly reinforcing clients for giving specific types of informa-

tion, an advantage if this is information that the clinician needs. The interviewer may decide to neither record nor take notes; but the interviewer then needs to rely more heavily on specific memory strategies, e.g., making frequent summary statements of known information, and later writing notes.

An interviewer may use tactics that initially result in accurate information, but the information quality will deteriorate throughout the interview if the interviewer does not maintain a relationship in which the client continues to want to give accurate information. Maintaining warmth, empathy, genuineness and person reinforcement may help maintain rapport. The interviewer must remain alert to changes in affect and change tactics to maintain an appropriate and culturally competent (Lesser, 1997) relationship.

Sources of interviewee error fall into categories of effects of developmental deficits, client perceptions of the nature and consequences of the interview, and fatigue. To the extent that the effects of these sources of error are under some control by the interviewer, they represent interviewer errors of control. Clinicians should be alert to signs of fatigue and other physiological effects; interview sessions should be a short as possible and conducted at times when the client is rested and least distractible. Children and developmentally delayed adults have deficits in their knowledge of vocabulary and conversational conventions (Conti & Camras, 1984; Dickson, 1981), in their understanding of what a listener needs to know (Flavell et al., 1968), and in the facility with which they can meet the cognitive demands of answering questions (Shatz, 1977). These sources of error can be partly controlled by ensuring that vocabulary used by the interviewer is familiar to the client, by keeping cognitive demands low (e.g., by asking for single bits of information at once rather than multiple bits), and by clearly explaining what information the interviewer knows and what information is needed. There is evidence that closed-ended or multiple-response format questions (e.g., "When the other kids call you that name, do you feel angry, sad, or something else?") obtain more reliable responses from developmentally younger persons than open-ended questions (e.g., "How do you feel when they call you that name?"), and some evidence that open-ended questions produce more refusals and less complete information than closed-ended ones (Ammons, 1950; Miller & Bigi, 1979). However, there is a tendency for developmentally delayed adults and children to give acquiescent responses to yes-no questions, and to give the last choice in multiple-response formats (Sigelman et al., 1981). There is a also a tendency for normal children under six to assume that they understand ambiguous questions and not ask clarifying questions (Robinson & Robinson, 1984). These deficits imply that when interviewing young children and developmentally delayed older persons, clinicians need to ask closed-ended questions, but avoid yes-no formats; clinicians should also be alert to a possible response bias. Sigelman et al. (1981) found a picture-choice format to be the most reliable, but nonverbal formats for interviewing may not always be available.

The interviewee's expectations about the interview and about what will be done with the information obtained is also likely to affect validity. Clinicians should ensure that clients understand what will happen during the interview, why the interview is being conducted, and how the information will be used, and should elicit any concerns the client has about the interview. In interpreting data, the clinician should consider the likelihood that the client may have been giving biased responses because of the demands of the setting; for example, when interviewing a client in a dormitory about involvement in an incident of stealing, it is likely that the client will give biased information, particularly if the client believes such information will be shared with houseparents. Bias owed to ecological demand characteristics can be reduced if the interview is designed so that the client believes the interview will be ecologically helpful. If the clinician begins the interview by asking whether there are problems in the setting that the client would like to have ameliorated, the client is more likely to be cooperative in sharing information.

The interview setting influences the interview, and can therefore be a source of error. Interviewer and interviewee should generally be alone unless the presence of other persons is expected to enhance the quality of the interview (e.g., a young child may be very fearful unless mother is present). The clinician needs to consider how the presence of other persons may affect the demand characteristics of the interview when interpreting the results. The client's prior experience with the clinician may also bias results; this problem is minimal in situations in which interviewer and interviewee have never met. The location of the interview may also affect the information that is elicited; interviewing a child in a classroom, for example, may generate a client expectation that the interviewer is a teacher; on the other hand, the setting can be used to prompt information that may not be normally accessible. It's possible, for example, that a child will give more reliable information about what has occurred in a classroom when the child is interviewed alone in the classroom. The setting for the interview should be carefully planned by the clinician.

REFERENCES

Abu-Saad, H., & Holzemer, W. L. (1981). Measuring children's self-assessment of pain. *Issues in Comprehensive Pediatric Nursing, 5,* 337–349.

Ammons, R. B. (1950). Reactions in a projective doll-play interview of white males two to six years of age to differences in skin color and facial features. *Journal of Genetic Psychology, 76,* 323–341.

Beiser, H. R. (1962). Psychiatric diagnostic interviews with children. *Journal of the American Academy of Child Psychiatry, 1,* 656–670.

Conti, D. J., & Camras, L. A. (1984). Children's understanding of conversational principles. *Journal of Experimental Child Psychology, 38,* 456–463.

Dickson, W. P. (1981). Introduction: Toward an interdisciplinary conception of children's communication abilities. In W. P. Dickson (Ed.), *Children's oral communication abilities* (pp. 1–10). New York: Academic.

Edelbrock, C., & Costello, A. J. (1984). *A review of structured psychiatric interviews for children.* Unpublished manuscript.

Flavell, J. H., Botkin, P. T., Fry, C. L., Wright, J. W., & Jarvis, P. E. (1968). *The development of role-taking and communication skills in children.* New York: Wiley.

Goodman, J., & Sours, J. (1967). *The child mental status examination.* New York: Basic Books.

Greenspan, S. I. (1981). *The clinical interview of the child.* New York: McGraw-Hill.

Haynes, S. N. (1978). The behavioral interview. In S. N. Haynes (Ed.), *Principles of behavioral assessment.* New York: Gardner Press.

Herjanic, B., & Campbell, W. (1977). Differentiating psychiatrically disturbed children on the basis of a structured interview. *Journal of Abnormal Child Psychology, 5,* 127–134.

Kanfer, F. H., & Saslow, G. (1969). Behavioral diagnosis. In C. M. Franks (Ed.), *Behavior theory: appraisal and status.* New York: McGraw-Hill.

Lazarus, A. (1973). Multimodal behavior therapy: Treating the BASIC ID. *Journal of Nervous and Mental Disease, 156,* 404–411.

Lesser, I. M. (1997). Cultural considerations using The Structured Clinical Interview for DSM-III for mood and anxiety disorder assessment. *Journal of Psyhopathology & Behavioral Assessment, 19,* 2, 149–160.

Miller, P. H., & Bigi, L. (1979). The development of children's understanding of attention. *Merrill-Palmer Quarterly, 25,* 235–250.

Orvaschel, H., Sholomskas, D., & Weissman, M. M. (1980). *The assessment of psychopathology and behavioral problems in children: A review of epidemiological and clinical research (1967–1979).* Rockville, MD: National Institute of Mental Health, Division of Biometry and Epidemiology (DHHS Publication No. (ADM)80-1037).

Robinson, E. J., & Robinson, W. P. (1984). Realizing you don't understand: A further study. *Journal of Child Psychology and Psychiatry, 25,* 621–627.

Shatz, M. (1977). The relationship between cognitive processes and the development of communication skills. *Nebraska Symposium on Motivation, 25,* 1–42.

Sigelman, C. K., Schoenrock, C. J., Winer, J. L., Spanhel, C. L., Hromas, S. G., Martin, P. W., Budd, E. C., & Bensberg, G. J. (1981). In R. H. Bruininks, C. E. Meyers, B. B. Sigford, & K. C. Lakin (Eds.), *Deinstitutionalization and community adjustment of mentally retarded people.* Washington, DC: American Association on Mental Deficiency.

Ventura, J., Liberman, R. P., Green, M. F., Shaner, A., & Mintz, J.

(1998). Training and quality assurance with Structured Clinical Interview for DSM-IV (SC ID-I/P). *Psychiatry Research, 19,* 2, 16–17.

JOHN MACDONALD
Eastern Kentucky University

ASSESSMENT
MENTAL STATUS EXAMS

CLINICAL PSYCHOLOGY

Clinical psychology is the branch of psychology devoted to the scientific study, assessment, diagnosis, and treatment of mental disorders. Clinical psychology has its origins in 1896 with the construction of the first psychological clinic by Lightner Witmer at the University of Pennsylvania (Benjamin, 1997). In 1907, Witmer founded and served as editor of *The Psychological Clinic*, a journal describing the types of problems and work performed at the clinic. Witmer wrote the initial article in the new journal and described his work with a child referred for treatment of bad spelling in school (Witmer, 1907). The article was titled "Clinical Psychology," wherein Witmer applied this name to his work, and became known as the founder of clinical psychology (Benjamin, 1997).

Initially, clinical psychology was most interested in the development and assessment of human abilities, and provided the government the means to test intelligence, achievement, vocational interests, and personality characteristics of recruits during both world wars. After World War II, the Veterans Administration hired large numbers of clinical psychologists to work with disabled veterans, and the psychologists' roles expanded beyond assessment to psychotherapy (Phares, 1979). During this time, clinical psychology gained professional status by obtaining licensure in most states, and establishing independent practice activities.

Training for clinical psychology is normally four years of graduate coursework followed by a full-time year of internship. Courses taken for the degree include basic psychological areas such as social, learning, methodology, and biological with advanced coursework in assessment and psychopathology (Matthews & Walker, 1997). The PhD (Doctor of Philosophy) degree is the traditional degree for clinical psychology and usually involves a scientist-practitioner model of training. The PsyD (Doctor of Psychology) is a newer degree focusing more on practitioner training with less emphasis on research productivity. Current requirements for licensure usually involves both a written and oral examination followed by a year of post-doctoral supervision. Additionally, the American Psychological Association provides accreditation for clinical psychology programs, allowing for common goals and training among diverse graduate programs.

At the present time, clinical psychologists are in ever-expanding positions committed to the advancement and promotion of mental health and human well-being. They serve in the traditional roles of providing diagnosis and assessment functions and psychotherapy, but are increasingly called upon to provide consultation, supervision, or assume administrative positions (Matthews & Walker, 1997). Current theoretical perspectives include psychodynamic, behavioral, cognitive, humanistic, and systemic. Clinical psychologists work with all age groups from infants to the elderly; and they are also developing specialty areas such as forensic psychology, health psychology, children, the aging, scientific research, psychology of women, child health problems and ethnic minority issues. Finally, clinical psychologists work in a wide range of settings such as individual practice, mental health clinics, hospitals, schools, universities, counseling centers, legal systems, government organizations, and the military services.

LINDA M. MONTGOMERY
*The University of Texas of the
Permian Basin*

REFERENCES

Benjamin, L. T., Jr. (1997). *A history of psychology: Original sources and contemporary research* (2nd ed.). New York: McGraw-Hill.

Matthews, J. R., & Walker, C. E. (1997). *Basic skills and professional issues in clinical psychology*. Boston: Allyn and Bacon.

Phares, E. J. (1979). *Clinical psychology: Concepts, methods, and profession* (Vols. 1–2). Homewood, IL: Dorsey Press.

Witmer, L. (1907). Clinical psychology. *The Psychological Clinic, 1,* 1–9.

CLINICAL INTERVIEW
DIAGNOSTIC AND STATISTICAL MANUAL OF MENTAL
DISORDERS (DSM-IV)
MENTAL STATUS EXAMS

CLINICAL TEACHING

Clinical teaching is teaching prescriptive (diagnosis → prescription → remediation), with the intent of matching the student's strengths and weaknesses to a specific type of instruction. Clinical teaching is therefore often called diagnostic-prescriptive teaching. It is a continuous test-teach-test process. This process was influenced by Johnson and Myklebust (1967), Smith (1968, 1974), Learner (1985), and many others. Teaching strategies in clinical teaching include task analysis and applied behavior analysis.

Learner (1985) views the clinical teaching process as a five-stage repetitive cycle of decision making that consists of assessment, planning, implementation, evaluation, and modification of the assessment. She further adds that the clinical teacher considers the student's ecological, home, social, and cultural environments.

Smith (1983) offers eight steps in the clinical teaching process: (1) the clinical teacher should objectively observe and analyze the student's classroom abilities; (2) the teacher should objectively observe and analyze the nature of the student's successes and difficulties on different types of tasks; (3) the teacher should scrutinize the characteristics of alternative tasks and settings; (4) compare and contrast how information gained from step (3) might interact with the observations in steps (2) and (1) so as to result in more favorable achievement; (5) the teacher should consult with the student whenever possible, present the choices for modification, and together decide which ones to try; (6) the teacher should set short-term goals, make the modifications; and (7) teach; (8) evaluate progress after a reasonable time interval; if successful, continue teaching similar but higher level objectives; if unsuccessful retrace steps 1–7 (p. 361).

REFERENCES

Johnson, D., & Mykelbust, H. (1967). Learning disabilities: Educational principles and practices. New York: Grune & Stratton.

Learner, J. (1985). Learning disabilities: Theories, diagnosis, and teaching strategies (4th ed.). Boston: Houghton Mifflin.

Smith, C. R. (1983). Learning disabilities: The intervention of learner, task and setting. Boston: Little, Brown.

Smith, R. M. (1968, 1974). Clinical teaching: Methods of instruction for the retarded. New York: McGraw-Hill.

MARIBETH MONTGOMERY KASIK
Governors State University

DIAGNOSTIC PRESCRIPTIVE TEACHING

CLOZE TECHNIQUE

The cloze technique is a procedure that is used for both the assessment and instruction of reading comprehension skills. Based on the psychological construct of closure, the technique was first developed by Taylor (1953), who believed that a person reading a narrative or expository selection psychologically endeavors to complete a pattern of thought and language that is left incomplete. With the cloze technique, such a language pattern is typically a reading passage from which words have been deleted. Typically, in a reading selection of approximately 250 words, e.g., every tenth lexical word would be deleted and it would be the reader's task to fill in the missing words.

According to Rye (1982), the cloze technique may be more appropriately considered a construction procedure, whereby the reader uses both linguistic knowledge and past experience to complete sentences in appropriate ways. Experience and language are used to choose the correct grammatical class of words.

Cloze exercises may be developed from basal reader texts, trade books, content area materials, and any other reading selections that are appropriate for a given population of readers. Often, the cloze procedure has been used as a device for the assessment of reading comprehension. As described by Smith and Johnson (1980), it may involve the use of a variety of cloze passages taken from the same reading material. For example, three different passages of approximately 100 words in length may be taken from the beginning, middle, and end of a selection. Then, certain words are deleted, e.g., every fifth or tenth lexical word. The reader's task is to read the passage and write in the missing word on a blank. Ekwall (1985) elaborated on this procedure by stating that the first and last sentences of the selection should be left intact, with every fifth word omitted to be replaced with a blank of 10 spaces in length. Again, the reader is required to read the selection and fill in blank spaces with a word that would seem to fit.

Cloze exercises can be used with either individual students or groups of students. As an assessment tool, there is usually no time limit for the completion of a cloze exercise. The evaluation or scoring of a cloze passage is usually based on a percentage of blank spaces that have been completed correctly. Furthermore, according to Smith and Johnson (1980), only the exact deleted word should be counted as correct. If a student is able to complete approximately 45 to 50% of the omitted spaces correctly, the reading material is judged to be at the reader's instructional level. If 60% or more of the blanks have been filled in correctly, the selection is probably at the reader's independent reading level. If fewer than 45% of the blanks are completed correctly, the material is at the reader's frustration reading level.

In addition to being used as a diagnostic measure, the cloze technique can also be used to improve reading comprehension in an instructional setting. In this manner, the technique can be used as a prereading activity to determine the reader's ability to deal with certain material, and as a postreading activity to develop certain comprehension skills and to practice various comprehension strategies, e.g., the use of context clues in understanding what has been read.

The cloze technique, therefore, based on the construct of perception and closure as defined by the gestalt psychologists, assumes the ability of a fluent reader to predict or anticipate what is coming next in a reading passage. This requires the use of various reading skills, including context clues, knowledge of linguistic patterns, and the ability to comprehend in general what is being read. As Rye (1982) describes, the activity involves a sampling of information from a contextual setting and the formation of hypotheses, a prediction of what will appear subsequently in the selection both linguistically and conceptually. The value of the cloze technique as both a diagnostic and instructional device lies in its demand on the reader's comprehension abilities and a variety of language skills.

REFERENCES

Ekwall, E. E. (1985). *Locating and correcting reading difficulties* (4th ed.). Columbus, OH: Merrill.

Miller, W. H. (1974). *Reading diagnosis kit*. New York: Center for Applied Research in Education.

Rye, J. (1982). *Cloze procedure and the teaching of reading*. Exeter, NH: Heinemann.

Smith, R. J., & Johnson, D. D. (1980). *Teaching children to read* (2nd ed.). Reading, MA: Addison-Wesley.

Taylor, W. L. (1953). Cloze procedure: A new tool for measuring readability. *Journalism Quarterly, 30*, 415–433.

JOHN M. EELLS
Souderton Area School District,
Souderton, Pennsylvania

READING DISORDERS
READING REMEDIATION

CLUTTERING

Cluttering is a speech disorder—or, more specifically, a fluency disorder—related to stuttering. Importantly, the two disorders are not the same. Cluttering is characterized by excessive breaks in the normal flow of speech that result from disorganized speech planning, talking too fast or in a jerky fashion, or simply being unsure of what one wants to say. By contrast, the person who stutters typically knows exactly what he or she wants to say but is temporarily unable to say it, thus repeating or prolonging sounds or syllables, blocking, and/or using accessory (secondary) devices (e.g., eye-blinks, synonyms for difficult words, or abnormal facial postures) (Daly, 1996; St. Louis & Myers, 1997). Because cluttering is not well-known, there is much ambiguity about the disorder. For example, the speech of many people who clutter is often described by themselves or others as stuttering. Moreover, cluttering frequently coexists with stuttering. And some authorities question whether or not a reliable definition of cluttering has been established (e.g., Curlee, 1996).

The definition of cluttering recently adopted by the fluency disorders division of the American Speech-Language-Hearing Association is "a fluency disorder characterized by a rapid and/or irregular speaking rate, excessive disfluen-

cies, and often other symptoms such as language or phonological errors and attention deficits" (St. Louis, Hanley, & Hood, 1998). Clutterers' speech does not sound fluent; in other words, they do not appear to be clear about either what they want to say or how to say it. They manifest excessive levels of normal disfluencies, such as interjections (e.g., "um," or "you know") and revisions (e.g., "We went over . . . we started to go to grandma's.") (St. Louis, Hinzman, & Hull, 1985); they manifest little or no physical struggle in speaking; and they have few, if any, accessory behaviors. A rapid and/or irregular speaking rate would be present in a speaker who shows symptoms of speaking to fast, whether based on actual syllable-per-minute counts or simply an overall impression; sounding jerky; or using pauses during speech that are too short, too long, or improperly placed.

These fluency and rate deviations are often considered to be the essential symptoms of cluttering (St. Louis, 1992). Other characteristics may also be present but are not mandatory. These include confusing, disorganized language or conversational skills, often with word-finding difficulties; limited awareness of fluency or rate problems; temporary improvement when asked to slow down or to pay attention to speech (or when being tape recorded); specific sound misarticulations, slurred speech, or deleting nonstressed syllables in longer words (e.g., "ferchly" for "fortunately"); speech that is difficult to understand; a family history of stuttering and/or cluttering; social or vocational problems; learning disabilities; attention deficit/hyperactivity disorder; sloppy handwriting; difficulty with organizational skills for daily activities; and/or auditory perceptual difficulties (Daly, 1992; St. Louis & Myers, 1995, 1997; Weiss, 1964).

A team approach to assessment and diagnosis with cluttering is often necessary. In addition to a standard speech evaluation by a speech-language pathologist (SLP), contributions or reports from classroom teachers, special educators, psychologists, or (possibly) neuropsychologists may also be warranted. The SLP evaluation will carefully assess the fluency problem, but also any coexisting oral-motor, language, or articulation problems. If the suspected clutterer is in school, special education personnel may be asked to provide information on learning, social problems, and attention or behavioral problems, and psychologists could be requested to provide test information on academic achievement or intelligence. The eventual diagnosis should specify whether or not cluttering is present and also what other problems are present, such as stuttering, a language disorder, or a learning disability (St. Louis & Myers, 1997).

Therapy for clutterers generally addresses the contributing problems before focusing directly on fluency. Ordinarily, one of the first goals of therapy is to reduce the speaking rate, although this may not be easy for the clutterer to achieve. Some clutterers respond well to "timing" their speech to a delayed auditory feedback (DAF) device; some do not. Another technique that has been found helpful with younger clutterers is to use the analogy of a speedometer wherein rapid speech is above the speed limit, and "speeding tickets" are given for exceeding the limit (St. Louis & Myers, 1995, 1997).

Articulation and language symptoms are often reduced if the clutterer can achieve a slower rate. Sometimes, however, these problems need to be addressed directly. One technique involves practice first in using short, highly structured utterances. It may also be helpful for clutterers to learn to exaggerate stressed syllables in longer words while being sure to include all the unstressed syllables (e.g., "par-tic´-u-lar," "con-di´-tion-al," or "gen-er-o´-si-ty") (St. Louis & Myers, 1997).

Some clutterers benefit from planning both the content (the "what") of a message as well as the delivery (the "how"). For example, the "what" can be taught as formulating a telegram (e.g., "Car won't start. I pump accelerator. Carburetor gets flooded."). The "how" then focuses on filling in the appropriate small words (e.g., "My car often won't start after it sits for a few minutes. I pump the accelerator a few times before trying again. Often, the carburetor gets flooded.") (Myers & Bradley, 1992).

As noted, many clutterers also stutter, and often the cluttering is masked by the stuttering. In some of these individuals, the cluttering emerges as the individual gets control of the stuttering or begins to stutter less (Van Riper, 1992). Yet, whether or not the clutterer also stutters (or previously stuttered), any therapy techniques that focus attention on fluency targets, such as easy onset of the voice, more prolonged syllables, or correct breathing, can also help the person to manage many of the cluttering symptoms. The important thing is that the clutterer learn to pay attention to—or monitor—his or her speech and do anything that makes it easier to remember to do so (Craig, 1996; Langevin & Boberg, 1996).

Lack of awareness is a particularly difficult clinical problem, for many clutterers are genuinely unaware of the extent of their cluttering behaviors. They must be taught to be careful observers of listener feedback. Some older clutterers are better able to monitor if they listen daily to a tape with a short sample of their disorganized cluttered speech and, immediately following, a sample of their clear, monitored speech (Daly, 1992).

It is currently impossible to predict with accuracy whether or not a clutterer will benefit from speech therapy. Most who benefit have become convinced from friends, family, or employers (or on their own) that they do have a significant speech problem. Also, motivation is a key element; successful clients typically have good reason for working hard to change, such as the likelihood of a job promotion. On the other hand, clutterers who are not sure that they have a problem, or are relatively unconcerned about it, tend not to improve as much or as easily from therapy (Daly, 1992; St. Louis & Myers, 1997).

REFERENCES

Craig, A. (1996). Long-term effects of intensive treatment for a client with both a cluttering and stuttering disorder. In K. O. St. Louis (Ed.), *Research and opinion on cluttering: State of the art and science*, Special issue of the *Journal of Fluency Disorders, 21,* 329–335.

Curlee, R. F. (1996). Cluttering: Data in search of understanding. In K. O. St. Louis (Ed.), *Research and opinion on cluttering: State of the art and science*, Special issue of the *Journal of Fluency Disorders, 21,* 315–327.

Daly, D. A. (1992). Helping the clutterer: Therapy considerations. In F. L. Myers & K. O. St. Louis. *Cluttering: A clinical perspective* (pp. 107–124). Kibworth, Great Britain: Far Communications. (Reissued in 1996 by Singular Press, San Diego, California.)

Langevin, M., & Boberg, E. (1996). Results of intensive stuttering therapy with adults who clutter and stutter. In K. O. St. Louis (Ed.), *Research and opinion on cluttering: State of the art and science*, Special issue of the *Journal of Fluency Disorders, 21,* 315–327.

Myers, F. L., & Bradley, C. L. (1992). Clinical management of cluttering from a synergistic framework. In F. L. Myers & K. O. St. Louis, *Cluttering: A clinical perspective* (pp. 85–105). Kibworth, Great Britain: Far Communications. (Reissued in 1996 by Singular Press, San Diego, California.)

St. Louis, K. O. (1992). On defining cluttering. In F. L. Myers & K. O. St. Louis, *Cluttering: A clinical perspective* (pp. 37–53). Kibworth, Great Britain: Far Communications. (Reissued in 1996 by Singular Press, San Diego, California.)

St. Louis, K. O., Hanley, J. M., & Hood, S. B. (1998). *Terminology pertaining to fluency and fluency disorders*. Final report of the Terminology Task Force of the Special Interest Division on Fluency and Fluency Disorders of the American Speech-Language-Hearing Association.

St. Louis, K. O., Hinzman, A. R., & Hull, F. M. (1985). Studies of cluttering: Disfluency and language measures in young possible clutterers and stutterers. *Journal of Fluency Disorders, 10,* 151–172.

St. Louis, K. O, & Myers, F. L. (1995). Clinical management of cluttering. *Language, Speech, and Hearing Services in Schools, 25,* 187–195.

St. Louis, K. O., & Myers, F. L. (1997). Management of cluttering and related fluency disorders. In R. Curlee & G. Siegel (Eds.), *Nature and treatment of stuttering: New directions* (pp. 313–332). New York: Allyn and Bacon.

Van Riper, C. (1992). Foreword. In F. L. Myers, & K. O. St. Louis, *Cluttering: A clinical perspective* (pp. vii–ix). Kibworth, Great Britain: Far Communications. (Reissued in 1996 by Singular Press, San Diego, California.)

Weiss, D. (1964). *Cluttering*. Englewood Cliff, NJ: Prentice Hall.

KENNETH O. ST. LOUIS
West Virginia University

COCKAYNE SYNDROME (CS)

Cockayne Syndrome (CS) is rare genetic disorder, autosomally recessive, of unknown prevalence. Males and females are equally affected. In CS, growth and development are normal for at least the first year followed by neurodevelopmental retardation that may not become especially prominent in many cases until 4 or 5 years of age.

In the early stages of CS, these children are often misdiagnosed with ADHD or with various coordination disorders. Typically, mental retardation develops in the childhood years and may be mild to severe. Photosensitivity is common and peripheral neuropathy develops. Small stature with large ears occurs routinely. Leukodystrophy occurs in all cases along with premature death. There is no cure, and the only treatment is symptom management. Diagnosis is by physical examination and CT or MRI (Gillberg, 1995). Symptoms are usually well-expressed by age 10 years.

Special education will typically be required for intellectual impairment and externalizing behavior problems. Dwarfism and emotional symptoms may occur as well, and may require special assistance. Thorough psychoeducational evaluations on a yearly basis are required due to the severity of the disorder and the rapid changes that may occur in behavior, intellect, and motor skills.

REFERENCE

Gillberg. C. (1995). *Clinical child neuropsychiatry*. Cambridge: Cambridge University Press.

CECIL R. REYNOLDS
Texas A & M University

COGENTIN

Cogentin is the proprietary name of benztropine mesylate, a skeletal muscle relaxant used in the treatment of Parkinson's disease (Modell, 1985). Cogentin acts on the basal ganglia of the brain. By restoring more normal chemical balance in the basal ganglia, specific movement disorders associated with parkinsonism are relieved. Cogentin reduces tremors, gait disturbances, and rigidity in afflicted individuals (Ellis & Speed, 1998; Long, 1982). Common side effects, especially during initial drug use, include blurred vision, nervousness, constipation, and dryness of the mouth. On rare occasions more serious side effects may occur, including confusion, hallucinations, nausea, and vomiting (Long, 1982). Common cold and cough remedies may interact unfavorably with Cogentin. The drug is not recommended for use in children under 3 years of age, and

should be used with caution in older children (Long, 1983; *Physician's Desk Reference*, 1983).

REFERENCES

Ellis, K. L., & Speed, J. (1998). Pharmacologic management of movement disorder after midbrain haemorrhage *Brain Injury, 12*, 7, 623–628.

Long, J. W. (1982). *The essential guide to prescription drugs*. New York: Harper & Row.

Modell, W. (Ed.). (1985). *Drugs in current use and new drugs* (31st ed.). New York: Springer.

Physician's desk reference (37th ed.). (1983). Oradell, NJ: Medical Economics.

CATHY F. TELZROW
*Cuyahoga Specific Education
Service Center*

DRUG THERAPY
MEDICATION

COGNITIVE ASSESSMENT SYSTEM (CAS)

The Cognitive Assessment System (CAS; Naglieri & Das, 1997a) is an individually administered test of ability for children ages 5 though 17 years that is given by psychologists and similarly trained professionals when conducting clinical, psychoeducational, or neuropsychological evaluations. The 1997 edition of the CAS is the first published version of the test, which was designed to measure Planning, Attention, Simultaneous, and Successive (PASS) cognitive processes. The PASS theory was used to identify subtests for the CAS, organize these tests into scales, and guide interpretation and intervention efforts. This test differs from traditional measures of ability because it (a) is built on a theory of ability reconceptualized as PASS cognitive processes; (b) is designed to measure specific cognitive processes rather than general ability; (c) was built to reflect contemporary understanding of cognitive processes that have been obtained from recent research in psychology and education; (d) does not include subtests that involve academic content, such as vocabulary and arithmetic; (e) was designed to be sensitive to the specific strengths and weaknesses of children that are related to academic success and failure; and (f) was built to have relevance to instruction and identification of specific interventions.

The PASS theory is based on the concept that these processes are very important to competent functioning and both influence and rely on the person's base of knowledge.

The processes are defined as follows: Planning–mental process by which the person determines, selects, and uses efficient solutions to problems; Attention–a mental process by which the person selectively attends to some stimuli and ignores others; Simultaneous processing–a mental activity by which the person integrates stimuli into groups; and Successive processing–a mental activity by which the person integrates stimuli in a specific serial order.

The CAS is comprised of a Planning, Attention, Simultaneous, and Successive scale, each of which represents the theory upon which the test was built. These four scales are further comprised of three subtests, each of which has undergone extensive development and validation (see Das, Naglieri, & Kirby, 1994; Naglieri & Das, 1997b). Each subtest yields a standardized score with a mean of 10 and standard deviation of 3. Subtests are combined into specific PASS Scales and a Full Scale, each of which are expressed as standard scores with a mean of 100 and standard deviation of 15. There are two versions of the test, a Standard Battery (12 subtests) and a Basic Battery (8 subtests), which are administered in 60 and 45 minutes, respectively. Each subtest is described by PASS Scale below.

Matching Numbers consists of four pages, each consisting of eight rows of numbers with six numbers per row. Children are instructed to underline the two numbers in each row that are the same. Numbers increase in length across the four pages from one digit to seven digits with four rows for each digit length. Each item has a time limit. The subtest score is based on the combination of time and number correct for each page. This score reflects the efficiency of the child's application of strategies to solve the task.

Planned Codes contains two pages, each with a distinct set of codes and arrangement of rows and columns. A legend at the top of each page shows how letters correspond to simple codes (e.g., A, B, C, D corresponds to OX, XX, OO, XO, respectively). Each page contains seven rows and eight columns of letters without codes. Children fill in the appropriate codes in empty boxes beneath each letter. On the first page, all the As appear in the first column, all the Bs in the second column, all the Cs in the third column, and so on. On the second page, letters are configured in a diagonal pattern. Children are permitted to complete each page in whatever fashion they desire. The subtest score is based on the combination of time and number correct for each page. This score measures the effects of the method(s) the child used to solve the task.

Planned Connections contains eight items. The first six items require children to connect numbers appearing in a quasi-random order on a page in sequential order. The last two items require children to connect both numbers and letters in sequential order alternating between numbers and letters (for example, 1-A-2-B-3-C). The items are constructed so that children never complete a sequence by crossing one line over the other. The score is based on the total amount of time in seconds used to complete the items. The score indicates how effective the child's strategies were in completing the items.

Expressive Attention uses two different sets of items, depending on the age of the child. Children 8 years and older are presented with three pages. On the first page, children read color words (i.e., Blue, Yellow, Green, and Red) presented in quasi-random order. Next, they name the colors of a series of rectangles (printed in blue, yellow, green, and red).

Finally, the words, Blue, Yellow, Green, and Red, are printed in a different color ink than the colors the words name. The child is instructed to name the color ink the word is printed in, rather than to read the word. Performance on the last page is used as the measure of attention. The subtest score is based on the combination of time and number correct. This score indicates how well the child was able to focus on the relevant variables and ignore competing stimuli.

Number Detection consists of pages of numbers that are printed in different formats. On each page, children are required to find a particular stimulus (e.g., the number 1, 2, and 3 printed in an open font) on a page containing many distractors (e.g., the same numbers printed in a different font). There are 180 stimuli with 45 targets (25% targets) on the pages. The score reflects the ratio of accuracy (total number correct minus the number of false detections) to total time for each item, summed across the items. This score reflects how well the child was able to identify target stimuli and ignore competing distracting stimuli.

Receptive Attention is a 2-page paper-and-pencil subtest. On the first page, letters that are physically the same (e.g., TT but not Tt) are targets, but on the second, letters that have the same name (e.g., Aa not Ba) are targets. Each page contains 200 pairs of letters with 50 targets (25% targets) and the same set of distractors. The score reflects the ratio of accuracy (total number correct minus the number of false detections) to total time for each page, summed across pages. This score indicates how successful the child was at identifying target stimuli and ignoring distracting stimuli.

Nonverbal Matrices is a 33-item subtest that utilizes shapes and geometric designs that are interrelated through spatial or logical organization. Children are required to decode the relationships among the parts of the item and choose the best of six options to occupy a missing space in the grid. The subtest score is based on the total number of items correctly answered.

Verbal-Spatial Relations is composed of 27 items that require the comprehension of logical and grammatical descriptions of spatial relationships. Children are shown items containing six drawings and a printed question at the bottom of each page. The items involve both objects and shapes that are arranged in a specific spatial manner. For example, the item, "Which picture shows a circle to the left of a cross under a triangle above a square?" includes six drawings with various arrangements of geometric figures, only one of which matches the description. The examiner reads the question aloud and the child is required to select the option that matches the verbal description. Children must indicate their answers within a 30-second time limit. The subtest score reflects the total number of items correctly answered.

Figure Memory is a 27-item subtest. Children are shown a two- or three-dimensional geometric figure for 5 seconds. The figure is then removed, and the child is presented with a response page that contains the original design embedded in a larger, more complex geometric pattern. Children are asked to identify the original design embedded within the more complex figure. To be scored correct, all lines of the design have to be indicated without any additions or omissions. The score reflects the total number of correct items.

Word Series requires the child repeat words in the same order as stated by the examiner. The test consists of the following nine single-syllable, high-frequency words: Book, Car, Cow, Dog, Girl, Key, Man, Shoe, Wall. There are 27 items that the examiner reads to the child. Each series ranges in length from 2 to 9 words, presented at the rate of 1 word per second. Items are scored as correct if the child reproduces the entire word series. The score is based on the total number of items correctly repeated.

Sentence Repetition requires the child repeat 20 sentences that are read aloud. Each sentence is composed of color words (e.g., "The blue is yellowing"). The children are required to repeat each sentence exactly as it was presented. Color words are utilized so that the sentences contain little semantic meaning, to help reduce the influence of simultaneous processing and accent the demands of the syntax of the sentence. Each item is scored correct if the sentence is repeated exactly as presented. The subtest score reflects the total number of sentences correctly repeated.

Sentence Questions is a 21-item subtest that uses the same type of sentences as those in Sentence Repetition. Children from ages 8 to 17 are read a sentence and then asked a question about the sentence. For example, the examiner says, "The blue is yellowing" and asks the following question: "Who is yellowing?" The correct answer is "The blue." Responses are scored correct if the child successfully answers the question regarding the sentence. The subtest score reflects the total number of questions answered correctly.

The CAS was standardized on 2,200 persons aged 5 years 0 months to 17 years 11 months who closely match the United States population on the basis of gender, race, region, community setting, classroom placement, educational classification, and parental education. The CAS Full Scale internal reliability is .96 and the separate PASS Scale reliabilities are as follows: Planning = .88; Sim-

ultaneous = .93; Attention = .88; and Successive = .93. The test meets or exceeds recognized standards for reliability.

There are a number of important validity studies of the CAS reported by Naglieri and Das (1997b). In summary, these authors have shown that the PASS scales are powerful predictors of achievement. Naglieri (1997) showed that the CAS Full Scale correlated .73 with the Woodcock-Johnson Tests of Achievement–Revised, in contrast to correlations between the WISC-III and WIAT correlation of .59 as well as the Woodcock-Johnson Cognitive Battery correlation of .62 with the Woodcock-Johnson Tests of Achievement. These data showed that the CAS accounted for more than 50% of the variance in achievement while the WISC-III and WJ-R Cognitive only accounted for about 35% of the variance. Importantly, Naglieri and Das (1997b) also showed that the CAS yields distinctive PASS profiles for children with Attention-Deficit Hyperactivity Disorders and reading disabilities. Finally, Naglieri and Gottling (1995, 1997) have clearly demonstrated that the CAS has important instructional implications. Thus, the CAS appears to offer a new way to conceptualize ability as well as a new way to measure it. Future research is needed to further explore these initial findings.

REFERENCES

Das, J. P., Naglieri, J. A., & Kirby, J. R. (1994). *The assessment of cognitive processes: The PASS theory of intelligence.* Boston: Allyn & Bacon.

Naglieri, J. A. (1997). *Relationships between achievement and the Cognitive Assessment System.* American Psychological Association, Chicago, IL.

Naglieri, J. A., & Das, J. P. (1997a). *Cognitive Assessment System.* Chicago: Riverside.

Naglieri, J. A., & Das, J. P. (1997b). *Cognitive Assessment System: Interpretive handbook.* Chicago: Riverside.

Naglieri, J. A., & Gottling, S. H. (1997). Mathematics instruction and PASS cognitive processes: An intervention study. *Journal of Learning Disabilities, 30,* 513–520.

Naglieri, J. A., & Gottling, S. H. (1995). A cognitive education approach to math instruction for the learning disabled: An individual study. *Psychological Reports, 76,* 1343–1354.

JACK A. NAGLIERI
The Ohio State University

COGNITIVE BEHAVIOR THERAPY

The term cognitive behavior therapy refers to a diverse assemblage of theoretical and applied orientations that share three underlying assumptions. First, a person's behavior is mediated by cognitive events (i.e., thoughts, images, expectancies, and beliefs). Second is a corollary to the first; it states that a change in mediating events results in a change in behavior. Third, a person is an active participant in his or her own learning. The third assumption recognizes the reciprocal relationships among a person's thoughts, behavior, and environment and runs counter to the behaviorist's unidirectional view of the individual as a passive recipient of environmental influences.

During the reign of behaviorism in American psychology, cognitions were banned from investigation because the earlier methods used in their investigation were methodologically unsound and because cognitions, which are not directly observable, were considered inappropriate subject matter for the scientific study of psychology. During the 1960s, an explosion of research into such cognitive processes as attention, memory, problem solving, imagery, self-referent speech, beliefs, attributions, and motivation heralded a cognitive revolution in American psychology. Behaviorists impressed with the rigor of experimental cognitive psychologists and alert to the limitations of traditional behaviorism increasingly considered the role of cognitive variables in the development of behavior and in the treatment of maladaptive behavior. Because Bandura's research in observational learning was couched in a learning theory framework, it provided a timely bridge between the cognitivists and behaviorists. Bandura's explanations for modeling became more cognitive as he introduced such cognitive constructs as attention, retention, and expectancies to explain observational learning. Bandura's view of the reciprocal relationships among cognitions, behavior, and environment remains a basic tenet of cognitive behavior therapy. The widely discussed *controversy* between the cognitivists and the behaviorists that was prevalent in the 1960s and early 1970s quieted. The compatibility of the two perspectives has been recognized and the advantages of the joint consideration of cognitions and behaviors in modifying behaviors has been demonstrated.

A variety of therapies derived from research in cognitive psychology and taking advantage of the broadened behavioral perspective were developed and subjected to empirical test. These therapies attempt to modify thinking processes as a mechanism for effecting cognitive and behavioral changes. Particular therapeutic approaches that are closely identified with cognitive behavior therapy include modeling, self-instructional training, problem-solving training, rational emotive therapy, cognitive therapy, self-control training, and cognitive skills training. Because self-instructional training and problem-solving training illustrate the dual focus on cognitions and behavior, have been researched in schools, and are particularly well suited to classroom application, they will be briefly described in this entry.

In self-instructional training, the child is taught to regulate his or her behavior through self-talk. The child is taught to ask and to answer covertly questions that guide his or her own performance. The questions are of four types:

1. Questions about the nature of the problem (OK. Now what is it I have to do? I have to find the two cars that are twins.)
2. Plans, or self-instructions for solving the task (How can I do it? I could look at each car carefully, looking at the hood first, and then the front wheels, until I get to the end.)
3. Self-monitoring (Am I using my plan?)
4. Self-evaluation. (How did I do? I did fine because I looked at each car carefully and I found the twins.)

The particular self-statements vary according to the type of task.

The steps in teaching children to use self-speech to guide problem-solving behavior are derived from research in the developmental sequence by which language regulates one's behavior. First, an adult talks out loud while solving a task, and the child observes (modeling). Next, the child performs the same task while the adult verbally instructs the child. Next, the child performs the task while instructing himself or herself out loud. Then the child performs the task while whispering. Finally, the child performs the task while talking silently to himself or herself, with no lip movements.

Research in self-instructional talk has demonstrated that it helps impulsive children to think before acting (Meichenbaum & Goodman, 1971). While treated children have improved on novel problem-solving tasks and academic performance (Camp, Blom, Hebert, & Van Doorninck, 1977; Douglas, Parry, Marton, & Garson, 1976; Meichenbaum & Goodman, 1971), results of treatment on classroom behavior have been inconclusive (Camp, 1980; Camp et al., 1977).

Problem-solving training is similar to self-instructional training in that the child is taught to think through problems following a systematic problem-solving process. In a series of studies, Spivack and Shure (Spivack, Platt, & Shure, 1976; Spivack & Shure, 1974) taught preschool children the following interpersonal cognitive problem-solving skills: problem identification, means-end thinking, alternative thinking, and consequential thinking. Means-end thinking includes the ability to plan, step-by-step, ways to reach an interpersonal goal. Alternative thinking includes the ability to generate different plans for solving a given interpersonal problem. Consequential thinking is the ability to anticipate and evaluate consequences of a given interpersonal solution. These skills are taught in game-type interactions involving pictures, puppets, and stories depicting interpersonal problem situations. Research on problem-solving training has demonstrated improvement on teacher ratings, academic performance, and behavior observations (Shure, 1981).

In terms of psychotherapeutic intervention, cognitive behavior therapy has been shown to be very helpful with pain control (Tan & Leucht, 1997), depression (Murphy, Carney, Kreserich, & Wetzel, 1995), body dysmorphic disorder (Neziroglu, McKay, Todaro, & Yaryura-Tobias, 1996), and eating disorders (Eldredge, Agras, Arnow, Telch, Bell, Castonguay, & Marnell, 1997). However, there are two caveats for using cognitive behavior therapy with school-aged populations. The first is including both the assessment of logical/analytical thought structures *and* social perspective-taking abilities of the child when planning a course of cognitive behavior therapy (Kinney, 1991). The second, (which pertains to any age of client/subject) is that multicultural influences and diversity must be taken into account and formally addressed if the course of treatment is to be successful (Hays, 1995).

REFERENCES

Camp, B. W. (1980). Two psychoeducational treatment programs for young aggressive boys. In C. K. Walen & B. Henker (Eds.), *Hyperactive children—The social psychology of identification and treatment*. New York: Academic.

Camp, B. W., Blom, G. E., Hebert, F., & Van Doorninck, W. J. (1977). "Think Aloud": A program for developing self-control in young aggressive boys. *Journal of Abnormal Child Psychology, 5,* 157–169.

Douglas, V. I., Parry, P., Marton, P., & Garson. C. (1976). *Journal of Abnormal Child Psychology, 4,* 389–410.

Eldredge, K. L., Agras, W. S., Arnow, B., Telch, C. F., Bell, S., Castonguay, L., & Marnell, M. (1997). The effects of extending cognitive-behavior therapy for binge eating disorder among initial treatment nonresponders. *International Journal of Eating Disorders, 21,* 4, 347–352.

Hays, P. A. (1997). Multicultural applications of cognitive behavior therapy. *Professional Psychology: Research & Practice, 26,* 3, 309–315.

Kinney, A. (1991). Cognitive-behavior therapy with children: Developmental considerations. *Journal of Rational-Emotive & Cognitive Behavior Therapy, 9,* 1, 51–61.

Meichenbaum, D. H., & Goodman, J. (1971). Training impulsive children to talk to themselves: A means of developing self-control. *Journal of Abnormal Psychology, 77,* 115–126.

Neziroglu, F., McKay, D., Todaro, J., & Yaryura-Tobias, J. A. (1996). Effect of cognitive behavior therapy on persons with body dysmorphic disorder and comorbid Axis II diagnosis. *Behavior Therapy, 27,* 1, 67–77.

Shure, M. B. (1981). Social competence as a problem-solving skill. In J. D. Wine & M. D. Smyne (Eds.), *Social competence* (pp. 158–185). New York: Guilford Press.

Spivack, G., Platt, J. J., & Shure, M. B. (1976). *The problem-solving approach to adjustment*. San Francisco: Jossey-Bass.

Spivack, G., & Shure, M. B. (1974). *Social adjustment of young children: A cognitive approach to solving real-life problems*. San Francisco: Jossey-Bass.

Tan, Siang-Yang, & Leucht, C. A., (1997). Cognitive-behavioral therapy for clinical pain control: A 15-year update and its relationship to hypnosis. *International Journal of Clinical & Experimental Hypnosis, 45,* 4, 396–416.

JAN N. HUGHES
Texas A & M University

COGNITIVE RETRAINING
COGNITIVE STRATEGIES
SELF CONTROL CURRICULUM

COGNITIVE DEVELOPMENT

Cognitive development consists of numerous overlapping conceptual and theoretical processes involving changes that occur in mental capacity and facility between birth and death. Cognition, the product of cognitive development, refers to mental processes by which individuals acquire knowledge. Moreover, cognition is the process of acquiring a conscious awareness that helps us to "know" and "understand" in a wide spectrum of activities such as remembering, learning, thinking, and attending. As a human phenomenon, cognition is comprised of unobservable events, their subsequent comprehension, and resultant response (Flavell, 1982). These covert behaviors characterize the activities of human thought processes.

In an effort to present general parameters of childhood cognitive development as it pertains to special education, several cognitive perspectives must be addressed. The human is an active problem solver who attempts to discriminate, extract, and analyze information; subsequently, directed planful action undergoes developmental change. Three contemporary theoretical orientations are consistent with the theme of the child as an active problem solver: Piaget's theory of cognitive development; information-processing approaches, and social learning theory.

One of the most influential descriptors of how development occurs is Piaget's theory of cognitive development (Piaget, 1970). In his work, cognitive structures are represented in the symbolic medium of formal logic, where each structure is regarded as a broad system of logical operations that mediates and unites a whole range of more specific intellectual behaviors and characteristics. Even though research with large samples of infants have confirmed Piaget's theories, certain aspects of his developmental accounts have come under scrutiny (Flavell, 1980; Gelman, 1978) and warrant revision or reinterpretation. Nevertheless, the Piagetian approach remains an important scientific paradigm on human intellectual development. The formative phases of the domain of study known as cognitive development are rooted in Piaget's theoretical formulations.

Piaget defines intelligence as a basic life function through which an individual adapts to the environment. In

Piaget's view, children do not simply receive information from the environment, they actively seek and achieve knowledge through their own efforts. This interaction, from Piaget's biological perspective, is viewed as adaptation. Organisms adapt by using their newly acquired information by processing and gaining understanding of the environment. Thus adaptation and construction of reality depend on a child's level of cognitive development.

Piaget views cognitive development as a process of the development of cognitive structures and intellectual functions. He uses the term schema to describe mental structures used by the individual to represent, organize, and interpret experience. Therefore, a schema is defined as a pattern of thought or action by which an individual constructs an "understanding" of some aspect of the environment. Three types of intellectual structures have been defined by Piaget: sensorimotor (organized behavior patterns used to represent or respond to objects or experiences), symbolic (internal cognitive images used to represent past experiences), and operational (internal cognitive images that organize thoughts logically).

According to Piaget's theory, cognitive development depends on maturation (genetically transmitted) and the child's interactions with the environment. Contingent on normal maturation are the organism's ability to adapt to environmental changes and demands. Thus, with maturation, assimilation, and accommodation (Piaget, 1970), the human organism tries to interpret new experiences in terms of existing information.

Analogously, through accommodation, the child modifies an existing schema to suit a novel experience. Hence, Piaget describes intellectual growth as an active process whereby children are repeatedly assimilating new experiences and accommodating their cognitive structures to their new experiences. The cognitive operations of adaptation and organization facilitate children's ability to construct a progressively better understanding of the world. A child's formulation of self and external world depend on the knowledge base acquired up to the particular point in time at which a response is necessary. Consequently, the greater immaturity of the child's cognitive system, the more limited the interpretation of environmental events.

Age ranges designated for each of Piaget's four stages are average estimates; nonetheless, the sequential emergence of hierarchical "stages" are believed to be absolutely constant or invariant. Piaget felt that earlier developmental stages are not skipped en route to later stages. Accomplishments for each stage are said to accumulate; i.e., skills achieved in earlier stages are not lost with the advent of latent stages.

Sensorimotor Stage

During the sensorimotor stage of development, birth to about 2 years of age, cognitive development originates with ability to organize and coordinate bodily sensations and perceptions with the child's own physical movements and actions. Throughout sensorimotor development, an infant progresses from instinctual reflexive actions at birth to symbolic reflexive actions toward the end of the second year.

Initial means of coordinating sensation and action are accomplished through instinctual reflexive behaviors such as sucking and rooting. These behaviors are exhibited during substage 1 simple reflexes (ages birth to 1 month).

Substage 2, first habits and primary circular reactions, is comprised of first acquired adaptations. For example, when orally stimulated by a bottle during the first substage (simple reflexes), an infant might suck; conversely, during the second substage, repetitions of sucking may commence when no bottle is present.

During substage 3 (4 to 8 months), secondary circular reactions, behaviors are also repetitious and pleasurable; however, they focus on events and objects in the external environment that occur by chance.

Throughout substage 4 (8 to 12 months), coordination of secondary schemata, cognitive thought is comprised of intentional combining previously unrelated stimuli, producing simple feats, solving simple problems, and imitating the behavior of others. Piaget suggests that throughout substage 4, an infant is applying known cognitive structures to new situations to produce coordinated, goal-directed, and independent imitative actions with his or her own body or environment.

Substage 5 (12 to 18 months), tertiary circular reactions, is evidenced by exploratory trial and error schematas in which the infant purposely discovers new procedures to solve problems or reproduce interesting outcomes. Piaget refers to this period as the developmental starting point for human curiosity and interest in novelty.

Finally, during the last sensorimotor substage (18 to 24 months), internalization of cognitive structures begins to develop. Mental functioning shifts from a purely sensorimotor plane to a symbolic plane in which infants develop the ability to use primitive symbols.

Object Permanence

Object permanence, considered one of the infant's most significant cognitive development achievements during the sensorimotor stage, is the idea that people, places, and things continue to exist when they are no longer visible or detectable through the senses. According to Piaget, the object concept first appears during substage 4, coordination of secondary schemata. During substage 5, tertiary circular reactions, an infant searches for and locates hidden objects in novel and familiar locations; nonetheless, this occurs only if movement of the objects is visible. In the final sensorimotor substage, object permanence is complete; invisible movement of objects can be followed in the imagination by means of mental representations. Thus the infant searches for and finds objects that have been hidden through visible displacements.

Contrary to Piaget, Bower's (1982) research suggests that infants understand object permanence earlier, during primary circular reactions, even though they will not search for objects during this substage. Evidence of object permanence in Bower's research is indicated by the infant's surprise or anticipation of perceived object location. Bower suggests that errors in spatial reasoning, rather than absence of the object concept, account for younger infants' failure to search in Piagetian tasks.

Preoperational Stage

In the preoperational stage (ages 2 to 7 years), a period when symbolic schemata predominates, a young child's symbolic system expands such that use of language and perceptual images moves well beyond abilities at the end of the sensorimotor period. The preoperational stage consists of two phases: the preconceptual period (ages 2 to 4 years) and the intuitive period (ages 5 to 7 years).

According to Piaget, deficits in logical reasoning are evident throughout the preconceptual period. For example, egocentrism, the most salient feature of preconceptual thought, is evidenced by an inability to distinguish easily between a child's own perspective and that of someone else. Another deficit exhibited during the preconceptual period is animism; the young child believes that inanimate objects have human qualities and are capable of human action. During the preconceptual period, pretend play develops to a level in which children are capable of creating fantasy worlds, inventing imaginary playmates, participating in role playing, and using play as a vehicle for coping with emotional crises.

The second phase of the preoperational stage, the intuitive period, is an extension of preconceptual thought where the use of symbolic thought improves. Perceptually based logic appears in class inclusion problems such as "a string of beads that has both blocks and beads," whereby the child focuses on one feature only. According to Piaget, the child has a hard time thinking about the subset.

To aid in the use of symbolic thought, two main systematic capabilities are necessary during the preoperational period: centration and irreversibility. Fundamentally, centration is a child's tendency to focus on a single aspect of a problem while ignoring other information that helps the child to answer correctly. Irreversibility is the inability to reverse or to undo an action mentally.

Recent research (Flavell, Everett, Croft, & Flavell, 1981; Mossler, Marvin, & Greenberg, 1976) suggests that preoperational children are less egocentric, take another's point of view, and can conserve, contrary to what Piaget found. Gelman (1978) found that preschoolers are capable of causal reasoning. Additional research (Beilin, 1980) indicates that conservation problems can be taught to preoperational children by methods such as identity training; i.e., objects or substances transformed in a conservation task are still the same regardless of their new appearance. Finally, the work of Acredolo and Acredolo (1979) suggests that reversibility and compensation are not absolutely necessary for conservation.

Concrete Operations Stage

Piaget's concrete operations stage, a period between ages 7 and 11 years, is a stage during which the child's thinking crystallizes into a coherent organization of cognitive operations. Cognitive deficits most evident in the preoperational stage completely fade during the concrete operations stage.

Cognitive operations shift to a more refined system of thought that leads to levels that facilitate previously unattainable competencies. During concrete operations development, children often display horizontal decalage meaning the child can solve some conservation problems but not others. For example, conservation skills such as reversibility develop such that the child can mentally reverse flow of action and thereby realize that a column of water can look the same when poured back into its original container. Ability to classify and reverse enables linguistic humor to develop. Another shift is the move from egocentrism to relativism. The child can now decenter, or operate with two or more aspects of a problem simultaneously.

Formal Operations Stage

The formal operations stage, the final stage of Piaget's cognitive development theory, is characterized by the ability to reason abstractly and hypothetically. Abstract quality of thought can be seen primarily in the adolescent's use of verbal propositions in problem solving. For example, the concrete thinker (sensorimotor stage) needs to see concrete elements A, B, and C to be able to make the logical inference that if $A > B$ and $B > C$, then $A > C$. Conversely, formal thinkers can solve the previous problem merely by having it presented as a verbal puzzle.

Although the transition to formal operations takes place gradually over several years, systematic and abstract thinking builds a foundation for considering morality, justice, beliefs, and values. Socially, the formal thinker no longer need rely on concrete experiences with people to form complex judgments about them.

Formal Thought in Adolescence

Since Piaget's classic experiments, many researchers have delved into the nature of adolescent thought. Their objective has been to specify the characteristics that distinguish this form of reasoning and problem solving from other more primitive forms.

One important characteristic of formal thought involves seeking explanations rather than mere descriptions of what has been observed. Another characteristic of formal thought involves the ability to remove oneself from the immediate context of a problem in order to get an additional perspective. One of the most socially significant characteristics of formal thought is the metacognitive ability to thinking about thinking; i.e., the ability to reflect on the thought process itself. In sum, formal thought is characterized by a relative freedom from the immediate constraints of a problem, which results in flexibility.

Late Adolescence and Adulthood

During this stage the most pronounced changes in cognitive development have taken place. Nonetheless, small but observable changes are still evident later in life. Young adults, from Erikson's (1963) theory of psychosocial development, experience a crisis of identity versus role confusion. Moreover, sex and romance influence the role of young adults.

Cognitive development continues to refine in its development as the young adult attempts to conceptualize a lifelong role in society by selecting an occupation. This mature realism about one's occupation is seen as a process that remains throughout one's life, sometimes leading to midlife career changes.

Information-Processing Approach to Cognitive Development

As a model of human cognitive development, information processing explains decision making, knowing, and remembering as processes. In this approach to the study of cognitive development, the mind is conceived of as a complex cognitive system, analogous in some ways to a computer. In essence, human cognition becomes what the computer must know in order to produce behavior y. Information from the environment is abstracted from sensory systems and "flows" through a variety of proposed information-processing components. Information is transformed and analyzed at each step; feedback and feedforward loops among the components influence these transformations and analyses. Planning and purposeful thinking are derived by executive functions. The executive system contains sets of elementary information-processing rules that construct, execute, and monitor the flow of information to achieve objectives.

Most of the information-processing research builds directly on Piaget's contributions to the understanding of cognitive development. Contrary to Piaget's structural explanation underlying the thought structure of logic in thought processes and operational reversibility, information processing accounts for and identifies specific mental processes by which cognition is processed. Some re-searchers, such as Pascual-Leone (1980) and Case (1978), have modified Piagetian theory to take into account information-processing considerations (also called neo-Piagetian theories). One such approach is Siegler's (1981) rule-assessment approach. In essence, Siegler's work examines a child's problem-solving skills within a domain at different ages. A child's pattern of responses across problems helps to determine which of information-processing rules the child is using.

Several other information-processing perspectives have examined cognitive development. For example, researchers have found that young children have limited attention and persistence at tasks (Wellman, Ritter, & Flavell, 1975) and that their curiosity interferes with systematic problem solving. Thus, contrary to Piagetian theory, very young children may fail to solve many problems because they are unable to sustain their attention long enough to gather the necessary information. By about age 5 children become more persistent in their attempts to solve problems. Hence younger children may know to look first at relevant stimuli and label them; whereas, older children are better at selectively attending without special training.

Social Learning Theory

Social learning theorists (e.g., Bandura, 1977b) suggest that cognitive development is much more than a result of some combination of individual characteristics and environmental influences. They view all three as existing within a mutually interdependent network; they exist as a set of reciprocal determinants. Thus cognitions, beliefs, and expectations influence behavior and vice versa. Behavior partially determines the nature of the environment, whereas cognitions determine the psychological definitions of the environment.

Learning takes place either directly (through association of behaviors and consequences) or through modeling. The direct consequences of behavior, or reinforcements, are not conceptualized in the more traditional fashion that ignores awareness of the contingencies on the part of the child. Hence consequences of behavior explicitly carry information and function to provoke the individual into formulating and testing hypotheses. Thus reinforcement influences whether or not a response will elicit cognitions or thoughts about stimulus associations.

Learning is thought to be acquired through modeling. All new behaviors are observed along with their consequences. Inherent symbolic abilities facilitate abstraction and representation of information and provide an efficient means for retaining that information. From a social learning perspective, the anticipation of reinforcement may serve as a stimulus to direct attention to a model's behavior; hence, reinforcement may facilitate learning.

In summary, social learning theory places a great deal

of emphasis on symbolic and self-regulatory processes. Cognitive development is important to the extent that changes in cognitive functioning influence changes in those processes. In children, development becomes more refined with experience and actual manipulation; consequently, children are better able to represent efficiently and retain observational experiences. Additionally, symbolic processes, attentional processes, and motivational processes change with observational learning.

Implications for Special Education

Traditional stages of cognitive development apply to individuals with and without disabilities alike. Handicapping conditions, however, may result in irregularities or delays in cognitive development, particularly in profoundly mentally retarded or multiply impaired persons. Some profoundly mentally retarded handicapped never progress into the higher stages of cognitive development such as preoperational or operational thought. Other handicapped children acquire skills by rote or through carefully structured instruction, but have difficulty in applying them to new situations (Brown, Campione, & Murphy, 1977).

Most mildly and moderately retarded children do progress through Piaget's lower stages of cognitive development; however, their rate of skill acquisition is much slower. As the child gets older, the gap between the age at which specific skills are expected to be learned and the age at which they are actually learned increases. The retarded child also performs cognitive tasks with less efficiency than the nonretarded child (Campione & Brown, 1978).

Individuals with learning disabilities (LD) represent the largest percentage of the handicapped population (U.S. Office of Special Education, 1996); they evidence a broad array of cognitive dysfunctions. These deficits emerge when academic learning lags with age. Children who are learning disabled may not exhibit specific cognitive problems early in development; however, skills acquired during Piaget's preoperational stage (intuitive thinking) are learned at a slower pace. Thus, problems in areas such as mathematics, reading, and memory are more prevalent.

During the primary years, children with LD have problems with seriation and classification tasks that are essential for mathematics. They cannot sort objects by size, match objects, or grasp the concept of counting and addition. In reading, LD children evidence word recognition errors (omissions, insertions, substitutions, reversals, and transpositions) and comprehension errors (inability to recall facts, sequences, or main ideas).

Word recognition difficulties suggest that LD children are unable to make a word or a letter stand for or represent something else. These are preconceptual skills (ages 2 to 7) of cognitive development in which symbolic thought develops. Problems with centration may inhibit reading comprehension.

Students with learning disabilities generally have problems with recalling auditory and visual stimuli. They also have problems with tasks requiring production or generation of specific learning or memorization strategies that influence the efficient organization of input for retrieval and recall. Bauer (1979) found that poor readers perform poorly on memory tasks that require complex organizational and retrieval strategies. Kauffman and Hallahan (1979) suggest that LD students fail to engage in strategies that enhance attention and recall. These deficits are evident when applied to academic tasks.

Cognitive development may be viewed from numerous perspectives and subsequently applied to academic problems encountered in the field of special education. The information-processing approach to cognitive development is still in the early stage. It is best described as a complement to, rather than a replacement for, Piaget's earlier framework. However, recent research suggests that infants and young children are more competent and adults less competent that once thought (Flavell, 1992). Growth and extension of the cognitive development literature continues and quite often fills in some of the gaps in Piaget's model (Siegler & Crowley, 1991); hence, advances in empirical findings will eventually aid in the development of successful school-based interventions.

REFERENCES

Acredolo, L., & Acredolo, L. T. (1979). Identity, compensation, and conservation. *Child Development, 50,* 524–535.

Bauer, R. H. (1979). Memory, acquisition, and category clustering in learning disabled children. *Journal of Experimental Child Psychology, 217,* 365–383.

Beilin, H. (1980). Piaget's theory: Refinement, revision, or rejection? In R. Kluwe & H. Spada (Eds.), *Developmental models of thinking.* New York: Academic.

Bower, T. G. R. (1982). *Development in infancy.* San Francisco: Freeman.

Brown, A., Campione, J., & Murphy, M. (1977). Maintenance and generalization of training meta-mnemonic awareness of educable retarded children. *Journal of Experimental Child Psychology, 24,* 191–211.

Campione, J. C., & Brown, A. (1978). Toward a theory of intelligence: Contributions from research with retarded children. *Intelligence, 2,* 279–304.

Case, R. S. (1978). Intellectual development from birth to adulthood: A neo-Piagetian interpretation. In R. W. Siegler (Ed.), *Children's thinking: What develops?* Hillsdale, NJ: Erlbaum.

Erikson, E. H. (1963). *Childhood and society* (2nd ed.). New York: Norton.

Flavell, J. (1980, Fall). A tribute to Piaget. *Society for Research in Child Development Newsletter.*

Flavell, J. (1982). On cognitive development. *Child Development, 53,* 1–10.

Flavell, J. (1992). Cognitive development. *Developmental Psychology, 28,* 998–1005.

Flavell, J., Everett, B. A., Croft, K., & Flavell, E. R. (1981). Young children's knowledge about visual perception: Further evidence for the Level 1-Level 2 distinction. *Developmental Psychology, 15,* 95–120.

Gelman, R. (1978). Cognitive development. *Annual Review of Psychology, 29,* 297–332.

Kauffman, J. M., & Hallahan, D. P. (1979). Learning disabled and hyperactivity. In B. B. Lahey & A. E. Kazdin (Eds.), *Advances in clinical child psychology* (Vol. 2). New York: Plenum.

Mossler, D. G., Marvin, R. S., & Greenberg, M. T. (1976). Conceptual perspective taking in 2- to 6-year-old children. *Developmental Psychology, 12,* 85–86.

Moynahan, E. D. (1973). The development of knowledge concerning the effect of categorization upon free recall. *Child Development, 44,* 238–246.

Pascual-Leone, J. (1980). Constructive problems for constructive theories: The current relevance of Piaget's work and a critique of information-processing simulation psychology. In R. H. Kluwe & H. Spada (Eds.), *Developmental models of thinking.* New York: Academic.

Piaget, J. (1970). Piaget's theory. In P. H. Mussen (Ed.), *Carmichael's manual of child psychology* (Vol. 1). New York: Wiley.

Siegler, R. S. (1981). Developmental sequences within and between concepts. *Monographs for the Society for Research in Child Development, 46* (Serial No. 189).

Siegler, R. S., & Crowley, K. (1991). The microgenetic method. *American Psychologist, 46,* 6, 606–620.

U.S. Office of Special Education. (1996). *Eighteenth annual report to Congress on the implementation of Public Law 94-142: The Education for All Handicapped Children Act.* Washington, DC: U.S. Department of Education.

Wellman, H. M., Ritter, K., & Flavell, J. (1975). Deliberate memory in the delayed reactions of very young children. *Developmental Psychology, 11,* 780–787.

JOSE LUIS TORRES
MICHAEL J. ASH
Texas A & M University

COGNITIVE STRATEGIES
COGNITIVE STYLES
INFORMATION PROCESSING
INTELLIGENCE
PIAGET, JEAN
SOCIAL LEARNING THEORY

COGNITIVE IMPAIRMENT AND METAL POLLUTANTS

It is well known that children who are exposed to high doses of lead and other metal pollutants may suffer permanent neurological sequelae and cognitive impairments (Hartman 1995; Moon, Marlow, Stellern, & Errera, 1985). The causes of metal pollution are often associated with substandard living conditions: e.g., living in dilapidated substandard housing with peeling lead-based paints or plaster, living with household dust carrying metal pollutants, and living in proximity to heavy traffic or factories with noxious emissions. Inadequate nutrition also contributes to the effects of metal pollution.

Some of the physical difficulties associated with metal pollution are loss of appetite, chronic abdominal pain, headache, and anemia. Reported behavior difficulties associated with high levels of such poisoning are decreased learning performance, deficient attention, irritability, and clumsiness. Investigators have implicated metal toxicity in nonadaptive behavior as manifested in classroom situations (Marlowe, Moon, Errera, Cossairt, McNeil, & Peak, in press), associated with learning-disabled children (Marlowe, Errera, Cossairt, & Welch, in press) and with emotional disturbances in children (Marlowe, Errera, & Jacoby, 1983).

The assessment of metal concentrations in humans is easily carried out through various bodily analyses, e.g., of blood, teeth, and hair. The study of hair is both easy and noninvasive: samples are subjected to the study of atomic absorption spectroscopy (Laker, 1982). Trace elements such as metals accumulate in hair at concentrations that are usually higher than in the blood serum. Hair thus can provide a record of a child's nutrient and mineral status. A method appropriate to classroom use to help teachers identify children who are potentially suffering from metal pollution is the Metal Exposure Questionnaire (Marlowe et al., 1983). This provides quantitative information about the possibility that a schoolchild is suffering significantly from metal pollutants.

Many of studies of metal pollutant effects suffer from methodological errors. One of the more significant of these is that while investigators study the effects of one toxic metal, they often fail to take into account the effects of other toxic metals on a child's behavior (Hartman, 1995; Moon et al., 1985).

While there is clear evidence indicating that high doses of metal pollution are physically and cognitively deleterious, there is less certainty as to whether low doses of such metals have significant effects. A number of studies have suggested that they do. Low levels of arsenic, cadmium, mercury, aluminum, and lead have been implicated in cognitive, perceptual, and behavioral childhood developmental deficits (Marlowe, Errera, J., Stellern, & Beck, 1983; Winneke et al, 1983). Some investigators also have hypothesized that metal combinations have interactive effects, thereby increasing the total toxicity in a child (Moon et al., 1985).

Among the more comprehensive reviews of literature concerning the behavioral effects of metal pollutants is that of Rimland and Larson (1983), who summarized studies of the relationship between incidence of learning disabilities and long-term, low-level metal exposure as measured through hair analysis. They found a total of nine studies. In five of the studies, learning-disabled subjects were found to have significantly more lead and/or cadmium than their controls. In the four remaining studies, the learning-disabled students were found to be somewhat higher in lead, cadmium, and/or aluminum concentrations.

The potential widespread nature of metal pollutants' toxic effects has been demonstrated by Moon, Marlowe, Stellern, & Errera (1985). These investigators, studying a randomly selected sample of elementary school children, found significant relationships between low metal concentrations and diminished performance on a variety of cognitive and academic tasks. They also discovered interactive effects. Thus, both increases in arsenic and its interaction with lead were significantly related to decreased reading and spelling achievement. Increases in aluminum and the interaction of aluminum with lead were associated with decreased visual motor performance. An excellent review of the neuropsychological segnelae of toxic substance exposure can be found by Hartman (1995).

REFERENCES

Hartman, D. E. (1995). *Neuropsychological Toxicology* (2nd ed.). New York: Plenum.

Laker, M. (1982). On determining trace element levels in man: The uses of blood and hair. *Lancet, 12,* 260–263.

Marlowe, M., Errera, J., Cossairt, A., & Welch, K. (in press). Hair mineral content as a predictor of learning disabilities. *Journal of Learning Disabilities.*

Marlowe, M., Errera, J., & Jacoby, J. (1983). Increased lead and cadmium levels in emotionally disturbed children. *Journal of Orthomollecular Psychiatry, 12,* 260–267.

Marlowe, M., Moon, C., Errera, J., Cossairt, A., McNeil, A., & Peak, R. (in press). Main and interaction effects of metallic toxins on classroom behavior. *Journal of Abnormal Child Psychology.*

Moon, C., Marlowe, M., Stellern, J., & Errera, J. (1985). Main and interaction effects of metallic pollutants on cognitive functioning. *Journal of Learning Disabilities, 18,* 217–220.

Rimland, B., & Larson, G. E. (1983). Hair mineral analysis and behavior: An analysis of 51 studies. *Journal of Learning Disabilities, 16,* 279–285.

Winneke, G., Kramer, U., Brockhaus, U., Evers, U., Kujanek, G., Lechner, H., & Janke, W. (1983). Neuropsyhological studies in children with elevated tooth-lead concentrations. *International Archives of Occupational environmental Health, 51,* 231–252.

LESTER MANN
Hunter College

LEAD POISONING
POVERTY, RELATIONSHIP TO SPECIAL EDUCATION

COGNITIVE RETRAINING

Cognitive retraining involves remediation of acquired cognitive dysfunction arising from brain injury, cerebrovascular accidents, or other less common neurological disorders. Referred to by different terms, cognitive retraining is synonymous with cognitive redevelopment, cognitive remediation, neurological retraining, and cognitive rehabilitation. In each case, the goal is to produce functional changes in verbal (e.g., verbal problem solving) and/or nonverbal (e.g., visual-spatial reasoning) skills or abilities. The approach attempts to strengthen premorbid patterns of mental functioning or the design of compensatory strategies to circumvent permanently impaired functions (i.e., return is unlikely). Cognitive retraining may involve remediation of deficits, capitalization on individual strengths, or the training of compensatory approaches. With dysfunction differing from one individual to the next, the therapist may design a program integrating more than one of these approaches. Indeed, rarely will a brain-damaged patient be presented with a specific area of impairment that is not reflected in other areas of cognitive functioning (e.g., abstract reasoning and memory).

As a precursor to such cognitive therapy, a complete neuropsychological assessment is often conducted to detail the patient's functional strengths and weaknesses. Moreover, neuropsychological assessment often relies on standardized observations of behavior that show a direct correspondence to the functional integrity of the brain. In this way, the examination provides a comprehensive picture of the patient's cognitive abilities; this is useful in planning retraining and rehabilitation in general. Neuropsychological assessment provides an objective baseline, from which success in treatment may be documented.

Cognitive retraining is a recent endeavor and therefore many of its methods continue to be developed. Most approaches involve controlling materials, such as computer programs, and strategies in therapy such that optimal conditions exist to facilitate task performance (Diller & Gordon, 1981; Nieman, Ruff, & Baser, 1990). The cognitive therapist seeks to move the patient in small enough steps to the final goal so that the opportunity for failure is rare. Although retraining packages have been developed, the majority of cognitive retraining involves a task analysis approach to the specific disorder (Dean, 1982). Task analysis involves (1) assessing the patient's modality specific cognitive functioning; (2) defining content elements necessary (terms, rules, and the like) to achieve the objective of therapy; (3) identifying the level of cognitive functioning and modality (visual memorization, etc.) necessary to master content; (4) specifying relationships between content and cognitive functions for the patient; (5) using small steps and correction feedback in retraining procedures; and (6) chaining small components together to encompass the final goal (Dean, 1982). Specific approaches may vary from teaching specific verbal strategies as compensation for spatial deficits to relearning phonetic skills necessary in reading.

From the above description, it should be clear that the present state of the art of cognitive retraining remains at a clinical level. Thus, most retraining procedures are applied without benefit of a consistent research base. In fact, the research that does address the effectiveness of cognitive training procedures is limited by a lack of control for spontaneous recovery. That is to say, following brain damage, a degree of functional recovery occurs without intervention. Clearly this recovery must be accounted for in evaluating the effectiveness of any retraining procedure (Dean, 1986).

REFERENCES

Dean, R. S. (1982). Neuropsychology and the rehabilitation process. *Bulletin of the National Academy of Neuropsychologists,* 161–162.

Dean, R. S. (1986). Neuropsychological assessment. In J. D. Cavenar & S. B. Guze (Eds.), *Psychiatry.* Philadelphia: Lippincott.

Diller, L., & Gordon, W. A. (1981). Rehabilitation and clinical neuropsychology. In S. B. Filskov & T. J. Boll (Eds.), *Handbook of clinical neuropsychology* (pp. 702–703). New York: Wiley.

Nieman, H., Ruff, R. M., & Baser, C. A. (1990). Computer-assisted attention retraining in head-injured individuals: A controlled efficacy study of an outpatient program. *Journal of Consulting & Clinical Psychology, 58,* 6, 811–817.

RAYMOND S. DEAN
Ball State University
Indiana University School
of Medicine

COGNITIVE STRATEGIES
NEUROPSYCHOLOGY

COGNITIVE STRATEGIES

Cognitive strategies are cognitive processes that we use to monitor, control, and manage our cognitive functioning. They mediate both learning and performance. While cognitive strategies have been studied under various names for a long time, credit should probably go to Bruner, Goodnow, and Austin (1956) for first using the construct in the modern-day sense of the term. During recent years, there has been considerable interest in the training and remediation of such strategies.

All of us, whether child, adult, gifted, or mentally retarded, constantly use cognitive strategies to control and direct our thinking and behavior. Word attack skills are strategic in nature, as are the carrying processes used in arithmetic. The ways students take notes or check test responses for accuracy are determined strategically. The manner in which an individual deports himself or herself during a job interview is strategically controlled.

While a variety of cognitive theories have influenced work on cognitive strategies, information processing theories have been the most influential of all. Defining cognitive strategies from an information processing point of view, Young has pointed out that most tasks and problems can be carried out and solved in a variety of different ways and that individuals "have at their command a number of different strategies from which to choose for these purposes . . . there is an analogy between strategies and the subroutines used by computer programmers to organize [their programs]" (1978, pp. 357–358).

Cognitive strategies are theoretically distinguished from cognitive capacities (abilities) and knowledge information). They are regarded as cognitive techniques that guide the ways our capacities are exercised and our knowledge is used. Strategies are learned both informally and formally. Most important from the standpoint of special education is that they are susceptible to training and improvement.

Apropos of this susceptibility is the distinction that has been made between fixed and modifiable cognitive characteristics (Baron, 1978). Fixed cognitive characteristics (i.e., cognitive capacities or abilities such as intelligence and memory) are difficult to influence environmentally or to change to any significant degree. Modifiable cognitive characteristics, such as cognitive strategies, however, are usually amenable to change and may be significantly improved by education and remediation. While fixed cognitive characteristics ultimately set limits on the development and expression of all cognitive processes, including cognitive strategy, some cognitive researchers believe that effective use of cognitive strategies can overcome "hard wired" cognitive limitations to a great degree: that students with mental retardation, for example, can approach normal cognitive achievement in certain areas if they are taught how to use strategies properly. One of the most important of intervention studies with the mentally retarded was carried out in the area of strategic training by Belmont and Butterfield (1975). These investigators found that with strategic training, mentally retarded learners were able to function on levels equivalent to those of nonretarded individuals in particular tasks.

Some cognitive strategies are general and can be applied across a broad spectrum of activities; e.g., checking one's work for accuracy on completion is a general strategy that is useful in most tasks. Other strategies are only applicable to specific situations, e.g., applying the processes of single-column addition.

There are short-term cognitive strategies and there are long-term ones. A student will apply certain strategies when taking a particular multiple choice quiz; these strategies serve a short-term purpose. The same student may develop a plan for gaining entry to professional school; in such a case, long-term strategies will be involved.

Cognitive strategies are sometimes used with full awareness of their application. At other times they operate automatically and with little or no consciousness of their use. We are usually most conscious of using them and laborious in their application when we are first learning them or when we attempt to correct or improve on them. As a rule, the more automatically cognitive strategies operate, and the less aware we are of their operations, the smoother and more effortless they will be. They are also likely to be more effective from the standpoint of freeing up our cognitive apparatuses to work on other aspects of a task or problem. Thus a concert pianist's efforts at interpreting music is at first consciously strategic in nature. The pianist plays with conscious intent to give the music certain nuances while practicing it. During the concert, however, such strategies, while still directing the pianist's playing, work at lower levels of awareness or entirely in an automatic fashion. Indeed, a high degree of awareness of any strategic intentions on the pianist's part would make it impossible to sustain smooth playing, particularly during passages of high velocity.

The particular cognitive strategies that an individual acquires and uses depend on that individual's experiences and instruction. They also depend on the individual's abilities and maturity. An adult will usually use more sophisticated and effective strategies than a 10-year-old child. A gifted child uses more complex strategies and has access to a wider range of strategies than does a retarded child. A deaf child will be limited in the use of certain strategies because of limited language capabilities but may learn to use still others more effectively than hearing children (Mann & Sabatino, 1985).

Not all cognitive strategies have the same degree of effectiveness. Some are effective for an appropriate age level or handicap but not for others; e.g., a first grader uses counting strategies that are effective for that age but may actually have negative effects if used in later grades. A child with learning disabilities may be ineffective at strategies that a good learner uses with ease.

Some strategies may even be harmful. A child who is a social isolate may use strategic approaches to other children that are intended to make friends but instead result in rejection. A child who is having trouble with advanced mathematics keeps using calculation strategies that are cumbersome and that interfere with understanding. If remedial cognitive strategy training is to succeed with such children, it will often require the unlearning of "bad" strategies prior to the acquisition of good ones.

Furthermore, it is not enough to know how to use a particular strategy well. It also is required that the user be skilled in its application and know when the strategy is appropriate or when another strategy should be used instead. Regular practice under varied conditions appears essential for most new strategies to become effective. Mentally retarded students will almost always be found to be deficient in their use of cognitive strategies and to require a great deal of rehearsal to master new strategies (Baron, 1978).

Success in school may ultimately depend on the number of effective strategies that a student can appropriately employ. Children with good abilities may fail academically because they do not know enough effective strategies to deal with their school work, or because they rely on inadequate or inappropriate strategies, or because they fail to effectively use the good strategies at their disposal. On the other hand, children with limited abilities may succeed academically because they have learned to use cognitive strategies to compensate for and minimize the impact of their deficiencies.

A number of classification systems have been suggested for cognitive strategies. Baron (1978) has suggested that we categorize them in three ways: (1) central strategies that are basic to the development of others strategies; (2) general strategies applicable to a variety of situations; and (3) specific strategies pertaining to particular types of applications.

Newell (1979) has addressed the classification of strategies using an analogy of an inverted cone of strategic skills. At the bottom of the cone are a large number of strategies that apply only to certain problems or situations, e.g., a carrying strategy for two-column addition. Such narrow strategies may be powerful and, if properly used, should effectively solve the problems to which they are applied. They are, however, limited to specific types of problems or work only under particular conditions.

As we move up Newell's inverted cone to its tip we find more generalizable but less effective strategies; there is a tradeoff between generalizability and effectiveness. At the very tip of the cone we find a few highly general strategies that are applicable to almost any problem or situation but that are weak and by themselves unable to solve any specific problem. Checking one's school work to see that it is accurate is an example of a general beneficial cognitive strategy, but it has weak effects and by itself can solve no specific problem. In between lie a variety of intermediate-level strategies that vary in specificity and power. It has been suggested that the most useful approach to cognitive strategy training from a general remedial standpoint might be to address such intermediate level strategies (Brown & Palincsar, 1982). Thus scanning written pages in a systematic left to right fashion is a strategy that has some specificity, i.e., it applies to reading; it also has some generality in that it applies to a wide range of reading.

In determining what type of strategies to use with special education students, the cognitive trainer is confronted with decisions as to optimal training programs. Teachers engaged in the cognitive training of learning-disabled children might well stick to specific and intermediate-level strategies that are directly applicable to particular types of school work. Psychologists might be interested in more general types of cognitive strategic training such as is involved in problem solving, test taking, etc.

A distinction has been made between blind and informed cognitive strategy training. Blind training programs are ones in which the subjects do not know the purpose of the training they are receiving. Informed cognitive strategy training not only trains the pupils strategically but helps them to understand the purpose of the training and the benefits to be derived from it. There is evidence that both types of training programs can be effective. However, students trained under informed conditions are likely to use their strategies more effectively and to continue to use them after their formal training is over (Kendall, Borkowski, & Cavanaugh, 1980).

A number of researchers have offered recommendations to guide cognitive strategy training with handicapped students (Belmont & Butterfield, 1979; Brown & Palinscar, 1982; Borkowski & Cavanaugh, 1980; Kreiner, 1992). Some investigators have advised that teachers of handicapped students may wish to use cognitive strategy curricula (Borkowski & Cavanaugh, 1979; Winschel & Lawrence, 1975).

The most active interest in cognitive strategies currently is in metacognition, which represents a supraordinate realm of executive cognitive strategies that monitor and regulate lower level strategies, and in cognitive behavioral interventions, which involve strategic training.

REFERENCES

Baron, J. (1978). Intelligence and general strategies. In G. Underwood (Ed.), *Strategies of information processing* (pp. 403–450). London: Academic.

Belmont, J. M., & Butterfield, E. C. (1979). Learning strategies as determinants of memory deficiencies. *Cognitive Psychology, 2,* 411–420.

Borkowski, J. G., & Cavanaugh, J. C. (1979). Maintenance and generalization of skills and strategies by the retarded. In W. R. Ellis (Ed.), *Handbook of mental deficiency* (2nd ed.). Hillsdale, NJ: Erlbaum.

Borkowski, J. G., & Kornarski, E. A. (1981). Educational implications of efforts to change intelligence. *Journal of Special Education, 15,* 289–306.

Brown, A. C. & Palincsar, A. S. (1982). Inducing strategic learning from texts by means of informed, self control training. *Topics in Learning & Learning Disabilities, 2,* 1–17.

Bruner, J. S., Goodnow, J. J., & Austin, G. A. (1956). A study of thinking. New York: Wiley.

Kendall, C. R., Borkowski, J. G., & Cavanaugh, J. C. (1980). Metamemory and the transfer of an interrogative strategy by EMR children. *Intelligence, 4,* 255–270.

Kreiner, D. S. (1992). Reaction times measures of spelling. *Journal of Experimental Psychology: Learning, Memory, & Cognition, 18,* 4, 765–776.

Mann, L., & Sabatino, D. A. (1985). *Foundations of cognitive processes in remedial and special education.* Rockville, MD: Aspen.

Newell, A. (1979). One final word. In D. T. Tuma & F. Reid (Eds.), *Problem solving and education: Issues in teaching and research.* Hillsdale, NJ: Erlbaum.

Winschel, J. F., & Lawrence, E. A. (1975). Short-term memory: Curricular implications for the mentally retarded. *Journal of Special Education, 9,* 395–408.

Young, R. M. (1978). Strategies and the structure of a cognitive skill. In G. Underwood (Ed.), *Strategies of information processing* (pp. 357–401). London: Academic.

Zigler, E., & Balla, D. (1971). Luria's verbal deficiency theory of mental retardation and performance on sameness, symmetry and opposition tasks: A critique. *American Journal of Mental Deficiency, 74,* 400–416.

Joni J. Gleason
University of West Florida

COGNITIVE STYLE
INFORMATION PROCESSING
METACOGNITION

COGNITIVE STYLES

Cognitive styles are constructs that help to explain the ways that personality variables affect cognition. Kogan has defined them as reflecting "individual variations in *modes* of attending, perceiving, remembering and thinking" (1980, p. 64). Two individuals who score identically on intelligence and other cognitive aptitude or achievement tests and are the same in information processing capabilities may nevertheless differ significantly in school work, success on the job, and other behaviors because they differ in their cognitive styles (Mann & Sabatino, 1985).

The study of cognitive styles began in earnest following World War II, urged on by concern about the psychiatric casualties of that war and postwar interest in personal self-development and psychotherapy. Personality assessment had become exceedingly popular. Thus interest developed respecting the ways that personality variables affect cognitive variables. Studies of what came to be known as cognitive styles emerged.

Interest in cognitive styles first appeared most prominently in the work of George Klein et al. at the Menninger clinic. While the original work was conceptualized in terms of perceptual attitudes (perceptual types of tests being used as the most prominent way of assessing cognitive styles), later research emphasized the cognitive aspects of the research and the term cognitive controls became the dominant descriptor applied to work seeking to determine how personality factors interact with and influence cognitive skills.

Many definitions of cognitive styles have been offered. They generally agree that cognitive styles should be thought of as personality characteristics or traits that are related to other personality characteristics. Furthermore, while cognitive styles cannot always be distinguished or separated from cognitive skills, they are distinct from cognitive contents.

A considerable number of different types of cognitive styles have been distinguished through research. Some are similar, but others are clearly different in their implications for cognitive functioning. It is not unusual to study children and adults from the standpoint of several different cognitive styles.

While the assessment of cognitive styles of schoolchildren is usually done through paper and pencil questionnaires and tests, problem-solving tasks and perceptual types of apparatus are also used. Among the most ingenious of the latter has been tilting-room chair test (Goldstein & Blackman, 1977). In this test, the subjects sit in a chair that is suspended in a small room. Both the chair and the room may be tilted either left or right in varying degrees. In one version, the Room-Adjustment Test (RAT), the room is tilted 56 degrees and chair 22 degrees. There are eight trials; in four of these trials the room and chair are tilted in the same direction; in the other four they are tilted in opposite directions. The object of the test is to determine the degree of effectiveness with which the subject can direct the examiner to reorient the room to an upright position under these circumstances. In the Body Adjustment Test (BAT), the room remains tilted and the subject directs the examiner to move him or her to an up-right position. The degree to which the subjects succeed on these orientation tasks was originally used to assess an individual's ability at field articulation and later to assess an individual's degree of field independence-dependence.

The scores assigned an individual on the basis of performance on cognitive-style assessments are usually used to place the subject somewhere on a bipolar continuum whose poles represent opposing stylistic types, e.g., leveling-sharpening, scanning-focusing. The more the individual's score is oriented toward one pole or another, the more he or she is characterized as being typified by the particular cognitive style associated with that pole. In the case of some cognitive styles, however, an individual will be characterized as belonging to one of several cognitive style categories, according to the means by which questions were answered or problems solved. This category is presumed to identify the way that an individual characteristically perceives, thinks, solves problems, etc. An example of this is provided by conceptual styles tasks that categorize children as to whether they tend to be analytic, categorical, or relational in their thinking.

Though there has been disagreement on the issue, Kogan has suggested that cognitive styles can be classified on the basis of whether the results obtained are judgmental, i.e., have positive or negative implications attached to particular styles and their scores. Thus certain cognitive styles clearly suggest good or poor cognitive performance, e.g., Witkin's field dependence-independence continuum. Other cognitive styles, however, only indirectly imply cognitive strength or weakness, while still others appear to be truly stylistic, i.e., inputing neither cognitive strength nor weakness but rather suggesting different ways of thinking. Still other cognitive styles can be interpreted either in terms of cognitive strengths and weaknesses or in purely stylistic terms, depending on the circumstances of usage and interpretation.

While the study of cognitive styles began with adult populations, it gradually moved over to juvenile populations as well, including those of children with learning problems and handicaps. This has been more for research rather than diagnostic purposes. The two most popular of cognitive-style study approaches to schoolchildren and special education students are those of field independence dependence and conceptual tempo. Blackman and Goldstein (1982) have suggested that a major reason for their popularity is the easy availability of instruments to assess them. Another reason seems to be that they appear to be cognitive styles that may have particular relevance to school work.

There have been many studies suggesting that field-independent students are better and more self-dependent learners than field-dependent ones; that they are better decoders in reading than field-dependent students; and that they are better at math and science as well. Field-independent students have been found to do better in "discovery" types of learning situations; while field-dependent students are benefited by structured learning situations. Gifted children are more likely to be field independent than mentally retarded ones (Mann & Sabatino, 1985). Learning-disabled pupils are more likely to be field dependent than normal readers.

In respect to conceptual tempo, this cognitive-style dimension characterizes children on the basis of their placement on a reflection-impulsivity dimension, according to their performance on problem-solving tests, etc. As might be expected, reflective children are usually better students, while impulsive ones are more likely to read inaccurately and to manifest behavior problems.

While the research into cognitive styles has been very

active, and results are regularly found indicating that cognitive styles are significantly related to school and academic variables that are important to both normal and handicapped children, the sum and substance of this research does not appear to support a position that knowledge of a handicapped child's particular cognitive style, in and of itself, is particularly helpful in respect to predicting school achievement (Swanson, 1980) or in guiding day-to-day instruction or management. Socioeconomic and general cognitive factors play roles of far greater importance in the school lives of special education students. Indeed, many of the significant differences found in the school performances of special education students who differ in cognitive style appear to be the result of consequences of investigators confounding their variables.

The most popular variant or offshoot of cognitive styles currently are identified as learning styles based on objective imaging and EEG examinations. (Riding, Glass, Butler, Pleydell-Pearce, 1997). Since learning styles tend to be educationally oriented, they have received a great deal of attention in educational circles. Learning style constructs, which emphasize learning preferences rather than personality characteristics, have taken much of the attention away from other types of cognitive styles among researchers concerned with school and academic achievement.

REFERENCES

Blackman, S., & Goldstein, K. M. (1982). Cognitive styles and learning disabilities. *Journal of Learning Disabilities, 15,* 106–113.

Goldstein, K. M., & Blackman, S. (1977). *Cognitive styles: Five approaches to theory and research.* New York: Wiley.

Kane, M. (1984). Cognitive styles of thinking and learning. Part one. *Academic Therapy, 19,* 527–536.

Kogan, N. (1980). Cognitive styles and reading performance. *Bulletin of the Orton Society, 39,* 63–77.

Mann, L., & Sabatino, D. A. (1985). *Foundations of cognitive processes in remedial and special education.* Rockville, MD: Aspen.

Riding, R. J., Glass, A., Butler, S. R., & Pleydell-Pearce, C. W. (1997). Cognitive style and individual differences in EEG alpha during information processing. *Educational Psychology, 17,* 219–234.

Swanson, L. (1980). Cognitive style, locus of control, and school achievement in learning disabled females. *Journal of Clinical Psychology, 36,* 964-967.

EMILY WAHLEN
LESTER MANN
Hunter College

LEARNING STYLES
PERSONALITY TESTS

SPERRY, R.
SPLIT BRAIN RESEARCH
TEMPERAMENT

COLITIS

Ulcerative colitis is a chronic inflammatory disease of the colon (large intestine). It is a progressive disease, spreading to include part or all of the colon and rectum. It is characterized by alternating remissions and relapses. The disease is usually more severe in children than adults, carrying an increased risk of malignancy because of the greater severity and duration of the disease (Dixon & Walker, 1984). A disease closely related to ulcerative colitis is Crohn's disease, which involves the small intestine as well as the large. Symptomatology and progression in Crohn's closely resembles that in ulcerative colitis.

The cause of ulcerative colitis is unknown. Symptoms of the disease include diarrhea with blood and mucous, abdominal pain preceding defecation, anemia, and rectal urgency. Weight loss is apparent in some children owing to reduced caloric intake or to limitation of food eaten to avoid discomforts of the disease (Dixon & Walker, 1984).

Treatment of colitis varies with severity and extent of the disease. The goal of treatment for children is to bring about remission to allow normal growth and development. Medical therapy includes use of corticosteroids to control inflammation and sulfasalazine to control flare-ups. Undesirable side effects of the two precipitate cautious use with children. Corticosteroids interfere with growth, increase susceptibility to infection, and cause temporary alterations in physical appearance. Sulfasalazine can cause headaches, nausea, vomiting, anorexia, and rash.

If the disease does not respond to medical therapy, or if it involves complications, surgery is required. Part or all of the colon is removed and then resected together or attached to the abdominal wall. If attached to the abdominal wall, a stoma is formed to allow excretion of waste products into an external collecting apparatus. With surgery, the effects of the disease disappear.

Children and their families need a great deal of emotional support and understanding in dealing with the manifestations of the disease and the effects of treatment (Burke, Neigut, Kocoshis, & Chandra, 1994). Children need special understanding and encouragement when dealing with side effects of steroid treatment or adjusting to the use of an external collecting apparatus. Advances in development of collection apparatus now make it possible for most children to participate in many activities and sports. Most individuals with colitis live a normal life under prolonged medical care.

REFERENCES

Bokey, E. L., & Shell, R. (1985). *Stomal therapy: A guide for nurses, practitioners and patients*. Sydney, Australia: Pergamon.

Burke, P. M., Neigut, D., Kocoshis, P. R., & Chandra, R. (1994). Correlates of depress in new onset pediatric bowel disease. *Child Psychiatry and Human Development, 24,* 4, 275–283.

Dixon, M. L., & Walker, W. A. (1984). Ulcerative colitis and Crohn's disease. In S. S. Gellis & B. M. Kagan (Eds.), *Current pediatric therapy* (pp. 195–198). Philadelphia: Saunders.

Goodman, M. J., & Sparberg, M. (1978). *Ulcerative colitis*. New York: Wiley.

Goulston, S. J., & McGovern, V. J. (1981). *Fundamentals of colitis*. Oxford, England: Pergamon.

Hanauer, S. B. (1984). Ulcerative colitis. In R. E. Rakel (Ed.), *Conn's current therapy* (pp. 410–415). Philadelphia: Saunders.

CHRISTINE A. ESPIN
University of Minnesota

FAMILY RESPONSE TO A HANDICAPPED CHILD PHYSICAL HANDICAPS

COLLABORATION

See INCLUSION.

COLLABORATIVE PERINATAL PROJECT

The main purpose of the Collaborative Perinatal Project is to evaluate factors in pregnancy that may relate to cerebral palsy and other abnormalities of the central nervous system. The project is sponsored by the National Institute of Neurological and Communicative Disorders and Strokes. Over 50,000 pregnant women were recruited (from January 1959 to December 1965) for the largest prospective study of its kind. Although readers of the study are urged to regard conclusions as tentative, it is generally agreed that this massive undertaking adds substantially to what is known about the general epidemiology of birth defects.

Data collected at the 14 university-affiliated hospitals include information on the mother's social and medical background; coexisting diseases; complications of pregnancy; current drug/medication use; and previous use of drugs (extending beyond the mother's last menstrual period). Each participant was interviewed at least monthly throughout pregnancy, at scheduled intervals during the infant's first 2 years, and annually until the child reached 8 years. Records on each child until the age of 8 years include birth and developmental history, diseases, noted congenital defects, and information on siblings and father. Infants received daily examinations for the first 7 days of life (and weekly for prolonged postnatal hospitalizations), with an extensive, standard pediatric exam at age one. Of the mortality rate (4.4% or 2227 stillborn or died before age 4), 81% came to autopsy.

A tangential purpose of this project was the epidemiological investigation of the possible teratogenic role of drugs (or those drugs that cause malformations): in other words, the relationship between drugs taken during pregnancy and malformations in offspring. Although frequent hypotheses are suggested, only a few such relationships are accepted universally as causal. Potent teratogens (e.g., thalidomide) are identified relatively easily. Less potent drugs with less dramatic outcomes are equally important but more difficult to isolate and detect. The Collaborative Perinatal Project provided the opportunity to use a battery of epidemiological and statistical method to screen a variety of drugs against a variety of malformation outcomes.

The study (1) provided quantitative information, much not previously available, on relationships among birth defects; (2) confirmed and elaborated on, in quantitative terms, factors such as single umbilical artery and birth defects; (3) raised, in quantitative terms, hypotheses concerning risk factors, some previously suspected but without quantitative information and some not previously suspected; and (4) concluded that birth defects are rarely attributable to a single cause and that many malformation outcomes appear to have multiple risk factors that are interrelated.

Heinonen et al. (1977) were commissioned by the National Institutes of Health to document all findings. Their text contains detailed information on methods, malformations, drugs used, etc. The data from the project continue to be analyzed (Friedman, Granick, Bransfield & Kreisher, 1995), and debated (James, 1996).

REFERENCE

Friedman, H. S., Granick, S., Bransfield, S., & Kreisher, C. (1995). Gender difference in early life risk factors for substance use/abuse: A Study of an African-American Sample. *American Journal of Drug & Alcohol Abuse, 21,* 4, 511–531.

Heinonen, O. P., Slone, D., & Shapiro, J. (1977). *Birth defects and drugs in pregnancy*. Littleton, MA: Publishing Sciences Group.

James, W. .H. (1996). Debate and argument: The sex ratio of the sibs of neurodevelopmentally disordered children. *Journal of Child Psychology & Psychiatry & Allied Disciplines, 37,* 5, 619.

C. MILDRED TASHMAN
College of St. Rose

CONGENITAL DISORDERS
LOW BIRTH WEIGHT INFANTS
PREMATURITY/PRETERM

COLLEGE PROGRAMS FOR DISABLED COLLEGE STUDENTS

Following the end of World War II, the majority of colleges and universities in the United States became more sensitive to the needs of students who would have been financially disabled without the original G.I. bill. This same sensitivity, however, on the part of colleges and universities for those who were physically, socially, and/or academically handicapped did not manifest itself to any major degree until the 1970s.

In April 1978 the Association on Handicapped Student Service Programs, in Post-Secondary Education (AHSSPPE) came into existence. This organization, along with others, provided professional support for full implementation of the Architectural Barriers Act of 1968 as upgraded and expanded on by Section 504 of the Vocational Rehabilitation Act of 1973, which became operational in April of 1977. The net effect of this act was to ensure the access and use of public schools (elementary through college) by the physically disabled through assurance that the schools would be constructed to accommodate the handicapped person.

Similarly, by the late 1970s a few colleges and universities began formal programs to serve college-bound students who had academic deficits resulting from either some innate and formal learning (language) disability and/or environmentally induced one. Those higher education institutions having programs for this population were identified in part by research projects sponsored by the National Association of College Admission Counselors (NACAC) (Mangrum, 1984). Two agencies that contributed to the development of the NACAC directory of college programs were the Post Secondary School Committee of the Association for Children with Learning Disabilities (ACLD) and the Loyola Academy of Wilmette, Illinois. Other references that identify colleges and universities having academic support services are Liscio's *A Guide to Colleges for Learning Disabled Students*; Mangrum and Strichart's *College and the Learning Disabled Student*; the *FCLD's Guide for Parents of Children with Learning Disabilities*; and *Peterson's Guide to Colleges with Programs for Learning Disabled Students*. These references suggest that the prospective user ask certain questions, as identified by Liscio (1984):

1. Is there a special program for learning-disabled students?
2. How many full-time learning-disabled students are enrolled in the program?
3. Is there a brochure or written description of the program available?
4. Do learning-disabled students in special programs take regular college courses?
5. Are special courses required of learning-disabled students? Do they carry college credit? Can credit be used toward graduation?
6. Are there additional tuition or fee requirements for learning-disabled students? (p. 12)

Additionally, the prospective users of these references and others like them, following a personal on-site examination of the institution and its services as listed, will probably determine that the primary thrust or intent of the institution's services falls into one of two categories: (1) assistance and support that is not necessarily remedial, and (2) assistance and support that is intended to be remedial. The former is specifically characterized by the use of books on tape (the same service used by blind students); oral presentations instead of written exams; cassette tapes in lieu of written papers; readers for reading textbooks and exams; and notetakers. These services allow the language-handicapped student to cope and to graduate in spite of unremediated reading and spelling deficits.

The college-aged learning-disabled student who is looking for a school to attend will find that the majority of two- and four-year higher education institutions (both public and private) that offer support services will be of the type just depicted; for example, those that provide assistance and support that is not necessarily intended to be remedial. The student who wishes to become language independent, academically as well as socially, might want to consider the other major type of service.

Those institutions that intend to remediate the student's language handicap and his or her accompanying social and psychological deficits, will be characterized by instruction that is designed to remediate the student's reading, spelling, written expression, and arithmetic deficits. The kind of instruction that would be most commonly used would directly reteach the basic or requisite information that must be known to read, spell, write, and carry out mathematical operations. Other probable aspects of this second service posture would be the use of tutors who have been trained to carry out direct remediation of the students academic deficits and formal support programs that deal directly with the student's social habilitation and psychological needs. Both types of schools offer their learning-disabled students the opportunity to take exams in a private setting without time constraints; use tape recorders to record lectures; take a reduced load as necessary; and partake in the institution's traditional student support services. Beyond the traditional academic assistance and/or remediation, most institutions of higher learning also offer counseling and testing support services.

REFERENCES

The FCLD guide for parents of children with learning disabilities. (1984). New York: Foundation for Children with Learning Disabilities.

Kavale, K., & Forness, S. (1985). *The science of learning disabilities*. San Diego, CA: College Hill.

Liscio, M. A. (1984). *A guide to colleges for learning disabled students*. Orlando, FL: Academic.

Mangrum, C. T., & Strichart, S. S. (1984). *College and the learning disabled student*. Orlando, FL: Grune & Stratton.

Nash, R. T. (1985). Remediation courses, Project Success, University of Wisconsin-Oshkosh. Unpublished raw data.

Peterson's guide to colleges with programs for learning disabled students. (1985). Princeton, NJ: Peterson's Guide.

ROBERT T. NASH
*University of Wisconsin
at Oshkosh*

CONTINUING EDUCATION FOR THE HANDICAPPED

COLOR BLINDNESS

The inability to perceive or discriminate colors is known as color blindness. There are four main types of color blindness, each containing a number of subtypes. The most rare type is known as *achromotopsia*. In this condition, the subject sees no color; everything is perceived as black, white, or shades of gray. This condition can result from a degenerative process. In the absence of such pathology, the condition is due to an autosomal recessive gene and is extremely rare.

The more common types of color vision disturbances are closely related to retinal physiology, specifically, to the structure and function of the cones. Since the cones are not evenly distributed in the retina, color vision in the visual field is somewhat variable. Color perception is not possible in the periphery of the visual field and diminishes as the object moves away from the point of fixation (Wald, 1968). The perception of color is dependent on not only the presence of different types of cone cells, but of complex chemical pigments thought to respond selectively to the different wavelengths of light.

Protanopia refers to the condition in which the individual has difficulty in distinguishing red. *Deuteranopia* is the condition in which the individual has difficulty in distinguishing green. *Tritanopia* is the condition in which the individual cannot distinguish blue; it is a severe and rare form of colorblindness, affecting less than .1% of the population. Tritanopia is considered to be an autosomal dominant trait.

Red-green color disturbances occur in both protanopia and deuteranopia. The former is more severe and less common than the latter. Both are sex-linked (X) recessive, traits, explaining their nearly exclusive presence in males. The prevalence of protanopia is about 1:100; deuteranopia about 1:20 (Linksz, 1964).

Determination of the condition is easily made using pseudoisochromatic plates (Isihara test) that present colored patterns or numbers to the individual. The normal person sees one pattern or number; those with color disturbances see the stimulus differently (Thuline, 1972).

Color blindness is not generally considered to be a significant handicap. Some authors (Cooley, 1977) feel that the tests are far too sensitive and that some persons have been needlessly denied employment. The classroom teacher, especially in the early grades, should expect to find at least one color-blind male in the classroom. Tasks involving color discrimination must be eliminated. The literature is replete with retinal changes owed to phenothiazine (Mellaril, Thorazine) administration (Apt, 1960; Weekly et al., 1960). Color vision anomalies may occur if a youngster is under phenothiazine therapy.

REFERENCES

Apt, R. (1960). Complications of phenothiazine tranquilizers ocular side effects. *Survey Ophthalmology, 5,* 550.

Cooley, D. (Ed.). (1977). *Family medical guide*. New York: Better Homes and Gardens.

Linksz, A. (1964). *An essay on color vision and clinical color vision tests*. New York: Grune & Stratton.

Thuline, H. (1972). Color blindness in children: The importance and feasibility of early recognition, *Clinical Pediatrics, 11*(5), 295–299.

Wald, G. (1968). The receptors of human color vision. *Science Magazine, 145,* 1007.

Weekly, R., Potts, A., Rebotem, J., & May, R. (1960). Pigmentary retinopathy in patients receiving high doses of a new phenothiazene. *Archives of Ophthalmology, 64,* 65.

JOHN E. PORCELLA
Rhinebeck Country School

**MELLARIL
THORAZINE
VISUAL PERCEPTION AND DISCRIMINATION
VISUALLY IMPAIRED**

COMMUNICATION AIDS, ELECTRONIC

See ELECTRONIC COMMUNICATION AIDS.

COMMUNICATION BOARDS

Communication boards are simple, nonelectronic, augmentative communication systems used by nonspeaking persons. They are usually made individually according to the skills and needs of the nonspeaking user. The advantages of communication boards are their flexibility and low cost. Any symbol system ranging from objects and pictures to written alphabet letters can be used as message symbols. The communication board can be accessed by direct selection, through scanning, or by an encoding process. As the nonspeaking person's skills change over time, the communication board can be easily adapted to reflect those changes.

The major disadvantage of communication boards is the lack of spoken or written output from the system. The listener who interacts with a nonspeaking communication board user must be able to physically see the communication board to receive a message. For long messages, the listener must remember each symbol selected and mentally sequence the symbols back together to understand the message. Communication boards are used frequently with children and adults who have limited vocabularies. In addition, they are often used as a secondary backup communication device for nonspeaking persons who rely primarily on sophisticated electronic augmentative systems.

REFERENCES

Goossens', C., Crain, S. S., & Elder, P. S. (1995). *Engineering the preschool environment for interactive symbolic communication*. Birmingham, AL: Southeast Augmentative Communication Conference Publications.

Musselwhite, C. R., & St. Louis, K. O. (1982). *Communication programming for the severely handicapped: Vocal and non-vocal strategies*. Houston, TX: College-Hill.

SHARON GLENNEN
Pennsylvania State University
First edition

SHEELA STUART
George Washington University
Second edition

AUGMENTATIVE COMMUNICATION DEVICES
COMPUTER USE WITH THE HANDICAPPED
ROBOTICS

COMMUNICATION DISORDERS

Communication disorders are defined as an observed disturbance in the normal speech, language, or hearing processes as determined by (1) objective signs (i.e., measurable characteristics that can be observed by other persons), (2) social signs (i.e., failing to understand a speaker's meaning and responding inappropriately resulting in mu-

tual embarrassment), and (3) personal signs (i.e., a person's reactions to a self-perceived disorder) (Plante & Beeson, 1999). Communication disorders may involve the processes of listening, speaking, reading, writing, and thinking. The American Speech-Language-Hearing Association (ASHA) estimates that about 10% of the population in the United States (approximately 25 million individuals of all ages) has some form of communication disorder involving speech, language, and/or hearing (Shames, Wiig, & Secord, 1994). Severity of communication disorders ranges from mild to severe/profound across different levels of communication (prelinguistic, sounds and letters, words, phrases and sentences, oral and literate discourse [conversation, narration, exposition] and discourse plus [nonliteral language, mathlanguage (including time and money), computer language, foreign language, and career or employment language]). Communication disorders are categorized as impairment (abnormality of structure or function at the organ level), disability (functional consequences of an impairment), or handicap (social consequences of impairment or disability) (Gelfer, 1996).

Communication disorders may be caused by (1) physical conditions (e.g., oral facial anomalies; cerebral palsy), (2) physiological conditions (e.g., neurological impairment), (3) psychological conditions (e.g., emotional/behavioral disorders such as neuroses and psychoses; learning, motivation), or (4) social conditions (e.g., lack of stimulation or communicative interaction with other humans) (Boone & Plante, 1993; Pressley & McCormick, 1995). Communication disorders affect not only the individuals who have the disorder, but others (family, peers, caregivers, colleagues) with whom the individuals need to communicate.

Because the purposes of communication are to regulate social interactions or interpersonal functions, as well as to transmit scientific or logically based knowledge and skills, communication disorders have a far-reaching effect on society. Communication rules and use vary from culture to culture and, therefore, differentiation is made among communication differences, communication delays, and communication disorders. It is generally recognized that to progress through life, humans must be able to understand and use, with some degree of competence, the cognitive, linguistic, and contextual conventions associated with oral, literate, and manually coded communication systems.

Speech Disorders

Speech disorders are variations from commonly used acoustic characteristics of the utterances one makes, rather than of the meaning of the utterances (Hegde, 1995; Silverman, 1995). Speech disorders include articulation (the process of producing vowels and consonants that result in meaningful language morphemes, words, phrases, sentences, and discourse), stuttering (the interruption of the flow of speech, characterized by sound or word repetitions, prolongations, and blocking of sound), and voice (production of the frequency and intensity of speech sounds that is atypical of sex, physical maturity, and age resulting in disorders of phonation and resonance). Associated features of speech disorders may be rate of speaking (too fast or too slow for communicative purposes) and dysphagia (disordered swallowing because of inflammation, compression, paralysis, weakness, or hypertonicity of the esophagus).

Language Disorders

Language disorders involve the impaired ability to receive, process, and use auditory, visual, and haptic (touch and movement) symbols in order to negotiate meaning for social interaction and/or academic/professional communication learning. Language disorders may involve nonverbal symbols or verbal language (phonologic, semantic, syntactic, morphologic, and pragmatic linguistic rule systems). Language disorders are often classified as receptive (watching, listening, reading), expressive (moving/gesturing, speaking, writing), or a combination of receptive and expressive (Palmer & Yantis, 1990). Language disorders include the problems associated with understanding and use of oral-aural language, braille, and manually coded communication systems (Nelson, 1998).

Auditory language disorders include problems making sense of speech sounds, single words, phrases, sentences, thoughts, concepts, and ideas. Visual language disorders include problems making sense of the nonverbal dimensions of communication that are critical in the pragmatic dimensions of communication (i.e., who can communicate what, with whom, how, when, where, and why), as well as decoding and encoding the graphemic and geometric visual symbols used for Augmentative/Alternative Communication (AAC) systems, reading, writing, mathematics, and the physical and technological sciences. Haptic language disorders include problems receiving, interpreting, and using nonverbal symbols involved in pragmatics, the linguistic symbols and motor acts associated with cursive and manuscript writing, and with specialized systems such as braille and manually-coded communication.

Language disorders and learning disabilities are integrally related. Preschool-aged children with a diagnosed language disorder (learning to communicate) will likely encounter problems with academic language (communicating to learn) when they enter a formal education system. Although the underlying problem is the encoding and decoding of symbols (language disorder), the disorder may be termed a learning disability because of the problems encountered learning academic material. The preferred term is language-learning disorder (Gelfer, 1996; Nelson, 1998; Plante & Beeson, 1999). Because individuals do not outgrow language-learning disorders, they continue to encounter social or academic problems as adults. The communication-learning deficits that are evident at the adult level are referred to as adaptive communication-learning disorders (Weller, Crelly, Watteyne, & Herbert, 1992).

Hearing Disorders

Hearing disorders stem from problems within the auditory system. Although this is usually associated with the ear, it may also be located in the areas of the peripheral and central nervous system where the perception of word meanings and associations occur. Individuals with ear infections or allergy/cold related symptoms may have temporary or chronic problems with hearing. Hearing impairments may slowly develop with advancing age. Irreversible impairment can occur following unusual levels of noise exposure, or from ototoxic drugs. Hearing impairments can easily lead to serious difficulties in the ability to perceive and understand the speech and language of others, resulting in speech and/or language disorders (Gelfer, 1996; Minifie, 1994; Plante & Beeson, 1999).

Early identification and intervention are important to maximize the successful management of both individuals with communication disorders and their families. Communication disorders should be assessed and treated by speech-language pathologists and audiologists who hold state licensure or who hold the certificate of clinical competence in speech-language pathology (CCC-SLP) or audiology (CCC-A) from the American Speech-Language-Hearing Association (ASHA). Speech-language pathologists and audiologists work in schools, hospitals, rehabilitation centers, long-term care facilities, through contract health care companies, and in private practice (Boone & Plante, 1993; Gelfer, 1996; Hegde, 1995; Minifie, 1994; Palmer & Yantis, 1990; Shames et al., 1994; Silverman, 1995).

The American Speech-Language-Hearing Association (ASHA) promotes aggressive prevention practices: primary (e.g., prenatal care to prevent a disorder from occurring), secondary (e.g., early identification and intervention to eliminate or minimize the effects of a disorder) and tertiary (decrease the possibility of further problems occurring because of an existing disorder, such as aspiration pneumonia related to dysphagia) (Plante & Beeson, 1999). The American Speech-Language-Hearing Association provides information through print and broadcast media. Contact can be made at: 10801 Rockville Pike, Rockville, MD 20852; (301) 897-5700 voice or TTY; FAX (301) 571-0481; or on the internet at http://www.asha.org/.

REFERENCES

Boone, D. R., & Plante, E. (1993). *Human communication and its disorders* (2nd ed.). Englewood Cliffs, NJ: Prentice Hall.

Gelfer, M. P. (1996). *Survey of communication disorders: A social and behavioral perspective*. New York: The McGraw-Hill Companies, Inc.

Hegde, M. N. (1995). *Introduction to communicative disorders* (2nd ed.). Austin, TX: Pro-Ed.

Minifie, F. D. (Ed.). (1994). *Introduction to communication sciences and disorders*. San Diego: Singular Publishing Group.

Nelson, N. W. (1998). *Childhood language disorders in context: Infancy through adolescence* (2nd ed.). Boston: Allyn and Bacon.

Palmer, J. M., & Yantis, P. A. (1990). *Survey of communication disorders*. Baltimore: Williams & Wilkins.

Plante, E., & Beeson, P. M. (1999). *Communication and communication disorders: A clinical introduction*. Boston: Allyn & Bacon.

Pressley, M., & McCormick, C. B. (1995). *Advanced educational psychology: For educators, researchers, and policymakers*. New York: HarperCollins.

Shames, G. H., Wiig, E. H., & Secord, W. A. (1994). *Human communication disorders: An introduction* (4th ed.). New York: Merrill/Macmillan College Publishing Co.

Silverman, F. H. (1995). *Speech, language, & hearing disorders*. Boston: Allyn & Bacon.

Weller, C., Crelly, C., Watteyne, L., & Herbert, M. (1992). *Adaptive language disorders of young adults with learning disabilities*. San Diego: Singular Publishing Group.

Stephen S. Farmer
New Mexico State University

APHASIA
AUDIOLOGY
AUDITORY ABNORMALITIES
LANGUAGE DEFICIENCIES AND DEFICITS
LANGUAGE DISORDERS
LANGUAGE DISORDERS, EXPRESSIVE
SPEECH AND LANGUAGE DISORDERS

COMMUNICATION METHODS IN SPECIAL EDUCATION, ALTERNATIVE

See ALTERNATIVE COMMUNICATION METHODS IN SPECIAL EDUCATION.

COMMUNICATION SPECIALIST

A communication specialist is any one of a number of professionals who deal with aspects of both normal and disordered human communication. Such an individual may have expertise in communication theory, small group communication, organizational communication, or rhetoric. This individual may call himself or herself a linguist, a psycholinguist, a sociolinguist, a cultural linguist, or a rhetorician. The specialist is concerned with the influence of such diverse disciplines as linguistics, psychology, and sociology on human communication in general and language and speech in particular. In addition, these professionals study the development of normal communication theories and processes.

The study of disordered communication can also be considered in the realm of the communication specialist. The individual typically has expertise in communication disorders, education of the hearing impaired, or neurolinguistics. Speech and language disorders in children and adults can be studied from an organic (anatomic and physiologic) or functional (psychological, learning) perspective. The specialist in disordered communication may be concerned with such problems as language delay in children from multiple articulation errors or delay in (or loss of) the acquisition of morphologic, syntactic, or semantic rules of language. The communication specialist will also be concerned with language disorders owed to neurologic factors (e.g., brain damage).

Harvey R. Gilbert
Pennsylvania State University

COMMUNICATION DISORDERS
SPEECH AND LANGUAGE HANDICAPS
SPEECH LANGUAGE PATHOLOGIST

COMMUNITY-BASED INSTRUCTION

Community-based instruction refers to the opportunity for students to have direct interaction with resources in the community while participating in educational programs. With the current emphasis on education in the least restrictive environment for all students with handicaps, community-based instruction has been implemented in many special education programs, especially in those that serve students with moderate to severe handicaps. For students with moderate and severe handicaps to perform adequately in normalized postschool environments, skills must be taught in locations where they will naturally occur (Brown et al., 1983). Indeed, community-based instruction is a more powerful predictor of education/adaptive gains than intelligence quotient, level of ambulation, or presence of behavior problems (McDonnell, 1993).

Community-based instruction may be implemented using a number of models (Brown et al., 1983). These include consecutive instruction, whereby skills are taught in a simulated setting within the school facility until a certain skill level is reached; instruction in nonschool settings then follows. Concurrent instruction can occur where instruction takes place in both school and nonschool settings at daily or weekly intervals. Nonschool instruction can be implemented with direct training in nonschool (community) settings only students must have current access or have contact with the setting in the future.

Community-based instruction may involve training in a number of areas. Ordering, purchasing, and eating food in a restaurant may be taught. Use of consumer services such as public transportation, banks, and laundromats may be emphasized during training. Recreation skills may be taught in natural community sites including parks, community gymnasiums, aerobics/fitness centers, and video arcades. Students may be taught to use stores and shops such as grocery stores, pharmacies, and department stores. Vocational skills may be taught in community vocational sites. Selection of community-based training sites can be determined by examining the current and future needs of particular students in community-referenced activities (Wehman, Renzaglia, & Bates, 1985). Certain skills such as street crossing, appropriate social interaction with nonhandicapped peers and adults, and nonvocal or vocal communication may be taught in more than one community-based training activity.

A number of advantages in using community-based instruction with students who have moderate to severe handicaps have been cited by professionals in the field of special education. If training takes place in heterogeneous, nonschool environments, student adaptive functioning will be more likely in current and subsequent community settings. Transfer and generalization of community skills will be more likely to occur when taught in natural rather than simulated settings (Brown et al., 1979; Brown et al., 1976; Council for Exceptional Children, 1990). In addition, handicapped students participating in community-based instruction will have frequent access to nonhandicapped peers who may serve as role models. In turn, the awareness by nonhandicapped people of their peers with handicaps will be enhanced. This will enable the nonhandicapped peers to be cognizant of the abilities of individuals with handicaps, thus promoting a smoother transition to postschool environments on the part of handicapped individuals. Parent and teacher expectations of student abilities may be increased when community-based instruction occurs. Finally, the opportunity for students to sample the reinforcing aspects of activities in the community can be an advantage in achieving acquisition of functional skills (Wehman & Hill, 1982; Wehman et al., 1985).

A number of factors need to be taken into account when considering community-based instruction. These include staffing, transportation, scheduling, costs, necessary curriculum changes, and modifications for severely physical handicapped students (Hamre-Nietupski et al., 1982). Considerations such as these require careful planning on the part of teachers and administrators to facilitate adequate community-based programming.

REFERENCES

Brown, L., Branston, M. B., Hamre-Nietupski, S., Pumpian, I., Certo, N., & Gruenwald, L. (1979). A strategy for developing chronological age-appropriate and functional curricular content for severely handicapped adolescents and young adults. *Journal of Special Education, 13,* 81–90.

Brown, L., Nietupski, M., & Hamre-Nietupski, S. (1976). Criterion of ultimate functioning. In M. A. Thomas (Ed.), *Hey, don't forget me!* Reston, VA: Council for Exceptional Children.

Brown, L., Nisbet, J., Ford, A., Sweet, M., Shiraga, B., York, J., & Loomis, R. (1983). The critical need for nonschool instruction in educational programs for severely handicapped students. *Journal of the Association for Persons with Severe Handicaps, 8*(3), 71–77.

Council for Exceptional Children (1990). Designing Community-based instruction. Research brief for teachers. Reston, VA: Author.

Hamre-Nietupski, S., Nietupski, J., Bates, P., & Maurer, S. (1982). Implementing a community-based educational model for moderately and severely handicapped students: Common problems and suggested solutions. *Journal of the Association for Persons with Severe Handicaps, 7*(4), 38–43.

McDonnell, J. (1993). Impact of Community-based instruction on the development of adaptive behavior of Secondary-Level students with mental retardation. *American Journal on Mental Retardation, 97,* 5, 575–584.

Wehman, P., & Hill, J. (1982). Preparing severely handicapped youth for less restrictive environments. *Journal of the Association for Persons with Severe Handicaps, 7*(1), 33–39.

Wehman, P., Renzaglia, A., & Bates, P. (1985). *Functional living skills for moderately and severely handicapped individuals.* Austin, TX: Pro-Ed.

CORNELIA LIVELY
University of Illinois

COMPETENCY EDUCATION
NON-SHELTERED EMPLOYMENT
SHELTERED WORKSHOPS
VOCATIONAL TRAINING OF HANDICAPPED

COMMUNITY-BASED JOB TRAINING FOR STUDENTS WITH AUTISM AND DEVELOPMENTAL DISABILITIES

In the past few years, the need to better prepare persons with disabilities for life after high school has become recognized by federal and local agencies and has been well documented in the professional literature. Now the development of programs to facilitate the transition from school to adult living has received substantial funding and attention. A major component of this transition movement involves vocational preparation of handicapped students.

Traditionally, vocational training efforts have centered on nonhandicapped and mildly handicapped students, with little or no related instruction being provided to persons having more severe handicaps. In fact, sheltered workshops and day treatment centers have served as the primary vehicles for the delivery of adult services for persons who are developmentally disabled, with few other placement alternatives (Schutz & Rusch, 1982). However, as generations of students served by the Individuals with Disabilities Education Act (IDEA) have begun to graduate from school, it has become clear that additional educational and vocational programs are required so that these individuals may also become employed.

The purpose of community-based job training is to prepare students for employment through the provision of instruction in actual job tasks at work sites within the local community. Research has shown that, because students with developmental disabilities often have difficulty transferring skills learned in one situation to another (Koegel, Rincover, & Egel, 1982), it is advantageous to assess and to teach job skills in the settings in which they will ultimately have to be performed (Berkell, 1985; Black & Langone, 1995). Through the provision of vocational training in job sites within the community, teachers can facilitate student mastery of specific job skills, as well as the development of interpersonal job-related skills required to maintain various employment positions.

There are five major phases involved in community-based job training: (1) student evaluation, (2) job development, (3) instruction at the work site, (4) supervision reduction, and (5) client follow-up. Each of these phases must be addressed by the vocational trainer regardless of the student's ability level.

Vocational training should begin with an assessment of a person's interests and aptitudes for different jobs. This involves the realistic assessment of learner needs and characteristics. Many of the vocational evaluation instruments commonly used by special educators and vocational rehabilitation counselors are useful for assessing mildly and moderately handicapped youths, but they provide less useful information when used with individuals with severe learning problems. For persons with developmental disabilities, assessment is most appropriately conducted through on-the-job evaluation, work samples, and interview techniques.

Vocational evaluation is both a student-centered and work-related assessment process. Prior to beginning a community-based job training program, the teacher must survey the local job market to become aware of the types of jobs available and plan the curriculum to prepare students for these types of work.

In order to match the student to a particular job, the evaluator requires information not only about student preferences, abilities, and behaviors, but also about the demands of the job and the behavioral characteristics required of workers on the job. Job analysis is the systematic study of an occupation in terms of what the worker does in relation to data, people, and things; the methodology and techniques employed; the machines, tools, equipment, and work aids used; the materials, products, subject matter, or services that result; and the traits required of the worker (McCray, 1982). This procedure is especially useful as a means of identifying essential job tasks; it provides much instructionally relevant information.

A comprehensive approach to vocational preparation involves both job skill development and the development of work-related skills. Job skills training generally focuses on use of equipment, production rate, and quality of the product produced. Work-related behaviors include self-care and grooming, communication skills, interpersonal social skills, leisure skills for break times, and travel skills.

Direct skill training and ongoing assessment are the major instructional requirements of a community-based job training program (Rusch & Mithaug, 1980). Instruction that is systematic and behavioral in nature tends to be most effective in vocational training.

The type and amount of supervision required by a student at a work site is often contingent on the nature of the handicapping condition and the complexity of the job task. Some autistic and developmentally disabled students may need ongoing supervision for an indefinite period of time, while others will require only a minimum of supervision following their initial training.

One key to increasing independence on the job is to fade, or reduce, supervision and assistance to the student as soon as possible in order to avoid the development of dependency on the teacher. Rotating supervisors during the training sessions is also beneficial in reducing such dependency, as well as in increasing generalization from the teacher to an actual job supervisor.

In contrast to job training programs for mildly handicapped persons, students with autism and developmental disabilities may require systematically planned job retention and follow-up services for many years following graduation from school. Methods of determining follow-up intervention strategies include periodic employee evaluations and progress reports, parent/guardian questionnaires, on-site visits, and telephone contacts with employers and family members or group home staff (Moon, Goodall, Barcus, & Brooke, 1985).

A problem or potential problem may be discovered through the use of such ongoing follow-up assessment procedures. When the client is in a new job situation, it is also helpful to request that the employer contact the job trainer with any concerns as soon as they arise. As the client and the employer become more comfortable with each other, the need for contact with the job trainer will become less frequent.

Preparation of students with developmental disabilities for productive employment has become a major educational concern. Issues regarding the selection of instructional locations and the types of assessment and training methods used in vocational preparation programs have received increased attention in the past decade. Research has shown that, because students with autism and developmental disabilities often have difficulty in transferring skills learned from one situation to another, it is advantageous to teach job skills in community-based settings rather than in the classroom even though inclusive educational settings may support generalization (Bang & Lamb, 1997). By providing vocational training in the job sites within the community, teachers can help students to master the necessary competencies for specific jobs and to learn job-related skills necessary to maintain various employment positions.

REFERENCES

Bang, Myong-Ye, & Lamb, P. (1997). *Impacts of an inclusive school-to-work program*. Paper presented at the Annual Convention of the Council for Exceptional Children, Salt Lake City, UT, April 9–13.

Black, R. S., & Langone, J. (1995). *Generalization of work-related social behavior for persons with mental retardation*. Paper presented at the Annual International Conference of the Division on Cancer Development and Transition. Raleigh, NC, October 19–21.

Koegel, R. L., Rincover, A., & Egel, A. I. (1982). *Educating and understanding autistic children*. San Diego, CA: College Hill.

Moon, S., Goodall, P., Barcus, M., & Brooke, V. (Eds.). (1985). *The supported work model of competitive employment for citizens with severe handicaps: A guide for job trainers*. Richmond, VA: Rehabilitation and Training Center, Virginia Commonwealth University.

Rusch, F. R., & Mithaug, D. E. (1980). *Vocational training for mentally retarded adults: A behavior analytic approach*. Champaign, IL: Research.

Schutz, R. P., & Rusch, F. R. (1982). Competitive employment: Toward employment integration for mentally retarded persons. In K. P. Lynch, W. E. Kiernan, & J. A. Stark (Eds.), *Prevocational and vocational education for special needs youth: A blueprint for the 1980's* (pp. 133–160). Baltimore, MD: Brookes.

Stodden, R. A., Casale, J., & Schwartz, S. E. (1977). Work evaluation and the mentally retarded: Review and recommendations. *Mental Retardation, 15,* 25–27.

Dianne E. Berkell
C.W. Post Campus, Long Island University

SHELTERED WORKSHOPS
UNEMPLOYMENT OF THE HANDICAPPED
VOCATIONAL REHABILITATION

COMMUNITY-BASED SERVICES

The concept of normalization has led to the current trend of serving individuals who might have been institutionalized in the community. These handicapped individuals must be provided with support services to help them successfully adjust to community life. To achieve the goal of normalization, the handicapped should be involved in developmental activities that are closely associated with those of nonhandicapped individuals. These activities should center around integration into the normal life of the community. To the maximum extent possible, each handicapped individual's developmental activities should focus on the following life cycle. During infancy and early childhood, skill development should be related to sensorimotor skills, communication, self-help, and socialization. During the stages of childhood and early adolescence, there should be application of basic academic skills in daily life activities; application of appropriate reasoning and judgment in mastery of the environment; and participation in interpersonal relationships. During late adolescence and adulthood, vocational and social activities should be the major areas of focus (Grossman, 1977). Intagliata, Kraus, and Willer (1980) conducted a study to determine the impact of deinstitutionalization on the community-based service system. Basic observations reported in this study include the following:

Agencies served a large portion of formerly institutionalized individuals

Agencies served individuals with low intellectual levels

Formerly institutionalized individuals required needed services to be more intensive

Special programs were needed to provide appropriate services for the lower functioning individuals

Pollard, Hall, & Kiernan (1979) state that there are many services available to the handicapped from various separate systems such as health, education, rehabilitation, recreation, employment, and housing. However, when these systems are working separately, there is little chance for them to solve the varied problems of the handicapped. There is a great need for these human services to work together to provide comprehensive community services (Pires, 1992). According to Schalock (1985), comprehensive community-based services for the handicapped include community living alternatives, habilitation programs, and support programs. Community living alternatives range from the highest level of independence, independent living, to congregate living, home care, supervised living, staffed apartments, and group homes, to the lowest level of independence, community institutional facilities. The habilitation programs in education range from the highest level of community integration, mainstreamed classes in public schools, to resource rooms, day training programs, and residential programs, to the lowest level of community integration, homebound instruction. The habilitation programs in employment range from the highest level of productivity, competitive employment, to transitional employment, sheltered workshop, and work activity, to the lowest level of activity, day training programs. The last category of comprehensive community services, support services, includes health and mental health care, legal services, home assistance (respite care), early identification/intervention, and transportation. In addition, the importance of the following points in designing and providing community living and habilitation alternatives are crucial:

Natural environments are the preferred service settings

Generic services should be used as much as possible

Assistance to the client should be provided only at the level actually needed to promote independence and self-sufficiency

Training should focus on increasing the client's independence, productivity, and community integration

Everyone has potential for growth regardless of his or her current functioning level (Schalock, 1985 p. 38).

Scheerenberger (1981) conducted a study of all superintendents of public residential facilities throughout the United States. All superintendents completed the questionnaire. The results indicated that the community variables that resulted in problems causing community placement failures included inadequacies in appropriate living settings, behavioral management programs, specialized services, and adult programs. Community services for the mildly and moderately retarded that were considered to be effective were transportation, medical services, educational opportunities, and advocacy. On the other hand, these same services for the severely and profoundly retarded were found to be less than adequate.

REFERENCES

Grossman, H. J. (Ed.). (1977). *Manual on terminology and classification in mental retardation* (Special Publication No. 2). Washington, DC: American Association on Mental Deficiency.

Intagliata, J., Kraus, S., & Willer, B. (1980). The impact of deinstitutionalization on a community-based service system. *Mental Retardation, 18,* 302–308.

Pires, S. (1992). *Issues related to community-based service delivery for children and adolescents with mental illness and their families*. Washington, DC: Georgetown University Child Development Center.

Pollard, A., Hall, H., & Kiernan, C. (1979). Community services planning. In P. R. Magrab & J. O. Elder (Eds.), *Planning services to handicapped persons: Community, education, health.* Baltimore, MD: Brookes.

Schalock, R. L. (1985). Comprehensive community services: A plea for interagency collaboration. In R. H. Bruininks & K. C. Lakin (Eds.), *Living and learning in the least restrictive environment.* Baltimore, MD: Brookes.

Scheerenberger, R. C. (1981). Deinstitutionalization: Trends and difficulties. In R. H. Bruininks, C. E. Meyers, B. B. Sigford, & K. C. Lakin (Eds.), *Deinstitutionalization and community adjustment of mentally retarded people.* Washington, DC: American Association on Mental Deficiency.

JANICE HARPER
*North Carolina Central
University*

DEINSTITUTIONALIZATION
NORMALIZATION
REHABILITATION

COMMUNITY PLACEMENT

The term community placement is generally used to denote those living, working, and recreational/leisure arrangements found in community environments as opposed to institutions. It refers to those environments in which persons with disabilities work, live, and recreate within a community. Community placement has received increased attention as the most appropriate and desirable treatment setting for persons with disabilities (Lakin et al., 1982; Prouty & Lakin, 1997; Larson & Lakin, 1991). As early as 1969 Wolfensberger stressed the importance of community services and facilities as a viable alternative to institutionalization. Others quickly recommended that such a movement be guided by the principle of normalization (Wolfensberger, 1972). The deinstitutionalization movement has created a need for a variety of community placement options. Community placement not only permits easier access to those experiences that lead to a more normal lifestyle, but also may sensitize nonhandicapped persons to those with handicapping conditions.

State-of-the-art community placement facilities share several common aspects. They are community-based, small in size, supervised by a social or private agency, and based on the principles of normalization and human management (Mamula & Newman, 1973). Training to allow persons increased access to, and participation in, existing community activities is a desirable characteristic. The physical location of the community placement should facilitate access to all community services enjoyed by persons without handicaps. These services would include access to parks, medical services, shopping facilities, federal and state support services, and other community services (e.g., post offices, banks).

The array of services provided in the community typically includes vocational opportunities, residential options, and recreational/leisure activities. Community vocational opportunities should include competitive employment (Hill & Wehman, 1983), long-term supported employment (Wehman & Kregel, 1985), small enterprise-contract shops (Wald & Rhodes, 1984), and mobile work crews (Wald & Rhodes, 1984).

Educational opportunities available in the community should consist of classes in age-appropriate regular education buildings (Brown, Ford et al., 1983). Curricular priorities should stress functional life skills with training conducted in the natural environments in which behaviors will ultimately be performed (Brown, Nisbet et al., 1983; Lynch, Kellow, & Willson, 1997). Residential options in the community range from natural homes or foster care (one to six persons) to group homes and domiciliary care facilities. The appropriateness of each option is determined by the individual needs of the residents.

The full range of recreational/leisure opportunities that are available to persons without handicaps should also be available to persons with handicaps. These should include recreational facilities (YMCA, YWCA, health clubs, etc.), sporting events (town leagues), and spectator sports. Other opportunities should include movies, concerts, and theater. In summary, it is important that whatever the recreational/leisure opportunities available in the community for persons without handicaps also be available to those with handicaps.

REFERENCES

Brown, L., Ford, A., Nisbet, J., Sweet, M., Donnellan, A., & Gruenewald, L. (1983). Opportunities available when severely handicapped students attend chronological age appropriate regular schools. *Journal of the Association for Persons with Severe Handicaps, 8*(1), 16–24.

Brown, L., Nisbet, J., Ford, A., Sweet, M., Shiraga, B., York, J., & Loomis, R. (1983). The critical need for nonschool instruction in educational programs for severely handicapped students. *Journal of the Association for Persons with Severe Handicaps, 8*(3), 71–78.

Hill, M., & Wehman, P. (1983). Cost benefit analysis of placing moderately and severely handicapped individuals into competitive employment. *Journal of the Association for the Severely Handicapped, 8*(1), 30–38.

Lakin, K. C., Krantz, G. C., Bruiniks, R. H., Clumpner, J. L., & Hill, B. K. (1982). One hundred years of data on populations of public residential facilities for mentally retarded people. *American Journal of Mental Deficiency, 87,* 1–8.

Larson, S. A., & Lakin, K. C. (1991). Parent attitudes about residential placement before & after deinstitutionalization. *Journal of the Association for Persons with Severe Handicaps, 16,* 1, 25–38.

Lynch, P., Kellow, J. T., Willson, V. L. (1997). The impact of deinstitutionalization on the adaptive behavior of adults with mental retardation: A meta-analysis. *Education and Training in Mental Retardation and Developmental Disabilities, 32,* 3, 255–262.

Mamula, R. A., & Newman, N. (1973). *Community placement of the mentally retarded.* Springfield, IL: Thomas.

Prouty, R., & Lakin, K. C. (1997). *Residential Services for Persons with Developments Disabilities: Status and Trends Through 1996, Report #49.* Minneapolis, MN: University of Minnesota.

Rhodes, L. E., & Valenta, L. (1985). Industry-based supported employment: An enclave approach. *Journal of the Association for Persons with Severe Handicaps, 10*(1), 12–20.

Wald, B. A., & Rhodes, L. E. (1984). *Developing model vocational programs in rural settings for adults with severe retardation: The mobile crew model.* Paper presented at the meeting of the Association for Persons with Severe Handicaps, Chicago, IL.

Wehman, P., & Kregel, J. (1985). A supported work approach to competitive employment of individuals with moderate and severe handicaps. *Journal of the Association for Persons with Severe Handicaps, 10*(1), 3–12.

Wolfensberger, W. (1969). Twenty predictions about the future of residential services in mental retardation. *Mental Retardation, 6*(7), 51–54.

Wolfensberger, W. (1972). *The principle of normalization in human services.* Toronto, Ontario: National Institute on Mental Retardation.

SUE ANN MORROW
EDGE, Inc.

LONNY W. MORROW
Northeast Missouri State University

**COMMUNITY-BASED SERVICES
COMMUNITY RESIDENTIAL PROGRAMS
DEINSTITUTIONALIZATION**

COMMUNITY RESIDENTIAL PROGRAMS

There is an array of community residential options available. Foster homes, also known as personal care homes or family care homes (McCoin, 1983), are private homes rented or owned by a family with one or more persons with disabilities living as family members (Hill & Lakin, 1984). The number of residents rarely exceeds six (Miller & Intagliata, 1984). These residences are licensed by a state agency or a local facility (e.g., a hospital). Foster homes are available for both children and adults. They tend to be homelike, with the person with the disability being "one of the family."

Group homes are residences with staff to provide care and supervision of one or more persons with disabilities (Hill & Lakin, 1984). Financial support comes from a variety of sources, including churches, states, private nonprofit organizations, and private for-profit organizations (Miller & Intagliata, 1984). It is not uncommon to find group homes staffed with house parents (a man and a woman who live in the residence, with one having an additional outside job) and one or two additional staff members for the hours when the majority of residents are home. The number of residents living in groups varies from home to home. Most of the research conducted has involved group homes serving under 20 residents (Miller & Intagliata, 1984).

Semiindependent living facilities are facilities having separate units or apartments with staff members living in one unit or apartment; however, staff members live in the same building to provide support services to those in need. Services might include assistance with budgeting or managing money, housework, or laundry. Currently, these facilities are mainly supported by nonprofit organizations (Hill, Lakin, & Bruininks, 1984).

Domicilary care facilities are community-based facilities whose primary function is to provide shelter and protection to the residents. There are no training or rehabilitation activities conducted (Miller & Intagliata, 1984). Since there is a lack of emphasis on training or rehabilitation, these types of facilities are deemed most appropriate for persons with high levels of independent living skills who need little or no additional training, or for those persons who, because of severe medical or physical needs or age, would not benefit from additional skill training (Miller & Intagliata, 1984). The number of residents in these facilities ranges from 5 to 200. Most of these facilities are operated by individual proprietors (Hill et al., 1984).

Although there are a variety of names given to domiciliary care facilities, there are generally two broad categories. Board and care facilities are also known as boarding homes and adult homes. As a general rule, these facilities provide a room and meals to the residents. Some also provide limited supervision. The major source of support for most residents is Social Security. (Miller & Intagliata, 1984). Health care facilities are also known as convalescent care homes, nursing homes, skilled nursing facilities, intermediate care facilities, and health-related facilities (Miller & Intagliata, 1984). In addition to providing a room and meals, these facilities also provide some level of nursing care to the residents. Generally, these facilities are funded through Medicare and Medicaid.

Halfway houses are short-term residential options available to persons leaving institutional settings (Katz, 1968). The setting is supervised with emphasis on facilitating the person's reentry into the community. The number of residents ranges from 12 to 25. An extensive report on residential services can be found by Prouty & Lakin, (1997).

REFERENCES

Hill, B. K., & Lakin, K. C. (1984). *Classification of residential facilities for mentally retarded people* (Brief No. 24). Minneapolis, MN: Center for Residential and Community Services, University of Minnesota, Department of Educational Psychology.

Hill, B. K., Lakin, K. C., & Bruininks, R. H. (1984). Trends in residential services for people who are mentally retarded 1977–1982. *Journal of the Association for Persons with Severe Handicaps, 9*(4), 243–251.

Katz, E. (1968). *The retarded adult in the community*. Springfield, IL: Thomas.

McCoin, J. M. (1983). Adult foster homes: *Their managers and residents*. New York: Human Sciences.

Miller, B., & Intagliata, T. (1984). *Promises and realities for mentally retarded citizens: Life in the community*. Baltimore, MD: University Park Press.

Prouty, R., & Lakin, K. (1997). *Residential Services for Persons with Development Disabilities: Status and Trends through 1996, Report #49*. Minneapolis, MN: University of Minnesota.

SUE ANN MORROW
EDGE, Inc.

LONNY W. MORROW
*Northeast Missouri State
University*

INDEPENDENT LIVING RESIDENTIAL FACILITIES

COMPAZINE

Compazine (prochlorperazine) is used for the short-term treatment of generalized nonpsychotic anxiety, the control of severe nausea and vomiting, and the management of the manifestations of psychotic disorders (Servis & Miller, 1997). Compazine may impair mental or physical abilities, especially during the first few days of therapy. Adverse reactions can include drowsiness, dizziness, blurred vision, restlessness, agitation, jitteriness, insomnia, and motor dysfunctions such as muscle spasms, pseudoparkinsonism, and tardive dyskinesia. Overdose can produce coma.

A brand name of Smith Kline and French, Compazine is available in tablets of 5, 10, and 25 mg, in sustained release capsules of 10, 15, and 30 mg in injectable ampuls, and in suppositories of 2½, 5, and 25 mg. Dosage may vary, ranging from 2½ mg, according to the symptom being treated. It is given one or two times per day for severe nausea and vomiting in young children to a maximum of 25 mg per day in children 6 to 12 years of age being treated for psychosis.

REFERENCE

Physicians' desk reference. (1984). (pp. 1874–1877). Oradell, NJ: Medical Economics.

Servis, M., & Miller, B. (1997). Treatment of psychosis with prochlorperazine in the ICU setting. *Psychosomatics, 38,* 6, 589–590.

LAWRENCE C. HARTLAGE
Evans, Georgia

ATARAX
BENADRYL
NAVANE

COMPENSATORY EDUCATION

Compensatory education usually refers to supplemental educational services provided through federal, state, or local programs to educationally disadvantaged children in schools with concentrations of children from low-income families.

The largest such program is that authorized by Chapter 1 of the Education Consolidation and Improvement Act, formerly known as Title I of the Elementary and Secondary Education Act. Federal grants are made through state education agencies to local school districts based on the number of children from families in poverty. About 90% of all districts, receive Chapter 1 funds.

Local educational agencies then allocate funds to schools based on poverty and educational criteria. Schools provide services to children based not on family income, but on extent of educational deprivation. This determination is made at the local level within broad federal guidelines. In general, schools with the greatest concentrations of children from poor families and children most in need of services receive priority in program delivery.

In the most recent year from which data are available (1983–1984), 4.8 million children received compensatory education through the federal program (Carpenter & Hopper, 1985). Additional children receive services from state and local compensatory education programs, and some Chapter 1 participants receive additional services from such programs. For the federal program, about 55% of participants are white, 27% black, 14% Hispanic, and 4% other (White, 1984). Service provision at the elementary level is emphasized: in 1983–1984, 7% of participants were in kindergarten or below, 69% of participants were in grades 1 to 6, and 24% were in grades 7 to 12. This distribution has been relatively constant over time (Carpenter & Hopper, 1985). Participants are concentrated in lower achievement quartiles; as the achievement quartile increases, percent participation in Chapter 1 decreases (White, 1984).

The law allows for a wide range of services to be provided: instructional services, purchase of materials and equipment, teacher training, construction, and social and health services. However, about 80% of funds are spent on instructional services (White, 1984), with particular emphasis on reading and math. About three-fourths of participants receive compensatory reading and almost one-half receive compensatory math, with language arts the next most common service (Carpenter & Hopper, 1985). Almost two-thirds of districts pull students out of regular classrooms to provide services in classes that are likely to be smaller and more personnel-intensive than regular classes. Title I average class size was about 10 children, with a 4.5 to 1 student to instructor ratio (White, 1984).

Chapter 1 programs resemble special education programs for learning-disabled children in several ways. They attempt to address a similar symptom: low or lower than expected achievement. There is a special concentration on attacking difficulties with reading and mathematics skills. Children are often removed from regular classrooms for part of the school day for more personnel-intensive services in smaller classes. That is not to suggest that children served, educational needs, or instructional content of programs for learning-disabled children and compensatory education are identical, or that learning-disabled children are interchangeable with children receiving compensatory education. They are not. But in terms of difficulty addressed, administrative design, or general approach to service delivery, there are important similarities.

Given the Chapter 1 eligibility criterion of educational disadvantagement, nothing prohibits a handicapped child who receives special education and related services from also being served as an educationally deprived child through compensatory education. Anecdotal evidence suggests this may not be common.

Evaluation of the federal compensatory education program has improved over the years. Findings from a large new federal study required by law are due in early 1987. This will be of particular interest to those in special education because the study includes the first school-based comparison of compensatory education, special education, bilingual education, and regular education programs.

It is also important to remember the many compensatory education programs run by state and local educational agencies complement and extend Chapter 1. Information on children served, services provided, and evaluation results of these programs is available from state and local education agencies.

REFERENCES

Carpenter, M., & Hopper, P. (1985). *Synthesis of state Chapter 1 data: Draft summary report.* Washington, DC: Advanced Technology.

Riddle, W. (1985). *Elementary and Secondary Education Act: A condensed history of the original law and major amendments.* Washington, DC: Congressional Research Service.

White, B. F. (1984). *Compensatory education*. Washington, DC: Office of Management and Budget.

JAMES R. RICCIUTI
*United States Office of
Management and Budget*

BILINGUAL SPECIAL EDUCATION
MIGRANT HANDICAPPED
SOCIOECONOMIC STATUS

COMPETENCY EDUCATION

Implementation of educational curricula in secondary special education programs requires a shift from traditional content-based curricula to more process-based approaches. Moore and Gysbers (1972) cautioned against viewing students as needing to be brought up to a grade level by the end of the school year, thereby creating passive-dependent students who may evidence apathy, irresponsibility, or rebellious behavior. A process-oriented approach, which relates curriculum directly to the outside world and focuses on each student's unique learning and motivational methods, is recommended for exceptional learners.

Competency education emphasizes developing skills; acquiring knowledge and information (or content) becomes secondary. In curriculum development and planning, the programming concerns revolve around what skills, or competencies, are essential to the student in order to make him or her a more effective person and community member. In competency-based education, the content of a curriculum is selected for its utility in bringing about and exercising those skills. The competencies become the goals, and the curriculum becomes the vehicle by which the goal of skill development may be realized (Cole, 1972).

A competency-based curriculum can assure that each student acquires competencies deemed essential to function adequately as a consumer, a producer, a learner, and a citizen. This means that some exceptional students may need to go beyond the traditional period of time allotted in a secondary program if they are to adequately gain desired competencies. The responsibility is fixed on the educational system to ensure that the student gains those skills, or competencies, essential for adequate community adjustment (Brolin, 1976). It is frequently proposed that a secondary-level educational curriculum that best meets the life career development needs of special education students should revolve around career education concepts that emphasize three primary curriculum areas and one support area. The three curriculum areas are daily living skills; occupational guidance and preparation; and personal-social skills. A fourth curriculum area that lends itself to competency-based educational programming and is supportive to the other three is academic skills. As many as 22 major competencies have been identified as important to acquire at the secondary level under one of these major areas (Brolin, 1974).

REFERENCES

Brolin, D. (1976). *Vocation preparation of the retarded citizen*. Columbus, OH: Merrill.

Brolin, D., & Kokaska, C. (1974). Critical issues in the job placement of the educable mentally retarded. *Rehabilitation Literature, 10*(2), 16–18.

Cole, H. P. (1972). *Process education: The new direction for elementary-secondary schools*. Englewood Cliffs, NJ: Educational Technology.

Moore, E. J., & Gysbers, N. C. (1972). Career development: A new focus. *Educational Leadership, 30*, 108.

CRAIG D. SMITH
Georgia College

CURRICULUM BASED ASSESSMENT
OUTCOME BASED EDUCATION
VOCATIONAL EVALUATION
VOCATIONAL TRAINING OF HANDICAPPED

COMPETENCY TEST

Testing for competence is a method of evaluating individuals to assess the attainment of minimal skills in a given area. Usually, this type of testing occurs in grade school (first through twelfth grade) for the purpose of advancement from one grade to another, as a condition of promotion from one level of schooling to another (e.g. elementary school to junior high school), or the conferring of a high school diploma. This diploma is the most common occasion for minimum competency testing, as it is often seen as the final hurdle in the schooling process. Widespread use of competency testing arose out of a concern regarding the low competence level of high school graduates in reading, writing, and arithmetic skills (Lazarus, 1988). Although competence is tested in many states, regulations are far from uniform.

There is no consensus on what constitutes "competency" or how to measure such a construct. The larger question of the nature of competency, leads back to a discussion of the point of schooling. Since there is no agreed-upon national standard for essential elements of education in the United States, each state is responsible for what ultimately constitutes "competence." It would seem that the traditional school skills of reading, writing, and arithmetic constitute competency from their widespread usage (Pipho, 1978). However, Anastasi posits that a common goal among many of the varying instruments used in minimum competency testing may be "the basic educational skills required to manage one's own life in a modern society" (1988, p. 425). For example, the items in a competency test may assess an examinee's ability to count change, tell time, read traffic signs, fill out a job application, and so forth. Without a uniform standard of contents, the reliability and validity of minimum competency testing is threatened. Anastasi suggests that those who employ minimum competency testing may want to seek the assistance of test publishers who can provide technically trained professionals and large item banks.

McClung (1977) has suggested that minimum competency tests should at least reflect the topics studied in the school curriculum (curriculum validity) and should ensure that the topics tested are actually taught (instructional validity). The legitimacy of minimum competency testing will be compromised until these issues are addressed.

In terms of content validity, the advent of computers has complicated the issue of minimum competency. Obviously, computers and computer skills are essential for the modern student, and most school systems recognize the importance of computers in our society by including computer classes in the curriculum. Despite this fact, there are very few, if any, minimum competency tests in the school systems designed to measure one's proficiency in computer usage.

The predictive validity of minimum competency tests is also at issue. The use of competency tests rests on the assumption that performance on such tests predicts later life success. Lazarus suggested that predicting life success would be a difficult, if not impossible, endeavor (1981).

Performance standards are another problematic issue of competency tests. Glass reviewed methods for establishing pass-fail cutoffs and found these methods to be arbitrary (1978). Milder critics concede that the process of establishing performance standards is subjective and vulnerable to social and political influences.

Minimum competency testing is supposed to be a means of improving the educational system. Currently there is too much variability among minimum competency tests in order to establish their worthiness as an improvement in education. In order to be truly worthy of their intention, minimum competency tests will need to resolve their deficits in validity.

REFERENCES

Anastasi, A. (1988). *Psychological testing* (6th ed.). New York: Macmillan.

Glass, G. V. (1978). Minimum competency and incompetence in Florida. *Phi Delta Kappan, 63*(2), 134–135.

Lazarus, M. (1981). *Goodbye to excellence: A critical look at minimum competency testing*. Boulder, CO: Westview.

McClung, M. (1977). Competency testing: Potential for discrimination. *Clearinghouse Review, 2,* 439–448.

Pipho, C. (1978). Minimum competency testing in 1978: A look at state standards. *Phi Delta Kappan, 59*(9), 585–588.

LIBBY GOODMAN
Pennsylvania State University
First edition

TRACY A. MUENZ
*California School of
Professional Psychology*
Second edition

ACHIEVEMENT TESTS
MINIMUM COMPETENCY TESTING

COMPETENCY TESTING FOR TEACHERS

Competency testing for teachers is an educational and political practice that has been implemented in some states but not others. While all states in the United States have certification requirements for teachers, many states have delegated decision-making and testing to teacher training institutions within the states. In other states, the decision has returned to state agencies in the form of competency tests administered at the completion of teacher training (Lines, 1985). Those states given the responsibility of determining competency have differing methods of evaluation. For example, Arkansas, along with other states, proposed a system of certifying teachers and then recertifying them at intervals to continue or withhold one's credentials. In Texas, prospective teacher trainees are tested prior to entry into teacher education programs for minimum competency in basic arithmetic, writing, and reading skills. In South Carolina, competency testing is also used to determine salary levels.

Generally, competency testing for prospective or active teachers is oriented toward basic skills content and knowledge of pedagogy. The most widely used test in this regard is the National Teacher Examination (NTE). Educational Testing Services (ETS) developed the NTE and stated that the test should be used only to test entering teachers on academic knowledge. ETS does not set cutoff scores for passing, as each state is given the responsibility of determining its own competency level.

The validity of the NTE is a major issue in competency testing for teachers. The NTE, along with other such tests, has been challenged in court cases regarding its validity.

Content validity has never been seriously challenged, mostly because the content being tested is fairly low in difficulty in arithmetic, spelling, grammar usage, and reading comprehension. Supreme Court decisions, notably *United States vs. South Carolina* (1976), have affirmed that a test such as the NTE may be used even though it does not have predictive validity of later job performance. The only validity reported for the NTE has been for performance in teacher training. The same decision affirmed that the test may be used as a basis for salary determination.

The effect of competency testing on minorities has been pointed out by several sources. Lies (1984) discussed a case in Alabama in which the school district using the NTE must show evidence for concurrent validity for its hiring and termination decisions whenever a disproportionate proportion of a minority group is affected. Also, Kauchak (1984) reported that the use of the NTE has greatly reduced the number of new black teachers in Louisiana. In fact, after 1978, only 23% of the prospective black teachers have taken the NTE since the testing program began, and the percentage of blacks attempting the test declined from 31% in 1978 to 13% in 1982. This reduction in the number of black teachers has been a major issue in competency testing for teachers, especially in southern states.

Minimum competency tests for teachers have not been able to produce respectable predictive validity estimates for effective teaching in the classroom. While some lawsuits have been based on this lack of validation, the South Carolina decision indicates that states may implement such a test without requiring predicative validity. The court uses the standard that it is reasonable that teachers possess knowledge such as that measured in such tests at the time of certification. Whether a minimum competency test is appropriate for continued certification of already-practicing teachers continues to be an issue.

REFERENCES

Kauchack, D. (1984). Testing teachers in Louisiana: A closer look. *Phi Delta Kappan, 65,* 626–628.

Lines, P. M. (1985). Testing the teacher: Are there legal pitfalls? *Phi Delta Kappan, 66,* 618–622.

VICTOR L. WILLSON
Texas A & M University
First edition

TRACY A. MUENZ
*California School of
   Professional Psychology*
Second edition

CRITERION-REFERENCED TESTING
TEACHER EFFECTIVENESS

COMPREHENSIVE RECEPTIVE AND EXPRESSIVE VOCABULARY TEST (CREVT)

The Comprehensive Receptive and Expressive Vocabulary Test (CREVT; Wallace & Hammill, 1994) measures both receptive and expressive oral vocabulary. The CREVT is used to identify students who are significantly below their peers in oral vocabulary proficiency, to note receptive vocabulary and expressive oral vocabulary strengths and weaknesses, and to document progress in oral vocabulary development as a consequence of intervention programs.

The CREVT was standardized on 1,920 students from 32 states. Characteristics of the normative sample approximate those provided in the 1990 Statistical Abstract of the United States with regard to gender, geographical region, ethnicity, race, urban/rural residence, and disability. Standard scores (mean = 100, SD = 15), percentiles, and age equivalents are provided in the Examiner's Manual. Internal consistency reliabilities (i.e., alphas), stability reliabilities (i.e., test-retest), and interscorer reliabilities for all scores exceed .8 at all ages. Criterion-related validity is reported, as are results of studies showing that the CREVT items have little gender or race bias.

A review of the CREVT by Kaufman (1998) found the test to be reliable and stable with good norms and attractive pictorial stimuli. He did find problems with specific items in Receptive Vocabulary, and cautions that additional research is needed to establish the instrument's validity. The CREVT is easy to use and nicely packaged, reports McLellan (1998). The test has reasonable statistical properties and conforms to standards of testing. An adult version of the instrument is available. The CREVT-A (Wallace & Hammill, 1997) was standardized on adults aged 18 through 89.

REFERENCES

Kaufman, A. S. (1998). Review of the Comprehensive Receptive and Expressive Vocabulary Test. In J. C. Impara & B. S. Plake (Eds.), *The thirteenth mental measurements yearbook* (pp. 301–304). Lincoln: Buros Institute of Mental Measurements, University of Nebraska Press.

McLellan, M. J. (1998). Review of the Comprehensive Receptive and Expressive Vocabulary Test. In J. C. Impara & B. S. Plake (Eds.), *The thirteenth mental measurements yearbook* (pp. 304–305). Lincoln: Buros Institute of Mental Measurements, University of Nebraska Press.

Wallace, G., & Hammill, D. D. (1994). *Comprehensive Receptive and Expressive Vocabulary Test.* Austin, TX: Pro-Ed.

Wallace, G., & Hammill, D. D. (1997). *Comprehensive Receptive and Expressive Vocabulary Test–Adult.* Austin, TX: Pro-Ed.

TADDY MADDOX
*Associate Director of Research,
   Pro-Ed, Inc.*

COMPREHENSIVE TEST OF NONVERBAL INTELLIGENCE (CTONI)

The *Comprehensive Test of Nonverbal Intelligence* (CTONI; Hammill, Pearson, & Wiederholt, 1996) is a test that measures nonverbal reasoning abilities of individuals aged 6 through 90 for whom most other mental ability tests are either inappropriate or biased. The CTONI measures analogical reasoning, categorical classifications, sequential reasoning in two different contexts: pictures of familiar objects (e.g., people, toys, and animals) and geometric designs (e.g., unfamiliar sketches and drawings).

Results of the CTONI are used to estimate the intelligence of individuals who experience undue difficulty in language or fine motor skills, including individuals who are bilingual, who speak a language other than English, or who are socioeconomically disadvantaged, deaf, language-disordered, motor-disabled, or neurologically impaired. No oral responses, reading, writing, or object manipulation are required to take the test. The subtests of the CTONI require students to look at a group of pictures or designs and to solve problems involving analogies, categorizations, and sequences. Individuals indicate their answer by pointing to alternative choices.

The CTONI is easy to administer and score. It can be administered orally to students who speak English or in pantomime to those who speak a language other than English or those who are deaf, aphasic, or neurologically impaired. The CTONI yields raw scores, standard scores, percentiles, and age equivalents. The subtests are combined into three composite scores: Geometric Nonverbal Intelligence Quotient, Pictorial Nonverbal Intelligence Quotient, and Nonverbal Intelligence Quotient.

The CTONI was standardized on more than 2,500 individuals from 25 U.S. states, Canada, and Panama. Characteristics of the normative sample have been stratified and approximate those provided in the 1996 *Statistical Abstract of the United States* with regard to gender, geographic region, ethnicity, race, urban/rural residence, and disability.

The reliability of the CTONI has been studied extensively, and evidence relating to content sampling, time sampling, and interscorer reliability is provided. The reliability coefficients are all .80 or greater, indicating a high level of test reliability. Evidence of content, criterion-related, and construct validity also is reported.

The test is also available in a computer administered format. The computer gives all the instructions to the person being tested in a clear, pleasant human voice. The examinee simply points the mouse and clicks it on the answer. When the testing is finished, the examiner can view a report of the results on the computer screen or print a copy.

The CTONI was reviewed in *The Thirteenth Mental Measurements Yearbook* by Aylward (1998) and von Lingen (1998). These reviewers state that the test seems particularly useful in testing bilingual students since there are fewer intervening variables than found on other tests or batteries.

REFERENCES

Aylward, G. P. (1998). Review of the Comprehensive Test of Nonverbal Intelligence. In J. C. Impara & B. S. Plake (Eds.), *The thirteenth mental measurements yearbook* (pp. 310–312). Lincoln: Buros Institute of Mental Measurements, University of Nebraska Press.

Hammill, D. D., Pearson, N. A., & Wiederholt, J. L. (1996). *Comprehensive Test for Nonverbal Intelligence.* Austin, TX: Pro-Ed.

van Lingen, G. (1998). Review of the Comprehensive Test of Nonverbal Intelligence. In J. C. Impara & B. S. Plake (Eds.), *The thirteenth mental measurements yearbook* (pp. 312–314). Lincoln: Buros Institute of Mental Measurements, University of Nebraska Press.

TADDY MADDOX
*Associate Director of Research,
Pro-Ed, Inc.*

COMPULSORY ATTENDANCE (AND STUDENTS WITH DISABILITIES)

Compulsory school attendance laws have been in effect in nearly every state and in most other parts of the western world for the bulk of the twentieth century. These laws require the parents or legal guardians of all children to send them to school or to provide an equivalent education. The ages of children for whom school attendance is compulsory varies as well, but includes children between the ages of 7 and 16 years in the vast majority of states. The courts have exempted some religious groups from the enforcement of compulsory attendance laws, notably the Amish nationwide and in some states the Mennonites. The states differ greatly in what constitutes a legal school under their compulsory attendance laws. Some states recognize only state certified and supervised schools (public or private), while some allow children to attend noncertified church-supported schools. Others are even more liberal and allow home schooling accomplished by lay parents. Compulsory attendance laws have been the subject of much litigation since their initial enactment.

Many consider compulsory attendance laws to be an infringement on various rights granted to the general populace in the first 10 amendments to the U.S. Constitution (the Bill of Rights). However, the courts have held, with minor religious exceptions, that the state has a compelling interest in the welfare of all children within its jurisdiction and that the provision for education under compulsory circumstances is an acceptable part of this compelling interest and is a legal extension of the police powers of the state. The full extent of the state's compelling interest in education has yet to be defined in adequate detail by the courts, but it is related to the provision of an education that allows individuals to become contributing members of society, preventing them from becoming burdens on the state.

Prior to the passage of the Education for All Handicapped Children Act of 1975 (PL 94-142), which required the states to make available to all handicapped children a free, appropriate, public education, few states enforced their compulsory attendance laws where handicapped children were involved. Many school districts throughout the country would not allow many handicapped children to attend, and in many such instances, encouraged parents to keep these children at home. Many states remain lax in the enforcement of compulsory attendance statutes with regard to the handicapped. With the growing problem of delinquency in the United States, there has been a recent trend away from strict enforcement of truancy laws.

In most states, children with disabilities are included in the compulsory attendance laws and the failure (or refusal) of the parents or legal guardians to present these children for school attendance is likely actionable on civil and/or criminal bases in most states. However, school officials or child welfare workers will, in the typical case, have to take the lead in seeking the enforcement of compulsory attendance laws for children with disabilities. It is clear, however, that unless specifically exempted by the wording of the state statute, handicapped children are required to attend school. What constitutes a school or an equivalent educational program may be different for the handicapped than the nonhandicapped given the broad authority granted to multidisciplinary teams to diagnose and prescribe educational plans.

CECIL R. REYNOLDS
Texas A & M University

INDIVIDUALS WITH DISABILITIES EDUCATION ACT (IDEA)

COMPUTER-ASSISTED INSTRUCTION

Computer-assisted instruction (CAI) refers to educational software that can be run by students with little or no teacher assistance. In CAI, the computer presents information, asks questions, and verifies responses in much the same way a teacher does. Unlike traditional means of instruction, however, CAI allows students to work at their own levels and paces. This mode of instruction can be beneficial to handicapped students who have difficulty in working at the same pace as their nonhandicapped peers. Because CAI can be geared toward students' needs, interests, and expertise, it is generally considered to increase students' motivation to learn.

There are six types of computer-assisted instruction: informational, drill and practice, tutorial, instructional gaming, simulation, and problem solving. The various types of CAI represent a continuum of instructional formats, ranging from the highly structured to the unstructured (Levy & Lahm, 1984).

Informational CAI presents text and graphics only and provides minimal interaction between the student and the computer program. The purpose of this type of CAI is to provide information that may be prerequisite to the acquisition of concepts and skills.

Drill and practice programs provide students with practice using materials they have already encountered. Because these programs cover various levels of many subject areas, they can be used for both remediation and acceleration. Good drill and practice programs include immediate corrective feedback to reinforce the acquisition of content; they also allow students to jump ahead when they encounter material they have already mastered.

Tutorials provide new information. Typically, a program presents a body of information and then questions the student accordingly. Good tutorials have the power of branching (the capability to assess the user's mastery of a concept and then go to an appropriate level of content presentation). If the student masters a concept, the program goes to the next step of instruction; if the student does not achieve mastery, the program goes to a remedial sequence.

Educational games should not be confused with arcade-type games. Educational games provide intellectual challenge, stimulate curiosity, and serve as a source of motivation. Well-designed computer games include variable-difficulty levels, multiple-level goals, hidden information, and randomness. Instructional games can be used individually or with small groups. Often, games are used for review or as a reward for a particular accomplishment.

Simulations and virtual reality programs are among the most powerful learning tools. They are based on the discovery approach to learning (i.e., learning by doing). Simulations provide situations that are analogous to real-life situations, but they control limiting factors that exist in the real situation such as danger, expense, time, and space. Some of the more popular simulations involve students in situations where they see the results of their attempts to solve difficult problems; for example, the meltdown of a nuclear reactor, going West in a covered wagon, or docking a spacecraft with an orbiting satellite (McClellan, 1984).

Problem-solving CAI focuses on the process of finding

an answer to a problem rather than the answer itself. One of the best-known problem-solving packages is Logo. Logo is a procedure-oriented language that provides students with concrete ways to think about problems systematically. Students divide problems into smaller ones by writing small procedures for each problem. The language is based on the learning theories of Jean Piaget and was developed in 1968 as a part of the National Science Foundation project (Papert, 1980). Learning to program in Logo transforms learning to a self-directed, active task.

In the past few years, as researchers have begun to explore the potential applications of artificial intelligence, they have pointed out some of the *shortcomings of CAI*. For example, with traditional CAI, students cannot ask questions. Further, CAI programs usually cannot handle unanticipated answers. Often, CAI programs do not have any information base of a particular subject; they simply offer questions and answers that have been preprogrammed. Researchers are now looking at ways of improving CAI by giving it the capability of responding to the idiosyncrasies of each student's learning style. In the future, educators can look forward to programs that combine the best features of traditional CAI with new developments in artificial intelligence. These programs are expected to include a problem-solving model appropriate for the target domain of knowledge; a tutoring or teaching model; and a model of the student, including individual student characteristics such as knowledge about the content to be learned (Roberts, 1984). Intelligent computer-assisted instruction programs will allow users to communicate with the computer in natural English sentences Borchardt & Johnson, 1993. Programs will be able to accommodate random student questions on a given topic. Intelligent computer-assisted instruction will be more teacherlike in that programs will keep track of what the student knows and needs to know. The program will also have the capability of understanding when and how to provide a student with information and when to ask a question (McGrath, 1984).

REFERENCES

Borchardt, F. L., & Johnson, E. M. (1993). *Assessment proceedings of the computer-assisted learning and instruction consortium (CALICO) Annual conference, March 8–13, 1993*. Durham, NC: Duke University.

Levy, S. A., & Lahm, E. A. (1984). Microcomputers in special education curriculum. In E. McClellan (Ed.), *Microcomputer applications in special education* (pp. 21–43). Reston, VA: Council for Exceptional Children.

McClellan, E. (1984). Introduction to microcomputers. In E. McClellan (Ed.), *Microcomputer applications in special education* (pp. 1–21). Reston, VA: Council for Exceptional Children.

McGrath, D. (1984). Artificial intelligence: A tutorial for educators. *Electronic Learning, 4*, 39–43.

Papert, S. (1980). *Mindstorms*. New York: Basic Books.

Roberts, F. C. (1984, June). *An overview of intelligent CAI systems*. Paper presented at the Special Education Technology Research and Development Symposium, Washington, DC.

ELIZABETH MCCLELLAN
Council for Exceptional Children

COMPUTER LITERACY
COMPUTER-MANAGED INSTRUCTION
COMPUTER USE WITH THE HANDICAPPED

COMPUTERIZED AXIAL TOMOGRAPHY

See CAT SCAN.

COMPUTER LITERACY

Because the state of the art of computer technology and the internet is constantly changing, so too is the definition of computer literacy. In the past, computer literacy was virtually synonymous with learning to write computer programs. Typically, computer novices gained an understanding of the machines by writing programs in BASIC (Beginner's All-Purpose Symbolic Instructional Code). The major thrust in computer literacy today has shifted away from programming and toward the applications of computer technology in various settings, particularly the home, school, and office. The primary reason for this shift has been the increased availability of good software, inexpensive hardware, and access to the internet.

The problem of defining computer literacy is compounded by the fact that individuals with different educational levels have differing computer needs. Meeting these needs requires varying levels of expertise. For example, for the high-school student, computer literacy encompasses the following areas: basic knowledge of how to operate a computer; an understanding of how computers are used in work and for leisure; an appreciation of the ethical, social, and economic ramifications of computer usage; and an ability to use computers and the internet for instruction, information collection and retrieval, word processing, decision making, and problem solving.

For teachers, computer literacy means being knowledgeable about the capabilities of hardware and software and understanding how computers and the internet can enhance students' educational experiences. For those who work with handicapped students, computer literacy also implies an understanding of the ways in which technology can be used to improve services to special needs learners. Specifically, to be computer literate, special educators should acquire the following competencies:

1. Understand the fundamental operation and care of computers and software.
2. Become fluent in the basic terminology of computer technology.
3. Be able to apply computer technology to improve instruction.
4. Be able to use computers for management of instruction.
5. Understand how microprocessor-based technology can compensate for motoric, sensory, and cognitive disabilities.
6. Become proficient in evaluating software and hardware.
7. Be able to use an authoring system or language to develop instructional programs.
8. Understand the principles of telecommunication, especially as they apply to the improvement of instruction and learning.
9. Be able to access and utilize information retrieved from the internet.

Educators continue to debate the inclusion of computer programming as a component of computer literacy. Many educators, particularly those who work with young children and/or gifted and talented children, believe that teaching students to write programs can help them to develop problem-solving skills that can be applied to real-life experiences. For example, Papert (1980) mentions that the language Logo was designed by Piagetian psychologists to help children "think about thinking" (i.e., to understand the steps they go through in solving a problem).

For teachers and teacher educators, however, the development of authoring systems and languages has reduced the need for learning an all-purpose language such as BASIC. An authoring system is a highly structured template that allows computer users with a minimal understanding of computer technology to develop computer-assisted tutorials and drill and practice routines. Proficiency in high-level languages such as PASCAL or "C" would be left to educators who are interested in designing state-of-the-art instructional and management software (Cartwright, 1984).

REFERENCES

Cartwright, G. P. (1984). Technology competencies for special education doctoral students. *Teacher Education and Special Education, 7,* 82–87.

Computer Competency. (1983, May). *Chronicle of higher education* (p. 5).

Papert, S. (1980). *Mindstorms.* New York: Basic Books.

Schery, T., & Spaw, L. (1993). *Computer talk: Helping young handicapped children communicate.* Paper presented at the CEC Conference, San Diego, CA, December 14, 1993.

ELIZABETH MCCLELLAN
Council for Exceptional Children

COMPUTER-ASSISTED INSTRUCTION
COMPUTER USE WITH THE HANDICAPPED

COMPUTER-MANAGED INSTRUCTION

Computer-managed instruction (CMI) refers to a category of computer programs that are used by educators to organize and manage data related to instruction. In the early days of microcomputers in the schools, CMI was limited to packages that helped teachers monitor students' grades or those that allowed administrators to keep track of students' schedules and records. In the past few years, however, sophisticated CMI packages have been created that not only facilitate recordkeeping but also aid in the diagnosis of students' strengths and weaknesses. In special education in particular, CMI is used to analyze test data, determine goals and objectives based on the data, generate individualized educational plans (IEPs) monitor student progress, and generate reports (Gibbons, 1993; McClellan, 1984).

Since 1975, when PL 94-142 was passed, the responsibilities of special education teachers and administrators have increased dramatically. Broader child-find programs have increased the number of children receiving special education services. Individualized educational programs are prepared annually. With larger numbers of students and increased individualization, the number of personnel who provide special education and related services has also grown. All of this growth calls for increased paperwork on the part of the teacher and administrator. Fortunately, computer programs have been developed to manage the paperwork.

The ERIC Clearinghouse on Handicapped and Gifted Children (1980) has published a list of tasks that computers can perform to assist in the management of instruction. These tasks include the following:

1. Generate IEPs from a large data base
2. Generate report cards
3. Generate quarterly student reports
4. Score tests
5. Recommend appropriate activities for students
6. Locate learning materials
7. Describe diagnostic materials

8. Report on student due-process status

9. Remind when notices are due or should be sent out

10. Report on student achievement and evaluation status

11. Store information on health history

In addition, software has been developed for the following administrative functions:

1. Reimburse computation according to state and federal formulas

2. Screen, assess, place, and review counts of students

3. Generate standardized reports

4. Report on compliance with IDEA

5. Cross-reference child counts by class, school, teacher, and handicap

6. Record testing and reports

7. Send personalized mailings to parents and service providers

8. Provide lists of incomplete information on student records

9. Audit trails for program placement and review

The key to the successful implementation of computer-managed instruction is not with single-purpose computer programs but with integrated packages. Software developers have created sophisticated, and often expensive, packages that can be customized to meet the specific needs of the teacher, administrator, or school system. These programs usually call for the creation of large data bases that integrate classroom and administrative information. Information stored in these master files might include student tracking data, assessment and diagnostic information, IEP goals and objectives, and classroom performance data. Integrated packages can also include instructional sequences and performance data (Lahm & Levy, 1984). The computer's capacity to analyze data rapidly and to present them in ways that are easily used suggests a tremendous potential for reducing the amount of time and paper work required to generate reports. More important, however, teachers and administrators can use the data compiled and analyzed by computer-managed instruction packages as a basis for making decisions that affect teaching and learning (Gibbons, 1993).

REFERENCES

ERIC Clearinghouse on Handicapped and Gifted Children. (1980). *Computers for special education management: Progress, potential, and pitfalls.* Reston, VA: Council for Exceptional Children.

Gibbons, A. S. (1993). The future of computer managed instruction (CMI). *Educational Technology, 33,* 5, 7–11.

Lahm, E. A., & Levy, S. A. (1984). Microcomputers in special education management. In E. McClellan (Ed.), *Microcomputer applications in special education* (pp. 44–59). Reston, VA: Council for Exceptional Children.

McClellan, E. (1984). Introduction to microcomputers. In E. McClellan (Ed.), *Microcomputer applications in special education* (pp. 1–21). Reston, VA: Council for Exceptional Children.

ELIZABETH MCCLELLAN
Council for Exceptional Children

COMPUTER LITERACY
COMPUTER USE WITH THE HANDICAPPED

COMPUTERS AND EDUCATION, AN INTERNATIONAL JOURNAL

Computers and Education is a scholarly journal published by the Pergamon division of Elsevier Publishing. Since 1977, the journal has provided a forum for communication in the use of all forms of computing. *Computers and Education* publishes papers in the language of the academic computer user on educational and training system development using techniques from and applications in many knowledge domains including: graphics, simulation, computer-aided design, computer integrated manufacture, and artificial intelligence and its applications. The journal is published 8 times a year and subscriptions can be ordered on-line from www.elsevier.nl/inca/publications/store/.

COMPUTERS IN HUMAN BEHAVIOR

Computers in Human Behavior is a scholarly journal devoted to research that attempts to articulate the relationship between psychology, the science of human behavior, and technological advances in computer science. Articles are concerned with advances in research design and the technology of research, but also with the effects of computers on the topics chosen for study by psychologists, such as the use of health promotion programs to promote behavioral change, and use of virtual reality programs. Changes in clinical practice, ethics, and standards related to computers are also examined. Articles appearing in the journal have also included studies of the equivalence of testing conditions (computerized vs. standard administration), computerized interpretation of tests. The latter two areas are of interest to special educators as several articles have addressed placement decisions and educational diagnosis using computer programs to interpret tests. *Computers in*

Human Behavior is a Pergamon Press journal; it began publication in 1985.

REFERENCES

Bosworth, K., Gustafson, D. H., & Hawkins, R. P. (1994). The BARN system and impact of adolescent health promotion via computer. *Computers in Human Behavior, 10,* 4, 467–482.

Riva, G. (1998). Virtual environment for body image modification: Virtual reality system for the treatment of body image disturbances. *Computers in Human Behavior, 14,* 3, 477–490.

CECIL R. REYNOLDS
Texas A & M University

COMPUTER USE WITH STUDENTS WITH DISABILITIES

For handicapped persons, computers have three main functions: compensation for disabilities, management, and instructional delivery.

In terms of compensation for disabilities, one of the most exciting aspects of computer technology is the use of augmentative devices for communication and control. Computers, particularly microcomputers, help users overcome communication problems associated with limited mobility and sensory impairment. To increase the speed and accuracy of using computers, engineers and educators have developed special input and output devices. Innovative input devices include voice recognition; speech synthesizers (Schery & Spaw, 1993), the mouse, joysticks and game paddles, mechanical keyboard aids such as guards, mouths, and headsticks, and splints. Examples of computer output devices are synthetic speech, Blissymbols, tactile display (Opticon), braille, and portable computer printers (Brady, 1982).

For individuals with cerebral palsy, amyotrophic lateral sclerosis, or severe paralysis, one of the biggest problems of computer usage is the multiple simultaneous key strokes required to run many pieces of standard software. To take advantage of the computer's capacity to control the environment, a person with limited mobility must have an adaptive firmware card. The card is a device that enables a person with limited mobility to run software by activating a single switch (Schwedja & Vanderheiden, 1982). Single switches and expanded keyboards require only slight movement, such as the blinking of an eye.

Access to standard software allows handicapped individuals to use the computer for information management. The four primary areas of information management are word processing, data base management, financial management, and telecommunication. Word processing packages allow users to draft, edit, and print text with relative ease. Changing margins and moving sentences or paragraphs are a matter of a few key strokes. Learning-disabled students can use word processing packages to overcome some of the problems associated with writing and spelling (Arms, 1984). Database management programs are used to store, sort, and retrieve large amounts of information. In special education, administrators and teachers use database management programs to file information such as students' names, addresses, birth dates, disabilities, and test scores. Financial management programs such as spreadsheets allow users to create, monitor, and change budgets. Other programs help with checkbook balancing and income tax preparation.

With the use of a modem and a telephone, computer users have access to virtually limitless sources of information. Users who subscribe to electronic networks such as SpecialNet can send messages to other users' electronic mailboxes, or they can review messages on electronic bulletin boards. Subscribers to information utility services (e.g., America online, The Source and CompuServe) can access stock market reports, make travel reservations, obtain up-to-the-minute weather reports, or search through large bibliographic data bases for information on a given topic.

Word processing, data base management, financial management, and telecommunications packages have reached a high level of sophistication. Users can now take the information from one program and load it into another. If, for example, a user wanted to include a budget in a manuscript, he or she could load the information from a spreadsheet program into the text of a word processing package. Or, a homebound individual could compose text on the word processor and send it to a teacher or other interested party by loading it into the telecommunication software.

In addition to the functions that allow the computer to aid in communication and information management, the computer has certain characteristics that enhance the delivery of instruction. Interaction means that the computer can perform many of the functions that are typically performed by the teacher such as providing immediate feedback. Software can be designed so that rates of response and level of difficulty can be varied according to the student. One of the characteristics that tends to motivate students is branching capability (i.e., the capability of moving from one part of a program to another). Branching allows learners to decide whether they need to repeat material or move on to new material. Moreover, the computer is tireless; it does not become irritated when asked to repeat information or activities.

REFERENCES

Arms, V. M. (1984). A dyslexic can compose a computer. *Educational Technology, 24,* 39–41.

Brady, M. (1982). The Trace Center International Hardware/Software Registry: Programs for handicapped students. *Journal of Special Education Technology, 5,* 16–21.

Gibbons, A. S. (1993). The future of computer-managed instruction (CMI). *Educational Technology, 33,* 5, 7–11.

McClellan, E. (1984). Introduction to microcomputers. In E. McClellan (Ed.), *Microcomputer applications in special education* (pp. 1–21). Reston, VA: Council for Exceptional Children.

Schery, T., & Spaw, L. (1993). Computer talk: Helping young handicapped children communicate. Paper presented at the Council for Exceptional Children Conference (San Diego, CA. December 14).

Schwejda, P., & Vanderheiden, G. (1982). Adaptive-firmware card for the Apple II. *Byte, 7,* 276–314.

ELIZABETH MCCLELLAN
Council for Exceptional Children

COMPUTER LITERACY
COMPUTER MANAGED INSTRUCTION

CONCEPT FORMATION

The term concept is used to describe one of the ways the human mind organizes the tremendous amounts of data with which it is bombarded. As Ausubel (1968) points out:

> Anyone who pauses long enough to give the problem some serious thought cannot escape the conclusion that man lives in a world of concepts, rather than a world of objects, events, and situations. . . . Reality, figuratively speaking, is experienced through a conceptual or categorical filter. (p. 505)

A concept would appear to be a mental construct that serves to group together similar entities. Having knowledge of a concept means having at least knowledge of the common elements that define inclusion or exclusion of an entity from a category. The presence of a concept is tested by observing which objects are placed in the same category or are acted on similarly. The individual carrying out such an activity may or may not have any idea what the concept is that he or she is using for categorization, nor what the common elements may be.

There are often confusions between the ideas of concept and language. It is not an uncommon approach to define a concept as "something about an idea expressed in words of our language" (Platt, 1963, p. 21). However, it is clear that animals as well as humans have concepts (Humphrey, 1984). A dog does not react to an unfamiliar cat each time it sees one as if it were a unique object. Rather, it behaves toward the cat based on its past experiences with other cats. The dog, then, must have some concept of cats.

The relationship between a concept and language is a culturally contextual and problematical one, however. Gagne (1970), for example, has argued that there are two types of concepts, concrete ones such as "dog," which are based on direct empirical experience, and those such as "uncle" or "democracy" which cannot exist without language. It is further argued by some that the way language organizes and categorizes information actually effects the way one perceives incoming data. For example, different languages break up the color spectrum differently. A number of studies have been conducted to determine whether individuals from different cultures actually perceive colors differently, based on their language.

Two general approaches for concept formation have been described (Martorella, 1972). The first is inductive, the second deductive. Concepts learned inductively start with a group of facts, data, or concepts that are already understood. Through the use of certain intellectual skills, new, more abstract concepts are developed. For example, to assist a child in learning the rule that "e" in a VCVe word usually makes the vowel long, the child could compare two lists of similar words, one containing the final "e," the other not. The deductive approach, on the other hand, begins by presenting the more abstract principle. The learner develops an understanding of the principle through repeated mental operations on examples pertinent to the concept. In this case, a child would be presented with the rule about the final "e" first, and then would be shown a number of examples. Research has not yet determined that teaching using either type of model is clearly superior. There is, in fact, some indication in cognitive style research that the success of one method over the other is at least to some degree dependent on a person's individual learning style (Witkin, Moore, Goodenough, & Cox, 1977).

Vygotsky (1962) made a similar distinction between two types of conceptual learning. He described two methods for learning concepts depending on whether the concept is spontaneous or scientific. Spontaneous concepts are learned from day-to-day concrete exposure to specific examples of the concept. An example of this type of concept would be that of "dog." The individual learns what a dog is by living with a dog and by seeing pictures of many different kinds of dogs. However, a term like exploitation is probably learned through a mediated situation in a formal learning environment. The individual is presented with only the beginning schematics of the term's meaning. A fuller understanding is gained over time with examples not directly experienced by the learner, but learned through discussion and reading.

In a sense, the development of spontaneous concepts is an upward process, the development of scientific ones a downward one. Concepts learned through an upward process start with a number of concrete examples, with the learner developing a general notion of the essence of "dogginess." Concepts learned through a downward process tend to start with definitions, with the learner gradually determining which specific instances are examples of the general notion.

Behaviorists have attempted to explain the development of concepts in strict stimulus-response terms. Vygotsky and others have objected to this explanation on the grounds that while the mental processes described by behaviorists are necessary, they are not sufficient for explaining how external phenomena become categorized into conceptual frameworks. These thinkers find the stimulus-response paradigm an inadequate explanation for how the brain arrives at the essence of concepts such as dogginess or exploitation.

Festinger (1957), in describing the process of concept formation, borrowed from the Piagetian notion of equilibrium. Festinger stated that if an organism has two cognitions that are perceived as being dissonant with one another, there is a tendency to attempt a modification of the cognitive structures to reduce the dissonance. This process, he states, creates new concepts. For example, if a child calls all animals doggie but notices others call some of those cats, the child will in time modify his or her notion of what characteristics identify members of the class of dogs.

DeCecco (1968) has proposed the following general model for teaching concepts:

1. Describe what performance is expected after the concept is taught.
2. For complex concepts, reduce the number of attributes to be taught; emphasize dominant attributes.
3. Provide clear verbal associations.
4. Give positive and negative examples of the concept.
5. Present the examples either in close succession or simultaneously.
6. Present a new positive example, asking the student to identify it.
7. Verify the student's understanding of the concept.
8. Ask the student to define the concept.
9. Provide opportunities for the student to practice the concept with appropriate reinforcement (p. 58).

There was considerable interest in the process of concept formation during the late 1960s and early 1970s, when new mathematics and social studies curricula were being developed. The back-to-basics movement led to a declining interest in this field of inquiry. Recently, with the introduction of problem solving into the curriculum, a renewed interest in concept formation has developed. The hope is that, particularly for students with special needs, understanding how concept formation occurs in a culturally competent Context (Gonzales & Schallert, 1993) will guide teachers in helping their students become more effective learners.

REFERENCES

Ausubel, D. P. (1968). *Educational psychology: A cognitive view.* New York: Holt, Rinehart, & Winston.

DeCecco, J. P. (1968). *The psychology of learning and instruction.* Englewood Cliffs, NJ: Prentice-Hall.

Festinger, L. (1964). The motivating factor of cognitive dissonance. In R. C. Harper, et al. (Eds.), *The cognitive processes.* Englewood Cliffs, NJ: Prentice-Hall.

Gagne, R. M. (1970). *The conditions of learning* (2nd ed.). New York: Holt, Rinehart, & Winston.

Gonzales, V., & Schallert, D. (1993). *Influence of Linguistic, and Cultural Variables on Conceptual Learning in Second Language Situations.* Paper presented at the Annual Meeting of the American Educational Research Association (Atlanta, GA, April 12–16, 1993).

Humphrey, N. (1984). *Consciousness regained: Chapters in the development of the mind.* Oxford, England: Oxford University Press.

Martorella, P. H. (1972). *Concept learning: Designs for instruction.* Scranton, PA: Intext Educational.

Platt, M. M. (1963). Concepts and the curriculum. *Social Education, 27,* 21.

Vygotsky, L. S. (1962). *Thought and language.* Cambridge, MA: MIT Press.

Witkin, H. A., Moore, C. A., Goodenough, D. R., & Cox, P. W. (1977). Field-dependent and field-independent cognitive styles and their educational implications. *Review of Educational Research, 47,* 1–64.

CAROLYN BULLARD
Lewis & Clark College

ABSTRACT THINKING, IMPAIRMENT IN THOUGHT DISORDERS VYGOTSKY, L. S.

CONCEPT OF ACTIVITY

See THEORY OF ACTIVITY; VYGOTSKY, L.S.

CONCRETE OPERATIONS

Concrete operations is the third of four invariant stages of Piaget's theory of cognitive development. According to Piaget, the distinctive features of children's thought occurring during the period of concrete operations are logic and objectivity that includes the ability to perform mental manipulations directly related to objects and events. These manipulations, which emerge between the ages of approximately 7 to 11 years, are termed operations by Piaget. To qualify as an operation, an action must be internalizable, reversible, and part of an overall system of actions. By internalizable Piaget meant that a child can think about the action "without losing their original character of actions" (1953, p. 8). An example of internalization during the concrete operations stage is the performance of mental arithmetic. Essential to understanding number and size relationships are transitivity and associativity. Transitivity, the basis for seriation, is the ability to arrange a series of events or objects in a continuum such as "less than," "greater than," "fewer than," or "more than." Associativity is demonstrated by understanding that parts of a whole may be combined in different ways without effecting a change on the whole.

Reversibility is another ability that characterizes a child's thought during the concrete operations stage. The child is able to reverse actions mentally; e.g., the child learns that the number of fingers on a hand counted sequentially from thumb to little finger is the same as counted from little finger to thumb, or the child imagines the effect weights will have when placed on or taken off a scale. Actions cannot be isolated manipulations. Instead, they are part of a coherent system of thinking. Concrete operational children develop a capacity to think about concept classes in equivalent and hierarchic forms; for example, oranges and bananas are both fruit, fruit is food, but all food is not fruit.

The classic measure of whether a particular child is capable of concrete operational thinking is provided by the task of conservation. There are more than 1000 published studies on conservation (Yussen & Santrock, 1982). In a classic study, a child is seated before two same size beakers equally filled with water and a taller empty beaker. The experimenter pours one of the beakers into the tall empty one and asks the child if the amounts in the tall beaker and the unpoured beaker are the same or different. The conserver, i.e., the concrete operational thinker, knows that the amount of liquid has not changed and that if it were poured back into the original container (internalization of a reversible action) it would be the same.

In recent years, several aspects of Piaget's theory of cognitive development have been challenged (Flavell, 1992). As early as 1964, Jerome Bruner showed that children who should not be able to conserve, according to Piaget, could do so if the transformation of the object (pouring the beaker of water) were hidden from view. Since then, there has been considerable debate as to the accuracy of Piaget's four-stage model. It now seems clear that many specifics of Piaget's theory such as the age of onset of concrete operations, are in doubt. Nonetheless, the elegance and insight that Piaget brought to the study of children's thinking was immense.

REFERENCES

Bruner, J. S. (1964). The course of cognitive growth. *American Psychologists, 19,* 1–15.

Flavell, J. H. (1992). Cognitive development: Past, present, and future. *Developmental Psychology, 28,* 6, 998–1005.

Piaget, J. (1953). *Logic and psychology.* Manchester, England: Manchester University.

Yussen, S. R., & Santrock, J. W. (1982). *Child development: An introduction.* Dubuque, IA: Brown.

MICHAEL ASH
JOSE LUIS TORRES
Texas A & M University

COGNITIVE DEVELOPMENT

CONDITIONING

Conditioning is a general term that describes a strengthening (through a predictive relationship) of an association between a stimulus and a response or between two stimuli. With conditioning, responses become increasingly likely to occur under appropriate circumstances. In operant conditioning, the probability of a response that has been followed by reinforcement increases. In Pavlovian (or respondent or classical) conditioning, the probability of a response to an initially neutral stimulus increases when that neutral stimulus is followed by one that reliably elicits a response in reflex fashion. Pavlovian conditioning is named after the great Russian physiologist Ivan Pavlov (1927), whose research established the basic phenomena associated with this type of conditioning. However, the phenomenon itself had been discovered and described some years earlier by an American psychologist, E. B. Twitmeyer.

Basic Aspects for Pavlovian Conditioning

The paradigm for Pavlovian conditioning is

$$CS \rightarrow UCS \rightarrow UCR \qquad \text{(before conditioning)}$$

$$CS \rightarrow CR \qquad \text{(after conditioning)}$$

Pairing of an initially neutral conditional stimulus (CS) with an unconditional stimulus (UCS) that reliably elicits a response (UCR) leads to a conditional response (CR) occurring to the CS. Frequently, but not always, the CR is similar to the UCR in form. For example, Pavlov would sound a bell (CS) and then give a dog food (UCS) that elicited salivation (UCR). After several pairings of the bell with food, the bell itself elicited salivation. Using the paradigm

$$CS \rightarrow UCS \rightarrow UCR \qquad \text{(before conditioning)}$$
(bell)   (food)   (sali-
vation)

$$CS \rightarrow CR \qquad \text{(after conditioning)}$$
(bell)   (sali-
vation)

we can see that through pairing, a response can occur to a stimulus that never occurred to it before.

Watson (1916) made Pavlovian conditioning the basic form of learning in his formulation of behaviorism. In 1920 Watson and Rayner published a classic article on conditioning of an emotional response in a human infant. While one experimenter held a white rat (CS) toward 11-month-old Albert, the other experimenter hit a bar with a hammer, making a very loud noise (UCR) that elicited crying (UCS) from Albert. After only five pairings, the rat itself elicited crying (CR).

The basic aspects of conditioning can be briefly described:

Acquisition. With repeated trials, strength of the CR increases to some maximum level.

Extinction. Presentation of the CS without the UCS leads to a decrease in intensity of the CR until no response is observed.

Spontaneous Recovery. Presenting the CS after some delay following extinction may revoke a CR, although it will be of relatively low intensity.

Reacquisition. Repairing of the CS and UCS generally leads to more rapid reconditioning than original conditioning.

Generalization. After conditioning, a CR will tend to occur, but at lower intensity, to similar stimuli.

Discrimination. Presentation of one CS (CS[1]) followed by a UCS and of another (CS[2]) not followed by a UCS will generally result in the subject developing a discrimination such that it produces a CR to CS[1] but not CS[2].

Some Important Issues

The nature of the CR. Pavlov proposed that the CS came to take the place of the UCS—stimulus substitution—in a mechanical process. Thus, the CR should be similar in form to the UCR. However, although dogs salivate to both bells and food, they do not try to eat the bell. Indeed, they look at and move toward the food dish, behaviors that suggest that conditioning produces a CR that anticipates the UCS (Zener, 1937). Recent research (Rescorla, 1966; Siegel, 1975) suggests that in at least some cases, conditioning indeed leads to the CS eliciting a CR that reflects expectancy of the UCS. For example, Siegel gave rats a se-

ries of insulin injections in which the hypodermic needle was the CS, the insulin was the UCS, and insulin-elicited hypoglycemia was the UCS. In response to a CS-only test, the rats showed hyperglycemia, as though they were compensating for the anticipated UCS, insulin. The influential Rescorla and Wagner (1972) model proposes that conditioning will occur only when the CS provides information ("expectancy") about the UCS.

Biological constraints on learning Although early theorists felt that all stimuli and responses should be equally conditionable, research shows that they are not. In their now classic study, Garcia and Koelling (1966) gave rats either "sweet water" or "bright-noisy water" (water paired with flashing lights and noise) and then either shocked them or made them ill. Of rats given sweet water, only those made ill subsequently avoided drinking the water; of rats given bright-noisy water, only those shocked subsequently avoided drinking. Similar results appear to hold in humans (Seligman, 1970). The specificity of "cue-consequence relations" is a topic of current interest. The implication is that some types of associations have particularly important adaptive value, and have been selected through evolution.

Consideration of biological factors helps to resolve the controversial question of whether or not young infants demonstrate classical conditioning. Although the existence of such conditioning had been generally accepted, Sameroff (1971) concluded that positive studies either could not be replicated or suffered from methodological problems, and that conditioning in newborns had not clearly been demonstrated. Sameroff and Cavenaugh (1979) later suggested that studies published since the initial review, which successfully demonstrated conditioning, had used CS and UCS pairings of biological relevance to the newborn. Indeed, by pairing biologically relevant stimuli, Blass, Ganchrow, and Steiner (1984) have obtained conditioning in infants of 2 to 48 hours of age. Tactile stimulation (CS) was followed by presentation of sucrose solution (UCS) that elicited sucking (UCR). Newborns sucked during CS in conditioning and showed extinction of sucking during subsequent CS-only trials. Further, seven of eight experimental infants cried during extinction trials at a time when the sucrose had been presented, suggesting an affective component of the conditioning.

Long-delay learning. Initially, research indicated that the CS and UCS had to be closely linked in time for conditioning to occur. However, in some circumstances, particularly where the UCS elicits illness, an association may be formed with a novel taste or olfactory CS encountered over 12 hours earlier (Revusky & Garcia, 1970). Thus, under circumstances such as food poisoning, a CR can occur to a stimulus removed in time from the UCS. Recently, some have suggested that aversions to food that develop in cancer patients undergoing chemotherapy may be classically conditioned since most chemotherapeutic agents induce intense symptoms of food poisoning (Braveman & Bronstein, 1985).

Higher-order conditioning. The potential role of Pavlovian conditioning is greatly extended by higher-order conditioning, originally described by Pavlov and recently studied in detail by Rescorla (1980). In such conditioning, a first CS (CS1) is paired with a UCS to establish a CR to CS1. Then, a second CS (CS2) is paired only with CS1, leading to the response conditioned to CS1 now occurring to CS2. Thus, once a response has been conditioned to a CS, other CSs may be tied to it that are not themselves directly associated with the UCS but are remote from it. If the original link between CS1 and the UCS is broken, as in extinction, the higher-order CRs also diminish.

Applications to Children's Development

Development of emotions. Since the time of Watson, Pavlovian conditioning has played an important role in accounting for the association of positive and negative emotional reactions with particular stimuli. Watson and Rayner demonstrated how conditioning could lead to negative emotions such as fear. Indeed, conditioning is viewed as a major process underlying the development of severe fears or phobias.

As conditioning may induce phobias, so it may be used to reduce them. As early as 1924, Jones "counterconditioned" a severe fear of rabbits in a child, Peter, by pairing a rabbit with pleasurable stimuli such as peer play and ice cream cones. By the end of the process, Peter no longer feared rabbits and, indeed, was petting them. This procedure, now called desensitization, is one of the most effective means of treating phobias in children and adults. Conditioning may also produce positive emotional responses, as shown, for example, in children's excitement at the sight of a favored food, person, or toy.

Development of meaning. Conditioning is one process thought to underlie the attachment of meaning to words (Mowrer, 1954). Pairing a word (CS) with the object (UCS) signified by the word will result in responses elicited by the object becoming attached to the word as a CR. Thus, pairing the word *doll* with an actual doll leads to responses elicited by the doll becoming associated with *doll*. Although a conditioning model cannot deal with all meaning, particularly that involving abstract concepts, it does provide a framework for understanding how reactions to stimuli can become attached to symbols for them. If an object comes to elicit an emotional response, then the word for the object may also elicit that response. If a child who has been painfully knocked to the ground by a large dog now fears all large dogs, he or she may show fear at the phrase *large*

dog. On the other hand, a child who likes ice cream cones might well show positive anticipation to the phrase *ice cream cone*.

Also important is the related concept of mediated or semantic generalization. Once a CR occurs to a word, it will occur to words similar in meaning if the individual has developed a concept involving that word. Thus, if conditioned to respond to the word *shoe*, an individual will respond more to *boot*, or other words similar in meaning, than *to shoot*, a word similar in physical characteristics. Already apparent by at least age eight semantic generalization becomes stronger with age (Osgood, 1953).

Implications for Educators

Those dealing with children need to be sensitive to the fact that they and the situation they are in are paired with what they say and do to the children. So is the situation paired with peers' reactions to children. Thus, teachers who use aversive means of classroom management may condition children to be anxious about them and their classrooms. Similarly, children who are ridiculed in class or on the playground or who experience much failure and little success may become conditioned to fear school itself and teachers generally. In extreme, a school phobia may result.

We should also be aware that children will arrive at school with conditioned likes and dislikes and emotional responses. Some may have been specifically food poisoned or have had gastric distress after eating and may have strong aversions to certain foods. Others may have strong fears. However controversial it may be, those in special education should consider the roles of conditioning when predicting the effects of inclusion on children with disabilities. Those children who succeed socially and academically will have a positive conditioning experience, whereas those who are not accepted and/or fail academically may suffer from negative conditioning and develop conditioned responses associated with anxiety and fear of failure.

REFERENCES

Blass, E. M., Ganchrow, J. R., & Steiner, J. E. (1984). Classical conditioning in new born humans 2–48 hours of age. *Infant Behavior and Development, 7,* 223–235.

Braveman, N. S., & Bronstein, P. (Eds.). (1985). Experimental assessments and clinical applications of conditioned food aversions. *Annuals of the New York Academy of Sciences, 443.*

Garcia, J., & Koelling, R. A. (1966). Relation of cue to consequence in avoidance learning. *Psychonomic Science, 4,* 123–124.

Jones, M. C. (1924). A laboratory study of fear: The case of Peter. *Pedagogical Seminary and Journal of Genetic Psychology, 31,* 308–315.

Mowrer, O. H. (1954). The psychologist looks at language. *American Psychologist, 9,* 660–694.

Osgood, C. E. (1953). *Method and theory in experimental psychology*. New York: Oxford University Press.

Pavlov, I. P. (1927). *Conditioned reflexes* (translated by G. V. Anrep). New York: Oxford University Press.

Rescorla, R. A. (1966). Predictability and number of pairings in Pavlovian fear conditioning. *Psychonomic Science, 4,* 383–384.

Rescorla, R. A. (1980). *Pavlovian second-order conditioning*. Hillsdale, NJ: Erlbaum.

Rescorla, R. A., & Wagner, A. R. (1972). A theory of Pavlovian conditioning: Variations in the effectiveness of reinforcement and nonreinforcement. In A. H. Black & W. F. Prokasy (Eds.), *Classical conditioning II: Current research and theory*. New York: Appleton-Century-Crofts.

Revusky, S. H., & Garcia, J. (1970). Learned associations over long delays. In G. H. Bower & J. T. Spence (Eds.), *The psychology of learning and motivation* (Vol. 4). New York: Academic.

Sameroff, A. J. (1971). Can conditioned responses be established in the newborn infant? *Developmental Psychology, 5,* 1–12.

Sameroff, A. J., & Cavenaugh, P. J. (1979). Learning in infancy: A developmental perspective. In J. D. Osofsky (Ed.), *Handbook of infant development* (pp. 344–392). New York: Wiley.

Seligman, M. E. P. (1970). On the generality of the laws of learning. *Psychological Review, 77,* 406–418.

Siegel, S. (1975). Conditioning insulin effects. *Journal of Comparative and Physiological Psychology, 89,* 189–199.

Watson, J. B. (1916). The place of the conditioned reflex in psychology. *Psychological Review, 23,* 89–116.

Watson, J. B., & Rayner, R. (1920). Conditioned emotional reactions. *Journal of Experimental Psychology, 3,* 1–14.

Zener, K. (1937). The significance of behavior accompanying conditioned salivary secretion for theories of the conditioned reflex. *American Journal of Psychology, 50,* 384–403.

ROBERT T. BROWN
*University of North Carolina
at Wilmington*

BEHAVIOR MODIFICATION
OPERANT CONDITIONING

CONDUCT DISORDER

Conduct disorder is a behavioral disorder in youth characterized by a "repetitive and persistent pattern of behavior in which the basic rights of others or major age-appropriate societal norms or rules are violated." (American Psychiatric Association, 1994, p. 85). The behaviors fall into four basic groups: (1) aggressive behaviors that cause or threaten physical harm to people or animals; (2) nonaggressive behaviors that cause harm to property; (3) deceitfulness or theft; and (4) serious violations of rules. Three or more of the characteristics must have been present for 12 months or more, and at least one of the charac-teristics for 6 months for a diagnosis to be made. Overall, the disturbance in conduct must significantly impair the youth's social, academic, or occupational functioning. The prevalence of conduct disorder has increased over the past few decades: For males under the age of 18, rates changed from 6% to 16%, and females from 2% to 9% (American Psychiatric Association, 1994).

Individuals with conduct disorder may not be the best informants about their own behavior; therefore, it is important that diagnosticians conduct assessments that are multi-setting, multi-modal, and multi-method to accurately assess functioning (Sommers-Flanagan & Sommers-Flanagan, 1998). Many individuals with conduct disorder have little empathy for the feelings of others, and may negatively distort the positive intentions of others. The disorder is also highly correlated with early and risky sexual behavior, substance abuse, recklessness, and illegal acts. The onset of conduct disorder may occur as early as age 5, but it usually begins in late childhood or early adolescence. Many youth diagnosed with this disorder continue to show similar behaviors in adulthood (Storm-Mathisen, & Valglum, 1994) and meet the criteria for Antisocial Personality Disorder (American Psychiatric Association, 1994). There is a significant overlap of other psychiatric disorders (such as depression) with conduct disorders (Offord, Boyle, & Racine, 1991), especially in incarcerated juvenile populations (Eppright, Kashani, Robison, & Reid, 1993). Substance abuse is a significant precursor for disorders of conduct (Storm-Mathisen, & Valglum 1994), especially in Hispanic populations (Steward, Brown, & Myers, 1997).

There is a great deal of research activity devoted to the treatment of youth with conduct disorders, and there are constant calls citing the need for new models of treatment delivery (Kazdin, 1997). Treatments include problem-solving skills training, parent management training, functional family therapy, and multisystemic therapy (Kazdin, 1997). The treatments are usually delivered in residential facilities and are subject to the common criticism of not being amenable to demonstrating clinically significant change that generalizes to every patient's situation. In addition, research about the treatments are not longitudinal in nature (Kazdin, 1993; 1997), which compromises the certainty of results. There have been some promising psychopharmacological treatments that are being researched (Shah, Seese, Abikoff, & Klein, 1994), but no conclusive results are available because of the multiple etiologies of conduct disorder (Stoewe, Kruesi, & Lelio, 1995). An exciting line of research stems from the field of neuropsychiatry where organic etiologists, such as early traumatic brain injury, are being studied with reasonable treatment success (Wood & Singh, 1994). Some researchers of conduct disorders, after reviewing treatment effectiveness, suggest that prevention is a far more an effective and economical use of resources (Dodge, 1993; Offord, 1994).

Special education services may be available to students with conduct disorders usually because of the comorbidity with handicapping conditions such as serious emotional disturbance, attention-deficit hyperactivity disorder, and learning disabilities. However, far too many of these students are underidentified and they subsequently enter the juvenile justice system where specific treatments that are linked to the etiology of the disorder are seldom available. School psychologists and support personnel can best serve these students by using multiple sources of information and assessment, not only for diagnosis, but also for treatment. Success in the demands of everyday living for these students requires that the school, community, and home work in unison.

REFERENCES

American Psychiatric Association. (1994). *Diagnostic and Statistical Manual of Mental Disorders* (4th ed.). Washington DC: Author.

Dodge, K. A. (1993). The future of research on the treatment of conduct disorder. *Development and Psychopathology, 5,* 1–2, 311–319.

Eppright, T. D., Kashani, J. H., Robison, B. D., & Reid, J. C. (1993). Comorbidity of conduct disorder and personality disorders in an incarcerated juvenile population. *American Journal of Psychiatry, 150,* 8, 1233–1236.

Kazdin, A. E. (1993). Treatment of conduct disorder: Progress and directions in psychotherapy research. *Development & Psychopathology, 5,* 1–2, 277–310.

Kazdin, A. E. (1997). Practitioner review: Psychosocial treatments for conduct disorder in children. *Journal of Child Psychology & Psychiatry & Allied Disciplines, 38,* 2, 161–178.

Offord, D. R., Boyle, M. H., & Racine, Y. A. (1991). *The epidemiology of antisocial behavior in childhood and adolescence.* Hillsdale, NJ: Erlbaum.

Offord, D. R., & Bennett, K. J. (1994). Conduct disorder: Long-term outcomes and intervention effectiveness. *Journal of the American Academy of Child & Adolescent Psychiatry, 33,* 8, 1069–1078.

Shah, M. R., Seese, L. M., Abikoff, H., & Klein, R. G. (1994). Pemoline for children and adolescents with conduct disorder: A pilot investigation. *Journal of Child & Adolescent Psychopharmacology, 4,* 4, 255–261.

Sommers-Flanagan, J., & Sommers-Flanagan, R. (1998). Assessment and diagnosis of conduct disorder. *Journal of Counseling & Development, 76,* 2, 189–197.

Stewart, D. G., Brown, S. A., & Myers, M. G. (1997). Antisocial behavior and psychoactive substance involvement among Hispanic and non-Hispanic Caucasian adolescents in substance abuse treatment. *Journal of Child and Adolescent Substance Abuse, 6,* 4, 1–22.

Storm-Mathisen, A., & Vaglum, P. (1994). Conduct disorder patients 20 years later: A personal follow-up study. *Acta Psychiatrica Scandinavica, 89,* 6, 416–420.

Stoewe, J. K., Kruesi, M. J. P., & Lelio, D. F. (1995). Psychopharmacology of aggressive states and features of conduct disorder. *Child & Adolescent Psychiatric Clinics of North America, 4,* 2, 359–379.

Wood, I. K., & Singh, N. N. (1994). The impact of neuropsychiatry upon forensic issues related to children and adolescents. In L. F. Koziol & C. E. Stout (Eds.), *The neuropsychology of mental disorders: A practical guide.* Springfield, IL: Charles C. Thomas.

ELAINE FLETCHER-JANZEN
University of Northern Colorado

ANTISOCIAL PERSONALITY
EMOTIONAL DISORDERS
SUBSTANCE ABUSE

CONDUCTIVE HEARING LOSS

Auditory functioning can be altered at several levels: the ear, the auditory nerve, or the brain. In the ear, there are two types of anatomical structures—those concerned with the mechanical transmission of sound (a physical process) and those concerned with the transformation of the sound waves into nervous impulses (a biological process). Conductive hearing loss (CHL) applies to the condition resulting from an alteration of the former in opposition to sensory-neural hearing loss, which results from pathology of the latter. The combination of CHL with sensory-neural hearing loss is called mixed hearing loss. For more details about terms and causes of the different types, see Davis and Silverman (1960).

The mechanical transmission of the sound vibrations obeys the laws of acoustics. It is effected by the external and middle ear, the fluids of the inner ear, and the combined displacements of the cochlea's basilar and tectorial membranes. These bring the vibrations to bear on the sensory cells of the organ of Corti, the hair cells. There the conduction process ends; the hair cells are the transducers that transform the acoustic phenomenon into a biochemical and bioelectrical event. The CHL alone is never greater than 60 dB hearing loss, for higher intensity sounds reach the inner ear directly through the skull (von Békésy, 1948). In small children, it is often superimposed on sensoryneural hearing loss, thereby producing an additional deficiency.

Interference with the conduction process most commonly occurs at the level of external or middle ear structures.

One of the most frequent causes of temporary CHL is the external obstruction of the external ear canal (the auditory meatus) by cerumen, a waxlike secretion, especially in individuals with mental retardation (Crandell & Roesner, 1993). Obstruction by foreign bodies is also relatively frequent, especially in children. Various malformations of the external ear can affect hearing, the most serious being nondevelopment of the external auditory meatus.

The tympanic membrane, or eardrum, located between the external and middle ear, is linked with the malleus, incus, and stapes. With these ossicles it constitutes the tympano-ossicular chain, which transmits the sound arriving through the external ear to the oval window, an orifice in the bony wall separating middle and inner ear. Numerous pathological processes can affect these structures and thus produce conductive hearing loss. The eardrum can be swollen by inflammation, stiffened by sclerosis, or perforated. The ossicles may be partly or totally absent or malformed. The mobility of the chain may be reduced by fixation of the stapes in the oval window owing to abnormal bone proliferation at that level. This occurs in otosclerosis (otospongiosis), a frequent condition in adults and a rare one in children.

The accumulation of fluid in the ear occurs in several different forms of otitis media. One of them, serous otitis media, is a frequent chronic or semichronic disease of small children up to 5 or 6 years of age. It is often associated with obstruction of the eustachian tube. These conditions can usually be alleviated or cured relatively easily by medical and/or surgical treatment. However, since the CHL caused by them is mild or moderate, it is often ignored or neglected: This could have serious consequences in later life. Animal studies by Webster and Webster (1979) have shown that temporary moderate auditory restriction in the rat produces changes in the auditory brain stem nuclei. Studies reviewed by Ruben (1984) indicate that language-related skills may be durably impaired, even after restoration of normal hearing, in children who had prolonged CHL during the early years of life. This is because the early years are a particularly sensitive period for language development.

Because CHL affects only the mechanical part of the auditory channel, it produces a decrease in the sound pressure level reaching the inner ear, but no qualitative deformation of that sound. Therefore, a hearing aid that amplifies the sound waves, inasmuch as it does not itself introduce distortions, is capable of restoring a practically normal hearing sensation. While most causes of CHL can be efficiently corrected by medical and/or surgical treatment, the latter may have to be delayed, especially in children where plastic reconstruction surgery can only be done at a certain age level. For these patients, as well as for those where medico-surgical therapy has failed, is contraindicated, is impossible for practical reasons, or is refused by the patient, a well-adapted hearing aid is an excellent solution.

While CHL alone does not prevent spoken language development, it may severely slow down its progression and affect speech skills if undiagnosed or inadequately treated. In the latter case, speech and hearing therapy, following the appropriate medical and/or surgical treatment and/or hearing aid fitting, may be required. Special education may also be necessary as a temporary measure for those children whose speech and language deficiencies prevent them from holding their own in a school for those who hear normally. The great majority of children with CHL, however, can follow their whole curriculum in a mainstream situation, for instance, in ordinary schools with hearing children.

REFERENCES

Crandell, C. C., & Roesner, R. J. (1993). Incidence of Excessive/ Impacted Cerumen in Individuals with mental retardation: A longitudinal study. *American Journal on Mental Retardation, 97,* 5, 568–574.

Davis, H., & Silverman, S. R. (1960). *Hearing and deafness.* New York: Holt, Rinehart and Winston.

Ruben, R. J. (1984). An inquiry into the minimal amount of auditory deprivation which results in a cognitive effect in man. *Acta Oto-Laryngological* (Suppl. 414), 157–164.

von G. Békésy, (1948). Vibration of the head in a sound field and its role in hearing by bone conduction. *Journal of the Acoustical Society of America, 20,* 749–760.

Webster, D. B., & Webster, M. (1979). Effects of neonatal conductive hearing loss on brain stem auditory nuclei. *Annals of Otology, Rhinology and Laryngology, 88,* 684–688.

OLIVIER PÉRIER
Université Libre de Bruxelles,
Centre Comprendre et Parler

DEAF
DEAF EDUCATION
DEPRIVATION, BIONEURAL RESULTS OF

CONFIDENTIALITY OF INFORMATION

One major right guaranteed all citizens under the U.S. Constitution is the right to privacy. Included within this privilege is the right to have certain information held confidential. Recent legislation specifically addresses the right to confidentiality of information as it applies to disabled individuals and students, including special education students (Overcast & Sales, 1982; Reynolds, Gutkin, Elliot, & Witt, 1984). Two basic forms of information are covered in the legislation: information held by educational or residential institutions; and certain information discussed by individuals with certain school officials.

Only since the 1970s have the legal rights of disabled individuals and parents of students, including handicapped students, been viewed as in need of regulation. Historically, parents and students had virtually no rights to monitor the information held in institutional files. Often this information was readily accessible to individuals not directly concerned with the educational welfare of the individual in question. In the event that important educational decisions were based on this information in the files, parents, for example, were afforded little if any input into the decisions made. Nor were parents aware of what, where, and when information regarding their children was released to others (Overcast & Sales, 1982).

The Buckley amendment (FERPA, 1976) was enacted in direct response to this practice by educational institutions or agencies that appeared to be in violation of their clients' constitutional rights. It now stands as the major legal document that provides parents and eligible students with the right to: review and inspect educational records; amend inaccurate records; and control disclosure of personally identifiable information in educational records. More specific to children with disabilities, parts of this document are reiterated in the Individual with Disabilities Education Act (IDEA). This act specifically extends parents of handicapped children the right to control or participate in major educational decisions directly affecting their child. Under this law, as in the Buckley amendment, consent must be given before certain filed information can be revealed to individuals outside the educational institution. In addition, under IDEA, parents must be able to inspect and amend all information in their child's file.

In addition to these legal documents that ensure the right to have recorded information held confidential, there are also certain guidelines intended to protect the confidentiality of information disclosed by students to certain educational personnel (e.g., counselors, school psychologists). The issue of what and how much information is confidential is not entirely clear. In general, professionals (e.g., psychologists) are bound by their particular ethical standards to protect the confidentiality of information revealed to them in private sessions. This information can usually be revealed without the individual's consent unless there is evidence that the information would result in harm or danger to the patient or others (Reynolds et al., 1984, p. 259). When this information is revealed to school personnel, there seems to be even more ambiguity regarding what is to be held confidential. Overcast and Sales (1982) state:

> It is simply not clear how much confidentiality a student may expect in dealing with school personnel. It depends on the nature of the communication, to whom the communication is directed, and the particular status of the state law. (p. 1089)

REFERENCES

Overcast, T. D., & Sales, B. D. (1982). The legal rights of students in the elementary and secondary public schools. In C. R. Reynolds & T. B. Gutkin (Eds.), *The handbook of school psychology.* New York: Wiley.

Reynolds, C. R., Gutkin, T. B., Elliot, S. N., & Witt, J. C. (1984). *School psychology: Essentials of theory and practice.* New York: Wiley.

JULIA A. HICKMAN
University of Texas

BUCKLEY AMENDMENT
INDIVIDUALS WITH DISABILITIES EDUCATION ACT (IDEA)

CONGENITAL DISORDERS

Two concepts are joined together in the expression congenital disorders, making it pertinent to begin this entry with a short comment on each. Congenital stands for present at birth. This definition does not imply any causal relationship. Nevertheless, for a long time, the terms congenital and hereditary have been confused. Indeed, some congenital disorders may be hereditary, but in many others heredity is not involved. Thus the clear recognition of the absence of any familial factor allows many couples to be reassured concerning the possible recurrence of congenital disorders.

Disorder (malformation or anomaly are also used) means any defect when compared with the normal. Earlier, mainly visible anomalies were detected; today, disorders are described at any level, on the surface or inside the organism, with the aid of sophisticated technical procedures. Therefore, according to Warkany (1971), "Congenital malformations are structural defects present at birth. They may be gross or microscopic, on the surface of the body or within it, familial or sporadic, hereditary or nonhereditary, single or multiple." Only the molecular level must be added to this definition to include all congenital disorders.

Estimations of the incidence of congenital disorders vary from report to report, depending heavily on the mode of ascertainment: external examination only at birth, X-rays, microscopic analyses of tissues, functional tests, inclusion or exclusion of stillbirths, distinction between major and minor defects, and even the personal interest of the examiner in charge at the birth of the child. Thus in a Belgian study, significantly more congenital heart anomalies were observed in two maternity wards participating in a concerted action project of the European Economic Community, probably because the neonatologist pediatricians had special training in cardiology (Borlée-Grimée, De Wals, & Vinçotte-Mols, 1985). Nevertheless, a mean figure could be 2 to 3%. This may seem very high, but it is well established that stillbirths show more congenital anomalies than live births, and that at least 50% of abortions of the first trimester show severe chromosome defects that are likely linked with expulsion (Boué & Boué, 1975). Therefore, the figure of 2 to 3% represents only a small proportion of all malformed embyros. Moreover, all disorders are included, from severe congenital heart malformations incompatible with life, to the partial fusion of two small toes. On the other hand, it is important to point out that congenital disorders are not so exceptional in our species and fortunately, not all are associated with a severe handicap. To our knowledge, there is no particular definition of major and minor anomalies; the interpretation is usually left to reporting authors.

There are many causes of congenital disorders. It is possible to distinguish three broad categories: (1) disorders genetically transmitted following classical Mendelian modes (McKusick, 1983), (2) disorders owed to anomalies of the genetic material but usually not transmitted (e.g., chromosome anomalies), and (3) disorders owed to environmental factors. Many can be recognized at birth by at least one characteristic symptom and some others are detected only later in life.

Dominant heredity is most frequently observed in the case of minor anomalies that do not impair normal life (e.g., supernumerary or fused fingers or toes). A dominant congenital defect is theoretically transmitted to half the offspring, and may be followed through many generations. Sometimes, one generation seems skipped over, or, on the contrary, more severely affected: this is due to variations in penetrance or expressivity of the gene. However, severe congenital disorders can be transmitted through a dominant mode. This is the case in Huntington's chorea, a disease of the nervous system (for a recent review, see Robert, 1985). Strictly speaking, Huntington's chorea is a congenital disorder, the gene responsible for it being present at birth. However, carriers of the mutation enjoy a normal life until 30 or 40 years of age and in reproduction transmit the gene to half their offspring. The onset of the disease is observed with a progressive neurological symptomatology (involuntary movements), and often a psychiatric component (depression sometimes ending in suicide). Death usually follows 10 to 15 years after the onset of symptoms.

Recessive heredity is characterized by the birth of affected children to normal parents. Indeed, the father and the mother are heterozygous for a common mutant gene, and 25% of their offspring are homozygous and affected. Hundreds of examples are found in McKusick's catalog of Mendelian diseases in man (1983). When the disorder is severe, people with the disease usually do not reproduce and the genes are eliminated: the reservoir of the disease is thus found in the heterozygous carriers. Many recessive disorders are rare: consanguineous marriages are a well-known favoring factor, as is a common ethnic background (e.g., Tay-Sachs disease is more frequent in Ashkenazi Jews, sickle-cell anemia in blacks, thalassemia in Mediterranean populations). However, this is not a general rule, and unrelated parents from different ethnic backgrounds

may be heterozygous for a common recessive gene (a well-known example is mucoviscidosis). When a recessive disorder is suspected, the diagnosis must first be firmly established with the use of appropriate techniques: X-rays, laboratory tests, pathologic and molecular studies. Genetic counseling then becomes possible.

Congenital disorders may be sex-linked, either dominant or recessive. In the first case, females and males are affected, in the second only males. Some common congenital malformations such as cleft lip and palate, clubfoot, spina bifida cystica, anencephaly, and pyloric stenosis are not transmitted through simple Mendelian inheritance, but nevertheless show a clear familial aggregation (Carter, 1976). In these cases, a particular genetic mechanism, called polygenism, is involved. In short, the anomaly is determined by more than one gene, all acting in the same direction and possibly interacting with environmental factors. Beyond a given threshold, the malformation is present. For instance, let us suppose a birth defect associated with the presence of five specific genes acting together in a specific environment. The intact father may possess four of them and the intact mother three. Unpredictably, they can transmit to one of their children five or more deleterious genes. Of course, they may also have non-affected children. The risk is not of the monogenic type; i.e., 50%, 25%, or sex-linked. Empirical tables have been proposed after tabulating direct observations. For example, in a determined population, the risk of having a child with a cleft lip is 1 in 1000 births. A couple who already has one affected child will have a risk increase of 40 times (4%; Carter, 1976). If one of the two parents is affected, the risk before any pregnancy is around 3%. If one of the parents is affected and one child is also affected, the risk is 11%. A major cause of congenital anomalies, usually associated with mental retardation, is chromosome anomalies. The malformations are undoubtedly of genetic origin, owed to anomalies of genetic material, but even if they are genetic and congenital, they are usually not hereditary.

A number of congenital disorders are due to environmental factors. The term environmental must, however, be understood in a broad sense: everything that alters the normal parameters of the body, the body being considered a conglomerate of cells. Clearly, this means that environmental factors can originate from the surrounding area in which the patient lives (e.g., radiation, viruses, drugs), or inside his or her own body (e.g., diabetes, hypothyroidism). This creates abnormal environmental conditions for the cells and, if the patient is a pregnant woman, for the fetus.

In experiments with animals, many agents are known to cause congenital disorders when they are administered to pregnant females (Warkany, 1971). The systematic study of these effects is called teratology. A catalog of teratogenic agents is regularly published and kept up to date (Shepard, 1983). Many drugs are known to be associated with fetal malformations. Pregnant women are usually warned to seek medical advice before taking any medication. Nevertheless, some compounds, although carefully tested before marketing, escape detection and are responsible for the birth of malformed babies. The case of thalidomide is well known. This sedative drug, used also by pregnant women for nausea and vomiting, was found to induce severe anomalies in the human fetus when ingested between the 35th and the 50th day after the last menstrual period (the 23rd to 38th day after conception). Rat and mouse embryos did not seem to suffer from thalidomide administered to pregnant females. However, when the relationship between human malformations and thalidomide was established, the effect of the drug was studied again on macaques. They showed the same sensibility as man. Rabbits also suffered, but to a lesser degree. This demonstrates the importance of selecting a good experimental model. All teratogenic agents cannot be reviewed here; only a few will be discussed.

Ionizing radiations have a well-known teratogenic effect. However fear of congenital malformations in the fetus must not stop pregnant women from having examinations needed for their health (and thus for their baby's health). The teratogenic effect is dose-dependent; it also depends on the site of irradiation and the advancement of the pregnancy. As all this has been extensively demonstrated, it is best to advise the radiologist about a pregnancy or to perform a pregnancy test in case of doubt. Some viruses, but not all, also present with teratogenic activity. The example of rubella is well known; however, the risk is not the same throughout pregnancy. The maximum fetal sensitivity is during the first trimester. Alcohol ingestion may be harmful and cause fetal alcohol syndrome. Heavy smoking is also responsible for fetal damage and low birth weight. Diseases of the mother may affect the fetus if not corrected. Diabetes causes the birth of large infants, higher mortality at birth, and a tendency to hypoglycemia and respiratory distress after delivery (Delaney & Ptacek, 1970). Moreover, some authors are convinced that congenital malformations are more frequent in children of diabetic mothers or at least that some diabetic mothers are more at risk than others. However, if the ingestion of some drugs is known to be teratogenic, the absence of other elements, like vitamins, is harmful. Nutritional deficiencies as a cause of congenital malformations in experimental animals are well documented (Warkany, 1971). These situations are seldom encountered under normal human living conditions, but they explain why a vitamin supplement is advised for pregnant women.

The prevention of congenital malformations has many aspects. An important and simple means of prevention is regular medical surveillance during pregnancy. Another mode of prevention is to avoid any known teratogenic agent and to have balanced nutritional intake. If the birth of a child with severe congenital disorder is followed by death, necropsy is of paramount importance to determine the recurrence risk for the parents. However, sophisticated means of surveillance have been developed for the at-risk mother to be. Prenatal diagnosis is offered, including chromosome analysis of the fetus, research on abnormal genes at the molecular level with recombinant DNA techniques, blood sampling or biopsy of the fetus, follow-up of the anatomical growth of the fetus with ultrasound, various biochemical dosages in the amniotic fluid, and direct viral research on fetal tissues. For some defects, no known treatment is possible, and interruption of pregnancy may appear as the most appropriate solution. For others, treatment is possible either directly with the fetus or just after birth. Thus if a curable congenital heart malformation is diagnosed before birth, the mother can be delivered in a hospital specializing in the correction of such an anomaly.

Neonatal screening is important in some metabolic or endocrine disorders. For instance, hypothyroidism at birth is responsible for future mental retardation of the child, known as cretinism. Nevertheless, after delivery, hypothyroidic children are potentially normal, the maternal thyroid having supplemented the fetus. Immediate substitution treatment allows normal intellectual development. Hypothyroidism can be diagnosed just after birth by the increase of the hormone stimulating the thyroid activity (the thyreostimulating hormone [TSH]) in the blood. Testing is possible on a few drops of blood taken in the perinatal period, and the affected babies, duly treated, enjoy normal development (Delange et al., 1979). Many other disorders can be detected by neonatal screening (Bickel et al., 1980), and progress in this area is promising. This compensates for the high incidence of congenital disorders at birth.

REFERENCES

Bickel, H., Guthrie, R., & Hammersen, G. (1980). *Neonatal screening for inborn errors of metabolism* (Vol. 1). Berlin: Springer-Verlag.

Borlée-Grimée, I., De Wals, P., & Vinçotte-Mols, M. (1985). Problems in the ascertainment of congenital heart disease. Review of 308 cases registered in Hainaut from 1979 to 1982. In P. De Wals, J. A. C. Weatherall, & M. F. Lechat (Eds.), *Registration of congenital anomalies in Eurocat Centers* 1979–1983. Louvain-la-Neuve, Cabay.

Boué, J., Boué, A., & Lazar, P. (1975). The epidemiology of human spontaneous abortions with chromosome anomalies. In R. J. Blondau (Ed.), *Aging gametes*. Basel, Switzerland: Karger.

Carter, C. O. (1976). Genetics of common single malformations. *British Medical Bulletin, 32,* 21–26.

Delange, F., Beckers, C., Höfer, R., König, M. P., Monaco, F., & Varrone, S. (1979). Neonatal screening for congenital hypothyroidism in Europe. *Acta Endocrinologica, 90* (Suppl. 223), 1–27.

Delaney, J. J., & Ptacek, J. (1970). Three decades of experience with diabetic pregnancies. *American Journal of Obstetrics & Gynecology, 106,* 550.

McKusick, V. (1983). *Mendelian inheritance in man* (6th ed.). Baltimore, MD: Johns Hopkins University Press.

Robert, J. M. (1985). La chorée de Huntington: Histoire naturelle de la maladie. *Journal de Genetique Humaine, 33,* 83–90.

Shepard, T. H. (1983). *Catalog of teratogenic agents* (4th ed.). Baltimore, MD: Johns Hopkins University Press.

Warkany, J. (1971). *Congenital malformations* (Vol. 1). Chicago: Year Book Medical.

L. KOULISCHER
*Institut de Morphologie
Pathologique, Belgium*

GENETIC COUNSELING
GENETIC VARIATIONS
HEREDITY

CONGENITAL WORD BLINDNESS, HISTORY OF

This term refers to "a condition in which, with normal vision and therefore seeing the letters and words distinctly, an individual is no longer able to interpret written or printed language" (Hinshelwood, 1917, p. 2). The term was the title of a book written by Hinshelwood (1917) in which he described case studies and intervention techniques with individuals who evidenced word blindness. Hinshelwood's clients showed such disability subsequent to strokes or brain damage induced by chronic alcoholism. He extended the use of this term to children who showed the same reading disability. However, "congenital word blindness" was originally used by Morgan (1896), whose paper was one of the first to document a clear case of severe reading disability in a 14-year-old boy of apparent brightness. The boy knew all his letters and could write and read them singly. However, except for some common sight words such as the, and, of, and that, he could not read any word, even words that he encountered daily, such as the name of his father's house. The boy's parents provided him with tutors and sent him to schools to teach him to read, but despite concerted teaching efforts, the boy's reading disability persisted.

Morgan and Hinshelwood were opthalmologists. They were intrigued by their clients and observed and recorded the details of severe reading disabilities. They both used the term congenital word blindness to describe adults and children with clear, pronounced reading disabilities. Specifically, Hinshelwood (1917) hypothesized that children with congenital word blindness sustained a brain defect in the left hemisphere, where he thought visual word and letter memories were stored. According to Hinshelwood, the inability to read was attributed to deficient visual memory, for he believed good readers recognize or remember words by activating a visual picture rather than by analyzing individual letters in the words. Additionally, both he and Morgan considered such a brain defect to be congenital (Smith, 1983).

Hinshelwood believed that intensive practice and the development of the brain's visual memory would enable individuals with congenital word blindness to reach reading proficiency (Mercer, 1983). Specifically, he suggested a three-stage approach to the remediation of deficits: teaching the individual letters for storage in the supposed visual-memory center of the brain; teaching word recognition by spelling the printed words aloud so as to use the individual's good auditory memory for letter sounds; and enabling storage of the reading words using oral and written practice. It has been suggested that Hinshelwood's emphasis on visual memory and generally visual interpretations of reading disability had a significant impact on subsequent visual-perceptual theories of learning disabilities (Smith, 1983).

REFERENCES

Hinshelwood, J. (1917). *Congenital word blindness.* London: Lewis.

Mercer, C. D. (1983). *Students with learning disabilities* (2nd ed.). Columbus, OH: Charles E. Merrill.

Morgan, W. P. (1896). A case of congenital word blindness. *British Medical Journal, 2,* 1378.

Smith, C. R. (1983). *Learning disabilities: The interaction of learner, task and setting.* Boston: Little, Brown.

BERNICE Y. L. WONG
Simon Fraser University

DYSLEXIA
READING DISORDERS

CONNERS' PARENT-RATING SCALES-REVISED, CONNERS' TEACHER-RATING SCALES-REVISED, CONNERS'-WELLS' ADOLESCENT SELF-REPORT SCALE

The revised Conners' rating scales follow the original aims of the earlier versions in assessing attention-deficit/hyperactivity disorder (ADHD) (Conners, 1997). Both the Conners' Parent-Rating Scale Revised (CPRS-R) and the Conners' Teacher-Rating Scales Revised (CTRS-R) are designed to assess attention-deficit ADHD and related behavioral problems for children ages 3 to 17. This measure should be used as an ancillary source of information rather than the sole means of diagnosing ADHD.

Both parent and teacher scales include Oppositional, Cognitive Problems, Hyperactivity, Anxious-Shy, Perfectionism, Social Problems, the Conners' Global Index, Restless-Impulsive, Emotional Liability, DSM-IV symptom subscale, DSM-IV Inattentive and DSM-IV Hyperactive-Impulsive. For the parent scale, there is an additional Psychosomatic scale. The parent form contains 80 items and the teacher form contains 59 items; both are rated using an adapted Likert 4 point scale (from never to very often) and both take approximately 20 minutes to complete.

CPRS Long Form was normed on parents or guardians of 2,482 children ages 3 to 17. Eighty-three percent of the children were Caucasian, but the normative sample also included African Americans, Hispanics, Asian Americans, Native Americans and others. Gender distribution was approximately equal. Internal reliability (Cronbach's alpha coefficient) are reported for each scale by gender and range from .73 to .94. Test-retest intervals between 6 and 8 weeks were studied for each subscale using 49 children (average age 11.8) and ranged from .47–.85.

CTRS Long Form was normed on teachers of 1,973 children ages 3–17. Seventy-eight percent of the adolescents were identified by teachers as Caucasian. Test-retest intervals between 6 and 8 weeks were studied for each subscale using 50 children (average age 11.2) and ranged from .47–.88. CTRS internal reliability (Cronbach's alpha coefficient) are reported for each scale, divided by gender range from .77 to .96. Test-retest reliability ranged from .62 to .87 (Danforth, et al., 1996).

The validity of this measure was determined by its ability to discriminate between clinically referred and nonreferred children. (Miller, et al., 1997). Correlations (concurrent validity) between parent and teacher ratings for individual subscales ranged from .12 to .47 for males, and .21 to .55 for females, indicating that teacher and parent raters often perceived the same children quite differently.

The Conners'-Wells' Adolescent Self-Report Scale (CASS) is a new addition to the parent and teacher rating scales. It contains 10 subscales including Family Problems, Emotional Problems, Conduct Problems, Cognitive Problems, Anger Control Problems, Hyperactivity, ADHD Index, DSM-IV Symptom Subscale, DSM-IV Inattentive, DSM-IV Hyperactive-Impulsive and takes approximately 20 minutes to complete.

The CASS long form contains 87 items that are rated using an adapted Likert 4 point scale (from never to very often) by adolescents between 12 and 17 years of age. The CASS long form was normed on 3,394 adolescents between the ages of 12 and 17 (1558 males and 1836 females). Sixty-two percent of this sample were Caucasian. Internal reliability (Cronbach's alpha coefficient) are reported for each scale, by gender and range from .75 to .92. Test-retest intervals between 6 and 8 weeks were studied for each subscale using 50 children (mean age 14.8) and ranged from .73–.89.

Until recently, only one form was available for the parent and teacher ratings. The revised version, however, now includes both long and short versions of these scales. The CPRS and CTRS short forms cover a smaller scope of problems (only the Oppositional, Cognitive Problems, Hyperactivity and ADHD Index are measured) then does the long form. The short forms can be completed in significantly less time than the long forms. The CASS is also available in a short form and includes only 4 subscales, Conduct Problems, Cognitive Problems, Hyperactivity-Impulsive, and the ADHD Index.

REFERENCES

Conners, C. K. (1997). *Conners' Rating Scales-Revised Technical Manual*. North Tonawanda, NY: Multi-Health Systems.

Danforth, J. S., & DuPaul, G. J. (1996). Interrater reliability of teacher rating scales for children with attention-deficit hyperactivity disorder. *Journal of Psychopathology & Behavioral Assessment, 3*, 227–237.

Miller, L. S., Koplewicz, H. S., & Klein, R. G. (1997). Teacher ratings of hyperactivity, inattention, and conduct problems in preschoolers. *Journal of Abnormal Child Psychology, 2*, 113–119.

ROSEANN BISIGHINI
The Salk Institute

ATTENTION DEFICIT DISORDER
HYPERKINESIS

CONSCIENCE, LACK OF IN HANDICAPPED

Society is particularly concerned that children develop the skills to regulate their own behavior or, stated differently, internalize moral principles. Situations often arise that pose a conflict between the individual desires of the person and the requirements of society. These circumstances call for the exercise of self-control as the person suppresses self-interested behavior in favor of actions that serve the needs of others. Two areas of research bear directly on this problem—altruism and resistance to temptation.

Altruism

Altruism refers to behavior that is carried out to benefit another in the absence of threat or expected reward. Altruism entails self-control since the helper must weigh the costs of helping (e.g., material loss or physical danger) against the benefits (e.g., self-satisfaction) of helping (Kanfer, 1979). Research with children has relied on several measures of altruism, including donating possessions to a charity or another child, willingness to rescue someone in trouble, peer ratings, and naturalistic observations of helping and sharing.

Most children show an increase in sharing during the

period of middle childhood. This change parallels children's decreasing egocentrism and increasingly sophisticated moral reasoning abilities. However, the relationship among these variables is not clearly understood. At least with children of average IQ, general level of cognitive development is unrelated to various measures of altruism (Rushton & Wiener, 1975). There does appear to be a weak relationship between generosity and level of moral reasoning among 7- to 11-year-old children, but it is not known if moral reasoning directly affects moral behavior (Rushton, 1975). Most studies fail to find a relationship between sex and altruism, but when differences are noted they tend to show females as more altruistic (Krebs, 1970). Finally, investigators have found a substantial degree of behavioral specificity across situations that offer an opportunity for altruistic behavior. For example, a child may donate a toy to a needy stranger but fail to volunteer time to help a peer. The correlation across measures is about .30 and may reflect the weak effect of an underlying personality variable or experimental or psychometric artifacts (Rushton, 1976).

One research finding that is unequivocal is that the altruistic behavior of children can be modified. Numerous studies have shown that children will imitate an altruistic model (Harris, 1971). In fact, the influence of a model was shown in one study to extend up to 4 months, even though posttesting was conducted under very different circumstances (Rushton, 1975). These results have obvious implications for child-rearing practices.

Resistance to Temptation

Resistance to temptation is another example of self-control. Here the child is required to exercise self-restraint in the absence of immediate surveillance. Several studies have examined variables that promote this form of self-control. From a developmental perspective, the emergence of language is important in that it allows the child to regulate his or her behavior by stating rules of conduct (Kanfer & Phillips, 1970). The ability to verbalize rules may be necessary but usually is not sufficient for resisting temptation.

Children who score high on resistance to temptation often make use of cognitive strategies (i.e., self-control techniques). A body of work by Kanfer (Hartig & Kanfer, 1973; Kanfer & Zich, 1974) and Mischel (Mischel, Ebbesen, & Zeiss, 1972; Mischel & Patterson, 1978) has shown that resistance to temptation is enhanced when children distract themselves (e.g., sing songs or thinking of a "fun activity"), repeatedly state a rule (e.g., "I'm a good girl if I don't look at the hampster"), or engage in mental transformations (e.g., "The pretzel is really just a log of wood"). The fact that older children are more successful in such situations is in part attributed to a greater facility in the use of language and a larger repertoire of cognitive strategies.

Researchers have just recently begun to extend these findings to retarded individuals. It has been noted that mildly retarded adolescents prefer immediate rewards even though by waiting they could receive twice as many of those rewards (Franzini, Litrownik, & Magy, 1978). In one study with moderately retarded adolescents, training in self-instruction ("I am gonna get more money if I wait to get paid . . . I sure am a good worker") reinforced practice and the provision of successful models led to a fivefold increase in the delay of gratification (Franzini, Litrownik, & Magy, 1980).

The importance of verbal controlling strategies in resistance to temptation is underscored by a study comparing Down's syndrome children to nonretarded children matched for level of cognitive development. On the average, the retarded children were less able to resist temptation than were the nonretarded children, a finding consistent with the Franzini et al. (1980) study. Interestingly, those Down's syndrome children that were most successful were observed to spontaneously engage in verbal and nonverbal behaviors that served to distract them from the desired object (Kopp, Krakow, & Johnson, 1983).

In considering the research in both the areas of altruism and resistance to temptation, a clear directive for teachers and parents is evident. In order to enhance self-control one should not think in terms of building the child's character. Instead, the child should be taught specific verbal and nonverbal behavioral skills that can be used for self-regulation in tempting situations.

REFERENCES

Franzini, L. R., Litrownik, A. J., & Magy, M. A. (1978). Immediate and delayed reward preferences of TMR adolescents. *American Journal of Mental Deficiency, 82,* 406–409.

Franzini, L. R., Litrownik, A. J., & Magy, M. A. (1980). Training trainable mentally retarded adolescents in delay behavior. *Mental Retardation, 18,* 45–47.

Harris, M. (1971). Models, norms and sharing. *Psychological Reports, 29,* 147–153.

Hartig, M., & Kanfer, F. H. (1973). The role of verbal self-instructions in children's resistance to temptation. *Journal of Personality & Social Psychology, 25,* 259–267.

Kanfer, F. H. (1979). Personal control, social control, and altruism: Can society survive the age of individualism? *American Psychologist, 34,* 231–239.

Kanfer, F. H., & Phillips, J. S. (1970). *Learning foundations of behavior therapy.* New York: Wiley.

Kanfer, F. H., & Zich, J. (1974). Self-control training: The effects of external control on children's resistance to temptation. *Developmental Psychology, 10,* 108–115.

Kopp, C. B., Krakow, J. B., & Johnson, K. L. (1983). Strategy production by young Down syndrome children. *American Journal of Mental Deficiency, 88,* 164–169.

Krebs, D. L. (1970). Altruism: An examination of the concept and a review of the literature. *Psychological Bulletin, 73,* 258–302.

Mischel, W., Ebbesen, E. B., & Zeiss, A. R. (1972). Cognitive and attentional mechanisms in delay of gratification. *Journal of Personality & Social Psychology, 21,* 204–218.

Mischel, W., & Patterson, C. J. (1978). Effective plans for self-control. In W. A. Collins (Ed.), *Minnesota symposia on child psychology* (Vol. 2). Hillsdale, NJ: Erlbaum.

Rushton, J. P. (1975). Generosity in children: Immediate and long term effects of modeling, preaching, and moral judgment. *Journal of Personality & Social Psychology, 31,* 459–466.

Rushton, J. P. (1976). Socialization and the altruistic behavior of children. *Psychological Bulletin, 83,* 898–913.

Rushton, J. P., & Wiener, J. (1975). Altruism and cognitive development in children. *British Journal of Social & Clinical Psychology, 14,* 341–349.

LAURENCE C. GRIMM
University of Illinois

IMPULSE CONTROL
MORAL REASONING
SELF-CONTROL CURRICULUM

CONSENT, INFORMED

Increased parental involvement through informed consent began with the Education for All Handicapped Children Act of 1975 and consistently has been supported and enforced by subsequent legislation in the firm of the Individuals with Disabilities Education Act (IDEA) and amendments. The intent of the informed consent requirement is to change the relationship between schools and parents from one of the schools as the primary authority in determining the appropriate education for handicapped students to one of shared decision making. Prior to the passage of PL 94-142, some schools consulted with parents and told them about their children's special education placement and some did not, carrying the doctrine of *in loco parentis* to an intolerable extreme. However, court decisions and decrees have stated that the consequences of possible labeling, segregation, and exclusion of handicapped children from other children, and changes in their curriculum, may infringe on their constitutional rights of life, liberty, or property, and that individuals who may be subject to such deprivation must consent to any process with these possible results.

To protect students from arbitrary changes in placement, parental consent must be received before conducting a preplacement evaluation, before placing a child in a program providing special education and related services and before re-valuation of services. If the parents refuse to give their consent to evaluation or placement, the school system may request a due process hearing to obtain the authority to proceed with the assessment and placement process without parental consent.

Bersoff (1978) argues that informed consent is more of a stated principle than a well-defined and agreed on concept. However, consensus exists that the principle of informed consent has three characteristics: knowledge, voluntariness, and capacity. First, parents must be "fully informed of all information relevant to the activity for which consent is sought." Bersoff (1978, 1982) argues that it is impossible for schools to present every technical detail of the evaluations to be performed or to anticipate every benefit and hazard that could arise from the evaluation or special education placement. There are guidelines on what needs to be provided at a minimum to parents such as a description of the actions to be taken by the school district and the rationale for those actions. In addition, the regulations make it clear that school personnel must make a good faith effort to communicate with parents; they must provide the notice in the parents' native language and must ensure that parents understand the content of the notice.

Second, consent is given voluntarily in the absence of any coercion, language problems, misrepresentation, or duress; consent is not permanently binding and can be withdrawn at any time. Finally, the law presumes that parents are competent to make decisions about their children's educational programs. If school districts believe that particular parents cannot make such decisions, they should then initiate procedures for the appointment of a substitute decision maker, typically in the form of a guardian ad litem. The American Educational Research Association, American Psychological Association, and the National Council on Measurement in Education have agreed on and endorsed a definition of informed consent that, although specific to the taking of educational and psychological tests, presents general principles applicable to nearly any special education circumstance. In the *Standards for Educational and Psychological Testing* (Committee to Revise the Standards, 1985), these organizations define informed consent as:

> The granting of consent by the test taker to be tested on the basis of full information concerning the purpose of the testing, the persons who may receive the test scores, the use to which the test scores may be put, and other such information as may be material to the consent process. (pp. 91–92)

Full disclosure of information necessary to the decision-making process and a full understanding of the information seem to be the key to obtaining informed consent.

Bersoff (1978, 1982), Overcast and Sales (1982), and Kotin (1978) suggest various procedures for securing informed consent and corresponding criteria and assessment techniques to determine the extent to which the informed consent principle has been implemented. Current practice in special education varies greatly from school district to school district. Ethics consultation (Heron, 1996) and specialized policies for students with handicapping conditions and aversive procedures are necessary (Braaten, 1991). Careful attention to obtaining informed consent is not just good professional practice, it is a requirement of federal law.

REFERENCES

Bersoff, D. N. (1978). Procedural safeguards. In L. G. Morra (Ed.), *Developing criteria for the evaluation of due process procedural safeguards provisions of Public Law 94-142* (pp. 63–142). Washington, DC: U.S. Office of Education.

Bersoff, D. N. (1982). The legal regulation of school psychology. In C. R. Reynolds & T. B. Gutkin (Eds.), *The handbook of school psychology*. New York: Wiley.

Braaten, S. (1991). A policy model for use of aversive and deprivation procedures to decrease problem behaviors of students in special education. *Preventing School Failure, 35,* 3, 27–31.

Committee to Revise the Standards. (1985). *Standards for educational and psychological testing*. Washington, DC: American Psychological Association.

Heron, T. E. (1996). Ethical and legal issues in consultation. *Remedial and Special Education, 17,* 6, 377–385.

Kotin, L. (1978). Recommended criteria and assessment techniques for the evaluation by LEAs of their compliance with the notice and consent requirements of PL 94-142. In L. G. Morra (Ed.), *Developing criteria for the evaluation of due process procedural safeguards provisions of Public Law 94-142* (pp. 143–178). Washington, DC: U.S. Office of Education.

Overcast, T. D., & Sales, B. D. (1982). The legal rights of students in the schools. In C. R. Reynolds & T. B. Gutkin (Eds.), *The handbook of school psychology*. New York: Wiley.

U.S. Department of Health, Education, and Welfare. (1977). Education of handicapped children: Implementation of Part B of the Education of Handicapped Act. *Federal Register, 42*(163), 42474–42518.

ROLAND K. YOSHIDA
Fordham University

INDIVIDUALS WITH DISABILITIES EDUCATION ACT (IDEA)

CONSENT AGREEMENT

See CONSENT DECREE.

CONSENT DECREE

A consent decree is a legal mandate or court order issued by a judiciary authority that has jurisdiction over the particular civil matter resolved in the decree. It is a legally en-

forceable order of that court. Consent decrees derive from the agreement of the adversarial parties to a civil lawsuit to end their disagreement provided that certain acts are performed by one or both parties and agreed to in order to avoid continuing litigation. The agreement is drawn up by the two parties, signed by the appropriate legal representatives, and submitted to the court for review. If the court decides the agreement is fair and entered into with appropriate understanding and representation by both parties, the court will then mandate and enforce the decree by court order.

Many special education cases are decided by consent agreements that become enforceable court decrees. Among the best known and most influential are *Diana and Guadalupe*. Consent decrees are binding only on the parties to the decree, however, and do not make case law or set legal precedent.

CECIL R. REYNOLDS
Texas A & M University

DIANA v. STATE BOARD OF EDUCATION

CONSTITUTIONAL LAW (IN SPECIAL EDUCATION)

Judicial interpretations of the Constitution and its amendments have played a major role in the comparatively recent efforts to obtain and maintain appropriate special education programs and services for handicapped children and youth and their families. The groundwork for this role was laid in the 1954 Supreme Court decision in *Brown v. Board of Education*; the decision made clear that separate education facilities for children of different races are inherently not equal (Lippman & Goldberg, 1973). This decision affirmed that, because of the importance of education today, education "is a right which must be available to all on equal terms" (*Brown v. Board*, 347 U.S. 483). Citing this decision almost 20 years later, attorneys in two class-action suits built their arguments for landmark special education cases that were resolved in federal district courts: *PARC v. Board* (*PARC v. Commonwealth*, 334 F. Supp. 1257, E.D. Pa., 1971), which made clear that mentally retarded children in Pennsylvania are entitled to free education programs appropriate for their needs; and *Mills v. Board* (*Mills v. Board of Education, District of Columbia*, 348 F. Supp. 866, 1972), which extended free and appropriate education to all handicapped children in the District of Columbia.

Both the *PARC and Mills* cases have been cited in subsequent litigation involving similar and related principles that eventually were incorporated into federal legislation. Of particular importance to special education are the Rehabilitation Act of 1973, which requires access to programs and facilities, and more recently the Individuals with Disabilities Education Act (IDEA) and subsequent amendments, the latest being in 1997 (Martin, 1996). They embody the principles of zero project, nondiscriminatory testing, individualized and appropriate education planning and programming, least restrictive alternative as preferred educational placement, and procedural due process. All of these principles can be found in the guarantees of the Fifth and Fourteenth amendments to the Constitution (Turnbull & Fiedler, 1985) which state:

No person shall...be deprived of life, liberty, or property, without due process of law. (Constitution of the United States, Amendment V, 1791)

No State shall make or enforce any law which shall abridge the privileges or immunities of citizens of the United States; nor shall any State deprive any person of life, liberty or property without due process of law, nor deny to any person within its jurisdiction the equal protection of the laws. (Constitution of the United States, Amendment XIV, 1868)

For a detailed discussion of litigation in special education and its reliance on constitutional guarantees and interpretations of the Supreme Court, see Turnbull and Fiedler (1984). Recent litigation has focused on the constitutionality of State financing systems (Verstegen, 1998).

REFERENCES

Ballard, J., Ramirez, B. A., & Weintraub, F. J. (1982). *Special education in America: Its legal and governmental foundations.* Reston, VA: Council for Exceptional Children.

Lippman, L., & Goldberg, I. (1973). *Right to education: Anatomy of the Pennsylvania case and its implications for exceptional children.* New York: Teachers College Press.

Martin, E. W. (1996). The legislative and litigation history of special education. *Future of Children, 6,* 1, 25–39.

Turnbull, J. R., III, & Fiedler, C. R. (1984). *Judicial interpretation of the Education for All Handicapped Children Act.* Reston, VA: Council for Exceptional Children.

Verstegen, D. A. (1998). Landmark court decisions challenge state special education funding. *Center for Special Education Brief.* Palo Alto, CA: American Institutes for Research.

Weintraub, F. J., Abeson, A., Ballard, J., & LaVor, M. L. (1977). *Public policy and the education of exceptional children.* Reston, VA: Council for Exceptional Children.

Weintraub, F. J., & Ramirez, B. A. (1985). *Progress in the education of the handicapped and analysis of PL 98-199.* Reston, VA: Council for Exceptional Children.

MARJORIE E. WARD
The Ohio State University

BROWN v. BOARD OF EDUCATION
LARRY P.

MILLS v. BOARD OF EDUCATION
PASE v. HANNON
THE PENNSYLVANIA ASSOCIATION FOR RETARDED CITIZENS v. PENNSYLVANIA

CONSULTATION

Consultation refers to a professional relationship in which a specialist attempts to improve the functioning of another professional. Although there are many models of school consultation, each with different sets of assumptions, techniques, and goals, Bergan and Tombari's definition (1976) is general enough to encompass the idiosyncrasies of these various models. "Consultation refers to services rendered by a consultant (e.g., school psychologist) to a consultee (e.g., teacher) who functions as a change agent with respect to the learning or adjustment of a client (e.g., a child) or a group of clients" (p. 4).

Consultation in school settings is an indirect model of providing broadly defined mental health services to children. The consultant attempts to effect a change in children's behavior and learning by attempting to change the teacher's (or administrator's) attitudes, perceptions, and behaviors. One of the rationales for consultation is the economy of resources it offers. By improving teacher and administrator functioning, the psychologist can affect many more children than possible in the traditional counseling and testing models of service delivery.

Certain key elements distinguish consultation from other professional activities. First, consultation is a professional-to-professional relationship that is focused on helping the consultee to do a job. Consultation is a voluntary relationship; thus the consultee is free to accept or reject the consultant's help and recommendations. In turn, the consultee is expected to contribute to the problem-solving process and is responsible for implementing action plans that result from the consultation. Finally, the consultant respects the confidential nature of the relationship.

One professional activity that shares similarities with consultation is supervision; however, consultation differs from supervision in several important ways. Because the supervisor is administratively responsible for the supervisee's work, the supervisee is obligated to accept the supervisor's advice. A supervisor is usually a senior professional in the same discipline as the supervisee, whereas the consultant is usually trained in a discipline different from that of the consultee. Thus supervision involves a hierarchical obligatory relationship, while consultation involves a egalatarian voluntary relationship.

Consultation has both remedial and preventive goals, but different consultation models emphasize one or the other goals. Thus when consulting with a teacher, the consultant attempts to improve both the learning and adjustment of the child about whom the teacher is concerned and the teacher's ability to cope effectively with similar children in the future. This latter, preventive goal of consultation allows psychologists to broaden their impact beyond the target child.

The goals of consultation listed by Conoley and Conoley (1982) are relevant to several consultation models and include (1) providing an objective point of view; (2) increasing problem-solving skills; (3) increasing coping skills; (4) increasing freedom of choice; (5) increasing commitment to choices made; and (6) increasing available resources.

The different models of school consultation do not have identical conceptual bases. For example, behavioral consultation is based on social learning theory, and the technology of applied behavioral analysis is used to change students' and teachers' behaviors. Process consultation is based on social, psychological, and general systems theory and assumes interpersonal and group processes affect educational outcomes. There are certain assumptions, or concepts, that are common to the various models. Two shared assumptions are that children's classroom behaviors and learning are determined by variables in the child and in the classroom setting and that the consultant must work jointly with the consultee to solve problems.

Considerable attention in the consultation literature is given to the task of entry as a consultant into an organization. Entry tasks include (1) obtaining approval for consultation from administrators; (2) establishing a shared set of expectations with administrators and teachers regarding consultation's purposes, the roles and responsibilities of the consultant and consultees, confidentiality, and the types of problems to be discussed in consultation; and (3) establishing the consultant as a credible and trustworthy resource person. If teachers are accustomed to receiving recommendations from psychologists, and the psychologist-consultant does not carefully lay the groundwork for the consultative relationship, the teacher and the psychologist will find themselves working at cross purposes, based on their differing expectations for the interaction.

Consultation involves two jobs: working on the content, or specific problem brought to consultation, and working on the process of helping the consultee improve his or her job-related performance. It is important for the consultant to have specialized knowledge that is relevant to the consultation content (e.g., the particular behavior, learning, or programmatic concern). Indeed, the reason the consultee asked for the consultant's help is that the consultee believes the consultant has such relevant knowledge. Knowledge bases the psychologist-consultant might draw from in teacher consultation include child development, theories of learning, childhood psychopathology, tests and measurements, diagnosis of learning and behavior, group processes, individual instructional programming, and treatment of childhood learning and behavioral disorders.

In addition to content skills, the consultant must have skills necessary for establishing and maintaining rapport with the consultee and for facilitating the consultee's professional growth. Thus the consultant (1) seeks clarification, encouraging consultees to see problems from new or broader perspectives; (2) supports the consultee while he or she is grappling with the problem, boosting consultee motivation and self-confidence; (3) asks questions that require consultees to validate information; (4) probes for feelings to help consultees accept their emotional reactions to children; (5) provides choices to increase consultee freedom to choose and commitment to choices made; and (6) confronts consultees either directly or indirectly to increase consultee objectivity. An example of an indirect confrontation is telling a female teacher who is inappropriately "mothering" a young girl that the girl is expecting the teacher to do too much for her and the girl needs to learn that the teacher cannot be her mother. An example of a direct confrontation is telling a male teacher that he seems to be apologizing to his students when he assumes an authoritative role, and that perhaps students are misbehaving because they are picking up on his discomfort in the authoritarian role.

Five models of school consultation are described with respect to their primary purpose and the roles and skills required of the consultant. Psychoeducational consultation is the type of consultation most frequently practiced in schools. After the psychologist has evaluated a child, the psychologist interprets the evaluation results to the teacher, presents recommendations to the teacher, and engages the teacher in a discussion of these recommendations so that the teacher will be able to choose and implement one or more recommendations. The primary purpose is remedial. The consultant's primary role is to diagnose the problem and recommend treatment.

Behavioral consultation is based on social learning theory. The behavioral consultant applies the technology of applied behavior analysis to the task of changing student and teacher behavior. The consultant observes the child as well as the teacher in the classroom to identify and count target behaviors, determine antecedents and consequences of those target behaviors, and recommend changes expected to result in a change in target behaviors. Because the teacher is ultimately responsible for making any changes that are recommended by the consultant, the consultant needs to establish a collaborative working relationship with the teacher. The primary goal in behavioral consultation is remedial; however, the consultant expects consultees will improve their skills in applied behavior analysis and will apply their new skills to similar problems in the future.

In educational consultation, the consultant presents new information or teaches new skills to consultees by conducting in-service workshops. The effective consultant-trainer carefully assesses educational needs of the workshop audience as well as the expectations of the administrators, and provides training that matches those needs and expectations. It is important, in cases of individual student consultation, that the question of needing informed consent from the parents is considered (Heron, 1996).

The mental health consultant's primary purpose is to improve the consultee's ability to effectively cope with similar problems in the future without the consultant's continued help. The particular problem discussed in consultation acts as leverage for changing the consultee's behavior. A secondary goal is to change the child's behavior. Because the focus is on the consultee, the consultant's process skills are especially important. The mental health consultant uses clinical interviewing skills to determine the reason a teacher is experiencing difficulty and employs different consultation approaches depending on the presumed reason for the consultee's difficulty. When the consultee's problem is presumed to be a lack of objectivity, the consultant uses specialized skills that require specialized training in consultation techniques. The consultant attempts to minimize the teacher's displacement of personal problems onto the work setting.

In program consultation, the consultant is requested by the administration to design or to evaluate a specific program such as a gifted education program, a race relations program, or a truancy program. The consultant must have experience and skills relevant to the particular program. The consultant issues a written report that contains recommendations for the school to implement.

Process consultation, like program consultation, is initiated by an administrator. It attempts to effect a change in the system rather than in the individual teacher or child. Process consultation is based on social psychological and general systems theory. The process consultant attempts to improve interpersonal and group processes used by administrators, teachers, parents, and students to reach educational objectives. Thus the consultant will involve the administrators and teachers in a mutual problem-solving effort aimed at diagnosing and changing such human processes as communication, leadership, decision making, and trust. The process consultant does not deal directly with the subject matter of the interactions of an organization. Rather, the consultant provides help with the methods of communication, problem solving, planning, and decision making (Schmuck, 1976).

Consultation is a term that encompasses a diverse set of models for delivering psychological services to a school (or other organization). The common thread is that the psychologist attempts to affect change in clients of the organization (e.g., students) by influencing the behaviors of persons who have a responsibility for client care.

REFERENCES

Bergan, J. R., & Tombari, M. L. (1976). Consultant skill and efficiency and the implementation and outcomes of consultation. *Journal of School Psychology, 14*(1), 3–14.

Conoley, J. C., & Conoley, C. W. (1982). *School consultation: A guide to practice and training*. New York: Pergamon.

Heron, T. E. (1996). Ethical and legal issues in consultation. *Remedial and Special Education, 17,* 6, 377–385.

Schmuck, R. A. (1976). *Process consultation and organization development*. Reading, MA: Addison-Wesley.

JAN N. HUGHES
Texas A & M University

CONSULTATION, MENTAL HEALTH
MULTIDISCIPLINARY TEAMS
PREREFERRAL INTERVENTIONS
PRESCHOOL SCREENING
PROFESSIONAL SCHOOL PSYCHOLOGY

CONSULTATION, INCLUSION AND

See INCLUSION.

CONSULTATION, MENTAL HEALTH

Mental health consultation is an indirect mode of providing mental health services to clients served by some agency. The mental health consultant attempts to improve the psychological adjustment of persons in the community (i.e., students, parishioners, probationers, or patients) by consulting with professional caregivers in the community (i.e., teachers, clergymen, probation officers, or doctors). Gerald Caplan's seminal book, *The Theory and Practice of Mental Health Consultation* (1970), summarized his most important writings on the subject and offered the first comprehensive coverage of this mode of providing mental health services. Caplan defined mental health consultation as "a process of interaction between two professional persons—the consultant, who is a specialist, and the consultee, who invokes the consultant's help in regard to a current work problem with which he is having some difficulty and which he has decided is within the other's area of specialized competence" (p. 19). Other persons have broadened this definition to include consultation with more than one consultee and consultation with nonprofessionals (Altrocchi, 1972).

The mental health consultant may be a psychiatrist, psychologist, or social worker, and the consultee may be any person whose ministrations to lay persons in the community have mental health implications. Mental health consultation is more prevalent in schools than in other settings. Reasons for its prevalence in schools include the opportunity provided in schools to affect the mental health of large numbers of children through consultation with a small number of teachers, the recognition of the importance of schooling on children's mental health, the presence of psychologists in schools, and the demonstrated relevance of psychological theories and knowledge to educational goals and practices. Consistent with the focus of this work, the following discussion of consultation will be specific to mental health consultation in schools.

There are several key elements in the previous definition of consultation that distinguish consultation from other professional activities. First, the consultee (teacher, principal, other administrator) invokes the consultant's help. Because consultation is a professional-to-professional interaction, the consultee is responsible for determining whether the assistance of the consultant would be helpful.

Second, the consultee retains responsibility for the problem. Thus, when teachers or administrators ask for a consultant's help, they do not diminish their responsibility for instructing the child or administering the program. Because the consultee retains responsibility for the problem and its handling, the consultee is an active participant in a joint problem-solving process. Responsibility for problem formulation and solution is shared between the consultant and consultee. Thus, consultation is different from referral of a child to a psychologist who then assumes sole responsibility for diagnosing the problem and prescribing treatment. In the referral model, the treatment may or may not be the teacher's responsibility to implement. By contrast, any recommendations that result from the consultation process are the responsibility of the consultee to implement. Moreover, the consultee is free to accept or to reject the consultant's advice, and the consultee may terminate the relationship at any point. The consultant has no authority over the consultee except the authority of the consultant's good ideas.

Consultation is a confidential relationship. By the time a teacher seeks a consultant's help, he or she may feel discouraged. Teachers would be reluctant to reveal their perceived failures in consultation if the relationship were not confidential. The active role of the teacher-consultee requires the teacher to communicate openly and honestly, with no fear that the consultant will disclose aspects of the communication to third parties. The active role is necessary because the consultant depends on the teacher's wealth of information regarding the problem, including past efforts to solve it. Furthermore, the teacher's values,

beliefs, role constraints, resources for solving the problem, instructional methods, interactional style, knowledge base, and skills are important variables for the consultant to consider in jointly designing a plan for solving the problem brought to consultation. If the consultation plan is not compatible with the unique characteristics of the teacher's work situation, either it will not be implemented as intended or it will result in a disruption of the teacher's functioning. The confidential nature of the consultation relationship enables the consultee to play the active role required in consultation.

Consultation is a collaborative relationship. The consultant's role is that of a facilitator. Although consultation includes giving expert advice, the consultant's primary method of assisting teachers includes offering observations, asking questions that clarify the problem or place the problem in a new perspective, suggesting information that needs to be obtained in order to understand the problem, serving as a springboard for the teacher's own ideas, and sharing pertinent knowledge from such fields as child development, learning theory, group processes, behavior analysis, child psychopathology, tests and measurements, or family systems theory.

The problems discussed in consultation are work-related problems. The consultant does not help the consultee solve personal problems. Although personal problems influence work performance, the professional-to-professional nature of consultation requires a focus on work-related concerns. When personal problems are brought up by the teacher, the consultant conveys an accepting attitude but refocuses the discussion on the teacher's professional functioning.

Caplan categorized mental health consultation as to the kind of problem dealt with (a case or an administrative problem) and as to the focus (the client or program on the one hand or the consultee on the other). This resulted in four categories of consultation.

In *client-centered case* consultation, the focus is on a child's problems. The goal of change in the teacher is secondary to the goal of formulating the problem. A written report to the teacher summarizes the diagnostic findings and recommendations for the teacher's handling of the problem.

In *consultee-centered case* consultation, the focus is on the student; however, the consultant's primary goal is change in the teacher's knowledge, skills, self-confidence, or objectivity. The problem case is a leverage point for effecting a change in the teacher that will enable the teacher to work more effectively, not only with the particular child who is the focus of consultation, but also with similar children in the future. This expected ripple effect in consultation extends the impact of consultation to an indefinite number of children. Because a change in the teacher is the primary goal, the consultant spends considerable time with the teacher, helping the teacher gain new perspectives, insights, knowledge, and skills that will generalize to similar problems in the future. Rather than offering an expert formulation of the problem and strategy for change, the consultant engages the teacher as a peer professional in a problem-solving process, facilitating the teacher's ability to solve the problem independently. As assumption in consultee-centered case consultation is that the teacher will generalize new learnings to future cases if the teacher accepts responsibility for the problem formulation and action plans in consultation. In this type of consultation, the task of assessing the child's problem is secondary to the task of assessing the nature of the teacher's work difficulty, which may involve a lack of knowledge, skills, self-confidence, or professional objectivity. The consultant's expertise is directed primarily to the task of helping the teacher remedy whichever of these shortcomings is present. It is this type of consultation about which the most has been written, and it is this type of consultation that has become nearly synonymous with the term mental health consultation.

In *program-centered administrative* consultation, the focus is on a particular program for which the administrator-consultee has responsibility. The primary goal is the assessment of obstacles to achieving goals of a particular program. After a site visit and interviews with persons in the school, a written report summarizing the consultant's findings and recommendations is prepared. As in client-centered case consultation, the goal of educating administrators to handle similar problems in the future is secondary.

In *consultee-centered administrative* consultation, the focus is on the administrator's skills in areas such as group processes, leadership, and interpersonal relationships. This model of consultation is frequently referred to as organizational development consultation. It assumes that change in social structures and human processes within a school will result in the greatest positive impact on the mental health of students and teachers.

Typically, the consultant has no line authority over consultees. Two sources of influence over consultees available to consultants are expert and referent power (Meyers, Parsons, & Martin, 1979.) Expert power is the influence the consultant has with a consultee based on the consultee's attribution of expertise to the consultant. Teachers seek out a consultant's help because they believe the consultant has special expert knowledge relevant to the problem for which consultation is sought. Referent power is influence the consultant has with consultees based on the consultee's identification with the consultant. When a consultee admires the consultant and identifies with the consultant's values, attitudes, and behaviors, the consultant is attributed referent power. Much of the consultation literature focuses on methods of building rapport, or referent power. While not using the term referent power, Caplan recommends such identification techniques as emphasizing the peer-professional relationship, "onedownsmanship," empathic listening, conveying respect for the consultee, accepting the consultee, emphasizing commonalities, being approachable, and engaging in informal social contacts with consultees.

Although consultation is different from teaching, the consultant has an educational role. As teacher, the consultant instructs, shares information, translates psychological theories into educationally relevant practices, models approaches, offers ideas, and interprets data. As facilitator, the consultant provides a model of professional objectivity, guides teachers in problem solving, encourages, helps consultees deal with affect that may decrease their ability to deal effectively with a problem, and helps consultees avoid displacement of personal problems in the work setting. The consultant also facilitates communication among different organizational units within the school (i.e., regular and special education teachers, grade level teachers, and administrators).

Empirical evidence derived from over 60 studies on the effectiveness of consultation services in alleviating special problems brought to consultation is positive (Mannino & Shore, 1975; Medway, 1979). Fewer studies on the preventive goals of consultation have been published; however, the results of these studies are positive (Gutkin & Curtis, 1982).

REFERENCES

Altrocchi, J. (1972). Mental health consultation. In S. Golann & C. Eisdorfer (Eds.), *Handbook of community mental health* (pp. 477–507). New York: Appleton-Century-Crofts.

Caplan, G. (1970). *The theory and practice of mental health consultation*. New York: Basic Books.

Gutkin, T. B., & Curtis, M. J. (1982). School-based consultation: Theory and techniques. In C. R. Reynolds & T. B. Gutkin (Eds.), *The handbook of school psychology* (pp. 796–828). New York: Wiley.

Mannino, F. V., & Shore, M. F. (1975). Effecting change through consultation. In F. V. Mannino, B. W. MacLennan, & M. F. Shore (Eds.), *The Practice of mental health consultation*. New York: Gardner.

Medway, F. J. (1979). How effective is school consultation: A review of recent research. *Journal of School Psychology, 17,* 275–282.

Meyers, J., Parsons, R. D., & Martin R. (1979). *Mental health consultation in the schools*. San Francisco: Jossey-Bass.

JAN N. HUGHES
Texas A & M University

CONSULTATION
PSYCHOLOGY IN THE SCHOOLS
SCHOOL PSYCHOLOGY

CONTINGENCY CONTRACTING

A contingency contract is a written agreement between parties that details specific behaviors that are expected and the various reinforcers or punishers that are associated with compliance or noncompliance with the terms of the contract. Contingency contracts have been used successfully with a wide variety of subjects to help manage diverse behaviors such as Attention-deficit/Hyperactivity Disorder (Gardill, 1996) homework compliance (Miller & Kelley, 1994) and reduction of suspension (Novell, 1994); they have become exceptionally popular management alternatives in special education.

Stuart (1971) has delineated five components that should be incorporated into an ideal contract. First, an exact explanation of the behaviors, rewards, punishers, and privileges must be provided. For example, if a teacher wanted a student to remain in his or her seat in exchange for extra time at the microcomputer, the time of in-seat behavior that must be exhibited before a specified amount of time at the computer can be earned must be detailed. Closely related to the first point is the second requirement: that all behaviors must be observable and measurable and that all terms must be specified. For example, once computer time has been earned, one should be able to refer to the contract to learn when the time may be claimed. Also, in-seat behavior can be operationally defined and measured accurately. However, a behavior such as "attending" is more nebulous and would be difficult to measure reliably enough for use in a contract. Third, contingencies for failure to meet with the terms of the contract should be specified for both parties. Just as a child must suffer the consequences if he or she does not perform as required, the manager must also be willing to suffer consequences (e.g., double reinforcement for the subject) if his or her part of the agreement is not fulfilled. Fourth, a bonus clause for consistent performance may be included if the subject or the manager feels it may be beneficial. This addition would help to stress the positive aspects of the contract. Finally, either the contract or the manager should provide a means of monitoring the effectiveness of the contract. By providing for this feedback, the contract can help to induce more positive comments on the part of the involved parties when each is in compliance with contract terms. Kazdin (1975) notes that well-developed contingency contracts offer a number of advantages over traditional management strategies: subject input into the contract can enhance performance and motivation; subject negotiation of contingencies will result in the contingencies being truly reinforcing; contracts can be flexible; contracts specify both behaviors and contingencies; and the logistics of contract implementation can help to structure interactions between parties and thus lead to more successful and lasting changes.

An interesting example of the effectiveness of a contract system was recently presented by Kelley and Stokes (1982). The subjects in their study were seven individuals who were being paid $2.35 an hour to attend a combination academic (GED preparation) and vocational training program. During baseline conditions the pay was based purely on attendance. During contract conditions, however, the subjects were paid contingent on their academic performance. Contracts were individually negotiated weekly by each subject and the teacher and reasonable performance minimums were accepted by each party. A withdrawal design was used, and the results clearly demonstrated that the contracting conditions were superior to the baseline conditions when academic performance was considered. Similarly, Bristol and Sloane (1974) used contracting in an attempt to increase the study time of undergraduate students enrolled in an introductory psychology course. Their results showed that the contracts were effective at increasing study time. However, while only the grades of the poorer students were affected, contracting did prove to be a viable alternative for helping these students to structure their study time and improve their performance.

Contingency contracting holds great promise as a useful management tool for special educators. Since contracts by nature enhance communication by specifying expectations on the part of both parties, compliance with the terms and performance can be easily measured and contingencies can be enforced. As with any behavioral strategy, however, consistent application of the procedures is mandatory. For further specific information on contracting, the reader is referred to the *Journal of Applied Behavior Analysis*. For information on implementation and examples of contracts, see Kerr and Nelson (1983).

REFERENCES

Bristol, M. M., & Sloane, H. (1974). Effects of contingency contracting on study rate and test performance. *Journal of Applied Behavior Analysis, 7,* 271–285.

Gardill, M. C. (1996). Classroom strategies for managing students with ADHD. *Intervention in School and Clinic, 32,* 89–94.

Kazdin, A. E. (1975). *Behavior modification in applied settings.* Homewood, IL: Dorsey.

Kelley, M. L., & Stokes, T. (1982). Contingency contracting with disadvantaged youths: Improving classroom performance. *Journal of Applied Behavior Analysis, 15,* 447–454.

Kerr, M. M., & Nelson, C. M. (1983). *Strategies for managing behavior problems in the classroom.* Columbus, OH: Merrill.

Miller, D. & Kelley, M. L. (1994). Use of goal setting and contingency contracting for improving children's homework performance. *Journal of Applied Behavior Analysis, 27,* 1, 73–84.

Novell, I. (1994). *Decreasing school suspension among middle school children by implementing a rehabilitative in-room suspension.* (ERIC Clearinghouse No. PSO 22397)

Stuart, R. B. (1971). Behavioral contracting within the families of delinquents. *Journal of Behavior Therapy and Experimental Psychiatry, 2,* 1–11.

ANDREW R. BRULLE
Eastern Illinois University

APPLIED BEHAVIOR ANALYSIS
BEHAVIOR MODIFICATION

CONTINUING EDUCATION FOR THE HANDICAPPED

Comparatively little is known about the continuing education needs or practices of handicapped persons. For the most part, it is presumed that handicapped persons take advantage of typical continuing and adult education programs afforded to nonhandicapped persons. Because the bulk of school-age, mildly/moderately handicapped persons are handicapped by virtue of their educational deficiencies, it is expected that these individuals blend into society on exit from the education program (Telford & Sawrey, 1977). Thus continuing education programs are seldom tailored to the unique needs of handicapped individuals.

The types of continuing education available to handicapped learners is dependent on the community in which an individual resides and the resources available. In general, however, programs of continuing education can include academic education, creative arts, economic education, basic and literacy education, home and family life education, human relations training, recreation education, and occupational education.

For those individuals exhibiting more severe handicapping conditions or requiring a unique form of assistance, continuing education consists of specific training/education in independent living, communication skills, or vocational employment. This type of continuing education is offered through public and private vocational rehabilitation facilities as well as social service organizations. For the most part, these programs of continuing education are supported by public funds intended to promote greater self-sufficiency and independence.

PATRICIA ANN ABRAMSON
Hudson Public Schools,
Hudson, Wisconsin

ADULT BASIC EDUCATION
ADULT PROGRAMS FOR THE DISABLED
VOCATIONAL REHABILITATION

CONTINUUM OF SPECIAL EDUCATION SERVICES

See INCLUSION.

CONTRACT PROCUREMENT

Contract procurement is a term used in vocational rehabilitation facilities, sheltered workshops, and work activities centers. The term is simply defined; however, the concept and process are more complex. The word contract refers to jobs that are used in the cited facilities to teach work habit skills or trade skills, or provide activities that result in reimbursement to persons with disabilities. The term procurement refers to the act of attaining contracts. The term contract procurement, as it relates to programs for the disabled, refers to the process of attaining work from businesses to be done by persons with disabilities. Subcontracts and prime manufacturing are two categories of contracts.

Subcontracts are jobs that are attained from businesses and that involve no purchases of materials or equipment. An example would be assembling circuit boards for microcomputers. Company A manufactures the parts to be assembled on the circuit boards. They purchase the boards and the boxes for shipping, and send a truck once a week to pick up the assembled and packaged product. The contract involves only labor; on completion of the contract, all surplus parts are returned to Company A.

Prime manufacturing contracts necessitate the purchase and inventory of materials to create a product. Attaining work is a sales function. In the process of selling the abilities of a work program, not only the equipment available but the manpower require legal protection. For example, Company A subcontracts the assembly of circuit boards to Work Program B. All assembly and packaging is done at Work Program B's site. However, Company A gets a special order for microcomputers with an additional resistor on the circuit boards that are already assembled into the microcomputers and boxed. The deadline is such that delivery and pickup of changes is too costly between Company A and Work Program B. Consequently, a labor force must be procured and attained by Company A if their business is to complete the work. They must open the boxes and add the resistor to each microcomputer circuit board, then repackage the unit.

Understanding that sales is a key concept in contract procurement is important. Often work programs fail to understand that attaining work is a process of identifying, attaining, working, and delivering. Some programs still use nonsales people to attain work and deliver a product, thus causing contract procurement for persons with disabilities to be thought of as cheap, subsidized labor.

The process of attaining work is subdivided into time and motion studies, and submitting a bid for subcontract or setting a price for prime manufacturing. Time and motion refers to setting up the work in the most efficient manner and then timing the steps in completing the work. The federal Department of Labor publications explain the rules for time and motion studies. A bid should include the following information: labor rate, overhead, materials, handling and waste, freight, and profit.

The bid also should include any conditions that may need to be included in the subcontract that concern the workshop regulations.

JEFF HEINZEN
Indianhead Enterprise

HABILITATION
REHABILITATION

CONTROL GROUPS

Control groups are aggregates of subjects who do not receive the treatment of interest in an experimental or quasi-experimental intervention. They are used in research and program evaluation to provide baselines against which to measure the impact of an experimental manipulation and as a means to rule out alternative explanations of "treatment" effects. Control groups are useful particularly in field settings, where there may be a number of plausible rival accounts for the meaning of the researcher's observations. Whether the study is an elaborate investigation or the simple introduction of classroom innovation, control groups are often crucial to the interpretation of results.

The logic of the use of control groups centers around the ability to equate subjects in the "treatment" (experimental) and control groups on all factors except the treatment of interest. Many studies are limited because the assignment of subjects to experimental and control groups is such that the assumption of equivalence is not tenable. In addition, the nature of the research setting may result in the contamination of the control groups by such factors as rivalries with the experimental group or imitation of the treatment by the control group (Cook & Campbell, 1979).

Control groups often involve a no-treatment control, where members engage in their activities with no intervention by the experimenter. Cook, Leviton, and Shadish (1985) note that rather than a no-treatment control group, it might be preferable to use a control that allows for comparison between the treatment of interest and another intervention. This might particularly be the case where practitioners are concerned with the relative efficacy of approaches or where ethical constraints prohibit withdrawal or denial of treatment.

Particularly in the case of quasiexperimental designs, where random assignment of subjects is not possible, a number of control groups are often used to rule out different competing interpretations. For example, members of a placebo control group receive an irrelevant treatment that gives an amount of time and attention similar to that of the experimental group (Cook & Campbell, 1979).

It is commonplace to introduce innovative programs in special education. By following proper control group design, one can judge the effectiveness of "reforms as experiments" and make policy decisions on a more rational basis (Campbell, 1969).

REFERENCES

Campbell, D. T. (1969). Reforms as experiments. *American Psychologist, 24,* 409–429.

Cook, T. D., & Campbell, D. T. (1979). *Quasiexperimentation: Design and analysis issues for field settings.* Chicago: Rand McNally.

Cook, T. D., Leviton, L. C., & Shadish, W. R. (1985). Program evaluation. In G. Lindzey & E. Aronson (Eds.), *Handbook of social psychology* (3rd ed.) (Vol. 1, pp. 699–777). New York: Random House.

LEE ANDERSON JACKSON, JR.
*University of North Carolina
at Wilmington*

MEASUREMENT
RESEARCH IN SPECIAL EDUCATION

CONVERGENT AND DIVERGENT THINKING

Emerging from Guilford's structure of intellect model of human intelligence, the concepts of convergent and divergent thinking are often applied to the education of gifted children. Both are viewed as high-level cognitive operations that individuals use when making decisions (Guilford, 1966, 1984).

Convergent thinking requires a narrowing process by which an individual develops classification rules that explain the relationships among objects and concepts. Essential to this process is the invocation of recall and recognition strategies. As such, the products of convergent thinking tend to be in the form of single "correct" answers. Critics have argued that typical school instruction demands an inappropriate proportion of convergent thinking at the expense of more creative (divergent) processes (Steffin, 1983).

Divergent thinking involves a broad scanning operation, enabling an individual to generate multiple possible solutions. It has received a major share of research attention in creativity, problem solving, and critical thinking (Steffin, 1983).

Guilford (1984) has discussed three aspects of divergent thinking. One aspect, fluency, relates to the breadth of associations available to an individual regarding a particular stimulus. A second, flexibility, is defined as the simultaneous consideration of multiple classes of information. In contrast to convergent processes, flexibility allows the individual to develop novel combinations. The third aspect, elaboration, is an integrative process that results in the formation of a broad theory. Here the thinker, demonstrating insight, is able to make predictions based on incomplete information.

Several studies have shown that young children's divergent productions can be increased by the use of open-ended questions in class discussions (Pucket-Cliatt, Shaw, & Sherwood, 1980; Thomas & Holcomb, 1981). These studies have also suggested that teachers can become increasingly comfortable using open-ended questions and that they can decrease their reliance on rote memory activities.

Steffin (1983) suggests that microcomputers offer new opportunities for fostering divergent thinking. Increasingly sophisticated computer simulations, with their capacity for user-controlled interaction and variability in presentation, can teach students to develop algorithms that can be generalized across learning situations.

While learning-disabled (Jaben, 1983) and language-deficient (Burrows & Wolf, 1983) children have shown gains in creativity following training in divergent thinking, the observation and development of creative thinking in gifted students continues to dominate the research literature at the present time (Hildebrand, 1991).

REFERENCES

Burrows, D., & Wolf, B. (1983). Creativity and the dyslexic child: A classroom view. *Annals of Dyslexia, 33,* 269–274.

Guilford, J. P. (1966). Basic problems in teaching for creativity. In C. W. Taylor & F. E. Williams (Eds.), *Instructional media and creativity.* New York: Wiley.

Guilford, J. P. (1984). Varieties of divergent production. *Journal of Creative Behavior, 18,* 1–10.

Hildebrand, V. (1991). Young children's care and education: Creative teaching and management. *Early Child Development and Care, 71,* 63–72.

Jaben, T. H. (1983). The effects of creativity training on learning disabled students' creative written expression. *Journal of Learning Disabilities, 16,* 264–265.

Pucket-Cliatt, M. J., Shaw, J. M., & Sherwood, J. M. (1980). Effects of training on the divergent thinking abilities of kindergarten children. *Child Development, 51,* 1061–1064.

Steffin, S. A. (1983). Fighting against convergent thinking. *Childhood Education, 59,* 255–258.

Thomas, E., & Holcomb, C. (1981). Nurturing productive thinking in able students. *Journal of General Psychology, 104,* 67–79.

GARY BERKOWITZ
Temple University

CREATIVE PROBLEM SOLVING
TEACHER EXPECTANCIES
TEACHING STRATEGIES

CONVULSIONS, FEBRILE

See FEBRILE CONVULSIONS.

CONVULSIVE DISORDERS

See SEIZURE DISORDERS.

COOPERATIVE TEACHING

See INCLUSION.

COPROLALIA

Coprolalia is a condition characterized by an irresistible urge to utter obscene words and phrases and uncontrollable performance of obscene gestures (Singer, 1997), which are frequently observed together. Obscenities are interspersed randomly within a dialogue, interrupting the normal flow of conversation. The cursing is usually uttered during a break between sentences and in a loud, sharp tone in contrast to normal voice. The frequency of obscene utterances has a tendency to vary from low to high frequencies for extended periods of time. Coprolalic episodes are positively associated with periods of anxiety and anticipation.

Coprolalia is most often associated with Gilles de la Tourette's syndrome (TS) and is evident in some patients following a stroke. As with other tics associated with TS, coprolalia can be controlled by TS patients for brief intervals. Lees, Robertson, Trimble, and Murray (1984) report that TS patients exhibiting coprolalia attempt to substitute euphemisms or somewhat disguised neologisms for obscenities. Early estimates of the prevalence of coprolalia in Tourette syndrome patients were approximately 60%, but more recently have been revised to approximately 33% (Lees et al., 1984). Coprolalia tends to peak in adolescence and to wane in adulthood (Singer, 1997).

Both medical and behavioral treatments have been used successfully to control coprolalic expressions. Erenberg, Cruse, and Rothner (1985) report that the preferred medical treatment is the use of dopamine-blocking agents such as haloperidol, a drug used in treating hyperkinetic and manic disorders. Comings and Comings (1985) recommend starting with low doses of haloperidol (.05 mg daily for 1 week) and increasing the dosage by .05 mg at weekly intervals until a 70 to 90% reduction of symptoms occurs. Because of the sedative side effects of haloperidol, stimulant drugs may be given simultaneously. Price, Lockman, Pauls, Cohen, and Kidd (1986) report, however, that stimulant drugs appear to be associated positively with increases in the frequency of tics.

Behavioral treatments have included the use of self-management and negative practice techniques. Friedman (1980), for instance, had a patient substitute socially acceptable utterances for obscenities whenever she had the urge to curse. Evans and Evans (1983) decreased the rate of utterances of an expletive using a self-counting procedure. The patient simply recorded each frequency of his use of the target expletive. Storms (1985) had patients practice their tics until they were tired, had them rest, and then repeated the practice.

Medical and behavioral treatments of coprolalia have been used in combination with each other as well as in isolation. Storms (1985), for instance, used doses of haloperidol in combination with negative practice to reduce the frequency of tics.

REFERENCES

Comings, D. E., & Comings, B. G. (1985). Tourette syndrome: Clinical and psychological aspects. *Human Genetics, 37,* 435–450.

Erenberg, G., Cruse, R. P., & Rothner, A. D. (1985). Gilles de la Tourette's syndrome: Effects of stimulant drugs. *Neurology, 35,* 1346–1348.

Evans, W. H., & Evans, S. S. (1983). Self-counting in the treatment of Gilles de la Tourette syndrome. *Journal of Precision Teaching, 4,* 14–17.

Friedman, S. (1980). Self-control in the treatment of Gilles de la Tourette's syndrome: Case study with 18-month follow-up. *Journal of Consulting & Clinical Psychology, 48,* 400–402.

Lees, A. J., Robertson, M., Trimble, M. R., & Murray, N. M. F. (1984). A clinical study of Gilles de la Tourette syndrome in the United Kingdom. *Journal of Neurology, Neurosurgery, & Psychiatry, 47,* 1–8.

Price, R. A., Leckman, J. F., Pauls, D. L., Cohen, D. J., & Kidd, K. K. (1986). Gilles de la Tourette syndrome: Tics and central nervous system stimulants in twins and non-twins. *Neurology, 36,* 232–237.

Singer, C. (1997). Coprolalia and other coprophenomena. *Neurologic Clinics, 15,* 2, 299–308.

Storms, L. (1985). Massed negative practice as a behavioral treatment for Gilles de la Tourette's syndrome. *American Journal of Psychotherapy, 39,* 277–281.

LAWRENCE J. O'SHEA
University of Florida

**STIMULANT DRUGS
TICS
TOURETTE'S SYNDROME**

COPROPRAXIA

See COPROLALIA.

CORE SCHOOL

The term core refers to an educational concept that first emerged in the United States in the 1930s and 1940s. The core school tries to provide a common background for all students and engineer a course of study that combines basic topics from school subjects that are usually taught separately. The intention of this concept was to make education more meaningful for students. Most popular in the 1950s, its popularity has declined in recent years, but it is still operational (Manning, 1971).

The core concept has two basic components: time and philosophy (Oliver, 1965). Time is usually administered through a "block time class," for example, two or more class periods are joined together in order to study a wide range of related subjects. The philosophy of core involves the breaking down of strict boundaries between disciplines. Thus, students may study a topic from literary, historical, mathematical, and artistic viewpoints concurrently rather than as separate topics in isolated classes (Manning, 1971; Oliver, 1965).

Beyond these two basic components, cores are identified as having the following characteristics (Hass, 1970; Manning, 1971; Oliver, 1965):

1. They are problem centered.
2. Learning is done through firsthand experiences by the learner.
3. Students are involved in the planning, teaching, and evaluation processes.
4. Students are provided with opportunities for total growth by way of lifelike environments.
5. The instruction is more personal, allowing for individual guidance.

6. There are opportunities for integrated knowledge across subject lines.

The core concept, when practiced, will probably be more student-oriented than may occur in other settings. The organization and overlapping of classes can be especially beneficial to the special education student needing structure and concentrated study. Student-oriented classes provide motivation for paying attention and becoming an active participant in the learning process.

REFERENCES

Hass, G., Wiles, K., & Bondi, J. (1970). *Reading in curriculum* (2nd ed.). Boston: Allyn & Bacon.

Manning, D. (1971). *Toward a humanistic curriculum*. New York: Harper & Row.

Oliver, A. I. (1965). *Curriculum improvement: A guide to problems, principles, and procedures*. New York: Dodd, Mead.

ROBERT T. NASH
*University of Wisconsin
at Oshkosh*

ECOLOGICAL EDUCATION FOR THE HANDICAPPED HOLISTIC APPROACH AND LEARNING DISABILITIES TEST-TEACH-TEST PARADIGM

CORNELIA DE LANGE SYNDROME

Cornelia De Lange syndrome is a developmental disability first reported by Brachman in 1916 and further investigated by De Lange in 1933 (Goodman & Gorlin, 1977). It may also be referred to as *Amsterdam dwarfism* (Clarke & Clarke, 1975). Currently, no definitive test or genetic analysis to confirm the diagnosis exists. However, it is suspected of being an autosomal dominant disorder associated with mutations on chromosome 3 (Gillberg, 1995). Diagnosis rests on the presence or absence of a number of physical, cognitive, and behavioral characteristics.

Cornelia De Lange infants show a lower than normal birth weight and length, and can be described as failing to thrive. The majority are found to be functioning in the lower reaches of the moderately retarded range. A few reported cases have shown functioning levels approaching the low average range. Motor problems are pronounced.

These children appear remarkably similar in appearance, substantiating the probability of a genetic etiology as well as a syndrome. Nearly all of the children show thick curly eyebrows, long eyelashes, and increased facial hair. They have thin lips forming a downward slanting mouth, with smaller than normal-sized limbs, hands, feet, and head. Many exhibit a characteristic low-pitched gravelly voice early in infancy (Smith & Jones, 1982).

Behaviorally, these children may demonstrate autistic-like behaviors as well as the potential for self-abusive behaviors. They may be stubborn and difficult to manage and may bruise easily, an observation that may be of particular interest to the special educator. The syndrome tends to be relatively uncommon, with reported incidence rates varying from 1:30,000 to 1:50,000 live births (Goodman, 1977). There is no syndrome-specific treatment and outcome is poor in many respects.

REFERENCES

Clarke, A., & Clarke, D. B. (1975). *Mental deficiency, the changing perspectives* (3rd ed.). New York: Free Press.

Gillberg, C. (1995). *Clinical child neuropsychiatry*. Cambridge: Cambridge University Press.

Goodman, R., & Gorlin, R. (1977). *Atlas of the face of genetic disorders*. St. Louis: Mosby.

Smith, D., & Jones, R. (1982). *Recognizable patterns of human malformation* (3rd ed.). Philadelphia: Saunders.

JOHN E. PORCELLA
Rhinebeck Country School

AUTISM

CORRECTIONAL EDUCATION

The Correctional Education Association (1983) defined correctional education as a coordinated system of individualized learning services and activities conducted within the walls of a correctional facility. Services are provided by certified educational staff and are designed to meet the identified needs of the inmate population in the areas of basic education leading to a high-school credential; vocational training geared toward obtaining entry-level skills and maintaining competitive employment; and development of attitudes, skills, and abilities in the context of sociopersonal development.

It is difficult to summarize the types of correctional education programs available in institutions because services vary among and within states. Few states provide comprehensive educational services to meet the identified educational needs. Usually, a state will focus on just a few program areas such as higher education or adult education.

Estimates indicate that 85 to 95% of the incarcerated adults do not have high-school diplomas. Many of them can neither read nor write after completing their sentences (Loeffler & Martin, 1982). From a survey conducted by Bell (1979), it was found that 50% of the adults in federal and state institutions were illiterate. Researchers such as

Roberts (1973) state that the average inmate is unable to complete a job application, read and understand newspapers, or apply for an automobile operator's license (Day & McCane, 1982). In addition, 70% of the inmates have had no vocational training prior to sentencing. The National Advisory Council on Vocational Education found that the typical inmate is male, poor, and with less than 10 years of schooling. Gehring (1980) described correctional students as frequently afflicted by special learning and/or drug-related problems, accustomed to violence, and lacking in academic skills.

According to the U.S. Department of Justice (1983), the incarceration rate for individuals not completing elementary school is 259 per 1000 for males between the ages of 20 to 29 years; for elementary school graduates, it is 83 per 1000; for those completing 9 to 11 years in school, it is 70 per 1000; for high-school graduates, it decreased to 11 per 1000; and for persons with 16 years of schooling, the rate drops to 1 per 1000.

Numerous research studies on correctional education programs have documented the effectiveness of both juvenile and adult correctional programs (Correctional Education Association, 1983). Correctional education programs have resulted in increased employment and improved quality of life for released inmates.

A major difficulty facing correctional educational administrators stems from the fact that the quantity of existing correctional education programs is insufficient to meet the needs of the hundreds of thousands of men, women, and children who are incarcerated in correctional institutions throughout the United States. The lack of public support and financial resources for correctional education programs severely limit the extent of correctional program effectiveness.

REFERENCES

Bell, R. (1979, June). *Correctional education program for inmates* (National Evaluation Programs, Phase I). Washington, DC: U.S. Department of Justice.

Correctional Education Association. (1983). Lobbying for correctional education: A guide to action. (Available from Correctional Education Association, 1400 20th Street, NW, Washington, DC 20009.)

Day, S. R., & McCane, M. R. (1982). *Vocational education in corrections* (Information Series 237, 11–12). Columbus, OH: State University, National Center for Research in Vocational Education.

Gehring, T. (1980, September). Correctional education and the U.S. Department of Education. *Journal of Correctional Education, 35*(4), 137–141.

Loeffler, C. A., & Martin, T. C. (1982, April). *The functional illiterate: Is correctional education doing its job?* Huntsville, TX: Marloe Research.

Roberts, A. R. (1973). *Readings in prison education.* Springfield, IL: Thomas.

U.S. Department of Justice. (1983, October). *Report to the nation on crime and justice. The data* (NCJ-87060, p. 37). Rockville, MD: Bureau of Justice Statistics.

Stan A. Karcz
University of Wisconsin at Stout

**CORRECTIONAL SPECIAL EDUCATION
JUVENILE DELINQUENCY
RIGHT TO EDUCATION**

CORRECTIONAL SPECIAL EDUCATION

Over 500,000 criminal offenders are currently housed in the nation's 559 state and federal prisons and 3493 local jails. Of this population, approximately 72,000 are incarcerated in state juvenile correctional facilities, jails, and group homes. In addition, almost 3 million persons are under community supervision instead of in confinement (Bureau of Justice Statistics, 1998). This rate of incarceration is among the highest in the world.

A large portion of the incarcerated population is handicapped for educational purposes. For example, Morgan's (1979) survey indicated that 42% of incarcerated juveniles meet IDEA definitional criteria as handicapped. Surveys of adult correctional facilities in Oregon (Hurtz & Heintz, 1979) and Louisiana (Klinger, Marshall, Price, & Ward, 1983) suggest similar proportions of handicapped persons in adult prisons, for example, between 30 and 50%.

Correctional education, which consists of formal educational programs ranging from basic literacy training to postsecondary vocational and university education, is offered in the vast majority of correctional facilities in the United States. Such programs typically are voluntary in adult facilities, but mandatory for juveniles. The administrative regulations for IDEA specifically include correctional education programs in the mandate for a free and appropriate public education for handicapped persons 21 years of age and under; however, less than 10% of the state departments of juvenile and adult corrections are in compliance (Coffey, 1983). States not in compliance are experiencing heightened pressure through litigation (Wood, 1984) and administrative sanction to provide special education programs. Increased interest in correctional special education is reflected in federally funded demonstration and training projects, receipt of PL 94-142 state flow-through monies by correctional education programs, and the development of training programs for correctional special educators.

In 1984 the Correctional/ Special Education Training (C/SET) Project staff (Rutherford, Nelson, & Wolford, 1985) surveyed the 85 state departments of juvenile and/or adult corrections and the 50 state departments of education to determine the number of handicapped offenders in juvenile and adult correctional facilities.

There are 33,190 individuals incarcerated in state juvenile correctional facilities. Of this number, 30,681 or 92%, are in correctional education programs. The estimated number of handicapped juvenile offenders is 9443, or 28% of the total incarcerated population. The number of juveniles receiving special education services is 7750, or 23% of the number of juveniles in corrections. Thus, according to state administrators' estimates, approximately 80% of handicapped juvenile offenders are being served.

In addition to the data collected concerning handicapped offenders in juvenile corrections, data were also collected relative to services for handicapped inmates in state adult correctional facilities. An estimated 117,000 of those in adult corrections are under the age of 22 (Gerry, 1985) and thus potentially eligible for special education services under IDEA.

Of the 399,636 adults in state corrections programs, approximately 118,158 or 30% are receiving correctional education services. Based on data reported by 31 states, the estimated number of handicapped offenders in adult corrections is 41,590 or 10%, 4313 of whom, or less than 1%, are receiving special education services.

Currently a need exists for correctional special education services in juvenile and adult correctional institutions, raising the question of what constitutes an effective correctional special education program. Some researchers (e.g., Gerry, 1985; Smith & Hockenberry, 1980; Smith, Ramirez, & Rutherford, 1983) have delineated essential compliance issues with regard to implementation of IDEA in correctional education programs. There are six factors that are important to the implementation of meaningful correctional special education programs. These are (1) procedures for conducting functional assessments of the skills and learning needs of handicapped offenders; (2) the existence of a curriculum that teaches functional academic and daily living skills; (3) the inclusion of vocational special education in the curriculum; (4) the existence of transitional programs and procedures between correctional programs and the public schools or the world of work; (5) the presence of a comprehensive system for providing institutional and community services to handicapped offenders; and (6) the provision of in-service and preservice training for correctional educators in special education.

REFERENCES

Bureau of Justice Statistics. (1998). *Justice statistics*. Washington, DC: U.S. Department of Justice.

Coffey, O. D. (1983). Meeting the needs of youth from a corrections viewpoint. In S. Braaten, R. B. Rutherford, & C. A. Kardash (Eds.), *Programming for adolescents with behavioral disorders* (pp. 79–84). Reston, VA: Council for Children with Behavioral Disorders.

Gerry, M. H. (1985). *Monitoring the special education programs of correctional institutions*. Washington, DC: U.S. Department of Education.

Hurzt, R., & Heintz, E. I. (1979). Incidence of specific learning disabilities at Oregon State Correctional Institution. Paper presented at the National Institute of Corrections Conference, Portland, OR.

Klinger, J. H., Marshall, G. M., Price, A. W., & Ward, K. D. (1983). A pupil appraisal for adults in the Louisiana Department of Corrections. *Journal of Correctional Education, 34*(2), 46–48.

Morgan, D. J. (1979). Prevalence and types of handicapping conditions found in juvenile correctional institutions: A national survey. *Journal of Special Education, 13,* 283–295.

Rutherford, R. B., Nelson, C. M., & Wolford, B. I. (1985). Special education in the most restrictive environment: Correctional/special education. *Journal of Special Education, 19,* 60–71.

Smith, B. J., & Hockenberry, C. M. (1980). Implementing the Education for All Handicapped Children Act, P.L. 94-142, in youth corrections facilities: Selected issues. In F. J. Weintraub, A. Abeson, J. Ballard, & M. L. LaVor (Eds.), *Public policy and the education of exceptional children* (pp. 1–36). Reston, VA: Council for Exceptional Children.

Smith, B. J., Ramirez, B., & Rutherford, R. B. (1983). Special education in youth correctional facilities. *Journal of Correctional Education, 34,* 108–112.

Wood, F. J. (1984). *The law and correctional education*. Tempe, AZ: Correctional Special Education Training Project.

ROBERT B. RUTHERFORD, JR.
Arizona State University

CORRECTIONAL EDUCATION
JUVENILE DELINQUENCY

COSTA RICA, SPECIAL EDUCATION IN

Costa Rica has the strongest public education system in Central America. The 1869 constitution mandated a free, obligatory, and state-supported educational system—making Costa Rica one of the first countries in the world to pass such legislation (Biesanz, Biesanz, & Biesanz, 1982; Creedman, 1991). Approximately 25% of the national budget is dedicated to education (United Nations Educational and Scientific Organization [UNESCO], 1997) and elementary schools can be found even in the most isolated regions of the country. As a result, Costa Rica's literacy rate of 93% is one of highest in all of Latin America (Economic Commission for Latin America and the Caribbean [ECLAC], 1996; UNESCO, 1997).

Costa Rica is equally progressive in the area of special education. Special education services were formally established in 1939 when the Fernando Centeno Güell School for children with mental retardation was created near the capital city of San José (Asesoría General de Educación Especial, 1992). Public special education services were first ensured through the Fundamental Law of Education of 1957, which declared that students had the right to a special education, if so needed, and the right to special didactic techniques and materials; and that parents had the right to information on how to care for their child. Costa Rica has continued to pass progressive legislation for individuals with disabilities. The recently enacted Equal Opportunity Law for Persons with Disabilities (1996) includes antidiscriminatory clauses and guarantees equal rights for individuals with disabilities across all sectors of public life. Special education has been redefined in this law as "the combination of assistance and services at the disposal of students with special educational needs, whether they be temporary or permanent" (Sección VI, Artículo 27). The Equal Opportunity Law also strongly suggests that students with disabilities should be integrated into regular education classrooms that are "preferentially in the educational center closest to their home" (Capítulo I, Artículo 18).

Special education services in Costa Rica have rapidly expanded in the last 25 years. Until the early 1970's, students with disabilities received instruction at one of 20 segregated special education campuses (Bulgarelli, 1971). However, in 1978, the Ministry of Education began to place special education classrooms on regular education campuses through a national integration program (Castillo & Stough, 1988). By 1984, 11 special education schools, 103 self-contained classrooms, and 15 resource rooms were in existence, most located in the heavily populated Central Valley (Castillo & Stough, 1988). In the late 1980's, the Ministry of Education was able to rapidly expand the number of resource rooms in the country by hiring teachers to instruct recargo, or an extra shift, each day (Stough & Aguirre-Roy, 1997). By 1988, the recargo model had become the predominate special education delivery model in elementary schools. At present, there are over 600 classrooms that are taught by recargo teachers (A. R. Aguirre-Roy, pers. comm., February, 1998).

Approximately 20,000 students with disabilities receive services through the public education system in Costa Rica (Asesoría General de Educación Especial, 1993). The Department of Special Education uses the diagnostic categories of learning disabilities, mental retardation, emotional disturbance, speech impaired, auditory impaired, visually impaired, physically disabled, psychosocially disordered, and multiply handicapped. Eligibility for services is determined through a psychological and educational assessment conducted by a diagnostic team consisting of a psychologist, social worker, educator, and psychiatrist (Mainieri Hidalgo & Méndez Barrantes, 1992). Children with disabilities are eligible to receive educational services beginning at birth and these services continue through age 18, when most Costa Ricans finish high school.

Early stimulation classes for children five and under are located in elementary schools in most large towns and in the Central Valley region surrounding San José. In rural areas, parents often take their children to the nearest town on a weekly or biweekly basis to attend class. At the elementary level, students with learning disabilities or mild mental retardation receive services in resource rooms. These are typically "pull-out" programs in which students receive instruction in small groups from a recargo teacher. These teachers usually deliver 20 hours of instruction a week, using one hour each day for planning and consulting with general education teachers (González Trejos, 1992). Students who are labeled as emotionally disturbed, who have sensory impairments, or who have moderate to severe disabilities are placed in self-contained classrooms or on separate school campuses. In rural areas, such as the Guanacaste region, several itinerant teachers have been hired to travel intermittently to schools that have small numbers of students with special needs. At the high-school level, students with mild disabilities usually attend a vocational, rather than academic, high school. There are also several special education high schools that serve students with more severe disabilities and focus on the development of vocational skills. The number of special education programs drops drastically at the high school level, however, and the great majority of students with disabilities, particularly moderate to severe disabilities, do not graduate from high school.

While the Ministry of Education promotes programs which are "integrated into the community, always using the least restrictive methods" (Asesoría General de Educación Especial, 1993), the reality is that the delivery of special education services usually segregates students with disabilities from their same-age peers. The Ministry is currently piloting a co-teaching model in which special educators teach in collaboration with general educators (Nieto, pers. comm., June 2, 1997); however, it is too early to speculate on how this new model might change the current special education practices.

Special education in Costa Rica suffers from the same obstacles that have been described in other developing countries: limited material resources, geographic isolation of large segments of the population, and insufficient training programs (see González-Vega & Céspedes, 1993; Marfo, Walker, & Charles, 1986). The greatest national need is for trained professionals. Few special education teacher training programs exist outside of the capital city and teachers in rural areas usually have had no formal training with students with disabilities (Stough, 1989; Villarreal, 1989). Physical therapists, speech therapists, and psychologists are also scarce and often have limited experience in the area of disabilities.

Recent educational initiatives have exponentially increased the number of students receiving special education in Costa Rica and the Ministry of Education is making a focused effort to coordinate these services. Undeniably progressive legislation now supports the rights of individuals with disabilities to work, receive public health services, and to be educated. While special education continues to expand in Costa Rica, untrained personnel limit the effectiveness of this instruction. The current challenge for Costa Rica is to ensure the quality of these special services, as well as the accessibility to them.

REFERENCES

Asesoría General de Educación Especial. (1992). *Estructura, principios, normas y procedimientos de la educación especial en Costa Rica* [Structure, principles, norms and procedures of special education in Costa Rica]. San José, Costa Rica: Ministerio de Educación Pública.

Asesoría General de Educación Especial. (1993, March). *La educación especial en Costa Rica* [Special education in Costa Rica]. Paper presented at the meeting of the Conferencia Hemisférica sobre Discapacidad, Washington, DC.

Biesanz, R., Biesanz, K. Z., & Biesanz, M. H. (1982). *The Costa Ricans*. Englewood Cliffs, NJ: Prentice Hall.

Bulgarelli, O. A. (Ed.). (1971). *El desarrollo nacional en 150 años de vida independiente* [National development in 150 years of independent life]. San José, Costa Rica: Publicaciones de la Universidad de Costa Rica.

Castillo, G., & Stough, L. M. (1988, May). *Informe a visita a Tegulcigalpa* [Report on a visit to Tegulcigalpa]. Unpublished manuscript.

Creedman, T. S. (1991). *Historical dictionary of Costa Rica* (2nd ed.). Metuchen, NJ: The Scarecrow Press.

Economic Commission for Latin America and the Caribbean [ECLAC]. (1996). *Statistical yearbook for Latin America and the Caribbean*. Chile: United Nations Publication.

González Trejos, F. (1992). *Información sobre el funcionamiento de las aulas recurso de problemas de aprendizaje* [Information on the functioning of resource rooms for learning disabilities]. San José, Costa Rica: Ministerio de Educación Pública.

González-Vega, C., & Céspedes, V. H. (1993). Costa Rica. In S. Rottenberg (Ed.), *A World Bank comparative study. The political economy of poverty, equity, and growth. Costa Rica and Uruguay*. New York: Oxford University Press.

Lara, S., Barry, T., & Simonson, P. (1995). *Inside Costa Rica*. Albuquerque, New Mexico: Interhemispheric Resource Center.

Ley de Igualdad de Oportunidades para las Personas con Discapacidad [Law of Equal Opportunity Law for Persons with Disabilities]. (1996).

Ley Fundamental de Educación de Costa Rica, Capítulo IV, Artículos 27, 28, y 29 [Costa Rican Fundamental Law of Education, Chapter IV, Articles 27, 28, and 29]. (1957).

Mainieri Hidalgo, A., & Méndez Barrantes, Z. (1992). *Detección de problemas de aprendizaje: Antología* [Detection of learning disabilities: Anthology]. San José, Costa Rica: Editorial Universidad Estatal a Distancia.

Marfo, K., Walker, S., & Charles, B. (1986). *Childhood disability in developing countries: Issues in habilitation and special education*. New York: Praeger.

Stough, L. M. (1990, January). *Special education and teacher training in the third world: Costa Rican and Honduran rural education programs*. Paper presented at the annual meeting of the Southwest Educational Research Association, Austin, TX.

Stough, L. M., & Aguirre-Roy, A. R. (1996). Learning disabilities in Costa Rica: Challenges for an "army of teachers." *Journal of Learning Disabilities, 30,* 566–571.

United Nations Educational and Scientific Organization [UNESCO]. *UNESCO Statistical Yearbook*. (1997). Lanham, MD: Bernan.

Villarreal, B. (1989). *An analysis of the special education services for children and youth in Costa Rica*. Unpublished doctoral dissertation, University of San Diego, CA.

LAURA M. STOUGH
Texas A & M University

COUNCIL FOR CHILDREN WITH BEHAVIORAL DISORDERS

Founded in 1961, the Council for Children with Behavioral Disorders (CCBD), a division of the Council for Exceptional Children (CEC), is the professional organization of teachers, teacher educators, administrators, parents, and mental health personnel concerned with the education and general welfare of children and youth with behavioral and emotional disorders. The goals of CCBD include: promoting quality educational services and program alternatives for persons with behavioral disorders; advocating for the needs of children and youth with behavioral disorders and their families; encouraging research and professional growth as vehicles for better understanding behavioral disorders; disseminating relevant and timely information through professional meetings, training programs, and publications; providing professional support for persons who are involved with and serve children and youth with behavioral disorders; and supporting the activities, policies, and procedures of CEC and other CEC divisions.

CCBD's major functions are coordinated by four standing committees of its executive committee: regional services and membership, advocacy/governmental relations, publications, and professional development. The regional services and membership committee coordinates state and provincial units of CCBD to further the professional development of members and provide advocacy activities for children and youth with behavioral and emotional disorders. The advocacy/governmental relations committee furthers these advocacy efforts at a national level through lobbying and legislative support efforts on behalf of these children and youth. The publications committee coordinates the publication efforts of the organization through the professional journal *Behavioral Disorders, Beyond Be-*

havior magazine, and the CCBD Newsletter. The professional development committee is responsible for conducting conferences and regional training events to support the professional needs of the division's members.

Currently, with a membership of 8,400, CCBD is the second largest of CEC's 17 divisions. CCBD has evolved into the primary advocacy organization for students whose behavioral and emotional problems bring them in conflict with the schools and the community. It is also the primary professional organization for those who educate and work with these students.

Membership inquiries should be made to the Council for Children with Behavioral Disorders, The Council for Exceptional Children, 1920 Association Drive, Reston, VA 20191-1589. Only members of The Council for Exceptional Children are eligible to join the Council for Children with Behavioral Disorders. Special membership categories for students, parents, and professionals are available for those who qualify for these discounted membership rates.

STAFF

COUNCIL FOR EXCEPTIONAL CHILDREN

The Council for Exceptional Children (CEC) is the world's largest professional organization dedicated to the welfare of exceptional children. The CEC was founded in 1922 at Teachers' College, Columbia University. Today, its United States and Canadian membership includes approximately 50,000 persons, including over 9,000 members of the organization's 288 student chapters. There are also 269 state, local, & provincial chapters in the U.S. & Canada. The organization is further divided into special interest groups, including divisions on the physically handicapped, behavior disorders, mental retardation, communication disorders, learning disabilities, visually handicapped, talented and gifted, early childhood education, special education administration, career development, technology and media, educational diagnostic services, teacher education, international special education, cultural and linguistic diversity, research, and pioneers of the CEC.

CEC members include educators, parents, students, and others concerned with the education of children with disabilities and gifted and talented children and youth. The CEC's membership is dedicated to increasing educational opportunities for all exceptional children and youth and to improving conditions for the professionals who work with them. The CEC advocates for appropriate governmental policies, sets professional standards, provides continual professional development, advocates for newly and historically underserved individuals with exceptionalities,

and helps professionals obtain conditions and resources necessary for effective professional practice.

CEC has been highly visible as an advocate for federal legislation and funding for the gifted and the handicapped. The organization issues two respected periodicals, *Exceptional Children and Teaching Exceptional Children*. The former is more research and policy oriented, while the latter is geared more toward practitioners' needs. In addition, several hundred books, multimedia packages, bibliographies, and fact sheets are available from CEC. Access to nearly one half a million references on handicapped and gifted children can be obtained from ERIC (Educational Resources Information Center) and CEC Information Services. Each year, a national convention sponsored by CEC attracts thousands of professionals, paraprofessionals, and parents. In the past few years, CEC has sponsored successful topical workshops devoted to areas such as microcomputer use in special education, black exceptional children, and early childhood special education. Periodic international conferences are also sponsored by CEC.

The CEC's founding in 1922 was predated by other organizations concerned with the handicapped; Convention of American Instructors of the Deaf, 1850; American Association of Instructors of the Blind, 1853; Conference of Executives of American Schools for the Deaf, 1863; American Association on Mental Deficiency, 1876; American Association to Promote the Teaching of Speech to the Deaf; 1890; and National Education Association's Department of Special Education, 1897. The CEC was founded the same year that a related organization, the National Association for the Study and Education of Exceptional Children, was disbanded. Four years earlier, the National Education Association (NEA) discontinued its Department of Special Education.

Elizabeth E. Farrell, who had been active in NEA's special education activities earlier, other Teachers' College faculty, and advanced students in the 1922 summer session at Columbia, formed CEC at a meeting on August 10 in a downtown New York restaurant. The early years found an organization without a true central office, limited funds, and a heavy reliance on volunteers for its existence. Various internal and external problems nearly ended CEC in its first two decades.

Wooden (1980) claims that one of the organization's strength was its system of local chapters. Grass-roots leadership was developed through planning and carrying out of professional activities at the local level. A sense of the *whole child* developed among members: since CEC's interests were broader than early groups with single-category interests. After the 1930s depression, CEC began to stabilize with the nation. Reorganization of the council's internal structure and a better financial situation allowed for expansion of CEC's role and activities. Today, despite some decline in membership from its peak in the 1970s, CEC is respected as a leader and advocate in its field. It works cooperatively with other organizations to promote the education and welfare of all exceptional children and youth. The Council for Exceptional Children's headquarters are now located at 1920 Association Drive, Reston, VA 20191, and may be reached by phone at (703) 620-3660.

REFERENCE

Wooden, H. Z. (1980a). Growth of a social concept. *Exceptional Children, 47*(1), 40–46.

JOHN D. WILSON
Elwyn Institutes

COUNCIL FOR LEARNING DISABILITIES

In 1968 educators formed the Division for Children with Learning Disabilities (DCLD) within the Council for Exceptional Children (CEC) (Hallahan, Kauffman, & Lloyd, 1985). Both groups believed that without a name to identify a group of children who did not fit into any other handicapping condition, there would be difficulty in obtaining needed funds for special services.

During the early 1980s emerged the realization that not only did children have learning disabilities but so did adults. Consequently, the Division for Children with Learning Disabilities became the Council for Learning Disabilities (CLD). Besides this change of name, CLD changed its affiliation: as it seceded from the Council for Exceptional Children (Lerner, 1985). The majority of CLD's membership voted to become a separate and independent organization.

Conferences and newsletters sponsored by CLD provide a valuable means of sharing information and serve as a stimulus for research, program development, and advocacy. In addition, CLD formed a strong national lobbying group to promote legislative recognition of learning disabilities.

REFERENCES

Hallahan, D. P., Kauffman, J. M., & Lloyd, J. W. (1985). *Introduction to learning disabilities.* Englewood Cliffs, NJ: Prentice-Hall.

Learner, J. W. (1985). *Learning disabilities.* Dallas: Houghton Mifflin.

JOSEPH M. RUSSO
Hunter College

COUNCIL OF ADMINISTRATORS OF SPECIAL EDUCATION (CASE)

The Council of Administrators of Special Education (CASE) was founded in 1952 as a division of the Council for Exceptional Children (CEC). The CASE membership of 5,200 includes administrators, directors, supervisors, and coordinators of local private and public special education programs, schools, or classes serving children and youth with special needs. There are also a number of members who are state department personnel as well as those who are university faculty engaged in the preparation of special education administrators. The purpose of CASE is to promote professional leadership, provide opportunity for the study of problems common to its members and to provide information for developing improved services to exceptional children. CASE has 41 Subdivisions in the U.S. and Canada.

CASE provides six newsletters and two issues of its refereed journal *CASE in POINT* to its members annually. Through its publications program the Council also offers publications of interest to administrators. CASE provides professional development opportunities to its members. Among those are an annual institute devoted to the study of a specific topic and an annual conference offering a wide range of topics for discussion and study. CASE maintains a web site at <http://www.members.aol.com/casecec/index.htm> where members may obtain current information on a variety of topics and activities of the Council.

The office staff is directed by the Executive Director, Dr. Jo Thomason. The office may be contacted at 615 16th St. NW, Albuquerque, New Mexico, 87104 or via e-mail through its web site.

JO THOMASON
Executive Director, CASE

COUNSELING THE HANDICAPPED

With so much emphasis placed on handicapped individuals' educational, adaptive behavior, and social skill needs, their emotional needs are often forgotten. Indeed, handicapped individuals often have issues that affect their lives that could be addressed and resolved through the counseling process. For example, some mentally retarded individuals experience feelings of frustration because of their handicap and its limitations and could benefit from counseling support. Learning-disabled students, given the peer rejection sometimes associated with their academic difficulties, also might benefit from therapeutic attention. And clearly, counseling should be a central intervention for behaviorally and emotionally disturbed persons.

While the need for counseling with the handicapped is apparent, the specific counseling techniques, or approaches that are most effective under defined circumstances are not empirically evident. From a comprehensive diagnostic and treatment perspective, the multimodal approach of Lazarus (1976) has been used with handicapped children. Using Lazarus's *BASIC ID* modalities (behavior, affect, sensation, images, cognition, interpersonal relationships, and drugs/biological functioning), handicapped children's comprehensive social-emotional needs are analyzed and a counseling and psychotherapy program is developed to address the modalities most critical to the identified issues. Keat (1979) has also proposed a multimodal therapy approach, which he has used with learning-disabled children, summarized by the acronym HELPING (health, emotions-feelings, learning-school, personal relationships, imagination-interests, need to know-think, guidance of antecedents-behaviors-consequences). Again, primary concerns in the modality areas are identified and then targeted for counseling support.

From a purely counseling perspective, a number of therapeutic approaches are available. Prout and Brown (1983) identified six major theoretical approaches to counseling and psychotherapy that can be adopted when handicapped individuals are the primary clients: behavior therapy, reality therapy, person-centered therapy, rational-emotive therapy, Adlerian therapy, and psychoanalytic/psychodynamic therapy. Behavior therapy has been especially useful with behaviorally disturbed individuals. Using operant or classical conditioning, cognitive, or social learning behavioral approaches, positive behaviors are taught and/or reinforced while disruptive or disturbing behaviors are altered or extinguished. The other psychotherapeutic approaches have been used, in addition to the behavioral, for emotionally disturbed individuals who manifest an assortment of affectively based difficulties and issues. Additionally, all of these approaches can be applied to the emotional issues that often coexist or result from other handicapping conditions.

Besides the psychotherapeutic approaches, a number of more specialized approaches are available when counseling handicapped individuals. Briefly reviewed in Reynolds and Gutkin (1982), these include family therapy approaches, sociodrama, developmental therapy, art therapy, music therapy, and holistic or milieu therapy. Again, these approaches often become part of a comprehensive program that addresses handicapped children's educational, social-emotional, affective, family, and adaptive needs. In many cases, the use of counseling occurs only as an afterthought to what is otherwise a comprehensive program. Clearly, the possibility that handicapped children have related or separate counseling needs must be emphasized in research programs and in applied settings.

REFERENCES

Keat, D. B. (1979). *Multimodal therapy with children*. New York: Pergamon.

Lazarus, A. A. (1976). *Multimodal behavior therapy*. New York: McGraw-Hill.

Prout, H. T., & Brown, D. T. (1983). *Counseling and psychotherapy with children and adolescents*. Tampa, FL: Mariner

Reynolds, C. R., & Gutkin, T. B. (1982). *The handbook of school psychology*. New York: Wiley.

HOWARD M. KNOFF
University of South Florida

BEHAVIOR MODIFICATION
FAMILY THERAPY
PSYCHOTHERAPY

CRATTY, BRYANT J. (1929–   )

As an assistant, associate, and full professor of kinesiology at the University of Southern California since 1961, Bryant Cratty has done research on perceptual and motor development and its relationship to the human personality. He developed programs for the neurologically impaired in the early 1960s that expanded to research of learning games to aid slow learners to acquire academic skills.

In 1970, Cratty published *Perceptual and Motor Development in Infants and Children*, which traced motor development from infancy to adolescence and gave specific teaching suggestions. In *Motor Activity and the Education of Retardates*, Cratty offered detailed curriculum guides, including relaxation and motor activities that would assist a child in gaining self-confidence. In 1991, Cratty, with Iranide Deoliveira, examined and assessed infants who had been exposed to cocaine prenatally: measurable delays were noted.

Bryant J. Cratty

Cratty has published over 55 books and monographs (many translated into 15 languages and braille) that range from graduate texts in motor development and learning to applied sports psychology. He has also published over 100 articles in domestic and foreign journals and lectured in 20 countries.

REFERENCES

Cratty, B. J. (1975). *Motor activity and the education of retardates* (2nd ed.). Philadelphia, PA: Lea and Febiger.

Cratty, B. J. (1980). *Adapted physical education for handicapped children and youth*. Denver, CO: Love.

Cratty, B. J. (1985). *Active learning* (2nd ed.). Englewood Cliffs, NJ: Prentice-Hall.

Cratty, B. J. (1986). *Perceptual and motor development in infants and children* (3rd ed.). Englewood Cliffs, NJ: Prentice-Hall.

Deoliveira, I. J. & Cratty, B. J. (1991) Survey of ten infants exposed prenatally to maternal cocaine use. *International Journal of Rehabilitation Research, 14*, 3, 265–274.

ELAINE FLETCHER-JANZEN
University of Northern Colorado

CREATIVE PROBLEM SOLVING (CPS)

Creative problem solving (CPS) is a structured model for using knowledge and imagination to arrive at a creative, innovative, or effective solution to a problem. Developed by Alex F. Osborn (1953), the original process consisted of three steps: fact finding, including problem definition and preparation; idea finding, including idea production and idea development; and solution finding, including evaluation and adoption. Parnes (1967) developed and refined this sequential problem-solving process into a five-step comprehensive model that incorporates findings from applied and theoretical research on creative thinking and behavior. The five steps are fact finding, problem finding, idea finding, solution finding, and acceptance finding.

Also known as the Osborn-Parnes Model, CPS is the most widely used method to encourage the application of creative thinking skills in the solving of problems. Fundamental to the CPS process is the principle of deferred judgment. This principle is based on Osborn's original notion that when judgment is withheld during ideation, at least 70% more good ideas are produced (Osborn, 1953). Throughout the process both divergent thinking and convergent thinking constantly occur as the problem solver moves from one step to the next. The CPS process proceeds in the following manner. Prior to the first step, there is the "mess" or preparation stage during which the identification or recognition of a situation of personal importance is determined. In fact finding, the emphasis is on gathering all possible background information that may help to define the real problem. Data are collected, facts about the situation are explored, and what is known about the situation is sought out and analyzed. Judgment is deferred until all alternatives have been exhausted. The next step focuses on the problem.

In problem finding, the emphasis is on restating the problem for solution. The problem is examined from a wide variety of perspectives, redefined, narrowed, and analyzed. As the problem is being defined, it is recommended that the phrase "In what ways might I . . ." (IWWMI) be used to encourage more ideas and further elaborations. Again, it is important that judgment be deferred so that thoughts about the problem may flow freely. Sometimes new facts or data will cause a return to step one for more fact finding.

Once the problem has been satisfactorily defined, step three, or idea finding, occurs. Here the intent is to generate many ideas and possible solutions. It is especially important during this phase to defer judgment. Many techniques may be used to generate a quantity of ideas. The most popular is brainstorming, or storming the mind, to generate new and frequently innovative ideas. Application of the four cardinal rules of brainstorming are a must to ensure that ideas flow freely before they are judged for their merits. The rules of brainstorming are (1) rule out criticism; (2) welcome freewheeling or wild ideas; (3) seek quantity; and (4) seek combination and improvement. Other techniques that may be used here and throughout the five steps to encourage the production of ideas are idea-spurring questions, morphological analyses, synectics, attribute listing, scampering, and free association.

In step four, solution finding, the goal is to choose those alternatives that seem to provide the greatest potential for solving the problem. Criteria for evaluating solutions are developed and applied to each possible solution. The best idea, or combination of ideas, to solve the problem is chosen. Ideas not chosen should not be discarded for they may be used later.

The final step, acceptance finding, involves preparations to put the idea into use. The challenge is to make it acceptable. This involves developing a plan for carrying out an idea and for selling and promoting it. Considerations must be given to all factors that may aid or hinder the implementation of the plan.

Parnes (1967) has emphasized the importance of knowledge and imagination in creative productivity. Through the Creative Problem Solving Institute, in university classes, and in many other settings, he has successfully demonstrated that the process is easy to learn and applicable to many situations. College students, government officials, business persons, artists, educators, parents, and children exemplify the types of people who have learned to apply the set of skills in CPS to the solution of practical problems.

The literature on CPS is extensive. Reviews of the CPS process have been completed by Parnes (1981) and Noller (1977), among others. Edwards (1986) has provided an extensive review of information on approaches to enhance creative thinking and ideation during the CPS process.

REFERENCES

Edwards, M. O. (1986). *Idea power: Time tested methods to stimulate your imagination*. Buffalo, NY: Bearly.

Noller, R. B. (1977). *Scratching the surface of creative problem solving*. Buffalo, NY: D.O.K.

Osborn, A. F. (1953). *Applied imagination*. New York: Scribner.

Parnes, S. J. (1967). *Creative behavior guidebook*. New York: Scribner.

Parnes, S. J. (1981). *The magic of your mind*. Buffalo, NY: Bearly.

MARY M. FRASIER
University of Georgia

CREATIVE PROBLEM SOLVING INSTITUTE
CREATIVITY
SOCIODRAMA
TORRANCE, E. PAUL

CREATIVE PROBLEM SOLVING INSTITUTE (CPSI)

The Creative Problem Solving Institute (CPSI) is a multidisciplinary, multilevel program designed to familiarize participants with the principles and techniques of creative problem solving (CPS). Founded in 1955 by Alex Osborn, the institute is sponsored by the Creative Education Foundation in cooperation with the State University College, Buffalo. In its first years the institute's program was based on brainstorming, a procedure introduced by Osborn to facilitate creative thinking in a group. Osborn's (1953) notion was that "most of us can work better creatively when teamed up with the right partner because collaboration tends to induce effort, and also to spur our automatic power of association" (p. 72). His conceptualization of the creative problem-solving process included three steps: (1) fact finding, (2) idea finding, and (3) solution finding (Osborn, 1953).

Sidney J. Parnes, who succeeded Osborn as the director of the institute, retained the basic principles of the original model while extending the process to encompass a more eclectic approach. Kitano and Kirby (1986) summarized Parnes's approach as follows: "The Model consists of six steps and incorporates a variety of research-supported techniques for stimulating creativity, including brainstorming, synectics, incubation, imaging, deferred judgment, forced relationships and practice" (p. 205). The six steps as outlined by Parnes (1977) are objective finding, fact finding, problem finding, idea finding, solution finding, and acceptance finding.

The annual summer institute has four major areas: (1) the Springboard Program, (2) the CPSI Youth Program, (3) the Extending Program, and (4) the Leadership Development Program Facilitating Creative Problem Solving. The Springboard Program and the CPSI Youth Program (ages 7 to 16) are designed for participants who have little or no previous experience in the study of creative problem solving. The Extending Program is designed to help participants expand their options through a variety of approaches to creativity. This program consists of different interest groups in which participants practice skills in the creative problem-solving process. The Leadership Development Program emphasizes self-growth and the development of skills for teaching creative problem solving to others.

In addition to annual summer institutes, regional Creative Problem Solving institutes, symposiums, and workshops are held throughout the year. The CPSI attracts people from business, education, and government to its summer institutes and other programs. Participants receive training from specialists with varied experiences in fields associated with creativity.

REFERENCES

Kitano, M. K., & Kirby, D. F. (1986). *Gifted education: A comprehensive review*. Boston: Little, Brown.

Osborn, A. F. (1953). *Applied imagination: Principles and procedures of creative problem-solving* (Rev. ed.). New York: Scribner.

Parnes, S. J. (1977). Guiding creative action. *Gifted Child Quarterly, 21*(4), 460–476.

MARY M. FRASIER
University of Georgia

CONCEPT FORMATION
CREATIVE PROBLEM SOLVING
OSBORN, ALEXANDER F.

CREATIVE STUDIES PROGRAM

The Creative Studies Program was inaugurated in September 1969 by Stanley J. Parnes at Buffalo (N.Y.) State University College to enhance various aspects of college students' present and future behaviors both in college and the general community (Parnes & Noller, 1972a). Parnes et al. developed the Creative Studies Program curriculum based on an earlier project, Creative Problem Solving.

The Creative Problem Solving curriculum is a five-step

process (fact finding, problem finding, idea finding, solution finding, and acceptance finding) that emphasizes the generation of a variety of alternatives prior to selecting or implementing a solution (Maher, 1982). The general purposes of the Creative Problem Solving Model are (1) to provide a sequential process that will enable an individual to work from an accumulation of information to arrive at a creative, innovative, or effective solution, and (2) to improve students' overall creative behavior (Maher, 1982).

In implementing the Creative Studies Project curriculum at Buffalo State, Noller and Parnes (1972) developed a 2-year, 4-semester curriculum. The first year of the curriculum provided the students with hands-on experience in creativity. Such experiences were provided through a variety of instructional procedures, including the use of discussions, creative media (e.g., sculpture, art, dance), films, and guest leaders (Noller & Parnes, 1972). The second year of the project provided the students an opportunity to lead others through the project's curriculum.

The Creative Studies Program appears to be a successful method to increase the creative performance of college students (Maher, 1982; Parnes & Noller, 1972b). These students do better in school, perform better on three out of five mental operations (cognition, divergent production, and convergent production) in Guilford's Structure of Intellect Model (Guilford, 1967), and are more productive in nonacademic settings calling for creative performance. Torrance (1972) notes that the Creative Problem Solving curriculum or its modifications (e.g., the Creative Studies Program) is successful in teaching children to think creatively 91 to 92% of the time.

REFERENCES

Guilford, J. P. (1967). *The nature of human intelligence*. New York: McGraw-Hill.

Maher, C. J. (1982). *Teaching models in the education of the gifted*. Rockville, MD: Aspen.

Noller, R. B., & Parnes, S. J. (1972). Applied creativity: The Creative Studies Project: Part III—The curriculum. *Journal of Creative Behavior, 6,* 275–294.

Parnes, S. J., & Noller, R. B. (1972a). Applied creativity: The Creative Studies Project: Part I—The development. *Journal of Creative Behavior, 6,* 11–22.

Parnes, S. J., & Noller, R. B. (1972b). Applied creativity: The Creative Studies Project: Part II—Results of the two-year program. *Journal of Creative Behavior, 6,* 164–186.

Torrance, E. P. (1972). Can we teach children to think creatively? *Journal of Creative Behavior, 6,* 114–143.

JOHN R. BEATTIE
*University of North Carolina
at Charlotte*

CREATIVITY
CREATIVITY TESTS

CREATIVITY

Creativity is a complex and multifaceted phenomenon of human behavior. Theories explaining creativity have ranged from those that define it as the innovative combination of knowledge and imagination applied to the solution of problems to those that view creativity as an "unconscious process through which libidinal or aggressive energies are converted into culturally sanctioned behaviors" (Freud, 1924).

MacKinnon (1978) has properly observed that one should not seek to choose from among the several meanings for the best single definition of creativity; it is a concept that carries all of the meanings that have been offered and will likely carry many more as investigations continue. Current positions on the meaning of creativity suggest a holistic view for, as Clark (1983) has observed, none of the theories thus far provide a complete picture. Her rationale for organizing the various theories into four areas of human functioning—thinking, feeling, sensing, and intuiting—is based on her perception that none of the theories provide a complete picture. The position she takes is that each perception may be only a fragment of the total. It is only through their integration that creativity is possible.

The creative process, person, product, and environment are the vantage points from which creativity is most often discussed. What happens in the creative process? Wallas (1926) described the process as consisting of four stages: preparation, incubation, illumination, and verification. Torrance defined the process as "one of becoming sensitive to or aware of problems . . . bringing together available information . . . searching for solutions . . . and communicating the results" (Torrance & Myers, 1970, p. 22).

While Taylor (1960) supported the notion of stages, he added that creativity exists at five levels with each level involving different psychological processes that may change the steps in the process. The five levels are (1) expressive creativity, a form of spontaneous expression without reference to originality and quality of the product; (2) technical or productive creativity, where the emphasis is on skill rather than spontaneity and novelty; (3) inventive creativity, with an emphasis on the new use of old things; (4) innovative creativity, where new ideas or principles are developed; and (5) emergentive creativity, which describes creative formulation using the most abstract ideational principles or assumptions underlying a body of art or science. Guilford (1959), emphasizing divergent thinking as the essence of creativity, identified generalized sensitivity to problems, fluency, flexibility, originality, redefinition, and elaboration as important components.

Research into hemispheric functioning has provided the most recent perspectives on creativity and the creative process. The notion that creative individuals are right-hemisphere dominant while logical, rational thinkers are left-hemisphere dominant has led to current theories that define the creative act as the result of interactions between hemispheres. For detailed reviews of current studies on hemisphericity, the reader is referred to Clark (1983) or Kitano and Kirby (1986).

Creative products may be ideas, works of art, scientific theories, or even building designs, provided certain criteria are met. According to MacKinnon (1978), these criteria include originality or novelty and relevance to a problem, situation, or goal. In addition, the answer that the product yields must be aesthetically pleasing and must create new conditions of human existence that transcend and transform traditional views and experiences.

Consistent among the many descriptions of creative persons are traits and behaviors such as unusual sensitivity to their environment, independence in thinking, nonconforming in their behaviors, and persistence at tasks. Creative people tend to be open to new ideas and experiences and less accepting of traditional points of view. Exploring ideas for their own sake, a marked sense of humor, a high tolerance for ambiguity, and strong self-confidence in their own work are other common traits of highly creative people.

An environment or situation that is open and accepting is critical for the release and development of creative potential. Kneller (1966) suggested that the main obstacles to creativity appear to be cultural and biological. Arieti (1976) presented the concept of the creativogenic society to describe his holistic view of cultural traits that support the development of creativity. Such a society is distinguished by its lack of emphasis on immediate gratification, its tolerance for and interest in divergent points of view, and its use of incentives and rewards for creativity. Torrance (1962) has suggested that other important variables are those that encourage unusual questions and ideas and those that allow performance to occur without constant threat of evaluation.

The debate regarding the nature of the relationship between creativity and intelligence has not been conclusively resolved. Kitano and Kirby (1986) contend that there is at least a conceptual agreement among researchers that creativity is distinguishable from general intelligence. That is, "an individual can be extremely bright but uncreative, or highly creative but not necessarily intellectually gifted" (Kitano & Kirby, 1986, p. 192). It has been estimated that an IQ of at least 120 is generally necessary for high creativity. IQ levels may vary according to the nature of the creative act.

Much of the discussion regarding the relationship between creativity and intelligence relates to assessment. There have been several measures developed to assess creativity, but questions still arise regarding whether creativity should be measured by recognized achievement or by tests of divergent or creative thinking. The most frequently used measure of creativity is the Torrance Tests of Creative Thinking (1974), which provides a single score index of creative potential on both the figural and verbal versions. Other measures of creativity are batteries developed by Guilford (1959) and by Wallach and Kogan (1965).

Leading proponents of the search for methods to teach creative thinking have been Parnes (1967) and Torrance (1979). Parnes developed the Creative Problem Solving Process, a five-step method combining knowledge and imagination in problem solving. Torrance (1979) created a three-stage instructional model—the Incubation Model—which integrates creativity objectives with content objectives. Clark (1983) and Kitano and Kirby (1986) provide further information on methods to teach creativity.

REFERENCES

Arieti, S. (1976). *Creativity: The magic synthesis*. New York: Basic Books.

Clark, B. (1983). *Growing up gifted* (2nd ed.). Columbus, OH: Merrill.

Freud, S. (1924). The relations of the poet to day-dreaming. In *Collected papers* (Vol. 2). London: Hogarth. (Original work published 1908.)

Guilford, J. P. (1959). Three faces of intellect. *American Psychology, 14,* 469–479.

Kitano, M. K., & Kirby, D. F. (1986). *Gifted education: A comprehensive view*. Boston: Little, Brown.

Kneller, G. F. (1966). *The art and science of creativity*. New York: Holt, Rinehart, & Winston.

MacKinnon, D. W. (1978). *In search of human effectiveness*. Buffalo, NY: Creative Education Foundation.

Parnes, S. J. (1967). *Creative behavior guidebook*. New York: Scribner.

Stein, M. I. (1974). *Stimulating creativity: Vol I. Individual procedures*. New York: Academic.

Taylor, I. A. (1960). The nature of the creative process. In P. Smith (Ed.), *Creativity: An examination of the creative process*. New York: Hastings House.

Torrance, E. P. (1962). *Guiding creative talent*. Englewood Cliffs, NJ: Prentice-Hall.

Torrance, E. P. (1974). *Torrance Tests of Creative Thinking: Norms-technical manual*. Bensenville, IL: Scholastic Testing Service.

Torrance, E. P. (1979). An instructional model for enhancing incubation. *Journal of Creative Behavior, 13*(1), 23–35.

Torrance, E. P., & Myers, R. E. (1970). *Creative learning and teaching*. New York: Dodd, Mead.

Wallach, M. A., & Kogan, N. (1965). *Modes of thinking in young children*. New York: Holt, Rinehart, & Winston.

Wallas, G. (1926). *The art of thought*. New York: Harcourt Brace Jovanovich.

MARY M. FRASIER
University of Georgia

CREATIVE STUDIES PROGRAM
GIFTED CHILDREN

INVESTMENT THEORY OF CREATIVITY
TORRANCE, PAUL

CREATIVITY TESTS

Creativity tests have been in widespread application for more than 50 years in research on cognitive skills and in the identification of gifted and talented children for participation in special education programs. However, it was the tremendous increase of interest in giftedness and creativity and concomitant funding of such research from about 1953 to 1963 that fueled research in the area. Major conceptual advances occurred during this period as Torrance began studying creativity in earnest and such classic and influential works as Guilford's (1959) *Three Faces of Intellect* and Getzels and Jackson's (1962) *Intelligence and Creativity* were published. Guilford was most influential in proposing the concept of convergent and divergent thinking, the latter being closely associated with creative thinking. Getzels and Jackson changed the dominant views of the relationship between IQ and creativity by postulating, based on their extensive study, that creativity was far more independent of IQ than previously believed, especially at the upper IQ levels. This work paved the way for the development of modern creativity tests. Creativity tests have changed very little since their growth spurt during the 1960s.

Most of the tests of creativity currently available were developed in the course of large-scale research projects on the nature of creativity. The two major batteries to be developed were the University of Southern California tests, devised by Guilford et al. as part of the Aptitude Research Project, and the Torrance Tests of Creative Thinking, devised by E. Paul Torrance in his efforts to design curriculum and teaching methods for the improvement of creative functioning in children. Torrance's research program has been designated the Georgia Studies of Creative Behavior since the late 1960s.

These tests and many others are commercially available and often used in the assessment of creativity; however, many psychometricians consider all such tests to be experimental (Anastasi, 1982). The items in creativity tests, with very few exceptions (such as the Welsh Figure Preference Test), are open-ended and thus on the subjective side of the scoring continuum. It is particularly important for this reason to assess the interscorer reliability of creativity tests before placing them into practice. Normative data for creativity tests generally fall significantly short of what has become the accepted psychometric standard for good tests of intelligence and achievement. Reliability and validity data are extensive for some tests such as the Torrance Tests of Creative Thinking, but for others they are extremely limited. The Torrance tests have been used in more than 1000 published studies and doctoral dissertations. Even with the large body of research on this scale, the relationship between measurement of creativity with existing tests and major variables of personality, intelligence, and creativity on the job or in other settings remains unclear.

The major creativity scales attempt to measure multiple dimensions of creativity, including such variables as fluency, originality, unusual responses, flexibility, resistance to premature closure, etc. It remains unclear whether these dimensions are sufficiently independent to warrant differentiation in the measurement process. The measurement of creativity also has been found to be relatively task specific; i.e., performance on creativity measures does not generalize well to tasks outside of the test and the test setting.

Despite these problems, the use of creativity tests continue to be a popular activity in programs for the gifted and talented. Creativity has proven a difficult concept to master and the state of the psychometric data regarding creativity tests generally reflects the nature of the concept. Creativity tests are probably better than most psychometricians believe (Bennett, 1972; Wallach, 1968). The relatively weak results of research on this genre of tests, compared with the outcome of research on tests of intelligence and academic achievement, are more reflective of the difficult nature of the concept than of any inherent weakness in the major scales in use today such as the Torrance Tests of Creative Thinking. Little progress has occurred in the development or refinement of creativity testing since the work of Torrance.

REFERENCES

Anastasi, A. (1982). *Psychological testing* (5th ed.). New York: Macmillan.

Bennett, G. K. (1972). Review of the Remote Associates Test. In O. K. Buros (Ed.), *Seventh mental measurements yearbook*. Highland Park, NJ: Gryphon.

Guilford, J. P. (1959). Three faces of intellect. *American Psychologist, 14,* 469–479.

Getzels, J. W., & Jackson, P. W. (1962). *Creativity and intelligence.* New York: Wiley.

Wallach, M. A. (1968). Review of the Torrance Test of Creative Thinking. *American Educational Research Journal, 5,* 272–281.

CECIL R. REYNOLDS
Texas A & M University

**CREATIVE PROBLEM SOLVING
TORRANCE, E. PAUL
TORRANCE TESTS OF CREATIVE THINKING
WELSH FIGURE PREFERENCE TEST
(SEE ALSO SPECIFIC TEST TITLES)**

CRETINISM

Cretinism is a metabolic endocrine abnormality that is caused by a thyroid gland disorder. It exists in many forms. Athyrotic hypothyroidism is the congenital absence or partial absence of the thyroid gland. Endemic cretinism is a dietary deficiency of iodine. Familial hypothyroidism is an inborn error of thyroid metabolism and iodine transport. Intrauterine hypothyroidism occurs in infants whose mothers were on antithyroid therapy during pregnancy. Prior to the advent of diets containing iodine and the addition of iodine to table salt within the last hundred years, the endemic form was most common in areas where iodine-rich seafoods were difficult to obtain, for example, the mountainous regions of western Europe and the midwestern United States.

Individuals with untreated congenital hypothyroidism have characteristic features: wide-set eyes, broad nose bridge, and protruding tongue. The head appears to be oversized. The abdomen is large and protrudes with frequent umbilical hernia. Extremities look as though they are shortened and there is general low muscle tone. Mental retardation is a frequent result of the untreated condition.

Felix Platter (1536–1614), a Swiss physician, was one of the first to note the existence of endemic cretinism. In the early part of the sixteenth century, a Swiss physician, Aureolus Theophrastus Bombastus Von Hohenheim, better known as Paracelsus (1493–1541), observed that cretinism was associated with mental retardation. Wolfgang Hoefer (1614–1681), a court physician in Vienna, offered the first extensive description of cretinism. He contended that cretinism could be attributed primarily to food and a poor education.

Throughout the nineteenth century, governments in central Europe expended resources and attention on the investigation and treatment of cretinism. Johann Jacob Guggenbuhl (1816–1863), a Swiss physician, devoted his life to the "cure and prophylaxis" of cretinism. During this time cretinism was viewed as typifying all forms of mental deficiency. The first journal on mental deficiency, which was published in 1850, was entitled *Beobachtungen tuber den Cretinismus (Observations of Cretinism)*.

Owing to the work of Thomas Curling in 1860 and Charles Fogge in 1870, cretinism was identified as related to hypothyroidism. The English physician George Murray developed the first thyroid treatment in 1891. However, etiological and pathological subtleties remained unknown and unappreciated until the twentieth century. In 1975, Dr. Jean H. Dussault from Quebec developed the screening test for neonatal hypothyroidism that is used in the United States today.

Treatment consists of replacement of the thyroid hormone, thyroxin, with synthetic preparations. The results of treatment depend not only on the length of time before treatment is begun but on the severity and type of hypothyroidism. Occurring in one in every 6000 children, hypothyroidism is one of the most common inborn errors of metabolism. The direct result of early identification is the opportunity for early treatment. This, in turn, allows children born with hypothyroidism to develop normally, obviating the need for special education.

REFERENCES

Dussault, J. H., Coulombe, P., Laberge, C., Letarte, J., Guyda, H., & Khoury, K., (1975). Preliminary report on a mass screening program for neonatal hypothyroidism. *Journal of Pediatrics, 86,* 670–674.

Gearheart, B. R., & Litton, F. W. (1975). *The trainable retarded: A foundations approach.* St. Louis: Mosby.

Kanner, L. (1967). Historical review of mental retardation (1800–1965). *American Journal of Mental Deficiency, 72,* 165–189.

Klein, A. H., Meltzer, S., & Kenny, F. M. (1972). Improved prognosis in congenital hypothyroidism treated before age 3 months. *Journal of Pediatrics, 81,* 912–915.

Prehem, H. J., & Cegelka, P. T. (1982). *Mental retardation: From categories to people.* Columbus, OH: Merrill.

Scheerenberger, R. C. (1983). *A history of mental retardation.* Baltimore, MD: Brookes.

CAROLE REITER GOTHELF
Hunter College

HYPOTHYROIDISM
INBORN ERRORS OF METABOLISM

CRI DU CHAT SYNDROME (CAT CRY SYNDROME)

Discovered by Jerome Lejeune, director of the department of genetics at the University of Paris, and his coworkers, Gautier and Turpin, in 1963, cri du chat syndrome is associated with a partial deletion of one of the chromosomes in the B group; specifically, there is a deletion of the short arm of chromosome 5 (5p-). Cri du chat syndrome is the most frequently reported of the autosomal deletion syndromes. The name was derived from the characteristic high-pitched, mewing cry, closely resembling the cry of a kitten, that is heard in the immediate newborn period, lasts several weeks, and then disappears with the exception of some cases, in which the catlike cry persists into adulthood. Incidence is estimated at 1:50,000 births (Hynd & Willis, 1987).

Affected infants show low birth weight, failure to thrive,

hypotonia, microcephaly, a round or moon-faced appearance with hypertelorism (wide-set eyes), antimongoloid or downward sloping palpebral fissures with or without epicanthal folds, strabismus, and a broad-based nose. Ears are low-set and abnormally shaped with malformations, including narrow external canals and preauricular tags. Micrognathia, a short neck, and varying degrees of syndactyly are present. Various types of congenital heart defects and abnormal dermatoglyphics are frequently noted. Major diagnostic features include severe mental retardation and markedly delayed motor development.

A significant number of cri du chat infants survive to adulthood and continue to demonstrate microcephaly. They also have short stature, facial asymmetry, dental malocclusions, skeletal problems such as scoliosis, eye defects, and a waddling gait. These individuals are at or below the trainable level. As school-aged children, they are found in classes for the moderately and severely retarded. According to Gearheart and Litton (1975), the incidence of cri du chat is not known. Berg et al. (1970) found that 7 of the 744 patients with IQs below 35 had this defect. Goodman and Gorlin (1970) reported that a preponderance of patients were female.

No treatment is presently available for this syndrome. As with other chromosome defects, prevention is associated with amniocentesis and genetic counseling. The possibility of a recurrence of the syndrome in another member of the family is rare unless the condition is due to a translocation chromosome. Most cases of cri du chat syndrome are sporadic, with about 13% originating from a balanced carrier parent who is phenotypically normal.

REFERENCES

Berg, J. M., McCreary, B. D., Ridler, M. A., & Smith, G. F., (1970). *The deLange syndrome*. Oxford, England: Pergamon.

Berkow, R. (Ed.). (1982). *The Merck manual of diagnosis and therapy* (14th ed.). Rahway, NJ: Merck Sharp & Dohme Research Laboratories.

Cegelka, P. T., & Prehn, H. J. (1982). *Mental retardation: From categories to people*. Columbus, OH: Merrill.

Gearheart, B. R., & Litton, F. W. (1975). *The trainable retarded: A foundations approach*. St. Louis, MO: Mosby.

Goodman, R. M., & Gorlin, R. J. (1970). *The face in genetic disorders*. St. Louis, MO: Mosby.

Holmes, L. B., Moses H. W., Halldorsson, S., Mack, C., Pavt, S. S., & Matzilevich, B. (1972). *Mental retardation: An atlas of diseases with associated physical abnormalities*. New York: Macmillan.

Hynd, G., & Willis, G. (1987). *Pediatric neuropsychology*. Boston: Allyn & Bacon.

Lejeune, J., Gautier, M., & Turpin, R. (1959). *Les chromosomes humains en culture des tissues: Competes rendus hebdomadaires des seances de l'Academie des Sciences* (pp. 248–602). Paris: l'Academie des Sciences.

Zellweger, H., & Ionasescu, V. (1978). Genetics of mental retardation. In C. H. Carter (Ed.), *Medical aspects of mental retardation* (2nd ed.). Springfield, IL: Thomas.

CATHERINE HALL RIKHYE
Hunter College

**CHROMOSOMAL ABNORMALITIES
MENTAL RETARDATION**

CRIME AND THE HANDICAPPED

Public Law 94-142 first mandated that educational services be provided to all handicapped youths no matter where they reside, a mandate continued by its successor, IDEA. Johnson (1979) indicates that about one third of incarcerated youths are thought to have serious learning disabilities, in contrast to only 16% of the unincarcerated population.

Morgan (1979) conducted a study to produce a national profile of handicapping conditions. He sent questionnaires to administrators of juvenile correctional facilities in 50 states and 5 U.S. territories. Among the respondents, only 6 did not provide most of the requested information; 204 institutions responded. Among the findings, Morgan reports that:

1. Compared to the national incidence of handicapped children (12.3%), 42.4% of delinquent children committed to correctional institutions were found to have some type of handicapping condition.
2. The handicapping conditions with the highest incidence rates in correctional facilities were emotional disturbance (16.23%), learning disabilities (10.59%), and educable mental retardation (7.69%).

Morgan (1979) indicates that the figure 42% is inflated. Keilitz and Miller (1980) combined results of several studies, including Morgan's (1979), and concluded that those studies suggest that (1) prevalence estimates of the major categories of emotional disorders, learning disabilities, and mental retardation are of greater magnitude than expected on the basis of estimates of prevalence among the general student population; and (2) the great difference in prevalence of handicapping conditions between those youths outside and inside the justice system remains even when study design problems and bias are minimized.

Much speculation exists as to the relationship between criminal behavior and handicapping conditions. Siegal and Senna (1981) assign theories that attempt to determine the cause of delinquency into four categories: individualized, social structure, social process, and social reaction. Unfortunately, the variables and factors that impact on these theories are the same that are used to describe the educable mentally retarded and the emotionally handicapped.

Keilitz and Miller (1980) present three rationales as the most prominent explanations of the disproportionate prevalence of handicapping conditions among youths in the justice system. The three are school failure, suspectibility, and differential treatment.

Despite these attempts to account for unexpectedly high prevalence, there is no definitive explanation for the disproportionate number of handicapped youths in the justice system. There is clear evidence that services (Johnson, 1979) mandated under PL 94-142 must be provided and that these services have not been fully implemented. The problem of handicapping conditions as they relate to crime is serious and needs much more attention, especially in the areas of research, programs, and prevention (Brown & Robbins, 1979).

REFERENCES

Brown, S., & Robbins, M. (1979). Serving the special education needs of students in correctional facilities. *Exceptional Children, 45,* 574–579.

Johnson, J. (1979). An essay on incarcerated youth: An oppressed group. *Exceptional Children, 45*(7), 566–571.

Keilitz, I., & Miller, S. L. (1980). Handicapped adolescents and young adults in the justice system. *Exceptional Education Quarterly, 1*(2), 117–126.

Morgan, D. I. (1979). Prevalence and type of handicapping conditions found in juvenile correctional institutions: A national survey. *Journal of Special Education, 13,* 283–295.

Siegal, L. J., & Senna, J. J. (1981). *Juvenile delinquency: Theory, practice, and law.* St. Paul, MN: West.

PHILIP E. LYON
College of St. Rose

EDUCATIONALLY DISADVANTAGED JUVENILE DELINQUENCY

CRISIS INTERVENTION

Crisis intervention is a service spontaneously available to individuals and students who are in need of immediate assistance (Kelly & Vergason, 1978). Caplan defines a crisis as a sudden onset of behavioral imbalance in a child where previous function was stable (Caplan, 1963). The intent of intervention in a crisis is to provide knowledge of coping behaviors of enduring value. According to Swanson and Reinert (1976), a child in conflict is one "whose manifested behavior has a deleterious effect on his/her personal or educational development and/or the personal or educational development of his peers" (p. 5).

Intervention at the point of disruption or crisis is not new. Traditionally, the crisis was handled by an administrator or teacher. According to Long, Morse, and Newman (1976):

> the problem is these are usually of a reflexive and haphazard type. From our analysis of acts and reactions in the school setting it appears that a good many leave much to be desired. Since they usually lack an awareness of the underlying conditions, they are reactions to symptoms, often with a curbing intention. (p. 232) also these crisis situations may be only "a crisis to the teacher who is the consumer of the behavior." (p. 325)

The crisis concept has changed in four ways. The first is in consultation, which has gone from supervisory to strategic planning. In other words, clinicians and teachers work together toward resolution. The second is in the use of the helping teacher, who becomes responsible for the disturbed child. The third change is in the style of interviewing proposed by Redl called life space interviewing (LSI). The fourth change occurs in a system to manage the confrontation situations that are found in secondary education.

The holding of crisis meetings is one way to develop a positive, success-oriented classroom. When disruptions such as fights, serious arguments, misunderstandings, and expressions of angry feelings (verbal or physical) occur, impromptu crisis meetings help students understand and resolve serious conflicts (Redl, 1959). These meetings, which involve only those students who were actually involved in the problem situation, can take place in the classroom, lunchroom, or playground. To conduct a crisis meeting, the following steps are usually taken:

1. *Cooling Off.* Students should be given a few minutes to cool off if they are very upset and not ready to engage in thoughtful discussion. If necessary, students can be sent to their desks, a quiet area, or the principal's office.

2. *Setting Rules.* The meeting is initiated by speaking in a calm manner. Ground rules for the discussion are set. These may include avoiding arguing and listening to what each person has to say.

3. *Listening Actively.* The student is asked to describe the incident, what led up to the incident, and how he or she feels. After listening carefully, the listener rephrases what the student has said to show understanding. Other students may be asked to summarize or repeat what the first student said. Then the second student is asked to give his or her recollection of the incident. During the active listening phase, the main goal is to obtain a clarification of what happened and how the participants are feeling. Helping

students clarify their feelings may also serve to drain off some anger or frustration.

4. *Exploring Problem.* At this step, the problem is considered at length. Questions such as how the problem could have been avoided, what can be done the next time the problem begins, and what consequences should be expected (Glass et al., 1982) can be addressed.

Another resource is the crisis or helping teacher. Gearheart and Weishahn find that this teacher

provides temporary support and control to troubled students when they are unable or unwilling to cope with the demands of the regular classroom. The type of service the Crisis Teacher provides requires that he/she be available at the time of the crisis. Working closely with the regular classroom teachers, he/she provides support, reassurance, and behavioral management strategies. Troubled students come and go on either a regular or an episodic basis, depending on the needs of the students. When the teacher is not dealing with a crisis, he/she can be helping less troubled students academically and behaviorally. He/she can make referrals to supportive services, provide the needed intensive assistance for the more severely troubled students, and follow up on specific recommendations. The crisis teacher becomes an active partner with the teacher, mental health personnel, and parents in helping this student. (p. 223)

Another form of crisis intervention is the life space interviewing (LSI) method which was developed to help teachers become effective in talking to children and to help teachers use these skills as a specific management tool (L'Abate & Curtis, 1975). There are two main goals: clinical exploitation of life events and immediate emotional first aid. There are both long-range and immediate goals. This kind of therapy may help the student to express hostility, frustration, or aggression; provide support while helping the student to avoid panic or guilt; help the student to maintain relationships; allow teachers to supervise behavior and ensure conformity to rules; and help teachers in settling complex situations (L'Abate & Curtis, 1975). Bernstein (1963) in L'Abate and Curtis (1975) provides some guidelines for LSI:

1. Be polite.
2. Do not tower above a child; bend down to him.
3. Be sure of yourself.
4. Use "why" sparingly.
5. Encourage talk about the actual situation.
6. Help the child to avoid being overwhelmed by shame or guilt by minimizing the problem.
7. Help the child to express his or her feelings about the situation.

8. Be aware of the kind of thinking demanded by a particular situation.
9. Work with the child to make the situation better.
10. Allow the child time to ask questions.

L'Abate and Curtis (1975) list some limitations of LSI:

1. It requires the teacher to have an ability to understand human behavior in more of an art than a science form.
2. It often requires more time than a regular classroom teacher with 30 students has to spare; this is where the helping teacher could assist.
3. It requires education and cooperation among all members of the school staff.

The resource classroom is yet another way to help exceptional children. Here the child is provided with instruction and emotional support by the resource teacher for part of the day. The child may move between the classrooms and receive instruction from both teachers. It is even possible that the child can be placed on a limited day schedule in cases where he or she cannot handle either the resource or regular classroom. In summary, crisis intervention can be the most appropriate kind of action if all psychological, sociological, and educational knowledge is applied at the correct moment in time.

REFERENCES

Caplan, G. (1963). Opportunities for school psychologists in the primary prevention. *Mental Hygiene, 47*(4), 525–539.

Gearheart, B. R., & Weishahn, M. W. (1980). *The handicapped student in the regular classroom.* St. Louis: Mosby.

Glass, R., Christiansen, J., & Christiansen, J. L. (1982). *Teaching exceptional students in the regular classroom.* Boston: Little, Brown.

Kelly, L. J., & Vergason, G. A. (1978). *Dictionary for special education and rehabilitation.* Denver: Love.

L'Abate, L., & Curtis, L. T. (1975). *Teaching the exceptional child.* Philadelphia: Saunders.

Long, H. J., Morse, W. C., & Newman, R. G. (1976). *Conflict in the classroom: The education of emotionally disturbed children.* Belmont, CA: Wadsworth.

Redl, F. (1959). Concept of the life space interview. *American Journal of Orthopsychiatry, 29*(1), 1–18.

Swanson, L. H., & Reinert, H. R. (1979). *Teaching strategies for children in conflict curriculum methods, and materials.* St. Louis: Mosby.

RICHARD E. HALMSTAD
University of Wisconsin at Stout

LIFE SPACE INTERVIEWING
REDL, FRITZ

CRISIS TEACHER

The concept of the crisis teacher/helping teacher was initiated, according to Long, Morse, and Newman (1976), as the result of the efforts of a staff of elementary teachers in a high problematic school. The crisis teacher is first an educator trained in psychoeducational theory and practice who provides direct assistance to regular classroom teachers and students that might exhibit disruptive (crisis) behaviors. Ultimately, this educator will enhance the learning environment by providing a liaison between the crisis teacher and the regular classroom teacher. This brings to the classroom teacher immediate peer help as opposed to the consultants, such as the school psychologist, school counselor, or principal, ordinarily sought out.

Historically, crises had been met by sending the students involved to the principal's office. Frequently, this procedure would yield less than adequate results for various reasons. First, the principal is often uninformed of the events leading up to the classroom crisis. Second, the principal's administrative responsibilities may make him or her unavailable when needed most. Third, the repressive nature of being sent to the principal's office may, in some instances, exacerbate the problem. In addition, resorting to this method of crisis resolution in some instances results in an inadvertent reinforcer being applied to the situation.

Regular classroom teachers are cognizant of the needs expressed by all students in their classrooms and as such understand that not all children manifest disruptive behaviors at all times. However, teachers are aware that every child in the classroom has the right to an equal share of his or her time. Since disruptive children cannot always be physically removed from the classroom and other students have educational needs to be met, the crisis teacher concept seems to meet the purpose of addressing the one who needs help, while keeping the classroom teacher in continuing interaction with other students.

Immediate help from a crisis teacher is also seen as an effort to interject a process that would promote a more expedient method of handling psychoeducational problems manifested by the disruptive student. Prior to such a process being developed, regular classroom teachers resorted to punishment and then waited until a staffing could be arranged to receive advice from a psychologist, nurse, counselor, special education teacher, or other team member. Again, the regular classroom teacher was faced with receiving well-meaning but delayed corrective suggestions that proved inappropriate to their needs. As cited by Reynolds and Birch (1977), such advice was often impractical. Teachers knew what to do but did not have the resources to implement the course of action advocated by a team to which the teacher was not always a contributing member.

If direct assistance is essential to the regular classroom teacher, then the training of the crisis teacher is crucial to the effectiveness of the position. It is suggested that the crisis teacher becomes a part of the school staff and, as such, an educator trained in psychoeducational programs that specifically qualify the individual to interact positively with regular classroom teachers and students during crises. This interaction requires the crisis teacher to possess a wealth of expertise concerning the theory and application of psychological concepts. Of equal importance, however, is the individual's ability to apply sound special education practices within the classroom setting. Here then, we have a new resource person to provide the regular classroom teacher with direct help (psychoeducational) in crisis situations.

While the crisis teacher's training encompasses a psychoeducational emphasis, it should be noted that the main thrust within this role remains one of service to the whole individual in his or her development. As such, the crisis teacher must be cognizant of a variety of specific interventions such as remedial instruction, tutoring, group activities, art, music, psychodrama, role-playing, "big brother" and "big sister" activities, and problem-solving activities (Shea, 1978). The crisis teacher must have competencies along with knowledge of behavioral, psychodynamic, and environmental interventions in order to adequately confront and correct most disruptive classroom dilemmas.

Of equal importance to offering direct assistance to students is the crisis teacher's responsibility to staff members, parents, and community-based agencies. Consultations with each group is essential. Acting as a liaison between child, teacher, parent, and community not only lends support through direct aid and remediation but will, through time, lead to provisions for the establishment of programs for future education and the therapeutic needs of troubled students. Modifications of the unhealthy aspects of the learning environment also becomes a responsibility of the crisis teacher, as well as generating plans to develop new programs to enhance a positive psychoeducational atmosphere that will foster sound mental health (Shea, 1978).

Long, Morse, and Newman (1976) has suggested the crisis/helping teacher model include the following features: (1) emphasizes direct assistance to pupils; (2) has an eclectic approach to intervention strategies; (3) is concerned with the prevention of problems as well as their remediation; (4) tends to be broadly concerned with the total life space of the child rather than targeted on specific discrepancies or deficits. It appears that the concept of the crisis teacher has had a positive effect in that it tends to promote healthy self-concepts and lends itself to future self-management and authentic human relationships.

An important footnote includes the crisis teacher's ability to know when an incident is not a crisis and does not warrant his or her attention. Of importance then is to avoid conceiving of all events of a disruptive nature as being catastrophic and in need of special attention. The following is a summary of the steps recognized by Morse in the development of the helping/crisis teacher model as presented by Reynolds and Birch (1977):

1. The majority of the faculty recognizes that the disruptive behavior of a number of pupils provides a barrier between the pupils and the teachers.

2. The teachers examine carefully the establishment of special classes for these children.

3. An in-depth analysis of needs results in the realization that what the faculty needs and what special education can provide are not compatible for the following reasons: the number of disruptive students that make teachers feel incompetent and discouraged usually is one or two per class; even the most difficult students are not that way all of the time; teachers have already learned to assess and thus anticipate problems; trials at repressing disruptive behavior through harsh verbal means, removal of privileges, and other forms of punishment have failed; advice from personnel such as psychologists, counselors, and administrators provide verbal encouragement but little in the way of actual help.

4. After an analysis of the classroom situation, the children, and teacher effectiveness, it is concluded that direct in-class help is needed in a form that provides a person capable of working with children who are in, or close to, a crisis. The training of this person should be that of a teacher and a specialist, with emphasis on learning disabilities and behavior disorders. Help should be present right in the school—not from an itinerant or central office base. The helping teacher should neither be under rigidly scheduled external control nor tied to a classroom of children. Flexibility for direct and timely cooperative work with a regular class teacher should have high priority. Sometimes the most helpful immediate action might be removal of a child from the regular class for conference or a quiet time under the visual supervision of the helping teacher. At other times, the helper might conduct the regular class while the teacher is attending to a problem in the class. The actual daily duties of the helping teacher must develop out of the needs of the particular school, its pupils, and community resources.

REFERENCES

Long, N. J., Morse, W. C., & Newman, R. G. (1976). *Conflict in the classroom: The education of emotionally, disturbed children* (3rd ed.). Belmont, CA: Wadsworth.

Reynolds, M. C., & Birch, J. W. (1977). *Teaching exceptional children in all America's schools*. Reston, VA: Council for Exceptional Children.

Shea, T. M. (1978). *Teaching children and youth with behavior disorders*. St. Louis: Mosby.

RICHARD E. HALMSTAD
University of Wisconsin at Stout

CRISIS INTERVENTION
RESOURCE ROOM
SPECIAL CLASS

CRISSEY, MARIE SKODAK (1910–   )

Born in Lorain, Ohio, Marie Skodak Crissey obtained her BS and MA degrees from Ohio State University in 1931. She was an Institute of International Education fellow at the University of Budapest in 1931–1932. Crissey became interested in factors influencing development of intelligence and school achievement partly through the influence of Henry H. Goddard and Sidney Pressey. Her PhD was in developmental psychology from the University of Iowa in 1938.

She is well known for her still frequently cited classic research (Skodak, 1939; Skodak & Skeels, 1949) on the heredity-environment issue, which countered the then widely held concept of genetically determined and fixed IQ. She found that the IQs of adopted children correlated more highly with the estimated intelligence of their biological rather than their adoptive parents, but that their actual level of intelligence was closer to that of their adoptive parents. Thus her research showed both hereditary and environmental influences on intelligence, and demonstrated that favorable home environment could raise levels of intelligence. From an applied standpoint, she emphasized the potential effectiveness of environmental intervention programs to stimulate the development of children from deprived backgrounds.

During her professional career, Crissey developed special education programs, intervention programs for handicapped and deprived children, vocational guidance programs for high school students, and vocational rehabilitation services for the handicapped. She was at the Child Guidance Center at Flint, Michigan, from 1938 to 1946 and was director of school psychology and special education at Dearborn, Michigan, from 1949 to 1969. She has had a private practice in psychology since 1942 (Anonymous, 1984). She is a fellow of the American Association of Mental Deficiency and of five divisions of the American Psychological Association. Among her numerous awards are the Joseph P. Kennedy International Award for research in mental retardation in 1968 and a citation for distinguished service from the American Psychological Association in 1972.

REFERENCES

Anonymous. (1984). Crissey, Marie Skodak. In R. Corsini (Ed.), *Encyclopedia of psychology* (Vol. 2). New York: Wiley.

Skodak, M. (1939). Children in foster homes: A study of mental development. *University of Iowa Studies in Child Welfare, 16*(1).

Skodak, M., & Skeels, H. M. (1949). A final follow-up study of one hundred adopted children. *Journal of Genetic Psychology, 75,* 85–125.

ROBERT T. BROWN
*University of North Carolina
at Wilmington*

CRITERION-REFERENCED TESTING

Criterion-referenced testing is a method for examining a person's performance with respect to a standard or criterion. It is commonly contrasted with norm-referenced testing, in which a person's performance is compared with that of other persons who make up a norm group. While this concept has been used in pedagogy for millennia, it has been most recently formalized by Glaser and Klaus (1962). In their conception, a criterion is a level of performance achieved only when the person being examined is able to perform certain tasks. These tasks have been determined to be necessary for learning. During the course of study there may be many criteria, which may be viewed as stages or intermediate steps. The assessment of the performance on the tasks necessary to achieve criteria is commonly called criterion referenced testing (CRT). A criterion referenced test is thus a test constructed to assess the performance level of examinees in relation to a well-defined domain of content (Hambleton, 1999).

In the late 1960s criterion-referencing became commonly associated with mastery (Popham & Husek, 1969; Glass, 1978), especially with minimum-competency testing. In this variant, CRT is intended to classify persons into those who can and those who cannot perform at some minimally acceptable level. Nearly all states in the United States require some form of minimum-competency testing (Hambleton, 1999). Purposes for the testing include issuing of high-school diplomas, passage to high school from junior high, and comparison of classes and schools for various political purposes. While the latter reason is almost never formally stated, it is common practice in many states to publish building- or district-level average test performance. These are then compared with state "competitors." There have been numerous proposals to link teacher salaries to their classrooms' performance on such tests. In only a few isolated school districts have such procedures been established.

The major issues in CRT are definition of the content, development of the tests, evaluation of test characteristics, and standard setting. A useful text on these issues has been compiled by Berk (1984a); more current thinking by researchers in the CRT field is reviewed by Hambleton (1999).

Definition of the content for criterion-referenced tests is closely tied to instruction. If one uses the Glaser and Husek concept of CRT, a careful analysis of the tasks being required of the students forms the basis for the test. Those tasks are separated either hierarchically or organizationally into stages or steps. Tests are constructed that sample the behaviors the student must exhibit to demonstrate knowledge or mastery for each step. In hierarchical content, the student must know certain content or be able to perform certain tasks before the next content or task can be attempted. Many courses in mathematics exhibit such structure. Other content may have an organizational sequence that is not inherent to it such as English literature. It may be studied historically, thematically, or by type such as poetry, novel, and essay. Criterion-referenced testing may be used to indicate level of achievement for each part. Nitko (1984) refers to ordering and definition for domains. A domain may be ordered or unordered and well-defined or ill-defined. He asserts that CRT should be used only with well-defined content domains.

There has been relatively little research on developing items or questions for CRTs, and most test developers have used item-writing technology developed for norm-referenced achievement tests. Roid and Haladyna (1980) have attempted to develop an item-writing technology using algorithms for sentence writing. Other proposed approaches are based on mapping and on factor analysis (Roid, 1984). Future efforts are certain to use computers in the generation of items for CRTs.

Analysis of item and test characteristics has received considerable attention from psychometricians. Both classical reliability theory and item characteristic curve theory have been applied to the analysis of items and of the entire test. Reliability of CRT tests has been derived for test scores (Berk, 1984b) and for the classification decision (Hambleton, 1999; Subkoviak, 1984).

A major debate erupted in the latter 1970s over the issue of standards setting: Can standards be set and who sets them? Glass (1978) argued that the arbitrariness of standard setting results in poor educational practice and that test scores should be interpreted in other, unspecified ways. Numerous authors argued for standard setting, and several techniques, notably owed to Nedelsky, Angoff, and Ebel, have been developed. Hambleton (1999) and Shepard (1984) give overviews of the issues and the techniques.

REFERENCES

Berk, R. A. (Ed.). (1984a). *A guide to criterion-referenced test construction*. Baltimore, MD: Johns Hopkins University Press.

Berk, R. A. (1984b). Conducting the item analysis. In R. A. Berk

(Ed.), *A guide to criterion-referenced test construction* (pp. 97–143). Baltimore, MD: Johns Hopkins University Press.

Glaser, R. (1963). Instructional technology and the measurement of learning outcomes. Some questions. *American Psychologist, 18,* 519–521.

Glaser, R., & Klaus, D. J. (1962). Proficiency measurement: Assessing human performance. In R. M. Gagne (Ed.), *Psychological Principles in Systems Development* (pp. 419–474) New York: Holt, Reinhart & Winston.

Glass, G. V. (1978). Standards and criteria. *Journal of Educational Measurement, 59,* 602–605.

Hambleton, R. (1999). Criterion-referenced testing: Principles, technical advances, and evaluation guidelines. In C. R. Reynolds & T. B. Gutkin (Eds.), *The Handbook of School Psychology* (3rd ed.) (pp. 409–433). NY: Wiley.

Nitko, A. J. (1984). Defining "Criterion-Referenced Test." In R. A. Berk (Ed.), *A guide to criterion-referenced test construction* (pp. 8–28). Baltimore, MD: Johns Hopkins University Press.

Popham, W. J., & Husek, T. R. (1969). Implications of criterion-referenced measurement. *Journal of Educational Measurement 6,* 1–9.

Roid, G. H. (1984). Generating the test items. In R. A. Berk (Ed.), *A guide to criterion-referenced test construction* (pp. 49–77). Baltimore, MD: Johns Hopkins University Press.

Roid, G. H., & Haladyna, T. M. (1980). The emergence of an item-writing technology. *Review of Educational Research, 50,* 293–314.

Shepard, L. A. (1984). Setting performance standards. In R. A. Berk (Ed.), *A guide to criterion-referenced test construction* (pp. 169–198). Baltimore, MD: Johns Hopkins University Press.

Subkoviak, M. J. (1984). Estimating the reliability of mastery nonmastery classifications. In R. A. Berk (Ed.), *A guide to criterion referenced test construction* (pp. 267–291). Baltimore, MD: Johns Hopkins University Press.

VICTOR L. WILLSON
Texas A & M University

MINIMUM COMPETENCY TESTING
NORM REFERENCED TESTING

CRONBACH, LEE J. (1916–   )

Lee J. Cronbach attended Fresno College, gaining his BA degree in 1934. After completing his MA degree at the University of California, Berkeley, in 1937, he attended the educational psychology program at the University of Chicago, gaining his PhD in 1940.

In 1940 Cronbach went to the State College of Washington as instructor in the department of psychology. He stayed there until 1946, advancing to the rank of assistant professor. During World War II, he was involved with the University of California division of War Research at San Diego, serving as research psychologist. After the war,

Cronbach spent three years (1946–1948) as assistant professor of education at the University of Chicago. In 1948 Cronbach went to the University of Illinois, where he remained until 1964.

Cronbach is well known for his work on tests and measurement in psychology. He served the American Psychological Association as chairman of its Committee on Test Standards (1950–1953) and served on the Committee on Psychological Tests. His book, *Essentials of Psychological Testing,* is considered a classic in the field.

Cronbach is also well known for his work as coinvestigator on the Terman Study of Children of High Ability, a project he joined in 1963. That study was a long-term longitudinal study of intellectually gifted students. The study has demonstrated much of what we know of the lives and productivity of the intellectually gifted. It has dispelled many of the common stereotypes surrounding the intellectually gifted.

REFERENCES

Cronbach, L. J. (1960). *Essentials of psychological testing* (2nd ed.). New York: Harper & Brothers.

Cronbach, L. J., & Gleser, G. C. (1965). *Psychological test and personnel decisions* (2nd ed.). Champaign: University of Illinois Press.

RAND B. EVANS
Texas A & M University

CROSS CATEGORICAL PROGRAMMING

Public Law 94-142 and its update, IDEA, identifies 11 categories of special-needs students. The categories include deaf, deaf-blind, hard of hearing, mentally retarded, multihandicapped, orthopedically impaired, other health impaired, emotionally disturbed, specific learning disability, speech impaired, and visually impaired (Federal Register, 1977). The most common practice is for educational agencies to group children and youth based on these categories of exceptionality. For example, a school district may have a resource program that serves learning-disabled adolescents. It may also have two self-contained classrooms, one for moderately mentally retarded youngsters and one for severely emotionally disturbed youths.

Alternately, it is becoming increasingly common for school districts and special education cooperatives to group students with diverse handicaps in a single classroom or program. One classroom, for example, may serve both moderately mentally retarded and severely emotionally disturbed youths. A resource program may serve both mildly mentally retarded and learning-disabled individuals. The practice of grouping children and youth with diverse handicaps is referred to as cross categorical programming.

The rationale for developing cross categorical programs is based on theoretical and practical issues. With reference to the theoretical basis, a number of experts have written that students with different exceptional labels are more alike than they are different (Gardner, 1977; Schloss, 1984). Consequently, many of the teaching methods used today with one group of exceptional students have been, and continue to be, used with other groups (Hallahan & Kauffman, 1976). Emphasizing this point, the vast majority of categorical special education methods and materials texts contain similar teaching strategies (Hallahan & Kauffman, 1976). There has been proliferation of generic methods texts that purport to contain instructional techniques suitable for a majority of handicapped individuals (Hammill & Bartell, 1986; Mercer & Mercer, 1985; Schloss & Sedlak, 1986).

Another compelling theoretical rationale for cross categorical instruction is provided by professionals with a behavioral orientation. These professionals emphasize that a common set of learning principles may be used to predict and influence the growth and development of individuals with a range of learning and behavioral features. As a result, the precise instructional needs of an individual should dictate instructional objectives and methodology, not general special education labels (Smith, Neisworth, & Hunt, 1984).

With reference to pragmatic issues, many school districts are not sufficiently large to staff separate classes for each category of exceptionality. For example, a rural school district may contain only 200 junior-high-school-aged students. Given current estimates, one would expect to find only nine learning-disabled youngsters, four mentally retarded youngsters, and one severely emotionally disturbed youth. It would not be feasible to staff three separate classrooms for each category. Consequently, the school district may choose to combine the 14 learners into one cross categorical classroom.

Cross categorical programs, or programs that serve students with diverse exceptional labels in the same setting, are becoming increasingly prevalent. Theoretically, categorical labels may be less useful for instructional grouping than for specific behavioral descriptions. Also, a common set of learning strategies may be useful for all handicapped persons. Many school districts find it to be administratively expedient to group children and youth with different exceptional labels.

REFERENCES

Federal Register. (1977, August). Washington, DC: U.S. Government Printing Office.

Gardner, W. I. (1977). Learning and behavioral characteristics of exceptional children and youth: A humanistic behavioral approach. Boston: Allyn & Bacon.

Hallahan, D. P., & Kauffman, J. M. (1976). Introduction to learning disabilities: A psycho-behavioral approach. Englewood Cliffs, NJ: Prentice-Hall.

Hammill, D. D., & Bartel, N. R. (1986). Teaching children with learning and behavior problems (6th ed.). Boston: Allyn & Bacon.

Mercer, C. D., & Mercer, A. R. (1985). Teaching students with learning problems. Columbus, OH: Merrill.

Schloss, P. J. (1984). Social development of exceptional children and youth. Rockville, MD: Aspen Systems.

Schloss, P. J., & Sedlak, R. (1986). Instructional methods for mildly handicapped children and youth. Boston: Allyn & Bacon.

Smith, B. M., Neisworth, J. T., & Hunt, F. M. (1984). The exceptional child: A functional approach. New York: McGraw-Hill.

PATRICK J. SCHLOSS
Pennsylvania State University

GENERIC SPECIAL EDUCATION
INDIVIDUALIZATION OF INSTRUCTION
LEAST RESTRICTIVE ENVIRONMENT

CROSS-CULTURAL ADAPTABILITY INVENTORY

The Cross-Cultural Adaptability Inventory (Kelly & Meyers, 1992) is a 50-item self-scored inventory that measures the ability of an individual to live and work in a cross-cultural environment. The CCAI is a self-assessment inventory. The instrument was first developed in 1987 by Dr. Colleen Kelly, a human resource specialist, and Dr. Judith Meyers, a clinical psychologist with a specialty in diagnostics. The instrument met the needs of cross-cultural specialists who needed a training tool to promote cross-cultural understanding and insight. The CCAI focuses on four skill areas which research has shown to be critical in adapting to other cultures. The CCAI is based on a cultural general approach, which purports that there are certain commonalties to all areas across cultural transitions, regardless of the culture of origin. It provides a frame of reference for evaluating individuals adapting from one culture to another or working in a multicultural setting.

The inventory is a self-report instrument that requires individuals to respond along a six-point Likert scale. Because of its high face validity, the questions can be transparent: Individuals who want to place themselves in a favorable light can slant their answers. However, respondents are encouraged to be honest about their responding style, so that the information will be useful. The instrument stanine scores on four dimensions associated with cross-cultural adaption. Scores are plotted on a circle graph, and the individual compares their four scores to one another. Follow-up training focuses on skill development in needed areas.

The Emotional Resilience scale is the largest of the four, with 18 items. The content focus involves coping with stress and ambiguity, rebounding from imperfections and mistakes, trying new things and experiences, and interacting with people in new or similar situations. People who are emotionally resilient tend to have a positive attitude, resourcefulness, and the ability to modulate negative emotions.

The next dimension, Flexibility/Openness, has 17 items and assesses the extent to which a person enjoys the different ways of thinking and behaving that are usually encountered in a cross-cultural experience. The items deal with openness toward those who are different from oneself, tolerance of others, and flexibility with regard to new experiences. It involves a nonjudgmental approach and flexibility in behavior.

The Perceptual Acuity scale has ten items and deals with attention to communication cues and the accurate perception of cues across cultures. It assesses behaviors as well as perceptions. Perceptual acuity is synonymous with cultural empathy. It is the ability to distinguish the logic and coherence of other cultures, and involves the ability to interpret nonverbal and social cues.

The final scale is Personal Autonomy, which has seven items. It deals with personal identity, confidence in one's values and beliefs, and a sense of empowerment in the context of an unfamiliar environment with different values. It measures a person's sense of identity and adherence to a strong set of cultural values, as well as respecting the values and traditions of another culture.

The CCAI is a popular instrument among trainers and cross-cultural specialists because it is research-based, easy to understand and administer, self-scoring, inexpensive, and easily available. It was normed on a population of 653 cross-cultural specialists, foreign students, educators, missionaries, and business people. The test underwent two revisions where factor analysis, principle components analysis, and item analysis were performed. The final version was published by NCS in 1992. The instrument has excellent alpha reliability, face validity, and construct validity. Predictive validity has not been established, and it is not recommended that the CCAI be used for selection purposes.

The CCAI is used to develop insight into the adaption process, increase awareness of cross-cultural issues, and provide training for individuals living and working in other cultures. It also has application for multicultural work groups. The CCAI has been used to train foreign students and to prepare business people and their families for relocation abroad. The CCAI has trained volunteer groups working abroad (such as missionaries) and has assisted social service groups working with immigrant populations. The CCAI is also an excellent tool for training counselors, teachers, and principals in the issues of cross-cultural competency. Psychotherapists have found the CCAI useful in working with foreign-born patients as a feedback tool.

The CCAI has a manual that provides thorough information on the development of the instrument, the theories underlying the instrument, and the statistical data supporting it. Training tools are available that provide a full-day training design, as well as follow-up materials in the form of action planning. A feedback form is also available.

REFERENCES

Kelly, C., & Meyers, J. (1992). *The Cross-Cultural Adaptability Inventory* (CCAI). Minneapolis, MN: National Computer Systems.

JUDITH MEYERS
San Diego, California

CROSS-CULTURAL SPECIAL EDUCATION

Public Law 94-142 was implemented to provide equal educational opportunities for all handicapped children. Legislation including IDEA and the ADA, and litigation continues to focus on educational opportunities for exceptional children, however, equal educational opportunity is not a reality for all. Many exceptional students continue to be discriminated against or receive inadequate services based solely on their race, social class, or creed (Heward & Orlansky, 1984).

In attempts to overcome these discriminating factors, it is necessary only to look at the basic premise on which special education relies; each individual student must be considered for his or her unique and special needs. Application of this premise across cultural boundaries will assist special educators in their attempt to provide equal educational opportunities for all exceptional children.

It seems unlikely that any teacher would possess the skills or background to deal adequately with the unique aspects of the many and varied cultures that may be encountered. As such, it may be useful to use as many community resources as possible in any attempt to meet these culturally diverse needs. King-Stoops (1980) devised a strategy for working with children of migrant farmers. She suggests that high school or college students with similar migrant backgrounds be used as aides or volunteers in the classroom setting. While King-Stoops speaks only to migrant children, it seems clear that such an approach could be easily and successfully used with a wide variety of cultures. While this may serve well in certain circumstances, this strategy may be impossible to implement in all settings. Heward and Orlansky (1984) suggest that the implementation of effective instructional techniques would likely benefit all students regardless of cultural background. It is important to note that effective instruction is based on and stems from effective assessment. Diversity in the provision of services in school also has began to receive special attention (e.g., Henning-Stout and Brown-Cheatham, 1999).

REFERENCES

Henning-Stout, M., & Brown-Cheatham, M. (1999). School psychology in a diverse world: Considerations for practice, research, and training. In C. R. Reynolds & T. B. Gutkin (Eds.), *The Handbook of School Psychology* (3rd ed.) (pp. 1041–1055). New York: Wiley.

Heward, W. L., & Orlansky, M. D. (1984). *Exceptional children.* Columbus, OH: Merrill.

King-Stoops, J. (1980). *Migrant education: Teaching the wandering ones.* Bloomington, IN: Phi Delta Kappa.

JOHN R. BEATTIE
*University of North Carolina
at Charlotte*

CULTURAL BIAS IN TESTING
SYSTEM OF MULTICULTURAL PLURALISTIC ASSESSMENT

CROSS MODALITY TRAINING

Cross modality training refers to teaching the neurological process of converting information received through one input modality to another system within the brain. The process is also referred to as intersensory integration, intermodal transfer, and transducing. Cross modality integration problems have been linked historically to learning disabilities. It has been hypothesized that certain learners may process visual and auditory information accurately when each type of information is presented distinctly, but that those students may be deficient in tasks requiring them to shift or cross information between sensory systems (Chalfant & Scheffelin, 1969).

Reading, where the learner must relate visual symbols to auditory equivalents, is one academic domain for which cross modal integration is required. Johnson and Myklebust (1978) proposed that some reading disorders are due to an inability to make such conversions within the neurosensory system. It also has been proposed that disabilities such as apraxia, or the inability to plan and execute appropriate motor action, are related to inadequate cross modality integration because the child must convert an auditory memory of a word into motor output (Lerner, 1985).

Cross modality training programs have been devised to address intersensory integration problems. For example, Frostig (1965, 1968) advocated cross modality exercises, including activities such as describing a picture (visual to auditory), following spoken directions (auditory to motor), and feeling objects through a curtain and drawing their shapes on paper (tactile to visual-motor). Scant research is available to support the use of cross modality training as a strategy to improve students' academic skills. Additionally, few, if any, tests are designed to assess cross-modal perception.

REFERENCES

Chalfant, J., & Scheffelin, M. (1969). *Central processing dysfunction in children* (NINDS Monograph NO. 9). Bethesda, MD: U.S. Department of Health, Education, and Welfare.

Frostig, M. (1965). Corrective reading in the classroom. *Reading Teacher, 18,* 573–580.

Frostig, M. (1968). Education for children with learning disabilities. In H. Myklebust (Ed.), *Progress in learning disabilities.* New York: Grune & Stratton.

Johnson, D., & Myklebust, H. (1967). *Learning disabilities: Educational principles and practices.* New York: Grune & Stratton.

Lerner, J. W. (1985). Learning disabilities: Theories, diagnosis, and teaching strategies. Boston: Houghton Mifflin.

DOUGLAS FUCHS
LYNN S. FUCHS
Vanderbilt University

DEVELOPMENTAL TEST OF VISUAL PERCEPTION-2
FROSTIG REMEDIAL PROGRAM
MULTISENSORY INSTRUCTION

CROUZON'S SYNDROME (CRANIOFACIAL DYSOSTOSIS) (CS)

Crouzon's syndrome (CS) is believed to be a congenital disability that follows a pattern of autosomal dominance. The major physical characteristics are a result of premature closing of the skull, which causes cranial deformity, widely spaced eyes (which may protrude), and a misshapened face. The nasal bridge may be flat and the nose beaked with underdeveloped nasal sinuses. Malformation of the ear canals and eyes as a result of hypertension and orbital deformity is said to occur in 70 to 80% of the cases (along with optic atrophy); this may cause visual and hearing problems. The upper jaw and bones of the midface may be underdeveloped and the lower jaw may be prominent. Crowding, misalignment of upper teeth, and an enlarged tongue may cause some problems with eating and speech development. Higher incidence of infections also may occur, and in some cases congenital heart disease has been reported. Mental retardation may be noted in some children, but most have average mental abilities. In rare instances, spina bifida may be present (Carter, 1978).

Some related services may be necessary if visual, aural, and motor problems exist. Speech therapy will probably be required. In addition, psychological and guidance counseling may be required because of the physical appearance of the child. Mainstreamed placement with support services is often the proper educational approach for CS children.

REFERENCES

Carter, C. (Ed.). (1978). *Medical aspects of mental retardation* (2nd ed.). Springfield, IL: Thomas.

Goodman, R., & Gorlin, R. (1977). *Atlas of the face in genetic disorders* (2nd ed.). St. Louis: Mosby.

SALLY L. FLAGLER
University of Oklahoma

CRUICKSHANK, WILLIAM M. (1915–1992)

William M. Cruickshank received his BA in 1937 from Eastern Michigan University, his MA in 1938 from the University of Chicago, and his PHD in 1945 from the University of Michigan.

Cruickshank was the founder and director of the Division of Special Education and Rehabilitation and distinguished professor at Syracuse University from 1946 to 1967. He subsequently became director of the Institute for the Study of Mental Health and Related Disabilities and professor of child and family health, psychology, and education at the University of Michigan from 1967 until his retirement.

Since 1937 Cruickshank's main interests have been in the area of brain-injured children, neurologically handicapped children, and the neurophysiological characteristics of accurately defined learning-disabled children. Author of over 200 books, articles, and edited books (some of which are translated in several languages), Cruickshank's major publications include *Teaching Methods for Brain-Injured and Hyperactive Children (1961)*, *Learning Disabilities in Home, School, and Community* (1977), and *Psychoeducational Foundations of Learning Disabilities* (1973).

Holder of six honorary degrees, he taught in many countries and remained active as a visiting professor and lecturer for a number of years following his retirement from the University of Michigan. As the founder, first president (1975–1985), and executive director of the International Academy for Research in Learning Disabilities, he was an international authority on the problems of learning-disabled children and youths. Dr. William Cruickshank passed away in 1992, after a long and productive career.

REFERENCES

Cruickshank, W. M. (1977). *Learning disabilities in home, school, and community* (Rev. ed.). Syracuse, NY: Syracuse University.

Cruickshank, W. M., et al. (1961). *Teaching methods for brain-injured and hyperactive children*. Syracuse, NY: Syracuse University.

KAY E. KETZENBERGER
*The University of Texas of the
Permian Basin*

William M. Cruickshank

CRYPTOPHASIA

Cryptophasia is a language disorder characteristic of twins. Twins often have delayed language development accompanied by what appears to be a jargon that only the twins understand. This jargon is a form of imitation of adult language with its own syntax, a type of "pidgin." The language may become elaborate and complex but remains, for the most part, understandable only to the twins. The language develops as they attempt to imitate the speech sounds of adults. Since twins spend an inordinate amount of time together, they begin to understand approximations of mature language and reinforce each other for use of this lesser form of communication. Cryptophasia retards normal language development.

CECIL R. REYNOLDS
Texas A & M University

LANGUAGE DELAYS
LANGUAGE DISORDERS
TWINS

CRYSTALLIZED v. FLUID INTELLIGENCE

The theory of fluid and crystallized intelligence was proposed over 40 years ago by Raymond Cattell. It is based on the work of Charles Spearman (1932), who concluded that intelligence has a unitary, comprehensive ability common to all tests. He called his universal factor "g" for general ability factor.

This factor was the basis for the two-factor theory proposed by Cattell. This theory states that every mental test measures two factors: a general factor g, which is common to all tests, and a specific factor s, which is peculiar to each test (Cattell, 1963). Cattell defined intelligence by dividing the general ability factor into two categories. These are now designated crystallized intelligence (Gc) and fluid intelligence (Gf).

Cattell and Horn (1978) suggested that Gf is the major measurable outcome of the influence of biological factors and that Gc is the primary manifestation of educational and cultural influence. They indicated that fluid intelligence pertains to the individual ability to perceive and extract rules and relationships, while crystallized intelligence arises from the individual application of fluid intelligence in learning symbols, language, and mathematics. Cattell and Horn suggested that Gf may be determined by heredity, and may be defined by tasks in which analytical ability is emphasized, while Gc is determined by education, and is similar to achievement in that it is the accumulated knowledge of an individual.

Fluid and crystallized intelligence may be measured by determining a person's ability for learning and problem solving. Gf can be measured with figure analogies, block designs, and memory span. Gc would be the product of Gf in content areas such as vocabulary, general information, authentic skill, and scholastic achievement (Cattell & Horn, 1978).

Research by Lansdell (1962) has indicated that Gc and Gf have been applicable in program planning for individuals with neurological impairment Lansdell found that the effects of general brain damage will be similar in both fluid and crystallized abilities, but more pronounced in fluid abilities. This may result in deficits in abstract reasoning as opposed to specific knowledge.

Other studies have attempted to link evidence and theory from cognitive psychology to individual differences. Kneif and James (1978) found that if students showed lower general ability, instruction focused on fluid ability would be more helpful for learning math concepts. If students showed higher general ability, instruction focused on crystallized ability would be more helpful. This indicates that we can, on occasion, capitalize on crystallized abilities.

Current research on Gf and Gc is focused on ability factors and cognitive processes (Lansman, 1982), primacy/recency components of short-term memory (Crawford & Stankov, 1983), and speed of information processing in sixth graders. This last study (Jenkinson, 1983) measured memory scanning and picture identification. It eliminated the effects of Gf and Gc and failed to support any causal relationship between fluid and crystallized abilities.

REFERENCES

Cattell, R. B. (1963). Theory of fluid and crystallized intelligence: A critical experiment. *Journal of Educational Psychology, 54,* 1–22.

Cattell, R. B., & Horn, J. L. (1978). A check on the theory of fluid and crystallized intelligence. *Journal of Educational Measurement, 15,* 139.

Crawford, J., & Stankov, L. (1983). Fluid and crystallized intelligence and primacy/recency components of short-term memory. *Intelligence, 7,* 227–252.

Jenkinson, J. L. (1983). Is speed of information processing related to fluid or to crystallized intelligence? *Intelligence, 7,* 91–106.

Kneif, L. M., & James, M. A. (1978). Interaction of general, fluid, and crystallized ability and instruction in 6th grade mathematics. *Journal of Educational Psychology, 70,* 319–323.

Lansdell, H. (1962). Laterality of verbal intelligence in the brain. *Science, 135,* 922–923.

Lansman, M., Donaldson, G., Hunt, E., & Yantis, S. (1982). Ability factors and cognitive processes. *Intelligence, 6,* 347–386.

Spearman, C. (1932). *The abilities of man.* London: Macmillan.

STEVEN GUMERMAN
Temple University

INTELLIGENCE
INTELLIGENCE QUOTIENT

CUED SPEECH

Cued speech was developed in 1967 by R. Orin Cornett at Gallaudet College in Washington, DC. It was designed to clarify ambiguity experienced by severely and profoundly hearing-impaired individuals relying on lipreading as a means of comprehending speech (Evans, 1982). During speechreading, hearing-impaired individuals may confuse many sounds such as /p/, /m/, and /b/, because they are visually similar. Users of cued speech attempt to overcome this confusion by providing a visual supplement to information presented through speechreading.

This system includes 12 hand signals or cues (presented in the Figure). Four cues are hand positions that differentiate between groups of vowel sounds. A hand can be placed at the side of the face, the throat, the chin, or the corner of the mouth. Eight cues, based on America Sign Language (ASL) hand shapes, are hand configurations used to visually differentiate between groups of consonants (Wilbur,

CUED SPEECH
English

CHART I
Cues for Vowel Sounds

	Side[1]	Throat	Chin	Mouth
open	ah (father) (got)[1]	a (that)	aw (dog)	
flattened-relaxed	u (but)[2]	i (is)	e (get)	ee (see)
rounded	oe (home)	oo (book)	ue (blue)	ur (her)

CHART II
Diphthongs

ie (my)　　ou (cow)　　ae (pay)　　oi (boy)

CHART III
Cues for Consonant Sounds

5	3	1	8	6	2	4	7
t	h	d	ng	l	k	b	g
m	s	p	y	sh	v	n	j
f	r	zh	ch	w	dh*	wh	th
					z		

(1) The side position is used also when a consonant is cued without a following vowel.
(2) This handshape is also used for a vowel without a preceding consonant.

*dh was formerly written tH

1 moves forward ½ inch
2 moves down

Cued speech—English.

1979). For example, a full hand represents the /m/, /f/, and /t/ sounds, whereas the extension of only the index finger represents the /d/, /p/, and /zh/ sounds. An auditory signal is visually supplemented by superimposing a consonant hand configuration on a vowel hand position. For example, the words *mitt* and *bit* may appear similar to the hearing-impaired speech reader; however, these words are cued differently. *Mitt* is cued with a full hand positioned at the throat, whereas *bit* is cued by placing a "b" hand shape at the throat.

Use of cued speech requires training for both the sender and the hearing-impaired individual. Cornett (1967) reports that an average of approximately 12 to 20 hours is required to develop proficient use of cued speech. Actually, time will vary with the individual learner and fluency comes with practice.

There are advantages and disadvantages associated with the use of cued speech. Its advantages include an adherence to the philosophy of oralism. Cued speech supplements information presented through speechreading; however, it cannot be used and understood in the absence of speech. In addition, use of cued speech has been associated with increases in speechreading accuracy (Clarke & Ling, 1976; Ling & Clarke, 1975), vocabulary, and intelligibility (Rupert, 1969). Disadvantages include the questionable phonetic competence of users, lack of transfer po-

tential to reading (Wilbur, 1979), and an overdependence on cues (Clarke & Ling, 1976).

REFERENCES

Clarke, B. R., & Ling, D. (1976). The effects of using cued speech: A follow-up study. *Volta Review, 78,* 23–34.

Cornett, R. O. (1967). Cued speech. *American Annals of the Deaf, 112,* 3–13.

Evans, L. (1982). *Total communication: Structure and strategy.* Washington, DC: Gallaudet College Press.

Ling, D., & Clarke, B. R. (1975). Cued speech: An evaluative study. *American Annals of the Deaf, 120,* 480–488.

Rupert, J. (1969). Kindergarten program using cued speech at the Idaho School for the Deaf. *Proceedings of the 44th Meeting of American Instructors of the Deaf.* Berkeley, CA.

Wilbur, R. B. (1979). *American Sign Language and sign systems.* Baltimore, MD: University Park Press.

Maureen A. Smith
Pennsylvania State University

SIGN LANGUAGE
TOTAL COMMUNICATION

CUISENAIRE RODS

Cuisenaire rods, named for the Belgian mathematician who designed them, consist of a set of small colored wooden rods of varying lengths. Gattegno, a British psychologist, popularized their use for both mathematics and language instruction through combinations of size and color. Karambelas (1971) described how the rods are used in language instruction.

There have been many studies of the use of Cuisenaire rods in mathematics instruction. Hawkins (1984) introduced the relationship in the Pythagorean theorem to low-ability seventh graders using Cuisenaire rods. Sweetland (1984) used the rods in teaching multiplication of fractions. LeBlanc (1976) designed a teacher preparation program in elementary school mathematics using Cuisenaire rods as the vehicle for actively engaging prospective teachers in mathematics with the goal of applying that mathematics in the elementary school. McDonald (1981) incorporated the rods in teaching binomial expressions and Ginther (1970) designed applications of the rods in advanced mathematics. Urion (1979) developed a Cuisenaire rod activity for generating approximations of pi. Knowles (1979) described the use of the rods and the calculator in examining decimals that result from division of whole numbers. Ewbank (1978) and Hater (1970) drew attention to the use of color in mathematics instruction including Cuisenaire rods, number lines, magic squares, and combinatorial problems.

Davidson (1977) suggested uses for the rods in teaching mathematics from basic arithmetic through algebra.

Brooks (1977) described a game for two teams that uses dice, meter sticks, and Cuisenaire rods. The games provide practice in number facts, regrouping, and use of the rods in relation to the metric system. Shively and Holz (1975) used the rods to illustrate finite mathematical systems. Steiner (1975) designed activities with Cuisenaire rods, Dienes Blocks, and Papy's minicomputer. Sheffelin and Seltzer (1974) described a workshop for 300 participants on the use of Cuisenaire rods with learning-disabled children. Kamps (1970) tested portions of Piaget's model for the development of operational conservation and measurement of length with 102 second-grade students from three different cities. One group had participated in the American Association for the Advancement of Science—A Process Approach science program in grades Kindergarten through 2, one group had received limited experience in linear measurement, and one group had used Cuisenaire rods in grades 1 and 2. A Kruskal-Wallis one-way analysis of variance revealed no significant difference at the .05 level among the three groups of students.

REFERENCES

Brooks, M. J. (1977). The one-meter dash. *Arithmetic Teacher, 24*(4), 327–328.

Davidson, P. S. (1977). Rods can help children learn at all grade levels. *Learning, 6*(3), 86–88.

Ewbank, W. A. (1978). The use of color for teaching mathematics. *Arithmetic Teacher, 26*(1), 53–57.

Ginther, J. L. (1970). An application of Cuisenaire rods in advanced mathematics. *School Science & Mathematics, 70*(3), 250–253.

Hater, M. A. (1970). Investigation of color in the Cuisenaire rods. *Perceptual & Motor Skills, 31*(2), 441–442.

Hawkins, V. J. (1984). The Pythagorean theorem revisited: Weighing the results. *Arithmetic Teacher, 32*(4), 36–37.

Kamps, K. G. (1970). An investigation of portions of a model for acquisition of conservation and measurement of length based on performance of selected second grade children on six Piaget-type tasks. *Research in Education* (Ann Arbor, MI: University Microfilms, SEO15002).

Karambelas, J. (1971). Teaching foreign languages "the silent way." *Association of Departments of Foreign Languages Bulletin, 3*(1), 41.

Knowles, F. (1979). Coloured rods, a calculator, and decimals. *Mathematics Teaching, 86,* 28–29.

LeBlanc, J. F. (1976). *Addition and subtraction Mathematics-methods program unit.* Bloomington, IN: Mathematics Education Development Center, Indiana University.

McDonald, J. R. (1981). Sharing teaching ideas: Factor cards: A device for GFC; A model of 3-space; Discovery in advanced algebra with concrete models. *Mathematics Teacher, 74*(5), 349–358.

Sheffelin, M. A., & Seltzer, C. (1974). Math manipulatives for learning disabilities. *Academic Therapy, 9*(5), 357–362.

Shively, J. E., & Holz, A. W. (1975). Finite operational systems for elementary students. *School Science & Mathematics, 75*(2), 191–196.

Steiner, H. G. (1975). Mathematical analysis of Piaget's grouping concept. Papy's minicomputer as a grouping. *International Journal of Mathematical Education in Science & Technology, 5*(2), 241–250.

Sweetland, R. D. (1984). Understanding multiplication of fractions. *Arithmetic Teacher, 32*(1), 48–52.

Urion, D. K. (1979). Using the Cuisenaire rods to discover approximations of pi. *Arithmetic Teacher, 27*(4), 17.

FREDRICKA K. REISMAN
Drexel University

CULTURAL ATTITUDES TOWARDS SPECIAL EDUCATION

The children and youth of the United States represent an increasingly diverse variety of cultural and linguistic groups. The 1990 Census (U.S. Bureau of the Census, 1990) determined that the school-age population within the United States included 6,914,000 African American children, 5,390,000 children of Hispanic descent (including children of Mexican, Cuban, and Puerto Rican origin), 1,550,000 children of Asian/Pacific Island descent (including children of Japanese, Chinese, Korean, and Filipino origin), and 522,000 Native American children (including American Indians, Eskimos, and Aleuts). This large number of school-age children (and the kaleidoscope of cultures and languages which they represent) offer unique challenges and opportunities for educational professionals.

Underscoring the need to appropriately address these challenges and opportunities is the rate at which the culturally and linguistically diverse school-age population is growing. Between 1995 and 2050 the overall U.S. population is forecast to grow by almost 50%, with the Anglo (White, Not of Hispanic Origin) population experiencing the smallest proportional increase (approximately 7%; U.S. Bureau of the Census, 1994). This is in sharp contrast to the proportional increase forecast for the African American population (70%), Native American population (83%), Hispanic population (258%), and the Asian/Pacific Islander population (269%) during the same time period.

In order to provide appropriate educational services for such a heterogeneous population, an understanding of cultural affiliation and corresponding cultural attitudes as related to special education is necessary. A cultural group, for the purpose of this entry, is defined as a group set apart from others because of its national origin or distinctive cultural patterns (Schaefer, 1990). It is furthermore recognized that although members of a cultural group may have common values, beliefs, and behaviors, no individual member exemplifies all of the groups modal practices (Wehrly,

1995). The following sections include a discussion of the literature related to cultural attitudes toward special education, a summary of common attitudes reported for various cultural groups, and an analysis of the benefits and limitations of our current knowledge base.

The present body of literature related to cultural attitudes towards special education is largely focused on suggestions for practice in the special education arena and can be generally categorized as either (a) theory-based (e.g., "best practice" papers in which general knowledge of specific cultural groups is applied to the school setting), or (b) research-based (i.e., the presentation of data to demonstrate specific relationships between cultural attitudes and educational strategies). Thus, cultural attitudes towards special education are presented within the framework of these two categories.

Theory-Based Literature

Throughout the last century two main theoretical perspectives have been employed when working with culturally and linguistically diverse children within the school setting (Bowman, 1994). These two perspectives may be simplistically categorized as uniformity and diversity. The theoretical perspective of uniformity, labeled by Kohlberg and Mayer (1972) as "cultural transmission," places an emphasis on socializing children into a uniform culture through standardized curricula, educational experiences, and achievement expectations. In contrast, the theoretical perspective of diversity emphasizes the uniquely individual nature of education and the need for schools to address the cultural, linguistic, and intellectual heterogeneity of children.

Special education service delivery as mandated by public law (e.g., P.L. 94-142 or IDEA) is based upon the theoretical perspective of diversity. In order to effectively meet the legal requirements set forth within the public law, it is necessary for school personnel to have a basic understanding of the attitudes and beliefs common to the different culturally and linguistically diverse groups which they serve. Numerous special education theorists have attempted to provide such an understanding through the application of specific cultural knowledge to the interpersonal interactions which take place within a school setting (e.g., Banks, 1994; Harry, 1992; Lynch & Hansen, 1992). The following is a synopsis of theory-based literature regarding the attitudes of culturally and linguistically diverse parents towards special education.

Parental Attitudes

The topic of parental attitudes towards special education as discussed in theory-based literature is typically focused on specific cultural groups.

Parents of African American origin. Literature regarding the attitudes of African American parents is limited and thus far suggests that parents may emphasize the role of immediate and extended family members (Seligman & Darling, 1989) and that attitudes towards severe disability may be often be related to a traditionally fatalistic interpretation of events (Harry, 1992). Common to many cultural groups, this fatalistic perception is described by Seligman and Darling (1989) as a seemingly passive acceptance of life circumstances which may in turn assist in the acceptance of a child's disability. African American parents of children with more mild forms of disability may display attitudes of caution and skepticism due to a well-documented history of group misdiagnosis and inappropriate special education service delivery (Harry, 1992).

Parents of Hispanic origin. Hispanic parents may also emphasize the role of immediate and extended family members and may be strongly tied to familism. This traditional view of the child as a reflection of the family unit may make acceptance of a severe disability more difficult for many Hispanic parents (Harry, 1992). A common cultural perception, in which developmental and intellectual disabilities are indistinguishable from mental disorders and mental illness, may add to the difficulty of acceptance (Adkins & Young, 1976). As a result of these two factors, the stigma associated with severe disabilities may be quite personal and significant for many Hispanic parents. On the other hand, a cultural emphasis on family relations and social interactions may assist parents in the acceptance of more mild forms of disability (Seligman & Darling, 1989). The mildly disabled child's ability to maintain their social role with immediate and extended family members may be a source of encouragement for parents and may even serve as a foundation for questioning the validity of the schools classification of their child. Common cultural attitudes of deference towards and respect for teachers and other school personnel may inhibit parental communication of concerns and expectations related to the special education process (Harry, 1992).

Parents of Asian/Pacific Island origin. Severe disabilities within the Asian/Pacific Islander culture have typically been viewed as the result of previous actions of parents or ancestors, the influence of spiritual forces (as in the case of some Southeast Asian groups), specific behaviors of the mother during pregnancy, or the imbalance of physiological functions (Chan, 1986). The potential cause of a disability may therefore be a source of shame for parents in that it is thought to reflect on the past or present behavior of family members. In addition, the inability of a child with a severe disability to represent the family through academic or occupational success may serve as a secondary source of embarrassment for some parents (Yano, 1986, as cited in Harry, 1992). A traditional Asian social structure which places the needs of the group before the needs of the individual may help influence acceptance of the situation and parental attitude towards special education service delivery (Dao, 1991). Asian/Pacific Islander parents of children with more mild forms of disability may tend to interpret the source of difficulty as "laziness" or ineffective training at home (Chan, 1986).

Parents of Native American origin. In accordance with traditional beliefs, many Native American parents view disabilities as having both a spiritual and physical etiology. The singular biological/psychoeducational viewpoint of the public schools in regard to disabilities may limit the course of action preferred by many Native American parents (Harry, 1992). Likewise, the public school procedure of interacting directly with parents may bypass the complex system of extended family communication shared by many Native Americans (Huang & Gibbs, 1992). The attitude of parents towards special education may also be influenced by the emphasis placed on childhood independence and the use of extended family members as caregivers. The extended support system available to the child and their freedom to find their own place in community relations is exemplified by the absence of words such as disabled and handicapped from most Native American languages (Harry, 1992).

Benefits and Limitations

The benefit of theory-based literature within this area is the increased awareness and improved communication which results from a basic understanding of a group's common beliefs and practices. Flanagan and Miranda (1995) note that the specific information generated about a given culture through theory-based literature aids in understanding the values, beliefs, and behaviors that are expressed in cross-cultural interactions. Unfortunately, the tendency to generalize cultural attitudes to all members of a particular group to the exclusion of individual traits and preferences may serve as its greatest limitation. This concern sparked Lynch and Hanson (1992) to caution against the use of theory-based literature as a cross-cultural "recipe book" which stereotypes individuals rather than providing a foundation for better understanding.

Research-Based Literature

There is a limited number of research-based studies addressing the attitudes of culturally and linguistically diverse groups within the United States towards special education. The few studies which are available tend to be ethnographic in nature and are focused on parental and teacher attitudes regarding (a) meanings attached to disabilities or special education labels, (b) the role of language

and culture in special education placements, (c) special education instruction format, and (d) parental participation in the special education process. The majority of researchers within this area employed naturalistic research methodologies such as interviews, surveys, or both, with not all studies including a quantitative analysis of results. The results from a sample of exemplary research-based studies are included in this section.

Parental Attitudes

Research-based studies regarding culturally and linguistically diverse parental attitudes towards special education have addressed various topics.

Meanings attached to labels. Studies on the meanings attached to special education labels by culturally and linguistically diverse parents reveal that (a) their concept and boundaries of "normal" may be different from that of the educational system (Bennett, 1988; Danseco, 1997; Harry, 1992; Rodriguez, 1995; Zetlin, Padron & Wilson, 1996); (b) they are often confused by the specific terminology or labels common to special education (e.g., handicapped, disabled, impaired, retarded) and may associate these labels with more severe, as opposed to mild, manifestations of impairments (Danseco, 1997; Harry, 1992); (c) they may perceive the label as somehow reflective of family inadequacies (Harry, 1992); and (d) may attach biomedical and sociocultural (e.g., spiritual) causes to the labels (Danseco, 1997; Rodriguez, 1995).

Perceived role of language and culture. Several studies (e.g., Harry, 1992; Rodriguez, 1995; Zetlin, Padron, & Wilson, 1996) revealed parental perceptions that their child was placed in special education as a result of a language and cultural difference and not because of a true handicapping condition. This sentiment was reported by parents from various cultural and linguistic backgrounds (e.g., Hispanic and Southeast Asian).

Instructional format concerns. While parents tend to report positive feelings regarding the smaller group size for instruction found in special education, they also expressed concern that the slower pace, and lack of actual individualization of instruction might hinder, rather than help, their children (Harry, 1992; Zetlin, Padron, & Wilson, 1996). Confusion seems to exist among some parents as to how native language and culture should be utilized in their child's instruction (Zetlin, Padron, & Wilson, 1996), while others felt that instruction should focus on English and reading (Harry, 1992; Rodriguez, 1995).

Factors affecting parental participation. Parental opportunities for participation in the special education process was often reported by parents as (a) impersonal and one-sided (e.g., during meetings), with school personnel underestimating parental capabilities and limiting parental voice and power in decision-making; (b) overwhelming with regard to the number of letters and forms involved; (c) constrained by the parents' limited knowledge of the special education process (e.g., legal rights and necessity of attendance at meetings) (Bennett, 1988; Danseco, 1997; Harry, 1992; Rodriguez, 1995); and (d) permeated with distrust (Bennett, 1988; Harry, 1992).

School Personnel Attitudes

Research-based studies within this area are generally focused on the attitudes of culturally and linguistically diverse school personnel, primarily teachers, towards special education. Two recent studies provide an example of this type of research. Rodriguez (1995) and Paez, Flores, & Trujillo (in press) surveyed culturally and linguistically diverse teachers employed in bilingual education programs. Both studies revealed that the teachers' knowledge of special education services and processes were limited and that the older the age group (Rodriguez, 1995) or the longer the time since college graduation (Paez, in press) the less informed they generally were.

According to Rodriguez (1995), there was significant variation among 100 teachers of Southeast Asian origin with regard to the belief that spiritual forces or destiny cause a child's disability with approximately one third agreeing, over one third disagreeing, and the rest being ambivalent on this point. Many of these teachers felt that children were often misplaced in special education and were discriminated against because of lower English proficiency. Moreover, they reported that lower levels of English proficiency among some students of Southeast Asian origin resulted in lower expectations for these students on the part of other school personnel.

Benefits and Limitations

The benefits of research-based literature in this area are that it provides for data-based decision making, often validates best practices literature, and supports a naturalistic or personalized approach to research. However, the current methodological approach in which surveys, interviews, or a combination of both are utilized is limited by subjectivity (e.g., in the generation of questions and consolidation of results) and the possible intrusion of the interviewer in the process. In addition, when the attitudes surveyed are those of culturally and linguistically diverse groups, the studies are ethnographic and have additional constraints, such as language and sociocultural barriers which are encountered whether the researcher is or is not a member of the cultural group.

Conclusion

It is clear that cultural attitudes play an important role in a family's adjustment to a child with a disability and the impact the situation has on the family's responsiveness and receptivity to sources of help (Fine & Gardner, 1994). The work of Harry (1992) serves as an example of the use of theory-based knowledge to construct data-based research. It is this type of application which will allow accurate and pertinent knowledge regarding cultural attitudes to be applied to the special education setting. Regardless of the informational source, whether it be theory- or research-based literature, the attitudes of culturally and linguistically diverse parents towards special education must be viewed within the context of the current life situation of the individual caregiver (Fracasso & Busch-Rossnagel, 1992). Dennis & Giangreco (1996) expand on this sentiment by noting that contextual considerations which should be considered include the emotional climate of racial or ethnic discrimination experienced by the individual, the implications of poverty, the neighborhood and living environment, and the degree and duration of acculturation into the dominant cultural group. Added to this list is the universal and very individual experience of caring for a child with special needs (Lynch & Hansen, 1992).

REFERENCES

Adkins, P. G., & Young, R. G. (1976). Cultural perceptions on the treatment of handicapped school children of Mexican-American parentage. *Journal of Research and Development in Education, 9*(4), 83–90.

Banks, J. A. (1994). *An introduction to multicultural education.* Boston: Allyn and Bacon.

Bennett, A. T. (1988). Gateways to powerlessness: Incorporating Hispanic deaf children and families into formal schooling. *Disability, Handicap, and Society, 3*(2), 119–151.

Bowman, B. T. (1994). The challenge of diversity. *Phi Delta Kappan, 76,* 218–224.

Chan, S. Q. (1986). Parents of exceptional Asian children. In M. K. Kitano & P. C. Chinn (Eds.), *Exceptional Asian children and youth* (pp. 36–53). Reston, VA: Council for Exceptional Children.

Danseco, E. R. (1997). Parental beliefs on childhood disability: Insights on culture, children development, and intervention. *International Journal of Disability, Development and Education, 44,* 41–52.

Dao, M. (1991). Designing assessment procedures for educationally at-risk Southeast Asian-American students. *Journal of Learning Disabilities, 24,* 594–601.

Dennis, R. E., & Giangreco, M. F. (1996). Creating conversation: Reflections on cultural sensitivity in family interviewing. *Exceptional Children, 63*(1), 103–113.

Fine, M. J., & Gardner, A. (1994). Collaborative consultation with families of children with special needs-why bother? *Journal of Educational and Psychological Consultation, 5,* 283–308.

Flanagan, D. P., & Miranda, A. H. (1995). Best practices in working with culturally different families. In A. Thomas & J. Grimes (Eds.), *Best Practices in School Psychology III* (pp. 1049–1060). Washington, D.C.: NASP.

Fracasso, M., & Busch-Rossnagel, N. (1992). Parents and children of Hispanic origin. In M. Procidano & C. Fisher (Eds.), *Contemporary families: A handbook for school professionals* (pp. 83–98). New York: Teachers College Press.

Harry, B. (1992). *Cultural diversity, families and the education system: Communication and empowerment.* New York: Teachers College.

Huang, L. N., & Gibbs, J. T. (1992). Partners or adversaries? Home-school collaboration across culture, race, and ethnicity, In S. L. Christenson & J. C. Conoley (Eds.), *Home-school collaboration* (pp. 81–109). Silver Spring, MD: National Association of School Psychologists.

Kohlberg, L. & Mayer, R. (1972). Development as the aim of education. *Harvard Educational Review, 42,* 449–469.

Lynch, E. W., & Hansen, M. J. (1992). *Developing cross-cultural competence: A guide for working with young children and their families.* Baltimore: Paul H. Brookes.

Paez, D., Flores, J., & Trujillo, T. (in press). Rural school personnel's conceptions of issues of diversity. *Rural Special Education Quarterly, 17.*

Rodriguez, J. (1995). *Southeast Asian's conception of disabilities and special education intervention in American schools.* Lowell, MA: University of Massachusetts, College of Education. (ERIC Document Reproduction Service No. 388 740)

Schaefer, R. T. (1990). *Racial and ethnic groups* (4th ed.). Glenview, Scott Foresman.

Seligman, M., & Darling, R. B. (1989). *Ordinary families, special children.* New York: Guilford.

U.S. Bureau of the Census. (1990). *1990 United States census.* Washington, D. C.: U.S. Department of Commerce, Economics and Statistics Administration.

U.S. Bureau of the Census. (1994). Population projections of the United States by age, sex, race, and Hispanic origin: 1995-2050. Washington, D.C.: U.S. Department of Commerce, Economics and Statistics Administration.

Wehrly, B. (1995). *Pathways to multicultural counseling competence: A developmental journey.* Pacific Grove, CA: Brookes/Cole.

Zetlin, A., Padron, M., & Wilson, S. (1996). The experience of five Latin American families with the special education system. *Education and Training in Mental Retardation and Developmental Disabilities, 31,* 22–28.

ROBERT L. RHODES
DORIS PAEZ
New Mexico State University

CULTURAL BIAS IN TESTING

The cultural test bias hypothesis is the contention that racial and ethnic group differences in mental test scores are the result of inherent flaws in the tests themselves. These flaws bias, or cause systematic error, in a manner that causes ethnic minorities to earn low scores. Mean differences in scores among groups are then interpreted as artifacts of the test and not as reflecting any real differences in mental abilities or skills.

Mean differences in mental test scores across race are some of the most well-established phenomena in psychological research on individual differences. One of the primary explanations of these differences is that they are produced by people who are reared in very different environments, with lower scoring groups having been relatively deprived of the quantity and quality of stimulation received in the formative years by higher scoring groups. Another explanation is that lower scoring groups reflect a difference in the genetic potential for intellectual performance. Most contemporary views take an environment X genetic interaction approach.

Cultural bias in testing has existed as a potential explanation at least since it was raised by Sir Cyril Burt (1921), with occasional papers on the issue appearing over the years. It was not widely accepted as a serious hypothesis until the late 1960s, when the Association of Black Psychologists (ABP) called for a moratorium on the use of psychological tests with minorities and disadvantaged students, particularly with regard to placement in special education programs. In 1969 the ABP issued an official policy statement encouraging parents of black children to refuse to allow their children or themselves to be evaluated on any achievement, intelligence, aptitude, or performance test.

The primary objections to the testing of minorities on the basis of race or cultural bias in the tests have been classified by Reynolds (1982a) into six categories as follows:

1. *Inappropriate Content.* Black or other minority children have not been exposed to the material on the test questions or other stimulus materials. The tests are geared toward white middle-class homes and values.

2. *Inappropriate Standardization Samples.* Ethnic minorities are underrepresented in the collection of normative reference group data. In the early years, it was not unusual for standardization samples of major tests to be all white.

3. *Examiner and Language Bias.* Since most psychologists are white and primarily speak only standard English, they intimidate blacks and other minorities. They are also unable to communicate accurately with minority children. Lower test scores for minorities, then, are said to reflect this intimidation and difficulty in the communication process, not lower ability levels.

4. *Inequitable Social Consequences.* As a result of bias in educational and psychological tests, minority

group members, who are already at a disadvantage in the educational and vocational markets because of past discrimination, are disproportionately relegated to dead-end educational tracks and thought unable to learn. Labeling effects also fall into this category.

5. *Measurement of Different Constructs.* Related to item (1), this position asserts that the tests are measuring significantly different attributes when used with children from other than the white middle-class culture.

6. *Differential Predictive Validity.* While tests may accurately predict a variety of outcomes for white middle-class children, they fail to predict at an acceptable level any relevant criteria for minority group members. Corollary to this objection is a variety of competing positions regarding the selection of an appropriate, common criterion against which to validate tests across cultural groupings. Scholastic or academic attainment levels are considered by a variety of black psychologists to be biased as to criteria.

Additionally, it has been argued (see Reynolds, Lowe, & Saenz, 1999, for a discussion) that minority and majority groups have qualitatively distinct forms of intelligence and personality and thus cannot be assessed with the same methods, negating any attempt to compare groups or test performance.

The actions by the ABP had several positive effects. Prior to the call for a moratorium on testing of minorities, little actual research existed in the area. Much research was prompted by the ABP position as it brought the race bias hypothesis to the forefront of explanations of race differences in intelligence. Also in response to this call for a moratorium, the American Psychological Association Board of Scientific Affairs had a committee appointed to study the use of tests with disadvantaged students. The committee, headed by T. Anne Cleary, gave its official report in the form of an article in American Psychologist (Cleary, Humphreys, Kendrick, & Wesman, 1975).

Research on race bias in testing was, and continues to be, of major importance to psychology as well as to society. The cultural test bias hypothesis is probably one of the most crucial scientific questions facing psychology (Reynolds, 1981). If this hypothesis ultimately is accepted as correct, then the past 100 years or so of research into the psychology of individual differences (or differential psychology, the basic psychological science underlying all fields of applied psychology) must be dismissed as artifactual, or at least as confounded, since such research is based on standard psychometric methodology. Race bias in testing is being tested in the judicial courts as well as in the scholarly court of open inquiry. Two major court decisions, known as *Larry P.* (1979) and *PASE* (1980), have given

conflicting opinions regarding the issues. Of two federal district courts, one decided that intelligence tests are racially biased and the other decided they are not biased.

Contrary to the position of the late 1960s, considerable research is now available regarding race bias in testing. For the most part, this research has failed to support the test bias hypothesis, revealing that (1) well-constructed, well-standardized educational and psychological tests predict future performance in an essentially equivalent manner across race for U.S.-born ethnic minorities; (2) the internal psychometric structure of the tests is essentially invariant with regard to race; and (3) the content of these tests is about equally appropriate across these groups (Reynolds, 1982a; Reynolds et al., 1999).

Race bias in testing is one of the most controversial and violently emotional issues in psychology. It will not be resolved entirely on the basis of research and data, as tests have unquestionably been abused in their past use with minority groups. Much of the controversy centers around the placement of minority children in special education programs. Thus, special consideration must be given to ensure that the misuses and abuses of the past are thwarted by "intelligent testing" (Kaufman, 1979). A general review of race bias in testing can be found in Jensen (1980). Specialty reviews of race bias in employment testing have been done by Hunter et al 1979), and of bias in the testing of children by Reynolds (1982a; Reynolds, et al, 1999). A book length debate of the issues can be found in Reynolds and Brown (1984). Methodology for investigating most aspects of cultural bias in testing relevant to special education is reviewed in Reynolds (1982b) and Reynolds, et al. (1999).

REFERENCES

Burt, C. (1921). *Mental and scholastic tests*. London: P. S. Kiy. Cleary, T. A., Humphreys, L. G., Kendrick, S. A., & Wesman, A. (1975). Educational uses of tests with disadvantaged students. *American Psychologist, 30*, 15–41.

Hunter, J. E., Schmidt, F. L., & Hunter, R. (1979). Differential validity of employment tests by race: A comprehensive review and analysis. *Psychological Bulletin, 86*, 721–735.

Jensen, A. R. (1980). *Bias in mental testing*. New York: Free Press.

Kaufman, A. S. (1979). Intelligence testing with the WISC-R. *Interscience*. New York: Wiley.

Reynolds, C. R. (1981). In support of bias in mental testing and scientific inquiry. *Behavioral & Brain Sciences, 3*, 352.

Reynolds, C. R. (1982a). The problem of bias in psychological assessment. In C. R. Reynolds & T. B. Gutkin (Eds.), *The handbook of school psychology*. New York: Wiley.

Reynolds, C. R. (1982b). Methods for detecting construct and predictive bias. In R. A. Berk (Ed.), *Handbook of methods for detecting test bias*. Baltimore, MD: Johns Hopkins University Press.

Reynolds, C. R., & Brown, R. T. (1984). *Perspectives on bias in mental testing*. New York: Wiley.

Reynolds, C. R., Lowe, P., & Saenz, A. (1999). The problem of bias in psychological assessment. In C. R. Reynolds & T. B. Gutkin (Eds.), *The Handbook of School Psychology* (3rd ed.) (pp. 549–595). New York: Wiley.

CECIL R. REYNOLDS
Texas A & M University

LARRY P.
MARSHALL v. GEORGIA
PASE v. HANNON

CULTURAL DEPRIVATION

See EARLY EXPERIENCE AND CRITICAL PERIODS; See SOCIO-ECONOMIC STATUS.

CULTURE FAIR TEST

Education and processes of socialization teach individuals cultural knowledge. Many standardized tests measure how well one has learned the information specific to a particular culture. The development of culture fair tests was begun to neutralize the culturally loaded information found in standardized tests (Lewis, 1998). A test used to assess diverse cultural groups cannot contain items specific to any one particular culture; otherwise, would not be considered to have content validity.

The Culture Fair Intelligence Test (Cattell, 1973) is a measure virtually devoid of verbal content (the test uses a paper and pencil format). It consists of novel problem-solving items that do not occur in any particular culture. The test format is multiple choice and includes four subtests: Series Completion, Classification, Matrices, and Conditions. Different levels are administered depending on the subject's age: 4 to 8 years, 8 to 14 years, or 14 to adult. Similar to other standardized tests, the results of the Culture Fair Intelligence Test are expressed as deviation IQs with a mean of 100 and a standard deviation of 16.

Lewis (1998) notes that there are some weaknesses of the Culture Fair Intelligence Test. One is that it uses fairly extensive verbal instructions during administration of the test. This causes difficulty for linguistically different clients. Therefore, although the test does not have culturally loaded information items or verbal components, the verbal nature of the directions themselves are problematic. Also, the subtests emphasize speed. This emphasis on speed can differ cross-culturally, and thereby reduces the cultural fairness of the instrument. These potential problems should be taken into account when assessing clients of different cultural backgrounds. Anastasi (1988) has

noted that the interpretation of test scores are "by far the most important considerations in the assessment of culturally diverse groups" (p. 66). Misinterpretation of scores with these groups is a serious concern.

REFERENCES

Anastasi, A. A. (1988). *Psychological testing* (6th ed.). New York: Macmillan.

Cattell, R. B. (1973). *Technical supplement for the Culture Fair Intelligence tests Scales 2 and 3*. Champaign, IL: Institute for Personality and Ability Testing.

Lewis, J. E. (1998). Nontraditional uses of traditional aptitude tests. In R. J. Samuda, R. Feurerstein, A. S. Kaufman, J. E. Lewis, & R. J. Sternberg (Eds.), *Advances in Cross Cultural Assessment*. Thousand Oaks, CA: Sage.

LIZ LICHTENBERGER
The Salk Institute

CULTURAL BIAS IN TESTING

CULTURAL-FAMILIAL RETARDATION

The term cultural-familial retardation has long been used to indicate mild retardation of unknown etiology that is associated with a family history of mild retardation, and a home environment that provides adverse experiences that are believed to inhibit mental development. The word cultural suggests an environmental basis; familial implies a genetic origin. Synonyms include sociocultural or psychosocial, intrinsic, subcultural, endogenous, and familial retardation. Individuals in this population usually have IQs in the range of mild retardation (about 55 to 70), have no demonstrable biological pathology to account for the retardation, usually have a parent or sibling who is retarded, and come from low socioeconomic status homes (Gillberg, 1995; Wrestling, 1986).

The specific cause of cultural-familial retardation is uncertain, but it probably involves interactive factors; each factor alone is not sufficient to explain the intellectual and behavioral deficits. The present consensus is that the interactions among psychosocial, environmental, and genetic factors are so great and begin so early in life that one cannot place responsibility on any single cause in individual cases (Grossman, 1983). A few decades ago it was believed that this type of retardation was inherited, and environmental factors were discounted. Polygenic inheritance is suggested because this type of retardation is not randomly distributed among the poverty stricken, but most often found in families where the mother is retarded.

Mild retardation is less common in children born to healthy, mature women than in children born to adolescent mothers, women who are malnourished, or women who get poor prenatal care and are thus especially vulnerable to infections, trauma, and prenatal intoxications. Children born to such mothers have a relatively high incidence of prematurity and/or low birth weight, factors that are related to problems in physical and intellectual development. However, most children born to such women, or born prematurely, are not retarded.

Specific environmental factors include extreme malnourishment during early infancy, severe early social isolation, very large families with closely spaced births, very harsh or abusive discipline, severe neglect, marked parental ignorance about health care, chaotic or highly disorganized family life, and extremely inadequate educational opportunities. However, the severe malnutrition during late pregnancy and early infancy that causes retardation in underdeveloped countries is virtually unknown in America and the other factors listed are found in families where there is no retardation.

Educable or mildly retarded (EMR) children without known biological cause for the retardation follow the normal sequence of physical and intellectual development. Retarded children go through the usual Piaget sequences of cognitive development, but more slowly. Very few reach the formal operations stage that normal children reach around age 12 (Inhelder, 1968; Zigler & Balla, 1982). Usually EMR students master basic academic skills. On intelligence and academic achievement tests they tend to have low scores on most subtests of the scales, in contrast to learning-disabled children, who may score low on one or two subtests (and who are more likely to come from middle-class families). The EMR students require more trials to learn new skills than normal children, perhaps because of attentional and short-term memory difficulties or failure to develop effective strategies for learning and problem solving (Warren & Taylor, 1984).

In the past, many dropped out of school early, but now most complete high school, usually in special education programs that focus on occupational skills during adolescence. It has been estimated that although poor children make up about 80% of the educable mentally retarded students in schools, only about 10% of American children living in poverty will be classified as mildly retarded (Haywood, Burns, Arbitman-Smith, & Delclos, 1984). Children from such families may also contribute to normal, slow-learning, and gifted populations (Richardson, 1968). Cultural–familial retardation accounts for about 29% of all cases of mild mental retardation but only 4% of moderate to severe cases of mental retardation (Gillberg, 1995).

Some psychologists and educators have proposed that much of the responsibility for retardation in culturally disadvantaged families is with the environment outside the home, particularly the educational system. Mildly retarded students have been called "six-hour retarded children," implying that they are retarded only during school hours; however, there is little evidence for assuming that those children cope as well as others outside of school. Criticism of schools is partially based on the fact that prevalence studies have shown a higher percentage of identified cases during school years than before or after those years (Richardson, 1968). School demands may tax the abilities of mildly retarded individuals more than some activities of later life; for example, good reading comprehension and high mathematics are important, but they are not essential for some occupations. If we classify as retarded any adults who are competitive and consistently employed full-time, many former EMR students would not be considered retarded as adults, whatever an earlier classification, and whatever their IQs as adults. Levine (1985) reported a high correlation between stress and anxiety, especially for unemployed mildly retarded adults; therefore, personality factors as well as job skills and IQ may be relevant in the classification of adults.

Some sociologists and educators have argued that children in this group are not really retarded, but that intelligence tests are biased against poor children, especially minority ones. This argument seems to ignore the fact that some children from the same families and communities are successful with the same test items that others fail. Careful empirical evaluations of tests and test items offer little support for claims of test bias in well-constructed, properly standardized tests (Reynolds, 1983; Reynolds, Lowe, & Saenz, 1999). Modifying (raising) scores because of economic disadvantages would merely make it more difficult for low-scoring and disadvantaged students to meet eligibility criteria for services they need.

Many misconceptions about cultural-familial retardation stem from interpretations and misinterpretations of the work of Henry Herbert Goddard. Publicity after the publication of *The Kallikaks* (Goddard, 1912) led to fear and prejudice toward retarded persons, especially those from poor families. The Kallikak study was part of a large study of over 300 families in which feeblemindedness was reported in two or more members of the same primary family for several generations. Goddard described an attractive young Caucasian woman to whom he gave the pseudonym of Deborah Kallikak (adapted from Greek words meaning good and bad) and her relatives in two lines of descent traced from Martin Kallikak, a Revolutionary War soldier. One line, from Martin's marriage to a prominent woman, was filled with outstanding citizens. Deborah's line, said to be from Martin's mating with a barmaid, had feeblemindedness, poverty, shiftlessness, illegitimacy, and alcoholism in each generation. Descriptions of Deborah's mental development and her skills as an adult make it clear that she functioned at a retarded level; she could do embroidery and simple carpentry, and manage second-grade academic work. Broad media coverage of Goddard's conclusion that retardation was hereditary was overgeneralized and assumed to apply to all persons from low-income families. Interpretations of Goddard's work influenced state sterilization laws and the placement of state schools for the retarded in remote areas as protection for the schools and for society. By 1950 practices and law had changed. Goddard's work was reevaluated by modern research criteria, and was sharply criticized (Smith, 1985). During the 1960s and 1970s, some psychologists took a strong environmentalist position.

Children in the cultural-familial group look much like other children and are usually not recognized as retarded by their families during preschool years. They are more likely than others to need eyeglasses and to have frequent illnesses or other health problems (perhaps related to inadequate health care and habits).

Follow-up studies of former students in EMR classes indicate that as adults, many meet the demands of society more easily than they did school demands. From 40 to 80% are employed as adults, but employment is likely to be in unskilled or semiskilled work and incomes may be at or below the poverty level. Whether similar adults who received no special education fare as well is uncertain, but the evidence suggests that they may not.

Edgerton et al. studied the community life of retarded adults. They used repeated interviews and direct observations in 1960–1961, 1972–1973, and 1983 (Edgerton, Bollinger, & Herr, 1984). Case histories and descriptions of the original 48 persons described in *The Cloak of Competence* (Edgerton, 1967) indicate that those studied belong to the cultural-familial group. Edgerton found them to be on the lower end of the continuum on almost every index of economic and social functioning. They lived in slum areas, under deplorable conditions, had very little job security and few marketable skills. Almost all had found a "benefactor" (spouse, relative, or friend) to help them cope with the stresses of everyday life such as losing jobs or friends, having illnesses and financial problems. Life was not easy for them, but many of the 15 adults (mean age 56) remaining in 1983 reported at least moderate satisfaction with life.

Since mid-century, extensive efforts have been made to interrupt the vicious cycle of poverty, social incompetence, and prejudice associated with cultural-familial retardation. The establishment of the federal Office of Economic Opportunity (OEO) in the 1960s illustrates a massive effort to provide health, educational, and social intervention. The OEO's most visible and enduring program is Project Head Start: a preschool program for young children. Federal and state programs have had impact, but have not even approached the goal of reducing mental retardation by half, as was predicted in 1962 by the President's Panel on Mental Retardation. Project Head Start is now one of the largest health service providers for young children in America. It has been very successful in health areas, but its effects on intellectual functioning and academic achievement are less certain. However, there have been positive results in federally funded research in rigorously controlled experimental preschool programs. In addition, a collaborative study of the pooled data from 11 major studies on the long-term effects of early educational intervention projects designed to prevent the progressive decline in cognitive skills of children from low-income families (primarily minorities) suggests that carefully planned early intervention may have a positive effect on school competence. The competence was measured by assignment to special education programs or repeated grades, the development of abilities as measured by standardized tests, and the effect of attitudes and values of children and on families, both measured by questionnaires (Lazar & Darlington, 1982).

Experimental educational interventions designed to reverse retardation and other severe learning problems in school-age students are exemplified by studies using the Instrumental Enrichment "mediated learning experience" approach developed in Israel (Feuerstein, Rand, Hoffman, & Miller, 1980) and used at several North American sites by Haywood of Vanderbilt University (Haywood & Arbitman-Smith, 1981). Both the American and the Israeli investigators reported positive effects from the use of Instrumental Enrichment, particularly for adolescents with severe educational disadvantages, but initial gains may not be sustainable.

Studies of socially competent children who are at high risk for retardation may provide especially useful information. Werner and Smith (1982) described the "resilient" children in a 20-year study of 698 multiracial children in Hawaii. The resilient children grew to successful, competent adulthood despite poverty, parents with little formal education, and a good deal of stress. Factors associated with resilience were fewer serious childhood illnesses, development of more internal locus of control, well-spaced families of less than five children, and high-achievement motivation.

Das (1973), who has lived in several cultures, has suggested that the technology and cultural demands of society may be important factors in determining whether individuals are classified as mildly retarded. He noted that "biases" in the West emphasize verbal abilities and reasoning, and that the educational systems selectively refer children showing deficiencies in these areas for special education. School experiences are an integral part of a child's growth and development; they transmit the values of the majority culture. Cultural-familial children generally are less adept in language and reasoning than those from higher socioeconomic status families; thus, they start school at a disadvantage. In a technological society in which high-level verbal and reasoning skills are needed and valued, these children begin at a disadvantage that might not be such a problem in a simpler society. It is unlikely that we will soon prevent cultural-familial retardation in America, but progress is being made in reducing associated medical problems and perhaps ameliorating some of the severe learning and educational problems of children from families in which the risk of cultural-familial retardation is high.

REFERENCES

Das, J. P. (1973). Cultural deprivation and cognitive competence. In N. R. Ellis (Ed.), *International review of research in mental retardation* (Vol. 6). New York: Academic.

Edgerton, R. B. (1967). *The cloak of competence: Stigma in the lives of the mentally retarded*. Berkeley: University of California Press.

Edgerton, R. B., Bollinger, M., & Herr, B. (1984). The cloak of competence: After two decades. *American Journal of Mental Deficiency, 88,* 345–351.

Feurerstein, R., Rand, Y., Hoffman, M. B., & Miller, R. (1980). *Instrumental enrichment*. Baltimore, MD: University Park Press.

Gillberg, C. (1995). *Clinical child neuropsychiatry*. Cambridge: Cambridge University Press.

Goddard, H. H. (1912). *The Kallikak family: A Study in the heredity of feeble-mindedness*. New York: Macmillan.

Grossman, H. J. (Ed.). (1983). *Classification in mental retardation*. Washington, DC: American Association on Mental Deficiency.

Haywood, H. C., & Arbitman-Smith, R. (1981). Modification of cognitive functions in slow learning adolescents. In P. Mittler (Ed.), *Frontiers of knowledge in mental retardation: Social, Educational, and behavioral aspects*. Baltimore, MD: University Park Press.

Haywood, H. C., Burns, S., Arbitman-Smith, R., & Delclos, V. R. (1984). Forward to fundamentals; Learning and the 4th R. *Peabody Journal of education, 61*(3), 6–35.

Inhelder, B. (1968). *The diagnosis of reasoning in the mentally retarded* (translated by W. B. Stephens). New York: Day.

Lazar, I., & Darlington, R. (1982). Lasting effects of early education: A report from the consortium for longitudinal studies. *Monographs of the Society for Research in Child Development, 47*(serial nos. 2–3).

Levine, H. G. (1985). Situational anxiety and everyday life experiences of mildly mentally retarded adults. *American Journal of Mental Deficiency, 90,* 27–83.

Reynolds, C. R. (1983). Test bias: In God we trust; all others must have data. *Journal of Special Education, 17,* 241–260.

Reynolds, C. R., Lowe, P., & Saenz, A. (1999). The problem of bias in psychological assessment. In C. R. Reynolds & T. B. Gutkin (Eds.), *The handbook of School Psychology* (3rd ed.) (pp. 549–595) New York: Wiley.

Richardson, S. A. (1968). The influence of social-environmental and nutritional factors on mental ability. In N. S. Scrimshaw & J. E. Gordon (Eds.), (1968). *Malnutrition, Learning, and behavior*. Cambridge, MA: MIT Press.

Smith, J. D. (1985). *Minds made feeble: The myth and legacy of the Kallikaks*. Rockville, MD: Aspen.

Warren, S. A., & Taylor, R. L. (1984). Education of children with learning problems. *Symposium on learning disorders, pediatric clinics of North America*. Philadelphia: Saunders.

Werner, E. E., & Smith, R. S. (1982). *Vulnerable but invincible: A longitudinal study of resilient children and youth*. New York: McGraw-Hill.

Westling, D. L. (1986). *Introduction to Mental Retardation*. Englewood Cliffs, NJ: Prentice-Hall.

Zigler, E., & Balla, D. (1982). Introduction: The developmental approach to mental retardation. In E. Zigler & D. Balla. *Mental retardation: The development-difference controversy*. Hillside, NJ: Erlbaum.

Sue Allen Warren
Boston University

ABCEDARIAN PROJECT
EDGERTON, R.
EDUCABLE MENTALLY RETARDED
GODDARD, H. H.
MENTAL RETARDATION
TRAINABLE MENTALLY RETARDED

CULTURALLY/LINGUISTICALLY DIVERSE ISSUES IN EARLY CHILDHOOD

See EARLY CHILDHOOD, CULTURALLY/LINGUISTICALLY DIVERSE ISSUES IN.

CULTURALLY/LINGUISTICALLY DIVERSE STUDENTS AND LEARNING DISABILITIES

Students who are culturally and linguistically diverse (CLD) who experience academic difficulties are often misidentified, misplaced, and misinstructed. Historically, these students been overrepresented in special education (Mercer & Rueda, 1991), although for many, their academic problems were more a result of limited English proficiency than a learning disability. More recently, some CLD students have been denied special education services as a reaction to the previous trend of misidentification, resulting in an underrepresentation of CLD students (Gersten & Woodward, 1994).

One critical issue for providing appropriate services for CLD students with learning disabilities is first determining if a student's academic difficulties are the result of a specific learning disability or other causal factors. Has the student had sufficient educational opportunity? Is the student literate in his or her native language? Does the student have the requisite English proficiency to successfully complete academic tasks in English? Is the student familiar with the content presented in academic subject areas? Is the student's behavior significantly different from peers from the same language and/or cultural group?

If the answer to any of these questions is no, then prereferral interventions are in order. Prereferral interventions are systematic, documented modifications suggested by a site based team, often called a Student Study Team, to ensure student success. Such interventions may include adapting assignments in ways that capitalize on the student's strengths, involving parents in the teaching and learning process, and using teaching approaches known to be effective with CLD learners.

If difficulties persist after appropriate interventions have been exhausted, a referral for special education services may be in order. Assessment of CLD students includes testing in the student's native language as well as English, to ensure the problem is evident in both languages. Also, informal measures should be used to support or refute the findings of standardized measures.

Once a learning disability has been diagnosed, a linguistically appropriate Individualized Education Plan, (IEP) is developed to reflect the student's cultural and language needs. The IEP addresses areas (such as language support options) that meet students' cultural and linguistic needs, including primary language support, ESL, and/or sheltered instruction. The IEP should also specify the language of instruction for each instructional goal, the specifics of the systematic development of English language skills, and how progress in these language-related areas will be measured.

Primary language support is best provided by the special education teacher who is proficient in the student's native language; however, shortage of bilingual special education teachers is critical. Other options for primary language support include a bilingual paraprofessional, community volunteer, or a peer from the same cultural group. Sheltered instruction is an effective instructional approach for students who have intermediate proficiency in English, or when primary language support is not available.

Sheltered instruction takes into linguistic needs of CLD learners by modifying the curriculum and delivery of instruction to make it understandable for them. CLD students with learning disabilities need extra support in acquiring content area concepts as well as developing English language skills (Echevarria & Graves, 1998).

The following issues in the education of CLD students with learning disabilities should be considered:

- Special educators must address the cognitive and language needs of English language learners who have learning disabilities.
- Instruction, including ESL teaching, may need to be more explicit for students with learning disabilities since they tend not to learn incidentally.
- Instruction must be meaningful and relevant to students' cultural and educational experiences.
- Learning environments must be culturally responsive, accommodating the learning needs of culturally diverse learners.
- Assessing whether students acquired the academic concepts and language development objectives of lessons is essential. This can be done by establishing relevant goals, carefully analyzing and documenting the

student's progress, or reteaching the lesson, based on the needs of the student.
- Modifications may include adapting the curriculum, using visuals to accompany oral presentation of information, and embedding activities in meaningful experiences that are linguistically and educationally rich.

Finally, special educators and paraprofessionals working with students with learning disabilities often are overlooked or excluded from general education professional development sessions that deal with culturally and linguistically diverse students. Special educators and paraprofessionals must be trained in current instructional practices in working with CLD students. Moreover, little interface occurs between special educators and those professionals who have expertise in working with CLD students (Gersten & Woodward, 1994). The focus needs to be on meeting the individual student's needs, not on purview. Increased communication and collaboration between programs and service providers, as well as support from administrators, would alleviate some of the issues relative to educating CLD students with learning disabilities.

REFERENCES

Echevarria, J., & Graves, A. (1998). *Sheltered content instruction: Teaching English-language learners with diverse abilities.* Boston: Allyn & Bacon.

Gersten, R., & Woodward, J. (1974). The language minority student and special education: Issues, trends and paradoxes. *Exceptional Children, 60*(4), 310-322.

Mercer, J., & Rueda, R. (1991, November). *The impact of changing paradigms of disabilities on assessment of special education.* Paper presented at the Council for Exceptional Children Topical Conference on At-Risk Children & Youth, New Orleans.

JANA ECHEVARRIA
AMITA EDRAN
*California State University
at Long Beach*

DISPROPORTIONALITY
LEARNING DISABILITIES

CULTURALLY/LINGUISTICALLY DIVERSE GIFTED STUDENTS

The immortal words of Harry Passow (1986) express concerns for the exclusion of various cultural and linguistic populations in gifted education programs:

> . . . these populations constitute the largest reservoir of untapped and underdeveloped talent available in our society. There is clear evidence that talent is not the prerogative of any racial or ethnic group, any social class, or any residential area.

It may lie untapped in some situations under some conditions, but no population has either a monopoly or an absence of giftedness. (p. 27)

The fact is that students with special gifts and talents come from all populations, and as society becomes increasingly diverse, educators are faced with a challenge in meeting the needs of students who have special gifts from all populations represented in society. However, government and media reports indicate that educators are not effectively identifying and serving minority students, particularly those who are either considered limited English proficient, or those who are from low socioeconomic status (SES) backgrounds and/or from other cultures out of the mainstream middle-class Anglo American culture. In fact, these groups are not fairly represented in programs for the gifted and talented (Irby, 1993; Ortiz & González, 1989; USDE, 1993).

In the early 1970s, the term culturally different was used to refer to children who were from low SES backgrounds and/or who were not members of the hegemonous society; however, in the later part of that decade, the term culturally diverse began to be used (Frasier, 1977). Zuke (1983) defined culturally diverse gifted children as those "who by reason of cultural identification and socioeconomic status have not been able to assimilate themselves into the dominant culture"; assimilation was a key term used in this definition. Later, Sheehy (1986) and Goffin (1988) suggested that cultural diversity is evidenced through any of an individual's traditional customs and sex-role behaviors that are different from those observed in the mainstream culture. Additionally, cultural differences may be found in learning styles, listening behaviors (Trueba, 1983), response patterns (Harris, 1988; Cohen, 1988) that are typically associated with mainstream giftedness.

Because cultural diversity, it has been defined, is closely associated with the language(s) one speaks, (García, 1994; Lara-Alecio & Irby, 1996), it is difficult to view cultural diversity apart from linguistic diversity when identifying and serving the gifted student. Linguistically and culturally diverse gifted students must then be defined within their own socio-linguistic-cultural context. Typically, school district personnel base definitions on the mainstream, Anglo middle-class gifted student, without taking into consideration cultural and linguistic diversity (Cohen, 1988; Bermúdez & Rakow, 1990). Borrowing from Renzulli's (1986) original definition of giftedness, a simple definition of the linguistically and culturally diverse gifted could be individuals who possess above average intelligence, task commitment, and creativity, with these three components being viewed solely within the individual's socio-linguistic-cultural context (Lara-Alecio & Irby, 1993). Other definitions, such as the multiple intelligence model promoted by Gardner (1983) may be applied, but all must be set within the same socio-linguistic-cultural context. Definitions of giftedness must be far more inclusive than they currently are, and far more adapted to a society defined by cultural and linguistic diversity.

There are a number of reasons that have been posed for the inequities in services provided to culturally and linguistically diverse gifted student populations. The challenge of providing appropriate services is particularly complex when native language and culture are conflicting with the child's new cultural and language environment. The exclusion of the culturally and linguistically diverse groups of underidentified and underserved children in programs for the gifted has at least three main implications. First, such exclusion sends a negative message to underrepresented populations and implies that they are somehow less able than those in mainstream populations. Many teachers hold opinions that there are just no gifted minorities, or that minority children are in need of academic, remediation, particularly those who are limited English proficient (Davis & Rimm, 1989). Additionally, when teachers equate giftedness with an IQ score of 130 (García, 1994), it further denigrates the diverse child's true abilities. Being fluent in English does not mean that the child has the same cultural experiences as the mainstream child; thus, identifying a limited English proficient child with standardized test scores based on majority culture may not be valid (González, Bauerie, & Félix-Holt, 1994).

Because of the misunderstandings among educators regarding this population (García, 1994), and furthermore, because Borland and Wright (1994) suggested that the potential for giftedness is present in roughly equal proportions in all groups of our society, there is a need to develop valid and reliable methods of screening and identifying culturally and linguistically diverse potentially gifted students (Irby, Hernandez, Torres, & González, 1997). Additionally, with increasing reliance on nominations from teachers who are guided by a checklist of behaviors commonly attributed to exceptional children (Strom, Johnson, Strom, & Strom, 1992), it becomes important for teachers to have valid, defining characteristics with which to screen culturally and linguistically diverse populations.

Several formal instruments or techniques for identifying potentially gifted individuals who are culturally and linguistically diverse have surfaced over the past two decades and include the child's cultural context. Among those are the Baldwin Matrix (Baldwin, 1977), the System of Multicultural Pluralistic Assessment (SOMPA; Mercer & Lewis, 1978), Kranz Talent Identification Instrument (KTII; Kranz, 1981), the Structure of the Intellect Test (Meeker, 1985), Torrance Tests of Creative Thinking (Solomon, 1974; Torrance, 1970; Torrance, 1977), Group Inventory for Finding Talent (Rimm, 1976), and Fraiser's Talent Assessment Profile (1990). For screening purposes, the Hispanic Bilingual Gifted Screening Instrument (Irby & Lara-Alecio, 1996) is under development and has been specifically designed for Hispanic linguistically and culturally diverse students (Irby, Hernandez, González, & Torres, 1997). Eleven characteristic aspects of gifted students have been determined to be significant for identifying potential within the population of diverse students: Motivation for Learning, Social and Academic Language, Cultural Sensitivity, Familial, Collaboration, Imagery, Achievement, Creative Performance, Support, Problem Solving, and Locus of Control (Lara-Alecio, Irby, & Walker, 1997).

A second implication for the culturally and linguistically diverse populations' underrepresentation in gifted programs is that the very exclusion of these groups is contradictory to the American principles of egalitarianism (Gintis, 1988). The task of providing equitable services for the gifted is made more difficult by the lack of uniformity in objective identification procedures and in appropriate needs-based curriculum services. Uniformity does not preclude the use of a multi-dimensional approach to identification of giftedness (Frasier, 1992; Irby & Lara-Alecio, 1997; Kitano, 1991; Maker & Schiever, 1989; Zappia, 1989). Furthermore, a study conducted by Irby, Henderson, and Berry (1992) determined that in many cases there was little or no match between the programmatic services being provided and a district's plan of gifted identification.

The third implication is that practitioners must learn how to change the programmatic services and/or the identification plans that merge at a point that respond to their particular populations within their communities. Curriculum cannot be discussed or developed in isolation to the definition of giftedness and identification of the particular cultural and language minority group. Currently there is a sufficient amount of theoretical claims regarding who these children are and what type of curricular programming they need, but there is little empirical data to support these claims (Zappia, 1989; Frasier, 1978; Irby & Lara-Alecio, 1993), and few teachers are trained at a level to make data-based decisions regarding the program structure for the culturally and linguistically diverse gifted child (Ford & Harris, 1990).

In summary, there are several principles that may be followed to improve the numbers of culturally and linguistically diverse students served in gifted education programs.

1. The definition used in the school district should be inclusive Renzulli (1986) noted that the definition of giftedness must be based on research about characteristics of gifted individuals; in this case, those individuals would be representative the diverse group to be served. Furthermore, researchers should identify ecological characteristics of the diverse group.

2. Definitions should be connected to the identification procedures and those identification procedures should be diverse (Fraiser, 1990). Look for the diversity.

3. Identification procedures should be multifaceted or multidimensional, including objective and subjective data. Data should also be gathered from those who know the child on a personal/cultural level (Frasier, 1990). Additionally, the instruments used should be based on sociocultural and linguistic characteristics of the referent population; seek out valid and reliable instruments in the child's native language or use nonverbal measures.

4. Implement an identification program early that includes a screening phase, an evaluation phase, and a recommendation phase (Frasier, 1990).

5. Make sure that all relevant information on a student has been reviewed prior to making a decision (Frasier, 1990).

6. Train teachers in general and specific diverse population characteristics of giftedness (Lara-Alecio & Irby, 1993; Rogers, 1986). Use a send-in model with the teacher of the gifted—send them into the classrooms and have them observe functional levels of children within the classroom on various types of activities. When observing, have them focus on products and performance. Additionally, have the teacher solicit products and performances demonstrated away from school.

7. Program options must match district definitions and identification procedures (Frasier, 1990; Lara-Alecio & Irby, 1993). The best learning environment should be provided for the student (Frasier, 1990).

8. Bilingual/bicultural instruction should be provided in early programming, in particular, which suggests a two-way bilingual campus program. Trained bilingual, biliterate, and bicultural teachers are needed for the gifted program (Lara-Alecio, & Irby, 1993). Curriculum for the general education program should have a multicultural perspective, which would urge educators to modify their opinions regarding cultural diversity (Kitano, 1991).

9. Include staff development for mainstream and gifted education teachers with a suggested model that includes workshops on research in this field, exploration of negative myths about the culturally and linguistically diverse, how to develop supportive environments, how to help alter attitudes about specific diverse populations, and how to utilize bilingualism in the classroom.

10. Come to a point of viewing cultural and linguistic diversity as an asset, not as a liability or as a need for remediation. Educators need to celebrate differences and develop a secure communicative environment in which the diverse gifted can thrive.

REFERENCES

Baldwin, A. Y. (1977). *Baldwin identification matrix inservice kit for the identification of gifted & talented students*. East Aurora, NY: Trillium.

Bermúdez, A., & Rakow, S. (1993). Analyzing teachers' perception of identification procedures for gifted & talented Hispanic limited English proficient students at risk. *The Journal of Educational Issues of Language Minority Students, 7,* 21–31.

Borland, J. H., & Wright, L. (1994). Identifying young, potentially gifted, economically disadvantaged students. *Gifted Child Quarterly, 38,* 164–171.

Cohen, M. (1988). Immigrant children need aid, study says. *The Boston Globe,* p. 25.

Davis, G., & Rimm, S. (1989). *Education of the gifted & talented* (2nd ed.). Englewood Clifs, NJ: Prentice Hall.

Ford, D. Y., & Harris, J. J. (1990). On discovering the hidden treasure of gifted and talented African American children. *Roeper Review, 13*(1), 27–37.

Frasier, M. (1977). Help for organizing productive experience (HOPE) for the culturally diverse gifted & talented. Reston, VA: Council for Exceptional Children. (ERIC Document Reproduction Service No. ED 141 981 & EC 101 227)

Frasier, M. (1978). Culturally different gifted/talented: Educational implications: Cognitive. In H. N. Rivlin (Ed.), Advantage: Disadvantaged gifted. Presentations from the Third National Conference on Disadvantaged Gifted (53–57). Ventura, CA: Ventura County Superintendent of Schools Office.

Frasier, M. (1990). *Frasier's Talent Assessment Profile*. Athens, GA: University of Georgia.

Frasier, M. (1992). Ethnic/minority children: Reflections & directions.

Gardner, H. (1983). *Frames of mind: The theory of multiple intelligences*. New York: Basic.

García, J. H. (1994). Nonstandardized instruments for the assessment of Mexican-American children for gifted/talented programs. In S. H. García (Ed.), *Addressing cultural & linguistic diversity in special education: Issues & trends*. Reston, VA: Council for Exceptional Children.

García, E. (1994). Understating & meeting the challenge of student cultural diversity. Boston: Houghton Mifflin.

Gintis, H. (1988). Education, personal development, & the human dignity. In H. Holtz et al. (Eds.), Education & the American dream. Conservatives, liberals & radicals debate the future education. Greenwood: Berging & Garrey.

Goffin, G. (1988). Putting our advocacy efforts into a new context. *The Journal of the National Association for the Education of Young Children, 43*(3), 52–56.

González V., Bauerie, P., & Félix-Holt, M. (1994). A qualitative assessment method for accurately diagnosing bilingual gifted children. In L. M. Malave (Ed.), *National Association for Bilingual Education*.

Harris, R. (1988). *Cultural conflict & patterns of achievement in gifted Asian-Pacific children*. Paper presented at the meeting of the National Association for Asian & Pacific American Education.

Irby, B. "Hispanic LEP Gifted Students." Education Week. May 1993.

Irby, B., Hernández, L., Torres, D., & González, C. The correlation between teacher perceptions of giftedness & the Hispanic bilingual screening instrument. Unpublished manuscript, Sam Houston State University.

Irby, B., Henderson, D., & Berry, K. (1992). State of gifted education in Texas. An unpublished manuscript submitted to the Texas Association of Gifted & Talented for a Grants in Excellence project. Huntsville, TX: Sam Houston State University.

Irby, B. & Lara-Alecio, R. (1997). Attributes of Hispanic gifted bilingual students as perceived by bilingual educators in Texas. *NYSABE Journal, 11,* 120–142.

Kitano, M. K. (1991). A multicultural education perspective on serving the culturally diverse gifted. *Journal for the Education of the Gifted, 15*(1), 4–19.

Kranz, B. (1981). *Kranz talent identification instrument*. Moorhead, MN: Moorhead State College.

Lara-Alecio, R., & Irby, B. (1993). Reforming identification procedures for the bilingual gifted child. Paper presented at BEAM, The Ninth Annual Bilingual/ESL Spring Conference, Denton, TX.

Lara-Alecio, R. & Irby. B. (1996). Bilingual education & multicultural education: An inclusively oriented educational delivery System. *The Journal of Educational Issues of Language Minority Students, 17,* 11–24.

Maker, C. J., & Scheiver, S. W. (Eds.). (1989). *Critical issues in gifted education: Defensible programs for cultural & ethnic minorities*. Austin, TX: Pro-Ed.

Mercer, J. R., & Lewis, J. F. (1978). Using the system of multicultural pluralistic assessment. (SOMPA) to identify the gifted minority child. In A. Y. Baldwin, G. H. Gear, & L. J. Lucito (Eds.), *Educational planning for the gifted* (pp. 7–14). Reston, VA: Council for Exceptional Children.

Meeker, M. N., Meeker, R., & Roid, G. (1985). Structure-of-intellect learning abilities test (SOI-LA). Los Angeles: Western Psychological Services.

Ortíz, V., & González, A. (1989). Validation of a short form of the WISC-R with accelerated & gifted Hispanic students. *Gifted Child Quarterly, 33,* 152–155.

Passow, H. *Educational programs for minority/disadvantaged gifted students*. Paper prepared for presentation in the Distinguished Lecture Series of the San Diego Unified School District, California, February 6, 1986.

Renzulli, J. S. (1986). The three-ring conception of giftedness: A developmental model for creative productivity. In R. J. Sternberg & J. E. Davidson (Eds.), *Conception of Giftedness*. Cambridge, MA: Cambridge University Press.

Rimm, S. B. (1976). *GIFT: Group Inventory for Finding Creative Talent*. Watertown, WI: Educational Assessment Service.

Rogers, K. (1986). *Review of research on the education of intellectually & academically gifted students*. Minnesota State Department of Education, St. Paul.

Strom, R., Johnson, A., Strom, S., & Strom, P. (1992). *Educating gifted children: Genetic studies of genius* (Vol. 1). Stanford CA: Stanford University Press.

Sheehy, G. (1986). *Spirit of survival*. New York: Bantam.

Torrance, E. P. (1970). *Encouraging creativity in the classroom*. Dubuque, IA: William C. Brown.

Torrance, E. P. (1997). *Discovery & nurturance of giftedness in the culturally different*. Reston: VA: Council for Exceptional Children.

Trueba, H. (1983). Adjustment problems of Mexican & Mexican-American students. An anthropological study. *Learning Disability Quarterly, 6*(4), 395–415.

U.S. Department of Education, Office of Educational Research & Improvement. (1993). *National excellence: A case for developing America's talented*. Washington, DC: U.S. Government Printing Office.

Zappia, I. A. (1989). Identification of gifted Hispanic students: A multidimensional view. In C. J. Maker & S. W. Schiever (Eds.), *Critical issues in gifted education, Vol. 2: Defensible programs for cultural & ethnic minorities* (pp. 19–26). Austin, TX: Pro-Ed.

Zuke, M. (1983). *Building bridges for culturally diverse gifted students*. (ERIC Document Reproduction Service No. ED 234570)

RAFAEL LARA-ALECIO
Texas A & M University

BEVERLY J. IRBY
Sam Houston State University

CREATIVITY
DISPROPORTIONALITY
GIFTED AND TALENTED CHILDREN
GIFTED HANDICAPPED

CULTURALLY AND LINGUISTICALLY DIVERSE STUDENTS IN SPECIAL EDUCATION, FAMILIES OF

School involvement by culturally and linguistically diverse families of children with disabilities should be seen in the context of the way parental roles have been conceptualized by professionals over the past three decades (for a comprehensive review, see Turnbull & Turnbull, 1996). Prior to the 1970s, the emphasis was on psychoanalytic approaches that (a) promoted a pathological view of families of children with disabilities, presenting the mother as victim or patient in severe psychological crisis, and (b) completely omitted the impact of differential cultural beliefs and practices on family reactions. The early seventies saw the advent of the "parent as teacher" approach, which sought to promote positive parental involvement through behavioral training programs, based predominantly on the childrearing practices and personal interaction styles prevalent among White, middle-class families. While some professionals failed to recognize or give credence to non-mainstream family patterns and practices, others interpreted parenting patterns that deviated from the mainstream as evidence of "deprivation" of culture.

The advent of PL 99-142 in 1975 brought into focus the ideal of the parent as collaborator with professionals. This concept of parent participation was based on the model of the middle-class advocate who would participate in formal conferences and, if necessary, draw on the availability of due process of law. Early studies of parent participation revealed that the advocacy role expected of parents was an ideal very difficult to achieve, even for middle-class parents. For low-income and minority parents, the challenge has been even more difficult.

The first direct attention to adaptations that might be needed for particular minority groups to participate effectively in the IEP process came from Marion (1979). Marion advocated adaptations that ought to have been considered basic requirements for interactions with all families, such as a personalized approach, respectful verbal and nonverbal interactions, simplification of educational jargon, and full, comprehensible explanation of rights, procedures, and test results. Overall, Marion's main point was that poor and minority parents stood at a disadvantage in terms of the stigma that had traditionally been attached to their ethnicity, culture, and social status, and that careless, even disrespectful, treatment of such parents was common. Marion's concerns have been echoed by researchers who studied the perceptions and experiences of families from various cultural backgrounds, such as American Indians (Connery, 1987), Chinese Americans (Smith & Ryan, 1987; Tran, 1982; Trueba, Jacobs, & Kirton, 1990), Mexican Americans (Lynch & Stein, 1987), African Americans (Harry, Allen, & McLaughlin, 1995; Patton & Braithwaite, 1984; Tomlinson, Acker, Canter, & Lindborg, 1977), Puerto Rican Americans (Harry, 1992) and a mixed nationality Hispanic group (Bennett, 1988). Other researchers have pointed to culturally based differences in interaction styles and levels of information, which tend to serve as barriers to effective parent-professional communication (Chan, 1986; Correa, 1989; Cunningham, Cunningham, & O'Connell, 1987; Harry, 1992; Leung, 1988; Sontag & Schact, 1994; Tran, 1982; Zetlin, Padron, & Wilson, 1996). Studies show that low levels of parental awareness of available services and their perceptions of their eligibility for such services are highly correlated with low income and geographic location (Huang & Van Horne, 1995; Sontag & Schact, 1994). Further, school personnel's strong identification with the culture of professionalism tends to dominate their interactions with parents (Bailey et al., 1992; Katz & Scarpatti, 1995, contributing to a "we-they posture by which parents are seen as adversaries rather than allies" (Harry, Allen, & McLaughlin, 1995, p. 374). Parental participation may also be negatively affected by differing cultural constructions of disability and developmental norms (Barnwell & Day, 1996; Harry & Kalyanpur, 1994). These differences often affect parental understanding of the assessment and diagnosis process as well as the setting of educational goals for students (Linan-Thompson &

Jean, 1997). With regard to more severe disabilities, cross-cultural studies indicate unequivocally that while all groups recognize gross developmental, behavioral, or sensory impairments, the attributions for their etiology or importance differ widely, as do the extent of the stigma or value attached to the condition (Fadiman, 1997; Scheer & Groce, 1988;). For children with milder disabilities, research reveals that culture and acculturation are strong predictors of parental expectations of children's cognitive and social development (Goodnow, Cashmore, Cotton, & Knight, 1984; Hess, Kashigawi, Azuma, Price, & Dickson, 1980; Quirk et al., 1986; Rosenthal, 1985). These variances in parental beliefs on children's development have implications for the classification of children as "mildly retarded," "behavior disordered," or "learning disabled." Studies show that many culturally diverse parents hold broader parameters of normalcy than allowed by the school-based evaluations by which children are classified (Harry, 1992; Harry, Allen, & McLaughlin, 1995).

In summary, attempts to examine parent participation among ethnic minorities reveal the following patterns: (a) lower levels of involvement than White counterparts, (b) lower awareness of procedures, rights, and services, (c) expressed sense of isolation and low self-confidence in dealing with professionals, (d) stressful life circumstances and lack of logistical supports such as transportation, child care, and respite, (e) culturally-based assumptions of deference to, and/or mistrust of school personnel, (f) professionals' implicit or explicit discouragement of parents' participation in the special education process, and (g) culturally-based dissonance between parental and professional understandings of the meanings and importance of disabilities.

Since the mid-1980s, because of PL 99-457, the ideal of parent participation has evolved into a vision of family-centered practice with issues of diverse family beliefs and practices becoming a crucial focus in the effort to address the problems listed above. Family-centered practice revolves around the concept of family empowerment, or the process of helping families increase control over their lives and take action to get what they want. Empowerment occurs when professionals (a) give families information about services and their rights; (b) facilitate their participation; for instance, by arranging transportation and/or childcare and scheduling meetings at times convenient to parents; and (c) develop collaborative relationships with families by affirming and building on family strengths, honoring cultural diversity, creative and cooperative problem-solving, and establishing trust and respect (Dunst & Trivette, 1987; Lynch & Hanson, 1992; Salend & Taylor, 1993; Turnbull & Turnbull, 1996). Evidence for the continuing centrality of this ideal is the 1997 re-authorization of IDEA. This current focus has generated the need for reconceptualizing culture—whether it is perceived as a static or discrete phenomenon—in order to prevent families from being presented in stereotypic ways. The original notion of culture as a process of stages (for instance, from traditional to bicultural to assimilation) through which individuals from minority groups might move, has gradually been superceded by a less discrete view of culture where boundaries are variable according to different dimensions of individual identity, thus acknowledging that an individual may assume multiple group memberships simultaneously (Banks & Banks, 1992).

This definition has also provided a need for context, which brings the focus of study to the precise realm of the individual family, rather than assuming that a generalized concept of the family's cultural tradition will be adequate. By applying Bronfenbrenner's theory of nested systems and Vygotsky's concept of the zone of proximal development, all development is seen as being based in participation in specific social and cultural settings or an individual's "ecocultural niche" (Tharp & Gallimore, 1988), combining the family's ecology and culture. This perspective takes into account more than just the ethnic status of the family by including contextual variables, such as education, acculturation, socioeconomic status, or geographic location, and the effects of these on the daily routines of families to describe a family in all its individuality, as opposed to generalizations about what a family from "this" or "that" cultural group would be expected to look like. The importance of examining contextual influences to avoid cultural stereotypes is well-illustrated, for instance, by Mardiros' (1989) study of Mexican-American parents which demonstrated that parents from a relatively homogenous cultural group, who held similar beliefs regarding the causation of a disability, still displayed a range of responses, some very proactive and creative, others passive and resigned. Similarly, Harry, Allen, & McLaughlin (1995) offer evidence of effective single parenting when they note that the six "living alone" mothers were the most proactive advocates in a sample of 24 African American families of preschoolers with mild disabilities.

Several writers have identified strategies that specifically accommodate this new concept of contextualized culture toward increasing the participation of culturally and linguistically diverse parents in the special education process.

1. Developing self-awareness as a first step towards understanding one's personal and professional values (Caple, Salsido, & di Cecco, 1995). This can involve examining genealogical records and asking oneself questions like "When I was growing up, what did my family say about people from different cultures?" (Hyun & Fowler, 1995), or "Why do I want 21-year-old Husain to move into a group home?" to recognize the cultural value that underlies one's professional recommendation (Kalyanpur & Harry, 1997).

2. Engaging in conversations with families to learn about their culture and values. This involves using naturalistic means for collecting information about families' situations, including open-ended interviewing (Harry, 1992), and identifying and involving key and/or extended members of the family (Linan-Thompson & Jean, 1997). Professionals should identify and accommodate the family's preferred method of communication, whether written or verbal, English or native language (Barnwell & Day, 1996); make time to listen to parents' stories (Caple, Salsido, & di Cecco, 1995; Kalyanpur & Rao, 1991; Thorp, 1997); and respect their input in the decision-making process (Correa, 1987; Harry, 1992).

3. Making available services and professional recommendations that are compatible with families' values. This involves working with the family to identify their resources and supports and modifying service options or developing creative, individualized alternatives (Correa, 1989; Harry, 1992; Rueda & Martinez, 1994). Comer and Haynes (1991) describe the successful efforts of the Yale Child Study Center Team to "change the ecology of a school" and empower low-income parents by improving parental status and meaningful collaboration between parents and professionals in special education. The program contained three mechanisms for change: a governance mechanism, the school planning and management team, that represented all the adult stakeholders in the school to develop a plan for restructuring the school; a mental health team to address the developmental and behavioral needs of students; and a parent program which focused on supporting the social program of the school restructuring plan and on the academic program as needed. The parent program created social occasions for families and professionals to meet, developing a sense of community, and encouraged parent volunteers to participate in a broad range of school activities from helping in classrooms to participation on the school planning and management team. The authors attribute the success of the entire program to allowing parents to participate in the way they were comfortable and effective and to play meaningful roles, with staff support, with a clear direction and purpose. Unfortunately, efforts to replicate this model have not been as successful in involving special education teachers and parents (Ware, 1994).

In conclusion, school involvement by families from culturally and linguistically diverse backgrounds continues to be problematic. However, parental participation can be enhanced when professionals use naturalistic collection of information about families' situations in order to find out where a family stands on a given issue, are aware of their own cultural influence in the decision-making process, and are committed to flexibility and responsiveness to the need for change.

REFERENCES

Bailey, D. B., Jr., Buysse, V., Edmondson, R., & Smith, T. (1992). Creating family-centered services in early intervention: Perceptions of professionals in four states. *Exceptional Children, 58,* 298–309.

Banks, J., & Banks, C. A. (1992). *Multicultural education: Issues and perspectives* (2nd ed.). Boston: Allyn & Bacon.

Barnwell, D. A., & Day, M. (1996). Providing support to diverse families. In P. J. Beckman (Ed.), *Strategies for working with families of young children with disabilities* (pp. 47–68). Baltimore: Brookes.

Bennett, A. T. (1988). Gateways to powerlessness: Incorporating Hispanic deaf children and families into formal schooling. *Disability, Handicap & Society, 3,* 119–151.

Caple, F. S., Salsido, R. M. & di Cecco, J. (1995). Engaging effectively with culturally diverse families and children. *Social Work in Education, 17*(3), 159–170.

Chan, S. (1986). Parents of exceptional Asian children. In M. K. Kitano & P. C. Chinn (Eds.), *Exceptional Asian children and youth* (pp. 36–53). Reston, VA: Council for Exceptional Children.

Comer, J. P. & Haynes, N. M. (1991). Parent involvement in schools: An ecological approach. *The Elementary School Journal, 91*(3), 271–277.

Connery, A. R. (1987). *A description and comparison of Native American and Anglo parents' knowledge of their handicapped children's rights.* Doctoral dissertation, Northern Arizona University.

Correa, V. I. (1989). Involving culturally diverse families in the educational process. In S. H. Fradd & M. J. Weismantel (Eds.), *Meeting the needs of culturally and linguistically different students: A handbook for educators* (pp. 130–144). Boston: College-Hill.

Cunningham, K., Cunningham, K., & O'Connell, J. C. (1987). Impact of differing cultural perceptions on special education service delivery. *Rural Special Education Quarterly, 8*(1), 2–8.

Dunst, C. J., & Trivette, C. M. (1987). Enabling and empowering families: Conceptual and intervention issues. *School Psychology Review, 16,* 443–456.

Fadiman, A. (1997). *The spirit catches you and you fall down: A Hmong child, her American doctors, and the collision of two cultures.* New York: Farrar, Strauss and Giroux.

Goodnow, J. J., Cashmore, J., Cotton, S., & Knight, R. (1984). Mothers' developmental timetables in two cultural groups. *International Journal of Psychology, 19,* 193–205.

Harry, B. (1992). *Cultural diversity, families, and the special education system: Communication and empowerment.* New York: Teachers College.

Harry, B. & Kalyanpur, M. (1994). The cultural underpinnings of special education: Implications for professional interactions with culturally diverse families. *Disability & Society, 9*(2), 145–165.

Harry, B., Allen, N., & McLaughlin, M. (1995). Communication versus compliance: African American parents' involvement in special education. *Exceptional Children, 61*(4), 364–377.

Hess, R. D., Kashigawi, K., Azuma, H., Price, G. G. & Dickson, W. P. (1980). Maternal expectations for the mastery of developmental tasks in Japan and the United States. *International Journal of Psychology, 15,* 259–271.

Huang, G. G., & Van Horn, P. (1995). Using child care services: Families with disabled children in nonmetropolitan areas. *Rural Special Education Quarterly, 14*(4), 27–36.

Hyun, J. K., & Fowler, S. A. (1995). Respect, cultural sensitivity, and communication: Promoting participation by Asian families in the Individualized Family Service Plan. *Teaching Exceptional Children, 28*(1), 25–28.

Kalyanpur, M. & Harry, B. (1997). A posture of reciprocity: A practical approach to collaboration between professionals and parents of culturally diverse backgrounds. *Journal of Child and Family Studies, 6*(4), 485–509.

Kalyanpur, M. & Rao, S. S. (1991). Empowering low-income, black families of handicapped children. *American Journal of Orthopsychiatry, 61,* 523–532.

Katz, L., & Scarpati, S. (1995). A cultural interpretation of early intervention teams and the IFSP: Parent and professional perceptions of roles and responsibilities. *The Transdisciplinary Journal, 5*(2), 177–192.

Leung, E. K. (1988). Cultural and acculturational commonalties and diversities among Asian Americans: Identification and programming considerations. In A. A. Ortiz & B. A. Ramirez (Eds.), *Schools and the culturally diverse student* (pp. 86–95). Reston, VA: ERIC.

Linan-Thompson, S. & Jean, R. E. (1997). Completing the parent participation puzzle: Accepting diversity. *Teaching Exceptional Children, 52*(6), 46–50.

Lynch, E. W. & Hanson, M. J. (1992). *Developing cross-cultural competence: A guide for working with young children and their families.* Baltimore: Brookes.

Lynch, E. W., & Stein, R. (1987). Parent participation by ethnicity: A comparison of Hispanic, Black, and Anglo families. *Exceptional Children, 54,* 105–11.

Mardiros, M. (1989). Conception of childhood disability among Mexican-American parents. *Medical Anthropology, 12,* 55–68.

Marion, R. (1979). Minority parent involvement in the IEP process: A systematic model approach. *Focus on Exceptional Children, 10*(8), 1–16.

Patton, J. M., & Braithwaite, R. L. (1984, August). Obstacles to the participation of Black parents in the educational programs of their handicapped children. *Centering Teacher Education,* 34–37.

Quirk, M., Ciottone, R., Minami, J., Wapner, S., Yamamoto, S., Ishii, S., Lucca-Irizarry, C., & Pacheco, A. (1986). Values mothers hold for handicapped and nonhandicapped preschool children in Japan, Puerto Rico, and the United States Mainland. *International Journal of Psychology, 21,* 463–485.

Rosenthal, D. (1985, July). *Child-rearing and cultural values: A study of Greek and Australian mothers.* Paper presented at the meeting of the International Society for the Study of Behavioural Development, Tours, France.

Rueda, R. & Martinez, I (1994). Fiesta educativa: One commu-
nity's approach to parent training in developmental disabilities for Latino families. *JASH, 17*(2), 95–103.

Salend, S. J. & Taylor, L. (1993). Working with families: A cross-cultural perspective. *Remedial and Special Education, 14*(5), 25–32.

Scheer, J. & Groce, N. (1988). *Impairment as a human constant: Cross-cultural and historical perspectives on variation. Journal of Social Issues, 44*(1), 23–37.

Smith, M. J., & Ryan, A. S. (1987). Chinese-American families of children with developmental disabilities: An exploratory study of reactions to service providers. *Mental Retardation, 25*(6), 345–350.

Sontag, J. C., & Schacht, R. (1994). An ethnic comparison of parent participation and information needs in early intervention. *Exceptional Children, 60*(5), 422–433.

Tharp, R. G. & Gallimore, R. (1988). *Rousing minds to life: Teaching, learning and schooling in social context.* Cambridge, MA: Cambridge University Press.

Thorp, E. K. (1997). Increasing opportunities for partnership with culturally and linguistically diverse families. *Intervention in School and Clinic, 32*(5), 261–269.

Tomlinson, J. R., Acker, N., Canter, A., & Lindborg, S. (1977). Minority status, sex and school psychological services. *Psychology in the Schools, 14*(4), 456–460.

Tran, X. C. (1982). *The factors hindering Indochinese parent participation in school activities.* San Diego, CA: San Diego State University, Institute for Cultural Pluralism. (ERIC Document Reproduction Service No. ED 245-018)

Trueba, H., Jacobs, L. & Kirton, E. (1990). *Cultural conflict and adaptation: The case of Hmong children in American society.* New York: Falmer Press.

Turnbull, A. P. & Turnbull, H. R. (1997). *Families, professionals, and exceptionality: A special partnership* (3rd ed.). Upper Saddle River, NJ: Merrill.

Ware, L. P. (1994). Contextual barriers to collaboration. *Journal of Educational and Psychological Consultation, 5*(4), 339–357.

Zetlin, A., Padron, M., & Wilson, S. (1996). The experience of five Latin American families with the special education system. *Education and Training in Mental Retardation and Developmental Disabilities, 31,* 22–28.

BETH HARRY
University of Miami

MAYA KALYANPUR
Towson University

FAMILY COUNSELING

CULTURALLY/LINGUISTICALLY DIVERSE STUDENTS, REPRESENTATION OF

Special educators have debated for decades about the disproportionate representation of ethnic and linguistic minority students in special and gifted education programs. This phenomenon refers to unequal proportions of culturally diverse students in these special programs. Two patterns are associated with disproportionality, namely over- and underrepresentation of minority students. The former tends to occur in special education; specifically, in the mild disability categories—i.e., mild mental retardation (MMR), specific learning disabilities (SLD), and serious emotional disturbances (SED). Underrepresentation is generally observed in programs for students with gifts and talents (G&T). Historically, certain ethnic minority groups (particularly African American) and poor and male students have been most affected by disproportionality.

Litigation (particularly placement bias cases) has been at the center of disproportionality discussions. For instance, some of the most important rulings in *Diana v. California Board of Education* (1970) and *Larry P. v. Riles* (1979) (which involved Latino and African American students respectively) included (a) intelligence tests were culturally and linguistically biased, (b) biased assessment resulted in the overrepresentation of Latino and African American students in MMR programs, (c) alternative procedures were needed to assess students' abilities (e.g., nonverbal tests, assessment in native language), and (d) many students needed to be retested and reclassified. These cases were very influential in the passage of federal legislation designed to protect the rights of individuals with disabilities, specifically in the inclusion of a requirement that identification and assessment procedures must be nondiscriminatory.

Although disproportionality patterns persisted throughout the 1970s and 1980s (Artiles & Trent, 1994), it was not until the 14th Report that the U.S. Department of Education (USDOE) provided enrollment data in disability programs by ethnic group. Interestingly, disproportionate representation has received more attention in the 1990s. For instance, the USDOE recently authorized the National Academy of Sciences to conduct a study on disproportionality (B. Ford, pers. comm., November 1997). It is ironic that this interest has emerged at a time when societal attitudes toward culturally diverse people are hostile and intolerant; two compelling examples being the anti-immigrant and the anti-Affirmative Action discourse, litigation, and policymaking.

Disproportionality: Patterns and Caveats

Formulas to estimate disproportionality typically aim to answer two questions: (a) "What proportion of students in a special education program is [say, Black]?" and (b) "What percent of the [Black] population is placed in a special education program?" (Reschly, 1997). The former is called the percent of program by group, and is calculated by contrasting the proportion of a particular ethnic group in the general education student population with the percentage of the same group of students enrolled in a special education program. The latter question is concerned with the percent of group in program. This figure is obtained by calculating the percent of, say, the Latino population that is enrolled in a special education program.

The percent of program by group is usually larger than the percent of group in program. To illustrate, Table 1 presents national enrollment data using both formulas on three ethnic groups at four points in time. These data suggest that Black students are overrepresented in MR and SED programs whereas Latinos are not overrepresented in any of the mild disability categories. A closer look at the total percent of ethnic group in mild disability program data presented in the B columns suggests that the difference between Black and White students with mild disabilities

Table 1. Percent of Mild Disability Program by Ethnic Group (A) and Percent of Ethnic Group in Mild Disability Program (B), 1986–1994

	1986[a]						1990[b]						1992[c]					
	Black (16)*		Latino (10)		White (70)		Black (16)		Latino (12)		White (68)		Black (16)		Latino (12)		White (67)	
	A	B	A	B	A	B	A	B	A	B	A	B	A	B	A	B	A	B
MMR**	35	2.30	5	0.56	58	0.87	35	2.10	8	0.65	56	0.81	32	1.62	5	0.39	61	0.75
SLD	17	4.43	10	4.31	71	4.29	17	4.95	11	4.68	70	4.97	18	5.79	12	5.29	68	5.32
SED	27	1.04	7	0.46	65	0.57	22	0.89	6	0.33	71	0.69	24	1.02	7	0.41	67	0.70
Total	—	7.77	—	5.33	—	5.73	—	7.94	—	5.66	—	6.47	—	8.43	—	6.09	—	6.77

[a,b] The data in the A columns are from Harry (1994) as presented in Reschly (1997, p. 54). The data in the B columns were obtained from Reschly (1997, p. 55).

[c] These data were obtained from USDOE (1997) (Table I-5, p. I-43).

[d] These date were obtained from OCR (1997, p. 1) (Revised data, July 22, 1997).

* Numbers in parenthesis are percents of the total student population.

A = percent of mild disability program by ethnic group; B = Percent of ethnic group in mild disability program.

**MMR = Mild mental retardation; SLD = Specific learning disabilities; SED = Serious emotional disturbances.

†The consulted 1994 OCR table (revised on July 22, 1997) only reported data for the whole mental retardation category.

declined from 1986 to 1990 but it has been increasing in the 1990s. Such differences were 2.04 (1986), 1.47 (1990), 1.66 (1992), and 1.77 (1994).

Interestingly, somewhat distinct patterns emerge when we disaggregate the data by disability category to examine Black/White differences in the 1986–1994 period. On the one hand, with the exception of 1994, Black/White differences decreased across time in the MR category (i.e., 1.43, 1.29, 0.87, and 1.40 respectively). However, similar to the national data, Black / White differences in the SED category decreased from 1986 to 1990 but it has increased in the 1990s—i.e., it was 0.47 in 1986, 0.20 in 1990, 0.32 in 1992, and 0.36 in 1994. It seems, therefore, that African Americans continue to be overrepresented in mild disability programs and that Black / White differences are increasing in the present decade.

A relation between the percent of minority students in the school population and disproportionality patterns was found in the 1970s and 1980s (Finn, 1982; Harry, 1992). Are disproportionality patterns observed in states with different levels of minority student enrollment in the 1990s? Table 2 presents enrollment data in four states with varying minority enrollment. Visual inspection of these data suggest (a) Blacks' overrepresentation in mild

disability programs is still observed at the state level and it seems to increase in states with large Black student enrollment; (b) Overrepresentation patterns for Latinos and American Indians vary from state to state and from category to category, and their proportion in the school population does not seem to affect overrepresentation patterns. Similarly to Black students, these groups tend to be underrepresented in G&T programs; (c) Asian students tend to be underrepresented in mild disability categories and overrepresented in some states in the G&T category (their proportion in the school population does not seem to affect disproportionality patterns); and (d) White students tend to be overrepresented in the G&T and SLD categories.

Causes of Disproportionate Representation

The most widely used explanation of this problem is based on the deficit thinking that has characterized theories about minority students' educational performance (Trent, Artiles, & Englert, in press): It has been concluded that many of these students lack the abilities and skills needed to succeed in the general educational system; hence, they need to receive specialized services. The most favored ar-

Table 2. Percent of Exceptionality Program by Ethnic Group and Percent of Ethnic Group in Exceptionality Program in Four States, 1994 (Office for Civil Rights, 1997).

State		American Indian		Asian/Pacific Islander		Black		Latino		White	
		A	B	A	B	A	B	A	B	A	B
AL (13)*	% Pop	0.70		0.60		36		0.39		63	
	G&T†	0.23	1.02	1.48	7.80	9	0.82	0.28	2.28	89	4.49
	MR	0.24	1.31	0.08	0.52	64	6.8	0.12	1.19	35	2.13
	SLD	0.45	3.27	0.08	0.67	27	3.85	0.25	3.32	72	5.9
	SED	0.14	0.13	0.06	0.07	34	0.66	0.33	0.59	65	0.73
CA (9)	% Pop	0.76		12		8		38		41	
	G&T	0.60	4.36	19	9.34	5	3.06	18	2.70	58	8.01
	MR	1.12	0.84	7.47	0.37	12	0.79	40	0.60	39	0.54
	SLD	1	6.98	4	1.82	13	7.95	35	4.85	47	6.06
	SED	1	0.23	3	0.04	24	0.43	16	0.06	56	0.20
HI (9)	% Pop	0.33		76		2		2		19	
	G&T	0.20	4.55	74	7.92	1	3.49	1	3.31	24	10.07
	MR	0.09	0.30	80	1.15	3	1.16	4	1.95	13	0.76
	SLD	0.40	5.45	70	4.06	3	4.77	4	6.83	23	5.30
	SED	1	2.42	61	0.69	3	0.88	5	1.87	30	1.35
NY (11)	% Pop	0.36		5		20		17		58	
	G&T	0.30	2.80	4	2.34	6	0.94	3	0.54	88	4.92
	MR	0.46	0.91	2	0.26	29	1	16	0.68	52	0.63
	SLD	0.40	7.28	1	2.12	23	8.20	19	8.19	56	6.89
	SED	0.44	1.53	1	0.20	41	2.50	20	1.47	38	0.79

A = Percent of exceptionality program by ethnic group; B = Percent of ethnic group in exceptionality program.

†G&T = Gifted and talented; MR = Mental retardation; SLD = Specific LD; SED = Serious emotional disturbances.

*Numbers in parenthesis are percents of students with disabilities (Nation's mean = 11%).

gument to explain minority students' deficits is the nefarious effects of poverty which is rampant among these groups. Because of their higher levels of poverty, the argument follows, we should expect a higher incidence of negative developmental outcomes (e.g., disabilities) among these groups. In this vein, research has linked poverty to placement in special education; however, we need more inquiries to understand (a) the complex nature of this association, (b) minorities' resilience to the negative effects of poverty, and (c) the role of structural factors in the production of higher rates of poverty among minority groups.

An alternative position posits that deficit explanations oversimplify this complex problem by blaming the student and disregarding the significant impact of contextual, technical, structural, and ideological factors. For example, a critical technical factor is related to the procedures used in the special education field. A case in point is the variability in the operationalization and implementation of eligibility and placement criteria: Analyses of the 1996 and 1997 USDOE reports to Congress indicate that students served in SED programs in Mississippi and Connecticut differ by a factor of 41 and 33 respectively. Similar, though less dramatic, variability patterns are observed in the MMR and SED categories (MacMillan & Reschly; in press, USDOE, 1997). Also, such patterns seem to vary according to school location. For example, it has been found that the psychometric profiles of students with LD in urban and suburban schools differ to the point that many identified students in urban schools did not fit the established eligibility criteria for LD (e.g., in terms of ability levels) (Gottlieb, Alter, Gottlieb, & Wishner, 1994).

Furthermore, we must be mindful of the nature of the disproportionality data. Many of these analyses draw from the Office for Civil Rights (OCR) survey data, which purportedly have several methodological limitations. For instance, the data are not based on a nationally representative sample, different surveys have sampled school districts with distinct demographic profiles, and distinct sampling procedures have been used over the different surveys, which complicates longitudinal and comparative analyses (Reschly, 1997). Hence, the question arises as to how we can assess the magnitude and causes of disproportionality given the potential confounding effect of the aforementioned technical aspects.

Another factor that complicates disproportionality analyses is our limited understanding of the role of culture in human development. For instance, an analysis of 22 years of research in four major special education journals showed a paucity of studies on ethnic minority students, a narrow scope of research topics, and a disregard for potential interactions between sociocultural variables (e.g., ethnicity and language, gender, or social class) (Artiles, Trent, & Kuan, 1997). How, then, can educators discern the influence of language, cognitions, social class, and ethnicity on students' competence and performance? How can educa-

tors make decisions about students' competence based on culturally-insensitive criteria? Indeed, this paucity of knowledge has enormous implications for the identification of students' needs and the provision of adequate educational services.

Other factors could impinge upon this predicament, though they have received scant attention by the research community. For instance, we need to investigate how disproportionality can be exacerbated, masked, or reduced in distinct contexts by (a) the quality of the instructional context, (b) the role of racism and discrimination, (c) the dismissal of alternative ways of knowing in the design and implementation of school rules, curricula, assessment practices, and expectations, (d) the inattention to the influence of sociocultural variables in researchers' labor (e.g., investigators' beliefs or values about cultural diversity), (e) the disregard for within-cultural-group variability, (f) the failure to include minority students' perspectives in investigations, and (g) the availability of alternative services (e.g., prereferral, bilingual education, and Chapter 1 programs).

Looking Ahead: Risks and Possibilities

We must transcend oversimplification of this problem so that we do not debate endlessly whether special education is harmful to minority students, whether disabilities exist or are social constructions, or whether minority students' poverty is the cause of the problem. By focusing on these oversimplifications we run the risk of losing generations of culturally diverse students, the future of our nation. At the same time, this multidimensional problem affords us the possibility to rethink the meaning and place of special education in our increasingly diverse society. For this purpose, we must acknowledge that implicit in this predicament are assumptions about human difference and about the role of education in a heterogeneous society. Hence, we must undertake two crucial tasks in the immediate future. First, we must conduct more and better studies that address the limitations of past research. Second, we must strengthen the theoretical grounding of the disproportionality discourse to begin grappling with equity issues in the education of culturally diverse students and with how our educational system meets the needs of an increasingly diverse society.

REFERENCES

Artiles, A. J., & Trent, S. C. (1994). Overrepresentation of minority students in special education: A continuing debate. *The Journal of Special Education, 27,* 410–437.

Artiles, A. J., Trent, S. C., & Kuan, L. A. (1997). Learning disabilities research on ethnic minority students: An analysis of 22 years of studies published in selected refereed journals. *Learning Disabilities Research & Practice, 12,* 82–91.

Finn, J. D. (1982). Patterns in special education placement as revealed by the OCR surveys. In K. A. Heller, W. H. Holtzman, &

S. Messick (Eds.), *Placing children in special education: A strategy for equity* (pp. 322–381). Washington, DC: National Academy Press.

Gottlieb, J., Alter, M., Gottlieb, B. W., & Wishner, J. (1994). Special education in urban America: It's not justifiable for many. *The Journal of Special Education, 27,* 453–465.

Harry, B. (1992). *Cultural diversity, families, and the special education system.* New York: Teachers College.

MacMillan, D., & Reschly, D. J. (in press). Overrepresentation of minority students: The case for greater specificity or reconsideration of the variables examined. *The Journal of Special Education.*

Office for Civil Rights. (1997). *Elementary and Secondary School Civil Rights Compliance Report* [Revised data, July 22, 1997]. Washington, DC: USDOE.

Reschly, D. J. (1997). *Disproportionate minority representation in general and special education: Patterns, issues, and alternatives.* Des Moines, IA: Iowa Department of Education.

Trent, S. C., Artiles, A. J., & Englert, C. S. (in press). From deficit thinking to social constructivism: A review of special education theory, research and practice. *Review of Research in Education.*

U.S. Department of Education. (1997). *Nineteenth annual report to Congress on the implementation of the Individuals with Disabilities Education Act.* Washington, DC: Author.

ALFREDO J. ARTILES
University of California

STANLEY O. TRENT
University of Virginia

CULTURAL PERSPECTIVES ON BEHAVIORAL DISORDERS

Children with behavioral disorders constitute one of the major national issues confronting the schools and society. There is increasing concern about the academic failure and school dropout rate of U.S. children and adolescents identified with behavioral disorders (BD). Observation, diagnosis, and intervention strategies for these students are poorly defined nationally (Sabatino, 1987). The current definition of BD may encourage the underidentification of students with behavioral disorders from the entire school-age population, while promoting an overrepresentation of students identified as BD from culturally diverse groups (Algozzine, Ruhl, & Ramsey, 1991). The rates of identification, placement, and achievement of children and adolescents with BD are strongly correlated with gender, race, and other cultural dimensions. However, these issues are often neglected in our educational system (Singh, Oswald, Wechsler, & Curtis, 1997).

In 1990, about one-third of school age children in the United States were children from nondominant cultures (Maag & Howell, 1992). The growing diversity in student population has increased the potential and practice for inappropriate educational placement of students. For example, in 1987, African Americans were 16% of the total enrollment in the nation's school system. However, in the same year, African Americans made up 27% of the students identified as having a behavioral/emotional disorder in the public schools. There is concern by many in this country that this 11% discrepancy is based on faulty thinking, biases, and inappropriate identification of culturally diverse students (Harry, 1992). Anglo American students are less likely to be identified as BD or placed in restrictive settings than are students from other cultures, particularly African American students. Hispanic American students are underrepresented in BD across most of the nation.

Overrepresentation of Culturally Diverse Students

Unfortunately, many culturally diverse groups of students are being misidentified as behaviorally disordered. This phenomenon is causing a misuse of services for other students who may need them but are not yet identified. Minority groups, other than ethnic minority children, are also affected by this situation. Students with limited English proficiency (LEP) are frequently misplaced in programs for students with BD. Students from nondominant cultural backgrounds should not be at risk for being labeled as BD simply for displaying traits reflecting their cultural upbringing.

The mismatch between schools and culturally diverse homes is a factor influencing the misidentification of students as BD. A home culture exists for all students, and this culture may be discrepant with the traditional Anglo middle-class public school culture. This discrepancy is often viewed by school personnel as a problem within the individual student instead of a cultural mismatch. The student may then be identified as having a behavioral problem and assigned a label, with a resulting loss of self-esteem (Algozzine et al., 1991).

Children of immigrant families and children from war-torn and politically repressive countries are vulnerable to being mislabeled as BD, yet often do not have their needs recognized by school personnel. Additionally, many students who are lesbian, gay, or bisexual are at risk for being identified as BD when they have no disability. The same scenario holds true for children raised in families with same-sex partners (McIntyre, 1996).

Preservice Training and Recruitment

Improved preservice training for future educators and improved recruitment of teachers of students with behavioral disorders may help solve the problem of inadequate education of culturally diverse students.

Preservice training. Most teachers do not have a solid grounding in multicultural education. Those that did receive multicultural training in college were trained about "culture within a cultural literacy model." This model teaches cultural diversity within the limited framework of race and ethnicity. Preservice teachers are often taught general characteristics and stereotypes regarding different minority groups. Research demonstrates that teacher sensitivity and general knowledge about a student's culture is correlated to student achievement; therefore, reevaluation of instructing preservice teachers needs to occur (Harry, 1992). In addition to preservice training, continued training inservice in the profession should also be provided on this topic.

Recruiting preservice teachers. Recruitment and retention of culturally diverse preservice teachers also needs to be addressed by colleges and universities. In special education classrooms, a disparity often exists between cultural background of students and teachers. This difference is even greater in programs involving students with BD. Gender issues are also important to consider. Female teachers refer students, particularly boys, for behavioral problems more often than male teachers. This problem will continue to increase as fewer males and culturally diverse individuals choose teaching as a career. This shortage of professionals from culturally diverse backgrounds leads to problems of isolation of majority students from teachers of culturally diverse backgrounds, reduces role models for culturally diverse students, and yields inadequate expertise in recommending multicultural changes and training to other school colleagues.

Aggressive recruitments of culturally diverse preservice teachers is necessary. While it is recognized that one's cultural background does not guarantee the ability to relate and work effectively with students exhibiting BD, the need for the recruitment of professionals from culturally diverse backgrounds is evident (McIntyre, 1996). Unfortunately, states such as California, Texas, and Michigan have been court-ordered to reduce or stop opportunities that would recruit underrepresented groups to meet a particular professional need. Practices such as these are hurting attempts to increase the cultural diversity of educators to serve students with BD.

Inadequately prepared professionals. To ensure that students with BD have access to a free appropriate public education, there must be an adequate supply of teachers and other instructional and noninstructional staff with appropriate training or certification (USDOE, 1996). There are 331,392 special education teachers in the United States, yet many of these teachers are not professionally certified (6.3%). In addition, there are inadequate numbers of teachers of special education, with a reported 3,643 special education teachers needed. These problems increase when we look at instructing students with BD. Many of the teachers (n = 30,151) who work with students with BD are not certified or not adequately trained to work with students with BD (Katsiyannis, Landrum, Bullock, & Vinton, 1997).

Cultural Mismatch of Teachers and Students

Behavioral patterns and values are often defined by and vary by culture. Also, behaviors and actions viewed as aberrant often vary by culture. Teachers who are unaware of cultural differences often misinterpret and judge culturally-determined behavior as being evidence of BD. In such a subjective climate, culturally diverse students identified as BD are set up for failure (Harry, 1992). Far too few educators realize that many culturally different youth view the school environment as alienating. Also, many African American, Mexican American, Native American, and Native Hawaiian students feel great pressure from their peers not to achieve (Ogbu, 1992). Due to numerous factors, such as historical oppression and an emphasis on cultural cohesion and cooperation rather than competition, individual success in schooling is often viewed as rejection of one's cultural group.

Cultural diversity misidentified as a behavioral disorder. The cultural mismatch between the teacher and the student often results in students from some cultures being misidentified as BD by teachers who are not aware or culturally competent. Educators generally have a more negative attitude towards students with BD, as a group, than towards students with other disabilities such as learning disabilities (Algozzine et al., 1991). By adding cultural diversity along with BD, the bias against these students by many teachers is exaggerated (Algozzine, et al., 1991). Because some teachers discriminate against students because of their racial, ethnic, political, or socioeconomic backgrounds, it is obvious that the coupling of BD with any of these traits has the potential for heightening the imbalance (Singh et al., 1997).

A continuation of this practice is present in the data collected in the area of student discipline. Some teachers' differential use of disciplinary practices with Anglo American students and those from other cultures is well-documented (Harry, 1992). African American students experience the most severe forms of discipline. The educational system is in the unfortunate position of having culturally inexperienced teachers from the dominant culture (over 80% European American females) teaching students of increasing diversity.

Cultural competence. Culturally competent teachers acknowledge, accept, and value cultural differences in their students. Teachers must be aware of their own culture as well as the culture of others and must acknowledge how it could bias their service towards students (Singh et al., 1997). A teacher should assess students with BD through their students' cultural backgrounds while acknowledging the expectations of the dominant culture.

Educators teach students prosocial norms for the public school setting usually from a middle class European-American perspective. Educators need to also incorporate values and behavioral standards from other cultural groups. Teachers must ensure that students have pride in their original culture as well as observing the determined norms for a particular setting. Modification of classroom practices can promote self-esteem and motivation for all students. (McIntyre, 1996).

Biased Assessment Practices

Most individuals truly understand only their own culture and frequently find it difficult to appreciate behavior that is different from their own. This fact influences not only the way educators teach, but also the way students are assessed. Culturally-based behavioral patterns often differ from what is considered normative on assessment instruments (Harry, 1992). Cultural biases and prejudices are often acknowledged to exist in many standardized instruments, particularly those measuring self-concept (McIntyre, 1996).

Complexity of cultural diversity and BD. The assessment of students for the possible presence of BD is a complex process that becomes more difficult when students are from a culturally diverse background. It has been demonstrated that assessment tools reflect cultural as well as school learning, but the invisible quality of many central aspects of culture makes the identification of cultural bias a challenging task (Harry, 1992). For example, it is easy to see that testing an LEP student in English would be unfair, but it is less obvious to many that standard English testing can be unfair to speakers of nonstandard varieties of the language. There is a pressing need for the development and implementation of more appropriate and accurate methods of assessment for culturally diverse students. This need is particularly noticeable in the area of behavioral disorders, since students who display culturally different behaviors are particularly susceptible to this diagnosis.

Assessment changes. The entire approach to assessment may need to change for students with BD who are culturally diverse. A more holistic method of assessment could be incorporated and framed within the context of a student's culture. The practice of using norm-referenced tests is problematic because these tests have often been shown to be based on middle-class Anglo American values and experiences (Singh et al., 1997). Assessment procedures should help to differentiate BD from cultural differences in be-havior. Also, a diverse multidisciplinary team reviewing students' assessments can help increase cultural awareness and decrease misidentification of students as BD.

The public school system needs to continue to move away from a cultural deficit model to a cultural difference model. A cultural difference model accepts that the cognitive, learning, and motivational styles of students are different from those often expected by the teacher, who is usually from the dominant culture (Singh et al., 1997) while a cultural deficit model uses the culture as the explanation for school failures. The idea that all students should assimilate and fit into the majority culture has been successfully challenged by the concept of cultural pluralism.

The United States is becoming a country where minority groups are becoming the majority (Robinson & Bradley, 1997). These demographic changes require adaptations in assessment and teaching in our public schools. Current trends lead to an overrepresentation of culturally diverse students being misidentified as emotionally or behaviorally disordered. In most cases, culturally divergent behaviors can be respected (McIntyre, 1996). Acknowledging culture as a predominant factor in shaping behaviors and values and respecting culturally defined traits will yield a more productive learning and teaching environment for culturally diverse students, students with BD, and teachers. This change also should result in more accurate identification of all students and more appropriate support for students who have BD, and it potentially will decrease the misdiagnosis of culturally diverse students (Singh et al., 1997).

REFERENCES

Algozzine, B., Ruhl, K., & Ramsey, R. (1991). *Behaviorally disordered? Assessment for identification and instruction.* Reston, VA: The Council for Exceptional Children.

Harry, B. (1992). *Cultural diversity, families, and the special education system: Communication and empowerment.* New York: Teachers College.

Katsiyannis, A., Landrum, T. J., Bullock, L., & Vinton, L. (1997). Certification requirements for teachers of students with emotional or behavioral disorders: A national survey. *Behavioral Disorders, 22*(3), 131–140.

Maag, J. W., & Howell, K. W. (1992). Special education and the exclusion of youth with social maladjustments: A cultural-organizational perspective. *Remedial and Special Education, 13*(1), 47–54, 59.

McIntyre, T. (1996). Guidelines for providing appropriate services to culturally diverse students with emotional and/or behavioral disorders. *Behavioral Disorders, 21*(2), 137–144.

Ogbu, J. U. (1992). Understanding cultural diversity and learning. *Educational Researcher, 21*(8), 5–14.

Robinson, B., & Bradley, L. J. (1997). Multicultural training for undergraduates: Developing knowledge and awareness. *Journal of Multicultural Counseling and Development, 25*(4), 281–289.

Sabatino, D. A. (1987). Behavior disorders. In C. R. Reynolds & Lester Mann (Eds.), *The Encyclopedia of Special Education* (Vol. 1). New York: Wiley.

Singh, N. N., Ellis, C. R., Oswald, D. P., Wechsler, H. A., & Curtis, W. J. (1997). Value and address diversity. *Journal of Emotional and Behavioral Disorders, 5*(1), 24–35.

U.S. Department of Education. (1996). *Eighteenth annual report to Congress on the implementation of the Individuals with Disabilities Education Act.*

NANCY E. ALGERT
LINDA H. PARRISH
Texas A & M University

CURRICULUM

Educational curriculum is what students learn, or the content of instruction. Historically, the curriculum of U.S. public education was specified in broad, global terms, addressing abstract notions such as Americanization and instilling of democratic values in youths (Mulhern, 1959). In the twentieth century, however, developments in learning theory such as Thorndike's demonstration of the specificity of transfer promoted a reconceptualization of learning from concurrent strengthening of global faculties to sequential mastery of numerous, definite, and particularized skills and knowledge (Fuchs & Deno, 1982). This reconceptualization has led to alternative ways of specifying school curricula for distinct behavioral outcomes (Bloom, Hastings, & Madaus, 1971). Current curriculum statements typically represent carefully sequenced, calibrated, and organized sets of tasks, regularly called objectives (Johnson, 1967).

In special education, as in regular education, curriculum is derived from an analysis of the needs of society. This analysis, however, renders considerably different instructional focuses for mildly and severely handicapped students. For the mildly handicapped, analysis of the needs of society results in a curriculum similar, if not identical, to that of normally developing pupils; it includes curricular tasks such as reading, writing, and mathematics. For the more severely handicapped, this analysis results in a curriculum that addresses basic survival skill requirements. These alternative educational focuses often are referred to as developmental curriculum (which identifies tasks for normally performing children) (Snell, 1983) and functional curriculum (which addresses skills necessary for ultimate attainment of self-sufficiency) (Holvoet, Guess, Mulligan, & Brown, 1980).

For the mildly handicapped student, the curriculum may be resequenced, broken down into smaller tasks, reorganized, or taught via dramatically different instructional strategies. Two alternative ways of addressing curriculum for the mildly handicapped have been referred to as the task analytic approach and the ability training model (Ysseldyke & Salvia, 1974). With the task analytic approach, the curriculum is approached by breaking down terminal tasks into sets of subskills, which are addressed separately and sequentially and ultimately synthesized into final tasks of the curriculum (Howell, in press). With the ability training model, hierarchies of abilities that are prerequisite to mastery of basic reading, writing, and mathematics skills such as perceptual-motor or psycholinguistic abilities are hypothesized. These abilities are addressed before the standard school curriculum is taught. In both cases, however, the ultimate curriculum, or the final educational objective, remains constant and is consonant with the curricular goals of the mainstream educational environment.

In contradistinction, the functional curriculum of the more severely handicapped population is determined more individually. It addresses objectives that (1) represent the practical or functional skills most likely to be needed currently or in the near future; (2) span the four instructional domains of domestic, leisure/recreational, community, and vocational skills; (3) are suitable for the student's chronological age; and (4) address the pupil's current performance levels and are reasonably thought to be attainable (Snell, 1983). The basic assumptions of a functional curriculum for the severely handicapped are that the school's responsibility is to teach skills that optimize a person's independent and responsible functioning in society (Hawkins & Hawkins, 1981). For the severely handicapped, these skills must be chosen from a group of tasks and activities that have a high probability of being required and that increase self-sufficiency (Brown et al., 1979).

REFERENCES

Bloom, B. S., Hastings, J. T., & Madaus, G. F. (1981). *Handbook on formative and summative evaluation of student learning.* New York: McGraw-Hill.

Brown, L., Branston, M. B., Hamre-Nietupski, S., Pumpian, I., Certo, N., & Gruenewald, L. (1979). A strategy for developing chronological age appropriate and functional curricular content for severely handicapped adolescents and young adults. *Journal of Special Education, 13,* 81–90.

Fuchs, L. S., & Deno, S. L. (1982). *Developing goals and objectives for educational programs.* Washington, DC: American Association of Colleges for Teacher Education.

Hawkins, R. P., & Hawkins, K. K. (1981). Parental observation on the education of severely retarded children: Can it be done in the classroom? *Analysis & Intervention in Developmental Disabilities, 1,* 13–22.

Holvoet, J., Guess, D., Mulligan, M., & Brown, F. (1980). The Individualized Curriculum Sequencing model (II): A teaching strategy for severely handicapped students. *Journal of the Association for the Severely Handicapped, 5,* 337–351.

Howell, K. W. (in press). Direct assessment of academic performance. In L. S. Fuchs & D. Fuchs (Eds.), Linking assessment to instruction. *School Psychology Review.*

Johnson, M. (1967). Definitions and models in curriculum theory. *Educational Theory, 7,* 127–140.

Mulhern, J. (1959). *A history of education* (2nd ed.). New York: Ronald.

Snell, M. E. (1983). *Systematic instruction of the moderately and severely handicapped* (2nd ed.). Columbus, OH: Merrill.

Ysseldyke, J. E., & Salvia, J. (1974). Diagnostic prescriptive teaching: Two models. *Exceptional Children, 41,* 181–185.

Lynn S. Fuchs
Vanderbilt University

ANNUAL GOALS
CURRICULUM FOR THE MILDLY HANDICAPPED
CURRICULUM FOR THE SEVERELY HANDICAPPED

CURRICULUM, AGE APPROPRIATE

See AGE APPROPRIATE CURRICULUM.

CURRICULUM-BASED ASSESSMENT (CBA)

Curriculum-based assessment (CBA) uses instructional materials and course content as the basis for testing. According to Shinn and Good, the prominence of CBA has grown in the last 10 years and within the last five years entire volumes of journals have been devoted to CBA (1993).

Although commercial norm-referenced tests continue as a mainstay in special education placement and program evaluation activity (Goh, Teslow, & Fuller, 1981), these traditional tests have been criticized regarding (1) poor psychometric properties and inadequate conceptualization (Ysseldyke, 1979), (2) poor relationship to instructional content and educational objectives (Jenkins & Pany, 1978; Zigmond & Silverman, 1984), and (3) insufficient alternative forms to permit ongoing progress monitoring.

As an alternative to commercial norm-referenced tests, CBA addresses at least the last two problems (Fuchs, 1986). With CBA, student's programmatic objectives are matched with measurement procedures. Alternative test forms are drawn directly from curricula specified in objectives and are administered repeatedly. Student progress data are evaluated with reference to the performance criteria specified in objectives and with respect to classroom peer's progress within the same curriculum. To ensure effective instructional programs and attainment of objectives, individualized programs are tested carefully and modified over time as required.

The following set of assumptions provide the basis for CBA: (1) the instructional and curricular validity of CBA is stronger than with traditional assessment methods, (2) each student's needs are defined best in terms of the context of local educational programs, (3) the essential measure of educational success is the student's progress in the school's curriculum, and (4) the appropriate reference group with which to judge the adequacy of students' rates of curricular progress is their local school district peers' progress through the same material (Deno, 1985).

Research indicates that at least some forms of ongoing CBA can be used effectively to address several different assessment functions. It can be used reliably to identify students in need of special education (Marston, Tindal, & Deno, 1984; Tindal & Marston, 1986), to clearly demarcate the criteria for entering special education (Shapiro, 1993), to specify target skills for students and write useful individual education program goals and objectives (Fuchs, Deno, & Mirkin, 1984), to monitor pupil progress toward goals and formatively develop effective instructional programs, and to evaluate the effectiveness of special education programs on an individual and district-wide basis (Tindal & Marston, 1986).

REFERENCES

Deno, S. L. (1985). Curriculum-based measurement: The emerging alternative. *Exceptional Children, 52,* 219–232.

Fuchs, L. S. (1986). Monitoring progress among mildly handicapped pupils: Review of current practice and research. *Remedial & Special Education, 7,* 5–12.

Fuchs, L. S., & Fuchs, D. (1984). Curriculum-based assessment of progress toward long- and short-term goals. *Journal of Special Education, 20,* 69–82.

Fuchs, L. S., Deno, S. L., & Mirkin, P. K. (1984). The effects of frequent curriculum-based measurement and evaluation on pedagogy, student achievement and student awareness of learning. *American Educational Research Journal, 21,* 449–460.

Goh, D. S., Teslow, C. J., & Fuller, G. B. (1981). The practices of psychological assessment among school psychologists. *Professional Psychology, 12,* 699–706.

Jenkins, J. R., & Pany, D. (1978). Standardized achievement tests: How useful for special education? *Exceptional Children, 44,* 448–453.

Martson, D., Tindal, G., & Deno, S. L. (1984). Eligibility for learning disability services: A direct and repeated measurement approach. *Exceptional Children, 50,* 554–555.

Shapiro, E. S. (1993). Curriculum-Based Assessment: Implications for psychoeducational practice. In J. J. Kramer (Ed.), *Curriculum based measurement* (pp. 123–138). Lincoln, NE: Buros Institute of Mental Measurements.

Tindal, G., & Martson, D. (1986). Approaches to assessment. In J. Torgeson & B. Wong (Eds.), *Psychological and educational perspectives on learning disabilities.* Orlando, FL: Academic.

Ysseldyke, J. E. (1979). Psychoeducational assessment of decision making. In J. E. Ysseldyke & P. K. Mirkin (Eds.), *Proceedings of the Minnesota Roundtable Conference on Assessment of Learning Disabled Children* (Monograph N. 8) (pp. 15–36). Minneapolis: University of Minnesota Institute for Research on Learning Disabilities.

Zigmond, N., & Silverman, R. (1984). Informal assessment for program planning and evaluation in special education. *Educational Psychologist, 19,* 163–171.

LYNN S. FUCHS
DOUGLAS FUCHS
Vanderbilt University
First edition

TRACY A. MUENZ
*California School of
    Professional Psychology*
Second edition

**AGE-APPROPRIATE CURRICULUM
ASSESSMENT
NORM-REFERENCED TESTING**

CURRICULUM FOR STUDENTS WITH MILD DISABILITIES IN SPECIAL EDUCATION

The definition of curriculum varies in the literature but in the broadest sense, it is used in the field in two ways: (1) to indicate a plan for the education of learners, and (2) to identify a field of study. The word curriculum comes from a Latin root meaning race course; it can be regarded as the standardized ground covered by students in their race for a diploma (Zais, 1976).

Special education curriculum for the mildly handicapped learner consists of learning tasks, activities, or assignments that are directed toward increasing a student's knowledge or skills in a specific content or subject area. It is the special educator's task to identify the differences between the regular and special education curriculum and to make educational decisions based on available assessment data.

The decision to provide variation in content may be less significant in educating mildly handicapped learners than the decision to provide variation in the conditions under which learning can be best facilitated. A critical issue involves the determination of the need for compensatory versus remedial curricula (Case, 1975). Many of the strategies and techniques used with mildly handicapped learners in special education overlap with Chapter I, other remedial programs, and regular education.

Mainstreaming has encouraged efforts to help the over 70% of special education students who spend at least part of the day in regular classrooms to master the regular curriculum or "face curricular isolationism" (O'Connell-Mason & Raison, 1982).

This special education curriculum must be coordinated with regular education curriculum, which in turn must be modified or changed at times to accommodate students with different learning styles. The curricula must be designed to meet the particular needs and characteristics of the individuals who are to learn various contents.

Howell, Kaplan, and O'Connell (1979) indicate that to date, the research has not demonstrated the superiority of one type of curriculum modification over another. However, there are a number of general types of modifications that have been found useful: (1) eliminate or reduce the subjects in the student's curriculum; (2) develop or identify an alternative curriculum; (3) alter expectations for the quantity or quality of work; (4) teach subject matter more slowly; (5) teach only the most essential subject matter; (6) develop a parallel curriculum; (7) provide a supplemented curriculum; or (8) adjust materials and/or response modes.

Growth in the field of special education curriculum for the mildly handicapped learner has become an integral part of regular education. It is clear that the similarities are greater than the differences. The same principles and procedures, with some modifications, can be used to instruct all children. All children can reach their potential given the opportunity, effective teaching, and proper resources (Berdine & Blackhurst, 1985).

REFERENCES

Berdine, W. H., & Blackhurst, A. E. (1985). *An introduction to special education.* Boston: Little, Brown.

Case, R. (1975). Gearing the demands of instruction to the developmental capacities of the learner. *Review of Educational Research, 45,* 3–9.

Howell, K. W., Kaplan, J. S., & O'Connell, C. Y. (1979). *Evaluating exceptional children: A task analysis approach.* Columbus, OH: Merrill.

O'Connell-Mason, C., & Raison, S. B. (1982). *Curriculum assessment and modification.* Washington, DC: American Association of Colleges for Teacher Education.

Zais, R. S. (1976). *Curriculum: Principles and foundations.* New York: Harper & Row.

DEBORAH A. SHANLEY
Medgar Evers College

**AGE-APPROPRIATE CURRICULUM
MAINSTREAMING
TASK ANALYSIS**

CURRICULUM FOR STUDENTS WITH SEVERE DISABILITIES

Educational curriculum is what students learn, or the content of instruction. Historically, the curriculum of U.S. public education was specified in broad, global terms, addressing abstract notions such as Americanization and instilling of democratic values in youths (Mulhern, 1959). In the twentieth century, however, developments in learning theory such as Thorndike's demonstration of the specificity of transfer promoted a reconceptualization of learning from concurrent strengthening of global faculties to sequential mastery of numerous, definite, and particularized skills and knowledge (Fuchs & Deno, 1982). This reconceptualization led to alternative ways of specifying school curricula for distinct behavioral outcomes (Bloom, Hastings, & Madaus, 1971). Current curriculum statements typically represent carefully sequenced, calibrated, and organized sets of tasks, regularly called objectives (Johnson, 1967).

In special education, as in regular education, curriculum is derived from an analysis of the needs of society. For the severely handicapped individual, this analysis results in curriculum that addresses basic survival skill requirements. This educational focus, which represents an alternative to the normal or developmental educational curriculum (Snell, 1983), is referred to as a functional curriculum. The basic assumptions of a functional curriculum for the severely handicapped are that the school's responsibility is to teach skills that optimize a person's independent and responsible functioning in society (Hawkins & Hawkins, 1981) and that, for the severely handicapped, these skills must be chosen from a group of tasks and activities that have a high probability of being required and that increase self-sufficiency (Brown et al., 1979).

This functional curriculum is determined individually and addresses objectives that (1) represent practical or functional skills most likely to be needed currently or in the near future; (2) are suitable for the student's chronological age; (3) address the pupil's current performance levels and are reasonably thought to be attainable; and (4) span four instructional domains (Snell, 1983).

The four domains of instructional content are domestic, leisure/recreational, community, and vocational. The domestic domain includes skills performed in and around the home, including self-care, clothing care, housekeeping, cooking, and yard work. In the leisure-recreational domain are skills needed to engage in spectator or participant activities performed for self-pleasure. Skills required in the community domain include street crossing, using public transportation, shopping, eating in restaurants, and using other public facilities such as parks. The vocational domain addresses skills necessary for employment such as appropriate work dress and demeanor, assembly line behavior, interviewing for jobs, completing work applications, and punctuality.

The process of determining appropriate functional curricula on an individual basis has been conceptualized as comprising five steps (Brown et al., 1979): (1) selecting curriculum domains; (2) identifying and surveying current and future natural environments; (3) dividing the relevant environments into subenvironments; (4) inventorying these subenvironments for the relevant activities performed there; and (5) examining the activities to isolate the skills required for their performance.

To address the functional curriculum for the severely handicapped, instructional strategies typically have been based on behavioral methodology. The instructional process begins with a descriptive analysis of the environmental events subsequent to, antecedent to, or during recurring behavioral events, with the purpose of identifying possible discriminative and reinforcing stimuli. Then, a task analysis of terminal objectives is conducted; in it subskills necessary for successful mastery of the final objectives are identified. Next, subskill instructional objectives are established and initial teaching strategies are specified. Then ongoing assessments of pupils' progress toward goals are collected as the instructional hypothesis is implemented. Finally, ongoing assessment data are evaluated and employed formatively to redesign instructional procedures in order to increase the probability of goal attainment.

REFERENCES

Bloom, B. S., Hastings, J. T., & Madaus, G. F. (1981). *Handbook on formative and summative evaluation of student learning.* New York: McGraw-Hill.

Brown, L., Branston, M. B., Hamre-Nietupski, S., Pumpian, I., Certo, N., & Gruenewald, L. (1979). A strategy for developing chronological age appropriate and functional curricular content for severely handicapped adolescents and young adults. *Journal of Special Education, 13,* 81–90.

Fuchs, L. S., & Deno, S. L. (1982). *Developing goals and objectives for educational programs.* Washington, DC: American Association of Colleges for Teacher Education.

Hawkins, R. P., & Hawkins, K. K. (1981). Parental observation on the education of severely retarded children: Can it be done in the classroom? *Analysis & Intervention in Developmental Disabilities, 1,* 13–22.

Holvoet, J., Guess, D., Mulligan, M., & Brown, F. (1980). The Individualized Curriculum Sequencing model (II): A teaching strategy for severely handicapped students. *Journal of the Association for the Severely Handicapped, 5,* 337–351.

Johnson, M. (1967). Definitions and models in curriculum theory. *Educational Theory, 7,* 127–140.

Mulhern, J. (1959). *A history of education* (2nd ed.). New York: Ronald.

Snell, M. E. (1983). *Systematic instruction of the moderately and severely handicapped* (2nd ed.). Columbus, OH: Merrill.

Lynn S. Fuchs
Vanderbilt University

CURRICULUM
CURRICULUM FOR THE MILDLY HANDICAPPED
FUNCTIONAL INSTRUCTION
FUNCTIONAL SKILLS

Bailey, D. B., Jr., & Wolery, M. (1984). *Teaching infants and preschoolers with handicaps*. Columbus, OH: Merrill.

Mary Murray
Journal of Special Education

EARLY IDENTIFICATION OF HANDICAPPED CHILDREN
PRESCHOOL ASSESSMENT
PRESCHOOL SPECIAL EDUCATION

CURRICULUM IN EARLY CHILDHOOD INTERVENTION

The curricula used in early intervention vary depending on the needs of the children served. Generally, however, they address developmental areas critical to the child's psychological/behavioral maturation and later school success (Bailey & Wolery, 1984). Early intervention curricula are likely to emphasize motor, cognitive, language, social, and self-help skill development. Early intervention instructors will likely address the development of gross and fine motor skills, eating and self-help skills, toileting, dressing, and undressing. A distinction has been made between developmental and functional approaches in early childhood curricula. The first emphasizes developmental progress; the second is more concerned with training for independent functioning (Bailey & Wolery, 1984).

The purposes of early intervention curricula are to develop, habilitate, or accelerate young children's development. In the case of handicapped children, the intent is to minimize the effects of children's disabilities on later development and learning and academic performance. With mildly to moderately handicapped children, early curriculum is more likely to emphasize developmental training. With more severely handicapped children, the emphasis is likely to be on functional training, for example, facilitating independent functioning.

There is considerable interaction between the various curriculum areas in any particular instructional approach. For example, eating training involves fine motor, social, and communication skill development as well as self-help training. A variety of curricula for early intervention are currently available. Few of them are distinguished by validation efforts. Bailey, Jens, and Johnson, (1983) have published a recent review of infant curricula.

REFERENCES

Bailey, D. B., Jens, K. G., & Johnson, N. (1983). Curricula for handicapped infants. In F. Fewell & S. G. Garwood (Eds.), *Educating handicapped infants*. Rockville, MD: Aspen.

CUSTODIAL CARE OF THE HANDICAPPED

Organized care for the handicapped goes back no more than 150 years. If we consider the handicapped to include the insane, mentally infirm, orphans, the poor, and those found to be criminal in nature, then we can easily locate the second American Revolution as during the Jackson presidency (Rothman, 1971). Prior to this period, care of handicapped individuals was managed primarily by families, neighbors, and friends of the handicapped. In the case of criminals, the offenders were put to death.

During the Jacksonian period large institutions were constructed in Boston, New York, and Philadelphia. Almshouses for the poor were constructed in smaller communities. Governmental agencies and the wealthy provided funds for the erection of insane asylums. Soon the medical profession was actively using the asylums as an integral part of care for the insane. It was also during this time that penitentiaries proliferated throughout the East Coast states. In addition, homes built with public funds and other types of asylums were constructed for orphans and delinquent children. In Rothman's (1971) *Discovery of the Asylum*, we find ample documentation of reform during the Jacksonian period. As Rothman has stated, this period could appropriately be referred to as "the age of the asylum."

Interested investigators have claimed that the growth of institutions in America for the insane, orphans, poor, criminals, and, one could hypothesize, the mentally retarded, paralleled the growth of psychiatry. It was 300 years prior to the advent of the first U.S. institutions that we find King Henry VIII taking the old monastery of St. Mary of Bethlehem in London, England, and reserving it solely for the care of the mentally ill. One can assume that at that time little was known about any differentiation of diagnosis between the mentally disturbed and the mentally retarded. Thus, the idiot and the insane were probably treated much the same. St. Mary's provided deplorable conditions and inadequate care for the infirm. Other asylums soon appeared in Mexico (1566), France (1641), Moscow (1764), and Vienna (the famous Lunatics' Tower, 1784). All of these institutions were the forerunners of similar edifices in America. Many of the first institutions were nothing more than a modification of a penal institution. An example of such early primitive care can be seen in the description of Lunatics' Tower:

> It was an ornately decorated tower within which were square rooms. The doctors and keepers lived in the square rooms, while the patients were confined in the spaces between the walls of the square rooms and the outside of the tower. The patients were put on exhibit to the public for a small fee. (Coleman, 1984)

An account (Coleman, 1984) of the LaBicetre Hospital in Paris is said to be representative of most institutions for the insane throughout the eighteenth century.

> The patients were ordinarily shackled to the walls of their dark, unlighted cells by iron collars which held them flat against the wall and permitting little movement. Oftimes, there were also iron hoops around the waists of the patients and both their hands and feet were chained. Although these chains usually permitted enough movement that the patients could feed themselves out of bowls, they often kept them from being able to lie down at night. Since little was known about dietetics, and the patients were presumed to be animals anyway, little attention was paid to whether they were adequately fed or to whether the food was good or bad. The cells were furnished only with straw and were never swept or cleaned; the patient remained in the midst of all the accumulated ordure. No one visited the cells except at feeding time, no provision was made for warmth, and even the most elementary gestures of humanity were lacking. (modified from Selling, 1943)

What is striking to the reader is the never ending stream of trends in the care of the handicapped, often instituted in the name of progress. In fact, care was generally for profit, coercion, incarceration, or medical validation. Historical accounts indicate that while benevolence was the primary motivation for the creation of institutional care, society also needed to seek stability from social disruption.

Humanitarian reform of institutions both in Europe and America occurred on a small scale during the eighteenth century. Pinel's experiments at LaBicetre included removing the chains, adding sunlit rooms, extending kindness, and including freedom to exercise. Reactions by patients were recorded as overwhelmingly positive by even the most seriously disturbed (Zilboorg & Henry, 1941, p. 3232). William Tuke, an English Quaker, also provided a humane environment, at the York Retreat in England, while in America Benjamin Rush, the founder of American psychiatry, provided care in a more benevolent manner. Such examples of humane treatment, however, are isolated, as most institutions continued to treat their residents much like animals and such labels as "snake pits" and "schools for unimprovable or unteachable idiots" were not uncommon.

Notable among Americans who created a moral cognizance of existing deplorable conditions was Dorothea Dix (1802–1887). In her famous *Memorial*, submitted to the U.S. Congress in 1848, she remarked that she had observed

> more than 9000 idiots, epileptics, and insane in the United States, destitute of appropriate care and protection . . . bound with galling chains; bowed beneath fetters and heavy iron balls attached to drag chains, lacerated with ropes, scourged with rods, and terrified beneath storms of execration and cruel blows; now subject to jibes and scorn and torturing tricks; now abandoned to the most outrageous violations. (Zilboorg & Henry, 1941, pp. 583–584)

This message was repeated often as Dix and her followers became instrumental in improving conditions throughout the United States, Canada, and Scotland. She is credited with establishing 32 hospitals. Unfortunately, most asylums continued to be unfit for humans.

It was not until the late 1800s that the mentally retarded were beginning to be seen as a group separate, at least in name, from other of society's deviant groups. There is reason to suspect that the mentally retarded had often been punished severely and in some instances hanged for criminal activities beyond their comprehension. The first institutions constructed solely for the mentally retarded seem to have been built for educational purposes. These temporary boarding school-type facilities were established primarily for the "improvables." The schools rejected admittance to those who could not be cured and returned to their families. Even the famed Fernald State School sought to create an institution that would not serve uncurables. When the effort to educate the mentally retarded and return them to society failed, retarded individuals' care deteriorated. The retarded were viewed as subhuman and unable to be taught productive skills. The failure was probably due to the unrealistically high expectations of complete recovery.

The perception of failure and disappointment prevailed after these early attempts at cure failed. Along with this perception came a dramatic change in the care of retarded individuals. People that had the potential to be developmentally changed were treated accordingly, while those thought of as having subhuman qualities were treated as animals.

State schools and institutions soon gave way to asylums. In 1893 the Custodial Asylum for Unteachable Idiots was founded in Rome, New York. Governor Butler of Massachusetts said:

> A well-fed, well-cared for idiot is a happy creature. An idiot awakened to his condition is a miserable one. . . . It is earnestly urged that the best disposal to be made of this large class of the permanently disabled is to place it in custodial departments of institutions for the feebleminded persons . . . under the same

merciful system that inspires hope and help for the lowest of humanity. (Kerlin, 1888 quoted in Kugel & Shearer, 1976)

It was also during this time (1885) that Illinois built a facility to provide for custodial care; the states of Iowa and Connecticut followed. Intentions were noble. There was an implied protectiveness associated with each state's appropriation for an asylum (Kugel & Shearer, 1976, p. 52). History, however, has recorded the opposite to have been the case.

In the early 1900s perceptions of the mentally retarded again changed and custodial care was said to have deteriorated. The moron and imbecile were soon made the source of all social ills. Leaders in the field such as M. W. Barr, a past president of the American Association for Mental Deficiency (AAMD), issued indictments of imbeciles as a threat to home and community. Calling for action, Johnson (1901) spoke bluntly when he stated that in order to prevent the propagation of idiocy and imbecility it might be "necessary to kill them or to resort to the knife" (Kugel & Shearer, 1976, p. 57). With attitudes such as these, it is little wonder that retarded individuals received deplorable care for the next 50 years.

The severely retarded were gradually dehumanized and moved to the back wards. These wards as well as other asylum cells were filthy and overcrowded. Such facilities were often referred to as the land of the living dead. In the fall of 1965 Senator Robert Kennedy visited several of his state's institutions; he was appalled at the conditions he encountered. Additional investigations by Blatt (1970) further delineated the horrors: "in toilets, I frequently saw urinals ripped out, sinks broken and toilet bowls backed up . . . I found incredible overcrowding" (p. 13). The national average cost of caring for the mentally retarded in 1962 was less than $5 per day per patient. Some states managed to lower that to less than $2.50 per day.

Blatt (1970) further described conditions in several institutions. He saw 7 foot by 7 foot isolation cells that seldom included beds, washstands, or toilets. Restraints were common. There were alarming shortages of staff and one supervisor for each 100 severely retarded individuals was not uncommon. It is small wonder that patients were locked up, restrained, or sedated. The odors of the wards and dayrooms were overpowering even though rooms were hosed down daily to move the human excretions to sewers located in the center of the rooms.

Blatt's (1966) photographic essay, "Christmas in Purgatory" did much to alert professionals and the general public to the deplorable conditions existing for the institutionalized retarded. Those pictures of the stark gray, high walls, barred windows, beds pushed head to head, patients lying unclothed in feces, and rooms full of young children, left their mark. The ensuing years have seen a movement away from those custodial conditions. Even in the 1960s, many institutions such as the Seaside, also chronicled by

Blatt, were providing residential treatment that encouraged more and better trained staff, family participation, fewer closed wards, sunlit areas, medical and dental attention, and daily hygienic care. Within the last 20 years, the mentally retarded have been part of a deinstitutionalization movement unlike that of any era in U.S. history. Residential homes for the handicapped are commonplace and the U.S. educational system now provides especially designed curricula to teach basic independent living skills. In addition, government-supported projects have proliferated throughout the United States and now include not only programs for assessment and training but opportunities in employment that were nonexistent only a few years ago.

REFERENCES

Blatt, B., & Kaplan, F. (1966). *Christmas in purgatory*. Boston: Allyn & Bacon.

Blatt, B. (1970). *Exodus from pandemonium*. Boston: Allyn & Bacon.

Coleman, J. C., Butcher, J. N., & Carson, R. C. (1984). *Abnormal psychology and modern life* (7th ed.). Glenview, IL: Scott, Foresman.

Kugel, R. B., & Shearer, A. (Eds.). (1976). *Changing patterns in residential services for the mentally retarded*. Washington, DC: President's Committee on Mental Retardation.

Rothman, D. J. (1971). *The discovery of the asylum*. Boston: Little, Brown.

Selling, L. S. (1943). *Men against madness*. New York: Garden City Books.

Zilboorg, G., & Henry, G. W. (1941). *A history of medical psychology*. New York: Norton.

RICHARD E. HALMSTAD
University of Wisconsin at Stout

DEINSTITUTIONALIZATION
INSTITUTIONALIZATION

CYLERT

Cylert (Pemoline) is a mild central nervous system stimulant medication that is used in the management of hyperactive children. While the onset of effectiveness of Cylert has been found to be slower than that of some other central nervous system stimulants, it also has been found to have a longer half-life, 12 hours compared with 4 hours for other stimulants (Ross & Ross, 1982). Because of this longer half-life, Cylert need be administered only on a once-daily basis. For hyperactive children, this eliminates the social stigma associated with taking medication at school. In addition, parents are better able to supervise drug administration, thereby reducing the possibility of drug abuse and increasing the probability of compliance. Another advantage of Cylert therapy over other psychostimulants in pediatric populations is its long duration of therapeutic action without sympathomimetic cardiovascular effects. In fact, therapeutic effects of Cylert have been found to be similar to those of amphetamines and methylphenidate (Ross & Ross, 1982). Clinical trials have yielded data to indicate that Cylert enhances short-term memory, attentiveness to cognitive and academic tasks, and social functioning (Ross & Ross, 1982).

As with other psychostimulants, one concern with Cylert administration has been the occurrence of side effects. While mild side effects, including insomnia, headaches, anorexia, abdominal pains, dizziness, and nausea have been reported, of greater concern is the elevation of liver enzymes, which sometimes necessitates the withdrawal of medication. Severe dysphoric effects following the cessation of Cylert also have been reported in some isolated cases (Brown, Borden, Spunt, & Medenis, 1985).

REFERENCES

Brown, R. T., Borden, K. A., Spunt, A. L., & Medenis, R. (1985). Depression following Pemoline withdrawal in a hyperactive child. *Clinical Pediatrics, 24,* 174.

Ross, D. M., & Ross, S. A. (1982). *Hyperactivity: Current issues, research and theory* (2nd ed.). New York: Wiley-Interscience.

RONALD T. BROWN
*Emory University School
of Medicine*

HYPERACTIVITY
MEDICAL MANAGEMENT

CYSTIC FIBROSIS

Cystic fibrosis is a fatal genetic disorder that involves almost all organ systems. Pulmonary infection and obstruction generally cause most of the complications and are ultimately the cause of death (Doershuk & Stern, 1982). Repeated hospitalizations and crises, financial burdens, as well as the fatal nature of the disease itself, have an extreme emotional impact on the child and his or her family. Parents must deal with the anxiety, depression, and self-blame associated with having a terminally ill child with an illness that is genetically determined. These parents may become overprotective and have difficulty allowing the child to engage in age-appropriate activities.

Frequent hospitalizations along with physical difficulties such as chronic cough, clubbed fingertips, shortness of breath, and short stature clearly set the cystic fibrosis child apart from his or her peers. Although the disease ap-

parently has little effect on intellectual functioning, the child may fall behind his or her peers academically if home instruction is not instituted during absences from school. Adolescence may be a particularly difficult period for both child and parents. The increasingly debilitating nature of the disease may thwart the child's natural striving for independence and make planning for the future difficult (Wright, Schaefer, & Solomons, 1979).

REFERENCES

Doershuk, C. F., & Stern, R. C. (1982). Cystic fibrosis. In S. S. Gellis & B. M. Kagan (Eds.), *Current pediatric therapy* (Vol. 10, pp. 207–218). Philadelphia: Saunders.

Wright, L., Schaefer, A. B., & Solomons, G. (1979). *Encyclopedia of pediatric psychology*. Baltimore, MD: University Park Press.

ALICE G. FRIEDMAN
*University of Oklahoma Health
Sciences Center*

LOGAN WRIGHT
University of Oklahoma

ADAPTED PHYSICAL EDUCATION
CYSTIC FIBROSIS FOUNDATION
HEALTH MAINTENANCE PROCEDURES

CYSTIC FIBROSIS FOUNDATION

The Cystic Fibrosis Foundation is a voluntary, nonprofit health organization that actively supports research and treatment for cystic fibrosis. Founded in 1955 by a small group of parents of children with cystic fibrosis, it was originally conceived to raise money for research to find a cure and improve the quality of life for individuals with the disease. With the help of more than 250,000 volunteers operating in 65 chapters and branch offices across the United States, the organization depends on public support to implement its programs.

The Foundation actively supports the advancement of medical science by funding research centers at leading universities and medical centers throughout the United States and providing a variety of grants to scientists for research on the disease. It also offers comprehensive diagnosis and treatment for people with cystic fibrosis through a nationwide network of 113 cystic fibrosis care centers. In addition to the research, diagnostic, and treatment services provided, the centers also offer professional medical education and training and conduct clinical trials testing new drug therapies. The Therapeutic Development Program, which provides matching funds to biotechnology companies to stimulate development of new therapies, furnishes the infrastructure needed to conduct these clinical trials in the early phases.

The Cystic Fibrosis Foundation influences public policy related to the disease by working closely with the U.S. Congress, the Food and Drug Administration, and pharmaceutical companies to speed the development of drugs to treat the disorder. The organization's efforts in this area also include advocating for increased funding for the National Institutes of Health and testifying before Congress to encourage more money for research.

Information on a variety of subjects related to cystic fibrosis, including updates on research, clinical trials, public policy issues, and ways to become involved with the Cystic Fibrosis Foundation may be obtained through its web site at www.cff.org. The Foundation may be contacted at its national offices at 6931 Arlington Road, Bethesda, MD 20814, by telephone at (800) FIGHTCF, (301) 951-4422, or fax at (301) 951-6378.

CYTOMEGALOVIRUS

The cytomegalovirus is a filterable DNA virus in the family of herpes viruses. It is responsible for the infectious disease known as cytomegalic inclusion disease. The virus is not easily eliminated and persists in host tissues for months, years, or even a lifetime. It produces a chronic infection with a variable incubation period, outcome, and course. The infection may be a significant form of congenital disease in newborns whose immune system is incompletely developed or in adults who are immunosuppressed.

There are two patterns of infection: localized and generalized. In the localized form, inclusion bodies are found only in the salivary glands; this clinical entity sometimes is referred to as generalized salivary gland disease. The second, generalized, form is represented in two principal types: that accompanied by necrotizing and calcifying encephalitis and that associated with enlargement of the spleen and the liver, lymphadenopathy, and blood dyscrasias. There is increasing recognition of the association of this infection with acquired immune deficiency syndrome (AIDS). Where there is significant cerebral damage, there is often ocular involvement.

It is generally agreed that the virus is widespread; the localized form of the disease is both frequent in occurrence and asymptomatic. Ten to thirty-two percent of autopsied infants show evidence of localized disease. Although the generalized form of the disease may occur in adults, it is characteristically seen in infants and children, occurring in up to 1% of children. Cytomegalovirus has been detected in up to 90% of immunosuppressed kidney transplant patients; active infection may predispose these patients to bacterial superinfection and transplant rejection. The virus also alters the immune system, although apparently only during the acute phase of infection; the mechanism for immunosuppression is not fully understood.

Because many organs may be affected in generalized disease, the clinical features are variable. Usually there is an acute or subacute febrile illness, and infants are likely to have been premature. There may be severe jaundice and bleeding tendencies, and enlargement of the spleen and liver is frequent. Pneumonia and renal involvement often are present. In the encephalitic form, hydrocephalus and chorioretinitis occur. Most infected infants succumb to encephalitic disease. Among those who survive, mental or motor retardation, microcephaly, seizures, and ocular involvement are common. Ocular lesions include microcornea, chorioretinitis, pseudocolobomas of the retina, retinal hemorrhage, pale optic discs, uveitis, keratoconjunctivitis, and dacryoadenitis.

The diagnosis is best established by recovery of the virus from the urine, saliva, or aqueous humor of the eye. Congenital toxoplasmosis is difficult to differentiate, but radiologic evidence of periventricular calcification suggests cytomegalic inclusion disease. Other diseases to be differentiated include generalized bacterial infection, herpes simplex encephalitis, congenital liver deformities, and diseases of the reticuloendothelial system. No treatment has been effective in controlling this disease. Several antiviral medications used to control the herpes virus have been tried with minimal success.

REFERENCES

Friedlaender, M. H. (1963). Immunology of infections systemic diseases that affect the eye. In T. D. Duane & E. A. Jaeger (Eds.), *Biomedical foundations of Ophthalmology*. Hagerstown, MD: Harper & Row.

Walsh, F. B., & Hoyt, W. F. (1969). *Clinical neuro-ophthalmology*. Baltimore, MD: Williams & Wilkins.

GEORGE R. BEAUCHAMP
Cleveland Clinic Foundation

HERPES

D

DAILY LIVING SKILLS

The term daily living skills refers to those skills that individuals use in their personal self-care and occasionally in their interactions with others. A wide range of specific behaviors may be included under each of these headings. The skills might appear to be very straightforward (e.g., grasping a brush handle) or extremely complex (e.g., developing healthy eating habits). The range of skills and behaviors that are often included under the rubric of daily living skills is best conceptualized as points along a continuum. At one end of the continuum essential daily living skills might include toileting, feeding, and dressing. Moving along the continuum toward increasing independence, a second level of skills could include hand washing, toothbrushing, etc. Daily living skills that might be taught at a higher level of independence include menstrual hygiene, shaving, and other more complex tasks.

As the student masters behaviors that are taught at fundamental levels, these newly acquired behaviors become the building material for future skill development. The end result of effective instruction in the skills that students use day to day is seen in the student's mastery of more complex conceptually oriented skills (e.g., sexual awareness, diet planning) that frequently subsume previously mastered skills. The goal in teaching these skills is to assist the exceptional needs learner in the development of more normative abilities. As these skills are taught and mastered, the student is more likely to gain access to more normative age-appropriate environments and interactions with others.

Nonexceptional children typically learn these skills (as a matter of course) through the instruction and modeling of parents, siblings, and peers, and through their own natural exploration of their environment. The exceptional child, however, often has handicaps that impair his or her ability to observe, explore, internalize, and use the skills that might otherwise be acquired. Physical handicaps may prevent the exceptional child from making use of information that he or she is able to absorb. The emotionally disordered child may exhibit problem behaviors that actively interfere with the learning of daily living skills. In addition, some exceptional children, notably those in institutions and segregated classrooms, may lack role models and/or access to the type of environments that allow the sort of exploration and experimentation necessary for the acquisition of daily living skills. Indeed, some environments actually discourage the development of such skills by prohibiting, in the interest of efficiency, neatness, etc., the exceptional individual from becoming involved in any aspect of his or her own care. Thus, the exceptional child often requires systematic instruction and/or various forms of environmental adaptation to enable him or her to reach the full development of potential in the area of daily living skills. As Bigge and O'Donnell (1976) have pointed out, not only is it necessary to teach exceptional children daily living skills in order to enable them to cope effectively with their present day-to-day experiences, but it is also necessary to provide them with the chance to survive in society and contribute to it. Failure to assist exceptional children in learning these skills can only result in their becoming unnecessarily dependent adults.

The following skills have been identified as essential to meet the demands of everyday adult living (Brolin, 1989):

MANAGING PERSONAL FINANCES
Count money and make correct change.
Manage a savings and checking account.
Maintain a personal budget and keep records.
Demonstrate personal finance decision-making skills.
Make responsible expenditures.
Calculate and pay taxes.
Use credit responsibly.
Pay bills.
Deal with renting or leasing.

SELECTING AND MANAGING A HOUSEHOLD
Perform or arrange for home maintenance.
Perform housekeeping tasks.
Plan and prepare meals.
Fill out warranty cards for new appliances and mail them.

CARING FOR PERSONAL NEEDS
Exhibit proper grooming and hygiene.
Dress appropriately.
Obtain health care.
Avoid substance abuse.
Demonstrate knowledge of common illnesses, prevention and treatment.
Maintain physical fitness, nutrition and weight.

SAFETY AWARENESS

Identify safety signs.

Identify unfamiliar odors.

Identify unfamiliar sounds.

Demonstrate knowledge and ability to evacuate a building in an emergency.

Read and understand basic safety procedures.

Obey safety rules when walking during the day or at night.

RAISING, PREPARING, AND CONSUMING FOOD

Purchase food and plan meals.

Clean food preparation areas.

Store food properly.

Prepare meals, read labels, and follow recipes.

Demonstrate appropriate eating habits.

Plan and eat balanced meals.

BUYING AND CARING FOR CLOTHING

Wash clothing.

Purchase clothing.

Demonstrate knowledge of prices and sales.

Iron, mend, and store clothing.

Demonstrate use of dry cleaner and laundromat.

EXHIBITING RESPONSIBLE CITIZENSHIP

Demonstrate knowledge of civil rights and responsibilities.

Get legal aid.

Report a crime.

Register with Selective Service at age 18.

Demonstrate knowledge of local, state, and federal governments.

Demonstrate knowledge of the law and ability to follow the law.

Demonstrate knowledge of citizen rights and responsibilities.

Vote.

USING RECREATIONAL FACILITIES AND ENGAGING IN LEISURE ACTIVITIES

Demonstrate knowledge of available community resources.

Choose and plan activities.

Demonstrate knowledge of the value of recreation.

Engage in group and individual activities.

Plan vacation time.

Plan a social event.

Engage in hobbies, sports, music, arts and crafts.

GETTING AROUND THE COMMUNITY

Differentiate between right side and left side, front and back, to demonstrate location.

Demonstrate knowledge of traffic rules and safety.

Demonstrate knowledge and use of many means of transportation including carpools.

Understand and use a map.

Drive a car; obtain a learner's permit, then a driver's license.

Obtain car insurance.

Accept and give criticism.

Develop confidence in self.

Identify and distinguish the proper way to answer and use the telephone.

Wear appropriate apparel, using clothes or uniforms to fit social and work situations.

ACHIEVING SOCIALLY RESPONSIBLE BEHAVIOR

Develop respect for the rights and properties of others.

Recognize authority and follow instructions.

Demonstrate appropriate behavior and social etiquette in public places and when dating or eating out.

Demonstrate knowledge of important character traits.

Recognize personal roles.

MAINTAINING GOOD INTERPERSONAL SKILLS

Demonstrate listening and responding skills.

Establish and keep close relationships.

Make and keep friendships.

ACHIEVING INDEPENDENCE

Do things without help.

Accept responsibility for actions.

Get around the community and be able to travel.

Cope with changes in travel schedule.

Cope with being lost.

Follow travel safety procedures.

Choose friends.

Get to school on time.

Decide what to wear.

ACHIEVING PROBLEM-SOLVING SKILLS

Seek assistance when needed.

Recognize problems.

Anticipate consequences.

Develop and evaluate alternatives.

Develop goals, solutions, and plans.

COMMUNICATING WITH OTHERS

Recognize and respond to emergency situations.

Communicate with understanding.

Demonstrate knowledge of social cues and the subtleties of conversation, both verbal and nonverbal.

Listen to others.

Owing to the complexity, the uniqueness of mental and physical conditions and limitations, and the variety of skills to be taught, a wide range of goals exists in the area of daily living skills. Some children may become self-reliant; others may be able to accomplish only the most basic of daily living tasks (Bigge & O'Donnell, 1976). In addition, the techniques used in teaching these skills will vary widely in accordance with the child's abilities, attention motor imitation, and verbal comprehension (Snell, 1978).

Prior to beginning training in daily living skills, there must be an initial period of assessment. At times it will be more efficient to first strengthen verbal skills, attending, and imitation. Likewise, behaviors such as those that are disruptive, aggressive, or nonresponsive may not only interfere with the teaching process but may lead to inaccurate test results and confused training methods. Thus, these behaviors are best decreased or eliminated before assessment begins. The assessment itself should produce not only a detailed analysis of existing daily living skills and needs, but also an estimate of additional factors that might affect training—current level of development and functioning in relevant areas, physical limitations, problem behaviors, and practical considerations such as accessibility of needed facilities and specialized equipment.

Once the assessment is complete, the child's individual needs can be clearly defined and appropriate goals set. A task analysis of the skill(s) to be taught can then be completed and any necessary adaptive equipment (e.g., a special spoon handle or clothing with velcro fastenings) can be obtained. Following this, the child is guided through the successive steps, with assistance being gradually cut back until the child is able to perform the task independently and across settings. The issues of generalization and maintenance are of utmost importance in the teaching of daily living skills. Teachers of exceptional students should consider, at all times, the learning characteristics of the students in conjunction with the potential for new behavior.

REFERENCES

Bigge, J. L., & O'Donnell, J. G. (1976). *Teaching individuals with physical and multiple disabilities.* Columbus, OH: Merrill.

Brolin, D. E. (1989). *Life Centered Career Education: A Competency Based Approach* (3rd ed.). Reston, VA: The Council for Exceptional Children.

Snell, M. E. (1978). *Systemic instruction of the moderately and severely handicapped.* Columbus, OH: Merrill.

ECOLOGICAL ASSESSMENT
FUNCTIONAL DOMAINS
FUNCTIONAL SKILLS TRAINING

DANCE THERAPY

Dance therapy is a method by which movement is incorporated into a therapeutic or educational program. As a therapy approach, dance has been used to enhance traditional methods of medical and verbal group therapies with numerous populations, including the aged, the mentally ill, and the mentally retarded. Dance especially useful with the retarded because it does not require verbal abilities (Rogers, 1977). Benefits noted through informal observations of dance therapy programs have included improvements in general motility, speech patterns, locomotion, and social ability (Barteneiff & Lewis, 1980). Dance therapy has also resulted in reduction of muscle tension and trait anxiety (Kline et al., 1978).

Dance has also been used in a broader context to promote physical and social development. Crain, Eisenhart, and McLaughlin (1984) implemented a dance program with mildly retarded adolescent students that included movement orientation, movement exploration, dance foundations, rhythms, and traditional dances. They noted improvements for 11 of 13 participants in areas of physical and social development.

Dance therapy is useful with special populations both as an adjunct to normal group verbal therapies and as a method to enhance physical, social, and educational development (Gladding, 1992).

REFERENCES

Barteneiff, I., & Lewis, D. (1980). *Body movement: Coping with the environment.* New York: Gordon & Breach.

Crain, C., Eisenhart, M., & McLaughlin, J. (1984). The application of a multiple measurement approach to investigate the effects of a dance program on educable mentally retarded adolescents. *Research Quarterly for Exercise & Sport, 55,* 231–236.

Gladding, S. T. (1992). *Counseling as an art: The creative arts in counseling.* Alexandria, VA: American Counseling Association.

Kline, F., Burgoyne, R. W., Staples, F., Moredock, P., Snyder, V., & Ioerger, M. (1978). A report on the use of movement therapy for chronic, severely disabled outpatients. *Art Psychotherapy, 5,* 181–183.

Rogers, S. B. (1977). Contributions of dance therapy in a treatment program for retarded adolescents and adults. *Art Psychotherapy, 4,* 195–197.

CHRISTINE A. ESPIN
University of Minnesota

RECREATION FOR THE HANDICAPPED
RECREATIONAL THERAPY

DANDY-WALKER SYNDROME (DWS)

DWS is a congenital anomaly that involves the formation of a large cyst in the posterior region of the brain (known as a Dandy-Walker Formation) that results in hydrocephalus and agenesis of the central region or vermis of the cerebellum (Greenspan, 1998). It is similar to Joubert Syndrome in the latter respect and has some overlapping symptoms. Etiology is unknown, but DWS is thought to be, not genetic, but related to some invasive organism, possibly cytomegalovirus. It is sometimes diagnosable via ultrasound in utero but is more likely to be detected in infancy and early childhood.

There are significant impairments associated with most cases of DWS including mental retardation of varying degrees (in about 50% of cases), nonverbal learning disabilities in higher functioning DWS patients, and many social and behavioral problems.

Specific psychoeducational recommendations cannot be made for all DWS patients due to the degree of variability in outcome. Most will require special education services, often as Other Health Impaired, but consistent assessment and modification of programming are typically necessary. The successfulness of the shunt for the hydrocephalus is crucial to a positive outcome, and the earlier the shunting takes place, the better the prognosis.

REFERENCE

Greenspan, S. (1998). Dandy-Walker syndrome. In L. Phelps (Ed.), *Health-related disorders in children and adolescents.* (pp. 219–223). Washington, DC: American Psychological Association.

DATA-BASED INSTRUCTION

Data-based instruction is a way of describing, measuring, and assessing behavior for instructional purposes. The system is based on the behavioral theories of B. F. Skinner (1938). Data-based instruction emerged from the concept of precision teaching. Precision teaching involves operationally defining behavior and measuring, recording, and assessing behavior to determine the success of an instructional program (Idol-Maestas 1983).

Lilly (1979) listed the eight basic steps of data-based instruction. The first step is to define the instructional problem in behavioral terms. The use of behavioral terms allows the teacher to pinpoint specific descriptions of behaviors that need addressing. The behavior should be defined in such a manner that anyone observing the child would be able to determine what the behavior is and when it occurs.

The second step involves assessing the problem so the teacher will have some idea of the student's present level of performance before intervention. There must be a pattern of behavior established during baseline. Therefore, one to five instances of baseline data of each behavior is required. Baseline data collected before intervention will serve as a measure of the student's progress after intervention has been implemented.

Once the behavior has been defined and baseline data collected, the next step is to state the objectives of the instructional program. What are the teacher's expectations as a result of the educational intervention? These objectives should be clear and specific. In breaking down instructional objectives into teachable components, instructional objectives may become simple and clear or complex and detailed. Therefore, some objectives may need to be broken down into small teachable steps. This process is called task analysis. In the determination of teaching-learning procedures, the teacher should determine the instructional strategies that will be used. In data-based instruction there are no specific instructional strategies that must be used. Any strategy that produces good results is acceptable. The emphasis is placed on determining the instructional objectives first; then instructional strategies and materials are selected based on the objectives.

Once the instructional program is implemented, it is very important to collect data on a continuous basis. This information is used to assess the effectiveness of the instructional program. The more often the data are collected, the more reliable and consistent the information. These data should be collected in the same manner as the baseline data to ensure appropriateness and the accuracy of the conclusions. Lilly (1977) states that it is important for the teacher to record the data so that it can be used for instructional decisions. Recording the data is done by charting the information on a graph. There are many formats used to chart data, however, the most important consideration is that the data display a visual presentation of the student's behavior for a specific amount of time.

The data that has been collected over time is used to make decisions concerning the effectiveness of the instructional program. The following guidelines are suggested by Lilly (1979).

1. Allow enough time for an instructional procedure to have an effect (at least 1 week).
2. Do not allow a student to continue more than 2 or 3 weeks without making progress.
3. When progress does not occur, blame the instruction program, not the child.
4. When progress does occur, celebrate with everyone involved.
5. Use progress charts in discussing school programs with parents.

In addition, Lilly (1977) states that it is essential to ask the following questions during instructional decision time.

1. Is progress sufficient to justify continuation of the present instructional procedures?
2. Do progress data indicate that the instructional objectives and/or methodology is appropriate or inappropriate for the student?
3. Is the criterion level appropriate for the instructional objective?
4. If the objective is reached, what is the appropriate next step?

At all times, precision teaching and data-based instruction involves "being aware of the relationship between teaching and learning, measuring student performance regularly and frequently, and analyzing the measurements to develop instructional and motivational strategies" (West, 1990).

REFERENCES

Idol-Maestas, L. (1983). *Special educator's consultation handbook.* Rockville, MD: Aspen.

Lilly, M. S. (1977). Evaluating individual education programs. In S. Torres (Ed.), *A primer on individualized education programs for handicapped children* (pp. 26–30). Reston VA: Council for Exceptional Children.

Lilly, M. S. (1979). Learning and behavior problems, current trends. In M. S. Lilly (Ed.), *Children with exceptional needs: A survey of special education.* New York: Holt, Rinehart & Winston.

Skinner, B. F. (1938). *The behavior of organisms.* New York: Appleton Century.

West, R. (1990). Precision teaching: An introduction. *Teaching Exceptional Children, 22,* 4–9.

JANICE HARPER
*North Carolina Central
University*

DIAGNOSTIC PRESCRIPTIVE TEACHING
PRECISION TEACHING

DAY-CARE CENTERS

Formal day-care programs originated during the Industrial Revolution with custodial care in factory rooms for young children of working mothers. Early in this century, the Salvation Army in Baltimore and Hull House in Chicago began day-care programs for infants and children of working mothers. Beginning in 1933, the Federal Work Relief Project supported Emergency Nursery Schools (ENS) as a way of providing jobs for unemployed teachers. The ENS programs were similar to the later Head Start programs in that they were for preschool children, offered medical services, emphasized nutrition, and provided in-service staff training; however, ENS emphasized nurturing care while Head Start emphasizes more formal education. When the ENS program ended, day care for mothers working in war industries was funded under the Lanham Act until 1946. Other day-care programs were supported by industry during World War II. None of those early programs were intended for handicapped children, but probably some with mild problems were admitted.

Programs exclusively for disabled children excluded from school began in the 1950s. Sponsored and conducted by parent groups, most were for moderately retarded children. In the 1960s the Massachusetts Department of Mental Health added a day-care program to its preschool program because many severely retarded children were excluded from schools. Very few private preschools, kindergartens, or public schools accepted children with severe handicaps until the late 1970s. Most blind, deaf, severely retarded, and severely physically impaired children could stay at home without day-care services or go to a state-supported residential facility. After implementation of PL 94-142 in 1977, school systems supported educational programs that replaced (and were often similar to) the private day-care facilities for school-age children. Then day-care services were developed for preschool- and postschool-age handicapped groups. This is noted in the American Association on Mental Deficiency's definition of day care: "extended care services provided on an ongoing basis for individuals residing in the community and not eligible for school programs or workshops; involves social, physical, recreational, and personal-care training and activity" (Grossman, 1983, p. 167).

Efforts at integrating handicapped and nonhandicapped preschool day-care programs have increased in recent years (Branca, 1988; Guralnick, 1978, 1994; 1995; Templeman, 1989). A national survey of day-care facilities for young children and infants showed that some handicapped children were eligible for integrated services. About 21% of the centers reported accepting physically and emotionally handicapped children; about 14% would accept retarded children (Coelen, Galantz, & Calore, 1979). The tendency for separation of handicapped from nonhandicapped children is still reflected in professional literature, with almost no mention of handicaps in day-care journals and books. A few booklets (e.g., Granato, 1972) offer common-sense suggestions for day-care providers working with integrated handicapped children.

Empirical studies evaluating the effects of day-care programs for handicapped children and adults are rare, but comments on scientific and social policy issues in a book by Zigler and Gordon (1982) suggest that the research trend is toward identifying factors associated with different outcomes rather than simply attempting to determine whether day care is good for children. Guralnick (1994, 1995) studied the parent's perception of early integration of exceptional preschoolers. Notwithstanding the parental concerns of peer rejection, most parents perceived positive gains for their children.

In addition, Zigler (1991, 1995) cites the 1990 Child Care and Development Act as a step towards the solutions of day/child care problems. Indeed, Zigler predicted the inclusion of integrated child care provided by the public schools and supported by parents and family. Community placements also give services for young children with severe disabilities that are successful (Branca, 1988). Best practices for the inclusion of preschoolers with moderate to profound disabilities can be found in Templeman (1989).

REFERENCES

Branca, R. A. (1988). Implementing a program of supportive services to severely handicapped preschool age children in community programs. (Eric Clearinghouse No. EC212115)

Coelen, C., Galantz, F., & Calore, D. (1979). *Day care centers in the United States: A national profile.* Cambridge, MA: Abt Associates.

Granato, S. (1972). *Day care: Serving children with special needs.* Washington, DC: U.S. Government Printing Office.

Grossman, H. J. (1983). *Classification in mental retardation.* Washington, DC: American Association on Mental Deficiency.

Guralnick, M. J. (1978). *Early intervention and the integration of handicapped and nonhandicapped children.* Baltimore, MD: University Park Press.

Guralnick, M. J. (1994). Mother's perceptions of the benefits and drawbacks of early childhood mainstreaming. *Journal of Early Intervention, 18,* 2, 168–38.

Guralnick M. J. (1995). Parent perspectives of peer relationships and friendships in integrated and specialized programs. *American Journal on Mental Retardation, 99,* 5, 457–476.

Templeman, T. P. (1989). Integration of children with moderate and severe handicaps into a daycare center. *Journal of Early Intervention, 13,* 4, 315–328.

Zigler, E. F., & Finn-Stevenson, M. (1995). The child care crisis: Implications for the growth and development of the nation's children. *Journal of Social Issues, 51,* 3, 215–231.

Zigler, E. F., & Gilman, E. (1991). Beyond academic instruction: The twenty-first century school model for preschoolers. *New Directions for Child Development, 53,* 75–82.

Zigler, E. F., & Gordon, E. W. (Eds.). (1982). *Day care: Scientific and social issues.* Boston: Auburn House.

SUE ALLEN WARREN
Boston University
First edition

ELAINE FLETCHER-JANZEN
University of Northern Colorado
Second edition

HEAD START
LEAST RESTRICTIVE ENVIRONMENT
MAINSTREAMING
RESPITE CARE

DAYDREAMING

The literature on daydreaming from the special educator's perspective tends to fall into three categories. In the first, daydreaming is seen as a symptom of disability. In the second, it is associated with creativity and giftedness. In the third, it is reported to be an effective therapeutic device. As a symptom of disability, daydreaming is associated with both physical and cognitive disorders. It has been suggested that a central nervous system dysfunction may cause a lag in brain structure development leading to behavior such as daydreaming that inhibits learning. Petite mal epileptic seizures are also often mistaken for daydreaming. As a result, medical screening might be appropriate for chronic daydreamers. Cognitively, Blanton (1983) and others classify daydreaming as an immature behavior—along with hyperactivity, distractibility, impulsivity, procrastination, messiness, and sloppiness—that becomes a problem in educational situations. Besides possible physiological causes, inordinate daydreaming may be due to shyness (Sheridan, Kratochwill, & Elliot, 1990) deep emotional problems, or to a student's inability to focus attention on a task for any length of time.

Suggested treatments for problem daydreaming vary as widely as suggested causes. Mock et al. (1982) found that among hyperactive students with distractible cognitive styles (characterized by daydreaming, slow response time, and high error rates), the use of ritalin improved performance on some school-related tasks, decreasing both decision time and error rates. Practical suggestions for teachers include calling the student's attention to the task at hand in some inconspicuous way such as placing a hand on the student's paper or using physical proximity to convey expectations. Operant conditioning can be effective as well, using reward points or some other positive reinforcement when students finish tasks. Allowing students to choose activities that are inherently interesting to them also fosters prolonged attention.

If daydreaming needs to be overcome in some students, it seems that it should be fostered in others. The connection between fantasy and creativity is widely recognized. Daydreaming seems to accompany the period of incubation that precedes creative production. Fred Kekule's discovery of the molecular structure of benzene is a common example of the power of relaxed, unguided fantasy. Guides for parents of gifted children consistently recommend allowing their children time to daydream, even though, like the learning disabled, gifted children must often be encouraged to stay on task. These two views of daydreaming—as a creative tool for gifted children and as an obstacle for the learning disabled—may be understood in light of recent findings by Kanter (1982). After controlling for IQ, Kanter found that frequent daydreamers are slow in response production and weak in verbal creativity, but gifted in visual creative abilities. Treatments vary as educators try to overcome the former with the learning disabled and foster the latter in the gifted.

Daydreaming itself has been used in a variety of ways as a clinical device. Programmed imaging, as McQueen (1983) describes it, is often used to develop skills in the psychomotor domain. Subjects practice basketball free throws in their mind's eye, for example, before going onto the court. Controlled experiments have shown this to be highly effective. Guided daydreaming, which until recently was a more common technique in Europe than in the United States, is controlled by someone who stays outside the activities of the participants. The leader, usually a teacher or therapist, talks the subjects through an experience. This is often useful for relaxation and as an aid to memory, self-awareness, and clarifying goals or realizing internal conflicts. Once a subject becomes adept at disciplined daydreaming, it can be used as a powerful tool. Therapists have reported decreased incidence of depression, phobias, and psychosomatic disorders in patients trained to use their imaginations. It has also aided those who have trouble making decisions. Subjects are encouraged to imagine possible scenarios that might occur in consequence of a variety of decisions and then choose the most desirable. Neurotic or otherwise undesirable behaviors have also been modified with clinical use of imagery. One technique is to have the subjects practice substitute behaviors mentally before incorporating them into their daily activities. A more extreme method is the use of aversive imagery techniques, in which highly negative mental pictures are evoked to discourage maladaptive behaviors such as compulsive stealing (Singer, 1974).

REFERENCES

Blanton, G. H. (1983, February). *Social and emotional development of learning disabled children.* Paper presented at the annual convention of the Association for Children and Adults with Learning Disabilities, (ERIC Document Reproduction Service No. ED 232 336), Washington, DC.

Kanter, S. (1982). Divergent thinking abilities as a function of daydreaming frequency. *Journal for the Education of the Gifted, 5*(1), 12–23.

McQueen, D. (1983, March). *Imaging as a heuristic.* Paper presented at the annual meeting of the Conference on College Composition and Communication, Detroit, MI. (ERIC Document Reproduction Service No. ED 234 429)

Mock, K. R., Swanson, J. M., & Kinsbourne, M. (1978, March). *Stimulant effect on matching familiar figures: Changes in impulsive and distractible cognitive styles.* Paper presented at the annual meeting of the American Educational Research Association, Toronto, Canada. (ERIC Document Reproduction Service No. ED 160 189)

Sheridan, S. T., Kratochwill, T., & Elliott, S. Behavioral Consultation with parents and teachers. *School Psychology Review, 19,* 33–52.

Singer, J. L. (1974). *Imagery and daydream methods in psychotherapy and behavior modification.* New York: Academic.

JANET S. BRAND
Hunter College

HYPNOSIS
IMAGERY

DEAF

The word deaf is applied to persons who cannot hear or have a major hearing impairment. In classical writings as well as in common talk, until only a few years ago, the word deaf frequently had a strongly pejorative connotation, either in its figurative sense of deaf to the word of God or in locutions such as deaf and dumb. The latter clearly indicated a belief that those who are deaf from birth also have an intellectual defect. The term deaf-mute (used either as an adjective or as a noun), carried the notion of a double infirmity, until it was realized that the absence of speech, in those born deaf, was not related to a deficiency of the vocal organs and was only the consequence of the lack of hearing. Deaf now is used alone mostly since a majority of deaf persons have no other infirmity aside from possibly an oral language deficiency.

There is as yet no universally accepted definition of the different categories of hearing impairment. All the existing classifications are based on the mean speech range frequency thresholds obtained for the best ear by pure tone. The classification of the Bureau International d'Audiophonologie (BIAP; International Office for Audiophonology) is based on the mean hearing loss for 500, 1000, and 2000 Hz (ISO standards). It uses the terms recommended by the World Health Organization for the grading of all types of impairments: mild (20–40 dB), moderate (40–70 dB), severe (70–90 dB), and profound (more than 90 dB). The last category is itself divided in three subgroups, because there are large differences in the possibilities of residual hearing use among those whose average loss is only slightly superior to 90 dB and those who have a more than 100 dB hearing loss. Other classifications use different gradings and terms for the less than 70 dB categories, but there is fair agreement concerning the definition of the severe and profound groups.

Pure-tone audiometry, however, provides only a partial picture of the residual hearing capacity. It does not reflect the variable potential gain that can be brought by adequate hearing aid fitting. Several authors such as Pollack (1964), advocate the aided audiogram as a more meaningful measure of functional hearing capacity. Even this, however, does not reflect the qualitative aspects of residual hearing, which may vary extensively among individuals with the same pure-tone audiometric thresholds. Some insight about the quality of hearing may be gained by investigation of psychoacoustic tuning curves (Harrison, 1984), but these measures cannot presently be applied to small children because they require the subjects' active and informed cooperation.

These difficulties in establishing a well-founded functional classification have led several authors to adopt simpler general definitions for educational purposes. According to the Conference of Executives of American Schools for the Deaf (Frisina, 1974), a deaf person is one whose hearing is disabled to an extent (usually 70 dB International Standards Organization or greater) that precludes the understanding of speech through the ear alone, without or with the use of a hearing aid; a hard-of-hearing person is one whose hearing is disabled to an extent (usually 35 to 69 dB International Standards Organization) that makes difficult, but does not preclude, the understanding of speech through the ear alone, without or with a hearing aid.

It is necessary to stress the importance in both of these definitions of the word usually because there is a large overlap in the degree of pure-tone hearing loss of people who functionally correspond to one or the other category. Recently, Quigley and Kretschmer (1982) stated that for educational purposes, "a deaf child or adult is one who sustained a profound (91 dB or greater) primarily sensorineural hearing impairment prelingually" (p. 2). This trend toward considering as deaf only those with a larger than 90 dB hearing impairment is probably related to development of early intervention programs and improvement of hearing aids, resulting in earlier and better spoken language acquisition for an increasing number of the less profoundly hearing impaired.

In addition to the former definitions, the definition that was adopted by a UNESCO experts' committee (1985) introduces the notion of relativity of deafness to prevalent socioeconomic conditions:

> To be considered as *deaf* those children whose spontaneous speech and language development have been very much retarded or is completely absent due to their severe hearing impairment or a hearing impairment combined with a lack of training and/or technical amplification. In countries with adequate resources for diagnosis, training, and provision of hearing aids, some children with hearing impairment would not be included in the above-mentioned group, whereas they would be regarded as functionally deaf in countries lacking these resources. (p. 5)

Other terms such as auditorially impaired or deficient, acoustically impaired, hypoacoustic, or, in French, demi-sourd (half deaf), are used either as synonyms for deaf and hearing impaired or to designate a category of the latter. The word cophotic, limited to the medical profession, is applied to those ears that have completely lost their auditory function.

The World Health Organization recommends that a distinction be made in all physical or mental defects, among impairment, disability, and handicap. Deaf children and adults are impaired in having a pathological auditory system. They are consequently disabled by difficulty in perceiving speech and environmental sounds. This disability can make them more or less severely handicapped by limiting their overall personal and social functioning. Some types of impairment, those owed to conductive hearing

loss, can be alleviated or cured by medical and/or surgical therapy. For most deaf persons, as defined by the Conference of Executives of American Schools for the deaf, the physical impairment is due to inner ear or nervous system damage and is irreversible. The disability can, however, be reduced by appropriate hearing aid fitting, training, and, in the case of children, education. The handicap can be lessened or even eliminated in two ways: through the reduction of the disability or through the functioning in a sociocultural group where hearing is not necessary.

Among deaf and hard-of-hearing children and adults, it is important to distinguish between those who were affected from birth or shortly thereafter (before language was established) and those who became hearing impaired later on. These groups are commonly called prelingually and postlingually deaf, respectively. The prelingually deaf child cannot acquire language by the same natural process as the normally hearing. Their auditory pathways in the brain, as well as those parts of the cerebral cortex concerned with the processing of spoken language, are not adequately stimulated in the early years most favorable for language development. This lack of adequate stimulation during the sensitive period not only results in great difficulties in the acquisition of spoken language skills, but may also produce permanent structural changes in the central nervous system. These changes could diminish the capacity of the brain to efficiently process speech-linked information later on, even if normal hearing could be restored, or artificial hearing produced (Périer et al., 1984).

Because of the interference of deafness with language acquisition prelingually deaf children and adults markedly differ from the postlingually deafened. The latter have a sensory impairment that interferes with their ability to perceive speech and other sounds, but they have a normally and completely developed language function. Although the quality of their speech may become distorted after some time because of the lack of auditory feedback, they usually remain intelligible. Their reading and writing capacities remain intact. By contrast, prelingually deaf children have such difficulties in acquiring spoken language that most of them, when they leave school as adolescents or young adults, have a linguistic insufficiency in addition to their sensory impairment (Conrad, 1979). Not only are they deficient in oral language skills, but also in reading and writing capacities. This linguistic insufficiency constitutes a serious handicap for their integration within the society of the normally hearing. It can, however, be attenuated and largely prevented by early and adequate education. When this includes sign language, a normal linguistic function may be developed in that modality, allowing full participation in the sociocultural life of the deaf community.

Deafness is related to a physical impairment, like other disabilities requiring rehabilitative and educational measures. It differs, however, from all these by a unique feature: the fact that this disability has given birth to a specific language, sign language (Bellugi 1972). Just as a wide variety of spoken languages have evolved among the normally hearing world population, different sign languages have originated among the scattered communities of deaf people (Stokoe, 1972). However, many western world sign languages have a partly common trunk because of the important influence of the Abbé de l'Epée, the first educator of the deaf to recognize, in the late eighteenth century in France, the sign language of the deaf. There are, therefore, more common or similar signs among western sign languages than there are common or similar words in spoken languages. This facilitates communication among deaf people of different nationalities.

The use of sign language eliminates all handicaps for those who are proficient in it. Indeed, it is the normally hearing individual who becomes handicapped when he or she tries to participate in a group where sign language is the principal or only mode of communication. The common language is a powerful bond that largely contributes to the creation of a group identity. This tendency is strengthened when the group is a minority subjected to strong social pressure. This is particularly true for the deaf, because sign language was not recognized as a proper language until several linguists such as William Stokoe (1972), Ursula Bellugi (1972), and others brought forward the convincing results of their research. They demonstrated that sign languages of the deaf are as worthy of esteem and respect as vocal languages, possessing all the attributes of the latter except oral realization. Among these attributes are not only grammatical correctness, arbitrariness, and double articulation, but also more affective qualities such as the capacity to express humor and poetry.

In the past, many deaf individuals did not themselves realize the value of their manual language (Meadow, 1980). They were influenced by the hearing society's contempt for what was regarded as a primitive and crude mode of communication, incapable of expressing abstraction and therefore unsuitable for high-level intellectual processes. The new status of sign language has done much not only to promote its diffusion and enrichment, but also to upgrade its users' self-confidence and self-esteem. This has given new impetus to deaf organizations and prompted the birth of such movements as Deaf Pride. This movement promulgates the notion that the deaf are equal but different and want this difference to be recognized and taken into account in the organization of society as a whole. Sign language supports deaf culture, mainly characterized by social and artistic events. It is, however, more appropriate to speak of cultural values rather than of a complete culture because the deaf share many ingredients of the hearing majorities' cultures such as their literature and their religions.

While some of the deaf reject spoken language and refuse to make any efforts at participation in sociocultural activities with the hearing, most of them aspire to bilingualism (i.e., the use of both sign and spoken languages) and biculturalism. Individuals who are deaf are considered bilingual if they are able to communicate effectively in both American Sign Language (ASL) and English or the spoken language of their country. They are considered bicultural if they are capable of functioning in both the deaf community and the majority culture (Baker & Baker, 1997). Bilingual-bicultural programs in the schools differ from other programs most notably by the approach to first language acquisition. These programs advocate for ASL to be the first language of children who are deaf because cognitive research indicates that "effective language has to be fast and clear. ASL is an efficient language for visual learning and is easier for deaf children to acquire as a first language than any form of English" (Finnegan, 1992, in Baker & Baker, 1997).

Bilingual-bicultural programs are generally found outside mainstream education and are relatively new. The gain in popularity may well be hampered or supported by achievement outcome studies. Baker and Baker (1997) suggest that students in rural areas may not have access to this approach, and classes for caregivers (especially in rural areas) are necessary for success.

Better information for society at large and sensitization to the rightful demands of the deaf has contributed in recent years to strengthening biculturalism. An important event in bringing the deaf to the attention of the hearing world was the success of Mark Medoff's play *Children of a Lesser God,* in which a deaf actress held the principal part. The play was awarded the Tony Award for best play of the year in 1980. In addition, the "Deaf Prez Now" or Gallaudet University protest in 1988 galvanized individuals who are deaf in ways that have not impacted the hearing community. In 1988 students at Gallaudet University protested the hiring of a hearing University President. They were successful in removing the President from office. The students removed hearing members of the board of trustees as well (McIntosh, 1996).

According to many psychologists and sociolinguists, it is important for the personality structure of severely and profoundly hearing-impaired individuals that they identify themselves as deaf. The realization that they are different, but not inferior, allows them to direct all their energies in a positive direction, rather than striving toward the unattainable goal of trying to be like the hearing. According to this view, deaf children of hearing parents (who represent more than 90% of deaf children) should be given the opportunity at an early age for social intercourse with deaf adults who can serve as realistic models. For many deaf adults, sign language is essential for the full expression of their personality. As a consequence, they deeply feel their belonging to the deaf community and cherish the values of deaf culture. The concept of "identity formation" is starting to be realized in the deaf and hearing communities. Professionals are being invited to take a more "ethical and positive view of sign language and the deaf community" (Carver, 1999). It is clearly felt that Deaf culture adds to, and does not detract from, a child's education and identity formation (Carver, 1999).

REFERENCES

Baker, S., & Baker, K. (1997). *Educating children who are deaf or hard-of-hearing: Bilingual-bicultural education.* Reston VA: ERIC Clearinghouse on Disabilities and Gifted Education. (ERIC Digest No. E 553)

Bellugi, U. (1972). Studies in sign language. In T. J. O'Rourke (Ed.), *Psycholinguistics and total communication: The state of the art. American Annals of the Deaf,* pp. 68–74.

Carver, R. (1999). Identity and deafness: Who am I? *Deaf World Web*: dww.org.

Conrad, R. (1979). *The deaf school child.* London: Harper & Row.

Finnegan, M. (1992). Bilingual-bicultural education. *The Endeavor, 3,* 1–8.

Frisina, R. (1974). *Report of the committee to redefine deaf and hard of hearing for educational purposes.* (Mimeo.)

Harrison, R. V. (1984). Objective measures of cochlear frequency selectivity in animals and in man. A review. *Acta Neurological Belgica, 84,* 213–232.

Meadow, K. P. (1980). *Deafness and child development.* London: Arnold.

Périer, O., Alegria, J., Buyse, M., D'Alimonte, G., Gilson, D., & Serniclaes, W. (1984). Consequences of auditory deprivation in animals and humans. *Acta Oto-Laryngologica* (Suppl. 411), 60–70.

Pollack, D. (1964). Acoupedics: A uni-sensory approach to auditory training. *Volta Review, 66,* 400–409.

Quigley, S. P., & Kretschmer, R. E. (1982). *The education of deaf children: Issues, theory and practice.* London: Arnold.

Stokoe, W. C. (1972). *Semiotics and human sign language.* Paris: Mouton.

UNESCO. (1985). *Consultation on alternative approaches for the education of the deaf.* Paris: UNESCO Headquarters.

OLIVIER PÉRIER
Université Libre de Bruxelles,
Centre Comprendre et Parler
First edition

ELAINE FLETCHER-JANZEN
University of Northern Colorado
Second edition

CONDUCTIVE HEARING LOSS
DEAF EDUCATION

DEAF, INTERPRETERS FOR

See INTERPRETERS FOR THE DEAF.

DEAF-BLIND

There exists a broad range of visual and auditory impairments among deaf-blind persons, indicating an enormous diversity in the severity of disabilities within this population. The term deaf-blind (also called dual sensory impairment) covers persons with severe visual and hearing disabilities who are unable to profit from special programs designed solely for deaf or blind children and youths (*Federal Register,* 1975).

It is estimated that there are over 5,000 children and youth who are deaf-blind in the United States (Arizona Deaf-Blind Project, 1998). Maternal rubella, CHARGE Association, Usher's Syndrome, and meningitis are among the top four causes of deaf-blindness in the United States. Additionally, deaf-blind persons often are afflicted with congenital heart disease, mental retardation (Vernon, Grieve, & Shaver, 1980), physical handicaps, social/emotional issues, and communication delays (Arizona Deaf-Blind Project, 1998).

Deaf-blindness has often been associated with Helen Keller and her teacher Anne Sullivan (Lash, 1980). Although some deaf-blind people function within or above normal intelligence, many require extraordinary educational training. The separate handicaps are not additive but multiplicative in nature (Warren, 1984), and often cause severe learning problems. Deaf-blind children have often been referred to as the most difficult group of children to educate (Sims-Tucker & Jensema, 1984). They frequently engage in stereotypic behaviors that interfere with learning and communication. In an attempt to meet the special needs of this population, Regional Centers for Services for Deaf-Blind Children was established in 1967 (Sims-Tucker & Jensema, 1984).

Educational programming for deaf-blind children, including assessment and evaluation, continues to be a difficult task. The trend in educating children with severe handicaps has emphasized a more functional curriculum (Brown et al., 1979). Similarly, educators of deaf-blind children are turning to these curricular approaches for developing intervention programs in such areas as self-help, prevocational and vocational skills, communication, and sensory development (Vadasy & Fewell, 1984). Programming developed by Van Dijk (1971) has provided teachers, parents, and therapists with an invaluable communication curriculum that incorporates movement theory, which is often associated with the coactive movement. In addition, the emphasis on visual as well as auditory training can be seen in educational programs developed by Goetz and Utley (undated) and Efron and DuBoff (1979).

The Arizona Deaf-Blind Program has recently been established as a federally-funded free resource for professionals and families working with deaf-blind individuals. It is housed at the Arizona School for the Deaf and Blind. The program provides consultation services for families of deaf-blind children, provides a lending library, and maintains an on-line interactive webpage. The project can be contacted at P.O. Box 87010, Tucson, AZ, 85754 or at www.azdb.org. Their telephone is 520-770-3680. Other resources are:

American Association of the Deaf-Blind, Inc.
Silver Spring, Maryland 20901
Telephone: 301-588-6545
TTY: 301-523-1265

Helen Keller National Center for Deaf-Blind
111 Middle Neck Road
Sands Point, New York 11050
Telephone: 516-944-8900
TTY: 516-944-8637

REFERENCES

Arizona Deaf-Blind Program. (1998). Deaf-blindness Fact Sheet. www.azdb.org.

Brown, L., Branston, M., Hamre-Nietupski, S., Pumpian, I., Certo, N., & Gruenewald, L. (1979). A strategy for developing chronological age appropriate and functional curricular content for severely handicapped adolescents and young adults. *Journal of Special Education, 13,* 81–90.

Efron, M., & DuBoff, B. (1979). *A vision guide for teachers of deaf-blind children.* Raleigh, NC: South Atlantic Regional Center for Services to Deaf-Blind Children.

Goetz, L., & Utley, B. (undated). *Auditory assessment and program manual for severely handicapped deaf-blind students.* Parsons, KS: Words & Pictures.

Lash, J. P. (1980). *Helen and teacher: The story of Helen Keller and Anne Sullivan Macy.* New York: Delacorte.

Lockett, T., & Rudolph, J. (1980). Deaf-blind children with maternal rubella: Implications for adult services. *American Annals of the Deaf, 125,* 1000–1006.

Sims-Tucker, B., & Jensema, C. (1984). Severely and profoundly auditorially/visually impaired students: The deaf-blind population. In P. Valletutti & B. Sims-Tucker (Eds.), *Severely and profoundly handicapped students: Their nature and needs* (pp. 269–317). Baltimore, MD: Brookes.

Vadasy, P., & Fewell, R. (1984). Predicting the futures of deaf-blind adolescents: Their living and vocational options. *Education of the Visually Handicapped, 16,* 12–19.

Van Dijk, J. (1971). Learning difficulties and deaf-blind children. *Proceedings of the Fourth International Conference on Deaf-*

Blind Children. Watertown, MA: Perkins School for the Blind.

Vernon, M., Grieve, B., & Shaver, K. (1980). Handicapping conditions associated with the congenital rubella syndrome. *American Annals of the Deaf, 125*(8), 993–997.

Warren, D. (1984). *Blindness and early childhood development.* New York: American Foundation for the Blind.

VIVIAN I. CORREA
University of Florida
First edition

ELAINE FLETCHER-JANZEN
University of Northern Colorado
Second edition

DEAF
KELLER, HELEN
MOVEMENT THERAPY
VISUALLY HANDICAPPED

DEAF EDUCATION

The history of deaf education is relatively short because no records exist of organized teaching in prehistoric times or in the ancient civilizations of Egypt, Greece, and Rome. Although a few records exist of previous isolated examples of deaf individuals reaching some degree of education, Pedro Ponce de Leon (1520–1584) is generally considered to be the first teacher of the deaf. A Benedictine monk, he was entrusted with the education of several deaf children of Spanish nobility, and received wide publicity as a result of his successes. The records concerning the first teachers of the deaf are full of information showing that many of the techniques used today find their roots in the work of those pioneers. The reader is referred to the excellent survey by Moores (1978) for a review. However, it is necessary to mention the Abbott de l'Epée and Samuel Heinicke, because confrontation between their methods was at the heart of the oral versus manual controversy that has profoundly divided deaf educators for two centuries.

De l'Epée established the first public school for the deaf in the world, in 1755, in his Paris home. He started it when he was asked to give religious instruction to deaf twin sisters who used signs to communicate between them. De l'Epée understood that gestures could express human thought as much as spoken language and believed sign language to be the natural language of the deaf. He, therefore, set out to learn it from his pupils, but felt compelled to supplement their natural signs by newly formed "methodical" signs in order to obtain a complete sign counterpart of French syntax and morphology. The teaching of articulation was regarded by him as of lesser importance than that of signs and written language.

Samuel Heinicke taught several deaf children as a private tutor in different parts of Germany and established a school in Leipzig in 1778. He prided himself on being able to teach his pupils to speak clearly, and was strongly opposed to the teaching of written before spoken language, which he considered the only appropriate vehicle of thought. Heinicke and his followers Graser and Hill bitterly criticized de l'Epée's method, considering speech to be the first priority of teaching and sign language detrimental to that cause.

Controversy between the advocates of oralism and manualism, which started with de l'Epée and Heinicke, was lively during most of the nineteenth century, not only in Europe, but also in the United States. The first school for the deaf in the United States was founded by Thomas Hopkins Gallaudet, in 1847, with Laurent Clerc, a deaf teacher trained in Paris by de l'Epée's successor, Sicard. Other manual schools were created along the same lines, most of them paying little or no attention to the teaching of speech and articulation. Other U.S. educators responded with the creation of strictly oral schools. The controversy between manual and oral methods was later embodied by two exceptional personalities: Edward Miner Gallaudet (Thomas's son) and Alexander Graham Bell. The former was convinced of the importance of spoken as well as sign language and was instrumental in establishing an oral-manual combined method in most American schools. Bell observed that education of the deaf in residential schools isolated them from the hearing society, and claimed that sign language was detrimental to the acquisition of English. He advocated the elimination of both sign language and the deaf teachers who used it.

In 1880 an international congress of educators of the deaf convened in Milan, Italy. It adopted two resolutions:

1. Considering the unquestionable superiority of speech over signs for the most perfect knowledge of language, the oral method must be preferred to the gestual method.

2. Considering that the simultaneous use of signs and speech has the disadvantage of being noxious to speech, to lip reading, and to the precision of ideas, the purely oral method must be preferred.

These resolutions were enforced in all European countries, but in the United States Edward Gallaudet opposed Bell and managed to restrict their application. Not only did he maintain a school system using the combined oral-manual method, but he was also able to educate teachers of the deaf in this method at the National Deaf Mute College, Washington, DC; that school was to become the present Gallaudet College. From that time on, the opposition between Bell and Gallaudet increased. It led to the formation of two rival groups of schools and teachers: the exclusively oral and the combined oral-manual.

In Europe, oral education continued to prevail, unchallenged, during more than half of the twentieth century. After World War II, progress in electroacoustic technology gave new impetus to oralism. Hopes arose that auditory training with sophisticated apparatus and efficient individual hearing aids combined with lip reading would enable hearing-impaired children to develop their speech skills, both receptively and expressively, to a much larger extent then previously. Whetnall and Fry in London (1964) and the John Tracy Clinic in Los Angeles (Thielman, 1970), among many others, considered that early intervention would allow most deaf children to attend ordinary schools for the normally hearing or special units attached to those schools. The integration—or mainstreaming—movement that they initiated progressively gathered more and more strength in Great Britain, then in the United States and continental Europe.

It is generally accepted today that many hearing-impaired children, with early education, proper hearing aid fitting, and continued support, can successfully be educated with the normally hearing (Nix, 1976; Webster & Ellwood, 1985). While the degree of hearing loss is an important factor in determining which hearing-impaired children can be mainstreamed, it is generally recognized that this factor is by no means decisive in itself. Some profoundly deaf children can succeed in ordinary schools, while others with more residual hearing may not be able to do so (Périer et al., 1980). There is, therefore, no consensus concerning the proportion of deaf and hard-of-hearing children that should be integrated. The present situation varies greatly among nations. In some such as Italy, the official policy is that all handicapped children should be mainstreamed. Other countries, like West Germany, maintain separate special school systems for the profoundly deaf and the hard of hearing, so that even the majority of the latter are not educated with the normally hearing. Several developing countries where special education has yet to be organized view mainstreaming as a tempting alternative to the building and maintaining of special schools. Caution against the excesses of such a trend is voiced by numerous educators of the deaf, who argue that most of the profoundly deaf will continue to need special education. The pros and cons of mainstreaming have been aptly described by Meadow (1980), who argues that the options should carefully be weighed for each child.

Sign language interpretation services for the deaf have been developed primarily in the United States to assist the deaf in all circumstances in which they may benefit from them. Legal provisions ensuring that a deaf child has the right to the best possible education has made it possible in some cases to provide support services in schools or universities, allowing more deaf children and students to be mainstreamed than was formerly possible. In addition to sign language interpretation, other forms of interpretation are beginning to be developed in some countries: oral interpretation and oral interpretation with cued speech.

While the trend toward mainstream education has steadily increased over the years, the hope that early speech and hearing training would solve the language and education difficulties of most hearing-impaired children has proved overly optimistic. Several studies, among them Conrad's (1979), demonstrated that whatever method was used, whether oral or manual, the majority of deaf school graduates reached a mean reading age equivalent only to that of 9- to 10-year-old hearing children. Thus, the existing methods had not prevented relative failure to develop good command of the societal language (English in this case), even in its written form. Other studies reviewed by Quigley & Kretschmer (1982) showed that deaf children of deaf parents who had had signs as their first language were not disadvantaged in the oral skills and had slightly but significantly better gradings in overall language evaluation when compared with deaf children of hearing parents.

These results, together with the rehabilitation of sign language, were largely instrumental in the birth and development of the total communication (TC) philosophy. This, as defined by Denton (1970), is the right of a deaf child to learn to use all forms of communication available to develop language competence. This includes the full spectrum: child-devised gestures, speech, formal sign language, finger spelling, speech reading, reading, writing, as well as any other methods that may be developed in the future. Every deaf child should also be provided with the opportunity to learn to use any remnant of residual hearing he or she may have by employing the best possible electronic equipment for amplifying sound. Many schools in the United States, and a growing number throughout the world, have adhered to the principle of TC, although there are various interpretations of its meaning. More and more infant programs throughout the world are using it from the earliest age; many are urging parents to learn to communicate with their children through signs in addition to speech. Such combination of signs and speech has been termed bimodal communication by Schlesinger (1978).

Several types of manual aids other than signs are used to facilitate the reception or the production of spoken language. While many educators are using these or some form of bimodal communication for the profoundly deaf, others continue to use exclusively oral methods.

The Table is an attempt at classification of the methods currently used. It must be borne in mind, however, that various combinations are possible; some techniques developed within the framework of a given method are applicable in other contexts. For instance, in some Belgian centers, cued speech (3.1) is used in combination with bimodal communication (4.1) and with the verbo-tonal method (1). Five groups can be distinguished: auditory, oral, oral plus manual aids, combined, and manual.

1. Auditory unisensory or acoupedic methods rely on

Classifications of Methods Used in Deaf Education

1. Auditory		Auditory unisensory or acoupedic
2. Oral		Oral-aural, multisensory
3. Oral + Manual Aids	3.1	Oral-aural + lip-reading complements
	3.2	Oral-aural + manual representation of phonemes
	3.3	Oral-aural + finger spelling
4. Combined	4.1	Unilingual bimodal communication or simultaneous method
	4.2	Bilingual bimodal communication
5. Manual		Visual unisensory communication by sign language alone

auditory training to develop spoken language. Speech reading is either not encouraged or suppressed during training periods (Pollack, 1964). In the verbo-tonal method (Guberina et al., 1972), perception of acoustic features through the tactile sense is used in addition to hearing. The auditory global approach of Calvert and Silverman (1975) stands at the margin between the acoupedic and the oral-aural, since "the primary, although not always the exclusive, channel for speech development is auditory."

2. Oral also called oral-aural (Simmons-Martin, 1972). Auditory perception and speech reading are used as well as other modalities, but signs are excluded. Ling (1976) describes systematic speech development procedure primarily based on audition though not neglecting tactile and visual support, as in Calvert and Silverman's multisensory approach, used when the auditory global is not sufficient. Van Uden's maternal reflective method (1970) insists on the necessity of active oral-aural dialogue and natural prosody.

3.1 Oral-aural plus lip-reading complements. In cued speech (Cornett, 1967) and related systems, the oral-aural approach is combined with a system of hand shapes executed near the mouth, synchronously with speech. The hand brings only that part of the information that is not supplied by lip reading. The combination of this information allows the deaf child to unequivocally identify by sight the speech sounds and syllables that the hearing identify through the ear (Nicholls & Ling, 1982; Périer et al., 1986).

3.2 Oral-aural plus manual representation of phonemes. In the French Borel-Maisonny method (1979), and in the German Phonembestimmte Manual System (PMS) of Schulte (1974), the oral-aural methodology is aided by contrived gestures that correspond to some of the characteristics of speech sounds and thus help in their identification and production. The gestures bring independent information that is not linked to lip reading.

3.3 Oral-aural plus finger spelling. These are the U.S. Rochester (Scouten, 1942) and U.S.S.R. neo-oralism (Morkovin, 1960) methods. Finger spelling is executed by the teacher simultaneously with speech; the child is asked to accompany his or her own speech by finger spelling. Since the latter is a representation of written language, reading and writing are strongly emphasized.

4.1 Unilingual bimodal communication or simultaneous method. One language, that of the hearing society and of most deaf children's parents, is simultaneously expressed in speech and signs. There are numerous varieties of signed representations of spoken language. Some are close to the regional sign language of the deaf, differing mostly in word order; others use additional signs to convey syntactical and morphological information; still others are wholly contrived (Crystal & Craig, 1978).

4.2 Bilingual bimodal communication. Spoken language in an oral-aural approach is used in certain situations by hearing persons, while sign language is used in other situations by deaf and hearing persons. In early education, it is often considered acceptable for hearing parents who have not yet mastered sign language to use those signs they have learned in combination with their spoken language (Bouvet, 1981; Erting, 1978).

5. Visual unisensory communication by sign language alone. While no educators advocate that deaf children should not learn the major societal language, a few favor the exclusive use of sign language for early education. Only when sign language is firmly established as a first language is the majority's societal language taught as a second language (Ahlgren, 1980). In some programs, teaching is first done in the written form, spoken language being delayed (Mali & Rickli, 1983).

The status of deaf education in 1985 is characterized by a great vitality and a large diversity, although the antagonism between methods has somewhat abated. The oral-manual controversy is not as bitter as before, with most people on each side now recognizing the merits of the other (Tervoort, 1982a, 1982b). The question today is not so much of a choice between exclusively oral and combined oral-manual methods as of deciding for whom, when, how, and how much each modality should be used. General agreement exists on the paramount importance of early detection, assessment, and intervention, including proper hearing aid fitting and maintenance. The role of parents as the first educators of their deaf children, already stressed by Whetnall and Fry and the John Tracy Clinic, is now widely recognized (UNESCO, 1985). Their full participation is essential for the success of any method. Parents should, therefore, be thoroughly informed about the different programs available so that they can make their own choices. The fact that more than 90% of deaf children's parents are normally hearing must be taken into account in any decision about education policy. Whichever method is adopted, and whether priority is given to speech or sign, educators of today all have common goals: to enable deaf children to acquire the mastery of language needed to assert their personalities and attain full accomplishment; to bring deaf children to complete literacy, through which

they will be able to reach the degree of academic achievement corresponding to their intellectual capacities and personal motivation.

REFERENCES

Ahlgren, E. (1980). The sign language group in Stockholm. In E. Ahlgren & Bengman (Eds.), Papers from the first international symposium on the sign language research (pp. 3–7). Leksand.

Borel-Maisonny, S. (1979). Absence d'expression verbale. Paris: A.R.P.L.O.E.

Bouvet, D. (1981). La Parole de l'enfant sourd. Paris: Presses Universitaires de France, Collection Le Fil Rouge.

Calvert, D. R., & Silverman, S. R. (1975). Speech and deafness: A text for learning and teaching. Washington, DC: A. G. Bell Association.

Conrad, R. (1979). The deaf school child. London: Harper & Row.

Cornett, R. O. (1967). Cued speech. American Annals of the Deaf, 112, 3–13.

Crystal, D., & Craig, E. (1978). Contrived sign language. In I. M. Schlesinger & L. Namir (Eds.), Sign language of the deaf (pp. 141–168). New York: Academic.

Denton, D. (1970). Remarks in support of a system of total communication for deaf children. Communication Symposium. Frederick, MD: Maryland School for the Deaf.

Erting, C. (1978). Language policy and deaf ethnicity in the United States. Sign Language Studies, 19, 139–152.

Guberina, P., Skaric, I., & Zaga, B. (1972). Case studies in the use of restricted bands of frequencies in auditory rehabilitation of the deaf. Zagreb, Yugoslavia: Institute of Phonetics Faculty of Arts.

Ling, D. (1976). Speech and the hearing-impaired child: Theory and practice. Washington, DC: A. G. Bell Association.

Malé, A., & Rickli, F. (1983). Introduction au bilinguisme: Langue des signes française—français oral, à l'école de Montbrillant. Geneva, Switzerland: Départment de l'Instruction Publique.

Moores, D. F. (1978). Educating the deaf: Psychology, principles, and practices. Boston: Houghton Mifflin.

Morkovin, B. (1960). Experiment in teaching deaf preschool children in the Soviet Union. Volta Review, 62, 260–268.

Nicholls, G. H., & Ling, D. (1982). Cued speech and the reception of spoken language. Journal of Speech and Hearing Research, 25, 262–269.

Nix, G. (1976). Mainstream education for hearing impaired children and youth. New York: Grune & Stratton.

Périer, O., Capouillez, J. M., & Paulissen, D. (1980). The relationship between the degree of auditory deficiency and the possibility of successful mainstreaming in schools for hearing children. In H. Hartmann (Ed.), 1st International Congress of the Hard of Hearing (pp. 348–353). Hamburg: Deutscher Schwerhorigenbund.

Périer, O., Charlier, B., Hage, C., & Alegria, J. (1986). Evaluation of the effects of prolonged cued speech practice upon the reception and internal processing of spoken language. Proceedings of the 1985 International Congress of Educators of the Deaf. Manchester, England.

Pollack, D. (1964). Acoupedics: An unisensory approach to auditory training. *Volta Review, 66,* 400–409.

Quigley, S. P., & Kretschmer, R. F. (1982). *The education of deaf children: Issues, theory and practice.* London: Arnold.

Schlesinger, H. S. (1978). The acquisition of bimodal language. In I. M. Schlesinger & L. Namir (Eds.), *Sign language of the deaf.* New York: Academic.

Schulte, K. (1974). *The phonemetransmitting manual system* (PMS). Heidelberg: Julius Verlag.

Scouten, E. (1942). *A revaluation of the Rochester method.* Rochester, NY: Rochester School for the Deaf.

Simmons-Martin, A. (1972). The oral/aural procedure: Theoretical basis and rationale. *Volta Review, 74,* 541–551.

Tervoort, B. T. (1982a). Communication and the deaf. *Proceedings of the International Congress on Education of the Deaf* (pp. 219–229). Hamburg. Heidelberg: Julius Verlag.

Tervoort, B. T. (1982b). The future: Oralism versus manualism? *Proceedings of the International Congress on Education of the Deaf* (pp. 544–547). Hamburg. Heidelberg: Julius Verlag.

Thielman, V. (1970). John Tracy Clinic correspondence course for parents of preschool deaf children. *Proceedings of the International Congress on Education of the Deaf* (pp. 156–158). Stockholm.

UNESCO (1985). Consultation on alternative approaches for the education of the deaf. Paris: UNESCO.

Van Uden, A. (1970). New realizations in the light of the pure oral method. *Volta Review, 72,* 524–536.

Webster, A., & Ellwood, J. (1985). *The hearing-impaired child in the ordinary school.* London: Croom Helm.

Whetnall, E., & Fry, D. (1964). *The deaf child.* Springfield, IL: Thomas.

OLIVIER PÉRIER
*Université Libre de Bruxelles,
and Centre Comprendre et
Parler*

AMERICAN SIGN LANGUAGE
DEAF
FINGERSPELLING
TOTAL COMMUNICATION

DEBORAH P. *v.* TURLINGTON

Deborah P. (1979) is the federal district court case that struck down the competency testing program requirements for high-school graduation in the state of Florida. Deborah P. represented the class of all students in the state who were in danger of failing the test, including students of all ethnic backgrounds. The federal district court found that the competency testing program was unconstitutional for two reasons. The program had failed to provide students with adequate notice of the changes in requirements for a diploma, and the program was held to be ra-

cially discriminatory under the Fourteenth Amendment. According to the court, the competency testing program tended to perpetuate preexisting patterns of racial discrimination within the Florida school system. Children in special education programs were not specifically addressed in *Deborah P.,* however, similar issues may be raised if special education students are required to pass competency tests or denied diplomas on the basis of testing programs that discriminate on the basis of race or handicapping condition.

REFERENCE

Deborah P. v. Turlington. (1979). #78-892-CIV-T-C, U.S. District Court, Middle District, Tampa Division, July 12 (slip opinion).

CECIL R. REYNOLDS
Texas A & M University

DECROLY, OVIDE (1871–1932)

Ovide Decroly, a Belgian physician whose hospital work brought him into contact with many handicapped children, reasoned that the best treatment for such children would be a sound educational program. He established a special school for "the retarded and abnormal" in 1901. A few years later, he founded a school for normal children, where he demonstrated that the methods he was using successfully with handicapped children were equally effective with the nonhandicapped.

Decroly's educational methods were unique. The cornerstone of his method was what he called the "center of interest." Centers of interest were developed around four basic needs: food, protection from the elements, defense against common dangers, and work. Emphasis was placed on learning through activities that grow out of the interests and needs of the students. As much as a year's study could grow out of one topic or theme.

Decroly's work profoundly influenced the European concept of education for both normal and handicapped children. Many of his ideas were similar to those of John Dewey, but Decroly was more a practitioner than a philosopher and his foremost contribution was the establishment of schools that served as models of education based on the needs of children.

REFERENCES

Hamaide, A. (1924). *The Decroly class.* New York: Dutton.
Kajava, K. (1951). *The traditional European school and some recent experiments in the new education.* Doctoral dissertation. New York: Columbia University.

PAUL IRVINE
Katonah, New York

DEFECTIVE SPEECH

See SPEECH.

DEFINITION OF HANDICAPPING CONDITIONS

See SPECIFIC HANDICAP.

DEINSTITUTIONALIZATION

Deinstitutionalization has been a movement based on the principles of normalization. Handicapped individuals, mostly the retarded and emotionally handicapped, have been moved out of institutions into alternative community living arrangements. Wolfensberger (1972), one of the most outspoken advocates of both deinstitutionalization and normalization, maintained that normalization referred not to treatment but to services, situations, and attitudes that would bring about humane care for the handicapped. The practice called for small, community-based group homes that permitted residents to participate in local activities and be closer to their families as opposed to long-term, total life care in institutions. Community residential facilities were small in size, house an equally small number of persons, and were meant to be either a permanent residence or a transitional training residence for retarded adults. These facilities ranged in design from loosely supervised apartments to group homes with live-in house parents (Baker, Seltzer, & Seltzer, 1977).

The trend toward deinstitutionalization of retarded persons began approximately 35 years ago when President Kennedy remarked that the practice of institutionalized segregation from the rest of society was immoral. In 1974 President Nixon announced the goal of returning half of all institutionalized retarded individuals to community settings (Braddock, 1977). The basic construct for the deinstitutionalization movement included: (1) the creation and maintenance of environments that did not impose excessive restrictions on disabled persons; (2) the creation of arrangements that brought persons as close as possible to the social and cultural mainstream; and (3) guaranteed that the human and legal rights of disabled citizens were protected (Neufeld, 1979, p. 115).

Numerous studies have been conducted over the past 35 years to assess outcomes for individuals who were a part of deinstitutionalization. The results of these studies are mixed. Many studies cite improvement in quality of life, adaptive behavior skills, and self-care skills (Fine, 1990; Larsen & Lakin, 1989; Lord & Pedlar, 1991).

Other studies present a more negative outcome, with deinstitutionalized mentally retarded individuals being overrepresented in the homeless (Roleff, 1996). Indeed, Craig and Paterson (1988) cited lack of long-term support for mentally ill individuals, and estimated that there are 300,000 mentally ill homeless persons in the United States. Perhaps the most disturbing of studies regarding deinstitutionalization is by Strauss and Kastner. In 1996 they compared risk-adjusted odds of mortality of people with mental retardation living in institutions or the community from 1980 to 1992 in California. It was estimated that the mortality was 72% higher in the community. It was suggested that the reason for the difference was the availability and adherence to health care (Strauss & Kastner, 1996).

For children, deinstitutionalization has had mixed results. Many children return to their families and research suggests that one-third will return to state schools. However, daily living skills training and vocational training are widely available, and many children who were originally placed in contained classrooms are included in the mainstream in less than a year (Laconia State School, 1987).

In summary, outcome studies for deinstitutionalization indicate that many individuals with mental retardation achieve much better self-help and daily living skills when living in the community. However, many do not receive the community support or health care that is necessary for day-to-day living. Indeed, many individuals who are psychiatrically disabled may live in homeless conditions.

For deinstitutionalization to produce effective results, several issues should be considered. Adequate alternatives that are properly designed, properly maintained, and properly supervised should be developed. In addition, comprehensive evaluations of the individual's ability to succeed in a community-based facility should be made.

REFERENCES

Baker, B. L., Seltzer, G. B., & Seltzer, M. M. (1977). *As close as possible. Community residences for retarded adults.* Boston: Little, Brown.

Braddock, D. (1977). *Opening closed doors: The deinstitutionalization of disabled individuals.* Reston, VA: Council of Exceptional Children.

Craig, R. T., & Paterson, A. (1988). The homeless mentally ill; No longer out of sight and out of mind. *State Legislative Report, 13,* 30; National Conference of State Legislatures, Denver, Co.

Fine, M. (1990). Changes in adaptive behavior of older adults with mental retardation following deinstitutionalization. *American Journal on Mental Retardation, 94,* 6, 661–668.

Laconia State School. (1987). Deinstitutionalization of minors with Mental retardation. *Abstract X: Research & Resources on Special Education.* Reston, VA: ERIC Clearinghouse on Handicapped and Gifted Children.

Larson, S. A., & Lakin, C. (1989). Deinstitutionalization of persons with mental retardation; The impact on daily living skills. *Policy Research Brief, 1,* 1.

Lord, J., & Pedlar, A. (1991). Life in the community: Four years after closure of an institution. *Mental Retardation, 29,* 4 213–221.

Roleff, T. L. (1996). *The homeless: Opposing viewpoints.* San Diego, CA: Greenhaven Press.

Strauss, D., & Kastner, T. A. (1996). Comparative mortality of people with mental retardation in institutions and the community. *American Journal on Mental Retardation, 101,* 1, 26–40.

Neufeld, G. R. (1979). Deinstitutionalization procedures. In R. Wiegerink & J. W. Pelosi (Eds.), *Developmental disabilities: The DD movement* (pp. 115–126). Baltimore, MD: Brookes.

Wolfensberger, W. (1972). *The principle of normalization in human services.* Toronto, Ontario: National Institute on Mental Retardation.

CECELIA STEPPE-JONES
*North Carolina Central
University*
First edition

ELAINE FLETCHER-JANZEN
University of Northern Colorado
Second edition

**COMMUNITY BASED SERVICES
NORMALIZATION
REHABILITATION**

Carl H. Delacato

DELACATO, CARL H. (1923–   )

Carl H. Delacato earned his BS in Education from West Chester State College in 1945. He continued his education, obtaining the MS (1948) and EdD (1952) from the University of Pennsylvania. From 1945 to 1964, he was assistant headmaster at Chestnut Hill Academy in Philadelphia, and in 1948, he founded and directed the Chestnut Hill Reading Clinic. During his distinguished career, he has served as associate director and instructor at the Institutes for the Achievement of Human Potential, Philadelphia, Pennsylvania (1953–1973); professor and chairman of the Department of Developmental Education, University of Plano, Plano, Texas; and director of the Institute for Rehabilitation of the Brain Injured, Morton, Pennsylvania (1974–1989).

Delacato (1968) has focused his study on neurological organization and patterning. The Doman-Delacato Treatment Method for children with neurological disabilities, developed by Delacato and Glenn Doman, is a remedy based on the neurological organization of the individual. Neurological organization is defined by Delacato as a physiologically optimum condition existing uniquely and most completely in man, resulting from total, uninterrupted ontogenetic development. Delacato contends that assessment and modification of neurological organization can be utilized for the diagnosis, treatment, and prevention of language problems.

Delacato's numerous awards include the Distinguished Alumnus award of West Chester College (1978), the Gold Medal Honor of Brazil (1960), and the first Trailblazer award of the University of Plano (1966). His major publications include *The Diagnosis and Treatment of Speech* (1968), *Neurological Organization and Reading* (1966), *A New Start for the Child with Reading Problems* (1970), and *The Ultimate Stranger: The Autistic Child* (1974). In addition, Delacato has contributed numerous articles on rehabilitation and education to professional journals, and has served as editor of *American Lectures in Education and Learning.*

REFERENCES

Delacato, C. H. (1966). *Neurological organization and reading.* Springfield, IL: Thomas.

Delacato, C. H. (1968). *The diagnosis and treatment of speech and reading problems.* Springfield, IL: Thomas.

Delacato, C. H. (1982). *A new start for the child with reading problems: A manual for parents* (Rev. ed.). Morton, PA: Morton.

Delacato, C. H. (1984). *The ultimate stranger: The autistic child.* Novato, CA: Arena.

ELIZABETH JONES
Texas A & M University
First edition

TAMARA J. MARTIN
*The University of Texas of the
Permian Basin*
Second edition

DELAYED LANGUAGE

See LANGUAGE DELAYS.

DE LEON, PEDRO

See PONCE DE LEON, PEDRO DE.

DE L'EPÉE, ABBÉ CHARLES MICHEL (1712–1789)

Abbé Charles Michel de l'Epée founded in Paris in 1755 the first public school for the deaf, the *Institution Nationale des Sourds Muets*. The Abeé developed a systematic language of signs based on the earlier work of Jacob Rodrigues Pereire. His system of signs was the basis of the instructional system in the United States' first school for the deaf, the American School for the Deaf. It is still in use today in modified form.

REFERENCE

Lane, H. (1984). *When the mind hears.* New York: Random House.

PAUL IRVINE
Katonah, New York

Abbé Charles Michel de l'Epée

DELINQUENCY, HANDICAPPING CONDITIONS AND

It has been estimated that between 30% and 60% of juvenile offenders have handicapping conditions that require special education services (OJJDP, 1998). This number may be low because many youths are identified with a handicapping condition before their incarceration (Perryman, DiGangi, & Rutherford, 1989). In addition, it is estimated that 22% of incarcerated youth have significant mental health problems (OJJDP, 1998). Estimates of prevalence of handicapping conditions among juvenile delinquents vary dramatically (Crawford, 1982; Murphy, 1986; Nelson & Rutherford, 1989; OJJDP, 1998). These disparities largely can be attributed to methodological inconsistencies in identification of the major handicapping conditions. Further methodological inconsistencies exist in the defining of juvenile delinquency. The criteria for identifying juvenile delinquents are not uniform across state departments of correction (Murphy, 1986). Indeed, differential diagnosis of handicapping conditions as well as juvenile delinquency appear, in part, to be a state phenomenon.

Though tenuous, the accumulated body of research indicates that the prevalence of handicapping conditions among juvenile delinquents is disproportionate to that reported in nondelinquent populations (Crawford, 1982; Keiltz & Dunivant, 1986; Murphy, 1986; OJJDP, 1998). However, the actual prevalence of the major handicaps among juvenile delinquents is difficult to establish. This difficulty can be attributed to the lack of uniform procedures in identifying handicapping conditions and juvenile delinquency. These findings have important implications concerning the identification and servicing of handicapped delinquents under the provision of the Individuals with Disabilities Education Act (IDEA, 1990) and its predecessor in 1975. Many states were slow to provide special education services to incarcerated youth, which resulted in more than 20 class action lawsuits involving special education over the years. Unfortunately, few of the cases went to court; therefore, very few published judicial opinions exist (OJJDP, 1998). The Office of Juvenile Justice and Delinquency Prevention has advocated for stronger links between correctional facilities and school districts, fiscal autonomy for cost-per-pupil budgeting, adherence to the standards for correctional education programs put out by the Correctional Education Association, and avoidance of litigation.

Leone (1991) suggests that the social disadvantages and characteristics associated with juvenile delinquents may lead to increased likelihood of contact with the criminal justice system. Although there is a correlation between poor social and conflict resolution skills and delinquent behavior, no causality can be inferred. Several studies are available that address the effectiveness of special education programs in corrections. Bachara and Zaba (1978) found that the juvenile offenders who were offered remediation in the form of special education, tutoring, or perceptual-motor training exhibited a significantly lower recidivism rate than those who were not offered these programs (Karcz, 1987). Other researchers of the juvenile delinquent population have found that there exists an overall impoverishment of adaptive skill behaviors for this population (Baerman & Siegal, 1976). More recent studies (Forbes, 1991; Grande & Koorland, 1988) suggest that the uniqueness of the correctional setting realizes special problems with staff training, special educator training for correctional settings, curriculum design, and interagency cooperation.

Several successful approaches to assisting special education students who are incarcerated utilize research-based reading instruction (Brunner, 1993), cite cooperative learning techniques as being successful with this population (Ragan, 1993), and have found support for Team-Assisted Individualization (TAI) (Salend & Washin, 1988).

The Office of Juvenile and Delinquency Prevention (1998) has suggested the following recommendations to parents or guardians of incarcerated youth who have handicapping conditions:

Discuss the need for appropriate services at the facility with:
 Teachers and tutors at the facility.
 A facility administrator.
 A special education attorney in the area or a law school clinical program.
 A professor of education.
 Parents.
Obtain the Correctional Education Association standards on correctional education programs.
Review the facility's educational standards.
Establish a committee of educators, advocates, and administrators to:
 Ensure that IEPs are conducted in a timely fashion by qualified personnel.
 Revise the educational standards of the facility.
 Simplify the eligibility determination for special education services.
 Ensure that the facility has qualified teachers.
Involve local advocacy groups that support children and persons with disabilities.
Contact an attorney who can assist you in bringing litigation against the facility if education services not improve.

REFERENCES

Bachara, G. H., & Zaba, J. N. (1978). Learning disabilities and juvenile delinquency. *Journal of Learning Disabilities, 11,* 58–62.

Berman, A., & Siegal, A. (1976). Adaptive and learning skills in juvenile delinquents: A neuropsychological analysis. *Journal of Learning Disabilities, 9,* 51–53.

Brunner, M. (1993). Reduced recidivism and increased employment opportunity through research-based reading instruction. Clearinghouse No. CS011379. Washington, D.C.: U.S. Department of Justice.

Crawford, D. (1982). *Prevalence of handicapped juveniles in the justice system: A study of the literature.* Phoenix, AZ: Research & Development Training Institutes.

Forbes, M. A. (1991). Special education in juvenile correctional facilities: A literature review. *Journal of Correctional Education, 42,* 1, 31–35.

Grande, C. G., & Koorland, M. A. (1988). A complex issue: Special education in corrections. *Children and Youth Services Review, 10,* 4, 345–350.

Karcz, S. A. (1987). Delinquency and special education. In C. R. Reynolds & Lester Mann (Eds.), *Encyclopedia of Special Education* (1st ed.). New York: Wiley.

Keiltz, I., & Duvinant, N. (1986). The relationship between learning disability and juvenile delinquency: Current state of knowledge. *Remedial & Special Education, 7,* 3, 18–26.

Leone, P. E. (1991). Juvenile corrections and the exceptional student. (ERIC Digest No. E509)

Murphy, D. A. (1986). The prevalence of handicapping conditions among juvenile delinquents. *Remedial and Special Education, 7,* 7–17.

Nelson, C. M. & Rutherford, R. B. (1989). Impact of the correctional special education training (C/SET) project on correctional special education. Paper presented at the CEC/CCBD National Topical Conference on Behavior Disorders, Charlotte, NC.

Office of Juvenile Justice and Delinquency Prevention (OJJDP). (1998). *Educational advocacy for youth with disabilities. Beyond the walls: Improving conditions of confinement for youth in custody.* Rockville, MD: Juvenile Justice Clearing House.

Perryman, P., DiGangi, S. A., & Rutherford, R. B. (1989). Recidivism of handicapped and nonhandicapped juvenile offenders: An exploratory analysis. Paper presented at the Learning Handicapped Offender Conference, Pittsburgh, PA.

Ragan, P. E. (1993). Cooperative learning can work in residential care settings. *Teaching Exceptional Children, 25,* 2, 48–51.

Salend, S. J., & Washin, B. (1988). Team-assisted individualization with handicapped adjudicated youth. *Exceptional Children, 55,* 2, 174–180.

HARRISON C. STANTON
Texas A & M University
First edition

ELAINE FLETCHER-JANSEN
University of Northern Colorado
Second edition

JUVENILE DELINQUENCY LEARNING DISABILITIES

DE LORENZO, MARIA E. G. E. (1927–　　)

Maria E. De Lorenzo is a noted Uruguayan special educator. She obtained her BA in education at Teacher's College, Montevideo, Uruguay (1941), and her MA in clinical psychology at the University of Michigan, Ann Arbor (1948). She served as director of School N.1 for mentally retarded children (1949–1967) and as a member of the National Board of Elementary Education in Uruguay from 1967 to 1972. From 1966 to the present, De Lorenzo has been chief of the Mental Retardation Unit of the Inter-American Children's Institute, a specialized agency of the Organization of American States.

She frequently acts as a consultant for numerous international organizations such as the United Nations, the Organization of American States, Partners of the Americas, the President's Committee on Mental Retardation (U.S.), and the International League of Societies for Persons with Mental Handicaps. Since 1967, De Lorenzo has been a member of various U.N. organizations, among them the World Health Organization, U.N. Educational, Scientific, and Cultural Organization, and U.N. International Children's Emergency Fund. She is a member of numerous professional associations and of the editorial boards of the *International Journal of Rehabilitation Research*, the *Journal of Learning, Disabilities*, and the *Infant Mental Health Journal*.

De Lorenzo received numerous honors and special appointments, e.g., the Joseph P. Kennedy Award (1966), the Leadership Award for Achievements in Mental Deficiency (1976), and the Award of Merit granted by the President's Committee on Mental Retardation (1977). She also received the associate researcher *honoris causa* at the Research Department of the Bureau of Child Research, University of Kansas (1972). In 1978, De Lorenzo was invited to be the main speaker at the opening session of the World Congress on Future Social Education, organized by Council for Exceptional Children in Sterling, Scotland. Her work was recently featured in the 1994 publication, *Comparative Studies in Special Education*, an examination of special education provisions throughout the world.

REFERENCE

Mazurek, K., & Winzer, M. A. (Eds.). (1994). *Comparative studies in special education*. Washington, DC: Gallaudet University.

Ivan C. Holowinsky
Rutgers University
First edition

Tamara J. Martin
The University of Texas of the Permian Basin
Second edition

DEMENTIA

Dementia is a generic term applied to a pattern of observable abnormalities in mental abilities, with impairment in at least three of the following five functions: memory, visuospatial skills, emotion or personality, language, and cognition. Combinations of symptoms are caused by many different etiologies (Hegde, 1994). Recent literature agrees that irreversible dementia can be subdivided into three major areas: primary degenerative dementia, multi-infarct dementia, and all other dementia diagnoses of terminal diseases collectively (Shekim, 1997). Dementia of the Alzheimer's type is the most common, and it is caused by structural and chemical changes in the brain. The second most common, multi-infarct dementia, is caused by repeated focal lesions from strokes. Dementia is associated with acquired immunodeficiency syndrome (AIDS), Pick's disease, Parkinson's disease, supranuclear palsy, Binswanger's disease, Creutzfeldt-Jakob disease, Huntington's disease, and Korsakoff's disease (Payne, 1997). In addition, reversible dementias arise from adverse drug interactions or toxicity, metabolic and endocrine disorders, infections, intracranial masses, normal-pressure hydrocephalus, alcohol abuse, vitamin deficiencies, neurosyphilis, arteriosclerotic complications, and epilepsy (Tonkovich, 1988).

Assessment and diagnosis of dementia is a team effort involving physicians, speech-language pathologists, psychologists, and other specialists. The final determination is made on the basis of case history, clinical examination, neurological tests, brain imaging, laboratory tests, communication assessment, and assessment of intellectual functions. Analysis of higher intellectual and language functions include verbal description of common objects, immediate and delayed story retelling, and verbal fluency ("Tell me all the words you can think of beginning with T.") (Hegde, 1994).

Language problems frequently observed in early stages of dementia are mild naming problems, verbal paraphasia (saying words that are similar to the target word), subtle problems in comprehending abstract meanings, impaired picture description, difficulty in topic maintenance, and repetitious speech. As the disease progresses, symptoms include severe memory problems in all forms of memory; generalized intellectual deterioration; profound disorientation to place, person, and time; speech at a rapid rate with echolalia (repeating what was said to them); pallilalia (repeating one's own utterances); jargon; and inattention to social conventions (Hegde, 1994).

REFERENCES

Hegde, M. N. (1994). *A coursebook on aphasia and other neurogenic language disorders*. San Diego: Singular.

Payne, J. C. (1997). *Adult neurogenic language disorders: Assessment and treatment*. San Diego: Singular.

Shekim, L. (1997). Dementia. In L. L. LaPointe (Ed.), *Aphasia and related neurogenic language disorders* (2nd ed.) (pp. 238–249). New York: Thieme.

Tonkovich, J. L. (1988). Communication disorders in the elderly. In B. B. Shadden (Ed.), *Communication behavior and aging: A sourcebook for clinicians* (pp. 197–218). Baltimore: Williams & Wilkins.

SHEELA STUART
George Washington University

DEMOGRAPHY OF SPECIAL EDUCATION

Demographic characteristics relating to handicapped children and youths include (1) the number and types of handicapped children and youths served; (2) the services received by these children and youths; (3) the personnel who provide services; and (4) the settings in which special education and related services are provided.

A total of 5,439,626 children and youth ages 3–21 were served under IDEA Part B during the 1994–95 school year. This figure was a 3.2 percent increase over the previous year, and a 12.7 percent increase since the 1990–91 school year. These figures do not include more than 100,000 infants and toddlers who were served under Part H of IDEA.

During the 1994–95 school year, approximately 12 percent of elementary and secondary students received special education services, and 95 percent of these students were served in regular school buildings. For several years in a row, the percentage of special education students served in the regular classroom increased and the percent served in resource rooms decreased.

Placement patterns vary by disability. The majority of students with speech and language impairments are served in regular classes. Students with learning disabilities, orthopedic impairments, serious emotional disturbance, and traumatic brain injury are generally placed in regular school buildings, but are then spread across regular classes, resource rooms, and separate classes. Separate classroom placements are most prevalent for students with mental retardation, autism, and multiple disabilities. However, resource room placements are also commonly used to serve students with mental retardation and multiple disabilities.

The category of disability that increased the most from 1990–91 to 1994–95 was Other Health Impaired. Much of the increase may be related to an increased number of students diagnosed with attention-deficit/hyperactivity disorder. Table 1 indicates the number of students age 6–21 served during the 1990–91 to 1994–95 school years by disability condition.

Table 1. Number of Students Ages 6–21 Served[a] During the 1990–91 Through 1994–95 School Years

Disability Condition	School Year					Change from 1990–91 through 1994–95	
	1990–91	1991–92	1992–93	1993–94	1994–95	Number	Percent
Specific learning disabilities	2,144,017	2,247,004	2,366,487	2,428,112	2,513,977	369,960	17.3
Speech or language impairments	987,778	998,904	998,049	1,018,208	1,023,665	35,887	3.6
Mental retardation	551,457	553,262	532,362	553,869	570,855	19,398	3.5
Serious emotional disturbance	390,764	400,211	401,652	415,071	428,168	37,404	9.6
Multiple disabilities	97,629	98,408	103,279	109,730	89,646	−7,983	−8.2
Hearing impairments	59,211	60,727	60,616	64,667	65,568	6,357	10.7
Orthopedic impairments	49,340	51,389	52,588	56,842	60,604	11,264	22.8
Other health impairments	56,349	58,749	66,063	83,080	106,509	50,160	89.0
Visual impairments	23,682	24,083	23,544	24,813	24,877	1,195	5.0
Autism	NA	5,415	15,580	19,058	22,780	22,780	—
Deaf-blindness	1,524	1,427	1,394	1,367	1,331	−193	12.7
Traumatic brain injury	NA	245	3,960	5,395	7,188	7,188	—
All disabilities	4,361,751	4,499,824	4,625,574	4,780,212	4,915,168	553,417	12.7

[a]The data for 1990–91 through 1993–94 include children 6 through 21 years of age served under IDEA, Part B and Chapter 1 Handicapped Program. For 1994–95 all children ages 6–21 are served under Part B, which includes children previously counted under the Chapter 1 Handicapped Program. Autism and traumatic brain injury were introduced as separate reporting categories in the 1991–92 school year as a result of PL 101-476, the 1990 Amendments to IDEA. SOURCE: U.S. Department of Education, Office of Special Education Programs, Data Analysis System (DANS).

The number of students ages 6–21 served increased by 12.7 percent (553,417) from 1990–91 through 1994–95. (See Table 1.) The increases within several disability categories were proportionately greater than the 12.7 percent increase across all categories. The largest increase occurred in the number of students with other health impairments, which increased by 89 percent (from 56,349 to 106,509). As noted earlier, much of the increase may be related to students with attention-deficit/hyperactivity disorder. A large increase also occurred in the category of students with orthopedic impairments (22.8 percent from 49,340 to 60,604). The increase in the percentage of students with orthopedic impairments and other health impairments is partly related to the relatively small number of students served in these categories. For a number of years, Michigan has combined the orthopedic impairments category with the other health impairments category. Students in both of these categories are reported under students with orthopedic impairments. Specific learning disabilities increased by 17.3 percent (from 2,144,017 to 2,513,977). There were also increases in the new categories of autism over a 4-year period (from 5,415 to 22,780) and traumatic brain injury (from 245 to 7,188). Two categories have decreased since 1990–91: deaf-blindness (–12.7 percent from 1,524 to 1,331) and multiple disabilities (–8.2 percent from 97,629 to 89,646). The decrease in the multiple disability category occurred in 1994–95 as a result of a decision by the Wisconsin SEA to report all students by their primary disability condition.

There are unique issues in the information available about inner city students' special education services. The Eighteenth Annual Report to Congress (1996) makes the following points:

- Inner-city and non-inner-city areas appear to have similar percentages of students in special education—10.4 percent and 10.8 percent, respectively. Little variation exists between the two types of areas by disability.

- Thirty percent of all inner-city students live in poverty, compared to 18 percent of students living outside inner cities. Data from the NLTS on secondary education students indicate that families of students with disabilities in urban areas are more likely to live in poverty than families of students with disabilities in suburban or rural areas.

- Inner-city districts enroll a greater percentage of limited English proficient students than non-inner-city districts, and data suggests that 5 percent of special education students in inner-city districts have limited English proficiency, compared to 1 percent in non-inner-city districts.

- Public schools in inner cities enroll almost twice as many African American and Hispanic students as do non-inner-city schools. The percentage of African American students enrolled in special education is generally high relative to their representation in the general student population. In some individual states and in some disability categories, Hispanics are over- and underrepresented relative to their proportion of the total population. In general, Asian American students are represented in special education at a lower rate proportional to the general population.

- Although a large number of African American and Hispanic students attend inner-city schools and are reportedly overrepresented in special education, two types of areas apparently enroll virtually the same percentage of students in special education. According to an analysis of NLTS data, the disproportionate representation of African Americans in special education is a function of relatively low income and the disabilities associated with poverty. When income is accounted for, disproportionate representation remains in the categories of speech or language impairments, visual impairments, and mental retardation.

- IDEA and its implementing regulations require that the special education assessment process be conducted in a nondiscriminatory manner. However, in inner-city schools and school districts, identification and assessment of students for special education is complicated by the effects of poverty, race/ethnicity, and limited English proficiency. A central concern over the disproportionate representation of minority students in special education is the role of intelligence tests in identifying students with disabilities.

- Current research suggests that for limited English proficient students, it is very difficult to distinguish between the effect of a disability on the student's achievement and the student's failure to understand the majority language and culture. This difficulty is a serious impediment to accurately assessing the student's disability.

- Data from the Office of Civil Rights suggest that students with disabilities living in inner cities are more likely to be placed in restrictive environments. NLTS data confirm that urban secondary students with disabilities spend less time in regular education classrooms than students living in nonurban areas.

- NLTS data indicate that secondary students with disabilities in urban areas spend a slightly higher percentage of their class time in academic subjects than students with disabilities in rural or suburban schools.

- Special education teachers are in particularly short supply in inner-city areas. Also, schools have failed to attract a sufficiently diverse work force, and over the past 20 years the proportion of African American college graduates entering teaching has declined to a lower level than that of whites.

- Two national datasets on parental reports of disability among their children provide inconsistent results. In the Current Population Survey data, which includes families of children ages 5–17, white families reported that their children had a disability at a higher rate (5.6 percent) than African American families (4.6 percent) or Hispanic families (2.7 percent). In the National Household Education Survey data, which includes families of children age 3 through grade 2, white and African American parents reported prevalence rates of 12.4 and 12.1 percent respectively, while Hispanics reported a prevalence rate of 14.4 percent. In both sets of data, reports of disability diminish as income increases, and rates by race/ethnicity become more similar in the higher income ranges.
- According to NLTS data, youth in urban areas were less likely than their peers in suburban and rural areas to graduate from high school and were more likely to drop out of school. Suburban youth with disabilities who were out of secondary school two years or more reported taking any postsecondary courses in the past year at a slightly higher rate (17 percent) than urban youth with disabilities (14 percent) or rural youth with disabilities (12 percent).
- Employed youth with disabilities in urban areas earned slightly more than youth in suburban or rural areas. A sizeable proportion of youth in urban, suburban, and rural areas were employed in manual labor and restaurant work.

It is clear that the disproportionality of ethnic minorities and inner-city youth in special education continues to be a source of investigation. Issues such as socioeconomic status and assessment bias are ongoing even after being subject to close scrutiny by researchers in the field and the U.S. Department of Education.

The demography of special education allows us to examine our advances in the understanding of handicapping conditions (such as the addition of Traumatic Brain Injury as a handicapping condition); it allows us to examine how we define disability from year to year; it allows us to track the impact of shifts in paradigms (such as inclusion); and it allows us to hold the field accountable for culturally competent services.

The Annual Report to Congress, written by Office of Special Education of the U.S. Department of Education, is published every year and is available on-line for inspection at www.ed.gov/pubs. The facts and table in this entry were taken verbatim from the *Eighteenth Annual Report to Congress* (1996).

REFERENCE

U.S. Department of Education. (1996). *Eighteenth annual report to Congress: To assure the free appropriate public education of all children with disabilities: Implementation of the Individuals with Disabilities Education Act (IDEA)*. Washington, DC: Author.

ELAINE FLETCHER-JANZEN
University of Northern Colorado

POLITICS AND SPECIAL EDUCATION
SPECIAL EDUCATION, FEDERAL IMPACT ON

DENDRITES

A typical neuron is depicted in the Figure on the following page. The nucleus of the cell, called the soma or perikaryon, has various protruding elements. The main protruding element is the axon.

Typically surrounding the soma, except where the axon exits, are a variety of smaller protruding elements that form the dendritic network of the neuron. The dendrites have an appearance somewhat akin to branches of a leafless tree and *dendron* is the Greek stem meaning tree. The dendrites serve as the neurotransmitter receptacle sites, as does the soma itself, from neurotransmitter release from the axon of a different neuron. The synaptic termination actually occurs on little spines that arise from the dendrite. These spines are numerous. For example, a single motor neuron may have as many as 4000 spines on its dendrites. Although it was originally assumed that the dendrite served a rather passive role in neuronal transmission, it is now speculated that the dendritic processes play a much more dynamic and active role in neurotransmission (Cooper, Bloom, & Roth, 1978; Cotman & McGaugh, 1980) and neurobehavioral (i.e., learning) functions.

REFERENCES

Cooper, J. R., Bloom, F. E., & Roth, R. H. (1978). *The biochemical basis of neuropharmacology* (3rd ed.). New York: Oxford University Press.

Cotman, C. W., & McGaugh, J. L. (1980). *Behavioral neuroscience*. New York: Academic.

ERIN D. BIGLER
Austin Neurological Clinic
University of Texas

CENTRAL NERVOUS SYSTEM
GLIAL CELLS

Sensory
neuron

Axon

Dendrite

Synapse

Capillary

Astrocytes
(glia)

Local
circuit
neuron

Axon

Oligodendrocyte
(glia)

Myelin
sheath

Synapse

Motor
neuron

(a)

(b)

(a) Left, a neural circuit. A large neuron with multiple dendrites receives synaptic contact from another neuron at upper left. It sends its myelinated axon into a synaptic connection with a third neuron at bottom. These neural surfaces are shown without the extensive investment of glia that envelop the branch extending toward the capillary at upper right. (b) Two views of synapses at different magnifications, as seen through the electron microscope.

DENO, EVELYN N. (1911–   )

As a developmental psychologist, Evelyn Deno has specialized in the design and delivery of helping services for handicapped children and their parents. As a preschool, elementary, and college teacher of 17 years, Deno earned her MA in 1950, and PhD in 1958, in child development and clinical psychology from the University of Minnesota, where she taught graduate-level classes in child development. She then went on to become director of special education and rehabilitation for the Minneapolis public schools. She returned to the University of Minnesota in 1967 as professor of educational psychology and director of the Psycho-Educational Center. She was also co-director of the Leadership Training Institute for the USOE Bureau of Professional Development.

Best known for her "cascade of special education services" concept and diagram, Deno has always seen the need for "helping service systems and political agents to promote a more compatible match between individual aspirations and the constraining social and physical environmental realities" (pers. comm., August 27, 1985). She has applied developmental theory to see

> how people with special adjustment problems can be helped to survive in a culture and society inclined to regard deviance from the "norm" (or what is expected) as a problem of the deviant one, not a challenge to society's ability and obligation to respect individual differences." (pers. comm., August 27, 1985)

Deno's current interests lie with the adjustment problems of older persons and the design and implementation of programs for them to serve as counselors to their peers, tutors, and as "special friends" to learning-disabled and emotionally disturbed children. She has received a number of awards for outstanding contributions in her field. Service delivery models designed and tested under her direction have been designated as national service prototypes. Her ideas on merging special and general education, labeling, and blaming students' failure to learn solely on teachers are analyzed in a recent article in the *Journal of Special Education* (Hallahan & Kauffman, 1994).

Deno retired from the University of Minnesota in the mid-70s, and resides in the Twin Cities area of Minnesota. She is currently editing an anthology of personal experiences of those involved in the major paradigm shift in 1955 in special education, when Minnesota passed into law the requirement that individual school systems provide educational services to all handicapped children, rather than placing them in residential state institutions.

REFERENCE

Hallahan, D. P., & Kauffman, J. M. (1994). Toward a culture of disability in the aftermath of Deno and Dunn. *Journal of Special Education, 27*, 496–508.

ELAINE FLETCHER-JANZEN
University of Northern Colorado
First edition

KAY E. KETZENBERGER
The University of Texas of the Permian Basin
Second edition

DENTISTRY AND THE HANDICAPPED CHILD

Dental disease represents a serious health problem for many handicapped children. A comprehensive survey by the National Center for Health Statistics (1979) estimated that oral disease is 40% higher among mentally retarded individuals, across all ages, than in the population at large. In a more recent report (Callahan, 1983a), the incidence of dental disease was almost 20% higher in the mentally retarded population than in comparably aged non-handicapped individuals.

The physical consequences and personal discomfort of dental disorders and untreated oral diseases for handicapped individuals are obvious; they include pain, oral abscesses, and loss of teeth. The educational and social implications are, perhaps, just as important. Bad teeth, gum disorders, etc. can cause bad breath and cosmetic disabilities and thus make the social acceptance of handicapped children and adults more difficult. The cosmetic implications of good dental health for the handicapped have been recognized by many states that provide dental care to vocational rehabilitation clients, though the need for services usually outstrips the resources available to meet them.

A number of diverse physiological social and economic factors have been identified as being responsible for the greater degree of dental and oral disorders in handicapped populations. Malformations and abnormal development of certain teeth are thus coincidental with certain types of handicapping conditions. Particular dental difficulties have been found to be associated with various types of handicapping conditions. Individuals with Down's syndrome have been found to experience a relatively low incidence of tooth decay but a high incidence of periodontal or gum disease (Pugliese, 1978); while the gums of many epileptic individuals have been found to overgrow as a consequence of dilantin use (Nowaka, 1976). Neurological seizures or motor disabilities may result in head injuries that cause serious damage to oral structures. Motor impairments, limited cognitive understanding of the importance of good dental habits, and poor motivation often limit the carrying out of oral hygiene practices by handicapped children and frustrate parents' training and monitoring efforts.

The strained economic conditions of many handicapped children is another reason for the high incidence of oral disease in special education populations. Many handicapped children come from socioeconomically disadvantaged families that are not likely to emphasize the precepts of oral hygiene in their daily living or to afford dental care. Furthermore, there has been a reduction of dental support for such families in Medicaid programs. Indeed, the federal government, under Title XIX, does not require that states provide any dental services to adult Medicaid recipients.

Additionally, until recently, barrier restrictions, difficulties in patient management, and negative attitudes have limited receptivity in dental professionals with regard to the provision of services to difficult patients. Difficulties in patient management and negative attitudes on the part of dental health professionals negatively affect the provision of dental care to difficult to treat handicapped patients. As recently as 1977, only 200 out of 1000 dentists in a metropolitan area were identified as either accepting or interested in accepting handicapped patients (Callahan, 1983b). Beyond such problems, even when willing and proficient service providers are available, parents of handicapped children and agencies serving them are often unaware of their availability.

Specific difficulties with respect to preventing or ameliorating dental problems and oral disease in handicapped students are attributable to the attitudes of school personnel generally and special education personnel in particular. There is very little attention paid to the dental/oral needs and problems of handicapped children in our schools currently. This is in part a consequence of changing conditions of service provision to handicapped children. Increasingly, as that provision has moved from segregated circumstances such as institutions in which health care considerations are predominant over educational ones, to the less restrictive environments of day and public school programs, there has been a decided shift from concern with the physical (care) needs of handicapped school-children to their specific instructional needs. While the health professionals and special education teachers serving special education populations undoubtedly recognize the needs of handicapped children for good oral training and dental health care, they are not likely to emphasize these in their day to day individualized education plan practices. Present-day special education requires the provision of so many mandated educational services that the laborious training of children in instructionally peripheral areas of brushing, flossing, etc. is likely to be neglected.

The 1970s were a particularly active period with respect to comprehensive investments of time and effort in improving dental care for handicapped individuals. One of the most important efforts in this respect was the funding by the Robert Wood Johnson Foundation during 1974–1978 of 11 dental schools across the country. This funding was to support the development of comprehensive dental school training programs relative to the provision of services to handicapped individuals; i.e., to develop specialized skills and technology, to create positive attitude change in dental professionals, to develop referral and service delivery capabilities at dental schools, and to institutionalize aspects of these programs at dental schools following funding.

Evaluation of these projects revealed decreased anxiety in faculty, staff, and students in working with handicapped students, increased ability to communicate with the handicapped regarding their dental problems, and improved dental care practices. Positive attitude changes were reported in persons affected by the program, e.g., decreased fear and anxiety, as well as a better understanding of handicapped dental patients. A comprehensive report on the Robert Wood Johnson Foundation's program, the most ambitious privately funded one to date, is available from the Educational Testing Service (Campbell et al., 1982).

Apropos of the Robert Wood Johnson Foundation's work, Stiefel and Truelove (1985) recently reported on the 5-year postgraduate program at the University of Washington that resulted in significant cognitive changes and gains in confidence respecting the treatment of handicapped individuals by dentists, dental hygienists, and assistants who participated in a postgraduate program. Curricula guidelines are also available (Jolly, 1990).

While there has been a steady if meager stream of publications concerning the dental management of handicapped children, a resurgence of interest is to be observed in the work of such investigators as Price (1978) and Pugliese (1978). Much of this interest, as might be expected, has been in the direction of preventive dentistry, and in the participation of home, school, and community in the dental management of handicapped individuals. The Association for Retarded Citizens' position is that dental treatment should "be of the same quality as received by other people, preserve or enhance the individual's health and be administered only with the *informed consent* of the person or his or her surrogate decision maker" (p. 1 ARC, 1992). Callahan (1983a, 1983b), among others, has emphasized that effective dental care for handicapped individuals must go beyond the improvement of dental services per se and improved technology to improving the willingness of dental practitioners to engage school and other service providers in the dental care of handicapped students. Callahan emphasizes the value of preventive services that will improve the dental status of the handicapped and reduce the costs of their dental care. For those handicapped individuals who will remain school and community based (this means most handicapped children and adults), programs of comprehensive preventive dental care should be emphasized over those of costly treatment.

What can be accomplished through preventive programs has been demonstrated through model outreach programs implemented by the National Foundation of Dentistry for the Handicapped (Callahan, 1983b). These programs have incorporated daily oral hygiene programs into the practices at a variety of special education schools, sheltered workshops, and group homes at relatively modest costs. They rely on periodic screening to detect dental disorders while they are still easily manageable. They use referral networks to coordinate the delivery of dental treatment to those handicapped individuals who require it. Most important, they use teachers, counselors, vocational rehabilitation personnel, houseparents, and other service personnel, in addition to those from the dental professions, on their service delivery teams. Similar concerted efforts might be valuable in bringing special education and special educators fully into the teaching and training of oral hygiene methods and precepts.

Recent interest in applying dental and oral hygiene principles in work with more severely handicapped populations is evidenced by the work of Feldman and Elliot (1981). Finally, because the vast majority of special education students these days reside at home, it is encouraging to observe recent efforts directed toward parents as oral hygiene trainers and monitors. Thus an article by Stark et al. (1985) provides guidelines to parents respecting their children's dental needs with regard to nutrition, medication, visits to the dentist, and the inculcation of proper dental care habits.

REFERENCES

Association for Retarded Citizens. (1992). *Position paper on Medical and dental treatment*. Arlington, Texas; ARC.

Callahan, W. P. (1983a). Dental disease: A continuing education problem for the disabled individual. *Journal of Special Education, 17,* 355–359.

Callahan, W. P. (1983b). The effectiveness of instructional programming on the reduction of dental diseases in mentally retarded individuals. *Mental Retardation, 21,* 260–262.

Campbell, J. Y., Esser, B. F., & Flaugher, R. L. (1982). *Evaluation of a program for training dentists in the care of handicapped patients* (Report No. QAT24225). Princeton, NJ: Educational Testing Service.

Dentistry and the handicapped. (1981). (Videotape). Denver: LA-DOCA.

Feldman, D., & Elliot, T. A. (1981). A multidimensional oral hygiene curriculum for the severely and profoundly handicapped. *Journal of Special Education Technology, 4,* 33–45.

Jolly, D. E. (1990). Curriculum guidelines for training general practice residents to treat the person with a handicap. *Journal of Dental Education, 54,* 5, 293–297.

Nowak, A. J. (1976). *Dentistry for the handicapped patient.* St. Louis: Mosby.

Price, J. H. (1978). Dental health education for the mentally and physically handicapped. *Journal of School Health, 48,* 171–173.

Pugliese, R. (1978). Oral health status in a group of mentally retarded patients. *Rhode Island Dental Journal, 11,* 6–9.

Stark, J., Markel, G., Black, C. M., & Greenbaum, J. (1985). Day to day dental care: A parents' guide. *Exceptional Parent, 15,* 15–17.

Stiefel, D. J. (1980). Dental care for the handicapped at the University of Washington. *Journal of Dental Medicine, 44,* 141–145.

Stiefel, D. J., & Truelove, E. L. (1985). A postgraduate dental training program for treatment of persons with disabilities. *Journal of Dental Education, 49,* 85–90.

U.S. Public Health Service. (1980). *Special report on dental care for handicapped people.* Arlington, VA: Rehabilitation Services Administration, U.S. Department of Health, Education, and Welfare.

U.S. Department of Health, Education, and Welfare, Public Health Service. (1979). *Basic data on dental examination findings of persons.* Hyattesville, MD: National Center for Health Statistics.

DAVID C. MANN
St. Francis Hospital

BRUXISM
INDIVIDUAL EDUCATION PLAN (IEP)
SELF-HELP TRAINING

DEPAKENE

Depakene is an antiepileptic agent known generically as valproic acid. Depakene is the most recently introduced anticonvulsant medication. It differs both chemically and in clinical action from most other anticonvulsants (Goldensohn, Glaser, & Goldberg, 1984). Generally this medication is used either as the sole or adjunctive treatment for simple (petit mal) and complex absence seizures as well as generalized seizure disorders. The precise mechanism by which Depakene works is unknown; however, some research has suggested that its activity is related to increased brain levels of gamma-aminobutyric acid.

While there is little research on the behavioral effects of Depakene, uncontrolled trials suggest that it may improve visual-motor coordination (Schlack, 1974), alertness, and school performance (Barnes & Bower, 1975). Nausea and gastrointestinal irritation are common side effects of Depakene, but these can be controlled through dosage or by giving the drug with food. If Depakene is given with other medications, particularly phenobarbital, there can be extreme, temporary sedation as well as awkward motor movements. Some of the more extreme side effects include a disruption of platelet functioning, liver damage, and pancreas failure, all of which have the potential to be fatal. For these reasons, Depakene typically is held in reserve as a medication of final resort for those individuals with seizures that cannot be controlled by other medication. For those who are using the ketogenic diet there may also be possible interactions (Ballaban-Gil, O'Dell, Pappo, Moshe, & Shinnar, 1998).

REFERENCES

Ballaban-Gil, K., Callahan, C., O'Dell, C., Pappo, M., Moshe, S., & Shinnar, S. (1998). Complications of the ketogenic diet. *Epilepsia, 39,* 7, 744–748.

Barnes, S. E., & Bower, B. D. (1975). Sodium valproate in the treatment of intractible childhood epilepsy. *Developmental Medicine and Child Neurology, 17,* 175–181.

Goldensohn, E. S., Glaser, G. H., & Goldberg, M. A. (1984). Epilepsy. In L. P. Rowland (Ed.), *Merritt's textbook of neurology* (7th ed.) (pp. 629–650). Philadelphia: Lea & Febiger.

Schlack, H. G. (1974). Ergenye in the treatment of epilepsy. *Therapiewoche, 24,* 39–42.

RICHARD A. BERG
West Virginia University
Medical Center

ANTICONVULSANTS
EPILEPSY

DEPRESSION

Depression has been considered to be the major psychiatric disease of the 20th century. Recent studies have indicated that greater than 20 percent of adolescents have emotional problems and one-third of adolescents attending psychiatric clinics suffer from depression (Blackman, 1995).

Depression is the leading cause of suicide (National Institute of Mental Health, 1998). The suicide rate for adolescents has increased more than 200 percent over the last decade (Blackman, 1995). Each year 250,000 teens attempt suicide, and 2,000 complete the act. Females are more likely to attempt suicide, but males kill themselves four times more often, usually with guns (Net-Health, 1998).

Symptoms of depression vary from individual to individual in terms of frequency, number, and intensity. Common symptoms are:

- Persistent sad, anxious, or "empty" mood
- Feelings of hopelessness, pessimism
- Feelings of guilt, worthlessness, helplessness

- Loss of interest or pleasure in hobbies and activities that were once enjoyed, including sex
- Insomnia, early-morning awakening, or oversleeping
- Appetite and/or weight loss or overeating and weight gain
- Decreased energy, fatigue, being "slowed down"
- Thoughts of death or suicide; suicide attempts
- Restlessness, irritability
- Difficulty concentrating, remembering, making decisions
- Persistent physical symptoms that do not respond to treatment, such as headaches, digestive disorders, and chronic pain

Many indicators of depression are atypical, especially in children. A diagnosis of depression in youth is often missed or misdiagnosed because the developmental issues associated with normal adolescence, mood lability, withdrawal, heightened emotions, acting-out behaviors, and so on create a challenge for the family and mental health professionals to distinguish between what is normal teenage behavior and what are serious indicators of depression.

The causes of depression are numerous. There is some indication that there is a genetic component; some 30 to 40 percent of depressed children will have a biologic parent who is also depressed at the time the child presents for initial evaluation (Weinberg, Harper, Emslie, & Brumback, 1995). Twin studies suggest that heredity partly determines how often normal children become mildly depressed and how their moods fluctuate. For both level of depression and fluctuations of symptoms, the correlation among identical twins in one study (Wierzbicki, 1987) was about .68 which suggested that up to two-thirds of the variance was genetic. Weinberg et al. (1995) has found that:

> "Depressed children who are oppositional and defiant or have a conduct disorder, have a positive family history of sociopathy, or alcoholism, along with depression or manic-depressive disease. Hallucinations during depression indicate a family member with schizophrenia. Depressed children with prominent somatic complaints frequently have a female family member with Briquet's syndrome (a disorder characterized by severe hypchondriasis and often multiple operations without recognizable underlying medical disease). Inherited traits of these other disorders become apparent as additional symptoms during the depressive episodes in young people. When that young person is free of depression or manic-depressive episodes, those traits become inapparent. Thus it is important to try to identify an underlying depression or manic-depressive state in any children presenting with an apparent conduct disorder, somatic complaints, or other behavior complexes." (p. 3)

Psychological makeup also plays a role in the possibility of developing depression. Children and adolescents who have low self-esteem and are easily overwhelmed by stress are prone to depression (NetHealth, 1998). Serious losses, chronic illness, or unwelcome changes in life patterns can also trigger depressive episodes.

Many adolescents and their families do not realize that depression is a treatable condition (NIMH, 1998). There are a variety of antidepressant medications which, when used in conjunction with psychotherapy, are very effective. The medication gives relatively quick symptom relief and the psychotherapy helps the individual and their family learn more effective ways to deal with life's problems (NIMH, 1998). Researchers have also been optimistic about light therapy for seasonal affective depression (Swedo, 1997).

In terms of the educational system, many times teachers are the first to notice that children and adolescents are having problems. Academic performance is very susceptible to disruption from depression. Teachers should receive training as to the unique symptomatology of depression in youth, and training to support the student who needs assistance (Willis, 1996).

Special education students may be particularly susceptible to depression. As mentioned previously, chronic illnesses such as diabetes, eating disorders, or cerebral palsy present long-term difficulties and problems that the child must overcome. The concurrent incidence of chronic illness and depression has been well established in the scientific literature. Learning disabilities are commonly diagnosed concurrently in youth with depression. Weinberg et al. (1995) report that 60 to 80 percent of learning-disabled children failing in school will fulfill criteria for depression at the time of initial clinical evaluation. School is a very frustrating place for many of these students, as repeated failure lowers motivation and self-esteem. This condition spirals downward as the child develops negative thinking about those academic tasks on which he or she cannot perform adequately. Weinberg et al. (1995) describes the affective responses that many learning-disabled children have:

"Young people with various specific learning disabilities often manifest poor attention, restlessness, daydreaming, and limited diligence when asked to do tasks that they are unable to do. It is postulated that continuous stimulation of a genetically maldeveloped area of the cerebral hemisphere makes that area, surrounding cerebral cortex, and homologous cerebral cortex in the opposite hemisphere all work less well. For example, language-impaired and dyslexic children (left hemisphere learning disability) often become moody, irritable, and angry when asked to speak, read, or recall works. Poor spellers (left hemisphere learning disability), practicing spelling for the spelling test, become increasingly dysphoric, anxious, irritable, and dysattentive as the school year progresses. Some will cry, show poor self-esteem and express death wishes." (p. 8)

Strength models of remediation in special education have primarily focused on the neurological and neuropsychological rationale for teaching to a child's strengths (Reynolds, 1992). The latter also focuses on the inherent positive feedback that a learner receives when the educational intervention matches the psychoeducational diagnosis. The child understands the material, performs to expectations, and receives positive feedback. This, in turn, enhances self-esteem and motivation, and recreates a positive and flexible mindset when the child approaches an academic task. Over a period of time, negative thoughts are not the norm for the child and depression can only exist when rigid and chronic negative thoughts are present. Therefore, for the special education learner, it is critical that any treatment for depression (psychopharmacology, family therapy, and/or individual therapy) also takes into account the individual education plan that is based on a strength model. The interplay between success in school and success in treatment is crucial for the special education student who is depressed.

Resources for individuals, families and educators about depression are offered by the National Institute of Mental Health as

D/ART/Public Inquiries
National Institute of Mental Health
Room 7C-02
5600 Fishers Lane
Rockville, MD 20857
1-800-421-4211
www.nimh.nih.gov

National Alliance for the Mentally Ill
200 North Glebe Road, Suite 1015
Arlington, VA 22203-3754
703-524-7600
1-800-950-NAMI

National Foundation for Depressive Illness, Inc.
P.O. Box 2257
New York, NY 10016
212-268-4260
1-800-248-4344

National Mental Health Association
1021 Prince Street
Alexandria, VA 22314-2972
703-685-7722
1-800-969-6642

REFERENCES

Blackman, M. (1995). Adolescent depression. *The Canadian Journal of CME*. Internet Mental Health: www.mentalhealth.com.

National Institute of Mental Health. (1998). *Plain talk about depression*. Washington DC.: Author.

NetHealth. (1995). *Depression.com*. www.depression.com.

Reynolds, C. R. (1992). Two key concepts in the diagnosis of learning disabilities and the habilitation of learning. *Learning Disability Quarterly, 15,* 1, 2–12.

Swedo, S. E. (1997). Light therapy may help kids with seasonal depression. *Journal of the American Academy of Child and Adolescent Psychiatry, 5,* 2, 112–115.

Weinberg, W. A., Harper, C. R., Emslie, G. J., & Brumback, R. A. (1995). Depression and other affective illnesses as a cause of school failure and maladaptation in learning disabled children, adolescents and young adults. *Secondary Education and Beyond.* Pittsburgh, PA: Learning Disabilities Association.

Wierzbicki, M. (1987). Similarity of monozygotic and dizygotic child twins in level and liability of subclinically depressed mood. *American Journal of Orthopsychiatry, 57,* 33–40.

Willis, S. M. (1996). Childhood depression in school age children. (ERIC Clearinghouse No. PS026156)

ELAINE FLETCHER-JANZEN
University of Northern Colorado

DRUG ABUSE
SERIOUS EMOTIONAL DISTURBANCE

DEPRIVATION

See NEGLECT; POST INSTITUTIONALIZED CHILD.

DEPRIVATION, BIONEURAL RESULTS OF

The term deprivation is usually used to mean the absence or reduction of normal sensory input to the nervous system. Its meaning is sometimes extended to include restriction or suppression of opportunities for normal motoric activities associated with exploration, play, and social intercourse. The bioneural results of deprivation have mostly been investigated through animal experiments.

The visual system has been studied extensively. Various changes reviewed by Vrensen and De Groot (1974) have been observed in the visual cortex of animals reared in the dark. Monocular deprivation has been shown to produce more salient changes than binocular; competition between the two sides seems to be a more important factor than deprivation per se. The changes are particularly marked, and largely irreversible, when deprivation occurs during a critical period of early life. The best known examples are the protracted loss of vision through one eye in kittens (Wiesel & Hubel, 1965) and monkeys (Hubel et al., 1976), resulting from a brief period of interference with that eye's function shortly after birth. Stimulation of the deprived eye no longer elicits normal activity in the visual area of the brain because this has become reorganized in favor of the other eye.

In the auditory system, complete suppression of input is impossible without destruction of both inner ears, since otherwise there is always some perception of the sounds produced in the animal's own body. Temporary restriction of auditory stimuli can be achieved by rearing in a sound-attenuated environment or by interfering with the external or middle ear structures that transmit sound to the inner ear. Both methods produce perturbations of the auditory function and neuronal alterations of brain stem auditory nuclei (Webster & Webster, 1979). Significant changes in the microscopic structure of the auditory cortex have been observed in mutant mice with hereditary deafness owed to inner ear degeneration (Périer et al., 1984). As in the visual system, there are critical or sensitive periods of development during which plasticity is greatest and the results of deprivation most evident (Eggermont, 1986).

Nonspecific reduction of sensory stimulation is achieved by rearing animals in standard or isolated laboratory conditions as opposed to environmental complexity. In these experiments, there is a reduction of the normal span of sensory experiences, motor activities, and social exchanges. Behavioral differences as well as differences in cerebral structures are observed. Both have been extensively reviewed by Walsch (1980, 1981a, 1981b).

In man, the counterpart of animal experiments on the visual system is functional amblyopia, a condition observed in some children who have suffered from unattended squinting or other conditions interfering with the vision of one eye. Even after correction of the pathological condition, the deprived eye may remain largely nonfunctional. Partial auditory deprivation is a frequent occurrence in small children as a result of serous otitis media. It seems to cause long-lasting learning difficulties, even after normal hearing has been restored. All degrees of hearing loss, from mild to profound, might affect the human auditory pathways and cortex, as shown in animals. These possible effects in man have been discussed by Ruben & Rapin (1980). Studies in language development indicate that infants possess a capacity for making phonetic distinctions which must, to persist, be confirmed by the corresponding sounds of language spoken in their environment. Some studies indicate that children with congenital or early acquired hearing loss might lose this early competence (Serniclaes, et al., 1984).

Examples of extreme multisensory and social deprivation in man are afforded by "wolf" children and exceptional cases such as that of Genie, a girl maintained in isolation for years by psychotic parents (Curtiss, 1977). The complexity of such cases as well as the lack of sufficient information about their early life make their interpretation difficult. Less severe but more frequent deprivation situations occur in hospitalism (Spitz, 1945) and in poorly stimulating familial background. It is probable, though yet unproven, that these have bioneural consequences in addition to the well-known psychological ones.

REFERENCES

Curtiss, S. (1977). *Genie, a psycholinguistic study of a modern day "wild child."* New York: Academic.

Eggermont, J. (1986). Critical periods in auditory development. Proceedings of the Nijmegen Workshop. *Acta Otolaryngologica* (Stockholm) (Suppl., in press).

Hubel, D. H., Wiesel, T. N., & LeVay S. (1976). Functional architecture of area 17 in normal and monocularly deprived Macaque monkeys. *Cold Spring Harbor Symposium on Quantitative Biology, 40,* 581–589.

Périer, O., Alegria, J., Buyse, M., D'Alimonte, G., Gilson, D., & Serniclaes, W. (1984). Consequences of auditory deprivation in animals and humans. *Acta Otolaryngologica* (Stockholm), *411,* 60–70.

Ruben, R. J., & Rapin, I. (1980). Plasticity of the developing auditory system. *Annals of Otology Rhinology and Laryngology, 89,* 303–311.

Serniclaes, W., D'Alimonte, G., & Alegria, J. (1984). Production and perception of French stops by moderately deaf subjects. *Speech Communication, 3,* 185–198.

Spitz, R. A. (1945). Hospitalism—An inquiry into the genesis of psychiatric conditions in early childhood. *Psychoanalytic Study of the Child, 1,* 53–74.

Vrensen, G., & De Groot, D. (1974). The effect of dark rearing and its recovery on synaptic terminals in the visual cortex of rabbits. A quantitative electron microscopic study. *Brain Research, 78,* 263–278.

Walsch, R. (1980). Effects of environmental complexity and deprivation on brain chemistry and physiology: A review. *International Journal of Neuroscience, 11,* 77–89.

Walsch, R. (1981a). Effects of environmental complexity and deprivation on brain anatomy and histology: A review. *International Journal of Neuroscience, 12,* 33–51.

Walsch, R. (1981b). Sensory environments, brain damage, and drugs: A review of interactions and mediating mechanisms. *International Journal of Neuroscience, 14,* 129–137.

Webster, D. B., & Webster, M. (1979). Effects of neonatal conductive hearing loss on brain stem auditory nuclei. *Annals of Otology Rhinology, & Laryngoly, 88,* 684–688.

OLIVIER PÉRIER
Université Libre de Bruxelles
Comprendre et Parler

EARLY EXPERIENCE & CRITICAL PERIODS
GENIE
LANGUAGE, ABSENCE OF
LANGUAGE DELAYS

DESENSITIZATION

Desensitization is a procedure that combines guided participation, modeling, and the graduated approach to a desired response (e.g., shaping). The technique has been used primarily with fear responses in children and adults, and its primary targets have been phobic reactions to various stimuli. While undergoing this therapy, the individual is first introduced to the process by beginning under the least demanding conditions. The therapist models the desired behavior and the individual is guided through his or her responses. These responses are gradually modified to approximate the real circumstances under which the feared stimuli might be encountered. The gradual modification takes place with the therapist modeling each successive response and guiding the student through the appropriate response. The therapist also makes encouraging statements and uses other reinforcing methods (Kratochwill, 1975). These supportive techniques are gradually withdrawn. The two procedures used are generally referred to as shaping a correct response and fading the prompts that have been used to support the acquisition of the behavior (Alberto & Troutman, 1982).

Desensitization, as a behavioral procedure, has a substantive body of research to support its feasibility in fear reduction treatment. As desensitization makes use of treatment technology (e.g., shaping, fading, prompting, modeling, and reinforcement), which is known to be effective with the acquisition of other adaptive behaviors, we would expect it to be effective in training individuals to respond in acceptable ways to stimuli that have in the past provoked maladaptive responses. Desensitization is currently used for many situations, such as test anxiety (Austin, 1995), math anxiety (Schneider, 1993), general school anxieties (Ross, 1990), and in attempts to control negative effects of mass media (Wilson, 1993). Therefore, desensitization is a procedure that combines several common behavioral techniques to assist in the development of appropriate responses to currently feared or anxiety-provoking situations (e.g., riding in a bus, entering a swimming pool, going to a movie).

REFERENCES

Alberto, P. A., & Troutman, A. C. (1982). *Applied behavior analysis for teachers.* Columbus, OH: Merrill.

Austin, J. S. (1995). Prevent school failure: Treat test anxiety. *Preventing School Failure, 40,* 1, 10–13.

Kratochwill, T. R. (1975). Contact desensitization. In A. S. Bellack & M. Hersen (Eds.), *Dictionary of behavior therapy techniques,* New York: Pergamon.

Ross, D. B. (1990). *Controlling School Anxiety: A practical guide for counselors and teachers.* Grayslake, IL: College of Lake County.

Schneider, W. J. (1993). Overcoming math anxiety: A comparison of stress inoclution training and systemic desensitization. *Journal of College Student Development, 34,* 4, 283–288.

Wilson, B. J. (1989). Densensitizing children's emotional reactions to the mass media. *Communicating Research, 16,* 6, 723–745.

LYLE E. BARTON
Kent State University

BEHAVIOR MODIFICATION
FEARS AND PHOBIAS

DES LAURIERS, AUSTIN M. (1917–)

Austin Des Lauriers earned his PhD in 1942 from the University of Montreal. From 1967 to 1970, he was professor and director of research and training at the University of Missouri Medical Center in Kansas City. He has also served as professor and director of the Child Study Center at Ottawa, where he maintained a private practice. He currently resides in Great Bend, Kansas.

Des Lauriers' work has primarily centered on school psychology, autism, and schizophrenia. However, his views on functional literacy in business have been featured in the quarterly publication *Learning in the Workplace* (Des Lauriers, 1990); and at the Working Conference on Vermont's Heritage for Teachers, his work contributed to the proceeding devoted to the development of teaching materials to be used in Vermont's classrooms (Des Lauriers, 1984).

Des Lauriers' research interests have focused on topics of childhood schizophrenia (Des Lauriers, 1962) and autism. He holds that the autistic child's condition and behavior (in an arrested form) involve the same conflicts that a normal child experiences. His book, *Your Child Is Asleep* (1969), is considered a classic in the field. The education of a child with autism is seen by Des Lauriers as an "awakening."

REFERENCES

Des Lauriers, A. M. (1962). The experience of reality in childhood schizophrenia. New York: I.V.P.

Des Lauriers, A. M., & Carlson, C. F. (1969). *Your child is asleep: Early infantile autism.* Homewood, IL: Dorsey.

Learning in the workplace. (1990). Toronto Frontier College.

True, M. (1984). Teaching Vermont's heritage. *Proceedings of the Working Conference on Vermont's Heritage for Teachers.* Burlington, VT: Vermont University.

RICK GONZALES
Texas A & M University
First edition

TAMARA J. MARTIN
The University of Texas of the Permian Basin
Second edition

DES LAURIERS–CARLSON HYPOTHESIS

In 1969 Austin Des Lauriers and Carole Carlson found that the reticular activating system was involved in the cause of early infantile autism. They proposed an imbalance in the relationship between the reticular activating system and the limbic system. The limbic system, which is involved in emotion, motivation, and reinforcement, is inhibited by the reticular activating system, rendering the autistic child unable to make associations between behavior and positive or negative consequences. The work of Des Lauriers and Carlson came after Kanner (1943) identified the behavioral characteristics of children who were qualitatively different from other childhood clinical populations. These symptoms included the inability to develop relationships, a delay in speech acquisition, echolalia, and repetitive play activities. These have become identifying characteristics of early infantile autism.

The etiology of early infantile autism was once thought to be based on abnormal family relationships and early parenting experiences (Kanner, 1943). There have since been many theories that attempt to understand the complicated disorder. Findings are mixed and tentative. The focus has included abnormal parenting and family relationships (a theory that has been recently eliminated; this act is seen as the most important improvement in treatment of autistic children (Schopler, 1990)), the social environment, and biochemical and organic deficits as contributing factors.

Although much of the early research focused on family and environmental causes, more recent research identifies possible involvement with neurochemistry, developmental biology, neurophysiology, and neuroanatomy (Hanson & Gottesman, 1976). In 1983 Gillberg and Gillberg reported an increase in pre and perinatal hazards that are suggestive of brain dysfunction in infantile autism. Recent advances in cytogenetics have resulted in the identification of a specific biological marker or fragile site on the X chromosome. These are indicators that there is a coexistence of autism with the fragile X chromosome, suggesting an etiological link (August & Lockhart, 1984). Sherman, Nass, and Shapiro (1984) researched cerebral blood flow in autistic children. Their research suggested depressed gray matter cerebral blood flow in autistic subjects; this may reflect their mental retardation. These findings lend support to the hypothesis of Damasio and Maurer (1978), who suggested that autism is the result of abnormalities of the mesolimbic dopaminergic system.

Currently, it is generally accepted that early infantile autism is a behavioral syndrome reflecting abnormal brain functioning (Sherman, Nass, & Shapiro, 1984) and multiple causes (Schopler, 1990). These findings present a challenge for special educators who are involved in the education and treatment of autistic persons. McDonald and Sheperd (1976) reported that teachers play a major role in educating autistic children using criterion-referenced assessment and behavior teaching practices in a comprehensive program. This work has led to the current involvement of special education in the treatment of autism.

REFERENCES

August, J. A., & Lockhart, H. L. (1984). Familial autism and the fragile X chromosome. *Journal of Autism & Developmental Disorders, 14,* 197–203.

Damasio, A. R., & Maurer, R. G. (1978). A neurological model for children with autism. *Archives of Neurology, 35,* 771–776.

Des Lauriers, A. M., & Carlson, C. F. (1969). *Your child is asleep: Early infantile autism.* Homewood, IL: Dorsey.

Gillberg, C., & Gillberg, C. I. (1983). Infantile autism: A total population study of reduce optimality in the pre-peri and neonatal period. *Journal of Autism & Developmental Disorders, 13,* 153–166.

Hanson, D. R., & Gottesman, I. I. (1976). The genetics, if any, of infantile autism and childhood schizophrenia. *Journal of Autism & Developmental Disorders, 6,* 209, 231.

Kanner, L. (1943). Autistic disturbances of affective contact. *Nervous Child, 2,* 217–250.

McDonald, J. E., & Sheperd, G. (1976). The autistic child, a challenge for educators. *Psychology in the Schools, 13,* 248–256.

Schopler, E. (1990). *Neurobiological correlates of autism.* Reston, VA: ERIC Publications. (ERIC Clearinghouse No. EC300540)

Sherman, M., & Nass, R., & Shapiro, T. (1984). Brief report: Regional cerebral blood flow in autism. *Journal of Autistic & Developmental Disorders, 14,* 439–446.

STEVEN GUMERMAN
Temple University

AUTISM
RETICULAR SYSTEM

DESPERT, JULIETTE L. (1892–1982)

Juliette L. Despert, MD, child psychiatrist and researcher, received her education in her native France and in the United States. During her many years as a practicing psychiatrist, she contributed numerous articles to professional journals and published over half a dozen books, including *The Emotionally Disturbed Child: An Inquiry into Family Patterns, Schizophrenia in Childhood,* and *Children of Divorce,* and developed the Despert Fables.

REFERENCES

Despert, J. L. (1953). *Children of divorce.* New York: Doubleday.

Despert, J. L. (1968). *Schizophrenia in childhood.* New York: Brunner.

Despert, J. L. (1970). *The emotionally disturbed child: An inquiry into family patterns.* New York: Doubleday.

PAUL IRVINE
Katonah, New York

DESTRUCTIVE BEHAVIORS

To specify all acts in which persons engage that could be considered destructive is impossible; the topography of various destructive behaviors is at least as diverse as the people who exhibit them. A number of factors mitigate against a universally acceptable definition of destructive behaviors and are generally accounted for in operational definitions of such acts. There are at least three elements that should be implicitly or explicitly incorporated into operational definitions of destructive behaviors. One element is that of intentionality. For example, a child who accidentally breaks a dish is not generally considered destructive, but one who deliberately breaks a dish is considered destructive. Second, characteristics of the behavior itself (e.g., intensity, frequency) play a definitional role. For instance, children who occasionally bite their fingernails are not considered to be self-destructive, while those who often bite their hands until they bleed generally are considered self-destructive. Third, situational factors influence definitions. Persons who intentionally break a glass in a restaurant are considered destructive; in contrast, in some wedding ceremonies the intentional breaking of a glass is a socially sanctioned event. Much has been asserted in recent years that society has redefined destructive behavior in a more innocuous fashion: a statement about society's increasing tolerance for deviant behaviors (Moynihan, 1994).

A multitude of treatment programs that have successfully reduced various types of destructive behaviors have been reported. These programs have ranged in scope from large district-wide programs to reduce vandalism to interventions that have reduced the destructive behavior of a single individual. Likewise, the programs have varied a great deal according to the procedures used. As in the case with selecting any procedure to reduce behavior, a host of ethical, moral, legal, empirical, and practical issues must be attended to (see Foxx, 1982; Polsgrove, 1983; Repp, 1983). In the following paragraphs, effective programs for reducing various destructive behaviors are briefly discussed in approximate order of increasing intrusiveness. It should be stressed, however, that ineffective programs, regardless of their level of intrusiveness, should never be perpetuated.

There have been many examples of positively-based programs to reduce destructive behaviors. An interesting large-scale program to reduce acts of vandalism was reported by Mayer, Butterworth, Nefpaktitis, and Sulzer-Azaroff (1983). Selected teachers in 18 schools participated in workshops and consultation sessions. Over the three-year study, the teachers significantly increased their rates of praise. Acts of vandalism were significantly reduced and decreases in other disruptive and destructive student behaviors were also observed. Russo, Cataldo, and Cushing (1981) reported that positively reinforcing compliance resulted in decreased acts of self-destruction among three children, although no contingencies were in effect for the self-destructive behaviors. Using a DRO procedure (reinforcement delivered for nonoccurrence of behavior), Frankel, Moss, Schofield, and Simmons (1976) eliminated aggressive and self-destructive acts.

Extinction combined with positive reinforcement was used by Martin and Treffry (1970) to eliminate poor posture and self-destructive behaviors in a 16-year-old partially paralyzed mentally retarded girl with cerebral palsy. She was positioned in such a manner that if she slouched she was not visible to the persons administering the reinforcers. If she was engaging in self-destructive behaviors, she was also not reinforced.

A variety of destructive behaviors exhibited by five mentally retarded boys were reduced by a nonexclusionary timeout procedure (Foxx & Shapiro, 1978). A number of advantages are associated with this technique compared with other forms of timeout procedures.

An overcorrection procedure (a punishment technique involving the correction of the undesirable behavior followed by practicing the desirable behavior) was used by Foxx and Azrin (1972) to eliminate the destructive behavior of a profoundly retarded adult female. Other punishment procedures (e.g., contingent electric shock, aromatic ammonia, citric acid, etc.) have also been used to decrease destructive behaviors.

Irrespective of the particular type of destructive behavior, these responses merit our best professional interventions. A variety of treatments (in addition to the ones mentioned here) have proven successful, but careful attention to aspects of individual cases is essential.

REFERENCES

Foxx, R. M. (1982). *Decreasing behaviors of severely retarded and autistic persons.* Champaign, IL: Research Press.

Foxx, R. M., & Azrin, N. H. (1972). Restitution: A method of eliminating aggressive-disruptive behavior of retarded and brain damaged patients. *Behavior Research and Therapy, 10,* 15–27.

Foxx, R. M., & Shapiro, S. T. (1978). The timeout ribbon: A nonexclusionary timeout procedure. *Journal of Applied Behavior Analysis, 11,* 125–136.

Frankel, F., Moss, D., Schofield, S., & Simmons, J. Q. (1976). Use of differential reinforcement to suppress self-injurious and aggressive behavior. *Psychological Reports, 39,* 843–849.

Martin, G. L., & Treffry, D. (1970). Treating self-destruction and developing self-care skills with a severely retarded girl: A case study. *Psychological Aspects of Disability, 17,* 125–131.

Mayer, G. R., Butterworth, T., Nafpaktitis, M., & Sulzer-Azaroff, B. (1983). Preventing school vandalism and improving discipline: A three-year study. *Journal of Applied Behavior Analysis, 16,* 355–369.

Moynihan, P. (1994). Defining deviancy down: How we've become accustomed to alarming levels of crime and destructive behavior. *American Educator, 17,* 10–18.

Polsgrove, L. (Ed.). (1983). Aversive control in the classroom. *Exceptional Education Quarterly, 3*(4).

Repp, A. C. (1983). *Teaching the mentally retarded.* Englewood Cliffs, NJ: Prentice-Hall.

Russo, D. C., Cataldo, M. F., & Cushing, P. J. (1981). Compliance training and behavioral covariation in the treatment of multiple behavior problems. *Journal of Applied Behavior Analysis, 14,* 209–222.

JAMES P. KROUSE
*Clarion University of
Pennsylvania*

ACTING OUT
APPLIED BEHAVIOR ANALYSIS
EMOTIONAL DISORDERS
REALITY THERAPY

DETROIT TESTS OF LEARNING APTITUDE—FOURTH EDITION (DTLA-4)

The Detroit Tests of Learning Aptitude—Fourth Edition (DTLA-4; Hammill, 1998) is an individually administered battery of tests assessing specific mental abilities. It is designed for use with children and adolescents ages 6 through 17. The first edition of the DTLA was published more than 60 years ago and served as one of the first batteries designed to measure a person's specific abilities, as opposed to the more traditional assessment of global mental ability.

The original DTLA was comprised of 19 subtests to be administered to persons ages 4 through 19. In 1985, the DTLA was revised (DTLA-2, Hammill, 1985). Eleven subtests were retained and domain composites were added. In 1991, there was a second revision of the DTLA which included changes in subtests (3 subtests were deleted and 3 new subtests were added), in addition to modifications to the domain composites (DTLA-3, Hammill, 1991). The most recent revision, the DTLA-4 (Hammill, 1998), retained all the items on the DTLA-3, while updating its norms using 1996 census data. The DTLA-4, like its predecessors, was designed to assess an individual's cognitive strengths and weaknesses and can be used to help identify children and adolescents with learning problems or special needs.

The DTLA-4 consists of ten discrete subtests that measure specific cognitive abilities. The subtests assess such areas as vocabulary, auditory and visual memory, visual closure, and visual problem solving. The DTLA-4 yields subtest scores, a global ability score, and six domain composite scores involving linguistic, attentional, and motoric aspects. Also, by regrouping the subtests in a variety of ways, theory-based composites can be generated that represent some of the major theories in intelligence, including Cattell and Horn's model of fluid and crystallized intelligence, Jensen's model of associative and cognitive levels, Das' model of simultaneous and successive processing, and Wechsler's verbal and performance scales. Each of the ten subtests yields a raw score that is converted to a standard score ($M = 10$, $SD = 3$). The global ability score is generated by combining all ten of the subtest standard scores, which are converted to a standard score or quotient ($M = 100$, $SD = 15$). The domain and theoretical composites are obtained by combining specific subtest standard scores, also converted to quotients ($M = 100$, $SD = 15$). Percentile ranks, age equivalents, and descriptive ratings (ranging from very superior to very poor) are provided for subtests and composites along with the above-mentioned standard scores.

Starting and stopping rules for the DTLA-4 vary by subtest, and specific information about administration is provided in the manual. For example, some subtests require that all items be administered; others have differing starting points corresponding to the examinee's age; some make use of the more traditional basal and/or ceiling rules (e.g., five consecutive failed items).

According to the author, the DTLA-4 improved the test in many significant ways (e.g., norms were stratified and keyed to the 1996 census data relative to gender, race, ethnicity, and family income). However, no critiques of the DTLA-4 have been published as of yet. The author contends that "because the DTLA-4 retained all the items on DTLA-3, the reviews of DTLA-3 have relevance to DTLA-4."

The primary criticisms raised in recent reviews of the DTLA-3 include statements concerning the norms, the factor structure of the test, and administration time. The DTLA-3 norms are based on a sample of 2,587 examinees, of which 1,532 of these examinees were tested as part of the 1984 normative group for the DTLA-2. However, the remaining 5 subtests were only normed on a sample of 1,055. Moreover, the demographics of this new sample is not discussed separately nor are "the specifics of how these two sets of data were combined to obtain the published norms" (Poteat, 1995). Regarding the factor structure of the DTLA-3, it was noted that factor analysis only supported the use of the global ability score and not any of the domain scores (Mehrens, 1995; Poteat, 1995). Hammill states that suggestions from critiques, such as having a confirmatory factor analysis to show validity of the com-

posites and including information about the socioeconomic status of the normative sample, were "incorporated into the DTLA-4." Finally, although the DTLA-3 took longer to administer than many other well-developed cognitive batteries, with the removal of one subtest, the administration time may be more similar to other batteries.

REFERENCES

Hammill, D. (1985). Detroit Tests of Learning Aptitude-2. Austin, TX: Pro-Ed.

Hammill, D. (1991). Detroit Tests of Learning Aptitude-3: Examiner's Manual. Austin, TX: Pro-Ed.

Hammill, D. (1998). Detroit Tests of Learning Aptitude-4. Austin, TX: Pro-Ed.

Mehrens, W. A. (1995). Detroit Tests of Learning Aptitude, Third Edition. In J. C. Conoley & J. C. Impara (Eds.), *The twelfth mental measurements yearbook*. Lincoln, NE: Buros Institute of Mental Measurements.

Poteat, G. M. (1995). Detroit Tests of Learning Aptitude, Third Edition. In J. C. Conoley & J. C. Impara (Eds.), *The twelfth mental measurements yearbook*. Lincoln, NE: Buros Institute of Mental Measurements.

DEBRA Y. BROADBOOKS
*California School of
Professional Psychology*

DEVELOPING UNDERSTANDING OF SELF AND OTHERS—REVISED (DUSO-R)

Developing Understanding of Self and Others—Revised (DUSO-R) is an improved version of the 1970 DUSO. Dinkmeyer and Dinkmeyer (1982) developed the DUSO program to increase understanding of social and emotional behavior in preschool and early primary age children. It is a program of activities and materials that uses puppets, songs, stories, discussion, and role playing to help children grow in their understanding of self and others as well as to recognize their needs and goals. Two different kits are provided, DUSO-1 for grades Kindergarten to 2 and DUSO-2 for grades 3 to 4; they differ only in the degree of complexity presented. There are 41 goals assessed in three major units. The units are (1) developing understanding of self; (2) developing understanding of others; and (3) developing understanding of choices. Each of the 41 goals uses songs, guided fantasies, dramatic play activities, problem situations, and feeling world activities (Goldman, 1984).

The DUSO-R has several improvements over the original DUSO. Stories and songs have been updated to be more reflective of current issues. Pictures featuring minority groups, handicapped persons, and the elderly are used to depict problem situations and show these people as responsible problem solvers. Also, males and females are portrayed as equal in capabilities. A new feature, Guided Fantasy, involves a combination of muscle relaxation and visual imagery to guide a child through presented situations. Another new feature is a set of activity sheets. These sheets can be sent home with the child to show to or do with the parents. Retained was the simplicity that allows easy administration with no special training. A guidebook is provided for the examiner; it is recommended that it be read thoroughly prior to administering the program. Teachers, counselors, and other guidance faculty are capable of administering the DUSO-R. Average administration time is 30 to 40 minutes.

The DUSO-R is a colorful, easily administered program that assesses three main subject areas (Krismann, 1983): affective education, guidance and counseling, and health. It is a based on an inquiry, experiential, and discussion approach to learning. The program can be used to teach appropriate social skills and problem-solving techniques, as well as to give insight into self-concept, interpersonal relationships and conflict resolution. As it is more of a teaching instrument than a testing instrument, objective interpretations are based on individual responses rather than norms. The DUSO-R can be a useful, valuable tool that can be added to a teacher's daily, weekly, or periodic schedule.

REFERENCES

Conn, E. J. R. (1989). *Conflict management techniques for kindergarten through fourth grade.* Reston, VA: ERIC. (ERIC Clearinghouse No. PS018340)

Dinkmeyer, D., & Dinkmeyer, D., Jr. (1984). *Developing Understanding of Self and Others-D-1* and *D-2* (Rev. eds.). Circle Pines, MN: American Guidance Services.

Goldman, S. J. (1984). Developing Understanding of Self and Others-Revised. *School Counselor, 31,* 486–488.

Krismann, C. (1983). Developing Understanding of Self and Others-Revised. *Social Science Education Consortium* (Suppl.), 39–40.

LISA J. SAMPSON
Eastern Kentucky University

COUNSELING THE HANDICAPPED
SOCIAL SKILLS

DEVELOPMENTAL APHASIA

See CHILDHOOD APHASIA; LANGUAGE DISORDERS.

DEVELOPMENTAL APRAXIA

Developmental apraxia is a childhood disorder of sensory integration interfering with ability to plan and execute skilled or non-habitual motor tasks in the absence of muscle weakness or paralysis (Davis, Jakielski, & Marquardt, 1998; Hall, Jordan, & Robin, 1993). Voluntary or purposeful motor acts are inconsistently produced while involuntary movements remain intact. The condition is characterized by difficulty in articulation of speech (oral, speech, or verbal apraxia); formation of letters in writing; difficulty with visual-spatial tasks such as drawing, block arrangements, assembling stick designs or shapes in drawing; or problems in sequential movements of gesture, pantomime, dressing, grooming, or eating (Hall et al., 1993; Shriberg, Aram, & Kwiatkowski, 1997). In less severe forms, apraxia may be referred to as dyspraxia (Dewey, 1995; Missiuna & Polatajko, 1995).

Developmental apraxia of speech (DAS) is a nonlinguistic sensorimotor disorder of articulation characterized by impaired capacity to program and position the speech musculature and the sequencing of muscle movements (respiratory, laryngeal, and oral) for the volitional production and sequencing of phonemes. Children with developmental apraxia of speech have more addition errors (producing extra phonemes), prolongation errors, repetitions of sounds and syllables, and nonphonemic productions such as glottal plosives, bilabial fricatives, nasal assimilation and distortions such as subtle voicing and devoicing errors that are not overt substitution errors (Davis et al., 1998; Hall et al., 1993; Shriberg et al., 1997).

Whereas speech-language pathologists may be more familiar with the term developmental apraxia of speech, occupational and physical therapists may use the term Developmental Coordination Disorders (DCD) (David, 1995; Willoughby & Polatajko, 1995). This condition is also referred to as clumsy child syndrome, mild motor problems, incoordination, developmental apraxia or dyspraxia, perceptual motor dysfunction, visual-motor problems and sensory-integrative dysfunction. The *Diagnostic and Statistical Manual of Mental Disorders* (DSM-IV) (American Psychiatric Association, 1994) description of DCD implicitly excludes the coordination disturbances affecting speech motor skill development, even though phonological awareness deficits are frequently found in children diagnosed with DCD. A consensus does not exist for etiology of the condition (Davis et al., 1998; Dewey, 1995; Hall et al., 1993; Shriberg et al., 1997). Developmental apraxia of speech and developmental coordination disorders can impact on the social and academic dimensions of the communication-learning process across the life course, but particularly do so in childhood.

REFERENCES

American Psychiatric Association. (1994). *Diagnostic and statistical manual of mental disorders* (4th ed.) (DSM-IV). Washington, CD: Author.

David, K. S. (1995). Developmental coordination disorders. In

S. Campbell (Ed.), *Physical therapy for children* (pp. 425–456). Philadelphia, PA: W. B. Saunders Co.

Davis, B. L., Jakielski, K. J., & Marquardt, T. P. (1998). Developmental apraxia of speech: Determiners of differential diagnosis. *Clinical Linguistics and Phonetics, 12*, 25–45.

Dewey, D. (1995). What is developmental dyspraxia? *Brain and Cognition, 29*, 254–274.

Hall, P. K., Jordan, L. S., & Robin, D. A. (1993). *Developmental apraxia of speech: Theory and clinical practice.* Austin, TX: Pro-Ed.

Missiuna, C., & Polatajko, H. (1995). Developmental dyspraxia by any other name: Are they all just clumsy children? *The American Journal of Occupational Therapy, 49*, 619–627.

Shriberg, L., Aram, D., & Kwiatkowski, J. (1997). Developmental apraxia of speech: I. Descriptive and theoretical perspectives. *Journal of Speech, Language and Hearing Research, 40*, 273–285.

Willoughby, C., & Polatajko, H. (1995). Motor problems in children with developmental coordination disorder: Review of the literature. *The American Journal of Occupational Therapy, 49*, 787–793.

STEPHEN S. FARMER
New Mexico State University

DEVELOPMENTAL DELAY

Historically, our understanding of human development as a dynamic, continuous process owes much to the pioneering research of Arnold Gesell (1925). Following years of clinical research observing and recording infant and child behavior, Gesell established a series of developmental norms. These age-related profiles described the sequence of normal motor development and adaptive, language, and personal-social behaviors of the average child. In addition, viewing school life from a developmental perspective, he emphasized maturational readiness as well as overall adjustment to school as a critical determinant of children's academic performance in reading, writing, and arithmetic (Gesell, 1946). Although urging conservation application of the developmental norms owing to the variable rate at which children normally develop, Gesell emphasized the value of developmental diagnosis as a means of identifying abnormal development (Gesell, 1925).

The concept of developmental delay refers to a maturational lag, an abnormal, slower rate of development in which a child demonstrates a functioning level below that observed in normal children of the same age (Thompson & O'Quinn, 1979). Suggesting no cerebral dysfunction or structural damage, proponents of the concept maintain that discrepant abilities manifested by the delayed child occur because of neurological immaturity associated with slower development (Golden & Wilkening, 1986; Lerner, 1985; Thompson & O'Quinn, 1979).

In the field of childhood exceptionalities, developmental delay is associated with theories of mental retardation, learning disabilities, and attention deficit disorder. Evidence supporting the existence of developmental delay and its relationship to exceptionality are found repeatedly in the literature. Although controversial and refuted by many, some researchers in each subfield support the concept.

In terms of handicapping conditions and eligibility for services, the term developmental delay was adapted in an amendment to the Individuals with Disabilities Education Act (IDEA) in 1986.

New PART H, which became PART C in 1998, addressed the needs of infants and toddlers with disabilities and their families through a "Statewide system of coordinated, comprehensive, multidisciplinary, interagency programs providing appropriate early intervention services to all infants and toddlers with disabilities and their families" (20 U.S.C. § 1476(a)).

The amendment was based on Congress' findings that services to families and children below the age of 2 were not organized, economic, or meeting the needs of initiatives designed to prevent the need for special education services. The criteria for eligibility in the Act laid the groundwork for clearer definitions of developmental delay to emerge. The Act states:

> Infants and toddlers from birth through age 2 are eligible for PART H services if they:
>
> (1) Are experiencing developmental delays, as measured by appropriate diagnostic instruments and procedures in one or more of the following areas:
>> (i) Cognitive development,
>> (ii) Physical development, including vision and hearing,
>> (iii) Communication development,
>> (iv) Social or emotional development,
>> (v) Adaptive development, or
>
> (2) Have a diagnosed physical or mental condition that has a high probability of resulting in developmental delay. (34 CFR 303.16)

States have the discretion to serve infants and toddlers and their families who are at risk of having substantial developmental delays if early intervention services are not provided (34 CFR 303.16). At this time, there are 13 states serving at-risk infants and toddlers (Nineteenth Annual Report, 1997).

Children eligible to receive these services under Part H must have an individualized family service plan (IFSP) in place. The IFSP is based on a family systems theoretical basis because infants and toddlers can only be assessed and assisted within the context of their environment. It is a requirement of the Act that professionals collaborate with the family (Nineteenth Annual Report, 1997).

Today, 50 states and 7 jurisdictions participate in the

Part H program. In general, the participants identify three categories of risk for adverse developmental outcomes: established risk, biological/medical risk, and environmental risk. Many state definitions of developmental delay address multiple risk factors (Shackelford, 1998).

The Council for Exceptional Children in 1996 made recommendations concerning the use of the developmental delay eligibility category:

> (1) that a **developmental delay** category of eligibility should be available for children in this age group; (2) that informed clinical opinion, culturally and linguistically appropriate test performance, and observation should be utilized in determining eligibility; (3) that a team process should be used as children move from IDEA Part H to Part B services; and (4) that personnel preparation programs should train professionals to use a multi-setting, multi-measure, and multi-informant model for identification and evaluation of **developmental delay**. (Abstract)

There have been many calls for clarification of eligibility criteria in the past few years (Larson, 1993; Harbin, 1991). In general, a 25% delay in one or more areas of development has been the most frequently used type of test-based criteria (Harbin, 1991). However, surveys of state consultants have shown a need for assessment instruments that assist with parental involvement and that are culturally competent (Harrington & Tongier, 1993).

In summary, the term developmental delay has a long history based in the understanding of normal developmental theory. In the mid 1980s the importance of serving infants and toddlers became patent, and service was mandated to these and at-risk children in a way that would maximize familial involvement. The current status of services to these children includes the evolution of a nationwide understanding of eligibility criteria, the establishment of appropriate assessment instruments, and a culturally competent awareness of the familial context of developmental delays.

REFERENCES

Council for Exceptional Children. (1996). *Developmental delay as an Eligibility Criteria*. Reston, VA: Council for Exceptional Children. (ERIC No. EC305927)

Gesell, A. (1925). *The mental growth of the pre-school child*. New York: Macmillan.

Gesell, A., & Ilg, F. L. (1946). *The child from five to ten*. New York: Harper & Brothers.

Golden, C. J., & Wilkening, G. N. (1986). Neuropsychological bases of exceptionality. In R. T. Brown & C. R. Reynolds (Eds.), *Psychological perspectives on childhood exceptionalities: A handbook* (pp. 61–90). New York: Wiley.

Harbin, G. L., & Maxwell, K. (1991). *Progress towards developing a definition for developmentally delayed: Report #2*. Carolina Institute for Child and Family Policy. Chapel Hill, NC: North Carolina University.

Harrington, R. G., & Tongier, J. (1993). The compatibility between State eligibility criteria for developmental delays and available early childhood assessment instrumentation. *Diagnostique, 18*, 3, 199–217.

Larson, L. (1993). *Part H of the Individuals with Disabilities Education Act: House research information brief*. St. Paul, MN: Minnesota House of Representatives Research Dept.

Lerner, J. (1985). *Learning disabilities: Theory, diagnosis & teaching strategies* (4th ed.). Boston: Houghton Mifflin.

Nineteenth Annual Report to Congress on the Implementation of the Individuals with Disabilities Education Act. (1997). Washington D.C.: U.S. Dept. of Education.

Shackelford, J. (1998). State and jurisdictional eligibility definitions for infants and toddlers with disabilities under IDEA. *NEC*TAS Notes, 5*.

Thompson, R. J., & O'Quinn, A. N. (1979). *Developmental disabilities*. New York: Oxford University Press.

SHIRLEY PARKER WELLS
University of North Carolina at Wilmington
First edition

ELAINE FLETCHER-JANZEN
University of Northern Colorado
Second edition

DEPRIVATION
INDIVIDUALS WITH DISABILITIES EDUCATION ACT (IDEA)
EARLY EXPERIENCES

DEVELOPMENTAL DISABILITIES

Developmental disabilities is a generic term that refers to "all of the lifelong disabling conditions that require similar treatment or helping services and that occurred prior to age 22" (Ehlers, Prothero, & Langone, 1982). According to Boggs (1972), the concept of developmental disabilities has no etiological basis and includes all children and adults with a substantial continuing disability originating in childhood. The term is not to include disabilities that effectively could be overcome with rehabilitation or that are not both apparent and disabling prior to age 18. This concept of developmental disabilities has evolved since its inception in 1969 from a coalition of representatives of the National Association for Retarded Children, American Association on Mental Deficiency (AAMD), National Association of Coordinators of State Programs for the Mentally Retarded, National Association of State Mental Health Program Directors, Council for Exceptional Children, and United Cerebral Palsy Association. The concept of developmental disabilities was introduced by this coalition because of three major concerns: (1) the emphasis on categories of exceptionality, (2) the narrow focus in federal legislation for the handicapped on mental retardation, and (3) the absence of any proposals by the Nixon administration for legislative action on behalf of the handicapped.

In regard to categorization, Boggs (1972) cites the following reasons for professional concern: (1) the high degree of coincidence in the same individuals of the most common disabling conditions (mental retardation, cerebral palsy, epilepsy, childhood schizophrenia, and other neurological and sensory disorders), (2) the exactitude of diagnostic semantics and the degree to which diagnosis could be manipulated when it was a factor in eligibility for service, and (3) the growing professional opinion against fragmenting services that call for similarly trained personnel. These concerns also are reflected in a report of the President's Committee on Mental Retardation (1968), which calls for people and organizations interested in specific handicapping conditions to work together to promote more effective services.

A second concern was that earlier legislation related to the handicapped focused primarily on persons with mental retardation while many persons with needs similar to the mentally retarded were being neglected (Ehlers et al., 1982). Also, training of professionals funded by previous legislation was primarily clinical and did not foster an interdisciplinary approach to providing services to the handicapped.

A third concern that influenced the coalition was the "vacillation and declining support from the Johnson administration" for programs for the mentally retarded and the lack of "any special thought . . . given to the needs in mental retardation by the" Nixon administration. (Boggs, 1972, pp. 184–185). While the coalition formed was, according to Boggs, "an ongoing legislative alliance" (p. 186), it represented professionals concerned not only with legislative issues but also with current thinking regarding provision of services for the handicapped. Consequently, members of the coalition sought to develop a legislative program with goals reflective of professional and consumer program objectives.

In 1969 the concept of developmental disabilities as previously described by Boggs was introduced by this coalition; its members developed an amendment to the Mental Retardation Facilities Act (PL 88-164). The reasons for amending PL 88-164, according to Boggs, were as follow: (1) to give states greater incentive to continue planning and greater authority to use federal funds in accordance with state plans, (2) to expand the list of eligible services and not have the services tied to a specialized facility, (3) to have available monies allocated in response to the same plan, and (4) to use a functional approach associating the handicapped by common service needs to define eligibility for service rather than categorization by diagnosis.

In the proposed legislation the term mental retardation was replaced by the term developmental disabilities. De-

velopmental disability was seen as a functional definition of a person needing specific services. According to a report issued by the President's Committee on Mental Retardation (1976), the rationale for use of the term developmental disability was to avoid categorical fractioning of service organizations and funding among similar and overlapping disabilities and to clearly distinguish developmental disabilities from the field of mental health. This concept as incorporated into the Developmental Disabilities Services and Facilities Construction Amendments of 1970 (PL 91-517) was broader than the one (mental retardation) used in previous legislation, but it did not reflect a truly functional definition of developmental disabilities. The definition is as follows:

> A disability attributable to mental retardation, cerebral palsy, epilepsy, or other neurological condition . . . closely related to mental retardation or to require treatment similar to that required for mentally retarded individuals, which disability originates before such individual attains age eighteen, which has continued or can be expected to continue indefinitely, and which constitutes a substantial handicap to such individuals.

The concept of developmental disabilities as reflected in this legislation was criticized because while expanding the population eligible for services, it was still essentially categorical. Neisworth and Smith (1974) point out that the definition as used in PL 91-517 lacked precision and included requirements based on assumptions that "invite inconsistent and tenuous interpretations and applications" (p. 345). They further point out the lack of functionality in the definition and suggest a redefinition of developmental disabilities that would, in their opinion, lead to more specificity and reliability of interpretation and implementation:

> Developmental disability refers to significantly deficient locomotor, communicative, adjustive, or academic functioning that is manifested during the developmental period, and that has continued or can be expected to continue indefinitely. (p. 346)

Since the introduction of the term developmental disability in federal legislation, it has been altered so that the definition used in recent legislation more clearly reflects the concept held by the coalition. The first alteration occurred when autism, any other condition closely related to mental retardation or requiring similar services and treatment, and dyslexia resulting from other disabilities included in the definition were added to the earlier definition and used in the Developmentally Disabled Assistance and Bill of Rights Act (PL 94-103). However, this altered definition still did not reflect the thinking of the coalition or address issues described by Neisworth and Smith.

A major alteration occurred when the National Task Force on the Definition of Developmental Disabilities was established in response to one of the requirements of PL 94-103. According to Thompson and O'Quinn (1979), members of this task force opposed the use of the term developmental disabilities as a "catch-all for an arbitrary collection of existing labels or conditions" (p. 14) and advocated a generic or functional definition be formulated to cut across specific categories or conditions. Members of this task force defined the developmentally disabled as "a group of people experiencing a chronic disability which substantially limits their functioning in a variety of broad areas of major life activity central to independent living" (p. 14). Subsequently, the thinking of the task force was reflected in the Rehabilitation Comprehensive Services and Developmental Disabilities Amendments of 1978 (PL 95-602) and retained in the Developmental Disabilities Act of 1984 (PL 98-527), and later Acts culminating in 1994. The definition reads as follows:

> The term developmental disability means a severe, chronic disability of a person which:
> —is attributable to a mental or physical impairment or combination of mental and physical impairments;
> —is manifested before the person attains age twenty-two;
> —is likely to continue indefinitely;
> —results in substantial functional limitations in three or more of the following areas of major life activities;
> (i) self-care, (ii) receptive and expressive language, (iii) learning, (iv) mobility, (v) self-direction, (vi) capacity for independent living, and (vii) economic sufficiency; and
> —reflects the person's need for a combination and sequence of special, interdisciplinary, or generic care, treatment, or other services which are of lifelong or extended duration and are individually planned and coordinated.

Seltzer (1983) describes this definition as functionally oriented with emphasis on chronicity, age-specific onset, multiple areas of functional limitations, and need for an extended array of long-term services from a multiplicity of service providers. Seltzer points to this functional orientation as an advantage of this latest definition but cites its lack of operational clarity as a disadvantage. However, Seltzer goes on to point out that with use and the development of operational guidelines, the disadvantages are hoped to diminish.

The term developmental disability has been incorporated into various classification systems. The American Association on Mental Deficiency (AAMD) includes developmental disability in the *Manual of Terminology and Classification in Mental Retardation* (Grossman, 1977) and *Classification in Mental Retardation* (Grossman, 1983). The definitions correspond to the one first introduced in 1970 (PL 91-602), which is categorical and restrictive. A major difference between these definitions is the concept of etiology of developmental disabilities. In the earlier edition, developmental disabilities are described as attributable to various disorders, while in the later definition developmental disabilities are described as associated with specific disorders. Developmental disability was added to the *Thesaurus of ERIC Descriptors* (Houston, 1984) in June 1977, and is defined as a

> category in federal legislation referring to disabilities resulting from mental retardation, cerebral palsy, epilepsy, autism or other neurological conditions closely related to mental retardation that originate before age 18 and are considered a substantial handicap to normal functioning. (p. 69)

Neither the AAMD nor the ERIC definitions are functional or reflective of the original concept proposed by the coalition or the definition incorporated into federal legislation in 1978.

The overlap in various definitions of developmental disabilities and other handicapping conditions has caused considerable confusion. Grossman (1983) points out that basic characteristics of mental retardation overlap with the legislative definition of developmental disabilities. Grossman goes on to say that the areas of limitations described in the legislative definition of developmental disabilities apply to more severe forms of mental retardation and to some mildly retarded individuals during certain periods of their lives. Grossman describes the parallel aspects of mental retardation and developmental disabilities as that of being developmental in origin and stressing impairment in adaptive behavior. He also indicates that the subgroup of persons with more severe forms of mental retardation will have a permanent and substantial handicap, as do many children with autism and cerebral palsy. Thus persons in this subgroup may be considered developmentally disabled. However, those with milder mental retardation and less severe conditions of cerebral palsy, epilepsy, and autism would fall outside the definition of developmental disability.

In summary, the concept of developmental disability is a generic one that evolved from the area of mental retardation and focuses on the needs of persons with serious and ongoing disabilities that originated before age 22. Thompson and O'Quinn (1979) point out that as the concept of developmental disabilities continues to evolve, efforts at defining developmental disabilities in cultural contexts are likely to continue as well.

REFERENCES

Boggs, E. M. (1972). Federal legislation 1966–1971. In J. Wortis (Ed.), *Mental retardation: An annual review* (Vol. 4). New York: Grune & Stratton.

Ehlers, W. H., Prothero, J. C., & Langone, J. (1982). *Mental retardation and other developmental disabilities* (3rd ed.). Columbus, OH: Merrill.

Grossman, H. J. (Ed.). (1977). *Manual of terminology and classification in mental retardation*. Washington, DC: American Association on Mental Deficiency.

Grossman, H. J. (Ed.). (1983). *Classification in mental retardation*. Washington, DC: American Association on Mental Deficiency.

Houston, J. E. (1984). *Thesaurus of ERIC descriptors.* Phoenix, AZ: Oryx.

Neisworth, J. T., & Smith, R. M. (1974). An analysis and redefinition of "developmental disabilities." *Exceptional Children, 40,* 345–347.

President's Committee on Mental Retardation. (1968). *MR68—The edge of change.* Washington, DC: U.S. Government Printing Office.

President's Committee on Mental Retardation. (1976). *MR76—Mental retardation past and present.* Washington, DC: U.S. Government Printing Office.

Seltzer, G. B. (1983). Systems of classification. In J. L. Matson & J. A. Mulick (Eds.), *Handbook of mental retardation.* New York: Pergamon.

Thompson, R. J., & O'Quinn, A. N. (1979). *Developmental disabilities.* New York: Oxford University Press.

ELEANOR BOYD WRIGHT
*University of North Carolina
at Wilmington*

AAMD
CEREBRAL PALSY
MENTAL RETARDATION
PHYSICAL HANDICAP

DEVELOPMENTAL DISABILITIES ASSISTANCE ACT AND BILL OF RIGHTS

The Developmental Disabilities Assistance and Bill of Rights Act Amendments of 1994 was originally enacted as Title 1 of the Mental Retardation Facilities and Construction Act of 1963, Public Law, 88-164 and was amended in 1981, 1987, 1990, and 1994. The purpose of the Act is to:

> assure that individuals with developmental disabilities and their families participate in the design of and have access to culturally competent services, supports, and other assistance and opportunities that promote independence, productivity, and integration and inclusion into the community. (Part A. p. 1)

This is carried out through the participation of State Developmental Disabilities Councils, the development of state protection and advocacy systems, the support of university-affiliated programs, and the support of national initiatives to collect data and provide technical assistance to state Councils.

The Act also states the rights of individuals with developmental disabilities as:

> (1) Individuals with developmental disabilities have a right to appropriate treatment, services, and habilitation for such disabilities.

> (2) The treatment services, and habilitation for an individual with developmental disabilities should be designed to maximize the developmental potential of the individual and should be provided the setting that is least restrictive of the individual's personal liberty.

> (3) The Federal Government and the States both have an obligation to assure that public funds are not provided to any institutional or other residential program for individuals with developmental disabilities that—

>> (A) does not provide treatment, services, and habilitation which is appropriate to the needs of such individuals, or

>> (B) does not meet the following minimum standards:

>>> (i) Provision of a nourishing, well-balanced daily diet to the individuals with developmental disabilities being served by the program.

>>> (ii) Provision to such individuals of appropriate and sufficient medical and dental services.

>>> (iii) Prohibition of the use of physical restraint on such individuals unless absolutely necessary and prohibition of the use of such restraint as a punishment or as a substitute for a habilitation program.

>>> (iv) Prohibition on the excessive use of chemical restraints on such individuals and the use of such restraints as punishments or as a substitute for a habilitation program or in quantities that interfere with services, treatment, or habilitation for such individuals.

>>> (v) Permission for close relatives of such individuals to visit them at reasonable hours without prior notice.

>>> (vi) Compliance with adequate fire and safety standards as may be promulgated by the Secretary.

> (4) All programs for individuals with developmental disabilities should meet standards which are designed to assure the most favorable possible outcome for those served, and—

>> (A) in the case of residential programs serving individuals in need of comprehensive health-related, habilitative, or rehabilitative services, which are at least equivalent to those standards applicable to intermediate care facilities for the mentally retarded promulgated in regulations of the Secretary on June 3, 1988, as appropriate when taking into account the size of the institutions and the service delivery arrangements of the facilities of the programs;

>> (B) in the case of other residential programs for individuals with developmental disabilities, which assure that care is appropriate to the needs of the individuals being served by such programs, assure that the individuals admitted to facilities of such programs are individuals whose needs can be met through services provided by such facilities, and assure that the facilities under such programs provide for the humane care of the residents of the facilities, are sanitary, and protect their rights; and

>> (C) in the case of nonresidential programs, which assure the care provided by such programs is appropriate to the individuals served by the programs. The rights of individuals with developmental disabilities described in findings made in this section are in addition to any constitutional or other rights otherwise afforded to all individuals. (Part A, Section 110)

Under Part B of the Act, the Developmental Disabilities Council program provides financial assistance to each state to support the activities of a Developmental Disabilities Council. The councils are made up of individuals who have developmental disabilities, family members, and representatives of State agencies that provide services to individuals with developmental disabilities. The Council develops and implements a state-wide plan to address employment (which is a federally mandated priority) and case management, child development and community living. Fiscal year 1998 appropriation provided $64,803,000 to support these plans.

The Administration on Developmental Disabilities receives annual reports from states and provides its own annual report on the implementation of the Act. The Administration is located at

U.S. Department of Health and Human Services
200 Independence Avenue
Room 329D
Washington, D.C. 20201
(202) 245-2897 (voice)
(202) 245-2890 (TDD)

The Administration on Developmental Disabilities also maintains an extensive webpage on the internet: http://www.acf.dhhs.gov/programs/add //.

ELAINE FLETCHER-JANZEN
University of Northern Colorado

INDIVIDUALS WITH DISABILITIES EDUCATION ACT (IDEA) OFFICE OF CIVIL RIGHTS

DEVELOPMENTAL DISABILITIES LEGAL RESOURCE CENTER

See PROTECTION AND ADVOCACY SYSTEM—DEVELOPMENTALLY DISABLED (P&A).

DEVELOPMENTAL DYSLEXIA

Developmental dyslexia is typically perceived as a complex heterogeneous reading disorder. It appears to stem from a selective disturbance of the maturation of neurological functions thought to be responsible for the acquisition of reading and writing skills. It is genetically determined and thus distinct from acquired alexia from traumatic brain injury (Gaddes, 1976). Critical components of the disorder that are relative to the individual's unique patterns of intrinsic abilities and extrinsic assets dictate that the dyslexic must have at least average intelligence; sufficient cultural and linguistic opportunity; emotional stability; access to appropriate instruction; and approximately normal sensory acuity (Rourke & Gates, 1981). Prognosis of relative success in compensating for the disorder's consequences is based on early identification, delineation of the individual's unique pattern of strengths and weaknesses, capitalization on unique educational strategies, and concomitant appropriate socio-cultural/familial support systems.

More than 80 years worth of published material (Benton, 1980) has been generated by the disorder; its history has been rich with conflicting information. To state that developmental dyslexia has been a confusing disorder would be diplomatic at best; however, continued research in the differentiation of subtypes, longitudinal studies on developmental changes, technological advances related to etiology, and empirical results from promising intervention programs continue to refine conceptualizations of dyslexia.

The origin of the term dyslexia has beep attributed to Kausmaul, who in 1877 defined the word *alexia* as word blindness. In 1891 Dejerine provided autopsy data on individuals who had suffered cerebrovascular injury and were left with reading disabilities. In 1896 Morgan described a famous dyslexic case study concerning an intelligent 14-year-old male who could not read or write but could perform algebra. These studies indicated specific deficits or abnormal development of the angular gyrus region in the dominant hemisphere (Dalby, 1979).

In 1900 Hinshelwood reported that the disorder caused partial or complete loss of visual memory for letters and words. In 1901 Nettleship observed that a disproportionate number of males had dyslexia, the disorder tended to run in families, and there was the presence of a linguistic factor. Four years later, Fisher recommended implementation of a "look and say" method of instruction for individuals who had a phonemic analysis deficit. This remediation used global word recognition. Interestingly, he also advocated teaching children to write with their left hands, based on the assumption that the right hemisphere subserved the learning process in children with faulty left hemispheres. Marie, in 1906, disagreed with the localizationalist theories of brain functioning, then the prevalent school of thought, which assumed specific behaviors were attributed to specific brain areas. He argued that there could not be specific centers for reading because reading was a new development in humans (Pirozzolo, 1981).

Educational and clinical psychologists' interest in dyslexia gained momentum during the first two decades of the twentieth century. Research focused on the basic underlying factors that presumably caused failure in learning to read, and two schools of thought emerged. The first emphasized the relation of perceptual and cognitive disabilities and the second concentrated on environmental factors (Benton, 1980). A new perspective on dyslexia was formulated by Orton toward the end of the second decade.

Orton related reading disability to a defective interhemispheric organization of cerebral function. It was assumed to be the result of a faulty maturational process of establishing specialization of function in a single hemisphere. The consequences of incomplete hemispheric dominance were said to lead to confusion and failure to read effectively (Johnson & Myklebust, 1967).

Behavioral and personality disorders in dyslexics were investigated in the 1930s. It was assumed that psychotherapy should be the primary mode of intervention before and during educational remediation. In the early 1940s, Werner and Strauss (Dalby, 1979) stated that brain damage was present, whether or not detectable by neurological means, as long as similar behavior patterns were exhibited. They initiated the term minimal brain damage (MBD), which, unfortunately, was embraced by zealous individuals who then attributed MBD to the entire population of persons with learning disorders. Without substantial evidence to support the conclusion that brain damage existed minimally, dissimilar disorders were erroneously lumped together (e.g., attention deficit disorders, developmental dyslexia). The devastating impact of these erroneous labels was unfortunately incurred by the child (Hobbs, 1975).

To complicate this picture further, incidence rates for dyslexics in the general population ranged from 10 to 30%, as reported in the voluminous post-World War II research on dyslexia. It became clear, however, that many researchers had failed to differentiate specific reading disability from failure to read owing to other factors (e.g., lack of normal intelligence, primary sensory impairments, lack of adequate educational and cultural opportunities, and emotional instability). The field of developmental dyslexia became clouded, and, as Benton and Pearl (1978) note, this large volume of research did little to differentiate distinct subtypes of dyslexia. The concept of dyslexia appeared to mean different things to different people. Adams (1967) found 23 definitions of dyslexia in the literature and he argued for abandonment of the term. It has been observed that the particular way in which research in developmental dyslexia is conducted stems directly from its definition, and if that definition is not one that is commonly accepted, researchers' results will differ accordingly (Rourke, 1976; Sawyer, 1992). It is currently estimated that 15% of the school population is dyslexic, as are over 85% of adult illiterates (Orton-Gillingham Practitioners and Educators, 1998).

From the 1960s to the present, research proceeded by varied means. Renewed interest in Orton's work followed advances in asymmetrical hemispheric specialization research (e.g., dichotic listening, dichaptic discrimination, and tachistoscopic methods). Medical technology has furthered investigations in the neurological basis of dyslexia by means of electroencephalography, computerized tomography scanning, cerebral blood flow studies, positron emission tomography, and autopsies on dyslexic and normal brains. Current research in the educational/neuropsychological literature (Hynd & Obrzut, 1981; Knights & Bakker, 1976) has supported the involvement of higher cortical impairment in developmental dyslexia. There are a select few that contend that dyslexia stems from subcortical impairment involving the cerebellar-vestibular system (Frank & Levinson, 1973); however, independent validation of this research has not yet been published.

Evidence from research on pre- and perinatal events in relation to dyslexia has demonstrated the importance of this period on the child's development. However, there is no strong evidence to substantiate that abnormalities in this period lead directly to specific reading disability. Extensive data from twin research (Herschel, 1978) showed a genetic basis to developmental dyslexia, although there is little evidence to support particular biochemical, physiological, or behavioral attributes linked specifically to dyslexia.

Sex differences are apparent in that males are disproportionately represented in reading-disabled populations. Data exist that indicate even normal girls are more adept at the learning-to-read process than normal boys. Anatomical data further substantiate those claims, since myelination occurred more rapidly in the left hemisphere for girls and the right hemisphere for boys (Dalby, 1979). Other sex differences have been hypothesized to be maturational lags in hemispheric specialization shifts in the learning-to-read process (Rourke, 1982), where girls pass through the stages faster than boys (Gaddes, 1976). These hypotheses suggest that the right hemisphere-mediated functions may have a critical role in the initial stages of the acquisition of the reading process, whereas the left hemisphere-mediated functions may be more efficient in using a routinized mode that stems from that acquisition. This right-to-left shift in hemispheric specialization may be a function of increased competence with the learning-to-read process.

The current perspective on developmental dyslexia has focused on more stringent methods of research in the identification of distinct subtypes (Rourke & Gates, 1981). Converging data from this body of research suggested a need for a multidimensional definition; it was clear that appropriate identification of dyslexics could not be made solely on the basis of poor reading achievement with approximately average intelligence (Yule & Rutter, 1976). The presence of differences in the types of dyslexia necessitates different strategies of educational interventions. Recognition of these differences became more pronounced following multivariate analyses of clinical neuropsychological methods (Petrauskas & Rourke, 1979) and important developmental changes, described in longitudinal research (Satz, Taylor, Friel, & Fletcher, 1978).

The neuropsychological evidence has suggested the presence of several subtypes of dyslexic readers, two of which are fairly distinct in older children and adults: auditory-linguistic deficient (dysphonetic) readers and visual-spatial deficient (dyseidetic) readers, as described by Pirozzolo (1981). Others have described a mixed dyslexic group (both dysphonetic and dyseidetic); an unspecified group (of which subcortical impairment cannot be completely ruled out), and a normal group; or linguistic, perceptual, and mixed groups (Masutto, 1994); and phonological and surface types (Murphy & Pollatsek, 1994).

Hartlage and Telzrow (1983) have elucidated various means of using neuropsychological data for successful educational intervention. They hypothesized that a child's neuropsychological strengths should be emphasized in matching complementary curricula to that pattern, without total rejection of tasks using weaker neuropsychological abilities. As an example, auditory-linguistic deficient dyslexics typically have stronger right hemisphere-mediated functions; thus, a "whole word" or "look and say" method of reading would be recommended. This would occur without rejecting the teaching of sounds of letters and blends when decoding new words. Other techniques (Aaron & Poostay, 1982) advocate a careful review of the individual child's functional behaviors. Task analysis of these behaviors indicates where the functional breakdown has occurred in the learning process and represents the focus of intervention. The most widely used teaching method is the Orton-Gillingham method, which uses a simultaneous association of visual, auditory, and kinesthetic language stimuli (Griesbach, 1993).

REFERENCES

Aaron, I. E., & Poostay, E. J. (1982). Strategies for reading disorders. In C. R. Reynolds & T. B. Gutkin (Eds.), *The handbook of school psychology* (pp. 410–435). New York: Wiley.

Adams, R. B. (1967). *Dyslexia: A discussion of its definition.* Paper prepared for the second meeting of the Federal Government's Attack on Dyslexia. Washington, DC: Bureau of Research, U.S. Office of Education.

Benton, A. L. (1980). Dyslexia: Evolution of a concept. *Bulletin of the Orton Society, 30,* 10–26.

Benton, A. L., & Pearl, D. (1978). *Dyslexia: An appraisal of current knowledge.* New York: Oxford University Press.

Dalby, J. T. (1979). Deficit or delay: Neuropsychological models of developmental dyslexia. *Journal of Special Education, 3,* 239–264.

Frank, J., & Levinson, H. (1973). Dysmetric dyslexia and dyspraxia: Hypothesis and study. *Journal of the American Academy of Child Psychiatry, 12,* 690–701.

Gaddes, W. H. (1976). Prevalence estimates and the need for definition of learning disabilities. In R. Knights & D. Bakker (Eds.), *The neuropsychology of learning disorders: Theoretical approaches* (pp. 3–24). Baltimore, MD: University Park Press.

Griesbach, G. (1993). *Dyslexia: It's history, etiology, and treatment.* (ERIC Clearinghouse No. CS011300)

Hartlage, L. C., & Telzrow, C. F. (1983). The neuropsychological basis of educational intervention. *Journal of Learning Disabilities, 16,* 521–523.

Herschel, M. (1978). Dyslexia revisted: A review. *Human Genetics, 40,* 115–134.

Hobbs, N. (1975). *The futures of children: Categories, labels, and their consequences.* San Francisco: Jossey-Bass.

Hynd, G. W., & Obrzut, J. E. (1981). *Neuropsychological assessment and the school-age child: Issues and procedures.* New York: Grune & Stratton.

Johnson, D. J., & Myklebust, H. R. (1967). *Learning disabilities: Educational principles and practices.* New York: Grune & Stratton.

Knights, R., & Bakker, D. (1976). *The neuropsychology of learning disorders: Theoretical approaches.* Baltimore, MD: University Park Press.

Orton-Gillingham Practitioners and Educators (1998). Dyslexia. www.ols.net./users/orton/index.htm

Masutto, C. (1994). Neurolinguistic differentiation of children with subtypes of dyslexia. *Journal of Learning Disabilities, 27,* 8, 520–526.

Murphy, L., & Pollatsek, A. (1994). Developmental dyslexia: Heterogeneity without discrete subgroups. *Annals of Dyslexia, 44,* 120–146.

Petrauskas, R. J., & Rourke, B. P. (1979). Identification of subtypes of retarded readers: A neuropsychological multivariate approach. *Journal of Clinical Neuropsychology, 1,* 17–37.

Pirozzolo, F. J. (1981). Language and brain: Neuropsychological aspects of developmental reading disability. *School Psychology Review, 3,* 350-355.

Rourke, B. P. (1976). Reading retardation in children: Developmental lag or deficit? In R. Knights & D. Bakker (Eds.), *The neuropsychology of learning disorders: Theoretical approaches* (pp. 125–137). Baltimore, MD: University Park Press.

Rourke, B. P. (1982). Central processing deficiencies in children: Toward a developmental neuropsychological model. *Journal of Clinical Neuropsychology, 4,* 1–18.

Rourke, B. P., & Gates, R. D. (1981). Neuropsychological research and school psychology. In G. W. Hynd & J. E. Obrzut (Eds.), *Neuropsychological assessment and the school-age child: Issue and procedures* (pp. 3–25). New York: Grune & Stratton.

Satz, P., Taylor, H. G., Friel, J., & Fletcher, J. M. (1978). Some developmental and predictive precursors of reading disabilities: A six year follow-up. In A. L. Benton & D. Pearl (Eds.), *Dyslexia: An appraisal of current knowledge* (pp. 313–347). New York: Oxford University Press.

Sawyer, D. J. (1992). Dyslexia: Introduction to Special Series. *Journal of Learning Disabilities, 25,* 1, 38.

Yule, W., & Rutter, M. (1976). Epidemiological and social implications of specific reading retardation. In R. Knights & D. Bakker (Eds.), *The neuropsychology of learning disorders: Theoretical approaches* (pp. 25–39). Baltimore, MD: University Park Press.

Scott W. Sautter
Vanderbilt University

DEVELOPMENTAL MILESTONES

Adults who have kept infant diaries have watched with pride as their children reached particular developmental milestones. The first responsive smile, the initial unsure steps, and the dawning of language are three of the most obvious milestones. Psychologists take an interest in these early milestones, but their perspective extends beyond the infant years to the whole life span. Their research includes a host of physical, biological, mental, emotional, and social milestones which, taken together, form a normative picture of the child's development.

Milestones that involve a physical or biological change are the most salient because the newly acquired behavior is so clear. One day infants are holding onto the coffee table investigating magazines or curios, and the next day they are launching themselves into a void where no support exists. This adventure constitutes the first step. The first step, typically achieved at 11.7 months is, however, a culmination of the series of physical milestones outlined in the Table below (Bayley, 1969). This table gives the average age when infants master the physical skills that precede walking as well as an age range when different children master the skills. Notice that these normal ranges are often several months apart. For example, occasionally children will pull themselves to a standing position at the age of 5 months. At the other end of the scale, some perfectly normal children do not accomplish this same feat until they are a year old. This range of normality attests to the individual differences that exist in attaining all developmental milestones.

Another physical sequence that psychologists have described in detail is the development of grasping (see Table). Newborns have a reflexive grasp and will close their palms around any object. In the first few months of life, infants bat at objects in their environment. By 4 months of age, infants have stopped batting at objects and have developed fluid eye-hand coordination (White, 1971). Now they can direct their hands efficiently to an object they see, open their fist en route and, once contact is made, grasp the object with their palms. The palmar grasp works well for handling wooden blocks and rattles, but it is not efficient for picking up small objects. The pincer grasp, where the thumb and forefinger are delicately opposed, will supplant the palmar grasp at approximately 9 months of age (Bayley, 1969).

Infants engage in a lot of rhythmical behaviors—repetitious kicking, rocking, waving, and bouncing. These rhythmical behaviors form a transition between reflexive, uncoordinated behavior and behaviors that are precise and controlled. Rocking on the hands, for example, can be observed shortly before the child begins to crawl. Bouncing on the legs precedes the first steps (Thelen, 1981). These progressions make sense if we view them as a consequence of the developments taking place in the brain.

At birth, the brain weighs about 12 ounces (350 grams). Most of this brain tissue is generated in the last 3 months of pregnancy. In fact, forming the 10 billion cells that comprise the human brain means that during the last months of pregnancy and the first months of life, about 250,000 neurons must be generated each minute (Cowan, 1979). In the first 2 years of life, the weight of the brain will triple, reflecting a surge in the number of dendrites (Conel, 1967). As the infant matures, the dendrites intertwine into more extensive networks, until each neuron is connected by its dendrites with thousands of other cells. When one cell is activated, the effect can be spread through the entire dendritic network.

This brief sketch of how the brain develops fits into Thelen's discussion of rhythmical behavior. She argues that the development of the brain presages the physical developments we regard as milestones. In newborns, the brain's neurons are relatively isolated, hence the child's behaviors are reflexive and uncoordinated. As the dendritic networks begin to form, the child's behavior takes on more rhythmical patterns. At this point, the child will practice activating

Physical Milestones

Walking	Mean Age for Mastery (Months)	Range of Ages for Mastery (Months)	Fine Motor Grasping	Mean Age for Mastery (Months)	Range of Ages for Mastery (Months)
Crawling movements	.4	.1–3	Holds onto red ring	.8	.3–3
Sits with support	2.3	1–5	Arm thrusts in play	.8	.3–2
Pulls self to sitting	5.3	4.–8	Opens hands	2.7	.7–6
Prewalking progression	7.1	5.–11	Grasps with palm	3.7	2–7
Pulls to standing position	8.1	5.–12	Partially opposes thumb	4.9	4–8
Walks with help	9.6	7–12	Reaches with one hand	5.4	4–8
Stands alone	11.0	9–16	Reaches for pellet	5.6	4–8
Walks alone	11.7	9–17	Thumb opposed to finger	6.9	5–9
			Finger prehension	7.4	6–10
			Pincer prehension	8.9	7–12

a particular part of the body in a rhythmical way. When neuronal networks for a particular area mature, physical skills will be controlled by the infant and will be integrated with the actions of other parts of the body (Hofer, 1981). Many of the milestones in physical development reflect, then, the developmental milestones of the brain.

Changes in the brain trigger other biological milestones. The hypothalamus, a small area of the brain that monitors and controls the release of hormones, can be characterized as the master controller for puberty (Grumbach, 1975). In males, the growth spurt, the deepening of the voice, and the appearance of secondary sex characteristics are obvious signals that the hormonal changes of puberty have begun. In females, menstruation is the most salient indication of the change from girlhood to womanhood, although girls also go through a growth spurt at the beginning of puberty. The female growth spurt peaks at approximately 12 years of age. In males, the period of fastest growth is approximately 14 years of age (Tanner & Eveleth, 1975). The timing of the growth spurt depends heavily on genetic factors, but is certainly influenced by a host of environmental variables such as diet and economic status (Tanner & Eveleth, 1975).

The impact of environmental factors on a biological milestone is most obvious in the case of menstruation. In many European countries, the age of menarch (first menstruation) during the late 1800s was approximately 16 years. In contemporary western cultures, menstruation typically begins 3 years earlier (Tanner & Eveleth, 1975). In the United States, for example, the mean age for menarche is 12.8 years (Warren, 1983). These marked changes in the age of menarch are attributed to better nutrition, more favorable socioeconomic conditions, and improvements in general health.

The physical and biological milestones that have been described are relatively easy to identify because they are characterized by unique or discrete changes. Many mental milestones appear gradually and are more difficult to identify because they are so subtle. To psychologists interested in cognitive development, however, these milestones have become as obvious as the pincer grasp of infancy or the growth spurt of puberty.

The sensory motor period of development refers to the first 2 years of life. During this period, the child changes dramatically, from a wordless newborn, whose behaviors are primarily reflexive, to a talking 2 year old who has developed an amazing mastery of the immediate environment. In these 2 growth-filled years, the biggest mental milestones are the development of the object concept and the beginnings of language.

The object concept, described by Piaget (1954), reflects the infant's growing mental awareness. In the first few months of life, the infant is unconcerned about the comings and goings of people and objects. "Out of sight, out of mind" is an appropriate description for the infant's understanding of objects. Shortly after the first 6 months, infants' behaviors begin to change. Now, when their mothers disappear, infants stare at the doorway. They may cry, hoping that the combination of looking and crying will make their mother reappear. This change in behavior signals the realization, on the infant's part, that their mother is a separate entity.

Piaget (1954) followed the development of the object concept in his own three children. Using an infant version of hide-and-seek, he hid his children's favorite toy under a cloth or pillow. The hiding involved no deception; the infant could follow the toy visually as Piaget slowly slid it under the cover. Prior to 8 months, Piaget's children often reached for the cloth, but abandoned the search in a moment or two. By 10 months, however, they quickly pulled the cloth away and grabbed the toy. Piaget interpreted this change as indicating that his children could hold an image of the toy in their memories long enough to search for the object. They had developed a concept of an object that endured even when the object disappeared.

The object concept is a landmark in the development of memory. Once infants can represent objects in their minds, they are no longer limited to a reacting role; they can plan a course of action. Combine this initiative with the fact that 8 to 10 month olds have some mobility and you have the foundation for the avid exploration and curiosity of the 2 year old. The exploration and action of the 2 year old may seem like play to adults, and it is; but it is play with a serious purpose. It serves as the foundation for the abstract logic that is still many years in the future (Langer, 1980).

It is not coincidental that the second milestones of infancy, the child's first word, appears shortly after the object concept. In order to name an object, you must have a clear concept of that object. In most children, the appearance of the first word occurs between 10 and 15 months (de Villiers & de Villiers, 1979). But these early words are tied to a specific context and really do not function as symbols. For example, Nicky at 13 months would wave and say "bye-bye" when his father left for work in the morning. But Nicky couldn't say "bye-bye" without waving. "Bye-bye" was associated with the morning, the waving, and the father leaving (Anisfeld, 1984). It took several more months for Nicky to use "bye-bye" in a symbolic way, to mean goodbye.

With the acquisition of language, the child moves into a period called the intuitive or preoperational stage of mental development. This stage of development, which lasts from approximately 2 to 5 years, stands in stark contrast to the sensory motor period because language begins to direct the child's behavior. The preoperational period begins with a child whose language skills are just emerging and ends with a child who relies on language instead of action to understand the world (Anisfeld, 1984). Two and 3 year olds buttress their beginning language skills by combining words and actions. These toddlers comprehend an airplane by saying "airplane," sticking out their arms, running around the room, and making sounds like a roaring engine. The action of imitating the airplane helps them form an image of an airplane and helps them attach the label "airplane" to the scene. Similarly, 3 and 4 year olds playing with blocks or dolls keep a running monologue going to describe the action they are orchestrating. By tying language to the action-based concepts that were developed during the sensory motor period, the child can gain confidence in the use of language. When language emerges as the primary means of understanding the world, the child's behavior changes dramatically. Four year olds who ask their parents endless questions about the car, the refrigerator, the dog, and the weather, are demonstrating that they can now learn about the world using language. When language skills are mature, the child is ready to transcend the constraints of time and space, to think about situations that cannot be experienced, and to let logic become the guide to mental operations.

Between 5 and 7 years of age, a third mental milestone is reached—concrete operational thought. Having mastered language and action, children begin to operate symbolically. They classify and order their environments and, in the process, enhance their awareness of the world. Understanding the days of the week and the months of the year allows adults to bring order to the daily chaos of life. Knowing that it is Monday supplies a great deal of information. It is the beginning of the week, tomorrow is Tuesday, and the weekend is 5 days away. The knowledge that today is Monday allows us to draw many other conclusions, because Monday is part of a larger organization of knowledge encompassing months, seasons, and years. Preoperational children lack these higher level organizations. But with the onset of concrete operational thought, children begin to sort out the world, order it for their use, and develop multilayered concepts (Kuhn, 1972). The baseball cards and coin collections that abound during the early elementary years are a testimony to the child's developing classification skills. Being able to order information is just as important as being able to classify. People can be tall, average, or short. Outdoor temperatures can range from over 100 degrees to well below zero. Students' examinations are ordered from "As" to "Fs." Establishing an order to information and assigning numbers to that order is a second way of organizing the world. This skill, called seriation, also emerges during the period of concrete operational thought.

The real hallmark of concrete operational thought, however, is not the skill of classification or seriation, but the ability to transform information. One woman can simultaneously be mother, Mrs. Lindsay, and Aunt Carol, and each of these classifications is appropriate. A pet can be Spot, an Irish Setter, a dog, and a mammal. Each label is understood as part of a larger organization. The concrete operational child not only uses language to guide actions, but co-ordinates different bits of information. We see this skill in a child's developing sense of humor (McGhee, 1979). Once children understand that words can be used in several contexts, they can appreciate the following joke:

Waiter, What's this fly doing in my soup?
It looks like the breaststroke, sir.

Mastering concrete operations moves the child toward more logical thought processes, but the advances of concrete operational thought are really a stepping stone to the culmination of mental development—formal operational thought. Formal thought processes are the final mental milestone; they begin between 12 and 16 years of age (Inhelder & Piaget, 1958). During this period of development, mental operations are completely integrated and thought attains a flexibility unrealized at the earlier stages. Students can abstract from the reality of a problem and consider alternatives to a problem. Furthermore, they can systematically test their ideas and discover which of several hypotheses is correct. As formal thought proceeds, adolescents can evaluate and transform hypothetical statements such as, "If this is Los Angeles, then the freeways are jammed." Most adolescents can logically extend this statement to include, "If the freeways are empty, this cannot be Los Angeles" (Moshman, 1979). As is obvious from this example, individuals who have reached the milestone of formal operations frequently move beyond the actual information given. As a result, they can speculate about worlds that do not exist, they can evaluate political systems they have not experienced, and they can predict technological advances that will not materialize for years. The thought processes foreshadowed by the toddler's exploration come to fruition in the balanced, flexible, cohesive thought of formal operations.

Human infants are helpless and need parental care and protection to survive. This evolutionary necessity may have prompted the development of the specific signs and signals that infants use to keep their mothers nearby (Bowlby, 1980). The first social smile, noticed by all parents, is part of a larger system known as the attachment behavioral system. The purpose of this system is to make sure the infant is safe. By using different attachment behaviors, infants signal their need for attention, express preferences for particular people, object angrily if they are separated from an attachment figure, and seek comfort from their attachment object when the environment is threatening (Main, 1981).

The newborn can signal the mother (or primary caretaker) by crying. Mothers are so tuned to this signal that their heart rate speeds up when their infant begins crying (Donovan, Leavitt, & Balling, 1978). Mothers all over the world respond to their infants' cries by going to their babies, picking them up, and cuddling them. Smiling is another attachment behavior. When the mother is near, the infant's smile strengthens and continues the social inter-action between mother and infant. From the second month of life, infants begin to smile broadly at their mothers and indicate their pleasure by bicycling movements of their arms and legs. Most parents find this combination irre-sistible and immediately interact with their child. Infants also signal their parents by reaching, clinging, crawling, and walking. Once toddlers are mobile, they can take a more active role in maintaining proximity to their moth-ers. The popular image of the child peeping from behind mother's skirts is an example of the child seeking the mother when the environment seems threatening.

The formation of strong caretaker-infant attachments during the first year of life bodes well for social develop-ment in the toddler and preschool years. When a secure attachment exists, toddlers seem competent and self-assured as they explore their environments. Infants who are securely attached become preschoolers who are re-garded as leaders and sought by other children as play-mates (Bronson, 1981). The continuing effects of a secure attachment are easily explained. A secure attachment in-dicates a caring, trusting relationship between the mother and infant. In all likelihood, this positive relationship will continue into the toddler, preschool, and school years (Bretherton & Waters, 1985).

The attachment behavioral system carries over into peer relationships. A positive relationship with the mother seems to set the stage for the development of friendships. Friendships that involve cooperation and communication typically begin to develop during the preschool years. In fact, preschoolers can engage in the full spectrum of social interaction—cooperation, competition, aggression, affili-ation, and altruism. Preschoolers can communicate, but more important, they can listen. If they need more infor-mation, they can ask questions. This ability to interact and carry on a dialogue is often the beginning of social rela-tionships.

Despite the existence of basic social skills, the pre-schooler's social repertoire looks rather meager when com-pared with the school-age child's. Whereas friendships in preschool are a matter of convenience, stable, long-term friendships exist among elementary school children. Whether children are skillful at making friends at this age period depends on their ability to establish a common ground and exchange information as well as their ability to resolve conflicts and communicate (Gottman, 1983).

By adolescence, friends become confidants. Typically, teenage friends are the same age, the same sex, the same race, and have some common interest (Berndt, 1982). Being a friend now carries a measure of responsibility. Friends demand loyalty and require support. This kind of interpersonal commitment was not part of friendships dur-ing earlier periods of development.

Developmental milestones take many forms. The rapid physical changes that occur during infancy and the biolog-ical milestones that herald a new period of life are readily identified because they represent an abrupt break with the past. Mental development is characterized by just as many milestones, but they tend to emerge gradually. The object concept, the first word, and concrete operational thought processes are each noticeable points on the continuous tableau of development. As with most milestones, cogni-tive advances represent both the culmination of earlier processes and the foundation for further development. So-cial and emotional milestones include attachment behav-iors and friendships. It is essential that these milestones are investigated and assessed in a culturally competent fashion. Family and social relationships are contextually and culturally-loaded concepts (Nissani, 1993; Rocco, 1993; Winborne & Randolf, 1991). The first cries for atten-tion and the devoted camaraderie of adolescence are both milestones that attest to the child's interactions with oth-ers. Examined together, the succession of physical, mental, and social milestones chart an individual's progress on the road of life.

REFERENCES

Anisfeld, M. (1984). *Language development from birth to three.* Hillsdale, NJ: Erlbaum.

Bayley, N. (1969). *Manual for the Bayley scales of infant develop-ment.* New York: Psychological Corporation.

Berndt, T. J. (1982). The features and effects of friendship in early adolescence. *Child Development, 53,* 1447–1460.

Bowlby, J. (1980). *Attachment and loss: (Loss, sadness, and de-pression)* (Vol. 3). New York: Basic Books.

Bretherton, I., & Waters, E. (1985). Growing points of attachment theory and research. *Monographs for the Society for Research in Child Development, 50,* (209).

Bronson, W. C. (1981). *Toddlers' behavior with agemates: Issues of interaction, cognition, and affect.* Norwood, NJ: Ablex.

Conel, J. L. (1967). *The postnatal development of the human cor-tex* (Vol. 8). Cambridge, MA: Harvard University Press.

Cowan, W. M. (1979). The development of the brain. *Scientific American, 241,* 112–133.

de Villiers, P. A., & de Villiers, J. G. (1979). *Early language.* Cam-bridge, MA: Harvard University Press.

Donovan, W. A., Leavitt, L. A., & Balling, J. D. (1978). Maternal physiological responses to infant signals. *Psychophysiology, 15,* 68–74.

Gottman, J. M. (1983). How children become friends. *Monographs of the Society for Research in Child Development, 48,* (201).

Grumbach, M. M. (1975). Onset of puberty. In S. R. Berenberg (Ed.), *Puberty: Biologic and psychosocial components.* Leiden, Netherlands: Stenfert Kroese.

Hofer, M. A. (1981). *The roots of human behavior.* San Francisco: Freeman.

Inhelder, B., & Piaget, J. (1958). *The growth of logical thinking from childhood to adolescence.* New York: Basic Books.

Kuhn, D. (1972). Mechanisms of change in the development of cognitive structures. *Child Development, 43,* 833–844.

Langer, J. (1980). *The origins of logic: Six to twelve months*. New York: Academic.

Main, M. (1981). Avoidance in the service of attachment. In K. Immelmann, G. W. Barlow, L. Petrinovich, & M. Main (Eds.), *Behavioral development: The Bielefeld Interdisciplinary Project*. London: Cambridge University Press.

McGhee, P. E. (1979). *Humor: Its origin and development*. San Francisco: Witt, Freeman.

Moshman, D. (1979). Development of formal hypothesis-testing ability. *Developmental Psychology, 15*, 104–112.

Nissani, H. (1993). Early childhood programs for language minority students. *ERIC clearinghouse on languages and linguistics*. (ERIC Digest No. ED355836)

Piaget, J. (1954). *The construction of reality in the child*. New York: Ballantine.

Rocco, S. (1993). *New visions for the developmental assessment of infants and young children*. (ERIC Clearinghouse No. EC302834)

Tanner, J. M., & Eveleth, P. B. (1975). Variability between populations in growth and development at puberty. In S. R. Berenberg (Ed.), *Puberty: Biologic and psychosocial components*. Leiden, Netherlands: Stenfert Kroese.

Thelen, E. (1981). Rhythmical behavior in infancy: An ethological perspective. *Developmental Psychology, 17*, 237–257.

Warren, M. P. (1983). Physical and biological aspects of puberty. In J. Brooks-Gunn and A. C. Petersen (Eds.), *Girls at puberty*. New York: Plenum.

White, B. L. (1971). *Human infants: Experience and psychological development*. Englewood Cliffs, NJ: Prentice-Hall.

Winborne, D. G., & Randolf, S. M. (1991). Developmental expectations and outcomes for African-American infants. (ERIC Clearinghouse No. PS019880)

CAROL TOMLINSON-KEASEY
University of California

DEVELOPMENTAL NORMS

Developmental norms describe the position of an individual along a continuum of development. Two fundamental types of developmental norms are age equivalents and grade equivalents. They are obtained by administering a test to several successive age or grade groups; the average, or typical, performance of each age or grade group is subsequently determined and becomes the norm for a particular age or grade group (Anastasi, 1982).

A number of human traits demonstrate growth with increasing age, including abstract intelligence, vocabulary or language acquisition, and motor skill development. Age equivalents have frequently been used to interpret performance for age-related traits. The average test score obtained by successive age or grade groups is determined based on the performance of a carefully selected sample of individuals. The age (in years and months) for which a particular test score was the average becomes the age equivalent for that particular test score; e.g., a child who answered 35 questions correctly on a receptive language test received an age equivalent of 4–6, meaning that 35 was the average, or typical, score for children aged 4 years, 6 months tested in the norming program. The term mental age refers to an age equivalent obtained from an intelligence test. A child with a mental age of 6 years, 3 months, for example, performed as well as the average child aged 6 years, 3 months.

Skills that develop as a direct result of school instruction such as reading or mathematics have frequently been assessed with tests that yield grade equivalents. The typical, or average, performance of successive grade groups is determined for a carefully selected sample of pupils. The grade for which a certain test score was the average becomes the grade equivalent for that particular test score (Thorndike & Hagen, 1977); e.g., a pupil who answered 40 questions correctly on a mathematics concepts test received a grade equivalent of 6.2, meaning that 40 was the average score for pupils in the second month of grade 6.

Age and grade equivalents have come into disfavor for a number of reasons:

1. They represent scales having unequal units because human traits typically develop faster in the earlier years and slow down in adolescence and adulthood. Thus, the difference in performance between ages 3 and 4, e.g., may be much greater than the difference in performance between ages 14 and 15 for a particular trait. Similarly, the difference in performance between grade equivalents 1.0 and 2.0 may be much greater than that between 8.0 and 9.0. This characteristic makes interpretation difficult.

2. They are not as rich in meaning as within-group norms (standard scores and percentile ranks) because they "match" the individual's performance to the age or grade group for which that performance was just average.

3. They can imply a level of functioning or skill development that is misleading. A fifth-grade pupil who receives a reading comprehension grade equivalent of 10.8 is not necessarily reading at the same level as a student in the eighth month of the tenth grade. The grade equivalent of 10.8 is to some extent a contrivance of the grade equivalent score scale and simply means the pupil is reading very well for a fifth grader (Cronbach, 1984). Grade equivalents are especially difficult to interpret when obtained from group achievement tests. Mental ages for adolescence and adulthood likewise do not describe actual performance at those ages and often represent an arbitrary and artificial extension of the mental age scale.

In summary, age and grade equivalents are developmental norms that, when interpreted cautiously, can sometimes provide useful information; however, within group norms such as standard scores and percentile ranks are the preferred method of test interpretation.

REFERENCES

Anastasi, A. (1982). *Psychological testing* (5th ed.). New York: Macmillan.

Cronbach, L. J. (1984). *Essentials of psychological testing* (4th ed.). New York: Harper & Row.

Thorndike, R. L., & Hagen, E. P. (1977). *Measurement and evaluation in psychology and education*. New York: Wiley.

GARY J. ROBERTSON
American Guidance Service

GRADE EQUIVALENTS
NORM REFERENCED TESTING

DEVELOPMENTAL OPTOMETRY

The relationship between vision, sight, and learning took on a new meaning in 1922 when A. M. Skeffington, an optometrist who help found the Postgraduate Optometric Extension Program, lectured on the concept that Snellen visual acuity (sight) and visual effectiveness (vision) were not one in the same. In the 1930s George Crow and Margaret Eberl expanded this concept by instituting the use of preventive lenses and visual training to enhance visual abilities, promote visual efficiency, and reduce or eliminate visual anomalies such as amblyopia, strabismus, and binocular dysfunction. At the same time, the American Optometric Association published a pamphlet, "It is a Cruel Test," stating that "Optometry is not interested in merely whether the child sees well—it is interested in whether he sees efficiently."

Clinical studies in the visual development of the school-age child took a dramatic step forward in the 1940s at the Clinic of Child Development at Yale University. Gesell, Ilg et al. established that the eye and the other sensory modalities take turns in the development of the mind. Gesell et al. stated that vision is so fundamental in the growth of the mind that the body takes hold of the physical world with his eyes long before he takes hold with his hands. The eyes lead in the patterning of behavior.

The team at the Clinic of Child Development Center observed visual behavior from the earliest stages. It was noted, for example, that the newborn eyes wander without a stimulus. However, after a few hours, the child can often fixate briefly. By 16 weeks the eyes are leading the other senses, but they also begin to team with the hands.

Through these observations, it was established that visual development began at birth despite the fact that vision appeared to be a "fleeting, discontinuous performance."

At the Child Development Center, Getman also developed, applied, and modified optometric techniques to test the visual development of the child from 21 to 48 months. These new tests and modifications were necessitated by the fact that adult testing procedures were of little value in the testing of children.

Getman found that monocular and binocular fixation, near and far point shifting of attention, and depth perception and spatial awareness develop and increase throughout childhood at varying rates. The studies revealed the importance of how the visual mechanism is involved in the total performance of the child. The concept of developmental vision that Getman and Kephart elaborated on also established a causal relationship between early motor patterns and the development of binocularity. Therefore, any delay or omission in development could result not only in binocular deficts but in amblyopias and anisometropias. According to Solan (1979) any deviation from the normal ontogeny of motor and sensory maturation is considered to be significant.

Renshaw, Getman, and Skeffington studied the retinoscopic reflex during reading in conjunction with the lie detector test. They noted that when reading, stress could be revealed by the blood pressure, respiration, galvanic skin response, and retinoscopic reflex. These studies, along with the work of Huebal, Wiesel, and others, established that vision is not just genetically endowed; it develops. The concept of function altering structure rather than structure altering function became embodied in developmental vision theory. Solan (1979) states that by integrating the concepts of Myklebust, Strauss, Werner, Birch, Kephart, Piaget, Jensen, and others, the developmental optometrist is able to construct a diagnostic and therapeutic regimen. Developmental and perceptual therapy provides a child experiencing a learning disability with those characteristics normally associated with good students who are efficient learners.

The optometrist specializing in the field of developmental vision includes in the basic vision examination a careful case history that covers any significant information on the prenatal, perinatal, and postnatal disorders and any delays in the developmental milestones. The visual examination includes the standard testing procedures such as visual acuity, ocular health status of the eyes, binocular status, refractive status, and accommodative facility. Additional tests may probe the child's concept of laterality, directionality, dominance, eye-hand coordination, and visual perception.

Training of the child with developmental vision problems encompasses the standard visual training procedures. These include enhancement of ocular motility, stereopsis, eye-hand coordination, and accommodation.

Additional techniques may emphasize bilateral and binocular integration. It is also important for the optometrist to collaborate with special services personnel to assist in the psychological conditions that sometimes exist with vision difficulties (Biaggo & Bittner, 1990).

The optometrist, as Solan (1979) states, blends professional and intellectual skills to develop in the learning-disabled child a suitable level of visual functional readiness for learning, the sensory-motor skills necessary for a child to respond to classroom instruction, and cognitive skills and conceptual tempo required for assimmilation and generalization in learning reasoning and problem solving.

REFERENCES

Barsch, R. H. (1964, January). The role of cognition in movement. *Optometric Child Vision Care & Guidance, 8*(4), 17–23.

Biaggio, M. K., & Bittner, E. (1990). Psychology and optometry: Interaction and collaboration. *American Psychologist, 45,* 12, 1313–1315.

Gesell, A., Halverson, A. Z., & Amstruda, C. (1940). *The first five years of life.* New York: Harper & Brothers.

Gesell, A., Ilg, F. L., & Bullis, G. E. (1949). *Vision: Its development in infant and child.* New York: Harper & Brothers.

Getman, G. (1960). *Techniques and diagnostic criteria for the optometric care of children's vision,* Duncan, OK: Occupational Education Programs.

Getman, G. (1962). *How to develop your child's intelligence.* Luverne, MI: Privately printed.

Getman, G., & Bullis, G. (1950). *Developmental vision* (Vol. 1). Duncan, OK: OEP.

Getman, G., & Kephart, N. (1957). *Developmental vision* (Vol. 2). Duncan, OK: OEP.

Kephart, N. C. (1960). *The slow learner in the classroom.* Columbus, OH: Charles E. Merril.

Lavatelli, C. (1973). *Piaget's theory applied to an early childhood curriculum.* Boston: Center for Media Development.

Piaget, J., & Inhelder, B. (1956). *The child's conception of space.* London: Routledge & Kegan Paul.

Skeffington, A. (1957). *Developmental vision* (Vol. 1). Duncan, OK: OEP.

Solan, H. (1979). *Learning disabilities: The role of the developmental optometrist, 50*(11), 1265. St. Louis: American Optometric Association.

BRUCE P. ROSENTHAL
State University of New York

DEVELOPMENTAL PSYCHOLOGY

Developmental Psychology is a publication of the American Psychological Association. Founded in 1968, its first editor was Boyd R. McCandless of Emory University.

The journal's primary purpose is to publish reports of empirical research on topics pertaining to developmental psychology. Developmental psychology is defined as including variables pertaining to growth and development broadly cast. Not only chronological age and physical growth variables are included, but also other factors, such as sex and socioeconomic status.

Developmental Psychology is published bimonthly. Manuscripts may be sent to *Developmental Psychology,* American Psychological Association, 1200 Seventeenth Street, NW, Washington, DC 20036.

ELIZABETH JONES
Texas A & M University

DEVELOPMENTAL TEST OF VISUAL PERCEPTION: SECOND EDITION (DTVP-2)

The *Developmental Test of Visual Perception: Second Edition* (DTVP-2) is the most recent revision of *The Marianne Frostig Developmental Test of Visual Perception* originally authored by Frostig, Maslow, Lefever, & Whittlesey (1963). The new edition includes numerous improvements, is suitable for children ages 4 to 10, measures both visual perception and visual-motor integration skills, has eight subtests, is based on updated theories of visual perception development, and can be administered to individuals in 35 minutes. The DTVP-2 subtests are Eye-Hand Coordination, Copying, Spatial Relations, Position in Space, Figure-Ground, Visual Closure, Visual-Motor Speed, and Form Constancy.

The DTVP-2 is unique among other tests of visual perception and visual-motor integration because (1) its subtests are reliable at the .8 or .9 levels for all age groups; (2) its scores are validated by many studies; (3) its norms are based on a large representative sample keyed to the 1990 census data; (4) it yields scores for both pure visual perception (no motor response) and visual-motor integration ability; and (5) it has been proven to be unbiased relative to race, gender, and handedness.

The DTVP-2 was standardized on 1,972 children from 12 states. Characteristics of the normative sample approximate those provided in the 1990 *Statistical Abstract of the United States* with regard to gender, geographical region, ethnicity, race, and urban/rural residence. Standard scores, NCEs, percentiles, and age equivalents are provided in the Examiner's Manual.

This test was reviewed in *The Twelfth Mental Measurements Yearbook* by Bologna (1995) and Tindal (1995). Bologna stated that the revised test was an impressive revision of a previously weak instrument; Tindal described the test as useful in determining General Visual Perception, Motor Reduced Visual Perception, and Visual-Motor Integration.

REFERENCES

Bologna, N. B. (1985). Review of the Developmental Test of Visual Perception: Second Edition. In J. C. Conoley & J. C. Impara (Eds.), *The twelfth mental measurements yearbook* (pp. 289–292). Lincoln, NE: Buros Institute of Mental Measurements, University of Nebraska Press.

Frostig, M., Maslow, P., Lefever, D. W., & Whittlesey, J. R. B. (1963). *The Marianne Frostig Developmental Test of Visual Perception*. Palo Alto, CA: Consulting Psychologists Press.

Hammill, D. D., Pearson, N. A., & Voress, J. K. (1993). *Developmental Test of Visual Perception-Second Edition*. Austin, TX: Pro-Ed.

Tindal, G. (1985). Review of the Developmental Test of Visual Perception: Second Edition. In J. C. Conoley & J. C. Impara (Eds.), *The twelfth mental measurements yearbook* (pp. 289–292). Lincoln, NE: Buros Institute of Mental Measurements, University of Nebraska Press.

NILS A. PEARSON
Pro-Ed, Inc.

DEVELOPMENTAL THERAPY

Developmental therapy is a method of educating severely socially, emotionally, and behaviorally handicapped children. It has normal social-emotional development as its goal. Developmental sequences in behavior, social communication, socialization, and cognition provide the framework for the curriculum. Devised by Mary M. Wood and associates (1979, 1986), developmental therapy links theory and research about normal social-emotional development to classroom practices. It was first demonstrated in 1970 at the Rutland Psychoeducational Center in Athens, Georgia, in a collaborative effort between the public school system, the mental health system, the University of Georgia, and the U.S. Department of Education.

Developmental therapy has been used successfully with severely emotionally disturbed and autistic children from age 2 to 16 years in preschool, elementary, middle school, and high-school classes. It also has been used effectively in day-treatment settings and residential facilities. Educators have adapted aspects of developmental therapy to resource rooms, self-contained classrooms, and regular education classes. It has extensive applications in the therapeutic arts, including art, music, and recreation therapies. It has also been adapted for use in camp settings and leisure programs, and for parents in home programs with autistic children. It was approved by the U.S. Office of Education, National Institute of Education Joint Dissemina-

tion Review Panel in 1975 as an exemplary educational program with documented effectiveness. It received validation again in 1981 from the same panel as an exemplary training model for teachers.

The foundation for developmental therapy is based on theory and research about social, emotional, cognitive, communication, and behavioral development. There is agreement that social knowledge, language, and judgment play important roles in governing behavior and that these are acquired through social experience. There also is agreement that the quality of interactions with others influences the form behavior will take. In addition, developmental theorists provide the concept of ordered, sequential processes in thinking, feeling, behaving, and relating from infancy through adolescence. Their work provides a reference for understanding the extent to which social and affective skills can be taught and the limitations that can be expected at any particular stage (Erikson, 1977; Flavell, 1977; Kohlberg, 1983; Piaget, 1977). Social learning and behavioral theorists provide knowledge about the impact of others on the development of self-control and self-regulated behavior. Studies of modeling, imitation, punishment, discipline, aggression by adults toward children, and the role of reasoning in behavioral management provide understanding about how social behavior emerges (Bandura, 1977; Turiel, 1983; Selman, 1980). Psychoanalytic theorists focus on feelings, anxieties, defense mechanisms, ego functions, and relationships with adults (Freud, 1965; Loevinger, 1976; Maccoby, 1980). These major constructs from different theoretical orientations have been integrated into the practices of developmental therapy.

Students are grouped for developmental therapy according to their stage of social-emotional development. Groups range in size from 4 to 12 students, with the smaller groups used for students at lower developmental stages and those with severe psychopathology. Each group is conducted by a lead teacher-therapist and a support teacher aide. The goals and specific program (treatment) objectives and procedures for each stage are based on individual assessment of each student's social-emotional development. Characteristic roles for adults and the activities, materials, schedules, and behavior management strategies are specified by the stage.

The instrument used to assess each student's social-emotional development is the Developmental Therapy Objectives Rating Form (DTORF). This instrument provides specific individual education plan (IEP) short-term objectives and long-range program goals. Since the first field testing, the DTORF has been used with several thousand students ages 2 to 16 with a range of handicapping conditions, including children who are autistic, mentally retarded, severely multihandicapped, deaf, schizophrenic, nonhandicapped, and gifted. Several studies provide adequate support for the effectiveness of developmental therapy (Kaufman, Paget, & Wood, 1981; Wood & Swan, 1978; Wood, 1997).

Developmental therapy has received contextual endorsement because of the directives for Part H of the Individuals with Disabilities Education Act and its amendments. Professionals working with young children with behavioral disorders and their families have adopted developmental therapy because it is based on the child's current level of performance rather than chronological age. This concept is conducive to the practicalities of working within the family system as mandated by IDEA (Hanft & Striffler, 1995; Zabel, 1991).

REFERENCES

Bandura, A. (1977). *Social learning theory*. Englewood Cliffs, NJ: Prentice-Hall.

Erikson, E. H. (1977). *Toys and reasons*. New York: Norton.

Flavell, J. H. (1977). *Cognitive development*. Englewood Cliffs, NJ: Prentice-Hall.

Freud, A. (1965). *Normality and pathology in childhood: Assessment of development*. New York: International Universities Press.

Hanft, B., & Striffler, N. (1995). Incorporating developmental therapy in early childhood programs: Challenges and promising practices. *Infants and Young Children, 8,* 2, 37–47.

Kaufman, A., Paget, C., & Wood, M. M. (1981). Effectiveness of developmental therapy for severely emotionally disturbed children. In F. H. Wood (Ed.), *Perspectives for a new decade: Education's responsibility for seriously emotionally disturbed and behaviorally disordered children and youth*. Reston, VA: Council for Exceptional Children.

Kohlberg, L. (1983). *Essays on moral development* (Vol. 2). San Francisco: Harper & Row.

Loevinger, J. (1976). *Ego development*. San Francisco: Jossey-Bass.

Maccoby, E. E. (1980). *Social development*. New York: Harcourt, Brace & Jovanovich.

Piaget, J. (1977). *The development of thought*. New York: Viking.

Selman, R. (1980). *The growth of interpersonal understanding*. New York: Holt, Rinehart & Winston.

Turiel, E. (1983). *The development of social knowledge*. Cambridge, MA: Cambridge University Press.

Wood, M. M. (1979). *The developmental therapy objectives: A self-instructional workbook*. Austin, TX: Pro-Ed.

Wood, M. M. (1986). *Developmental therapy in the classroom*. Austin, TX: Pro Ed.

Wood, M. M. (1997). *Social competence for young children: An outreach project for inservice training*. (ERIC Clearinghouse No. EC305787)

Wood, M. M., & Swan, W. W. (1978). A developmental approach to educating the disturbed young child. *Behavioral Disorders 3,* 197–209.

Zabel, M. K. (1991). Teaching young children with behavior disorders: Working with behavior disorders. *ERIC Clearinghouse on Handicapped and Gifted Children*. Reston, VA: Council for Exceptional Children. (ERIC Document No. EC300413)

Mary M. Wood
University of Georgia
First edition

Elaine Fletcher-Janzen
University of Northern Colorado
Second edition

EMOTIONAL DISORDERS
SOCIAL DEVELOPMENT
SOCIAL LEARNING THEORY

DEVEREUX FOUNDATION, THE

The Devereux Foundation was founded in 1912 by Helena T. Devereux (1885–1975), a public school teacher who resigned her position to begin a school for emotionally disturbed and mentally retarded children. Devereux was considered a pioneer in the field of education, operating on the premise that every student can learn and grow in an environment tailored to his or her needs. In 1938, the school was chartered as a Pennsylvania nonprofit foundation and currently maintains its headquarters in Devon, Pennsylvania. With locations in 12 states and the District of Columbia, today's Foundation is the largest independent nonprofit provider of treatment services for individuals with emotional, behavioral, and developmental disabilities in the United States.

The purpose of the Devereux Foundation is to provide high quality human services to children, adults, and families with special needs which derive from behavioral, psychological, intellectual, or neurological impairments. With children, adolescents, and adults coming to Devereux from forty-three states and five foreign countries, services are provided in a way that fosters human potential and contributes to the person's health and social, psychological, and educational well-being. The four general groups of individuals provided services are (1) at-risk children with serious emotional disturbances or problems with their families, communities, and schools; (2) adolescents with behavior disorders; (3) children with multiple diagnoses and other complications of emotional and behavioral health; and (4) adults with mental illness, mental retardation, and/or developmental disabilities preparing for their appropriate level of independence. The Foundation employs a wide variety of educational and treatment programs which are conducted in diverse settings, including hospital, campus-based, community, and outpatient.

In addition to the provision of educational and treatment services, Devereux was involved in various research and publishing efforts, such as publication of the *Devereux Behavior Rating Scale* and the *Individual Motor Achieve-*

ment Guided Education (IMAGE) program (Sargent, 1984). The Foundation may be contacted via email at info@devereux.org.

REFERENCE

Sargent, J. K. (1984). *The directory for exceptional children* (10th ed.). Boston: Porter Sargent.

JOHN D. WILSON
Elwyn Institutes
First edition

TAMARA J. MARTIN
*The University of Texas of the
Permian Basin*
Second edition

DEVIATION IQ

A standard score, known as a deviation IQ, was introduced to overcome the technical problems inherent in the ratio IQ. A standard score is obtained by converting raw test scores from a standardization sample to a normalized score distribution with a fixed mean and standard deviation. Deviation IQs typically have a mean of 100 and a standard deviation of the authors' choosing such as 15 for Wechsler tests and 16 for the Stanford-Binet. There is no difference between Wechsler and Binet IQs in the 90 to 110 range, but the further the score from average, the greater the difference, as illustrated in the Table above. Standard scores are used to convert ordinal to interval data. Standard (normalized) scores provide equal variability at each age level and standard scores from one test can be directly compared with standard scores from another. In individual assessment, David Wechsler introduced the deviation IQ with his Wechsler-Bellevue scale in 1939. (The deviation IQ had been used with some group tests earlier.) Wechsler chose to use a standard score with a standard deviation of 15 (instead of 16, the median standard deviation of the contemporary Binet) because most people are more familiar with units of 5 (i.e., 5, 10, 15) than of 4 (i.e., 4, 8, 12, 16). Today most test authors use a deviation IQ with a standard deviation of either 15 or 16, but some use 20 and even 24.

Because of the popularity among professionals of the concept of the standard score with a mean of 100 and a standard deviation of 15 or 16, and because of the lack of popularity of the letters I and Q, some contemporary test authors have changed the name of the score from IQ to Learning Quotient (LQ), General Cognitive Index (GCI), Mental Processing Composite, etc. Whatever standard scores may be called, when they are derived from a test of mental ability, they are interpreted in the same way as deviation IQs, i.e., as indicating where the individual stands in relation to others of his or her age on the content of the test.

Percentile Rank Equivalents for Deviation IQs with Standard Deviations of 15, 16, and 20[a]

Percentile Rank	Wechsler 15z + 100	Stanford-Binet 16z + 100	ASVAB 20z +100
0.1	55	52	40
0.9	65	62	53
2.0	69	67	59
2.9	72	70	62
5.0	75	74	67
9.7	81	79	74
14.7	84	83	79
25.8	90	90	87
40.1	96	96	95
50.0	100	100	100
59.9	104	104	105
74.2	110	110	113
84.1	115	116	120
90.3	120	121	126
95.0	125	126	133
97.1	129	130	138
98.0	131	133	141
98.9	135	137	146
99.9	145	148	160

[a]Wechsler refers to Wechsler Preschool and Primary Scale of Intelligence, Wechsler Intelligence Scale for Children—Revised, and the Wechsler Adult Intelligence Scale—Revised. Stanford-Binet refers to the 1972 and 1985 editions only. ASVAB is the common abbreviation for the Armed Services Vocational Assessment Battery.

It should be noted that the Wechsler-Bellevue (predecessor of the Wechsler Adult Intelligence Scale) was developed for adults rather than children/adolescents and that mental test raw scores for average adults are very little higher than those of adolescents. Since the average raw score at age 50 is actually a little lower than of age 20, it makes no sense to refer to someone as having reached a mental age of 50 or to divide such a score by chronological age. With adults, as with children, a deviation IQ is a convenient index for indicating the current level of intellectual development and functioning (as later qualified). By mid-adolescence and for many predictions, tests with norms based on educational status may be better than those based on age.

Since an IQ is a score from a test and since the content of tests of mental ability differ not only from each other but also within a test from childhood to adolescence, the term IQ should be preceded by the name of the test from which it was derived and accompanied by the age at which it was obtained. As a score, an IQ indicates both an individual's ability level at a given point in time and the relationship of the individual's score to those obtained by others of his or her age. As such, an IQ should be considered as a descriptive rather than an explanatory term. An IQ can be used to help understand a person's current level of cognitive functioning associated with learning in the mainstream culture. Scores from mental ability scales are to some extent reflections of previous learning within the culture in which the test was standardized, and they are predictors of subsequent educational performance in that culture over the next few years.

IQs are often thought of as indicators of scholastic or educational aptitude. However, they do not reflect important variables such as mechanical, motor, musical, and artistic aptitudes. IQs do not reflect skills in building or maintaining inter- or intrapersonal relationships. Only to a limited extent do IQs reflect such catalytic variables as persistence, enthusiasm for a particular kind of effort, or divergent thinking. Decisions about an individual need to be based on more than scores from one test of cognitive ability.

JOSEPH L. FRENCH
Pennsylvania State University

INTELLIGENCE QUOTIENT
RATIO IQ

DEXEDRINE

(Dextroamphetamine sulfate), an amphetamine, is used in the treatment of attention deficit disorder with hyperactivity (Rxlist, 1997), narcolepsy, and as short-term therapy for exogenous obesity. Although amphetamines are known to work as central nervous stimulants, the mechanism whereby they produce mental and behavioral effects in children is not known. Adverse reactions can include palpitations and rapid heartbeat; euphoria, restlessness, and insomnia; and exacerbation of motor and vocal tics and Tourette's syndrome. Overdose may result in assaultiveness, confusion, hallucinations, and panic states usually followed by fatigue and depression.

A brand name of Smith Kline and French, Dexedrine is available in 5 mg tablets; 5, 10, and 15 mg sustained released capsules, and elixir. Recommended dosage for attention deficit disorder with hyperactivity in children 6 years of age and older is to start with 5 mg once or twice daily, with daily dosage to be raised, if needed, in increments of 5 mg at weekly intervals, typically not to exceed a total of 40 mg per day.

REFERENCE

Physicians' desk reference. (1984). (pp. 1878–1880). Oradell, NJ: Medical Economics.

RXLIST. (1997). Internet Drug Index. www.rxlist.com/.

LAWRENCE C. HARTLAGE
Evans, Georgia

ATTENTION DEFICIT DISORDER
HYPERACTIVITY
RITALIN

DIABETES

Diabetes is a chronic metabolic disease affecting approximately 12 million Americans. Common symptoms of diabetes include extreme hunger and thirst, frequent urination, irritability, weakness, fatigue, nausea, and high blood and urine sugar levels. Two major types of diabetes have been identified. Type I, or insulin dependent diabetes, was formerly called juvenile-onset because it usually occurred in children and adolescents. Type II, or non-insulin dependent, was formerly called maturity-onset. In Type I diabetes, the pancreas does not function properly, resulting in little to no insulin production and a build-up of sugar in the bloodstream. Treatment involves insulin injections, diet, and regular exercise. Approximately 1 million Americans are Type I diabetics. It is thought that there is a genetic predisposition for diabetes. At present there is no known cure. Obesity and stress can contribute to the onset of diabetes.

Hypoglycemia (low blood sugar) and hyperglycemia (high blood sugar) are the two most common emergencies encountered by diabetics. Hypoglycemia occurs when the blood sugar drops too low because of too much insulin, not enough food, or too much exercise. Symptoms include anger or bad temper, sudden staggering and poor coordination, pale color, disorientation, confusion, and sweating, eventually leading to stupor or unconsciousness, also called insulin shock. This condition is treated by administering some form of sugar such as fruit juice or candy. If unconsciousness occurs, a child should receive emergency medical care.

Hyperglycemia occurs when there is too little insulin, when infection or illness is present, or when too much food or drink is consumed. Symptoms of hyperglycemia include drowsiness, extreme thirst and frequent urination, fruity or wine-smelling breath, heavy breathing, flushed skin, vomiting, and eventually stupor or unconsciousness, called a diabetic coma. Treatment of this condition is usually the administration of insulin with the supervision of a healthcare professional.

Some diabetics develop complications such as retinopathy, that sometimes result in blindness, diabetic neuropathy or nerve disease, diabetic nephropathy or kidney disease, cardiovascular disease, or respiratory failure. Diabetes and its complications is the number three cause of nonaccidental death among children in the United States (Wright, Schafer, & Solomons, 1979).

It has been suggested by researchers that by the time a child reaches the developmental age of 12, he or she should be able to take the lead by doing his or her own urine or blood sugar tests and administration of insulin. Keep in mind that children in special education classes may reach these developmental ages at slower rates and thus may be more reliant on teachers and parents for assistance in complying with their diabetic regimen. In such cases teachers must be aware of the regimen. Parents should inform teachers about their child's needs, which may include a special diet, especially at lunch and snack time, time to run tests and take insulin injections, exercise, and signs of emergency, especially hyperglycemia and hypoglycemia. However, teachers should make every effort not to separate the child from the peer group. The diabetic child has the same needs for support, encouragement, and understanding as other children and should be encouraged to participate in all activities. When treats are offered, the teacher might offer a "diabetic" treat such as raisins, peanuts, or sugarless candy or gum.

Compliance with the diabetic treatment regimen is usually difficult for a child and it may be more difficult for a child in special education who does not understand all of the rules of diabetes. It is important in this case that the teacher and school staff work with the child's parents to understand the special needs and restrictions diabetes places on the child. Teachers need to be aware of the diabetic child's developmental age and work with the child to develop responsibility, independence, and self-reliance compatible with his or her age of development. Should parents prove either unsophisticated or unresponsive, direct teacher-physician contact becomes essential. Indeed, school districts have been found in violation of the Americans with Disabilities Act (1990) with respect to their treatment of students with diabetes (Vennum, 1995). In addition, most parents surveyed by the American Diabetes Association (1996) indicate dissatisfaction with their child's diabetes management in school. Certainly, higher expectations for school involvement are the current trend.

REFERENCES

American Diabetes Association. (1984). *A word to . . . teachers and school staff*. Alexandria, VA: Author.

American Diabetes Association. (1984). *Your child has diabetes: What you should know*. Alexandria, VA: Author.

American Diabetes Association. (1984). An introduction: *What you need to know about diabetes*. Alexandria, VA: Author.

American Diabetes Association. (1996) This can't be happening in our schools! *Diabetes Forecast, 49*, 2, 61–66.

Carpenter, J. (1976). *Diabetes: A handicap*. Unpublished manuscript.

Vennum, M. K. (1995). Students with diabetes: Is there legal protection? *Journal of Law and Education, 24*, 1, 33–69.

Wright, L., Schafer, A., & Solomons, G. (1979). *Encyclopedia of pediatric psychology*. Baltimore, MD: University Park Press.

JANET CARPENTER
LOGAN WRIGHT
University of Oklahoma

**FAMILY RESPONSE TO HANDICAP
HEALTH PROBLEMS OF THE HANDICAPPED**

DIAGNOSIS IN SPECIAL EDUCATION

Diagnosis or evaluation is an essential step in the process of identifying those children in need of special education services. Matarazzo and Pankratz (1984) define psychological diagnosis as "(1) the process of classifying information relevant to an individual's emotional and behavioral state, and (2) the name assigned the state, taken generally from a commonly accepted classification system (p. 369)." Based on this definition, diagnosis in special education involves taking the information obtained through the assessment of a student's emotional, behavioral, academic, and intellectual functioning and classifying that information based on some accepted diagnostic system. The specific diagnostic system used determines the specific classification or name given to that student's level of functioning or condition.

The diagnostic procedure traditionally employed in special education has been one based on a medical model (Reynolds, 1984; Ysseldyke & Algozzine, 1982). This model is one borrowed from psychological diagnostic systems. It consists of preparing catalogs of systems of various special and remedial conditions and determining the extent to which an individual has characteristics similar to those of the known condition (Ysseldyke & Algozzine, 1982). According to Reynolds (1984), the focus has been on "intrapsychic causes of psychological dysfunction to the exclusion of extrapersonal factors, and on the deficiencies and weaknesses of individuals rather than on their strengths (p. 453)."

There have been many problems associated with the use of this type of a diagnostic model in special education. One problem centers around the fact that a wide variety of diagnostic systems have been developed. This has resulted in a situation in which the assessment of one student can produce very different diagnoses depending on the diagnostic system being referred to. There also tends to be considerable variations among the diagnoses of individuals classified under the same diagnostic system (Edgar & Hayden, 1985; Reynolds, 1984). These inconsistencies have made the process of special education diagnosis complicated and controversial.

The passage of PL 94-142, the Education for All Handicapped Children Act of 1975, began the formal process of diagnosis in special education. Subsequent amendments defined and redefined the different handicapping conditions; and as the Act changed its name in 1990 to the Individuals with Disabilities Education Act (IDEA), so did the idea of "handicaps" change to "disabilities." Under current law disability is defined as

(A) In general.—The term "child with a disability" means a child—

(i) with mental retardation, hearing impairments (including deafness), speech or language impairments, visual impairments (including blindness), serious emotional disturbance (hereinafter referred to as "emotional disturbance"), orthopedic impairments, autism, traumatic brain injury, other health impairments, or specific learning disabilities; and

(ii) who, by reason thereof, needs special education and related services.

(B) Child aged 3 through 9.—The term "child with a disability" for a child aged 3 through 9 may, at the discretion of the State and the local educational agency, include a child—

(i) experiencing developmental delays, as defined by the State and as measured by appropriate diagnostic instruments and procedures, in one or more of the following areas: physical development, cognitive development, communication development, social or emotional development, or adaptive development; and

(ii) who, by reason thereof, needs special education and related services. (Section 602, Part A, IDEA)

Disabilities that are defined under IDEA are:

- autism
- hearing impairments (includes deafness)
- mental retardation
- multiple disabilities
- orthopedic impairments
- other health impairments
- emotional disturbance
- specific learning disabilities
- speech or language impairments
- traumatic brain injury
- visual impairments (includes blindness)

The evaluations and diagnoses of children with disabilities that determine eligibility for special education services must adhere to guidelines according to IDEA that include the following points.

1. Individual testing. The student must be tested individually, not as part of a larger group. [Section 614(a)(1)(A)]

2. Evaluation in the native language. The evaluation must be conducted in the child's native language (for example, Spanish) or other mode of communication (for example, sign language for a student who is deaf), unless it is clearly not feasible to do so. [Section 614(b)(3)(A)(ii)]

3. Nondiscriminatory evaluations. Tests and other evaluation materials must be selected and administered so as not to be discriminatory on a racial or cultural basis. [Section 614(b)(3)(A)(i)]

4. Using tests correctly. Any standardized tests given to the child must be validated for the specific purpose for which they are being used. [Section 614(b)(3)(B)(i)]

5. Appropriate evaluation. Any standardized tests given to the child must be administered by trained and knowledgeable personnel, in keeping with the instructions provided by the producer of the test. [Section 614(b)(3)(B)(ii) and (iii)] (NICHCY, 1998).

The emphasis on cultural competency in diagnosis is not new, but it is much more emphasized in the scientific literature and in the law. Cultural competence also refers to the individual who is conducting the evaluation. The individual must have professional training in multicultural issues and demonstrate competence in assessment and diagnosis of children and adolescents of different socioeconomic status, gender, ethnicity, handicapping condition, and acculturation.

School psychologists traditionally have been the gatekeeper in the diagnosis/eligibility process. School psychology emphasized classification. Rosenfield and Nelson (1995) state:

But as the current ethical, political, legal and educational context has evolved, there has been a re-examination of the purposes and applications of data gathered during assessment process (Taylor, et al., 1993). In a position paper on the Role of the School Psychologist in Assessment (1994), the National Association of School Psychologists endorsed the proposition that assessment practices must be linked to prevention and intervention to provide positive outcomes for students. Thus, there is an increasing emphasis on information that is "useful in designing, implementing, monitoring, and evaluating interventions" (Reschly, Kicklighter, & McKee, 1988, p. 9–50).

Diagnosis in special education therefore, has taken on a broader definition and is linked much more to intervention than ever before. Rosenfield and Nelson (1995) suggest that there are three purposes of school psychological assessment: informing/entitlement/classification decisions, planning interventions, and evaluating outcomes. Diagnosis and outcome are on the same continuum as opposed to being discrete entities. This shift in paradigm has also changed assessment instrument usage. The use of more natural and dynamic forms of assessment that directly impact instructional delivery and behavior management are common (Rosenfield & Nelson, 1995).

It is obvious that there is much diversity in the diagnosis of the mildly mentally retarded, learning disabled, and emotionally disturbed. According to Edgar and Hayden (1985), these handicapping conditions belong to a large percent of the total handicapped population and are the ones that are most difficult to quantify. These categories are basically indistinguishable from one another, and the population of children within these categories is indistinguishable from the larger group of children with general learning problems (e.g., disadvantaged, slow learner, etc.).

Each of these nonquantifiable categories has a history of problems in terms of the criteria used in their identification. For example, mild retardation is defined based on an IQ; there has been continual criticism of the use of IQ tests with minority population (Edgar & Hayden, 1985). The high percentage of minority students diagnosed as mentally retarded has brought charges from some that the traditional IQ tests cannot be reliably used to diagnose mental retardation. It has also been virtually impossible to define the distinction between seriously emotionally disturbed and socially maladjusted. There are no quantitative measures available for determining who is seriously emotionally disturbed. Emotional disturbance tends to be a socially defined condition, as does mild mental retardation and learning disabilities. Many of the problems associated with the diagnosis of learning disabilities have already been discussed. Edgar and Hayden (1985) feel that the only quantifiable aspect of the learning disabled definition is low achievement, which could classify 20 to 30% of all school-age children. Reynolds (1984) concludes that a large segment of children being served as learning disabled may not, in fact, be learning disabled. These are usually the intellectually borderline and low average children. According to Reynolds (1984), this is due, in part, to the diversity of models of severe discrepancy as well as to biases in the referral process favoring low IQ, low-achieving children.

Diagnosis in special education has attempted and failed to follow the traditional model of psychological diagnosis. This model has not been proven to be an effective one for special education. One of the main criticisms of this diagnostic system has been its inability to provide reliable and valid classifications of the conditions involved in special education diagnosis. Conditions such as mental retardation, emotional disturbance, and learning disabilities have not been quantifiably defined and are therefore difficult to classify. Despite these serious flaws, the concept of formal diagnosis is still considered to be of vital importance, and has changed to fit the current demands of IDEA and intervention and outcome-focused needs of special education.

REFERENCES

Edgar, E., & Hayden, A. H. (1985). Who are the children special education should serve? And how many children are there? *Journal of Special Education, 18,* 523–539.

Grossman, H. J. (Ed.). (1983). *Classification in mental retardation.* Washington, DC: American Association on Mental Deficiencies.

Hammill, D. D., Larsen, S. C., Leigh, J., & McNult, G. (1981). A new definition of learning disabilities. *Learning Disabilities Quarterly, 4,* 336–342.

Matarazzo, J. D., & Pankratz, L. D. (1984). Diagnosis. In R. J. Corsini (Ed.), *Encyclopedia of psychology* (pp. 369–372). New York: Wiley.

Mercer, C. D., Hughes, C., & Mercer, A. R. (1985). Learning disabilities definitions used by state education departments. *Learning Disabilities Quarterly, 8,* 45–55.

National Information Center for Children and Youth with Disabilities (1998). Evaluation and Testing Guidelines. Washington DC: Author.

Reynolds, C. R. (1984). Critical measurement issues in learning disabilities. *Journal of Special Education, 18,* 451–475.

Reynolds, C. R., Gutkin, T. B., Elliot, S. N., & Witt, J. C. (1984). *School psychology: Essentials of theory and practice.* New York: Wiley.

Rosenfield, S., & Nelson, D. (1995). *The school psychologist's role in school assessment.* (ERIC Digest No. ED391985)

Ysseldyke, J. E., & Algozzine, B. (1982). *Critical issues in special and remedial education.* Boston: Houghton Mifflin.

Lori E. Unruh
Eastern Kentucky University

AAMD
DIAGNOSTIC & STATISTICAL MANUAL
MENTAL STATUS
SEVERE DISCREPANCY ANALYSIS

DIAGNOSTIC ACHIEVEMENT BATTERY— SECOND EDITION (DAB-2)

The *Diagnostic Achievement Battery—Second Edition* (DAB-2; Newcomer, 1990) uses 12 subtests divided into five areas: listening (Story Comprehension, Characteristics), speaking (Synonyms, Grammatic Completion), reading (Alphabet/Word Knowledge, Reading Comprehension), writing (Capitalization, Punctuation, Spelling, Writing Composition), and mathematics (Mathematics Calculation, Mathematics Reasoning) for children between the ages of 6 and 14. Subtest raw scores convert to standard scores (M = 10, SD = 3) and percentile ranks. By combining subtests, composite scores (M = 100, SD = 15) are generated that reliably assess global strengths and weaknesses. The composites are Listening, Speaking, Reading, Writing,

Mathematics, Spoken Language, Written Language, and Total Achievement.

The test was normed on 2,623 students residing in 40 states. The sample is representative of the nation as a whole with regard to gender, race, ethnicity, geographic region, and urban/rural residence. Reliability coefficients are high. Evidence of content, concurrent, and construct validity also is provided.

Compton (1996) reports that the DAB-2 measures a wide variety of skills that are directly related to classroom performance. Bernier and Hebert (1995) find that the DAB-2 is a well-designed individual diagnostic test. Brown (1995) reports that the subtests seem to measure common constructs.

REFERENCES

Bernier, J., & Hebert, M. (1995). Review of the Diagnostic Achievement Battery, Second Edition. In J. C. Conoley & J. C. Impara (Eds.), *The twelfth mental measurements yearbook* (pp. 294–295). Lincoln: Buros Institute of Mental Measurements, University of Nebraska Press.

Brown, R. (1995). Review of the Diagnostic Achievement Battery, Second Edition. In J. C. Conoley & J. C. Impara (Eds.), *The twelfth mental measurements yearbook* (pp. 295–296). Lincoln: Buros Institute of Mental Measurements, University of Nebraska Press.

Compton, C. (1996). *A guide to 100 tests for special education.* Upper Saddle River, NJ: Globe Fearon.

Newcomer, P. L. (1990). *Diagnostic Achievement Battery: Second Edition.* Austin, TX: Pro-Ed.

TADDY MADDOX
Pro-Ed, Inc.

DIAGNOSTIC AND STATISTICAL MANUAL OF MENTAL DISORDERS (DSM-IV)

The most widely used system for psychiatric diagnosis and classification in the United States is the fourth edition of the Diagnostic and Statistical Manual of Mental Disorders (DSM-IV; American Psychiatric Association, 1994). The first edition of the DSM was published in 1952, with the first revision appearing in 1968. All revisions of the DSM were developed for use with children, adolescents, and adults. The revision process included literature reviews, data reanalyses, and field trials. The APA also publishes the DSM-IV Sourcebook, which provides a comprehensive and convenient reference record of the clinical and research support for the various revision decisions.

The purpose of the DSM "is to provide clear descriptions of diagnostic categories in order to enable clinicians and investigators to diagnose, communicate about, study, and treat people with various mental disorders" (APA, 1994). The DSM uses a multiaxial classification system. Each axis refers to a different domain of information that may help the professional plan treatment plans and advice, and predict outcomes for the patient or student.

Axis I: Clinical Disorders
           Other Conditions that May Be a Focus of Clinical Attention
Axis II: Personality Disorders
           Mental Retardation
Axis III: General Medical Conditions
Axis IV: Psychosocial and Environmental Problems
Axis V: Global Assessment of Functioning

The multiaxial system assists the clinician in making a diagnosis that is biopsychosocial in nature. In other words, the information given is holistic and takes the mental, physical, and social aspects of the individual's life into consideration. This is particularly appropriate for the 1990s, where the field of psychology has recognized the need for cultural competence in diagnosis.

The DSM-IV includes a section on "Disorders Usually First Diagnosed in Infancy, Childhood, or Adolescence." The diagnoses included in this section are: Mental Retardation, Learning Disorders, Motor Skills Disorder, Communication Disorders, Pervasive Developmental Disorders, Attention-Deficit and Disruptive Behavior Disorders, Feeding and Eating Disorders of Infancy or Early Childhood, Tic Disorders, Elimination Disorders, and a category of Other Disorders of Infancy Childhood or Adolescence. The latter diagnoses include Separation Anxiety Disorder, Selective Mutism, Reactive Attachment Disorder of Infancy or Early Childhood, Stereotypic Movement Disorder and Disorder of Infancy, Childhood, or Adolescence NOS.

The current DSM-IV defines "mental disorder" in much the same way as its predecessors:

> a clinically significant behavioral or psychological syndrome or pattern that occurs in an individual and that is associated with present distress (e.g., a painful symptom) or disability (i.e., impairment in one or more important areas of functioning) or with a significantly increased risk of suffering death, pain, disability, or an important loss of freedom. In addition, this syndrome or pattern must not be merely an expectable and culturally sanctioned response to a particular event, for example, the death of a loved one. Whatever its cause, it must currently be considered a manifestation of a behavioral, psychological, or biological dysfunction in the individual." (p. xxi, APA, 1984)

A criticism of this definition of mental disorder that is particularly relevant to children is that it includes areas not typically regarded as mental disorders such as developmental disorders and learning disabilities. Concerns have been expressed that children diagnosed with specific developmental or learning problems will be diagnosed and stigmatized as having a mental disorder (Rutter & Schaffer, 1980). The issue of labeling children for special education placement decisions has been controversial over the years, and it continues to be a source of frustration for many students, professionals, and parents. Therefore, the DSM-IV is probably best used in clinical settings where specific psychiatric treatment plans follow the specific psychiatric diagnoses. The DSM-IV provides at best only, a basis for diagnosis and treatment for learning problems. In educational settings, special education professionals have the expertise to specify learning strengths and weaknesses and develop individual academic treatment plans that are carried out in the most appropriate learning environment.

A DSM-IV for primary care physicians has been developed, DSM-IV Primary Care Version (APA, 1995), which is a volume devised to assist the primary care physician during routine patient visits. This version focuses on common conditions such as anxiety, depression, and substance abuse; diagnoses that the primary care physician is likely to encounter and to need specialized knowledge. The volume also assists in communication between primary care physicians and psychiatrists. Children and adolescents presenting with the more common mental disorders may be identified by their primary physicians, and this may help in prevention and the availability of treatment.

REFERENCES

American Psychiatric Association. (1994). *Diagnostic and Statistical Manual of Mental Disorders* (4th ed.). Washington, DC: Author.

American Psychiatric Association. (1995). *Diagnostic and Statistical Manual of Mental Disorders* (4th ed.). *Primary Care Version*. Washington, DC: Author.

Lawrence J. Siegal
*University of Texas Medical
Branch, Galveston*
First edition

Elaine Fletcher-Janzen
University of Northern Colorado
Second edition

CLINICAL PSYCHOLOGY
MENTAL ILLNESS
MENTAL STATUS EXAMS

DIAGNOSTIC ASSESSMENTS OF READING WITH TRIAL TEACHING STRATEGIES (DARTTS)

The Diagnostic Assessments of Reading with Trial Teaching Strategies (DARTTS; Roswell & Chall, 1992) program is designed to assess students' relative strengths and weaknesses in reading and to discover methods and materials that will be effective in helping students grow as readers. The development of DARTTS was guided by two different but complementary perspectives on reading: (1) that good readers possess not only the ability to translate alphabetic symbols into words but also have good language skills and the ability to understand ideas (Carroll, 1977); and (2) that in becoming good readers over a period of time, individuals experience a series of qualitative changes in their skills (Chall, 1983).

DARTTS is intended for use in regular classrooms, Title I programs, special education, reading clinics, placement situations, adult education, and other settings where a detailed diagnostic picture of reading achievement is needed. It is appropriate for use with students of all ages—from first grade students who are just beginning to fall behind their classmates, to adults who have come to realize that improved reading would enhance the quality of their lives.

The two components of DARTTS are the Diagnostic Assessments of Reading (DAR) and the Trial Teaching Strategies (TTS). The DAR is comprise of six formal individually-administered tests in reading and language: Word Recognition, Word Analysis, Oral Reading, Silent Reading Comprehension, Spelling, and Word Meaning. Administration of the DAR is untimed and takes about 20 minutes. The questions are primarily open-ended, with the test administrator noting students' correct responses and recording incorrect responses verbatim. Scoring is based on mastery criteria. The subtests are multilevel, and each student is administered only the portion of each subtest that is needed to determine mastery. Because of the nature of the questions and administration procedures, standard Kuder-Richardson Formula 20 (K-R 20) reliability data were not published in the Technical Manual (Roswell & Chall, 1994). Unpublished K-R 20 data for Silent Reading Comprehension, the only DAR subtest that uses multiple-choice questions, are provided below. Validity information in the Technical Manual includes a description of the test development process. Validity data are provided in the form of correlations with a nationally standardized norm-referenced reading test and intercorrelations between the DAR and the TTS and among the DAR subtests.

The TTS is a group of informal lessons designed to explore effective reading comprehension strategies with the student. The timing of the TTS is completely flexible depending on the needs of the student, but basic information can be obtained in about 30 minutes. The DAR and TTS may be used together or separately, depending on circumstances.

During the 1990–91 school year, a year-long validation study was conducted to establish the statistical characteristics of the DAR and the effectiveness of the TTS. Participating teachers were asked to identify six students in their group whom they believed were not reading up to potential, including students with extreme reading difficulties.

Kuder-Richardson Formula 20 (K-R 20) Reliability Data for the Silent Reading Comprehension Subtest of the Diagnostic Assessments of Reading

Subtest Level	3	4	5	6	7	8	9/10	11/12
K-R 20	.856	.916	.838	.877	.790	.888	.909	.874

In fall 1990, the DAR was administered to the students, immediately followed by the appropriate TTS. For the validation research, the teachers first administered a standardized norm-referenced reading test (NRT) along with the DAR; then an alternate form of the NRT immediately after the TTS to measure short-term gains; and finally, at the end of the school year, the first form of the NRT to determine long-term stability of gains.

The NRT results suggest both short-term gains and long-term stability of gains. At grade 6, for example, the mean grade equivalent scores of the participating students were 3.5 in October, 3.8 immediately following the TTS, and 4.3 as the end of the school year. The grade 6 students who participated in the validation study started the school year far behind their academic peers. They made immediate gains of 0.3 GE points and a total of 0.8 GE points during the seven months of the research. Data from the validation study are provided in the Technical Manual.

Two reviews of the DAR, including brief mention of the TTS, can be found in the Buros Institute's *Twelfth Mental Measurements Yearbook* (Conoley & Impara, 1995). A paper describing the validation research was presented at the 1992 meeting of the American Educational Research Association in San Francisco (Hennings & Hughes, 1992).

REFERENCES

Carroll, John B. (1977). Developmental parameters of reading comprehension. *Cognition, curriculum, and comprehension.* Newark, DE: International Reading Association.

Chall, Jeanne S. (1983). *Stages of reading development.* New York: McGraw-Hill.

Conoley, J. C. and Impara, J. C. (Eds.). (1995). *Twelfth mental measurements yearbook.* Lincoln, NE: Buros Institute of Mental Measurements.

Hennings, S. S., and Hughes, K. E. (1992). Building a performance-based assessment system to diagnose strengths and weaknesses in reading achievement. Paper presented at meeting of the American Educational Research Association. (ERIC Document Reproduction Service No. TM 018521)

Roswell, Florence G., and Chall, Jeanne S. (1992) *Diagnostic Assessments of Reading with Trial Teaching Strategies.* Itasca, IL: The Riverside Publishing Company.

Roswell, Florence G., and Chall, Jeanne S. (1994). *Technical manual: DARTTS.* Itasca, IL: The Riverside Publishing Company.

KAY E. HUGHES
*The Riverside Publishing
Company*

DIAGNOSTIC PRESCRIPTIVE TEACHING

Diagnostic prescriptive teaching "refers to the practice of formulating instructional prescriptions on the basis of differential diagnostic results" (Arter & Jenkins, 1979, p. 518). Although any educational plan for an individual learner should spring from assessment, diagnostic prescriptive teaching has had a more specific meaning. The key idea underlying diagnostic prescriptive teaching is that a given diagnostic pattern is linked differentially to a specific instructional strategy (methods, materials, techniques, etc.). That a given set of assessment findings implies an accompanying set of instructional strategies is assumed.

In the early 1970s, when ability training began to receive criticism from within the field of learning diabilities (Hammill, 1972; Hammill, Goodman, & Wiederholt, 1974), Ysseldyke and Salvia (1974) suggested that diagnostic prescriptive teaching should be based on one of two theoretical models. The first model is the ability training model. From this perspective, the diagnosed strengths and weaknesses are conceptualized primarily as perceptual or psycholinguistic in nature and understood to be the basis for academic skills. Training programs are then differentially prescribed to improve the underlying abilities demonstrating weaknesses. For example, if a student is diagnosed as expressing figure-ground errors, the prescribed educational plan would include remedial figure-ground activities, without any "advice" from the diagnostic pattern to suggest how teaching the ability will or should relate to the level of academic skill. The second model is the task analysis model. From this perspective, the diagnosis or assessment targets are the specific academic skills for the purpose of identifying the skills within the learner's repertoire. The goal of instruction is then the attainment of those new or missing skills. For example, if assessment identifies a student knows only 75% of the addition facts through 10, the prescription is that the student should be taught the remaining 25% without any "advice" from the assessment results of how those skills should be taught.

Since the early 1970s, diagnostic prescriptive teaching has taken on a meaning broader than the two theoretical models. Smead and Schwartz (1982) have developed a model that is integrative in nature. Moving beyond the ability training model with its focus nearly completely on perceptual or psycholinguistic processes. They have identified three learner-focused areas from which diagnostic information has relevance for instruction: motivational-emotional, cognitive-perceptual, and neurological-physical. In a similar manner, they have focused on a greater variety of dimensions than did those previously concerned solely with the application of task analysis to special education. In addition, they have suggested that a third set of factors must be considered: the environmental characteristics of the learning situation, which include sociological, emotional, pedagological, contingency, standing patterns of behavior, and physical factors. Finally, they have suggested that the interactions among these three sets of factors—learner focused, task focused, and environmental focused—must also be diagnosed and related to the instructional prescription.

Thus, diagnostic prescriptive teaching has become better understood with the realization that a series of diagnostic patterns with related prescribed activities is simplistic given the complexity and variety of learners, tasks, and environments—and how they interact. Prescribed instructional goals must flow from assessment, addressing the learner and his/her style of learning, the skills or abilities that must be learned, and the situation and contingencies under which learning will be best facilitated. Recent studies (Covey, 1991; Fox & Thompson, 1994) suggest that diagnostic-prescriptive teaching techniques such as multisensory approaches, mapping strategies, peer learning, and process writing have achieved good outcomes with learning disabled students.

REFERENCES

Arter, J. A., & Jenkins, J. R. (1979). Differential diagnosis-prescriptive teaching: A critical appraisal. *Review of Educational Research, 49,* 517–555.

Covey, D. G. (1991). *The influence of teaching the main idea, drawing conclusions, and making inferences on the improvement of writing skills.* (ERIC Clearinghouse No. CS213114)

Fox, L. H., & Thompson, D. L. (1994). *Bringing the lab school method to an inner-city school.* (ERIC Clearinghouse No. EC304266)

Hammill, D., (1972). Training visual perceptual processes. *Journal Learning Disabilities, 5,* 39–44.

Hammill, D., Goodman, L., & Wiederholt, J. L. (1974). Visual-motor processes: Can we train them? *Exceptional Children, 41,* 5–14.

Smead, V. S., & Schwartz, N. H. (1982, August). *An integrative model for instructional planning.* Paper presented at the 19th Annual Meeting, of the American Psychological Association, Washington, DC.

Ysseldyke, J. E., & Salvia, J. (1974). Diagnostic-prescriptive teaching: Two models. *Exceptional Children, 41,* 17–32.

STEVEN R. TIMMERMANS
*Mary Free Bed Hospital and
Rehabilitation Center*

DIAGNOSTIC REMEDIAL APPROACH
DIAGNOSTIC TEACHING
DIRECT INSTRUCTION

DIAGNOSTIC TEACHING

Diagnostic teaching is the name given an instructional process used to discover the instructional and environmental conditions under which student learning is most productive. Diagnostic teaching is also referred to as clinical teaching and data-based instructional decision making.

Diagnostic teaching differs from a diagnostic-prescriptive model of instruction. In a diagnostic-prescriptive approach, a student's achievement and learning characteristics are assessed. Subsequently, recommendations for instructional delivery are drawn from this information. This model relies on inference from a static data base (e.g., test information) for prediction of optimal instructional arrangements. In common use, such a model often fails to make use of information gained during the instructional process.

Diagnostic teaching, although sometimes included as a step in a diagnostic-prescriptive model of instruction (Reynolds & Birch, 1977), is more commonly viewed as an alternative assessment system. Like a diagnostic-prescriptive approach, diagnostic teaching makes use of test information about a student's achievement and learning characteristics, but it differs from a diagnostic-prescriptive model in a number of significant ways.

Diagnostic teaching is a process of systematic discovery rather than prediction. Reisman (1982), in discussing application of diagnostic teaching to mathematics, describes a process with five steps: (1) identify strengths and weaknesses in mathematics; (2) hypothesize reasons for achievement and nonachievement; (3) formulate instructional objectives; (4) teach to the objectives; and (5) evaluate student learning.

Zigmond, Vallecorsa, and Silverman (1983) propose a model of diagnostic teaching that is similar to that of Reisman but that is more detailed; it contains 12 discrete steps. Other and different models of diagnostic teaching are available (Walker, 1988). Differences tend to be in the thoroughness of description. Most have a set of common characteristics.

Diagnostic teaching is a cyclical process that is continued throughout the duration of student instruction. It involves planning, executing and evaluating teaching hypotheses (Wixson, 1991). It is used to find the most effective match of learner characteristics and instructionally relevant variables. However, there is a recognition that because the difficulty of material and the demands of schooling change over time, the most appropriate combinations of instructional variables will change over time as well.

Since diagnostic teaching is an ongoing process, the diagnostician is most properly a skilled teacher rather than a diagnostic specialist who does not have continual contact with the student. The child's teacher is also in the best position to judge whether student performance or a particular instructional interchange is typical and of significance or merely an exception to the norm. The teacher's ability to note student habits and learning strategies, likes and dislikes, reactions to grouping arrangements, etc., provides the basis on which trial modifications in instruction can be made.

Diagnostic teaching requires the diagnostician to be familiar with a variety of different curricular approaches. For any given approach, the diagnostician must be able to determine where the student might encounter difficulty. This allows the teacher to provide instruction at an appropriate level of difficulty using curricula that require different student behaviors, capacities, and experiences. Howell & Kaplan (1980) demonstrate how basic skills can be analyzed for use in diagnostic teaching.

Diagnostic teaching also requires the diagnostician to be culturally competent (Baca & Valenzuela, 1994) and familiar with instructional variables that can be used differently in conjunction with various curricular approaches. Among these are engaged time, the immediacy and nature of performance feedback, grouping practices, and presentation and questioning techniques. For example, one exploratory combination within the diagnostic teaching process might be an increase in the engaged time a student spends being directly taught (instructional variables) phonics (curricular approach). If student learning did not meet expectations, one or more of the critical variables would be systematically altered.

Historically, the effects of different instructional combinations have been judged subjectively by the diagnostic teacher. The decision whether to continue instruction or to test another combination of variables was equally subjective. During the past decade, there has been a growing sophistication in the use of student performance data to judge instructional effect more effectively. There has also been an increase in the sophistication of decision rules that can be used to guide the course of diagnostic teaching.

Procedures for the collection of student performance data are integral to most models of diagnostic teaching. These range from the use of special recording paper and elaborate techniques for performance analysis (White & Haring, 1980) to the use of checklists and behavioral tallies (Zigmond, Vallecorsa, & Silverman, 1983). Decision rules are usually presented within the context of a particular model but generally indicate what to do if student performance is deficient and how long instruction should continue before some systematic modification in instruction is made.

REFERENCES

Baca, L., & de Valenzuela, J. S. (1994). Reconstructing the bilingual special education interface. Washington DC: National Clearinghouse for Bilingual Education.

Howell, K. W., & Kaplan, J. S. (1980). *Diagnosing basic skills.* Columbus, OH: Merrill.

Reisman, F. K. (1982). *A guide to the diagnostic teaching of arithmetic.* Columbus, OH: Merrill.

Reynolds, M. C., & Birch, J. W. (1977). *Teaching exceptional children in all. America's schools.* Reston, VA: Council for Exceptional Children.

Walker, B. J. (1988). *Diagnostic teaching of reading; Techniques for instruction and assessment.* (ERIC Clearinghouse No. CS0103329)

White, 0. R., & Haring, N. G. (1980). *Exceptional teaching.* Columbus, OH: Merrill.

Wixson, K. K. (1991). Dignostic teaching. *Reading Teacher, 44,* 6, 420–422.

Zigmond, N., Vallecorsa, A., & Silverman, R. (1983). *Assessment for instructional planning in special education.* Englewood Cliffs, NJ: Prentice-Hall.

STEVEN A. CARLSON
Beaverton Schools, Beaverton, Oregon

DIAGNOSTIC PRESCRIPTIVE TEACHING
DIRECT INSTRUCTION
TEACHER EFFECTIVENESS

DIALYSIS AND SPECIAL EDUCATION

Dialysis, the process of flushing kidney wastes by artificial means in cases of acute or chronic renal failure, has been increasingly used with children during the last 25 years. Dialysis methodology is viewed as a drastic mode of treatment for children, necessitated in advanced cases of kidney disease prior to, or as the result of, failed transplantation (Czaczkes & De-Nour, 1979).

While individual differences make generalization difficult, Whitt (1984) indicates that the complex and time-consuming dialysis schedule places most children at educational and emotional risk, as the time spent in hemodialysis treatment interrupts the normal pace and progress of the child's schooling. Hobbs and Perrin (1985) found the result of this loss of school time and educational opportunity to be academic underachievement and missed and splintered basic skills. In addition, the disruption of normal school progress and success weakens children's emotional stability and their feelings of competence and control (Stapleton, 1983).

During periods of school attendance, the primary role of special education is to maintain the independence of the child in dialysis. This is best accomplished by providing resource assistance to allow that child to function effectively within the regular classroom whenever possible while remediating educational weaknesses and gaps (Kleinberg, 1982). As the school experience for the dialysis child represents one of the few opportunities for that child to be in control of the environment, to gain competence and skill, and to prepare for the future in a normalized setting, special education must be used to modify programs, instruction, and the learning environment to ensure optimal educational progress (Sirvis, 1989; Van Osdol, 1982).

Special education services are also required for those periods of time (each week) during which a child is undergoing hemodialysis. Children in such treatment report concerns with the boredom imposed by the length of the sessions and the anxiety associated with the process and its discomforts (Amonette, 1984). Special education must provide instructional materials and programs for children to be used during treatment to relieve anxiety and boredom and effective home and hospital instructors to apply them. Recent technological advances in microcomputer and telecommunication strategies hold promise for upgrading the educational experience for the dialysis student during nonattendance periods.

REFERENCES

Amonette, L. (1984). *Kidney dialysis patients discover new hope through ABE Program.* Paper presented at the National Adult Education Conference, Louisville, KY.

Czaczkes, J. W., & De-Nour, A. K. (1979). *Chronic hemodialysis as a way of life.* New York: Brunner/Mazel.

Hobbs, N., & Perrin, J. M. (Eds.). (1985). *Issues in the care of children with chronic illness.* San Francisco: Jossey-Bass.

Kleinberg, S. (1982). *Educating the chronically ill child.* Baltimore, MD: Aspen Systems.

Sirvis, B. (1989). Students with specialized health care needs. *ERIC Clearinghouse on Handicapped and Gifted Children:* Reston, VA: Council for Exceptional Children. (ERIC Digest No. 458)

Stapleton, S. (1983). Recognizing powerlessness: Causes and indicators in patients with chronic renal failure. In J. F. Miller (Ed.), *Coping with chronic illness: Overcoming powerlessness.* Philadelphia: Davis.

Van Osdol, W. R. (1982). *Introduction to exceptional children* (3rd ed.). Dubuque, LA: Brown.

Whitt, J. K. (1984). End stage renal disease. In M. G. Eisenberg, L. C. Sutkin, & M. A. Jansen (Eds.), *Chronic illness and disability through the life span: Effects on self and family.* New York: Springer.

RONALD S. LENKOWSKY
Hunter College

ADAPTIVE PHYSICAL EDUCATION
PHYSICAL DISABILITIES

DIANA v. STATE BOARD OF EDUCATION

Diana (1970) and *Guadalupe* v. *Tempe Elementary School District* (1972) were highly similar cases that were never actually brought to trial but that have nevertheless had a significant impact on special education assessment and placement procedures. In each case, civil rights organizations filed suit in federal courts on behalf of all bilingual students attending classes for the mildly mentally retarded (or the respective state's cognate designation). Both cases noted disproportionate representation of bilingual, Spanish-surnamed children in programs for the mentally retarded. Additionally, the plaintiffs in each case argued that intelligence tests administered in English to Spanish-speaking children were the principal reason for the overrepresentation. Other charges were made raising concerns about the quality of programs for the mentally retarded in both cases and violations of the equal protection clause of the Fourteenth Amendent to the U.S. Constitution, including lack of due process considerations. As Reschly (1979) has noted, in both cases the school districts involved were engaged in unsound, unprofessional assessment procedures and had developed much of their special education processes around what most in the field would consider bad professional practice.

Each case was resolved on the basis of similar consent decrees, agreements entered into by each party and then certified by the court to avoid further litigation. Issues regarding the quality of direct service were virtually ignored in the decrees, which centered on assessment and placement procedures. In *Diana*, for example, the consent decree certified by the court required assessment of each child's primary language competence; if the primary language was found to be other than English, tests used in the assessment had to be nonverbal, translated, or administered using an interpreter. The decree also required that unfair portions of English language tests were to be deleted and more influence accorded to the results of nonverbal intelligence tests when placement decisions were being made.

Guadalupe, in the consent decree, mandated the same changes in testing practices as *Diana*. *Guadalupe* went on to add four additional statements:

1. IQ tests were not to be the exclusive or the primary basis for the diagnosis of mild mental retardation.

2. Adaptive behavior in other than school settings would be assessed.

3. Due process procedures were to be developed and instituted before individual assessment or any movement toward diagnosis and placement could occur.

4. Special education would be provided to each child in the most normal setting or environment possible.

Since *Diana* and *Guadalupe* were settled by consent decrees, no judicial opinion is available and there are no findings to be reviewed and discussed. Neither case set legal precedent. Both were strongly influential, however, in subsequent legislation passed at the state and federal levels. Wording from the two decrees is now commonplace in many state and federal regulations governing the education of the handicapped.

REFERENCE

Reschly, D. J. (1979). Nonbiased assessment. In G. Phye & D. Reschly (Eds.), *School psychology. Perspectives and issues.* New York: Academic.

CECIL R. REYNOLDS
Texas A & M University

CONSENT DECREE
EDUCATION FOR ALL HANDICAPPED CHILDREN ACT
   OF 1975
EQUAL PROTECTION
LARRY P.
MARSHALL *v.* GEORGIA

DIAZEPAM

Diazepam (Valium) is a minor tranquilizer with relatively few side effects compared with other psychotropic medications. It is prescribed primarily with adult populations for symptoms of anxiety. Although the use of diazepam continues to be widespread (i.e., 77 million prescriptions were filled in retail pharmacies in one year) (Yaffe & Danish, 1977), few studies regarding its therapeutic efficacy can be found in pediatric literature. Clinically, diazepam seems to be prescribed infrequently as a psychotropic, particularly as an antianxiety drug in children.

While diazepam is used only infrequently as a psychotropic agent in pediatric populations, it is often used as an adjunct in the treatment of seizure disorders. When administered intravenously in repeated dosages as deemed necessary, diazepam has been found to be effective in the initial management of uncontrolled, continuous seizures, or status epilepticus (Behrman, Vaughn, Victor, & Nelson, 1983). In general, diazepam is not used in the long-term management of seizure disorders because of the likelihood of the development of tolerance to the drug. Tolerance often develops very rapidly, sometimes as quickly as 3 to 14 days after initiation of therapy (Behrman et al., 1983). Increasing the dosage when the tolerance develops may help control the seizures, but, frequently, side effects such as drowsiness, ataxia, and slurred speech make the increased dosage intolerable. Occasionally, diazepam may be indicated therapeutically in the treatment of petit mal seizures, refractory to Zarontin and other agents, and in combination with phenobarbital and phenytoin in the treatment of seizures associated with central nervous system disease (Behrman et al., 1983).

Diazepam has been used to some extent in the treatment of sleep disturbances in children. It should be noted that insomnia and night waking, although common in childhood, are typically transitory. The practitioner must carefully rule out other dysfunctions such as phobic and separation disorders, as well as psychosocial stressors that may result in sleep disturbances. Further, psychostimulant medications used during the day for the treatment of hyperactivity may also cause sleep disturbances (Brown & Borden, in press). However, if the etiology of the sleep disturbance is an identifiable stressor that cannot be alleviated, the short-term use of diazepam at low dosages, administered in a single dose at bedtime, may be a temporary treatment for both the child and the parent (Shaffer & Ambrosini, 1985). Diazepam may also be particularly effective for those sleep disturbances termed parasomnias, they include nightmares, sleep terrors, and sleepwalking. Because these disorders typically dissipate with age, the need for continued medication must be reassessed frequently.

The side effects attributed to diazepam are often further elaborations of the desired therapeutic effects. Those of primary concern include disinhibition, incoordination, drowsiness, and depression (Jaffe & Magnuson, 1985; Rapoport, Mikkelsen, &. Werry, 1978). Both physiological and psychological dependence may also develop as a function of prolonged usage (Rapoport et al., 1978). Following prolonged usage, diazepam should be discontinued slowly with decreasing dosages because seizures may occur in response to abrupt withdrawal.

REFERENCES

Behrman, R. E., Vaughn, V. C., Victor, B., & Nelson, W. E. (1983). Convulsive disorders. In R. Behrman & V. Vaughn (Eds.), *Nelson textbook of pediatrics* (pp. 1531–1545). Philadelphia: Saunders.

Brown, R. T., & Borden, K. A. (in press). Neuropsychological effects of stimulant medication on children's learning and behavior. In C. R. Reynolds (Ed.), *Child neuropsychology: Techniques of diagnosis and treatment.* New York: Plenum.

Jaffe, S., & Magnuson, J. V. (1985). Anxiety disorders. In J. Wiener (Ed.), *Diagnosis and psychopharmacology of childhood and adolescent disorders* (pp. 199–214). New York: Wiley.

Rapoport, J. L., Mikkelsen, E. J., & Werry, J. S. (1978). Antimanic, antianxiety, hallucinogenic, and miscellaneous drugs. In J. Werry (Ed.), *Pediatric psychopharmacology* (pp. 316–355). New York: Brunner/Mazel.

Shaffer, D., & Ambrosini, P. J. (1985). Enuresis and sleep disorders. In J. Wiener (Ed.), *Diagnosis and psychopharmacology of childhood and adolescent disorders* (pp. 305–331). New York: Wiley.

Yaffe, S. J., & Danish, M. (1977). The classification and pharmacology of psychoactive drugs in childhood and adolescence.

In J. Wiener (Ed.), *Psychopharmacology in childhood and adolescence* (pp. 41–57). New York: Basic Books.

RONALD T. BROWN
SANDRA B. SEXON
*Emory University School
of Medicine*

ANTICONVULSANTS
PHENOBARBITAL
TRANQUILIZERS
ZARONTIN

DICHOTIC LISTENING

Dichotic listening involves the simultaneous presentation of similar stimuli to both ears. An advantage of one ear over another is assumed by faster or more correct recall for a given ear. This technique has been used to draw conclusions concerning an individual subject's auditory asymmetry and cerebral lateralization for a given stimuli. Originally devised by Broadbent (1954) to examine auditory attention and memory deficits, the dichotic listening paradigm was later adapted by Kimura (1961) to examine hemispheric lateralization of language.

The method involves the presentation of stimulus pairs (e.g., sentences, digits, words, consonant-vowel-consonant [CVC] syllables) with equal intensity to both ears. At the end of the sequence, the subject is instructed to select from a known set of alternatives or to recall what was heard. The subject is not typically required to report the ear to which the signal was presented.

Research using a dichotic listening task has typically focused on "ear advantages" or the number of correct responses for each ear. Most normal (nonbrain injured) individuals demonstrate a right ear advantage (REA) (left-hemisphere) for verbal material and a left ear advantage (LEA) for nonverbal material (Kimura, 1961). This effect is thought to reflect the functional specialization of the cerebral hemisphere opposite the favored ear. Neurologically, this favored access is due to greater numbers of contralateral ear to hemisphere connections and a blocking of ipsilateral signals.

The dichotic listening paradigm has been demonstrated to have both clinical and research application. Clinical use of dichotic listening tasks attempt to differentiate disorders that involve the central auditory system (at the cerebral level) from those that are primarily peripheral (sensory organs). It is expected that achieved scores will be lower for input presented to the ear that is contralateral to a temporal lobe lesion than scores for input presented to the ear ipsilateral to the lesion. This difference in scores is referred to as the lesion or contralateral effect (Speaks, Niccum, & Van Tasell, 1985).

The majority of the research has examined functional lateralization in normal subjects. Dichotic listening is useful in such study because it is noninvasive and hence it allows the investigation of functioning in normal subjects. Attempts have also been made to associate reading disorders with reversed or incomplete cerebral lateralization based on performance on dichotic listening tasks. Findings, however, have been inconsistent, with some researchers suggesting incomplete cerebral dominance for poor readers (Chyczij, 1993; Zurif & Carson, 1970) and others indicating a REA for both normal and reading-disabled students (Sparrow & Satz, 1970; Hynd, Obrzut, Weed, & Hynd, 1979). These differences may be attributed to the methodological and conceptual difficulties that have plagued research in this area (Lamm & Epstein, 1997; Satz, 1976). Clearly, caution must be observed when inferring cerebral lateralization from dichotic listening tasks for children with reading disorders.

REFERENCES

Broadbent, D. E. (1954). The role of auditory localization in attention and memory span. *Journal of Experimental Psychology, 47,* 191–196.

Chyczij, M. A. (1993). Self-report measures of perceived difficulty and strategies used in dichotic listening. *Canadian Journal of Special Education, 9,* 2, 160–170.

Hynd, G. W., Obrzut, J. W., Weed, W., & Hynd, C. R. (1979). Development of cerebral dominance: Dichotic listening asymmetry in normal and learning disabled children. *Journal of Experimental Child Psychology, 28,* 445–454.

Kimura, D. (1961). Cerebral dominance and the perception of verbal stimuli. *Canadian Journal of Psychology, 15,* 166–171.

Lamm, O., & Epstein, R. (1997). Dichotic listening in children: The reflection of verbal and attentional changes with age. *Journal of Experimental Child Psychology, 65,* 1, 25–42.

Satz, P. (1976). Cerebral dominance and reading disability: An old problem revisited. In R. M. Knights & D. J. Bakker (Eds.), *The neuropsychology of learning disorders:* theoretical approaches (pp. 273–297). Baltimore, MD: University Park Press.

Sparrow, S., & Satz, P. (1970). Dyslexia, laterality and neuropsychological development. In D. J. Bakker and P. Satz (Eds.), *Specific reading disability: Advances in theory and method* (pp. 41–60). Rotterdam: Rotterdam University Press.

Speaks, C., Niccum, N., & Van Tasell, D. (1985). Effects of stimulus material on the dichotic listening performance of patients with sensorineural hearing loss. *Journal of Speech & Hearing Research, 28,* 16–25.

Zurif, E. F., & Carson, G. (1970). Dyslexia in relation to cerebral dominance and temporal analysis. *Neuropsychologia, 8,* 351–361.

ARLENE L. RATTAN
Ball State University

RAYMOND S. DEAN
*Ball State University
Indiana University School
of Medicine*

CEREBRAL FUNCTION, LATERALIZATION OF DEVELOPMENTAL DYSLEXIA

DICTIONARY OF OCCUPATIONAL TITLES

The *Dictionary of Occupational Titles* (DOT) is prepared and published by the U.S. Department of Labor, Employment and Training Administration. It provides comprehensive occupational information to serve the labor market in job placement, employment counseling, and guidance. Concise standardized definitions (12,741) are alphabetized by title with coding arrangements for occupational classifications. Blocks of jobs are assigned to one of 550 occupational groups using 5- or 6-digit code. Skilled, semiskilled, or unskilled categories are specified. The format for each definition is occupational code number; occupational title; industry designation; alternate title (if any); body of the definitional lead statement; task element statement; undefined related title (if any).

Consumers may reproduce any part of this public document without special permission from the federal government. Source credit is requested but not required. The *Dictionary of Occupational Titles* has 1,404 pages. A new computerized version of the DOT is available and provides the benefit of a searchable database.

REFERENCE

U.S. Department of Labor, Employment, and Training Administration. (1996). *Dictionary of occupational titles* (4th ed.). Washington, DC: Author.

C. MILDRED TASHMAN
College of St. Rose

DIFFERENTIAL ABILITIES SCALES (DAS)

The Differential Abilities Scales (DAS; Elliott, 1990) is an individually administered battery of cognitive and achievement tests designed to be administered to children and adolescents between the ages of 2 years, 6 months through 17 years, 11 months. The British Ability Scales (BAS; 1979, Elliott) was published in Great Britain and was the forerunner to the DAS. In 1984, Colin Elliott began development of the DAS, an American version of the BAS.

The DAS cognitive battery consists of 17 subtests that divide into three levels: Preschool Level (ages 2:6 to 3:5), Upper Preschool Level (3:6 to 5:11), and School-Aged Level (ages 6:0 to 17:11). Depending on the child's age, the core battery consists of four to six subtests. The cognitive battery yields a composite score or General Conceptual Ability score (GCA), in addition to lower-level composite scores, called Cluster scores. For preschool-aged children, two Cluster scores, Verbal Ability and Nonverbal Ability, are yielded from 4 to 6 subtests. For school-aged children, three cluster scores, Verbal Ability, Nonverbal Reasoning Ability and Spatial Ability, are yielded from 6 subtests. The composite scores are comprised of "core" subtests, only those subtests with relatively high g loadings. There are also 2 to 5 "diagnostic" subtests for each level, which measure specific abilities that are less related to g, such as speed of information processing and short-term memory; however, the diagnostic subtests do not contribute to the composites. The cognitive battery takes approximately 25 to 65 minutes to administer. The brief school achievement battery consists of 3 subtests that measure basic skills of spelling, arithmetic, and word reading. It is administered only to school-aged children and takes approximately 15 to 25 minutes to administer.

There are some key differences between the DAS and other widely used cognitive batteries such as the Wechsler tests, Kaufman tests, and Stanford-Binet. First, in the DAS, an estimate of the child's ability is based on performance on a set of targeted items, or item set. The DAS does not assume that the child would pass all items below the item set or fail all items above the item set. Thus, children may take different sets of items ranging in difficulty. Second, administration differs in that there is not the use of traditional basal and ceiling rules (e.g., five consecutive failures for ceiling). Rather, if a child passes more than two items and fails more than two items in the item set, the item set would be considered an accurate set of items for the child and the test would be discontinued. A third difference in the DAS concerns scoring. Raw scores are converted to ability scores, which take into account both the difficulty of the items and the number of items answered correctly. However, ability scores are not norm-referenced. Therefore, ability scores for cognitive subtests must then be converted to T-scores (M = 50, SD = 10) in order to make comparisons with other children or between subtests. T-scores are then summed and converted to a standard score (M = 100, SD = 15) for both cluster scores and the GCA. Achievement tests yield raw and ability scores, but are directly converted to standard scores (no T-scores). Percentiles and age equivalents are also available for all subtests and composite scores.

The DAS was standardized on a sample of 3,475 children and adolescents. There were 175 children for each age group from 2:6 to 4:11, and 200 children per group for ages 5:00 to 17:11. There were approximately equal distributions of girls and boys per group. Data from the 1988 U.S. Census Bureau was used to stratify the sample on variables including age, sex, race/ethnicity, parent education, geographic location, and (for preschool children) enrollment in preschool. *The Differential Ability Scales Introductory and Technical Handbook* (Elliott, 1990b) contains specific characteristics of the sample.

Reliability and validity data appear to be good and are described in detail in two full chapters of the DAS handbook. Additional studies not included in the handbook have shown high correlations between the DAS and WISC-III, with the highest correlations between DAS GCA and WISC-III FSIQ, DAS Verbal Composite and WISC-III VIQ, DAS Spatial Composite and WISC-III PIQ (correlations ranging from .82 to .92; Wechsler, 1991).

The DAS was designed as a classification and diagnostic tool. For classification purposes, it is intended to provide a single overall score of conceptual and reasoning abilities, in combination with other data, to determine if a child falls into a category such as learning disabled, mentally retarded, or gifted. For diagnostic purposes, the child's profile of cognitive strengths and weaknesses should be examined. The DAS has several strengths that are noteworthy: its division of fluid ability into two factors, nonverbal reasoning and spatial ability; its measurement of nonverbal reasoning without using time limits or requiring visual-motor coordination; and its use of subtests that load high on *g* for the overall GCA score. The most notable limitations of the DAS relate to the difficult scoring and conversion system. Five subtests have open-ended responses requiring some judgment by the examiner. Additionally, converting cognitive subtest scores from a raw score to an ability score to a T-score to a standard score is tedious for examiners. The utility of the ability score, which uses an arbitrary numbering system and does not allow for norm-referenced comparisons, does not appear to warrant the "extra" step involved in converting the raw score to its final norm-referenced score.

REFERENCES

Elliott, C. D., Murray, D. J., & Pearson, L. S. (1979). *British Ability Scales.* Windsor, England: National Foundation for Educational Research.

Elliott, C. D. (1990a). *DAS: Administration and scoring manual.* San Antonio, TX: Psychological Corporation.

Elliott, C. D. (1990b). *Differential Ability Scales: Introductory and technical handbook.* San Antonio, TX: Psychological Corporation.

Wechsler, D. (1991). *Manual for the Wechsler Intelligence Scale for Children–Third Edition (WISC-III).* San Antonio, TX: Psychological Corporation.

DEBRA Y. BROADBOOKS
California School of
Professional Psychology

RONALD V. SCHMELZER
Eastern Kentucky University

DIGEORGE SYNDROME

See VELOCRANIAL FACIAL SYNDROME.

DILANTIN

Dilantin is an antiepileptic drug that can be useful in the treatment of seizure disorders. Generically, it is known as phenytoin. It was introduced in 1938 by Merritt and Putnam, who discovered its anticonvulsant activity in animals. It has proven remarkably effective in treating both partial seizures and generalized tonic-clonic seizure activity. Dilantin appears to work primarily in the motor cortex of the brain; it acts to inhibit the spread of seizure activity by preventing the extension of seizure activity from abnormally discharging neurons to surrounding cells. (Mosby, 1997) It is thought that Dilantin tends to stabilize the threshold of neurons against the hyperexcitability caused by excessive stimulation or environmental changes that can lead to seizures. Additionally, Dilantin appears to reduce brain stem center activity responsible for the tonic phase of tonic clonic (grand mal) seizures.

Some minor toxic symptoms such as gastric discomfort and nausea are frequent at the onset of Dilantin therapy. These tend to disappear rapidly. In children, a common effect of chronic use is gingival hyperplasia, which may cause bleeding gums. This condition generally can be prevented by good oral hygiene. Hirsutism occurs frequently, and may be aesthetically distressing, especially in girls. Toxic reactions to Dilantin include blurring of vision or ataxia. The onset of pruritus (severe itching), rash, or fever is an indication for immediate drug withdrawal, as liver damage or bone marrow suppression may occur, as may a syndrome resembling systemic lupus. However, drug withdrawal should always be done on physician's orders. Abrupt withdrawal of Dilantin may precipitate status epilepticus (Mosby, 1997).

REFERENCES

Goldensohn, E. S., Glaser, G. H., & Goldberg, M. A. (1984). Epilepsy. In L. P. Rowland (Ed.), *Merritt's textbook of neurology* (7th ed.) (pp. 629–650). Philadelphia: Lea & Febiger.

Mosby's GenRx. (1997). Phenytoin Sodium. Rx List Monographs. Linn, MO: Mosby.

RICHARD A. BERG
West Virginia University
Medical Center, Charleston
Division

ANTICONVULSANTS
EPILEPSY

DIPLEGIA

Diplegia is a topographic term used to describe a movement disorder predominantly affecting the lower extremities, with only mild involvement of the upper extremities. The term diplegia frequently is used as a description of a kind of cerebral palsy in which the arms are less involved than in a quadriplegia and more involved than in a paraplegia. The term quadriplegia indicates both arms and both legs are involved to a similar degree, and the term paraplegia denotes involvement of both legs only.

Clinical practice suggests the term diplegia is somewhat misleading, as the primary emphasis truly is on the movement disorder of the lower extremities; however, the upper extremities show so little involvement that a casual observer may not detect deficits that could impair function seriously. Often these deficits are sensory-motor-vestibular in nature and interfere with acquisition of fine motor skills such as dressing and handwriting.

The etiology of diplegia may be developmental delay, anoxia, trauma, jaundice, neonatal seizures, reflex suppression, or other factors that suggest the possibility of certain progressive biochemical disorders or spinocerebellar degenerative diseases. Differential diagnosis by a skilled pediatric neurologist, with ongoing follow-up by appropriate therapists, is essential to provide appropriate medical and educational intervention for children with diplegia.

REFERENCE

Berkow, R. (Ed.). (1982). *The Merck manual of diagnosis and therapy* (14th ed.). Rahway, NJ: Merck, Sharp & Dohme.

RACHAEL J. STEVENSON
Bedford, Ohio

CHOREA
DYSKINESIA
NEUROPSYCHOLOGY

DIPLOPIA

The basis for understanding diplopia (double vision) requires an appreciation of the physiologic mechanisms of binocularity within the visual cortex (Records, 1979). Evidence suggests there are four classes of cortical neuronal receptive fields for common visual direction—monocular left eye, monocular right eye, binocular corresponding, and binocular disparate. Presumably, each neuron derives stimulation from a specific visual direction; the visual direction is unambiguous for all classes except binocular disparate, where it falls between the visual directions of the two monocular receptive fields for that neuron. Consider stimuli to two eyes, presented on corresponding retinal points and moved gradually away in disparity; in time, fusion breaks and diplopia is perceived. When stimuli are presented to corresponding points only, as with a point of light, binocular corresponding neurons and monocular right and left neurons are stimulated. All three types have the same visual direction label and there is no conflict, resulting in single vision. When a small disparity is introduced, some binocular disparate neurons are stimulated and binocular corresponding neurons should cease responding. However, the monocular right and left neurons each are stimulated for a visual direction slightly to either side of the mean visual direction for binocular disparate neurons. These are integrated with a third set of responses from the binocular disparate neuron; therefore there should be a range of small disparities for which binocular response gives a unitary perception of a fused stimulus. In essence, it is this disparity that permits stereopsis, a specialized form of depth perception.

Diplopia may be physiologic or pathologic (Von Noorden, 1985). Physiologic diplopia is normal and results from stimulation and appreciation of objects simultaneously with the area of disparities that may be fused within the cortex and those outside. Object points in visual space stimulating corresponding retinal elements may be constructed to form a plane known as horopter. Both in front of and behind this plane is Panum's fusional space, an area in space that can be integrated cortically without perceiving objects as double. Physiologic diplopia occurs outside this space, and may be appreciated by observing an object in the distance and holding a pencil near. While attending to the distant object, the pencil will be seen as double. Most of the time, physiologic diplopia is cortically suppressed and not appreciated. Its clinical significance is twofold. Occasionally, schoolchildren become aware of and concerned about physiologic diplopia; reassurance is warranted. Second, diplopia may be useful from a diagnostic and therapeutic perspective in the presence of strabismus.

Pathological diplopia may be characterized as either monocular or binocular. Monocular diplopia results from defects in the refractive media or retinal pathology. Examples are high astigmatic refractive error, cataract, ectopic lens position, or macular edema. If diplopia is binocular, image positions may be separated horizontally, vertically, or obliquely; may vary with different directions of gaze and head position; and may be constant or variable.

Extraocular muscle paresis in adults almost always yields diplopia. However, patients with strabismus from early life rarely perceive diplopia. A series of adaptive mechanisms in infancy and childhood avoid this symptom: abnormal head position, binocular rivalry, suppression, and abnormal retinal correspondence. In the presence of a weak extraocular muscle, moving the head to a position that avoids the field of action of the paretic muscle often will prevent diplopia; therefore, an abnormal head position may be an indicator of extraocular muscle paresis. Binocular rivalry is a function that can be present normally or abnormally. When viewing with one eye through a monocular telescope or microscope, it often is unnecessary to close the other eye to avoid confusion of images. This cortical phenomenon, known as retinal rivalry, is a normal adaptation to avoid diplopia. In the presence of strabismus, particularly in a strabismic circumstance where there is alternation of fixation from one eye to the other, retinal rivalry is apparently the operant mechanism. In a constant strabismic circumstance, one eye assumes fixation to the exclusion of the other, and the image from the deviating eye is suppressed. Suppression is a mechanism, largely limited to infancy and youth, one consequence of which is decreased vision (amblyopia). Thus, amblyopia develops and is treatable in infancy and early childhood; however, once maturation of the system is complete (about age 9 years), amblyopia is neither a threat nor effectively treated.

Where strabismus is of early onset and longstanding duration, the cortical adaptation of abnormal retinal correspondence may ensue. In this instance, noncorresponding retinal points are cortically integrated, presumably to avoid diplopia. Thus diplopia may be monocular or binocular, physiologic or pathologic. The presence of diplopia may be detrimental to school performance. It is generally avoidable by closing one eye, and this behavior may be observed. Generally, however, adaptations are readily achieved to conditions producing diplopia in children, and the symptom does not represent a significant barrier to learning.

REFERENCES

Records, R. E. (1979). *Physiology of the human eye and visual system*. Hagerstown, MD: Harper & Row.

Von Noorden, G. K. (1985). *Binocular vision and ocular motility*. St. Louis: Mosby.

GEORGE R. BEAUCHAMP
Cleveland Clinic Foundation

DIRECT INSTRUCTION

The term direct instruction arose from two complementary lines of research and development. Rosenshine (1976) introduced the term into the mainstream of educational research. His synthesis of many classroom observation studies indicated that students consistently demonstrate higher reading achievement scores when their teachers do the following:

1. Devote substantial time to active instruction
2. Break complex skills and concepts into small, easy-to-understand steps and systematically teach in a step-by-step fashion
3. Ensure that all students operate at a high rate of success
4. Provide immediate feedback to students about the accuracy of their work
5. Conduct much of the instruction in small groups to allow for frequent student-teacher interactions

The other source of direct instruction derives from the work of curriculum developers rather than researchers. In the early 1960s in Israel, Smilarsky taught preschoolers from peasant immigrant families from surrounding Arab nations. The method, called direct promotion, taught in a direct manner toward specific goals. In the mid-1960s Bereiter and Engelmann (1966) formed an academically oriented preschool based on direct-instruction principles. In the late 1960s, Engelmann articulated the concept of direct instruction in the form of specific curricular materials and in a comprehensive model for teaching low-performing students. Direct instruction was incorporated as part of the acronym for DISTAR (Direct Instruction System for Teaching and Remediation) and as part of the title of the direct instruction model that took part in the U.S. Office of Education Follow Through Project. The key to direct instruction, as envisioned by Engelmann and his colleagues, is a comprehensive intervention, addressing teacher expectations for student learning, the curriculum, teaching skills, time spent engaged in academic activities, administrative support, and parental involvement.

At the heart of the direct instruction intervention was the conviction that student failure could be prevented or at least remedied, regardless of the label placed on the child. The empirical basis for this conviction is found in a number of sources, ranging from an annotated bibliography of 188 articles and books on direct instruction in special education (Fabre, 1983) to an article reviewing 20 direct instruction studies in special education in Australia (Maggs & Maggs, 1979). Other sources include a review of special education studies in the United States (Gersten, 1985) and an overview of articles on direct instruction (Carnine, 1983). These various reports frequently emphasize the academic gains of students in direct instruction (ABT Associates, 1977).

The national evaluation of the Follow Through (FT) Project yielded another finding that surprised many educators:

> The performance of FT children in direct instruction sites on the affective measures is an unexpected result. The direct instruction model does not explicitly emphasize affective outcomes of instruction, but the sponsor has asserted that they

will be the consequence of effective teaching. Critics of the model have predicted that the emphasis on tightly controlled instruction might discourage children from freely expressing themselves, and thus inhibit the development of self-esteem and other affective skills. In fact, this is not the case. (ABT Associates, 1977, p. 73)

These outcomes reflect the basic philosophy of direct instruction: student failures are school failures. School failures are not remedied by showing teachers research findings in an attempt to increase teacher expectations; however, teachers need well-designed curricular materials, substantial instructional time to teach students, and teaching techniques for motivating and helping students who are making numerous mistakes.

Curricular materials guide teachers in explaining, reviewing, and giving practice on academic content. Direct instruction materials are designed in part to minimize student confusions. In a simple example, subtracting 3942 from 6000 often confuses students as they try to rename in one column at a time. In direct instruction, students rewrite 600 tens as 599 tens and 1 ten in a single step:

$$\begin{array}{r} 599+1 \\ 6000 \\ -3942 \end{array}.$$

Recognizing that $600 = 599 + 1$ is much less confusing than crossing out successive zeroes and rewriting the value represented by each renamed zero.

Direct instruction materials also teach students strategies that allow them to handle a wide range of tasks. In intermediate spelling, students learn a few rules and 655 word roots; they then can spell over 10,000 words. The instructional design principles are articulated in several books: *Theory of Instruction* (Engelmann & Carnine, 1982), *Direct Instruction Reading* (Carnine & Silbert, 1979), *Direct Instruction Mathematics* (Silbert, Carnine, & Stein, 1981), and *Applied Psychology for Teachers: A Behavioral Cognitive Approach* (Becker, in press).

Direct instruction teaching techniques are designed to maximize the quality and amount of academic engaged time. The amount of time is increased by showing teachers how to schedule instructional time more effectively and how to keep students attending by using reinforcement, rapid pacing, challenges, etc. The quality of learning is particularly influenced by how teachers react to student errors. For memorization errors, teachers give the answers and periodically review the missed questions. For errors reflecting inappropriate strategy selection or application, the teacher asks questions based on prior instruction to guide the student in using the strategy to arrive at an appropriate answer.

Familiarity with direct instruction curriculas and teaching techniques requires intensive staff development.

Staff development occurs primarily in individual teachers' classrooms. A supervisor observes and sets priorities for training on teaching techniques. A supervisor might model a correction procedure with a teacher's students one day, observe the teacher applying the procedure immediately, and then return a few days later to see whether the teacher is comfortable with the procedure. If the teacher has mastered the correction procedure, the supervisor will commence training in the next teaching technique on the priority list.

Supervision of direct instruction can be difficult. Supervisors must have tact as well as skill in diagnosing teaching deficiencies, identifying and prioritizing remedies, modeling and prompting remedies, and managing their time efficiently in order to spend sufficient time making classroom observations.

Although some sources point to the success (broadranged) of direct instruction (Adams & Siegfried, 1996), others have suggested that there are no significant differences between direct instruction and regular classroom reading outcomes (Mosley, 1997). Findings suggest that students have to be taught by direct instruction for 2 years before effects are noted (Mosley, 1997).

REFERENCES

ABT Associates. (1977). *Education as experimentation: A planned variation model* (Vol. 4). Cambridge, MA: Authors.

Adams, G. L., & Siegfried, L. (1996). *Research on direct instruction: 25 years beyond DISTAR*. Seattle, Washington: Educational Achievement Systems.

Bereiter, C., & Engelmann, S. (1966). *Teaching disadvantaged children in the preschool*. Engelwood Cliffs, NJ: Prentice-Hall.

Carnine, D. W., & Silbert, J. (1979). *Direct instruction reading*. Columbus, QH: Merrill.

Carnine, D. (1983). Direct instruction: In search of instructional solutions for educational problems. In D. Carnine, D. Elkind, D. Melchenbaum, R. Lisieben, & F. Smith (Eds.), *Interdisciplinary voices in learning disabilities and remedial education* (pp. 1–66). Austin, TX: Pro-Ed.

Engelmann, S., & Carnine, D. W. (1982). *Theory of instruction*. New York: Irvington.

Fabre, T. (1983). *The application of direct instruction in special education: An annotated bibliography*. University of Oregon.

Gersten, R. (1985). Direct instruction with special education students: A review of evaluation research. *Journal of Special Education, 19*, 42–58.

Maggs, A., & Maggs, R. K. (1979). Direct instruction research in Australia. *Journal of Special Education Technology, 81*(3), 26–34.

Mosley, A. M. (1997). *The effectiveness of direct instruction on reading achievement*. (ERIC Clearinghouse No. CS012664)

Rosenshine, B. (1976). Classroom instruction. In N. L. Gage (Ed.), *Psychology of teaching. The 77th yearbook of the National Society for the Study of Education*. Chicago, IL: National Society for the Study of Education.

Silbert, J., Carnine, D. W., & Stein, M. (1981). *Direct instruction mathematics*. Columbus, OH: Merrill.

DOUGLAS CARNINE
University of Oregon
First edition

ELAINE FLETCHER-JANZEN
University of Northern Colorado
Second edition

DISTAR
READING REMEDIATION

DISABILITY

The term disability is derived from the Latin prefix *dis-*, meaning negation, separation, lack of, or opposite of; and the Latin *habilitas*, meaning fitness, and *habere*, indicating to have or to be easily handled. Disability today indicates the lack of power or ability to do something. It is usually regarded as a negative attribute. The prefix contributes to our English word some of the connotations of its association with Dis, the god of the underworld in Roman mythology with whom the Greeks identified Pluto, and with Hades and the realm of the dead.

Some writers distinguish disability from impairment and handicap. Wright (1960) views a disability as mainly a medical condition; however, she sees a handicap reflecting the demands placed on an individual in a particular situation. An individual may indeed have a disability but may not have a handicap except in certain situations. Wright's elaboration on the significance of physical disability is essential reading for persons interested in a psychological perspective of body physique.

Stevens (1962) has formulated a taxonomy for special education in which he distinguishes among disability, impairment, and handicap. Stevens regards disability as a loss of function, impairment as tissue damage or disease, and handicap as "the burden which is imposed on the learner when confronted with educational situations which cannot be resolved by reason of body dysfunction or impairment" (p. 65). While the progression may be from tissue damage to loss of function to certain situational difficulties, Stevens argues that the extent or severity of any disability cannot be directly predicted from evaluation of the impairment only. Nor can the behavior one exhibits, or the burden that one elects to carry or that is assigned by society to a person with a certain disability or impairment, be accurately determined from knowledge about the disability only. Disabilities in motion, sensation, intelligence, emotion, and physiological processes do not necessarily translate into specific handicaps in situations requiring mobility, communication, healthy self-concept, or social interaction skills.

The World Health Organization (WHO) has made efforts to clarify terms and extend the medical model of disease per se to account for the consequences of disease (1980). In 1980, the International Classification of Impairments, Disabilities, and Handicaps (ICIDH) was formed. The ICIDH bridged the former medical model with a social model and facilitated the recognition of the contributions of medical services, rehabilitation agencies, and social welfare personnel to the care of people with conditions that interfere with everyday life, especially those people who have chronic, progressive, and irreversible conditions. The medical model of disease may be illustrated as:

$$\text{etiology} \rightarrow \text{pathology} \rightarrow \text{manifestation}$$
(WHO, 1980, p. 10).

The extended model, a biopsychosocial model, may be presented as:

$$\text{disease} \rightarrow \text{impairment} \rightarrow \text{disability} \rightarrow \text{handicap}$$
(WHO, 1980, p. 11).

Disability in the WHO classification system denotes the "consequences of impairment in terms of functional performance and activity by the individual" (p. 14). An impairment is defined as "any loss or abnormality of psychological, physiological, or anatomical structure or function" (p. 47). Handicap is defined as "a disadvantage for a given individual, resulting from an impairment or a disability, that limits or prevents the fulfillment of a role that is normal (depending on age, sex, and social and cultural factors) for that individual" (p. 183). Thus impairment represents "exteriorization of a pathological state" (p. 47) and occurs at the tissue level; disability refers to "excesses or deficiencies of customarily expected activity, performance, and behavior" (p. 142) and is located at the level of the person; and handicap "reflects the consequences for the individual—cultural, social, economic, and environmental—that stem from the presence of impairment and disability" (p. 183).

The ICIDH is again, in the process of revision. Suggested revisions include:

the need to keep in mind users who are not health professionals, the presentation of handicap as a set of circumstances that individuals encounter as part of an interaction between their impairments and disabilities and their physical and social environment, the reflection of the major revision in the mental health sections of the ICD in the ICIDH as this is especially important for legislation and the protection of human rights, newer understanding of the biology of illness mechanisms and ensure that the classification is appropriate across cultures and no inappropriate gender references are made. (p. 1, WHO, 1998)

The emphasis on cultural competence is noted. The draft of the revision has been renamed the "International Classification of Impairments, Activities and Participation–A Manual for Dimensions of Disablement and Functioning" (WHO, 1998). The term disability has been replaced by "limitation in activity" and the term handicap has been replaced by "restriction in participation" (WHO, 1998). The revision is currently undergoing extensive field testing and the final draft will be presented in 1999.

In the present context of special education and rehabilitation, the term disability is frequently changed to the adjectival form and used to describe individuals. Thus we hear talk about disabled persons. Note, however, the affect of this change; instead of considering a disability or the lack of power to act, attention is directed to people who are characterized as not having power to act, with no distinction as to what actions might be limited. Wright (1960), in her discussion of physical disabilities, has pointed out the distinction between calling someone a physically disabled person as opposed to a person with a physical disability: "it is precisely the perception of a person with a physical disability as a *physically disabled person* that has reduced all his life to the disability aspects of his physique. The short cut distorts and undermines" (p. 8). Consider the impact of further streamlining our language when we talk about the disabled and characterize as disabled an entire group of people who may share nothing other than their membership in the amorphous group labeled disabled. A common example is the group called the learning disabled (LD); the extreme heterogeneity among the individual group members is obscured by the blanket term or its abbreviation to LD.

Attempts to define the term disability and differentiate it from related terms is more than an exercise in semantics. Precise definitions are needed for determining who is eligible for services; what the incidence and prevalence of conditions are; what projected health care, educational, rehabilitation, and welfare assistance may be required from a local, state, national, or international perspective; and what efforts might facilitate the development of appropriate housing and employment opportunities. It seems likely that as long as the term disability carries a strong pejorative connotation, attempts will be made to limit its denotation and increase the objectivity of its meaning.

REFERENCES

Stevens, G. D. (1962). *Taxonomy in special education for children with body disorders*. Pittsburgh: Department of Special Education and Rehabilitation, University of Pittsburgh.

World Health Organization. (1980). *International classification of impairments, disabilities, and handicaps: A manual of classification relating to the consequences of disease*. Geneva, Switzerland: Author.

World Health Organization. (1998). *ICIDH-2 Beta 1 Field Trials*. www.who.org.

Wright, B. (1960). *Physical disability—A psychological approach*. New York: Harper & Row.

MARJORIE E. WARD
The Ohio State University
First edition

ELAINE FLETCHER-JANZEN
University of Northern Colorado
Second edition

HANDICAPPED, DEFINITION
INDIVIDUALS WITH DISABILITIES EDUCATION
**   ACT (IDEA)**
LABELING

DISADVANTAGED CHILD

Most writings about disadvantaged children first gained attention during the 1940s and 1950s; lower-class youths and racial minorities were identified as the populace of this educationally disenfranchised group of learners. Historically we can identify the roots of this population in terms of their educational needs, but it was not until the mid 1960s that writers such as Riessman and Havighurst had their turns at defining the characteristics that constitute this deprived population. As indicated by Riessman (1962), the terms culturally deprived, educationally deprived, deprived, underprivileged, disadvantaged, lower class, and lower socioeconomic group, could all be used interchangeably.

Ornstein (1976) has presented an interesting and basic critique of the attempts made by Havighurst and Riessman to provide us with the characteristics of the disadvantaged. Havighurst began by attempting to provide the traditional conceptualization of the disadvantaged that grew out of the earliest of writings. The disadvantaged youth is seen as coming primarily from a low-income family and most likely from a racial minority. Havighurst emphasizes the social, economic, and personal handicaps of the disadvantaged and sees this youth at the lowest end of several strata. Ornstein interprets this as providing the unwary reader with a convenient label that is essentially laden with negativism.

On the other hand, we have Ornstein's interpretation of what he refers to as a positive trend exemplified in Riessman's (1962) classic book. *The Culturally Deprived Child*, in which he views the disadvantaged youth as having many positive characteristics. With the emphasis now on a more positive outlook, readers are encouraged to note and develop qualities within this population such as physical orientation, hidden verbal ability, creative potential, group cohesiveness informality, and sense of humor.

Although Riessman has made great efforts to identify some characteristics that might be construed as potentially positive qualities, he also is cognizant of the negative criteria used by Havighurst and others. An examination of *The Culturally Deprived Child* (1962), results in the reader's awareness that Reissman understood the enormity of the problems encountered by the deprived children of our nation.

Karnes, Reid, & Jones (1971), in the Guidance Monograph Series, provide us with an approach to the identification process in that they refer to a difference between middle class and lower class in only the six areas of (1) self-concept, (2) motivation, (3) social behavior, (4) language, (5) intellectual functioning, and (6) physical fitness. With such broad categories, each educator can conceivably provide us with information applicable to either the Havighurst or Riessman model. In addition, the term disadvantaged youth is also seen as being too nebulous and having a degree of relativism that in turn reduces the selection process for innovative educational programs to confront this issue. Loss of objectivity in the identification and ultimate selection of students for educational enrichment often results in failure to meet the program's goals.

Without many of the precise criteria needed to identify the disadvantaged population, the educational community moved ahead with special programs with a financial base from congressional legislation. In 1965 Congress passed the Elementary and Secondary Education Act (ESEA) and for the first time in U.S. history, federal financial support was provided to both public and nonpublic schools. From this legislation came Title I—Education of Children of Low-Income Families. Title I was designed to support and provide financial incentives for special programs to meet the special needs of socially and educationally deprived children of low-income families. Congress amended and expanded the ESEA many times over the next 30 years. The major criticism of the Act was that funds were spread thinly instead of being focused in areas of most need (Department of Education, 1993). In addition, a crisis developed in urban schools, where an exodus of White middle-class families from the city to private and/or suburban schools created a buildup of educationally disadvantaged minority students (Ornstein, 1989). Issues of cultural competence have also been included recently to the evaluation of services to disadvantaged children. There have been requests (Lake, 1990) to distinguish between the terms "culturally disadvantaged" and "culturally different."

Specific learning characteristics of the deprived or disadvantaged student might include many of the following: (1) oriented to the physical and visual rather than to the oral; (2) content-centered rather than form-centered; (3) externally oriented rather than introspective; (4) prob-lem-centered rather than abstract-centered; (5) inductive rather than deductive; (6) spatial rather than temporal; (7) slow, careful, patient, and persevering (in areas of importance) rather than quick, clever, facile, and flexible; (8) inclined to communicate through actions rather than words; (9) deficient in auditory attention and interpretation skills; (10) oriented toward concrete application of what is learned; (11) short attention span; (12) characteristic gaps in knowledge and learning; (13) lacking experiences of receiving approval for success in tasks (Conte & Grimes, 1969).

Meeting the needs of the disadvantaged child is a relatively new educational approach when viewed within the context of America's education history. Efforts to define this population have not been without conflict, and massive expenditures of monies by the federal government has also stirred controversy. However, studies indicate that enrichment programs (Kaniel & Richtenberg, 1992), mentoring (Shaughnessy, 1992), and appropriate curricula design (Gemma, 1989) have very positive outcomes with children who are disadvantaged.

REFERENCES

Conte, J. M., & Grimes, G. H. (1969). *Media and the culturally different*. Washington, DC: National Education Association.

Department of Education. (1993). *Improving America's Schools Act of 1993: The Reauthorization of the Elementary and Secondary Education Act*. Washington, DC: U.S. Department of Education.

Gemma, A. (1989). *A comparison of the child-centered curriculum model, the direct instruction curriculum model, and the open-framework curriculum model: Three curriculum models for disadvantaged preschool children*. (ERIC Clearinghouse No. PS018905)

Kaniel, S., & Richtenberg, R. (1992). Instrumental enrichment: Effects of generalization and durability with talented adolescents. *Gifted Education International, 8,* 3, 128–35.

Karnes, M. B., Reid, J., & Jones, G. R. (1971). The culturally disadvantaged student and guidance. Boston: Houghton Mifflin.

Lake, R. (1990). An Indian father's plea: *Teacher Magazine, 2,* 1, 48–53.

Ornstein, A. C. (1976). Who are the disadvantaged? In J. H. Cull & R. E. Hardy (Eds.), *Problems of disadvantaged and deprived youth* (pp. 5–15). Springfield, IL: Thomas.

Ornstein, A. C. (1989). Enrollment trends in big city schools. *Peabody Journal of Education, 66,* 4, 64–71.

Riessman, F. (1962). *The culturally deprived child*. New York: Harper & Row.

Shaughnessy, M. .F. (1992). *Mentoring disadvantaged gifted children and youth*. (ERIC Clearinghouse No. UD028765)

RICHARD E. HALMSTAD
University of Wisconsin at Stout

DISCIPLINE

The noun discipline comes from the Latin word *disciplina*, meaning teaching, learning. However, a more common use of the word connotes either training that corrects or molds or punishment for transgressions against societal or parental rules.

Discipline begins with the efforts of parents to teach the mores of their culture. Almost all of this early discipline begins when the infant becomes mobile and can therefore behave in ways that parents believe need to be changed. Early parental discipline usually focuses on behavioral control, e.g., not touching the untouchable or not running in the street. Difficulties can arise if parents think that the child can control a behavior that the child in fact cannot— at least not at that age. A good example of this is toilet training of toddlers. Parents continue to carry the responsibility for disciplining children until they enter school. From the time children enter school until they leave, teachers endeavor to discipline children as well.

Parents seem to discipline their children either through power-assertion techniques or through love-oriented techniques (Hoffman, 1970). In the former style of parental discipline, power-assertion, the parent uses physical punishment, deprives the child of material objects or privileges, directly applies force, or threatens. Control is exercised by taking advantage of greater physical strength and/or control of home environment.

Love withdrawal, a form of love-oriented discipline, uses direct but nonphysical expressions of anger or disappointment when the child misbehaves. For example, the parent may discipline by explicitly stating negative feelings, ignoring, isolating, or turning away from the child.

The use of power-assertive discipline such as spanking or love-oriented techniques such as withdrawal of affection may produce resentment or anxiety and cause the child to focus attention on his or her own negative consequences. These procedures are punitive rather than altruistic, i.e., they decrease the child's appreciation of another person's distress.

Through induction, another form of love-oriented parental discipline, the parent appeals to the child's affection or respect for another. In essence, the child may be reminded that someone else will be hurt, disappointed, or suffer from his or her actions.

In comparison, inductive discipline is a nonpunitive technique that communicates the harm caused by a child's actions and encourages the child to place himself or herself in the victim's place. Hoffman (1975) believes that children are likely to develop a strong altruistic orientation if their parents often use inductive disciplinary techniques.

Another perspective on discipline is espoused by William Glasser (1969). Glasser suggests that children be allowed to determine their own discipline and to set conse-

quences for their behavior. Adults (parents, teachers, etc.) who use Glasser's style of discipline often play a low-key role that reduces immediate application of reward and punishment and supplants both with discussion in which the adult serves as mediator for decision making.

While Glasser's approach may be effective with bright, middle-class, high-school students, it may not be effective with young children or with older adolescents who have grown up in a lower-class setting. If children have not developed the requisite skills for deciding on a socially competent course of action when disciplinary decisions are required, this approach is not suggested. The effectiveness of each technique varies, perhaps influenced most by such factors as the age and cultural background of the child.

On entering the school setting, previously learned behavior patterns emerge when children are faced with adapting to participating in a room where waiting, sharing, instruction, and learning must take place. The term control is often viewed as a convenient catch all for what should be termed classroom management. One is never sure whether the meaning is intended in the broad sense (to cover all of classroom management), or the literal sense, that of keeping pupil behavior so curbed that the classroom is totally teacher-dominated.

Discipline, like control, is often incorrectly used to mean various aspects of classroom management. Good discipline may be considered maintaining an orderly classroom. A classroom and/or school environment that supports good student behavior must also expect the student to make good choices. Students that only respond to external structures such as rewards or punishments learn very little self-discipline and the gains are usually only short-term (Short, 1994).

A more acceptable use of the term in the educational setting would describe discipline as an imposition of self-control in order to promote efficient habits of learning, proper conduct, consideration for others, and a positive learning environment. From the educator's point of view, preventing misbehavior is much more important than imposing control after the fact (Baron, 1992). Teachers working in teams to create positive classroom climates have much better support and success than individual efforts (Bell-Ruppert, 1994). In addition, democratic rather than authoritarian values have emerged in recent classroom discipline models. However, democratic values require flexible problem-solving skills that both the teacher and the students must value (Lewis, 1997).

To maintain discipline in the classroom, the student must be given as much independence as the teacher and child can tolerate. Classroom management should yield neither highly structured teacher-dominated environments nor completely permissive ones. To facilitate the development of self-control and discipline, a teacher's managerial style should attempt to promote active participation and a positive learning environment.

REFERENCES

Baron, E. B. (1992). *Discipline strategies for teachers*. (ERIC Clearinghouse No. SP034413)

Bell-Ruppert, N. (1994). *Discipline plans in middle schools*. Paper presented at the Annual Conference and Exhibit of the National Middle School Association, November, 1994.

Glasser, W. (1969). *Schools without failure*. New York: Harper & Row.

Hoffman, M. L. (1970). Moral development. In P. H. Mussen (Ed.), *Carmicheal's manual of child psychology* (3rd ed.) (Vol. 2). New York: Wiley.

Hoffman, M. L. (1975). Altruistic behavior and the parent-child relationships: *Journal of Personality & Social Psychology, 40,* 121–137.

Lewis, R. (1997). *The discipline dilemma: Control Management, Influence* (2nd ed.). Melbourne, Australia: Australian Council for Educational Research.

Short, P. (1994). *Rethinking student discipline: Alternatives that work*. (ERIC Clearinghouse No. EA026417)

MICHAEL J. ASH
JOSE LUIS TORRES
Texas A & M University
First edition

ELAINE FLETCHER-JANZEN
University of Northern Colorado
Second edition

CLASSROOM MANAGEMENT
SELF-CONTROL CURRICULUM
SELF-MONITORING

DISCOURSE

Discourse, oral and literate units of language that are usually larger than a sentence, show a common theme as well as local and global cohesion and coherence patterns (Schiffrin, 1994). It creates representation of events, objects, beliefs, personalities, and experiences. Discourse includes a variety of cues that include not only words and sentences, but also the tone, the overall purpose, and the relative formality of a communication event. In addition, oral discourse involves gestures, body positions, facial expressions of the speaker, and context (Brownell & Joanette, 1993). Two major types of discourse exist: Basic Interpersonal Communication Skills (BICS) or "everyday language," and Cognitive-Academic Language Proficiency (CALP) or "instructional language" (Cummins, 1983; Chamot & O'Malley, 1994). Both BICS and CALP con-

tribute to education success. Characteristics of discourse associated with BICS and CALP are divided into three categories that occur across a developmental continuum: Conversation, Narration, and Exposition (Larson & McKinley, 1995; Merritt & Culatta, 1998; Naremore et al., 1995; Nelson, 1998; Wallach & Butler, 1994).

Conversation is used to request and report concrete items and actions (informal or personal oral or written interactions) (Halliday, 1975; Hoskins, 1996; Naremore, Densmore, & Harman, 1995; Nelson, 1998; Tough, 1979). Conversation is a type of BICS that can be oral (e.g., social group, family conferences, telephone calls, "rap" sessions, gossip) or literate (e.g., personal notes, a diary, e-mail). Conversational discourse is context-embedded and has a structure of topics, initiations, responses, turns, exchanges, topic maintenance, reaction time latency, breakdowns, repairs, pacing/leading, and closure. Conversation competence is measured by quantity, quality, relationship, and manner, as well as nonverbal dimensions of communication. Individuals who do not develop conversational skills may experience difficulty with the second level of discourse, narration.

Narration is used to report what happened, to talk or write about, or to read about the there and then (recounts, eventcasts, accounts, fictional stories) (Esterreicher, 1995; Hedberg & Westby, 1993; Hughes, McGillivray, & Schmidek, 1997; Naremore et al., 1995; Nelson, 1998). Narrative competence includes the understanding and use of *story grammars* (characters, place, time, initiating event, problem, internal response, resolution, and ending). Story grammars develop through the process of centering and chaining involved in learning *story types* (heaps, sequences, primitive narratives, unfocused chains, focused chains, and eventually true narratives represented by complex, multiple, embedded, or interactive episodes). Narration, a combination of BICS and CALP discourse, is a bridge between conversation and exposition because narration develops the cognitive, linguistic, and contextual structures introduced in conversation and required by exposition. For some individuals, reading problems may be related to poorly developed productive narrative abilities.

Exposition, an oral and literate CALP communication form, is a context-reduced and abstract form of language used to generalize about and infer what happens in the there and then (Chamot & O'Malley, 1994; Cummins, 1983; Larson & McKinley, 1995; Merritt & Culatta, 1998; Naremore et al., 1995; Nelson, 1998; Ripich & Creaghead, 1994; Wallach & Butler, 1994). Expository language includes understanding and producing speeches, lectures, discussions, classroom discourse, textbooks, reaction papers, essays, and technical, (research, or term papers). Expository forms are structured through genres such as description, collection, sequence/procedure, compare-contrast, cause-effect, problem-solution, and argue-persuade. Exposition competence requires the understanding and use of precise vocabulary (often associated with academic content or career areas), pronunciation, grammar, organization, sequencing, transitions, cohesion, coherence, spelling, proofreading, and editing. Individuals who have not developed the oral and literate communication skills associated with narration may experience difficulties with expository language.

Critical elements that serve as building blocks for successful discourse abilities include *communication-learning functions* (instrumental, regulatory, interactional, personal, heuristic, imaginative, informational/representational, performatives, responsives, expressive; Halliday, 1975), *language-thinking functions* (maintaining, reporting, applying, analyzing, logical reasoning, evaluating, synthesizing, imagining, projecting, predicting, inferencing; Tough, 1979), and *executive functions* (awareness, goal setting, planning, self-initiating, self-inhibiting, self-monitoring, self-evaluating, ability to change set, strategic behavior; Ylvisaker & Szekeres, 1989). These various communication-learning functions are used in the process of *heuristics*, the reciprocal system of requesting information (asking questions) and responding (answering questions).

Discourse problems may be caused by developmental or acquired conditions. Oral and literate discourse rules and use vary from culture to culture (Hedberg & Westby, 1993). However, the consensus is that for social and academic success throughout life, individuals must be able to understand and use the communication-learning conventions associated with conversation, narration, and exposition (Nelson, 1998; Wallach & Butler, 1994).

REFERENCES

Brownell, H. H., & Joanette, Y. (Eds). (1993). *Narrative discourse in neurologically impaired and normal aging adults*. San Diego: Singular.

Chamot, A. U., & O'Malley, J. M. (1994). *The CALLA handbook: Implementing the cognitive academic language learning approach*. Reading, MA: Addison-Wesley.

Cummins, J. (1983). Language proficiency and academic achievement. In Oller, J. W., Jr. (Ed.), *Issues in language testing research*. Boston, MA: Newbury House.

Esterreicher, C. A. (1995). *Scamper Strategies: FUNdamental activities for narrative development*. Eau Claire, WI: Thinking Publications.

Halliday, M. A. K. (1975). *Learning how to mean: Explorations in the development of language*. London: Edward Arnold.

Hedberg, N. L., & Westby, C. E. (1993). *Analyzing Storytelling skills: Theory to practice*. Tucson, AZ: Communication Skill Builders.

Hoskins, B. (1996). *Conversations: A framework for language intervention*. Eau Claire, WI: Thinking Publications.

Hughes, D., McGillivray, L., & Schmidek, M. (1997). *Guide to narrative language*. Eau Claire, WI: Thinking Publications.

Larson, V. L., & McKinley, N. (1995). *Language disorders in older students: Preadolescents and adolescents*. Eau Claire, WI: Thinking Publications.

Merritt, D. D., & Culatta, B. (1998). *Language intervention in the classroom*. San Diego, CA: Singular.

Naremore, R. C., Densmore, A. E., & Harman, D. R. (1995). *Language intervention with school-aged children: Conversation, narrative, and text*. San Diego: Singular.

Nelson, N. W. (1998). *Childhood language disorders in context: Infancy through adolescence* (2nd ed.). Boston: Allyn and Bacon.

Ripich, D. N., & Creaghead, N. A. (Eds.). (1994). *School discourse problems* (2nd ed.). San Diego, CA: Singular.

Schiffrin, D. (1994). *Approaches to discourse*. Cambridge, MA: Blackwell.

Tough, J. (1979). *Talk for teaching and learning*. Portsmouth, NJ: Heinemann.

Wallach, G. P., & Butler, K. G. (1994). *Language learning disabilities in school-age children and adolescents: Some principles and applications*. New York: Merrill/Macmillan College.

Ylvisaker, M., & Szekeres, S. (1989). Metacognitive and executive impairments in head injured children and adults. *Topics in Language Disorders, 9,* 34–49.

STEPHEN S. FARMER
New Mexico State University

DISCREPANCY ANALYSIS

See LEARNING DISABILITIES, SEVERE DISCREPANCY ANALYSIS IN.

DISCREPANCY FROM GRADE

Discrepancy model analysis is used in the assessment of learning disabilities to determine if a difference exists between the level of achievement and ability. Levels of achievement and intelligence are measured reliably by using standardized tests. Results, however, may not always be accurate owing to error in measurement (Connell, 1991). Attempts to measure discrepancy may also be complicated by age or grade level. A discrepancy of one year at the third grade for a 9 year old is more severe than a similar discrepancy for a 16 year old. In addition, cognitive language relationships change over time, which may make eligibility decision-making inappropriate using these models (Cole, 1992).

Several techniques using expectancy analysis are used in quantifying learning disabilities (Mercer, 1983). They are the mental grade method, the learning quotient method, and the Harris method. Harris (1961) provided a method to determine an individual's reading expectancy grade (RE). The examiner subtracts five years from the individual's mental age:

$$RE = MA - 5$$

To determine if a discrepancy exists, a comparison is made between the individual's reading expectancy and the present reading level. The learning quotient method was developed by Myklebust (1968); it includes mental age, chronological age, and grade age (GA). The learning quotient is the ratio between the present achievement age and expectancy age with a score of 89 or below resulting in classification as learning disabled.

A third technique once commonly used to determine discrepancy in learning disabilities was proposed by Harris (1970). This method includes both mental age and chronological age but gives priority to mental age:

$$EA = \frac{2MA + CA}{3}$$

These methods for determining discrepancy have been criticized in that difference scores between two tests were less reliable than each score separately (Salvia & Clark, 1973). It has also been noted that a large number of children might exhibit discrepancy by pure chance. These techniques were also criticized because of their failure with nonreaders.

REFERE3NCES

Cole, K. (1992). Stability of the intelligence quotient-language quotient relation. *American Journal of Mental Retardation, 97,* 2, 131–143.

Connell, P. H. (1991). *An analysis of aptitude-achievement discrepancy formulas in learning disability assessment.* (ERIC Clearinghouse No. TM017793)

Harris, I. (1961). *Emotional blocks to learning.* New York: Free Press.

Harris, A. J. (1970). *How to increase reading ability* (5th ed.). New York: McKay.

Mercer, C. D. (1983). *Students with learning disabilities* (2nd ed.). Columbus, OH: Merrill.

Myklebust, H. (1968). Learning disabilities: Definition and overview. In H. Myklebust (Ed.), *Progress in learning disabilities.* New York: Grune & Stratton.

Salvia, J., & Clark, J. (1973). Use of deficits to identify the learning disabled. *Exceptional Children, 39,* 305–308.

Craig D. Smith
Georgia College

DISCRIMINANT ANALYSIS

Discriminant analysis is a statistical technique used to predict group membership from two or more interval dependent variables. It is similar to multiple regression in conception. For example, a researcher might be interested in determining if dyslexic students are distinguishable from other learning-disabled students using the subtests of the WISC-R. Discriminant analysis can be used to determine the optimal set of weights for the WISC-R subtests that maximally separate the two groups on a new variable composed of the weighted sum of the WISC-R subtests.

Discriminant analysis may also be viewed as a data reduction technique. Instead of needing a large number of variables to categorize subjects, the researcher applies discriminant analysis so that a new variable or set of variables is created that uses the information of the original variables. The new variables are linear combinations, or weighted sums, of the original variables. It is anticipated that fewer new variables are needed than in the original set, hence the idea of data reduction. Mathematically, more than one unique solution to the problem is possible. The number of solutions will be equal to the smaller of two numbers: the number of predictors or the degrees of freedom for groups (number of groups minus one). Each solution corresponds to a new variable independent statistically of all the other new solution variables. For two groups there is only one solution since the smaller of the two numbers is equal to one (two groups minus one). This solution is also equal to the multiple regression of the group variable (mathematically defined as, for example, one or two on the predictor variables. The regression weights and the discriminant analysis weights in this case are identical.

For three or more groups, there will be two or more solutions to the problem of maximally distinguishing between the groups. Each solution corresponds to constructing a straight line on which the groups differ most in the sense of squared distance from the mean of the groups on the line. Each solution line is perpendicular in a Euclidean geometric sense from each other solution line. Computer programs are used to solve these problems, and the programs are designed to find the best solution first. The best solution is one in which the variance between the groups is greatest in relation to average variance within the groups for all possible lines. Once this solution is found, the next one is found from the residuals of fit to the first solution. A statistical test, Wilks lambda, is a multivariate analog to the ratio of the sum of squares within groups to the sum of the squares' total. An F-test may be used to test significance. For each new solution, test the additional error reduced in a manner similar to that employed in multiple regression to test a new predictor's additional contribution to prediction. Also, stepwise procedures can be employed in discriminant analysis to select the subset of predictors that maximally separate the groups. Predictors that do not contribute to separation in a given solution are dropped.

Discriminant analysis is widely used in both social and physical sciences. Its mathematical solutions are straightforward for a computer; discriminant analysis programs for microcomputers are widely used (Huberty & Lowman, 1997).

REFERENCES

Cohen, J., & Cohen, P. (1983). *Applied multiple regression / correlation analysis for the social sciences* (3rd ed.). Hillsdale, NJ: Erlbaum.

Huberty, C., & Lowman, L. L. (1997). Discriminant analysis via statistical packages. *Educational and Psychological Management, 57,* 759–784.

Pedhazur, E. (1982). *Multiple regression in behavioral research* (2nd ed.). New York: Holt, Rinehart & Winston.

VICTOR L. WILLSON
Texas A & M University

FACTOR ANALYSIS
MULTIPLE REGRESSION
WISC-WISC-R

DISCRIMINATION LEARNING

Discrimination learning refers to the process of learning to respond differentially to relevant dimensions of a stimulus event. As a fundamental construct of behaviorally oriented learning explanations, this type of learning emphasizes events that occur before a behavior(s); the relationship of these events to the strength and contextual appropriateness of the behavior(s); and the resulting consequences that serve to maintain, strengthen, or punish the behavior(s).

During the teaching of discriminations, a stimulus event is presented to the student. Following this presentation, the student independently or, if necessary, with prompts, exhibits a behavioral response. If the behavior that the individual engages in is appropriate relative to the stimulus event, the learner is rewarded with a potentially reinforcing outcome. If the behavior is not appropriate with regard to the stimulus event, the consequent alternatives might include not attending to the response (ignoring), or systematic presentation of consequences aimed at reducing the future probability of the behavior occurring (punishment).

As a function of the consequences that occur in this S > R > C relationship, the stimulus events that have historically led to reinforcement become cues for the learner to engage in particular behaviors that will result in rewarding consequences. These stimulus events are referred to as discriminative stimuli (S^D). Conversely, those stimulus events that have not resulted in reinforcement (S^Δ) do not cue the individual to respond. Discrimination learning, then, teaches an individual when to engage in a particular behavior to obtain desirable outcomes, and by contrast clarifies when behavior will not lead to desirable consequences.

The teaching of discriminations constitutes one of the major tasks for individuals who are involved in educating the exceptional needs learner. While this type of learning is often assumed to take place in an almost incidental fashion, with most exceptional learners this outcome is not as likely. A host of variables, including diverse cognitive skills, inconsistent learning opportunities, and nefarious reinforcement contingencies, may interact to limit such individuals' development of accurate discriminations. Effective educational service delivery for the exceptional child or youth often necessitates the use of more systematic methods of teaching discriminations.

Planned teaching of discriminations has involved simple to complex presentations of the attributes of the stimulus events (e.g., size, shape, volume, color, or combinations of these) and varied reinforcement schedules (e.g., movement from fixed to variable schedules of reinforcement) aimed at strengthening the discriminative potential of the stimulus event. Following accurate individualized assessment, discriminations are taught beginning at a level that increases the opportunity for success. Based on continuing assessment, teaching complexity is systematically moved in the direction of more normative skill development.

Teaching of discriminated responses has been used in vocationally oriented, curricula, social skills programs, and many other curriculum areas targeted for the exceptional needs learner. By teaching individuals to exhibit specified behaviors under certain stimulus conditions, many of the inconsistent and inappropriate behaviors exhibited by this diverse group have been strengthened or replaced with more environmentally appropriate responses. For a comprehensive explanation of discrimination learning, the reader is referred to texts by Alberto and Troutman (1977) and Sulzer-Azaroff and Mayer (1977). Both texts provide clear examples of the application of this learning principle to educational programming. McDonald and Martin (1993) recommend the use of the Assessment of Basic Learning Abilities Test to assess discrimination acquisition with individuals who have profound disabilities.

REFERENCES

Alberto, P. A., & Troutman, A. C. (1977). *Applied behavior analysis for teachers: Influencing student performance.* Columbus, OH: Merrill.

McDonald, L., & Martin, G. L. (1993). Facilitating discrimination learning for persons with developmental disabilities. *International Journal of Rehabilitation Research, 16,* 2, 160–164.

Sulzer-Azaroff, B., & Mayer, G. R. (1977). *Applying behavior-analysis procedures with children and youth.* New York: Holt, Rinehart & Winston.

J. TODD STEPHENS
University of Wisconsin
at Madison

APPLIED BEHAVIOR ANALYSIS
BEHAVIOR MODIFICATION
DATA BASE INSTRUCTION
PRECISION TEACHING

DISPROPORTIONALITY

Disproportionality in special education denotes unequal percentages of students with various demographic characteristics in special education classifications and programs. Disproportionality most often occurs in the mildly handicapping classifications of mild mental retardation (MMR), emotionally disturbed (ED), and specific learning disability (SLD), or in programs for the talented and gifted (TAG). The demographic variables in which disproportionality is most often observed, and sometimes seen as a problem, are ethnic/ racial status, sex, and socioeconomic status. Disproportionality related to these student characteristics is well known, but highly controversial (Reschly, 1986; 1991; 1997).

The most widely studied disproportionality phenomenon is the overrepresentation of minorities, males, and economically disadvantaged students in the exceptional child classification of MMR. The same groups are also overrepresented, according to some studies, in programs for the SLD and ED. However, the overrepresentation in SLD and ED is rarely of the same magnitude as in MMR.

In the Table, data compiled from a Federal Office of

National Projections from 1978 OCR Survey

	Minority (%)	White (%)	Hispanic (%)	Black (%)
Classification				
Mildly mentally retarded	2.54	1.07	0.98	3.46
Seriously emotionally disturbed	0.42	0.29	0.29	0.50
Learning disabled	2.29	2.32	2.58	2.23
Speech impaired	1.82	2.04	1.78	1.87
Totally (mildly handicapped)	7.07	5.72	5.63	8.06

Source: Based on Finn (1982), Table 1, p. 324 and Table 3, p. 330.

Civil Rights (OCR) survey of school districts in the United States, reported in a National Academy of Sciences monograph (Heller, Holtzman, & Messick, 1982), are presented. In 1978, these national results indicated that the only significant area of disproportionality was MMR, where the percentage of black students classified as MMR was three times the percentage of white students so classified. Relatively equal percentages of black, white, and Hispanic students were found in all other classifications except for ED, where black students were again overrepresented, but the numbers of students were small. The national results also indicated that Hispanic students were not overrepresented in special education programs for the mildly handicapped, an apparent reversal of a phenomenon that led earlier to placement bias litigation in Arizona and California.

Other studies have indicated minority disproportionality in SLD and ED. For example, data for the state of Florida presented in the *S1 v. Turlington* trial (1986) indicated that black students were overrepresented in SLD, ED, and MMR.

Males and economically disadvantaged students generally are overrepresented in special education programs for the MMR. This overrepresentation sometimes approaches a ratio of two males for every female in SLD, ED, and MMR programs. Although studied far less frequently, overrepresentation of economically disadvantaged students is at least as ubiquitous as minority overrepresentation. Indeed, minority overrepresentation is probably best understood as reflecting the effects of poverty circumstances (Reschly, 1986).

The disproportionate representation of students in TAG programs is a virtual mirror image of representation in programs for the mildly handicapped. Economically disadvantaged minority students are underrepresented in programs for the gifted. The degree of underrepresentation is highly variable, but for black students, it is approximately the same as the degree of overrepresentation in programs for the mildly handicapped. The representation of males and females is approximately equal in TAG programs except in very specialized programs that attempt to select the markedly gifted (IQ greater than 150) or in programs for markedly advanced students in the areas of science and mathematics. In the latter kinds of programs, there is considerable underrepresentation of females, a phenomenon that also evokes considerable controversy.

Disproportionality statistics are easily confused and often distorted. In the *Larry P. case,* undisputed facts established that black students constituted 10% of the total enrollment in California, but 25% of the MMR enrollment. However, only 1% of all California black students were in MMR programs. These seeming disparities arise from the low base rate of MMR (and other exceptional conditions) and the failure to clearly distinguish between percent of group in the general population (10%), percent of group in the program (1%), and percent of the program by group (25%) (Reschly, 1986). Interpretation of disproportionality statistics must carefully distinguish among these different percentages.

The two general causes of disproportionality suggested in the literature are bias or discrimination and genuine individual differences. In short, the disproportionality is seen by some as a reflection of genuine differences among students and by others as a reflection of pernicious bias and discrimination from a variety of sources.

Allegations of bias or discrimination generally implicate the processes and procedures in which students are selected to be considered for placement in various kinds of programs. Thus bias or discrimination has been alleged in referral procedures, in the assessment process and assessment instruments (especially in intelligence tests), and in decision making by persons responsible for classification and placement decisions. Results of research on referral, assessment process and procedures, and decision making are far from definitive or unequivocal. Thus far, there is little evidence that intentional bias or discrimination is a primary cause of disproportionality (Bickel, 1982; Reschly, 1986).

There is ample evidence establishing an association between extreme poverty and the incidence of mild mental retardation. This evidence has been gathered over the past 80 years with different racial or ethnic groups throughout western Europe and the United States. The MMR is to a large degree a phenomenon of poverty, but the vast majority of poor persons are not mildly mentally retarded (Reschly, 1986; 1991). The mechanisms whereby poverty increases risk for mild mental retardation are not clearly understood, but a variety of conditions are implicated (Robinson & Robinson, 1976).

Explanations for the sex disproportionality within the mildly handicapped and in certain types of programs for the gifted are far less clear, but no less controversial. These explanations range from constitutional factors (e.g., suggesting that the greater susceptibility of males to various constitutional disorders explains the overrepresentation of males in the mildly handicapped classifications) to the hypothesis that lower amounts of testosterone in females might account for the underrepresentation of women in programs for extremely advanced students in science and mathematics. Experiential or environmental influences are also suggested for sex disproportionality, e.g., suggestions that sex-typed behavior accounts for greater male referral for learning problems as well as fewer females excelling in math and science. Again, definitive, unequivocal results have not been established, and probably cannot be established in the foreseeable future.

Disproportionality, whether it involves overrepresentation of black students in programs for the mildly retarded or underrepresentation of women in programs for mathematically precocious youths, should be seen as a symptom, but only a symptom. Factors that might lead to disproportionality should be investigated, including possible bias or discrimination in procedures and processes whereby students are selected or placed in various programs.

Disproportionality, particularly overrepresentation of minority students in programs for the mildly mentally retarded, has provoked extensive and enormously expensive litigation beginning in about 1968 and continuing through present day (Bersoff, 1982; Prasse & Reschly, 1986; Reschly, 1986; 1991). The common features of the placement bias cases are (1) overrepresentation of minority students, usually blacks, in self-contained MMR special classes; (2) class-action suits filed in federal district courts; and (3) allegations of bias in various aspects of the referral, pre-placement evaluation, and classification/placement decision making. The outcomes of these cases have been extremely diverse, ranging from judicial decrees banning overrepresentation and forbidding the use of individually administered intelligence tests in certain circumstances to judicial decrees indicating that overrepresentation as such is not discriminatory and upholding the use of IQ tests along with other measures as an important protection for all children in the referral and classification/placement process. Federal circuit courts have upheld trial decisions in two cases, *Larry P.* v. *Riles* (1984) and *Marshall* v. *Georgia* (1985). However, the *Larry P.* and *Marshall* opinions reached opposite conclusions on a similar set of issues. Further litigation is likely.

Research methods designed to develop valid ways to screen, refer, and classify/place students that also eliminate disproportionality have been unsuccessful to date. However, inclusive programming (Kovach, 1997; Markowitz, 1997) has reduced many instances of placement from service provision to special education outcomes. Processes and procedures that maintain the integrity of programs in meeting the needs of students, apply reliable and valid screening, referral, and classification/placement procedures, and are being consistently implemented and assessed. Centers such as COMRISE (Center of Minority Research in Special Education) are attempting to increase the number and research capacity of minority scholars in institutions of higher education with high minority enrollments. They are building a community of minority scholars within the larger special education research community and are trying to improve the quality and effectiveness of culturally competent special education services for minority students (COMRISE, 1998). The U.S. Department of Education reports disproportionality statistics on an annual basis, and is currently focusing much attention to the less than adequate special education services delivered to inner-city students (U.S. Dept. of Education, 1996). The Office of Civil Rights conducts compliance reviews on such issues as ensuring nondiscriminatory practices are followed in the placement of minority students in special education and low-track courses, ensuring that access to

English language instruction as well as content courses and other educational benefits are afforded to limited-English proficient students, ensuring student assessment practices are nondiscriminatory and providing nondiscriminatory access to gifted and talented and other high ability programs (OCR, 1998). There also has been a national shift towards prereferral intervention, better interventions in regular education, orienting assessment procedures towards intervention rather than classification, the use of court orders, and the use of alternative criteria and assessment procedures (Reschly, 1991; 1997).

REFERENCES

Bersoff, D. N. (1982). The legal regulation of school psychology. In C. R. Reynolds & T. B. Gutkin (Eds.), *The handbook of school psychology* (pp. 1043–1074). New York: Wiley.

Bickel, W. E. (1982). Classifying mentally retarded students: A review of placement practice in special education. In K. A. Heller, W. H. Holtzman, & S. Messick (Eds.), *Placing children in special education: A strategy for equity* (pp. 182–229). Washington, DC: National Academy.

COMRISE. (1998). *Center of Minority Research in Special Education*. Charlottesville, VA: University of Virginia, Curry School of Education.

Finn, J. D. (1982). Patterns in special education placement as revealed by OCR surveys. In R. A. Heller, W. H. Holtzman, & S. Messick (Eds.), *Placing children in special education: A strategy for equity* (pp. 322–381). Washington, DC: National Academy.

Heller, K., Holtzman, W., & Messick, S. (Eds.). (1982). *Placing children in special education: A strategy for equity*. Washington, DC: National Academy.

Kovach, J. A., & Gordon, D. E. (1997). Inclusive education: A modern-day civil-rights struggle. *Educational Forum, 6,* 3, 247–257.

Markowitz, J. (1997). *Addressing the disproportionale representation of students from racial and ethnic minority groups in special education: A resource document*. Alexandria, VA: National Association of State Directors of Special Education.

Office of Civil Rights. (1998). Annual report to Congress, Fiscal Year 1996. Washington, DC: Department of Education.

Prasse, D. P., & Reschly, D. J. (1986). *Larry P*: A case of segregation, testing, or program efficacy? *Exceptional Children, 52,* 333–346.

Reschly, D. J. (1986). Economic and cultural factors in childhood exceptionality. In R. T. Brown & C. R. Reynolds (Eds.), *Psychological perspectives on childhood exceptionality: A handbook* (pp. 423–466). New York: Wiley-Interscience.

Reschly, D. J. (1991). Bias in cognitive assessment: Implications for future litigation and professional practices. *Diagnostique, 17,* 1, 86–90.

Reschly, D. J. (1997). *Disproportionate minority representation in general and special education: Patterns, issues, and alternatives*. Des Moines, IA: Iowa State Department of Education.

Robinson, N., & Robinson, H. (1976). *The mentally retarded child* (2nd ed.). New York: McGraw-Hill.

U.S. Department of Education. (1996). *Eighteenth annual report to Congress: To assure the free appropriate public education of all children with disabilities: Implementation of the Individuals with Disabilities Education Act (IDEA)*. Washington, DC: Author.

DANIEL J. RESCHLY
Iowa State University

CULTURAL BIAS IN TESTS
CULTURALLY/LINGUISTICALLY DIVERSE STUDENTS, REPRESENTATION OF
LARRY P.
MARSHALL *v.* GEORGIA
NONDISCRIMINATORY ASSESSMENT

DISTAR

DISTAR (Direct Instructional System for Teaching and Remediation) is a product name for an instructional system published by Science Research Associates Inc. (SRA). From 1964 to 1966, Siegfried Engelmann and Carl Bereiter developed the teaching methods used in the DISTAR program, which is based on a task analysis of basic skills and presentation of materials in a direct teaching model. In 1967 SRA contracted with Engelmann to develop, write, and test DISTAR reading, language, and arithmetic materials. His coauthors were Elaine Bruner, reading; Douglas Carnine, arithmetic; and Jean Osborn and Therese Engelmann, language. In 1968 Wesley Becker joined Engelmann's Follow-Through Project and in 1969 they formed the Engelmann-Becker Corporation, a private non-profit organization providing teacher training in the Engelmann-Becker instructional model and the production of materials for Follow-Through sites. Although developmental work took place at the Engelmann-Becker Corporation, product development for DISTAR per se was and is performed under contract between SRA and the individual authors involved. Siegfried Engelmann became and remains professor of special education at the University of Oregon and codirector of the Direct Instruction Follow-Through Program (Brinckerhoff, 1983; Guinet, 1971; Kim, Berger, & Kratochvil, 1972; Moodie & Hoen, 1972).

The DISTAR system was originally designed to teach basic skills and concepts in reading, arithmetic, and language to disadvantaged preschoolers (Guinet, 1971). However, the scope has broadened to include average, above average, learning-disabled, and educable and trainable mentally retarded children (Kim et al., 1972). Current reviews of research (Cotton & Savard, 1982; Gersten, 1981) have revealed that the direct instruction method has proven successful with socioeconomically disadvantaged primary age children and special education students through age 13.

The system is grounded in the ideas that children learn what they are taught, that the necessary basic skills and concepts are the same for all children, that IQ is a function of teaching, and that it is possible to teach all of the necessary skills and concepts by means of a suitable instructional program. The required small group instruction ensures maximum student participation. Immediate reinforcement or correction ensures the prevention of error patterns (*Direct Instruction Management Handbook*, 1981; Guinet, 1971; Kim et al., 1972; Moodie & Hoen, 1972). The 30-minute lessons consisting of verbal interaction between teacher and students provide immediate teacher feedback. Lessons are carefully sequenced in a step-by-step fashion requiring mastery of basic skills before presentation of more complex ones. The well-defined small learning stages ensure daily successes that reinforce student self-concept. Limited visuals control distractions and are provided only at the end of lessons as rewards. The rewards are similar to the worksheets completed in class and taken home in recognition of doing well (Williamson, 1970). The presentation of tasks and the use of praise is highly structured. The teacher's manual instructs the teacher how to present the tasks, what to say, what signals and cues to use, what to expect from the children, and how to correct errors. Research results comparing the DISTAR program with other direct instruction curricula indicate that DISTAR is comparable in outcomes (Kuder, 1990; Traweek & Berniger, 1997).

REFERENCES

Brinckerhoff, L. (1983, Spring). Siegfried Engleman-Prophet or Profiteer. *ADI NEWS*, p. 1.

Cotton, K., & Savard, W. G. (1982). *Direct instruction: Research on school effectiveness project*. Portland, OR: Northwest Regional Educational Lab. (ERIC Document Reproduction Service No. ED 214 909)

Direct instruction management handbook. (1981). Chicago: Science Research Associates.

Gersten, R. M. (1981, April). *Direct instruction programs in special education settings: A review of evaluation research findings*. Paper presented at the annual international convention of the Council for Exceptional Children, New York. (ERIC Document Reproduction Service No. ED 204 957)

Guinet, L. (1971). *Evaluation of DISTAR materials in three junior learning assistance classes* (Report No. 71–16). Vancouver, BC: Board of School Trustees, Department of Planning and Evaluation. (ERIC Document Reproduction Service No. ED 057 105)

Kim, Y., Berger, B. J., & Kratochvil, D. W. (1972). *DISTAR instructional system* (Report No. OEC-0-70-4892). Washington, DC: Office of Education, Office of Program Planning and Evaluation. (ERIC Document Reproduction Service No. ED 061 632)

Kuder, S. J. (1990). Effectiveness of the DISTAR reading program for children with learning disabilities. *Journal of Learning Disabilities, 23*, 1, 69–71.

Moodie, A., & Hoen, R. (1972). *Evaluation of DISTAR programs in learning assistance classes of Vancouver 1971–72* (Report No. 72–18). Vancouver, BC: Board of School Trustees, Department of Planning and Evaluation. (ERIC Document Reproduction Service No. ED 088 911)

Traweek, D., & Berniger, V. (1997). Comparisons of beginning literacy programs. *Learning Disability Quarterly, 20*, 2, 160–168.

Williamson, F. (1970). *DISTAR Reading—Research and Experiment*. Urbana: University of Illinois. (ERIC Document Reproduction Service No. ED 045 318)

MARY D'IPPOLITO
*Montgomery County
Intermediate Unit,
Norristown, Pennsylvania*

DIRECT INSTRUCTION FOLLOW THROUGH

DISTRACTIBILITY

Attention is considered the most basic prerequisite for learning (Hewett, Taylor, & Artuso, 1969). As a disorder of attention, distractibility has been extensively studied by special educators and psychologists. Distractibility represents a construct that cannot be directly measured but rather must be based on inferences from gross behavioral observations of a child's behavior or performance on a particular task. Operational definitions of distractibility therefore differ and measurement is often imprecise. For example, some researchers and practitioners define distractibility as poor performance on an attentionally demanding task such as matching similar figures, while others define it as diminished performance when a distraction is introduced. Whether a child who is observed to be looking away from a task is inferred to be distractible or rather contemplating the task by considering a relevant idea illustrates the difficulty with precise measurement. Despite these definitional and methodological problems, research has advanced our understanding of the diagnosis, etiology, and treatment of distractibility.

Definitions of distractibility include difficulty in tuning out or forced responsiveness to unessential or extraneous stimulation such as environmental noises or stimuli such as hunger pangs, that may produce a motor activity within the individual (Cruickshank, Bentzen, Ratzeburg, & Tannhauser, 1961). In a classroom setting, distractibility typically refers to behavior that reflects the child's interest in things other than those on which the child should be concentrating (Bryan, 1974).

In the research literature, distractibility has been assessed by a variety of methods in a number of different settings (Whalen, 1983). Methods have included assessing performance as a child works in a room containing colorful and interesting distractors or, after introducing extraneous auditory or visual stimuli, while performing the task. The administration of a variety of laboratory games and procedures, the use of standardized behavior rating scales such as the Connors Teacher and Parent Rating Scale (Goyette, Connors, & Ulrich, 1978), and the analysis of results from individually administered intelligence tests (Kaufman, 1979) represent other methods reported in the research literature. Assessments have been conducted in the home, classroom, playground, playroom, and during the administration of individual intelligence and achievement tests (Bryan, 1974; Milich, Loney, & Landau, 1982).

Behaviors that reflect distractibility vary greatly depending on the task, type of distraction, setting, and the individual child. Evidence suggests that children are differentially distracted by some environmental stimuli or tasks but not others, and that they are distracted in some settings but not others (Tarver & Hallahan, 1974). Relating to the task variable, tasks that require a high degree of voluntary attention or those characterized as being less interesting to the child such as attending to a math or reading lesson are more likely to elicit distractible behavior than those tasks that require a low degree of voluntary attention such as playing with toys or drawing a picture of the child's choice. A difference also exists between auditory and visual tasks in the amount of distractibility that may be induced. In addition, a distraction that is more central to a task is more likely to interfere with a child's performance than a distraction that is more peripheral (Ricks & Mirsky, 1974). For example, children working independently at their desks completing reading worksheets are more likely to be distracted by the oral reading of a small reading group across the room than by a classmate sitting next to them jostling papers. The setting is also an important interacting variable in the eliciting of distractible behavior. A child may be distracted by a certain stimulus in one setting but not in another. For example, the noise from an overhead fluorescent light may distract a child in art class but not during math. The degree of structure provided in a particular setting is also related to the eliciting of distractible behavior, with distractibility more likely to occur in more unstructured settings.

Various characteristics of the child are also associated with whether distractible behavior occurs. The very same task and distracting stimuli in the identical setting may elicit distractible behaviors in one child but not another. Based on teacher and parent ratings in the home and classroom and observations during individual testing sessions, children with a wide variety of learning handicaps are found to exhibit greater distractibility than their non-handicapped peers (Krupski, 1981). These groups include all functioning levels of the mentally retarded (Zigler, 1973), low achievers (Soli & Devine, 1976), and children with centrencephalic epilepsy (Campanelli, 1970). Distractibility is often associated with hyperactivity. However, investigators (Douglas, 1972, 1974) have failed to support the assumption that all hyperactive children are distractible.

The presumed causes of distractibility are many and varied. There exists some evidence for a developmental trend in distractibility, with children becoming less distractible as they grow older (Well, Lorch, & Anderson, 1980). Distractibility in boys has also been associated with congenital characteristics such as minor, physical anomalies as well as gross motor incoordination (O'Donnell, O'Neill, & Staley, 1979). Other suspected etiologies include metabolic disturbances interacting with diet (Wunderlich, 1981), gross brain damage or an underlying neurological condition such as minimal brain dysfunction, and environmental variables such as child-rearing practices. Ross (1976) postulates that distractibility is due to a delayed development in selective attention.

Selective attention refers to a child's age-appropriate ability to focus on relevant information in the environment while excluding irrelevant or distracting information. As a child is listening to a teacher-directed lesson in the classroom, numerous stimuli impinge on the child's senses such as the noise from the overhead lights, the child's classmate across the row shifting in his or her chair, or a feeling of hunger. In order for the child to learn and attend to the teacher, the child must screen out all the irrelevant stimuli and focus on the relevant stimuli. The ability to screen out the irrelevant while focusing on the relevant stimuli requires selective attention.

Although there exists wide agreement that attention/distractibility and learning are strongly related, the precise nature of this relationship remains unclear. Distractibility has been demonstrated to negatively affect memory (Torgesen, 1981), and achievement in arithmetic and reading (Stedman, Lawlis, & Cortner, 1978). The exhibiting of distractible behaviors also affects adult behavior, with distractible children eliciting greater amounts of attention and instruction from adults in a one-to-one setting but less attention and interaction in a group setting (Ianna, Hallahan, & Bell, 1982). Distractibility typically occurs following head trauma in children and in adults.

The most common types of interventions for distractibility are pharmacotherapy, consisting of the administration of stimulant medication such as Ritalin and Mellaril (Gadow, 1981), and behavior-management techniques. Behavior-management techniques include making rewards contingent on attentive behaviors and cognitive behavioral interventions such as self-instruction, self-correction, and self-monitoring (Kneedler & Hallahan, 1981). Other types of interventions have included reducing distracting input by environmental modifications such as changing the seating arrangement (Sandoval, 1982), having youngsters work in plain, nonstimulating cubicles, changing the student's diet (Wunderlich, 1981), introducing sensory integrative therapy, which involves gross, fine and visual-motor activities (Ainsa, 1983) and introducing attentional skills as learning objectives (Wolfson, 1995). Although all of these interventions have enjoyed some success, the most successful are pharmacotherapy and behavior management. Further, although these two types of interventions have often reduced distractibility in particular children, they frequently do not produce increases in learning unless they are combined with increased direct academic instruction, and interventions that require various degrees of monitoring and supervision (Faison & Barniskis, 1993).

REFERENCES

Ainsa, T. (1983). Sensory integration: A home intervention program. *Academic Therapy, 18,* 495–498.

Bryan, T. S. (1974). An observational analysis of classroom behaviors of children with learning disabilities. *Journal of Learning Disabilities, 7,* 35–43.

Capanelli, P. (1970). Sustained attention in brain damaged children. *Exceptional Children, 36,* 317–323.

Cruickshank, W. M., Bentzen, F. A., Ratzeburg, F. H., & Tannhauser, R. (1961). *A teaching method for brain-injured and hyperactive children.* Syracuse, NY: Syracuse University Press.

Douglas, V. I. (1972). Stop, look and listen: The problem of sustained attention and impulse control in hyperactive and normal children. *Canadian Journal of Behavioral Science, 4,* 259–282.

Douglas, V. I. (1974). Sustained attention and impulse control: Implications for the handicapped child. In J. A. Swets & L. L. Elliott (Eds.), *Psychology and the handicapped child* (DHEW, Pub. No. (OE) 73-05000). Washington, DC: U.S. Department of Education and Welfare.

Faison, M. W., & Bernikis E. A. (1993). *A systematic approach to the treatment of ADHD: An intervention model.* (ERIC Clearinghouse No. EC30311)

Gadow, K. (1981). Effects of stimulant drugs on attention and cognitive deficits. *Exceptional Child Quarterly, 2*(3), 83–93.

Goyette, C. H., Connors, C. K., & Ulrich, R. F. (1978). Normative data on revised Connors parent and teacher rating scales. *Journal of Abnormal and Child Psychology, 6,* 221–236.

Hewett, F. M., Taylor, F. D., & Artuso, D. A. (1969). The Santa Monica Project. Evaluation of an engineered classroom design with emotionally disturbed children. *Exceptional Children, 33,* 523–529.

Ianna, S. O., Hallahan, D. P., & Bell, R. Q. (1982). The effects of distractible child behavior on adults in a problem-solving setting. *Learning Disabilities Quarterly, 5,* 126–132.

Kaufman, A. S. (1979). *Intelligent testing with the WISC-R.* New York: Wiley.

Kneedler, R. D., & Hallahan, D. P. (1981). Self-monitoring of on-task behavior with learning-disabled children: Current studies and directions. *Exceptional Child Quarterly, 2*(3), 73–82.

Krupski, A. (1981, August). *Variations in attention as a function of classroom task demands.* Paper presented at the meeting of the American Psychological Association, Los Angeles, CA.

Milich, R., Loney, J., & Landau, S. (1982). Independent dimensions of hyperactivity and aggression: A validation with playroom observation data. *Journal of Abnormal Psychology, 91,* 183–198.

O'Donnell, J. P., O'Neill, S. O., & Staley, A. (1979). Congenital correlates of distractibility. *Journal of Abnormal Child Psychology, 7,* 465–470.

Ricks, N. L., & Mirsky, A. F. (1974). Sustained attention and the effects of distraction in underachieving second grade children. *Journal of Education, 156,* 4–17.

Ross, A. O. (1976). *Psychological aspects of learning disabilities and reading disorders.* New York: McGraw-Hill.

Sandoval, J. (1982). Hypreactive children. 12 Ways to help them in the classroom. *Academic Therapy, 18,* 107–113.

Soli, S. D., & Devine, V. T. (1976). Behavioral correlates of achievements: A look at high and low achievers. *Journal of Educational Psychology, 68,* 335–341.

Stedman, J. M., Lawlis, G. F., & Cortner, R. H. (1978). Relationships between WISC-R factors, Wide Range Achievement Test scores, and visual-motor maturation in children referred for psychological evaluation. *Journal of Consulting & Clinical Psychology, 46,* 869–872.

Tarver, S. G., & Hallahan, D. P. (1974). Attention deficits in children with learning disabilities: A review. *Journal of Learning Disabilities, 1,* 560–569.

Torgesen, J. K. (1981). Relationship between memory and attention in learning disabilities. *Exceptional Child Quarterly, 2*(3), 51–59.

Well, A. D., Lorch, E. P., & Anderson, D. R. (1980). Developmental trends in distractibility: Is absolute or proportional decrement the appropriate measure of interference? *Journal of Experimental Child Psychology, 30,* 109–124.

Whalen, C. K. (1983). Hyperactivity, learning problems, and the attention deficit disorders. In T. H. Ollendick & M. Hersen (Eds.), Handbook of child psychopathology (pp. 151–199). New York: Plenum.

Wolfson, L. (1995). Attentional skills and 5–14. *Scottish Educational Review, 27,* 2, 138–145.

Wunderlich, R. C. (1981). Nutrition and learning. *Academic Therapy, 16,* 303-307.

Zigler, C. (1973). Why retarded children do not perform up to the level of their ability. In R. M. Allen, A. D. Cortazzo, & R. P. Toister (Eds.), *Theories of cognitive development: Implications for the mentally retarded* (pp. 13–35). Coral Cables, FL: University of Miami Press.

MARK E. SWERDLIK
Illinois State University

DIVISION OF INTERNATIONAL SPECIAL EDUCATION AND SERVICES (DISES)

In June, 1978, the Council for Exceptional Children held the first World Congress on Future Special Education in Stirling, Scotland (Fink, 1978). Following that meeting in order to preserve the momentum created by this Congress, some university faculty members organized a special interest group within the CEC's Teacher Education Division. This group was concerned primarily with the international aspects of delivery of special education services to children with disabilities. Since the scope of interest went beyond teacher education, a separate division of the CEC, known as the Division of International Special Education and Services (DISES), was formed in 1990 with the mission of assisting in the improvement of the quality of special education and services to individuals with disabilities throughout the world.

With the breakup of the USSR and the movement away from communism in the former Soviet republics, DISES established relations with several organizations serving children with disabilities, especially in St. Petersburg and Moscow, Russia; Latvia; Lithuania; and Kazakhstan. In 1993, working with Project Concern International, DISES identified special educators to assist adolescents who had been institutionalized in Romania to function independently. Also during 1993, DISES served as the international portion of a COSMOS Corporation project to identify trends in the delivery of special education services, and to anticipate how educational technology could be used effectively for students with disabilities throughout the world. In 1995, DISES, working with the Citizen Ambassador Program of People to People International, led a special education delegation visiting programs in China.

DISES has also been active in disseminating information about special education programs worldwide through its newsletter and special publications. Four monographs have been published, and a professional journal, *The Journal of International Special Needs Education (JISNE)* began publication in 1998. The editors of the DISES newsletter are Bob Henderson of the University of Illinois (bob-h@uiuc.edu), Lisa Dieker of the University of Wisconsin-Milwaukee (dieker@csd.uwm.edu), and Yash Bhagwanj (bhagwanj@students.uiuc.edu); and the editor of *JISNE* is Robert Michael (michaelr@npvm.newpaltz. edu).

Another major activity of DISES has been the organization of the Special Education World Congress 2000 (SEWC 2000), held in Vancouver, British Columbia during April 2–5, 2000. Building on previous conferences, SEWC 2000 involves partnerships with the other CEC divisions; professional organizations dealing with various disabilities, such as the American Association on Mental Retardation and the American Foundation for the Blind; international groups such as UNESCO, the World Health Organization, the International Association of Special Education, and Rehabilitation International; and special education offices in various Ministries of Education. A unique feature of SEWC 2000 has been the use of the internet to conduct "cyber seminars," in which participants read and commented on professional papers that were published on the SEWC 2000 web page (http://cid.unomaha.edu/~wwwsped/wc/2000.html).

REFERENCE

Fink, A. H. (1978.) *International Perspectives on Future Special Education*. Reston, VA: Council for Exceptional Children.

DIVORCE AND SPECIAL EDUCATION

Since the mid 1970s, the impact of parental divorce on children has been an area of concern for professionals in psychology and education. This interdisciplinary consensus has been generated in part by alarming Census descriptions of rapidly changing adult lifestyles. For example, Census reports indicate that the divorce rate more than quadrupled from 1970 to 1994. Since these figures do not account for those who were divorced and remarried at the time of the survey, they actually underestimate the total incidence of divorce in our society. Similarly, the incidence of single-parent child rearing has also increased markedly, from 11.9% in 1970 to 29% in 1994. These figures do not include those who have previously experienced a single-parent situation but are now living in reconstituted two-parent families.

A central issue is whether adjustment to divorce represents a transitory stressor or is associated with long-term disorders. Longitudinal studies provide a consensus that divorce should be conceptualized as a multistage process (Hetherington, Cox, & Cox, 1978, 1985; Wallerstein, 1985; Wallerstein & Kelly, 1974). These studies, conducted over periods of 6 and 10 years, respectively, reveal complex interactions and altered family relationships that result in long-term maladjustment for children. They also illustrate substantial age and sex differences in adjustment.

Wallerstein and Kelly (Kelly & Wallerstein, 1976; Wallerstein, 1984, 1985; Wallerstein & Kelly, 1974, 1975, 1976, 1980a, 1980b) conducted a 10-year longitudinal study of 131 children residing in Marin County, California, whose parents were divorced. This was a nonclinical sample of children, ages 2½ to 18 years, from white, middle-class families. Clinical interviews were conducted just after separation, and at 1-, 5-, and 10-year intervals following divorce. Initial results revealed that children responded differently by age. At the 1-year follow-up, adjustment problems persisted, although most adolescents had made adequate adjustments (attributed to distancing from parents and successful mastery experiences during the past year). At the 5-year follow-up, variables that mediate children's adjustment to divorce were identified—resolution of parental conflict, child's relationship with noncustodial parent, quality of parenting by custodial parent, personality and coping skills of the child, child's support system, diminished anger and depression in the child, and age and sex of the child. A positive relationship with the father was more important for boys than girls. Results of the 10-year follow-up (of 113 original subjects) confirmed the long-term impact of divorce. Difficulties at 10 years were characterized by poor parenting (diminished capacity to parent) and an overburdened child (taking on of adult responsibility).

Hetherington, Cox, and Cox (Hetherington, 1979; Hetherington, Cox, & Cox, 1978, 1979a, 1979b, 1982, 1985) used a sample of 96 divorced- and intact-family preschoolage children from white, middle-class families in Virginia. Children were assessed at 2 months, and 1, 2, and 6 years after divorce. A comprehensive, multifactored, multisource approach to assessment was used to assess sex-role typing and cognitive and social development of the child.

Results indicated severe disorganization and stress during the first year. Difficulties were evident in parenting behavior and child adjustment. Divorced parents were less able than nondivorced parents to cope with parenting. They made fewer maturity demands, were less consistent in discipline, used less reasoning, communicated less with the child, and displayed less interaction with and affection toward the child. Children were more dependent, disobedient, aggressive, demanding, unaffectionate, and whining. Mother-son relationships were particularly affected, characterized by a cycle of poor parenting, child aggression, coercive parenting, increased negative child behavior, and parental feelings of helplessness and incompetence. By 2 years, most of the negative effects had abated. Factors that facilitated adjustment included low parental conflict and parental agreement on child rearing. Results at 6 years (which included a remarried sample) indicated that divorce had a more negative impact on boys and remarriage had a more negative impact on girls. Externalizing problems were more stable across time for boys and internalizing problems more stable for girls. Divorced-family children experienced more negative life changes, which were, in turn, related to more behavior problems at follow-up.

Kurdek et al. (Kurdek, 1981, 1983, 1985, 1987; Kurdek & Berg, 1983; Kurdek, Blisk, & Siesky, 1981; Kurdek & Siesky, 1980a, 1980b; Kurdek & Sinclair, 1985) examined the role of cognitive mediators in children's adjustment to divorce. Their initial study included a sample of 70 divorced-family children, mean age of 9.92 years, from white middle-class families in Dayton, Ohio, whose parents were members of Parents Without Partners. Results revealed that children's adjustment to divorce was facilitated by an internal locus of control, accurate perceptions of social situations (i.e., understanding of interpersonal relations), low interpersonal stress, and good father-child relation-

ships. They found that children's reasoning about divorce was linked to the development of logical and social reasoning. Further, level of cognitive understanding determined whether the child's thinking about divorce was nonegocentric; focused on parents' thoughts, feelings, and intentions; and was grounded in an appreciation of the complex dynamics of interpersonal relations.

Using a national sample of 18,000 elementary and secondary students from 14 states, Brown (1980) compared one-parent (divorced, separated, widowed, unmarried) and two-parent families. Global measures of adjustment such as grade point average, attendance, suspensions, truancy, and referral for discipline problems were obtained from school records. Findings indicated that the impact for elementary-aged children was evident on behavioral (e.g., suspensions and truancy) and academic indexes. For high-school children, differences were evident on behavioral indexes (e.g., expulsions, tardiness, suspensions); however, there appeared to be little impact on academic achievement.

The research of Stolberg et al. (Stolberg, 1987; Stolberg & Anker, 1983; Stolberg & Bush, 1985; Stolberg & Cullen, 1983; Stolberg, Kiluk, & Garrison, 1986) has focused on environmental factors that mediate children's adjustment to divorce, including such factors as parenting skills, visitation, and family changes associated with divorce. Local samples obtained through Parents Without Partners, newspaper ads, and schools were used. They found parenting skills, frequency of life changes, and marital hostility to be successful predictors of prosocial skills and psychopathology of divorced-family children. Parenting skills (of the mother/custodial parent) were found to be the single most significant influence on child adjustment, particularly affecting prosocial skills. There was no direct relationship between parent and child adjustment when effects of parenting skills were removed.

Furstenberg et al. (Furstenberg et al., 1983; Furstenberg & Spanier, 1984) used data from a national sociological study of children's well being. The representative sample included 1300 U.S. children (ages 11 to 16) and their families, and subsequent subsamples of divorced and remarried families. Findings from this study revealed a racial difference in divorce and remarriage rates, with blacks one and a half times as likely to divorce but less likely to remarry than whites (remarriage rate: one out of eight for blacks, four out of seven for whites). Frequent contact (at least once per week) of the child with the noncustodial parent was evident in only 17% of the divorced sample. Those variables that best predicted amount of contact with the noncustodial parent, irrespective of the child's sex, included provision of child support and residential propinquity, which were positively related to amount of contact, and length of time since separation, which was negatively related.

Findings from other studies relevant to determinants of

children's postdivorce adjustment indicate that adjustment is facilitated by availability of the noncustodial parent and a positive relationship with the custodial parent (Hess & Camara, 1979); parent-child discussion of divorce-related topics (Jacobson, 1978a, 1978b); low interpersonal hostility prior to separation (Berg & Kelly, 1979; Jacobson, 1978a, 1978b, 1978c); and more time spent with the father (Jacobson, 1978a, 1978c).

In reviewing the literature on remarriage, Kurdek and Sinclair (1985) conclude that similarities exist between children's adjustment to divorce and to remarriage in that children from both situations (compared with those in intact families) exhibit higher deviance rates, more difficulty in management, and lower self-esteem, as do their parents. Although findings are conflicting, past research generally indicates that (1) remarriage does not necessarily stabilize the family; (2) children reexperience the disruption associated with divorce when parents remarry; and (3) the parent's situation in reference to role strain does not necessarily improve with remarriage.

Critical reviews of past research have consistently indicated severe methodological limitations (Atkeson, Forehand, & Rickard, 1982; Clingempeel & Reppucci, 1982; Kurdek, 1981, 1983). Major limitations include (1) small and biased samples that limit generalizability of the findings; (2) inadequate or nonexistent control groups, which precludes the study of divorce-specific effects; (3) failure to control for socioeconomic status in comparisons between divorced and intact families; and (4) failure to include multimethod, multifactored criteria to control for measurement bias.

The NASP-KSU (National Association of School Psychologists—Kent State University) Impact of Divorce Project was directed at minimizing the limitations of the cited research in order to provide more definitive conclusions about the long-term impact of divorce on children (Guidubaldi, 1983, 1985; Guidubaldi & Cleminshaw, 1985; Guidubaldi, Cleminshaw, & Perry, 1985; Guidubaldi, Cleminshaw, Perry, & Mcloughlin, 1983; Guidubaldi, Cleminshaw, Perry, & Nastasi, 1984; Guidubaldi, Cleminshaw, Perry, Nastasi, & Lightel, 1986; Guidubaldi & Nastasi, 1984; Guidubaldi & Perry, 1985, 1987, Guidubaldi, Perry, & Cleminshaw, 1984; Guidubaldi, Perry, & Nastasi, 1986. Results on 699 children from 38 states at the initial data-gathering period (Time-1) demonstrated more conclusively than previous studies that, during middle childhood (ages 6 to 11), youths are adversely affected by divorce. Because the average length of time in a single-parent home at Time-1 was 3.98 years (sd = 2.54), these effects were interpreted as long term. Specific criteria on which children from divorced homes performed more poorly than those from intact homes are as follows: (1) social-behavioral measures from parent and teacher ratings of peer popularity status, anxiety, dependency, aggression, withdrawal, inattention, and locus of control;

(2) Wechsler IQ scores; (3) Wide Range Achievement Test scores in reading, spelling, and math; (4) school performance indexes, including grades in reading and math and repeating of a school grade; (5) adaptive behaviors (measured by the Vineland Teacher Rating Scale) in the areas of daily living, social skills, and communication; and (6) physical health ratings of the children in the study as well as of parents and siblings. Intact-family children showed superior performance on 21 of 27 social competence criteria and 8 of 9 academic competence criteria. Additionally, analyses revealed that divorced-family children were far more likely to have been previously referred to a school psychologist, to have been retained in grade, and to be in special class placements, including programs for reading difficulties.

Definition of the sequelae of divorce is a complex process, and assessment must therefore include not only multidimensional aspects of child and parent adjustment but also a longitudinal-ecological approach. The NASP-KSU study thus included follow-up samples of 229 children at 2- and 3-year intervals, and examined environmental factors as mediators of children's postdivorce adjustment. Major findings from this nationwide study are as follows:

1. The negative, differential effects of divorce on children and young adolescents are long term where the average length of time since divorce was 6.41 years (sd = 2.35) at Time-2 of this study.

2. Children's reactions to divorce are especially influenced by sex and age, with boys during late childhood and early adolescence being more adversely affected on multiple criteria than 6- and 7-year-old boys. Late childhood and young adolescent girls were much better adjusted than those at the 6- and 7-year age levels.

3. Single-parent, divorced-family households have significantly less income than intact families. This difference accounts for significant academic achievement variance between divorced- and intact-family children.

4. The socioeconomic measures of parents' educational and occupational levels moderate some of children's divorce adjustment. This is especially apparent in regard to the educational level of the same sex parent.

5. A positive relationship with both the custodial and noncustodial parent predicted positive adjustment for both girls and boys of divorce concurrently and across time. The noncustodial parent-child relationship was noticeably more important for boys.

6. More frequent and reliable visitation with the noncustodial parent (typically, the father) was associated with better adjustment for both girls and boys.

7. Diminished degree of conflict between parents predicted improved children's adjustment, especially for boys across time to early adolescence.

8. Authoritarian (i.e., punitive) child-rearing styles in comparison with authoritative (i.e., more democratic) and permissive styles predicted more adverse child adjustment, especially for boys.

9. The home routines of less television viewing, regular bedtimes, maternal employment, and helpfulness of maternal grandfather predict positive adjustment for both boys and girls.

10. Family support factors that promote positive postdivorce adjustment are availability of helpful relatives, including in-laws, availability of friends, paid child care assistance such as nursery schools and babysitters, and participation in occupational and educational endeavors by the custodial parent.

11. When the total sample of male and female divorcedfamily children are considered, school environment variables of smaller school population, safe and orderly atmosphere, fewer miles bused to school, and traditional rather than open classroom structure are associated with better adjustment. However, several school and classroom climate factors relate to better adjustment for girls only. These include safe and orderly environment, frequent monitoring of student progress, high expectations for academic achievement, and time on task.

The impact of divorce on children has appropriately become a central concern of mainstreamed education. Special educators perhaps need to focus even more on this rapidly increasing disruption of children's lives. As evidenced in the NASP-KSU nationwide study and in Beattie & Maniscalo (1985), children in special education programs disproportionately come from divorced, single-parent homes. Income levels, home routines, and parental supports are adversely affected by this condition and children from these homes, particularly boys, show overwhelming evidence of maladjustment in both academic and socialemotional areas of performance. Understanding conditions that can ameliorate the negative impact of divorce on children may be one of the most critical bases for development of preventive mental health interventions as well as remedial techniques for children already identified as special.

REFERENCES

Atkeson, B. M., Forehand, R. L., & Rickard, K. M. (1982). The effects of divorce on children. In B. B. Lahey & A. E. Kazdin (Eds.), *Advances in clinical child psychology* (Vol. 5). New York: Plenum.

Baumrind, D. (1972). Socialization and instrumental competence in young children. In I. B. Weiner & D. Elkind (Eds.), *Readings in child development* (pp. 178–195). New York: Wiley.

Beattie, J. R., & Maniscalo, G. O. (1985). Special education and divorce. Is there a line? *Techniques, 1,* 5, 342–345.

Berg, B., & Kelly, R. (1979). The measured self-esteem of children from broken, rejected, and accepted families. *Journal of Divorce, 2,* 263–369.

Brown, B. F. (1980). A study of the school needs of children from one-parent families. *Phi Delta Kappan, 62,* 537–540.

Clingempeel, W. G., & Reppucci, N. D. (1982). Joint custody after divorce: Major issues and goals for research. *Psychological Bulletin, 91,* 102–127.

Furstenberg, F. F., Nord, C. W., Peterson, J. L., & Zill, N. (1983) The life course of children of divorce: Marital disruption and parental contact. *American Sociological Review, 48,* 656–668.

Furstenberg, F. F., & Spanier, G. B. (1984). *Recycling the family.* Beverly Hills, CA: Sage.

Glick, P. C., & Norton, A. J. (1977). Marrying, divorcing and living together in the U.S. today. *Population Bulletin, 5,* 32.

Guidubaldi, J. (1983, July). Divorce research clarifies issues: A report on NASP's nationwide study. *Communique, 10,* 1–3.

Guidubaldi, J. (1985). Differences in children's divorce adjustment across grade level and gender: A report from the NASP-Kent State University Nationwide Project. In S. Wolchik & P. Karoly (Eds.), *Children of divorce: Perspectives on adjustment.* Lexington, MA: Lexington.

Guidubaldi, J., & Cleminshaw, H. (1985). Divorce, family health and child adjustment. *Family Relations, 34,* 35–41.

Guidubaldi, J., Cleminshaw, H., & Perry, J. (1985). The relationship of parental divorce to health status of parents and children. *Special Services in the Schools, 1,* 73–81.

Guidubaldi, J., Cleminshaw, H. K., Perry, J. D., & Mcloughlin, C. S. (1983). The impact of parental divorce on children: Report of the nationwide NASP study. *School Psychology Review, 12,* 300–323.

Guidubaldi, J., Cleminshaw, H. K., Perry, J., & Nastasi, B. (1984). Impact of family support systems on children's academic and social functioning after divorce. In G. Rowe, J. DeFrain, H. Lingrin, R. MacDonald, N. Stinnet, S. Van Zandt, & R. Williams (Eds.), *Family strengths 5: Continuity and diversity* (pp. 191–207). Newton, MA: Education Development Center.

Guidubaldi, J., Cleminshaw, H. K. Perry, J. D., Nastasi, B. K., & Lightel, J. (1986). The role of selected family environment factors in, children's post-divorce adjustment. *Family Relations, 35,* 141–151.

Guidubaldi, J., & Nastasi, B. (1984, April). Classroom climate and post-divorce child adjustment. In J. Guidubaldi (Chair), *Factors related to academic and social adjustment of elementary grade divorced-family children.* Symposium conducted at the annual convention of the American Educational Research Association, New Orleans.

Guidubaldi, J., & Perry, J. D. (1985). Divorce and mental health sequelae for children: A two-year follow-up of a nationwide sample. *Journal of the American Academy of Child Psychiatry, 24,* 531–537.

Guidubaldi, J., & Perry, J. D. (1987) Assessment of adolescents' divorce adjustment and custody arrangements. In R. G. Harrington (Ed.), *Testing adolescents*. Kansas City: Test Corporation of America.

Guidubaldi, J., Perry, J. D., & Cleminshaw, H. K. (1984). The legacy of parental divorce: A nationwide study of family status and selected mediating variables on children's academic and social competencies. In B. B. Lahey & A. E. Kazdin (Eds.), *Advances in clinical child psychology* (Vol. 7, pp. 109–151). New York: Plenum.

Guidubaldi, J., Perry, J. D., & Nastasi, B. K. (1986). Growing up in a divorced family: Initial and long-term perspectives on children's adjustment. In S. Oskamp (Ed.), *Annual review of social psychology*. Beverly Hills, CA: Sage.

Hess, R. D., & Camara, K. A. (1979). Post-divorce family relationships as mediating factors in the consequences of divorce for children. *Journal of Social Issues, 35*(4), 79–96.

Hetherington, E. M. (1979). Divorce: A child's perspective. *American Psychologist, 34,* 851–858.

Hetherington, E. M., Cox, M., & Cox, R. (1978). The aftermath of divorce. In J. H. Stevens, Jr., & M. Mathews (Eds.), *Mother-child, father-child relationships* (pp. 149–176). Washington, DC: National Association for Education of Young Children.

Hetherington, E. M., Cox, M., & Cox, R. (1979a). Family interaction and the social-emotional and cognitive development of children following divorce. In V. Vaughn & T. Brazelton (Eds.), *The family setting priorities*. New York: Science and Medicine.

Hetherington, E. M., Cox, M., & Cox, R. (1979b). Play and social interaction in children following divorce. *Journal of Social Issues, 35,* 26–49.

Hetherington, E. M., Cox, M., & Cox, R. (1982). Effects of divorce on parents and children. In M. E. Lamb (Ed.), *Nontraditional families: Parenting and child development* (pp. 233–288). Hillsdale, NJ: Erlbaum.

Hetherington, E. M., Cox, M., & Cox, R. (1985). Long-term effects of divorce and remarriage on the adjustment of children. *Journal of the American Academy of Child Psychiatry, 24,* 518–530.

Jacobson, D. S. (1978a). The impact of marital separation/divorce on children. I. Parent-child separation and child adjustment. *Journal of Divorce, 1*(4), 341–360.

Jacobson, D. S. (1978b). The impact of marital separation/divorce on children: II. Interparent hostility and child adjustment. *Journal of Divorce, 2,* 3–19.

Jacobson, D. S. (1978c). The impact of marital separation/divorce on children: III. Parent-child communication and child adjustment, and regression analysis of findings from overall study. *Journal of Divorce, 2,* 175–194.

Jenkins, J. E., & Guidubaldi, J. (1997). Nature-Nurture Controversy Revisited: Divorce and gender as factors in children's racial group differences. *Child Study Journal, 27,* 2, 145–160.

Kelly, J. B., & Wallerstein, J. S. (1976). The effects of parental divorce: Experiences of the child in early latency. American *Journal of Orthopsychiatry, 46,* 20–23.

Kurdek, L. A. (1981). An integrative perspective on children's divorce adjustment. *American Psychologist, 36,* 856–866.

Kurdek, L. A. (Ed.). (1983). *Children and divorce*. San Francisco: Jossey-Bass.

Kurdek, L. A. (1985). Children's reasoning about parental divorce. In R. D. Ashmore & D. M. Brodzinsky (Eds.), *Perspectives on the family* (pp. 1–48). Hillsdale, NJ: Erlbaum.

Kurdek, L. A. (1987). Cognitive mediators of children's adjustment to divorce. In S. Wolchick & D. Karoly (Eds.), *Children of divorce: Perspectives on adjustment*. New York: Gardner.

Kurdek, L. A., & Berg, B. (1983). Correlates of children's adjustment to their parents' divorces. In L. A. Kurdek (Ed.), *Children and divorce* (pp. 47–60). San Francisco: Jossey-Bass.

Kurdek, L. A., Blisk, D., & Siesky, A. E. (1981). Correlates of children's long-term adjustment to their parents' divorce. *Developmental Psychology, 17,* 565–579.

Kurdek, L. A., & Siesky, A. E. (1980a). Sex role self-concepts of single divorced parents and their children. *Journal of Divorce, 3,* 249–261.

Kurdek, L. A., & Siesky, A. E. (1980b). Children's perceptions of their parents' divorce. *Journal of Divorce, 3,* 339–378.

Kurdek, L. A., & Sinclair, R. (1985). *The relation between adolescent adjustment and family structure, grade, and gender*. Unpublished manuscript, Wright State University, Department of Psychology, Dayton, OH.

Stolberg, A. L. (1987). Prevention programs for divorcing families. In L. Bond (Ed.), *Vermont Conference on the Primary Prevention of Psychopathology*.

Stolberg, A., & Anker, J. (1983). Cognitive and behavioral changes in children resulting from parental divorce and consequent environmental changes. *Journal of Divorce, 7,* 23–41.

Stolberg, A. L., & Bush, J. P. (1985). A path analysis of factors predicting children's divorce adjustment. *Journal of Clinical Child Psychology, 14,* 49–54.

Stolberg, A. L., & Cullen, P. M. (1983). Preventive interventions for families of divorce: Divorce Adjustment Project. In L. A. Kurdek (Ed.), *Children and divorce* (pp. 71–82). San Francisco: Jossey-Bass.

Stolberg, A. L., Kiluk, D., & Garrison, K. M. (1986). A temporal model of divorce adjustment with implications for primary prevention. In S. M. Auerbach & A. L. Stolberg (Eds.), *Issues in clinical and community psychology: Crisis intervention with children and families*. Washington, DC: Hemisphere.

U.S. Bureau of the Census. (1979). *Divorce, child custody, and child support* (Current Population Reports, Series P-23, No. 84). Washington, DC: U.S. Government Printing Office.

U.S. Bureau of the Census. (1982a). *Household and family characteristics: March 1981* (Current Population Reports, Series P-20, No. 371). Washington, DC: U.S. Government Printing Office.

U.S. Bureau of the Census. (1982b). *Marital status and living arrangements: March 1981* (Current Population Reports, Series P-20, No. 372). Washington, DC: U.S. Government Printing Office.

U.S. Bureau of the Census. (1984). *Marital status and living arrangements: March 1983* (Current Population Reports, Series P-20). Washington, DC: U.S. Government Printing Office.

Wallerstein, J. S. (1984). Children of divorce: Preliminary report of a ten-year follow-up of young children. *American Journal of Orthopsychiatry, 54,* 444–453.

Wallerstein, J. S. (1985). Children of divorce: Preliminary report of a ten-year follow-up of older children and adolescents. *Journal of the American Academy of Child Psychiatry, 24,* 545–553.

Wallerstein, J. S., & Kelly, J. B. (1974). The effects of parental divorce: The adolescent experience. In E. Anthony & C. Koupanik (Eds.), *The child and his family* (Vol. 3, pp. 479–505). New York: Wiley.

Wallerstein, J. S., & Kelly, J. B. (1975). The effects of parental divorce: Experiences of the preschool child. *Journal of the American Academy of Child Psychiatry, 14,* 600–616.

Wallerstein, J. S., & Kelly, J. B. (1976). The effects of parental divorce experiences of the child in later latency. *American Journal of Orthopsychiatry, 46,* 256–267.

Wallerstein, J. S., & Kelly, J. B. (1980a). California's children of divorce. *Psychology Today, 13,* 66–67.

Wallerstein, J. S., & Kelly, J. B. (1980b). *Surviving the break-up: How children and parents cope with divorce.* New York: Basic Books.

JOHN GUIDUBALDI
BONNIE K. NASTASI
Kent State University

DIX, DOROTHEA L. (1802–1887)

Dorothea Dix, a humanitarian and social reformer, was responsible for major reforms in the care of the mentally ill in the United States and abroad. Shocked by the common practice of incarcerating mentally ill people in jails with criminals, she spent a year and a half investigating conditions in her home state of Massachusetts and, in 1843, reported her findings to the state legislature. Her description of the abhorrent conditions that existed (including the use of chains for restraint) and her argument that mentally ill

Dorthea L. Dix

persons could be properly treated and cared for only in hospitals, resulted in substantial enlargement of the state hospital at Worcester, which was one of only eight mental hospitals in the United States at that time. Capitalizing on her success in Massachusetts, Dix turned her attention to other states and countries. She was responsible for the construction of 32 hospitals in the United States and others in Canada, Europe, and Japan.

During the Civil War, Dix served as superintendent of women nurses, the highest office held by a woman during the war. After the war she returned, at age 65, to her work with hospitals. In 1881 she retired to the New Jersey State Hospital at Trenton, the first hospital established through her efforts, where she remained until her death.

REFERENCE

Marshall, H. E. (1937). *Dorothea Dix, forgotten samaritan.* Chapel Hill, NC: University of North Carolina Press.

PAUL IRVINE
Katonah, New York

DOCTORAL TRAINING IN SPECIAL EDUCATION

Over 80 special education programs in colleges and universities in the United States award the doctoral degree (Sindelar & Schloss, 1986). The common purpose of these programs is to prepare leaders for the field, but the programs themselves are as diverse as the roles their graduates assume. Many local, state, and federal administrators, college and university teacher trainers, scholars, and researchers hold the doctorate in special education. Both the doctor of philosophy (PhD) and the doctor of education (DEd or EdD) are awarded. Although the PhD is considered an academic degree and the DEd a professional degree, this distinction does not hold up in practice because many prominent scholars hold the DEd and many practitioners the PhD.

Students are typically selected for doctoral training on the basis of their potential for success in advanced graduate training and the potential they exhibit as special education leaders. Programs frequently use the previous academic achievement of their applicants and Graduate Record Examination scores (or both) to predict success in advanced graduate work. Leadership potential is evaluated through previous professional experience, professional references, and, occasionally, statements of professional goals (by which the seriousness of an applicant's intent may be judged). Typically, admission is competitive.

A program of study is planned under the direction of an advisor (or major professor) and a supervisory committee.

The program typically derives from the aspirations of the student and the strengths of the program offerings. In addition to special education course work, doctoral programs may include concentrations in a related field of study or cognate area and work in research methodology and statistics. The successful completion of coursework, however, represents only a fraction of the formal requirements that a doctoral candidate must meet. Many programs require a qualifying examination before formal admission to candidacy and, later in the program, a comprehensive examination to determine mastery of the program of studies. Doctoral programs culminate with the completion of an independent research project and the preparation and defense of the dissertation. The supervisory committee evaluates the student's performance at each of these checkpoints.

These formal requirements represent only part of what students learn during their doctoral studies. Many have the opportunity (often as graduate assistants) to develop skills in teaching, supervision, administration, and research. Initially, their participation in these activities is guided by the faculty. With experience, candidates may take on more responsibility and operate with greater independence. Many programs provide financial support for graduate assistants with funds from leadership preparation grants awarded by the U.S. Department of Education's Office of Special Education and Rehabilitative Services.

The importance of these informal experiences in the full preparation of doctoral students was established in an analysis of the credentials of recent graduates. Rose, Cullinan, and Heller (1984) reported that recent graduates who were considered competitive applicants for college and university positions had published at least three articles, presented more than four papers at national conferences, written or assisted in the writing of two grant applications, taught at least one course independently, and conducted numerous workshops and consultancies. Clearly, there is much to be accomplished beyond the formal requirements of a doctoral program for its graduates to compete successfully in the academic job market.

Finally, it must be emphasized that leadership preparation programs have undertaken a critical self-evaluation in response to the common and difficult problems they face: the quantity and quality of students, the poor focus of their offerings, faculty dissatisfaction, and low faculty productivity (Prehm, 1984). With regard to this final concern, recent research (Schloss & Sindelar, 1985) has shown that productive researchers are the exception and not the rule, even for faculties of doctoral-granting programs. The recent efforts of the Higher Education Consortium for Special Education, an organization representing institutions with comprehensive programs in special education, in developing indicators of quality in leadership training represent a positive first step in addressing these issues. There

has been a call for a national data collection system to address a critical shortage of doctoral-level specialists (Smith, 1990).

REFERENCES

Prehm, H. J. (1984). Preparation for leadership in personnel preparation. *Teacher Education & Special Education, 7,* 59–65.

Rose, T. L., Cullinan, D., & Heller, H. W. (1984). A consumer's report of special education doctoral programs. *Teacher Education & Special Education, 7,* 88–91.

Schloss, P. J., & Sindelar, P. T. (1985). Publication frequencies of departments conferring the PhD in special education. *Teacher Education and Special Education.*

Sindelar, P. T., & Schloss, P. J. (1986). The reputations of doctoral training program in special education. *Journal of Special Education, 20,* 49–59.

Smith, D. D. (1990) *History and future needs of doctoral training in special education.* (ERIC Clearinghouse No. EC301042)

PAUL T. SINDELAR
Florida State University

SPECIAL NET
SUPERVISION IN SPECIAL EDUCATION
TEACHER CENTERS

DOG GUIDES FOR THE BLIND

The use of dogs to guide blind persons has a long history. However, it was not until after World War I that the dog was systematically trained to guide blinded German veterans. The veterans were taught to follow the trained dog's movements through the use of a specially designed harness.

An American, Dorothy Harrison Eustis, living in Switzerland, described the use of German shepherds as dog guides for the blind in a 1927 article published in the *Saturday Evening Post.* One of the Americans who got in touch with Eustis after the publication of the article was Morris Frank, a young man from Tennessee who had been recently blinded. He persuaded Eustis to have a dog trained for him and traveled to Switzerland to be trained with the dog.

After Frank's success with the first American dog guide, the legendary Buddy, Eustis returned to the United States in 1929 and established The Seeing Eye Inc., the first school to train dog guides for the blind in America. The twenty-second edition of the American Foundation for the Blind *Directory of Agencies Serving the Blind in the United States* lists eight programs in the United States that prepare dog guides. There are similar training programs throughout the world.

The dog guide, because of a variety of limitations, provides mobility assistance to only about 1% of the blind population (Whitstock, 1980). However, the introduction of guide dogs has led to a greater acceptance of blind travelers and has helped a shift in perception of the blind (Blasch & Stuckey, 1995). Personal preferences, remaining vision, vocation, and life circumstances often dictate the advisability of the use of a dog guide. Very few school-aged visually impaired persons use dog guides, although the practice is not prohibited.

REFERENCES

American Foundation for the Blind. (1984). *Directory of agencies serving the visually handicapped in the U.S.* (22nd ed.). New York: Author.

Blasch, B. B., & Stuckey, R. A. (1995). Accessibility and mobility of persons who are visually impaired: A historical analysis. *Journal of Visual Impairment, 89,* 5, 417–422.

Whitstock, R. H. (1980). Dog guides. In R. L. Welsh & B. B. Blasch (Eds.), *Foundations of orientation and mobility.* New York: American Foundation for the Blind.

GIDEON JONES
Florida State University

AMERICAN FOUNDATION FOR THE BLIND
MOBILITY TRAINING

DOLCH WORD LIST

The Dolch Word List of 220 common words constitutes over 65% of the words found in elementary reading materials and 50% of all reading materials (Dolch, 1960). These high-frequency words form the framework for all reading materials. The list, developed by Edward W. Dolch, includes prepositions, conjunctions, pronouns, adjectives, adverbs, and the most common verbs. There are no nouns included in this list since each noun, according to Dolch, is tied to subject matter (Johns, 1971). The list is comprised of structure words, words that hold language together, as opposed to content words.

The average third-grade reader should be able to identify these 220 service words at sight. Many of the words have irregular spellings and cannot be learned by picture cues. Dolch (1939) reports that if the reader is able to recognize more than half the words at the sight reading rate of 120 words per minute, he or she will have confidence and will be able focus on the meaning of the material.

The Dolch Word List is frequently used as a diagnostic tool to identify poor readers (Elmquist, 1987). Many retarded readers are deficient in recognizing and understanding the proper use of these words. The list also serves as the basis of remedial instruction. Garrard Publishers produces several materials, Popper Words, Basic Sight Vocabulary Cards, and Basic Sight Word Test, based on the list.

REFERENCES

Dolch, E. W. (1939). *A manual of remedial reading.* Champaign, IL: Garrard.

Dolch, E. W. (1960). *Teaching primary reading.* Champaign, IL: Garrard.

Elmquist, E. (1987). Improving reading skills and attitudes through the reading and writing connection. (ERIC Clearinghouse No. CS010210)

Johns, J. L. (1971). The Dolch Basic Word List—Then and now. *Journal of Reading Behavior, 3,* 35–40.

JOYCE E. NESS
*Montgomery County
Intermediate Unit,
Norristown, Pennsylvania*

READING DISORDERS
READING REMEDIATION

DOLL, EDGAR A. (1889–1968)

Edgar A. Doll joined the staff of the Training School at Vineland, New Jersey, as research and clinical psychologist in 1913. There he worked with E. R. Johnstone and H. H. Goddard in the Vineland Laboratory: the first laboratory devoted solely to the study of mental retardation.

Following service in World War I, three years with New

Edgar A. Doll

Jersey's State Department of Classification and Education, completion of the doctorate in psychology at Princeton University, and two years of teaching at Ohio State University, Doll returned to Vineland as director of research. His studies of social competence led to the publication, in 1935, of the *Vineland Social Maturity Scale*, a revolutionary instrument that provided an objective basis for measuring social functioning which was more useful than mental age for classifying people for purposes of training and care.

Doll left Vineland in 1949 to serve as coordinator of research for the Devereux Schools. He was later consulting psychologist for the Bellingham, Washington, public schools. He served as president of the American Association of Applied Psychology, the American Association on Mental Deficiency, and the American Orthopsychiatric Association.

REFERENCES

Doll, E. A. (1953). *The measurement of social competence: A manual for the Vineland Social Maturity Scale*. Minneapolis: Educational Test Bureau.

Doll, E. E. (1969). Edgar Arnold Doll, 1889–1968. *American Journal of Mental Deficiency, 73*, 680–682.

PAUL IRVINE
Katonah, New York

DOMAN, GLENN (1919–   )

Glenn Doman is internationally known for his interest and pioneering work in child brain development and function. He attended Drexel Institute in 1938, graduated from the University of Pennsylvania in 1940, and in 1965 went on to graduate from the University of Pennsylvania School of Physical Therapy. He was certified at the perceptor level in human brain development in 1969.

Doman has studied children for over 40 years. He founded The Institutes for the Achievement of Human Potential in 1955 and served as its director until 1981, subsequently, he has served as the chairman of its board. He is known for the formulation of the Doman-Delacato treatment method for children with neurological disabilities, a treatment which was popular during the 1960's. The theory stresses that an individual's development in mobility, vision, audition, and language follows specific neurological stages that are correlated with anatomical progress. The Institutes have worked with thousands of brain-injured children.

Doman's publications include *How to Teach Your Baby to Read* (1964/1994), *What to Do About Your Brain-Injured Child* (1974/1994), *How to Teach Your Baby Math* (1979/

Glenn Doman

1994), *How to Multiply your Baby's Intelligence* (1984/1994), and *How to Teach Your Baby to be Physically Superb* (1988/1994). These books are available in 20 languages.

Among his numerous honors, Doman was knighted by the Brazilian government for his work on behalf of the children of the world. In 1994, he was presented with the European prize "Lorenzo, the Magnificent" by the Accademia Internazionale Medicea for his work in the field of science. In 1996 The Institutes for Functional Medicine awarded Doman the first annual Linus Pauling Functional Medicine Award.

REFERENCES

Doman, G. (1994). *How to teach your baby to read* (2nd ed.). New York: Avery.

Doman, G. (1994). *What to do about your brain-injured child* (2nd ed.). New York: Avery.

Doman, G. (1994). *How to teach your baby math* (2nd ed.). New York: Avery.

Doman, G. (1994). *How to multiply your baby's intelligence* (2nd ed.). New York: Avery.

Doman, G. (1994). *How to teach your baby to be physically superb* (2nd ed.). New York: Avery.

ROBERTA C. STOKES
Texas A & M University
First edition

TAMARA J. MARTIN
The University of Texas of the Permian Basin
Second edition

DOPAMINE

Dopamine (DA) is a catecholamine class neurotransmitter. Dopamine has been one of the most studied neurotransmitters because of observed roles for DA in schizophrenia, obessive-compulsive behavior (Lewis, 1996), conduct disorder (Galvin, 1995) tardive dyskinesia, and Parkinson's disease. Dopaminergic pathways are located throughout the limbic system (area of the brain often associated with emotional reactivity and memory), the basal ganglia (area of the brain associated with motor timing and complex integration), and frontal brain areas. Animal studies of DA depletion and studies of neurological disorders with motor manifestations (i.e., Parkinson's disease) produce results supportive of DA's contributory role in brain systems involved in normal locomotion (Seiden & Dykstra, 1977). Similarly, researchers working with drugs that stimulate DA in animal brains have noted increases in spontaneous aggression during chemical stimulation of DA receptor sites (Senault, 1970). Introduction of haloperidol (Haldol), a DA-blocking agent, reduces the frequency of such fighting (Leavitt, 1982). The role of DA in sexual activity appears similar; that is, increased availability of DA increases sexual behavior in rats. In humans, however, the latter effect appears more indirect. When L-Dopa, a precursor of DA, was administered to male Parkinson's patients, its observed effect on sexual potency appeared more the result of removing other disabling motor symptoms than a result of direct stimulation of libido (Leavitt, 1982). In addition, DA appears to play a role in the regulation of food intake. Investigators (Seiden & Dykstra, 1977) also have noted a role for DA in the maintenance of avoidance behavior and in the facilitation of behavior on positive reinforcement schedules.

REFERENCES

Galvin, M. (1995). Serum dopamine beta Hydroxylase and maltreatment in psychiatrically hospitalized boys. *Child Abuse & Neglect: The International Journal, 19*, 7, 821–832.

Leavitt, F. (1982). *Drugs and behavior.* New York: Wiley.

Lewis, M. H. (1996). Plasma HVA in adults with mental retardation and stereotyped behaviors: Biochemical evidence for a dopamine deficiency model. *American Journal on Mental Retardation, 100*, 4, 413–418.

Seiden, L. S., & Dykstra, L. A. (1977). *Psychopharmocology: A biochemical and behavioral approach.* New York: Van Nostrand Reinhold.

Senault, B. (1970). Comportement d'aggressivité intraspécifique induit par l'apomorphine chez le rat. *Psychopharmocologia, 18*, 271–287.

ROBERT F. SAWICKI
Lake Erie Institute of
Rehabilitation

HALDOL

See TRANQUILIZERS

DOUBLE-BLIND DESIGN

One frequently encountered problem in research involving the administration of medication, particularly psychotropic drugs, is that some children or adults may be improved solely as a function of their knowledge that a drug has been administered. The degree to which this effect, frequently referred to as a placebo effect, is present and affecting the outcome of research is unknown and uncontrolled in any specific situation. Experimenters may also be influenced by administration of medication, particularly if the researcher developed the pharmaceutical agent or has other subjective reasons to be biased toward a particular outcome. In such cases, investigators may observe differential rates of behavioral or physiological change in those subjects receiving medication in comparison with those individuals receiving no drug therapy (Babbie, 1979). In either of these cases, the subject's or experimenter's expectation of a certain outcome represents a threat to the validity of the research design. Validity is compromised when the effect of the drug administered is confounded with the expectation of what, if any, the effects of the drug might be.

To control for the effect of patients merely taking medication, as would be the case if those taking medication were compared with a nonmedicated control group, subjects who are not receiving an active drug substance are administered a placebo that appears identical to the active medication in every regard, with the exception that its active ingredients are inert. Thus, the drug under study is not present in the placebo dose and the patients are unaware of whether their medication is in fact active or a placebo. In research terminology, then, the patients are blind to their own drug condition. In order to control for the effect of experimenter bias, it is also necessary for the investigators who administer medication and those who evaluate the outcome (the presence or absence of the drug effect) to be blind to the drug condition of the patients. When these precautions are followed, the research design is said to employ a double-blind procedure, since neither the patients nor the researchers are cognizant of the drug condition to which patients may be assigned (Sprague, 1979).

Obviously, there must be records of which patients have received active medication and which have received placebos in order for the results of the study to be interpretable. However, it is critical that this information not be available to researchers who may have contact with the patients or to the patients themselves until after the study has been completed. Thus, by following a strict double-blind research design, drug effects may be distinguished from actual patient and experimenter expectations regarding the drug under investigation (Sprague, 1979). Unless these two types of effects can be separated, the validity of such a study would be compromised seriously (Sprague, 1979; Sprague & Werry, 1971).

In summary, the double-blind condition exists when neither the subject involved nor the investigator evaluating the drug trial is cognizant of the control condition (placebo) or the active pharmacological intervention. Such a procedure precludes the investigator's expectations and hopes from influencing any physiological or behavioral changes that may occur as a function of active pharmacotherapy (Sprague, 1979).

In reviews of the massive literature pertaining to the psychopharmacology of hyperactive and mentally retarded populations, Sprague (Sprague, 1979; Sprague & Werry, 1971) has underscored that the use of double-blind procedures is a minimum requisite in evaluating psychotropic drugs for these groups. Nonetheless, ethical considerations may preclude withholding an effective medication for a child despite the requirements of rigorous empirical research. Thus, investigators must carefully weigh the mandates of controlled clinical trials research with the special needs of some children. Moreover, some research (Whalen & Henker, 1980) in the field of pediatric psychopharmacology has provided rather convincing evidence to suggest that the notion of being administered any pill, whether placebo or active medication, exerts a specific effect on children's views of personal causality (Margraf, 1991). This is particularly true for hyperactive or conduct-disordered children (Ross & Ross, 1982). Should these findings be upheld in future research, the use of active medication as well as both a placebo and a no-pill condition will in fact be necessary in clinical trials, particularly those that involve stimulant medications or other psychotropic drugs prescribed for behavior disorders in children.

REFERENCES

Babbie, E. R. (1979). *The practice of social research*. Belmont, CA: Wadsworth.

Margraf, J. (1991). How "blind" are doubled blind studies? *Journal of Consulting and Clinical Psychology, 59*, 1, 184–187.

Ross, D. M., & Ross S. A. (1982). *Hyperactivity*. New York: Wiley.

Sprague, R. L. (1979). Assessment of intervention. In R. L. Trites (Ed.), *Hyperactivity in children: Etiology, measurement and treatment implications* (pp. 217–229). Baltimore, MD: University Park Press.

Sprague, R. L., & Werry, J. S. (1971). Methodology of psychopharmacological studies with the retarded. In N. R. Ellis (Ed.), *International review of research in mental retardation* (Vol. 5). New York: Academic.

Whalen, C. K., & Henker, B. (1980). *Hyperactive children: The social ecology of identification and treatment*. New York: Academic.

MARTHA ELLEN WYNNE
Loyola University of Chicago

RONALD T. BROWN
Emory University School of Medicine

ABAB DESIGN
HAWTHORNE EFFECT
RESEARCH

DOWN, J. (JOHN) LANGDON, (1828–1896)

J. (John) Langdon Down, an English physician, in 1866 described the condition that he called mongolism and that is now known as Down syndrome or Down's syndrome. Although there had been earlier descriptions in the medical literature of individuals who appeared to belong to the same category, Down is credited with the discovery and description of this clinical entity.

Down was concerned with the prevention of mental retardation. He recommended attention to good parental health and sound prenatal care and child-rearing practices. He advocated education for mentally retarded individuals and recognized the efficacy of early training.

REFERENCES

Down, J. L. (1866). Observations on an ethnic classification of idiots. *London Hospital Clinical Lecture Reports, 3*, 259–262.

Down, J. L. (1887). *Mental affectations of childhood and youth*. London: Churchill.

Penrose, L. S., & Smith, G. F. (1966). *Down's anomaly*. Boston: Little, Brown.

PAUL IRVINE
Katonah, New York

DOWN'S SYNDROME

Down's syndrome, a chromosomal anomaly, accounts for one-third of all cases of genetic-origin mental retardation (Hayden & Beck, 1981). Zarfas and Wolf (1979) reported a frequency of 2/1000 live births. The Centers for Disease Control in Atlanta currently report statistics of 1/1000. In 1866 J. Langdon Down, the first person to describe the characteristics of the syndrome, believed that the condition was a regression to a more primitive racial type. He

Figure 1. Children with Down's syndrome often, but not always, have appealing features as do these children.

coined the term mongolism. The term is derogatory to both the individual with Down's syndrome and the Mongolian race. However, Down's recognition of the pattern of characteristics clearly delineated the condition as a distinct and separate entity (Pueschel, Canning, Murphy, & Zausmer, 1978).

Of the more than 50 known characteristics (Koch & Koch, 1974), the most common are a small skull with a flat back of head; slanting, almond-shaped eyes; white speckled irises; flat-bridged nose and ears slightly smaller than average; small mouth with protruding, fissured tongue; drooping corners of the mouth; shortness of stature; stubby hands; little finger curved inward; a single crease along the palm of the hand rather than the average double palm crease; fingerprints and footprints differing from the norm; hypotonia (too little muscle tone); and an unsteady, jerky gait (See Figure 1). Not all characteristics are present in each Down's syndrome individual and some of the symptoms may be less pronounced. Some level of mental retardation is inevitable but the degree of mental retardation may vary greatly. Studies have shown that cognitive development advances steadily until it levels off at mental ages of about 3½ to 5 years (Cornwell & Birch, 1969; Zeaman & House, 1962). Connally (1978) suggests that despite the generally found IQ deficit, the abilities of Down's syndrome children are not as limited as once suggested. Some IQs may be as high as borderline normal. Skill development may continue well into the third and fourth decade but abstract abilities may remain severely limited (Cornwell, 1974).

Lejeune, Gautur, and Turpin (1963) discovered that individuals with Down's syndrome had 47 rather than 46 chromosomes in each cell. All of the types of chromosomal abnormalities that cause Down's syndrome result in an extra 21 chromosome, or trisomy 21. Hereditary types account for less than 4%. In such cases, genetic counseling can be given. Amniocentesis may be helpful, as Down's syndrome is detectable in utero.

Nondisjunction, the most common form of Down's syndrome, found in 95% of afflicted persons, is not inherited. Trisomy 21 occurs when in place of the chromosome 21 pair, there is a trisomy (three individual 21 chromosomes). Nondisjunction can occur during formation of the egg or the sperm, or during the first few cell divisions after conception. The older the female, the more likely Down's syndrome will occur (See Figure 2). During aging, the ova are exposed to stressors that may damage the chromosomes. Recent studies that examined chromosomes from both parents indicate that there may be a link between the age of the male and Down's syndrome as well (Pueschel, 1982).

Translocation, the inherited form of Down's syndrome, occurs during normal cell reproduction when two chromosomes overlap and break at the point of contact. Instead of reuniting properly, the broken ends unite with the wrong chromosome. The translocation usually occurs between the 14th and 21st chromosomes. A 14th may break and unite with a 21st or may become attached to a 21st without breaking, resulting in an abnormal chromosome (a 14–21 combination). The abnormal chromosome will reproduce itself. Therefore, an individual who inherits it will be a carrier of translocation Down's syndrome. Either a male or female can be a carrier, but it is more common in the female (Koch & Koch, 1974).

Mosaicism is the least common type of Down's syndrome. The mosaic has some normal 46 chromosome cells and some abnormal 47 chromosome cells, as detailed by

Figure 2. Incidence of Down's syndrome as a function of mother's age at birth.

Koch and Koch (1974). At some point during prenatal cell division (mitosis), and after a number of normal cells are produced, a mutation occurs. Generally, the result is a milder form of Down's syndrome. In some cases, a mosaic may have normal intelligence and exhibit few or no Down's syndrome characteristics. This type of Down's syndrome is not initially hereditary and there is little chance that it will occur in a second birth to the same parents. However, mosaics can pass on Down's syndrome to their offspring.

Although the exact cause of Down's syndrome is unknown, possible causes include radiation, gene mutation, viruses, drugs and other chemicals, autoimmune mechanisms, existing aberrations, aged gametes, and factors such as economic, thermal, temporal, and geographic conditions (American Association of Mental Deficiency, 1983). Advances in technology have made it possible to photomicrograph and more accurately study chromosomes.

Careful medical attention using a preventive medical approach is important as there are a number of medical problems associated with Down's syndrome. Common are the following: respiratory infections, thyroid disorders, congenital heart disease, intestinal obstruction of the duodenum, underdeveloped sex organs, and skeletal abnormalities (Pueschel et al., 1978; Smith & Berg, 1976). Life expectancy for Down's syndrome individuals is much higher today than in the past. These individuals may survive into their 60s and 70s (Kasparyan, 1977).

Parent support is a vital need (Turnbull & Turnbull, 1978) to ensure that infant stimulation programs emphasizing self-help skills, motor training (Sanz & Menendez,

1992) language acquisition, feeding, toilet training, and positive socialization, are provided. Down's syndrome individuals are educable and should have exposure to their nonhandicapped peers from their early years. Generally, there is no reason that most Down's syndrome individuals cannot attend regular preschools and later local neighborhood schools. In the past, professionals advised parents to place their Down's syndrome child in 24-hour institutional care based on the false assumption that the Down's syndrome individual would be severely or profoundly retarded. Custodial care is seldom warranted unless severe medical, psychological, or social problems occur. Carefully supervised, comprehensive special education, K–12, should include inclusion (Cheney & Demchak, 1996) and prevocational and vocational skill development. Adult living may include working in a sheltered workshop or in a well-organized and supervised private work place in business or industry. The greatest general development is found in Down's syndrome individuals who are reared at home and well stimulated (Connally, 1978). Optimum progress occurs when facilities are positive, view Down's syndrome as a part of a rich inheritance, (Stratford, 1994) and training begins early and is comprehensive.

REFERENCES

American Association of Mental Deficiency. (1983). Classification in mental retardation (Rev. ed.). *American Journal of Mental Deficiency, 89*, 242–256.

Centers for Disease Control. (1985, September). *Birth defect monitoring progress data* (Congenital Malformation Survey Report). Washington, DC: Department of Health and Human Services.

Cheney, C., & Demchak, M. (1996) *Providing appropriate education in inclusive settings: A rural case study.* (ERIC Clearinghouse No. RC020560)

Connally, J. (1978). Intelligence levels of Down's syndrome children. *American Journal of Mental Deficiency, 83,* 193–196.

Cornwell, A. C. (1974). Development of language abstraction and numerical concept formation in Down's syndrome children. *American Journal of Mental Deficiency, 79,* 179–190.

Cornwell, A. C., & Birch, H. G. (1969). Psychological and social development in home reared children with Down syndrome (mongolism). *American Journal of Mental Deficiency, 74,* 314–350.

Hayden, A. H., & Beck, G. R. (1981). Finding and educating high risk infants. In R. Meyer, C. Ramsey, & P. Throames (Eds.), *Finding and educating high risk infants* (pp. 19–51). Baltimore, MD: University Park.

Kasparyan, A. (1977). Prolonged survival in Down syndrome. *Journal of American Medical Association, 237*(17), 1827.

Koch, R., & Koch, K. (1974). *Understanding the mentally retarded child. A new approach.* New York: Random House.

Lejeune, J., Gautur, M., & Turpin, R. (1963). Study of the somatic chromosomes of nine mongoloid idiot children. In S. H. Bayer (Ed.), *Papers on human genetics* (pp. 238–240). Englewood Cliffs, NJ: Prentice-Hall.

Pines, M. (1982). Infant stimulation. *Psychology Today, 7,* 48–53.

Pueschel, S. (1982). *A study of the young child with Down syndrome.* New York: Human Science.

Pueschel, S., Canning, C., Murphy, A., & Zausmer, E. (1978). *Down syndrome growing and learning.* Fairway: Andrews, McMeel, & Parker.

Sanz, M. T., & Menendez, F. J. (1992). *Early motor training in Down's Syndrome babies: Results of an intervention program.* (ERIC Clearinghouse No. EC301660)

Smith, G. F., & Berg, J. M. (1976). *Down's anomaly.* New York: Churchill Livingstone.

Stratford, B. (1994). Down syndrome is for life. International *Journal on disability, development & Education, 41,* 1, 3–14.

Turnbull, A., & Turnbull, H. (1978). *Parents speak out: Growing with a handicapped child.* Columbus, OH: Merrill.

Zarfas, D. E., & Wolf, L. C. (1979). Maternal age patterns and the incidence of Down's syndrome. *American Journal of Mental Deficiency, 83,* 353–359.

Zeaman, D., & House, B. (1962). Mongoloid mental age is proportional to log cognitive age. *Child Development, 33,* 481–488.

SALLY E. PISARCHICK
*Cuyahoga Special Education
Service Center*

**GENETIC COUNSELING
MENTAL RETARDATION
MOSAICISM
TRISOMY 21**

DRAW-A-PERSON TEST

The draw-a-person (DAP) is an assessment technique used with both children and adults for a variety of purposes. Harris (1963) provided a set of instructions, a scoring system, and norms for using the technique as a measure of children's intelligence. The test has also been widely used as a projective personality assessment technique following a suggestion by Machover (1949). Although specific instructions vary, the examinee is typically asked to draw a picture of a person. The examiner provides as little structure as possible; however, if necessary, the subject is encouraged to draw an entire person and not to use stick figures. The subject is then asked to draw a person of the opposite sex. These basic instructions are often embellished to include a drawing of oneself and an inquiry phase during which the subject may be asked to make up a story about the person in the drawing or to explain various details included in the picture. Several scoring systems are available (Naglieri, 1988; Shaffer, Duszynski, & Thomas, 1984), and they have moderate to high test-retest reliability based on global quantitative ratings (Naglieri, 1988; Swenson, 1968).

However, the DAP, along with other projective tests, has serious validity problems as a tool for diagnosing emotional disorders. The problems have two sources. First, subjects are drawing the person at only one point in time, and their drawings may vary from one test to another owing to a variety of circumstances. Second, clinical interpreters or researchers may be biased owing to their own theoretical perspective (e.g., psychoanalysis) or desired outcome.

Even with its drawbacks, the DAP is still popular and may provide a reasonable estimate of the cognitive abilities of people across a wide age range. Unfortunately, its effectiveness in diagnosing emotional disorders is limited at best (Groth-Marnat, 1997). Commonly used with standardized tests such as the MMPI, the DAP can be used alone as a means of initiating a conversation with a child or adult in a counseling situation (Groth-Marnat, 1997).

REFERENCES

Groth-Marnat, G. (1997). *Handbook of psychological assessment* (3rd ed.). New York: Wiley.

Harris, D. B. (1963). *Children's drawings as measures of intellectual maturity.* New York: Harcourt, Brace, & World.

Machover, K. (1949). *Personality projection in the drawing of the human figure.* Springfield, IL: Thomas.

Naglieri, J. A. (1988). *Draw a person: A quantitative scoring system.* San Antonio, TX: The Psychological Corporation.

Shaffer, J., Duszynski, K., & Thomas, C. (1984). A comparison of three methods for scoring figure drawings. *Journal of Personality Assessment, 48,* 245–254.

Swenson, C. H. (1968). Empirical evaluation of human figure drawings. 1957–1966. *Psychological Bulletin, 70,* 20–44.

ROBERT G. BRUBAKER
Eastern Kentucky University
First edition

WENDY L. FLYNN
Staffordshire University
Second edition

BENDER GESTALT
HOUSE TREE PERSON
KINETIC FAMILY DRAWING

DROPOUT

A dropout is generally considered to be an individual who leaves school before graduation. Yet, Block, Covill-Servo, and Rosen (1978) found a serious problem with this definition and the reporting of dropouts. They found many inconsistencies in the way school districts define and report dropouts. New York defines a dropout as "any pupil who leaves school prior to graduation for any reason except death and does not enter another school" (Block, Covill-Servo, & Rosen, 1978, p. 15). Under this definition, an average of 25% of the students entering high school drop out.

In recent year the dropout rate has been declining. For example, the event dropout rate for ages 15 through 24 in grades 10 through 12 has fallen from 6.1% in 1972 to 4.5% in 1993. However, these figures still constitute a large number of individuals. In 1993, approximately 381,000 students in grades 10 through 12 dropped out of school (National Center for Education Statistics, 1993).

For special education students and children with disabilities, the dropout rate is twice that of their non-disabled peers (OSERS, 1997). In addition, dropouts with disabilities do not return to school, and females became unwed mothers at a much higher rate than non-disabled peers (OSERS, 1997).

One of the six national education goals for the United States is to achieve a 90% graduation rate by the year 2000 (Dorn, 1996). Reasons for leaving school include a dislike of school, involuntary exclusion, academic problems, problems with teachers, marriage, and pregnancy. These reasons are determined ex post facto and do not have a high predictive value in identifying potential dropouts. Most dropouts are 16 years old and from families with lower socioeconomic status where parental attitudes toward education and parental supervision are low. Dropouts generally are of lower intellectual ability, have poor personal-social skills, and have academic problems.

The consequences of dropping out of school are seen when compared with the results of graduating. Dropouts generally earn significantly less money and are more likely to be unemployed. Contributing to these effects is the finding that dropouts have no postsecondary training because, as an entrance requirement, most postsecondary training programs require a high-school diploma or equivalent.

Dorn (1996) argues that "instead of seeing different educational outcomes as evidence of remaining equities in schooling, Americans have focused instead on the social costs of dropping out". Schools are expected to ameliorate problems that are essentially socioeconomic in nature and many times beyond their scope and jurisdiction.

REFERENCES

Block, E. E., Covill-Servo, J., & Rosen, M. F. (1978). *Failing students—Failing schools: A study of dropouts and discipline in New York State.* Rochester, NY: Statewide Youth Advocacy Project.

Dorn, S. (1996). *Creating the dropout: An institutional and social history of school failure.* Westport, CT: Praeger.

Office of Special Education. (1997). *An overview of the bill to provide a broad understanding of some of the changes in IDEA '97.* http://www.ed.gov/offices/OSERS/IDEA/overview.html.

U.S. Department of Education National Center for Education Statistics. (1993). *High School Dropout Rates.* Washington D.C.: National Institute on the Education of at-risk students.

DANIEL R. PAULSON
University of Wisconsin at Stout
First edition

ELAINE FLETCHER-JANZEN
University of Northern Colorado
Second edition

DRUG ABUSE

Drug abuse, or more currently substance abuse, is defined by the Diagnostic and Statistical Manual of Mental Disorders Fourth Edition (DSM-IV; American Psychiatric Association, 1994) as "a maladaptive pattern of substance use manifested by recurrent and significant adverse consequences related to the repeated use of substances" (p. 182). The criteria for a substance abuse diagnosis are the following:

A. A maladaptive pattern of substance use leading to clinically significant impairment or distress, as manifested by one (or more) of the following, occurring within a 12-month period:

(1) recurrent substance use resulting in a failure to fulfill major role obligations at work, school, or home (e.g., repeated absences or poor work performance related to substance use; substance-related absences,

suspensions, or expulsions from school; neglect of children or household)

(2) recurrent substance use in situations in which it is physically hazardous (e.g., driving an automobile or operating a machine when impaired by substance use)

(3) recurrent substance-related legal problems (e.g., arrests for substance-related disorderly conduct)

(4) continued substance use despite having persistent or recurrent social or interpersonal problems caused or exacerbated by the effects of the substance (e.g., arguments with spouse about consequences of intoxication, physical fights)

B. The symptoms have never met the criteria for Substance Dependence for this class of substance (pp. 182–183)

Drug abuse is one of the six categories of behaviors that contribute to the leading causes of morbidity and mortality in the United States (National Clearinghouse for Alcohol and Drug Information [NCADI], 1998). It has only been in the 1980s and 1990s that the neuropsychological effects of drug abuse have started to be understood. This new understanding has been due to technological advances in the study of the brain, and the rise and development of pediatric neurology and neuropsychology. It is during adolescence that the more abstract and sophisticated cognitive skills develop in the human brain. Planning, evaluation, flexibility, internalized behavioral controls, higher-level abstracting skills, and higher levels of moral awareness are some of these sophisticated skills. The use of drugs during this period many have long-lasting effects on frontal and pre-frontal regions of the brain (Elliott, 1998). For each insult to the brain there is a concomitant negative consequence for cognitive functions and behavior; therefore, the prevention of drug abuse in youth is extremely important if individual and social consequences are to be avoided.

The Centers for Disease Control (CDC) has developed a Youth Risk Behavior Surveillance System (YRBSS) to monitor the health-risk behaviors among youth and young adults (CDC, 1996). The system includes national, state, and local school-based surveys of high school students and gives a shocking picture of how students in the United States are involved in drug abuse.

According to the 1995 YRBSS, over 80% of high school students have used alcohol; over 40% have used marijuana; 16% have used cocaine, crack, or freebase; and over 20% have sniffed or inhaled intoxicating substances. Of the students who had experienced drug abuse, 40% initiated drug-related behaviors before the age of 13. Over 30% of the students reported using alcohol or drugs at the last episode of sexual intercourse. In addition, over 40% of the students had ridden with a driver who had been drinking alcohol.

For the past twenty years, significant efforts have been made with private and public monies to prevent drug abuse. Schools have been a primary vehicle for prevention monies because education has been shown to assist in prevention, and education is a compatible goal with school missions (Bosworth, 1997). Education programs begin as early as the elementary years, and try to eliminate myths that support student use (such as "everybody is doing it") with normative information that gives students statistics. There is no conclusive evidence on what types of programs or strategies are effective or ineffective; however, there is some evidence that scare tactics, providing only information on drugs and their effects, self-esteem building, values clarification, large assemblies, and didactic presentation of material have not been shown to be particularly effective (Tobler & Stratton, 1997, cited in Bosworth, 1997). Skill building and experiential teaching techniques (role-playing, simulations, and so on) have been successful in helping students utilize positive approaches to avoiding drug use (Bosworth, 1997).

The following resources are cited in Bosworth (1997):

For educators exploring possible drug prevention approaches and curricula, several excellent guides to curriculum selection are available from the National Clearinghouse for Alcohol and Drug Information (NCADI), P.O. Box 2345, Rockville, MD 20852, (800) 729-6686. [NCADI is the public information arm of the U.S. Department of Health and Human Services. Free titles include:

Drug prevention Curricula: A Guide to Selection and Implementation

Community Creating Change: Exemplary Alcohol and Other Drug Prevention Programs

Prevention Plus II: Tools for Creating and Sustaining Drug-Free Communities

Learning to Live Drug Free: A Curriculum Model for Prevention

Prevention Resource Guide's for Elementary Youth and Secondary School Students

Also serving as a programming resource are the Drug-Free Schools and Communities Regional Centers established in 1986 as part of the Drug-Free Schools and Communities Act to help schools and communities eliminate drug and alcohol use among youth. The five regional centers are:

Northeast Regional Center, Sayville, NY, (516) 589-7022

Southeast Regional Center, Louisville, KY, (502) 588-0052

Midwest Regional Center, Oak Brook, IL, (708) 571-4710

Southwest Regional Center, Norman, OK,
(800) 234-7972

Western Regional Center, Portland, OR,
(503) 275-9480

Two organizations, dedicated to the promotion and improvement of peer leader programs may also be of help:

The National Peer Helpers Association
P.O. Box 3783
Glendale, California 91221-0783
(818) 240-2926

The Peer Counseling Project
University of Victoria
Victoria, British Columbia
V8W 3N4, CANADA
(604) 721-7812

REFERENCES

American Psychiatric Association. (1994). *Diagnostic and statistical manual of mental disorders* (4th ed.). Washington D.C.: Author.

Bosworth, K. (1997). Drug abuse prevention: School-based strategies that work. *ERIC Clearinghouse on Teaching and Teacher Education*, Washington D.C. (ERIC Digest No. ED409316)

Centers for Disease Control. (1996). *Youth Risk Behavior Surveillance United States, 1995.* 45, SS-4.

Elliot, R. (1998). Neuropsychological sequelae of substance abuse by youths. In C. R. Reynolds & E. Fletcher-Janzen (Eds.), *Handbook of Clinical Child Neuropsychology* (pp. 311–331). New York Plenum.

National Clearinghouse for Alcohol and Drug Information. (1998). *Youth risk Behavior Surveillance United States, 1995.* http://www.health.org/pubs/yrbbs/index.htm

ELAINE FLETCHER-JANZEN
University of Northern Colorado

AL-ANON
ALCOHOL AND DRUG ABUSE PATTERNS
CHEMICALLY DEPENDENT YOUTH
SUBSTANCE ABUSE

DRUGS

See SPECIFIC DRUGS.

DRUG THERAPY

Drug therapy may be broadly described as the administration of medications designed to alter behaviors, thoughts, or moods that interfere with adaptive functioning. A voluminous amount has been written on the topic of drug therapy with children; no attempt is made to review this literature in depth here. Excellent sources may be found in the reviews by Barkley (1983), Campbell and Small (1978), Conners and Werry (1979), Gadow (1979), Sprague and Ullmann (1981), and Sroufe (1975) and in meta-analyses by Kavale (1982) and Kavale and Nye (1984). Drug therapy is the most common medical intervention for altering the behavior of children. Despite its relatively short history (usually traced to the mid-1930s), drug treatment is widely practiced today. Exact prevalence data do not exist, yet most estimates indicate that in any given year about 2% of all schoolchildren receive medication for hyperactivity alone.

It is important to recognize limitations inherent in general discussions of drug effects. A variety of factors, such as the nature of the dependent measures used in particular studies, control of placebo and expectancy effects, the effects of situational factors, dosage level, and numerous individual subject variables (e.g., metabolism, severity of problem, etc.), preclude the possibility of listing universal effects of various drugs. Neither the intended effects nor the undesirable side effects discussed here are seen in all persons receiving drug therapy. The major categories of drugs most often used with handicapped children are anticonvulsants, stimulants, antipsychotics, and antidepressants. Of these classes of drugs, stimulants are the most frequently prescribed.

Anticonvulsants are used in the treatment of disorders such as epilepsy. Beyond their use as antiepileptics, there is little evidence indicating desirable effects of these drugs. In fact, research indicates that adverse short-term side effects such as anxiety, nausea, and increased disorganization may result from these medications.

Ritalin (methylphenidate), Dexedrine (dextroamphetamine), and Cylert (magnesium pemoline) are the stimulants most often prescribed for hyperactivity. Used for this purpose, these drugs have sparked the most controversy and also have been the most thoroughly researched of all psychoactive medications. Many earlier researchers referred to the calming effects of stimulants with hyperactive children as paradoxical, and suggested this response had diagnostic merit. However, because increased sustained attention is seen in both hyperactive and non-hyperactive children who are given stimulants, the paradoxical effect and its diagnostic implications have been seriously questioned.

Other frequently reported effects of stimulants include improvement in impulse control, increased compliance, and decreased disruptive behavior. The learning of new skills or improvements in memory or intelligence test performance are generally not influenced beyond that which can be ascribed to improvements in attention. Adverse side effects associated with stimulants include increases in heart rate and blood pressure, insomnia, decreases in appetite, heightened emotionality, nervous habits, and assorted somatic complaints (e.g., headaches, stomach aches). One potential side effect, although rare, is the risk of producing an irreversible form of Tourette's syndrome.

Antipsychotics are most often used to treat extreme excitability, stereotypic behavior, delusions, hallucinations, and other schizophrenic characteristics. Among a number of possible negative side effects of antipsychotics are impairments in learning, enuresis, drowsiness, retarded speech and movement, rashes, sensitivity to sunlight, drooling, and tardive dyskinesia.

Antidepressants are generally prescribed to children to treat hyperactivity (when the use of stimulants is not appropriate), enuresis, and anxiety. In reports of the efficacy of antidepressants, it is generally concluded that both enuresis and anxiety (e.g., school phobia) respond to drug therapy but only while the drug is administered. Reported side effects include dry mouth, decreased appetite, nausea, seizures, and even death in rare instances.

Drug therapy has perhaps engendered more controversy and polemics than any other single type of treatment for children. Although beneficial in some instances as an adjunct to other treatments, there are a number of valid considerations regarding drug therapy: (1) Although they may be moderated by changes in dose or type of drug given, side effects do occur. (2) Many children do not respond to drug therapy. (3) Drugs are not as specific in their effects as are other available treatments. (4) Important questions concerning generalization and maintenance of improvements made during drug therapy as well as long-term effects of receiving medication need to be answered. (5) Reliance on external controls may not be desirable. (6) A host of ethical concerns are inherent in the administration of drugs. (7) Court decisions and state regulations have influenced the use of drugs.

In sum, the following conclusions appear justified. Alternative treatments must be attempted before drug therapy is initiated; drug therapy alone is insufficient; careful monitoring by both physicians and persons in the child's daily environment of both intended and unintended effects is essential; the prolonged use of psychoactive medications should be minimized; medications should not be used as punishment, as an alternative for active programming, or in dosages larger than necessary.

REFERENCES

Barkley, R. A. (1983). Hyperactivity. In R. J. Morris & T. R. Kratochwill (Eds.), *The practice of child therapy* (pp. 87–112). New York: Pergamon.

Campbell, M., & Small, A. M. (1978). Chemotherapy. In B. B. Wolman, J. Egan, & A. O. Ross (Eds.), *Handbook of treatment of mental disorders in childhood and adolescence* (pp. 9–27). Englewood Cliffs, NJ: Prentice-Hall.

Conners, C. K., & Werry, J. S. (1979). Pharmacotherapy. In H. C. Quay & J. S. Werry (Eds.), *Psychopathological disorders of childhood* (2nd ed.) (pp. 336–386). New York: Wiley.

Gadow, K. D. (1979). *Children on medication: A primer for school personnel.* Reston, VA: Council for Exceptional Children.

Kavale, K. A. (1982). The efficacy of stimulant drug treatment for hyperactivity: A meta-analysis. *Journal of Learning Disabilities, 15,* 280–289.

Kavale, K. A., & Nye, C. (1984). The effectiveness of drug treatment for severe behavior disorders: A meta-analysis. *Behavioral Disorders, 9,* 117–130.

Sprague, R. L., & Ullmann, R. (1981). Psychoactive drugs and child management. In J. M. Kauffman & D. P. Hallahan (Eds.), *Handbook of special education* (pp. 749–766). Englewood Cliffs, NJ: Prentice-Hall.

Sroufe, L. A. (1975). Drug treatment of children with behavior problems. In F. Horowitz (Ed.), *Review of child development research* (Vol. 4, pp. 347–407). Chicago: University of Chicago Press.

JAMES P. KROUSE
*Clarion University of
Pennsylvania*

ANTICONVULSANTS, SEE SPECIFIC DRUG

DUE PROCESS

Due process is the shorthand term applied to the procedural safeguard and due process procedures stated in the Individuals with Disabilities Education Act (IDEA) reauthorizations and regulations. These procedures offer parents the right to share with schools in decision making that could result in their children's being found eligible for and placed in special education classes. Because these placements may segregate children from the typical school environment, courts and laws have mandated that schools follow particular procedures to ensure that parents have the opportunity to review and give their consent to changes in their child's educational program. Bersoff (1978) and Kotin (1978) provide a discussion of the legal theory underlying the due process requirements.

The due process requirements can be classified under six headings: prior notice, opportunity to examine records, independent educational evaluation, informed consent, impartial due process hearing and appeal, and surrogate parents. First, the educational agency must provide written notice a reasonable time before any action is initiated to propose or reject (e.g., when parents request special education for their child) a change in the identification, evaluation, or educational placement of a child. The notice must be written in the parents' native language or other mode of communication such as braille and in a way that results in parents understanding the notice. The notice must contain a description of the action proposed or refused by the agency, an explanation of why such action was considered, a description of any options to be considered in making a decision, and a full explanation of all procedural safeguards available to the parents. These procedural safeguards allow the parents, at no cost, the opportunity to inspect and review all education records of their child and to obtain an independent educational evaluation conducted by a qualified examiner who is not employed by the agency. The intent of these provisions is to fully inform parents.

With this information, the parents are presumed able to give voluntary informed consent to the actions proposed. Consent must be obtained before the agency conducts a preplacement evaluation and before initial special education placement.

When parents and schools disagree about any issue concerning the evaluation, placement, or educational program for a special education student, either party may request an impartial due process hearing. A hearing officer is presented evidence under conditions that are similar to those in a court. Either party can call witnesses and cross-examine. A verbatim record is taken of the proceedings. The hearing officer writes a decision that may be appealed to the state education agency and, if desired, to a civil court. Given the emotional and financial costs of this procedure, several states have initiated a mediation process as an alternative for settling disputes before a due process hearing is conducted; however, mediation is not a substitute for a due process hearing. Recent U.S. Department of Education Reports to Congress (up to 1996) have reported on the extent to which mediations are used and have described issues concerning implementation.

Finally, public agencies are required to identify surrogate parents to represent a handicapped child when no parent or guardian can be located. Several issues have been raised about this requirement, such as qualifications to be a surrogate parent, training for this role, and liability protection, among others (U.S. Department of Education, 1977).

REFERENCES

Bersoff, D. N. (1978). Procedural safeguards. In L. G. Morra (Ed.), *Developing criteria for the evaluation of due process procedural safeguards provision of Public Law 94-142* (pp. 63–142). Washington, DC: U.S. Office of Education.

Kotin, L. (1978). Recommended criteria and assessment techniques for the evaluation by LEAs of their compliance with the notice and consent requirements of P.L. 94-142. In L. G. Morra (Ed.), *Developing criteria for the evaluation of due process procedural safeguards provision of Public Law 94-142* (pp. 143–178). Washington, DC: U.S. Office of Education.

U.S. Department of Education. (1984). *Fifth annual report to Congress on the implementation of Public Law 94-142: The Educa-*
tion for All Handicapped Children Act. Washington DC: Author.

U.S. Department of Education. (1985). *Sixth annual report to Congress on the implementation of Public Law 94-142: The Education for All Handicapped Children Act.* Washington, DC: Author.

U.S. Department of Education. (1986). *Seventh annual report to Congress on the implementation of Public Law 94-142: The Education for All Handicapped Children Act.* Washington, DC: Author.

U.S. Department of Health, Education, and Welfare. (1977). Education of handicapped children: Implementation of Part B of the Education of the Handicapped Act. *Federal Register, 42*(163), 42474–42518.

Roland K. Yoshida
Fordham University

INFORMED CONSENT
LEGAL REGULATIONS OF SPECIAL EDUCATION
PUBLIC LAW 94-142
SURROGATE PARENTS

DUNN, LLOYD M. (1917–   )

Lloyd Dunn was born in Saskatchewan, Canada, and received his U. S. citizenship in 1963. He obtained his BEd (1949) and MEd (1950) from the University of Saskatchewan, later earning his PhD in special education at the University of Illinois. From 1953 to 1969, he was a faculty member of Peabody College, now part of Vanderbilt University. Dunn has served as affiliate professor of education at the University of Hawaii, and was past president and recipient of the Wallin Award of the Council for Exceptional Children.

His major works are in the areas of psychometrics, language development, and education of the mentally retarded. Dunn (1968) has taken the position that much of the past and present practices of special education for minority children who are labeled mildly retarded are morally and educationally wrong. He believes that regular class placement without special education services is needed for most such children (Dunn, 1968). He was an early advocate of small, special-purpose residential facilities for the more severely retarded, rather than large, impersonal state residential institutions (Dunn, 1963).

Dunn is best known for the textbook, *Exceptional Children in the Schools;* the article, "Special Education for the Mildly Retarded–Is Much of It Justifiable!"; and various assessment tools and instructional programs, including the Peabody Picture Vocabulary Test, the Peabody Individual Achievement Test, and the Peabody Early Languages Kit. His work, outlining a progressive plan to improve special education by merging it with general education, has been extensively analyzed and very influential on policy change and legislation in Canada and the United States (Snell & Drake, 1994; Hallahan & Kauffman, 1994; Dahl & Sanche, 1997).

REFERENCES

Dahl, H., & Sanche, R. (1997). *Special education policy: A retrospective and future prospective–A view from Saskatchewan.* Salt Lake City, UT: Council for Exceptional Children.

Dunn, L. M. (1963). *Exceptional children in the schools.* New York: Holt, Rinehart, & Winston.

Dunn, L. M. (1968). Special education for the mildly retarded–Is much of it justifiable! *Exceptional children, 35,* 5–22.

Dunn, L. M. & Dunn, L. M. (1981). *Peabody Picture Vocabulary Test-Revised.* Circle Pines, MN: American Guidance Service.

Hallahan, D. P., & Kaufmann, J. M. (1994). *Toward a culture of disability in the aftermath of Deno and Dunn. Journal of Special Education, 27*(4), 496–508.

Snell, M. E., & Drake, George, P. (1994). Replacing cascades with supported education. *Journal of Special Education, 27*(4), 393–409.

ELIZABETH JONES
Texas A & M University
First edition

TAMARA J. MARTIN
The University of Texas of the Permian Basin
Second edition

DUSO

See DEVELOPING UNDERSTANDING OF SELF AND OTHERS.

DWARFISM

Dwarfism is a condition of extreme smallness of stature in an individual. There are several kinds of dwarfism, and systems of categorization vary. In general, however, two distant types exist: dwarfism, usually seen in specific groups such as pygmies, in which individuals have normal psychic development, physiological functioning, and regular physical proportions; and dwarfism owed to a disorder of the pituitary gland, also called hypopituitarism (Guyton, 1977).

Guyton (1977) describes several kinds of pituitary disorders in which the rate of secretion of one or more of the eight hormones produced by this gland is affected. Disorders in the production of human growth hormone during childhood can lead to childhood dwarfism. Hypopituitarism can be caused by genetic factors in which normal parents may produce an individual with dwarfism. In this type of dwarfism, the individual usually is of normal intelligence with disproportionate growth of body parts, usually the legs. Some of these cases are marked by sexual immaturity as well.

A variety of metabolic disturbances owed to organic disease may also result in hypopituitarism, and may result in mental deficiency as well as suppressed growth. In recent years, experimentation with human growth hormone obtained from cadavers has resulted in near normal growth in children with hypopituitarism. Various organizations have been formed recently to promote acceptance and understanding of "little people" (as they prefer to be called) and to dissipate stereotypical ideas that have arisen from the centuries of sideshow ostracism that little people have received (Ablon, 1984).

REFERENCES

Ablon, J. (1984). *Little people in America: The social dimension of dwarfism.* New York: Praeger.

Guyton, A. C. (1977). *Basic human physiology.* Philadelphia: Saunders.

BERNICE ARRICALE
Hunter College

PHYSICAL ANOMALIES

DYSCALCULIA

Dyscalculia is a term that applies to disturbances of quantitative thinking stemming from dysfunction of the central nervous system. The term precludes limited intellectual capacity, primary language disorders, anxiety, or poor teaching as causes of arithmetic failure. Kosc (1974) describes developmental dyscalculia as a disorder owed to heredity or congenital impairment of the brain centers that are the organic substrates of mathematical abilities. In cases of developmental dyscalculia, these abilities fail to develop within the normal limits of time and sequence. The term acalculia generally is used to describe an acquired disorder of calculating ability resulting from traumatic brain damage (Gaddes, 1980).

Studies of traumatically brain-damaged adults indicate that specific areas of damage are associated with specific arithmetical disabilities. Lesions of the parieto-occipital areas of the left hemisphere are likely to be related to disabilities in counting, ordering, or reading numbers. Posterior right hemisphere lesions may result in spatial difficulties associated with poor computation skills (Lezak, 1983). While these studies give insight into the organic origins of developmental dyscalculia, precise localization is difficult to ascertain. However, limited postmortem study suggests that developmental dyscalculia is related to abnormality or underdevelopment of parietal, temporal, and occipital cortices of both hemispheres and the intracerebral mechanisms associated with hearing and language (Gaddes, 1980).

Kosc identifies specific disturbances that may be indicative of dyscalculia. These may occur in clusters or individually and include verbal disturbances in which students cannot designate numerals or mathematical terms by name; disturbances of visuo-spatial organization in which students are unable to manipulate objects abstractly to determine relative sizes, shapes, and amounts; disturbances related to reading and writing numerals and operational symbols; disturbances of concept formation in which students are unable to understand mathematical concepts and relationships among numbers; and operational disturbances in which students are unable to compute.

The symptoms of dyscalculia frequently appear with other impaired symbolic functions of the brain, including dyslexia and dysgraphia. Gaddes classifies these disturbances as deficits in language (auditory-gnostic), reading (reading-gnostic), or spatial imagery. He suggests that developmental problems in auditory language probably are more devastating to arithmetic competence than deficiencies in any of the other psychological processes because inner language, conceptual growth, and incidental learning are impaired.

Johnson and Myklebust (1967) describe additional nonverbal behavioral correlates that occur frequently in the dyscalculic population. Many dyscalculic children are deficient in visual-spatial organization and nonverbal integration. They may have excellent auditory abilities and excel in word reading; however, it is not unusual for these children to encounter difficulty in higher levels of reading comprehension (Rourke & Strang, 1983). Johnson and Myklebust suggest this is due to an inability to integrate certain types of nonverbal experience, some dyscalculics have a disturbance in body image and lack a strong sense of direction (Badian, 1983). They may have disturbances in visual-motor integration, either for writing or for nonverbal motor skills (Cohn, 1971). Frequently, dyscalculics are poor in social perception and in making judgments; they may be unable to pick up or give nonverbal cues, often a part of social communication (Bryan, 1977). Badian reports a high correlation of sociability with arithmetic achievement.

Rourke and Strang (1983) and Rourke (1997) suggest the existence of subtypes of arithmetical disabilities on the basis of neuropsychological characteristics. Research has demonstrated that children who have similarly low levels of performance in arithmetic may differ widely in neuropsychological abilities and deficiencies (Rourke & Finlayson, 1978; Rourke & Strang, 1978). Children who performed poorly on most measures of verbal and auditory-perceptual abilities made arithmetical errors involving memory for number facts, sequencing steps necessary to do complex written computation, and word problems. Their deficient language skills were reflected in these errors. Conversely, those children who performed poorly on visual-spatial, visual-perceptual, complex psychomotor, and bilateral tactile-perceptual tasks showed an impoverished understanding of mathematical concepts; difficulty with column alignment, number formation, and directionality; and general visual-spatial disorganization. It is possible that different and additional subtypes may emerge as a result of further research in this area.

The existence of different sets of central processing skills in dyscalculic children points to the importance of differential diagnosis and the selection of appropriate methods of intervention and instruction. Johnson and Myklebust stress the use of auditory verbalization as a mediating process to help children with visual-spatial problems learn numerical relationships they are unable to generalize through observation and manipulation. This theory is consistent with recent data suggesting that teaching approaches emphasizing neuropsychological strengths in the instruction of specific academic subjects may result in the greatest gains for individual students (Hartlage & Telzrow, 1983, Reynolds, 1992).

REFERENCES

Badian, N. A. (1983). Dyscalculia and nonverbal disorders of learning. In H. R. Myklebust (Ed.), *Progress in learning disabilities* (Vol. 5, pp. 235–264). New York: Grune & Stratton.

Bryan, T. (1977). Learning disabled children's comprehension of nonverbal communication. *Journal of Learning Disabilities, 10,* 501–506.

Cohn, R. (1971). Arithmetic and learning disabilities. In H. R. Myklebust (Ed.), *Progress in learning disabilities* (Vol. 2, pp. 322–389). New York: Grune & Stratton.

Gaddes, W. H. (1980). *Learning disabilities and brain function: A neuropsychological approach* (2nd ed.). New York: Springer-Verlag.

Hartlage, L. C., & Telzrow, C. F. (1983). The neuropsychological bases of educational intervention. *Journal of Learning Disabilities, 16*(9), 521–528.

Johnson, D. J., & Myklebust, H. R. (1967). *Learning disabilities. Educational principles and practices.* New York: Grune & Stratton.

Kosc, L. (1974). Developmental dyscalculia. *Journal of Learning Disabilities, 7*(3), 164–177.

Lezak, M. D. (1983). *Neuropsychological assessment* (2nd ed.). New York: Oxford University Press.

Reynolds, C. R. (1992). Two key concepts in the diagnosis of learning disabilities and the habilitation of learning. *Learning Disability Quarterly, 15,* 1, 2–12.

Rourke, B., & Conway, J. A. (1997). Disabilities of arithmetic and mathematical reasoning; Perspectives from neurology and neuropsychology. *Journal of Learning Disabilities, 30,* 1, 34–46.

Rourke, B. P., & Finlayson, M. A. J. (1978). Neuropsychological significance of variations in patterns of academic performance: Verbal and visual-spatial abilities. *Journal of Abnormal Child Psychology, 6,* 121–133.

Rourke, B. P., & Strang, J. D. (1978). Neuropsychological significance of variations in patterns of academic performance: Motor, psychomotor, and tactile-perceptual abilities. *Journal of Pediatric Psychology, 3,* 62–66.

Rourke, B. P., & Strang, J. D. (1983). Subtypes of reading and arithmetical disabilities: A neuropsychological analysis. In M. Rutter (Ed.), *Developmental neuropsychiatry analysis* (pp. 473–488). New York: Guilford Press.

BARBARA S. SPEER
*Shaker Heights City School
District, Ohio*

ARITHMETIC REMEDIATION
MATHEMATICS, LEARNING DISABILITIES AND

DYSCOPIA

See APRAXIA.

DYSFLUENCY

See STUTTERING.

DYSGRAPHIA

Dysgraphia is the impaired ability to express ideas in writing (Gaddes, 1980). The ability to communicate thoughts to others through the written word is a highly complex process involving the integration of auditory, visual, and motor skills (Myklebust, 1965). The nature of the underlying deficits in dysgraphia is related to one or more of these factors. Writing disturbances are commonly observed when children are required to copy written or printed material, write words and sentences to dictation, or write spontaneously (Luria, 1966).

To learn to write, children must have developed many prerequisite skills in language, perception, sequencing, memory, and motor coordination. Slowed or delayed development interferes with the acquisition of readiness skills needed for writing (Myklebust, 1965). Writing requires a variety of verbal functions, including verbal comprehension and expression, auditory phonetic discrimination, oral sequencing, and verbal memory. A deficit in any one of these functions may result in impaired ability to convey ideas in spontaneous writing while the ability to copy accurately remains unimpaired (Johnson & Myklebust, 1967).

Children who have acquired a limited vocabulary, have poor reading skills, and have difficulty using grammar and syntax usually are unable to organize and translate their thoughts into writing. Written selections tend to be short and concrete. Words frequently are omitted or poorly organized into sentences; verbs and pronouns are misused; and errors in grammar, capitalization, and punctuation are displayed (Johnson & Myklebust, 1967).

Children with auditory discrimination deficits have difficulty distinguishing the sounds in words and confuse similarly sounding letters. Spontaneous writing and writing to dictation frequently reveal misspellings characterized by the omission and insertion of letters and syllables (Luria, 1973). Children who cannot hear the sequence of sounds in words are unable to write letters in the correct order. Auditory memory problems often are associated with this difficulty (Gaddes, 1980).

Writing also requires many nonverbal functions, including visual discrimination, visual-spatial orientation, visual memory, motor control, and visual-motor integration. Impairments in these skills not only are evidenced in writing to dictation and writing spontaneously, but are manifested in difficulty reproducing and copying written or printed materials (Johnson & Myklebust, 1967). Writing requires children to visually recognize and distinguish the differences between letters and words. Children with visual-spatial disturbances frequently confuse letters of the same shape but different orientation, make directional errors, and have difficulty maintaining horizontal and vertical positions.

Impaired visual memory is reflected in an inability to recall and reproduce the visual image or sequence of letters and words. Children with memory problems often can copy but lack the ability to write spontaneously or from dictation because they cannot visually remember letter and word forms (Johnson & Myklebust, 1967). Visual skills must be integrated and coordinated with motor skills. Children with disorders of motor control may be able to read and may possess the auditory and visual skills needed for writing but are unable to make the appropriate motor movements needed to produce letters and words (Luria, 1973; Myklebust, 1965; Smits-Engelsman & Van Galen, 1997). Motor dysfunction is revealed in two different ways. Some children write so rapidly and carelessly that the quality of their writing is poor, perhaps even illegible. In contrast, other children write very slowly and with considerable effort but are able to produce well-formed letters and acceptable writing. These children typically have difficulty with written assignments because they require an unusual amount of time to complete their work (Orton, 1937). Computers have helped dysgraphic students with word processing capabilities and are now used in the classroom and at home (NEC Foundation, 1994).

REFERENCES

Gaddes, W. H. (1980). *Learning disabilities and brain function: A neuropsychological approach.* New York: Springer-Verlag.

Johnson, D. J., & Myklebust, H. R. (1967). *Learning disabilities: Educational principles and practices.* New York: Grune & Stratton.

Luria, A. R. (1966). *Higher cortical functions in man.* New York: Basic Books.

Luria, A. R. (1973). *The working brain.* New York: Basic Books.

Myklebust, H. R. (1965). *Development and disorders of written language* (Vol. I). New York: Grune & Stratton.

NEC Foundation (1994). *Adaptive technology that provides access to computers.* Seattle, WA: Author.

Orton, S. T. (1937). *Reading, writing, and speech problems in children.* New York: Norton.

Smits-Engelsman, B. C. M., & Van Galen, G. P. (1997). Dysgraphia in children: Lasting psychomotor deficiency of transient developmental delay? *Journal of Experimental Child Psychology, 67,* 2, 164-168.

MARILYN P. DORNBUSH
Atlanta, Georgia

VISUAL-MOTOR AND VISUAL-PERCEPTUAL PROBLEMS
WRITING DISORDERS
WRITING REMEDIATION

DYSKINESIA

Dyskinesia refers to a difficulty in performing voluntary movements. Dyskinetic syndromes refer to a large group of different problems that interfere with the performance of voluntary motion. When used in descriptions of cerebral palsy, the dyskinetic syndrome may include the slow writing movements of athetosis, which affects extremities; the proximal and trunk movements (dystonia); or the abrupt, sudden, unpatterned choreiform movements. In this context, the dyskinesia is most apparent with emotional tension and disappears during sleep. Such movements are felt to be due to pathological states of the basal ganglion and associated neurological systems (Berkow, 1982).

Tardive dyskinesia sometimes is used to describe a kind of involuntary movement of the jaw or other tremors, including rigidity that contributes to difficulty in performance of voluntary movements. Tardive dyskinesia may result from adverse side effects of certain antipsychotic drugs (Berkow, 1982). Dyskinesis intermittens sometimes is used to describe a movement difficulty owed to poor circulation (Hensyl, 1982). Since all of the aforementioned terms are medical and imply special cause/effect relation-

ships, the use of these terms is most appropriate within a medical context. Observations of such movement disorders by teachers or therapists should be communicated to appropriate medical personnel in a clear, descriptive manner.

REFERENCES

Berkow, R. (Ed.). (1982). *The Merck manual of diagnosis and therapy* (14th ed.). Rahway, NJ: Merck, Sharp & Dohme.

Hensyl, W. R. (Ed.). (1982). *Stedman's medical dictionary* (24th ed.). Baltimore, MD: Williams & Wilkins

RACHAEL J. STEVENSON
Bedford, Ohio

CEREBRAL PALSY
CHOREA

DYSLEXIA

See DEVELOPMENTAL DYSLEXIA.

DYSLOGIC SYNDROME

Dyslogia refers to an impairment in the ability to express ideas in speech (*Blakiston's,* 1979; Hinsie & Campbell, 1960). Most authors, however, use the term to denote an impairment in the ability to use language that is of a central nervous system etiology and cannot be explained by specific sensory deficits (e.g., deafness) or mental deficiency (Nicolosi, Harryman, & Kresheck, 1978). Hence dyslogia is a seldom used synonym for aphasia. Eisenson (1972) used the term dyslogia to describe youngsters with congenital or developmental aphasia. He argued that by definition aphasia denotes a loss of language function, and thus use of this term to describe children who had never developed language would not be accurate. Hence, in the strictest use, dyslogic syndrome refers to children with congenital or developmental aphasia (Eisenson, 1972).

Eisenson (1972) indicates such children are not mentally retarded, deaf, or hard of hearing, and not severely autistic, although at times children with dyslogic syndrome may exhibit behaviors indicative of all these conditions. Perceptual deficits, particularly in the auditory modality, are evident, and these may be uniquely related to the processing of speech. Impairments in the ability to sequence, particularly of a temporal nature, are present. Performance on nonverbal tests of intelligence is reported to be within normal limits (Eisenson, 1972).

Rapin and Allen (1983) described seven developmental language syndromes identified from their clinical samples:

phonologic-syntactic syndrome; severe expressive syndrome with good comprehension; verbal auditory agnosia; mute autistic syndrome; autistic syndrome with echolalia; semantic-pragmatic syndrome without autism; and syntatic pragmatic syndrome. The authors state that all syndromes are characterized by delayed onset of expressive speech and impaired communicative intent (pragmatics). Three of Rapin and Allen's syndrome may be similar to Eisenson's description of the dyslogic syndrome: phonologic-syntactic syndrome; severe expressive syndrome with good comprehension; and syntactic-pragmatic syndrome. Each of these is characterized by severe expressive language deficits in absence of autisticlike behavior.

REFERENCES

Blakiston's Gould medical dictionary (4th ed.). (1979). New York: McGraw-Hill.

Eisenson, J. (1972). *Aphasia in children.* New York: Harper & Row.

Hinsie, L. E., & Campbell, R. J. (1960). *Psychiatric dictionary* (3rd ed.). New York: Oxford University Press.

Nicolosi, L., Harryman, E., & Kresheck, J. (1978). *Terminology of communication disorders.* Baltimore, MD: Williams & Wilkens.

Rapin, I., & Allen, D. A. (1983). Developmental language disorders: Nosologic considerations. In U. Kirk (Ed.), *Neuropsychology of language, reading, and spelling* (pp. 155–184). New York: Academic.

CATHY F. TELZROW
*Cuyahoga Special Education
Service Center*

APHASIA
DEVELOPMENTAL APHASIA
DYSPHASIA
LANGUAGE DISORDERS

DYSMETRIA

Dysmetria is a term derived from the Greek *dys-* (difficult) and *metron* (measure). It refers to a condition in which an individual has difficulty in gauging distance for bodily movements. Dysmetria is a form of dysergia, in which an individual is unable to stop muscular movement at a desired point. Signs of dysmetria are elicited by asking the afflicted individual to raise both arms rapidly, stopping at the shoulders so the arms are extended horizontally. Difficulty in controlling the range of movement in such a task may be indicative of dysmetria. In some expressions of dysmetria, the individual may overshoot the intended goal (hypermetria). Undershooting the intended goal is referred to as hypometria. Individuals with dysmetria may perform rapid, brusque movements with more force than is typically seen in voluntary movement. Dysmetria may be associated with cerebellar dysfunction.

REFERENCES

Blakiston's Gould medical dictionary (4th ed.). (1979). New York: McGraw-Hill.

Dorland's illustrated medical dictionary (26th ed.). (1981). Philadelphia: Saunders.

Mosby's medical and nursing dictionary (1983). St. Louis: Mosby.

CATHY F. TELZROW
*Cuyahoga Special Education
Service Center*

ATAXIA
GAIT DISTURBANCES

DYSMORPHIC FEATURES

Dysmorphic features are those physical anomalies that identify the presence of congenital syndromes or acquired disabilities. Dysmorphic features may be present in a variety of body parts, including the head, face, hands, and feet. Most congenital syndromes are associated with dysmorphic features that are specific to and, in fact, represent signs of the condition. Dysmorphic features associated with Down's syndrome, for example, include a single palmar crease (Simian crease) on one or both hands, epicanthus, and microcephaly (Kelly, 1975). Apert's syndrome, another condition frequently associated with mental retardation, is characterized by syndactyly (webbing) of the hands and feet and a flat, narrow head owing to closure of the bony sutures (Batshaw & Perret, 1981). Some dysmorphic features (e.g., anencephaly or absence of the cortical brain tissues) are severe and typically result in death (Batshaw & Perret, 1981).

While dysmorphic features may occur in the absence of any known syndrome and without apparent mental or physical impairment, in most cases such anomalies are suggestive of moderate to severe impairment. Dysmorphic features may represent malformations that occur during the first trimester (Batshaw & Perret, 1981). Malformations may result from genetic abnormalities (e.g., Down's syndrome, phenylketonuria); cell migration defects (e.g., cleft palate, spina bifida); maternal infection (e.g., rubella, cytomegalovirus); drugs (e.g., fetal alcohol syndrome, fetal dilantin syndrome); and other teratogens (Batshaw & Perret, 1981; Casey & Collie, 1984). The presence of dysmorphic features often is used to infer level and type of associated impairment. A study of the relationship between physical appearance and mental retardation syndromes reported that atypical appearance increases with the severity of mental retardation; greater atypical appearance is associated with more severe organic impairment in populations of severely and profoundly retarded persons; and mildly retarded persons with positive neurologic findings demonstrated greater degrees of atypical appearance (Richardson, Koller, & Katz, 1985).

Dysmorphic features of a less severe nature also have been identified in populations of mildly handicapped children. Waldrop and Halverson (1971) described findings from five separate studies in which congenital anomalies such as epicanthus, curved fifth digits, and a wide gap between the first and second toes were associated with hyperactive behavior in children. The authors suggest that "the same factors operating in the first weeks of pregnancy influenced the occurrence of *both* the morphological aberrations and the predisposition for impulsive, fast-moving behavior" (Waldrop & Halverson, 1971, p. 343). Subsequent studies demonstrated such minor physical anomalies could be identified in infants, were stable overtime, and were associated with infant irritability (Quinn, Renfield, Burg, & Rapaport, 1977). While these and other authors (e.g., Rosenberg & Weller, 1973) suggest minor congenital anomalies may be useful in predicting at-risk status for mild learning problems, other findings suggest the quality of the child's environment may represent an important intervening variable (LaVeck, Hammond, Telzrow, LaVeck, 1983).

REFERENCES

Batshaw, M. L., & Perret, Y. M. (1981). *Children with handicaps: A medical primer*. Baltimore, MD: Brooks.

Casey, P. H., & Collie, W. R. (1984). Severe mental retardation and multiple congenital anomalies of uncertain cause after extreme parental exposure to 2, 4-D. *The Journal of Pediatrics, 104,* 313–315.

Kelly, T. E. (1975). The role of genetic mechanisms in childhood handicaps. In R. H. A. Haslam & P. J. Valletutti (Eds.), *Medical problems in the classroom* (pp. 193–215). Baltimore: University Park Press.

LaVeck, F., Hammond, M. A., Telzrow, R., & LaVeck, G. D. (1983). Further observations on minor anomalies and behavior in different home environments. *Journal of Pediatric Psychology, 8,* 171–179.

Quinn, P. O., Renfield, M., Burg, C., & Rapaport, J. L. (1977). Minor physical anomalies: A newborn screening and 1-year follow-up. *Journal of Child Psychiatry, 16,* 662–669.

Richardson, S. A., Koller, H., & Katz, M. (1985). Appearance and mental retardation: Some first steps in the development and application of a measure. *American Journal of Mental Deficiency, 89,* 475–484.

Rosenberg, J. B., & Weller, G. M. (1973). Minor physical anomalies and academic performance in young school-children. *Developmental Medicine & Child Neurology, 15,* 131–135.

Waldrop, M. F., & Halverson, C. F. (1971). Minor physical anomalies and hyperactive behavior in young children. In J. Hellmuth (Ed.), *The exceptional infant* (Vol. 2, pp. 343–380). New York: Brunner/Mazel.

CATHY F. TELZROW
Cuyahoga Special Education Service Center

CONGENITAL DISORDERS
MINOR PHYSICAL ANOMALIES
PHYSICAL ANOMALIES

DYSNOMIA

Dysnomia and anomia are used interchangeably to denote problems in finding and using an intended word. Eisenson (1973) defines dysnomia as "difficulty in invoking an appropriate term regardless of its part of speech" (p. 19). It is frequently evidenced in dysphasic patients as a residual of central nervous system dysfunction. The dysphasic individual may substitute a word related by class or function to the intended word (e.g., knife for fork, (Eisenson, 1973). Fewer problems were noted on common words than those used less frequently in the language (Jenkins, Jiménez-Pabón, Shaw, & Sefer, 1975).

A dysphasic individual tends to talk around the elusive word and sometimes may remark that he or she knows it but cannot say it. He or she may attempt a gesture to illustrate the word's meaning or may give several functional cues, sometimes achieving successful recall through associations. Some dysphasics recognize the word when it is said to them. Word-finding difficulties also have been found among learning-disabled children with language disorders (Wiig & Semel, 1984) and among children diagnosed as being developmentally dysphasic (Myklebust, 1971). In such cases, the child cannot name an object or picture, but is aware of the error and can recognize the intended word when it is supplied because auditory monitoring processes are intact (Myklebust, 1971).

Dysnomic difficulties are evident in picture-naming tasks, characterized by use of an associated word (e.g., door for key). Use of an opposite such as "brother" for "sister" also is a common error in both children and adults. Verbal association tasks that require a child to name items within categories (e.g., animals) may produce rapid naming of several items and then either silence or incorrect responses. Errors may occur on words that a child has evidenced knowing on previous occasions (Wiig & Semel, 1984). German (1982) studied 8-to-11-year-old learning-disabled children to identify types of substitutions unique to this group when the children were unable to retrieve words. The strongest pattern noted was the substitution of a word of lesser complexity and with wider application (e.g., "string" for "rein"); the weakest pattern was the repetition of initial sound(s) of a related word before the target word was uttered (e.g., "br, br, comb").

Word-finding problems in spontaneous speech may be signaled by inappropriate pauses, use of filler ("um" and "er") and nonmeaningful phrases ("whatchama call it"), substitution of a functional description (circumlocution), or overuse of nonspecific words ("stuff," "place," "something," "thing") (Wiig & Semel, 1984). Classroom tasks involving rhyming words, silent picture naming, matching initial-, medical-, and final-consonant sounds, and look-say methods of reading may prove troublesome for dysnomic children (Wiig, Semel, & Nystrom, 1982). German (1982) suggests that a thorough evaluation of a child's pattern of word substitutions may prove helpful in intervention techniques.

REFERENCES

Eisenson, J. (1973). *Adult aphasia: Assessment and treatment.* New York: Appleton-Century-Crofts.

German, D. (1982). Word-finding substitutions in children with learning disabilities. *Language, Speech & Hearing Services in Schools, 13,* 223–230.

Jenkins, J. J., Jiménez-Pabón, E., Shaw, R. E., & Sefer, J. W. (1975). *Schuell's aphasia in adults: Diagnosis, prognosis, and treatment.* Hagerstown, MD: Harper & Row.

Myklebust, H. (1971). Childhood aphasia: An evolving concept. In L. E. Travis (Ed.), *The handbook of speech pathology and audiology* (pp. 1181–1201). New York: Appleton-Century-Crofts.

Wiig, E., & Semel, E. (1984). *Language assessment and intervention for the learning disabled* (2nd ed.). Columbus, OH: Merrill.

Wiig, E., Semel, E., & Nystrom, L. A. (1982). Comparison of rapid naming abilities in language learning disabled and academically achieving eight-year olds. *Language, Speech & Hearing Services in Schools, 13,* 11–25.

K. Sandra Vanta
Cleveland Public Schools,
Cleveland, Ohio

APHASIA
SPEECH AND LANGUAGE HANDICAPS

DYSPHAGIA

Dysphagia is difficulty in swallowing (Arvedson & Brodsky, 1993; Logemann, 1998). It is specifically defined as difficulty moving food from the mouth through the pharynx and esophagus and into the stomach. Recently, some clinicians and investigators have suggested that the act of eating and swallowing actually begins with the development of appetite, the increase in oral secretions prior to eating, as well as the action of placing food in the mouth (Logemann, 1998).

Dysphagia can occur in a variety of different populations as a result of structural or neurologic damage (Perlman & Schulze-Delrieu, 1997). Infants can be born with various disturbances in swallowing, including difficulty controlling the oral musculature, difficulty in triggering the pharyngeal stage of swallowing, problems in the motor movements characteristic of the pharyngeal stage of swallowing, as well as either anatomic or physiologic abnormalities in the esophagus.

Children and adults of all ages may acquire swallowing difficulty as a result of stroke; head injury; head and neck cancer and its treatment; degenerative neurologic diseases such as motor or neuron disease, multiple sclerosis, or Parkinson's disease; dementias such as Alzheimer's disease; and a wide range of other medical problems. Almost all neurologic diseases can result in changes in the swallow in any of its various stages.

Normal swallowing is a set of neuromuscular behaviors resulting in moving food from the mouth to the stomach safely and efficiently. This set of behaviors varies systematically with the nature of the food being swallowed (its volume, viscosity, and so on) and the volitional control the individual exerts over the process. Some patients are aware of their swallow disorder and can describe it quite accurately, while many others, especially those with a language impairment, are unable to identify that they have a swallow problem or to communicate the nature of the problem.

Typical management of dysphagia begins with a screening to identify patients at significant risk. Speech-language pathologists are usually the professionals providing both the evaluation and treatment of the patient's dysphagia (Sonies, 1997). The screening procedure usually involves observation of the patient eating (if they are taking oral nutrition), review of the patient's medical chart or educational history, and observation of the patient's management of their own saliva. If the patient appears to be at significant risk for dysphagia or exhibits symptoms such as coughing or choking while eating, change in vocal quality to a more gurgly sound during or after eating, or repetitive swallowing of a single amount, the patient is typically assessed in more depth. These in-depth assessments may involve a detailed oral motor examination looking at lip, tongue, palate, pharyngeal and laryngeal function in a variety of tasks. Following this clinical bedside examination, the patient may receive an instrumental assessment, which is a radiographic study usually known as a modified barium swallow (MBS). This test visualizes movement of food through the oral cavity, pharynx, and esophagus and also observes the structural movements as the food is moved through the system. This assessment can define the types of food the patient can swallow most safely, the patient's efficiency in moving food from the mouth to the stomach, and the effectiveness of treatment strategies to improve the swallow. If the patient is unsafe in swallowing—that is, food or liquid enters their airway on a regular basis—they are at risk for development of pneumonia as a result. If the individual is inefficient in their swallowing and is not able to swallow most of the food given to them, they may become malnourished or dehydrated. All of these are serious medical problems which can result from dysphagia.

As the health care system has changed and encouraged sick children to be treated in schools, many children must receive their swallowing assessment and treatment in public school systems. This has expanded the scope of practice of school speech-language pathologists.

Treatment for dysphagia typically involves a variety of compensatory and direct exercise programs. Compensatory strategies are designed to eliminate the symptoms of the problem (such as food entering the airway) without necessarily changing or eliminating the underlying disorder. Included in compensatory strategies are postural techniques, sensory enhancement techniques, swallowing maneuvers, and dietary changes. Direct therapy strategies include exercise programs to improve the range, rate, and coordination of movements of structures in the oral cavity and pharynx, as well as swallowing maneuvers. Swallowing maneuvers are voluntary controls over selected aspects of the oropharyngeal swallow.

REFERENCES

Arvedson, J. C., & Brodsky, L. (Eds.). (1993). *Pediatric swallowing and feeding: Assessment and management*. San Diego: Singular.

Logemann, J. A. (1998). *Evaluation and treatment of swallowing disorders* (2nd ed.). Austin, TX: Pro-Ed.

Perlman, A. L., & Schulze-Delrieu, K. S. (Eds.). (1997). *Deglutition and its disorders*. San Diego: Singular.

Sonies, B. C. (Ed.). (1997). *Dysphagia*. Gaithersburg, MD: Aspen.

JERI A. LOGEMANN
Northwestern University

DYSPEDAGOGIA

Dyspedagogia refers to poor teaching. It has been cited as a major cause of reading retardation and other learning disorders. Though the term is used as one of the etiological agents for a wide array of problems, dyspedagogia is most commonly associated with the field of learning disabilities (Epstein et al., 1980).

Early research in reading disorders and learning disabilities looked for psychophysiological dysfunctions or psychological information-processing deficits as the cause of a child's inefficient learning. Once various forms of testing established a supposed etiology, specific treatment regimens were to flow directly from the diagnosis. Although this approach to special and remedial education, often referred to as ability training, has been questioned (Ysseldyke, 1973), it remains a dominant force in practice. Learning problems were seen as based in the individual child, whether because of psychoneurological dysfunction or sociocultural disadvantage. Improper choice of teaching materials or methodology, or an inappropriate match between learning style and pedagogy, were rarely viewed as contributing factors in a student's academic retardation.

Cohen (1971) cites Harris's research (1968) on teaching beginning reading as an early example of dyspedagogia as an etiological agent in poor reading achievement. When comparisons were made between different beginning reading programs, matching classrooms across and within each program, the achievement discrepancies were greater between classrooms using the same program than across the different types of beginning reading programs. This was generally interpreted to indicate that the teacher variable is a more powerful determinant of student achievement than the actual programs or materials employed.

Cohen (1971) believes that dyspedagogia is the norm for most children, both in regular and special education. Many children, however, learn well enough despite poor or inappropriate teaching. The problem lies in the fact that those children who come to the educational setting with negatively predisposing social, psychological, neurological, or linguistic differences need effective, intensive teaching, and will suffer inordinately from dyspedagogia (Wertsch, 1985). The presenting background problems are not ignored, but the burden falls on educators to minimize their deleterious effects on learning by providing sound, skill-oriented instruction.

Currently, as a result of recent research in regular education on effective teaching (e.g., Brophy, 1979; Rosenshine, 1978), a good deal of attention is being given to issues such as direct instruction, time on task, academically engaged time, instructional management, performance monitoring, success-oriented learning, feedback, reflective teaching, and related practices. This research may offer promise for special education (Englert, 1984; Goodman, 1985; Rieth et al., 1979).

REFERENCES

Brophy, J. E. (1979). Teacher behavior and its effects. *Journal of Educational Psychology, 71,* 733–750.

Cohen, S. A. (1971). Dyspedagogia as a cause of reading retardation: Definition and treatment. In B. Bateman (Ed.), *Learning disorders* (Vol. 4). Seattle, WA: Special Child Publications.

Englert, C. S. (1984). Effective direct instruction practices in special education settings. *Remedial & Special Education, 5*(2), 38–47.

Epstein, M. H., Cullinan, D., Hessen, E. L., & Lloyd, J. (1980). Understanding children with learning disabilities. *Child Welfare, 59*(1), 3–14.

Goodman, L. (1985). The effective schools movement and special education. *Teaching Exceptional Children, 17,* 102–105.

Harris, A., Morrison, C., Serwa, B., & Gold, L. (1968). *A continuation of the craft project: Comparing approaches with disadvantaged urban Negro children in primary grades* (U.S.O.E. #6-10-063). New York: City University of New York.

Rieth, H. J., Edsgrove, L., & Semmel, M. I. (1979). Relationship between instructional time and academic achievement: Implications for research and practice. *Education Unlimited, 1*(6), 53–56.

Rosenshine, B. (1978). *Academic engaged time, content covered and direct instruction* (ERIC Document No. 152 776). Champaign, IL: University of Illinois.

Wertsch, J. (1985). *Vygotsky and the social formation of mind.* London, England: Harvard University Press.

Ysseldyke, J. E. (1973). Diagnostic-prescriptive teaching: The search for aptitude-treatment interactions. In L. Mann & D. Sabatino (Eds.), *First review of special education.* New York: Grune & Stratton.

JOHN D. WILSON
Elwyn Institutes

DYSPHASIA

See LANGUAGE DISORDERS.

DYSPHONIA

See VOICE DISORDERS.

DYSPRAXIA

See APRAXIA.

DYSTONIA MUSCULORUM DEFORMANS (DMD)

Dystonia musculorum deformans (DMD) is a progressive neurological disease primarily reflected in movement disorders. In addition to impaired motor function, twisting of the limbs is often seen. In its early stages, DMD may be mistaken for hysteria or psychosomatic movement disturbances. Well learned, previously smooth, coordinated movements become difficult and awkward in appearance. Individuals in the early stages of DMD may lose the previously acquired ability to write legibly; one hand may be affected prior to the other, even more confusing in the early stages of the disorder. Other apparently confusing symptoms appear; some children may be able to walk backward and even run without visible difficulty, but ordinary forward walking may be severely impaired (Hartlage & Hartlage, 1986). Children with DMD are often misdiagnosed as having emotional disorders. Proper diagnosis requires not only a psychological assessment but a thorough evaluation by a pediatric neurologist. Children with DMD have a serious orthopedic neuromuscular disorder that requires adaptive physical education and other accommodations at school in order for the child to function successfully in formal educational environments. Placement in a special education classroom is not typically required.

Families and professionals may find support and information from the Dystonia Society at Weddel House, 13–14 West Smithfield, London ECIA 9HY, United Kingdom. Their telephone number is 0 (171) 329-0797, and they can be faxed at 0 (171) 329-0689.

REFERENCE

Hartlage, P. L., & Hartlage, L. C. (1986). Epilepsy and other neurological and neuromuscular handicaps. In R. T. Brown & C. R. Reynolds (Eds.), *Psychological perspectives on childhood exceptionality*. New York: Wiley-Interscience.

CECIL R. REYNOLDS
Texas A & M University

ADAPTIVE PHYSICAL EDUCATION